U0906961

HENAN STATISTICAL YEARBOOK 2020

河南统计年鉴

河南统计年鉴

HENAN STATISTICAL YEARBOOK

河 南 省 统 计 局
国家统计局河南调查总队 编
Compiled by Henan Statistics Bureau Henan
General Team of Investigation under the NBS

总第37期 NO.37

©中国统计出版社有限公司2020
版权所有。未经许可，本书的任何部分不得以任何方式在世界任何地区以任何文字翻印、拷贝、仿制或转载。

© 2020 China Statistics Press Co.,Ltd.
All rights reserved. No part of the publication may be reproduced or transmitted in any form or by any means, electronic or mechanical, including photocopying, recording, or any information storage and retrieval system, without written permission from the publisher.

图书在版编目（CIP）数据

河南统计年鉴. 2020 = Henan Statistical Yearbook 2020 ： 汉英对照 / 河南省统计局, 国家统计局河南调查总队编. -- 北京 ： 中国统计出版社, 2020.9
ISBN 978-7-5037-9208-3

I. ①河… II. ①河…②国… III. ①统计资料－河南－2020－年鉴－汉、英 IV. ①C832.61-54
中国版本图书馆CIP数据核字（2020)第120636号

河南统计年鉴-2020

作　　者/ 河南省统计局　国家统计局河南调查总队
责任编辑/ 钟　钰 熊　威
装帧设计/ 梁裕宇
出版发行/ 中国统计出版社有限公司
地　　址/ 北京市丰台区西三环南路甲6号
邮政编码/ 100073
电　　话/ 邮购 (010)63376909　书店 (010)68783171
网　　址/ http://www.zgtjcbs.com
印　　刷/ 河南豫统印刷有限公司
经　　销/ 新华书店
开　　本/ 890mm×1240mm　1/16
字　　数/ 1600千字
印　　张/ 51
版　　别/ 2020年9月第1版
版　　次/ 2020年9月第1次印刷
定　　价/ 398.00元　Price:398.00yuan(RMB)

本书附同版本CD-ROM一张，光盘内容以书面文字为准。
如有印装差错，由本社发行部调换。

《河南统计年鉴－2020》
编委会和编辑部工作人员名单

编 委 会

主　　　编：陈红瑜　夏雨春

副　主　编：（按姓氏笔划排序）

王传健　冯文元　冯建中　朱怀安　李贵峰　罗勤礼
季红梅　武　洁　陈建设　赵德友　郭学来　袁祖霞

编　　　委：（按姓氏笔划排序）

王予荷　王有社　王松林　王宪彬　王　超　王　超
（调查总队）　司曼珈　冯保安　朱启明　田晓更
刘朝阳　刘建功　刘录林　孙　磊　乔西宏　安巧枝
李跃苏　李素香　李　鑫　李先锋　杨冠军　张亚民
张喜峥　张旭建　张俊芝　张　龙　张广宇　张　静
张　杰　赵　杨　赵祖亮　郝　兵　顾俊龙　徐　良
海向阳　常冬梅　梁景予　梁文海　梁修群　温素清

编辑工作人员

总　编　辑：朱启明

副总编辑：韩军平　朱　涛　徐委乔　杨　屹

编辑部主任：朱　涛

编辑部副主任：李　湛

责任编辑：钟　钰　熊　威

编　　　辑：（按姓氏笔划排序）

孔令惠　王　思　王晓燕　王姣慧　左俊勇　乔旭明
刘　佳　朱　娜　宋谊晴　谷永翔　吴　娜　杨　琳
杨　青　杨　争　张　静　李　丽　陈　哲　陈　琛
金民伟　周文瑞　呼晓飞　郑文革　郑　洁　郑　霞
赵文献　赵　霞　赵国顺　胡昶昶　秦红涛　袁　勇
贾　梁　贾云静　高　彦　常伟杰　郭婷婷　彭　敏
靳伟莉　雷茜茜　潘　勇　樊福顺　冀寒阳

英文校订：李　湛

2020 河南统计年鉴

Editorial Board and Staff

I. Editorial Board

Chairman: Chen Hongyu Xia Yuchun

Vice-chairmen: (in order of strokes of Chinese character of the surname)

Wang Chuanjian	Feng Wenyuan	Feng Jianzhong	Zhu Huaian
Li Guifeng	Luo qinli	Ji Hongmei	Wu Jie
Chen Jianshe	Zhao Deyou	Guo Xuelai	Yuan Zuxia

Editorial Board: (in order of strokes of Chinese character of the surname)

Wang Yuhe	Wang Youshe	Wang Songlin	Wang Xianbin	Wang Chao
Wang Chao(General Team of Investigation)			Si Manjia	Feng Baoan
Zhu Qiming	Tian Xiaogeng	Liu Chaoyang	Liu Jiangong	Liu Lulin
Sun Lei	Qiao Xihong	An Qiaozhi	Li Yuesu	Li Suxiang
Li Xin	Li Xianfeng	Yang Guanjun	Zhang Yamin	Zhang Xizheng
Zhang Xujian	Zhang Junzhi	Zhang Long	Zhang Guangyu	Zhang Jing
Zhang Jie	Zhao Yang	Zhao Zuliang	Hao Bing	Gu Junlong
Xu Liang	Hai Xiangyang	Chang Dongmei	Liang Jingyu	Liang Wenhai
Liang Xiuqun	Wen Suqing			

II. Editorial Staff

Editor-in-chief: Zhu Qiming

Associate Editors-in-chief: Han Junping Zhu Tao Xu Weiqiao Yang Yi

Directors of Editorial Department: Zhu Tao

Deputy Directors of Editorial Department: Li Zhan

Coordinators: Zhong Yu Xiong Wei

Editorial Staff:(in order of strokes of Chinese character of the surname)

Kong Linghui	Wang Si	Wang Xiaoyan	Wang Jiaohui	Zuo Junyong
Qiao Xuming	Liu Jia	Zhu Na	Song Yiqing	Gu Yongxiang
Wu Na	Yang Lin	Yang Qing	Yang Zheng	Zhang Jing
Li Li	Chen Zhe	Chen Chen	Jin Minwei	Zhou Wenrui
Hu Xiaofei	Zheng Wenge	Zheng Jie	Zheng Xia	Zhao Wenxian
Zhao Xia	Zhao Guoshun	Hu Changchang	Qin Hongtao	Yuan Yong
Jia Liang	Jia Yunjing	Gao Yan	Chang Weijie	Guo Tingting
Peng Min	Jin Weili	Lei Xixi	Pan Yong	Fan Fushun
Ji Hanyang				

English Proofreaders: Li Zhan

编辑说明

一、《河南统计年鉴—2020》是一部全面反映河南省经济和社会发展情况的资料性年刊。本书收录了全省和各市(县)2019年以及重要历史年份的经济和社会各方面大量的统计数据，并收录了全国及各省市区2019年的主要统计数据。

二、全书内容分为27个部分，即，1．综合；2．国民经济核算；3．人口；4．从业人员和职工工资；5．固定资产投资；6．对外贸易和旅游；7．能源；8．财政；9．物价；10．人民生活；11．城市概况；12．农业；13．工业；14．建筑业；15．房地产业；16．批发和零售业、住宿和餐饮业；17．金融业；18．其他服务业；19．运输和邮电；20．资源和环境；21．科技；22．教育；23．卫生和社会工作；24．文化和体育；25．公共管理、社会保障和社会组织；26．各县（市、区）主要统计指标；27．全国及各省市区主要统计指标。

三、为方便读者使用，各篇章前设有《简要说明》，对本篇章的主要内容、资料来源、统计范围、统计方法以及历史变动情况予以简要概述。篇末附有《主要统计指标解释》。

四、资料中所使用的度量衡单位均采用国际统一标准计量单位。

五、本年鉴部分数据合计数或相对数由于单位取舍不同而产生的计算误差均未作机械调整。

六、本年鉴各表中，有关对全表的注解均在该表上方，对表中部分指标的注解则在该表下方。凡带续表的资料，对部分指标的注解一律在最后一张续表的下方。

七、本年鉴表中的符号使用说明："空格"表示该项统计指标数据不详或无该项数据；"#"表示其中的主要项。

Editor's Notes

I. *Henan Statistical Yearbook 2020* is an annual statistical publication, which reflects comprehensively the economy and society development of Henan. It covers data for 2019 and key statistical data in some historically important years at the provincial level and city(couty) level of Henan. It also covers data for 2019 and key statistical data at the national level and the local level of other provinces.

II. The yearbook contains the following 27 parts, 1. General Survey; 2.National Accounts; 3.Population; 4.Employment and Wages; 5.Investment in Fixed Assets, 6. Foreign Trade and Tourism; 7. Energy; 8.Government Finance; 9.Prices; 10.People's Living Conditions; 11.General Survey of Cities; 12.Agriculture; 13.Industry; 14.Construction; 15. Real Estate; 16. Wholesale and Retail Sale Trades, Hotels and Catering Services; 17. Financial Intermediation; 18.Other Services; 19. Transport, Postal and Telecommunication Services; 20. Resources and Environment; 21.Science and Technology; 22.Education; 23.Public Health and Social Work; 24.Culture and Sports; 25. Public Management, Social Security and Social Organizations;26.Main Indicators of County （City, municipal districts）; 27.Main Indicators of the Whole Nation and 31 Provinces (Municipality, Autonomous Regions).

III. To facilitate readers, the Brief Introduction at the beginning of each chapter provides a summary of the main contents of the chapter, data sources, statistical scope, statistical methods and historical changes. At the end of each chapter, Explanatory Notes on Main Statistical Indicators are included.

IV. The units of measurement used in this yearbook are internationally standard measurement units.

V. Statistical discrepancies on totals and relative figures due to rounding are not adjusted in this yearbook.

VI. The notes concerning the whole table are placed at the upper part of the table, while the notes concerning individual indicators are placed at the lower part of the table. If the table occupied more than one page, the notes of the individual indicators are placed at the end of the last page.

VII. Notations used in this yearbook: "(Blank)" indicates that the data are unknown or are not available; "#"Indicates a major breakdown of the total.

目　　录

CONTENTS

一、综合

General Survey

简要说明

Brief Introduction

1-1 全省行政区划(2019 年底)……………………………………………………………… (3)

Administrative Divisions of Henan Province (End of 2019)

1-2 各市、县(市、区)名称(2019 年底)……………………………………………………… (4)

Names of Administrative Areas (End of 2019)

1-3 河南省主要统计指标居全国位次……………………………………………………… (5)

The Rank of Main Indicators of Henan in Nation

1-4 河南省主要统计指标占全国比重……………………………………………………… (5)

The Poroportion of Main Indicators of Henan in Nation

1-5 国民经济和社会发展总量和速度指标………………………………………………… (6)

Principal Aggregate Indicators and Growth Rates of National Economic and Social Development

1-6 国民经济和社会发展结构指标………………………………………………………… (12)

Structural Indicators on National Economic and Social Development

1-7 国民经济和社会发展比例和效益指标………………………………………………… (14)

Indicators on Proportions and Efficiency in National Economic and Social Development

1-8 按三次产业分的基本单位数及构成…………………………………………………… (16)

Institutional Units and Composition By Industry

1-9 分行业法人单位数……………………………………………………………………… (17)

Number of Institutional Unit by Sector

1-10 各市按三次产业和机构类型分法人单位数(2018 年)………………………………… (18)

Number of Institutional Unit by orgniztion type and City (2018)

1-11 各市按三次产业和机构类型分法人单位数(2019 年)………………………………… (19)

Number of Institutional Unit by orgniztion type and City (2019)

1-12 各市分行业法人单位数(2018 年)……………………………………………………… (20)

Number of Institutional Unit by Sector and City (2018)

1-13 各市分行业法人单位数(2019 年)……………………………………………………… (22)

Number of Institutional Unit by Sector and City (2019)

1-14 各市按登记注册类型分企业法人单位数(2018 年)…………………………………… (24)

Number of Business Entities by City and Status of Registration (2018)

1-15 各市按登记注册类型分企业法人单位数(2019 年)…………………………………… (26)

Number of Business Entities by City and Status of Registration (2019)

1-16 “四上”法人单位数(2018 年底)……(28)
Number of Institutional Unit of industry, construction, wholesale and retail trades, hotels and catering enterprises above designated size (End of 2018)
1-17 “四上”法人单位数(2019 年底)……(29)
Number of Institutional Unit of industry, construction, wholesale and retail trades, hotels and catering enterprises above designated size (End of 2019)
1-18 航空港主要经济指标……(30)
Main Economic Indicators of Zhengzhou Airport
主要统计指标解释 ……(31)
Explanatory Notes on Main Statistical Indicators

二、国民经济核算

National Accounts

简要说明
Brief Introduction
2-1 生产总值……(43)
Gross Domestic Product
2-2 生产总值指数(上年=100) ……(44)
Indices of Gross Domestic Product (Preceding year=100)
2-3 生产总值指数(1978=100) ……(45)
Indices of Gross Domestic Product (1978=100)
2-4 生产总值分产业构成………(46)
Industrial Composition of Gross Domestic Product
2-5 三次产业贡献率………(47)
Share of the Contributions of Three Strata of Industry to the Increase of the GDP
2-6 三次产业对生产总值增长的拉动……(48)
Contribution of the Three Strata of Industry to GDP Growth
2-7 全员劳动生产率………(49)
Overall Labor Productivity
2-8 各市生产总值(2018 年)………(50)
Gross Domestic Product by City (2018)
2-9 各市生产总值(2019 年)………(51)
Gross Domestic Product by City (2019)
2-10 各市生产总值指数(2018 年)………(52)
Indices of Gross Domestic Product by City (2018)
2-11 各市生产总值指数(2019 年)………(53)
Indices of Gross Domestic Product by City (2019)
2-12 支出法生产总值………(54)
Gross Domestic Product by Expenditure Approach
2-13 最终消费支出指数……(55)
Indices of Final Consumption Expenditure

2-14 资本形成总额指数…… (56)
Indices of Gross Capital Formation
2-15 支出法生产总值构成…… (57)
Components of Gross Domestic Product by Expenditure Approach
2-16 居民消费水平及指数…… (58)
Household Consumption Expenditure and Indices
2-17 投入产出表(2017 年)…… (60)
Input-Output Table (2017)
主要统计指标解释…… (72)
Explanatory Notes on Main Statistical Indicators

三、人口
Population

简要说明
Brief Introduction
3-1 总人口(年底数)…… (83)
Total Population (Year-end)
3-2 人口自然变动情况…… (84)
Natural Changes of Population
3-3 各市常住人口数…… (85)
Resident Population by City
3-4 各市城镇常住人口数…… (86)
Urban Resident Population by City
3-5 各市户数、人口数(2019 年底)…… (87)
Number of Households and Population by City (End of 2019)
3-6 各市人口出生率、死亡率、自然增长率(2019 年底)…… (88)
Birth Rate, Death Rate, and Natural Growth Rate by City (End of 2019)
3-7 河南省人口预期寿命…… (89)
Life Expectancy of Henan
3-8 各市常住人口年龄结构(2019 年底)…… (90)
Age Composition of Population by City (End of 2019)
3-9 各市常住人口抚养系数(2019 年底)…… (91)
Dependency Ratio of Population by City (End of 2019)
3-10 分年龄、性别的人口结构(2019 年)…… (92)
Population Construction by Age and Sex (2019)
3-11 6 岁及 6 岁以上分年龄、性别、受教育程度的人口结构(2019 年)…… (93)
Population Age 6 and over by Age, Sex and Educational Attainment (2019)
3-12 15 岁及以上分年龄、性别、婚姻状况的人口结构(2019 年)…… (94)
Population Aged 15 and over by Age, Sex and Marital Status (2019)
3-13 育龄妇女分年龄、孩次的生育状况(2019 年)…… (95)
Age-specific Fertility Rate of Childbearing Women by Age of Mother and Birth Order (2019)

3-14 六次人口普查主要指标…… (96)
Main Indicators of National Population Censuses in 1953, 1964, 1982, 1990, 2000, 2010
主要统计指标解释 …… (97)
Explanatory Notes on Main Statistical Indicators

四、就业人员与职工工资
Employment and Wages

简要说明
Brief Introduction
4-1 按城乡分的就业人员数…… (101)
Number of Employed Persons in Urban and Rural Areas
4-2 各市分城乡的就业人员数(2019 年底)…… (102)
Number of Employed Persons in Urban and Rural Areas by City (End of 2019)
4-3 分三次产业的就业人员数…… (104)
Number of Employed Persons by Three Strata of Industry
4-4 各市分三次产业的就业人员数(2019 年底)…… (105)
Number of Employed Persons by Three Strata of Industry and City (End of 2019)
4-5 分行业就业人员数…… (106)
Number of Employed Persons by Sector
4-6 各市分行业就业人员数(2019 年底)…… (108)
Number of Employed Persons by Sector (End of 2019)
4-7 分行业城镇非私营单位就业人员数…… (110)
Number of Employed Persons in Urban Non-private Units by Sector
4-8 城镇非私营单位就业人员数(2019 年底)…… (112)
Number of Employed Persons in Urban Non-private Units by City (End of 2019)
4-9 各种分组的城镇非私营单位就业人员数(2019 年底)…… (113)
Number of Employed Persons in Urban Non-private Units by Groups (End of 2019)
4-10 各种分组的城镇非私营单位女性就业人员数(年底数)…… (114)
Number of Female Employed Persons in Urban Non-private Units by Groups (Year-end)
4-11 城镇非私营单位就业人员平均工资…… (115)
Average Wage of Employed Persons in Urban Non-private Units
4-12 城镇非私营单位职工工资及指数…… (116)
Wages and Related Indices of Staff and Workers in Urban Non-private Units
4-13 各种分组的城镇非私营单位就业人员平均工资(2019 年)…… (117)
Average Wage of Employed Persons in Urban Npn-private Units by Groups (2019)
4-14 各市城镇非私营单位就业人员平均工资(2019 年)…… (118)
Average Wage of Employed Persons in Urban Non-private Units by City (2019)
4-15 分行业城镇非私营单位就业人员平均工资(2019 年)…… (120)
Average Wage of Employed Persons in Urban Non-private Units by Sector and City (2019)
4-16 城镇私营单位就业人员平均工资…… (122)
Average Wage of Employed Persons in Urban Non-private Units

4-17 各市城镇私营单位就业人员平均工资…………(123)
Average Wage of Empleyed Persons in Urban Non-private Units by City
4-18 各市城镇登记失业人数及失业率…………(124)
Registered Unemployed Persons and Unemployment Rate in Urban Area by City
主要统计指标解释…………(125)
Explanatory Notes on Main Statistical Indicators

五、固定资产投资

Investment in Fixed Assets

简要说明
Brief Introduction
5-1 固定资产投资增速…………(133)
Growth Rate of Investment in Fixed Assets in the whole Province
5-2 固定资产投资结构…………(134)
Structure of Investment in Fixed Assets in the whole Province
5-3 按行业分固定资产投资增速及比重(2019 年)…………(135)
Growth Rate and Proportion of Investment in Fixed Assets by Registration Status and Sector (2019)
5-4 各市分行业固定资产投资增速(2019 年)…………(138)
Growth Rate of Investment in Fixed Assets by Sector and City (2019)
5-5 各市分行业固定资产投资比重(2019 年)…………(140)
Proportion of Investment in Fixed Assets by Sector and City (2019)
5-6 各市固定资产投资增速(2019 年)…………(142)
Growth Rate of Investment in Fixed Assets by City (2019)
5-7 各市固定资产投资比重(2019 年)…………(143)
Proportion of Investment in Fixed Assets by City (2019)
5-8 各市固定资产投资增速(2019 年)…………(144)
Growth Rate of Investment in Fixed Assets by City(2019)
5-9 固定资产投资增速及结构…………(145)
Growth Rate and Structure of Investment in Fixed Assets
5-10 工业主要产业投资增速及结构…………(146)
Growth Rate and Structure of Investment in Fixed Assets in Major Industries
5-11 能源原材料工业投资增速及结构…………(147)
Growth Rate and Structure of Energy Raw Material Industry
5-12 各市工业固定资产投资增速及比重(2019 年)…………(148)
Growth Rate and Proportion of Investment in Fixed Assets of Industry by City (2019)
5-13 分行业农村农户固定资产投资增速及结构(2019 年)…………(149)
Investment in Fixed Assets of Households in Rural Area by Sector (2019)
主要统计指标解释…………(150)
Explanatory Notes on Main Statistical Indicators

六、对外经济贸易和旅游

Foreign Trade and Tourism

简要说明

Brief Introduction

6-1 对外经济贸易基本情况…………(159)

Foreign Trade and Economic Cooperation

6-2 进出口总额…………(160)

Total Value of Imports and Exports

6-3 各种分组的进出口总值…………(161)

Total Value of Imports and Exports by Group

6-4 河南向一些国家(地区)进出口总值…………(162)

Total Value of Imports and Exports To Related Countries and Regions

6-5 人民币汇率(年平均价)…………(163)

Exchange Rate of Renminbi (Annual Average)

6-6 外商和港澳台商直接投资情况…………(164)

Foreign, Hong Kong, Macao and Taiwan's Direct Investments

6-7 外商和港澳台商在豫直接投资(2019 年)…………(165)

Direct Investment From Foreign, Hong Kong, Macao and Taiwan Businessmen in Henan (2019)

6-8 各市外商和港澳台商在豫直接投资金额…………(166)

Direct Investment from Foreign, Hong Kong, Macao and Taiwan in Henan by City

6-9 外商和港澳台商投资企业(单位)注册登记情况…………(167)

Registration Status of Foreign, Hong Kong, Macao and Taiwan Funded Enterprises

6-10 各市外商和港澳台商投资企业登记注册情况(2019 年)…………(168)

Registration Status of Foreign, Hong Kong, Macao and Taiwan Funded Enterprises by City (2019)

6-11 对外国和港澳台地区投资…………(169)

Investment to Foreign, Hong Kong, Macao and Taiwan

6-12 对外承包工程和劳务合作…………(169)

Contracted Projects and Labor Cooperation with Foreign Countries or Regions

6-13 各市利用省外资金情况…………(170)

Direct Investment by Other Provinces in Henan by City

6-14 旅游业基本情况…………(171)

Basic Information of International Tourism

6-15 各市入境旅游情况(2019 年)…………(171)

Basic Information of International Tourism by City (2019)

6-16 接待国内游客人数和收入…………(172)

Number and Income of Domestic Tourists Received

6-17 各市国内旅游基本情况(2019 年)…………(172)

Basic Information of Domestic Tour by City (2019)

主要统计指标解释…………(173)

Explanatory Notes on Main Statistical Indicators

七、能源
Energy

简要说明
Brief Introduction
7-1 一次能源生产总量及构成…………(181)
Total Production of Primary Energy and Its Composition
7-2 能源消费总量及构成…………(182)
Total Consumption of Energy and Its Composition
7-3 能源生产弹性系数…………(183)
Elasticity Ratio of Energy Production
7-4 能源消费弹性系数…………(184)
Elasticity Ratio of Energy Consumption
7-5 能源加工转换效率…………(185)
Efficiency of Energy Conversion
7-6 综合平衡表…………(186)
Overall Energy Balance Sheet
7-7 平均每天能源消费量…………(187)
Average Daily Energy Consumption by Type of Energy
7-8 人均生活能源消费量…………(188)
Average Per Capita Energy Consumption of Households
7-9 规模以上工业企业分品种能源购进、消费及库存(2019 年)…………(189)
Purchase, Consumption, and Stock of Energy in above Designated Size Industrial Enterprises by Catalog (2019)
7-10 规模以上工业企业分行业主要能源消费量(2019 年)…………(190)
Consumption of Main Energy in above Designated Size Industrial Enterprises by Sector (2019)
7-11 规模以上工业分部门主要能源消费量(2019 年)…………(192)
Consumption of Main Energy in above Designated Size Industrial Enterprises by Sector (2019)
7-12 各市规模以上工业企业分品种主要能源消费量(2019 年)…………(193)
Consumption of Main Energy Sources in above Designated Size Industrial Enterprises by Industrial Sector and City (2019)
7-13 规模以上工业企业分行业水消费总量(2019 年)…………(194)
Computation of Water in above Designated Size Industrial Enterprises by Sector (2019)
7-14 各市规模以上工业企业水消费量(2019 年)…………(196)
Computation of Water in above Designated Size Industrial Enterprises by City (2019)
7-15 各市年耗能万吨标准煤以上工业企业个数…………(197)
Number of Industrial Enterprises of Consumption of Energy Above 10 000 tons by City
7-16 各行业年耗能万吨标准煤以上工业企业单位数…………(198)
Number of Industrial Enterprises of Consumption of Energy Above 10 000 tons by Sector
7-17 主要耗能工业企业单位产品能源消耗情况…………(199)
Energy Consumption per Unit of Product in Major Energy Consuming Industrial Enterprises
7-18 主要耗能工业企业单位产品电力消耗情况…………(200)
Electric Power Consumption per Unit of Product in Major Energy Consuming Industrial Enterprises

7-19 各市全社会用电量…………………………………………………………………………………………（201）
Electricity Consumption by City
7-20 平均每万元地区生产总值能耗情况…………………………………………………………………………（202）
Basic Imformation of Energy Consumption
主要统计指标解释 ………………………………………………………………………………………………（203）
Explanatory Notes on Main Statistical Indicators

八、财政
Government Finance

简要说明
Brief Introduction
8-1 一般公共预算收支额…………………………………………………………………………………………（209）
General Public Budget Revenue and Expenditure of the Local Government
8-2 各项税收……………………………………………………………………………………………………（210）
Taxes
8-3 一般公共预算收入……………………………………………………………………………………………（210）
General Public Budget Revenue of the Local Government
8-4 一般公共预算支出……………………………………………………………………………………………（211）
General Public Budget Expenditure of the Local Government
8-5 各级一般公共预算收入(2019 年)…………………………………………………………………………（212）
General Public Budget Revenue of the Local Government by Rank (2019)
8-6 各级一般公共预算支出(2019 年)…………………………………………………………………………（213）
General Public Budget Expenditure of the Local Government by Rank (2019)
8-7 各市一般公共预算收入………………………………………………………………………………………（214）
General Public Budget Revenue of the Local Government by City
8-8 各市一般公共预算支出………………………………………………………………………………………（216）
General Public Budget Expenditure of the Local Government by City
主要统计指标解释 ………………………………………………………………………………………………（218）
Explanatory Notes on Main Statistical Indicators

九、物价
Prices

简要说明
Brief Introduction
9-1 各种物价总指数…………………………………………………………………………………………………（227）
General Price Indices
9-2 各种物价定基指数………………………………………………………………………………………………（228）
Fixed-base Price Indices
9-3 居民消费价格指数(2019 年)………………………………………………………………………………（229）
Consumer Price Indices (2019)
9-4 分类商品零售价格指数…………………………………………………………………………………………（230）
Retail Price Indices by Category

9-5 农业生产资料价格指数…………………………………………………………………………………………（230）
Price Indices for Means of Agricultural Production
9-6 各市(县)居民消费价格指数(2019 年)…………………………………………………………………………（231）
Consumer Price Indices by City (2019)
9-7 各市商品零售价格指数(2019 年)……………………………………………………………………………（232）
Retail Price Indices by City (2019)
9-8 各市居民消费价格指数(2019 年)……………………………………………………………………………（234）
Consumer Price Indices by City (2019)
9-9 各市商品零售价格指数(2019 年)……………………………………………………………………………（235）
Retail Price Indices by City (2019)
9-10 工业生产者出厂价格指数……………………………………………………………………………………（237）
Producer Price Index for Industrial Products
9-11 工业生产者购进价格指数……………………………………………………………………………………（238）
Purchasing Price Index for Industrial Producers
9-12 固定资产投资价格指数………………………………………………………………………………………（238）
Price Index for Investment in Fixed Assets
主要统计指标解释…………………………………………………………………………………………………（239）
Explanatory Notes on Main Statistical Indicators

十、人民生活

People's Living Conditions

简要说明
Brief Introduction
10-1 城乡居民家庭人均收支……………………………………………………………………………………（243）
Per Capita Income, Expenditure in Urban and Rural Areas
10-2 家庭平均每人收入、支出及结构(2019 年)………………………………………………………………（244）
Per Capita Income and Expenditure and Structure in Households (2019)
10-3 各市居民家庭人均收支情况(2019 年)……………………………………………………………………（245）
Per Capita Income and Expenditure in Urban and Rural Areas by City (2019)
10-4 城镇居民家庭人口及居住情况……………………………………………………………………………（246）
Population and Living condition of Urban Households
10-5 城镇居民家庭人均收支及结构(2019 年)…………………………………………………………………（247）
Per Capita Income, Expenditure and Structure in Urban Areas (2019)
10-6 城镇居民家庭人均购买生活消费品及服务现金支出(2019 年)…………………………………………（249）
Per Capita Cash Expenditure of Urban Households to Purchase Living Goods and Services (2019)
10-7 城镇居民家庭平均每人购买食品数量(2019 年)…………………………………………………………（250）
Food Consumption Per Person of Urban Households (2019)
10-8 城镇居民家庭平均每百户主要消费品年末拥有量(2019 年)……………………………………………（251）
Main Consumer Goods Owned Per 100 Urban Households in the year end (2019)
10-9 各市城镇居民家庭人均全年可支配收入情况(2019 年)…………………………………………………（252）
Per Capita Annual Disposable Income of Urban Households by City (2019)

10-10 各市城镇居民家庭消费支出情况(2019 年)…… (253)
Per Capita Consumption Expenditure of Urban Households by City (2019)
10-11 各市按收入等级分的城镇居民家庭人均全年消费支出(2019 年)…… (254)
Per Capita Annual Consumption Expenditure of Urban Households by Level of Income By City (2019)
10-12 各市城镇居民家庭平均每人主要食品消费量(2019 年)…… (255)
Per Capita Consumption of Major Food of Urban Households by City (2019)
10-13 按收入分组的农民家庭人口，劳动力及居住状况(2019 年)…… (256)
Status of the Peasant Family Population, Labor Force and Housing Conditions by Income Level (2019)
10-14 按收入分组的农民家庭人均总收支及结构(2019 年)…… (258)
Per Capita Total Income and Expenditure in Rural Households by Level of Income (2019)
10-15 按收入分组的农民家庭人均可支配收入及消费性支出(2019 年)…… (260)
Per Capita Disposable Income and Consumption Expenditure of Rural Households by Income Level (2019)
10-16 按收入分组的农民家庭人均现金收入及支出(2019 年)…… (261)
Per Capita Cash Income and Expenditure of Rural Households by Income Level (2019)
10-17 按收入分组的农民家庭主要食品消费量(2019 年)…… (262)
Consumption of Major Food in Rural Households by Income Level (2019)
10-18 按收入分组的农民家庭平均每百户主要耐用消费品及生产性固定资产年末拥有量(2019 年)…… (263)
Main Durable Goods and Productive Fixed Assets Owned Per hundred Rural Households at Year-end by Income Level (2019)
10-19 各市农村居民家庭人均全年可支配收入按收入来源分组情况(2019 年)…… (265)
Per Capita Annual Disposable Income of Rural Household by Source and City (2019)
10-20 各市农村居民家庭人均全年可支配收入分组情况(2019 年…… (266)
Per Capita Annual Disposable Income of Rural Household by City (2019)
10-21 各市农村居民家庭平均每人生活消费总支出(2019 年)…… (267)
Per Capita Consumption Expenditure of Rural Households by City (2019)
10-22 各市农村居民家庭平均每人生活消费现金支出(2019 年)…… (268)
Per Capita Cash Consumption Expenditure of Rural Households by City (2019)
10-23 各市农村居民家庭平均每人主要食品消费量(2019 年)…… (269)
Per Capita Consumption of Major Food of Rural Households by City (2019)
10-24 各市农村居民家庭住房情况(2019 年)…… (270)
Housing Conditions of Rural Households by City (2019)
主要统计指标解释 …… (271)
Explanatory Notes on Main Statistical Indicators

十一、城市概况

General Survey of Cities

简要说明
Brief Introduction
11-1 城市社会经济主要指标 …… (275)
Major Social and Economic Indicators of Cities

11-2 省辖市市区社会经济主要指标(2019 年) …… (276)
Major Social and Economic Indicators of Districts in Cities Directly Under the Province (2019)

11-3 城市建设基本情况 …… (278)
Basic Statistics on City Construction

11-4 城市市政公用设施水平情况(2019 年) …… (279)
Statistics on Level of Public Facilities by City (2019)

11-5 城市供、排水情况(2019 年) …… (281)
Basic Statistics on Tap Water Supply and Drainage in Cities (2019)

11-6 城市天然气、石油液化气供应情况(2019 年) …… (282)
Basic Statistics on Supply of Natural Gas and Liquefied Gas in Cities (2019)

11-7 城市道路、园林和绿化情况(2019 年) …… (283)
Basic Statistics on Road, Botanical Garden and Green Coverage Area in Cities (2019)

11-8 城市市容环境卫生情况(2019 年) …… (284)
Basic Statistics on Urban Sanitation in Cities (2019)

主要统计指标解释 …… (285)
Explanatory Notes on Main Statistical Indicators

十二、农业
Agriculture

简要说明
Brief Introduction

12-1 农林牧渔业总产值 …… (293)
Gross Output Value of Agriculture, Forestry, Animal Husbandry and Fishery

12-2 农林牧渔业总产值指数(上年=100) …… (294)
Gross Output Value and Related Indices of Agriculture, Forestry, Animal Husbandry and Fishery (Preceding year=100)

12-3 农林牧渔业增加值 …… (295)
Value-Added of Agriculture, Forestry, Animal Husbandry and Fishery

12-4 农林牧渔业增加值指数(上年=100) …… (296)
Value-Added Related Indices of Agriculture, Forestry, Animal Husbandry and Fishery (Preceding year=100)

12-5 河南省十大优势特色农业产值 …… (297)
Output Value of Ten Dominant Characteristic Agriculture in Henan Province

12-6 农业生产条件 …… (298)
Conditions of Agriculture

12-7 各市耕地面积 …… (299)
Arable Land Area by City

12-8 各市农业机械和农产品加工机械年末拥有量(2019 年) …… (300)
Number of Agricultural Machinery and Machinery for Processing Farm Products at Year-end by City (2019)

12-9 各市农田水利情况 …… (302)
Condition of Irrigation and Conservancy Project by City

12-10 各市农用物资消耗情况(2019 年)…… (303)
Consumption of Agricultural Materials by City (2019)
12-11 水库、灌区和除涝治水情况 …… (304)
Reservoirs，Irrigation, Flood Prevention, Water and Soil Conservation
12-12 各市水库和除涝治水情况(2019 年)…… (304)
Reservoirs, Flood Prevention, Water and Soil Conservation by City (2019)
12-13 农业生产情况 …… (305)
Agriculture Production
12-14 农作物播种面积 …… (306)
Total Sown Areas of Farm Crops
12-15 主要农产品产量 …… (308)
Output of Major Farm Products
12-16 蔬菜瓜果播种面积 …… (310)
Total Sown Areas of Vegetables and Fruits
12-17 蔬菜及食用菌、瓜果产量 …… (312)
Output of Vegetables, Edible Fungis and Fruits
12-18 各市茶园、果园面积 …… (314)
Area of Tea Garden and Orchard
12-19 茶叶、园林水果及食用坚果产量 …… (315)
Output of Tea, Garden Fruit and Edible Nuts
12-20 各市林业生产情况(2019 年)…… (316)
Conditions of Forestry Production by City (2019)
12-21 牧渔业产量 …… (318)
Output of Animal Husbandry and Fishery
12-22 畜禽产品年末存栏数量及产量 …… (319)
Number of Livestock and Output of Livestock Products at Year-end
12-23 各市牲畜饲养情况(2019 年底)…… (320)
Number of Livestock by City (End of 2019)
12-24 各市畜产品产量(2019 年)…… (321)
Output of Livestock Products by City (2019)
主要统计指标解释 …… (322)
Explanatory Notes on Main Statistical Indicators

十三、工业
Industry

简要说明
Brief Introduction
13-1 各种分组的规模以上工业增加值指数 …… (331)
Indices of Value-added of Industrial Enterprises above Designated Size
13-2 规模以上工业企业主要指标(2019 年)…… (332)
Main Indicators of Industrial Enterprises above Designated Size by Sector (2019)

13-3 规模以上国有控股工业企业主要指标(2019 年)…………………………………………………………………… (334)
Main Indicators of State-holding Industrial Enterprises above Designated Size (2019)
13-4 规模以上公有制工业企业主要指标(2019 年)…………………………………………………………………… (336)
Main Indicators of Public-owned Industrial Enterprises above Designated Size (2019)
13-5 分行业规模以上私营工业企业主要指标(2019 年)……………………………………………………………… (338)
Main Indicators of Private Industrial Enterprises above Designated Size (2019)
13-6 规模以上工业主要产业单位数及增加值(2019 年)……………………………………………………………… (340)
Main indicators of Industrial Enterprises above Designated Size (2019)
13-7 规模以上能源原材料工业增加值结构 ……………………………………………………………………… (341)
Struction of Added value on Raw Energy Material Industries Above Designated Size
13-8 各市规模以上工业企业主要财务指标(2019 年)………………………………………………………………… (342)
Main Financial Indicators of Industrial Enterprises above Designated Size by City (2019)
13-9 各市规模以上国有控股工业企业主要财务指标(2019 年)…………………………………………………… (344)
Main Financial Indicators of State-holding Industrial Enterprises above Designated Size by City (2019)
13-10 各市规模以上公有制工业企业主要财务指标(2019 年)……………………………………………………… (346)
Main Financial Indicators of Public-owned Industrial Enterprises above Designated Size by City (2019)
13-11 各市规模以上私营工业企业主要财务指标(2019 年)………………………………………………………… (347)
Main Financial Indicators of Private Industrial Enterprises above Designated Size by City (2019)
13-12 分行业规模以上工业企业主要经济效益指标(2019 年)……………………………………………………… (348)
Main Economic Efficiency Indicators of Industrial Enterprises above Designated Size by Sector (2019)
13-13 分行业规模以上国有控股工业企业主要经济效益指标(2019 年)…………………………………………… (350)
Main Economic Efficiency Indicators of State-holding Industrial Enterprises above Designated Size by Sector (2019)
13-14 分行业规模以上公有制工业企业主要经济效益指标(2019 年)……………………………………………… (351)
Main Economic Efficiency Indicators of Public-owned Industrial Enterprises above Designated Size by Sector (2019)
13-15 分行业规模以上私营工业企业主要经济效益指标(2019 年)………………………………………………… (352)
Main Economic Efficiency Indicators of Private Industrial Enterprises above Designated Size by Sector (2019)
13-16 各市规模以上工业企业主要经济效益指标(2019 年)………………………………………………………… (353)
Main Economic Efficiency Indicators of Industrial Enterprises above Designated Size by City (2019)
13-17 各市规模以上国有控股工业企业主要经济效益指标(2019 年)……………………………………………… (354)
Main Economic Efficiency Indicators of State-holding Industrial Enterprises above Designated Size by City (2019)
13-18 各市规模以上公有制工业企业主要经济效益指标(2019 年)………………………………………………… (355)
Main Economic Efficiency Indicators of Public-owned Industrial Enterprises above Designated Size by City (2019)
13-19 各市规模以上私营工业企业主要经济效益指标(2019 年)…………………………………………………… (356)
Main Economic Efficiency Indicators of Private Industrial Enterprises above Designated Size by City (2019)
13-20 各市主要工业产品产量(2019 年)……………………………………………………………………………… (357)
Output of Major Industrial Products by City (2019)

主要统计指标解释 …………………………………………………………………………… (361)
Explanatory Notes on Main Statistical Indicators

十四、建筑业
Construction

简要说明
Brief Introduction
14-1 建筑业企业主要统计指标 ………………………………………………………………… (371)
Main Indicators on Construction Enterprises
14-2 建筑业企业主要经济指标 ………………………………………………………………… (372)
Main Economic Indicators on Construction Enterprises
14-3 建筑业企业房屋建筑竣工面积及竣工价值(2019 年)……………………………………… (373)
Floor space and Value of Building completed of Construction Enterprises (2019)
14-4 建筑业企业生产情况(2019 年)…………………………………………………………… (374)
Main Indicators on Construction Enterprises (2019)
14-5 建筑业企业主要财务指标(2019 年)……………………………………………………… (376)
Main Financial Indicators on Construction Enterprises by Registration Status (2019)
14-6 各市建筑业企业总产值 …………………………………………………………………… (378)
Total Output Value of Construction by City
14-7 各市建筑业企业利税总额 ………………………………………………………………… (379)
Total Pre-Tax Profits of Construction Enterprises by City
14-8 各市建筑业企业利润总额 ………………………………………………………………… (379)
Total Profits of Construction Enterprises by City
14-9 各市建筑业企业主要指标(2019 年)……………………………………………………… (380)
Main Indicators of Construction Enterprises by City (2019)
14-10 各市建筑业企业个数(2019 年)…………………………………………………………… (382)
Number of Construction Enterprises by City (2019)
14-11 各市建筑业企业总产值(2019 年)………………………………………………………… (384)
Total Output Value of Construction Enterprises by City (2019)
14-12 各市建筑业企业资产总计(2019 年)……………………………………………………… (386)
Total Assets of Construction Enterprises by City (2019)
14-13 各市建筑业企业负债合计(2019 年)……………………………………………………… (388)
Total Liabilities of Construction Enterprises by City (2019)
14-14 各市建筑业企业主营业务收入(2019 年)………………………………………………… (390)
Revenue from Principal Business of Construction Enterprises by City (2019)
14-15 各市建筑业企业利润总额(2019 年)……………………………………………………… (392)
Total Profits of Construction Enterprises by City (2019)
14-16 各市建筑业企业利税总额(2019 年)……………………………………………………… (394)
Total Pre-tax Profits of Construction Enterprises by City (2019)
主要统计指标解释 …………………………………………………………………………… (396)
Explanatory Notes on Main Statistical Indicators

十五、房地产业

Real Estate

简要说明

Brief Introduction

15-1 房地产开发企业主要指标 …… (401)

Main Indicators of Enterprises for Real Estate Development

15-2 房地产开发企业(单位)个数和从业人员数 …… (402)

Number of Employed Persons and Enterprises for Real Estate Development

15-3 各市房地产开发企业(单位)个数(2019 年) …… (403)

Number of Enterprises for Real Estate Development by City (2019)

15-4 各市房地产开发企业从业人员(2019 年) …… (404)

Number of Employed Persons in Enterprises for Real Estate Development (2019)

15-5 房地产开发投资额 …… (405)

Completed Investment in Real Estate Development

15-6 房地产开发企业(单位)建设房屋建筑面积和造价 …… (406)

Floor Space and Cost of Buildings Developed by Enterprises for Real Estate Development

15-7 房地产开发企业开发情况 …… (407)

Operating Statistics of Enterprises for Real Estate Development

15-8 房地产开发企业施工、销售和待售情况(2019 年) …… (408)

Situation of Construction, Sale and for Sale of Real Estate Enterprises (2019)

15-9 各市房地产开发投资情况(2019 年) …… (410)

Development and Investment Completed for Real Estate by City (2019)

15-10 各市房地产开发企业实际到位资金(2019 年) …… (411)

Actual Funds in Place of Enterprises for Real Estate Development (2019)

15-11 各市房地产开发施工房屋面积(2019 年) …… (412)

Floor Space of Buildings under Construction by City (2019)

15-12 各市房地产开发竣工房屋面积(2019 年) …… (413)

Floor Space of Buildings Completed by City (2019)

15-13 各市房地产开发竣工房屋价值(2019 年) …… (414)

Value of Buildings Completed by City (2019)

15-14 房地产开发企业房屋销售情况 …… (415)

Selling of Enterprises for Real Estate Development

15-15 各市房地产开发商品房屋销售面积(2019 年) …… (416)

Floor Space of Commercialized Buildings Sold by City (2019)

15-16 各市房地产开发商品房屋销售额(2019 年) …… (417)

Total Sales of Commercialized Buildings Commercial Houses by City (2019)

15-17 房地产开发企业(单位)财务状况 …… (418)

Financial Conditions of Enterprises for Real Estate Development

15-18 房地产开发企业(单位)经营状况 …… (419)

Operating Statistics on Enterprises for Real Estate Development

主要统计指标解释 …… (420)

Explanatory Notes on Main Statistical Indicators

十六、批发和零售业、住宿和餐饮业

Wholesale and Retail Sale trades, Hotels and Catering Services

简要说明

Brief Introduction

16-1 社会消费品零售总额 …… (427)

Total Retail Sale of Consumer Goods

16-2 各市社会消费品零售总额(2019 年)…… (428)

Total Retail Sale of Consumer Goods by City (2019)

16-3 限额以上批发和零售业法人基本情况(2019 年)…… (429)

Basic Conditions of Corporation in Wholesale and Retail Trades above Designated Size (2019)

16-4 限额以上住宿和餐饮业法人基本情况(2019 年)…… (431)

Basic Conditions of Corporation of Hotels and Catering Services above Designated Size (2019)

16-5 各市批发和零售、住宿和餐饮业法人企业单位数(2019 年)…… (433)

Number of Corporations in Wholesale and Retail Sale, Hotels and Catering Services by City (2019)

16-6 各市批发和零售、住宿和餐饮业法人企业从业人员(2019 年)…… (434)

Number of Persons Employed in Wholesale and Retail Sale, Hotels and Catering Services by City (2019)

16-7 各市批发和零售、住宿和餐饮业限额以上企业(单位)单位数(2019 年)…… (435)

Number of Corporation in Wholesale and Retail Sale, Hotels and Catering Services Above Designated Size by City (2019)

16-8 各市批发和零售、住宿和餐饮业限上企业(单位)从业人员(2019 年)…… (437)

Number of Persons Employed in Wholesale and Retail Sale, Hotels and Catering Services Above Designated Size by City (2019)

16-9 限额以上批发和零售企业(单位)商品分类销售总额(2019 年)…… (439)

Total Sales of Enterprises above Designated Size of Wholesale and Retail Trade by Category of Main Commodities (2019)

16-10 各市限额以上批发和零售企业(单位)商品分类批发总额(2019 年)…… (440)

Total Wholesale Value of Enterprises above Designated Size of Wholesales and Retail Trades by City and Sort (2019)

16-11 各市限额以上批发和零售企业(单位)商品分类零售总额(2019 年)…… (441)

Retail Trades Value of Enterprises above Designated Size in Wholesales and Retail Trades by City and Sort (2019)

16-12 限额以上批发和零售企业(单位)商品购销存总额(2019 年)…… (442)

Total Purchases, Sales and Inventory above Designated Size of Wholesale and Retail Trades (2019)

16-13 各市限额以上批发和零售企业(单位)商品购、销、存总额(2019 年)…… (444)

Total Purchases, Sales and Inventory of Enterprises above Designated Size of Wholesale and Retail Trades by City (2019)

16-14 限额以上住宿和餐饮业企业(单位)经营情况(2019 年)…… (445)

Management of Enterprises above Designated Size of Star-rated Hotels and Catering Services (2019)

16-15 各市限额以上住宿和餐饮企业(单位)经营情况(2019 年)…… (447)

Operation Conditions of Enterprises above Designated Size of Star-rated Hotels and Catering Services by City (2019)

16-16 各市限额以上住宿企业(单位)经营情况(2019 年)…………………………………………………………… (448)
Operation Conditions of Star-rated Hotels above Designated Sized by City (2019)
16-17 各市限额以上餐饮企业(单位)经营情况(2019 年)…………………………………………………………… (449)
Operation Conditions of Catering Services above Designated Size by City (2019)
16-18 限额以上批发和零售、住宿和餐饮法人企业主要财务指标(2019 年)……………………………………… (450)
Main Financial Indicators of Enterprises in Wholesale and Retail Trades, Hotels and Catering Services above Designated Size (2019)
16-19 各市限额以上批发和零售法人企业主要财务指标(2019 年)…………………………………………………… (451)
Main Financial Indicators of Enterprises in Wholesale and Retail Trades above Designated Size by City (2019)
16-20 各市限额以上住宿和餐饮法人企业主要财务指标(2019 年)…………………………………………………… (453)
Main Economic Indicators of Enterprises in Hotels and Catering Services above Designated Size by City (2019)
16-21 各种分组的连锁企业单位数(2019 年)………………………………………………………………………… (455)
Number of Chain Enterprise By variety of Group (2019)
16-22 各种分组的连锁企业基本情况(2019 年)……………………………………………………………………… (456)
Basic Conditions of Chain Enterprise By variety of Group (2019)
16-23 连锁企业商品购进和配送情况(2019 年)……………………………………………………………………… (457)
Conditions of Purchase and Delivery of Chain Enterprise (2019)
16-24 各种分组的住宿餐饮业连锁企业主要指标(2019 年)………………………………………………………… (458)
Main Indicators of Chain Hotels and Catering Services Enterprise By variety of Group (2019)
16-25 亿元以上商品交易市场情况 ……………………………………………………………………………………… (459)
Statistics on Commodity Exchange Market of Turnover above 100 million yuan
16-26 各市亿元以上商品交易市场情况 ………………………………………………………………………………… (460)
Statistics on Commodity Exchange Market of Turnover above 100 million yuan by City
16-27 按行业分企业信息化及电子商务情况（2019） ………………………………………………………………… (461)
Informationization and E-commerce Situation by Sector (2019)
16-28 按地区分企业信息化及电子商务情况(2019） …………………………………………………………………… (463)
Informationization and E-commerce Situation by Region (2019)
主要统计指标解释 ……………………………………………………………………………………………………… (464)
Explanatory Notes on Main Statistical Indicators

十七、金融业
Financial Intermediation

简要说明
Brief Introduction
17-1 金融机构和保险业主要指标 ……………………………………………………………………………………… (471)
Main Indicators of Financial Institutions and Insurance
17-2 金融机构人民币存贷款情况 ……………………………………………………………………………………… (472)
Deposits and Loans of Financial Institutions

17-3 各类银行人民币存贷款情况(2018 年)…… (472)
Deposits and Loans of Financial Institutions (2018)
17-4 各市金融机构贷款年底余额 …… (473)
Loans of Financial Institutions by City
17-5 个人贷款总额 …… (473)
Total Amount of Personal Loans
17-6 各市证券交易额 …… (474)
Stock Turnover by City
17-7 各市国债发行情况 …… (475)
Issuance of National Debt by City
17-8 证券市场情况 …… (476)
Basic Statistics on Securities Market
17-9 河南 A 股股票发行情况(1993-2018 年)…… (477)
Issuance of A Shares (1993-2018)
17-10 保险业务情况 …… (479)
Main Indicators of Insurance Business
17-11 各市国内保险业务主要指标(2019 年)…… (480)
Main Indicators of Domestic Insurance Business by City (2019)
主要统计指标解释 …… (481)
Explanatory Notes on Main Statistical Indicators

十八、其他服务业

Other Services

简要说明
Brief Introduction
18-1 规模以上服务业企业主要财务指标(2019 年)…… (485)
Main indictors of Enterprises Above Designated size in Service Industry (2019)
18-2 各市规模以上服务业企业单位数(2019 年)…… (486)
Number of Enterprises Above Designated size in Service Industry by Sector and City (2019)
18-3 各市规模以上服务业企业营业收入(2019 年)…… (488)
Operating income of Everage Employed Persons of Enterprises Above Designated size in Service Industry by Sector and City (2019)
18-4 各市规模以上服务业企业营业利润(2019 年)…… (490)
Profit of Enterprises Above Designated size in Service Industry by Sector and City (2019)
18-5 各市规模以上服务业企业应付职工薪酬(2019 年)…… (492)
Wages Payable of Enterprises Above Designated size in Service Industry by Sector and City (2019)
18-6 各市规模以上服务业企业平均从业人员人数(2019 年)…… (494)
Number of Everage Employed Persons of Enterprises Above Designated size in Service Industry by Sector and City (2019)

十九、运输和邮电

Transport, Postal and Telecommunication Services

简要说明

Brief Introduction

19-1 交通运输基本情况 …… (501)

Basic Conditions of Transport

19-2 旅客和货物运输量 …… (502)

Passenger and Freight Traffic

19-3 旅客和货物周转量 …… (503)

Passenger-Kilometers and Freight Ton-Kilometers

19-4 铁路、公路、内河通车通航里程(年底数) …… (504)

Length of Railways, Highways and Navigable Inland Waterways (Year-end)

19-5 交通运输工具拥有量(年底数) …… (504)

Possession of Means of Transportation (Year-end)

19-6 各市公路线路里程(2019 年底)…… (505)

Length of Highways by City (End of 2019)

19-7 各种民用车辆拥有量(2019 年底)…… (507)

Possession of Civil Vehicles (End of 2019)

19-8 各市民用车辆拥有量(2019 年底)…… (508)

Possession of Civil Vehicles by City (End of 2019)

19-9 各市私人车辆拥有量(2019 年底)…… (509)

Possession of Private Vehicles by City (End of 2019)

19-10 客货运量及周转量 …… (510)

Passenger and Freight Traffic, Turnover Volume

19-11 各市公路客货运输量(2019 年)…… (511)

Passenger and Freight Traffic of Highway by City (2019)

19-12 铁路主要站客货发送量(2019 年)…… (512)

Number of Passengers and Volume of Freight Dispatched from Principal Railway Stations (2019)

19-13 铁路分货类运输量 …… (513)

Freight Traffic of Railway by Category

19-14 铁路运输主要技术经济指标 …… (514)

Major Economic and Technical Indicators of Railway Transport

19-15 民航基本情况 …… (515)

Main Indicators of Civil Aviation

19-16 邮政行业基本情况及邮政水平(年底数) …… (515)

Basic Conditions and Level of Post Services (Year-end)

19-17 邮电通信行业基本情况 …… (516)

Basic Conditions of Postal and Telecommunication Services Level of Telecommunication Service

19-18 通信行业基本情况及通信水平(年底数) …… (518)

Basic Conditions and s (Year-end)

19-19 各市邮政网和业务量(2019 年)…… (519)

Network and Business Volume of Post by City (2019)

19-20 各市电信网和业务量(2019 年)…… (520)
Network of Telecommunications and Business Volume by City (2019)
主要统计指标解释 …… (522)
Explanatory Notes on Main Statistical Indicators

二十、资源和环境
Resources and Environment

简要说明
Brief Introduction
20-1 生态环境保护情况 …… (529)
Basic Conditions of Environmental Protection
20-2 自然资源 …… (529)
Natural Resources
20-3 水资源情况 …… (530)
Water Resources
20-4 废水中主要污染物排放情况 …… (530)
Main Pollutant Emission in Waste Water
20-5 各市年平均气温和平均年降水量(2019 年)…… (531)
Annual Average Temperature and Average Annual Precipitation by City (2019)
20-6 大气环境情况 …… (532)
Basic Conditions of Atmosphere Environment
20-7 固体废物的产生及利用情况 …… (532)
Production and Utilization of Industrial Solid Wastes
20-8 农村环境基本情况 …… (533)
Basic Condition of Rural Enviroment
20-9 自然灾害情况 …… (533)
Conditions of Natural Disasters
20-10 各市农村改厕情况(2019 年)…… (534)
Condition of Rural Compost toilets by City (2019)
20-11 各市农村可再生能源利用情况(2019 年)…… (535)
Condition of Rural Renewable energy utilization by City (2019)
20-12 工业重点调查单位分行业工业废水排放及处理利用情况(2017 年)…… (536)
Industrial waste water discharge, treatment and utilization in Key research Industrial unit by Sector (2017)
20-13 工业重点调查单位分行业工业废气排放及处理情况(2017 年)…… (537)
Industrial Wastes gas discharge and treatment and utilization in Key research Industrial unit by Sector (2017)
20-14 工业重点调查单位分行业工业固体废物产生及处理利用情况(2017 年)…… (538)
Industrial Solid Wastes Produced discharge and treatment and utilization in Key research Industrial unit by Sector (2017)
主要统计指标解释 …… (539)
Explanatory Notes on Main Statistical Indicators

二十一、科学技术

Science and Technology

简要说明

Brief Introduction

21-1 研究与试验发展(R&D)主要指标 ········· (547)

Basic Statistics on R&D Activities

21-2 研究与试验发展(R&D)活动概况 ········· (548)

Basic Statistics on R&D Activities

21-3 研究与试验发展(R&D)活动概况(2019 年) ········· (549)

Basic Statistics on R&D Activities (2019)

21-4 研究与试验发展(R&D)经费支出情况(2019 年) ········· (551)

Statistics on Appropriation Expenditure for R&D (2019)

21-5 研究与试验发展(R&D)活动机构情况(2019 年) ········· (552)

Basic Statistics on Institutions Having R&D Activities (2019)

21-6 研究与试验发展(R&D)人员情况(2019 年) ········· (553)

Basic Statistics on Personnel Engaged in R&D Activities (2019)

21-7 研究与试验发展(R&D)产出情况(2019 年) ········· (554)

Statistics on Achievements for R&D (2019)

21-8 规模以上工业企业研究与试验发展(R&D)人员活动情况(2019 年) ········· (556)

Basic Statistics on R&D Activities in Enterprises above Designated Size (2019)

21-9 规模以上工业企业研究与试验发展(R&D)经费支出活动情况(2019 年) ········· (558)

Basic Statistics on R&D Activities in Enterprises above Designated Size (2019)

21-10 规模以上工业企业研究与试验发展(R&D)活动情况(2019 年) ········· (560)

Basic Statistics on R&D Activities in Enterprises above Designated Size (2019)

21-11 研究与试验发展(R&D)项目(课题)情况(2019 年) ········· (561)

Statistics on R&D Projects (Topics) (2019)

21-12 各市研究与试验发展(R&D)人员情况(2019 年) ········· (562)

Basic Statistics on Personnel Engaged in R&D Activities by City (2019)

21-13 各市研究与试验发展(R&D)经费支出情况(2019 年) ········· (563)

Statistics on Appropriation Expenditure for R&D by City (2019)

21-14 各市研究与试验发展(R&D)产出情况(2019 年) ········· (564)

Statistics on Achievements for R&D by City (2019)

21-15 各市规模以上工业企业研究与试验发展(R&D)活动情况(2019 年) ········· (566)

Basic Statistics on R&D Activities in Enterprises above Designated Size by City (2019)

21-16 大中型工业企业研究与试验发展(R&D)活动情况 ········· (571)

Basic Statistics on R&D Activities in Large and Medium-Sized Industrial Enterprises

21-17 三种专利申请受理量及授权量 ········· (571)

Three Types of Patent Application Accepted and Granted

21-18 规模(限额)以上企业创新活动情况 ········· (572)

Innovative Activities in Enterprises above Designated size

21-19 各市规模(限额)以上企业创新活动情况(2019 年) ········· (574)

Innovative Activities in Enterprises above Designated size by City (2019)

21-20 技术市场成交合同情况(2019 年)…… (575)
Statistics on Transaction of Technology (2019)
21-21 各市技术市场成交合同情况 …… (576)
Statistics on Transaction of Technology by City
21-22 软科学基本情况 …… (577)
Statistics on Soft science
21-23 产品质量监督抽查情况(2019 年)…… (577)
Results of Sampling Check under State Supervision on the Quality of Products (2019)
21-24 国家和地方标准、计量基本情况 …… (578)
National and local standards, measuring basic situation
21-25 测绘行业单位、人员及测绘成果提供情况 …… (579)
Statistics on Unit,Persons Engaged and Output in Certificated Units in Surveying and Mapping Industry
21-26 气象部门基本情况 …… (580)
Basic Statistics on Meteorological Department
21-27 各市地震台(网)基本情况(2019 年)…… (581)
Basic Statistics on Earthquake Station (Net) by City (2019)
主要统计指标解释 …… (582)
Explanatory Notes on Main Statistical Indicators

二十二、教育
Education

简要说明
Brief Introduction
22-1 各级各类学校数 …… (587)
Number of Schools by Level and Type
22-2 各级各类学校专任教师数 …… (588)
Number of Full-time Teachers by Level and Type of school
22-3 各级各类学校在校学生数 …… (589)
Student Enrollment by Level and Type of school
22-4 各级各类学校招生数 …… (590)
New Student Enrollment by Level and Type of school
22-5 各级各类学校毕业生数 …… (591)
Graduates by Level and Type of school
22-6 各级各类学校、教职工和专任教师情况(2019 年)…… (592)
Basic Statistics on Schools, Teachers and Staff and Full-time Teachers (2019)
22-7 各级各类学校专任教师分学历的人数与构成(2019 年)…… (593)
Number and Composition of Full-time Teachers in Schools by Educational Level (2019)
22-8 各级各类学历教育学生情况(2019 年)…… (594)
Basic Statistics on Students by Level and Type of Education (2019)
22-9 各级教育入学率及升学率情况 …… (595)
Enrolment Ratio and Promotion Rate by Levels

22-10 成人学校基本情况(2019 年)…………………………………………………………………… (596)
Basic Statistics on Adult Schools (2019)

22-11 分学科研究生情况(2019 年)…………………………………………………………………… (597)
Number of Postgraduate Students by Academic Field (2019)

22-12 分学科本科学生情况(2019 年)…………………………………………………………………… (598)
Number of Undergraduate Students by Academic Field (2019)

22-13 分学科专科学生情况(2019 年)…………………………………………………………………… (599)
Number of Students in Junior College by Field (2019)

22-14 中等职业学校分学科学生情况(2019 年)…………………………………………………………… (600)
Number of Students in Secondary Vocational Schools by Field (2019)

22-15 网络教育学生情况(2019 年)…………………………………………………………………… (601)
Statistics on Web-based Education Students (2019)

22-16 网络教育学生情况(2019 年)…………………………………………………………………… (601)
Statistics on Web-based Education Students (2019)

22-17 进城务工子女和农村留守儿童在校情况(2019 年)…………………………………………………… (602)
Statistics on Children of Migrant Workers and Rural Left-behind Children in Schools (2019)

22-18 普通高等学校办学条件 …………………………………………………………………………… (602)
Running Conditions of Regular Institutions of Higher Education

22-19 各市普通高等学校情况(2019 年)…………………………………………………………………… (603)
Basic Statistics on Regular Institutions of Higher Education by City (2019)

22-20 各市普通高中情况(2019 年)…………………………………………………………………… (605)
Statistics on Regular Senior Secondary Schools by City (2019)

22-21 各市中等职业学校情况(2019 年)…………………………………………………………………… (606)
Statistics on Secondary Vocational Schools by City (2019)

22-22 各市普通初中教育情况(2019 年)…………………………………………………………………… (607)
Statistics on Regular Junior Secondary Schools by City (2019)

22-23 各市普通小学教育情况(2019 年)…………………………………………………………………… (609)
Statistics on Regular Junior Secondary Schools by City (2019)

22-24 各市特殊教育情况(2019 年)…………………………………………………………………… (611)
Statistics on Special Education by City (2019)

22-25 各市技工学校基本情况(2019 年)…………………………………………………………………… (612)
Basic Statistics on Technical Schools by City (2019)

22-26 各市成人高等教育基本情况(2019 年)……………………………………………………………… (613)
Basic Statistics on Adult Education Schools by City (2019)

22-27 各市学前教育情况(2019 年)…………………………………………………………………… (614)
Statistics on Pre-school Education by City (2019)

22-28 各市各级普通学校生师比(2019 年)……………………………………………………………… (615)
Student-Teacher Ratio by Level of Regular Schools by City (2019)

22-29 各市每十万人口各级学校平均在校生数(2019 年)…………………………………………………… (616)
Number of Average Students Enrollment by Level of school per 10 0000 Population by City (2019)

22-30 各市教育经费情况(2019 年)…………………………………………………………………… (617)
Basic Statistics on Educational Funds by City (2019)

22-31 外国留学生情况(2019 年)…… (618)
Basic condition of International student (2019)
主要统计指标解释 …… (619)
Explanatory Notes on Main Statistical Indicators

二十三、卫生和社会工作
Public Health and Social Work

简要说明
Brief Introduction
23-1 卫生事业基本情况 …… (625)
Basic Statistics on Public Health
23-2 卫生事业发展情况 …… (626)
Basic Statistics on Public Health Development
23-3 卫生机构、床位、人员数(2019 年)…… (627)
Number of Health Institutions, Beds and Persons (2019)
23-4 卫生机构各类人员 …… (628)
Employed Persons In Health Institutions by Types of Occupation
23-5 卫生总费用 …… (628)
Total Health Expenditure
23-6 卫生部门医院住院病人前十位疾病构成(ICD-10)(2019 年) …… (629)
Percentage of 10 Main Diseases of Inpatients in Hospitals of Health Sector (ICD-10) (2019)
23-7 部分市、县前十位主要疾病死亡率(2019 年)…… (630)
Death Rate of Ten Major Diseases in Partial Cities and Counties (2019)
23-8 甲乙类法定报告传染病发病及死亡情况(2019 年)…… (631)
Incidence and Death from Class A and B Infectious Diseases (2019)
23-9 防病工作情况 …… (631)
Basic Condition of Disease Prevention and Cure
23-10 各市医疗卫生机构情况(2019 年)…… (632)
Conditions of Health Institutions by City (2019)
23-11 各市医疗卫生机构床位情况(2019 年)…… (633)
Number of Beds in Health Institutions by City (2019)
23-12 各市卫生人员情况(2019 年)…… (634)
Employed Persons in Health Care Institutions by City (2019)
23-13 农村乡镇卫生院医疗服务情况 …… (635)
Situations of Medical Services in Township Health Centers
23-14 妇女儿童卫生保健状况 …… (636)
Basic Statistics on Health Care of Women and Children
23-15 社会服务机构基本情况(2019 年)…… (637)
Statistics on Social Service Institutions (2019)
23-16 各市孤儿和家庭收养基本情况(2019 年)…… (638)
Statistics on Orphans and Children Adopted by Families by City (2019)

23-17 各市社会救助情况(2019 年)…………………………………………………………………………………………（639）
Statistics on Social Relief by City (2019)
23-18 各市医疗救助基本情况(2019 年)……………………………………………………………………………………（640）
Basic Statistics on Medical Aid by City (2019)
23-19 各市社区服务基本情况(2019 年)……………………………………………………………………………………（641）
Statistics on Community Service Facilities by City (2019)
23-20 各市婚姻服务基本情况(2019 年)……………………………………………………………………………………（642）
Statistics on Marriages and Divorces by City (2019)
23-21 残疾人事业基本情况(2019 年)………………………………………………………………………………………（643）
Basic Information of Person with Disabilities (2019)
主要统计指标解释 ……………………………………………………………………………………………………（645）
Explanatory Notes on Main Statistical Indicators

二十四、文化和体育

Culture and Sports

简要说明
Brief Introduction
24-1 文化及相关产业增加值 ………………………………………………………………………………………………（649）
Value-Added of Cultural and Related Industry
24-2 文化及相关产业规模以上企业分类主要指标(2018 年)……………………………………………………………（650）
Main Indicators of Culture and Related Industry above Designated Size by Type (2018)
24-3 文化及相关产业规模以上企业分类主要指标(2019 年)……………………………………………………………（650）
Main Indicators of Culture and Related Industry above Designated Size by Type (2019)
24-4 文化及相关产业规模以上企业主要经济指标(2018 年)……………………………………………………………（651）
Main Economic Indicators of Culture and Related Industry Enterprises above Designated Size (2018)
24-5 文化及相关产业规模以上企业主要经济指标(2019 年)……………………………………………………………（652）
Main Economic Indicators of Culture and Related Industry Enterprises above Designated Size (2019)
24-6 各市文化及相关产业规模以上企业主要指标(2018 年)……………………………………………………………（653）
Main Indicators of Enterprises in Culture and Related Industry above Designated Size by City (2018)
24-7 各市文化及相关产业规模以上企业主要指标(2019 年)……………………………………………………………（654）
Main Indicators of Enterprises in Culture and Related Industry above Designated Size by City (2019)
24-8 各市文化及相关产业规模以上文化制造业企业主要指标(2018 年)…………………………………………………（655）
Main Indicators of Cultural Manufacturing Enterprises above Designated Size by City (2018)
24-9 各市文化及相关产业规模以上文化制造业企业主要指标(2019 年)…………………………………………………（656）
Main Indicators of Cultural Manufacturing Enterprises above Designated Size by City (2019)
24-10 各市文化及相关产业限额以上文化批零业企业主要指标(2018 年)…………………………………………………（657）
Main Indicators of Cultural wholesale and Retail Enterprises above Designated Size by City (2018)
24-11 各市文化及相关产业限额以上文化批零业企业主要指标(2019 年)…………………………………………………（658）
Main Indicators of Cultural wholesale and Retail Enterprises above Designated Size by City (2019)
24-12 各市文化及相关产业规模以上文化服务业企业主要指标(2018 年)…………………………………………………（659）
Main Indicators of Culture Service Enterprises above Designated Size by City (2018)

24-13 各市文化及相关产业规模以上文化服务业企业主要指标(2019 年)…… (660)
Main Indicators of Culture Service Enterprises above Designated Size by City (2019)
24-14 文化文物机构和人员情况(2019 年)…… (661)
Number of Institutions and Employed persons in Cultural Industry (2019)
24-15 艺术表演场馆基本情况(2019 年)…… (662)
Basic Statistics of Arts Performance Places (2019)
24-16 艺术表演团体基本情况(2019 年)…… (663)
Basic Statistics of Arts Performance Troupes (2019)
24-17 娱乐场所基本情况 …… (664)
Basic Statistics on Entertainment
24-18 公共图书馆基本情况(2019 年)…… (665)
Basic Statistics on Libraries (2019)
24-19 分地区公共图书馆基本情况(2019 年)…… (666)
Basic Statistics on Public Libraries by City (2019)
24-20 文物业、博物馆和文物管理机构基本情况 …… (667)
Statistics on Cultural Relics, Museums and Agencies of cultural relics Preservation
24-21 国家综合档案馆基本情况(2019 年底)…… (668)
Basic Statistics on the National comprehensive Archives (End of 2019)
24-22 新闻出版业主要指标 …… (669)
Main Indicators of Press and Publication Industry
24-23 课本出版情况(2019 年)…… (670)
Basic Statistics of Publication of Textbook (2019)
24-24 音像制品及电子出版物情况 …… (670)
Basic Statistics of Audio-video Products and Electronic Publications
24-25 各市出版物发行网点数和从业人数(2019 年)…… (671)
Issuing Institutions and Spots of Publication by City (2019)
24-26 广播电视业基本情况 …… (672)
Basic Statistics on Radio and Television Industry
24-27 广播电视业经营情况 …… (672)
Basic Statistics on Radio and Television Operation
24-28 分市广播电视覆盖率 …… (673)
Coverage Rate of Radio and TV
24-29 运动员人数 …… (674)
Number of Athletes
24-30 体育彩票发行情况 …… (674)
Issue of Sports Lottery Ticket
主要统计指标解释 …… (675)
Explanatory Notes on Main Statistical Indicators

二十五、公共管理、社会保障和社会组织

Public Management, Social Security and Social Organizations

简要说明

Brief Introduction

25-1 公安机关立案的刑事案件情况 …… (679)

Criminal Case of Register in Public Security Organs

25-2 公安机关受理和查处治安案件情况(2019 年)…… (679)

Cases of Offence Against Public Order Handled by Public Security Organs (2019)

25-3 交通事故情况(2019 年)…… (680)

Basic Statistics on Traffic Accidents (2019)

25-4 各市火灾事故情况(2019 年)…… (680)

Basic Statistics on Fires by City (2019)

25-5 人民检察院审查逮捕、审查起诉情况(2019 年)…… (681)

Arrests and Prosecution Approved by People's Procuratorate (2019)

25-6 人民检察院处理申诉案件情况(2019 年)…… (681)

Appeals Handled by People's Procuratorate (2019)

25-7 人民检察院出庭公诉情况(2019 年)…… (682)

Public Prosecutions Appearing in Court by People's Procuratorate (2019)

25-8 人民检察院办理刑事抗诉案件情况(2019 年)…… (682)

Criminal Appeals Handled by People's Procuratorate (2019)

25-9 人民检察院办理民事、行政抗诉案件情况(2019 年)…… (683)

Civil and Administrative Appeals Handled by People's Procuratorate (2019)

25-10 人民检察院办理公益诉讼案件情况(2019 年)…… (683)

Information on Public Interest Litigation Cases Handled by the people's procuratorate (2019)

25-11 人民检察院受理举报、控告和申诉案件情况(2019 年)…… (684)

Case of Reporting, Accusation and Petition Handled by People's Procuratorate (2019)

25-12 人民检察院纠正违法情况 …… (684)

Law-breaking Cases Rectified by People's Procuratorate

25-13 人民检察院检察官基本情况 …… (685)

Basic Statistics on Procurator

25-14 人民法院审理刑事一审案件收结案情况 …… (685)

Basic Statistics on Criminal Case at First Trial by People’s Court

25-15 各市人民法院审理刑事案件罪犯情况(2019 年)…… (686)

Criminal Offenders Heard by Courts by City (2019)

25-16 人民法院审理婚姻家庭、继承一审案件收结案情况(2019 年)…… (687)

First Trial Civil Cases of Marriage, Family Affairs and Inheritance Accepted and Settled by Courts (2019)

25-17 人民法院审理合同纠纷一审案件收结案情况(2019 年)…… (687)

First Trial Cases of Contract Disputes Accepted and Settled by Courts (2019)

25-18 人民法院审理民事一审案件收结案情况(2019 年)…… (688)

First Trial Civil Affairs Cases Accepted and Settled by Courts (2019)

25-19 人民法院审理行政一审案件收结案情况(2019 年)…………(689)
First Trial Administrative Cases Accepted and Settled by Courts (2019)
25-20 全省法官及建立少年法庭情况 …………(689)
Statistics on Judges and Juvenile Courts
25-21 律师、公证和调解工作基本情况 …………(690)
Basic Statistics on Lawyers, Notarization and Mediation
25-22 法律援助工作情况 …………(690)
Statistics on legal aid
25-23 法律服务基本情况(2019 年)…………(691)
Basic Statistics on Legal Services (2019)
25-24 劳动人事仲裁委员会受理及处理案件情况(2019 年)…………(692)
Cases Accepted and Heard by Board of Labor Arbitration (2019)
25-25 工会组织情况 …………(694)
Basic Statistics on Trade Unions
25-26 全省工会组织基本情况 …………(695)
Basic Statistics on Trade Unions
25-27 各市基层工会劳动法律监督工作情况(2019 年)…………(696)
Statistics on Labor Law Supervision Work of Primary Trade Union by City (2019)
25-28 参加各类保险人数 …………(697)
Persons Covered of Insurans
25-29 社会保险基金 …………(698)
Social Insurance Fund
25-30 各市城镇职工参加基本养老保险人数 …………(699)
Number of People Participated in Basic Pension Insurance by City
25-31 各市参加基本医疗保险人数 …………(700)
Number of People Participated in Basic Medical Insurance by City
25-32 各市参加失业保险人数 …………(701)
Number of People Participated in Unemployment Insurance by City
25-33 各市参加工伤保险人数 …………(702)
Number of People Participated in Work Injury Insurance by City
25-34 各市参加生育保险人数 …………(703)
Number of People Participated in Maternity Insurance by City
25-35 安全生产基本情况 …………(704)
Basic Statistics on safetyin production
主要统计指标解释 …………(705)
Explanatory Notes on Main Statistical Indicators

二十六、各县（市、区）主要统计指标

Main Indicators of County（City, municipal districts）

26-1 各县(市、区)人口及就业人员(2019 年)…………(713)
Population and Employed Person by County and District (2019)

26-2 各县(市、区)生产总值和指数(2019 年)…… (718)
Gross Domestic Product and Its indices by County and District (2019)
26-3 各县(市、区)固定资产投资、建筑业及规模以上工业主要指标(2019 年)…… (726)
Main Indicators on Investment in Fixed Assets、Construction and Enterprises above Designated Size Industry by County and District (2019)
26-4 各县(市、区)城镇单位就业人员和工资(2019 年)…… (730)
Number and Wages of Employed Person in Urban Units by County and District (2019)
26-5 各县(市、区)城乡居民收入和社会消费品零售总额(2019 年)…… (734)
Per Capita Net Income of Rural and Urban Residents, Total Retail Sales of Consumer Goods by County and District (2019)
26-6 各县(市)农业生产条件(2019 年)…… (738)
Agricultural Conditions by County and City (2019)
26-7 各县(市)主要农作物播种面积(2019 年)…… (741)
Sown Area of Major Farm Products by County and City (2019)
26-8 各县(市)主要农作物产量(2019 年)…… (744)
Output of Major Farm Products by County and City (2019)
26-9 各县(市)畜牧业生产情况(2019 年)…… (747)
Statistics on Animal Husbandry by County and City (2019)
26-10 各县(市、区)财政、金融主要指标(2019 年)…… (750)
Main Indicators of Finance by County and Distict (2019)
26-11 各县(市)义务教育主要指标(2019 年)…… (754)
Main Indicators of Compulsory Education by County and City (2019)
26-12 各县(市)卫生主要指标(2019 年)…… (757)
Main Indicators of Sanitation by County and City (2019)
26-13 各县(市)社会保险和低保参保人数(2019 年)…… (760)
Number of People Participated in Basic Insurance and Lowest Cost-of-Living by County and City (2019)

二十七、全国及各省、区、市主要统计指标
Main Indicators of the whole Nation and 31 Provinces (Municipality, Autonomous, Regions)
27-1 全国及各省区市人口、工资及投资(2019 年)…… (765)
Population, Wage and Investment by Province and Region (2019)
27-2 全国及各省区市生产总值(2019 年)…… (766)
Gross Domestic Product by Province and Region (2019)
27-3 全国及各省区市物价指数(2019 年)…… (767)
Price Indices by Province and Region (2019)
27-4 全国及各省区市城乡居民收支(2019 年)…… (768)
Income and Expenditure of Urban and Rural Residents by Province and Region (2019)
27-5 全国及各省区市主要农产品产量(2019 年)…… (769)
Output of Major Farm Products by Province and Region (2019)
27-6 全国及各省区市规模以上工业主要统计指标(2019 年)…… (770)
Main Indicators of Enterprises Above Designed Size by Province and Region (2019)

27-7 全国及各省区市贸易外经和财政主要指标(2019 年)…… (771)
Main Indicators of Internal and Foreign Trade、Government Finance by Province and Region (2019)
27-8 全国及各省区市教育、卫生情况(2018 年)…… (772)
Main Indicator on Education and Public Health by Province and Region (2018)

综合

General Survey

1

◉ 资料整理：赵霞　李湛　乔旭明　常伟杰

简要说明

一、主要内容

本篇包括行政区划资料，国民经济综合资料，基本单位资料，产业集聚区、航空港区和商务两区资料。

二、资料来源

行政区划资料，是截止上年末经国务院批准的行政区划变更情况，由河南省民政厅提供。

国民经济综合资料是通过对各篇章主要统计指标及其速度、结构和效益等加工计算的，由河南省统计局综合处编辑整理。

基本单位资料主要包括所有法人单位和产业活动单位数，是根据名录库中各部门的单位审批登记资料和经常性统计调查中查到的新增、变动和消亡单位情况，本部分由河南省统计局普查中心编辑整理。

产业集聚区、航空港区和商务两区资料由河南省统计局监测评价考核处编辑整理。

Brief Introduction

I. Main Contents

This chapter consists of following parts: summary data on the national economy and social development, Institutional unit, Main economic indicators of industry gathering area, zhengzhou Airport and two business areas.

II. Sources of Data

Data on divisions of administrative areas in Henan are prepared and provided by the Henan Province Bureau of Civil Affairs on the basis of the changes in the divisions of administrative areas as approved by the State Council at the end of the previous year.

The summary data on the national economy and social development reflect the overall situation by presenting further processed statistics including growth, structure, ratio, and efficiency data derived from other chapters. Data in this part are prepared by Comprehensive Department of Henan provincial Bureau of statistics.

Data on institutional unit include legal and establishment units, which are calculated on directory library and increase, change and reduce unit in regular surreys. Data in this part are prepared by Census Center of Henan provincial Bureau of statistics.

Data on industry gathering area, zhengzhou Airport and two business areas is prepared by Assessment of monitoring and evaluation of Henan provincial Bureau of Statistics.

1-1 全省行政区划(2019年底)

Administrative Divisions of Henan Province (End of 2019)

单位：个 (unit)

市 City	市 City	省辖市 Cities Under the Jurisdi-cation of Province	县级市 Cities at County Level	县 Counties	市辖区 Districts Under the Juris-dication of City	镇 Town-ships	乡 Town-ships	街道办事处 Urban Subdi-strict Offices	居民委员会 Neighbo-urhood Commi-ttees	村民委员会 Village Commi-ttees
全省 Total	**39**	**17**	**22**	**83**	**53**	**1173**	**618**	**660**	**6083**	**45595**
郑州市 Zhengzhou	6	1	5	1	6	73	13	91	862	2222
开封市 Kaifeng	1	1		4	5	34	45	38	420	2128
洛阳市 Luoyang	2	1	1	8	6	106	24	58	493	2703
平顶山市 Pingdingshan	3	1	2	4	4	53	33	57	248	2532
安阳市 Anyang	2	1	1	4	4	66	23	46	264	3257
鹤壁市 Hebi	1	1		2	3	14	5	25	210	779
新乡市 Xinxiang	4	1	3	5	4	77	41	36	218	3561
焦作市 Jiaozuo	3	1	2	4	4	34	18	56	167	1826
濮阳市 Puyang	1	1		5	1	42	33	14	124	2963
许昌市 Xuchang	3	1	2	2	2	60	16	27	871	1610
漯河市 Luohe	1	1		2	3	37	9	6	77	1269
三门峡市 Sanmenxia	3	1	2	2	2	29	33	12	127	1270
南阳市 Nanyang	2	1	1	10	2	159	45	39	375	4515
商丘市 Shangqiu	2	1	1	6	2	97	70	30	238	4542
信阳市 Xinyang	1	1		8	2	83	86	40	512	2855
周口市 Zhoukou	2	1	1	7	2	101	67	38	382	4643
驻马店市 Zhumadian	1	1		9	1	97	57	42	423	2467
济源市 Jiyuan	1		1			11		5	72	453

1-2 各市、县(市、区)名称(2019年底)
Names of Administrative Areas (End of 2019)

市 Cities	县(市、区)数(个) Counties (unit)	市辖县 Counties Under the Jurisdiction of Cities	市辖区 Districts Under the Jurisdiction of Cities	县级市 Cities at County Level
郑州市 Zhengzhou	12	中牟 Zhongmou	中原区、二七区、管城回族区、金水区、上街区、惠济区 Zhongyuan,Erqi,Guancheng Huizu,Jinshui,Shangjie,Huiji	巩义市 Gongyi 荥阳市 Xingyang 新郑市 Xinzheng 登封市 Dengfeng 新密市 Xinmi
开封市 Kaifeng	9	杞县、通许、尉氏、兰考 Qixian,Tongxu,Weishi,Lankao	龙亭区、顺河回族区、鼓楼区、禹王台区、祥符区 Longting,Shunhe Huizu,Gulou,Yuwangtai,Xiangfu	
洛阳市 Luoyang	15	孟津、新安、栾川、嵩县、汝阳、宜阳、洛宁、伊川 Mengjin,Xin'an,Luanchuan,Songxian,Ruyang,Yiyang,Luoning,Yichuan	老城区、西工区、瀍河回族区、涧西区、吉利区、洛龙区 Laocheng,Xigong,Chanhe Huizu,Jianxi,Jili,Luolong	偃师市 Yanshi
平顶山市 Pingdingshan	10	宝丰、叶县、鲁山、郏县 Baofeng,Yexian,Lushan,Jiaxian	新华区、卫东区、湛河区、石龙区 Xinhua,Weidong,Zhanhe,Shilong	汝州市 Ruzhou 舞钢市 Wugang
安阳市 Anyang	9	安阳、汤阴、滑县、内黄 Anyang,Tangyin,Huaxian,Neihuang	文峰区、北关区、殷都区、龙安区 Wenfeng,Beiguan,Yindu,Longan	林州市 Linzhou
鹤壁市 Hebi	5	浚县、淇县 Xunxian,Qixian	鹤山区、山城区、淇滨区 Heshan,Shancheng,Qibin	
新乡市 Xinxiang	12	新乡、获嘉、原阳、延津、封丘 Xinxiang,Huojia,Yuanyang,Yanjin,Fengqiu,Changyuan	红旗区、卫滨区、凤泉区、牧野区 Hongqi,WeiBin,Fengquan,Muye	卫辉市Weihui 辉县市Huixian 长垣市Changyuan
焦作市 Jiaozuo	10	修武、博爱、武陟、温县 Xiuwu,Boai,Wuzhi,Wenxian	解放区、中站区、马村区、山阳区 Jiefang,Zhongzhan,Macun,Shanyang	沁阳市Qinyang 孟州市Mengzhou
濮阳市 Puyang	6	清丰、南乐、范县、台前、濮阳 Qingfeng,Nanle,Fanxian,Taiqian,Puyang	华龙区 Hualong	
许昌市 Xuchang	6	鄢陵、襄城 Yanling,Xiangcheng	魏都区、建安区 Weidu,Jianan	禹州市Yuzhou 长葛市Changge
漯河市 Luohe	5	舞阳、临颍、 Wuyang,Linying	源汇区、郾城区、召陵区 Yuanhui , Yancheng, Zhaoling	
三门峡市 Sanmenxia	6	渑池、卢氏 Mianchi,Lushi	湖滨区、陕州区 Hubin，Shanzhou	义马市Yima 灵宝市Lingbao
南阳市 Nanyang	13	南召、方城、西峡、镇平、内乡、淅川、社旗、唐河、新野、桐柏 Nanzhao,Fangcheng,Xixia,Zhenping,Neixiang Xichuan,Sheqi,Tanghe,Xinye,Tongbai	卧龙区、宛城区 Wolong,Wancheng	邓州市 Dengzhou
商丘市 Shangqiu	9	虞城、民权、宁陵、睢县、夏邑、柘城 Yucheng,Minquan,Ningling,Suixian,Xiayi,Zhecheng	梁园区、睢阳区 LiangYuan,Suiyang	永城市 Yongcheng
信阳市 Xinyang	10	息县、淮滨、潢川、光山、固始、商城、罗山、新县 Xixian,Huaibin,Huangchuan,Guangshan,Gushi,Shangcheng,Luoshan,Xinxian	浉河区、平桥区 Shihe,Pingqiao	
周口市 Zhoukou	10	扶沟、西华、商水、太康、鹿邑、郸城、沈丘 Fugou,Xihua,Shangshui,Taikang,Luyi,Dancheng,Huaiyang,Shenqiu	川汇区、淮阳区 Chuanhui,Huaiyang	项城市 XiangCheng
驻马店市 Zhumadian	10	确山、泌阳、遂平、西平、上蔡、汝南、平舆、新蔡、正阳 Queshan,Biyang,Suiping,Xiping,Shangcai Runan,Pingyu,Xincai,Zhengyang	驿城区 Yicheng	
济源市 Jiyuan	1			济源市 Jiyuan

1-3 河南省主要统计指标居全国位次
The Rank of Main Indicators of Henan in Nation

指　标	Indicator	2000	2005	2010	2015	2017	2018	2019
生产总值	Gross Domestic Product	5	5	5	5	5	5	5
生产总值增速	Growth of Gross Domestic Product	14	5	21	13	11	11	10
居民消费价格指数	General Consumer Price Index	26	9	13	20	23	11	8
一般公共预算收入	General Public Budget Revenue of the Local Government	9	8	9	8	8	8	8
一般公共预算支出	General Public Budget Expenditure of the Local Government	7	7	5	5	5	5	5
规模以上工业增加值增速	Growth Rate of Industrial Enterprises above Designated Size	17	4	14	7	11	14	7
社会消费品零售总额	Total Retail Sales of Consumer Goods	5	5	5	5	5	5	5
进出口总额	Total Exports and Imports	18	16	16	11	10	11	12
出口	Exports	14	13	17	11	8	8	9
居民可支配收入	Disposable Income				24	24	24	23
城镇	Disposable Income of Urban Households				24	24	25	26
农村	Disposable Income of Rural Households				17	17	15	16

1-4 河南省主要统计指标占全国比重
The Poroportion of Main Indicators of Henan in Nation

单位：%　　　　(%)

指　标	Indicator	1952	1978	1990	2000	2010	2015	2017	2018	2019
生产总值	Gross Domestic Product	5.3	4.4	5.0	5.0	5.6	5.4	5.4	5.3	5.5
第一产业	Primary Industry	6.6	6.4	6.5	7.9	8.1	6.9	6.3	6.6	6.6
第二产业	Secondary Industry	5.8	4.0	4.3	5.0	6.7	6.4	6.3	6.0	6.1
第三产业	Tertiary Industry	2.8	3.2	4.5	4.0	3.9	4.3	4.5	4.6	4.9
人均生产总值	Per Capita GDP		60.3	65.6	68.6	79.6	78.4	78.2	77.6	79.5
一般公共预算收入	General Public Budget Revenue of the Local Government	2.5	3.5	4.3	3.8	3.4	3.6	3.7	3.8	4.0
一般公共预算支出	General Public Budget Expenditure of the Local Government	1.0	4.7	4.3	4.3	4.6	4.5	4.7	4.9	5.0
粮食产量	Output of Grain	6.3	6.9	7.4	8.9	9.9	9.8	9.9	10.1	10.1
社会消费品零售总额	Total Retail Sales of Consumer Goods	3.9	4.6	3.8	4.8	5.1	5.2	5.4	5.4	5.5
进出口总额	Total Exports and Imports	0.1(1957年)	0.6	0.9	0.5	0.6	1.9	1.9	1.8	1.8
#出口	Exports	0.3(1957年)	1.0	1.4	0.6	0.7	1.9	2.1	2.2	2.2
居民可支配收入	Disposable Income						78.0	77.7	77.8	77.8
城镇	Disposable Income of Urban Households						82.0	81.2	81.2	80.7
农村	Disposable Income of Rural Households						95.0	94.7	94.6	94.7

1-5　国民经济和社会发展总量和速度指标

指　　标	Item	1978	2000	2005	2010
人口与就业	**Population and Employment**				
人口(万人)	**Population (10 000 persons)**				
年底总人口	Population (year-end)	7067	9488	9768	10437
#城镇人口	Urban	963	2201	2994	4052
常住人口	Residents popolation			9380	9405
就业(万人)	**Employment (10 000 persons)**				
年底就业人员	Employment (year-end)	2807	5572	5662	6042
#在岗职工	Staff and Workers	420	718	681	723
城镇登记失业人数	Registered Unemployed Persons in Urban Areas	15.74	21.40	33.02	38.20
宏观经济	**Macroeconomy**				
国民核算	**National Accounts**				
生产总值(亿元)	Gross Domestic Product (100 million yuan)	162.92	5052.99	10243.47	22655.02
第一产业	Primary Industry	64.86	1124.93	1844.04	3127.14
第二产业	Secondary Industry	69.45	2282.48	5202.27	12173.51
第三产业	Tertiary Industry	28.61	1645.59	3197.16	7354.38
人均生产总值(元)	Per Capita GDP (yuan)	232	5450	10978	23984
固定资产投资(亿元)	**Investment in Fixed Assets (100 million yuan)**				
全社会固定资产投资	Investment in Fixed Assets in the Whole Country				
#固定资产投资	Investment in Fixed Assets				
#工业投资	Industry				
#房地产开发投资	Real Estate Development				
#基础设施投资	Infrastructure				
#民间投资	Civilian				
对外贸易	**Foreign Trade**				
进出口总额(亿元)	Total Exports and Imports (100 million yuan)	1.99	188.36	626.54	1204.40
进口额	Imports	0.27	64.71	213.42	491.27
出口额	Exports	1.72	123.65	413.12	713.13
利用外资(万美元)	**Utilization of Foreign Capital (USD 10 000)**				
实际利用外商直接投资	Actually Utilized Foreign Direct Investments	565(1985年)	53999	122960	624670
能源(万吨标准煤)	**Energy (10 000 tons of SCE)**				
能源生产总量	Total Energy Production	4434	6591	14522	17438
能源消费总量	Total Energy Consumption	3353	7919	14625	18964
财政(亿元)	**Public Finance (100 million yuan)**				
一般公共预算收入	General Public Budget Revenue of the Local Government	33.73	246.47	537.65	1381.32
一般公共预算支出	General Public Budget Expenditure of the Local Government	27.67	445.53	1116.04	3416.14
物价总指数(以上年为100)	**Price Indices (preceding year=100)**				
居民消费价格总指数	General Consumer Price Index	100.1	99.2	102.1	103.5
商品零售价格总指数	Producer Price Indices for Industrial Products	100.1	98.5	101.7	103.7
农业生产资料价格总指数	Purchasing Price Indices for Industrial Producers	97.9	99.6	107.9	103.1
人民生活	**People's Living Conditions**				
居民可支配收入(元)	Disposable Income (yuan)				9520
城镇	Urban Households	315	4766	8668	15930
农村	Rural Households	105	1986	2871	5524
居民消费支出(元)	Living Expenditure (yuan)				
城镇	Urban Households	274	3831	6038	10838
农村	Rural Households	82	1316	1892	3682

Principal Aggregate Indicators and Growth Rates of National Economic and Social Development

2015	2018	2019	2019年为以下各年% 2019as % of the Following years				年均增长速度(%) Average Annual Growth Rate		
			1978	2000	2010	2018	1979-2019	2001-2019	2011-2019
10722	10906	10952	155.0	115.4	104.9	100.4	1.1	0.8	0.5
5023	5639	5828	605.2	264.8	143.8	103.4	4.5	5.3	4.1
9480	9605	9640			102.5	100.4			0.3
6636	6692	6562	233.8	117.8	108.6	98.1	2.1	0.9	0.9
1077	920	922	219.6	128.5	127.6	100.2	1.9	1.3	2.7
42.46	48.60	49.43	314.0	231.0	129.4	101.7	2.8	4.5	2.9
37084.10	49935.90	54259.20	6316.4	663.2	213.3	107.0	10.6	10.5	8.8
4015.56	4311.12	4635.40	868.8	235.5	140.9	102.3	5.4	4.6	3.9
17947.86	22038.56	23605.79	12184.2	856.1	214.9	107.5	12.4	12.0	8.9
15120.68	23586.21	26018.01	12366.8	694.7	238.1	107.4	12.5	10.7	10.1
39209	52114	56388	4602.9	639.0	209.4	106.5	9.8	10.3	8.6
				4031.9	355.7	108.1		24.0	15.0
				4381.4	287.8	102.0		24.7	10.0
				9004.6	331.7	98.9		28.4	15.0
				2055.1	521.4	118.5		21.4	24.9
				7969.7	342.7	103.2		28.7	13.4
4600.19	5512.71	5711.63	287016.6	3032.3	474.2	103.6	21.4	19.7	18.9
1916.16	1933.73	1956.99	724811.1	3024.2	398.4	101.2	24.2	19.7	16.6
2684.03	3578.99	3754.64	218293.0	3036.5	526.5	104.9	20.6	19.7	20.3
1608637	1790214	1872727		3468.1	299.8	104.6		20.5	13.0
11173	9731	10304	232.4	156.3	59.1	105.9	2.1	2.4	-5.7
22343	22659	22300	665.1	281.6	117.6	98.4	4.7	5.6	1.8
3016.05	3766.02	4041.89	11983.1	1639.9	292.6	107.3	12.4	15.9	12.7
6799.35	9217.73	10163.93	36732.7	2281.3	297.5	110.3	15.5	17.9	12.9
101.3	102.3	103.0							
99.8	102.9	102.4							
100.3	104.3	103.8							
17125	21964	23903			251.1	108.8			10.8
25576	31874	34201	10857.5	717.6	214.7	107.3	12.1	10.9	8.9
10853	13831	15164	14441.7	763.5	274.5	109.6	12.9	11.3	11.9
11835	15169	16332				107.7			
17154	20989	21972	8018.8	573.5	202.7	104.7	11.3	9.6	8.2
7887	10392	11546	14080.5	877.4	313.6	111.1	12.8	12.1	13.5

1-5　续表 1

指　标	Item	1978	2000	2005	2010
城市概况	**General Conditions of Cities**				
供水总量(万立方米)	Water Supply (10 000 cu.m)		191706	183436	179122
排水管道长度(公里)	Length of Sewer Pipelines (km)		6070	10201	14733
城市煤气、天然气家庭用量(万立方米)	Consumption of Coal Gas and Natural Gas for Residential Use (10 000 cu.m)		30100	31384	63663
公共汽(电)车总数(标台)	Total Number of Public Buses and Trolley Buses (unit)		12514	12514	18912
道路长度(公里)	Length of Roads (km)		4920	7090	9413
公园绿地面积(公顷)	Areas of Green Land (hectare)		6286	12644	18361
产　业	**Industry**				
农林牧渔业	**Farming, Forestry, Animal Husbandry and Fishery**				
主要农产品产量	Output of Major Farm Products				
粮食(万吨)	Grain (10 000 tons)	2097.40	4101.50	4582.00	5581.82
棉花(万吨)	Cotton (10 000 tons)	22.42	70.38	67.70	33.89
油料(万吨)	Oil-bearing Crops (10 000 tons)	24.16	392.55	449.60	515.66
烟叶(万吨)	Tobacco (10 000 tons)	29.95	27.60	28.84	28.75
园林水果(万吨)	Fruits (10 000 tons)	47.11	364.73	555.69	797.50
年底大牲畜存栏头数(万头)	Large Animals (year-end) (10 000 heads)	515.03	1445.73	1508.80	719.19
年底生猪存栏头数(万头)	Hogs (year-end) (10 000 heads)	1724.90	3787.69	4439.00	4540.55
年底羊存栏只数(万只)	Sheep and goats (year-end) (10 000 heads)	989.70	2961.40	3988.00	1895.40
肉类(万吨)	Meat (10 000 tons)	45.64	517.00	689.00	608.96
工业	**Industry**				
规模以上工业增加值增速(%)	Growth Rate of Value-added of Industrial Above Designated Size (%)		11.6	23.3	19.0
建筑业	**Construction**				
建筑业总产值（亿元）	Gross Output Value of Construction (100 million yuan)		357.34	1066.15	4400.61
施工房屋面积(万平方米)	Floor Space of Buildings Under Construction (10 000 sq.m)		5308.29	10813.15	28677.13
竣工房屋面积(万平方米)	Floor Space of Buildings Completed (10 000 sq.m)		2629.33	4787.12	13156.03
交通运输、仓储、邮政业	**Transport, Storage and Post**				
客运量(万人)	Passengers (10 000 persons)	11177	83912	98099	167804
#铁路	Railways	4319	4727	5842	8399
公路	Highways	6781	79017	91920	158630
货运量(万吨)	Freight (10 000 tons)	18206	60678	78827	202470
#铁路	Railways	6722	10172	14806	14224
公路	Highways	11321	50133	62684	183291
邮电业务总量(亿元)	Business Volume of Post and Telecommunications Service (100 million yuan)	0.71	130.06	556.50	486.11

continued

2015	2018	2019	2019年为以下各年% 2019as % of the Following years				年均增长速度(%) Average Annual Growth Rate		
			1978	2000	2010	2018	1979-2019	2001-2019	2011-2019
196709	216305	221104		115.3	123.4	102.2		0.8	2.4
20467	25027	27932		460.2	189.6	111.6		8.4	7.4
110929	157939	216839		720.4	340.6	137.3		11.0	14.6
27355	37833	39149		312.8	207.0	103.5		6.2	8.4
12318	14538	15766		320.4	167.5	108.4		6.3	5.9
25201	31934	35361		562.6	192.6	110.7		9.5	7.6
6470.22	6648.91	6698.36	319.4	163.3	120.0	100.7	2.9	2.6	2.6
6.77	3.79	2.71	12.1	3.9	8.0	71.5	-5.0	-15.8	-30.3
538.99	631.03	645.45	2671.6	164.4	125.2	102.3	8.3	2.7	3.3
28.85	25.31	22.76	76.0	82.5	79.2	89.9	-0.7	-1.0	-3.3
919.68	907.39	950.74	2018.1	260.7	119.2	104.8	7.6	5.2	2.5
411.70	377.01	388.27	75.4	26.9	54.0	103.0	-0.7	-6.7	-8.4
4361.95	4337.15	3170.76	183.8	83.7	69.8	73.1	1.5	-0.9	-5.0
1926.00	1734.07	1898.81	191.9	64.1	100.2	109.5	1.6	-2.3	0.0
647.22	669.41	560.06	1227.1	108.3	92.0	83.7	6.3	0.4	-1.2
8.6	7.2	7.8							
8047.65	11360.52	12700.97		3554.3	288.6	111.8		20.7	12.5
53132.48	63789.69	64256.07		1210.5	224.1	100.7		14.0	9.4
18026.91	20624.12	20736.33		788.7	157.6	100.5		11.5	5.2
126812	112611	111458	2018.4	268.1	125.5	95.6	7.6	5.3	2.6
13068	17095	18278	423.2	386.7	217.6	113.0	3.6	7.4	9.0
112535	93707	91281	2882.8	247.4	114.9	92.4	8.5	4.9	1.6
192715	259461	218647	2367.4	709.1	251.6	122.5	8.0	10.9	10.8
9802	10012	10502	156.2	103.2	73.8	111.7	1.1	0.2	-3.3
172431	235183	190883	3617.3	816.9	268.3	122.4	9.1	11.7	11.6
1317.28	4383.72	6589.24	928061.4	5066.4	1355.5	150.3	25.0	22.9	33.6

1-5　续表 2

指　　标	Item	1978	2000	2005	2010
批发、零售业和旅游业	**Wholesale and Retail Trades、Hotels and Catering Services**				
接待旅游者人数(万人次)	Number of Tourists (10 000 person-times)		32.50	60.05	146.84
旅游外汇收入(万美元)	Foreign Exchange Earnings from Tourism (USD 10 000)		12390	21604	49877
社会消费品零售总额(亿元)	Total Retail Sales of Consumer Goods (100 million yuan)	71.79	1858.46	3362.58	7922.66
金融业(亿元)	**Finance (100 million yuan)**				
金融机构人民币年底存款余额	Deposits of Financial Institutions	45.71	4753.41	10003.96	23148.83
金融机构人民币年底贷款余额	Loans of Financial Institutions	99.99	4356.94	7434.53	15871.32
科学研究、技术服务和地质勘查业	**Scientific Research, Technical Services and Geologic Prospecting**				
R&D经费内部支出(亿元)	Internal Expenditures on R&D (100 million yuan)		24.80	55.61	211.38
技术市场成交额(亿元)	Volume of Transaction in Technical Markets (100 million yuan)		21.16	26.37	27.69
三种专利授权量(项)	Three Types of Patent Application Granted (item)		2766	3748	16539
教育	**Education**				
专任教师数(万人)	Number of Full-time Teachers (10 000 persons)				
普通高等学校	Regular Institutions of Higher Education	0.54	2.02	4.63	7.75
普通中学	Regular Secondary School	29.34	30.86	37.30	38.10
小学	Primary Schools	42.88	45.93	47.55	49.04
在校学生数(万人)	Students Enrollment (10 000 persons)				
普通高等学校	Regular Institutions of Higher Education	2.73	26.24	85.19	145.67
普通中学	Regular Secondary School	521.62	638.14	758.22	661.56
小学	Primary Schools	1140.26	1130.63	986.84	1070.53
卫生、社会保障和社会福利业	**Health, Social Security and Social Welfare**				
卫生机构床位数(万张)	Number of Beds in Health Institutions (10 000 units)	10.20	19.86	21.40	32.76
#医院、卫生院	Hospitals	9.73	18.34	20.23	30.44
卫生技术人员数(万人)	Number of Medical Technical Personnel (10 000 persons)	11.44	26.84	28.92	37.28
#执业（助理）医师	Doctors	4.38	11.11	11.11	15.48
文化、体育和娱乐业	**Culture**				
图书出版总印数(万册)	Number of Books Published (10 000 copies)		35077	27260	20150
期刊出版总印数(万册)	Number of Magazines Issued (10 000 copies)		10721	9323	8524
报纸出版总印数(万份)	Number of Newspapers Issued (10 000 copies)		129104	197896	214158

注：1.本表价值量指标除邮电业务总量2001年以来为2000年不变价，1990-2000年按1990年不变价格计算，以前年度按1980年不变价格计算，其他价值量指标均按当年价格计算。生产总值、工业增加值、邮电业务总量发展(增长)速度均按可比价格计算(下同)。
2.2000年以后生产总值相关数据已按新的行业划分办法和第四次经济普查数据调整(下同)。
3.2000年以后财政收入为分税制后新口径数据，发展(增长)速度按可比口径计算。
4.进出口总额2000年及以后年度为海关数，1978年为有关部门数。
5.2010年客货运输量为公路水路运输量专项调查数据，2015年、2019年客货运输量按交通部新统计方法测算(下同)。
6.从2013年起，国家统计局开展了城乡一体化住户收支与生活状况调查，2015年以后数据来源于此调查，与以前年份的调查范围、方法和口径有所不同。

continued

2015	2018	2019	2019年为以下各年% 2019as % of the Following years				年均增长速度(%) Average Annual Growth Rate		
			1978	2000	2010	2018	1979-2019	2001-2019	2011-2019
268.29	321.73	351.47		1081.4	239.4	109.2		13.3	10.2
84948	103362	130401		1052.5	261.4	126.2		13.2	11.3
15475.80	21267.96	23476.13	32701.1	1263.2	296.3	110.4	15.2	14.3	12.8
47629.91	63867.63	69508.66	152073.8	1462.3	300.3	108.8	19.6	15.2	13.0
31432.62	47834.76	55659.00	55662.2	1277.5	350.7	116.4	16.7	14.3	15.0
435.04	671.52	793.04		3197.4	375.2	118.1		20.0	15.8
45.56	149.74	234.07		1106.1	845.3	156.3		13.5	26.8
47766	82318	86247		3118.1	521.5	104.8		19.8	20.1
9.80	11.54	12.40	2296.3	613.9	160.0	107.5	7.9	10.0	5.4
42.87	49.24	52.04	177.4	168.6	136.6	105.7	1.4	2.8	3.5
47.21	50.02	51.03	119.0	111.1	104.1	102.0	0.4	0.6	0.4
176.69	214.08	231.97	8497.1	884.0	159.2	108.4	11.4	12.2	5.3
599.12	661.94	684.36	131.2	107.2	103.4	103.4	0.7	0.4	0.4
937.05	994.60	1012.48	88.8	89.6	94.6	101.8	-0.3	-0.6	-0.6
48.96	60.85	64.00	627.5	322.3	195.4	105.2	4.6	6.4	7.7
45.65	57.04	60.05	617.2	327.4	197.3	105.3	4.5	6.4	7.8
51.96	62.13	65.39	571.6	243.6	175.4	105.2	4.3	4.8	6.4
19.86	23.55	25.14	574.0	226.3	162.4	106.8	4.4	4.4	5.5
23224	31068	37473		106.8	186.0	120.6		0.3	7.1
8602	8351	7752		72.3	90.9	92.8		-1.7	-1.0
204783	167782	157481		122.0	73.5	93.9		1.1	-3.4

a) Figures in value terms in this table are Calculated at current prices, except that on the business transaction of post and telecommunications service since 2001 were calculated at 2000 constant prices. Data on 1990~2000 were calculated at 1990 constant prices.Figures on postal and telecommunication services before 1990 were calculated at 1980 constant prices, and those since 1991 were calculated at constant prices. The indices and growth rates of the follow indicators are calculated atcomparable prices:GDP, value added of industry, Business volume of post and telecommunications (the same as following tables).

b) Since 2000,the data of GDP were adjusted by new industry classification method and the fourth economic census (the same as following tables).

c) Total financial revenue since tax reform began to be implemented since 2000. The indices in this table are calculated at comparable prices.

d) Since 2000, the data of imports and exports in foreign trade begin to be obtained from custom statistics (the same as following tables).

e) Data on passenger and freight Volume in 2010 were calculated on basis of Highway and waterway traffic special investigation, Data on passenger and freight Volume in 2015 and 2019 were calculated on new statistical methods of Ministry of Communications, and data in the brakfets are original data.

f) Since 2013, the national bureau of statistics (NBS) caries out the integration of urban and rural residents income and expenditure survey and living conditions survey. After 2015, the data comes from this survey, which is different from the survey scope, method and caliber of previous years.

1-6 国民经济和社会发展结构指标

Structural Indicators on National Economic and Social Development

单位：%

指 标	Item	2000	2005	2010	2015	2018	2019
人口	**Population**						
城乡结构	Urban and Rural Structure						
市镇	Urban	23.2	30.7	38.8	46.9	51.7	53.2
乡村	Rural	76.8	69.3	61.2	53.2	48.3	46.8
性别结构	Sexual Structure						
男	Male	51.6	51.6	51.8	51.8	51.7	51.6
女	Female	48.4	48.4	48.2	48.2	48.3	48.4
就业	**Employment**						
就业人员产业结构	Industrial Structure						
第一产业	Primary Industry	64.0	55.4	44.9	39.0	35.4	34.7
第二产业	Secondary Industry	17.5	22.1	29.0	30.8	30.6	29.2
第三产业	Tertiary Industry	18.5	22.5	26.1	30.2	34.0	36.0
国民核算	**National Accounts**						
生产总值产业结构	Industrial Structure						
第一产业	Primary Industry	22.3	18.0	13.8	10.8	8.6	8.5
第二产业	Secondary Industry	45.2	50.8	53.7	48.4	44.1	43.5
第三产业	Tertiary Industry	32.6	31.2	32.5	40.8	47.2	48.0
固定资产投资	**Investment**						
固定资产投资产业结构	Structure of Investment in Fixed Assets						
第一产业	Primary Industry			4.4	4.2	4.6	3.7
第二产业	Secondary Industry			51.1	48.6	28.6	28.9
第三产业	Tertiary Industry			44.5	47.1	66.8	67.4
重点行业占工业投资比重	Structure of Industry Investment						
#五大主导产业	Five-Leading Industry				48.7	38.2	37.0
#传统产业	Traditional Pillar Industry				35.1	40.3	42.9
#高耗能工业	High Energy Consumable Industry				25.8	29.9	32.2
能源	**Energy Sources**						
能源消费总量结构	Structure of Energy Sources Composition						
原煤	Coal	87.6	87.2	82.8	76.4	69.9	67.4
原油	Base oil	9.6	8.7	9.3	13.3	15.3	15.7
天然气	Gas	1.7	2.2	3.4	5.2	5.8	6.1
一次电力及其他能源	Primary Electricity	1.1	1.9	4.5	5.1	9.0	10.7
财政	**Government Finance**						
一般公共预算收入结构	Structure of General Public Budget Revenue						
#各项税收	Taxes	79.1	68.0	73.6	69.7	70.5	70.3
一般公共预算支出结构	Structure of General Public Budget Expenditure						
#农林水事务	Supporting Agricultural Production and Agricultural Operating Expenses	7.7	7.4	11.7	11.6	10.9	10.4
教科文卫	Culture Education Science and Health Care	24.3	24.2	28.7	32.0	30.9	30.9
#科学技术	Science	1.5	1.2	1.3	1.2	1.7	2.1

1-6 续表 continued

单位：%

指标	Item	2000	2005	2010	2015	2018	2019
生活	**People's Living Conditions**						
城镇居民消费结构	Consumption Structure of Urban Residents						
食品烟酒	Food, Alcohol and tobacco				28.1	25.7	25.3
衣着	Clothing				10.5	8.1	7.8
居住	Residence				19.8	23.9	23.6
生活用品及服务	Articles for Daily Use and Others				8.1	7.1	7.0
交通通信	Traffic Communication				10.9	12.0	12.2
教育文化娱乐	Education, Culture and Entertainment				11.6	11.6	12.2
医疗保健	Health Care				8.0	9.2	9.5
其他用品和服务	Others				3.1	2.4	2.5
农村居民消费结构	Consumption Structure of Rural Residents						
食品烟酒	Food, Alcohol and tobacco				29.2	26.7	26.2
衣着	Clothing				8.3	7.1	7.1
居住	Residence				20.8	21.9	21.5
生活用品及服务	Articles for Daily Use and Others				7.1	6.7	6.4
交通通信	Traffic Communication				12.3	12.4	11.9
教育文化娱乐	Education, Culture and Entertainment				10.8	11.8	12.6
医疗保健	Health Care				9.7	11.8	12.7
其他用品和服务	Others				1.7	1.6	1.6
工业	**Industry**						
重点行业增加值比重	Structure of Value-added of the Industry						
#五大主导产业	Five-Leading Industry				44.0	45.2	45.5
#传统产业	Traditional Pillar Industry				45.3	46.6	46.7
#高技术产业	High-technology Industry				8.8	10.0	9.9
运输业	**Transportation**						
货运量运输方式结构	Structure of Freight Traffic						
#铁　路	Railways	16.8	18.8	7.0	5.1	3.9	4.8
公　路	Highways	82.6	79.5	90.5	89.5	90.6	87.3
水　运	Waterways	0.6	1.7	2.4	5.4	5.5	7.9
客运量运输方式结构	Structure of Passenger Traffic						
#铁　路	Railways	5.6	6.0	5.0	10.3	15.2	16.4
公　路	Highways	94.2	93.7	94.5	88.7	83.2	81.9
水　运	Waterways	0.1	0.1	0.2	0.2	0.3	0.3
批发零售贸易、住宿和餐饮业	**Wholesale and Retail Trades, Hotels and Catering Services**						
社会消费品零售总额结构	Structure of Retail Sales of Consumer Goods						
批发零售和贸易业	Wholesale and Retail Trade	90.8	89.6	88.0	88.3	88.3	88.2
住宿和餐饮业	Hotels and Catering Services	9.2	10.4	12.0	11.7	11.7	11.8

1-7 国民经济和社会发展比例和效益指标

Indicators on Proportions and Efficiency in National Economic and Social Development

本表价值量指标均按当年价格计算。

The data in value terms in the table are calculated at current prices.

指　标	Item	2000	2010	2015	2018	2019
人口	**Population**					
出生率(‰)	Birth Rate (‰)	13.07	11.52	12.70	11.72	11.02
死亡率(‰)	Death Rate (‰)	5.93	6.57	7.05	6.80	6.84
自然增长率(‰)	Natural Growth Rate (‰)	7.14	4.95	5.65	4.92	4.18
就业	**Employment**					
城镇户均就业人口(人)	Number of Dependents per Urban Employee (person)	1.94	1.95	1.76	1.75	1.64
城镇登记失业率(%)	Registered Unemployment Rate in Urban Areas (%)	2.60	3.38	3.00	3.02	3.17
国民核算	**National Accounting**					
经济增长贡献率(%)	Contribution Rate to GDP (%)					
第一产业	Primary Industry	9.7	4.9	5.8	4.5	3.2
第二产业	Secondary Industry	61.2	65.3	50.0	43.1	50.9
第三产业	Tertiary Industry	29.1	29.7	44.2	52.4	45.9
全社会劳动生产率(元/人.年)	Overall Labor Productivity (yuan/person.year)	9377	37787	56376	74204	81876
第一产业	Primary Industry	3275	11419	15329	17741	19967
第二产业	Secondary Industry	24153	71024	88895	106159	119011
第三产业	Tertiary Industry	16309	47663	77942	106101	112074
对外经济贸易和国际旅游	**Foreign Trade and International Tourism**					
进出口总额相当于生产总值比例(%)	Proportion of Total Imports & Exports to GDP (%)	3.7	5.3	12.4	11.0	10.5
境外每一来豫游客支出(美元)	Expenditure per International Tourist in Henan (USD)	381	340	317	321	371
能源	**Energy**					
能源生产弹性系数	Elasticity Ratio of Energy Production		0.21			0.84
能源消费弹性系数	Elasticity Ratio of Energy Consumption	0.77	0.69	0.14	0.29	
单位GDP能耗降低率(%)	Reduction Rate of Energy Consumption per 10 000 yuan GDP (%)		-3.53	-6.57	-5.02	-7.98
单位GDP电耗降低率(%)	Reduction Rate of Electricity Consumption per 10 000 yuan GDP (%)		0.80	-8.98	0.29	-7.96
单位工业增加值能耗降低率(%)	Reduction Rate of Energy Consumption per 10 000 yuan Add-value Industry (%)		-10.75	-11.54	-7.97	-14.13
财政	**Finance**					
一般公共预算收入占GDP比重(%)	Proportion of General Public Budget Revenue to GDP (%)	4.9	6.1	8.1	7.5	7.4
家庭	**Family**					
少儿抚养系数(%)	Dependency Ratio of Children (%)		29.7	30.7	31.6	34.1
老年抚养系数(%)	Dependency Ratio of the Aged (%)		11.8	13.9	15.6	20.6
生活	**Family**					
城乡居民收入比例(农民人均可支配收入为1)	Proportion of Per Capita Annual Disposable Income of Urban Residents to Rural Residents (Rural Residents=1)	2.40	2.88	2.36	2.30	2.26

1-7 续表 continued

指 标	Item	2000	2010	2015	2018	2019
农业	**Agriculture**					
主要农产品单产(千克/亩)	Per Unit Yield of Main Agricultural Products (kg/mu)					
粮食	Grain	303	372	394	406	416
棉花	Cotton	60	64	70	69	53
油料	Oil-bearing Crops	175	230	250	288	281
工业	**Industry**					
成本费用利润率(%)	Ratio of Profits to Industrial Cost (%)	4.5	10.2	7.2	8.6	7.7
资产负债率(%)	Assets Liability Ratio (%)	66.4	55.2	47.0	54.9	55.8
总资产贡献率(%)	Ratio of Total Assets to Industrial Output Value (%)	8.6	22.4	13.9	12.3	11.0
产品销售率(%)	Proportion of Products Sold (%)	98.0	98.7	98.2	98.3	98.2
建筑业	**Construction**					
劳动生产率(元/人)	Overall Labor Productivity (yuan/person)		183639	287604	373130	403962
技术装备率(元/人)	Value of Machinery per Laborer (yuan/person)	5302	10173	13294	11893.97	10328
金融	**Financial**					
金融机构存款相当于	Bank Deposits as Percentage of					
生产总值比例（%）	GDP (%)	94.1	102.2	128.4	127.9	128.1
金融机构存贷比	Bank Loans as Percentage of Deposits					
（存款=100）	(Deposits=100)	91.7	68.6	66.0	74.9	80.1
科技	**Science and Technology**					
R&D经费投入强度（%）	Proportion of R&D Expenditure to GDP (%)	0.5	0.93	1.17	1.34	1.46
教育	**Education**					
九年义务教育巩固率	Percentage of Student Enrollment Consolidated					
	of Nine-year Compulsory Education			94.0	94.6	95.5
高中阶段毛入学率	The Gross enrollment rate of higher stage			90.3	91.2	91.6
高等教育毛入学率	The Gross enrollment rate of higher education			36.5	45.6	49.3
每万人拥有大学生	Number of University Students per 10 000 Persons					
(含研究生)(人)	(Include Postgraduates) (person)	28	149	228	279	303
卫生	**Health Care**					
每万人拥有卫生机构	Number of Hospital Beds per 10 000					
院床位(张)	Persons (unit)	20.9	34.8	51.6	63.4	66.4
每万人拥有执业医师(人)	Number of Doctors per 10 000 Persons (person)	11.7	16.5	21.0	24.5	26.1

1-8 按三次产业分的基本单位数及构成

Institutional Units and Composition By Industry

年 份 Year	单位数 (个) Number of Enteprised (unit)	第一产业 Primary Industry		第二产业 Secondary Industry		第三产业 Tertiary Industry	
		绝对数 Value	构成(%) Composition (%)	绝对数 Value	构成(%) Composition (%)	绝对数 Value	构成(%) Composition (%)
法人单位 **Institutional Units**							
2000	225806	5035	2.2	90865	40.3	129906	57.5
2001	267883	4782	1.8	88965	33.2	174136	65.0
2002	266230	4604	1.7	87495	32.9	174131	65.4
2003	272024	10803	4.0	89839	33.0	171382	63.0
2004	277950	8660	3.1	91370	32.9	177920	64.0
2005	286207	8334	2.9	97446	34.1	180427	63.0
2006	305722	8600	2.8	106732	34.9	190390	62.3
2007	322828	9570	3.0	114560	35.5	198698	61.5
2008	362427	11406	3.1	123219	34.0	227802	62.9
2009	379992	13022	3.4	128949	33.9	238021	62.6
2010	400767	14317	3.6	136646	34.1	249804	62.3
2011	412772	15179	3.7	139539	33.8	258054	62.5
2012	426534	15923	3.7	142556	33.4	268055	62.9
2013	511887	10713	2.1	121078	23.7	380096	74.2
2014	623773	34473	5.5	139985	22.4	449315	72.1
2015	763212	45042	5.9	158963	20.8	559207	73.3
2016	816779	46778	5.7	149863	18.4	620138	75.9
2017	964946	76844	8.0	174156	18.0	713946	74.0
2018	1360376	81169	6.0	223621	16.4	1055586	77.6
2019	1418827	122389	8.6	231248	16.3	1065190	75.1
产业活动单位 **Establishments Units**							
2000	336330	5755	1.7	97001	28.8	233574	69.5
2001	374810	5386	1.5	94602	25.2	274822	73.3
2002	371791	5159	1.4	92909	25.0	273723	73.6
2003	374699	13518	3.6	94607	25.3	266574	71.1
2004	383093	10811	2.8	96284	25.1	275998	72.1
2005	387463	9924	2.6	101636	26.2	275903	71.2
2006	403819	10054	2.5	110784	27.4	282981	70.1
2007	421567	10957	2.6	118568	28.1	292042	69.3
2008	453789	12071	2.7	126048	27.8	315670	69.6
2009	471512	13655	2.9	131829	28.0	326028	69.1
2010	492300	14941	3.1	139509	28.3	337850	68.6
2011	503248	15806	3.1	142386	28.3	345056	68.6
2012	517217	16540	3.2	145425	28.1	355252	68.7
2013	587177	10922	1.9	123681	21.1	452574	77.0
2014	724050	34770	4.8	144347	19.9	544933	75.3
2015	861422	45342	5.3	163283	18.9	652797	75.8
2016	912907	47073	5.2	153299	16.8	712535	78.0
2017	1074783	77231	7.2	180181	16.8	817371	76.0
2018	1504762	81443	5.4	235057	15.6	1188262	79.0
2019	1544165	122776	8.0	240381	15.6	1181008	76.5

1-9 分行业法人单位数

Number of Institutional Unit by Sector

单位：个 (unit)

年份 Year	合计 Total	农林牧渔业 Agriculture, Forestry, Animal Husbandry and Fishery	采矿业 Mining	制造业 Manufacturing	电力、燃气及水的生产和供应业 Production and Supply of Electricity,Gas and Water	建筑业 Construction	交通运输仓储及邮政业 Transport, Storage and Post	信息传输、软件和信息技术服务业 Information Transmission, Software and Information Technology	批发和零售业 Wholesale and Retail Trade	住宿和餐饮业 Hotels and Catering Services
2003	272024	10803	5893	77783	794	5369	2471	1486	26052	4666
2004	277950	8660	6853	77694	938	5885	2462	1699	27384	4402
2005	286207	8334	7482	82822	946	6196	2430	1704	28669	4546
2006	305722	8600	7800	90965	1025	6942	2652	2156	33862	5181
2007	322828	9570	7893	97862	1090	7715	2882	2497	37450	5882
2008	362427	11406	7454	105315	1367	9083	4885	4631	47472	8809
2009	379992	13022	7774	109908	1450	9817	5300	4892	52698	9092
2010	400767	14317	7955	115652	1556	11483	5787	5267	58780	8240
2011	412772	15179	7951	117629	1605	12354	6112	5564	63176	8411
2012	426534	15923	7882	119770	1629	13275	6319	6451	67778	8688
2013	511887	10713	5741	100313	2181	12843	9409	4809	99916	11136
2014	623773	45427	6353	116185	2402	15511	11185	6306	118451	12223
2015	763212	57525	6487	127692	2892	22490	14401	11964	172393	14547
2016	816779	58830	4761	110992	2778	32006	16364	18203	206121	12911
2017	964946	90759	4746	124077	3753	42317	18979	25564	257404	15029
2018	1360376	116564	3588	138461	4971	78034	26433	56112	408979	21284
2019	1418827	156665	3314	140759	4965	83586	26724	56385	415432	21297

年份 Year	金融业 Finance	房地产业 Real estate	租赁和商务服务业 Leasing and Business Services	科学研究和技术服务业 Scientific Research and Technical Service	水利、环境和公共设施管理业 Management of Water Conservancy, Environment and Public Facilities	居民服务、修理和其他服务业 Resident Services, Repair and Other Services	教育 Education	卫生和社会工作 Health and Social Work	文化、体育和娱乐业 Culture, Sports and Entertainment	公共管理、社会保障和社会组织 Public Management, Social Security and Social Organization
2003	3248	2455	4952	4366	2193	1370	14180	25428	3445	75070
2004	1907	3467	5759	4038	1913	1813	16623	29686	2542	74225
2005	1679	3610	6468	4189	1942	1920	16705	29715	2599	74251
2006	1755	4210	7820	4341	1915	2298	16917	29660	2685	74938
2007	1796	5111	8620	4527	1979	2556	17127	30031	2814	75426
2008	1076	6765	9821	5266	2206	3700	22536	26057	3492	81086
2009	1368	7464	11318	5577	2323	4173	22751	26114	3607	81344
2010	1695	9328	13304	6221	2418	4448	22900	26174	3751	81491
2011	1983	10550	15093	6574	2510	4568	22940	25221	3876	81476
2012	2034	11420	16400	7053	2604	4814	23074	25239	4608	81573
2013	1369	14387	22923	24110	4033	6898	40079	34020	13048	93959
2014	3226	17160	29737	27150	4614	8029	42309	37933	15757	103815
2015	4159	22377	45465	36962	6094	11089	44940	38881	17609	105245
2016	4891	27501	57916	39894	7072	13368	45623	36862	15552	105134
2017	4921	31673	71012	47284	7865	15432	46326	36494	18163	103148
2018	3001	46303	126282	75709	9631	25048	60451	20369	34229	104927
2019	2727	47075	129596	77074	11121	24305	60178	20560	33538	103526

1-10 各市按三次产业和机构类型分法人单位数(2018年)
Number of Institutional Unit by orgniztion type and City (2018)

单位：个 (unit)

市(县) City(County)	合计 Total	第一产业 Primary Industry	第二产业 Secondary Industry	第三产业 Tertiary Industry	企业法人 Business Entity	事业法人 Institution Entity	机关法人 Government Entity	社会团体 Social Organization	其他 Others
全省 Total	**1360376**	**81169**	**223621**	**1055586**	**1067819**	**72608**	**14120**	**10688**	**195141**
省辖市 City									
郑州市 Zhengzhou	389198	3912	51056	334230	369511	6110	1230	1263	11084
开封市 Kaifeng	60530	3443	12470	44617	47662	2769	751	358	8990
洛阳市 Luoyang	95172	5556	18156	71460	75637	5881	1176	1281	11197
平顶山市 Pingdingshan	55383	3600	8496	43287	42398	3480	886	594	8025
安阳市 Anyang	55712	1839	11192	42681	42217	3573	891	340	8691
鹤壁市 Hebi	22383	1821	4860	15702	17821	996	383	263	2920
新乡市 Xinxiang	76738	5352	17696	53690	55197	4808	1021	611	15101
焦作市 Jiaozuo	43275	2395	10242	30638	33455	3146	717	421	5536
濮阳市 Puyang	40428	2645	7862	29921	28992	3265	563	320	7288
许昌市 Xuchang	62078	2958	13551	45569	50317	2211	521	454	8575
漯河市 Luohe	21896	711	3698	17487	16543	1625	362	194	3172
三门峡市 Sanmenxia	27075	2401	3629	21045	18901	2405	561	466	4742
南阳市 Nanyang	123261	14936	14745	93580	82736	9218	1205	1116	28986
商丘市 Shangqiu	74397	4422	12999	56976	51475	5227	938	635	16122
信阳市 Xinyang	61904	4995	9240	47669	39829	4819	1001	851	15404
周口市 Zhoukou	69887	8233	11972	49682	43199	6407	933	673	18675
驻马店市 Zhumadian	70414	11514	10032	48868	43712	6252	901	545	19004
济源市 Jiyuan	10645	436	1725	8484	8217	416	80	303	1629
省直管县 County Directly Administrated by Province									
巩义市 Gongyi	10942	294	3940	6708	9243	612	117	82	888
兰考县 Lankao	10559	562	2811	7186	8648	411	74	62	1364
汝州市 Ruzhou	11750	1089	1714	8947	8799	806	91	114	1940
滑县 Huaxian	10398	466	2339	7593	6825	605	81	69	2818
长垣市 Changyuan	11591	469	3132	7990	8814	772	99	96	1810
邓州市 Dengzhou	10422	2153	1394	6875	5280	1086	82	100	3874
永城市 Yongcheng	12218	612	1472	10134	8388	273	80	79	3398
固始县 Gushi	7683	382	1574	5727	5506	602	108	128	1339
鹿邑县 Luyi	8561	1311	1512	5738	4926	876	124	42	2593
新蔡县 Xincai	6613	969	1124	4520	4214	271	82	48	1998

1-11 各市按三次产业和机构类型分法人单位数(2019年)

Number of Institutional Unit by orgniztion type and City (2019)

单位：个 (unit)

市(县) City(County)	合计 Total	第一产业 Primary Industry	第二产业 Secondary Industry	第三产业 Tertiary Industry	企业法人 Business Entity	事业法人 Institution Entity	机关法人 Government Entity	社会团体 Social Organization	其他 Others
全省 Total	**1418827**	**122389**	**231248**	**1065190**	**1097825**	**71380**	**13960**	**10360**	**225302**
省辖市 City									
郑州市 Zhengzhou	388161	5121	51682	331358	368160	5943	1194	1238	11626
开封市 Kaifeng	72592	11985	13161	47446	53238	2739	738	362	15515
洛阳市 Luoyang	97120	8521	18556	70043	75777	5779	1163	1235	13166
平顶山市 Pingdingshan	58143	5137	8717	44289	44277	3481	843	541	9001
安阳市 Anyang	55317	4020	10721	40576	40221	3529	870	320	10377
鹤壁市 Hebi	22721	2184	5002	15535	17930	990	382	258	3161
新乡市 Xinxiang	83277	7309	19332	56636	60111	4685	1002	585	16894
焦作市 Jiaozuo	43432	4626	9879	28927	31709	3114	742	422	7445
濮阳市 Puyang	40937	3459	7938	29540	29029	3204	538	306	7860
许昌市 Xuchang	65128	4041	13904	47183	52938	2208	529	452	9001
漯河市 Luohe	21545	1439	3764	16342	15906	1653	367	179	3440
三门峡市 Sanmenxia	28975	3241	3878	21856	20125	2339	551	474	5486
南阳市 Nanyang	131847	18459	16194	97194	88759	8902	1194	1054	31938
商丘市 Shangqiu	78652	5595	13615	59442	55351	5142	933	600	16626
信阳市 Xinyang	63684	6227	9625	47832	41066	4770	1008	859	15981
周口市 Zhoukou	74510	12286	12153	50071	44634	6340	920	635	21981
驻马店市 Zhumadian	81085	17980	11223	51882	49552	6150	905	537	23941
济源市 Jiyuan	11701	759	1904	9038	9042	412	81	303	1863
省直管县 County Directly Administrated by Province									
巩义市 Gongyi	12000	587	4197	7216	10106	586	112	79	1117
兰考县 Lankao	12915	2328	3097	7490	9659	411	74	60	2711
汝州市 Ruzhou	13084	1841	1794	9449	9661	803	91	112	2417
滑县 Huaxian	12533	1360	2588	8585	8167	609	80	71	3606
长垣县 Changyuan	13001	475	3734	8792	10243	762	98	89	1809
邓州市 Dengzhou	12119	3541	1436	7142	5937	1074	84	92	4932
永城市 Yongcheng	12166	594	1593	9979	8686	248	81	74	3077
固始县 Gushi	9764	2242	1700	5822	6857	589	110	124	2084
鹿邑县 Luyi	9567	2491	1455	5621	4738	857	124	42	3806
新蔡县 Xincai	7720	1444	1379	4897	4781	277	89	58	2515

1-12 各市分行业法人单位数(2018年)

单位：个

市(县) City(County)	合计 Total	农林牧渔业 Agriculture Forestry, Animal Husbandry and Fishery	采矿业 Mining	制造业 Manufacturing	电力、燃气及水的生产和供应业 Production and Supply of Electricity, Gas and Water	建筑业 Construction	交通运输仓储及邮政业 Transport, Storage and Post	信息传输、软件和信息技术服务业 Information Transmission, Software and Information Technology Services
全　　省 Total	**1360376**	**116564**	**3588**	**138461**	**4971**	**78034**	**26433**	**56112**
省　辖　市 City								
郑　州　市 Zhengzhou	389198	5099	427	19499	408	31094	6113	31099
开　封　市 Kaifeng	60530	4978	4	8493	197	3834	1168	1581
洛　阳　市 Luoyang	95172	6500	667	11531	463	5645	1653	4025
平顶山市 Pingdingshan	55383	4563	440	4999	320	2835	1054	1408
安　阳　市 Anyang	55712	3243	134	6881	386	3861	1278	1411
鹤　壁　市 Hebi	22383	2103	62	3347	155	1350	495	644
新　乡　市 Xinxiang	76738	8163	46	13321	303	4089	1483	2031
焦　作　市 Jiaozuo	43275	2948	129	8006	222	1939	1377	1473
濮　阳　市 Puyang	40428	3479	32	5157	200	2547	1126	1093
许　昌　市 Xuchang	62078	4441	159	10267	187	3064	1076	1569
漯　河　市 Luohe	21896	1066	4	2540	66	1098	691	666
三门峡市 Sanmenxia	27075	2721	414	1716	239	1305	793	555
南　阳　市 Nanyang	123261	20146	528	10878	524	2905	2073	3014
商　丘　市 Shangqiu	74397	6936	11	10000	384	2648	1812	1939
信　阳　市 Xinyang	61904	11643	256	5401	313	3310	1182	1223
周　口　市 Zhoukou	69887	12085	5	9112	321	2557	1538	803
驻马店市 Zhumadian	70414	15723	208	6111	231	3528	1180	1094
济　源　市 Jiyuan	10645	727	62	1202	52	425	341	484
省直管县 County Directly Administrated by Province								
巩　义　市 Gongyi	10942	341	33	3465	43	410	249	222
兰　考　县 Lankao	10559	813	2	2122	44	654	206	161
汝　州　市 Ruzhou	11750	1394	140	1048	63	473	186	244
滑　　县 Huaxian	10398	969		1803	34	507	126	97
长　垣　县 Changyuan	11591	586		2307	36	806	150	133
邓　州　市 Dengzhou	10422	2886	5	857	65	475	119	107
永　城　市 Yongcheng	12218	1345	8	1066	43	366	289	415
固　始　县 Gushi	7683	488	73	1082	56	367	233	143
鹿　邑　县 Luyi	8561	1503	1	1192	42	279	192	96
新　蔡　县 Xincai	6613	1563		684	19	423	76	56

Number of Institutional Unit by Sector and City (2018)

(unit)

批发和零售业 Wholesale and Retail Trade	住宿和餐饮业 Hotels and Catering Services	金融业 Finance	房地产业 Real Estate	租赁和商务服务业 Leasing and Business Services	科学研究和技术服务业 Scientific Research, and Technical Service	水利、环境和公共设施管理业 Management of Water Conservancy, Environment and Public Facilities	居民服务、修理和其他服务业 Resident Services, Repair and Other Services	教育 Education	卫生和社会工作 Health and Social Work	文化、体育和娱乐业 Culture, Sports and Entertainment	公共管理、社会保障和社会组织 Public Management, Social Security and Social Organization
408979	**21284**	**3001**	**46303**	**126282**	**75709**	**9631**	**25048**	**60451**	**20369**	**34229**	**104927**
141836	6272	960	16447	61544	30980	1660	8206	7516	2021	9466	8551
17844	1285	129	2134	4723	2620	352	1140	2885	710	1748	4705
26743	1635	191	3118	7690	5429	885	1717	4183	2270	2962	7865
18446	999	168	2069	3332	2075	627	967	3102	953	1413	5613
16447	720	138	1551	4601	2094	562	1170	3163	553	1257	6262
5711	343	50	872	1741	837	326	419	1111	218	549	2050
19970	777	132	2448	4985	2227	529	1310	4207	2184	1364	7169
12052	513	126	1156	2368	1290	289	709	2145	590	1246	4697
10092	389	106	1264	2650	2030	331	817	2637	468	912	5098
20157	936	117	1700	3502	3491	662	918	2688	1354	1451	4339
6838	456	67	881	1912	870	211	353	1159	275	341	2402
8734	424	65	852	1731	886	317	512	874	382	788	3767
37941	2004	199	2763	9005	5789	927	2051	6950	2541	2436	10587
16987	980	107	2505	5269	5111	471	1411	4765	1679	3304	8078
12875	1055	186	2281	4130	3800	481	1000	2368	1064	1540	7796
16107	1192	111	1568	2935	2604	331	1041	5974	1799	1658	8146
17083	1191	119	2373	3364	3107	469	1113	4335	1032	1496	6657
3116	113	30	321	800	469	201	194	389	276	298	1145
3596	107	11	244	325	124	78	102	361	128	233	870
2987	178	11	325	797	415	83	237	535	72	232	685
3782	228	8	269	703	361	169	212	868	345	319	938
3225	89	8	162	535	261	53	107	811	101	189	1321
3645	117	9	232	768	336	55	172	632	435	182	990
1740	171	8	268	491	208	39	153	934	636	197	1063
2589	141	11	371	920	470	117	276	442	590	1686	1073
1890	142	13	231	511	281	83	175	421	180	172	1142
1618	141	2	224	373	202	58	150	805	501	258	924
1696	110	7	256	260	217	37	106	211	112	147	633

1-13 各市分行业法人单位数(2019年)

单位：个

市(县) City(County)	合计 Total	农林牧渔业 Agriculture Forestry, Animal Husbandry and Fishery	采矿业 Mining	制造业 Manufacturing	电力、燃气及水的生产和供应业 Production and Supply of Electricity,Gas and Water	建筑业 Construction	交通运输仓储及邮政业 Transport, Storage and Post	信息传输、软件和信息技术服务业 Information Transmission, Software and Information Technology Services
全省 Total	**1418827**	**156665**	**3314**	**140759**	**4965**	**83586**	**26724**	**56385**
省辖市 City								
郑州市 Zhengzhou	388161	6215	365	19652	422	31608	6149	30448
开封市 Kaifeng	72592	13485	5	8835	200	4180	1166	2053
洛阳市 Luoyang	97120	9464	635	11718	449	5892	1661	3798
平顶山市 Pingdingshan	58143	6102	396	5078	305	3029	1083	1495
安阳市 Anyang	55317	5382	83	6599	372	3722	1119	1274
鹤壁市 Hebi	22721	2463	56	3343	145	1505	487	659
新乡市 Xinxiang	83277	10063	43	14135	304	4916	1568	2149
焦作市 Jiaozuo	43432	5171	124	7717	206	1885	1330	1250
濮阳市 Puyang	40937	4235	34	5056	202	2710	1113	1055
许昌市 Xuchang	65128	5493	147	10269	206	3406	1156	1737
漯河市 Luohe	21545	1785	3	2675	76	1021	666	584
三门峡市 Sanmenxia	28975	3553	359	1837	233	1490	813	601
南阳市 Nanyang	131847	23363	540	11486	515	3742	2172	3261
商丘市 Shangqiu	78652	8109	11	10189	390	3069	1856	2183
信阳市 Xinyang	63684	12633	261	5440	317	3647	1179	1249
周口市 Zhoukou	74510	15999	4	8957	328	2889	1547	893
驻马店市 Zhumadian	81085	22108	190	6551	239	4291	1293	1220
济源市 Jiyuan	11701	1042	58	1222	56	584	366	476
省直管县 County Directly Administrated by Province								
巩义市 Gongyi	12000	635	33	3651	45	481	255	213
兰考县 Lankao	12915	2571	2	2355	51	700	200	221
汝州市 Ruzhou	13084	2123	128	1080	53	545	203	281
滑县 Huaxian	12533	1898		1944	32	617	134	116
长垣县 Changyuan	13001	587	1	2660	36	1055	159	159
邓州市 Dengzhou	12119	4212	5	883	64	494	121	113
永城市 Yongcheng	12166	1322	8	1153	44	401	283	379
固始县 Gushi	9764	2350	74	1109	53	469	226	142
鹿邑县 Luyi	9567	2767	1	1145	42	269	192	84
新蔡县 Xincai	7720	2086	3	791	21	566	95	69

Number of Institutional Unit by Sector and City (2019)

(unit)

批发和零售业 Wholesale and Retail Trade	住宿和餐饮业 Hotels and Catering Services	金融业 Finance	房地产业 Real Estate	租赁和商务服务业 Leasing and Business Services	科学研究和技术服务业 Scientific Research, and Technical Service	水利、环境和公共设施管理业 Management of Water Conservancy, Environment and Public Facilities	居民服务、修理和其他服务业 Resident Services, Repair and Other Services	教育 Education	卫生和社会工作 Health and Social Work	文化、体育和娱乐业 Culture, Sports and Entertainment	公共管理、社会保障和社会组织 Public Management, Social Security and Social Organization
415432	**21297**	**2727**	**47075**	**129596**	**77074**	**11121**	**24305**	**60178**	**20560**	**33538**	**103526**
141676	6182	729	16112	61526	30860	1953	7735	7274	2019	8886	8350
19119	1340	133	2176	5486	2845	410	1157	2938	723	1706	4635
26361	1621	193	3097	7289	5232	1002	1627	4154	2303	2850	7774
19141	996	126	2104	3537	2154	693	944	3094	964	1374	5528
15607	671	125	1471	4297	1954	549	1030	3115	551	1166	6230
5559	336	52	863	1715	894	331	391	1095	215	571	2041
21511	788	138	2534	5717	2567	622	1296	4257	2201	1420	7048
11079	486	123	1136	2208	1223	299	624	2130	580	1164	4697
9929	366	107	1249	2717	2092	349	776	2590	475	864	5018
20674	938	115	1769	3900	3652	886	924	2701	1362	1443	4350
6396	417	68	857	1754	780	205	355	1122	285	316	2180
9065	457	57	897	1851	994	392	508	974	395	798	3701
39903	2034	204	3108	9616	6381	1123	2004	6917	2565	2534	10379
17961	1003	116	2708	5704	5413	558	1483	4769	1712	3424	7994
13038	1065	175	2372	4317	3670	595	985	2347	1083	1545	7766
16553	1205	108	1665	2955	2575	371	1039	5906	1792	1636	8088
18508	1278	127	2616	4041	3266	561	1228	4384	1057	1534	6593
3352	114	31	341	966	522	222	199	411	278	307	1154
3975	109	9	255	391	154	104	123	371	126	232	838
3086	184	13	340	890	431	90	256	533	80	230	682
4142	246	9	287	782	359	197	208	861	347	305	928
3875	104	9	200	650	284	71	118	832	110	178	1361
4328	109	9	249	828	333	62	175	658	433	183	977
1903	203	6	313	595	200	70	134	928	610	234	1031
2599	140	11	364	897	454	109	277	443	587	1632	1063
1897	148	12	270	565	269	91	177	418	191	177	1126
1524	131	2	213	360	188	58	136	789	498	248	920
1741	160	16	288	280	242	52	155	216	118	164	657

1-14　各市按登记注册类型分企业法人单位数(2018年)

单位：个

市(县)	City(County)	企业单位数 Number of Enterprises	内资企业 Domestic Funded Enterprises	#国有企业 State-owned Enterprises	#集体企业 Collective-owned Enterprises	#股份合作企业 Cooperative Enterprises
全省	**Total**	**1067819**	**1066284**	**3836**	**5599**	**422**
省辖市	**City**					
郑州市	Zhengzhou	369511	368972	497	548	64
开封市	Kaifeng	47662	47568	213	305	19
洛阳市	Luoyang	75637	75509	315	336	15
平顶山市	Pingdingshan	42398	42324	244	235	16
安阳市	Anyang	42217	42159	158	324	11
鹤壁市	Hebi	17821	17804	67	158	30
新乡市	Xinxiang	55197	55104	217	448	31
焦作市	Jiaozuo	33455	33405	135	197	9
濮阳市	Puyang	28992	28958	151	147	24
许昌市	Xuchang	50317	50268	85	185	2
漯河市	Luohe	16543	16499	95	94	6
三门峡市	Sanmenxia	18901	18864	130	191	4
南阳市	Nanyang	82736	82639	493	569	114
商丘市	Shangqiu	51475	51416	210	328	11
信阳市	Xinyang	39829	39796	310	782	15
周口市	Zhoukou	43199	43147	263	430	30
驻马店市	Zhumadian	43712	43650	225	280	21
济源市	Jiyuan	8217	8202	28	42	
省直管县	**County Directly Administrated by Province**					
巩义市	Gongyi	9243	9232	27	89	7
兰考县	Lankao	8648	8638	16	10	1
汝州市	Ruzhou	8799	8777	27	27	
滑县	Huaxian	6825	6813	23	67	2
长垣县	Changyuan	8814	8804	18	23	2
邓州市	Dengzhou	5280	5271	36	50	2
永城市	Yongcheng	8388	8378	32	39	1
固始县	Gushi	5506	5503	25	42	1
鹿邑县	Luyi	4926	4920	17	43	18
新蔡县	Xincai	4214	4213	29	29	1

Number of Business Entities by City and Status of Registration (2018)

(unit)

#联 营 Joint Ownership	#有限责任公司 Limited Liability Corporations	#股份有限公司 Share-holding Corporations Ltd.	#私 营 Private	#其他内资 Others	港、澳、台商投资企业 Enterprises with Funds from Hong Kong, Macao and Taiwan	外商投资企业 Enterprises with Foreign Investment
606	**180516**	**13917**	**861193**	**195**	**649**	**886**
36	82842	2215	282766	4	262	277
20	5651	1153	40193	14	40	54
35	9913	809	64076	10	49	79
18	7708	831	33250	22	24	50
28	8264	724	32648	2	23	35
9	2562	265	14709	4	7	10
29	6028	866	47477	8	32	61
24	5561	568	26902	9	16	34
15	4292	397	23925	7	14	20
33	7335	463	42161	4	29	20
11	4093	403	11797		15	29
21	1819	342	16356	1	15	22
157	9869	1400	70024	13	44	53
47	6585	744	43466	25	21	38
38	5229	1059	32337	26	10	23
54	5385	771	36178	36	18	34
29	6341	800	35944	10	27	35
2	1039	107	6984		3	12
4	1485	89	7531		2	9
1	981	107	7520	2	2	8
1	1268	126	7320	8	3	19
9	477	86	6149		5	7
5	1497	80	7178	1	2	8
2	861	118	4197	5	5	4
4	371	52	7874	5	2	8
10	1375	243	3807			3
4	859	122	3846	11	4	2
	584	133	3436	1		1

1-15 各市按登记注册类型分企业法人单位数(2019年)

单位：个

市(县) City(County)	企业单位数 Number of Enterprises	内资企业 Domestic Funded Enterprises	#国有企业 State-owned Enterprises	#集体企业 Collective-owned Enterprises	#股份合作企业 Cooperative Enterprises
全省 Total	**1097825**	**1095974**	**3769**	**5226**	**431**
省辖市 City					
郑州市 Zhengzhou	368160	367440	532	584	86
开封市 Kaifeng	53238	53132	249	345	22
洛阳市 Luoyang	75777	75625	246	272	10
平顶山市 Pingdingshan	44277	44200	252	258	15
安阳市 Anyang	40221	40164	151	308	10
鹤壁市 Hebi	17930	17897	55	138	25
新乡市 Xinxiang	60111	60002	213	390	28
焦作市 Jiaozuo	31709	31649	118	198	5
濮阳市 Puyang	29029	28988	150	151	23
许昌市 Xuchang	52938	52872	97	207	2
漯河市 Luohe	15906	15862	98	102	6
三门峡市 Sanmenxia	20125	20083	145	186	3
南阳市 Nanyang	88759	88658	489	463	117
商丘市 Shangqiu	55351	55290	182	306	13
信阳市 Xinyang	41066	41027	292	562	13
周口市 Zhoukou	44634	44573	242	441	28
驻马店市 Zhumadian	49552	49488	233	295	25
济源市 Jiyuan	9042	9024	25	20	
省直管县 County Directly Administrated by Province					
巩义市 Gongyi	10106	10094	29	86	6
兰考县 Lankao	9659	9651	20	13	1
汝州市 Ruzhou	9661	9654	28	28	
滑县 Huaxian	8167	8157	13	57	4
长垣县 Changyuan	10243	10230	23	26	3
邓州市 Dengzhou	5937	5926	42	39	4
永城市 Yongcheng	8686	8680	14	6	1
固始县 Gushi	6857	6851	24	41	2
鹿邑县 Luyi	4738	4732	20	53	19
新蔡县 Xincai	4781	4778	30	28	12

Number of Business Entities by City and Status of Registration (2019)

(unit)

#联　营 Joint Ownership	#有限责任公　司 Limited Liability Corporations	#股份有限公　司 Share-holding Corporations Ltd.	#私　营 Private	#其他内资 Others	港、澳、台商投资企业 Enterprises with Funds from Hong Kong, Macao and Taiwan	外商投资企　业 Enterprises with Foreign Investment
292	**68416**	**5352**	**1010970**	**1518**	**782**	**1069**
16	21836	851	343352	183	332	388
12	3460	405	48449	190	45	61
12	3636	250	71148	51	53	99
10	4057	315	39181	112	31	46
13	2976	196	36470	40	22	35
1	1215	104	16330	29	15	18
12	3305	336	55633	85	40	69
10	2323	243	28737	15	21	39
6	2303	162	26182	11	19	22
8	3251	252	48731	324	33	33
8	1536	163	13931	18	18	26
7	1270	148	18284	40	19	23
93	3501	387	83453	155	46	55
29	3736	352	50639	33	24	37
16	2399	282	37425	38	10	29
19	3192	433	40128	90	18	43
20	3859	438	44515	103	31	33
	561	35	8382	1	5	13
3	692	43	9226	9	3	9
2	706	52	8824	33	4	4
	485	22	9072	19	4	3
5	313	28	7722	15	5	5
1	899	38	9237	3	3	10
2	258	19	5553	9	7	4
1	165	13	8477	3	3	3
2	359	35	6386	2		6
	650	52	3914	24	4	2
	619	102	3916	71	1	2

1-16 “四上”法人单位数(2018年底)

Number of Institutional Unit of industry, construction, wholesale and retail trades, hotels and catering enterprises above designated size (End of 2018)

单位：个 (unit)

市(县) City(County)	合 计 Total	工 业 Industry	建筑业 Construction	批发和零售业 Wholesale and retail trade	住宿和餐饮业 Hotels and Catering Services	房地产业 Real estate	重点服务业 Key Services
全 省 Total	**57215**	**20992**	**8082**	**9790**	**2277**	**7536**	**8538**
省 辖 市 City							
郑 州 市 Zhengzhou	10514	2686	2337	1816	403	1457	1815
开 封 市 Kaifeng	2780	1164	347	485	120	254	410
洛 阳 市 Luoyang	4605	1882	628	806	221	558	510
平 顶 山 市 Pingdingshan	2822	844	407	516	130	480	445
安 阳 市 Anyang	2222	872	443	351	69	306	181
鹤 壁 市 Hebi	985	461	156	113	21	135	99
新 乡 市 Xinxiang	3346	1224	703	505	101	531	282
焦 作 市 Jiaozuo	2540	1207	254	439	60	241	339
濮 阳 市 Puyang	1888	817	296	251	47	204	273
许 昌 市 Xuchang	3400	1573	176	439	113	465	634
漯 河 市 Luohe	1283	559	116	226	60	182	140
三 门 峡 市 Sanmenxia	1328	418	198	293	55	209	155
南 阳 市 Nanyang	4752	1878	532	1034	239	496	573
商 丘 市 Shangqiu	3679	1368	279	784	124	562	562
信 阳 市 Xinyang	3459	1147	333	603	185	541	650
周 口 市 Zhoukou	3351	1305	328	518	156	347	697
驻 马 店 市 Zhumadian	3621	1351	445	503	163	495	664
济 源 市 Jiyuan	640	236	104	108	10	73	109
省 直 管 县 County Directly Administrated by Province							
巩 义 市 Gongyi	862	541	40	86	16	49	130
兰 考 县 Lankao	618	247	56	151	24	16	124
汝 州 市 Ruzhou	614	196	33	164	8	33	180
滑 县 Huaxian	467	221	75	87	10	31	43
长 垣 县 Changyuan	727	192	263	105	35	67	65
邓 州 市 Dengzhou	504	165	57	136	28	62	56
永 城 市 Yongcheng	528	227	58	77	24	59	83
固 始 县 Gushi	634	204	44	175	45	45	121
鹿 邑 县 Luyi	541	185	31	82	37	37	169
新 蔡 县 Xincai	529	143	51	124	37	70	104

1–17 "四上"法人单位数(2019年底)

Number of Institutional Unit of industry, construction, wholesale and retail trades, hotels and catering enterprises above designated size (End of 2019)

单位：个 (unit)

市(县)	City(County)	合计 Total	工业 Industry	建筑业 Construction	批发和零售业 Wholesale and retail trade	住宿和餐饮业 Hotels and Catering Services	房地产业 Real estate	重点服务业 Key Services
全省	**Total**	**58351**	**19496**	**8530**	**11097**	**2565**	**7930**	**8733**
省辖市	**City**							
郑州市	Zhengzhou	11248	2420	2268	2446	560	1438	2116
开封市	Kaifeng	2685	1038	364	506	128	292	357
洛阳市	Luoyang	4742	1793	669	906	218	602	554
平顶山市	Pingdingshan	2775	822	422	457	121	517	436
安阳市	Anyang	2078	756	458	336	68	304	156
鹤壁市	Hebi	948	387	174	131	20	136	100
新乡市	Xinxiang	3657	1338	787	583	96	550	303
焦作市	Jiaozuo	2505	1101	286	457	59	283	319
濮阳市	Puyang	1750	687	335	243	48	185	252
许昌市	Xuchang	3394	1529	194	439	138	445	649
漯河市	Luohe	1332	571	117	266	65	202	111
三门峡市	Sanmenxia	1380	369	202	362	73	208	166
南阳市	Nanyang	4337	1546	527	970	237	536	521
商丘市	Shangqiu	3828	1400	308	804	139	584	593
信阳市	Xinyang	3663	1134	372	732	208	594	623
周口市	Zhoukou	4015	1334	449	769	197	468	798
驻马店市	Zhumadian	3384	1051	496	570	179	511	577
济源市	Jiyuan	630	220	102	120	11	75	102
省直管县	**County Directly Administrated by Province**							
巩义市	Gongyi	810	487	41	96	16	58	112
兰考县	Lankao	613	224	72	158	31	37	91
汝州市	Ruzhou	555	191	37	127	7	43	150
滑县	Huaxian	473	232	82	65	12	37	45
长垣县	Changyuan	790	232	309	116	28	40	65
邓州市	Dengzhou	506	142	62	151	34	60	57
永城市	Yongcheng	591	271	62	76	29	60	93
固始县	Gushi	649	199	44	189	45	51	121
鹿邑县	Luyi	638	236	38	88	43	41	192
新蔡县	Xincai	529	137	50	157	42	68	75

1-18 航空港主要经济指标

Main Economic Indicators of Zhengzhou Airport

指 标	Item	2018 绝对数 Absolute value	2018 增长速度(%) Growth Rate (%)	2019 绝对数 Absolute value	2019 增长速度(%) Growth Rate (%)
生产总值(亿元)	Gross Domestic Product (100 million yuan)	800.24	12.0	980.80	10.2
第一产业	Primary Industry	9.10	-10.9	9.00	-6.7
第二产业	Secondary Industry	567.57	12.0	697.00	10.1
第三产业	Tertiary Industry	223.58	13.6	274.80	11.5
规模以上工业增加值(亿元)	value-added of Industrial Above Designated Size (100 million yuan)		11.7		10.1
固定资产投资(亿元)	Investment in Fixed Assets		0.1		1.4
#民间投资	Civilian		-29.9		172.8
#工业	Industry		-52.6		53.7
#房地产业	Real Estate		21.3		-26.6
社会消费品零售总额(亿元)	Total Retail Sales of Consumer Goods (100 million yuan)	126.94	12.2	142.49	12.2
#限上企业(单位)消费品零售额	above Designated Size	9.10	-18.8	8.01	-4.0
外商实际投资额(亿美元)	Actually Amount of Foreign Investment (USD 100 million)	5.66	4.8	5.84	3.1
引进省外境内资金(亿元)	Domestic Capital from other Provinces (100 million yuan)	45.10	5.6	46.60	3.3
一般公共预算收入(亿元)	General Public Budget Revenue of the Local Government (100 million yuan)	42.37	16.8	46.72	10.0
#税收收入	Tax Revenue	30.54	18.6	38.88	26.9
一般公共预算支出(亿元)	Genenral Public Budget Expenditure of the Local Government (100 million yuan)	101.37	36.7	88.69	-12.5
民航旅客吞吐量(万人次)	Passenger Throughput of Civil Aviation (10 000 person-time)	2733.47	12.5	2912.93	6.6
民航货邮吞吐量(万吨)	Freight Throughput of Civil Aviation (10 000 tons)	51.49	2.4	52.20	1.4
航空运输飞行架次(万架次)	Air Transport Flight Vehicles (10 000 vehicles)	20.89	7.1	21.57	3.3

主要统计指标解释

行政区划 指国家对行政区域的划分。根据有关法规规定，我国的行政区域划分如下：(1)全国分为省、自治区、直辖市；(2)省、自治区分为自治州、县、自治县、市；(3)自治州分为县、自治县、市；(4) 自治区、自治州、自治县都是民族自治的地方；县、自治县分为乡、民族乡、镇；(5)直辖市和较大的市分为区、县；(6)国家在必要时设立的特别行政区。

可比价格 指计算各种总量指标所采用的扣除了价格变动因素的价格，可进行不同时期总量指标的对比。按可比价格计算总量指标有两种方法：一种是直接用产品产量乘某一年的不变价格计算；另一种是用价格指数进行缩减。

不变价格 指以同类产品某年的平均价格作为固定价格，用于计算各年的产品价值。按不变价格计算的产品价值消除了价格变动因素，不同时期对比可以反映生产的发展速度。新中国成立后，随着工农业产品价格水平的变化，国家统计局先后五次制定了全国统一的工业产品不变价格和农业产品不变价格。从 1952 年到 1957 年使用 1952 年工（农）业产品不变价格，从 1957 年到 1970 年使用 1957 年不变价格，从 1971 年到 1980 年使用 1970 年不变价格，从 1981 年到 1990 年使用 1980 年不变价格，从 1991 年开始使用 1990 年不变价格。

平均增长速度 平均增长速度表明社会经济现象在一个较长的时期内逐期平均增长变化的程度，它不能根据各个环比增长速度直接求得，但与平均发展速度之间存在着一定的数量关系：平均增长速度＝平均发展速度－1。

平均发展速度是一种根据环比发展速度计算的序时平均数，由于各时期对比的基础不同，所以计算平均发展速度不能采用一般的序时平均数的计算方法，计算方法分为水平法和累计法。水平法，又称几何平均法，即将环比发展速度按连乘法用几何平均数公式计算。累计法，也称方程法，根据一段时期内各年发展水平总和与基期水平的关系，列出方程式计算平均发展速度。水平法着重考虑最后一年所达到的发展水平；累计法着重考虑整个时期累计发展水平的总量。

本《年鉴》内所列的平均增长速度，除固定资产投资用“累计法”计算外，其余均用“水平法”计算。从某年到某年平均增长速度的年份，均不包括基期年在内。如建国四十三年以来的平均增长速度是以 1949 年为基期计算的，则写为 1950-1992 年平均增长速度，其余类推。

国民经济行业分类 自 2012 年定期报表开始使用新的《国民经济行业分类》(GB/T4754-2011)。该分类是由国家统计局组织修订，国家质量监督检验检疫总局和中国国家标准化管理委员会于 2011 年 4 月 29 日发布。这次修订是在 2002 年分类标准的基础上，参照联合国《全部经济活动的国际标准产业分类》(ISIC/Rev.4）进行的。修订后的《国民经济行业分类》（GB/T4754-2012）共有门类 20 个，大类 96 个，中类 432 个，小类 1094 个。

企业（单位）登记注册类型 是以在工商行政管理机关登记注册的各类企业为划分对象，以工商行政管理部门对企业登记注册的类型为依据，将企业登记注册类型分为内资企业、港澳台商投资企业和外商投资企业三大类。内资企业包括国有企业、集体企业、股份合作企业、联营企业、有限责任公司、股份有限公司、私营公司和其他企业；港澳台商投资企业和外商投资企业分别包括合资经营企业、合作经营企业、独资经营企业和股份有限公司。对不在工商行政管理部门进行登记注册的行政机关、事业单位和社会团体，主要按其经费来源和管理方式进行划分。

国有企业 指企业全部资产归国家所有，并按《中华人民共和国企业法人登记管理条例》规定登记注册的非公司制的经济组织。不包括有限责任公司中的国有独资公司。

集体企业 指企业资产归集体所有，并按《中华人民共和国企业法人登记管理条例》规定登记注册的经济组织。

股份合作企业 指以合作制为基础，由企业职工共同出资入股，吸收一定比例的社会资产投资组建，实行自主经营，自负盈亏，共同劳动，民主管理，按劳分配与按股分红相结合的一种集体经济组织。

联营企业 指两个及两个以上相同或不同所有制性质的企业法人或事业单位法人，按自愿、平等、互利的原则，共同投资组成的经济组织。联营企业包括国有联营企业、集体联营企业、国有与集体联营企业和其他联营企业。

有限责任公司 指根据《中华人民共和国公司登记管理条例》规定登记注册，由两个以上、五十个以下的股东共同出资，每个股东以其所认缴的出资额对公司承担有限责任，公司以其全部资产对其债务承担责任的经济组织。有限责任公司包括国有独资公司以及其他有限责任公司。

股份有限公司 指根据《中华人民共和国公司登记管理条例》规定登记注册，其全部注册资本由等额股份构成并通过发行股票筹集资本，股东以其认购的股份对公司承担有限责任，公司以其全部资产对其债务承担责任的经济组织。

私营企业 指由自然人投资设立或由自然人控股，以雇佣劳动为基础的营利性经济组织。包括按照《公司法》、《合伙企业法》、《私营企业暂行条例》规定登记注册的私营有限责任公司、私营股份有限公司、私营合伙企业和私营独资企业。

其他内资企业 指上述企业之外的其他内资经济组织。

合资经营企业（港或澳、台资） 指港澳台地区投资者与内地企业依照《中华人民共和国中外合资经营企业法》及有关法律的规定，按合同规定的比例投资设立、分享利润和分担风险的企业。

合作经营企业（港或澳、台资） 指港澳台地区投资者与内地企业依照《中华人民共和国中外合作经营企业法》及有关法律的规定，依照合作合同的约定进行投资或提供条件设立、分配利润和分担风险的企业。

港澳台商独资经营企业 指依照《中华人民共和国外资企业法》及有关法律的规定，在内地由港澳台地区投资者全额投资设立的企业。

港澳台商投资股份有限公司 指根据国家有关规定，经外经贸部依法批准设立，其中港、澳、台商的股本占公司注册资本的比例达25%以上的股份有限公司。凡其中港、澳、台商的股本占公司注册资本的比例小于25%的，属于内资企业中的股份有限公司。

中外合资经营企业 指外国企业或外国人与中国内地企业依照《中华人民共和国中外合资经营企业法》及有关法律的规定，按合同规定的比例投资设立、分享利润和分担风险的企业。

中外合作经营企业 指外国企业或外国人与中国内地企业依照《中华人民共和国中外合作经营企业法》及有关法律的规定，依照合作合同的约定进行投资或提供条件设立、分配利润和分担风险的企业。

外资企业 指依照《中华人民共和国外资企业法》及有关法律的规定，在中国内地由外国投资者全额投资设立的企业。

外商投资股份有限公司 指根据国家有关规定，经外经贸部依法批准设立，其中外资的股本占公司注册资本的比例达25%以上的股份有限公司。凡其中外资股本占公司注册资本的比例小于25%的，属于内资企业中的股份有限公司。

行政机关、事业单位和社会团体 参照企业登记注册类型，主要按其经费来源和管理方式划分。具体规定如下：

⑴行政机关：包括国家机关和政党机关，原则上均列为“国有”。但有特殊规定的，如供销社等，则列为“集体”。

⑵事业单位：包括经国家机构编制部门和有关业务主管部门批准成立的各类事业单位，不包括实行企业化管理的事业单位。事业单位的划分办法如下：

①由国家财政预算拨款或列入财政预算外资金管理以及经费主要来源于国有主管部门或国有上级单位的事业单位，列为“国有”。

②经费主要来源于集体单位的事业单位，列为“集体”。

③公民个人（或个人合伙）开办的事业单位，列为“私营”。

④上述以外的其他事业单位，如果其经费来源不明确，按管理方式进行归类。

⑶社会团体：包括经民政部门批准成立以及未纳入社会团体管理条例范围的工会、妇联等各类社会团体。社会团体的划分办法如下：

①未纳入民政部社会团体管理条例范围的工会、妇联、共青团、青联、工商联、科协、侨联等社会团体，国家拨款设立的基金会或基金管理组织以及经费主要来源于国有业务主管部门或国有上级单位的社会团体，列为“国有”。

②经费主要来源于集体单位的社会团体，列为“集体”。

③公民个人（或个人合伙）开办的社会团体，划为“私营”。

④上述以外的其他社会团体，如果其经费来源不明确，改按管理方式进行归类。

法人单位 指具备：

⑴依法成立、有自己的名称、组织机构和场所、能够独立承担民事责任；

⑵独立拥有和使用（或授权使用）资产、承担负债、有权与其它单位签订合同；

⑶会计上独立核算、能够编制资产负债表。法人单位包括企业法人、事业单位法人、机关法人、会团体法人和其他法人。

产业活动单位　是法人单位的附属单位。产业活动单位应具备下列条件：

⑴在一个场所从事一种或主要从事一种社会经济活动；

⑵相对独立组织生产经营和业务活动；

⑶能够掌握收入和支出等业务核算资料。

Explanatory Notes on Main Statistical Indicators

Divisions of Administrative Areas refers to the division of administrative areas by the State. The relative laws stipulate that 1) the whole country is divided into provinces, autonomous regions and municipalities directly under the Central Government; 2) provinces and autonomous regions are further divided into autonomous prefectures, counties, autonomous counties and cities; 3) autonomous prefectures are further divided into counties, autonomous counties and cities; 4) counties and autonomous counties are further divided into townships, ethnic townships and towns; 5) municipalities directly under the Central Government and large cities are divided into districts and counties, 6) the State shall, when necessary, establish special administrative regions.

Comparable Prices refer to prices that are used to remove the factors of price change in calculating economic aggregates, so as to facilitate comparison of aggregates over time. Two methods are used for calculating economic aggregates at comparable prices:

One is Multiplying the output of products by their constant prices of certain year, and other is Deflation of data at current prices by relevant price index.

Constant Price refers to the average price of a given product in certain year, which is used for comparison of over output value time. As the output value at constant prices removes the factor of price changes, it reflects the trend of production development over time. Since 1949,with the changes in general price level, the State Statistical Bureau has issued nationally unified constant prices five times: the 1952 constant prices for 1949-1957;the 1957 constant prices for 1957-1971; the 1970 constant prices for 1971-1981; the 1980 constant prices for 1981-1990;and the 1990 constant prices have been used since 1991.

Average Annual Growth Rate shows the average growth rate of social and economic development during a longer period. It can not be directly calculated by chain based growth rate. The relation is:

Average Annual Growth Rate = Average Speed of Development – 1

Average speed of development is the time series average of speed which calculated by chain based. Because the reference bases during the different periods are not same, average speed of development can not be calculated by the general method. Level approach and accumulative approach for calculating average speed of development rate are applied. The “level approach”, or the method of calculating the geometric average, is derived by the formula of geometric average of the chain-based speeds of development, or comparing the level of the last year of the interval with that of the beginning year; the other is called the “accumulative approach” or the “algebraic average”, “equation” method, which is derived by the summation of the actual figure of each year in the interval divided by the figure in the base year. The level approach focuses on the level of the last year, while the accumulative approach emphasizes the aggregate development in the duration.

The average annual growth rates listed in the Yearbook are calculated by the level approach except for the growth rate of investment in fixed assets. The base year is not listed in the duration for which average annual growth rates are computed. For instance, the average annual growth rate of the 43 years since 1949 is shown as the average annual growth rate of 1950-1992 without showing the base year 1949.

Industrial Classification of the National Economy The new Industrial Classification of the National Economy (GB/T 4754-2011) is introduced starting from the compilation of 2012 annual statistics. The revision, based on the 2002 classification, was organized by the National Bureau of Statistics taking into consideration of the International Standards of the Industrial Classification of All Economic Activities (ISIC/Rev.4) of the United Nations. The new Classification was promulgated by the National Administration of Quality Supervision, Inspection and Quarantine and the Standardization Administration of the People's Republic of China on April 29, 2011. The revised version of the Industrial Classification of the National Economy (GB/T 4754-2012) is composed of 20 sections, 96 divisions, 432 groups and 1094 classes.

Registration Status of Enterprises Enterprises are classified into 3 categories, namely domestic-funded enterprises, enterprises with investment from Hong Kong, Macau and Taiwan, and enterprises with foreign investment, in the light of the registration status of an enterprise in industrial and commercial administration agencies. Domestic-funded enterprises include state-owned enterprises, collective-owned enterprises, cooperative enterprises, joint ownership enterprises, limited liability corporations, share-holding corporations Ltd., private enterprises and other enterprises. Included in the enterprises with investment from Hong Kong, Macau and Taiwan and enterprises with foreign investment are joint-venture enterprises, cooperative enterprises, sole investment enterprises and share-holding corporations Ltd. For government agencies, institutions and social organizations which are not requested to be registered in industrial and commercial administration agencies, they are classified mainly by their sources of funds and way of management.

State-owned Enterprises refer to non-corporation economic units where the entire assets are owned by the state and which have registered in accordance with the Regulation of the People's Republic of China on the Management of Registration of Corporate Enterprises. Excluded from this category are sole state-funded corporations in the limited liability corporations.

Collective-owned Enterprises refer to economic units where the assets are owned collectively and which have registered in accordance with the Regulation of the People's Republic of China on the Management of Registration of Corporate Enterprises.

Cooperative Enterprises refer to a form of collective economic units (enterprises) where capitals come mainly from employees as their shares, with certain proportion of capital from the outside, where production is organized on the basis of independent operation, independent accounting for profits and losses, joint work, democratic management, and a distribution system that integrates remuneration according to work with dividend according to capital share.

Joint Ownership Enterprises refer to economic units established by two or more corporate enterprises or corporate institutions of the same or different ownership, through joint investment on the basis of equality, voluntary participation and mutual benefits. They include state joint ownership enterprises, collective joint ownership enterprises, joint state-collective enterprises, and other joint ownership enterprises.

Limited Liability Corporations refer to economic units established with investment from 2-50 investors and registered in accordance with the Regulation of the People's Republic of China on the Management of Registration of Corporations, each investor bearing limited liability to the corporation depending on its share of investment, and the corporation bearing liability to its debt to the maximum of its total assets. Limited liability corporations include exclusive state-funded limited liability corporations and other limited liability corporations.

Share-holding Corporations Ltd. refer to economic units registered in accordance with the Regulation of the People's Republic of China on the Management of Registration of Corporations, with total registered capitals divided into equal shares and raised through issuing stocks. Each investor bears limited liability to the corporation depending on the holding of shares, and the corporation bears liability to its debt to the maximum of its total assets.

Private Enterprises refer to profit-making economic units invested and established by natural persons, or controlled by natural persons using employed labor. Included in this category are private limited liability corporations, private share-holding corporations Ltd, private partnership enterprises and private-funded enterprises registered in accordance with the Corporation Law, Partnership Enterprises Law and Interim Regulations on Private Enterprises.

Other Domestic-funded Enterprises refer to domestic-funded economic units other than those mentioned above.

Joint Venture Enterprises（Funds are from Hong Kong, Macau or Taiwan) refer to enterprises jointly established by investors from Hong Kong, Macau and Taiwan with enterprises in the mainland of China in accordance with the Law of the People's Republic of China on Sino-foreign Joint Venture Enterprises and other relevant laws, where the share of investment, profits and risks is stipulated in the contract.

Cooperative Enterprises(Funds are from Hong Kong Macao or Taiwan) established by investors from Hong Kong, Macao and Taiwan with enterprises in the mainland of China in accordance with the Law of the People's Republic of China on Sino-foreign Cooperative Enterprises and other relevant laws, where the investment or provision of facilities, and the share of profits and risks is stipulated in the cooperative contract.

Enterprises with Sole (exclusive) Investment from Hong Kong, Macao and Taiwan refer to enterprises established in the mainland of China with exclusive investment from investors from Hong Kong, Macao and Taiwan in accordance with the Law of the People's Republic of China on Foreign-Funded Enterprises and other relevant laws.

Share-holding Corporations Ltd. with Investment from Hong Kong, Macao and Taiwan refer to share-holding corporations Ltd. established with the approval from the Ministry of Foreign Trade and Economic Relations in line with relevant state regulations, where the share of investment from Hong Kong, Macau or Taiwan businessmen exceeds 25% of the total registered capital of the corporation. In case the share of investment from Hong Kong, Macao or Taiwan is less than 25% of the total registered capital, the enterprise is to be classified as domestic-funded share-holding corporation Ltd.

Joint-venture Enterprises with Foreign Investment refer to enterprises jointly established by foreign enterprises or foreigners with enterprises in the mainland of China in accordance with the Law of the People's Republic of China on Sino-foreign Joint Venture Enterprises and other relevant laws, where the share of investment, profits and risks is stipulated in the contract.

Cooperation Enterprises with Foreign Investment refer to enterprises jointly established by foreign enterprises or foreigners with enterprises in the mainland of China in accordance with the Law of the People's Republic of China on Sino-foreign Cooperative Enterprises and other relevant laws, where the investment or provision of facilities, and the share of profits and risks is stipulated in the cooperative contract.

Enterprises with Sole (exclusive) Foreign Investment refer to enterprises established in the mainland of China with exclusive investment from foreign investors in accordance with the Law of the People's Republic of China on Foreign-Funded Enterprises and other relevant laws.

Share-holding Corporations Ltd. with Foreign Investment refer to share-holding corporations Ltd. Established with the approval from the Ministry of Foreign Trade and Economic Relations in line with relevant state regulations, where the share of investment from foreign investors exceeds 25% of the total registered capital of the corporation. In case the share of foreign investment is less than 25% of the total registered capital, the enterprise is to be classified as domestic-funded share-holding corporation Ltd.

Government Agencies, Institutions and Social Organizations are classified into following categories by source of funds and way of management taking reference of the registration status of enterprises:

(1) Government agencies: include state and party agencies, classified in principle as "state-owned". There are exceptions, such as supply and marketing cooperatives, which are classified, as "collective".

(2) Institutions: include institutions of various types established with the approval by organization and staffing departments of the government, but exclude institutions where enterprise management system is introduced. Institutions are further classified as follows:

(a) Institutions whose main budget is listed in the government budget appropriations or extra-budget funds, or allocated from the budget of their competent government agencies. Such institutions are classified as "state-owned".

(b) Institutions whose budget mainly comes from collective units. Such institutions are classified as "collective".

(c) Institutions other than those mentioned above whose source of budget is not clear. Such institutions are classified by way of management.

(3) Social organizations: include social organizations established with the approval from the Ministry of Civil Affairs, and organizations that are not covered by social organization management regulations such as trade unions, women's federations etc. Social organizations are further classified as follows:

(a) Social organizations that are not covered by social organization management regulations of the Ministry of Civil Affairs such as trade unions, women's federations, communist youth leagues, youth associations, industrial and commerce associations, scientists associations, overseas Chinese associations, etc., foundations and fund management organizations established with funds from the state, and social organizations whose funds mainly come from the budget of their competent government agencies. Such institutions are classified as "state-owned".

(b) Social organizations whose budget mainly comes from collective units. Such institutions are classified as "collective".

(c) Social organizations established by individual or a group of citizens, which are classified as "private".

(d) Social organizations other than those mentioned above whose source of budget is not clear. Such organizations are classified by way of management.

Artificial person Refer to unit that have following conditions:

(1) legally Established, have own name, organization ,location and can undertake a civil case responsibility independently by law.

(2) independently Own and use(or authorizable usage) a property, undertake liabilities and can make a bargain with other units.

(3) can independently account and workout balance sheet. artificial person unit includes business artificial person, artificial person, organization artificial person, meeting group artificial person and other.

Establishments unit Refer to the subsidiary unit of artificial person unit. it should have following conditions:

(1) Be engaged in only one kind of social economic activities in exclusive condition.

(2) Opposite independently organize management and business activity.

(3) predominate data of businesses, such as income and expenditure...etc.

国民经济核算
National Accounts

● 资料整理：胡昶昶　雷茜茜

简要说明

一、主要内容

本篇包括生产总值资料和资金流量表。

二、资料来源

生产总值资料是根据不同产业部门、不同支出构成的特点和资料来源情况而采用不同方法计算的。本年鉴公布的地区生产总值以及与之有关的指标数据，如果遇到普查，在能够获得更详细的基础资料的情况下，地区生产总值历史数据还会发生变动。根据第三次经济普查资料，重新修订了2004年以来的地区生产总值数据。2017年国家统计局在实施研发支出核算方法改革，讲研发支出计入地区GDP核算中，研发支出核算改革后，对以前年度GDP历史数据进行了系统修订。根据第三次农业普查资料，对以前年度GDP历史数据进行了系统修订。本年鉴中的数据是修订以后的数据。本年鉴所列分省辖市、省直管县数据来自各省辖市、省直管县统计局的国民经济核算资料。由于采取分级核算，各省辖市数据相加不等于全省数据。由河南省统计局国民经济核算处编辑整理。

资产负债表采用国际上通用的矩阵结构。主栏为资产和负债项目，包括三个部分：非金融资产项目、金融资产与负债项目和资产负债差额项目。宾栏为机构部门和经济总体，并下设使用项和来源项，其中使用项目记录资产，来源项目记录负债和资产负债差额。由河南省统计局国民经济核算处编制。

资金流量表表式与国际上通用的表式相似，是机构部门与交易项目的矩阵表式。主栏为交易项目，主要反映分配方式和融资工具；宾栏按机构部门分类。机构部门分类是根据机构单位具有的基本特征所进行的部门分类。资金流量表把参与资金活动的主体分为非金融企业、金融机构、政府、住户、国内省外和国外六个部门。每一部门下设资金来源与资金运用两栏。现行的资金流量表分为两大部分，一部分为实物交易，另一部分为金融交易，本年鉴登录的为实物交易部分。由河南省统计局国民经济核算处编制。

Brief Introduction

I. Main Contents

Statistics on national accounts include mainly four parts: gross domestic product, balance sheet, Flow of Funds Table and Input-output table.

II. Sources of Data

Data on GDP are computed by the Department of National Accounts of the Henan provincial Bureau of Statistics based on different approaches in the light of the different features of various sectors, various expenditure structures and different data sources. Data on GDP and related indicators of the most recent year published in the Yearbook are not final, Where a census has been conducted, historical data of GDP of the previous years may also undergo change. GDP since 2004 is adjusted on the basis of the Third Economic Census. In 2007, the National Bureau of Statistics carried out the reform of the research and development expenditure accounting method, and the research and development expenditure is included in the regional GDP calculation. After the reform, the historical data on GDP has been revised. According to the third agricultural census data, the historical data of GDP in previous years were systematically revised. Data in this yearbook has been revised.Regional data in this Yearbook are prepared from the national accounts data provided by the statistical bureaus of the 18 cities and province administrating county. The sum of the regional data is not equal to the provincial total due to the decentralized accounting approach. Municipal data of Statistics on national accounts are computed by the Department of National Accounts of the Henan provincial Bureau of Statistics.

Similar to internationally accepted format, the Balance Sheet of Henan constitutes a matrix. Items of transactions are expressed as assets and liabilities, including three parts: non-financial assets, financial assets and liabilities, the difference between assets and liabilities. Institutional sectors are column headings and macroeconomic, grouped by utilization and source, utilization record the item of project assets , and source record the item of liabilities and difference between assets and liabilities. Balance Sheet of Henan province is compiled by the Department of National Accounts of the Henan provincial Bureau of Statistics.

Similar to internationally accepted format, the Flow of Funds table of China constitutes a matrix of institutional sectors by transaction items. Items of transactions are expressed as row headings representing forms of distribution and methods of financing. Institutional sectors are shown as column headings, grouped by the characteristics of the transactions. There are 6 groups of institutional sectors in the flow of funds table, namely, non-financial corporations, financial institutions, general governments, households, other provinces and the rest of the world. Under each sector there are 2 headings: sources of funds and uses of funds. The current flow of funds table is composed of two parts: the first part, comprising the physical (real) transactions, and the second part, refers to comprising financial transactions, and data in this yearbook is the physical (real) transactions, which compiled by the Department of National Accounts of the Henan provincial Bureau of Statistics.

2-1 生产总值
Gross Domestic Product

本表按当年价格计算。
Data in this table are calculated at current prices.
单位：亿元 (100 million yuan)

年份 Year	生产总值 Gross Domestic Product	第一产业 Primary Industry	第二产业 Secondary Industry	第三产业 Tertiary Industry	人均生产总值(元) Per Capita GDP (yuan)
1978	162.92	64.86	69.45	28.61	232
1979	190.09	77.30	80.52	32.27	267
1980	229.16	93.23	94.44	41.49	317
1981	249.69	106.04	95.79	47.86	340
1982	263.30	108.18	102.76	52.36	353
1983	327.95	143.49	116.36	68.10	433
1984	370.04	155.28	136.29	78.47	482
1985	451.74	173.43	170.07	108.24	580
1986	502.91	179.02	202.15	121.74	635
1987	609.60	220.22	230.25	159.13	756
1988	749.09	240.72	299.83	208.54	910
1989	850.71	289.95	317.13	243.63	1012
1990	934.65	325.77	331.85	277.03	1091
1991	1045.73	334.61	388.09	323.03	1201
1992	1279.75	342.75	542.40	394.60	1452
1993	1660.18	397.50	760.24	502.44	1865
1994	2216.83	529.43	1053.35	634.05	2467
1995	2988.37	738.91	1387.65	861.81	3297
1996	3634.69	908.05	1668.88	1057.75	3978
1997	4041.09	976.73	1851.70	1212.66	4389
1998	4308.24	1037.58	1927.95	1342.70	4643
1999	4517.94	1087.70	1970.98	1459.26	4832
2000	5052.99	1124.93	2282.48	1645.59	5450
2001	5533.01	1195.39	2497.71	1839.91	5959
2002	6035.48	1207.11	2881.60	1946.77	6487
2003	6942.41	1198.70	3348.63	2395.08	7376
2004	8411.19	1647.57	4080.74	2682.88	9047
2005	10243.47	1844.04	5202.27	3197.16	10978
2006	11977.87	1869.82	6316.19	3791.86	12761
2007	14824.49	2156.69	7904.01	4763.80	15811
2008	17735.93	2575.81	9713.40	5446.72	18879
2009	19181.00	2665.66	10324.57	6190.77	20280
2010	22655.02	3127.14	12173.51	7354.38	23984
2011	26318.68	3349.25	14021.59	8947.84	28009
2012	28961.92	3577.15	15042.55	10342.21	30820
2013	31632.50	3827.20	15995.37	11809.92	33618
2014	34574.76	3988.22	17139.61	13446.93	36686
2015	37084.10	4015.56	17947.86	15120.68	39209
2016	40249.34	4063.64	18986.89	17198.81	42341
2017	44824.92	4139.29	20940.33	19745.30	46959
2018	49935.90	4311.12	22038.56	23586.21	52114
2019	54259.20	4635.40	23605.79	26018.01	56388

注：1.三次产业结构已执行《国民经济行业分类》(GB/T4754-2017) 行业分类标准；2000年以来人均GDP按常住人口计算(以下相关表格同)。
2.根据第四次经济普查结果对1992年以来的GDP及三次产业数据进行了调整(以下相关表格同)。

a) The industrial structure has been executed the industry classification standard of the "national economy industry classification "(GB/T4754-2017). The data on Per capita GDP since 2000 are calculated at resident population.(the same as the following related tables).

b) According to the results of the fourth economic census, the data of GDP have been adjusted since 1992 (the same as the following related tables).

2-2 生产总值指数(上年=100)

Indices of Gross Domestic Product (Preceding year=100)

本表按可比价格计算。
The indices in this table are calculated at comparable prices.

(上年=100) (preceding year=100)

年 份 Year	生产总值 Gross Domestic Product	第一产业 Primary Industry	第二产业 Secondary Industry	第三产业 Tertiary Industry	人 均 生产总值 Per Capita GDP
1978	111.3	110.6	112.1	111.3	109.5
1979	108.7	101.7	112.6	119.7	106.9
1980	115.4	109.2	117.2	126.9	113.7
1981	107.8	111.7	101.3	113.7	106.3
1982	104.3	100.5	106.1	109.0	102.7
1983	123.8	130.2	113.5	131.3	121.9
1984	110.1	105.5	115.0	110.7	108.5
1985	113.5	100.8	117.0	131.9	111.9
1986	104.6	92.1	114.0	108.6	103.0
1987	115.0	116.9	108.6	123.5	112.9
1988	109.8	97.4	120.1	109.4	107.6
1989	107.0	109.2	103.5	110.3	104.8
1990	104.5	105.4	102.3	106.8	102.5
1991	106.9	97.4	113.3	110.4	105.2
1992	113.7	101.5	125.4	111.1	112.3
1993	115.6	110.4	122.0	111.7	114.3
1994	113.5	101.3	121.5	112.6	112.5
1995	114.7	111.9	117.1	113.2	113.8
1996	113.9	111.3	116.1	112.5	113.0
1997	110.5	107.6	111.0	111.8	109.7
1998	108.8	107.0	109.2	109.3	107.9
1999	108.1	107.2	107.8	109.2	107.3
2000	109.1	104.2	111.5	108.8	110.1
2001	108.7	104.9	109.5	110.1	108.5
2002	109.1	104.8	116.6	101.6	108.9
2003	110.9	97.2	115.7	112.5	109.6
2004	112.8	113.6	113.3	111.6	114.2
2005	114.3	107.6	117.1	113.7	113.9
2006	114.5	107.4	117.8	113.3	113.8
2007	114.6	103.7	117.9	115.0	114.7
2008	112.0	105.5	114.2	111.5	111.8
2009	111.0	104.1	111.9	112.4	110.2
2010	112.4	104.5	114.7	111.8	112.5
2011	112.0	103.6	113.9	112.4	112.6
2012	110.1	104.4	111.2	110.6	110.1
2013	109.0	104.2	109.5	109.9	108.9
2014	108.9	104.0	109.3	110.0	108.7
2015	108.4	104.4	107.6	111.1	108.0
2016	108.2	104.3	107.1	110.6	107.7
2017	107.8	104.3	107.0	109.7	107.4
2018	107.6	103.4	106.9	109.5	107.2
2019	107.0	102.3	107.5	107.4	106.5

2-3 生产总值指数(1978=100)

Indices of Gross Domestic Product (1978=100)

本表按可比价格计算。
The indices in this table are calculated at comparable prices.

年 份 Year	生产总值 Gross Domestic Product	第一产业 Primary Industry	第二产业 Secondary Industry	第三产业 Tertiary Industry	人均生产总值 Per Capita GDP
1978	100.0	100.0	100.0	100.0	100.0
1979	108.7	101.7	112.6	119.7	106.9
1980	125.4	111.1	132.0	151.9	121.5
1981	135.2	124.0	133.7	172.7	129.2
1982	141.0	124.7	141.8	188.3	132.7
1983	174.6	162.3	161.0	247.2	161.8
1984	192.2	171.2	185.1	273.6	175.5
1985	218.2	172.6	216.6	360.9	196.4
1986	228.2	159.0	246.9	391.9	202.3
1987	262.5	185.8	268.2	484.1	228.4
1988	288.2	181.0	322.1	529.6	245.7
1989	308.4	197.7	333.3	584.1	257.5
1990	322.2	208.3	341.0	623.8	264.0
1991	344.5	202.9	386.4	688.7	277.7
1992	391.7	206.0	484.5	765.1	311.8
1993	452.6	227.4	590.9	854.3	356.5
1994	513.9	230.3	718.1	962.3	401.0
1995	589.6	257.8	841.2	1089.3	456.2
1996	671.8	286.9	976.4	1225.6	515.6
1997	742.4	308.7	1084.3	1370.6	565.4
1998	807.5	330.3	1184.5	1497.9	610.2
1999	872.8	354.1	1276.9	1635.8	654.5
2000	952.5	369.0	1423.1	1780.1	720.3
2001	1035.0	387.2	1558.5	1959.1	781.7
2002	1129.2	405.8	1816.5	1990.7	851.1
2003	1252.5	394.4	2102.3	2240.0	933.1
2004	1412.8	447.9	2381.0	2500.0	1065.6
2005	1615.0	481.7	2788.0	2842.8	1213.7
2006	1849.4	517.4	3283.3	3221.0	1381.6
2007	2119.7	536.8	3870.2	3705.7	1585.3
2008	2374.6	566.5	4418.3	4132.8	1772.4
2009	2634.8	590.0	4945.3	4646.0	1953.5
2010	2961.5	616.7	5670.9	5193.6	2198.4
2011	3316.7	639.1	6459.3	5837.4	2475.1
2012	3653.4	667.4	7183.7	6456.9	2726.2
2013	3982.9	695.4	7869.1	7097.8	2968.2
2014	4336.7	723.5	8597.1	7804.4	3226.6
2015	4700.9	755.5	9246.4	8673.3	3485.3
2016	5087.9	787.6	9906.9	9591.2	3753.2
2017	5486.7	821.6	10600.0	10520.2	4030.6
2018	5905.9	849.3	11334.7	11514.5	4322.0
2019	6316.4	868.8	12184.2	12366.8	4602.9

2-4 生产总值分产业构成

Industrial Composition of Gross Domestic Product

本表按当年价格计算。
Data in this table are calculated at current prices.
单位：% (%)

年份 Year	生产总值 Gross Domestic Product	第一产业 Primary Industry	第二产业 Secondary Industry	第三产业 Tertiary Industry
1978	100.0	39.8	42.6	17.6
1979	100.0	40.7	42.3	17.0
1980	100.0	40.7	41.2	18.1
1981	100.0	42.5	38.3	19.2
1982	100.0	41.1	39.0	19.9
1983	100.0	43.7	35.5	20.8
1984	100.0	42.0	36.8	21.2
1985	100.0	38.4	37.6	24.0
1986	100.0	35.6	40.2	24.2
1987	100.0	36.1	37.8	26.1
1988	100.0	32.1	40.0	27.9
1989	100.0	34.1	37.3	28.6
1990	100.0	34.9	35.5	29.6
1991	100.0	32.0	37.1	30.9
1992	100.0	26.8	42.4	30.8
1993	100.0	23.9	45.8	30.3
1994	100.0	23.9	47.5	28.6
1995	100.0	24.7	46.4	28.8
1996	100.0	25.0	45.9	29.1
1997	100.0	24.2	45.8	30.0
1998	100.0	24.1	44.8	31.2
1999	100.0	24.1	43.6	32.3
2000	100.0	22.3	45.2	32.6
2001	100.0	21.6	45.1	33.3
2002	100.0	20.0	47.7	32.3
2003	100.0	17.3	48.2	34.5
2004	100.0	19.6	48.5	31.9
2005	100.0	18.0	50.8	31.2
2006	100.0	15.6	52.7	31.7
2007	100.0	14.5	53.3	32.1
2008	100.0	14.5	54.8	30.7
2009	100.0	13.9	53.8	32.3
2010	100.0	13.8	53.7	32.5
2011	100.0	12.7	53.3	34.0
2012	100.0	12.4	51.9	35.7
2013	100.0	12.1	50.6	37.3
2014	100.0	11.5	49.6	38.9
2015	100.0	10.8	48.4	40.8
2016	100.0	10.1	47.2	42.7
2017	100.0	9.2	46.7	44.0
2018	100.0	8.6	44.1	47.2
2019	100.0	8.5	43.5	48.0

2-5 三次产业贡献率

Share of the Contributions of Three Strata of Industry to the Increase of the GDP

本表按可比价格计算。
Data in this table are calculated at constant prices.
单位：% (%)

年 份 Year	生产总值 Gross Domestic Product	第一产业 Primary Industry	第二产业 Secondary Industry	第三产业 Tertiary Industry
1981	100.0	61.5	6.9	31.6
1982	100.0	4.9	55.3	39.8
1983	100.0	51.7	22.4	26.0
1984	100.0	23.5	54.1	22.4
1985	100.0	2.6	47.6	49.9
1986	100.0	-62.4	117.2	45.2
1987	100.0	36.0	24.2	39.8
1988	100.0	-8.8	82.4	26.4
1989	100.0	37.8	22.0	40.2
1990	100.0	35.5	21.8	42.7
1991	100.0	-13.0	69.8	43.2
1992	100.0	3.4	72.2	24.3
1993	100.0	18.3	58.2	23.4
1994	100.0	2.5	69.2	28.3
1995	100.0	18.9	54.2	26.9
1996	100.0	18.5	54.9	26.6
1997	100.0	16.1	51.0	32.9
1998	100.0	17.3	51.3	31.4
1999	100.0	19.0	47.2	33.8
2000	100.0	9.7	61.2	29.1
2001	100.0	12.7	49.6	37.8
2002	100.0	11.4	82.8	5.9
2003	100.0	-5.3	70.1	35.2
2004	100.0	19.2	52.6	28.3
2005	100.0	9.6	60.8	29.5
2006	100.0	9.2	62.2	28.6
2007	100.0	4.3	63.9	31.8
2008	100.0	7.0	63.3	29.7
2009	100.0	5.5	59.6	35.0
2010	100.0	4.9	65.3	29.7
2011	100.0	4.2	62.3	33.5
2012	100.0	5.6	60.4	34.1
2013	100.0	5.6	58.4	36.0
2014	100.0	5.3	57.8	37.0
2015	100.0	5.8	50.0	44.2
2016	100.0	5.6	42.0	52.4
2017	100.0	5.7	42.8	51.5
2018	100.0	4.5	43.1	52.4
2019	100.0	3.2	50.9	45.9

注：产业贡献率指各产业增加值增量与GDP增量之比。
a) Share of the contributions of three strata of industry refers to the proportion of the increment of value-addede of each industry to the increment of GDP.

2-6 三次产业对生产总值增长的拉动

Contribution of the Three Strata of Industry to GDP Growth

本表按可比价格计算。

Data in this table are calculated at current prices.

单位：百分点 (percent)

年 份 Year	生产总值 Gross Domestic Product	第一产业 Primary Industry	第二产业 Secondary Industry	第三产业 Tertiary Industry
1981	7.8	4.8	0.5	2.5
1982	4.3	0.2	2.4	1.7
1983	23.8	12.3	5.3	6.2
1984	10.1	2.4	5.5	2.3
1985	13.5	0.3	6.4	6.7
1986	4.6	-2.9	5.4	2.1
1987	15.0	5.4	3.6	6.0
1988	9.8	-0.9	8.1	2.6
1989	7.0	2.6	1.5	2.8
1990	4.5	1.6	1.0	1.9
1991	6.9	-0.9	4.8	3.0
1992	13.7	0.5	9.9	3.3
1993	15.6	2.8	9.1	3.7
1994	13.5	0.4	9.3	3.8
1995	14.7	2.7	8.0	4.0
1996	13.9	2.6	7.6	3.7
1997	10.5	1.6	5.4	3.5
1998	8.8	1.5	4.5	2.8
1999	8.1	1.5	3.8	2.8
2000	9.1	0.9	5.6	2.6
2001	8.7	1.1	4.3	3.3
2002	9.1	1.0	7.5	0.6
2003	10.9	-0.5	7.6	3.8
2004	12.8	2.5	6.7	3.6
2005	14.3	1.4	8.7	4.2
2006	14.5	1.3	9.0	4.2
2007	14.6	0.7	9.3	4.6
2008	12.0	0.8	7.6	3.6
2009	11.0	0.6	6.6	3.8
2010	12.4	0.6	8.1	3.7
2011	12.0	0.5	7.5	4.0
2012	10.1	0.6	6.1	3.4
2013	9.0	0.5	5.3	3.2
2014	8.9	0.5	5.1	3.3
2015	8.4	0.5	4.2	3.7
2016	8.2	0.5	3.4	4.3
2017	7.8	0.4	3.3	4.1
2018	7.6	0.3	3.3	4.0
2019	7.0	0.2	3.6	3.2

注：产业拉动指GDP增长速度与各产业贡献率之乘积。

a) Contribution of the three strata of industry to GDP growth refers to the growth rate of GDP multiplied by the contribution share of every industry.

2-7 全员劳动生产率

Overall Labor Productivity

单位：元/人.年 (yuan/person.year)

年　份 Year	全员劳动 生产率 Over all Labor Productivity	第一产业 Primary Industry	第二产业 Secondary Industry	第三产业 Tertiary Industry
1979	669	334	2748	1385
1980	790	393	3180	1788
1981	837	437	3120	1892
1982	851	433	3288	1870
1983	1019	560	3548	2092
1984	1115	600	3802	2115
1985	1316	674	3784	2646
1986	1413	696	3706	2761
1987	1652	852	3889	3102
1988	1946	918	4703	3538
1989	2165	1080	4812	4150
1990	2328	1174	4990	4831
1991	2519	1163	5707	5438
1992	2994	1167	7677	6268
1993	3803	1355	9925	7527
1994	5011	1834	12600	9051
1995	6673	2602	15478	11607
1996	7947	3222	17411	13272
1997	8545	3409	18526	14035
1998	8774	3544	19543	13488
1999	8854	3480	21024	14045
2000	9377	3275	24153	16309
2001	9979	3395	25306	17751
2002	10935	3511	28320	18297
2003	12556	3562	31561	21714
2004	15124	5009	36664	23128
2005	18212	5776	43479	25867
2006	21049	6042	48549	29281
2007	25800	7225	55701	35498
2008	30558	8933	63674	39045
2009	32554	9500	63752	42215
2010	37787	11419	71024	47663
2011	43004	12446	77768	55030
2012	46391	13504	79759	60569
2013	49913	14746	80907	66931
2014	53575	15295	85039	73440
2015	56376	15329	88895	77942
2016	60244	15720	92664	83999
2017	66442	16306	100675	92788
2018	74204	17741	106159	106101
2019	81876	19967	119011	112074

2-8 各市生产总值(2018年)

Gross Domestic Product by City (2018)

本表按当年价格计算。
Data in this table are calculated at current prices.

市(县)	City(County)	生产总值(亿元) Gross Domestic Product (100 million yuan)	第一产业 Primary Industry	第二产业 Secondary Industry	第三产业 Tertiary Industry	人均生产总值(元) Per Capita GDP (yuan)
省辖市	**City**					
郑州市	Zhengzhou	10670.14	150.95	4335.24	6183.94	106611
开封市	Kaifeng	2157.70	279.69	879.56	998.46	47350
洛阳市	Luoyang	4613.49	243.40	2152.40	2217.70	67294
平顶山市	Pingdingshan	2170.86	164.56	1014.70	991.61	43302
安阳市	Anyang	2141.87	199.84	983.12	958.91	41574
鹤壁市	Hebi	921.18	61.52	551.22	308.44	56718
新乡市	Xinxiang	2671.60	231.50	1235.26	1204.85	46209
焦作市	Jiaozuo	2501.76	138.14	1349.02	1014.60	69972
濮阳市	Puyang	1442.65	168.16	540.76	733.73	39806
许昌市	Xuchang	3140.93	151.98	1719.68	1269.26	71010
漯河市	Luohe	1435.90	113.57	676.80	645.53	54029
三门峡市	Sanmenxia	1319.01	121.74	650.84	546.43	58082
南阳市	Nanyang	3500.56	535.96	1177.24	1787.36	34895
商丘市	Shangqiu	2659.52	390.67	1113.92	1154.93	36371
信阳市	Xinyang	2534.47	457.46	950.97	1126.04	39209
周口市	Zhoukou	2939.59	460.20	1302.45	1176.94	33711
驻马店市	Zhumadian	2485.26	422.55	1008.46	1054.25	35409
济源市	Jiyuan	630.46	19.31	393.36	217.79	86146
省直管县	**County Directly Administrated by Province**					
巩义市	Gongyi	753.61	12.42	444.78	296.41	90199
兰考县	Lankao	343.06	41.25	161.53	140.28	53180
汝州市	Ruzhou	432.90	35.40	180.35	217.15	45242
滑县	Huaxian	343.00	60.18	134.80	148.02	31996
长垣县	Changyuan	425.93	42.62	228.33	154.98	55062
邓州市	Dengzhou	418.00	90.93	135.65	191.41	30257
永城市	Yongcheng	548.89	62.03	243.23	243.63	44410
固始县	Gushi	365.58	75.54	115.49	174.54	33439
鹿邑县	Luyi	360.50	51.62	154.48	154.39	41190
新蔡县	Xincai	247.08	48.96	76.69	121.44	29197

注：人均生产总值按常住人口计算。
a) Per Capita GDP are calculated at resident population.

2-9 各市生产总值(2019年)

Gross Domestic Product by City (2019)

本表按当年价格计算。
Data in this table are calculated at current prices.

市(县) City(County)	生产总值(亿元) Gross Domestic Product (100 million yuan)	第一产业 Primary Industry	第二产业 Secondary Industry	第三产业 Tertiary Industry	人均生产总值(元) Per Capita GDP (yuan)
省辖市 City					
郑州市 Zhengzhou	11589.72	140.88	4617.07	6831.77	113139
开封市 Kaifeng	2364.14	318.24	949.24	1096.66	51733
洛阳市 Luoyang	5034.85	245.13	2330.55	2459.16	72912
平顶山市 Pingdingshan	2372.64	173.67	1092.59	1106.38	47201
安阳市 Anyang	2229.29	198.00	998.41	1032.89	43002
鹤壁市 Hebi	988.69	63.83	593.17	331.68	60678
新乡市 Xinxiang	2918.18	253.62	1338.57	1325.99	50277
焦作市 Jiaozuo	2761.11	149.78	1480.18	1131.16	76828
濮阳市 Puyang	1581.49	193.12	570.89	817.48	43810
许昌市 Xuchang	3395.68	162.27	1834.42	1398.99	76312
漯河市 Luohe	1578.44	137.80	729.93	710.71	59190
三门峡市 Sanmenxia	1443.82	136.18	704.89	602.76	63473
南阳市 Nanyang	3814.98	569.46	1267.78	1977.73	38064
商丘市 Shangqiu	2911.20	428.92	1193.48	1288.80	39719
信阳市 Xinyang	2758.47	497.71	1008.89	1251.87	42641
周口市 Zhoukou	3198.49	474.53	1406.01	1317.95	36891
驻马店市 Zhumadian	2742.06	467.92	1101.90	1172.25	38943
济源市 Jiyuan	686.96	24.36	421.89	240.71	93693
省直管县 County Directly Administrated by Province					
巩义市 Gongyi	801.21	11.91	470.98	318.32	95260
兰考县 Lankao	389.87	58.21	176.43	155.23	59942
汝州市 Ruzhou	475.73	39.80	194.37	241.57	49077
滑县 Huaxian	372.60	67.40	143.78	161.42	34677
长垣县 Changyuan	469.32	49.14	252.57	167.62	59847
邓州市 Dengzhou	450.04	94.62	146.19	209.23	33159
永城市 Yongcheng	615.79	77.95	265.80	272.04	49654
固始县 Gushi	409.55	85.80	126.69	197.07	37249
鹿邑县 Luyi	398.88	57.36	169.05	172.46	45278
新蔡县 Xincai	272.25	50.81	85.49	135.95	32088

注：人均生产总值按常住人口计算。
a) Per Capita GDP are calculated at resident population.

2-10 各市生产总值指数(2018年)
Indices of Gross Domestic Product by City (2018)

本表按可比价格计算。
The indices in this table are calculated at comparable prices.
(上年=100) (preceding year=100)

市(县) City(County)	生产总值 Gross Domestic Product	第一产业 Primary Industry	第二产业 Secondary Industry	第三产业 Tertiary Industry	人均生产总值 Per Capita GDP
省辖市 City					
郑州市 Zhengzhou	108.1	102.1	106.2	110.0	105.9
开封市 Kaifeng	107.0	103.9	106.5	108.8	106.8
洛阳市 Luoyang	107.9	103.6	106.8	109.8	107.3
平顶山市 Pingdingshan	107.5	103.3	107.5	108.6	107.1
安阳市 Anyang	106.7	103.2	104.8	110.0	106.3
鹤壁市 Hebi	105.9	103.4	105.3	107.9	105.5
新乡市 Xinxiang	107.1	103.5	108.5	106.4	106.6
焦作市 Jiaozuo	106.3	103.7	105.7	107.8	105.7
濮阳市 Puyang	105.8	102.9	104.4	107.8	106.1
许昌市 Xuchang	108.6	103.4	108.1	110.4	107.9
漯河市 Luohe	107.7	100.4	107.9	109.4	107.1
三门峡市 Sanmenxia	108.0	104.1	107.9	109.3	107.6
南阳市 Nanyang	107.2	103.8	106.4	109.3	107.5
商丘市 Shangqiu	108.7	103.9	106.8	113.2	108.4
信阳市 Xinyang	108.3	103.0	106.5	113.1	108.1
周口市 Zhoukou	108.2	103.4	107.9	111.4	109.1
驻马店市 Zhumadian	108.5	103.7	109.0	110.6	108.1
济源市 Jiyuan	108.3	103.8	108.5	108.5	108.3
省直管县 County Directly Administrated by Province					
巩义市 Gongyi	108.1	102.7	108.0	108.7	107.4
兰考县 Lankao	108.1	103.9	108.7	108.9	107.2
汝州市 Ruzhou	108.5	103.8	108.4	109.7	106.7
滑县 Huaxian	107.0	103.5	109.0	107.3	108.2
长垣县 Changyuan	107.4	103.6	109.3	105.6	105.8
邓州市 Dengzhou	108.1	103.2	108.3	111.5	111.5
永城市 Yongcheng	109.6	103.6	109.2	112.2	109.2
固始县 Gushi	109.1	104.1	111.0	110.7	108.7
鹿邑县 Luyi	109.2	103.0	108.4	113.0	109.9
新蔡县 Xincai	109.1	103.6	109.9	111.6	108.8

2-11 各市生产总值指数(2019年)

Indices of Gross Domestic Product by City (2019)

本表按可比价格计算。

The indices in this table are calculated at comparable prices.

(上年=100) (preceding year=100)

市(县)	City(County)	生产总值 Gross Domestic Product	第一产业 Primary Industry	第二产业 Secondary Industry	第三产业 Tertiary Industry	人均生产总值 Per Capita GDP
省辖市	**City**					
郑州市	Zhengzhou	106.5	95.1	106.2	107.1	104.0
开封市	Kaifeng	107.2	103.6	108.6	107.0	106.9
洛阳市	Luoyang	107.8	103.7	108.8	107.3	107.0
平顶山市	Pingdingshan	107.5	102.3	108.5	107.4	107.2
安阳市	Anyang	102.7	97.7	101.5	105.4	102.1
鹤壁市	Hebi	107.1	103.1	108.6	104.8	106.7
新乡市	Xinxiang	107.0	103.1	108.6	105.8	106.6
焦作市	Jiaozuo	108.0	104.2	108.7	107.5	107.4
濮阳市	Puyang	106.8	103.5	105.8	108.4	107.2
许昌市	Xuchang	107.1	102.0	107.8	106.9	106.5
漯河市	Luohe	107.5	102.6	108.9	106.7	107.2
三门峡市	Sanmenxia	107.5	103.8	108.5	107.0	107.3
南阳市	Nanyang	107.0	103.2	108.0	107.6	107.1
商丘市	Shangqiu	107.4	102.4	107.9	108.9	107.1
信阳市	Xinyang	106.3	102.2	106.7	108.1	106.2
周口市	Zhoukou	107.5	102.4	108.5	108.7	108.1
驻马店市	Zhumadian	107.4	102.5	109.2	107.8	107.0
济源市	Jiyuan	107.8	103.9	108.5	107.1	107.6
省直管县	**County Directly Administrated by Province**					
巩义市	Gongyi	105.8	96.8	107.0	104.1	105.1
兰考县	Lankao	108.0	102.8	109.8	107.6	107.1
汝州市	Ruzhou	107.6	102.2	108.2	108.1	106.2
滑县	Huaxian	105.8	102.3	107.4	106.3	105.6
长垣县	Changyuan	108.1	103.1	110.3	105.8	106.3
邓州市	Dengzhou	105.6	101.3	107.7	106.5	107.5
永城市	Yongcheng	108.4	103.8	109.8	108.1	108.0
固始县	Gushi	107.7	103.1	109.6	108.8	107.1
鹿邑县	Luyi	108.5	103.0	109.7	109.3	107.8
新蔡县	Xincai	108.2	103.4	110.7	108.9	107.9

2-12 支出法生产总值

Gross Domestic Product by Expenditure Approach

本表按当年价格计算。

Data in this table are calculated at current prices.

单位：亿元 (100 million yuan)

年 份 Year	支出法生产总值 Gross Domestic Product by Expenditure Approach	最终消费支出 Final Consumption	居民消费支出 Household Consumption	城镇居民 Urban Households	农村居民 Rural Households	政府消费支出 Government Consumption	资本形成总额 Gross Capital Formation	固定资本形成总额 Fixed Capital Formation	存货变动 Changes in Inventories	货物和服务净流出 Net Export of Good and Services
1978	162.92	107.07	94.34	23.89	70.45	12.73	52.49	40.66	11.83	3.36
1979	190.09	127.10	113.01	26.91	86.10	14.09	60.46	46.37	14.09	2.53
1980	229.16	151.48	135.23	30.87	104.36	16.25	69.20	57.70	11.50	8.48
1981	249.69	164.83	147.09	34.47	112.62	17.74	76.12	55.20	20.92	8.74
1982	263.30	183.01	159.95	36.62	123.33	23.06	71.15	66.10	5.05	9.14
1983	327.95	194.43	165.43	39.80	125.63	29.00	115.21	88.14	27.07	18.31
1984	370.04	222.17	187.89	48.57	139.32	34.28	130.82	101.87	28.95	17.05
1985	451.74	275.95	231.11	64.95	166.16	44.84	173.43	138.19	35.24	2.36
1986	502.91	307.91	256.87	74.19	182.68	51.04	184.00	158.84	25.16	11.00
1987	609.60	344.68	285.09	84.04	201.05	59.59	223.78	174.20	49.58	41.14
1988	749.09	410.63	348.87	113.53	235.34	61.76	307.85	222.33	85.52	30.61
1989	850.71	466.33	395.47	130.65	264.82	70.86	345.19	209.62	135.57	39.19
1990	934.65	527.43	447.97	138.64	309.33	79.46	364.81	225.73	139.08	42.41
1991	1045.73	572.63	479.04	153.74	325.30	93.59	421.32	279.06	142.26	51.78
1992	1279.75	641.79	531.59	173.70	357.89	110.20	571.96	346.67	225.29	66.00
1993	1660.18	878.69	672.23	220.37	451.86	206.46	682.64	485.98	196.66	98.85
1994	2216.83	1196.17	927.84	334.29	593.55	268.33	879.39	670.84	208.55	141.27
1995	2988.37	1590.89	1251.49	437.39	814.10	339.40	1235.62	877.41	358.21	161.86
1996	3634.69	1936.99	1537.04	535.52	1001.52	399.95	1485.58	1079.31	406.27	212.12
1997	4041.09	2146.53	1694.84	622.23	1072.61	451.69	1677.86	1254.89	422.97	216.70
1998	4308.24	2217.62	1717.39	665.78	1051.61	500.23	1845.87	1413.55	432.32	244.75
1999	4517.94	2347.13	1781.18	751.37	1029.81	565.95	1924.38	1469.87	454.51	246.43
2000	5052.99	2745.80	2090.01	900.75	1189.26	655.79	2104.00	1641.43	462.57	203.19
2001	5533.01	3086.15	2266.65	992.74	1273.91	819.50	2257.24	1790.76	466.48	189.62
2002	6035.48	3386.68	2446.93	1105.70	1341.23	939.75	2474.19	2018.58	455.61	174.61
2003	6867.70	3891.70	2870.19	1625.12	1245.07	1021.51	2786.46	2431.76	354.70	189.54
2004	8579.42	4567.78	3370.21	1928.42	1441.79	1197.57	3771.87	3243.47	528.40	239.77
2005	10621.56	5352.68	3817.86	2263.64	1554.22	1534.82	5054.94	4541.88	513.06	213.94
2006	12412.86	6100.82	4251.50	2609.65	1641.85	1849.32	6374.34	6053.02	321.32	-62.30
2007	15064.73	6829.42	4820.00	3051.32	1768.68	2009.42	8420.49	8097.47	323.02	-185.18
2008	18068.47	7757.05	5521.46	3567.66	1953.80	2235.59	10765.75	10353.89	411.86	-454.33
2009	19547.60	8739.50	6248.92	4142.02	2106.90	2490.58	13374.37	13066.40	307.97	-2566.27
2010	22655.02	10647.86	7560.97	4907.05	2653.91	3086.89	14023.46	13797.90	225.56	-2016.30
2011	26318.68	12606.65	9013.77	5869.60	3144.17	3592.88	16343.90	15971.03	372.87	-2631.87
2012	28961.92	14095.77	10076.59	6646.70	3429.89	4019.18	18101.20	17696.20	405.00	-3235.05
2013	31632.50	16069.31	11389.95	7585.31	3804.64	4679.36	19991.74	19532.00	459.74	-4428.55
2014	34574.76	17676.36	12634.61	8337.37	4297.24	5041.75	22058.70	21459.83	598.87	-5160.29
2015	37084.10	19657.49	14076.10	9405.33	4670.77	5581.38	22806.72	22268.25	538.47	-5380.11
2016	40249.34	21851.29	15653.75	10536.28	5117.46	6197.54	23787.36	23822.81	-35.45	-5389.31
2017	44824.92	24922.66	17888.29	12246.43	5641.87	7034.36	25639.85	25576.09	63.77	-5737.59
2018	49935.90	28183.19	20258.01	13947.94	6310.07	7925.18	27014.87	26780.16	234.71	-5262.16

2-13 最终消费支出指数

Indices of Final Consumption Expenditure

本表按可比价格计算。
The indices in this table are calculated at comparable prices.

年份 Year	以1978年为100 (1978=100)					以上年为100 (preceding year=100)				
	最终消费支出 Final Consumption	居民消费支出 Household Consumption	城镇居民 Urban Households Consumption	农村居民 Rural Households Consumption	政府消费支出 Government Consumption	最终消费支出 Final Consumption	居民消费支出 Household Consumption	城镇居民 Urban Households Consumption	农村居民 Rural Households Consumption	政府消费支出 Government Consumption
1978	100.0	100.0	100.0	100.0	100.0	118.3	118.7	119.9	118.3	115.7
1979	118.6	119.6	112.6	122.1	110.7	118.6	119.6	112.6	122.1	110.7
1980	134.8	136.6	121.0	142.1	121.1	113.7	114.2	107.5	116.4	109.4
1918	145.0	146.8	131.7	152.2	130.1	107.5	107.5	108.8	107.1	107.4
1982	158.9	157.5	137.5	164.7	166.7	109.6	107.3	104.4	108.2	128.2
1983	166.3	160.7	145.2	166.3	206.1	104.7	102.0	105.6	101.0	123.6
1984	189.0	181.4	173.8	184.5	241.5	113.6	112.9	119.7	110.9	117.2
1985	224.5	213.7	218.5	212.5	299.8	118.8	117.8	125.7	115.2	124.1
1986	239.1	226.8	234.2	224.6	324.9	106.5	106.1	107.2	105.7	108.4
1987	252.5	237.6	245.7	235.4	356.8	105.6	104.8	104.9	104.8	109.8
1988	263.3	248.1	271.7	240.6	370.0	104.3	104.4	110.6	102.2	103.7
1989	268.9	253.3	278.0	245.4	377.4	102.1	102.1	102.3	102.0	102.0
1990	281.5	263.4	296.6	252.5	407.6	104.7	104.0	106.7	102.9	108.0
1991	298.4	276.6	313.2	264.1	458.1	106.0	105.0	105.6	104.6	112.4
1992	322.3	295.4	345.4	276.3	527.3	108.0	106.8	110.3	104.6	115.1
1993	395.1	353.3	418.3	327.7	730.8	122.6	119.6	121.1	118.6	138.6
1994	445.3	383.0	458.1	352.9	966.2	112.7	108.4	109.5	107.7	132.2
1995	495.1	425.1	503.9	394.2	1082.1	111.2	111.0	110.0	111.7	112.0
1996	560.5	485.5	545.7	465.9	1183.8	113.2	114.2	108.3	118.2	109.4
1997	609.3	521.9	611.7	487.8	1340.1	108.7	107.5	112.1	104.7	113.2
1998	644.0	543.3	649.0	501.5	1492.8	105.7	104.1	106.1	102.8	111.4
1999	696.1	576.5	725.0	513.0	1716.8	108.1	106.1	111.7	102.3	115.0
2000	798.5	660.0	832.3	585.9	1977.7	114.7	114.5	114.8	114.2	115.2
2001	891.9	711.5	903.0	628.7	2454.3	111.7	107.8	108.5	107.3	124.1
2002	986.4	777.0	1031.3	656.9	2810.2	110.6	109.2	114.2	104.5	114.5
2003	1116.7	892.0	1303.5	674.7	3065.9	113.2	114.8	126.4	102.7	109.1
2004	1219.6	974.9	1454.7	717.9	3341.9	109.2	109.3	111.6	106.4	109.0
2005	1335.1	1054.4	1630.2	738.7	3781.6	109.5	108.2	112.1	102.9	113.2
2006	1522.7	1191.0	1881.2	808.2	4415.9	114.1	113.0	115.4	109.4	116.8
2007	1642.0	1297.6	2105.9	843.3	4643.4	107.8	109.0	111.9	104.3	105.2
2008	1734.7	1381.0	2323.9	842.9	4814.9	105.6	106.4	110.3	99.9	103.7
2009	1967.2	1571.8	2722.4	908.2	5409.9	113.4	113.8	117.1	107.7	112.4
2010	2221.7	1790.6	3183.8	980.4	5971.0	112.9	113.9	116.9	107.9	110.4
2011	2465.1	1994.5	3545.1	1092.7	6562.9	111.0	111.4	111.3	111.5	109.9
2012	2747.0	2199.6	3958.0	1177.5	7500.6	111.4	110.3	111.6	107.8	114.3
2013	3056.5	2420.9	4406.3	1263.3	8579.3	111.3	110.1	111.3	107.3	114.4
2014	3299.4	2635.6	4746.7	1404.0	9079.6	107.9	108.9	107.7	111.1	105.8
2015	3640.3	2920.1	5320.3	1520.6	9918.8	110.3	110.8	112.1	108.3	109.2
2016	3972.1	3191.5	5843.8	1645.3	10777.5	109.1	109.3	109.8	108.2	108.7
2017	4341.7	3499.2	6475.1	1764.9	11687.7	109.3	109.6	110.8	107.3	108.4
2018	4746.6	3805.5	7022.0	1930.8	12950.1	109.3	108.8	108.4	109.4	110.8

2-14 资本形成总额指数

Indices of Gross Capital Formation

本表按可比价格计算。
The indices in this table are calculated at comparable prices.

年份 Year	以1978年为100 (1978=100)			以上年为100 (preceding year=100)		
	资本形成总额 Gross Capital Formation	固定资本形成总额 Fixed Capital Formation	存货变动 Changes in Inventories	资本形成总额 Gross Capital Formation	固定资本形成总额 Fixed Capital Formation	存货变动 Changes in Inventories
1978	100.0	100.0		103.9	111.6	
1979	108.3	104.1		108.3	104.1	
1980	123.4	128.6		113.9	123.5	
1981	134.6	122.5		109.1	95.3	
1982	125.7	146.2		93.4	119.3	
1983	200.6	191.6		159.6	131.1	
1984	210.0	200.4		104.7	104.6	
1985	249.3	241.3		118.7	120.4	
1986	253.8	268.1		101.8	111.1	
1987	271.1	257.1		106.8	95.9	
1988	387.4	350.2		142.9	136.2	
1989	402.1	317.6		103.8	90.7	
1990	406.9	318.3		101.2	100.2	
1991	452.1	359.0		111.1	112.8	
1992	550.2	424.3		121.7	118.2	
1993	585.9	489.3		106.5	115.3	
1994	660.9	585.7		112.8	119.7	
1995	806.3	694.6		122.0	118.6	
1996	936.1	820.3		116.1	118.1	
1997	1051.3	944.2		112.3	115.1	
1998	1180.6	1078.3		112.3	114.2	
1999	1266.8	1145.1		107.3	106.2	
2000	1364.3	1253.9		107.7	109.5	
2001	1459.8	1360.5		107.0	108.5	
2002	1613.1	1537.3		110.5	113.0	
2003	1782.5	1815.6		110.5	118.1	
2004	2141.7	2162.4		120.2	119.1	
2005	2626.8	2815.4		122.6	130.2	
2006	3167.9	3583.1		120.5	127.2	
2007	3904.5	4478.7		123.3	125.0	
2008	4691.5	5392.1		120.2	120.5	
2009	6031.8	7024.7		128.5	130.2	
2010	6930.3	8126.2		114.9	115.7	
2011	7940.9	9272.0		114.6	114.1	
2012	9098.1	10607.2		114.6	114.4	
2013	10299.0	11996.7		113.2	113.1	
2014	11311.1	13124.4		109.8	109.4	
2015	12016.9	13990.7		106.2	106.6	
2016	12723.7	15198.8		105.9	108.6	
2017	13425.8	15971.7		105.5	105.1	
2018	14126.5	16706.4		105.2	104.6	

2-15 支出法生产总值构成

Components of Gross Domestic Product by Expenditure Approach

本表按当年价格计算。
Data in this table are calculated at current prices.

年份 Year	比重（支出法生产总值=100） Proportion (Gross Domestic Product by Expenditure Approach=100)			比重（最终消费支出=100） Proportion (Final Consumption Expenditure=100)	
	最终消费支出 Final Consumption	资本形成总额 Gross Capital Formation	货物和服务净流出 Net Export of Good and Services	居民消费支出 Household Consumption	政府消费支出 Government Consumption
1978	65.7	32.2	2.1	88.1	11.9
1979	66.9	31.8	1.3	88.9	11.1
1980	66.1	30.2	3.7	89.3	10.7
1981	66.0	30.5	3.5	89.2	10.8
1982	69.5	27.0	3.5	87.4	12.6
1983	59.3	35.1	5.6	85.1	14.9
1984	60.0	35.4	4.6	84.6	15.4
1985	61.1	38.4	0.5	83.8	16.2
1986	61.2	36.6	2.2	83.4	16.6
1987	56.5	36.7	6.7	82.7	17.3
1988	54.8	41.1	4.1	85.0	15.0
1989	54.8	40.6	4.6	84.8	15.2
1990	56.4	39.0	4.5	84.9	15.1
1991	54.8	40.3	5.0	83.7	16.3
1992	50.1	44.7	5.2	82.8	17.2
1993	52.9	41.1	6.0	76.5	23.5
1994	54.0	39.7	6.4	77.6	22.4
1995	53.2	41.3	5.4	78.7	21.3
1996	53.3	40.9	5.8	79.4	20.6
1997	53.1	41.5	5.4	79.0	21.0
1998	51.5	42.8	5.7	77.4	22.6
1999	52.0	42.6	5.5	75.9	24.1
2000	54.3	41.6	4.0	76.1	23.9
2001	55.8	40.8	3.4	73.4	26.6
2002	56.1	41.0	2.9	72.3	27.7
2003	56.7	40.6	2.8	73.8	26.2
2004	53.2	44.0	2.8	73.8	26.2
2005	50.4	47.6	2.0	71.3	28.7
2006	49.1	51.4	-0.5	69.7	30.3
2007	45.3	55.9	-1.2	70.6	29.4
2008	42.9	59.6	-2.5	71.2	28.8
2009	44.6	68.5	-13.1	71.5	28.5
2010	47.0	61.9	-8.9	71.0	29.0
2011	47.9	62.1	-10.0	71.5	28.5
2012	48.7	62.5	-11.2	71.5	28.5
2013	50.8	63.2	-14.0	70.9	29.1
2014	51.1	63.8	-14.9	71.5	28.5
2015	53.0	61.5	-14.5	71.6	28.4
2016	54.3	59.1	-13.4	71.6	28.4
2017	55.6	57.2	-12.8	71.8	28.2
2018	56.4	54.1	-10.5	71.9	28.1

2-16 居民消费水平及指数

本表绝对数按当年价格计算，指数按可比价格计算。
Value items in this table are calculated at current prices, while indices are calculated at comparable prices.

年 份 Year	居民消费水平(元) Household Consumption (yuan)			城乡消费水平对比 (农民=1) Urban/Rural Consumption Ratio (Rural Household=1)
	全体居民 All Household	城镇居民 Urban Household	农村居民 Rural Household	
1978	135	428	109	3.9
1979	159	447	132	3.4
1980	187	471	159	3.0
1981	200	496	169	2.9
1982	214	502	183	2.7
1983	218	524	184	2.8
1984	245	605	202	3.0
1985	297	750	240	3.1
1986	324	817	261	3.1
1987	353	895	282	3.2
1988	424	1147	325	3.5
1989	471	1256	360	3.5
1990	523	1274	413	3.1
1991	550	1362	429	3.2
1992	603	1478	469	3.2
1993	755	1769	590	3.0
1994	1032	2493	776	3.2
1995	1381	3045	1067	2.9
1996	1682	3548	1313	2.7
1997	1841	3963	1404	2.8
1998	1851	4106	1373	3.0
1999	1905	4521	1339	3.4
2000	2215	5090	1551	3.3
2001	2381	5562	1647	3.4
2002	2553	5986	1734	3.5
2003	3083	6585	1819	3.6
2004	3625	7394	2156	3.4
2005	4092	8145	2372	3.4
2006	4530	8810	2556	3.4
2007	5141	9743	2833	3.4
2008	5877	10797	3208	3.4
2009	6607	11884	3528	3.4
2010	8004	13578	4551	3.0
2011	9593	15736	5549	2.8
2012	10723	17043	6239	2.7
2013	12105	18697	7108	2.6
2014	13406	19879	8216	2.4
2015	14883	21606	9149	2.4
2016	16467	23249	10288	2.3
2017	18740	26006	11665	2.2
2018	21142	28576	13423	2.1

Household Consumption Expenditure and Indices

居民消费水平指数 Indices of Household Consumption Expenditure					
以上年为100 (preceding year=100)			以1952年为100 (1952=100)		
全体居民 All Household	城镇居民 Urban Household	农村居民 Rural Household	全体居民 All Household	城镇居民 Urban Household	农村居民 Rural Household
116.9	116.3	116.7	100.0	100.0	100.0
117.6	104.4	120.8	117.6	104.4	120.8
112.5	98.6	115.5	132.3	102.9	139.5
106.0	102.7	106.1	140.2	105.7	148.0
105.6	99.4	106.9	148.1	105.1	158.2
100.4	101.4	99.7	148.7	106.6	157.8
111.3	113.3	109.8	165.5	120.7	173.2
116.2	116.4	114.5	192.3	140.5	198.4
104.4	102.2	104.5	200.8	143.6	207.3
102.9	101.4	103.0	206.6	145.6	213.5
102.3	105.0	100.6	211.3	152.9	214.8
100.0	97.3	100.3	211.3	148.8	215.4
102.0	102.0	101.3	215.6	151.8	218.2
103.3	101.9	103.3	222.7	154.6	225.4
105.5	105.9	103.8	234.9	163.8	234.0
118.4	114.2	118.3	278.1	187.0	276.8
107.4	101.7	107.8	298.7	190.2	298.4
110.1	102.7	111.9	328.9	195.3	333.9
113.3	103.0	118.2	372.6	201.2	394.7
106.7	107.7	104.5	397.6	216.7	412.5
103.3	102.7	102.5	410.7	222.5	422.8
105.3	109.0	101.9	432.5	242.6	430.8
113.5	111.8	113.6	490.9	271.2	489.4
106.9	108.0	106.1	524.7	292.9	519.2
108.6	109.9	105.1	569.9	321.9	545.7
108.6	109.3	104.7	618.9	351.8	571.4
109.5	105.6	108.8	677.7	371.5	621.6
107.7	105.2	105.1	729.9	390.8	653.3
112.3	108.3	111.6	819.6	423.3	729.1
109.1	105.8	107.3	894.2	447.8	782.4
114.3	110.8	113.2	1022.1	496.2	885.6
112.4	110.1	110.0	1148.8	546.3	974.2
114.1	113.1	110.3	1310.8	617.9	1074.5
112.0	107.9	114.7	1467.7	666.6	1232.6
110.3	106.8	111.1	1618.6	711.8	1369.2
109.9	107.0	110.2	1779.0	761.8	1508.7
108.7	104.2	113.7	1933.7	793.8	1715.8
110.4	108.0	111.0	2134.9	857.2	1904.0
108.7	105.5	111.0	2321.5	904.4	2114.4
109.2	106.6	110.3	2534.8	964.4	2332.6
108.3	104.6	112.6	2746.2	1009.0	2625.4

2-17 投入产出表(2017年)

单位：万元

投入 Input	产出 Output	中间使用 农林牧渔产品和服务 Farming 、Forestry、Animal Husbandry and Fishery	中间使用 煤炭采选产品 Coal Mining and Processing
农林牧渔产品和服务	Products and Service of Farming 、Forestry、Animal Husbandry and Fishery	9671540	97498
煤炭采选产品	Products of Coal Mining and Processing	70271	3338951
石油和天然气开采产品	Products of Petroleum and Natural Gas Extraction	0	21487
金属矿采选产品	Products of Metals Mining and Dressing		1
非金属矿和其他矿采选产品	Nonmetal Minerals Mining and Dressing	115	18561
食品和烟草	Food and Tobacco	5539561	4119
纺织品	Textile Products	6811	24129
纺织服装鞋帽皮革羽绒及其制品	Manufacture of Leather, Fur, Feather and Its Products	21499	109656
木材加工品和家具	Timber Processing and Furniture	68129	58062
造纸印刷和文教体育用品	Papermaking, Printing, Cultural and Educational Goods	142574	14957
石油、炼焦产品和核燃料加工品	Processing of Petroleum, Coking, Processing of Nucleus Fuel	804831	193466
化学产品	Chemical Products	7955360	336212
非金属矿物制品	Nonmetal Mineral Products	2757	79701
金属冶炼和压延加工品	Products of Smelting and Pressing of Metals	265985	386089
金属制品	Metal Products	985136	260599
通用设备	General Machinery	44574	223135
专用设备	Special Purpose Machinery	585033	231248
交通运输设备	Transport Equipment Machinery	163405	9384
电气机械和器材	Electric Equipment and Machinery	13766	196377
通信设备、计算机和其他电子设备	Communication Equipment, Computer and other Electronic Equipment	19790	16186
仪器仪表	Instruments and Meters	671	18608
其他制造产品和废品废料	Other Manufacture, Waster and Flotsam	3643	17964
金属制品、机械和设备修理服务	Repair Services of Metal Products Equipment and Machinery	40401	291987
电力、热力的生产和供应	Production and Supply of Electric Power, Steam and Hot Water	387997	1005271
燃气生产和供应	Production and Supply of Gas	17668	132
水的生产和供应	Production and Supply of Tap Water	3584	102146
建筑	Construction	93980	37439
批发和零售	Wholesale and Retail Trade	1663646	506234
交通运输、仓储和邮政	Traffic, Transport, Storage and Mail	750063	227403
住宿和餐饮	Accommodation and Restaurants	68035	33214
信息传输、软件和信息技术服务	Information Transfer, Computer and Software Services	48294	10102
金融	Banking	1388355	1379539
房地产	Real Estate Trade	248	47775
租赁和商务服务	Renting and Leasing, Business Services	78783	702150
研究和试验发展	Research and Development		
综合技术服务	Technical Service	535620	8892
水利、环境和公共设施管理	Management of Water Conservancy, Environment and Public Establishment	764780	679
居民服务、修理和其他服务	Resident Services, Repair and Other Services	125860	191298
教育	Education	74618	8192
卫生和社会工作	Health Care and Social Work Activities	1697	80
文化、体育和娱乐	Culture, Sports and Entertainment	1783	4371
公共管理、社会保障和社会组织	Public Management, Social Security and Social Organization	108939	1057
中间投入合计	**Intermediate Input**	**32519800**	**10214350**
劳动者报酬	Compensation of Laborers	42080900	3106567
生产税净额	Net Taxes on Production	105300	1998373
固定资产折旧	Depreciation of Fixed Assets	919300	579003
营业盈余	Operating Surplus		1741365
增加值合计	**Total Value-added**	**43105500**	**7425308**
总投入	**Total Input**	**75625300**	**17639658**

Input-Output Table (2017)

(10 000 yuan)

Intermediate Use Part						
石油和天然气开采产品 Petroleum and Natural Gas Extraction	金属矿采选产品 Metals Mining and Dressing	非金属矿和其他矿采选产品 Nonmetal MineralsMining and Dressing	食品和烟草 Food Production and Tobacco Processing	纺织品 Textile Industry	纺织服装鞋帽皮革羽绒及其制品 Leather, Fur, Feather and Its Products	木材加工品和家具 Timber Processing and Furniture Manufacturing
17	11861	1619	39503881	4520441	990074	2427344
2615	621580	91366	798617	109493	75324	47905
25130	20144	1758				
	1458237					
94759	223130	134610	168477	478	14169	55448
220	22765	41528	43275902	137063	1604762	72456
316	39865	13961	209816	12325243	10084962	226310
5527	24022	13177	218824	58014	5931888	87078
260	43920	6123	487022	38841	84821	6590794
575	29649	21073	2404781	147675	310367	329120
15227	1134786	401258	336968	79588	146742	119458
11274	2587122	544300	2829225	2865560	2792056	1672737
1395	189021	103520	835312	27063	22466	109935
10544	297115	57937	54491	29896	57952	180448
4197	905772	156741	769426	69735	99288	275288
1975	524487	131935	468839	86609	36291	101801
22765	154336	299869	315699	122851	96846	86835
614	30193	67126	12620	9301	3900	4889
1949	183247	68779	79637	28016	16170	9809
1208	3628	4012	31730	6596	16168	16026
4368	22078	12192	11540	2152	705	3363
523	622	8630	31248	12095	235877	80443
12096	1553432	7655	1286474	24525	375354	11612
59426	842484	433306	2777355	810850	781083	652240
544	171	4064	25422	5845	10933	2312
1088	28876	5232	350944	57994	40467	47711
1357	20100	3059	132084	14583	36304	52749
7156	593821	164154	8330912	1039252	2881338	1821982
11544	310320	54456	2121142	380159	377405	502705
1993	47866	42439	489622	74024	114161	117442
1215	12352	7649	121143	17555	23950	72327
14517	1263027	210594	2318186	470411	393065	350550
296	95	2541	43070	2321	14807	15141
75222	692101	151548	2733604	270807	382012	196720
276	3489	94608	184509	18400	54875	147514
124	1191	19959	43183	31540	5949	4887
3420	33412	30002	279231	39053	70836	61181
261	4903	1218	40831	8776	16898	9412
14	53	4811	8545	2454	8384	3222
121	4311	5607	76446	21045	36058	23812
17	1302	3200	16059	4766	8179	4838
396147	**13940885**	**3427615**	**114222814**	**23971072**	**28252885**	**16595845**
116180	2314886	1202243	8217730	2138946	2164601	1268228
263166	2336446	372099	4993370	418032	226059	260366
199168	768942	317662	2392264	399103	396842	472375
55840	2144289	79175	13026872	1450610	3721696	2315137
634354	**7564562**	**1971179**	**28630236**	**4406690**	**6509199**	**4316106**
1030501	**21505447**	**5398794**	**142853051**	**28377762**	**34762084**	**20911951**

2-17 续表 1

单位：万元

投入 Input	产出 Output	中间使用 造纸印刷和文教体育用品 Papermaking, Printing, Cultural and Educational Goods Manufacturing	中间使用 石油、炼焦产品和核燃料加工品 Processing of Petroleum, Coking,Processing of Nucleus Fuel
农林牧渔产品和服务	Products and Service of Farming 、Forestry、Animal Husbandry and Fishery	1360554	200
煤炭采选产品	Products of Coal Mining and Processing	238131	3751312
石油和天然气开采产品	Products of Petroleum and Natural Gas Extraction	4732	3091366
金属矿采选产品	Products of Metals Mining and Dressing		3131
非金属矿和其他矿采选产品	Nonmetal Minerals Mining and Dressing	156882	554
食品和烟草	Food and Tobacco	80703	42931
纺织品	Textile Products	823411	707
纺织服装鞋帽皮革羽绒及其制品	Manufacture of Leather, Fur, Feather and Its Products	65826	7478
木材加工品和家具	Timber Processing and Furniture	763430	374
造纸印刷和文教体育用品	Papermaking, Printing, Cultural and Educational Goods	8787394	2558
石油、炼焦产品和核燃料加工品	Processing of Petroleum, Coking, Processing of Nucleus Fuel	130469	710767
化学产品	Chemical Products	3938799	160269
非金属矿物制品	Nonmetal Mineral Products	102516	402549
金属冶炼和压延加工品	Products of Smelting and Pressing of Metals	1871873	6455
金属制品	Metal Products	305377	4198
通用设备	General Machinery	369537	56069
专用设备	Special Purpose Machinery	415150	9051
交通运输设备	Transport Equipment Machinery	1671	1062
电气机械和器材	Electric Equipment and Machinery	248879	5392
通信设备、计算机和其他电子设备	Communication Equipment, Computer and other Electronic Equipment	169745	659
仪器仪表	Instruments and Meters	5821	5455
其他制造产品和废品废料	Other Manufacture, Waster and Flotsam	996317	4222
金属制品、机械和设备修理服务	Repair Services of Metal Products Equipment and Machinery	247069	159567
电力、热力的生产和供应	Production and Supply of Electric Power, Steam and Hot Water	883420	130741
燃气生产和供应	Production and Supply of Gas	32758	27847
水的生产和供应	Production and Supply of Tap Water	43076	8629
建筑	Construction	15776	3924
批发和零售	Wholesale and Retail Trade	2092082	343121
交通运输、仓储和邮政	Traffic, Transport, Storage and Mail	343989	141647
住宿和餐饮	Accommodation and Restaurants	47576	9925
信息传输、软件和信息技术服务	Information Transfer, Computer and Software Services	19577	1244
金融	Banking	682425	303133
房地产	Real Estate Trade	9231	19
租赁和商务服务	Renting and Leasing, Business Services	400278	84083
研究和试验发展	Research and Development		
综合技术服务	Technical Service	17480	941
水利、环境和公共设施管理	Management of Water Conservancy, Environment and Public Establishment	46785	8819
居民服务、修理和其他服务	Resident Services, Repair and Other Services	51801	42175
教育	Education	4868	3437
卫生和社会工作	Health Care and Social Work Activities	5620	9918
文化、体育和娱乐	Culture, Sports and Entertainment	22914	5567
公共管理、社会保障和社会组织	Public Management, Social Security and Social Organization	4276	1160
中间投入合计	**Intermediate Input**	**25808213**	**9552656**
劳动者报酬	Compensation of Laborers	2030766	617629
生产税净额	Net Taxes on Production	427545	1194062
固定资产折旧	Depreciation of Fixed Assets	1003945	556284
营业盈余	Operating Surplus	3172572	900574
增加值合计	**Total Value-added**	**6634828**	**3268548**
总投入	**Total Input**	**32443041**	**12821204**

continued

(10 000 yuan)

Intermediate Use Part						
化学产品 Chemical Industry	非金属矿物制品 Nonmetal Mineral Products	金属冶炼和压延加工品 Smelting and Pressing of Metals	金属制品 Metal Products	通用设备 General Equipment	专用设备 Special Equipment	交通运输设备 Transport Equipment
3948151	23427	3961	24727	1678	28929	9620
2477470	5620450	2415025	23616	60332	11379	6356
1454650	1277939	559621	69187	27271	184946	95026
147214	1677206	22765706	648896			
1426191	9197316	390568	264242	41693	68149	72176
2774734	75913	89168	17536	18183	36123	93438
906041	198214	42316	25646	42278	26812	75447
147070	108913	57659	41821	78160	43506	137696
424992	155457	41751	356889	141817	67441	185384
1510181	868971	148331	492356	317303	154479	380379
4056868	3862131	4113755	271341	245224	275651	276564
44573878	8130265	2710954	590290	1530076	2018507	3062543
565821	24778473	1429672	288176	602085	587943	227836
1206989	5984133	22635589	16179457	7461362	6605595	4084137
676891	2000160	242577	5788416	2024960	2147562	970585
874370	2136593	282598	577574	10473682	6512353	2399293
274089	535053	187112	31877	1193955	6837074	504717
8344	167357	45089	95949	908061	3337877	15504587
338028	457848	75171	642302	1860376	2393800	2673037
135619	52329	25226	15226	1404647	1195843	848749
76579	23636	26569	30963	135077	202978	269104
172521	153164	4275731	1340307	10551	16059	20002
897449	1632316	495054	86350	722354	982734	131823
4814886	4631126	6183285	2333024	1358597	1265808	883070
191510	37461	796	40656	47001	23618	4680
141404	88816	96309	32459	40940	39673	40994
136530	99529	48118	48908	60880	48524	115014
5479142	5151529	1933126	577610	841089	831273	2086243
1937925	2485210	789752	800535	602646	871792	609382
482024	455997	138407	94163	146915	206374	186087
80989	92437	12231	22653	37554	27210	15430
2709337	3624277	2787105	384660	564221	698545	323245
32702	27425	3074	33490	31298	118553	9810
1909494	1505169	462170	331967	553882	888573	791218
419483	183629	83190	90234	131730	166265	351900
38183	37456	41339	7241	11502	9254	10764
333656	209470	136743	92074	220092	181701	633871
48836	43742	6178	6707	12091	19496	9260
12958	28770	22610	18555	23361	22178	14010
116418	125149	71184	27467	59196	46219	22153
15867	21909	8764	5882	9004	5903	5036
87975485	**87966367**	**75883584**	**32851428**	**34053125**	**39206696**	**38140667**
4889031	6245046	3385656	2010779	2732312	3151070	2506820
1235338	1555176	1569013	1374968	479902	521794	375301
2947078	3102364	3617443	986884	1413663	1357242	946175
11944055	14775826	4061278	1662358	3712386	3675309	3284326
21015502	**25678412**	**12633390**	**6034989**	**8338263**	**8705415**	**7112622**
108990987	**113644779**	**88516974**	**38886417**	**42391388**	**47912111**	**45253289**

2-17 续表 2

单位：万元

投入 Input	产出 Output	中间使用 电气机械和器材 Electric Equipment and Machinery	中间使用 通信设备、计算机和其他电子设备 Communication Equipment, Computer and other Electronic Equipment
农林牧渔产品和服务	Products and Service of Farming 、Forestry、Animal Husbandry and Fishery	3538	15
煤炭采选产品	Products of Coal Mining and Processing	14926	49
石油和天然气开采产品	Products of Petroleum and Natural Gas Extraction	110611	
金属矿采选产品	Products of Metals Mining and Dressing		
非金属矿和其他矿采选产品	Nonmetal Minerals Mining and Dressing	91956	333
食品和烟草	Food and Tobacco	124004	18652
纺织品	Textile Products	133263	7789
纺织服装鞋帽皮革羽绒及其制品	Manufacture of Leather, Fur, Feather and Its Products	31625	23659
木材加工品和家具	Timber Processing and Furniture	109055	30276
造纸印刷和文教体育用品	Papermaking, Printing, Cultural and Educational Goods	242884	68043
石油、炼焦产品和核燃料加工品	Processing of Petroleum, Coking, Processing of Nucleus Fuel	195913	19372
化学产品	Chemical Products	3031798	980267
非金属矿物制品	Nonmetal Mineral Products	2048080	1106244
金属冶炼和压延加工品	Products of Smelting and Pressing of Metals	9972458	1041450
金属制品	Metal Products	1522123	492087
通用设备	General Machinery	1857252	943599
专用设备	Special Purpose Machinery	965789	571182
交通运输设备	Transport Equipment Machinery	555280	231328
电气机械和器材	Electric Equipment and Machinery	9044824	3149185
通信设备、计算机和其他电子设备	Communication Equipment, Computer and other Electronic Equipment	2589118	26516879
仪器仪表	Instruments and Meters	242346	45607
其他制造产品和废品废料	Other Manufacture, Waster and Flotsam	35081	233639
金属制品、机械和设备修理服务	Repair Services of Metal Products Equipment and Machinery	709500	38637
电力、热力的生产和供应	Production and Supply of Electric Power, Steam and Hot Water	836709	253671
燃气生产和供应	Production and Supply of Gas	12584	2704
水的生产和供应	Production and Supply of Tap Water	44497	59270
建筑	Construction	20492	26654
批发和零售	Wholesale and Retail Trade	1946545	2058422
交通运输、仓储和邮政	Traffic, Transport, Storage and Mail	421149	120746
住宿和餐饮	Accommodation and Restaurants	176844	22247
信息传输、软件和信息技术服务	Information Transfer, Computer and Software Services	21585	14718
金融	Banking	469689	571740
房地产	Real Estate Trade	62747	128787
租赁和商务服务	Renting and Leasing, Business Services	426983	1329516
研究和试验发展	Research and Development		
综合技术服务	Technical Service	113822	335855
水利、环境和公共设施管理	Management of Water Conservancy, Environment and Public Establishment	8770	5389
居民服务、修理和其他服务	Resident Services, Repair and Other Services	131192	157808
教育	Education	17542	1906
卫生和社会工作	Health Care and Social Work Activities	14951	4409
文化、体育和娱乐	Culture, Sports and Entertainment	43155	31964
公共管理、社会保障和社会组织	Public Management, Social Security and Social Organization	6981	4108
中间投入合计	**Intermediate Input**	**38407659**	**40648204**
劳动者报酬	Compensation of Laborers	2186751	3529024
生产税净额	Net Taxes on Production	554787	131643
固定资产折旧	Depreciation of Fixed Assets	755296	475484
营业盈余	Operating Surplus	4248295	887650
增加值合计	**Total Value-added**	**7745129**	**5023802**
总投入	**Total Input**	**46152787**	**45672006**

continued

(10 000 yuan)

Intermediate Use Part						
仪器仪表 Instruments and Meters	其他制造产品和废品废料 Other Manufacture，Waster and Flotsam	金属制品、机械和设备修理服务 Repair Services of Metal Products Equipment and Machinery	电力、热力的生产和供应 Production and Supply of Electric Power, Steam and Hot Water	燃气生产和供应 Production and Supply of Gas	水的生产和供应 Production and Supply of Tap Water	建　筑 Construction
	110666		49980	60	15	834412
1097	4363	1424	5357050	80544	20571	341034
			345617	1642701	419557	
	311	0	0			
344	757	2	257032			967577
10863	7058	1351	13439	7677	1961	246653
6775	147091	407	1167	12	3	149341
15396	28631	2365	33276	393	100	162482
16065	56407	827	1040	405	103	1347085
24101	36758	10868	9333	2504	640	423330
9868	18128	5504	444268	71355	18224	1702264
172838	286790	14065	108835	12199	3116	4660273
131735	9076	4186	78004	1173	300	20028999
279026	143800	54287	48682	1980	506	9152946
240576	46933	43046	23348	1056	270	3984884
197733	16094	16172	153238	4334	1107	2167011
7962	12933	1018	11641	14	4	813989
79632	46890	109943	1120	761	194	1202558
261227	14250	15766	2490016	3012	769	4556065
1081004	16456	17987	6222	428	109	443192
824160	10040	448	24887	4794	1224	476465
8185	241447	103	1640	635	162	612930
7311	7401	32342	668503	11405	2913	76275
94133	19011	12208	8364061	86954	22209	1391600
526	7168	2871	41	508923	129982	1106
7864	1007	841	105971	3655	934	394903
18686	3120	2276	59427	1009	258	3068265
243516	111921	28725	567045	66275	16927	3473602
93524	44055	4149	622966	19039	4863	1202614
36729	6080	17352	22541	4506	1151	322237
3526	1134	3214	5628	977	250	100700
21878	56013	6487	1799909	30461	7780	4357926
9072	2480	130	3116	19154	4892	31084
59617	43179	80210	162176	38810	9912	2635495
14349	9953	782	41463	79	20	9374768
965	1375	424	114195	383	98	81305
48402	4952	3459	132579	4546	1161	659504
2446	2277	4356	5066	1047	267	47583
1563	278	114	11513	970	248	28570
3341	2200	2905	19740	3247	829	141654
635	3132	406	3140	541	138	9518
4036672	**1581611**	**503017**	**22168918**	**2638020**	**673768**	**81672200**
458269	445672	214009	3284764	232144	204413	15104900
66343	151340	14188	603302	29442	31468	4659600
109439	59922	24064	5239364	82996	125275	1130900
722412	645494	-75477	-2241883	397637	47471	6045700
1356462	**1302428**	**176783**	**6885547**	**742219**	**408627**	**26941100**
5393134	**2884039**	**679800**	**29054465**	**3380239**	**1082396**	**108613300**

2-17 续表 3

单位：万元

投入 Input	产出 Output	中间使用 批发和零售 Wholesale and Retail Trade	中间使用 交通运输、仓储和邮政 Traffic, Transport, Storage and Mail
农林牧渔产品和服务	Products and Service of Farming 、Forestry、Animal Husbandry and Fishery	1020	81325
煤炭采选产品	Products of Coal Mining and Processing	1675	2526
石油和天然气开采产品	Products of Petroleum and Natural Gas Extraction		10
金属矿采选产品	Products of Metals Mining and Dressing		0
非金属矿和其他矿采选产品	Nonmetal Minerals Mining and Dressing	1891	4775
食品和烟草	Food and Tobacco	20984	73083
纺织品	Textile Products	30831	61876
纺织服装鞋帽皮革羽绒及其制品	Manufacture of Leather, Fur, Feather and Its Products	32876	82880
木材加工品和家具	Timber Processing and Furniture	20256	65439
造纸印刷和文教体育用品	Papermaking, Printing, Cultural and Educational Goods	116831	274158
石油、炼焦产品和核燃料加工品	Processing of Petroleum, Coking, Processing of Nucleus Fuel	363537	3845985
化学产品	Chemical Products	96505	954970
非金属矿物制品	Nonmetal Mineral Products	6438	28631
金属冶炼和压延加工品	Products of Smelting and Pressing of Metals	1056	24790
金属制品	Metal Products	45596	151056
通用设备	General Machinery	44577	779574
专用设备	Special Purpose Machinery	8623	44709
交通运输设备	Transport Equipment Machinery	1661	5264270
电气机械和器材	Electric Equipment and Machinery	116218	515577
通信设备、计算机和其他电子设备	Communication Equipment, Computer and other Electronic Equipment	194960	166631
仪器仪表	Instruments and Meters	654	28986
其他制造产品和废品废料	Other Manufacture, Waster and Flotsam	2619	13990
金属制品、机械和设备修理服务	Repair Services of Metal Products Equipment and Machinery	139394	420407
电力、热力的生产和供应	Production and Supply of Electric Power, Steam and Hot Water	589483	1274146
燃气生产和供应	Production and Supply of Gas	3179	5554201
水的生产和供应	Production and Supply of Tap Water	57349	44164
建筑	Construction	102402	308690
批发和零售	Wholesale and Retail Trade	1455515	2242343
交通运输、仓储和邮政	Traffic, Transport, Storage and Mail	1619984	9042592
住宿和餐饮	Accommodation and Restaurants	345521	217578
信息传输、软件和信息技术服务	Information Transfer, Computer and Software Services	85154	154918
金融	Banking	3764915	4393461
房地产	Real Estate Trade	1809885	1108593
租赁和商务服务	Renting and Leasing, Business Services	3281701	2226950
研究和试验发展	Research and Development		
综合技术服务	Technical Service	88473	103183
水利、环境和公共设施管理	Management of Water Conservancy, Environment and Public Establishment	18729	35604
居民服务、修理和其他服务	Resident Services, Repair and Other Services	364440	1093450
教育	Education	152704	60955
卫生和社会工作	Health Care and Social Work Activities	11022	39466
文化、体育和娱乐	Culture, Sports and Entertainment	46849	91042
公共管理、社会保障和社会组织	Public Management, Social Security and Social Organization	76021	21771
中间投入合计	**Intermediate Input**	**15121523**	**40898755**
劳动者报酬	Compensation of Laborers	14006100	17286809
生产税净额	Net Taxes on Production	6915600	1115107
固定资产折旧	Depreciation of Fixed Assets	928700	5101796
营业盈余	Operating Surplus	10780200	5783033
增加值合计	**Total Value-added**	**32630600**	**29286745**
总投入	**Total Input**	**47752123**	**70185500**

continued

(10 000 yuan)

Intermediate Use Part							
住宿和餐饮 Accommodation and Restaurants	信息传输、软件和信息技术服务 Information Transfer, Computer and Software Services	金融 Banking	房地产 Real Estate Trade	租赁和商务服务 Tenancy and Business Services	研究和试验发展 Research and Development	综合技术服务 Technical Service	水利、环境和公共设施管理 Management of Water Conservancy, Environment and Public Establishment
1495668	22290	26388	20143	14702	14313	82482	130665
15975		2056	3938	12	976	270	547
0					12		
					1119		
312	2	389	291	237	74	26	248
7711692	60882	114737	91443	29055	18708	11400	19744
289234	671	1191	5123	6123	6431	4244	13576
48484	42148	286738	85890	24944	4272	117383	11762
20458	210409	92703	56975	17084	189	30675	13224
659918	171543	3120950	1554548	205013	10556	502323	46441
44552	43295	79637	175615	11399	4883	25675	74449
453865	30725	255087	77464	11987	72118	228785	24387
80877	3949	256	10975	2672	9411	77	2512
461	171	11	864	361	1308	5909	2693
29098	48249	2608	84193	407631	19522	371019	13853
37452	27911	180094	63707	10454	954	12397	5724
13390	13605	276436	43505	1542	168	322	2873
1569	3264	41381	11319	247499	1864	13502	37642
25839	135950	16799	170807	82081	28411	253861	7634
36425	1607708	169679	94191	167052	69790	39436	11143
518	13505	629	16826	146086	56766	309583	5718
30027	8585	301	14326	641273	6585	633100	11813
84361	163206	151114	616443	249214	649	38421	17220
943520	330261	1217900	1280761	764686	12438	81534	45341
503272	1146	1866	73884	4087	727	17411	6057
133656	15493	137490	145668	43186	1830	21622	7595
141651	34291	528391	816947	130505	1510	6040	23410
1486186	139639	418580	154050	342646	24334	233241	45725
98157	114902	617057	223080	384981	21646	776628	83969
110527	71686	1175578	452576	71076	4900	338643	52524
104601	1976236	678207	69292	12443	392	16108	4262
553521	83849	3474766	4021922	1273913	37750	153493	156289
1479022	193787	4440835	1260542	409760	1364	105226	16911
946943	901305	7939920	3793541	982608	50206	1053842	134511
					3318		
822	17112	2910	2259	1158	11890	1108334	1164
9155	4202	50779	19270	5060	516	3634	65441
235070	47907	693637	194173	502411	6242	67977	48272
29242	19590	497079	45257	9564	721	8488	4585
585	320	19621	113	49	60	628	489
42337	21451	170585	91682	11226	1128	17399	5997
8559	22513	63396	22399	41217	116	6067	2130
17907000	**6603756**	**26947782**	**15866002**	**7266998**	**510167**	**6697204**	**1158542**
9692600	2276999	9606352	4386512	9974850	110186	3272576	755568
450400	755955	3612466	5818553	1070840	12901	475562	115946
937400	5361958	2045919	1871910	633125	182063	720462	423003
2066100	1294674	9827180	5139954	545486	180483	2452095	304241
13146500	**9689585**	**25091918**	**17216929**	**12224302**	**485633**	**6920696**	**1598758**
31053500	**16293341**	**52039700**	**33082931**	**19491300**	**995800**	**13617900**	**2757300**

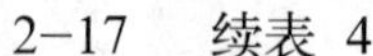
2-17 续表 4

单位：万元

投入 Input \ 产出 Output		中间使用	
		居民服务、修理和其他服务 Resident Services and Other services	教育 Education
农林牧渔产品和服务	Products and Service of Farming 、Forestry、 Animal Husbandry and Fishery	291334	195608
煤炭采选产品	Products of Coal Mining and Processing	17659	141050
石油和天然气开采产品	Products of Petroleum and Natural Gas Extraction		
金属矿采选产品	Products of Metals Mining and Dressing		
非金属矿和其他矿采选产品	Nonmetal Minerals Mining and Dressing	405	264
食品和烟草	Food and Tobacco	271400	965019
纺织品	Textile Products	364717	7245
纺织服装鞋帽皮革羽绒及其制品	Manufacture of Leather, Fur, Feather and Its Products	176646	218219
木材加工品和家具	Timber Processing and Furniture	386489	413673
造纸印刷和文教体育用品	Papermaking, Printing, Cultural and Educational Goods	395503	1513415
石油、炼焦产品和核燃料加工品	Processing of Petroleum, Coking, Processing of Nucleus Fuel	169537	11135
化学产品	Chemical Products	672441	1150280
非金属矿物制品	Nonmetal Mineral Products	2872	25309
金属冶炼和压延加工品	Products of Smelting and Pressing of Metals	12002	6845
金属制品	Metal Products	509791	25477
通用设备	General Machinery	69360	50676
专用设备	Special Purpose Machinery	3107	3596
交通运输设备	Transport Equipment Machinery	389506	14349
电气机械和器材	Electric Equipment and Machinery	244365	53299
通信设备、计算机和其他电子设备	Communication Equipment, Computer and other Electronic Equipment	566947	496154
仪器仪表	Instruments and Meters	95914	115485
其他制造产品和废品废料	Other Manufacture, Waster and Flotsam	427672	13095
金属制品、机械和设备修理服务	Repair Services of Metal Products Equipment and Machinery	68444	44527
电力、热力的生产和供应	Production and Supply of Electric Power, Steam and Hot Water	533833	473407
燃气生产和供应	Production and Supply of Gas	362200	38543
水的生产和供应	Production and Supply of Tap Water	61835	515356
建筑	Construction	183631	621737
批发和零售	Wholesale and Retail Trade	570155	467174
交通运输、仓储和邮政	Traffic,Transport, Storage and Mail	575284	716403
住宿和餐饮	Accommodation and Restaurants	208041	493959
信息传输、软件和信息技术服务	Information Transfer, Computer and Software Services	40814	165933
金融	Banking	536583	679448
房地产	Real Estate Trade	1806983	480469
租赁和商务服务	Renting and Leasing, Business Services	803568	929175
研究和试验发展	Research and Development		
综合技术服务	Technical Service	567	50907
水利、环境和公共设施管理	Management of Water Conservancy, Environment and Public Establishment	18997	17844
居民服务、修理和其他服务	Resident Services, Repair and Other Services	722568	1141040
教育	Education	20826	1221758
卫生和社会工作	Health Care and Social Work Activities	5977	14932
文化、体育和娱乐	Culture, Sports and Entertainment	38606	199500
公共管理、社会保障和社会组织	Public Management, Social Security and Social Organization	11002	11993
中间投入合计	**Intermediate Input**	**11637577**	**13704296**
劳动者报酬	Compensation of Laborers	4995007	6810513
生产税净额	Net Taxes on Production	280543	31911
固定资产折旧	Depreciation of Fixed Assets	451192	1714726
营业盈余	Operating Surplus	1280681	622053
增加值合计	**Total Value-added**	**7007423**	**9179204**
总投入	**Total Input**	**18645000**	**22883500**

continued

(10 000 yuan)

Intermediate Use Part				最终使用 Final used		
卫生和社会工作 Sanitation and Social Work	文化、体育和娱乐 Culture, Sports and Entertainment	公共管理和社会组织 Public Management and Social Organization	中间使用合计 Total of Intermediate Use Part	最终消费支出 Final Consumption 居民消费支出 Household Consumption		
				农村居民消费支出 Rural Households	城镇居民消费支出 Urban Households	合计 Total
34410	15132		66049690	4277661	8165516	12443177
13130	338	4429	25785829	60268	11931	72199
1369	48	1644	9354826			
			26701821			
84	245	228	13654990			
93762	149782	130187	64120642	12069468	16787797	28857265
306044	47775	30347	26693559	365890	956274	1322164
5025	99337	267665	8960010	848525	6402274	7250800
56359	21883	90495	12573081	613879	2202156	2816035
203792	338367	1203698	27198238	856709	1917612	2774321
8203	20996	41418	24580305	179690	130258	309948
4218762	27227	253524	106107736	1848615	4451183	6299798
14181	338	935	53953470	90938	224507	315445
36	128	741	88128557			
2090	26260	438	25778111	64440	178702	243142
6811	9701	12298	31969943	13933	25514	39447
501127	572	167	15201833	53037	52534	105572
12101	3117	63930	28706111	2692984	7326065	10019049
19230	8044	18611	30524421	1027901	2707555	3735456
13016	48545	135236	38451696	882640	3073413	3956053
36130	4336	6407	3319372	139583	695958	835540
4100	22020	252	10343501	98425	290277	388703
27535	14768	58911	12607155			
202465	47803	420840	49532946	559950	2956015	3515965
15759	16012	2023	7739691	142395	997034	1139428
153557	19785	166783	3314654	189957	563507	753464
80690	29480	504471	7682890			
822609	124957	279893	53663732	3133681	6377571	9511252
198556	114926	855763	31295107	540508	1401012	1941520
476629	78002	1401111	8864302	1299196	6036862	7336058
251728	19405	542103	4897241	1056940	2522543	3579482
73406	187488	1579217	48157096	2299354	9470661	11770015
180252	81970	512572	14541527	5570000	12767418	18337418
114161	275994	352338	40782442	198398	2646011	2844409
			3318			
34666	444	1802	13809814	55101	178201	233303
12864	7355	8385	1574373	18562	138784	157346
178659	78570	936800	10190694	2036961	5394076	7431038
27731	13217	238165	2752096	3525612	6515623	10041235
67213	1427	40743	452501	2783914	5564500	8348414
68409	278518	161748	2165331	143402	1112030	1255432
15383	2354	1055169	1614846	42481	274925	317406
8552038	**2236666**	**11381489**	**1053799500**	**49781000**	**120516300**	**170297300**
5275567	2564960	14583664	221437600			
108575	284259	77159	47074200			
699190	652107	1071575	53173600			
309330	764108	92314	123842900			
6392662	**4265434**	**15824711**	**445528300**			
14944700	**6502100**	**27206200**	**1499327800**			

2-17 续表 5

单位：万元

投入 Input	产出 Output	最终使用 最终消费支出 Final Consumption 政府消费支出 Government Consumption	合计 Total
农林牧渔产品和服务	Products and Service of Farming 、Forestry、 Animal Husbandry and Fishery	1285411	13728588
煤炭采选产品	Products of Coal Mining and Processing		72199
石油和天然气开采产品	Products of Petroleum and Natural Gas Extraction		
金属矿采选产品	Products of Metals Mining and Dressing		
非金属矿和其他矿采选产品	Nonmetal Minerals Mining and Dressing		
食品和烟草	Food and Tobacco		28857265
纺织品	Textile Products		1322164
纺织服装鞋帽皮革羽绒及其制品	Manufacture of Leather, Fur, Feather and Its Products		7250800
木材加工品和家具	Timber Processing and Furniture		2816035
造纸印刷和文教体育用品	Papermaking, Printing, Cultural and Educational Goods		2774321
石油、炼焦产品和核燃料加工品	Processing of Petroleum, Coking, Processing of Nucleus Fuel		309948
化学产品	Chemical Products		6299798
非金属矿物制品	Nonmetal Mineral Products		315445
金属冶炼和压延加工品	Products of Smelting and Pressing of Metals		
金属制品	Metal Products		243142
通用设备	General Machinery		39447
专用设备	Special Purpose Machinery		105572
交通运输设备	Transport Equipment Machinery		10019049
电气机械和器材	Electric Equipment and Machinery		3735456
通信设备、计算机和其他电子设备	Communication Equipment, Computer and other Electronic Equipment		3956053
仪器仪表	Instruments and Meters		835540
其他制造产品和废品废料	Other Manufacture, Waster and Flotsam		388703
金属制品、机械和设备修理服务	Repair Services of Metal Products Equipment and Machinery		
电力、热力的生产和供应	Production and Supply of Electric Power, Steam and Hot Water		3515965
燃气生产和供应	Production and Supply of Gas		1139428
水的生产和供应	Production and Supply of Tap Water		753464
建筑	Construction		
批发和零售	Wholesale and Retail Trade		9511252
交通运输、仓储和邮政	Traffic, Transport, Storage and Mail	1067448	3008969
住宿和餐饮	Accommodation and Restaurants		7336058
信息传输、软件和信息技术服务	Information Transfer, Computer and Software Services		3579482
金融	Banking	3637	11773653
房地产	Real Estate Trade		18337418
租赁和商务服务	Renting and Leasing, Business Services	70694	2915103
研究和试验发展	Research and Development	506661	506661
综合技术服务	Technical Service	1012311	1245614
水利、环境和公共设施管理	Management of Water Conservancy, Environment and Public Establishment	3979915	4137261
居民服务、修理和其他服务	Resident Services, Repair and Other Services		7431038
教育	Education	15358091	25399326
卫生和社会工作	Health Care and Social Work Activities	19331152	27679566
文化、体育和娱乐	Culture, Sports and Entertainment	1173426	2428858
公共管理、社会保障和社会组织	Public Management, Social Security and Social Organization	17210154	17527560
中间投入合计	**Intermediate Input**	**60998900**	**231296200**
劳动者报酬	Compensation of Laborers		
生产税净额	Net Taxes on Production		
固定资产折旧	Depreciation of Fixed Assets		
营业盈余	Operating Surplus		
增加值合计	**Total Value-added**		
总投入	**Total Input**		

continued

(10 000 yuan)

Final used					省外购进 Domestic inflow outside the province	总产出 gross output
资本形成总额 Gross Capital Formation			销往省外 Sold to Other province	最终使用合计 Total Final used		
固定资本形成总额 Fixed Capital Formation	存货变动 Changes in Inventories	合计 Total				
324658	877846	1202504	15013999	17786266	1202504	75625300
	-6688	-6688	72199	5317916	-6688	17639658
	17099	17099		3431661	17099	1030501
	-2374	-2374		2489694	-2374	21505447
	44877	44877		370516	44877	5398794
	365043	365043	28857265	94634992	365043	142853051
	32153	32153	1322164	6277388	32153	28377762
	50561	50561	7250800	25990266	50561	34762084
3351650	45797	3397447	2816035	9622091	3397447	20911951
553269	194449	747719	2774321	13196122	747719	32443041
	185645	185645	309948	12180817	185645	12821204
	511248	511248	6299798	41639759	511248	108990987
	308672	308672	315445	63500298	308672	113644779
	475987	475987		53758575	475987	88516974
5919725	2451	5922176	243142	15119636	5922176	38886417
15373671	160983	15534653	39447	24022497	15534653	42391388
55742689	291438	56034127	105572	72185601	56034127	47912111
8160739	175230	8335969	10019049	33673076	8335969	45253289
4348120	203795	4551914	3735456	27211382	4551914	46152787
2325005	1351989	3676993	3956053	36136041	3676993	45672006
961106	273979	1235085	835540	3988728	1235085	5393134
	358584	358584	388703	1841373	358584	2884039
				1976792		679800
			3515965	3535566		29054465
	155672	155672	1139428	3524675	155672	3380239
	12111	12111	753464	1483504	12111	1082396
180809454		180809454		182725262	180809454	108613300
769082	175915	944997	9511252	13465806	944997	47752123
58153	62041	120194	4076417	44478251	120194	70185500
			7336058	22316955		31053500
12760148		12760148	3579482	23200422	12760148	16293341
			11777290	22022577		52039700
9241562		9241562	18337418	28911931	9241562	33082931
			2985797	3107334		19491300
3263234		3263234	1013322	3829461	3263234	995800
190435		190435	2257926	1839070	190435	13617900
			8117175	4197998		2757300
			7431038	10446084		18645000
			40757417	25421603		22883500
			47010717	31965081		14944700
	0	0	3602283	5486939	0	6502100
	0	0	34737714	28876345	0	27206200
304152700	**6324500**	**310477200**	**292295100**	**1027186349**	**310477200**	**1499327800**

主要统计指标解释

国内生产总值（GDP） 指按市场价格计算的一个国家(或地区)所有常住单位在一定时期内生产活动的最终成果。国内生产总值有三种表现形态，即价值形态、收入形态和产品形态。从价值形态看，它是所有常住单位在一定时期内生产的全部货物和服务价值超过同期投入的全部非固定资产货物和服务价值的差额，即所有常住单位的增加值之和；从收入形态看，它是所有常住单位在一定时期内创造并分配给常住单位和非常住单位的初次收入之和；从产品形态看，它是所有常住单位在一定时期内最终使用的货物和服务价值减去货物和服务进口价值。在实际核算中，国内生产总值有三种计算方法，即生产法、收入法和支出法。三种方法分别从不同的方面反映国内生产总值及其构成。

三次产业 三次产业的划分是世界上较为常用的产业结构分类，但各国的划分不尽一致。根据《国民经济行业分类》(GB/T 4754-2011）和《三次产业划分规定》，我国的三次产业划分是：

第一产业是指农、林、牧、渔业（不含农、林、牧、渔服务业）。

第二产业是指采矿业（不含开采辅助活动），制造业（不含金属制品、机械和设备修理业），电力、热力、燃气及水生产和供应业，建筑业。

第三产业即服务业，是指除第一产业、第二产业以外的其他行业。

支出法国内生产总值 是从最终使用的角度反映一个国家（或地区）一定时期内生产活动最终成果的一种方法，包括最终消费支出、资本形成总额及货物和服务净出口三部分。计算公式为：

支出法国内生产总值=最终消费支出+资本形成总额+货物和服务净出口

最终消费支出 指常住单位为满足物质、文化和精神生活的需要，从本国经济领土和国外购买的货物和服务的支出。它不包括非常住单位在本国经济领土内的消费支出。最终消费支出分为居民消费支出和政府消费支出。

居民消费支出 指常住住户在一定时期内对于货物和服务的全部最终消费支出。居民消费支出除了直接以货币形式购买的货物和服务的消费支出外，还包括以其他方式获得的货物和服务的消费支出，即所谓的虚拟消费支出。居民虚拟消费支出包括如下几种类型：单位以实物报酬及实物转移的形式提供给劳动者的货物和服务；住户生产并由本住户消费了的货物和服务，其中的服务仅指住户的自有住房服务；金融机构提供的金融媒介服务；保险公司提供的保险服务。

政府消费支出 指政府部门为全社会提供的公共服务的消费支出和免费或以较低的价格向居民住户提供的货物和服务的净支出，前者等于政府服务的产出价值减去政府单位所获得的经营收入的价值，后者等于政府部门免费或以较低价格向居民住户提供的货物和服务的市场价值减去向住户收取的价值。

资本形成总额 指常住单位在一定时期内获得减去处置的固定资产和存货的净额，包括固定资本形成总额和存货变动两部分。

固定资本形成总额 指常住单位在一定时期内获得的固定资产减处置的固定资产的价值总额。固定资产是通过生产活动生产出来的，且其使用年限在一年以上、单位价值在规定标准以上的资产，不包括自然资产、耐用消费品、小型工器具。固定资本形成总额包括住宅、其他建筑和构筑物、机器和设备、培育性生物资源、知识产权产品（研发支出、矿藏的勘探、计算机软件）的价值获得减处置。

存货变动 指常住单位在一定时期内存货实物量变动的市场价值，即期末价值减期初价值的差额，再扣除当期由于价格变动而产生的持有收益。存货变动可以是正值，也可以是负值，正值表示存货上升，负值表示存货下降。存货包括生产单位购进的原材料、燃料和储备物资等存货，以及生产单位生产的产成品、在制品和半成品等存货。

货物和服务净出口 指货物和服务出口减货物和服务进口的差额。出口包括常住单位向非常住单位出售或无偿转让的各种货物和服务的价值；进口包括常住单位从非常住单位购买或无偿得到的各种货物和服务的价值。由于服务活动的提供与使用同时发生，一般把常住单位从非常住单位得到的服务作为进口，非常住单位从常住单位得到的服务作为出口。货物的出口和进口都按离岸价格计算。

劳动者报酬 指劳动者因从事生产活动所获得的全部报酬。包括劳动者获得的各种形式的工资、奖金和津贴，既包括货币形式的，也包括实物形式的，还包括劳动者所享受的公费医疗和医药卫生费、上下班交通补贴、单位支付的社会保险费、住房公积金等。

生产税净额 指生产税减生产补贴后的差额。其中，生产税指政府对生产单位从事生产、销售和经营活动，以及因从事生产活动使用某些生产要素（如固定资产和土地等）所征收的各种税收、附加费和其他规费。生产税分为产品税和其他生产税，产品税主要有：增值税、消费税、进口关税、出口税等；其他生产税主要有：房产税、车船使用税、城镇土地使用税等。生产补贴则相反，它是政府为影响生产单位的生产、销售及定价等生产活动而对其提供的无偿支付，包括农业生产补贴、政策亏损补贴、进口补贴等。生产补贴作为负生产税处理。

固定资产折旧 指由于自然退化、正常淘汰或损耗而导致的固定资产价值下降，用以代表固定资产通过生产过程被转移到其产出中的价值。原则上，固定资产折旧应按照固定资产的重置价值计算。

营业盈余 指常住单位创造的增加值扣除劳动者报酬、生产税净额和固定资产折旧后的余额。

机构单位 指能够以自己的名义拥有资产和承担负债，能够独立地从事经济活动并与其他主体进行交易的经济主体。

机构部门 将相同性质的机构单位归并在一起，就形成机构部门。资金流量核算将常住机构单位划分为以下四个机构部门：非金融企业部门、金融机构部门、政府部门、住户部门。与常住单位发生经济往来关系的非常住单位组成国外部门，在资金流量核算中也视同机构部门。

非金融企业与非金融企业部门 非金融企业指主要从事市场货物生产和提供非金融市场服务的常住企业，它主要包括从事上述活动的各类法人企业。所有非金融企业归并在一起，就形成非金融企业部门。

金融机构与金融机构部门 金融机构指主要从事金融媒介以及与金融媒介密切相关的辅助金融活动的常住单位，它主要包括中央银行、商业银行和政策性银行、非银行信贷机构和保险公司。所有金融机构组成金融机构部门。

政府机构与政府部门 政府机构指在设定区域内对其他机构单位拥有立法、司法或行政权的法律实体及其附属单位。政府机构的主要职能是利用征税和其他方式获得的资金向社会和公众提供货物和服务；通过转移支付，对社会收入和财产进行再分配；从事非市场性生产。它主要包括各级党政机关、群众团体、事业单位、基层群众的自治组织等。所有政府机构组成政府部门。

住户与住户部门 住户指共享同一生活设施、部分或全部收入和财产集中使用、共同消费住房、食品和其他消费品与消费服务的常住个人或个人群体。所有住户组成住户部门。

非常住单位与国外部门 所有不具有常住性的机构单位都是非常住单位。与我国常住单位发生交易的所有非常住单位称为国外部门。

初次分配总收入 收入初次分配是生产活动创造的价值在参与生产活动的生产要素所有者及政府之间的分配。生产活动的最终成果是增加值。生产要素主要包括劳动力、资本、自然资源。劳动力所有者因提供劳动而获得劳动报酬；资本的所有者因提供资本而获得不同形式的收入，如借贷资本所有者获得利息收入；股权所有者获得红利或参与利润分配；自然资源所有者因出让自然资源使用权而获得地租；政府因国家管理需要对生产活动或生产要素征收生产税同时也因扶持有关生产活动而支付生产补贴。初次分配的结果形成各个机构部门的初次分配总收入。各部门的初次分配总收入之和就等于国民总收入，亦即国民生产总值。

经常转移 转移是一个机构单位向另一个机构单位提供货物、服务或资产，而同时并没有从后一机构单位获得任何货物、服务或资产作为回报的一种交易。经常转移指交易的一方或双方都不涉及获得或处置资产（除存货和现金外）的转移。其形式有所得税、财产税等经常税、社会保险缴款、社会保险福利、社会补助和其他经常转移。

可支配总收入 在初次分配总收入的基础上，通过经常转移的形式对初次分配总收入进行再次分配。再分配的结果形成各个机构部门的可支配总收入。各部门的可支配总收入之和称为国民可支配总收入。

总储蓄 指可支配总收入用于最终消费后的余额。各部门的总储蓄之和称为国民总储蓄。

资本转移 指交易的一方或双方涉及获得或处置资产（除存货和现金外）的转移。资本转移包括资本税、投资性补助和其他资本转移。

净金融投资 它反映各机构部门或经济总体非金融投资过程中资金富余或短缺的状况。从非金融交易角度看，它是指总储蓄加资本转移收入减资本转移支出减非金融投资后的差额。从金融交易角度看，它是金融资产的增加额减金融负债的增加额之后的差额。

通货 指以现金形式存在于市场流通中的货币，包括纸币和硬币。

存款 以各种形式存在存款类金融机构的存款，包括活期存款、定期存款、财政存款、外汇存款和其他存款等。

贷款 指金融机构发放的各类贷款，包括短期贷款、票据融资、中长期贷款、外汇贷款、委托贷款和其他贷款等。

证券 包括债券和股票。由债券购买者承购的或因销售产品而拥有的，可在金融市场上交易并代表一定债权的书面证明。包括政府债券、金融债券、企业债券、商业票据、支付固定收入但不提供法人企业残余价值分享权的优先股等。股票购买者及直接投资者对其投资企业净资产所拥有的权益。股票是股份公司签发的证明股东投资并按其所持股份享有权益和承担义务的权益性证券。其他股权是机构单位以直接投资的方式用除股票、债权性证券以外的土地、房屋及建筑物、机器设备、存货、资源资产等实物资产，商标、专利权、土地使用权、特许使用权、商誉等无形资产及货币资金直接向其他单位进行的投资。通常以股权证、出资证明书、参与证或类似的单据为凭证。

保险准备金 指社会保险和商业保险基金的净权益、保险费预付款和未结索赔准备金。

结算资金 指金融机构用于结算目的汇兑在途的资金。

金融机构往来 指金融机构部门子部门之间发生的同业存放、同业拆借和债券回购等。

准备金 指各金融机构在中央银行的存款及缴存中央银行的法定准备金。

中央银行贷款 指中央银行向各金融机构的贷款。

经常项目 包括货物、服务、收益及经常性转移。

货物进出口 指通过我国海关进出口的货物。货物的进出口值都按离岸价格估价。离岸价格可视为进口商在出口商边境领取货物时支付的购买者价格。当进口商领取该货物时，该货物已装载到进口商自己的运载工具或其他运载工具，出口商已为该货物支付了出口税或获得了出口退税。

服务进出口 指常住单位与非常住单位之间相互提供的服务。包括运输服务、旅游服务、通讯服务、建筑服务、保险服务、金融服务、计算机和信息服务、咨询服务、广告、宣传服务、电影音像服务、专有权力使用费和特许费、其他商务服务、政府服务。

收益 指常住单位与非常住单位之间因相互提供生产要素而产生的收入，包括劳动者报酬和投资收益。其中投资收益包括直接投资、证券投资和其他投资的收益和支出，以及直接投资收益的再投资。

资本项目 包括移民转移、债务减免等资本性转移。

金融项目 包括直接投资、证券投资和其它投资。

直接投资 以投资者寻求在本国以外运行企业获取有效发言权为目的的投资，包括直接投资资产和直接投资负债两部分。相关投资工具可划分为股权和关联企业债务。股权包括股权和投资基金份额，以及再投资收益。关联企业债务包括关联企业间可流通和不可流通的债权和债务。

证券投资 包括证券投资资产和证券投资负债，相关投资工具可划分为股权和债券。股权包括股权和投资基金份额，记录在证券投资项下的股权和投资基金份额均应可流通（可交易）。股权通常以股份、股票、参股、存托凭证或类似单据作为凭证。投资基金份额指投资者持有的共同基金等集合投资产品的份额。债券指可流通的债务工具，是证明其持有人（债权人）有权在未来某个（些）时点向其发行人（债务人）收回本金或收取利息的凭证，包括可转让存单、商业票据、公司债券、有资产担保的证券、货币市场工具以及通常在金融市场上交易的类似工具。

其它投资 除直接投资、证券投资、金融衍生工具和储备资产外，居民与非居民之间的其他金融交易。包括其他股权、货币和存款、贷款、保险和养老金、贸易信贷和其他。

储备资产增减额 指我国在黄金储备、外汇储备、在国际货币基金组织的储备头寸、特别提款权、使用基金信贷等方面本年末与上年末余额之间的差额。负号表示储备资产增加，正号表示储备资产减少。

Explanatory Notes on Main Statistical Indicators

Gross Domestic Product (GDP) refers to the final products at market prices produced by all resident units in a country (or a region) during a certain period of time. Gross domestic product is expressed in three different perspectives, namely value, income, and products respectively. GDP in its value perspective refers to the total value of all goods and services produced by all resident units during a certain period of time, minus the total value of input of goods and services of the nature of non-fixed assets; in other words, it is the sum of the value-added of all resident units. GDP from the perspective of income includes the primary income created by all resident units and distributed to resident and non-resident units. GDP from the perspective of products refers to the value of all goods and services for final consumption by all resident units minus the net exports of goods and services during a given period of time. In the practice of national accounting, gross domestic product is calculated from three approaches, namely production approach, income approach and expenditure approach, which reflect gross domestic product and its composition from different angles.

Three Industries Classification of economic activities into three strata of industry is a common practice in the world, although the grouping varies to some extent form country to country. In China economic activities are categorized into the following three strata of industry:

Primary industry refers to agriculture, forestry, animal husbandry and fishery and services in support of these industries.

Secondary industry refers to mining and quarrying, manufacturing, production and supply of electricity, water and gas, and construction.

Tertiary industry refers to all other economic activities not included in the primary or secondary industries.

GDP by Expenditure Approach refers to the method of measuring the final results of production activities of a country (region) during a given period from the perspective of final uses. It includes final consumption expenditure, gross capital formation and net export of goods and services. The formula for computation is

GDP by expenditure approach = final consumption expenditure + gross capital formation + net export of goods and services

Final Consumption Expenditure refers to the total expenditure of resident units for purchases of goods and services from both the domestic economic territory and abroad to meet the needs of material, cultural and spiritual life. It does not include the expenditure of non-resident units on consumption in the economic territory of the country. The final consumption expenditure is broken down into household consumption expenditure and government consumption expenditure.

Household Consumption Expenditure refers to the total expenditure of resident households on the final consumption of goods and services. In addition to the consumption of goods and services bought by the households directly with money, the household consumption expenditure also includes expenditure on goods and services obtained by the households in other ways, i.e. the so-called imputed consumption expenditure, which includes the following: (a) the goods and services provided to households by employers in the form of payment in kind and transfer in kind; (b) goods and services produced and consumed by the households themselves, in which the services refer only to the owner-occupied housing; (c) financial intermediate services provided by financial institutions; (d) insurance services provided by insurance companies.

Government Consumption Expenditure refers to the consumption expenditure spent for the provision of public services provided by the government to the whole country and the net expenditure on the goods and services provided by the government to households free of charge or at reduced prices. The former equals to the output value of the government services minus the value of operating income obtained by the government departments. The latter equals to the market value of the goods and services provided by the government free of charge or at reduced prices to the households minus the value received by the government from the households.

Gross Capital Formation refers to the fixed assets acquired less disposals and the net value of inventory, thus including gross fixed capital formation and changes in inventories.

Gross Fixed Capital Formation refers to the value of acquisitions less those disposals of fixed assets during a given period. Fixed assets are the assets produced through production activities with unit value above a specified amount and which could be used for over one year. Natural assets, consumer durables, small instruments are not included. Gross Fixed Capital Formation includes the value of housing, other buildings and structure, equipment and machinery, breeding biological resources, intellectual property right product (expenditure for R&D, the prospecting of minerals and the acquisition of computer software) minus the disposal of them.

Changes in Inventories refers to the market value of the change in the physical volume of inventory of resident units during a given period, i.e. the difference between the values at the beginning and at the end of the period minus the gains due to the change in prices. The changes in inventories can have a positive or a negative value. A positive value indicates an increase in inventory while a negative value indicates a decrease in inventory. The inventory includes raw materials, fuels and reserve materials purchased by the production units as well as the inventory of finished products, semi-finished products and work-in-progress.

Net Export of Goods and Services refers to the exports of goods and services subtracting the imports of goods and services. Exports include the value of various goods and services sold or gratuitously transferred by resident units to non-resident units. Imports include the value of various goods and services purchased or gratuitously acquired resident units from non-resident units. Because the provision of services and the use of them happen simultaneously, the acquisition of services by resident units from abroad is usually treated as import while the acquisition of services by non-resident units in this country is usually treated as export. The exports and imports of goods are calculated at FOB.

Laborers Remuneration refers to the total payment of various forms to labourers for the productive activities they are engaged in. It includes wages, bonuses and allowances, which the labourers earn in cash and in kind. It also includes the free medical services provided to the labourers and the medicine expenses, transport subsidies and social insurance, and housing fund paid by the employers.

Net Taxes on Production refers to taxes on production less subsidies on production. The taxes on production refers to the various taxes, extra charges and fees levied on the production units on their production, sale and business activities as well as on the use of some factors of production, such as fixed assets, land etc. in the production activities they are engaged in. Taxes on production are divided into product tax and other kinds of taxes on production, product tax mainly includes: value-added tax, consumption tax, import duty, export duty; other taxes on production mainly include: House Property Tax, Tax on Vehicles and Boat Operation, Urban Land Use Tax, etc. In contrast to taxes on production, subsidies on production refer to the payment by the government for free to the production units to influence production activities of production units such as production, sales and pricing, which include agricultural production subsidies, subsidies for policy losses, import subsidies, etc. Subsidies on production are therefore regarded as negative taxes on production.

Depreciation of Fixed Assets refers to the decline of the value of fixed assets due to natural deterioration, normal elimination or loss, it reflects the value of transfer of the fixed assets in the production of the current period. In principle, the depreciation of fixed assets should be calculated on the basis of the re-purchased value of the fixed assets.

Operating Surplus refers to the balance of the value added created by the resident units after deducting the labourers remuneration, net taxes on production and the depreciation of fixed assets.

Institutional Units refer to economic subjects that can be in a position to own assets and incur liabilities in one's own name; to engage independently in economic activities; and to conduct transactions with other subjects.

Institutional Sectors refer to groups of institutional units that are homogenous in nature and have been grouped together. The following 4 institutional sectors are identified in the flow of funds accounts: non-financial corporations, financial institutions, general government and households. and also treated as an institutional sector is the rest of the world, which is composed of non-resident units that have economic relations with resident units.

Non-Financial Corporations and the Sector of Non-Financial Corporations refer to resident corporations that are engaged in the production of goods and the provision of non financial services in the market, mainly covering corporate enterprises of various types engaged in the above-mentioned activities. All non-financial corporations make up the sector of non-financial corporations.

Financial Institutions and the Sector of Financial Institutions refer to resident institutions that are engaged in the financial intermediary services or auxiliary financial activities that are closely related with financial intermediary services, mainly covering the Central Bank, commercial banks, policy banks, non-banking credit institutions and insurance companies. All financial institutions together make up the sector of financial institutions.

Government and the Sector of Governments Government refer to legal entities and their auxiliary units that are established through the political process and are empowered with legislative, administrative or judicial rights over other institutional within specific regions. The main function of government is to acquire funds through taxation or other means in order to provide goods and services to society and households; and to conduct redistribution of income and properties of society through transfer payment; and engaged in non-market production. Government cover mainly: Party and government organizations at all levels, mass organizations, institutional units, grass roots self-governing organizations, etc. All governments together make up the sector of governments.

Households and the Sector of Households refer to resident individuals or groups of resident individuals who share common living facilities, pool together entire or part of their income and properties for their common disposal, and share their housing, food and other consumer goods and services. All households together make up the sector of households.

Non-resident Units and the Rest of the World Non-resident units refer to units that are of a non-resident nature. All non-resident units that have transactions with resident units together make up the rest of the world.

Total Income from Primary Distribution Primary distribution of income refers to the distribution of the value created from production activities among the owners of factors of production and the governments. The final result from production activities is the value-added. Factors of production mainly include labour force, capital, natural resources. Owners of labour force gain remuneration by providing labour. Owners of capitals get income of various forms by providing capital: owners of loan capital receive income from interests. Share holders receive dividends or participation in profit distribution. Owners of natural resources obtains rents for assign the use right of natural resources. Government levies production tax on production activities or factors of production for state administration needs and pay production subsidies for supporting related production activities. Results of primary distribution generate the total income from primary distribution of each sector, and the sum of the total income of primary distribution of all sectors make up the Gross National Income, or the Gross National Product. Owners of land receive rents from leasing of land.

Current Transfers to the transaction in the form of provision of goods, services or assets by an institutional unit to another institutional unit without receiving any goods, services or assets in return from the recipient. Current transfers that don't involve obtaining or disposing property (except inventory and cash) of one side or both sides. They include regular tax such as income tax and property tax, payment to social securities, social security benefits, social allowances and other current transfers.

Total Disposable Income Total income from primary distribution is re-distributed through current transfer, resulting in the total disposable income of various institutional sectors. The sum of total disposable income of all institutional sectors makes up the total national disposable income.

Total Savings refer to total disposable income subtracting final consumption. Total savings of all sectors make up the total national savings.

Capital Transfer refers to the transfer that don't involve obtaining or disposing property (except inventory and cash) of one side or both sides. Capital transfer includes: capital tax, investment subsidy and other capital transfer.

Net Financial Investment reflects the surplus or shortage of capitals of institutional sectors or of the economy in general in the process of non-finanical investment. It refers to total savings plus the income from capital transfer minus payment for capital transfer and minus non-financial investment from the point of view of non-financial transaction. In terms of monetary transaction, it is the difference between the increase in financial assets minus the increase of the financial liabilities.

Currency refers to currency that is in circulation in the market, including paper money and coin.

Deposits refer to deposits in depository financial institutions in various forms, which mainly include demand deposit, time deposit, fiscal deposit, foreign exchange deposit and other deposit, etc.

Loans refer to various types of loans granted by financial institutions, which mainly include short-term loan and bill finacing, medium- and long-term loan, foreign exchange loan, entrusted loans and other loans.

Securities Include Shares and bond. refer to written certificates representing creditors' rights as purchased by bond holders or as acquired by selling products, which can be transacted at the financial markets. They include government bonds, financial bonds, corporation bonds, commercial drafts, preferential stocks that provide fixed income without the right to share the residual value of corporations, and so on. the rights of stockholders and direct investors on the net assets of corporations they have invested in. Shares refer to negotiable securities on creditor's rights, issued by share companies certifying the investment by stockholders and their rights and duties in accordance with the amount of stocks that they hold. Other holding rights refer to the direct investment by institutional units in other units with currency capital or with assets, in forms other than shares and negotiable securities on creditor's rights, including such tangible assets such as land, buildings, machines and equipment, inventory, resources, etc., and such intangible assets as trade marks, patents, monopolies, rights on land use, licenses, commercial reputation, etc.. Documents of proof of holding rights usually include certificates on creditor's right, certificates on investment or on participation, etc.

Insurance Reserve Funds consists of net equity of social insurance and commercial insurance, prepayments of insurance premiums, and reserves for outstanding claims, and bond repurchase.

Settlement Fund refers to fund in float of financial institutions for settlement.

Inter- financial Institutions Accounts refer to flow of capital between financial institutions, consisting of nostro & vostro accounts, inter-bank lending.

Required and Excessive Reserves refer to financial institutions' deposits with the People's Bank of China.

Central Bank Lending refer to lending to financial institutions by the People's Bank of China

Current Account includes goods, services, income and current transfers.

Import and Export of Goods refer to imported or exported goods through Chinese customs. Both import and export of goods are valued at free on board (f.o.b.) prices. Free on board prices can be regarded as the purchaser's prices paid by importers when claiming goods at the border of the exporters. When the importer claim the imported goods, the goods have been loaded in importer's carriers or other carriers, and the exporter has paid export duty or received export redeem.

Import and Export of Services refer to services provided between resident and non-resident units, including services on transportation, tourism, communications, construction, insurance, finance, computer and information, consultancy, advertising and publicity, as well as film, audio and video services, royalty for patents, trademarks and other special rights, other commercial services, and government services.

Income refers income from provision of factors of production between resident and non-resident units, including compensation of labour and earnings from investment. Earnings from investment include earnings from and expenses on direct investment, security investment and other investment, as well as reinvestment of earnings from direct investment.

Capital Account includes capital transfers such as immigration transfer, reduction or exemption of debts, etc.

Financial Account includes direct investment, security investment and other investments.

Direct Investment is an investment aimed at investors seeking effective voice for enterprises operating outside their own country. It includes two parts: direct investment assets and direct investment liabilities. Related investment instruments can be divided into equity and related enterprise debt. Equity includes equity and investment fund shares, as well as reinvestment returns. The liabilities of affiliated enterprises include negotiable and non-negotiable creditor's rights and liabilities among affiliated enterprises.

Security Investment includes securities investment assets and securities investment liabilities, and related investment instruments can be divided into equity and bonds. Equity rights include share rights and investment fund shares. Shares recorded under securities investment and investment fund shares should be negotiable (tradable). Equity rights are usually evidenced by shares, stocks, shares, depository receipts or similar documents. Investment fund share refers to the share of collective investment products such as mutual funds held by investors. A bond is a negotiable debt instrument, which is a certificate proving that its holder (creditor) has the right to recover principal or interest from its issuer (debtor) at some point in the future, including negotiable deposits, commercial instruments, corporate bonds, asset-backed securities, money market instruments, and a similar tool for usually trading on the financial market.

Other Investment refer to other financial transactions between residents and non-residents except direct investment, securities investment, financial derivatives and reserve assets. They include other equity, currency and deposits, loans, insurance and pensions, trade credit and others.

Reserve Assets, Net Increase refers to the difference between the end of the reference year and the end of the previous year, in gold reserve, foreign exchange reserve, special drawing rights in the International Monetary Fund, and the use of the Fund's credits. An increase in reserve assets is expressed in a negative figure and a decrease in the reserve assets is expressed in a positive figure.

人口

Population

3

• 资料整理：谷永翔

简要说明

一、主要内容

本篇包括历年人口及自然变动资料，城镇化资料、人口结构主要分类资料，历次人口普查主要指标。

二、资料来源

1971—1981年、1983—1989年、2000年和2010年总人口数是根据1982年、1990年、2000年和2010年人口普查数据调整推算的；1990—1999、2001—2009年数据是人口变动抽样调查调整数；市镇、乡村人口1953、1964、1982、1990、1995、2000、2005、2010年数据是根据当年人口普查（或抽样调查）数据调整推算的，普查年度之间年份是根据两次普查间平均每年增幅调整的；2004年后非普查年份是根据当年人口抽样调查推算的。由河南省统计局人口和就业统计处编辑整理。

三、统计调查方法

在逢“0”的年份进行全国人口普查；在逢“5”的年份进行全国1%人口抽样调查；其余年份进行全国人口变动情况抽样调查。人口抽样调查是以全国为总体，各省为次总体，采用分层、多阶段、整群概率比例抽样方法抽取样本。

Brief Introduction

I. Main Contents

This chapter include the size of Henan population and natural change, urban proportion, classification of the population structure, data of All previous National Population Census, marriage registration.

II. Sources of Data

Figures for 1971-1981, 1983-1989, 2000,2010 have been adjusted on the basis of the 1982, 1990, 2000,2010 National Population Census. Figures for 1990-1999, 2001-2009 are estimated from the National Sample Survey on Population Changes. Figures of Urban and rural population in 1953,1964,1982,1990,1995,2000,2005,2010 are adjusted on the basis of the current year National Population Census or National Sample Survey, Figures for the years between National Population Census are adjusted on the basis of the growth rate of two National Population Census. Data of years without Population Census since 2014 were calculated on the basis of the Spot Check of population in the current year. Tables in this part are compiled by the Department of Population and Employment Statistics of the Henan provincial Bureau of Statistics.

III. Sampling Methodology

The national population census is conducted in the year ending with 0; the national 1 percent population sample survey is conducted in the year ending with 5; sample surveys on population changes are conducted in the rest of the years. The sample survey on population change takes the whole nation as the population and each province, autonomous region or municipality as sub-populations, and the stratified multi-stage systematic PPS cluster sampling scheme is used.

3-1 总 人 口(年底数)

Total Population (Year-end)

单位：万人 (10 000 persons)

年份 Year	总人口数 Total Population	按性别分 By Sex 男 Male	女 Female	性别比 (女=100) Sex Ratio (Female=100)	按城乡分 By Residence 城镇 Urban	乡村 Rural	城镇化率 (%) Urbanization Proportion (%)	人口密度 (人/平方公里) Population Density (person/sq.km)	常住人口 Resident Population
1978	7067	3599	3468	103.8	963	6104	13.6	423	
1979	7189	3662	3527	103.8	994	6195	13.8	431	
1980	7285	3710	3575	103.8	1021	6264	14.0	436	
1981	7397	3768	3629	103.8	1050	6347	14.2	443	
1982	7519	3835	3684	104.1	1084	6435	14.4	450	
1983	7632	3902	3730	104.6	1111	6521	14.6	457	
1984	7737	3960	3777	104.9	1137	6600	14.7	463	
1985	7847	4022	3825	105.2	1164	6683	14.8	470	
1986	7985	4097	3888	105.4	1196	6789	15.0	478	
1987	8148	4184	3964	105.5	1232	6916	15.1	488	
1988	8317	4272	4045	105.6	1269	7048	15.3	498	
1989	8491	4366	4125	105.9	1308	7183	15.4	508	
1990	8649	4440	4209	105.5	1342	7307	15.5	518	
1991	8763	4501	4262	105.6	1389	7374	15.9	525	
1992	8861	4554	4307	105.7	1434	7427	16.2	531	
1993	8946	4602	4344	105.9	1477	7469	16.5	536	
1994	9027	4643	4384	105.9	1520	7507	16.8	541	
1995	9100	4651	4449	104.5	1564	7536	17.2	545	
1996	9172	4715	4457	105.8	1687	7485	18.4	549	
1997	9243	4751	4492	105.8	1811	7432	19.6	553	
1998	9315	4787	4528	105.7	1937	7378	20.79	558	
1999	9387	4825	4562	105.8	2064	7323	21.99	562	
2000	9488	4895	4593	106.6	2201	7287	23.20	568	
2001	9555	4915	4640	105.9	2334	7221	24.43	572	
2002	9613	4946	4667	105.9	2480	7133	25.80	576	
2003	9667	4980	4687	106.3	2630	7037	27.20	579	
2004	9717	5000	4717	106.0	2809	6908	28.90	582	
2005	9768	5045	4723	106.8	2994	6774	30.65	585	9380
2006	9820	5074	4746	106.9	3189	6631	32.50	588	9392
2007	9869	5100	4769	106.9	3389	6480	34.34	591	9360
2008	9918	5125	4793	106.9	3573	6345	36.03	594	9429
2009	9967	5150	4817	106.9	3758	6209	37.70	597	9487
2010	10437	5407	5030	107.5	4052	6385	38.82	625	9405
2011	10489	5417	5072	106.8	4255	6234	40.57	628	9388
2012	10543	5456	5087	107.2	4473	6070	42.43	631	9406
2013	10601	5487	5114	107.3	4643	5958	43.80	635	9413
2014	10662	5523	5139	107.5	4819	5843	45.20	638	9436
2015	10722	5552	5170	107.4	5023	5699	46.85	642	9480
2016	10788	5576	5212	107.0	5232	5556	48.50	646	9532
2017	10853	5607	5246	106.9	5444	5409	50.16	650	9559
2018	10906	5633	5273	106.8	5639	5267	51.71	653	9605
2019	10952	5654	5298	106.7	5828	5124	53.21	655	9640

注：1. 1982、1990、2000、2010年以来总人口数为当年人口普查推算数；其余年份数据为年度人口抽样调查推算数据。(下同)

2. 2010年以来总人口数据为以2010年人口普查登记的户籍人口为基础，结合年度人口抽样调查的推算数据。(下同)

a) Data of the total population on 1982, 1990,2000, 2010 are calculated on the basis of National Population Census, and data on other year are calculated on the basis of population sample survey (the same as following tables).

b) Data of the total population since 2010 are calculated on the basis of the Registered population of the 2010 National Population Census and the estimates of the population sampling survey each year (the same as following tables).

3-2 人口自然变动情况
Natural Changes of Population

单位：万人 (10 000 persons)

年 份 Year	年平均人口数 Annual Average Population	出生人口数 Number of Birth	出生率(‰) Birth Rate (‰)	死亡人口数 Number of Death	死亡率(‰) Death Rate (‰)	自然增加人口数 Number of Natural Growth	自然增长率(‰) Natural Growth Rate (‰)
1978	7012	154	21.92	44	6.30	110	15.62
1979	7128	153	21.51	45	6.35	108	15.16
1980	7237	145	20.00	46	6.32	99	13.68
1981	7341	151	20.64	48	6.57	103	14.07
1982	7458	153	20.62	46	6.21	107	14.41
1983	7576	154	20.38	48	6.30	106	14.08
1984	7685	145	18.89	48	6.26	97	12.63
1985	7792	157	20.09	48	6.13	109	13.96
1986	7916	187	23.65	51	6.44	136	17.21
1987	8067	212	26.22	51	6.32	161	19.90
1988	8233	214	25.95	48	5.83	166	20.12
1989	8404	223	26.51	48	5.76	175	20.75
1990	8570	214	24.92	56	6.52	158	18.40
1991	8706	172	19.78	58	6.63	114	13.15
1992	8812	159	18.13	61	6.99	98	11.14
1993	8904	141	15.87	56	6.35	85	9.52
1994	8987	138	15.36	57	6.34	81	9.02
1995	9064	130	14.41	57	6.28	73	8.13
1996	9136	130	14.28	58	6.44	72	7.84
1997	9208	129	13.97	58	6.30	71	7.67
1998	9279	131	14.17	59	6.37	72	7.80
1999	9351	132	14.07	60	6.35	72	7.72
2000	9438	123	13.07	56	5.93	67	7.14
2001	9522	126	13.20	59	6.26	67	6.94
2002	9584	119	12.41	61	6.38	58	6.03
2003	9640	116	12.10	62	6.46	54	5.64
2004	9692	113	11.67	63	6.47	50	5.20
2005	9743	112	11.55	61	6.30	51	5.25
2006	9794	113	11.59	61	6.27	52	5.32
2007	9845	111	11.30	62	6.30	49	4.90
2008	9893	113	11.42	64	6.45	49	4.97
2009	9943	113	11.45	64	6.46	49	4.99
2010	10202	117	11.52	67	6.57	50	4.95
2011	10463	121	11.56	69	6.62	52	4.94
2012	10516	125	11.87	71	6.71	54	5.16
2013	10572	130	12.27	72	6.76	58	5.51
2014	10631	136	12.80	75	7.02	61	5.78
2015	10692	136	12.70	75	7.05	60	5.65
2016	10755	143	13.26	77	7.11	66	6.15
2017	10820	140	12.95	75	6.97	65	5.98
2018	10880	127	11.72	74	6.80	53	4.92
2019	10929	120	11.02	75	6.84	46	4.18

3-3 各市常住人口数
Resident Population by City

单位：万人 (10 000 persons)

市(县) City(County)	2005	2006	2007	2008	2009	2010	2011	2012	2013	2014	2015	2016	2017	2018	2019
全 省 Total	**9380**	**9392**	**9360**	**9429**	**9487**	**9405**	**9388**	**9406**	**9413**	**9436**	**9480**	**9532**	**9559**	**9605**	**9640**
省 辖 市 City															
郑 州 市 Zhengzhou	716	724	736	744	752	866	886	903	919	938	957	972	988	1014	1035
开 封 市 Kaifeng	471	469	468	469	471	468	466	465	465	455	454	455	455	456	457
洛 阳 市 Luoyang	635	636	634	642	642	655	657	659	662	668	674	680	682	689	692
平顶山市 Pingdingshan	484	484	484	487	490	491	492	493	496	496	496	498	500	503	503
安 阳 市 Anyang	521	522	519	521	522	517	515	508	509	509	512	513	513	518	519
鹤 壁 市 Hebi	146	144	142	143	144	157	158	159	161	160	161	161	162	163	163
新 乡 市 Xinxiang	557	555	552	551	552	571	566	567	568	571	572	574	577	579	581
焦 作 市 Jiaozuo	340	340	339	341	342	354	353	352	351	352	353	355	356	359	360
濮 阳 市 Puyang	355	353	349	350	352	360	356	360	358	360	361	363	364	361	361
许 昌 市 Xuchang	425	428	429	431	431	431	430	430	430	432	434	438	441	444	446
漯 河 市 Luohe	249	250	247	248	250	255	255	256	258	260	263	264	265	267	267
三门峡市 Sanmenxia	228	226	221	222	223	223	224	223	224	225	225	226	227	227	228
南 阳 市 Nanyang	996	997	995	1004	1013	1027	1013	1015	1009	999	1002	1007	1005	1001	1003
商 丘 市 Shangqiu	761	765	764	777	781	735	736	732	728	726	727	728	730	733	733
信 阳 市 Xinyang	663	663	663	669	679	610	611	640	638	641	640	644	645	647	646
周 口 市 Zhoukou	994	994	990	996	1004	894	895	881	878	880	881	882	876	868	866
驻马店市 Zhumadian	777	777	764	768	770	723	709	694	690	693	696	699	700	704	705
济 源 市 Jiyuan	66	67	68	68	68	68	68	70	72	72	73	73	73	73	73
省直管县 County Directly Administrated by Province															
巩 义 市 Gongyi	80	80	81	81	81	81	81	81	82	82	82	83	83	84	84
兰 考 县 Lankao	73	73	75	75	76	68	67	67	66	63	63	64	64	65	65
汝 州 市 Ruzhou	93	93	93	93	93	93	93	93	93	93	93	94	95	97	97
滑 县 Huaxian	115	114	113	114	114	126	120	114	111	111	111	110	107	107	108
长 垣 市 Changyuan	80	80	79	79	78	81	80	75	74	76	75	76	77	78	79
邓 州 市 Dengzhou	132	133	131	133	137	147	145	145	143	141	143	143	141	135	137
永 城 市 Yongcheng	127	126	122	127	127	124	123	123	123	121	123	123	123	124	124
固 始 县 Gushi	124	128	128	129	131	102	102	106	107	107	108	109	109	110	110
鹿 邑 县 Luyi	107	107	106	107	108	91	90	89	89	89	89	89	87	88	88
新 蔡 县 Xincai	94	95	92	93	93	85	84	83	83	84	84	84	85	85	85

3-4 各市城镇常住人口数
Urban Resident Population by City

单位：万人 (10 000 persons)

市(县)	City(County)	2005	2006	2007	2008	2009	2010	2011	2012	2013	2014	2015	2016	2017	2018	2019
全省	**Total**	**2875**	**3050**	**3214**	**3397**	**3577**	**3651**	**3809**	**3991**	**4123**	**4265**	**4441**	**4623**	**4795**	**4967**	**5129**
省辖市	**City**															
郑州市	Zhengzhou	424	436	451	463	477	551	574	599	617	641	667	691	714	744	772
开封市	Kaifeng	154	160	168	177	187	168	176	185	191	194	201	209	216	223	230
洛阳市	Luoyang	242	252	261	273	284	291	303	316	327	340	355	370	382	397	409
平顶山市	Pingdingshan	169	179	187	196	205	203	212	222	230	237	244	253	262	271	279
安阳市	Anyang	169	179	185	195	203	200	209	216	223	230	240	249	257	268	276
鹤壁市	Hebi	62	64	65	68	71	75	79	82	85	86	89	92	95	98	100
新乡市	Xinxiang	187	197	206	216	226	235	243	253	261	272	280	290	300	309	319
焦作市	Jiaozuo	136	142	148	154	161	167	172	179	183	188	194	200	206	213	219
濮阳市	Puyang	102	107	112	118	125	113	119	127	132	139	146	152	159	163	169
许昌市	Xuchang	136	145	153	162	169	169	176	184	190	197	207	216	225	234	242
漯河市	Luohe	79	83	88	93	98	100	104	110	114	119	125	130	135	140	144
三门峡市	Sanmenxia	89	92	94	97	101	99	103	106	110	113	116	120	124	128	131
南阳市	Nanyang	299	315	331	351	371	339	353	374	386	395	414	433	449	463	479
商丘市	Shangqiu	199	215	230	245	261	219	232	245	255	265	278	291	304	317	329
信阳市	Xinyang	182	195	207	218	232	210	221	244	253	263	274	286	297	308	317
周口市	Zhoukou	189	208	258	275	296	266	282	295	306	319	333	348	361	372	384
驻马店市	Zhumadian	145	160	198	213	227	215	223	232	241	252	265	278	291	303	314
济源市	Jiyuan	26	28	30	32	34	33	35	38	39	41	42	44	45	46	47
省直管县	**County Directly Administrated by Province**															
巩义市	Gongyi	29	32	33	34	36	37	38	39	40	41	43	45	47	49	50
兰考县	Lankao	14	16	19	20	21	18	19	20	21	21	22	24	25	27	28
汝州市	Ruzhou	21	26	28	30	31	30	32	34	35	37	38	41	43	46	48
滑县	Huaxian	17	22	25	27	29	23	24	25	26	28	30	32	33	35	38
长垣市	Changyuan	17	19	20	21	23	26	27	27	28	30	31	33	35	37	39
邓州市	Dengzhou	34	38	40	43	47	42	44	46	48	49	52	55	57	57	60
永城市	Yongcheng	36	37	39	43	46	42	44	46	48	49	53	55	58	60	63
固始县	Gushi	30	34	37	38	39	29	31	34	36	38	40	43	45	47	49
鹿邑县	Luyi	14	19	28	31	33	26	28	29	30	32	34	35	36	38	40
新蔡县	Xincai	17	19	22	24	26	19	20	21	22	24	25	27	29	30	32

3-5 各市户数、人口数(2019年底)

Number of Households and Population by City (End of 2019)

分市数据是根据全省2019年人口抽样调查数据及公安年报数据推算。
Data by city were estimated on the basis of the 2019 National Sample Survey of Population and annual reports of the Bureau of Public Security.

市(县) City(County)	总户数(万户) Total Number of Households (10 000 households)	总人口数(万人) Total Population (10 000 persons)	常住人口(万人) Resident Population (10 000 persons)	男 Male	女 Female	城镇 Urban	乡村 Rural	年平均人口数(万人) Average Population (10 000 persons)	城镇化率(%) Urban Proportion (%)	年平均常住人口(万人) Average Resident Population (10 000 persons)
全　省 Total	**3301**	**10952**	**9640**	**4885**	**4755**	5129	4511	**10929**	**53.21**	**9622**
省辖市 City										
郑州市 Zhengzhou	235	795	1035	512	523	772	263	791	74.58	1024
开封市 Kaifeng	167	528	457	224	234	230	227	527	50.28	457
洛阳市 Luoyang	217	717	692	353	340	409	283	715	59.10	691
平顶山市 Pingdingshan	161	555	503	248	255	279	224	554	55.50	503
安阳市 Anyang	185	595	519	265	254	276	243	594	53.25	518
鹤壁市 Hebi	49	167	163	79	84	100	63	166	61.31	163
新乡市 Xinxiang	181	620	581	289	293	319	262	619	54.91	580
焦作市 Jiaozuo	102	378	360	179	181	219	141	378	60.94	359
濮阳市 Puyang	120	401	361	184	177	169	192	400	46.80	361
许昌市 Xuchang	157	500	446	221	225	242	205	499	54.13	445
漯河市 Luohe	75	285	267	132	135	144	123	285	53.97	267
三门峡市 Sanmenxia	73	231	228	113	115	131	96	231	57.70	227
南阳市 Nanyang	364	1202	1003	499	504	479	524	1200	47.73	1002
商丘市 Shangqiu	305	930	733	371	363	329	405	928	44.83	733
信阳市 Xinyang	281	888	646	320	326	317	330	886	48.98	647
周口市 Zhoukou	338	1166	866	442	424	384	482	1164	44.36	867
驻马店市 Zhumadian	268	923	705	357	348	314	390	921	44.63	704
济源市 Jiyuan	21	72	73	35	38	47	27	72	63.61	73
省直管县 County Directly Administrated by Province										
巩义市 Gongyi	21	86	84	41	43	50	34	85	59.81	84
兰考县 Lankao	29	87	65	33	32	28	37	87	43.59	65
汝州市 Ruzhou	31	110	97	49	48	48	49	110	49.16	97
滑县 Huaxian	47	140	108	57	51	38	70	139	35.03	107
长垣市 Changyuan	26	88	79	39	40	39	40	88	49.81	78
邓州市 Dengzhou	50	180	137	67	69	60	77	180	43.99	136
永城市 Yongcheng	47	158	124	63	61	63	61	158	50.50	124
固始县 Gushi	56	179	110	53	57	49	61	179	44.85	110
鹿邑县 Luyi	40	124	88	46	42	40	48	124	45.59	88
新蔡县 Xincai	33	115	85	43	42	32	53	115	37.71	85

3-6　各市人口出生率、死亡率、自然增长率(2019年底)
Birth Rate, Death Rate, and Natural Growth Rate by City (End of 2019)

市(县) City(County)	出生人口(万人) Birth (10 000 person)	出生率(‰) Birth Rate (‰)	死亡人口(万人) Death (10 000 person)	死亡率(‰) Death Rate (‰)	自然增长人口(万人) Natural Growth (10 000 person)	自然增长率(‰) Natural Growth Rate (‰)
全　　省 Total	**120.44**	**11.02**	**74.76**	**6.84**	**45.68**	**4.18**
省辖市 City						
郑州市 Zhengzhou	11.40	11.22	5.78	5.69	5.62	5.53
开封市 Kaifeng	5.70	10.86	3.47	6.53	2.23	4.33
洛阳市 Luoyang	7.98	11.15	4.62	6.46	3.36	4.69
平顶山市 Pingdingshan	6.22	11.23	3.59	6.48	2.63	4.75
安阳市 Anyang	6.35	10.70	3.83	6.46	2.52	4.24
鹤壁市 Hebi	1.79	10.80	1.05	6.31	0.74	4.49
新乡市 Xinxiang	6.77	10.94	4.30	6.95	2.47	3.99
焦作市 Jiaozuo	4.00	10.57	2.41	6.36	1.59	4.21
濮阳市 Puyang	4.54	11.35	2.81	7.03	1.73	4.32
许昌市 Xuchang	5.70	11.41	3.45	6.92	2.25	4.49
漯河市 Luohe	3.00	10.54	1.80	6.32	1.20	4.22
三门峡市 Sanmenxia	2.24	9.68	1.49	6.44	0.75	3.24
南阳市 Nanyang	12.07	10.06	8.26	6.88	3.81	3.18
商丘市 Shangqiu	10.79	11.62	6.56	7.07	4.23	4.55
信阳市 Xinyang	8.91	10.05	6.15	6.94	2.76	3.11
周口市 Zhoukou	12.67	10.89	8.21	7.06	4.46	3.83
驻马店市 Zhumadian	9.42	10.22	6.49	7.03	2.93	3.19
济源市 Jiyuan	0.89	12.50	0.49	6.85	0.40	5.65
省直管县 County Directly Administrated by Province						
巩义市 Gongyi	0.98	11.48	0.54	6.34	0.44	5.14
兰考县 Lankao	1.09	12.52	0.57	6.56	0.52	5.96
汝州市 Ruzhou	1.25	11.34	0.75	6.84	0.50	4.50
滑县 Huaxian	1.58	11.35	0.95	6.81	0.63	4.54
长垣市 Changyuan	0.93	10.57	0.58	6.62	0.35	3.95
邓州市 Dengzhou	1.98	11.02	1.27	7.08	0.71	3.94
永城市 Yongcheng	1.54	9.75	1.03	6.55	0.51	3.20
固始县 Gushi	1.53	12.98	1.05	7.03	0.48	5.95
鹿邑县 Luyi	1.55	12.50	0.89	7.20	0.66	5.30
新蔡县 Xincai	1.19	10.38	0.81	7.01	0.38	3.37

3-7 河南省人口预期寿命

Life Expectancy of Henan

单位：岁 (age)

年龄 Age	1990			2000			2010		
	合计 Total	男 Male	女 Female	合计 Total	男 Male	女 Female	合计 Total	男 Male	女 Female
	70.0	**68.1**	**72.0**	**72.8**	**71.0**	**74.7**	**74.6**	**71.8**	**77.6**
1	70.5	68.4	72.8	73.5	71.2	75.9	74.3	71.6	77.4
5	67.1	64.9	69.4	69.7	67.4	72.2	70.5	67.7	73.5
10	62.3	60.1	64.6	64.9	62.6	67.3	65.5	62.8	68.6
15	57.4	55.3	59.7	60.0	57.7	62.4	60.6	57.9	63.6
20	52.7	50.6	54.9	55.2	52.9	57.5	55.7	53.0	58.7
25	48.0	45.9	50.2	50.4	48.2	52.7	50.9	48.3	53.8
30	43.3	41.2	45.5	45.7	43.5	47.9	46.1	43.5	48.9
35	38.6	36.5	40.8	40.9	38.8	43.1	41.3	38.8	44.0
40	33.9	31.9	36.1	36.2	34.2	38.3	36.6	34.2	39.2
45	29.3	27.3	31.4	31.6	29.7	33.6	32.0	29.7	34.4
50	24.9	23.0	26.9	27.1	25.2	29.0	27.5	25.4	29.8
55	20.7	18.9	22.6	22.8	21.0	24.6	23.2	21.3	25.4
60	16.8	15.2	18.4	18.7	17.0	20.3	19.1	17.3	21.1
65	13.4	11.9	14.7	15.0	13.4	16.4	15.4	13.7	17.1
70	10.3	9.1	11.3	11.7	10.3	12.8	12.0	10.6	13.5
75	7.8	6.8	8.5	9.1	7.9	9.9	9.4	8.1	10.6
80	5.5	4.8	6.0	6.9	5.9	7.4	7.2	6.0	8.1
85	3.6	3.2	3.8	5.4	4.6	5.7	5.8	4.8	6.5
90	1.5	1.4	1.6	3.9	3.6	4.0	4.8	3.9	5.3
95	1.3	1.1	1.3	2.8	3.0	2.8			
100	1.1	1.0	1.2	0.5	0.5	0.5			

注：本表数据是根据普查数据计算。

a) Data in this table are calculated on the basis of the National Population Census.

3-8 各市常住人口年龄结构(2019年底)

Age Composition of Population by City (End of 2019)

全省数据是根据2019年人口抽样调查汇总数据推算，分市数据是2019年人口抽样调查数据(下表同)。
Data of total in this table are estimated from the national sample survey of population in 2019. Data by city are from the provincial sample survey of population in 2019 (same as the next table).

市 City	常住人口数(万人) Resident Population (10 000 persons)				比重 (%) Proportion		
		0-14岁 Age 0-14	15-64岁 Age 15-64	65岁及以上 Age 65+	0-14岁 Age 0-14	15-64岁 Age 15-64	65岁及以上 Age 65+
全 省 Total	**9640**	**2050**	**6514**	**1076**	**21.3**	**67.6**	**11.2**
省辖市 City							
郑州市 Zhengzhou	1035	211	705	118	20.4	68.1	11.4
开封市 Kaifeng	457	99	296	62	21.7	64.8	13.5
洛阳市 Luoyang	692	146	454	93	21.0	65.6	13.4
平顶山市 Pingdingshan	503	119	319	64	23.7	63.5	12.8
安阳市 Anyang	519	122	333	64	23.6	64.1	12.3
鹤壁市 Hebi	163	33	111	18	20.5	68.2	11.3
新乡市 Xinxiang	581	133	376	72	22.9	64.7	12.4
焦作市 Jiaozuo	360	63	252	45	17.6	70.0	12.4
濮阳市 Puyang	361	92	225	44	25.4	62.3	12.2
许昌市 Xuchang	446	95	290	61	21.3	65.0	13.7
漯河市 Luohe	267	50	178	39	18.7	66.6	14.6
三门峡市 Sanmenxia	228	37	161	29	16.2	70.9	12.9
南阳市 Nanyang	1003	250	613	140	24.9	61.1	14.0
商丘市 Shangqiu	733	161	474	98	21.9	64.7	13.4
信阳市 Xinyang	646	138	408	100	21.4	63.2	15.4
周口市 Zhoukou	866	204	537	125	23.5	62.1	14.4
驻马店市 Zhumadian	705	163	434	108	23.1	61.7	15.3
济源市 Jiyuan	73	14	49	10	19.2	67.4	13.4
省直管县 County Directly Administrated by Province							
巩义市 Gongyi	84	15	58	12	17.3	68.6	14.0
兰考县 Lankao	65	17	39	9	25.5	60.1	14.4
汝州市 Ruzhou	97	28	59	11	28.4	60.6	11.0
滑县 Huaxian	108	31	62	15	28.9	57.1	14.0
长垣市 Changyuan	79	19	50	11	23.6	62.9	13.5
邓州市 Dengzhou	137	36	83	17	26.2	61.0	12.8
永城市 Yongcheng	124	28	78	19	22.5	62.5	15.0
固始县 Gushi	110	25	66	20	22.6	59.6	17.8
鹿邑县 Luyi	88	21	53	14	23.9	60.1	16.0
新蔡县 Xincai	85	21	50	14	24.6	59.4	16.0

3-9 各市常住人口抚养系数(2019年底)

Dependency Ratio of Population by City (End of 2019)

单位：% (%)

市 City	少儿系数 Ratio of Children	老年系数 Ratio of the aged	老少比 Ratio of the aged to Children	少儿抚养系数 Children Dependency Ratio	老年抚养系数 The Aged Dependency Ratio	总抚养系数 Gross Dependency Ratio
全　省 Total	**21.3**	**11.2**	**52.5**	**31.5**	**16.5**	**48.0**
省辖市 City						
郑州市 Zhengzhou	20.4	11.4	56.0	30.0	16.8	46.8
开封市 Kaifeng	21.7	13.5	62.2	33.6	20.9	54.4
洛阳市 Luoyang	21.0	13.4	63.9	32.1	20.5	52.6
平顶山市 Pingdingshan	23.7	12.8	54.1	37.3	20.2	57.4
安阳市 Anyang	23.6	12.3	52.3	36.7	19.2	56.0
鹤壁市 Hebi	20.5	11.3	54.9	30.1	16.5	46.6
新乡市 Xinxiang	22.9	12.4	54.2	35.4	19.2	54.5
焦作市 Jiaozuo	17.6	12.4	70.7	25.1	17.8	42.9
濮阳市 Puyang	25.4	12.2	48.1	40.8	19.6	60.4
许昌市 Xuchang	21.3	13.7	64.2	32.8	21.0	53.8
漯河市 Luohe	18.7	14.6	78.2	28.1	22.0	50.1
三门峡市 Sanmenxia	16.2	12.9	79.7	22.8	18.2	41.0
南阳市 Nanyang	24.9	14.0	56.3	40.7	22.9	63.6
商丘市 Shangqiu	21.9	13.4	61.2	33.9	20.7	54.6
信阳市 Xinyang	21.4	15.4	72.1	33.9	24.4	58.3
周口市 Zhoukou	23.5	14.4	61.4	37.9	23.3	61.2
驻马店市 Zhumadian	23.1	15.3	66.2	37.4	24.8	62.2
济源市 Jiyuan	19.2	13.4	70.0	28.5	20.0	48.5
省直管县 County Directly Administrated by Province						
巩义市 Gongyi	17.3	14.0	81.0	25.3	20.5	45.7
兰考县 Lankao	25.5	14.4	56.4	42.4	23.9	66.3
汝州市 Ruzhou	28.4	11.0	38.6	46.9	18.1	65.1
滑县 Huaxian	28.9	14.0	48.5	50.5	24.5	75.0
长垣市 Changyuan	23.6	13.5	57.4	37.5	21.5	59.0
邓州市 Dengzhou	26.2	12.8	48.9	42.9	21.0	63.9
永城市 Yongcheng	22.5	15.0	66.8	35.9	24.0	59.9
固始县 Gushi	22.6	17.8	78.6	38.0	29.8	67.8
鹿邑县 Luyi	23.9	16.0	66.9	39.8	26.6	66.4
新蔡县 Xincai	24.6	16.0	65.0	41.5	27.0	68.4

3-10　分年龄、性别的人口结构(2019年)

Population Construction by Age and Sex (2019)

本表数据为2019年人口抽样调查汇总样本数据。抽样比为1.50%。(3-11，3-12表同)
Data in this table are the sumed data obtained from the provincial sample survey of population in 2019.The sampling fraction is 1.50%. (3-11, 3-12 are the same)

年龄	Age	占常住人口比重 (%) Percentage to Resident Population (%)	男 Male	女 Female	性别比 (女=100) Sex Ratio (Female=100)
合 计	**Total**	**100.0**	**50.7**	**49.3**	**102.7**
0-4岁	0-4 Age	6.3	3.4	3.0	114.5
5-9岁	5-9 Age	7.3	4.0	3.3	119.7
10-14岁	10-14 Age	7.6	4.3	3.4	126.6
15-19岁	15-19 Age	6.4	3.6	2.8	129.1
20-24岁	20-24 Age	5.0	2.6	2.3	113.7
25-29岁	25-29 Age	8.1	4.0	4.1	98.2
30-34岁	30-34 Age	7.4	3.6	3.8	94.2
35-39岁	35-39 Age	5.9	2.9	3.0	97.1
40-44岁	40-44 Age	6.1	3.0	3.1	97.8
45-49岁	45-49 Age	8.1	4.0	4.1	98.0
50-54岁	50-54 Age	8.2	4.0	4.3	93.5
55-59岁	55-59 Age	6.6	3.1	3.4	91.1
60-64岁	60-64 Age	5.7	2.8	2.9	97.7
65-69岁	65-69 Age	4.7	2.3	2.4	95.9
70-74岁	70-74 Age	3.0	1.4	1.5	96.6
75-79岁	75-79 Age	1.8	0.8	0.9	88.4
80-84岁	80-84 Age	1.1	0.5	0.6	78.7
85-89岁	85-89 Age	0.5	0.2	0.3	62.3
90-94岁	90-94 Age	0.2	0.1	0.1	49.7
95岁及以上	Above 95 Age	0.0	0.0	0.0	31.6

3-11 6岁及6岁以上分年龄、性别、受教育程度的人口结构(2019年)

Population Age 6 and over by Age, Sex and Educational Attainment (2019)

单位：% (%)

年龄	Age	未上过学 No-Schooling	男 Male	女 Female	小学 Primary Schools	男 Male	女 Female	初中 Junior Secondary Schools	男 Male	女 Female	高中 Senior Secondary Schools	男 Male	女 Female
合 计	**Total**	**5.4**	**3.4**	**7.4**	**26.5**	**25.4**	**27.6**	**42.0**	**43.4**	**40.6**	**17.7**	**19.2**	**16.1**
6-9岁	6-9 Age	10.6	10.6	10.7	89.4	89.4	89.3						
10-14岁	10-14 Age	0.5	0.5	0.5	52.5	52.4	52.7	45.5	45.8	45.2	1.4	1.3	1.5
15-19岁	15-19 Age	0.2	0.2	0.2	0.6	0.7	0.6	32.9	34.4	31.1	55.8	55.7	55.9
20-24岁	20-24 Age	0.3	0.3	0.2	1.2	1.3	1.1	32.2	33.1	31.2	31.8	33.2	30.4
25-29岁	25-29 Age	0.3	0.3	0.3	1.8	1.8	1.8	45.0	44.4	45.6	30.3	31.8	28.9
30-34岁	30-34 Age	0.4	0.4	0.5	2.7	2.7	2.8	50.8	49.9	51.7	28.0	29.0	27.0
35-39岁	35-39 Age	0.6	0.6	0.6	4.3	3.8	4.7	54.9	53.5	56.2	24.7	25.9	23.6
40-44岁	40-44 Age	0.9	0.8	1.0	8.3	7.2	9.4	58.9	58.3	59.6	21.3	22.3	20.3
45-49岁	45-49 Age	1.4	0.8	1.9	13.9	11.3	16.3	60.8	61.3	60.3	17.3	18.9	15.8
50-54岁	50-54 Age	2.6	1.3	3.7	23.1	18.7	27.2	57.7	60.3	55.3	12.7	14.9	10.7
55-59岁	55-59 Age	3.8	1.7	5.7	26.9	21.1	32.0	50.8	54.2	47.7	15.1	18.4	12.0
60-64岁	60-64 Age	8.1	4.0	12.0	37.8	32.4	43.0	40.3	46.2	34.7	11.4	14.3	8.6
65岁及以上	Above 65 Age	22.9	13.2	31.4	46.3	46.0	46.5	24.0	31.3	17.6	5.2	7.2	3.5

年龄	Age	大学专科 College Students	男 Male	女 Female	大学本科 Undergraduates	男 Male	女 Female	研究生 Graduates	男 Male	女 Female
合 计	**Total**	**5.3**	**5.4**	**5.1**	**3.0**	**3.0**	**2.9**	**0.2**	**0.2**	**0.2**
6-9岁	6-9 Age									
10-14岁	10-14 Age									
15-19岁	15-19 Age	6.4	5.7	7.2	4.0	3.3	5.0			
20-24岁	20-24 Age	20.0	18.8	21.3	13.8	12.7	15.0	0.7	0.6	0.9
25-29岁	25-29 Age	14.0	13.6	14.4	7.6	7.2	7.9	1.0	0.9	1.0
30-34岁	30-34 Age	11.5	11.4	11.5	5.9	6.0	5.9	0.6	0.6	0.6
35-39岁	35-39 Age	9.3	9.6	9.0	5.6	5.9	5.3	0.7	0.7	0.6
40-44岁	40-44 Age	6.8	7.3	6.3	3.4	3.7	3.2	0.3	0.3	0.2
45-49岁	45-49 Age	4.3	4.9	3.8	2.2	2.6	1.7	0.2	0.2	0.1
50-54岁	50-54 Age	2.5	3.0	2.0	1.3	1.6	1.0	0.1	0.1	0.0
55-59岁	55-59 Age	2.3	2.9	1.8	1.1	1.5	0.7	0.1	0.2	0.1
60-64岁	60-64 Age	1.7	2.1	1.2	0.6	0.8	0.4	0.0	0.1	0.0
65岁及以上	Above 65 Age	1.1	1.6	0.7	0.5	0.7	0.3	0.0	0.0	0.0

注：1. 分年龄段受教育程度为本年龄段受教育程度人口占本年龄段全部人口的比重。
2. 其中项中"男"为各年龄段各种教育程度的男性人数占本年龄段全部男性的比重，"女"为各年龄段各种教育程度的女性人数占本年龄段全部女性的比重。

a) The education level of different age groups is the proportion of the population with education level in the whole population of this age group.
b) Among them, "male" refers to the proportion of males with various educational levels in each age group, and "female" refers to the proportion of females with various educational levels in all females of this age group.

3-12 15岁及以上分年龄、性别、婚姻状况的人口结构(2019年)

Population Aged 15 and over by Age, Sex and Marital Status (2019)

单位：% (%)

年龄	Age	未 婚 Never married	男 Male	女 Female	有配偶 Married	男 Male	女 Female
合 计	**Total**	**17.3**	**20.7**	**14.1**	**74.8**	**73.5**	**76.0**
15-19岁	15-19 Age	98.9	99.1	98.7	1.1	0.9	1.3
20-24岁	20-24 Age	81.0	85.5	75.9	18.7	14.1	23.9
25-29岁	25-29 Age	34.6	40.6	28.9	64.0	57.7	70.0
30-34岁	30-34 Age	11.0	14.0	8.2	86.3	82.8	89.6
35-39岁	35-39 Age	3.7	5.2	2.3	92.9	90.7	95.0
40-44岁	40-44 Age	2.2	3.6	0.8	94.1	92.6	95.6
45-49岁	45-49 Age	1.5	2.7	0.3	94.6	93.6	95.5
50-54岁	50-54 Age	1.1	2.1	0.1	94.1	93.7	94.4
55-59岁	55-59 Age	0.9	1.8	0.1	92.6	93.3	92.0
60-64岁	60-64 Age	1.3	2.6	0.1	88.6	90.1	87.2
65岁及以上	Above 65 Age	1.6	3.4	0.1	70.4	78.3	63.5

年龄	Age	离 婚 Divorced	男 Male	女 Female	丧 偶 Widowed	男 Male	女 Female
合 计	**Total**	**1.5**	**1.8**	**1.3**	**6.4**	**4.0**	**8.6**
15-19岁	15-19 Age	0.0	0.0	0.0	0.0	0.0	0.0
20-24岁	20-24 Age	0.3	0.4	0.2	0.0	0.0	0.0
25-29岁	25-29 Age	1.3	1.7	1.0	0.1	0.1	0.1
30-34岁	30-34 Age	2.4	3.0	1.9	0.2	0.1	0.3
35-39岁	35-39 Age	2.9	3.8	2.1	0.4	0.3	0.6
40-44岁	40-44 Age	2.8	3.3	2.3	0.9	0.6	1.2
45-49岁	45-49 Age	2.3	2.8	1.9	1.6	1.0	2.3
50-54岁	50-54 Age	1.8	2.2	1.4	3.1	2.1	4.0
55-59岁	55-59 Age	1.5	1.7	1.3	5.0	3.2	6.6
60-64岁	60-64 Age	1.0	1.2	0.9	9.0	6.1	11.8
65岁及以上	Above 65 Age	0.8	0.8	0.7	27.2	17.6	35.6

注：1. 分年龄段婚姻状况为本年龄段各婚姻状况人口占本年龄段人口的比重。
2. 其中项中"男"为各年龄段各种婚姻状况的男性人数占本年龄段全部男性的比重，"女"为各年龄段各种婚姻状况的女性人数占本年龄段全部女性的比重。

a) The marriage status of different age groups is the proportion of the population with different marital status in this age group.

b) Among them, "male" refers to the proportion of males with various marital status in each age group, and "female" refers to the proportion of females with various marital status in all females of this age group.

3-13 育龄妇女分年龄、孩次的生育状况(2019年)

Age-specific Fertility Rate of Childbearing Women by Age of Mother and Birth Order (2019)

本表数据为2019年人口抽样调查汇总样本数据。抽样比为1.50%。

Data in this table are the sumed data obtained from the provincial sample survey of population in 2019. The sampling fraction is 1.50%.

年龄	平均育龄妇女人数(人) Average Number of Childbearing Women (person)	出生人数(人) Births (person)	一孩 1st Birth	二孩 2nd Birth	三孩及以上 3rd Birth and Above	生育率(‰) Fertility Rate (‰)	一孩 1st Birth	二孩 2nd Birth	三孩及以上 3rd Birth and Above
总计 Total	**293859**	**10408**	**3993**	**4922**	**1493**	**35.42**	**13.59**	**16.75**	**5.08**
15-19	**34815**	**209**	**173**	**35**	**1**	**6.00**	**4.97**	**1.01**	**0.03**
15	7813	1	1			0.13	0.13		
16	7387	12	10	2		1.63	1.35	0.27	
17	6950	24	20	4		3.45	2.88	0.58	
18	6547	53	46	7		8.10	7.03	1.07	
19	6118	119	96	22	1	19.46	15.69	3.60	0.16
20-24	**28019**	**1891**	**1200**	**637**	**54**	**67.50**	**42.83**	**22.74**	**1.93**
20	5706	239	191	45	3	41.89	33.48	7.89	0.53
21	5587	292	207	78	7	52.27	37.06	13.96	1.25
22	5456	373	246	119	8	68.37	45.09	21.81	1.47
23	5649	479	281	185	13	84.81	49.75	32.76	2.30
24	5622	508	275	210	23	90.37	48.92	37.36	4.09
25-29	**46833**	**4407**	**1817**	**2090**	**500**	**94.10**	**38.79**	**44.63**	**10.68**
25	6150	631	329	261	41	102.61	53.50	42.45	6.67
26	7731	752	346	325	81	97.28	44.76	42.04	10.48
27	8678	878	389	402	87	101.18	44.82	46.33	10.03
28	10771	1047	389	521	137	97.20	36.11	48.37	12.72
29	13503	1099	364	581	154	81.38	26.95	43.02	11.41
30-34	**49519**	**2854**	**649**	**1601**	**604**	**57.63**	**13.10**	**32.33**	**12.20**
30	12071	878	248	484	146	72.73	20.54	40.09	12.10
31	11909	785	191	433	161	65.91	16.04	36.36	13.52
32	10369	560	106	325	129	54.00	10.22	31.34	12.44
33	8099	367	53	223	91	45.31	6.54	27.53	11.24
34	7070	264	51	136	77	37.34	7.21	19.23	10.89
35-39	**38967**	**849**	**129**	**461**	**259**	**21.79**	**3.31**	**11.83**	**6.65**
35	7393	237	39	142	56	32.05	5.27	19.20	7.58
36	7985	231	34	122	75	28.93	4.26	15.28	9.39
37	8132	166	22	85	59	20.41	2.70	10.45	7.26
38	7378	119	21	55	43	16.13	2.85	7.45	5.83
39	8077	96	13	57	26	11.88	1.61	7.06	3.22
40-44	**39469**	**176**	**23**	**87**	**66**	**4.46**	**0.58**	**2.20**	**1.67**
40	7739	56	11	28	17	7.23	1.42	3.62	2.20
41	7468	43	2	21	20	5.76	0.27	2.81	2.68
42	7556	30	5	12	13	3.97	0.66	1.59	1.72
43	7787	29	4	16	9	3.72	0.51	2.05	1.16
44	8917	18	1	10	7	2.02	0.11	1.12	0.79
45-49	**56237**	**22**	**2**	**11**	**9**	**0.39**	**0.04**	**0.20**	**0.16**
45	9869	5		2	3	0.51		0.20	0.30
46	11073	11		7	4	0.99		0.63	0.36
47	10848	2		1	1	0.18		0.09	0.09
48	11746	2	2			0.17	0.17		
49	12702	2		1	1	0.16		0.08	0.08

3-14　六次人口普查主要指标

Main Indicators of National Population Censuses in 1953, 1964, 1982, 1990, 2000, 2010

单位：万人　　(10 000 persons)

项　目	Item	1953	1964	1982	1990	2000	2010
全省总人口	**Total Population**	**4379**	**5033**	**7442**	**8553**	**9256**	**9403**
按性别分的人口	**Population By Sex**						
男　性	Male	2232	2549	3795	4380	4775	4749
女　性	Female	2147	2484	3647	4173	4481	4654
按年龄分的人口	**Population By Age**						
0岁-6岁	Age 0-6	914	920	1027	1269	765	981
7岁-12岁	Age 7-12	511	846	1165	943	1211	760
育龄妇女(15-49岁)	Women at Childbearing Age (Age 15-49)	1017	1109	1781	2279	2496	2623
劳动年龄人口	Working Age Population						
(男16-59　女16-54)	(Male Age 16-59 and Female Age 16-54)	2290	2482	3927	4985	5601	5819
男60岁女55岁以上人口	Males Aged 60 and over and Females Aged 55 and Over	458	449	739	899	1105	1483
按民族分的人口	**Population By Nationality**						
汉　族	Han Nationality	4338	4981	7362	8453	9143	9291
各少数民族	Minority Nationality	41	52	80	101	113	112
按城乡分的人口	**Population By Residence**						
城镇总人口	Urban Population	311	552	1173	1303	2145	3622
乡村总人口	Rural Population	4068	4481	6270	7251	7111	5781
按文化程度分的人口	**Population By Educational Level**						
#大学和相当于大学	University and Equivalent		9	25	73	248	602
高中	Senior Secondary School		44	470	606	928	1242
初中	Junior Secondary School		209	1427	2270	3646	3993
小学	Primary School		1230	2322	2972	3073	2267
文盲和半文盲(12周岁以上)	Illiterate and Semi-literate (Age 12 and Over)		2147	2015	1396	543	399

注：1.第五次人口普查数据为快速汇总数据，其中文盲和半文盲人口是指15岁及以上。
2.第五次人口普查总人口指根据《第五次人口普查办法》规定的常住人口。
3.第六次人口普查数据为常住人口，其中文盲和半文盲人口是指15岁及以上。

a) Data of the fifth Population Census were fast collected results,and illiterate and semi-literate were age 15 and over.
b) Total population of the fifth Population Census refers to population of resident according to "Way of the fifth National Population Census".
c) Data of the sixth Population Census is resident population, and illiterate and semi-literate were age 15 and over.

主要统计指标解释

人口数 指一定时点、一定地区范围内的有生命的个人总和。

年度统计的年末人口数指每年 12 月 31 日 24 时的人口数。

常住人口 指实际经常居住在某地区一定时间（指半年以上）的人口。按人口普查和抽样调查规定，主要包括：1、在本地居住，户口也在本地的人口；2、户口在外地，但在本地居住半年以上者，或离开户口地半年以上而调查时在本地居住的人口；3、调查时居住在本地，但在任何地方都没有登记常住户口，如手持户口迁移证、出生证、退伍证、劳改劳教释放证等尚未办理常住户口的人，即所谓“口袋户口”的人。

出生率（又称粗出生率） 指在一定时期内(通常为一年)一定地区的出生人数与同期内平均人数(或期中人数)之比，用千分率表示。本资料中的出生率指年出生率，其计算公式为：

出生率＝年出生人数／年平均人数×1000‰

式中：出生人数指活产婴儿，即胎儿脱离母体时(不管怀孕月数)，有过呼吸或其他生命现象。年平均人数指年初、年底人口数的平均数，也可用年中人口数代替。

死亡率（又称粗死亡率） 指在一定时期内（通常为一年）一定地区的死亡人数与同期平均人数（或期中人数）之比，一般用千分率表示。计算公式为：

死亡率＝年死亡人数／年平均人数×1000‰

人口自然增长率 指在一定时期内（通常为一年）人口自然增加数（出生人数减死亡人数）与该时期内平均人数（或期中人数）之比，一般用千分率表示。计算公式为：

人口自然增长率＝（本年出生人数－本年死亡人数）／年平均人数×1000‰＝人口出生率－人口死亡率

性别比 总人口中男性人数与女性人数之比。通常用每 100 个女性人口相应有多少男性人口表示。其计算公式为：

性别比＝男性人口数/女性人口数×100%

总抚养系数 指被抚养人口（0-14岁和65岁或60岁以上人口）与15-64岁或15-59岁人口的比例。计算公式为:

总抚养系数＝被抚养人口/15-64岁或15-59岁人口×100

老年抚养系数 指老年人口（65岁或60岁以上人口）与15-64岁或15-59岁人口的比例。计算公式为:

老年抚养系数＝老年人口/15-64岁或15-59岁人口×100

少年抚养系数 指少年儿童与 15-64 岁或 15-59 岁人口的比例。计算公式为:

少年抚养系数＝少年儿童人口/15-64 岁或 15-59 岁人口×100（修改）

Explanatory Notes on Main Statistical Indicators

Total Population refers to the total number of people alive at a certain point of time within a given area.

The annual statistics on total population is taken at midnight, the 3lst of December.

Resident Population refers to the population actual living in a certain area for six months or more. According to the census and sample surveys, it includes the following main items : 1, Population live in this area, with the local resident registered; 2, Population with the resident registered of other area, live this area over half a year or Less than half a year but Leaving the area where they resident registered over half a year; 3, Population live in the local area, but have no resident registered, only have Migration Certificate、Birth certificate、Legionnaires card、Release card from Re-education through labor or haven not yet requisition the resident registered ,so-called "pocket-registered "population.

Birth Rate (or Crude Birth Rate) refers to the ratio of the number of births to the average population (or mid-period population) during a certain period of time (usually a year), expressed in ‰. Birth rate in the chapter refers to annual birth rate. The following formula is used:

Birth Rate=Number of Births/Average Number of Population×1000‰

Number of births refers to live births i.e. the births when babies had showed any vital phenomena regardless of the length of pregnancy.

Annual Average Number of Population is the average of the number of population at the beginning of the year and that at the end of the year. Sometimes it is substituted for with the mid year population.

Death Rate (or Crude Death Rate) refers to the ratio of the number of deaths to the average population (or mid year population) during a certain period of time (usually a year), which is often expressed in‰. The following formula is used:

Death Rate umber of Deaths=Number of Deaths/Annual Average Number of Population×1000‰

Natural Growth Rate of Population refers to the ratio of natural increase in population (number of births minus number of deaths) in a certain period of time (usually a year) to the average population (or mid year population) of the same period, which is often expressed in‰. The following formulas are applied:

Natural Growth of Population= (Number of Births－Number of Deaths) /Average Number of Population×1000‰

Natural Growth Rate of Population=Birth Rate－Death Rate

Sex Ratio Refers to the Proportion of Male to Female Among the Total Population Which is often described as the proportion of 100 females to males. the following formula is used:

Sex Ratio = Number of Males/Number of Females×100％

Total Dependency Ratio refers to the ratio of number of dependents to the total population aged 15-64, the number of dependents being population aged 0-14 and population aged 65 and over. The total dependency ratio is calculated as follows:

Total Dependency Ratio = Number of Dependents/Population Aged 15-64×100%

The Aged Dependency Ratio refers to the ratio of the number of the aged population to the total population aged 15-64, the aged being population aged 65 and over. The aged dependency ratio is calculated as follows:

The Aged Dependency Ratio = Number of the Aged Population/ Population Aged 15-64×100%

The Juvenile and Children Dependency Ratio refers to the ratio of the number of the juvenile and children to the total population aged 15-64, the juvenile and children being population aged 0-14. The juvenile and children dependency ratio is calculated as follows:

The Juvenile and Children Dependency Ratio = Number of Juvenile and Children/ Population Aged 15-64 or 15-59×100%

就业人员与职工工资

Employment and Wages

◉ 资料整理：吴娜

简要说明

一、主要内容

本篇资料反映从业人员就业情况、城镇登记失业情况，平均工资及指数变化情况等。

二、统计范围

《劳动统计报表制度》的调查范围为法人单位（不包括乡镇企业和个体工商户）；私营企业及个体工商业统计范围为城镇。1998年及以后城镇单位就业人员、平均工资等指标中不再包括离开本单位仍保留劳动关系职工及其生活费。

本篇"城镇单位"均指"城镇非私营单位"。

三、资料来源

就业基本情况及分组、工资总额和平均工资等资料，由河南省统计局人口和就业统计处根据《劳动统计报表制度》编辑整理。城镇私营企业及个体工商业就业人员，由河南省市场监督管理局提供。城镇登记失业人数，由河南省人力资源和社会保障厅提供。

四、调查方法

劳动统计报表采用全面调查方法，由各级统计部门逐级上报。培训、就业统计及私营企业和个体工商业统计利用行政登记资料加工整理。

Brief Introduction

I. Main Contents

Data in this chapter include employment situation, the registered urban unemployment situation, average wages and index change situation, etc.

II. Scope of Statistics

Statistics Scope of "Labor statistics system" is investigation units (not including township enterprises and individual); Statistics Scope of private enterprises and individual industrial refers town. Data on employment personnel, total wages, average wage of town unit no-include leaving this unit but still keep working relationship worker and the cost of living since 1998.

"Urban units" in this chapter refer to "Urban Non-private units".

III. Sources of Data

Data on employment, Earnings and wages of staff and workers is used in the labor statistics, are compiled by the Department of population and employment of the Henan provincial Bureau of Statistics. Data on the number of employed persons in private enterprises and self-employed individuals are provided by the Administration for market regulation of Henan province. Data on the number of registered unemployed persons in urban areas are collected provided by the Henan provincial Bureau of Human Resources and Social Security.

IV. Sampling Methodology

Labor statistics using comprehensive investigation method, statistical departments at various levels shall report to higher level. Training, employment statistics, private enterprises, individual industrial and commercial statistics are collected through administrative registration data.

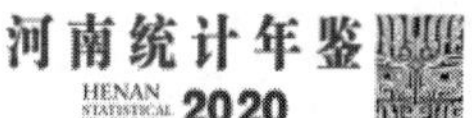

4-1 按城乡分的就业人员数

Number of Employed Persons in Urban and Rural Areas

单位：万人 (10 000 persons)

年份 Year	合计 Total	城镇 Urban Areas	#国有经济 State-owned Units	#集体经济 Collective-owned Units	#有限责任公司 Limited Liability Corporations	#港澳台投资经济 Units with Funds from Hong Kong, Macao and Taiwan	#外商投资经济 Foreign Funded Units	乡村 Rural Areas
1978	2807	423	346	74				2384
1979	2873	444	363	78				2429
1980	2929	469	379	83				2460
1981	3039	508	407	90				2531
1982	3146	516	407	95				2630
1983	3289	542	425	99				2747
1984	3346	574	419	129				2772
1985	3520	627	454	139				2893
1986	3598	649	469	149				2949
1987	3782	686	488	156				3096
1988	3916	704	508	161				3212
1989	3943	717	512	168				3226
1990	4086	727	521	171				3359
1991	4216	774	544	177				3442
1992	4332	811	571	172				3521
1993	4400	865	599	162				3535
1994	4448	890	604	158				3558
1995	4509	931	617	162				3578
1996	4638	981	640	161				3657
1997	4820	1002	603	177				3818
1998	5000	933	485	149				4067
1999	5205	894	475	146	66	9	6	4311
2000	5572	860	464	143	69	10	6	4712
2001	5517	829	448	134	69	8	5	4688
2002	5522	831	417	123	99	8	5	4691
2003	5536	841	399	117	121	8	6	4695
2004	5587	869	409	96	121	8	7	4718
2005	5662	910	405	91	132	7	8	4752
2006	5719	942	402	86	147	8	10	4777
2007	5773	958	397	83	154	10	11	4815
2008	5835	976	391	68	160	10	10	4859
2009	5949	1067	381	49	192	10	11	4882
2010	6042	1127	389	50	192	11	12	4915
2011	6198	1287	400	52	238	28	16	4911
2012	6288	1383	409	51	287	19	17	4905
2013	6387	1535	370	46	435	53	20	4851
2014	6520	1713	368	43	450	55	18	4807
2015	6636	1839	366	39	493	57	19	4798
2016	6726	1924	367	34	520	52	19	4803
2017	6767	1960	362	28	526	52	17	4807
2018	6692	2017	354	21	416	35	13	4675
2019	6562	2145	313	19	378	31	15	4417

4–2 各市分城乡的就业人员数(2019年底)

单位：万人

市(县) City(County)	合计 Total	城镇 Urban Areas	#国有经济 State-owned Units	集体经济 Collective-owned Units	股份合作经济 Cooperative Units	联营经济 Joint Ownership Units
省辖市 City						
郑州市 Zhengzhou	635.01	408.23	44.37	1.46	0.61	0.32
开封市 Kaifeng	322.71	92.60	12.96	1.49	0.07	0.00
洛阳市 Luoyang	421.75	167.67	23.20	1.23	0.05	0.09
平顶山市 Pingdingshan	318.85	100.26	17.85	1.46	0.25	0.07
安阳市 Anyang	356.86	103.20	15.79	0.81	0.00	0.02
鹤壁市 Hebi	97.42	38.26	5.18	0.18	0.06	0.00
新乡市 Xinxiang	350.16	116.96	16.37	1.40	0.23	0.03
焦作市 Jiaozuo	235.23	95.53	11.13	0.51	0.04	0.01
濮阳市 Puyang	242.53	108.55	12.35	0.59	0.14	0.01
许昌市 Xuchang	275.94	91.85	12.44	0.68	0.06	0.12
漯河市 Luohe	176.29	65.35	6.63	0.50	0.14	0.05
三门峡市 Sanmenxia	136.09	52.90	8.17	0.30	0.08	0.00
南阳市 Nanyang	654.11	173.09	30.90	2.40	0.70	0.25
商丘市 Shangqiu	549.60	144.78	22.45	0.92	0.21	0.06
信阳市 Xinyang	479.94	96.19	25.11	1.47	0.20	0.02
周口市 Zhoukou	687.11	137.83	23.38	1.89	0.26	0.16
驻马店市 Zhumadian	576.30	131.59	22.12	1.69	0.13	0.14
济源市 Jiyuan	45.85	20.41	2.44	0.12		0.00
省直管县 County Directly Administrated by Province						
巩义市 Gongyi	51.77	23.31	2.00	0.32	0.10	0.00
兰考县 Lankao	62.31	17.13	1.81	0.07	0.17	0.01
汝州市 Ruzhou	69.56	18.39	2.56	0.21	0.00	0.04
滑县 Huaxian	77.24	14.50	2.51	0.14	0.07	0.01
长垣市 Changyuan	53.25	22.37	1.51	0.10	0.00	0.00
邓州市 Dengzhou	88.04	16.13	3.52	0.11	0.07	0.01
永城市 Yongcheng	93.75	22.05	3.17	0.03	0.05	
固始县 Gushi	101.83	24.70	3.97	0.28		0.00
鹿邑县 Luyi	76.90	8.31	1.82	0.09	0.00	0.00
新蔡县 Xincai	68.91	10.64	1.96	0.03	0.01	0.01

Number of Employed Persons in Urban and Rural Areas by City (End of 2019)

(10 000 persons)

有限责任公司 Limited Liability Corporations	股份有限公司 Share Holding Corporations	港澳台投资经济 Units with Funds from Hong Kong, Macao and Taiwan	外商投资经济 Foreign Funded Units	私营经济 Urban Private	城镇个体 Urban Selfemployed Individuals	乡　村 Rural Areas
87.90	17.46	23.57	3.77	133.78	85.21	226.78
2.77	0.06	0.27	0.15	27.25	27.84	230.11
31.87	7.54	0.89	0.86	43.37	55.98	254.08
15.50	11.37	0.53	1.00	17.93	32.76	218.59
10.35	1.29	0.21	0.21	15.35	38.60	253.66
9.56	1.89	0.14	0.30	11.19	9.39	59.16
20.75	4.10	0.49	0.84	31.56	37.75	233.20
17.51	5.90	0.32	1.36	33.30	23.75	139.70
14.71	3.79	0.25	0.12	15.71	58.87	133.99
20.35	4.90	0.63	0.76	19.14	30.34	184.09
12.61	4.18	1.01	1.06	8.56	29.90	110.94
7.32	4.00	0.14	0.32	10.14	21.80	83.19
24.80	7.60	0.67	0.24	32.82	69.20	481.03
36.52	4.48	0.67	0.74	22.33	54.11	404.82
15.93	4.09	0.05	0.28	22.42	21.11	383.75
24.09	6.42	1.01	2.57	35.03	39.21	549.28
25.36	5.98	0.40	0.51	38.07	34.46	444.71
0.50	0.13		0.00	5.03	6.19	25.44
1.85	0.60	0.01	0.03	8.88	8.88	28.46
3.18	0.17	0.02	0.06	6.44	4.97	45.18
2.43	0.58	0.04	0.00	6.20	5.85	51.17
2.91	0.16	0.12	0.02	1.36	6.78	62.74
5.44	0.50	0.01	0.08	6.72	7.21	30.88
2.03	0.26	0.17		2.77	6.95	71.91
5.57	0.16	0.00	0.05	4.83	8.01	71.70
3.14	0.21		0.11	4.06	12.62	77.12
2.69	0.61	0.02	0.04	0.65	1.83	68.59
2.31	0.35		0.00	2.88	2.77	58.27

4-3 分三次产业的就业人员数

Number of Employed Persons by Three Strata of Industry

年 份 Year	就业人员 (万人) Number of Employed Persons (10 000 persons)	第一产业 Primary Industry	第二产业 Secondary Industry	第三产业 Tretiary Industry	就业人员构成(以就业人员为100) Composition in Percentage (Total=100) 第一产业 Primary Industry	第二产业 Secondary Industry	第三产业 Tretiary Industry
1952	1683	1511	74	98	89.8	4.4	5.8
1957	1829	1577	111	141	86.2	6.1	7.7
1962	2021	1698	82	241	84.0	4.1	11.9
1965	2172	1796	91	285	82.7	4.2	13.1
1970	2481	2037	150	294	82.1	6.0	11.9
1975	2689	2279	230	180	84.8	8.6	6.7
1978	2807	2262	296	249	80.6	10.5	8.9
1979	2873	2366	290	217	82.4	10.1	7.6
1980	2929	2378	304	247	81.2	10.4	8.4
1981	3039	2470	310	259	81.3	10.2	8.5
1982	3146	2530	315	301	80.4	10.0	9.6
1983	3289	2598	341	350	79.0	10.4	10.6
1984	3346	2578	376	392	77.0	11.2	11.7
1985	3520	2571	523	426	73.0	14.9	12.1
1986	3598	2574	568	456	71.5	15.8	12.7
1987	3782	2596	616	570	68.6	16.3	15.1
1988	3916	2648	659	609	67.6	16.8	15.6
1989	3943	2719	659	565	69.0	16.7	14.3
1990	4086	2833	671	582	69.3	16.4	14.2
1991	4216	2921	689	606	69.3	16.3	14.4
1992	4332	2955	724	653	68.2	16.7	15.1
1993	4400	2910	808	682	66.1	18.4	15.5
1994	4448	2865	864	719	64.4	19.4	16.2
1995	4509	2814	929	766	62.4	20.6	17.0
1996	4638	2822	988	828	60.8	21.3	17.9
1997	4820	2909	1011	900	60.4	21.0	18.7
1998	5000	2947	962	1091	58.9	19.2	21.8
1999	5205	3305	913	987	63.5	17.5	19.0
2000	5572	3564	977	1031	64.0	17.5	18.5
2001	5517	3478	997	1042	63.0	18.1	18.9
2002	5522	3398	1038	1086	61.5	18.8	19.7
2003	5536	3332	1084	1120	60.2	19.6	20.2
2004	5587	3246	1142	1200	58.1	20.4	21.5
2005	5662	3139	1251	1272	55.4	22.1	22.5
2006	5719	3050	1351	1318	53.3	23.6	23.0
2007	5773	2920	1487	1366	50.6	25.8	23.7
2008	5835	2847	1564	1424	48.8	26.8	24.4
2009	5949	2765	1675	1509	46.5	28.2	25.4
2010	6042	2712	1753	1577	44.9	29.0	26.1
2011	6198	2670	1853	1675	43.1	29.9	27.0
2012	6288	2628	1919	1740	41.8	30.5	27.7
2013	6387	2563	2035	1789	40.1	31.9	28.0
2014	6520	2652	1996	1873	40.7	30.6	28.7
2015	6636	2587	2042	2007	39.0	30.8	30.2
2016	6726	2583	2056	2088	38.4	30.6	31.0
2017	6767	2494	2104	2168	36.9	31.1	32.0
2018	6692	2366	2048	2278	35.4	30.6	34.0
2019	6562	2277	1919	2365	34.7	29.2	36.0

4-4 各市分三次产业的就业人员数(2019年底)

Number of Employed Persons by Three Strata of Industry and City (End of 2019)

市(县) City(County)	就业人员(万人) Number of Employed Persons (10 000 persons)	第一产业 Primary Industry	第二产业 Secondary Industry	第三产业 Tretiary Industry	就业人员构成(以从业人员为100) Composition in Percentage (Total=100) 第一产业 Primary Industry	第二产业 Secondary Industry	第三产业 Tretiary Industry
省辖市 City							
郑州市 Zhengzhou	635.01	91.07	171.55	372.39	14.3	27.0	58.6
开封市 Kaifeng	322.71	130.51	84.14	108.07	40.4	26.1	33.5
洛阳市 Luoyang	421.75	117.39	123.74	180.62	27.8	29.3	42.8
平顶山市 Pingdingshan	318.85	127.41	84.49	106.95	40.0	26.5	33.5
安阳市 Anyang	356.86	113.88	127.53	115.45	31.9	35.7	32.4
鹤壁市 Hebi	97.42	27.35	32.48	37.59	27.3	32.4	40.2
新乡市 Xinxiang	350.16	111.04	121.62	117.50	31.7	34.7	33.6
焦作市 Jiaozuo	235.23	67.53	88.15	79.55	28.7	37.5	33.8
濮阳市 Puyang	242.53	84.53	62.31	95.70	34.9	25.7	39.5
许昌市 Xuchang	275.94	99.46	84.81	91.66	36.0	30.7	33.2
漯河市 Luohe	176.29	68.39	47.18	60.72	38.8	26.8	34.4
三门峡市 Sanmenxia	136.09	53.98	27.56	54.55	39.7	20.3	40.1
南阳市 Nanyang	654.11	295.53	161.22	197.37	45.2	24.6	30.2
商丘市 Shangqiu	549.60	190.84	157.28	201.48	34.7	28.6	36.7
信阳市 Xinyang	479.94	211.30	116.05	152.58	44.0	24.2	31.8
周口市 Zhoukou	687.11	254.53	238.28	194.30	37.0	34.7	28.3
驻马店市 Zhumadian	576.30	219.09	174.04	183.17	38.0	30.2	31.8
济源市 Jiyuan	45.85	13.60	16.65	15.61	29.7	36.3	34.0
省直管县 County Directly Administrated by Province							
巩义市 Gongyi	51.77	11.75	20.39	19.63	22.7	39.4	37.9
兰考县 Lankao	62.31	22.75	10.99	28.57	36.5	17.6	45.8
汝州市 Ruzhou	69.56	30.20	17.94	21.41	43.4	25.8	30.8
滑县 Huaxian	77.24	30.03	24.32	22.89	38.9	31.5	29.6
长垣市 Changyuan	53.25	8.70	26.15	18.40	16.3	49.1	34.6
邓州市 Dengzhou	88.04	49.09	17.83	21.12	55.8	20.3	24.0
永城市 Yongcheng	93.75	22.45	43.04	28.26	24.0	45.9	30.2
固始县 Gushi	101.83	30.48	31.72	39.63	29.9	31.2	38.9
鹿邑县 Luyi	76.90	19.14	35.11	22.66	24.9	45.7	29.5
新蔡县 Xincai	68.91	18.92	25.84	24.14	27.5	37.5	35.0

4–5 分行业就业人员数

单位：万人

年 份 Year	合 计 Total	农 林 牧渔业 Agriculture Forestry, Animal Husbandry and Fishery	采矿业 Mining	制造业 Manufacturing	电力、燃气及水的生产和供应业 Production and Supply of Electricity,Gas and Water	建筑业 Construction	批发和零售业 Wholesale and Retail Trades	交通运输仓储及邮政业 Transport, Storage, and Post	住宿和餐饮业 Hotels and Catering Services	信息传输、软件和信息技术服务业 Information Transmission, software and Information Technology
2003	5535.67	3331.86	49.44	614.84	23.14	396.13	318.00	166.37	44.47	6.63
2004	5587.44	3245.66	49.27	652.80	22.90	417.15	315.33	180.37	106.05	17.98
2005	5662.44	3138.83	49.96	732.53	22.66	446.55	343.71	187.29	123.50	17.14
2006	5718.70	3050.00	50.20	800.40	22.20	477.80	362.30	188.90	129.10	20.70
2007	5772.72	2920.29	51.33	884.14	21.61	529.90	378.70	198.65	139.50	24.25
2008	5835.45	2847.31	51.27	933.43	20.99	558.23	406.10	204.46	147.07	25.63
2009	5948.78	2764.86	55.49	1006.00	21.23	592.00	443.94	207.70	157.12	31.34
2010	6041.56	2711.72	54.43	1053.52	21.66	623.76	481.71	213.14	165.97	34.25
2011	6197.85	2670.45	65.17	1109.32	22.01	656.00	535.44	217.80	176.52	35.74
2012	6287.50	2628.01	64.48	1155.66	23.20	675.97	565.80	222.77	186.60	35.73
2013	6386.57	2562.60	63.40	1222.81	24.98	723.88	575.91	242.80	184.76	38.58
2014	6520.03	2651.74	57.25	1211.15	26.06	701.11	639.70	234.71	189.51	39.62
2015	6636.08	2586.93	52.59	1256.30	26.07	707.45	692.51	242.84	209.46	45.29
2016	6726.39	2582.92	46.15	1274.75	27.36	707.69	714.67	245.65	227.38	49.43
2017	6766.86	2494.27	41.49	1286.70	28.18	748.12	621.91	268.68	255.21	88.99
2018	6692.00	2366.29	36.17	1229.92	28.04	753.61	718.29	261.54	266.96	88.30
2019	6561.76	2277.42	48.16	1141.53	17.14	712.25	805.59	267.33	291.08	76.75

Number of Employed Persons by Sector

(10 000 persons)

金融业 Financial Intermediation	房地产业 Real Estate	租赁和商务服务业 Leasing and Business Services	科学研究和技术服务业 Scientific Research, and Technical Services	水利、环境和公共设施管理业 Management of Water conservancy, Environment and Public Facilities	居民服务、修理和其他服务业 Services to Households, Repair and Other Services	教育 Education	卫生和社会工作 Health and social service	文化、体育和娱乐业 Culture, Sports and Enterta-inment	公共管理、社会保障和社会组织 Public Management, Social Security and Social Organization
21.11	4.56	8.34	10.73	10.37	294.74	103.84	31.80	7.00	92.30
21.19	6.04	11.21	11.09	10.45	278.48	104.75	33.27	7.70	95.75
20.92	7.68	13.98	11.09	10.58	291.37	107.22	33.43	6.92	97.08
20.70	8.80	15.30	11.40	11.30	301.90	109.60	34.40	8.20	95.50
22.32	9.82	16.29	11.56	11.70	300.75	111.60	35.51	8.22	96.58
21.58	10.87	20.08	13.07	11.78	310.18	109.81	36.50	8.28	98.81
22.48	15.06	26.85	13.88	11.98	314.83	112.58	39.21	8.43	103.80
23.47	17.18	29.04	14.92	12.82	314.08	114.27	41.27	8.62	105.72
25.15	21.98	32.15	16.30	13.53	323.86	117.59	43.75	8.99	106.11
24.75	24.43	33.06	18.65	13.90	330.46	119.17	46.66	9.79	108.40
25.35	26.02	31.05	20.00	13.00	345.34	117.30	49.07	11.27	108.48
25.44	31.23	41.90	23.66	13.99	340.83	119.60	50.90	11.06	110.56
25.90	35.02	51.69	26.98	14.48	357.56	125.86	56.49	12.89	109.75
31.56	36.57	57.39	29.88	14.12	367.35	125.64	59.93	14.17	113.79
30.83	38.49	70.17	30.13	14.74	414.30	125.92	62.03	30.95	115.73
33.38	39.12	69.22	29.30	16.57	410.52	127.76	65.87	30.22	120.92
36.61	43.42	73.54	60.97	60.17	291.99	132.61	75.24	18.17	131.80

4-6 各市分行业就业人员数(2019年底)

单位：万人

市（县） City(County)	合计 Total	农林牧渔业 Agriculture Forestry, Animal Husbandry and Fishery	采矿业 Mining	制造业 Manufacturing	电力、燃气及水的生产和供应业 Production and Supply of Electricity, Gas and Water	建筑业 Construction	批发和零售业 Wholesale and Retail Trades	交通运输仓储及邮政业 Transport, Storage, and Post	住宿和餐饮业 Hotels and Catering Services	信息传输、软件和信息技术服务业 Information Transmission, software and Information Technology
省辖市 City										
郑州市 Zhengzhou	635.01	91.07	3.23	112.05	1.64	54.64	79.41	78.45	34.24	11.04
开封市 Kaifeng	322.71	130.51	0.00	49.47	0.57	34.10	34.60	9.93	11.02	1.87
洛阳市 Luoyang	421.75	117.39	4.49	82.46	1.49	35.30	64.92	12.85	23.91	7.77
平顶山市 Pingdingshan	318.85	127.41	9.87	50.27	1.96	22.40	38.15	10.83	13.02	2.07
安阳市 Anyang	356.86	113.88	0.55	55.99	0.79	70.20	41.33	12.55	14.45	4.16
鹤壁市 Hebi	97.42	27.35	2.51	18.72	0.25	10.99	10.32	4.22	4.76	0.60
新乡市 Xinxiang	350.16	111.04	0.01	67.03	0.79	53.79	41.76	12.25	13.51	2.70
焦作市 Jiaozuo	235.23	67.53	2.56	70.58	0.54	14.48	27.91	10.44	8.68	2.27
濮阳市 Puyang	242.53	84.53	3.66	33.51	1.77	23.37	34.72	9.38	10.83	1.04
许昌市 Xuchang	275.94	99.46	0.81	66.19	0.56	17.26	33.73	8.86	11.52	2.91
漯河市 Luohe	176.29	68.39		33.08	0.36	13.74	31.61	4.74	5.74	0.89
三门峡市 Sanmenxia	136.09	53.98	13.02	5.79	0.73	8.02	20.75	5.10	7.32	1.21
南阳市 Nanyang	654.11	295.53	1.23	107.36	1.10	51.52	74.76	18.11	24.49	3.50
商丘市 Shangqiu	549.60	190.84	1.81	101.27	0.63	53.56	90.51	18.41	23.65	5.60
信阳市 Xinyang	479.94	211.30	2.19	42.88	2.30	68.68	50.52	28.31	15.47	1.05
周口市 Zhoukou	687.11	254.53		138.40	0.62	99.26	67.14	4.81	33.73	14.93
驻马店市 Zhumadian	576.30	219.09	1.68	93.94	0.73	77.70	58.70	15.84	32.98	12.96
济源市 Jiyuan	45.85	13.60	0.54	12.55	0.32	3.24	4.76	2.26	1.75	0.17
省直管县 County Directly Administrated by Province										
巩义市 Gongyi	51.77	11.75	0.34	17.29	0.11	2.64	7.65	2.06	2.98	0.30
兰考县 Lankao	62.31	22.75	0.00	4.46	0.14	6.39	5.58	2.02	1.75	0.23
汝州市 Ruzhou	69.56	30.20	0.81	13.00	0.06	4.07	8.25	2.33	2.19	0.46
滑县 Huaxian	77.24	30.03	0.00	11.39	0.06	12.87	7.97	2.74	3.55	1.29
长垣市 Changyuan	53.25	8.70		12.20	0.09	13.85	7.83	1.02	2.54	0.35
邓州市 Dengzhou	88.04	49.09	0.02	12.71	0.09	5.02	8.96	1.68	2.84	0.46
永城市 Yongcheng	93.75	22.45	1.81	27.84	0.06	13.33	10.79	2.36	3.91	0.80
固始县 Gushi	101.83	30.48	0.12	19.14	0.12	12.34	16.33	9.90	4.84	1.06
鹿邑县 Luyi	76.90	19.14		22.48	0.03	12.60	7.30	4.57	0.62	0.14
新蔡县 Xincai	68.91	18.92		16.02	0.05	9.78	6.49	0.80	4.46	2.57

Number of Employed Persons by Sector (End of 2019)

金融业 Financial Intermediation	房地产业 Real Estate	租赁和商务服务业 Leasing and Business Services	科学研究和技术服务业 Scientific Research, and Technical Services	水利、环境和公共设施管理业 Management of Water conservancy, Environment and Public Facilities	居民服务、修理和其他服务业 Services to Households, Repair and Other Services	教育 Education	卫生和社会工作 Health and social service	文化、体育和娱乐业 Culture, Sports and Entertainment	公共管理、社会保障和社会组织 Public Management, Social Security and Social Organization
11.77	8.37	13.62	37.35	18.94	22.18	18.29	12.19	2.65	23.91
1.16	2.38	4.01	1.48	2.79	23.49	4.91	3.59	0.94	5.92
1.84	3.31	9.16	5.01	4.76	21.57	8.32	5.81	1.51	9.89
2.08	1.85	2.48	1.08	2.80	15.26	5.58	3.68	0.84	7.22
1.17	1.22	2.98	0.85	4.57	15.24	6.86	3.59	0.66	5.82
0.59	0.96	2.11	0.68	1.05	6.60	1.86	1.22	0.44	2.19
0.99	2.21	3.74	1.15	3.22	16.32	7.26	4.06	0.98	7.35
1.17	1.73	2.31	1.54	2.23	8.11	4.28	2.45	1.00	5.41
0.76	2.04	5.60	2.41	1.18	7.37	9.64	3.99	1.65	5.10
0.88	1.61	2.12	1.19	2.98	11.65	5.11	2.81	0.82	5.49
1.03	0.90	1.48	0.39	1.39	5.61	1.98	1.57	0.42	2.98
1.22	0.64	1.28	0.67	1.41	6.59	2.71	1.69	0.56	3.41
3.62	2.03	5.77	2.25	4.43	26.09	13.45	6.88	1.41	10.58
0.97	5.18	4.32	1.66	3.18	23.95	8.68	4.71	1.34	9.33
1.63	3.10	5.34	1.12	0.81	16.08	11.93	7.87	0.79	8.59
1.44	1.62	3.48	0.89	1.12	39.13	10.92	4.57	0.76	9.75
4.11	4.11	3.42	1.16	3.02	23.83	9.92	3.95	1.28	7.90
0.18	0.17	0.35	0.11	0.31	2.95	0.89	0.61	0.13	0.96
0.06	0.28	0.42	0.13	0.58	2.10	1.28	0.57	0.25	0.98
0.07	0.49	0.80	0.26	0.61	14.22	0.67	0.77	0.14	0.95
0.08	0.33	0.76	0.14	0.55	3.34	0.98	0.83	0.23	0.95
0.08	0.14	0.31	0.07	0.40	3.27	1.36	0.67	0.05	0.99
0.05	0.43	0.48	0.18	0.63	2.29	1.14	0.47	0.22	0.78
0.07	0.25	0.33	0.10	0.67	2.45	1.68	0.74	0.10	0.78
0.02	0.38	0.78	0.30	0.23	5.07	1.42	0.72	0.41	1.07
0.09	0.59	0.50	0.28	0.26	1.00	2.81	0.85	0.15	0.97
0.00	0.20	0.21	0.11	0.05	7.10	1.06	0.35	0.07	0.89
0.02	0.42	0.42	0.11	0.22	6.56	0.77	0.33	0.13	0.86

4-7 分行业城镇非私营单位就业人员数

单位：万人

市(县) City(County)	合计 Total	农林牧渔业 Agriculture Forestry, Animal Husbandry and Fishery	采矿业 Mining	制造业 Manufacturing	电力、燃气及水的生产和供应业 Production and Supply of Electricity,Gas and Water	建筑业 Construction	批发和零售业 Wholesale and Retail Trade	交通运输仓储及邮政业 Transport, Storage and Post	住宿和餐饮业 Hotels and Catering Services	信息传输、软件和信息技术服务业 Information Transmission, Software and Information Technology
全　省 Total	**967.97**	**2.06**	**29.60**	**222.08**	**23.54**	**153.06**	**36.82**	**41.19**	**7.79**	**16.63**
省辖市 City										
郑州市 Zhengzhou	189.24	0.13	3.18	44.48	1.61	32.58	9.36	7.34	2.85	7.54
开封市 Kaifeng	37.52	0.04		9.02	0.49	6.29	1.35	0.80	0.34	0.36
洛阳市 Luoyang	68.33	0.05	0.98	21.36	1.18	7.46	1.95	1.77	0.59	1.65
平顶山市 Pingdingshan	49.57	0.07	9.79	9.14	1.86	3.90	1.14	1.18	0.32	0.36
安阳市 Anyang	49.24	0.03	0.55	6.14	0.67	19.12	0.80	0.92	0.21	0.39
鹤壁市 Hebi	17.69	0.01	2.50	5.29	0.21	1.48	0.47	0.28	0.08	0.23
新乡市 Xinxiang	47.65	0.08		8.94	0.52	12.36	1.65	1.12	0.26	0.51
焦作市 Jiaozuo	38.48	0.03	2.53	14.52	0.40	2.23	1.30	1.75	0.24	0.37
濮阳市 Puyang	33.97	0.05	3.47	3.01	1.36	6.99	0.90	1.04	0.17	0.29
许昌市 Xuchang	42.37	0.10	0.79	16.12	0.53	2.84	1.60	0.86	0.31	1.19
漯河市 Luohe	26.89	0.05		12.12	0.32	2.05	1.60	0.75	0.16	0.20
三门峡市 Sanmenxia	20.95	0.05	2.45	3.94	0.63	2.11	0.78	0.38	0.25	0.30
南阳市 Nanyang	71.06	0.28	1.07	12.92	0.62	11.31	2.67	2.18	0.51	0.50
商丘市 Shangqiu	68.23	0.07	1.81	15.85	0.40	9.96	4.37	3.37	0.31	0.75
信阳市 Xinyang	52.66	0.12	0.09	8.17	0.62	10.26	2.35	1.67	0.45	0.62
周口市 Zhoukou	63.59	0.68		16.50	0.40	9.08	2.53	2.28	0.29	0.82
驻马店市 Zhumadian	59.06	0.24		10.76	0.59	11.84	1.86	2.13	0.42	0.49
济源市 Jiyuan	8.43	0.00	0.40	2.65	0.13	1.21	0.16	0.49	0.04	0.06
省直管县 County Directly Administrated by Province										
巩义市 Gongyi	5.55	0.00	0.33	1.16	0.09	0.38	0.20	0.19	0.06	0.04
兰考县 Lankao	5.73	0.02		1.72	0.11	0.36	0.31	0.06	0.04	0.02
汝州市 Ruzhou	6.34	0.01	0.78	1.35	0.04	0.27	0.10	0.25	0.03	0.02
滑县 Huaxian	6.36	0.00		0.59	0.05	2.05	0.11	0.11	0.02	0.04
长垣市 Changyuan	8.45	0.01		1.10	0.08	3.82	0.45	0.08	0.03	0.01
邓州市 Dengzhou	6.42	0.01	0.01	1.33	0.06	0.86	0.15	0.17	0.01	0.01
永城市 Yongcheng	9.20	0.01	1.81	1.97	0.03	1.37	0.29	0.19	0.03	0.04
固始县 Gushi	8.02	0.02	0.00	0.75	0.07	1.64	0.23	0.27	0.06	0.01
鹿邑县 Luyi	5.83	0.02		1.47	0.03	1.22	0.18	0.10	0.04	0.02
新蔡县 Xincai	4.99	0.02		1.02	0.04	0.87	0.25	0.11	0.09	0.04

Number of Employed Persons in Urban Non-private Units by Sector

(10 000 persons)

金融业 Financial Intermediation	房地产业 Real Estate	租赁和商务服务业 Leasing and Business Services	科学研究和技术服务业 Scientific Research, and Technical Services	水利、环境和公共设施管理业 Management of Water Conservancy, Environment and Public Facilities	居民服务、修理和其他服务业 Services to Households, Repair and Other Services	教　育 Education	卫生和社会工作 Health and Social Service	文化、体育和娱乐业 Culture, Sports and Enterta-inment	公共管理、社会保障和社会组织 Public Management, Social Security and Social Organization
29.51	**28.01**	**26.41**	**17.57**	**13.57**	**2.74**	**121.46**	**66.05**	**6.78**	**123.09**
6.00	7.89	9.88	7.65	2.35	0.50	16.83	11.64	1.90	15.55
1.10	1.13	0.69	0.51	0.75	0.11	4.77	3.56	0.30	5.90
1.77	2.07	0.94	2.29	0.98	0.06	7.79	4.97	0.60	9.87
2.02	0.99	0.90	0.46	0.70	0.21	5.52	3.53	0.27	7.22
1.09	0.76	0.95	0.42	0.90	0.05	6.77	3.48	0.19	5.82
0.46	0.27	0.91	0.12	0.29	0.01	1.67	1.12	0.11	2.18
0.90	1.01	0.97	0.27	0.48	0.12	7.08	3.87	0.19	7.33
1.11	0.75	0.59	0.25	0.51	0.07	4.00	2.30	0.19	5.37
0.70	0.72	2.17	0.41	0.52	0.08	4.55	2.22	0.22	5.10
0.82	1.15	0.70	0.72	0.78	0.17	5.05	2.78	0.37	5.49
1.02	0.61	0.75	0.20	0.35	0.11	1.95	1.55	0.15	2.96
1.19	0.32	0.23	0.22	0.31	0.08	2.59	1.57	0.15	3.39
3.51	0.99	1.35	1.16	1.19	0.16	13.02	6.49	0.56	10.57
0.91	3.94	2.01	0.79	0.84	0.33	8.41	4.58	0.31	9.21
1.38	1.52	1.03	0.78	0.67	0.18	10.04	3.76	0.40	8.55
1.38	1.47	0.95	0.55	1.05	0.20	10.77	4.48	0.41	9.75
3.98	2.26	1.18	0.66	0.65	0.29	9.80	3.61	0.42	7.88
0.18	0.13	0.21	0.09	0.25	0.02	0.86	0.55	0.03	0.96
0.05	0.16	0.08	0.04	0.04	0.02	1.13	0.55	0.05	0.98
0.05	0.19	0.12	0.06	0.25	0.02	0.65	0.77	0.03	0.94
0.07	0.10	0.27	0.06	0.13	0.09	0.96	0.80	0.07	0.95
0.08	0.11	0.11	0.03	0.03	0.01	1.35	0.67	0.01	0.99
0.05	0.21	0.11	0.04	0.08	0.01	1.12	0.44	0.04	0.78
0.06	0.11	0.07	0.07	0.30	0.02	1.64	0.73	0.02	0.78
	0.13	0.12	0.04	0.12	0.04	1.21	0.69	0.04	1.07
0.09	0.35	0.22	0.22	0.16	0.05	2.17	0.61	0.11	0.97
	0.17	0.13	0.07	0.04	0.02	1.06	0.34	0.03	0.89
0.02	0.20	0.17	0.07	0.04	0.07	0.76	0.31	0.04	0.86

4-8 城镇非私营单位就业人员数(2019年底)

Number of Employed Persons in Urban Non-private Units by City (End of 2019)

单位：万人 (10 000 persons)

市(县) City(County)	合计 Total	在岗职工 Staff and Workers	#劳务派遣 Labor Dispatching	其他就业人员 Others	国有单位 State-owned Units	城镇集体单位 Urban Collective-owned Units	其他单位 Units of Other Types of Ownership
全省 Total	**967.97**	**922.28**	**56.11**	**45.69**	**323.83**	**19.06**	**625.08**
省辖市 City							
郑州市 Zhengzhou	189.24	178.88	22.09	10.37	44.37	1.46	143.42
开封市 Kaifeng	37.52	35.69	2.01	1.83	12.96	1.49	23.07
洛阳市 Luoyang	68.33	65.78	7.81	2.54	23.20	1.23	43.90
平顶山市 Pingdingshan	49.57	47.56	2.80	2.01	17.85	1.46	30.26
安阳市 Anyang	49.24	44.78	3.10	4.46	15.79	0.81	32.64
鹤壁市 Hebi	17.69	17.03	1.41	0.66	5.18	0.18	12.34
新乡市 Xinxiang	47.65	44.21	2.76	3.44	16.37	1.40	29.88
焦作市 Jiaozuo	38.48	36.87	2.31	1.61	11.13	0.51	26.84
濮阳市 Puyang	33.97	31.37	1.90	2.60	12.35	0.59	21.04
许昌市 Xuchang	42.37	40.40	1.15	1.97	12.44	0.68	29.25
漯河市 Luohe	26.89	26.00	0.86	0.88	6.63	0.50	19.76
三门峡市 Sanmenxia	20.95	19.74	0.69	1.21	8.17	0.30	12.49
南阳市 Nanyang	71.06	67.05	1.79	4.02	30.90	2.40	37.77
商丘市 Shangqiu	68.23	66.30	1.33	1.93	22.45	0.92	44.86
信阳市 Xinyang	52.66	50.14	1.23	2.53	25.11	1.47	26.09
周口市 Zhoukou	63.59	62.50	0.65	1.08	23.38	1.89	38.33
驻马店市 Zhumadian	59.06	57.30	1.26	1.75	22.12	1.69	35.25
济源市 Jiyuan	8.43	7.83	0.65	0.60	2.44	0.12	5.88
省直管县 County Directly Administrated by Province							
巩义市 Gongyi	5.55	5.38	0.20	0.17	2.00	0.32	3.23
兰考县 Lankao	5.73	5.41	0.12	0.31	1.81	0.07	3.86
汝州市 Ruzhou	6.34	6.14	0.43	0.20	2.56	0.21	3.57
滑县 Huaxian	6.36	5.92	0.22	0.44	2.51	0.14	3.71
长垣市 Changyuan	8.45	8.00	0.65	0.45	1.51	0.10	6.84
邓州市 Dengzhou	6.42	5.89	0.09	0.53	3.52	0.11	2.79
永城市 Yongcheng	9.20	8.98	0.31	0.21	3.17	0.03	6.00
固始县 Gushi	8.02	7.65	0.15	0.37	3.97	0.28	3.78
鹿邑县 Luyi	5.83	5.73	0.00	0.10	1.82	0.09	3.92
新蔡县 Xincai	4.99	4.95	0.04	0.04	1.96	0.03	3.00

4-9 各种分组的城镇非私营单位就业人员数(2019年底)

Number of Employed Persons in Urban Non-private Units by Groups (End of 2019)

单位：万人 (10 000 persons)

类别	Type	合计 Total	在岗职工 Staff and Workers	#劳务派遣 Labor Dispatching	其他就业人员 Others	国有单位 State-owned Units	城镇集体单位 Urban Collective-owned Units	其他单位 Units of Other Types of Ownership
总 计	**Total**	**967.97**	**922.28**	**56.11**	**45.69**	**323.83**	**19.06**	**625.08**
按执行会计标准类别分组	**by Performing Accounting Standard Category**							
企业	Enterprises	654.17	619.15	44.54	35.02	50.12	11.59	592.46
事业	Institutions	200.98	193.95	4.03	7.02	171.98	6.95	22.05
机关	Agencies and Organizations	99.15	95.84	7.39	3.31	98.01	0.17	0.97
按国民经济行业分组	**by Sector**							
农、林、牧、渔业	Agriculture, Forestry, animal Husbandry and Fishery	2.06	1.97	0.01	0.10	1.35	0.16	0.55
采矿业	Mining	29.60	29.26	1.12	0.34	0.31	0.02	29.27
制造业	Manufacturing	222.08	219.39	9.10	2.69	1.83	1.61	218.63
电力、热力、燃气及水生产和供应业	Production and Distribution of Electricity, Gas and Water	23.54	23.23	0.57	0.30	14.21	0.08	9.24
建筑业	Construction	153.06	134.42	19.24	18.64	3.82	5.10	144.15
批发和零售业	Wholesale and Retail Trade	36.82	36.03	1.07	0.79	4.00	1.02	31.80
交通运输、仓储和邮政业	Transport, Storage and Post	41.19	40.01	2.60	1.18	10.03	0.95	30.21
住宿和餐饮业	Hotels and Catering Services	7.79	7.58	0.21	0.21	1.07	0.18	6.54
信息传输、软件和信息技术服务业	Information Transmission and Information Technology services	16.63	13.30	1.29	3.32	1.06	0.28	15.28
金融业	Finance	29.51	25.61	0.49	3.90	4.47	0.34	24.70
房地产业	Real estate	28.01	27.08	1.68	0.93	0.70	0.26	27.05
租赁和商务服务业	Leasing and Business Services	26.41	25.48	5.74	0.93	4.98	0.63	20.79
科学研究和技术服务业	Scientific Research and Technical Service	17.57	16.94	0.92	0.63	7.68	0.34	9.55
水利、环境和公共设施管理业	Management of Water Conservancy, Environment	13.57	11.49	0.68	2.07	6.80	0.10	6.68
居民服务、修理和其他服务业	Service to Households, Repair and other Services	2.74	2.62	0.08	0.12	0.46	0.13	2.16
教育	Education	121.46	118.57	0.84	2.89	87.53	4.73	29.20
卫生和社会工作	Health and Social Work	66.05	63.98	1.89	2.07	49.63	2.50	13.93
文化、体育和娱乐业	Culture, Sports and Entertainment	6.78	6.50	0.15	0.27	3.99	0.07	2.72
公共管理、社会保障和社会组织	Public Management, Social Security and Social Organization	123.09	118.80	8.45	4.29	119.92	0.56	2.61

4-10 各种分组的城镇非私营单位女性就业人员数(年底数)

Number of Female Employed Persons in Urban Non-private Units by Groups (Year-end)

单位：万人

项 目	Item	2018	2019
合 计	**Total**	**360.76**	**371.16**
按国民经济行业分	**by Sector**		
农、林、牧、渔业	Agriculture, Forestry, animal Husbandry and Fishery	0.45	0.74
采矿业	Mining	6.17	5.04
制造业	Manufacturing	95.57	85.76
电力、燃气及水的生产和供应业	Production and Distribution of Electricity, Gas and Water	7.13	6.89
建筑业	Construction	21.21	19.93
批发和零售业	Wholesale and Retail Trade	17.99	18.57
交通运输、仓储和邮政业	Transport, Storage and Post	11.23	11.78
住宿和餐饮业	Hotels and Catering Services	4.68	4.65
信息传输、软件和信息技术服务业	Information Transmission and Information Technology services	5.31	6.01
金融业	Finance	13.02	16.19
房地产业	Real estate	8.89	10.86
租赁和商务服务业	Leasing and Business Services	4.26	7.81
科学研究和技术服务业	Scientific Research and Technical Service	4.27	5.55
水利、环境和公共设施管理业	Management of Water Conservancy, Environment	5.46	5.77
居民服务、修理和其他服务业	Service to Households, Repair and other Services	1.06	1.34
教育	Education	69.74	76.51
卫生和社会工作	Health and Social Work	40.47	43.66
文化、体育和娱乐业	Culture, Sports and Entertainment	3.25	3.14
公共管理、社会保障和社会组织	Public Management, Social Security and Social Organization	40.60	40.96
按三次产业分	**by Three Strata of Industry**		
第一产业	Primary Industry	0.45	0.74
第二产业	Secondary Industry	130.07	117.62
第三产业	Tertiary Industry	230.23	252.81
按注册类型分	**by Status of Registration**		
#国有单位	State-owned Units	159.56	149.77
城镇集体单位	Urban Collective Owned Units	8.55	7.56
股份合作单位	Cooperative Units	2.62	1.82
联营单位	Joint Ownership Units	0.99	0.85
有限责任公司	Limited Liability Corporations	121.85	126.69
股份有限公司	Share-holding Corporations Ltd.	31.07	34.40
港澳台商投资单位	Units with Funds from Hong Kong, Macao & Taiwan	18.99	15.55
外商投资单位	Foreign Funded Units	5.77	6.67

4-11 城镇非私营单位就业人员平均工资

Average Wage of Employed Persons in Urban Non-private Units

单位：元 (yuan)

年份 Year	合计 Total	国有单位 State-owned Units	城镇集体单位 Urban Collective-owned Units	股份合作单位 Cooperative Units	联营单位 Joint Ownership Units	有限责任公司 Limited Liability Corporations Units	股份有限公司 Share Holding Corporations	港、澳、台商投资单位 Units with Funds from Hong Kong, Macao and Taiwan	外商投资单位 Foreign Funded Units	其他 Others
1998	5641	6103	4050	4026	5270	6201	5342	6009	8503	2213
1999	6136	6562	4524	5201	3897	6637	5895	6997	7502	4017
2000	6877	7408	4840	5640	5084	6910	7515	9267	7997	5521
2001	7868	8518	5669	5685	5661	7811	8077	9596	9070	5512
2002	9714	9791	6607	7208	6370	9148	10003	10482	9992	7507
2003	10639	11280	7828	9285	8482	10789	11862	12091	13363	8718
2004	11970	12562	8582	9586	9211	12150	13629	14278	14045	9864
2005	14119	14740	10248	11722	10386	14796	14986	14937	15437	10886
2006	16791	17702	12377	13075	12247	17051	17034	17710	17452	14811
2007	20639	22044	15674	17581	13370	19728	21771	20133	21371	17488
2008	24438	26222	16873	21493	17581	24012	24740	23315	25237	18435
2009	26906	28503	18006	26731	20665	25701	29628	25153	27120	22135
2010	29819	31470	20385	29928	25245	28775	32377	27257	29620	25087
2011	33634	35386	24220	32982	32881	33136	34884	31948	32674	28909
2012	37338	39344	27682	36536	33885	36386	38581	36814	36053	31329
2013	38301	42270	33135	41673	34299	34323	41388	42801	36985	32572
2014	42179	46604	37601	49356	38770	38334	44432	46005	39721	37188
2015	45403	49978	41511	52724	46112	41188	47676	50235	42546	45290
2016	49505	56609	45608	60727	53879	43560	53519	52300	46116	45946
2017	55495	65958	51882	69275	59803	47586	59685	55195	49448	52433
2018	63174	73330	57617	77381	96181	53626	69184	57775	61550	58620
2019	67268	76547	57405	88113	58858	58283	78759	60664	63728	68555

注：2013年后工资数据为联网直报平台汇总(下同)。

a) Data in 2013 are collected from network platform (the same as following tables).

4-12 城镇非私营单位职工工资及指数
Wages and Related Indices of Staff and Workers in Urban Non-private Units

年份 Year	工资总额(亿元) Total Wages (100 million yuan)				平均工资(元) Average Wage (yuan)				平均工资指数(以上年为100) Index of Average Wage (Preceding year=100)			
		国有单位 State-owned Units	城镇集体单位 Urban Collective-owned Units	其他单位 Units of Other Types of Ownership		国有单位 State-owned Units	城镇集体单位 Urban Collective-owned Units	其他单位 Units of Other Types of Ownership	全部职工 Total Staff and Workers	国有单位 State-owned Units	城镇集体单位 Urban Collective-owned Units	其他单位 Units of Other Types of Ownership
1978	24.30	20.65	3.64		590	609	496		104.8	105.4	99.8	
1979	27.63	23.60	4.03		644	668	533		108.8	109.4	107.1	
1980	32.93	28.14	4.79		730	759	597		106.9	107.2	105.7	
1981	35.43	30.33	5.09		742	772	604		99.3	99.3	98.8	
1982	37.40	31.82	5.59		754	789	604		99.8	100.4	98.2	
1983	39.19	33.36	5.82		767	805	606		98.9	99.2	97.5	
1984	46.24	37.76	8.47	0.01	866	921	686	809	110.5	111.9	110.8	
1985	57.85	47.06	10.76	0.02	1015	1080	804	1014	110.1	110.1	110.0	117.7
1986	69.57	56.97	12.57	0.03	1159	1245	882	1079	106.9	107.9	102.7	99.6
1987	78.98	64.34	14.58	0.06	1258	1347	974	1559	100.7	100.4	102.4	134.0
1988	95.90	78.66	17.18	0.07	1470	1582	1110	1520	96.2	96.7	93.8	80.2
1989	108.70	89.48	19.12	0.09	1628	1767	1191	1724	96.4	97.2	93.4	98.7
1990	123.86	102.52	21.19	0.15	1825	1997	1288	2128	111.5	112.5	107.6	122.8
1991	138.18	113.58	24.33	0.27	1964	2132	1433	2477	102.4	101.6	105.9	110.8
1992	165.51	138.38	26.51	0.62	2269	2473	1583	2544	107.3	107.7	102.6	95.4
1993	200.82	168.89	28.90	3.03	2646	2860	1821	3097	105.4	104.6	104.0	110.1
1994	275.18	229.87	35.66	9.66	3545	3851	2295	4038	105.2	105.7	98.9	102.3
1995	347.70	284.17	47.79	15.75	4344	4677	3007	4644	104.8	103.9	112.1	98.4
1996	407.43	332.03	54.77	20.63	4924	5265	3485	5197	103.5	102.8	105.8	102.2
1997	434.08	336.34	66.05	31.69	5225	5643	3797	5209	103.6	104.7	106.4	97.9
1998	431.01	299.76	63.36	67.88	5781	6204	4258	5976	119.9	120.4	117.5	117.2
1999	445.61	307.17	62.31	76.13	6194	6594	4639	6384	110.9	110.0	112.8	110.6
2000	495.66	338.39	66.44	90.84	6930	7453	4913	7212	112.9	114.1	106.9	114.0
2001	553.40	381.92	75.73	95.75	7916	8573	5726	7889	113.4	114.2	115.7	108.6
2002	622.42	400.42	80.84	141.15	9174	9864	6664	9335	116.1	115.3	116.6	118.5
2003	720.52	436.31	88.51	195.69	10749	11397	7894	11160	115.2	113.6	116.5	117.5
2004	801.95	497.47	79.62	224.86	12114	12701	8686	12588	106.9	105.7	104.4	107.0
2005	949.97	575.63	90.29	284.05	14282	14877	10383	14852	115.5	114.7	117.1	115.6
2006	1152.05	690.58	103.21	358.26	16981	17886	12483	17088	117.5	118.8	118.8	113.7
2007	1431.35	849.87	125.01	456.48	20935	22345	15850	20333	117.0	118.5	120.5	112.9
2008	1702.22	1008.08	111.75	582.39	24816	26536	17118	24189	110.8	111.0	100.9	111.2
2009	1918.14	1066.34	85.52	766.28	27357	28914	18352	26817	110.9	109.6	107.9	111.5
2010	2171.69	1200.07	98.62	873.00	30303	31924	20769	29770	107.1	106.8	109.5	107.4
2011	2721.42	1390.91	119.85	1210.66	34203	35894	24397	33719	107.1	106.6	111.3	107.5
2012	3146.25	1575.98	134.27	1436.00	37958	39948	28103	37145	111.0	111.3	115.2	110.2
2013	4048.73	1556.02	149.02	2343.68	38804	42831	33954	36765	102.2	107.2	120.8	99.0
2014	4432.94	1667.53	152.34	2613.08	42670	47258	38288	40435	108.2	110.6	107.8	103.7
2015	4862.54	1786.62	151.60	2924.32	45920	50662	42058	43633	107.6	107.2	109.8	107.9
2016	5365.62	2026.18	144.86	3194.58	50028	57333	46168	46451	108.9	113.2	109.8	106.5
2017	5903.60	2313.85	136.91	3452.84	55997	66685	52788	50676	111.9	116.3	114.3	109.1
2018	5972.87	2566.64	121.64	3284.59	64148	74649	58339	57824	114.6	111.9	110.5	114.1
2019	6189.46	2406.07	103.48	3679.90	68305	78036	58287	63439	106.5	104.5	99.9	109.7

注：1998年及以后年度工资总额为在岗职工口径，与以前年度不尽可比。

a) Total wages funds since 1998 were totalized by all employed staff and workers, the data are not comparable with previous years.

4-13 各种分组的城镇非私营单位就业人员平均工资(2019年)
Average Wage of Employed Persons in Urban Npn-private Units by Groups (2019)

单位：元 (yuan)

类别	Type	平均工资 Average Wage	在岗职工 Staff and Workers	#劳务派遣 Labor Dispatching	其他就业人员 Others	国有单位 State-owned Units	集体单位 Collectiveowned Units	其他单位 Units of Other Types of Ownership
总　计	**Total**	**67268**	**68305**	**49767**	**45740**	**76547**	**57405**	**62719**
按执行会计标准类别分组	**by Performing Accounting Standard Category**							
企业	Enterprises	63278	64049	52386	49176	80258	49590	62082
事业	Institutions	76230	77674	45585	35958	75524	70602	83523
机关	Agencies and Organizations	75755	77260	36177	31996	75862	67408	66408
按国民经济行业分组	**by Sector**							
农、林、牧、渔业	Agriculture, Forestry, animal Husbandry and Fishery	47272	47980	57615	33510	49232	41762	44010
采矿业	Mining	71822	72344	71950	28489	63501	59214	71916
制造业	Manufacturing	56691	56831	50220	45083	49226	55304	56764
电力、热力、燃气及水生产和供应业	Production and Distribution of Electricity, Gas and Water	88544	89052	51216	49440	99853	50094	71285
建筑业	Construction	54972	55381	54588	51964	52353	45945	55367
批发和零售业	Wholesale and Retail Trade	56584	56901	46582	42170	97839	41025	51752
交通运输、仓储和邮政业	Transport, Storage and Post	75865	76534	60244	51609	65967	43303	80159
住宿和餐饮业	Hotels and Catering Services	43111	43176	49194	40772	42730	41126	43229
信息传输、软件和信息技术服务业	Information Transmission and Information Technology services	79992	88613	70828	39220	69368	70704	80962
金融业	Finance	124240	135357	66278	50622	101977	88343	128903
房地产业	Real estate	60973	61570	44985	44419	65448	45342	61010
租赁和商务服务业	Leasing and Business Services	49706	49637	39259	51506	51761	46028	49316
科学研究和技术服务业	Scientific Research and Technical Service	89322	90494	61253	59854	93408	60418	87070
水利、环境和公共设施管理业	Management of Water Conservancy, Environment	49073	52636	31596	28797	57519	64148	40292
居民服务、修理和其他服务业	Service to Households, Repair and other Services	46858	46858	32159	46869	60950	41353	44173
教育	Education	73598	74545	40818	34705	77059	71089	63506
卫生和社会工作	Health and Social Work	81520	82561	54724	49546	82237	69305	81163
文化、体育和娱乐业	Culture, Sports and Entertainment	73108	74319	45155	41632	67698	47432	81654
公共管理、社会保障和社会组织	Public Management, Social Security and Social Organization	73221	74726	36227	31439	73544	57193	61783

4-14 各市城镇非私营单位就业人员平均工资(2019年)

单位：元

市(县)	City(County)	平均工资 Average Wages	在岗职工 Staff and Workers	#劳务派遣 Labor Dispatching	其他就业人员 Others	#国有单位 State-owned Units
省辖市	**City**					
郑州市	Zhengzhou	85901	88030	52640	46647	106466
开封市	Kaifeng	58589	59288	56878	44646	68460
洛阳市	Luoyang	71195	72457	51512	38497	80912
平顶山市	Pingdingshan	60911	62154	55664	32332	63024
安阳市	Anyang	61668	62727	36807	50013	74988
鹤壁市	Hebi	56048	57039	35014	34861	70340
新乡市	Xinxiang	60507	61149	49390	52104	70183
焦作市	Jiaozuo	61074	61831	43372	42080	72586
濮阳市	Puyang	66983	68852	48340	44891	74280
许昌市	Xuchang	63355	64380	51848	40662	77173
漯河市	Luohe	60838	60787	43711	62316	78537
三门峡市	Sanmenxia	63836	66132	43917	30198	79750
南阳市	Nanyang	57531	58160	43635	46450	66276
商丘市	Shangqiu	59272	59489	45961	51465	68911
信阳市	Xinyang	59800	60256	50187	50655	64254
周口市	Zhoukou	56562	56667	51699	50676	66003
驻马店市	Zhumadian	58448	58957	44385	42225	66631
济源市	Jiyuan	64138	65324	43970	49726	90152
省直管县	**County Directly Administrated by Province**					
巩义市	Gongyi	62399	63291	47638	32041	83791
兰考县	Lankao	59289	59877	67984	48829	68171
汝州市	Ruzhou	51250	51816	58033	34793	57904
滑县	Huaxian	57925	59499	42609	37223	68844
长垣市	Changyuan	56875	57082	54837	52567	62992
邓州市	Dengzhou	53134	54199	41132	41135	59073
永城市	Yongcheng	57520	57942	45005	37983	62969
固始县	Gushi	64332	64708	62179	55219	75529
鹿邑县	Luyi	55003	54997	60476	55348	67977
新蔡县	Xincai	53183	53240	43576	46462	57736

Average Wage of Employed Persons in Urban Non-private Units by City (2019)

(yuan)

#集体单位 Urban Collective-owned Units	#股份合作单位 Cooperative Units	#联营单位 Joint Ownership Units	#有限责任公司 Limited Liability Corporations	#股份有限公司 Share Holding Corporations Ltd	#港澳台投资 Units with Funds from Hong Kong, Macao and Taiwan	#外商投资 Foreign Funded Units
69680	139963	81415	70441	136179	60686	84371
53058	40411	36462	45135	58339	44032	60461
63804	59109	21137	61739	85863	57036	61391
56695	108419	47226	51085	71164	67067	46026
55087	25167	58764	60879	77397	85133	62763
48160	95931	27286	46980	56579	81423	71303
46970	64937	50512	52676	59590	73707	59156
58939	74606	57451	54467	60985	46028	64504
49327	76249	33452	55839	96538	65536	98626
59320	65206	44661	54319	70599	52418	67283
71496	77980	58528	50443	64720	49964	60266
42387	91777	30000	51665	54134	95580	68582
54906	76920	58360	46981	57890	46445	49090
58727	73919	53346	53738	55605	57076	56599
72154	100931	53630	53250	59908	65172	55140
56785	71047	59396	48846	53075	76210	43056
46573	87806	62036	49557	68360	51359	75662
79949		85349	51007	108101		80818
66755	69101	38714	44757	57944	50296	53458
60454	77720	56316	53095	67019	73566	49634
40956	34000	39111	43692	55469	65547	56704
55743	45299	38500	48459	63773	66670	52952
54367	37000	49444	54876	52937	51795	61514
45831	109896	52564	43010	49330	43424	
47073	68487		55260	38740	60526	34107
74426		52875	47827	79457		49943
70694	36909	42000	48449	47589	43515	39098
54781	68938	47278	45908	65483		57000

4-15 分行业城镇非私营单位就业人员平均工资(2019年)

单位：元

市(县)	City(County)	合计 Total	农林牧渔业 Agriculture Forestry, Animal Husbandry and Fishery	采矿业 Mining	制造业 Manufacturing	电力、燃气及水的生产和供应业 Production and Supply of Electricity,Gas and Water	建筑业 Construction	批发和零售业 Wholesale and Retail Trade	交通运输仓储及邮政业 Transport, Storage and Post	住宿和餐饮业 Hotels and Catering Services
全　　省	**Total**	**67268**	**47272**	**71822**	**56691**	**88544**	**54972**	**56584**	**75865**	**43111**
省 辖 市	**City**									
郑 州 市	Zhengzhou	85901	53135	54139	66134	95592	69559	65885	86807	49892
开 封 市	Kaifeng	58589	52501		48867	80802	51933	56990	46888	47578
洛 阳 市	Luoyang	71195	58073	58601	63373	69082	65671	62349	50633	39382
平顶山市	Pingdingshan	60911	44640	67490	52038	78506	46114	70233	42028	36501
安 阳 市	Anyang	61668	55105	78173	63950	78316	50958	56360	55588	30256
鹤 壁 市	Hebi	56048	26327	67041	43148	64268	39420	41553	48067	35023
新 乡 市	Xinxiang	60507	60792		50926	61126	53239	53235	68901	34638
焦 作 市	Jiaozuo	61074	36391	78884	54538	68217	46823	41809	50389	35012
濮 阳 市	Puyang	66983	42800	106950	54169	87702	53736	48269	56767	42561
许 昌 市	Xuchang	63355	43304	89561	59130	43328	51230	57772	56025	43802
漯 河 市	Luohe	60838	54605		55346	65799	44030	52422	51227	34680
三门峡市	Sanmenxia	63836	53109	55807	47209	80821	51694	65202	60846	37287
南 阳 市	Nanyang	57531	40376	105491	45869	44995	44512	53965	47175	36532
商 丘 市	Shangqiu	59272	54270	61716	52273	55263	54268	45829	56493	39551
信 阳 市	Xinyang	59800	54700	53117	56112	53680	50750	45916	50482	38088
周 口 市	Zhoukou	56562	45602		44248	54519	51773	54829	52863	44126
驻马店市	Zhumadian	58448	46005		52277	57149	46001	58475	47330	43119
济 源 市	Jiyuan	64138	116667	41113	52486	75684	45477	53365	55166	38806
省直管县	**County Directly Administrated by Province**									
巩 义 市	Gongyi	62399	32347	38512	45989	51048	54358	43301	47599	31171
兰 考 县	Lankao	59289	56155		53214	87120	56531	52368	58743	58848
汝 州 市	Ruzhou	51250	29226	58382	45986	56418	39817	38495	43895	31015
滑 县	Huaxian	57925	38321		53114	56343	50096	39586	53676	29014
长 垣 市	Changyuan	56875	52500		49728	72256	55005	50910	46654	42861
邓 州 市	Dengzhou	53134	62041	36938	40652	57107	46668	46844	33166	31042
永 城 市	Yongcheng	57520	34157	61716	58080	55977	49050	42389	38701	40595
固 始 县	Gushi	64332	75058	44867	47477	35595	55022	37277	52964	34789
鹿 邑 县	Luyi	55003	50405		38851	45524	62656	36445	46281	41950
新 蔡 县	Xincai	53183	49656		49634	76417	46548	46442	45225	53922

Average Wage of Employed Persons in Urban Non-private Units by Sector and City (2019)

(yuan)

信息传输、软件和信息技术服务业 Information Transmission, Software and Information Technology Services	金融业 Financial Intermediation	房地产业 Real Estate	租赁和商务服务业 Leasing and Business Services	科学研究和技术服务业 Scientific Research, and Technical Services	水利、环境和公共设施管理业 Management of Water Conservancy, Environment and Public Facilities	居民服务、修理和其他服务业 Services to Households, Repair and Other Services	教育 Education	卫生和社会工作 Health and Social Work	文化、体育和娱乐业 Culture, Sports and Entertainment	公共管理、社会保障和社会组织 Public Management, Social Security and Social Organization
79992	**124240**	**60973**	**49706**	**89322**	**49073**	**46858**	**73598**	**81520**	**73108**	**73221**
76237	259346	77679	55580	104209	59716	56668	105725	121284	115003	105849
68758	83350	60062	44406	62038	33445	50241	67992	70842	53583	65872
104153	117816	50474	48327	131529	43567	54302	80598	79206	62654	72876
71831	81149	48761	40655	66281	55774	42348	66311	65528	51388	61219
95687	89131	50395	34678	77869	46930	48342	75768	66599	68689	73442
76119	98863	46511	39317	68136	37017	51811	71056	63923	56343	73308
103449	95714	55941	39532	65937	56214	39223	71027	70161	58944	66713
70419	87897	49197	43039	58196	50847	40890	71390	62145	55629	75834
88596	89930	49634	57258	68163	42284	40179	70445	69055	65883	66508
48482	90061	57893	56178	53842	39574	51577	70588	72090	58096	78736
73458	86954	69352	39979	63247	41969	26401	76308	90427	63755	73993
64579	66102	44596	54531	70404	44771	41769	80027	74232	50095	82074
86667	83819	44292	39949	56225	46765	43616	63867	75338	51545	61889
76044	78951	62978	51384	55839	44449	45490	63475	79632	57124	69400
88732	91068	52013	46692	63207	58863	40527	66093	72175	51904	64560
90335	107253	49542	46356	63835	48140	44360	63070	76927	58982	60305
86154	87033	51683	45190	57274	55927	53568	61685	70198	55364	69047
84978	107002	53603	35466	82838	49127	27535	100562	84601	67077	92502
55738	152549	47237	37302	56233	58459	46322	72567	84172	57229	80767
64943	91377	59379	60120	61218	11029	56262	66666	70901	48478	67090
53469	103079	40264	33824	38857	29503	30697	59797	55055	37662	56120
56894	88955	47103	48332	55710	16736	30410	68359	69780	61193	63291
42083	106819	44835	43434	47437	47883	38950	60054	80154	47661	64199
20543	124855	51756	41346	52034	44789	46704	55751	71527	55155	63147
32997		45494	36765	29662	21971	29549	66155	67742	42324	62341
52043	98976	50706	47302	70670	68095	35348	73911	88660	43802	74241
50917		50291	40341	60451	41396	40610	58387	85978	43589	65557
64992	70488	52335	50930	55793	42611	63276	54447	58004	51087	61448

4-16 城镇私营单位就业人员平均工资
Average Wage of Employed Persons in Urban Non-private Units

单位：元 (yuan)

项　　目	Item	2012	2013	2014	2015	2016	2017	2018	2019
从业人员总计	**Total Employed persons**	**21255**	**23936**	**27414**	**30546**	**33312**	**36730**	**40209**	**43194**
按国民经济行业分	**By Sector**								
农、林、牧、渔业	Agriculture, Forestry, Animal Husbandry and Fishery	17071	19869	23179	25526	27450	28690	29889	35305
采矿业	Mining	22361	24314	27319	29201	33175	34662	36853	39199
制造业	Manufacturing	20844	23142	26867	30554	33157	36479	39704	42325
电力、燃气及水的生产和供应业	Production and Supply of Electricity, Gas and Water	21024	23711	25437	25060	30413	34239	38131	42889
建筑业	Construction	24054	27104	31471	34154	36021	40547	43665	47650
批发和零售业	Wholesale and Retail Trade	19339	23086	26384	27570	30965	34855	40076	41171
交通运输、仓储和邮政业	Transport, Storage and Post	19581	24919	26689	29940	35533	38041	40226	43009
住宿和餐饮业	Hotels and Catering Services	19352	21798	25552	28682	33817	33425	34371	37370
信息传输、软件和信息服务业	Information Transmission, Software and Information Technology	19111	22215	25343	30674	31976	37911	42472	46679
金融业	Financial Intermediation	21652	20682	24345	28828	30091	33822	39414	37287
房地产业	Real Estate	22621	26746	29808	32428	38208	40484	43995	47397
租赁和商务服务业	Leasing and Business Services	21498	24655	26967	28815	32661	37514	42797	45119
科学研究、技术服务业	Scientific Research and Technical Services	26399	28898	32733	31556	33106	39085	46650	48029
水利、环境和公共设施管理业	Management of Water Conservancy, Environment and Public Facilities	20480	24411	27333	29130	33090	34878	37145	39829
居民服务、修理和其他服务业	Services to Households, Repair and Other Services	18705	21372	24484	26621	30215	32040	35164	39395
教育	Education	21028	24772	27354	29957	32784	36190	39035	41339
卫生和社会工作	Health and Social Work	24293	25966	29323	30145	34318	39014	40083	44777
文化、体育和娱乐业	Culture, Sports and Entertainment	19982	22177	25405	26439	30192	30962	34377	39115

4-17　各市城镇私营单位就业人员平均工资

Average Wage of Empleyed Persons in Urban Non-private Units by City

单位：元　　　　　　　　　　　　　　　　　　　　　　　　　　　　　　(yuan)

市	City	2010	2011	2012	2013	2014	2015	2016	2017	2018	2019
郑　州　市	Zhengzhou	18832	22326	24686	27533	30853	33495	37998	43085	49488	51357
开　封　市	Kaifeng	16049	19153	21609	24902	28671	32628	35249	38030	41226	43304
洛　阳　市	Luoyang	16363	20583	23271	25208	29500	31613	34139	36510	37282	41828
平顶山市	Pingdingshan	17091	19374	21514	23807	25853	27980	29925	32821	35797	37563
安　阳　市	Anyang	16226	18477	20324	23003	26824	28357	31081	33038	36369	38297
鹤　壁　市	Hebi	13023	16635	18662	20581	24440	31292	34392	37548	39529	42646
新　乡　市	Xinxiang	16014	18852	21116	23552	26455	28837	30935	34669	38784	41373
焦　作　市	Jiaozuo	14171	16736	19511	22369	24714	31142	31837	33968	33975	37475
濮　阳　市	Puyang	13536	16222	18807	20489	22789	25077	27898	30357	34668	33664
许　昌　市	Xuchang	17407	20224	22378	27662	30760	37665	39601	41790	43502	43509
漯　河　市	Luohe	13692	16244	19022	23882	30471	30565	32859	35228	37919	40562
三门峡市	Sanmenxia	15659	17296	21909	23899	28835	29296	30764	32933	34115	37136
南　阳　市	Nanyang	14379	15880	18115	20263	23325	27095	30955	34106	37162	39616
商　丘　市	Shangqiu	13101	15265	18338	21696	26111	31229	35401	38705	41681	44176
信　阳　市	Xinyang	16510	18750	20649	22838	27972	29744	32190	35658	39406	43135
周　口　市	Zhoukou	14525	16912	19033	21881	25159	28005	29690	32311	35461	38958
驻马店市	Zhumadian	13968	16192	18847	22500	26155	29342	31679	34240	36947	39150
济　源　市	Jiyuan	15379	19733	25678	29938	30082	30603	33539	37216	41038	45630

4-18 各市城镇登记失业人数及失业率

Registered Unemployed Persons and Unemployment Rate in Urban Area by City

市(县) City(County)	年底登记失业人数(万人) Unemployed Persons at year-end (10 0000 person)							登记失业率(%) Registered Unemployment Rate (%)						
	2005	2010	2015	2016	2017	2018	2019	2005	2010	2015	2016	2017	2018	2019
全省 Total	**33.02**	**38.20**	**42.46**	**43.58**	**40.67**	**48.60**	**49.43**	**3.5**	**3.4**	**3.0**	**3.0**	**2.8**	**3.0**	**3.2**
省辖市 City														
郑州市 Zhengzhou	4.64	2.95	4.92	5.68	6.66	7.09	5.56	3.5	2.8	1.6	1.9	2.3	2.5	1.8
开封市 Kaifeng	2.15	2.54	1.85	1.81	2.71	2.59	3.07	3.0	3.9	2.9	2.9	2.8	2.6	3.0
洛阳市 Luoyang	2.53	2.80	4.60	4.86	4.88	8.01	8.44	3.9	3.3	3.9	4.0	3.9	4.0	3.8
平顶山市 Pingdingshan	1.93	2.01	2.82	2.64	2.18	1.69	1.21	3.6	3.2	3.3	3.1	2.7	3.1	2.2
安阳市 Anyang	1.96	2.09	2.99	3.08	2.85	2.75	2.96	3.3	3.3	3.3	3.3	3.1	3.0	3.4
鹤壁市 Hebi	0.47	0.70	0.42	0.43	0.42	0.46	0.42	4.0	3.7	1.7	2.1	1.8	1.7	1.8
新乡市 Xinxiang	2.07	2.45	4.32	4.36	4.43	4.59	3.21	2.9	3.9	4.0	3.8	3.8	3.8	3.7
焦作市 Jiaozuo	1.36	2.17	3.15	3.06	2.38	2.01	1.77	3.3	3.9	4.0	3.9	3.0	3.0	2.9
濮阳市 Puyang	1.28	0.94	1.53	1.72	1.52	1.67	1.62	3.8	2.6	2.6	2.3	2.1	2.3	3.0
许昌市 Xuchang	0.95	0.99	0.81	1.02	1.05	2.57	2.74	4.1	3.3	2.9	3.0	3.0	3.0	3.0
漯河市 Luohe	0.60	0.62	0.78	0.42	0.38	0.50	0.37	3.1	2.5	2.0	2.5	2.1	2.2	1.3
三门峡市 Sanmenxia	1.07	0.90	0.80	0.84	0.80	1.38	0.88	3.1	3.3	2.8	2.8	2.8	2.8	2.6
南阳市 Nanyang	3.31	3.70	4.02	4.21	1.70	3.84	4.10	3.8	3.3	2.8	2.7	1.2	2.6	2.8
商丘市 Shangqiu	2.42	2.52	2.70	2.83	2.63	2.45	2.26	3.4	3.6	3.7	3.7	3.6	3.5	2.3
信阳市 Xinyang	1.75	1.19	0.87	0.76	0.72	1.27	1.80	3.8	2.9	2.8	2.7	2.0	3.0	2.5
周口市 Zhoukou	2.64	3.17	3.61	3.43	3.28	3.17	2.92	3.4	4.0	2.9	3.7	3.8	3.7	3.5
驻马店市 Zhumadian	1.56	1.50	1.51	1.59	1.28	1.66	1.83	3.7	3.4	3.1	3.2	2.6	2.8	2.0
济源市 Jiyuan	0.33	0.69	0.77	0.83	0.82	0.89	0.95	3.3	3.3	2.9	2.9	2.8	3.0	3.0
省直管县 County Directly Administrated by Province														
巩义市 Gongyi	0.19	0.47	0.58	0.58	0.58	0.26	0.26	0.8	2.0	2.7	2.7	2.7	3.0	2.3
兰考县 Lankao	0.48	0.10	0.02	0.01	0.01	0.17	0.14	4.4	3.2	0.6	0.1	0.2	2.8	1.5
汝州市 Ruzhou	0.16	0.21	0.28	0.27	0.25	0.57	0.31	3.4	3.8	3.2	3.5	3.1	3.4	3.0
滑县 Huaxian	0.19	0.13	0.25	0.28	0.23	0.22	0.24	3.9	3.7	4.0	4.0	4.0	3.5	2.2
长垣县 Changyuan	0.14	0.23	0.21	0.21	0.21	0.22	0.44	4.2	3.8	3.3	3.4	3.4	3.6	2.7
邓州市 Dengzhou	0.18	0.14	0.87	0.83	0.66	0.15	0.18	3.4	2.4	3.6	3.5	3.3	0.8	1.0
永城市 Yongcheng	0.14	0.27	0.27	0.27	0.26	0.26	0.34	3.9	4.0	3.9	3.9	3.8	3.8	2.3
固始县 Gushi	0.16	0.17	0.07	0.05	0.04	0.48	0.48	3.2	3.2	1.3	0.9	0.4	4.0	3.9
鹿邑县 Luyi	0.21	0.15	0.35	0.35	0.35	0.30	0.22	4.1	3.8	3.9	3.9	3.9	3.8	3.8
新蔡县 Xincai	0.15	0.08	0.21	0.22	0.21	0.22	0.16	3.1	2.8	2.9	3.0	2.9	3.1	3.0

注：本表数据来源于河南省人力资源和社会保障厅。

a) Data in this table are from the Department of Human Resources and Social Security of Henan Province.

主要统计指标解释

就业人员　指在一定年龄以上，有劳动能力，为取得劳动报酬或经营收入而从事一定社会劳动的人员。具体指年满16周岁，为取得报酬或经营利润，在调查周内从事了1小时（含1小时）以上劳动的人员；或由于学习、休假等原因在调查周内暂时处于未工作状态，但有工作单位或场所的人员；或由于临时停工放假、单位不景气放假等原因在调查周内暂时处于未工作状态，但不满三个月的人员。

单位就业人员　指报告期末最后一日24时在本单位工作，并取得工资或其他形式劳动报酬的人员数。该指标为时点指标，不包括最后一日当天及以前已经与单位解除劳动合同关系的人员，是在岗职工、劳务派遣人员及其他就业人员之和。就业人员不包括：

(1)离开本单位仍保留劳动关系，并定期领取生活费的人员；

(2)利用课余时间打工的学生及在本单位实习的各类在校学生；

(3)本单位因劳务外包而使用的人员。

城镇私营和个体就业人员　城镇私营就业人员指在工商管理部门注册登记，其经营地址设在县城关镇(含县城关镇)以上的私营企业就业人员，包括私营企业投资者和雇工。城镇个体就业人员指在工商管理部门注册登记，并持有城镇户口或在城镇长期居住，经批准从事个体工商经营的就业人员，包括个体经营者和在个体工商户劳动的家庭帮工和雇工。

在岗职工　指在本单位工作且与本单位签订劳动合同，并由单位支付各项工资和社会保险、住房公积金的人员，以及上述人员中由于学习、病伤、产假等原因暂未工作仍由单位支付工资的人员。在岗职工还包括：

(1)应订立劳动合同而未订立劳动合同人员(如使用的农村户籍人员)；

(2)处于试用期人员；

(3)编制外招用的人员；

(4)派往外单位工作，但工资仍由本单位发放的人员(如挂职锻炼、外派工作等情况)。

工资总额　指根据《关于工资总额组成的规定》(1990年1月1日国家统计局发布的一号令)进行修订，本单位在报告期内(季度或年度)直接支付给本单位全部就业人员的劳动报酬总额。包括计时工资、计件工资、奖金、津贴和补贴、加班加点工资、特殊情况下支付的工资，是在岗职工工资总额、劳务派遣人员工资总额和其他就业人员工资总额之和。

工资总额是税前工资，包括单位从个人工资中直接为其代扣或代缴的房费、水费、电费、住房公积金和社会保险基金个人缴纳部分等。

工资总额不论是计入成本的还是不计入成本的，不论是以货币形式支付的还是以实物形式支付的，均应列入工资总额的计算范围。

平均工资　指单位就业人员在一定时期内平均每人所得的货币工资额。它表明一定时期职工工资收入的高低程度，是反映就业人员工资水平的主要指标。计算公式为：

$$平均工资=\frac{报告期实际支付的全部就业人员工资总额}{报告期全部就业人员平均人数}$$

平均工资指数　指报告期就业人员平均工资与基期就业人员平均工资的比率，是反映不同时期就业人员货币工资水平变动情况的相对数。计算公式为：

$$平均工资指数=\frac{报告期就业人员平均工资}{基期就业人员平均工资}\times100\%$$

平均实际工资指数　就业人员平均实际工资指扣除物价变动因素后的就业人员平均工资。就业人员平均实际工资指数是反映实际工资变动情况的相对数，表明就业人员实际工资水平提高或降低的程度。计算公式为：

$$平均实际工资指数=\frac{报告期就业人员平均工资指数}{报告期城镇居民消费价格指数}\times100\%$$

城镇登记失业人员　指有非农业户口，在一定的劳动年龄内(16 周岁至退休年龄)，有劳动能力，无业而要求就业，并在当地劳动保障部门进行失业登记的人员。

城镇登记失业率　城镇登记失业人员与城镇单位就业人员(扣除使用的农村劳动力、聘用的离退休人员、港澳台及外方人员)、城镇单位中的不在岗职工、城镇私营业主、个体户主、城镇私营企业和个体就业人员、城镇登记失业人员之和的比。

城镇单位为城镇非私营单位；由于城镇非私营单位数调整，有不可比因素。

Explanatory Notes on Main Statistical Indicators

Employed Persons refers to persons above a specified age who had labour capacity and performed some social work for compensation or business gains. Specifically, it refers to persons, aged 16 and over, who performed some work for compensation or business gains for one hour or more during the reference period; or persons who do not work for the reasons of study or on holiday, but had work units or sites during the reference period; or persons temporary absence from a job for disorganization or suspension of work, recession, etc, but not exceeding three months during the reference period.

Persons Employed in Various Units refer to the total number of employees who work at his unit and obtain wages or other forms of payment at the end of the reporting period. This indicator is a kind of time point index and it equals to the sum of the number of employed staff and workers, labor dispatch personnel and other employed persons. Employed persons do not include:

1) persons who have left their working units while keeping their labour contract (employment relation) unchanged and receiving regular alimony;

2) students who do part-time jobs in spare time and all kinds of enrolled students who do internship in various units;

3) persons employed due to labor outsourcing;

4) persons who dissolve labor contracts with their units on the last day of reporting period or before.

Persons Employed in Private Enterprises and Self-Employed Individuals in Urban Areas Persons employed in private enterprises refer to the persons employed in the private enterprises which have been registered at the departments of industrial and commercial administration for which the business operation are situated at a county town (i.e. a town where the county government is located), or at urban areas with administrative hierarchy higher than a county town. The self-employed individuals in urban areas refer to persons who hold the certificates of residence in urban areas or have resided in the urban areas for a long time and have been registered at the departments of industrial and commercial administration and approved to be engaged in individual industrial or commercial business, including self-employed persons as well as helpers and hired laborers who work in individual households.

Employed Staff and Workers refer to persons who signed labor contracts with working units and working units would pay wages, social insurance and housing funds for them. Persons who have their work posts but are temporarily absent from work for reasons of study or on sick, injury or maternal leave and still receive wages from their working units are also included. Employed staff and workers also include:

1) Persons who should have signed the labor contracts but not (like people with rural household registration);

2) Employees on probation;

3) Employees beyond the staffing quota;

4) Employees who are sent to other working units but still obtain wages from their original units (situations like on-the-job placement, expatriated assignment, etc.)

1) Employed Staff and Workers do not include: Dispatched personnel who work and are paid directly by the working units; they shall be counted into "labour dispatch personnel" of the working units;

2) Personnel through labor outsourcing, they shall be counted into "employed staff and workers" of the units which contracted them.

Total Wage Bill It is revised according to the "Provision of Composition of Total Wages" (Order No.1 by National Bureau of Statistics on January, 1st, ,1990), total wage bill refers to the total remuneration payment to all employed persons in various units during the reporting period (by quarter or by year), including hourly-paid wages, piece-rate wages, bonuses, allowance and subsidies, overtime wages and wages paid under special circumstances. It equals to the sum of total wages of employed staff and workers, dispatch labors and other employed persons.

Total wage bill is pre-tax wages, including the room charges, utility bills, housing funds and social insurance paid or withheld by employee's units.

Total wage bill, whether or not included in cost, whether or not paid in money or in kind, shall be included in the calculation of total wage.

Average Wage refers to the average per capita wage in money terms during a certain period of time for employed persons. It shows the general level of wage income of staff and worker during a certain period of time, one major indicator to reflect the wage level. It is calculated as follows:

$$\text{Average Wage} = \frac{\text{Total Wage Bill of Employed Persons at Reference Time}}{\text{Average Number of Persons Employed at Reference Time}}$$

Average Wage Indices refers to the ratio of average wage of employed persons the reporting period to that at the base period, which reflects the change of wage of employed persons at the different period. It is calculated as follows:

$$\text{Average Wage Indices} = \frac{\text{Average Wage of Employed Persons at Reference Time}}{\text{Average Wage of Persons Employeds at Base Period}} \times 100\%$$

Average Real Wage Indices average real wage of employed persons refers to the average wage of employed persons after removing the effects of the price changes and average real wage indices of employed persons refers to the change of real wage, which reflects the relative increasing or decreasing level of real wage of employed persons ,which is calculated as follows:

$$\text{Average Real Wage Indices} = \frac{\text{Average Wage Indices of Employed Persons at the Reference Time}}{\text{Urban Consumer Price Indices at Reference Time}} \times 100\%$$

Registered Unemployed Persons in Urban Areas refer to the persons with non-agricultural household registration at certain working ages (16 years old to retirement age), who are capable of working, unemployed and willing to work, and have been registered at the local employment service agencies to apply for a job.

Registered Unemployment Rate in Urban Areas refers to the ratio of the number of the registered unemployed persons to the sum of the number of persons employed in various units (minus the employed rural labour force, re-employed retirees, and Hong Kong, Macao, Taiwan or foreign employees), laid-off staff and workers in urban units, owners of private enterprises in urban areas, owners of self-employed individuals in urban areas, employees of private enterprises in urban areas, employee of self-employed individuals in urban areas, and the registered unemployed persons in urban areas.

Urban units are non-private units in urban area, and due to the adjustment of the number of non-private units in urban area,there are non-comparable factors.

固定资产投资

Investment in Fixed Assets

5

● 资料整理：呼晓飞

简要说明

一、主要内容

本篇包括固定资产投资的规模、结构和比例关系、资金来源、投资效果及大型项目等资料。

二、统计范围

固定资产投资统计范围包括：城乡计划总投资500万元及500万元以上建设项目投资，房地产开发投资,不包括农户投资。

三、统计口径的变化

自1997年起，除房地产开发投资、农村非农户投资、个人投资及城镇和工矿区私人建房投资外，固定资产投资的统计起点由5万元提高到50万元。自2006年起，非农户固定资产投资统计改为按项目统计，调查方法由抽样调查改为全面统计报表，起点提高到50万元。城镇和工矿区私人建房投资改为按项目统计，起点为50万元。自2011年起，固定资产投资的统计起点由50万元提高到500万元,2010年新口径数据与2011年标准一致；取消“城镇固定资产投资”指标。

四、资料来源

农村农户投资数据来源于农村住户抽样调查，除此以外的固定资产投资统计资料均为全面统计报表，由河南省统计局固定资产投资统计处编辑整理。

Brief Introduction

I. Main Contents

Statistics in this chapter include the size, growth, structure, ratio, financing and results of the investment in fixed assets and major projects.

II. Scope of Statistics

Statistics on the investment in fixed assets cover investments in capital construction projects investment 5 million yuan and over , investments in real estate development. Farm household investment are not included.

III. Changes in Statistical Scope

Since 1997, the cut-off point of projects covered by statistics of investment in fixed assets are raised from an investment of 50,000 yuan to 500,000 yuan, except investment in real estate development, farm household investment, non-farm household investment and private investment in housing construction in urban areas and industrial and mining areas. Since 2006, statistics on investments in fixed assets of rural non-farm households are changed to project-based, the sample survey method changed from Sampling survey to comprehensive statistics, investments in private investment in housing construction in urban areas and industrial and mining areas The cut-off point has been raised to 500,000 yuan. Since 2011, the cut-off point of projects covered by statistics of investment in fixed assets are raised from an investment of 500,000 yuan to 5 million yuan, and the same as New caliber data on 2010Index of investment in fixed assets in unban areas was canceled.

IV. Sources of Data

Data on individual investments in fixed assets in rural areas are collected through sample surveys, Other data on investment in fixed assets are collected by the system of reporting form with complete enumeration, which are provided by the Department of investment in fixed assets of the Henan provincial Bureau of Statistics.

5-1 固定资产投资增速

Growth Rate of Investment in Fixed Assets in the whole Province

单位：% (%)

年 份 Year	固定资产投资 Investment	#工业投资 Industry Investment	#民间投资 Private Investment	#基础设施投资 Infrastructure Investment
1986	11.4		8.4	
1987	12.1		6.4	
1988	30.2		37.7	
1989	-7.3		-13.2	
1990	11.9		24.8	21.6
1991	25.9	31.5		29.6
1992	42.6	15.9	95.9	44.4
1993	58.0	35.9	64.8	95.4
1994	41.8	31.1	47.3	51.8
1995	27.4	26.5	43.9	37.3
1996	23.5	18.7	43.8	29.7
1997	11.1	2.1	26.7	12.9
1998	6.9	-7.6	3.9	16.3
1999	2.5	19.8	6.4	10.1
2000	9.6	10.4	3.6	21.0
2001	11.0	7.5	14.0	14.2
2002	13.6	9.3	21.8	8.1
2003	33.7	58.8	47.1	31.9
2004	38.7	54.5	29.9	27.0
2005	42.8	50.6	68.5	26.5
2006	37.4	39.5	55.8	22.7
2007	37.4	50.9	61.1	3.7
2008	32.4	32.0	40.3	16.4
2009	31.6	29.1	39.9	36.2
2010	22.2	18.2	25.1	19.4
2011	27.0	34.0	29.0	18.1
2012	21.4	21.0	24.8	16.2
2013	22.5	19.1	24.2	18.3
2014	19.2	17.1	23.2	19.1
2015	16.5	10.7	16.6	35.1
2016	13.7	8.9	5.9	29.0
2017	10.4	3.5	9.1	30.4
2018	8.1	2.0	2.9	18.5
2019	8.0	9.7	6.7	16.1

5-2 固定资产投资结构

Structure of Investment in Fixed Assets in the whole Province

单位：% (%)

年份 Year	固定资产投资 Investment	#工业投资 Industry Investment	#民间投资 Private Investment	#基础设施投资 Infrastructure Investment
1985	100.0		21.9	
1986	100.0		21.3	
1987	100.0		20.2	
1988	100.0		21.4	
1989	100.0		20.0	
1990	100.0	63.0	22.3	21.1
1991	100.0	65.8	17.7	21.7
1992	100.0	53.5	24.4	22.0
1993	100.0	46.0	25.4	27.2
1994	100.0	42.6	26.4	29.1
1995	100.0	42.3	29.8	31.4
1996	100.0	40.6	34.7	33.0
1997	100.0	37.3	39.6	33.5
1998	100.0	32.3	38.4	36.5
1999	100.0	37.7	39.9	39.2
2000	100.0	38.0	37.7	43.3
2001	100.0	36.8	38.7	44.5
2002	100.0	35.4	41.5	42.4
2003	100.0	42.0	45.7	41.8
2004	100.0	46.8	42.8	38.3
2005	100.0	49.3	50.5	33.9
2006	100.0	50.1	57.3	30.3
2007	100.0	55.0	67.2	22.8
2008	100.0	54.8	71.2	20.1
2009	100.0	53.8	75.7	20.8
2010	100.0	52.1	77.4	20.3
2011	100.0	53.8	78.6	14.0
2012	100.0	53.6	80.9	13.4
2013	100.0	52.1	81.9	12.9
2014	100.0	51.2	84.7	12.9
2015	100.0	48.7	84.9	15.0
2016	100.0	46.6	79.0	17.0
2017	100.0	43.7	78.1	20.1
2018	100.0	28.5	71.2	22.5
2019	100.0	28.9	70.3	19.8

5-3 按行业分固定资产投资增速及比重(2019年)

Growth Rate and Proportion of Investment in Fixed Assets by Registration Status and Sector (2019)

单位：% (%)

指 标	Item	增速 Growth Rate	比重 Proportion
总 计	**Total**	**8.0**	**100.0**
农、林、牧、渔业	**Agriculture, Forestry, animal Husbandry and Fishery**	**-10.9**	**4.0**
农业	Agriculture	-19.4	2.2
林业	Forestry	25.5	0.5
畜牧业	Animal Husbandry	-13.9	0.9
渔业	Fishery	128.8	0.1
农、林、牧、渔服务业	Services in Support of Agriculture, Forestry, Animal Husbandry and Fishery	16.4	0.2
工业	**Industry**	**9.7**	**28.9**
采矿业	Mining	47.2	0.9
煤炭开采和洗选业	Mining and Washing of Coal	31.9	0.2
石油和天然气开采业	Extraction of Petroleum and Natural Gas	60.8	0.1
黑色金属矿采选业	Mining of Ferrous Metal Ores	840.9	
有色金属矿采选业	Mining of Non-ferrous Metal Ores	22.8	0.3
非金属矿采选业	Mining and Processing of Nonmetal Ores	76.5	0.3
开采辅助活动	Support Activities for Mining	92.7	0.1
其他采矿业	Mining of Other Ores	-16.8	
制造业	Manufacturing	8.2	23.8
农副食品加工业	Processing of Food from Agricultural Products	2.6	1.4
食品制造业	Manufacture of Foods	4.5	1.0
酒、饮料和精制茶制造业	Manufacture of Liquor, Beverevges and Refined Tea	20.9	0.6
烟草制造业	Manufacture of Tobacco	-87.3	
纺织业	Manufacture of Textile	8.4	0.7
纺织服装、服饰业	Manufacture of Textile, Wearing Apparel and Accessories	-0.3	0.9
皮革、毛皮、羽毛及其制品和制鞋业	Manufacture of Leather, Fur, Feather and Its Products, Footwear	6.0	0.6
木材加工及木、竹、藤、棕、草制品业	Processing of Timbers, Manufacture of Wood, Bamboo, Rattan, Palm, and Straw Products	-11.8	0.4
家具制造业	Manufacture of Furniture	-2.9	0.8
造纸及纸制品业	Manufacture of Paper and Paper Products	-1.7	0.3
印刷和记录媒介复制业	Printing,Reproduction of Recording Media	3.0	0.1
文教、工美、体育和娱乐用品制造业	Manufacture of Articles for Culture, Arts and Crafts, Sport and Entertainment Activities	-8.5	0.2
石油加工、炼焦及核燃料加工业	Processing of Petroleum ,Coking, Processing of Nucleus Fuel	24.1	0.3

5-3 续表 1 continued

单位：% (%)

指 标	Item	增速 Growth Rate	比重 Proportion
化学原料及化学制品制造业	Manufacture of Raw Chemical Material and Chemical Products	9.1	1.6
医药制造业	Manufacture of Medicines	-11.7	0.7
化学纤维制造业	Manufacture of Chemical Fiber	87.2	0.2
橡胶和塑料制品业	Manufacture of Rubber and Plastic Products	0.0	0.7
非金属矿物制品业	Manufacture of Non-metallic Mineral Products	29.7	3.4
黑色金属冶炼和压延加工业	Smering and pressing of Ferrous Metals	7.2	0.2
有色金属冶炼及压延加工业	Smelting and Pressing of Non-ferrous Metals	23.0	0.9
金属制品业	Manufacture of Metal Products	-0.1	1.3
通用设备制造业	Manufacture of General Purpose Machinery	16.7	1.5
专业设备制造业	Manufacture of Special Purpose Machinery	-6.7	1.3
汽车制造业	Manufacture of Automobile	7.8	1.2
铁路、船舶、航空航天和其他运输设备制造业	Manufacture of Railway, Ship, Aerospace, and other Transport Equipment	-9.4	0.3
电气机械及器材制造业	Manufacture of Electrical Machinery and Equipment	0.9	1.4
计算机、通信和其他电子设备制造业	Manufacture of Computer, Communication and Other Electronic Equipment	15.2	1.0
仪器仪表制造业	Manufacture of Measuring Instrument and Machinery	0.2	0.2
其他制造业	Manufacture of Others	20.2	0.2
废弃资源综合利用业	Comprehensive Utilization of Waste Resources	45.8	0.5
金属制品、机械和设备修理业	Repairing of Metal Products, Machinery and Equipment	470.8	0.0
电力、燃气及水的生产和供应业	Production and Distribution of Electricity, Gas and Water	12.0	4.2
电力、热力生产和供应业	Production and Supply of Electric Power and Heat Power	10.3	3.1
燃气生产和供应业	Production and Supply of Gas	62.7	0.5
水的生产和供应业	Production and Supply of Water	-5.7	0.6
建筑业	**Construction**	**-92.3**	**0.0**
#房屋建筑业	Building Construction	-88.3	0.0
批发和零售业	**Wholesale and Retail Trade**	**-26.5**	**1.4**
#批发业	Wholesale	-9.9	0.5
交通运输、仓储和邮政业	**Transport, Storage and Post**	**4.8**	**6.1**
#铁路运输	Transport via Railway	41.1	0.4
道路运输业	Transport via road	7.8	4.5
装卸搬运和仓储业	Loading, Unloading and Storage	-0.5	0.9
邮政业	Post	31.1	0.0

5-3 续表 2 continued

单位：% (%)

指　　标	Item	增速 Growth Rate	比重 Proportion
住宿和餐饮业	**Hotels and Catering Services**	**-3.3**	**0.5**
#住宿业	Hotels	0.5	0.4
信息传输、软件和信息技术服务业	**Information Transmission and Information Technology services**	**-10.6**	**0.4**
#电信、广播电视和卫星传输服务业	Telecom,Radio,Television and Satellite Transmission Service	-26.0	0.1
互联网和相关服务	Internet and Related Services	-16.7	0.1
金融业	**Finance**	**6.7**	**0.1**
#货币金融服务	Monetary and Financial Services	68.7	0.1
保险业	Insurance	102.1	0.0
房地产业	**Real Estate**	**5.8**	**35.9**
租赁和商务服务业	**Leasing and Business Services**	**44.9**	**1.7**
#商务服务业	Business Service	44.8	1.6
科学研究和技术服务业	**Scientific Research and Technical Service**	**-3.0**	**0.7**
#研究和试验发展	Research and Experimental Development	-0.8	0.2
专业技术服务业	Professional Technique Services	-21.4	0.2
水利、环境和公共设施管理业	**Management of Water Conservancy, Environment and Public Facilities**	**21.5**	**14.4**
水利管理业	Management of Water Conservancy	4.2	1.3
生态保护和环境治理业	Ecological Protection and Environmental Management	67.4	1.0
公共设施管理业	Management of Public Facilities	20.8	12.1
居民服务、修理和其他服务业	**Service to Households, Repair and other Services**	**-11.4**	**0.2**
#居民服务业	Service to Households	-1.0	0.1
教育	**Education**	**24.6**	**2.2**
卫生和社会工作	**Health and Social Work**	**21.6**	**1.4**
#卫生	Health	29.6	1.0
文化、体育和娱乐业	**Culture, Sports and Entertainment**	**23.1**	**1.8**
#广播、电视、电影和影视录音制作业	Broadcasting,Movies,Television and Audiovisual Activities	99.6	0.1
文化艺术业	Culture and Art	9.6	0.6
公共管理、社会保障和社会组织	**Public Management,Social welfare and Social Organization**	**-38.3**	**0.3**
国家机构	Organ of State	-38.6	0.3
社会保障	Social welfare	-81.9	0.0

5-4 各市分行业固定资产投资增速(2019年)

单位：%

市(县) City(County)	合计 Total	农林牧渔业 Agriculture Forestry, Animal Husbandry and Fishery	工业 Industry	建筑业 Construction	批发和零售业 Wholesale and Retail Trade	交通运输仓储及邮政业 Transport, Storage and Post	住宿和餐饮业 Hotels and Catering Services	信息传输、软件和信息技术服务业 Information Transmission, Software and Information Technology Services
全　省 Total	**8.0**	**-10.9**	**9.7**	**-92.3**	**-26.5**	**4.8**	**-3.3**	**-10.6**
省辖市 City								
郑州市 Zhengzhou	2.8	-26.2	1.6	-80.6	-33.9	-14.9	290.4	-12.1
开封市 Kaifeng	10.8	69.9	2.8		-79.3	4.4	-55.2	
洛阳市 Luoyang	10.2	-27.0	9.0	-69.3	2.9	28.2	13.2	-21.8
平顶山市 Pingdingshan	9.1	-34.6	17.0		-11.5	2.5	-20.1	-35.2
安阳市 Anyang	-11.5	-41.5	-20.8		-63.6	-16.2	-79.1	-57.3
鹤壁市 Hebi	11.3	-25.4	38.0		-14.6	78.8	74.0	-59.0
新乡市 Xinxiang	11.3	-29.1	-1.2		24.9	62.8	-25.4	-32.7
焦作市 Jiaozuo	12.0	23.9	10.3		-24.3	10.2	45.7	36.8
濮阳市 Puyang	5.5	29.8	-3.7		-26.2	-2.3		-99.4
许昌市 Xuchang	5.2	37.8	0.4		9.3	-15.9	-44.6	3.5
漯河市 Luohe	11.4	-59.8	4.4		-3.3	62.7	-2.1	4.8
三门峡市 Sanmenxia	10.2	-2.2	28.9		-37.5	11.8	29.1	-34.0
南阳市 Nanyang	10.4	-19.2	25.1		-28.0	18.0	63.0	-29.0
商丘市 Shangqiu	10.9	-13.2	11.3		-32.8	-7.5	86.9	-19.3
信阳市 Xinyang	10.6	5.1	13.1		2.4	40.8	-29.2	42.7
周口市 Zhoukou	9.8	4.0	-10.1		-30.0	-4.4	-19.4	-13.6
驻马店市 Zhumadian	11.7	2.8	19.6		-31.2	23.8	-45.1	115.7
济源市 Jiyuan	12.0	-19.4	21.9		-56.0	-15.2	-14.8	-6.3
省直管县 County Directly Administrated by Province								
巩义市 Gongyi	9.1	172.3	-2.6		-38.9	-25.5	1202.8	
兰考县 Lankao	10.0	69.9	-35.6		-8.4	-99.4	238.8	
汝州市 Ruzhou	-14.5	-4.4	-18.2		-2.8	-11.6		
滑县 Huaxian	-33.5	-60.2	-47.6		-78.5	-18.8	-62.4	
长垣市 Changyuan	10.0	-10.6	-11.7		-81.3	-17.8	96.3	
邓州市 Dengzhou	5.3	8.0	14.8		3.6	-2.1		-60.3
永城市 Yongcheng	10.0	-62.1	19.0		-51.9	131.4	176.8	33.3
固始县 Gushi	10.0	-2.7	12.3		-17.5	-46.8	-75.3	
鹿邑县 Luyi	10.0	12.1	30.5		65.7	-5.8		
新蔡县 Xincai	10.0	-35.2	6.1		-56.8	68.7		225.4

Growth Rate of Investment in Fixed Assets by Sector and City (2019)

(%)

金融业 Finance	房地产业 Real Estate	租赁和商务服务业 Leasing and Business Services	科学研究和技术服务业 Scientific Research, and Technical Service	水利、环境和公共设施管理业 Management of Water Conservancy, Environment and Public Facilities	居民服务、修理和其他服务业 Service to Households, Repair and other Services	教育 Education	卫生和社会工作 Health and Social work	文化、体育和娱乐业 Culture, Sports and Entertainment	公共管理、社会保障和社会组织 Public Management, Social Security and Social Organization
6.7	**5.8**	**44.9**	**-3.0**	**21.5**	**-11.4**	**24.6**	**21.6**	**23.1**	**-38.3**
-23.6	-0.6	75.2	13.8	33.0	-26.6	20.5	-14.2	-7.9	67.5
486.2	26.2	90.8	102.7	20.4	-71.1	-37.1	59.2	-22.8	-45.9
-74.1	2.9	2.2	-15.8	23.0	-19.2	52.7	11.4	66.3	20.9
-84.2	8.0	32.7	-21.2	24.5	8.1	36.1	68.6	10.5	-81.7
	9.2	-71.1	21.3	-32.3	-87.4	171.9	-22.3	10.4	15.4
	2.7	75.7	-78.8	11.4	77.8	25.3	56.5	11.3	176.3
	0.9	115.2	15.6	56.6	-11.4	37.6	63.5	42.0	112.5
	1.2	15.4	35.9	13.8	39.0	14.7	9.9	18.8	-98.1
	16.5	43.7	165.8	-9.2		38.6	83.1	23.1	-76.9
	25.3	87.3	-67.7	12.3		-49.2	-2.7	8.8	-83.0
	16.9	15.5	400.0	27.5		9.6	57.1	-58.8	-10.5
	2.1	35.7	20.4	7.9	6.8	-2.8	-24.8	108.8	-72.8
	10.1	45.7	29.2	6.3	25.8	53.7	11.2	-40.0	-56.7
	13.2	93.8	68.2	40.6	-46.3	-18.2	9.8	20.3	-82.8
	-3.9		25.9	8.3	85.6	34.1	153.0	154.2	-17.4
	38.9	-16.1	-54.9	55.7	47.1	124.5	43.6	-16.1	-50.0
-22.8	9.7	-0.8	23.7	7.4	-90.5	22.0	17.5	-5.1	58.4
	-6.8	-2.7	-71.8	55.3	1.2	124.8	-80.7	21.2	
	3.5	338.3	1.5	84.6	69.1	27.4	-58.1	-70.6	-84.4
	51.1	117.8	-90.7	58.3		-21.6		349.2	-18.7
	8.5	-44.2		-13.2	-86.4	-11.5	56.7	-48.2	-95.0
	24.5	218.1	64.7	-26.6		101.2	-81.2	273.5	
	-11.6	69.8	23.7	40.9		40.9	439.9		
-96.2	-2.4	45.7	-86.3	8.6		2.5	-66.2	18.3	45.6
	-29.0	-34.4	-61.3	77.1	160.1	326.0	316.7		-10.6
	31.0	96.1	-11.1	-5.2		55.3	286.1	-8.3	205.3
	18.2	-21.8	111.3	-33.9		-25.9	-45.6		-58.8
	22.0	-80.0	-27.3	31.3	-44.2	180.8	118.4	-10.4	-92.7

5-5 各市分行业固定资产投资比重(2019年)

单位：%

市(县) City(County)	合 计 Total	农 林 牧渔业 Agriculture Forestry, Animal Husbandry and Fishery	工 业 Industry	建筑业 Constru-ction	批发和 零售业 Whole-sale and Retail Trade	交通运输 仓 储 及 邮 政 业 Transport, Storage and Post	住宿和 餐饮业 Hotels and Catering Services	信息传输、 软件和信息 技术服务业 Information Transmission, Software and Information Technology Services
全 省 Total	**100.0**	**4.0**	**28.9**	**0.0**	**1.4**	**6.1**	**0.5**	**0.4**
省 辖 市 City								
郑 州 市 Zhengzhou	100.0	0.4	10.6	0.0	0.5	6.4	0.1	0.7
开 封 市 Kaifeng	100.0	3.6	33.3	0.1	0.8	1.3	1.0	
洛 阳 市 Luoyang	100.0	5.4	34.6	0.0	1.2	7.9	1.0	0.3
平 顶 山 市 Pingdingshan	100.0	4.7	32.6		2.2	6.5	0.7	0.2
安 阳 市 Anyang	100.0	3.0	30.7		0.6	4.9	0.1	0.2
鹤 壁 市 Hebi	100.0	2.8	41.3		2.2	5.0	0.8	0.8
新 乡 市 Xinxiang	100.0	1.7	33.4		1.6	4.1	0.6	0.0
焦 作 市 Jiaozuo	100.0	1.3	45.1		2.9	6.7	1.3	1.3
濮 阳 市 Puyang	100.0	3.6	31.0		1.9	6.7		0.0
许 昌 市 Xuchang	100.0	2.7	32.9		0.8	5.1	0.4	0.5
漯 河 市 Luohe	100.0	0.5	42.5		4.3	6.5	0.6	0.4
三 门 峡 市 Sanmenxia	100.0	16.7	39.6		2.0	6.8	0.6	0.3
南 阳 市 Nanyang	100.0	8.0	37.7		2.8	7.3	0.7	0.4
商 丘 市 Shangqiu	100.0	1.2	39.3		1.9	3.4	0.3	0.0
信 阳 市 Xinyang	100.0	7.3	24.0		0.9	7.5	0.7	0.6
周 口 市 Zhoukou	100.0	5.6	36.8		1.8	4.4	0.5	0.4
驻 马 店 市 Zhumadian	100.0	4.1	30.8		1.0	5.6	0.4	0.1
济 源 市 Jiyuan	100.0	3.1	46.4		1.8	11.8	1.3	1.2
省 直 管 县 County Directly Administrated by Province								
巩 义 市 Gongyi	100.0	1.6	41.9		1.1	4.3	1.5	
兰 考 县 Lankao	100.0	13.6	26.9	0.4	1.3	0.0	0.3	
汝 州 市 Ruzhou	100.0	1.9	23.6		3.3	6.6		
滑 县 Huaxian	100.0	7.1	45.4		1.0	2.6	0.4	
长 垣 市 Changyuan	100.0	3.4	34.4		0.1	0.2	1.6	
邓 州 市 Dengzhou	100.0	10.7	31.8		1.3	5.0		0.0
永 城 市 Yongcheng	100.0	1.0	63.4		0.8	7.2	0.2	0.1
固 始 县 Gushi	100.0	4.6	27.3		2.0	1.7	0.4	
鹿 邑 县 Luyi	100.0	3.8	52.7		0.1	8.2		
新 蔡 县 Xincai	100.0	4.4	29.3		1.4	6.9		0.3

Proportion of Investment in Fixed Assets by Sector and City (2019)

(%)

金融业 Finance	房地产业 Real Estate	租赁和商务服务业 Leasing and Business Services	科学研究和技术服务业 Scientific Research, and Technical Service	水利、环境和公共设施管理业 Management of Water Conservancy, Environment and Public Facilities	居民服务、修理和其他服务业 Service to Households, Repair and other Services	教育 Education	卫生和社会工作 Health and Social work	文化、体育和娱乐业 Culture, Sports and Entertainment	公共管理、社会保障和社会组织 Public Management, Social Security and Social Organization
0.1	**35.9**	**1.7**	**0.7**	**14.4**	**0.2**	**2.2**	**1.4**	**1.8**	**0.3**
0.2	60.7	1.9	0.7	14.1	0.3	1.7	0.4	0.9	0.3
0.5	40.3	2.9	0.8	10.2	0.1	0.9	1.6	2.3	0.2
0.0	15.7	1.8	1.4	23.1	0.3	1.6	1.6	3.7	0.5
0.0	24.6	2.9	0.8	15.6	0.3	3.7	2.2	2.9	0.2
	40.6	0.8	0.3	10.0	0.0	5.1	1.2	2.3	0.2
	25.1	1.4	0.7	10.4	0.6	2.3	1.3	4.6	0.8
0.1	34.3	5.3	0.6	11.8	0.1	2.5	1.7	1.2	0.8
0.1	22.0	2.2	0.7	9.4	0.3	3.5	1.5	1.8	0.0
	41.4	0.8	1.2	8.5	0.0	2.0	1.0	1.6	0.2
	36.4	1.4	0.4	13.5	0.1	1.7	2.2	1.7	0.4
0.1	30.0	1.7	0.2	8.7	0.0	2.4	1.5	0.3	0.4
	14.3	0.6	0.7	14.3	0.1	1.5	1.0	1.5	0.1
0.1	17.4	1.4	0.6	15.4	0.1	4.1	2.6	1.1	0.4
	35.4	1.1	0.9	12.2	0.1	2.0	1.1	0.8	0.1
0.1	33.3	0.2	0.2	16.1	0.2	3.4	2.0	3.3	0.2
	31.6	0.8	0.2	11.2	0.2	2.4	2.6	1.2	0.3
0.1	38.2	0.5	0.7	13.6	0.0	1.3	1.5	1.1	1.0
	7.6	1.8	0.1	20.5	0.4	2.5	0.1	1.3	0.1
	23.9	2.6	1.3	19.1	1.2	0.7	0.2	0.3	0.3
	30.5	2.7	0.1	17.0	0.3	2.2	2.7	0.4	1.4
	31.2	3.8	0.5	19.5	0.1	3.7	2.9	2.6	0.2
	26.1	1.9	0.2	6.5		5.1	0.2	3.4	
	18.1	14.9	1.6	17.4		4.6	1.0	2.7	
0.0	25.6	0.6	0.1	19.5		3.2	0.4	0.5	1.2
	15.8	0.1	0.1	6.2	0.1	1.5	1.4	1.5	0.5
0.6	31.2	0.2	0.2	21.0		4.0	4.2	2.4	0.1
	22.1	2.4	0.2	7.1		1.1	2.1		0.2
	29.1	0.5	1.7	16.7	0.1	5.3	2.8	1.2	0.1

5-6 各市固定资产投资增速(2019年)
Growth Rate of Investment in Fixed Assets by City (2019)

单位：% (%)

市(县) City(County)	固定资产投资 Investment in Fixed Assets	第一产业 Primary Industry	第二产业 Secondary Industry	第三产业 Tertiary Industry
全　　省 Total	**8.0**	**-12.1**	**9.0**	**9.0**
省 辖 市 City				
郑　州　市 Zhengzhou	2.8	-26.1	1.2	3.2
开　封　市 Kaifeng	10.8	75.0	2.9	13.0
洛　阳　市 Luoyang	10.2	-25.9	8.4	16.2
平 顶 山 市 Pingdingshan	9.1	-34.3	15.3	11.5
安　阳　市 Anyang	-11.5	-50.9	-21.1	-3.6
鹤　壁　市 Hebi	11.3	-29.1	38.0	-0.2
新　乡　市 Xinxiang	11.3	-28.4	-1.4	21.1
焦　作　市 Jiaozuo	12.0	-10.3	10.1	14.2
濮　阳　市 Puyang	5.5	32.1	-3.7	9.3
许　昌　市 Xuchang	5.2	38.5	-0.6	7.4
漯　河　市 Luohe	11.4	-55.5	3.9	19.3
三 门 峡 市 Sanmenxia	10.2	-4.3	26.2	4.1
南　阳　市 Nanyang	10.4	-23.7	25.1	8.3
商　丘　市 Shangqiu	10.9	-24.5	9.7	12.6
信　阳　市 Xinyang	10.6	3.4	13.1	10.5
周　口　市 Zhoukou	9.8	5.0	-10.2	28.7
驻 马 店 市 Zhumadian	11.7	7.9	19.1	8.8
济　源　市 Jiyuan	12.0	-26.5	21.8	7.0
省 直 管 县 County Directly Administrated by Province				
巩　义　市 Gongyi	9.1	172.3	-2.6	17.5
兰　考　县 Lankao	10.0	70.3	-34.7	43.8
汝　州　市 Ruzhou	-14.5	-4.4	-18.9	-13.2
滑　　　县 Huaxian	-33.5	-55.6	-48.1	0.2
长　垣　市 Changyuan	10.0	-10.6	-11.7	29.1
邓　州　市 Dengzhou	5.3	6.3	14.4	0.7
永　城　市 Yongcheng	10.0	-62.1	13.6	9.7
固　始　县 Gushi	10.0	-3.0	12.3	10.1
鹿　邑　县 Luyi	10.0	12.1	30.5	-7.7
新　蔡　县 Xincai	10.0	-39.5	5.3	18.3

5-7 各市固定资产投资比重(2019年)
Proportion of Investment in Fixed Assets by City (2019)

单位：% (%)

市(县) City(County)	固定资产投资 Investment in Fixed Assets	第一产业 Primary Industry	第二产业 Secondary Industry	第三产业 Tertiary Industry
全省 Total	**100.0**	**3.7**	**28.9**	**67.4**
省辖市 City				
郑州市 Zhengzhou	100.0	0.4	10.6	89.0
开封市 Kaifeng	100.0	3.6	33.4	63.0
洛阳市 Luoyang	100.0	5.2	34.5	60.3
平顶山市 Pingdingshan	100.0	4.7	31.6	63.7
安阳市 Anyang	100.0	2.2	30.7	67.1
鹤壁市 Hebi	100.0	2.8	41.3	55.9
新乡市 Xinxiang	100.0	1.7	33.4	64.9
焦作市 Jiaozuo	100.0	1.0	45.1	53.8
濮阳市 Puyang	100.0	3.5	31.0	65.5
许昌市 Xuchang	100.0	2.4	32.6	64.9
漯河市 Luohe	100.0	0.5	42.5	57.0
三门峡市 Sanmenxia	100.0	15.7	39.3	44.9
南阳市 Nanyang	100.0	7.4	37.6	54.9
商丘市 Shangqiu	100.0	1.0	39.3	59.7
信阳市 Xinyang	100.0	6.9	24.0	69.1
周口市 Zhoukou	100.0	5.3	36.8	57.9
驻马店市 Zhumadian	100.0	3.8	30.8	65.4
济源市 Jiyuan	100.0	2.5	46.3	51.2
省直管县 County Directly Administrated by Province				
巩义市 Gongyi	100.0	1.6	41.9	56.5
兰考县 Lankao	100.0	13.5	27.3	59.3
汝州市 Ruzhou	100.0	1.9	23.6	74.5
滑县 Huaxian	100.0	6.6	45.4	47.9
长垣市 Changyuan	100.0	3.4	34.4	62.2
邓州市 Dengzhou	100.0	10.3	31.6	58.0
永城市 Yongcheng	100.0	1.0	63.4	35.6
固始县 Gushi	100.0	4.5	27.3	68.1
鹿邑县 Luyi	100.0	3.8	52.7	43.5
新蔡县 Xincai	100.0	4.1	29.3	66.6

5-8 各市固定资产投资增速(2019年)

Growth Rate of Investment in Fixed Assets by City(2019)

单位：% (%)

市(县)	City(County)	固定资产投资 Investment in Fixed Assets	建筑安装工程 Construction and Installation	设备、工器具购置 Purchase of Equipments and Tools	其他费用 Others
全　　省	**Total**	**8.0**	**9.6**	**-5.5**	**15.2**
省 辖 市	**City**				
郑　州　市	Zhengzhou	2.8	5.3	-23.5	5.5
开　封　市	Kaifeng	10.8	5.2	-16.2	293.3
洛　阳　市	Luoyang	10.2	15.9	-9.2	-7.6
平 顶 山 市	Pingdingshan	9.1	19.9	-10.7	-20.0
安　阳　市	Anyang	-11.5	-21.6	-5.8	80.0
鹤　壁　市	Hebi	11.2	3.3	91.5	189.4
新　乡　市	Xinxiang	11.3	14.6	-4.7	17.3
焦　作　市	Jiaozuo	12.0	7.4	28.2	5.9
濮　阳　市	Puyang	5.5	10.1	-20.7	49.6
许　昌　市	Xuchang	5.2	-0.2	-9.2	118.7
漯　河　市	Luohe	11.4	13.8	10.7	-10.4
三 门 峡 市	Sanmenxia	10.2	15.9	3.2	-12.3
南　阳　市	Nanyang	10.4	9.0	13.8	34.5
商　丘　市	Shangqiu	10.9	9.8	5.1	78.6
信　阳　市	Xinyang	10.6	14.0	-25.2	24.9
周　口　市	Zhoukou	9.8	12.7	-25.9	71.8
驻 马 店 市	Zhumadian	11.7	11.1	12.4	18.6
济　源　市	Jiyuan	12.0	23.2	-12.5	4.1
省 直 管 县	**County Directly Administrated by Province**				
巩　义　市	Gongyi	9.1	20.7	-12.9	-3.8
兰　考　县	Lankao	10.0	10.0	-33.7	159.3
汝　州　市	Ruzhou	-14.5	-9.3	-37.5	-71.0
滑　　　县	Huaxian	-33.5	-42.5	51.2	11.0
长　垣　市	Changyuan	10.0	14.0	-11.2	484.2
邓　州　市	Dengzhou	5.3	14.1	-20.0	-41.4
永　城　市	Yongcheng	10.0	10.2	17.6	-86.9
固　始　县	Gushi	10.0	21.6	-51.5	-57.8
鹿　邑　县	Luyi	10.0	9.9	21.0	-64.3
新　蔡　县	Xincai	10.0	15.5	-27.9	296.8

5-9 固定资产投资增速及结构
Growth Rate and Structure of Investment in Fixed Assets

单位：% (%)

项 目	Item	2018		2019	
		增 速 Growth Rate	比 重 Proportion	增 速 Growth Rate	比 重 Proportion
总 计	**Total**	**8.1**	**100.0**	**8.0**	**100.0**
#工业投资	Industry Investment	2.0	28.5	9.7	28.9
#基础设施投资	Infrastructure Investment	18.5	22.5	16.1	19.8
#民间投资	Private Investment	2.9	71.2	6.7	70.3
按产业分	by Sector				
第一产业	Primary Industry	16.9	4.6	-12.1	3.7
第二产业	Secondary Industry	1.7	28.6	9.0	28.9
第三产业	Teriary Industry	10.6	66.8	9.0	67.4
按隶属关系分	by Administrative Relationship				
中央项目	Central	-6.0	1.2	75.9	1.9
地方项目	Local	8.3	98.8	7.2	98.1
按建设性质分	by Type of Construction				
#新 建	New Construction	15.0	60.2	6.0	59.1
扩 建	Expansion	13.1	5.0	24.8	5.7
改建与技术改造	Reconstruction	-13.3	2.5	51.6	3.5
按构成分	by Composition				
建筑安装工程	Construction and Installation	9.5	74.1	9.6	75.2
设备工器具购置	Purchase of Equipments and Tools	7.6	14.7	-5.5	12.8
其他费用	Others	0.3	11.2	15.2	11.9
本年实际到位资金	Actual Funds	12.6	100.0	8.7	100.0
国家预算资金	State Budgetary	42.7	4.4	17.3	4.7
国内贷款	Domestic Loans	-12.3	9.1	-3.4	8.1
债 券	Bond				
利用外资	Foreign Investment	51.7	0.2	55.1	0.3
自筹资金	Self-raised Funds	16.1	73.6	6.4	72.0
其他资金来源	Others	7.8	12.7	27.3	14.9

5-10 工业主要产业投资增速及结构

Growth Rate and Structure of Investment in Fixed Assets in Major Industries

单位：% (%)

行 业	Sector	2018年增 速 Growth Rate	占工业投资比重 Percentage of Industry Investment	2019年增 速 Growth Rate	占工业投资比重 Percentage of Industry Investment
五大主导产业	**High-growth industries**	**2.5**	**38.2**	**6.2**	**37.0**
装备制造	Electronic Information Industry	0.5	18.7	2.1	17.4
食品制造	Equipment Manufacturing Industry	10.3	10.6	5.2	10.1
新型材料制造	Automobile and Parts Industry	0.8	1.3	43.9	1.7
电子制造	Food Industry	-11.7	3.4	15.2	3.6
汽车制造	Modern Furniture Industry	7.4	4.2	7.8	4.2
传统产业	**Traditional Pillar Industries**	**-1.3**	**40.3**	**16.9**	**42.9**
冶金工业	Metallurgical Industry	-23.1	3.5	10.1	6.8
建材工业	Building Materials Industry	6.9	9.5	19.9	3.8
化学工业	Chemical Industry	8.8	6.7	30.5	11.3
轻纺工业	Textile Industry	1.5	7.9	4.6	7.5
能源工业	Energy Industry	-5.6	12.7	17.1	13.6
高技术产业(制造业)	**High-tech Industries(Manufacturing)**	**-4.3**	**9.3**	**-2.0**	**8.3**
高载能工业	**Six Carrying Energy Industrial**	**-1.7**	**29.9**	**18.0**	**32.2**
煤炭开采和洗选业	Mining and Washing of Coal	-17.4	0.5	31.9	0.6
化学原料及化学制品制造业	Manufacture of Raw Chemical Material and Chemical Products	11.8	5.4	9.1	5.4
非金属矿物制品业	Manufacture of Non-metallic Mineral Products	7.2	9.8	29.7	11.6
黑色金属冶炼及压延加工业	Smelting and Pressing of Ferrous Metals	17.6	0.7	7.2	0.7
有色金属冶炼及压延加工业	Smelting and Pressing of Non-ferrous Metals	-28.9	2.8	23.0	3.1
电力、热力的生产和供应业	Production and Supply of Electric Power and Heat Power	-5.1	10.7	10.3	10.8
工业技术改造投资	**Investment in Industrial Technological Transformation**	**21.5**	**21.1**	**55.0**	**29.9**

5-11 能源原材料工业投资增速及结构

Growth Rate and Structure of Energy Raw Material Industry

单位：% (%)

行业	Sector	2018年增速 Growth Rate	占工业投资比重 Percentage of Industry Investment	2019年增速 Growth Rate	占工业投资比重 Percentage of Industry Investment
能源原材料工业(亿元)	**Energy and raw material industrial (100 million)**	**0.3**	**40.1**	**19.0**	**43.5**
煤炭开采和洗选业	Mining and Washing of Coal	-17.4	0.5	31.9	0.6
石油和天然气开采业	Extraction of Petroleum and Natural Gas	-16.8	0.2	60.8	0.3
黑色金属矿采选业	Mining of Ferrous Metal Ores	-52.2	0.0	840.9	0.1
有色金属矿采选业	Mining of Non-ferrous Metal Ores	-50.4	0.9	22.8	1.0
非金属矿采选业	Mining of Nonmetal Ores	131.4	0.6	76.5	0.9
石油加工、炼焦和核燃料加工业	Processing of Petroleum ,Coking, Processing of Nucleus Fuel	11.0	0.9	24.1	1.0
化学原料和化学制品制造业	Manufacture of Raw Chemical Material and Chemical Products	11.8	5.4	9.1	5.4
橡胶和塑料制品业	Manufacture of Rubber and Plastic	5.0	2.8		2.5
非金属矿物制品业	Manufacture of Non-metallic Mineral Products	7.2	9.8	29.7	11.6
黑色金属冶炼和压延加工业	Smelting and Pressing of Ferrous Metals	17.6	0.7	7.2	0.7
有色金属冶炼和压延加工业	Smelting and Pressing of Non-ferrous Metals	-28.9	2.8	23.0	3.1
废弃资源综合利用业	Comprehensive Utilization of Waste Resources	81.3	1.3	45.8	1.7
电力、热力生产和供应业	Production and Supply of Electric Power and Heat Power	-5.1	10.7	10.3	10.8
燃气生产和供应业	Production and Distribution of Gas	-0.5	1.2	62.7	1.8
水的生产和供应业	Production and Distribution of Water	22.7	2.4	-5.7	2.1

5-12 各市工业固定资产投资增速及比重(2019年)

Growth Rate and Proportion of Investment in Fixed Assets of Industry by City (2019)

单位：% (%)

年份 市(县) Year City(County)	工业投资比上年同期增长 Growth Rate	采矿业 Mining	制造业 Manufacturing	电力、热力、燃气及水生产和供应业 Electricity, Heat, Gas and Water Production and Supply	工业投资结构 Structure	采矿业 Mining	制造业 Manufacturing	电力、热力、燃气及水生产和供应业 Electricity, Heat, Gas and Water Production and Supply
全 省 Total	**9.7**	**47.2**	**8.2**	**12.0**	**100.0**	**3.2**	**82.1**	**14.6**
省辖市 City								
郑州市 Zhengzhou	1.6	-17.4	0.8	7.0	100.0	1.7	78.9	19.4
开封市 Kaifeng	2.8		3.3	-1.8	100.0		89.7	10.3
洛阳市 Luoyang	9.0	69.4	8.9	-4.5	100.0	5.4	81.5	13.1
平顶山市 Pingdingshan	17.0	55.4	13.3	18.7	100.0	7.9	69.7	22.4
安阳市 Anyang	-20.8		-33.7	17.9	100.0	2.1	65.4	32.4
鹤壁市 Hebi	38.0		25.1	223.1	100.0	3.6	86.2	10.2
新乡市 Xinxiang	-1.2	103.8	-7.3	52.1	100.0	2.2	85.1	12.7
焦作市 Jiaozuo	10.3	31.3	12.6	10.1	100.0	0.4	88.8	10.8
濮阳市 Puyang	-3.7		-4.0	-23.0	100.0	5.8	75.2	19.0
许昌市 Xuchang	0.4	65.7	0.2	-9.4	100.0	3.5	85.0	11.5
漯河市 Luohe	4.4		10.4	-33.8	100.0		91.4	8.6
三门峡市 Sanmenxia	28.9	4.7	36.2	7.3	100.0	9.3	80.0	10.7
南阳市 Nanyang	25.1	25.6	16.2	77.7	100.0	3.9	76.3	19.8
商丘市 Shangqiu	11.3	270.0	7.8	32.4	100.0	1.2	86.5	12.3
信阳市 Xinyang	13.1	19.0	15.9	-2.0	100.0	1.9	84.1	13.9
周口市 Zhoukou	-10.1	-100.0	-15.1	36.2	100.0		85.4	14.6
驻马店市 Zhumadian	19.6	136.6	23.6	-5.8	100.0	0.5	88.1	11.4
济源市 Jiyuan	21.9	-13.2	21.1	33.5	100.0	2.2	82.0	15.8
省直管县 County Directly Administrated by Province								
巩义市 Gongyi	-2.6	33.2	-5.6	43.3	100.0	1.4	90.6	7.9
兰考县 Lankao	-35.6		-47.1	25.9	100.0		69.3	30.7
汝州市 Ruzhou	-18.2		-8.5	-59.7	100.0	1.1	88.8	10.2
滑县 Huaxian	-47.6		-57.9	-19.9	100.0		58.8	41.2
长垣市 Changyuan	-11.7		-20.3	108.6	100.0		84.2	15.8
邓州市 Dengzhou	14.8		19.5	-0.2	100.0		79.3	20.7
永城市 Yongcheng	19.0	270.0	8.6	86.7	100.0	4.2	81.9	13.8
固始县 Gushi	12.3	156.1	8.6	22.8	100.0	1.7	78.1	20.3
鹿邑县 Luyi	30.5		13.1		100.0		84.8	15.2
新蔡县 Xincai	6.1		-5.6	128.2	100.0		81.2	18.8

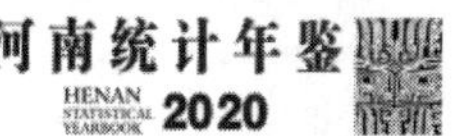

5-13 分行业农村农户固定资产投资增速及结构(2019年)
Investment in Fixed Assets of Households in Rural Area by Sector (2019)

单位：% (%)

产业	Sector	增速 Growth Rate	结构 Structure
总计	**Total**	**-7.8**	**100.0**
农、林、牧、渔业	Agriculture, Forestry, Animal Husbandry and Fishery	-26.8	14.4
工业	Industry	28.7	0.8
采矿业	Mining		
制造业	Manufacturing	27.6	0.7
电力、热力、燃气及水的生产和供应业	Production and Distribution of Electricity, Gas and Water	36.3	0.1
建筑业	Construction	-25.5	1.0
交通运输、仓储和邮政业	Transport, Storage and Post	293.6	9.6
批发和零售业	Wholesale and Retail Trade	-22.1	1.1
住宿和餐饮业	Hotels and Catering Services	-11.8	0.8
房地产业	Real estate	-10.9	71.6
居民服务和其他服务业	Service to Households and Other Services	-63.3	0.6

主要统计指标解释

固定资产投资（不含农户） 指城镇和农村各种登记注册类型的企业、事业、行政单位及城镇个体户进行的计划总投资500万元及以上的建设项目投资和房地产开发投资，包括原口径的城镇固定资产投资加上农村企事业组织项目投资，该口径自2011年起开始使用。

民间固定资产投资 指具有集体、私营、个人性质的内资企事业单位以及由其控股（包括绝对控股和相对控股）的企业单位在中华人民共和国境内建造或购置固定资产的投资。

基础设施投资 指为社会生产和生活提供基础性、大众性服务的工程和设施，是社会赖以生存和发展的基本条件。包括以下行业投资：铁路运输业、道路运输业、水上运输业、航空运输业、管道运输业、多式联运和运输代理业、装卸搬运业、邮政业、电信广播电视和卫星传输服务业、互联网和相关服务业、水利管理业、生态保护和环境治理业、公共设施管理业。

实际到位资金 指用于固定资产投资的各种货币资金。包括国家预算资金、国内贷款、利用外资、自筹资金和其他资金。

国家预算资金 国家预算包括一般预算、政府性基金预算、国有资本经营预算和社保基金预算。各类预算中用于固定资产投资的资金全部作为国家预算资金填报，其中一般预算中用于固定资产投资的部分包括基建投资、车购税、灾后恢复重建基金和其他财政投资。各级政府债券也应归入国家预算资金。

国内贷款 指报告期固定资产投资项目单位向银行及非银行金融机构借入用于固定资产投资的各种国内借款，包括银行利用自有资金及吸收存款发放的贷款、上级拨入的国内贷款、国家专项贷款（包括煤代油贷款、劳改煤矿专项贷款等），地方财政专项资金安排的贷款、国内储备贷款、周转贷款等。

利用外资 指报告期收到的境外（包括外国及港澳台地区）资金(包括设备、材料、技术在内)。包括对外借款(外国政府贷款、国际金融组织贷款、出口信贷、外国银行商业贷款、对外发行债券和股票)、外商直接投资、外商其他投资(包括利用外商投资收益在国内进行固定资产再投资活动的资金)。不包括我国自有外汇资金(国家外汇、地方外汇、留成外汇、调济外汇和国内银行自有资金发放的外汇贷款等)。各类外资按报告期的外汇牌价（中间价）折成人民币计算。

自筹资金 指固定资产投资单位在报告期收到的，由各企、事业单位筹集用于固定资产投资的资金，包括各类企事业单位的自有资金和从其他单位筹集的用于固定资产投资的资金，但不包括各类财政性资金、从各类金融机构借入资金和国外资金。

其他资金来源 指在报告期收到的除以上各种资金之外的用于固定资产投资的资金。包括社会集资、个人资金、无偿捐赠的资金及其他单位拨入的资金等。

固定资产投资按国民经济行业分 指根据其从事的社会经济活动性质对各类单位进行的分类。应根据建设项目建成投产后的主要产品种类或主要用途及社会经济活动种类来划分，不能根据项目单位本身的行业类别来划分。如果项目投产后有几种产品，应根据主要产品来确定行业类别。一般情况下，一个建设项目只能属于一种国民经济行业。

固定资产投资按隶属关系分 是按建设单位或企业、事业、行政单位的主管上级机关确定的。

（1）中央 是指中共中央、人大常委会和国务院各部、委、局、总公司以及直属机构直接领导的建设项目和企业、事业、行政单位。这些单位的固定资产投资计划由国务院各部门直接编制和下达，统一组织或委托下级实施。包括有中央垂直管理的部门（如国家统计局各级调查队）和中央直属企业、事业单位（如工商银行、中国电信、中国石油）等。

（2）地方 是由省（自治区、直辖市）、地（区、市、州、盟）、县（区、市、旗）三级政府及业务主管部门直接领导和管理的建设项目、企业、事业、行政单位。地方项目还包括不隶属以上各级政府及主管部门的建设项目和企业、事业单位，如外商投资企业和无主管部门的企业等。

固定资产投资按建设性质分 按整个建设项目情况来确定。建设项目的性质一般分为新建、扩建、改建和技术改造、单纯建造生活设施、迁建、恢复、单纯购置。农户投资不划分建设性质。

（1）新建　指从无到有“平地起家”开始建设的项目。现有企业、事业、行政单位投资的项目一般不属于新建。但如有的单位原有基础很小，经过建设后新增的固定资产价值超过该企业、事业、行政单位原有固定资产价值（原值）三倍以上的，也应作为新建。

（2）扩建　指在厂内或其他地点，为扩大原有产品的生产能力（或效益）或增加新的产品生产能力，而增建的生产车间（或主要工程）、分厂、独立的生产线等项目。行政、事业单位在原单位增建业务性用房（如学校增建教学用房、医院增建门诊部、病房等）也作为扩建。

现有企、事业单位为扩大原有主要产品生产能力或增加新的产品生产能力，增建一个或几个主要生产车间（或主要工程）、分厂，同时进行一些更新改造工程的，也应作为扩建。

（3）改建和技术改造　指现有企业、事业单位对原有设施进行技术改造或更新（包括相应配套的辅助性生产、生活福利设施）的建设项目。改建项目包括企业、事业单位为适应市场变化的需要，而改变企业的主要产品种类（如军工企业转民用产品等）的建设项目；原有产品生产作业线由于各工序（车间）之间能力不平衡，为填平补齐充分发挥原有生产能力而增建但不增加主要产品生产能力的建设项目。技术改造是指企业、事业单位在现有基础上用先进的技术代替落后的技术，用先进的工艺和装备代替落后的工艺和装备，以改变企业落后的技术经济面貌，实现以内涵为主的扩大再生产，达到提高产品质量、促进产品更新换代、节约能源、降低消耗、扩大生产规模、全面提高社会经效益的目的。技术改造具体包括以下内容：机器设备和工具的更新改造；生产工艺改革、节约能源和原材料的改造；厂房建筑和公共设施的改造；保护环境进行的“三废”治理改造；劳动条件和生产环境的改造等。

固定资产投资按构成分

（1）建筑工程　指各种房屋、建筑物的建造工程。这部分投资额必须兴工动料，通过施工活动才能实现，是固定资产投资额的重要组成部分。

（2）安装工程　指各种设备、装置的安装工程。

在安装工程中，不包括被安装设备本身价值。

（3）设备工器具购置　指报告期内购置或自制的，达到固定资产标准的设备、工具、器具的价值。新建单位及扩建单位的新建车间，按照设计或计划要求购置或自制的全部设备、工具、器具，不论是否达到固定资产标准均计入“设备工器具购置”中。

（4）其他费用　指在固定资产建造和购置过程中发生的，除建筑安装工程和设备、工器具购置投资完成额以外的应当分摊计入固定资产投资的费用，不指经营中财务上的其他费用。

Explanatory Notes on Main Statistical Indicators

Investment in Fixed Assets (Excluding Rural Households) refers to the investment in construction projects with a total planned investment of 5 million yuan and over by enterprises of various ownerships, institutions, administrative units and urban self-employed individuals, and the investment in real estate development in both urban and rural areas. Since 2011, it covers the urban investment in fixed assets under the previous statistical coverage plus project investments by rural enterprises and institutions.

Non-governmental Investment in Fixed Assets refers to the investment in the construction or purchase of fixed assets in the territory of the People's Republic of China by domestic-funded enterprises and institutions with collective, private and personal nature and by enterprises and institutions controlled by them (including absolute and relative holding).

Infrastructure Investment refers to projects and facilities that provide basic and popular services for social production and life. It is the basic condition for the survival and development of society. It includes: railway transport, road transport, water transport, air transport, pipeline transport, multimodal transport and transport agent Intermodality and Forwarding Agency, loading and unloading, posts, telecommunications, radio and television and satellite transmission services, Internet and related services, water management industry, ecological protection and environmental governance, public facilities management.

Actual Funds for Investment refer to all kinds of monetary funds used for fixed assets investment. It includes state budget funds, domestic loans, foreign capital utilization, self-raising funds and other funds.

Fund from the State Budget State budget consists of general budget, government fund budget, operation budget of state-owned assets and social security fund budget. Funds for investment in fixed assets from various budgets are reported as fund from the state budget, of which, the general budget utilized on fixed assets investment includes investment on infrastructure construction, vehicle purchase tax, post-disaster restoration and reconstruction funds and other financial investment. Government bonds at all levels should also be included.

Domestic Loans refer to loans of various forms borrowed by investing units from banks and non-bank financial institutions during the reference period for the purpose of investment in fixed assets, including loans issued by banks from their self-owned funds and deposit, loans appropriated by higher responsible authorities, special loans by government (including loan for substituting petroleum with coal, special loans for reform-through-labour coal mines), loans arranged by local government from special funds, domestic reserve loan, and revolving loan, etc.

Foreign Investment refers to overseas (including foreign countries, Hongkong, Macao and Taiwan) funds received during the reference period (covering equipment, materials and technology), including foreign borrowings (loans from foreign governments and international financial institutions, export credit, commercial loans from foreign banks, issue of bonds and stocks overseas), foreign direct investment and other foreign investments (including funds from foreign direct investment income that are reinvested in fixed assets domestically). Excluded from this category is capital in foreign exchanges owned by China (foreign exchanges owned by the central and local governments, foreign exchanges retained by enterprises, foreign exchanges by enterprises through the regulating mechanism, loans in foreign exchanges issued by the Bank of China with its own fund, etc.). In calculating the utilization of foreign capital, foreign currencies are converted into Chinese Renminbi applying the exchange rate (central parity rate) at the end of the reference period.

Self-raised Funds refer to funds for investment in fixed assets received during the reference period by investing units, including investment in fixed assets using own funds of various enterprises and institutions or funds raised from other units other than financial funds, funds borrowed from financial institutions and overseas funds.

Other Funds refer to funds for investment in fixed assets received from sources other than those listed above, including funds raised from individuals and through donations, and funds transferred from other units.

Investment in Fixed Assets by Sector refers to the classification of investment by the nature of social economic activities the investing units are engaged in. The classification of construction projects by sector is determined by the major products or the purpose of the projects when they are put into production or use, and by the nature of their social economic activities, instead of being determined by industrial classification of the project enterprises. The project will be classified according to major product if there are several kinds of products yielded. In general, one project can only be classified into one sector.

Investment in Fixed Assets by Jurisdiction of Management refers to the classification of investment by the competent authorities under which investment is made by construction units, enterprises, institutions or administrative units.

(1) Central investment refers to the investment in projects or by enterprises, institutions or administrative units which are under the direct leadership and management of the State Council and of the national commissions, ministries, agencies and State-owned large corporations. Various ministries and departments of the State Council prepare and implement plans through unified organization or lower-level commissions, which include departments direct under central government (i.e. survey offices at all level of the National Bureau of Statistics) and enterprises and institutions directly under central government (like the Industrial and Commercial Bank of China, China Telecom and China National Petroleum Corporation).

(2) Local investment refers to the investment in projects or by enterprises, institutions or administrative units which are under the direct leadership and management of competent departments and governments at the level of province (autonomous regions and municipalities directly under the Central Government), prefecture （prefectures, cities and leagues） and county (districts, cities and banners). Also included are projects by foreign-invested enterprises and enterprises without competent managing authorities.

Investment in Fixed Assets by Type of Construction Construction projects in general can be classified, by the type of construction, into new construction, expansion, reconstruction and technical transformation, purely construction of living facilities, moving, restoration and purely purchasing. However, investment by type of construction is not applied to investment by real-estate development units and investment by rural households.

(1) New construction in general refers to construction projects, which start from scratch. The existing projects invested by enterprises, institutions and administrative agencies cannot be classified as new construction. In case the size of the existing unit is quite small, and the value of newly added fixed assets is more than three times of the original value, the expansion will be considered as new construction.

(2) Expansion refers to projects of construction of new production workshop, branch factory or independent production line within a factory or in other locations, for the purpose of increasing the production capacity (or improving efficiency) or adding new production capacity. Newly constructed accommodation for the operation of institutions and administrative organizations (such as newly constructed buildings for teaching in schools, buildings for clinics or wards in hospitals, etc.) are also classified as expansion.

Also included in expansion are investments by existing enterprises or institutions in building major production line(s) or branch factory (ies) along with some work on innovation, for the purpose of expanding the production capacity of original products or producing new products.

(3) Reconstruction and technical transformation refers to construction projects by existing enterprises or institutions in innovation or technical transformation of the old facilities (including auxiliary production equipment and welfare facilities). Also considered as reconstruction is the construction of new workshops by the existing enterprises or institutions to change the variety of products to meet the market demand (such as the production of civil products by defence industries), or to bring the designed production capacity into full play through a more balanced production process on production lines. Technical transformation refers to replacement of old technology or equipment by new technology or equipment, in order to expand the reproduction through improvement of technology contents in production, to improve product quality, to promote new products, to save energy, to reduce

consumption, to expand the production scale and to improve overall social-economic efficiency. Contents of technical transformation include: updating of machinery, equipment and tools; reforming production process by using energy or materials saving technology; construction of factory workshops and transformation of public facilities; treatment transformation of "three wastes" (waste gas, waste water and industrial residue) aiming at environmental protection; improvement of working conditions and environment, etc.

Investment in Fixed Assets by Structure

(1) Construction refers to the construction of houses and buildings, also known as work volume of construction. This part of investment can only be achieved through construction activities, it is the major component of the total investment in fixed assets.

(2) Installation refers to the installation of various kinds of equipment and instruments, also known as work volume of installation.

The value of equipment installed itself is not included in the value of installation projects.

(3) Purchase of equipment and instruments refers to the total value of equipment, tools, and instruments purchased or self-produced which come up to the cut-off point for fixed assets during the reference period. Equipment, tools and instruments purchased or self-produced for new workshops by newly established or expanded units are categorized as "purchase of equipment and instruments" no matter whether they come up to the cut-off point for fixed assets.

(4) Other expenses refer to expenses arising during the construction or purchase of fixed assets other than those expenses on construction, installation and purchase of equipment and instruments. Other financial expenses arising in operation are not included.

对外经济贸易和旅游

Foreign Trade and Tourism

6

◉ 资料整理：周文瑞

简要说明

一、主要内容

本篇包括河南对外贸易资料，利用外资资料，对外经济合作以及旅游等资料。

二、统计范围

对外贸易统计的范围是全省各进、出口贸易公司和有进出口经营权的生产企业、外商及港澳台商投资企业、科研机构等辖区内全部有进出口经营权的企业；利用外资统计的范围是辖区内全部外商投资企业、港澳台商投资企业和有外商其他投资的单位；对外经济合作统计范围是经各级商务部门批准的从事对外承包和劳务合作业务并具有法人地位的对外承包劳务企业。对外直接投资统计范围是境内投资主体通过直接投资在境外设立的各类公司型企业和非公司型企业。

三、资料来源

对外贸易、外商投资企业的登记注册情况、对外经济合作和对外直接投资资料采用全面调查方法。对外贸易资料1992年及以后为海关进出口统计数字，由郑州海关提供；利用外资资料中外商投资企业的登记注册情况资料由河南省市场监督管理局提供,其他由河南省商务厅提供；对外经济合作资料和对外直接投资资料由河南省商务厅提供。本篇资料由河南省统计局贸易外经处编辑整理。

旅游资料由河南省文化和旅游厅等有关部门提供，由河南省统计局贸易外经处编辑整理。

Brief Introduction

I. Main Contents

Data in this chapter provide summary data of Henan provincial foreign trade, utilization of foreign capital, economic cooperation with foreign countries or territories and Tourists.

II. Statistical Scopes

The statistics of foreign trade cover the Henan provincial import and export corporation, the manufacturing enterprises that have right to operate import and export, foreign and Hong Kong, Macao and Taiwan-invested enterprises and scientific research institutions. The statistics of utilization of foreign capital cover the foreign direct investments and other foreign investments, and the basic condition of registration of foreign funded enterprises. The statistics of economic cooperation with foreign countries or territories cover the corporate enterprise engaged in contracted projects and labour services cooperation with foreign countries and has been approved by the department of commerce at various levels. The statistics of foreign direct investment cover overseas corporate and non-corporate enterprises of various forms established by domestic investors through their investment operation.

III. Data Sources

Data on foreign trade, utilization of foreign capital, economic cooperation with foreign countries or territories are calculated through a comprehensive reporting system. Data on foreign trade since 1992 and later are calculated by Zhengzhou Customs. Data on utilization of foreign capital are calculated by the Henan provincial bureau of Commerce, data on registered cases of foreign-invested enterprises are calculated by the administration for market regulation of Henan Province. Data on overseas direct investment and economic cooperation with foreign countries or territories are calculated by the Henan provincial bureau of Commerce. Data in this chapter are provided by the Department of Trade and External Economic Relations of the Henan provincial bureau of Statistics.

Data on tourism are calculated by the culture and tourism department of Henan Province. Data on tourism are provided by the Department of Trade and External Economic Relations of the Henan provincial bureau of Statistics.

6-1 对外经济贸易基本情况
Foreign Trade and Economic Cooperation

指　　标	Item	2005	2010	2015	2017	2018	2019
货物进出口总值(亿元)	**Total Value of Imports and Exports (100 million yuan)**	**626.54**	**1204.40**	**4600.19**	**5232.79**	**5512.71**	**5711.63**
出口总额	Total Exports	413.12	713.13	2684.03	3171.81	3578.99	3754.64
进口总额	Total Imports	213.42	491.27	1916.16	2060.98	1933.73	1956.99
进出口差额	Balance	199.71	221.86	767.86	1110.84	1645.26	1797.65
货物进出口总额(亿美元)	**Total Value of Imports and Exports (USD 100 million)**	**77.36**	**177.92**	**737.81**	**776.13**	**828.19**	**824.45**
出口总额	Total Exports	51.01	105.34	430.61	470.29	537.67	541.93
进口总额	Total Imports	26.35	72.57	307.19	305.84	290.52	282.52
进出口差额	Balance	24.66	32.77	123.42	164.45	247.16	259.41
外商直接投资合同项目(个)	**Number of Projects for Contracted Foreign Direct Investment (unit)**	472	362	272	210	217	214
实际使用外资额(亿美元)	**Total Amount of Foreign Investment Actually Utilized (USD 100 million)**	**23.52**	**62.47**	**160.86**	**172.24**	**179.02**	**187.27**
#外商直接投资	Foreign Direct Investments	12.30	62.47	160.86	172.24	179.02	187.27
外资企业基本情况	**Registered Foreign-funded Enterprises**						
年末实有企业数(户)	Number of Registered Enterprise in the Year-end (unit)	2877	2459	2154	2348	2466	2629
投资总额(亿美元)	Total Investment (USD 100 million)	206.41	378.66	687.10	1045.38	1106.28	1163.07
注册资本(亿美元)	Registered Capital (USD 100 million)	112.29	205.35	348.16	555.29	593.98	713.09
#外方	Capital from Foreign Investors	75.34	148.66	248.44	408.69	446.98	507.86
对外经济合作(亿美元)	**Economic Cooperation with Foreign Countries & Regions (USD 100 million)**						
合同金额	Contracted Value	6.29	25.26	43.35	37.48	37.44	44.27
完成营业额	Value of Turnover Fulfilled	4.99	23.23	48.32	47.71	34.48	41.63

6-2 进出口总额
Total Value of Imports and Exports

年 份 Year	美元(万美元) USD (10 000 dollors)				人民币(万元) RMB (10 000 yuan)			
	进出口总额 Total Imports & Exports	出口总额 Total Exports	进口总额 Total Imports	顺 差 Balance	进出口总额 Total Imports & Exports	出口总额 Total Exports	进口总额 Total Imports	顺 差 Balance
1978	11843	10231	1612	8619	19896	17188	2708	14480
1979	15406	13422	1984	11438	23879	20804	3075	17729
1980	22644	20448	2196	18252	33966	30672	3294	27378
1981	28487	24948	3539	21409	42855	37531	5324	32207
1982	28761	25471	3290	22181	54358	48140	6218	41922
1983	30418	27963	2455	25508	60228	55367	4861	50506
1984	38203	34174	4029	30145	89013	79625	9388	70237
1985	44991	36710	8281	28429	167367	136561	30806	105755
1986	50671	45263	5408	39855	188496	168378	20118	148260
1987	74732	65434	9298	56136	278003	243414	34589	208825
1988	84961	75052	9909	65143	316055	279193	36862	242331
1989	98539	81897	16642	65255	335157	304657	30500	274157
1990	100385	86689	13696	72993	481848	416107	65741	350366
1991	121489	104297	17192	87105	643892	552774	91118	461656
1992	116194	81632	34562	47070	633257	444894	188363	256532
1993	131423	75546	55877	19669	756996	435145	321852	113293
1994	163193	102242	60951	41291	1398564	876214	522350	353864
1995	222918	135759	87159	48600	1861365	1133588	727778	405810
1996	196855	124001	72854	51147	1631928	1027968	603960	424009
1997	189699	128663	61036	67627	1572604	1066616	505988	560628
1998	173196	118675	54521	64154	1435795	983816	451979	531837
1999	175044	112889	62155	50734	1449364	934721	514643	420078
2000	227486	149338	78148	71190	1883584	1236519	647065	589453
2001	279256	171548	107708	63840	2311339	1419864	891475	528389
2002	320351	211876	108475	103401	2652506	1754333	898173	856160
2003	471640	298041	173599	124442	3905179	2467779	1437400	1030380
2004	661346	417610	243736	173874	5475945	3457811	2018134	1439677
2005	773604	510093	263511	246582	6265419	4131243	2134176	1997067
2006	979594	663497	316097	347400	7809094	5289240	2519853	2769387
2007	1280493	839145	441347	397798	9803869	6424771	3379098	3045673
2008	1747934	1071890	676044	395846	12238006	7504743	4733263	2771481
2009	1343839	734648	609191	125457	9179764	5018380	4161384	856997
2010	1779157	1053447	725710	327737	12044003	7131309	4912694	2218616
2011	3264212	1924040	1340172	583868	20711951	12208344	8503607	3704736
2012	5175027	2967788	2207239	760549	32602703	18697083	13905620	4791463
2013	5995687	3598710	2396977	1201733	37165081	22312067	14853013	7459054
2014	6503288	3938370	2564918	1373452	39943605	24188066	15755539	8432527
2015	7378063	4306142	3071921	1234221	46001884	26840255	19161629	7678626
2016	7122554	4283385	2839169	1444215	47146980	28353441	18793539	9559902
2017	7761339	4702929	3058410	1644519	52327904	31718144	20609760	11108384
2018	8281923	5376745	2905178	2471567	55127145	35789861	19337284	16452577
2019	8244529	5419325	2825204	2594121	57116270	37546362	19569908	17976454

注：本表1991年及以前年度为有关部门统计数据，从1992年开始为海关进出口数据。
a) Data before 1991 are obtained from the related Department, and the data since 1992 are obtained from the customs statistics.

6−3 各种分组的进出口总值

Total Value of Imports and Exports by Group

单位：万元 (10 000 yuan)

项　目	Item	进出口总值 Total Value of Imports and Exports		#出口总值 Exports Trade	
		2018	2019	2018	2019
合　计	**Total**	**55127145**	**57116270**	**35789861**	**37546362**
按贸易方式分	**By trade system**				
一般贸易	General Trade	18560869	20055303	12765711	13583505
援助物资	Aid Material		533		
加工贸易	Processing Trade	35635030	35875540	22679672	23419536
#来料加工贸易	Processing Trade with Customer's Materials	107685	100123	72920	63490
进料加工贸易	Processing Trade with Imported Materials	35527345	35775417	22606752	23356046
对外承包工程出口	Export of Contracted Projects	183861	145078	183861	145078
三资企业投资设备进口	Import of Machines Invested by Equrty Joint Venture, Contractual Joint Venture, Wholly Foreign-owned Enterprise	9102	10931		
保税监管场所进出境货物	Inbound and Outbound Goods in Bounded Areas	91935	756576	19711	234373
其他贸易方式	Other Trade System	646348	272309	140906	163870
按注册类型分	**By Registration**				
国有企业	State-owned Enterprises	4468265	4528781	2113072	1791841
外商投资企业	Foreign Investment	35623911	35432203	22831427	23220879
合作	Cooperative Operation	4805	21572	4477	7275
合资	Equity Joint Ventures	34725219	34669759	22167950	22686913
独资	Sole Proprietorship	893887	740872	659000	526691
民营企业	Private Enterprise	15012394	16963649	10828506	12362514
其他企业	Others	6436	191637		171128

6-4 河南向一些国家(地区)进出口总值

Total Value of Imports and Exports To Related Countries and Regions

单位：万元 (10 000 yuan)

国家(地区)名称	Country (Region)	进出口总值 Total Imports & Exports		#出口 Exports	
		2018	2019	2018	2019
合 计	**Total**	**55127145**	**57116270**	**35789861**	**37546362**
亚洲	**Asia**	**25737831**	**26787236**	**11480254**	**12836172**
韩国	South Korea	3269347	3734088	797120	1333548
日本	Japan	3574099	2936087	2468578	1999415
中国	China	2418200	1779708		
台湾省	Taiwan	4604535	4575239	252771	340724
越南	Vietnam	3408517	3370996	840729	676186
中国香港	Hong Kong, China	1857874	2106091	1856567	2103083
非洲	**Africa**	**1835469**	**2101388**	**1537946**	**1608451**
南非	South Africa	392512	330175	303927	272450
贝宁	Benin	257014	169790	257014	165398
欧洲	**Europe**	**7501109**	**8618024**	**6235339**	**7355962**
荷兰	Holland	1879797	2228432	1846209	2183200
德国	Germany	907691	1099886	501863	817080
英国	United Kingdom	1194487	1447359	1094937	1356741
俄罗斯联邦	Russia	890307	962048	731450	746494
意大利	Italy	678892	562646	614428	498993
拉丁美洲	**Latin America**	**3531249**	**3932290**	**1579365**	**1671409**
巴西	Brazil	1017288	1038513	397724	577605
墨西哥	Mexico	1141373	1208373	466261	417055
智利	Chile	404190	556139	187732	160797
北美洲	**North America**	**14744194**	**13756091**	**14041826**	**13256775**
美国	United States	13826648	12712854	13260209	12355410
加拿大	Canada	917540	1043211	781612	901338
大洋洲	**Oceania**	**1763102**	**1895987**	**907790**	**817593**
澳大利亚	Australia	1628526	1757278	823404	764719
新西兰	New Zealand	109321	86716	76166	41708

6−5 人民币汇率(年平均价)

Exchange Rate of Renminbi (Annual Average)

单位：元 (yuan)

年 份 Year	100美元 100 US Dollars	100日元 100 Japanese Yen	100港元 100 Hong Kong Dollars	100欧元 100 Euros
1985	293.66	1.2457	37.57	
1986	345.28	2.0694	44.22	
1987	372.21	2.5799	47.74	
1988	372.21	2.9082	47.70	
1989	376.51	2.7360	48.28	
1990	478.32	3.3233	61.39	
1991	532.33	3.9602	68.45	
1992	551.46	4.3608	71.24	
1993	576.20	5.2020	74.41	
1994	861.87	8.4370	111.53	
1995	835.10	8.9225	107.96	
1996	831.42	7.6352	107.51	
1997	828.98	6.8600	107.09	
1998	827.91	6.3488	106.88	
1999	827.83	7.2932	106.66	
2000	827.84	7.6864	106.18	
2001	827.70	6.8075	106.08	
2002	827.70	6.6237	106.07	800.58
2003	827.70	7.1466	106.24	936.13
2004	827.68	7.6552	106.23	1029.00
2005	819.17	7.4484	105.30	1019.53
2006	797.18	6.8570	102.62	1001.90
2007	760.40	6.4632	97.46	1041.75
2008	694.51	6.7427	89.19	1022.27
2009	683.10	7.2986	88.12	952.70
2010	676.95	7.7279	87.13	897.25
2011	645.88	8.1050	82.97	900.11
2012	631.25	7.9037	81.38	810.67
2013	619.32	6.3323	79.85	822.19
2014	614.28	5.8196	79.22	816.51
2015	622.84	5.1543	80.34	691.41
2016	664.23	6.1243	85.58	734.26
2017	675.18	6.0200	88.64	763.03
2018	661.74	5.9890	84.43	780.16
2019	689.85	6.3347	88.05	772.55

注：数据来源于国家外汇管理局。

a) Data are from State Administration of Foreign Exchange.

6-6 外商和港澳台商直接投资情况

Foreign, Hong Kong, Macao and Taiwan's Direct Investments

单位：万美元 (USD 10 000)

年份 Year	签订协议(合同) New Signed Agreement		实际利用外资额 Actually Utilized Foreign Value	#独资经营 Foreign Investment Enterprises	#合资经营 Equity Joint Venture	#合作经营 Contractual Joint Venture
	个数 Number of Projects(unit)	金额 Value				
1985	29	6870	565		541	24
1986	14	2724	605		542	63
1987	31	12562	467	31	244	192
1988	38	1986	6436		6268	168
1989	36	1681	4266	37	4199	30
1990	50	2107	1049	75	708	266
1991	154	12716	3791	294	3214	283
1992	1053	88327	10691	717	9655	319
1993	1727	157768	34197	5190	27338	1669
1994	1011	79168	42488	7168	32008	3312
1995	815	86748	47981	5064	42121	796
1996	478	92166	52566	7543	36831	8192
1997	423	86799	64735	14096	30159	20480
1998	353	57333	61794	6198	36356	19240
1999	264	61832	49527	8185	32317	9025
2000	237	69921	53999	4459	27292	6248
2001	224	62188	35861	9510	20685	5666
2002	290	101964	45165	9860	29592	5713
2003	324	182560	56149	16628	32970	5911
2004	478	205383	87367	39866	36071	11430
2005	472	235176	122960	48312	54698	10267
2006	497	336788	184526	89313	81926	8702
2007	516	483538	306162	150935	97847	18572
2008	364	604146	403266	203739	94822	14715
2009	274	492055	479858	284554	163957	27023
2010	362	578385	624670	366770	191196	58545
2011	355	767752	1008209	593537	322191	84563
2012	363	1172936	1211777	766291	368604	76373
2013	344	1154233	1345659	888056	411544	28321
2014	328	1183590	1492688	893738	537869	25846
2015	272	737323	1608637	963356	536546	33182
2016	196	875349	1699312	989249	628254	10981
2017	210	864691	1722428	1056063	575019	8140
2018	217	682233	1790214	1089743	630272	733
2019	214	413554	1872727	1117947	687365	16375

6-7 外商和港澳台商在豫直接投资(2019年)

Direct Investment From Foreign, Hong Kong, Macao and Taiwan Businessmen in Henan (2019)

项目	Item	新签协议 New Signed Agreement 合同个数(个) Number of Contracts (unit)	投资额(万美元) Investments Value (USD 10 000)	实际投资(万美元) Actually Investments (USD 10 000)
总计	**Total**	**214**	**413554**	**1872727**
按登记注册类型分	**By Registration**			
#合资经营	Equity Joint Venture	108	135582	687365
合作经营	Contractual Joivt Venture	1	255	16375
独资	Foreign Investment Enterprises	102	241294	1117947
股份有限公司	FDI Shareholding Inc	3	36423	51039
按国民经济行业分	**By Sector**			
#农、林、牧、渔业	Agriculture, Forestry, Animal Husbandry and Fishery	10	9039	51748
采矿业	Mining		743	24125
制造业	Manufacturing	48	123245	920237
电力、燃气及水的生产和供应业	Production and Supply of Electricity,Gas and Water	18	28422	277045
建筑业	Construction	2	-68	10649
交通运输、仓储及邮政业	Transport, Storage and Post	6	8462	29784
信息传输、计算机服务和软件业	Information Transimission, Computer Services and Software	8	8381	5853
批发和零售业	Wholesale and Retail Trade	33	8865	33276
住宿和餐饮业	Hotels and Catering Sevrices	8	284	10644
金融业	Financial Intermediation	3	16185	50105
房地产业	Real Estate	11	108358	288456
租赁和商务服务业	Leasing and Business Services	17	24150	68529
科学研究、技术服务和地质勘查业	Scientific Research, Technical Service and Geologic Perambulation	40	59723	20364
水利、环境和公共设施管理业	Management of Water Conservancy, Environment and Public Facilities	4	15169	6200
居民服务和其他服务业	Services to Households and Other Services	2	-3	
教育	Education	2	568	
卫生、社会保障和社会福利业	Health, Social Security and Social Welfare	1	540	8744
文化、体育和娱乐业	Culture, Sports and Entertainment	1	1491	66968
按地区、国别分	**By Country or Region**			
香港	Hong Kong, China	87	297354	1131852
台湾	Taiwan	22	23890	127526
加拿大	Canada	9	8295	15440
日本	Japan	4	-131	46408
英国	United Kingdom	3	3348	136128
美国	America	9	5383	77260
新加坡	Singapore	7	11195	64791
德国	Germany	5	974	33241
韩国	South Korea	13	2015	9563

6-8 各市外商和港澳台商在豫直接投资金额

Direct Investment from Foreign, Hong Kong, Macao and Taiwan in Henan by City

单位：万美元 (USD 10 000)

市 City	新签协议(合同)金额 Value of New Signed Agreement (Contract)		实际利用外资 Actually Utilized Foreign Capital	
	2018	2019	2018	2019
全　　省 Total	**682233**	**413554**	**1790214**	**1872727**
省　辖　市 City				
郑　州　市 Zhengzhou	115032	239298	421080	440542
开　封　市 Kaifeng	4559	17955	69026	71810
洛　阳　市 Luoyang	232022	12011	279750	290822
平顶山市 Pingdingshan	55830	7786	45901	50488
安　阳　市 Anyang	37862	692	52723	55175
鹤　壁　市 Hebi	7581	4746	84408	87812
新　乡　市 Xinxiang	105891	10488	114141	121560
焦　作　市 Jiaozuo	1038	1533	85349	88414
濮　阳　市 Puyang	8108	2730	66390	69031
许　昌　市 Xuchang	4727	10905	75868	79165
漯　河　市 Luohe	12013	53940	93852	97880
三门峡市 Sanmenxia	40112	1192	111438	115904
南　阳　市 Nanyang	8938	4651	62622	65302
商　丘　市 Shangqiu	19347	11757	38474	42108
信　阳　市 Xinyang	3180	2830	55419	57480
周　口　市 Zhoukou	8956	9434	56192	58604
驻马店市 Zhumadian	14981	20350	42211	44024
济　源　市 Jiyuan	2056	1256	35370	36606
省直管县 County Directly Administrated by Province				
巩　义　市 Gongyi	54	822	33300	34350
兰　考　县 Lankao			6725	8065
汝　州　市 Ruzhou	2268	3020	7000	7664
滑　　县 Huaxian	15289		1197	1250
长　垣　市 Changyuan	1013	2530	17248	20680
邓　州　市 Dengzhou		20	1740	1800
永　城　市 Yongcheng		11520	4468	4796
固　始　县 Gushi			2961	3098
鹿　邑　县 Luyi			601	746
新　蔡　县 Xincai	1027	2973		554

6-9 外商和港澳台商投资企业(单位)注册登记情况

Registration Status of Foreign, Hong Kong, Macao and Taiwan Funded Enterprises

指　　标	Item	2005	2010	2015	2016	2017	2018	2019
年末实有企业数(户)	**Number of Registered Enterprise in the Year-end (unit)**	**2877**	**2459**	**2154**	**2272**	**2348**	**2466**	**2629**
与外商和港澳台商合资经营	Equity Joint Venture	1717	1251	974	1016	1026	1082	1151
与外商和港澳台商合作经营	Contractual Joint Venture	292	181	118	120	114	108	108
外商和港澳台商独资	Wholly owned Enterprise	860	1006	1027	1092	1159	1231	1325
外商和港澳台商投资股份有限公司	FDI Shareholding Inc	8	21	35	44	47	45	45
年末实有企业投资总额(亿美元)	**Total Investments (100 million USD)**	**206.41**	**378.66**	**687.10**	**822.49**	**1045.38**	**1106.28**	**1163.07**
注册资本(亿美元)	**Registered Capital (100 million USD)**	**112.29**	**205.35**	**348.16**	**449.00**	**555.29**	**593.98**	**713.09**
#外方	Capital Invested by Foreign Partner	75.34	148.66	248.44	331.63	408.69	446.98	507.86
本年登记企业数(户)	**Number of Registered Enterprise in the Year (unit)**	**420**	**252**	**154**	**186**	**251**	**226**	**244**
中外合资	Joint-venture Enterprises	212	91	52	79	104	96	97
中外合作	Cooperation Enterprises	39	19	3	6	6	1	1
外商独资	Wholly Foreign-owned Enterprise	169	142	98	100	138	129	145
中外股份公司	Share-holding Corporations			1	1	3		1
本年注册企业投资总额(亿美元)	**Total Investments of Registered Enterprise in the Year (100 million USD)**	40.10	50.75	41.21	92.66	261.48	125.99	80.34
本年注册资本(亿美元)	**Registered Capital ih the Year (100 million USD)**	20.18	27.00	21.62	47.11	138.42	97.12	55.71
#外方	Capital Invested by Foreign Partner	15.28	22.55	18.64	40.28	104.44	67.33	48.86

6-10 各市外商和港澳台商投资企业登记注册情况(2019年)
Registration Status of Foreign, Hong Kong, Macao and Taiwan Funded Enterprises by City (2019)

市 City	年末实有企业数(个，含分公司) Real Number of Enterprises by the end of the year (unit, including branch company)	年末实有企业投资总额(万美元) Realized Investment by the end of the year (USD 10 000)	本年登记企业数(个，含分公司) Registered Enterprises in the year (unit, including branch company)	本年注册企业投资总额(万美元) Total Value of Investment by Registered Enterprises This Year (USD 10 000)	累计注销企业数(个) Accumulative Number of Deregistered Enterprises (unit)
全省 Total	**10145**	**11630706**	**634**	**634182**	**6710**
河南省(省级) Provincial	**205**	**1175777**	**4**	**1455**	**1963**
郑州市 Zhengzhou	2542	3914899	276	268018	1067
开封市 Kaifeng	462	314127	18	20199	397
洛阳市 Luoyang	863	1179628	41	14206	694
平顶山市 Pingdingshan	397	578172	26	98240	226
安阳市 Anyang	422	404195	16	141	185
鹤壁市 Hebi	177	161034	11	22859	75
新乡市 Xinxiang	606	943597	32	8307	334
焦作市 Jiaozuo	428	310008	14	5123	165
濮阳市 Puyang	225	102920	30		214
许昌市 Xuchang	385	239823	21	7787	270
漯河市 Luohe	252	202098	12	66617	223
三门峡市 Sanmenxia	217	371453	13	2885	133
南阳市 Nanyang	740	568457	30	1911	356
商丘市 Shangqiu	576	257540	25	33362	95
信阳市 Xinyang	563	385345	18	5846	102
周口市 Zhoukou	471	189760	13	24344	83
驻马店市 Zhumadian	500	261898	23	50759	108
济源市 Jiyuan	114	69977	11	2123	20
省直管县 County Directly Administrated by Province					
巩义市 Gongyi	78	27883	3		
兰考县 Lankao	46	113718	1	624	2
汝州市 Ruzhou	54	94330	5	80754	2
滑县 Huaxian	39	98623	2		1
长垣市 Changyuan	53	27741	4	2440	
邓州市 Dengzhou	51	27679	4	20	
永城市 Yongcheng	92	33648	4	4169	3
固始县 Gushi	73	4886	3		
鹿邑县 Luyi	57	18318			
新蔡县 Xincai	44	7204	3	14	

6-11 对外国和港澳台地区投资

Investment to Foreign, Hong Kong, Macao and Taiwan

项　目	Item	2010	2012	2013	2014	2015	2016	2017	2018	2019
对外投资项目备案个数	Number of Foreign Investment Projects on Record	62	69	81	87	92	121	210	126	110
中方新签协议(合同)	Investments of New Agreement (Contract)									
投资额(万美元)	Signed by China (USD 10 000)	53132	108405	130207	159014	232461	436751	175780	223682	143358
年末已建成投产(开业)企业数(个)	Number of Business Completed and Put into Use in the Year-end (unit)	288	360	382	442	561	682	759	827	638

6-12 对外承包工程和劳务合作

Contracted Projects and Labor Cooperation with Foreign Countries or Regions

指　标	Item	2010	2012	2013	2014	2015	2016	2017	2018	2019
签订合同数(个)	Number of Contracts Signed (unit)	860	229	315	128	151	127	232	231	258
签订合同金额(亿美元)	Contracted Value (USD 100 million)	25.26	34.71	40.58	42.29	43.35	40.70	37.48	37.44	44.27
营业额(亿美元)	Value of Business (USD 100 million)	23.23	37.09	42.09	47.08	48.32	45.10	47.71	34.48	41.63
派出人员(人次)	Person Send Abroad (person-time)	32350	16492	68877	69703	70243	60942	57708	31761	28580
年底在外人员(人)	Number of Abroad Person at Year-end (person)	56251	57103	81751	88825	101289	116302	61622	63336	56608

6-13 各市利用省外资金情况

Direct Investment by Other Provinces in Henan by City

单位：亿元 (100 million yuan)

市 City	新签协议(合同)金额 Value of New Signed Agreement (Contract)		实际利用省外资金 Actually utilized Foreign Capital	
	2018	2019	2018	2019
全　　省 Total	**23495.7**	**24136.1**	**9647.1**	**9993.8**
省 辖 市 City				
郑 州 市 Zhengzhou	2832.6	3421.7	1134.7	1175.9
开 封 市 Kaifeng	1152.1	1219.8	618.3	638.1
洛 阳 市 Luoyang	1468.3	1228.7	811.6	838.4
平顶山市 Pingdingshan	2993.5	2290.4	579.3	599.1
安 阳 市 Anyang	1172.9	1142.4	719.2	744.9
鹤 壁 市 Hebi	626.9	1169.4	328.4	342.9
新 乡 市 Xinxiang	1322.1	1511.2	674.6	700.4
焦 作 市 Jiaozuo	1376.9	1362.9	657.5	679.9
濮 阳 市 Puyang	634.7	634.0	244.0	254.3
许 昌 市 Xuchang	1530.8	1296.5	508.7	528.5
漯 河 市 Luohe	527.9	687.6	255.7	265.1
三门峡市 Sanmenxia	714.4	791.0	401.8	417.9
南 阳 市 Nanyang	1146.9	932.1	589.1	609.6
商 丘 市 Shangqiu	2356.2	2362.4	736.3	759.2
信 阳 市 Xinyang	763.6	884.0	281.7	293.2
周 口 市 Zhoukou	1228.6	1148.7	585.7	606.4
驻马店市 Zhumadian	1259.6	1664.4	302.9	315.9
济 源 市 Jiyuan	396.7	388.9	217.6	224.1
省直管县 County Directly Administrated by Province				
巩 义 市 Gongyi	62.2	79.2	82.0	85.1
兰 考 县 Lankao	209.7	182.2	71.5	74.1
汝 州 市 Ruzhou	114.4	164.5	78.9	81.4
滑 县 Huaxian	152.1	83.3	71.5	74.0
长 垣 市 Changyuan	259.5	403.3	54.9	57.0
邓 州 市 Dengzhou	92.7	37.9	55.8	57.7
永 城 市 Yongcheng	192.7	113.8	69.9	72.2
固 始 县 Gushi	43.6	46.1	36.3	37.4
鹿 邑 县 Luyi	151.1	129.0	72.2	74.9
新 蔡 县 Xincai	93.5	76.7	22.8	23.5

6-14 旅游业基本情况
Basic Information of International Tourism

项 目	Item	2010	2011	2012	2013	2014	2015	2016	2017	2018	2019
接待入境游客人数	**Number of International Tourists**										
（万人次）	**Received (10 000 person-times)**	**146.84**	**168.29**	**190.77**	**207.33**	**227.20**	**268.29**	**293.95**	**307.32**	**321.73**	**351.47**
外国人	Foreigner	96.09	104.29	118.74	125.27	139.75	172.62	191.98	195.42	198.09	219.64
香港同胞	Compatriots from Hongkong	17.91	23.40	26.48	29.38	32.56	31.00	35.50	37.69	41.75	39.41
澳门同胞	Compatriots from Macao	8.07	10.00	11.25	11.62	11.72	14.54	14.31	16.15	16.00	18.35
台湾同胞	Compatriots from Taiwan	24.77	30.16	34.30	41.06	43.17	50.13	52.15	58.06	65.89	74.07
旅游创汇收入	**Income from International Tourists**										
（万美元）	**(USD 10 000)**	**49877**	**54902**	**61141**	**65997**	**72530**	**84948**	**89542**	**98182**	**103362**	**130401**

注：1. 本表接待入境旅游者人数包括不过夜人数(下表同)。
2. 旅游创汇收入为旅游部门抽样调查数。
a) Number of international tourists received exclude persons who didn't stay for night. (same as the following table).
b) Data on the income of international tourists received are obtained from sample survey by tourism administration.

6-15 各市入境旅游情况(2019年)
Basic Information of International Tourism by City (2019)

市	City	星级饭店数（个）Total Number of Starred Hotels (unit)	接待入境游客人数（人次）Number of International Tourists Received (person-time)	#外国人 Foreigner	旅游创汇收入（万美元）Income from International Tourists (USD 10 000)
郑州市	Zhengzhou	71	598412	429953	20603
开封市	Kaifeng	13	342612	174972	8992
洛阳市	Luoyang	50	1500616	960157	64170
平顶山市	Pingdingshan	21	59190	33590	1947
安阳市	Anyang	12	86956	85533	2678
鹤壁市	Hebi	9	9919	2536	245
新乡市	Xinxiang	11	123643	111774	3564
焦作市	Jiaozuo	20	395201	230396	12817
濮阳市	Puyang	10	60000	36000	3391
许昌市	Xuchang	16			
漯河市	Luohe	10	9980	6910	240
三门峡市	Sanmenxia	17	117169	58403	3700
南阳市	Nanyang	70	29920	3558	880
商丘市	Shangqiu	10	7382	1835	170
信阳市	Xinyang	28	28983	5890	1214
周口市	Zhoukou	16	89594	32247	3290
驻马店市	Zhumadian	20	41447	16022	2200
济源市	Jiyuan	2	13660	6586	300

6-16 接待国内游客人数和收入

Number and Income of Domestic Tourists Received

本表为抽样调查数。
Date in this table are obtained from the sample survey.

项 目	Item	2018	省内游客 Local Tourists	省外游客 Non-local Tourists	2019	省内游客 Local Tourists	省外游客 Non-local Tourists
接待国内游客人数 (万人次)	Number of Domestic Tourists Received (10 000 person-time)	78261	49148	29113	89803	55139	34664
#一日游	One Day Tour	27986	20429	7557	46787	28727	18060
接待国内游客收入 (亿元)	From Domestic Tourists (100 million yuan)	8052	5073	2979	9517	5843	3674

6-17 各市国内旅游基本情况(2019年)

Basic Information of Domestic Tour by City (2019)

市	City	总人次数(万人次) Number of Person-time (10 000 person-times)	总花费(亿元) Total Cost (100 million yuan)	人均花费(元) Per Capita Cost (yuan)
郑州市	Zhengzhou	20928	2531.27	1210
开封市	Kaifeng	8328	661.32	794
洛阳市	Luoyang	13996	1647.69	1177
平顶山市	Pingdingshan	3249	301.13	927
安阳市	Anyang	5597	443.48	792
鹤壁市	Hebi	1529	128.82	842
新乡市	Xinxiang	5190	353.74	682
焦作市	Jiaozuo	6546	542.15	828
濮阳市	Puyang	2912	236.72	813
许昌市	Xuchang	3197	213.55	668
漯河市	Luohe	1492	95.15	638
三门峡市	Sanmenxia	4379	378.43	864
南阳市	Nanyang	4670	379.69	813
商丘市	Shangqiu	2714	172.76	637
信阳市	Xinyang	4827	281.41	583
周口市	Zhoukou	2552	180.47	707
驻马店市	Zhumadian	5414	385.15	711
济源市	Jiyuan	1624	79.60	490

主要统计指标解释

货物进出口总额 指实际进出我国国境的货物总金额。包括对外贸易实际进出口货物，来料加工装配进出口货物，国家间、联合国及国际组织无偿援助物资和赠送品，华侨、港澳台同胞和外籍华人捐赠品，租赁期满归承租人所有的租赁货物，进料加工进出口货物，边境地方贸易及边境地区小额贸易进出口货物(边民互市贸易除外)，中外合资企业、中外合作经营企业、外商独资经营企业进出口货物和公用物品，到、离岸价格在规定限额以上的进出口货样和广告品(无商业价值、无使用价值和免费提供出口的除外)，从保税仓库提取在中国境内销售的进口货物，以及其他进出口货物。进出口总额用以观察一个国家在对外贸易方面的总规模。我国规定出口货物按离岸价格统计，进口货物按到岸价格统计。

利用外资 指我国各级政府、部门、企业和其他经济组织通过对外借款、吸收外商直接投资以及用其他方式筹措的境外现汇、设备、技术等。

外商直接投资 是指外国投资者在我国境内通过设立外商投资企业、合伙企业、与中方投资者共同进行石油资源的合作勘探开发以及设立外国公司分支机构等方式进行投资。外国投资者可以用现金、实物、无形资产、股权等投资，还可以用从外商投资企业获得的利润进行再投资。

外商其他投资 指除对外借款和外商直接投资以外的各种利用外资的形式。包括企业在境内外股票市场公开发行的以外币计价的股票（目前主要是在香港证券市场发行的H股和在境内证券市场发行的B股）发行价总额，国际租赁进口设备的应付款，补偿贸易中外商提供的进口设备、技术、物料的价款，加工装配贸易中外商提供的进口设备、物料的价款。

对外承包工程 指各对外承包公司以招标议标承包方式承揽的下列业务：⑴承包国外工程建设项目，⑵承包我国对外经援项目，⑶承包我国驻外机构的工程建设项目，⑷承包我国境内利用外资进行建设的工程项目，⑸与外国承包公司合营或联合承包工程项目时我国公司分包部分，⑹对外承包兼营的房屋开发业务。对外承包工程的营业额是以货币表现的本期内完成的对外承包工程的工作量，包括以前年度签订的合同和本年度新签订的合同在报告期内完成的工作量。

对外劳务合作 指以收取工资的形式向业主或承包商提供技术和劳动服务的活动。我国对外承包公司在境外开办的合营企业，中国公司同时又提供劳务的，其劳务部分也纳入劳务合作统计。劳务合作营业额按报告期内向雇主提交的结算数(包括工资、加班费和奖金等)统计。

旅游人数

(1)入境旅游人数：指报告期内来我国观光、度假、探亲访友、就医疗养、购物、参加会议或从事经济、文化、体育、宗教活动的外国人、港澳台同胞等入境游客。统计时，外国人、港澳台同胞每入境一次统计 1 人次。

(2)出境人数：指中国（大陆）居民因公或因私出境前往其他国家、中国香港特别行政区、澳门特别行政区和台湾省观光、度假、探亲访友、就医疗养、购物、参加会议或从事经济、文化、体育、宗教活动的人数，即出境游客。统计时，按每出境一次统计 1 人次。

(3)国内旅游人数：指在报告期内在中国（大陆）观光游览、度假、探亲访友、就医疗养、购物、参加会议或从事经济、文化、体育、宗教活动的中国（大陆）居民人数，其出游的目的不是通过所从事的活动谋取报酬。统计时，国内游客按每出游一次统计 1 人次。

国际旅游(外汇)收入 指入境游客在中国（大陆）境内旅行、游览过程中用于交通、参观游览、住宿、餐饮、购物、娱乐等全部花费。

国内旅游收入 指国内游客在国内旅行、游览过程中用于交通、参观游览、住宿、餐饮、购物、娱乐等全部花费。

星级饭店 指设备、设施、服务符合《旅游饭店星级的划分与评定》(GB/T14308-2010)，通过相关旅游管理部门评定，并取得星级饭店称号的饭店。

Explanatory Notes on Main Statistical Indicators

Total Imports and Exports of Goods refer to the real value of commodities imported into and exported from the boundary of China. They include the actual imports and exports through foreign trade, imported and exported goods under the processing and assembling trades and materials, supplies and gifts as aid given gratis between governments and by the United Nations and other international organizations, and contributions donated by overseas Chinese, compatriots in Hong Kong and Macao and Chinese with foreign citizenship, leasing commodities owned by tenant at the expiration of leasing period, the imported and exported commodities processed with imported materials, commodities trading in border areas(excluding mutual exchange goods), the imported and exported commodities and articles for public use of the Sino-foreign joint ventures, cooperative enterprises and ventures exclusively with foreign own investment. Also included are import or export of samples and advertising goods for whose CIF or FOB value are beyond the permitted ceiling (excluding goods of no trading or use value and free commodities for export), imported goods sold in China from bonded warehouses and other imported or exported goods. The indicator of the total imports and exports at customs can be used to observe the total size of external trade in a country. In accordance with the stipulation of the Chinese government, imports are calculated at CIF, while exports are calculated at FOB.

Utilization of Foreign Capital refers to remittance, equipment and technology financed from abroad, by loans, foreign direct investment and other forms undertaken by the Chinese governments at all levels, by various departments, enterprises and other economic units.

Direct Investment by Foreign Entrepreneurs refers to foreign investment in China through the establishment of foreign invested enterprises, cooperative exploration and development of petroleum resources with domestic investors and the establishment of branch organizations of foreign enterprises. Foreign investment can be made in forms of cash, physical investment, intangible assets and equity, in addition with reinvestment of the foreign enterprises with the profits gained from the investment.

Other Investment by Foreign Entrepreneurs refers to all forms of utilization of foreign capitals other than foreign borrowings and foreign direct investment. It includes the total value of stock shares in foreign currencies issued by enterprises at domestic or foreign stock exchanges (now mainly consisting of H shares issued at Hong Kong Security Market and B shares issued at domestic security markets), rent payable for the imported equipment through international leasing arrangement, cost of imported equipment, technology and materials provided by foreign counterparts in compensation trade and processing and assembly trade.

Contracted Projects with Foreign Countries refer to projects undertaken by Chinese contractors (project contracting companies) through bidding process. They include: (1) overseas civil engineering construction projects financed by foreign investors; (2) overseas projects financed by the Chinese government through its foreign aid programs; (3) construction projects of Chinese diplomatic missions, trade offices and other institutions stationed abroad; (4) construction projects in China financed by foreign investment; (5)sub-contracted projects to be taken by Chinese contractors through a joint umbrella project with foreign contractor's); (6)housing development projects. The business income from international contracted projects is the work volume of contracted projects completed during the reference period, expressed in monetary terms, including completed work on projects signed in previous years.

Service Cooperation with Foreign Countries refers to the activities of providing technology and labor services to employers or contractors in the forms of receiving salaries and wages. Labor services providing by contractual joint ventures of Chinese international contracting corporations should be included in the statistics of service co-operation with foreign countries. The business income of labor service co-operation is the income in the form of wages and salaries, overtime pay, bonuses and other remuneration received from the employers during the reference period.

Number of Tourists

(1) Visitor arrivals refer to the number of foreigners, Chinese compatriots from Hong Kong, Macao and Taiwan Chinese (mainland) who come to China (mainland) for sight-seeing, vacation, visiting relatives, medical treatment, shopping, attending conference, or to engage in economic, cultural, sports and religious activities. In compiling statistics, each time of entering China is counted as one person-time.

(2) Number of Chinese residents going abroad refer to the number of Chinese (mainland) residents going to other countries, Hong Kong Special Administrative region, Macao Special Administrative region and Taiwan for on official or private purposes, for sight-seeing, vacation, visiting relatives, medical treatment, shopping, attending conference, or to engage in economic, cultural, sports and religious activities. In compiling statistics, each time of leaving is counted as one person-time.

(3) Number of domestic tourists refers to the number Of Chinese (mainland) residents who travel within China (mainland) for sight-seeing, vacation, visiting relatives, medical treatment, shopping, attending conference, or to engage in economic, cultural, sports and religious activities. In compiling statistics, each time of traveling is counted as one person-time.

Foreign Exchange Earnings from International Tourism refer to the total expenditure of foreigners, overseas Chinese, Chinese compatriots from Hong Kong, Macao and Taiwan during their stay in the mainland of China on transportation, sighting, accommodation, food, shopping and entertainment.

Income from Domestic Tourism refer to expenditure of domestic tourists on transportation, sighting, accommodation, food, shopping and entertainment while they travel.

Star-rated Hotels refer to hotels rated with stars as assessed by the relevant tourism authorities according to GB/T14308-2010 standard with reference to their infrastructure, facilities and service levels.

能源

Energy

● 资料整理：杨琳

简要说明

一、主要内容

本篇包括能源生产、消费及品种构成，能源生产和消费弹性系数、能源加工转换效率、单位能耗、规模以上工业分行业主要能源品种的购进、消费及库存，主要耗能工业企业单位产品能源消耗，水资源消耗和电力消耗等资料。

二、统计范围

本篇统计范围为全社会或规模以上工业法人企业(年主营业收入达到2000万元及以上)。

三、资料来源

本篇数据来自能源平衡表以及规模以上工业企业能源购进、消费、库存统计年报、主要耗能工业企业单位产品能源消费情况表、工业企业用水情况年报。7-19表数据来自省电力公司。四、关于计算方法与数据修订的说明

1.能源生产与消费弹性系数分别以能源生产、消费增长速度与国内生产总值增长速度相比求得。

2.能源平衡表中，电力折算标准煤系数按平均发电煤耗计算。

3.能源加工转换效率表中，电力折算标准煤系数采用当量值计算，每千瓦小时折0.1229千克标准煤。

4.GDP按可比价格计算。

5.2010年、2015年以来相关数据根据第三、第四次经济普查结果进行修订。

Brief Introduction

I. Main Contents

Data in this chapter cover mainly energy production, consumption, and composition; elasticity ratio of energy production and consumption; efficiency of energy processing and conversion; energy consumption per unit; Purchase, consumption and Stock of enterprises above designated size by sector, Energy consumption per unit of product, consumption of water and electric.

II. Scope of Statistics

The scope of data in this chapter is the whole province, and Industrial enterprises above designated size (annual main business income reaches 20 million yuan and above)).

III. Sources of Data

Data in this part comes from the energy balance sheets and annual report on energy purchase, consumption and Stock by industrial enterprises above designated size, energy consumption per unit product of major energy consuming industrial enterprises, and annual report of water consumption of industrial enterprises. The data in table 7-19 are from the electric power of HeNan.

IV. Notes on Coverage and Compilation of Data

(1) The elasticity ratio of energy production is calculated as the quotient of the growth rate of energy production divided by the growth rate of GDP; and the elasticity ratio of energy consumption is calculated as the quotient of the growth rate of energy consumption divided by the growth rate of GDP.

(2) In the energy balance sheet, the coefficient for conversion of electric power into the standard coal equivalent is calculated according to the average consumption of coal for generating electricity.

(3) In the table on the efficiency of energy conversion, the coefficient for the conversion of electric power into the standard coal equivalent is calculated on the basis of the heat value equivalent. One kilowatt is equal to 0.1229 kg SCE.

(4) Gross domestic product are calculated at constant prices.

(5) Data on 2010 and 2015 have been revised according to the results of the third and fourth national economic census.

7-1 一次能源生产总量及构成
Total Production of Primary Energy and Its Composition

年 份 Year	一次能源生产总量（万吨标准煤）Total Primary Energy Production (10 000 tons of SCE)	占能源生产总量的比重（%）As Percentage of Total Energy Production			
		原 煤 Coal	原 油 Crude Oil	天然气 Natural Gas	一次电力及其他能源 Primary Electricity and Other Energy
1978	4434	93.7	5.4		0.9
1979	4536	91.9	7.1		1.0
1980	4402	91.3	7.5	0.1	1.1
1981	4760	87.4	11.1	0.5	1.0
1982	4998	85.3	12.8	0.7	1.2
1983	5456	83.8	14.1	0.9	1.2
1984	5981	82.8	15.3	0.9	1.0
1985	6909	81.5	16.4	1.2	0.9
1986	7261	80.3	17.3	1.6	0.8
1987	7361	79.3	18.1	1.9	0.7
1988	7624	78.6	18.3	2.3	0.8
1989	8031	80.0	17.0	2.2	0.8
1990	8071	81.3	15.6	2.3	0.8
1991	7999	81.9	15.2	2.2	0.7
1992	8058	82.8	14.4	2.1	0.7
1993	8037	83.7	13.6	1.9	0.8
1994	8085	85.0	12.1	2.0	0.9
1995	8454	87.5	10.2	1.6	0.7
1996	8757	88.1	9.6	1.6	0.7
1997	8558	87.9	9.8	1.7	0.6
1998	8080	87.4	10.4	2.0	0.2
1999	6947	85.6	11.6	2.5	0.3
2000	6591	83.7	12.2	2.8	1.4
2001	7238	84.0	11.2	2.9	1.9
2002	8321	85.2	9.8	2.8	2.3
2003	10634	88.3	7.4	2.3	2.0
2004	13079	90.4	5.7	1.7	2.2
2005	14522	91.3	5.0	1.8	1.9
2006	15002	91.7	4.7	1.7	2.0
2007	14604	91.8	4.8	1.4	2.0
2008	15487	92.6	4.4	1.2	1.8
2009	17002	93.4	4.0	0.8	1.8
2010	17438	92.4	4.1	0.5	3.0
2011	15786	91.3	4.4	0.4	3.9
2012	12224	90.2	5.6	0.5	3.7
2013	13133	90.6	5.2	0.5	3.7
2014	11796	89.8	5.7	0.6	3.9
2015	11173	89.3	5.3	0.5	4.9
2016	9695	89.0	4.7	0.5	5.9
2017	10254	87.2	3.9	0.4	8.5
2018	9731	84.8	3.8	0.4	11.0
2019	10304	82.3	3.5	0.4	13.8

注：电力折算标准煤数根据当年平均发电煤耗计算。

a) The coefficient for conversion of electric power into SCE is calculated on the basis of the data on average coal consunption in generating electric power in the same year.The same applies to the tables following.

7-2 能源消费总量及构成

Total Consumption of Energy and Its Composition

年 份 Year	能源消费总量 (万吨标准煤) Total Energy Consumption (10 000 tons of SCE)	占能源消费总量的比重 (%) As Percentage of Total Energy Consumption			
		煤 炭 Coal	石 油 Crude Oil	天然气 Natural Gas	一次电力及其他能源 Primary Electricity and Other Energy
1978	3353	92.3	6.8		0.9
1979	3228	92.1	6.9		1.0
1980	3389	91.6	7.0	0.2	1.2
1981	3612	91.3	6.9	0.6	1.2
1982	3560	91.1	6.5	0.9	1.5
1983	4035	90.9	6.5	1.1	1.5
1984	4474	91.0	6.5	1.2	1.3
1985	4618	89.9	7.0	1.8	1.3
1986	4709	88.3	8.4	2.2	1.1
1987	5006	88.4	8.4	2.2	1.0
1988	5292	87.7	8.8	2.5	1.0
1989	5112	87.7	8.7	2.3	1.3
1990	5206	87.8	8.4	2.6	1.2
1991	5363	88.3	8.5	2.2	1.0
1992	5583	88.4	8.4	2.3	0.9
1993	5862	88.2	8.8	2.0	1.0
1994	6225	87.7	9.0	2.2	1.1
1995	6473	87.6	9.6	1.8	1.0
1996	6654	87.5	9.8	1.7	1.0
1997	6711	87.8	9.6	1.7	0.9
1998	7244	87.6	9.8	1.6	1.0
1999	7380	87.5	9.8	1.7	1.0
2000	7919	87.6	9.6	1.7	1.1
2001	8367	87.0	9.5	1.9	1.6
2002	9005	86.6	9.3	2.0	2.1
2003	10595	86.7	9.4	1.9	2.0
2004	13074	86.6	9.2	2.0	2.2
2005	14625	87.2	8.7	2.2	1.9
2006	16234	87.4	8.0	2.5	2.1
2007	17838	87.7	7.9	2.5	1.9
2008	18976	87.2	8.0	2.6	2.2
2009	19751	87.0	7.9	2.8	2.3
2010	18964	82.8	9.3	3.4	4.5
2011	20462	81.6	10.4	3.6	4.4
2012	20920	80.0	11.5	4.7	3.8
2013	21909	77.2	12.9	4.8	5.2
2014	22890	77.7	12.6	4.5	5.3
2015	22343	76.4	13.3	5.2	5.1
2016	22323	75.3	14.3	5.2	5.0
2017	22162	71.6	14.6	5.8	8.0
2018	22659	69.9	15.3	5.8	9.0
2019	22300	67.4	15.7	6.1	10.7

7-3 能源生产弹性系数
Elasticity Ratio of Energy Production

年 份 Year	能源生产比上年增长 (%) Growth Rate of Energy Production over Preceding Year (%)	电力生产比上年增长 (%) Growth Rate of Electricity Production over Preceding Year (%)	生产总值比上年增长 (%) Growth Rate of Gross Domestic Product(GDP) over Preceding Year (%)	能源生产弹性系数 Elasticity Ratio of Energy Production	电力生产弹性系数 Elasticity Ratio of Electricity Production
1980	-3.0		15.4		
1981	8.1	13.6	7.8	1.04	1.74
1982	5.0	4.1	4.3	1.16	0.95
1983	9.2	5.6	23.8	0.39	0.24
1984	9.6	5.8	10.1	0.95	0.57
1985	15.5	5.3	13.5	1.15	0.39
1986	5.1	12.3	4.6	1.11	2.67
1987	1.4	12.0	15.0	0.09	0.80
1988	3.6	0.1	9.8	0.37	0.01
1989	5.3	5.6	7.0	0.76	0.80
1990	0.5	5.4	4.5	0.11	1.20
1991	-0.9	11.3	6.9		1.64
1992	0.7	16.2	13.7	0.05	1.18
1993	-0.3	8.8	15.6		0.56
1994	0.6	10.3	13.5	0.04	0.76
1995	4.6	12.8	14.7	0.31	0.87
1996	3.6	8.5	13.9	0.26	0.61
1997	-2.3	6.2	10.5		0.59
1998	-5.6	0.0	8.8		
1999	-14.0	4.4	8.1		0.55
2000	-5.1	6.6	9.1		0.73
2001	9.8	12.8	8.7	1.13	1.47
2002	15.0	14.4	9.1	1.64	1.59
2003	27.8	12.7	10.9	2.55	1.17
2004	23.0	24.2	12.8	1.80	1.89
2005	11.0	11.3	14.3	0.77	0.79
2006	3.3	12.6	14.5	0.23	0.87
2007	-2.7	19.9	14.6		1.36
2008	6.1	2.2	12.0	0.50	0.18
2009	9.8	4.9	11.0	0.89	0.45
2010	2.6	10.4	12.4	0.21	0.84
2011	-9.5	13.8	12.0		1.15
2012	-22.6	1.9	10.1		0.18
2013	7.4	8.3	9.0	0.83	0.90
2014	-10.2	-4.9	8.9		
2015	-4.8	-4.3	8.4		
2016	-13.2	1.5	8.2		0.18
2017	5.8	4.1	7.8	0.74	0.53
2018	-5.1	10.0	7.6		1.32
2019	5.9	-5.3	7.0	0.84	

7-4 能源消费弹性系数
Elasticity Ratio of Energy Consumption

年 份 Year	能源消费比上年增长（%） Growth Rate of Energy Consumption over Preceding Year (%)	电力消费比上年增长（%） Growth Rate of Electricity Consumption over Preceding Year (%)	生产总值比上年增长（%） Growth Rate of Gross Domestic Product(GDP)over Preceding Year (%)	能源消费弹性系数 Elasticity Ratio of Energy Consumption	电力消费弹性系数 Elasticity Ratio of Electricity Consumption
1980	5.0		15.4	0.32	
1981	6.6	5.6	7.8	0.85	0.72
1982	-1.4	32.3	4.3		7.51
1983	13.3	-3.2	23.8	0.56	
1984	10.9	6.5	10.1	1.08	0.64
1985	3.2	5.6	13.5	0.24	0.41
1986	2.0	7.0	4.6	0.43	1.52
1987	6.3	10.6	15.0	0.42	0.71
1988	5.7	12.1	9.8	0.58	1.23
1989	-3.4	9.8	7.0		1.40
1990	1.8	2.2	4.5	0.40	0.49
1991	3.0	9.3	6.9	0.43	1.35
1992	4.1	15.7	13.7	0.30	1.15
1993	5.0	7.5	15.6	0.32	0.48
1994	6.2	8.8	13.5	0.46	0.65
1995	4.0	13.2	14.7	0.27	0.90
1996	2.8	8.3	13.9	0.20	0.60
1997	0.9	6.5	10.5	0.09	0.62
1998	7.9	-0.5	8.8	0.90	
1999	1.9	3.4	8.1	0.23	0.42
2000	7.3	6.8	9.1	0.80	0.74
2001	5.7	12.7	8.7	0.65	1.45
2002	8.2	14.7	9.1	0.90	1.62
2003	17.0	13.7	10.9	1.56	1.26
2004	23.4	22.3	12.8	1.83	1.74
2005	11.9	7.6	14.3	0.83	0.53
2006	11.0	10.6	14.5	0.76	0.73
2007	9.9	21.5	14.6	0.68	1.47
2008	6.4	12.0	12.0	0.53	1.00
2009	4.1	5.6	11.0	0.37	0.51
2010	8.5	13.1	12.4	0.69	1.06
2011	7.9	13.0	12.0	0.66	1.08
2012	2.2	3.3	10.1	0.22	0.33
2013	4.7	5.5	9.0	0.53	0.61
2014	4.5	0.7	8.9	0.50	0.08
2015	1.2	-1.4	8.4	0.14	
2016	-0.1	3.8	8.2		0.46
2017	-0.7	5.9	7.8		0.76
2018	2.2	7.9	7.6	0.29	1.04
2019	-1.6	-1.6	7.0		

7-5 能源加工转换效率
Efficiency of Energy Conversion

单位：% (%)

年 份 Year	总效率 Total Efficiency	发电及供热 Electricity Generation and Heating by Power Stations	炼 焦 Coking	炼 油 Petroleum Refining
1995	59.73	33.58	93.35	96.93
1996	61.21	35.64	91.90	97.71
1997	61.61	36.27	94.79	95.69
1998	67.84	35.41	99.40	99.40
1999	63.57	36.54	95.44	95.44
2000	61.78	36.03	96.71	96.71
2001	61.26	35.49	96.06	96.06
2002	59.47	36.36	98.31	98.31
2003	58.34	34.34	97.90	97.90
2004	58.36	33.45	94.38	94.38
2005	60.97	34.18	96.81	96.81
2006	64.94	36.10	99.08	99.08
2007	66.22	38.10	89.43	99.67
2008	65.96	39.49	91.89	95.43
2009	70.15	39.62	91.97	99.16
2010	72.64	40.85	93.24	87.14
2011	73.74	41.96	91.22	97.01
2012	72.24	41.99	91.62	97.66
2013	73.09	42.61	97.40	96.25
2014	74.30	43.51	96.33	97.88
2015	73.46	43.84	94.32	98.18
2016	75.03	44.60	94.11	98.92
2017	73.79	44.94	93.90	98.80
2018	68.95	45.58	94.62	98.62
2019	69.75	46.33	95.77	98.55

7-6 综合平衡表
Overall Energy Balance Sheet

单位：万吨标准煤 (10 000 tons of SCE)

项 目	Item	2015	2016	2017	2018	2019
可供量	**Total Energy Available for Consumption**	**22416.32**	**22283.65**	**22112.83**	**22603.14**	**22123.20**
一次能源生产量	Primary Energy Output	11172.53	9695.33	10253.90	9731.22	10303.95
外省(区、市)调入量	Transfer from Other Provinces (Districts, Cities)	18145.73	19345.28	19319.34	19006.72	20004.24
进口量	Imports					
本省(区、市)调出量(－)	Transfer to Other Provinces (Districts, Cities)	6288.50	6748.94	7801.73	5365.86	8201.37
出口量(–)	Exports (-)					
年初年末库存差额	Stock Changes in the Year	-613.44	-8.02	341.34	-768.94	16.38
年初库存量	Stock at the beginning of the year	578.46	1188.36	1196.38	855.04	1623.99
年末库存量(–)	Stock at the end of the year	1191.90	1196.38	855.04	1623.99	1607.61
消费量	**Total Energy Consumption**	**22342.93**	**22322.82**	**22162.09**	**22658.52**	**22299.65**
在总量中：	Consumption by Sector					
农、林、牧、渔业	Agriculture, Forestry, Animal Husbandry, Fishery	471.86	473.60	476.06	556.76	571.57
工 业	Industry	15757.20	15441.67	14896.83	14691.09	13930.75
建筑业	Construction	348.34	265.49	353.05	387.34	451.26
交通运输、仓储和邮政业	Transport, Storage and Post	1577.08	1686.24	1700.83	1801.14	1806.32
批发、零售业和	Wholesale and Retail Trades,					
住宿、餐饮业	Hotels and Catering Services	788.85	859.08	853.03	1042.32	1196.42
其他	Other Sectors	726.69	821.56	796.84	869.18	892.67
生活消费	Household Consumption	2672.90	2775.17	3085.45	3310.71	3450.66
在总量中：	Consumption by Usage					
终端消费	End-use Consumption	21387.12	21557.91	21369.65	21701.36	21368.85
#工业	Industry	14813.61	14684.87	14127.51	13760.04	13026.96
加工转换损失	Losses During the Process of Energy Conversion	288.93	92.98	107.47	204.97	180.76
#火力发电损失	Power Generation	0.00				0.00
供热损失	Heating	226.53	217.10	264.63	292.27	324.67
洗选煤损失	Coal Cleaning	295.67	145.81	155.75	334.51	340.23
炼焦损失	Coking	197.63	204.78	165.79	148.92	105.96
炼油及煤制油损失	Petroleum Refining	16.86	11.50	12.36	17.84	18.14
制气损失	Gas Production	52.87	42.54	39.04	41.89	52.00
天然气液化损失	Gas Liquidation	0.04	0.30	0.80	6.63	10.08
煤制品加工损失	Coal Products Processing	4.39			0.29	1.93
回收能	Recovery of Energy	-505.06	-529.05	-530.91	-637.38	-672.25
损失量	**Energy Losses**	**666.88**	**671.93**	**684.97**	**752.19**	**750.04**
平衡差额	**Balance**	**73.40**	**-39.17**	**-49.25**	**-55.38**	**-176.45**

7-7 平均每天能源消费量
Average Daily Energy Consumption by Type of Energy

能源品种	Item	1995	2000	2005	2010	2015	2016	2017	2018	2019
合计 （万吨标准煤）	**Total (10 000 tons of SCE)**	**17.73**	**21.70**	**40.07**	**50.94**	**61.21**	**61.16**	**60.72**	**62.08**	**61.10**
原煤 （万吨）	Coal (10 000 tons)	23.33	26.58	55.38	73.33	77.96	75.84	75.77	66.11	60.91
焦炭 （万吨）	Coke (10 000 tons)	1.08	1.17	2.72	4.78	3.87	3.68	3.38	3.90	3.92
原油 （万吨）	Crude Oil (10 000 tons)	1.10	1.67	1.83	2.29	1.66	1.88	1.78	2.27	2.19
汽油 （万吨）	Gasoline (10 000 tons)	0.39	0.33	0.64	0.81	1.87	1.92	2.03	2.09	2.11
煤油 （万吨）	Kerosene (10 000 tons)	0.04	0.04	0.04	0.08	0.19	0.20	0.20	0.22	0.25
柴油 （万吨）	Diesel Oil (10 000 tons)	0.37	0.42	0.90	1.54	2.36	2.54	2.67	2.72	2.76
燃料油 （万吨）	Fuel Oil (10 000 tons)	0.14	0.16	0.21	0.05	0.11	0.11	0.08	0.09	0.03
天然气 （亿立方米）	Natural Gas (100 million cu.m)	0.03	0.03	0.06	0.13	0.24	0.24	0.27	0.29	0.29
电力 （亿千瓦小时）	Electricity (100 million kwh)	1.57	1.97	3.80	7.00	9.22	9.32	9.28	10.03	9.88

7-8 人均生活能源消费量

Average Per Capita Energy Consumption of Households

能源品种	Item	1995	2000	2005	2010	2015	2016	2017	2018	2019
平均每人生活消费	**Annual Per Capita Consumption**									
能源（千克标准煤）	**for Households (kg of SCE)**	**112.97**	**121.27**	**161.29**	**179.79**	**282.61**	**291.94**	**323.24**	**345.51**	**358.60**
煤炭　（千克）	Coal (kg)	119.76	95.36	112.90	53.89	40.91	38.45	36.84	34.97	34.46
液化石油气　（千克）	Liquefied Petroleum gas (kg)	0.91	2.18	2.62	3.40	8.37	10.77	12.68	13.19	13.90
天然气　（立方米）	Natural Gas (cu.m)	2.63	2.00	5.49	6.45	23.45	24.76	27.66	33.50	35.26
热力　（百万千焦）	Heat (million kJ)	0.02	0.09	0.17	0.24	0.60	0.63	0.65	0.68	0.88
电力　（千瓦小时）	Electricity (kwh)	46.28	80.05	128.91	288.20	472.91	515.92	555.24	629.62	634.56

注：2010年以后使用常住人口计算人均生活能源消费量。
a) Per capita energy consumption is calculated on resident population since 2010.

7-9 规模以上工业企业分品种能源购进、消费及库存(2019年)

Purchase, Consumption, and Stock of Energy in above Designated Size Industrial Enterprises by Catalog (2019)

项 目	Item	年初库存 Stock of Year Beginning	购进量 Purchase Capacity	消费量 Total Energy Consumption	工业生产消费 Consumption of Industry Production	非工业生产消费 Consumptin of Industry Nonindustry Production	年末库存 Stock at Year-end
原煤(万吨)	Coal (10 000tons)	1239.20	20554.55	21609.45	21568.87	40.59	1200.38
洗精煤(万吨)	Clean Coal (10 000tons)	129.96	2527.27	2702.89	2702.89		119.64
其他洗煤(万吨)	Other Clean Coal (10 000tons)	15.16	325.11	374.86	374.82	0.04	12.31
煤制品(万吨)	Coal Products (10 000tons)	0.02	2.91	2.91	2.91		0.01
焦炭(万吨)	Coke (10 000tons)	33.88	1160.61	1431.85	1431.85	0.00	33.24
其他焦化产品(万吨)	Other Coking Products (10 000 tons)	0.62	13.98	25.97	25.97		0.43
焦炉煤气(亿立方米)	Coking Gas (100 million cu.m)		13.80	49.44	49.44		
高炉煤气(亿立方米)	Blast furnace Gas (100 million cu.m)		22.34	344.42	344.42		
其他煤气(亿立方米)	Other Gas (100 million cu.m)		18.98	71.55	71.55		
天然气(亿立方米)	Natural Gas (100 million cu.m)	0.06	49.14	53.70	53.36	0.33	0.03
液化天然气(万吨)	Liquefied Gas (10 000 tons)	0.13	11.17	11.04	11.02	0.02	0.18
原油(万吨)	Crude Oil (10 000 tons)	24.23	786.66	799.61	799.61		20.04
汽油(万吨)	Gasoline (10 000 tons)	0.04	9.58	9.66	7.36	2.30	0.03
煤油(万吨)	Kerosene (ton)	0.01	0.31	0.31	0.31	0.00	0.02
柴油(万吨)	Diesel Fuel Oil (10 000 tons)	1.93	39.42	37.68	36.23	1.45	3.74
燃料油(万吨)	Fuel Oil (10 000 tons)	0.34	6.13	6.37	6.37	0.00	0.23
液化石油气(万吨)	Liquefied Petroleum Gas (10 000 tons)	0.08	60.24	59.20	59.19	0.00	1.08
炼厂干气(万吨)	Net Gas of Plant (10 000 tons)		1.76	27.13	27.13		
其他石油制品(万吨)	Other Petroleum Products (10 000 tons)	2.41	98.64	107.29	107.29		0.19
热力(万百万千焦)	Heat (10 billion kilo-joule)		7341.76	16720.80	16550.99	169.80	
电力(亿千瓦时)	Power (100 million kwh)		1468.73	1842.65	1832.11	10.54	
其他燃料(万吨标准煤)	Other Fuel (10 000 tons of SCE)	0.02	2.32	2.30	2.30	0.00	0.08

7-10 规模以上工业企业分行业主要能源消费量(2019年)

行 业	Sector	综合能源消费量（万吨标准煤）Total Energy Consumption (10 000 tons of SCE)
总 计	**Total**	**12988.75**
采矿业	**Mining**	**775.71**
煤炭开采和洗选业	Mining and Washing of Coal	642.78
石油和天然气开采业	Extraction of Petroleum and Natural Gas	65.47
黑色金属矿采选业	Mining and Processing of Ferrous Metal Ores	7.15
有色金属矿采选业	Mining and Processing of Non-ferrous Metal Ores	19.42
非金属矿采选业	Mining and Processing of Nonmetal Ores	5.09
开采辅助活动	Support Activities for Mining	35.80
其他采矿业	Mining of Other Ores	
制造业	**Manufacturing**	**8107.08**
农副食品加工业	Processing of Food from Agricultural Products	114.00
食品制造业	Manufacture of Foods	102.99
酒、饮料和精制茶制造业	Manufacture of Liquor, Beverages and Refined Tea	57.32
烟草制造业	Manufacture of Tobacco	5.60
纺织业	Manufacture of Textile	71.93
纺织服装、服饰业	Manufacture of Textile, Wearing, Apparel and Accessories	11.58
皮革、毛皮、羽毛及其制品和制鞋业	Manufacture of Leather, Fur, Feather and Related Products and Footwear	12.14
木材加工及木、竹、藤、棕、草制品业	Processing of Timbers, Manufacture of Wood, Bamboo, Rattan, Palm, and Straw Products	26.50
家具制造业	Manufacture of Furniture	5.22
造纸及纸制品业	Manufacture of Paper and Paper Products	188.10
印刷和记录媒介复制业	Printing,Reproduction of Recording Media	8.07
文教、工美、体育和娱乐用品制造业	Manufacture for Culture, Education, Arts and Crafts Sport and Entertainment Activities	8.02
石油加工、炼焦及核燃料加工业	Processing of Petroleum, Coking, and Processing of Nucleus Fuel	521.77
化学原料及化学制品制造业	Manufacture of Raw Chemical Materials and Chemical Products	1936.01
医药制造业	Manufacture of Medicines	62.67
化学纤维制造业	Manufacture of Chemical Fibers	45.88
橡胶和塑料制品业	Manufacture of Rubber and Plastics Products	45.67
非金属矿物制品业	Manufacture of Non-metallic Mineral Products	1142.91
黑色金属冶炼和压延加工业	Smelting and Pressing of Ferrous Metals	1830.58
有色金属冶炼及压延加工业	Smelting and Pressing of Non-ferrous Metals	1584.69
金属制品业	Manufacture of Metal Products	90.06
通用设备制造业	Manufacture of General Purpose Machinery	37.41
专业设备制造业	Manufacture of Special Purpose Machinery	37.00
汽车制造业	Manufacture of Automobiles	48.69
铁路、船舶、航空航天和其他运输设备制造业	Manufacture of Railway, Ship, Aerospace, and other Transport Equipments	8.67
电气机械及器材制造业	Manufacture of Electrical Machinery and Apparatus	50.34
计算机、通信和其他电子设备制造业	Manufacture of Computer, Communication and Other Electronic Equipment	45.91
仪器仪表制造业	Manufacture of Measuring Instrument and Machinery	2.54
其他制造业	Others Mannfacture	0.87
废弃资源综合利用业	Utilization of Waste Resources	3.35
金属制品、机械和设备修理业	Repairing Services of Metal Products, Machinery and Equipment	0.60
电力、燃气及水的生产和供应业	**Production and Supply of Electric Pouver Gas and Water**	**4105.96**
电力、热力生产和供应业	Production and Supply of Electric Power and Heat Power	4079.84
燃气生产和供应业	Production and Distribution of Gas	12.30
水的生产和供应业	Production and Distribution of Water	13.82

Consumption of Main Energy in above Designated Size Industrial Enterprises by Sector (2019)

原　煤 (万吨) Coal (10 000tons)	焦　炭 (万吨) Coke (10 000tons)	原　油 (万吨) Crude Oil (10 000tons)	柴　油 (万吨) Diesel Fuel Oil (10 000tons)	燃料油 (万吨) Fuel Oil (10 000tons)	热　力 (万百万千焦) Heat (10 billion Kilo Joule)	电　力 (亿千瓦时) Electricity (100 million kwh)
21609.45	**1431.85**	**799.61**	**37.68**	**6.37**	**16720.80**	**1842.65**
6271.65	**0.00**	**8.90**	**22.49**	**5.09**	**756.72**	**112.05**
6244.70		0.05	1.53	0.00	144.66	72.61
9.83		8.76	1.77	5.09	593.97	14.35
0.01			0.25			3.99
0.00			0.64			14.36
0.00	0.00		0.72			3.06
17.09		0.09	17.57		18.09	3.66
5908.58	**1431.85**	**790.72**	**11.39**	**0.99**	**15619.33**	**1426.88**
53.17			0.39	0.01	515.39	38.20
32.86			0.34	0.01	841.60	20.18
34.88			0.16		165.99	11.39
			0.01		28.47	1.67
1.90			0.03	0.01	71.14	49.45
0.01			0.15	0.03	21.04	6.00
5.20			0.01		1.61	5.11
0.20			0.12	0.00	65.38	10.99
0.02			0.03			2.40
142.97	0.22		0.26	0.01	1566.72	37.40
			0.12		14.27	4.95
			0.02		57.84	3.97
577.76		790.72	0.52	0.13	1423.39	36.29
1775.41	84.89		0.56	0.10	5661.66	229.32
13.90			0.63		403.47	19.96
44.05			0.02	0.09	535.62	11.83
16.36	0.00		0.10	0.01	288.14	20.01
842.60	13.62		2.97	0.50	85.89	179.37
341.57	1274.02	0.00	0.79			169.96
2020.72	28.04		2.09	0.08	3545.14	394.16
4.01	30.78		0.13	0.00	13.49	30.10
	0.03		0.18		12.41	25.04
0.02	0.09		0.47		80.52	19.04
	0.01		0.64		16.95	28.92
			0.02		7.19	4.75
			0.43	0.00	51.65	31.14
0.00			0.02		138.50	31.62
			0.01		1.03	1.80
0.04			0.01			0.60
0.94	0.15		0.09			1.08
			0.06		4.82	0.18
9429.22			**3.81**	**0.30**	**344.75**	**303.72**
9429.22			3.74	0.30	344.58	289.12
			0.02			3.50
			0.05		0.17	11.10

7-11 规模以上工业分部门主要能源消费量(2019年)

Consumption of Main Energy in above Designated Size Industrial Enterprises by Sector (2019)

部 门	Sector	综合能源消费量(万吨标准煤) Total Energy Consumption (10 000 (tons of SCE)	原 煤(万吨) Coal (10 000 tons)	焦 炭(万吨) Coke (10 000 tons)	原 油(万吨) Crude Oil (10 000 tons)	柴 油(万吨) Diesel Fuel Oil (10 000 tons)	燃料油(万吨) Fuel Oil (10 000 tons)	热 力(万百万千焦) Heat (10 billion Kilo Joule)	电 力(亿千瓦时) Electricity (100 million kwh)
全省总计	**Total**	**12988.75**	**21609.45**	**1431.85**	**799.61**	**37.68**	**6.37**	**16720.80**	**1842.65**
煤 炭	Coal	646.54	6261.76		0.05	1.53	0.00	144.66	72.62
石油石化	Petroleum	234.83	60.39		799.56	19.51	5.22	1377.14	32.37
冶 金	Metallurgy	2244.75	868.82	1274.02	0.00	1.42		663.68	205.59
有 色	coloured Coherer	1604.11	2020.72	28.04		2.73	0.08	3545.14	408.53
建 材	Construction Material	1119.46	842.02	13.62		3.62	0.50	85.89	175.08
化 工	Chymic Industry	1959.68	1791.77	84.90		0.59	0.11	5923.57	235.82
轻 工	Light Industry	578.90	269.68	0.22		1.59	0.03	3209.64	164.64
烟 草	Tobacco	5.60				0.01		28.47	1.67
纺 织	Textile	129.38	45.96			0.20	0.13	627.80	67.28
医 药	Medication	64.70	13.90			0.71		403.47	21.20
机 械	Machinery	166.85	0.11	0.12		1.67	0.00	162.70	98.61
电 子	Electron	45.91	0.00			0.02		138.50	31.62
电 力	Electric Power	4050.34	9366.87			2.80	0.30	209.12	285.11
其 他	Other	137.71	67.45	30.93		1.27	0.00	201.01	42.51

7-12 各市规模以上工业企业分品种主要能源消费量(2019年)

Consumption of Main Energy Sources in above Designated Size Industrial Enterprises by Industrial Sector and City (2019)

市(县) City(County)	综合能源消费量(万吨标准煤) Total Energy Consumption (10 000 tons of SCE)	原煤(万吨) Coal (10 000 tons)	焦炭(万吨) Coke (10 000 tons)	原油(万吨) Crude Oil (10 000 tons)	柴油(万吨) Diesel Fuel Oil (10 000 tons)	燃料油(万吨) Fuel Oil (10 000 tons)	热力(万百万千焦) Heat (10 billion Kilo Joule)	电力(亿千瓦时) Electricity (100 million kwh)
全　　省 Total	**12988.75**	**21609.45**	**1431.85**	**799.61**	**37.68**	**6.37**	**16720.80**	**1842.65**
省辖市 City								
郑州市 Zhengzhou	1371.23	2066.79	23.73		3.34	0.53	1556.40	239.93
开封市 Kaifeng	309.74	413.00	0.45		0.46		59.22	38.60
洛阳市 Luoyang	1338.52	1894.71	2.60	549.47	2.53	0.04	1151.47	303.43
平顶山市 Pingdingshan	1042.93	4489.10	107.77		2.11	0.08	2229.42	145.50
安阳市 Anyang	1537.85	1073.23	676.16		0.71	0.00	844.15	154.52
鹤壁市 Hebi	454.36	1224.11			0.38	0.07	236.53	31.59
新乡市 Xinxiang	901.85	1234.79	30.33		0.68	0.10	1455.31	125.61
焦作市 Jiaozuo	1011.06	1338.02	4.47		0.91	0.02	2632.96	171.55
濮阳市 Puyang	567.30	394.59		224.43	18.81		742.85	53.18
许昌市 Xuchang	405.37	1055.77			0.67	0.08	262.90	71.46
漯河市 Luohe	222.45	290.34			1.55	0.00	389.64	37.85
三门峡市 Sanmenxia	691.27	1324.73	0.24		1.50	0.11	1915.36	71.97
南阳市 Nanyang	674.15	705.96	107.28	25.66	1.46	5.23	2109.36	110.79
商丘市 Shangqiu	715.71	2044.50	124.06	0.05	0.34	0.01	499.63	63.68
信阳市 Xinyang	429.33	433.44	136.30		0.45		6.30	47.89
周口市 Zhoukou	166.03	212.58	0.03		0.89			41.47
驻马店市 Zhumadian	424.02	547.31	26.17		0.23	0.05	338.14	49.34
济源市 Jiyuan	725.57	866.47	192.25		0.67	0.04	291.16	84.30
省直管县 County Directly Administrated by Province								
巩义市 Gongyi	323.05	387.85	18.29		0.31	0.05	21.89	62.86
兰考县 Lankao	13.62	0.17			0.08		8.63	4.26
汝州市 Ruzhou	219.09	988.93	23.10		0.46	0.00	23.75	26.93
滑县 Huaxian	60.90	75.00			0.01			11.99
长垣市 Changyuan	90.91	206.88			0.10			5.59
邓州市 Dengzhou	25.38	15.41			0.03			4.36
永城市 Yongcheng	532.28	1722.53	124.06	0.05	0.24	0.01	449.49	37.24
固始县 Gushi	3.71	0.20			0.03			1.72
鹿邑县 Luyi	10.18	2.16			0.01			2.42
新蔡县 Xincai	1.69	0.02						1.20

7-13 规模以上工业企业分行业水消费总量(2019年)

单位：万立方米

行 业	Sector	取水总量 Water consumption
总 计	**Total**	**346475**
轻工业	Light Industry	30614
重工业	Heavy Industry	315861
采矿业	**Mining**	**23623**
煤炭开采和洗选业	Mining and Washing of Coal	20916
石油和天然气开采业	Extraction of Petroleum and Natural Gas	1094
黑色金属矿采选业	Mining and Processing of Ferrous Metal Ores	217
有色金属矿采选业	Mining and Processing of Non-ferrous Metal Ores	1238
非金属矿采选业	Mining and Processing of Nonmetal Ores	135
开采辅助活动	Support Activities for Mining	24
其他采矿业	Mining of Other Ores	
制造业	**Manufacturing**	**87713**
农副食品加工业	Processing of Food from Agricultural Products	4880
食品制造业	Manufacture of Foods	3663
酒、饮料和精制茶制造业	Manufacture of Liquor Beverages and Refined Tea	4068
烟草制造业	Manufacture of Tobacco	213
纺织业	Manufacture of Textile	2584
纺织服装、服饰业	Manufacture of Textile, Wearing, Apparel and Accessories	521
皮革、毛皮、羽毛及其制品和制鞋业	Manufacture of Leather, Fur, Feather and Related Products and Footwear	1051
木材加工及木、竹、藤、棕、草制品业	Processing of Timbers, Manufacture of Wood, Bamboo, Rattan, Palm, and Straw Products	294
家具制造业	Manufacture of Furniture	147
造纸及纸制品业	Manufacture of Paper and Paper Products	4996
印刷和记录媒介复制业	Printing,Reproduction of Recording Media	184
文教、工美、体育和娱乐用品制造业	Manufacture for Culture, Education, Arts and Crafts, Sport and entertainment Activities	480
石油加工、炼焦及核燃料加工业	Processing of Petroleum ,Coking, and Processing of Nucleus Fuel	3772
化学原料及化学制品制造业	Manufacture of Raw Chemical Material and Chemical Products	18932
医药制造业	Manufacture of Medicines	3019
化学纤维制造业	Manufacture of Chemical Fibers	2559
橡胶和塑料制品业	Manufacture of Rubber and Plastics Products	915
非金属矿物制品业	Manufacture of Non-metallic Mineral Products	8404
黑色金属冶炼和压延加工业	Smelting and Pressing of Ferrous Metals	7057
有色金属冶炼及压延加工业	Smelting and Pressing of Non-ferrous Metals	11211
金属制品业	Manufacture of Metal Products	894
通用设备制造业	Manufacture of General Purpose Machinery	1456
专业设备制造业	Manufacture of Special Purpose Machinery	981
汽车制造业	Manufacture of Automobiles	1206
铁路、船舶、航空航天和其他运输设备制造业	Manufacture of Railway, Ship, Aerospace, and other Transport Equipment	167
电气机械及器材制造业	Manufacture of Electrical Machinery and Apparatus	1407
计算机、通信和其他电子设备制造业	Manufacture of Computer Communication and Other Electronic Equipment	2249
仪器仪表制造业	Manufacture of Measuring Instrument and Machinery	160
其他制造业	Others Manufacture	158
废弃资源综合利用业	Utilization of Waste Resources	47
金属制品、机械和设备修理业	Repair Services of Metal Products, Machinery and Equipment	37
电力、燃气及水的生产和供应业	**Production and Supply of Electric Power Gas and Water**	**235139**
电力、热力生产和供应业	Production and Supply of Electric Power and Heat Power	41549
燃气生产和供应业	Production and Distribution of Gas	132
水的生产和供应业	Production and Distribution of Water	193459

Computation of Water in above Designated Size Industrial Enterprises by Sector (2019)

(10 000 cubic meters)

地表水 Surface Water	地下水 Ground-water	自来水 Tap water	其它水 Others	重复用水 Volume of Repeated Consumption
189230	**84137**	**43453**	**29656**	**2770783**
2410	16056	11922	227	23265
186821	68081	31531	29429	2747518
4725	**9729**	**1676**	**7493**	**37513**
3342	8579	1531	7464	28158
44	945	104		
207	8		2	959
1083	120	10	26	8359
49	76	8	2	38
		24		
25152	**31605**	**24920**	**6037**	**1138797**
108	2509	2225	38	168
25	2077	1561		74
345	2030	1679	15	586
	1	212		41
4	1961	619		744
31	294	197		52
491	503	56	1	25
39	234	21		3
1	102	44		
1218	3078	635	65	6283
4	112	69		1
42	278	160		1
1703	704	1080	285	74994
7714	4255	3078	3886	560098
98	1158	1674	90	6521
5	514	2021	18	8412
7	619	145	144	6277
1858	4179	2309	59	11697
4573	618	1336	531	246055
6626	3227	570	788	198729
47	474	372	1	62
108	847	500	1	2855
19	311	635	17	3340
29	291	786	100	9669
13	46	109		2
30	503	875		226
3	473	1772		1549
9	45	107		295
	152	5		
3	10	35		7
		37		30
159354	**42803**	**16857**	**16126**	**1594472**
19796	2004	3653	16095	1594303
	32	100		
139558	40767	13103	30	169

7-14 各市规模以上工业企业水消费量(2019年)

Computation of Water in above Designated Size Industrial Enterprises by City (2019)

单位：万立方米 (10 000 cubic meters)

市(县) City(County)	取水总量 Water consumption	地表水 Surface Water	地下水 Ground-water	自来水 Tap Water	其它水 Others	重复用水 Volume of Repeated Consumption
全 省 Total	**346475**	**189230**	**84137**	**43453**	**29656**	**2770783**
省 辖 市 City						
郑 州 市 Zhengzhou	82475	57498	6927	10397	7652	328433
开 封 市 Kaifeng	14167	11824	1134	842	367	202619
洛 阳 市 Luoyang	28763	7176	14377	4363	2848	223673
平 顶 山 市 Pingdingshan	25540	16075	1517	5038	2910	219578
安 阳 市 Anyang	16161	11059	1805	1818	1479	209035
鹤 壁 市 Hebi	6841	1831	894	2950	1166	139963
新 乡 市 Xinxiang	21612	14042	2990	2820	1760	154011
焦 作 市 Jiaozuo	24299	6185	13592	2000	2523	213944
濮 阳 市 Puyang	13477	10155	1523	1616	183	161215
许 昌 市 Xuchang	10112	6157	1747	343	1865	144419
漯 河 市 Luohe	8564	5258	1712	1232	362	41667
三 门 峡 市 Sanmenxia	19179	6418	7830	3070	1861	130844
南 阳 市 Nanyang	13840	5812	6852	1098	78	40768
商 丘 市 Shangqiu	11132	3691	4753	494	2194	162426
信 阳 市 Xinyang	25471	17717	3515	2798	1441	27376
周 口 市 Zhoukou	8429	436	7298	201	495	48
驻 马 店 市 Zhumadian	6819	3227	1898	1485	208	99737
济 源 市 Jiyuan	9593	4670	3771	889	263	271028
省 直 管 县 County Directly Administrated by Province						
巩 义 市 Gongyi	3954	1390	212	2275	76	112760
兰 考 县 Lankao	156	1	30	125		
汝 州 市 Ruzhou	1049	493	448	65	42	3389
滑 县 Huaxian	768		89	334	345	1600
长 垣 市 Changyuan	1058	530	87	29	412	14670
邓 州 市 Dengzhou	213	87	82	18	26	51
永 城 市 Yongcheng	4887	256	2812	29	1790	119607
固 始 县 Gushi	1206	1091	92	21	1	119
鹿 邑 县 Luyi	1337		1332	6		4
新 蔡 县 Xincai	233	3	204	26		3

7-15 各市年耗能万吨标准煤以上工业企业个数

Number of Industrial Enterprises of Consumption of Energy Above 10 000 tons by City

单位：个 (unit)

市(县)	City(County)	2005	2010	2011	2012	2013	2014	2015	2016	2017	2018	2019
全省	**Total**	**849**	**1071**	**1118**	**1003**	**978**	**958**	**907**	**857**	**751**	**673**	**648**
省辖市	**City**											
郑州市	Zhengzhou	165	212	212	191	189	167	165	145	133	105	87
开封市	Kaifeng	21	36	36	31	27	27	24	22	15	13	10
洛阳市	Luoyang	64	76	74	63	65	69	72	68	65	58	60
平顶山市	Pingdingshan	49	79	92	86	86	84	81	75	78	75	69
安阳市	Anyang	64	72	98	85	90	93	82	86	72	66	70
鹤壁市	Hebi	42	41	30	27	26	26	22	24	17	20	17
新乡市	Xinxiang	63	62	68	61	61	63	63	61	50	44	45
焦作市	Jiaozuo	106	113	108	84	77	68	70	62	62	60	59
濮阳市	Puyang	23	54	60	48	40	35	30	28	23	22	21
许昌市	Xuchang	38	92	91	95	94	97	82	71	49	40	34
漯河市	Luohe	23	28	22	23	19	17	21	20	18	17	20
三门峡市	Sanmenxia	36	46	65	56	51	54	53	53	44	33	33
南阳市	Nanyang	59	46	45	51	52	55	53	56	47	43	44
商丘市	Shangqiu	11	22	21	19	17	16	12	10	8	12	13
信阳市	Xinyang	21	22	24	20	20	21	19	19	16	12	12
周口市	Zhoukou	13	21	20	21	22	21	16	16	14	10	11
驻马店市	Zhumadian	27	22	26	20	19	20	21	20	16	12	14
济源市	Jiyuan	24	27	26	22	23	25	21	21	24	31	27
省直管县	**County Directly Administrated by Province**											
巩义市	Gongyi	38	36	36	34	33	32	30	30	24	25	20
兰考县	Lankao		1						1	1	2	2
汝州市	Ruzhou	12	26	36	36	30	29	29	26	24	25	22
滑县	Huaxian	3	3	2			1	1	2	2	2	2
长垣市	Changyuan	1	1	2	2	3	3	3	2	1	1	1
邓州市	Dengzhou	10	2	2	5	4	6	4	4	3	4	4
永城市	Yongcheng	6	4	6	6	5	7	3	3	3	4	5
固始县	Gushi			1	1	3	3	3	2	1		
鹿邑县	Luyi	1	5	5	5	7	7	3	4	4	3	3
新蔡县	Xincai											

注：2019年全省合计数包含2家省直管企业。

a) The total number of 2019 includes 2 enterprises directly under the jurisdiction of the province.

7-16 各行业年耗能万吨标准煤以上工业企业单位数

Number of Industrial Enterprises of Consumption of Energy Above 10 000 tons by Sector

单位：个 (unit)

行 业	Sector	2018	2019
总 计	**Total**	**673**	**648**
采矿业	**Mining**	**62**	**61**
煤炭开采和洗选业	Mining and Washing of Coal	52	50
石油和天然气开采业	Extraction of Petroleum and Natural Gas	2	2
黑色金属矿采选业	Mining and Processing of Ferrous Metal Ores	3	3
有色金属矿采选业	Mining and Processing of Non-ferrous Metal Ores	3	4
非金属矿采选业	Mining and Processing of Nonmetal Ores		
开采辅助活动	Support Activities for Mining	2	2
其他采矿业	Mining of Other Ores		
制造业	**Manufacturing**	**513**	**475**
农副食品加工业	Processing of Food from Agricultural Products	17	18
食品制造业	Manufacture of Foods	18	20
酒、饮料和精制茶制造业	Manufacture of Liquor, Beverages and Refined Tea	10	13
烟草制造业	Manufacture of Tobacco	1	1
纺织业	Manufacture of Textile	10	8
纺织服装、服饰业	Manufacture of Textile, Wearing Apparel and Accessories		1
皮革、毛皮、羽毛及其制品和制鞋业	Manufacture of Leather, Fur, Feather and Related Products and Footwear	1	1
木材加工及木、竹、藤、棕、草制品业	Processing of Timbers, Manufacture of Wood, Bamboo, Rattan, Palm, and Straw Products	6	2
家具制造业	Manufacture of Furniture		
造纸及纸制品业	Manufacture of Paper and Paper Products	30	28
印刷和记录媒介复制业	Printing,Reproduction of Recording Media	1	1
文教、工美、体育和娱乐用品制造业	Manufacture of Articles for Culture, Education, Arts and Crafts, Sport and entertainment Activities	1	
石油加工、炼焦及核燃料加工业	Processing of Petroleum ,Coking, Processing of Nucleus Fuel	25	27
化学原料及化学制品制造业	Manufacture of Raw Chemical Material and Chemical Products	88	75
医药制造业	Manufacture of Medicines	12	11
化学纤维制造业	Manufacture of Chemical Fiber	2	2
橡胶和塑料制品业	Manufacture of Rubber and Plastics Products	3	3
非金属矿物制品业	Manufacture of Non-metallic Mineral Products	158	137
黑色金属冶炼和压延加工业	Smelting and Pressing of Ferrous Metals	38	40
有色金属冶炼及压延加工业	Smelting and Pressing of Non-ferrous Metals	46	43
金属制品业	Manufacture of Metal Products	8	9
通用设备制造业	Manufacture of General Purpose Machinery	4	4
专业设备制造业	Manufacture of Special Purpose Machinery	4	3
汽车制造业	Manufacture of Automobile	8	8
铁路、船舶、航空航天和其他运输设备制造业	Manufacture of Railway, Ship, Aerospace, and other Transport Equipment	2	2
电气机械及器材制造业	Manufacture of Electrical Machinery and Spparatus	11	10
计算机、通信和其他电子设备制造业	Manufacture of Computer, Communication and Other Electronic Equipment	8	7
仪器仪表制造业	Manufacture of Measuring Instrument		
其他制造业	Others Manafacture		
废弃资源综合利用业	Utilization of Waste Resaurces	**1**	**1**
金属制品、机械和设备修理业	Repairing of Metal Products, Machinery and Equipment		
电力、燃气及水的生产和供应业	**Production and Distribution of Electricity, Gas and Water**	**98**	**112**
电力、热力生产和供应业	Production and Supply of Electric Power and Heat Power	94	107
燃气生产和供应业	Production and Supply of Gas	2	3
水的生产和供应业	Production and Supply of Water	2	2

7-17 主要耗能工业企业单位产品能源消耗情况
Energy Consumption per Unit of Product in Major Energy Consuming Industrial Enterprises

单位：千克标准煤/吨 (kg SEC/ton)

指标名称	Item	2015	2016	2017	2018	2019
吨原煤生产综合能耗	Overall Energy Consumption per ton of Machining Coal	6.75	6.70	6.18	6.22	7.25
单位油气产量综合能耗	Overall Energy Consumption of Manufacturing Oil and Gas	186.87	198.82	211.57	226.77	233.44
铁矿采矿工序单位能耗	Energy Consumption per Uint of Mining of Iron ore	4.62	4.16	4.11	4.01	3.98
铁矿选矿工序单位能耗	Energy Consumption per Uint of Milling run Iron ore	4.48	4.35	4.39	4.16	4.32
每吨涤纶综合能耗(短纤)	Overall Energy Consumption per ton of Terylene (short fibre)	129.97	137.79	126.79	146.03	147.40
每吨纱(线)混合数综合能耗	Overall Energy Consumption per ton of Mixed Yarn (Cotton)	376.62	381.00	368.41	384.49	374.04
机制纸及纸板综合能耗	Overall Energy Consumption of Machinemade Paper and Paperboard	325.06	331.31	337.26	376.05	377.07
炼焦工序单位能耗	Energy Consumption per Unit of Coking plant	132.04	126.65	130.83	117.50	123.26
原油加工单位综合能耗	Overall Energy Consumption of Machining Base oil	70.24	67.46	68.44	59.28	56.23
单位烧碱生产综合能耗	Overall Energy Consumption of Manufacturing Caustic Soda	326.20	327.57	330.48	340.34	326.44
单位烧碱生产综合能耗(离子膜法30%)	Overall Energy Consumption per Unit of Manufacturing Caustic Soda (Ion Film 30%)	326.20	327.44	330.48	340.34	326.44
单位纯碱生产能耗	Overall Energy Consumption per Unit of Manufacturing Sodium carbonate	281.27	292.11	293.23	337.27	315.37
联碱法纯碱双吨产品生产综合能耗	Overall Energy Consumption per Unit of Sodium carbonate in Joint Alkali	249.59	244.89	246.61	292.44	255.39
天然碱法单位纯碱生产综合能耗	Overall Energy Consumption per Unit of Sodium carbonate in Natural Law	319.97	345.87	343.06	393.63	392.69
单位电石生产综合能耗	Overall Energy Consumption per Unit of Manufacturing Calcium carbide	989.45	901.82	927.81	929.04	938.47
单位乙烯生产综合能耗	Overall Energy Consumption per Unit of Manufacturing Ethylene	1047.85	978.49	886.77	838.90	885.42
单位合成氨生产综合能耗	Overall Energy Consumption per Unit of Manufacturing Compound Ammonia	1227.06	1159.24	1181.97	1171.67	1120.43
吨水泥熟料综合能耗	Energy Consumption per ton of Cement Ripe-material	105.56	103.96	100.35	105.06	102.83
吨水泥综合能耗	Energy Consumption per ton of Cement	74.48	74.70	72.14	76.37	69.21
每重量箱平板玻璃综合能耗(千克标准煤/重量箱)	Energy Consumption per weight case of Plate Glass (Kg SEC/weight Case)	17.67	16.57	14.22	14.41	14.43
硅铁工序单位能耗	Energy Consumption per Unit of Ferrosilicon Processes	545.58	540.48	514.49	482.37	481.94
吨钢综合能耗	Energy Consumption per ton of Steel	496.80	499.02	483.01	506.42	480.18
吨钢耗新水(吨/吨)	Fresh Water Consumption per ton of Steel (ton/ton)	3.02	2.92	2.92	2.47	2.21
单位氧化铝综合能耗	Energy Consumption per Unit of Coking Alumina	463.64	456.60	457.80	451.78	410.40
单位电解铝综合能耗	Energy Consumption per Unit of Coking Aluminum	1649.35	1641.27	1612.78	1594.81	1576.31
单位粗铅综合能耗	Energy Consumption per Unit of Coking Lead	325.44	310.18	292.40	284.46	265.20
单位铅冶炼综合能耗	Energy Consumption per Unit of Lead smelting	381.80	377.33	367.33	364.26	341.28
吨铝加工材消耗能源量	Energy Consumption per ton of Machining Aluminium	132.39	126.94	126.78	117.16	104.48
电厂火力发电标准煤耗(克标准煤/千瓦时)	SEC Consumption of Firepower Generate Electricity (g SEC/kwh)	300.76	299.70	296.70	294.39	294.14

7-18 主要耗能工业企业单位产品电力消耗情况

Electric Power Consumption per Unit of Product in Major Energy Consuming Industrial Enterprises

单位：千瓦时/吨 (kwh/ton)

指标名称	Item	2015	2016	2017	2018	2019
吨原煤生产耗电	Electric Power Consumption per ton of Machining Coal	38.03	38.72	37.82	39.70	41.78
选煤电力单耗	Electric Power Consumption per ton of Milling run Coal	8.85	8.54	8.24	8.68	6.97
单位油气产量耗电	Electric Power Consumption per ton of Manufacturing Oil and Gas	360.27	418.94	457.97	497.01	502.56
每吨粘胶纤维用电量(长丝)	Electric Power Consumption per ton of Pectic-fibre (long silk)	7207.63	7139.79	7238.91	7265.68	6601.90
每吨涤纶用电量(短纤)	Electric Power Consumption per ton of Terylene (short fibre)	222.47	192.81	168.83	169.33	166.39
每吨纱(线)混合数生产用电量	Electric Power Consumption per ton of Gauze and Line	2641.64	2791.52	2661.13	2294.29	2340.39
机制纸及纸板耗电	Electric Power Consumption per ton of Machinemade Paper and Paperboard	523.10	526.93	531.31	654.29	703.22
原油加工单位耗电	Electric Power Consumption per ton of Machining Base oil	73.59	76.96	71.70	73.99	70.46
单位烧碱耗电	Electric Power Consumption per unit of Manufacturing Caustic Soda	2297.69	2304.90	2338.20	2316.93	2255.56
单位烧碱生产耗交流电(离子膜法30%)	Electric Power Consumption per ton of Manufacturing Caustic Soda (Ion Film 30%)	2297.69	2304.34	2338.20	2316.93	2255.56
单位纯碱耗电	Electric Power Consumption per ton of Manufacturing Sodium carbonate	303.70	292.50	294.12	285.32	289.97
联碱法纯碱双吨产品生产耗电	Electric Power Consumption per Unit of Sodium carbonate in Joint Alkali	299.52	289.92	301.49	315.77	317.16
天然碱法单位纯碱生产耗电	Electric Power Consumption per Unit of Sodium carbonate in Natural Law	308.79	295.46	286.16	247.03	254.91
单位电石生产电力消耗	Electric Power Consumption per ton of Manufacturing Calcium carbide	3381.20	2940.74	3105.32	3090.98	3062.91
单位乙烯生产耗电	Electric Power Consumption per ton of Manufacturing Ethylene	94.65	127.11	149.13	142.29	150.87
单位合成氨耗电	Electric Power Consumption per ton of Manufacturing Compound ammonia	1023.10	917.09	932.33	864.03	897.21
吨水泥熟料综合电耗	Overall Electric Power Consumption per ton of Cement Ripe-material	66.49	63.56	61.21	63.45	60.42
吨水泥综合电耗	Overall Electric Power Consumption per ton of Cement	76.38	76.98	75.47	76.91	73.28
每重量箱平板玻璃耗电(千瓦时/重量箱)	Electric Power Consumption per ton of Plate Glass (kwh/weight case)	11.61	10.59	7.73	7.60	8.65
吨钢耗电	Electric Power Consumption per ton of Steel	357.52	348.03	355.58	417.29	413.14
电炉炼钢综合电力消耗	Electric Power Consumption per ton of Electric Cooker Ferroalloy-making	325.80	320.01	329.06	232.07	336.86
轧钢工序单位电力消耗	Electric Power Consumption per ton of Steel rolling	129.91	129.93	97.32	104.30	107.42
单位铝锭综合交流电耗	Overall Alternating Current Electric Power Consumption per ton of Aluminium	13740.03	13732.71	13664.39	13669.01	13701.18
析出铅直流电单耗	DC Electric Power Consumption per ton of Separate out Aluminium	108.76	107.76	107.86	108.91	107.38
析出锌(湿法)直流电单耗	DC Electric Power Consumption per ton of Separate out Zn	2920.92	2898.24	2897.02	2907.97	2896.30
吨铝加工材消耗电量	Electric Power Consumption per ton of Machining Aluminium	448.65	442.04	444.62	465.32	421.05
发电厂用电率(%)	Electro-rate of Power plant (%)	6.05	6.04	6.11	6.01	5.81

7-19 各市全社会用电量
Electricity Consumption by City

单位：亿千瓦时 (100 million kwh)

市(县)	City(County)	2008	2009	2010	2011	2012	2013	2014	2015	2016	2017	2018	2019
省辖市	**City**												
郑州市	Zhengzhou	366.67	365.84	410.09	455.99	479.52	504.92	496.85	500.65	502.89	543.22	560.32	564.63
开封市	Kaifeng	42.89	51.78	59.71	68.00	75.13	85.64	95.47	95.59	99.01	104.48	114.93	119.76
洛阳市	Luoyang	287.74	294.67	349.42	408.29	392.98	390.33	395.13	382.44	397.00	418.10	435.43	442.23
平顶山市	Pingdingshan	124.12	126.14	131.70	149.98	159.11	161.32	161.05	157.17	159.24	170.72	193.87	202.22
安阳市	Anyang	125.73	131.45	164.93	193.84	179.44	196.57	216.17	214.53	215.74	211.03	222.88	210.52
鹤壁市	Hebi	35.48	34.24	38.93	41.82	43.80	49.56	52.58	52.40	50.31	52.17	55.99	59.81
新乡市	Xinxiang	117.88	128.06	144.02	162.23	173.70	186.07	196.41	196.32	206.32	225.87	250.81	261.02
焦作市	Jiaozuo	186.50	182.03	186.31	207.59	197.91	210.90	213.96	215.23	205.87	226.63	238.73	243.65
濮阳市	Puyang	46.33	51.71	56.85	60.03	73.84	83.92	89.85	90.37	94.22	88.89	102.28	111.60
许昌市	Xuchang	55.77	65.89	76.16	84.11	93.70	103.57	109.13	104.53	107.15	121.39	137.43	145.11
漯河市	Luohe	33.89	36.51	41.17	46.92	50.59	53.62	58.21	57.87	59.37	63.49	69.93	76.68
三门峡市	Sanmenxia	105.11	117.86	141.72	140.91	133.97	130.90	127.36	114.68	99.69	112.73	114.12	116.66
南阳市	Nanyang	124.55	132.38	160.69	190.25	203.87	215.92	211.69	180.13	188.23	204.57	231.47	242.98
商丘市	Shangqiu	114.56	121.83	134.34	152.56	156.04	173.92	170.95	158.02	167.82	180.44	193.76	177.74
信阳市	Xinyang	50.53	62.10	69.22	78.24	87.59	95.77	95.25	95.86	103.36	109.66	120.47	136.21
周口市	Zhoukou	41.84	47.41	53.92	59.88	70.54	81.94	83.82	86.56	94.45	99.16	114.33	125.42
驻马店市	Zhumadian	53.89	59.89	66.32	80.10	91.77	100.48	108.68	111.44	114.60	124.41	140.10	151.08
济源市	Jiyuan	48.28	53.44	59.68	67.61	75.10	80.30	82.97	82.12	81.27	86.82	84.97	91.08
省直管县	**County Directly Administrated by Province**												
巩义市	Gongyi	79.67	83.21	94.79	105.07	103.67	100.72	100.66	94.17	86.54	80.33	83.77	78.98
兰考县	Lankao	3.04	3.67	5.07	5.85	7.18	9.59	11.11	10.34	11.03	12.05	14.61	16.46
汝州市	Ruzhou	13.57	12.70	13.47	16.43	19.60	20.07	19.41	19.63	21.98	25.01	28.34	29.96
滑县	Huaxian	6.22	6.96	7.52	10.22	11.07	13.29	14.92	16.30	18.81	25.59	26.52	30.40
长垣市	Changyuan	5.60	6.40	7.50	8.90	9.76	10.58	11.34	13.48	15.16	16.59	19.35	21.48
邓州市	Dengzhou	5.45	6.91	7.58	8.34	10.81	12.11	12.76	13.32	15.56	16.34	18.36	19.35
永城市	Yongcheng	55.08	50.50	52.54	55.23	61.34	74.71	74.51	72.42	74.09	81.07	82.63	55.50
固始县	Gushi	4.44	5.34	5.96	6.94	8.31	9.43	9.76	10.21	11.74	12.28	14.26	16.72
鹿邑县	Luyi	3.05	3.48	4.12	4.92	5.87	7.09	7.58	7.80	8.89	9.24	10.25	11.39
新蔡县	Xincai	1.67	2.10	2.48	2.95	3.75	4.27	4.37	4.64	5.72	6.31	8.38	9.50

7-20 平均每万元地区生产总值能耗情况
Basic Imformation of Energy Consumption

市(县) City(County)	万元地区生产总值能耗上升或下降(±%) Change of Energy Consumption for GDP (%)	能源消费总量增速(%) Growth Rate of Total Consumption (%)	万元地区生产总值电耗上升或下降(±%) Change of Energy Consumption for GDP (%)	万元工业增加值能耗上升或降低(±%) Change of Energy Consumption for Value-added of Industry (%)
2006	-2.98	10.99	-1.58	-5.93
2007	-4.11	9.89	3.55	-7.08
2008	-5.10	6.38	-2.77	-10.83
2009	-6.16	4.10	-4.79	-11.56
2010	-3.53	8.50	0.80	-10.75
2011	-3.57	7.91	1.27	-8.60
2012	-7.14	2.24	-6.42	-14.75
2013	-3.92	4.73	-3.16	-8.32
2014	-4.06	4.48	-7.53	-11.29
2015	-6.57	1.20	-8.98	-11.54
2016	-7.69	-0.09	-3.95	-10.98
2017	-7.94	-0.72	-1.72	-9.10
2018	-5.02	2.24	0.29	-7.97
2019	-7.98	-1.58	-7.96	-14.13
省辖市 City				
郑州市 Zhengzhou	-6.06	0.10	-2.79	-16.14
开封市 Kaifeng	-19.54	-13.92	-3.77	-34.13
洛阳市 Luoyang	-10.80	-3.86	-5.78	-18.98
平顶山市 Pingdingshan	-10.72	-4.09	-3.13	-18.64
安阳市 Anyang	-2.52	-0.46	-10.17	-3.49
鹤壁市 Hebi	6.94	14.51	-0.24	10.48
新乡市 Xinxiang	-10.53	-4.48	-3.06	-15.87
焦作市 Jiaozuo	-12.00	-5.00	-5.46	-16.51
濮阳市 Puyang	-8.75	-2.59	2.21	-12.52
许昌市 Xuchang	-6.65	-0.02	-1.41	-12.47
漯河市 Luohe	-4.72	2.47	1.96	-12.10
三门峡市 Sanmenxia	-18.20	-12.09	-9.02	-26.21
南阳市 Nanyang	-5.16	1.66	-2.10	-6.68
商丘市 Shangqiu	-2.60	4.25	2.76	6.35
信阳市 Xinyang	-3.69	2.16	6.07	-10.87
周口市 Zhoukou	-2.80	4.30	2.10	2.04
驻马店市 Zhumadian	-3.97	3.01	0.20	-15.43
济源市 Jiyuan	-7.02	0.27	-0.61	-14.19
省直管县 County Directly Administrated by Province				
巩义市 Gongyi	-20.94	-16.37	-18.33	-16.35
兰考县 Lankao	-4.20	3.47	4.31	-15.14
汝州市 Ruzhou	-8.14	-1.19	-1.72	-12.17
滑县 Huaxian	-3.01	2.63	8.33	-5.33
长垣市 Changyuan	-3.53	4.27	2.68	-4.52
邓州市 Dengzhou	-0.42	5.20	-0.21	1.40
永城市 Yongcheng	-13.36	-6.07	-38.04	-8.86
固始县 Gushi	-2.60	4.87	8.85	-2.78
鹿邑县 Luyi	-4.71	3.38	2.42	-18.40
新蔡县 Xincai	-3.36	4.60	4.52	-9.17

注：本表中，省辖市数据不包含直管县(市)。
a) In this table, the data of cities do not include the data of counties directly administrated by province.

主要统计指标解释

能源生产总量 指一定时期内全国(地区)一次能源生产量的总和。该指标是观察全国(地区)能源生产水平、规模、构成和发展速度的总量指标。一次能源生产量包括原煤、原油、天然气、水电、核能及其他动力能(如风能、地热能等)发电量，不包括低热值燃料生产量、生物质能、太阳能等的利用和由一次能源加工转换而成的二次能源产量。

能源消费总量 是指一定地域内，国民经济各行业和居民家庭在一定时间消费的各种能源的总和。包括：原煤、原油、天然气、水能、核能、风能、太阳能、地热能、生物质能等一次能源；一次能源通过加工转换产生的洗煤、焦炭、煤气、电力、热力、成品油等二次能源和同时产生的其他产品；其他化石能源、可再生能源和新能源。其中水能、风能、太阳能、地热能、生物质能等可再生能源，是指人们通过一定技术手段获得的，并作为商品能源使用的部分。在核算过程中，一次能源、二次能源消费不能重复计算。能源消费总量分为终端能源消费量、能源加工转换损失量和能源损失量三部分。

（1）终端能源消费量：指一定时期内，生产和生活消费的各种能源在扣除了用于加工转换二次能源消费量和损失量以后的数量。

（2）能源加工转换损失量：指一定时期内，投入加工转换的各种能源数量之和与产出各种能源产品之和的差额。该指标是观察能源在加工转换过程中损失量变化的指标。

（3）能源损失量：指一定时期内，能源在输送、分配、储存过程中发生的损失和由客观原因造成的各种损失量，不包括各种气体能源放空、放散量。

能源生产弹性系数 研究能源生产增长速度与国民经济增长速度之间关系的指标。计算公式为：

能源生产弹性系数=能源生产总量年平均增长速度/国民经济年平均增长速度

国民经济年平均增长速度，可根据不同的目的或需要，用国民生产总值、国内生产总值等指标来计算，本年鉴是采用国内生产总值指标计算的。

电力生产弹性系数 是研究电力生产增长速度与国民经济增长速度之间关系的指标。一般来说，电力的发展应当快于国民经济的发展，也就是说电力应超前发展。计算公式为：

电力生产弹性系数=电力生产量年平均增长速度/国民经济年平均增长速度

能源消费弹性系数 反映能源消费增长速度与国民经济增长速度之间比例关系的指标。计算公式为：

能源消费弹性系数=能源消费量年平均增长速度/国民经济年平均增长速度

电力消费弹性系数 反映电力消费增长速度与国民经济增长速度之间比例关系的指标。计算公式为：

电力消费弹性系数=电力消费量年平均增长速度/国民经济年平均增长速度

能源加工转换效率 指一定时期内能源经过加工、转换后，产出的各种能源产品的数量与同期内投入加工转换的各种能源数量的比率。该指标是观察能源加工转换装置和生产工艺先进与落后、管理水平高低等的重要指标。计算公式为：

能源加工转换效率=能源加工转换产出量/能源加工转换投入量×100%

单位GDP能耗 指一定时期内，一个国家或地区每生产一个单位的生产总值所消耗的能源。计算公式为：

单位GDP能耗=能源消费总量/GDP（可比价）

单位GDP电耗 指一定时期内，一个国家或地区每生产一个单位的国内生产总值所消耗的电力。计算公式为：

单位GDP电耗=全社会用电量/GDP（可比价）

单位工业增加值能耗 指一定时期内，一个国家或地区每生产一个单位的工业增加值所消耗的能源。计算公式为：

单位工业增加值能耗=工业能源消耗量/工业增加值

Explanatory Notes on Main Statistical Indicators

Total Energy Production refers to the total production of primary energy by all energy producing enterprises in the country in a given period of time. It is a comprehensive indicator to show the capacity, scale, composition and development of energy production of the country. The production of primary energy includes that of coal, crude oil, natural gas, hydro-power and electricity generated by nuclear energy and other means such as wind power and geothermal power. However, it excludes the production of fuels of low calorific value, bio-energy, solar energy and the secondary energy converted from the primary energy.

Total Energy Consumption refers to the total consumption of energy of various kinds by the production sectors of the economy and the households in a given period of time. It includes the primary kinds of energy such as coal, crude oil, natural gas, hydro-power, nuclear power, wind power, solar power, geothermal power and bio-energy; the secondary kinds of energy and their products which are transformed from the primary energy such as washed coal, coke, coal gas, electricity, heating, and petroleum products; and other kinds of fossil energy, renewable energy and new energy. The renewable energy, including hydro-power, wind power, solar power, geothermal power and bio-energy, refers to the part attained with some given technical means and used for commercial purpose. Total energy consumption can be divided into three parts: end-use energy consumption, loss during the process of energy conversion, and energy loss.

(1) End-use Energy Consumption: It refers to the total energy consumption by the production sectors and the households in the country (region) in a given period of time. It does not include the consumption during the conversion of primary energy into secondary energy and the loss in the process of energy conversion.

(2) Loss During the Process of Energy Conversion: It refers to the total input of various kinds of energy for conversion, minus the total output of various kinds of energy in the country in a given period of time. It is an indicator to show the loss that occurs during the process of energy conversion.

(3) Energy Loss: It refers to the total of the loss of energy during the course of energy transport, distribution and storage and the loss caused by any objective reason in a given period of time. The loss of various kinds of gas due to gas discharges and stocktaking is not included.

Elasticity Ratio of Energy Production the indicator to show the relationship between the growth rate of energy production and the growth rate of the national economy. The formula is:

Elasticity Ratio of Energy Production = Average Annual Growth Rate of Energy Production / Average Annual Growth Rate of National Economy

The average annual growth rate of the national economy can be shown by the gross national product, gross domestic product and other indicators, depending upon the purposes or needs. The gross domestic product is used in calculation of the ratio in this chapter.

Elasticity Ratio of Electricity Production is an indicator to show the relationship between the growth rate of electricity production and the growth rate of the national economy. Generally speaking, the growth rate of electricity production should be higher than that of the national economy.

Its formula is:

$$\text{Elasticity Ratio of Electricity Production} = \frac{\text{Average Annual Growth Rate of Electricity Production}}{\text{Average Annual Growth Rate of National Economy}}$$

Elasticity Ratio of Energy Consumption the indicator to show the relationship between the growth rate of energy consumption and the growth rate of the national economy. The formula is:

Elasticity Ratio of Energy Consumption = Average Annual Growth Rate of Energy Consumption / Average Annual Growth Rate of National Economy

Elasticity Ratio of Electricity Consumption is an indicator to show the relationship between the growth rate of electricity consumption and the growth rate of the national economy. The formula is:

$$\text{Elasticity Ratio of Electricity Consumption} = \frac{\text{Average Annual Growth Rate of Electricity Consumption}}{\text{Average Annual Growth Rate of National Economy}}$$

Efficiency of Energy Processing and Conversion refers to the ratio of the total output of energy products of various kinds after processing and conversion and the total input of energy of various kinds for processing and conversion in the same reference period. It is an important indicator to show the current conditions of energy processing and conversion equipment, production technique and management. The formula is:

Efficiency of Energy Processing & Conversion = (Output of Energy After Processing & Conversion / Input of Energy for Processing & Conversion)×100%

Energy Consumption per Unit of GDP refers to the energy consumption per unit of gross domestic production in a country or the gross region production in a region in the same reference period.

The formula is:

Energy Consumption per Unit of GDP = Total Energy Consumption / Gross Domestic Production

Electricity Consumption per Unit of GDP refers to the electricity consumption per unit of gross domestic production in a country or the gross region production in a region in the same reference period. The formula is:

Electricity Consumption per Unit of GDP = Total Electricity Consumption / Gross Domestic Production

Energy Consumption per Unit of Industrial Value-added refers to the energy consumption per unit of industrial value-added in a country or region in the same reference period. The formula is:

Energy Consumption per Unit of Industrial Value-added = Total Energy Consumption / Industrial Value-added

财政
Government Finance

8

● 资料整理：赵国顺

简要说明

一、主要内容

本篇包括地方财政收支和预算外资金收支资料。

二、统计口径

2007年起，财政收支科目实施了较大改革，特别是财政支出项目口径变化很大，与往年数据不可比，2015年开始，财政收支指标改为财政一般公共预算收支，财政部门对指标口径进行相应调整。

三、资料来源

资料来源于河南省财政厅的财政总决算，由河南省统计局国民经济核算处编辑整理。

Brief Introduction

I. Main Contents

The data in this chapter present the government revenue and expenditure situation, the extra-budgetary revenue and expenditure.

II. Scope of Statistics

Because of the classifications of revenue and expenditure accounts have been adjusted largely since 2007, especially the government expenditure, the relative data are not compared with data in preceding years.

III. Sources of Data

The data are based on final Henan provincial financial accounts, which are provided by the Department of National Accounts of the Henan provincial Bureau of Statistics.

8-1 一般公共预算收支额

General Public Budget Revenue and Expenditure of the Local Government

单位：亿元 (100 million yuan)

年 份 Year	财 政 总收入 Total Revenue	一般公共 预算收入 General Public Budget Revenue of Local Government	#税收收入 Taxes	一般公共 预算支出 General Public Budget Expenditure of Local Government	#农林水事务 Agriauture Forestry Water Conservancy Operating	#社会保障和就业 Social Security and Employment	#教科文卫 Culture, Education, Science & Health Care	#科学技术 Technology	#教育 Education	#医疗卫生 Medical Treatment and Public Health
1978		33.73	23.04	27.67	4.20		5.77	0.43		
1979		33.68	23.62	29.86	5.28		7.05	0.53		
1980		31.86	24.86	26.74	4.66		8.31	0.59		
1981		34.23	29.73	25.84	4.25		8.84	0.61		
1982		33.49	30.96	29.81	4.57		9.83	0.67		
1983		36.49	30.69	30.06	4.73		10.45	0.91		
1984		39.26	34.54	36.79	4.86		11.83	1.08		
1985		48.93	44.57	49.51	5.01		13.93	1.16		
1986		54.92	49.71	69.20	5.92		15.78	1.31		
1987		63.15	56.10	65.26	6.90		16.67	1.18		
1988		70.98	65.09	76.22	8.64		19.47	1.35		
1989		80.97	75.50	87.67	10.85		22.76	1.49		
1990		83.59	78.85	89.53	10.74		24.54	1.53		
1991		91.36	84.61	97.88	12.18		26.99	1.70		
1992		104.03	95.41	116.49	13.29		33.22	1.93		
1993		139.20	126.36	147.73	14.34		39.28	2.01		
1994		(171.38)								
		93.35	81.77	169.62	15.09		50.64	2.54		
1995		124.63	103.45	207.28	17.59		58.30	3.24		
1996		162.06	126.63	255.29	21.12		69.49	3.75		
1997		192.63	152.09	290.84	23.47		75.43	4.52		
1998		208.20	160.60	323.63	25.71		82.89	5.05		
1999		223.35	176.12	384.32	28.39		95.57	6.01		
2000		246.47	195.04	445.53	34.19		108.46	6.86		
2001		267.75	226.70	508.58	36.94		131.35	7.25		
2002		296.72	242.24	629.18	44.77		166.56	7.95		
2003		338.05	264.40	716.60	47.92		188.27	9.06		
2004	789.05	428.78	307.12	879.96	65.99		220.81	10.40		
2005	967.16	537.65	365.67	1116.04	82.28		270.22	13.85		
2006	1202.96	679.17	471.80	1440.09	(99.12)		(344.21)	(18.84)		
					111.34		362.82	17.37		
2007	1530.48	862.08	625.02	1870.61	152.51	281.22	523.51	25.23	366.12	98.78
2008	1781.89	1008.90	742.27	2281.61	209.59	330.23	661.40	30.44	444.03	145.47
2009	1921.80	1126.06	821.50	2905.76	361.60	403.62	843.47	35.52	526.14	223.15
2010	2293.70	1381.32	1016.55	3416.14	399.19	461.22	979.24	44.67	609.37	270.21
2011	2851.91	1721.76	1263.10	4248.82	480.48	547.96	1332.75	56.59	857.14	361.48
2012	3282.48	2040.33	1469.57	5006.40	551.73	631.61	1671.77	69.64	1106.51	425.99
2013	3686.81	2415.45	1764.71	5582.31	629.85	731.41	1824.78	80.00	1171.52	492.48
2014	4094.78	2739.26	1951.46	6028.69	661.94	790.87	1976.74	81.25	1201.38	602.95
2015	4426.96	3016.05	2101.17	6799.35	791.63	945.83	2177.38	83.25	1270.99	717.74
2016	4706.96	3153.48	2158.45	7453.74	807.06	1067.40	2315.19	96.10	1343.76	778.01
2017	5238.35	3407.22	2329.31	8215.52	916.81	1160.23	2565.23	137.94	1493.11	836.66
2018	5875.82	3766.02	2656.65	9217.73	1001.08	1298.45	2852.33	155.67	1664.67	928.95
2019	6187.23	4041.89	2841.34	10163.93	1059.70	1457.14	3136.43	211.07	1810.71	986.78

注：1. 财政收入1993年以前为分税制前老口径，1994年以后为分税制后新口径，括号内为分税制前老口径。

2. 1994-2006年,财政收支均为地方财政一般预算收支。2007年以后，财政收支项目按新科目列支。2011-2014年财政一般预算收支改称公共财政预算收支，2015年以后为一般公共预算收支口径（括号里为老口径）。

a) Before 1993, government revenue are calculated on old caliber. Data on 1994 and after are calculated on new caliber, and the data in parentheses are calculated on old caliber.

b) From1994 to 2006, financial revenue and expenditure refer to generalpublic budget revenue and expenditure of local government.Data of revenue and expenditure based on new system since 2007.Data of financial general budget revenue and expenditure changed to public financial revenue and expenditure from 2011 to 2014,and changed to general public budget revenue and expenditure since 2015.Data in parentheses are calculated on old caliber.

8-2 各项税收
Taxes

单位：亿元 (100 million yuan)

年 份 Year	一般公共预算收入 General Public Budget Revenue of Local Government	#增值税 Value-added Tax	#企业所得税 Corporate Income Tax	#个人所得税 Individual Income Tax	#城市维护建设税 City Maintenance and Construction Tax
1995	124.63	25.57	18.64	3.44	8.39
1996	162.06	30.00	19.83	4.92	10.13
1997	192.63	32.80	28.43	6.38	11.18
1998	208.20	36.07	22.68	8.84	12.28
1999	223.35	36.72	29.47	10.83	12.69
2000	246.47	42.24	39.60	12.88	13.64
2001	267.75	44.35	60.85	19.25	13.73
2002	296.72	49.25	31.97	17.82	17.24
2003	338.05	57.95	29.14	15.60	20.54
2004	428.78	65.78	38.43	19.32	24.60
2005	537.65	87.97	51.56	22.05	29.18
2006	679.17	105.84	70.21	24.05	35.02
2007	862.08	129.96	103.06	30.26	42.87
2008	1008.90	153.89	116.76	32.30	49.06
2009	1126.06	140.82	114.81	33.33	51.93
2010	1381.32	155.79	136.63	40.29	61.35
2011	1721.76	181.38	185.21	48.38	80.22
2012	2040.33	187.79	209.13	41.41	89.77
2013	2415.45	202.66	235.60	47.63	98.57
2014	2739.26	256.47	261.00	58.01	106.67
2015	3016.05	263.73	281.41	62.03	112.72
2016	3153.48	550.61	297.31	71.75	117.09
2017	3407.22	888.93	332.02	86.31	131.43
2018	3766.02	1007.46	370.23	102.74	152.50
2019	4041.89	1076.10	382.13	77.15	158.92

8-3 一般公共预算收入
General Public Budget Revenue of the Local Government

单位：亿元 (100 million yuan)

项 目	Item	2018 绝对数 Absolute Value	2018 比重(%) Proportion (%)	2019 绝对数 Absolute Value	2019 比重(%) Proportion (%)
收入合计	**Total Revenue**	**3766.02**	**100.0**	**4041.89**	**100.0**
税收收入	Tax Revenue	2656.65	70.5	2841.34	70.3
增值税	Value-added Tax	1007.46	26.8	1076.10	26.6
企业所得税	Corporate Income Tax	370.23	9.8	382.13	9.5
个人所得税	Individual Income Tax	102.74	2.7	77.15	1.9
资源税	Resources Tax	60.29	1.6	68.88	1.7
城市维护建设税	City Maintenance and Construction Tax	152.50	4.0	158.92	3.9
房产税	House Property Tax	71.52	1.9	76.17	1.9
印花税	Stamp Tax	41.13	1.1	43.52	1.1
城镇土地使用税	Urban Land Use Tax	126.84	3.4	153.83	3.8
土地增值税	Land Appreciation Tax	237.40	6.3	295.81	7.3
车船税	Tax on Vehicles and Boat Operation	45.56	1.2	48.29	1.2
耕地占用税	Farm Land Occupation Tax	175.73	4.7	166.87	4.1
契税	Deed Tax	246.79	6.6	274.94	6.8
烟叶税	Tobacco Leaf Tax	18.47	0.5	7.54	0.2
环境保护税	Environment Protection Tax			10.67	0.3
其他税收收入	Other Tax Revenue			0.53	0.0
非税收入	Non-Tax Revenue	1109.36	29.5	1200.54	29.7
专项收入	Special Program Receipts	350.07	9.3	373.49	9.2
行政事业性收费收入	Charge of Adiministrative and Institutional Units	224.06	5.9	225.41	5.6
罚没收入	Penalty Receipts	140.57	3.7	159.50	3.9
国有资本经营收入	Operating Income from Goverment Capital	45.27	1.2	66.91	1.7
国有资源(资产)有偿使用收入	Income from Use of Stated-owned Resources(Assets)	235.28	6.2	247.63	6.1
其他收入	Other Revenue	114.12	3.0	127.60	3.2

8-4 一般公共预算支出

General Public Budget Expenditure of the Local Government

单位：亿元 (100 million yuan)

项　目	Item	2018 绝对数 Absolute Value	2018 比重(%) Proportion (%)	2019 绝对数 Absolute Value	2019 比重(%) Proportion (%)
本年支出合计	**Total Expenditure**	**9217.73**	**100.0**	**10163.93**	**100.0**
一般公共服务	General Public Service	972.55	10.6	1097.40	10.8
国防	National Defense	7.08	0.1	9.26	0.1
公共安全	Public Security	460.18	5.0	496.79	4.9
教育	Education	1664.67	18.1	1810.71	17.8
科学技术	Science and Technology	155.67	1.7	211.07	2.1
文化旅游体育与传媒	Culture, Tourism, Sport and Media	103.04	1.1	127.87	1.3
社会保障和就业	Social Security and Employment	1298.45	14.1	1457.14	14.3
卫生健康	Heaith	928.95	10.1	986.78	9.7
节能环保	Energy Conservation and Environment Protection	358.70	3.9	352.29	3.5
城乡社区事务	Urban and Rural Community Affairs	1152.43	12.5	1381.48	13.6
农林水事务	Agriculture, Forestry and Water Conservancy	1001.08	10.9	1059.70	10.4
交通运输	Transportation	283.19	3.1	383.82	3.8
资源勘探信息等事务	Affairs of Resource Exploration and Information	119.67	1.3	106.40	1.0
商业服务业等事务	Affairs of Commerce and Services	41.89	0.5	30.14	0.3
金融支出	Financial Affairs	19.83	0.2	12.99	0.1
援助其它地区支出	Other Regional Assistance	5.01	0.1	4.03	0.0
自然资源海洋气象等支出	Natural Resources, Marine Meteorology	68.60	0.7	82.92	0.8
住房保障支出	Housing Security	359.62	3.9	284.71	2.8
粮油物资储备支出	Grain and Oil Reserves Management	42.45	0.5	42.01	0.4
灾害防治及应急管理支出	Disaster Prevention and Emergency Management			34.04	0.3
债务付息支出	Interest Payment on Debts	128.39	1.4	144.15	1.4
债务发行费用支出	Issuing Debts	0.66	0.0	0.76	0.0
其他支出	Others	45.63	0.5	47.47	0.5

8-5 各级一般公共预算收入(2019年)

General Public Budget Revenue of the Local Government by Rank (2019)

单位：亿元 (100 million yuan)

项　目	Item	合计 Total	省级 Province	市级 City	县市级 County	乡镇级 Town & Township
收入合计	**Total Revenue**	**4041.89**	**193.41**	**1487.10**	**1583.41**	**777.97**
税收收入	Tax Revenue	2841.34	90.11	1025.98	988.72	736.54
增值税	Value-added Tax	1076.10	34.45	378.07	322.03	341.56
企业所得税	Corporate Income Tax	382.13	47.61	156.87	106.47	71.18
个人所得税	Individual Income Tax	77.15		40.07	25.30	11.77
资源税	Resources Tax	68.88	5.51	12.20	28.82	22.35
城市维护建设税	City Maintenance and Construction Tax	158.92	0.44	72.60	55.09	30.80
房产税	House Property Tax	76.17		26.43	36.14	13.60
印花税	Stamp Tax	43.52		15.23	16.85	11.44
城镇土地使用税	Urban Land Use Tax	153.83		34.17	66.50	53.16
土地增值税	Land Appreciation Tax	295.81		95.75	126.12	73.93
车船税	Tax on Vehicles and Boat Operation	48.29		18.92	18.34	11.04
耕地占用税	Farm Land Occupation Tax	166.87		25.79	95.35	45.73
契税	Deed Tax	274.94		148.08	84.85	42.01
烟叶税	Tobacco Leaf Tax	7.54		0.04	1.75	5.75
环境保护税	Environment Protection Tax	10.67	2.13	1.63	5.07	1.84
其他税收收入	Other Tax Revenue	0.53	-0.03	0.14	0.05	0.37
非税收入	Non-Tax Revenue	1200.54	103.30	461.12	594.69	41.44
专项收入	Special Program Receipts	373.49	49.59	200.91	118.07	4.92
行政事业性收费收入	Charge of Adiministrative and Institutional Units	225.41	18.02	64.35	137.64	5.40
罚没收入	Penalty Receipts	159.50	3.35	55.23	100.71	0.21
国有资本经营收入	Operating Income from Goverment Capital	66.91		28.00	28.34	10.57
国有资源(资产)有偿使用收入	Income from Use of Stated-owned Resources (Assets)	247.63	30.68	55.04	150.31	11.60
其他收入	Other Revenue	127.60	1.66	57.59	59.61	8.73

8-6 各级一般公共预算支出(2019年)

General Public Budget Expenditure of the Local Government by Rank (2019)

单位：亿元 (100 million yuan)

项目	Item	合计 Total	省级 Province	市级 City	县市级 County	乡镇级 Town & Township
本年支出合计	**Total Expenditure**	**10163.93**	**1090.76**	**2653.20**	**5717.68**	**702.29**
一般公共服务	General Public Service	1097.40	63.78	231.49	519.05	283.09
国防	National Defense	9.26	2.03	4.25	2.94	0.04
公共安全	Public Security	496.79	64.21	180.20	250.49	1.89
教育	Education	1810.71	231.71	375.33	1180.43	23.24
科学技术	Science and Technology	211.07	27.73	85.98	85.08	12.28
文化旅游体育与传媒	Culture, Tourism, Sport and Media	127.87	16.14	51.91	53.76	6.05
社会保障和就业	Social Security and Employment	1457.14	380.08	240.53	806.88	29.64
卫生健康	Heaith	986.78	48.24	133.95	788.44	16.16
节能环保	Energy Conservation and Environment Protection	352.29	19.49	152.34	156.09	24.37
城乡社区事务	Urban and Rural Community Affairs	1381.48	0.76	704.16	532.94	143.61
农林水事务	Agriculture, Forestry and Water Conservancy	1059.70	77.85	89.21	754.63	138.01
交通运输	Transportation	383.82	51.01	149.43	181.27	2.12
资源勘探信息等事务	Affairs of Resource Exploration and Information	106.40	14.65	47.30	38.26	6.19
商业服务业等事务	Affairs of Commerce and Services	30.14	0.53	13.27	16.24	0.10
金融支出	Financial Affairs	12.99	7.73	2.67	1.62	0.96
援助其它地区支出	Other Regional Assistance	4.03	2.03	1.38	0.61	0.02
自然资源海洋气象等支出	Natural Resources, Marine Meteorology	82.92	13.08	13.12	52.44	4.28
住房保障支出	Housing Security	284.71	18.69	80.44	178.73	6.84
粮油物资储备支出	Grain and Oil Reserves Management	42.01	16.81	8.09	17.09	0.01
灾害防治及应急管理支出	Disaster Prevention and Emergency Management	34.04	6.12	10.02	17.56	0.34
债务付息支出	Interest Payment on Debts	144.15	26.79	58.15	59.11	0.10
债务发行费用支出	Issuing Debts	0.76	0.76			
其他支出	Others	47.47	0.53	19.99	24.01	2.94

8-7 各市一般公共预算收入

单位：亿元

市（县） City(County)	收入合计 Total Revenue	税收收入 Tax Revenue	增值税 Value-added Tax	企业所得税 Corporate Income Tax	个人所得税 Individual Income Tax
2010	1381.32	1016.55	155.79	136.63	40.29
2011	1721.76	1263.10	181.38	185.21	48.38
2012	2040.33	1469.57	187.78	209.13	41.41
2013	2415.45	1764.71	202.66	235.60	47.63
2014	2739.26	1951.46	256.47	261.00	58.01
2015	3016.05	2101.17	263.73	281.41	62.03
2016	3153.48	2158.45	550.61	297.31	71.75
2017	3407.22	2329.31	888.93	332.02	86.31
2018	3766.02	2656.65	1007.46	370.23	102.74
2019	4041.89	2841.34	1076.10	382.1324	77.15
省辖市 City					
郑州市 Zhengzhou	1222.53	892.94	315.13	145.83	35.93
开封市 Kaifeng	154.86	113.30	52.63	10.75	1.76
洛阳市 Luoyang	369.78	248.27	79.46	28.69	5.82
平顶山市 Pingdingshan	171.39	124.94	51.78	7.78	2.19
安阳市 Anyang	164.06	121.42	55.57	16.73	2.03
鹤壁市 Hebi	69.45	48.65	12.59	3.20	0.58
新乡市 Xinxiang	187.21	133.88	58.80	18.50	3.08
焦作市 Jiaozuo	156.47	109.59	34.09	10.36	2.55
濮阳市 Puyang	100.48	73.22	29.15	6.26	1.89
许昌市 Xuchang	179.86	123.41	48.03	11.29	3.61
漯河市 Luohe	95.91	73.25	27.97	8.71	3.16
三门峡市 Sanmenxia	131.37	92.16	34.46	6.15	1.43
南阳市 Nanyang	196.15	135.44	55.07	13.67	3.58
商丘市 Shangqiu	171.71	118.84	44.86	9.11	2.30
信阳市 Xinyang	119.00	83.83	38.07	8.89	2.29
周口市 Zhoukou	140.92	100.25	43.51	9.03	1.80
驻马店市 Zhumadian	160.27	113.18	37.79	11.50	2.15
济源市 Jiyuan	57.07	44.66	22.69	8.08	1.01
省直管县 County Directly Administrated by Province					
巩义市 Gongyi	48.21	33.92	13.32	1.66	0.39
兰考县 Lankao	25.20	19.25	11.96	2.07	0.13
汝州市 Ruzhou	33.20	26.08	8.50	1.71	0.26
滑县 Huaxian	13.82	9.92	4.62	1.25	0.32
长垣市 Changyuan	30.30	25.92	15.17	3.23	0.30
邓州市 Dengzhou	18.02	11.91	2.87	0.95	0.22
永城市 Yongcheng	45.00	31.84	13.34	1.45	0.39
固始县 Gushi	15.57	11.16	4.66	1.09	0.30
鹿邑县 Luyi	15.53	10.92	4.56	0.71	0.13
新蔡县 Xincai	12.07	8.49	2.67	0.69	0.13

General Public Budget Revenue of the Local Government by City

(100 million yuan)

				非税收入			
城市维护建设税 City Maintenance and Construction Tax	城镇土地使用税 Urban Land Use Tax	契税 Deed Tax	其他各项税收 Other Tax	Non-Tax Revenue	#专项收入 Special Program Receipts	#行政事业性收费收入 Charge of Adiministrative and Institutional Units	#国有资本经营收入 Operating Income from Goverment Capital
61.35	48.96	88.98	165.20	364.77	89.04	122.42	60.36
80.22	61.18	98.06	204.39	458.65	90.60	161.33	71.97
89.77	78.15	120.21	217.40	570.77	87.89	199.92	88.48
98.57	102.62	185.29	310.55	650.74	90.25	224.78	90.17
106.67	125.31	142.01	374.66	787.80	101.42	263.90	108.25
112.72	184.74	138.75	398.64	914.88	201.29	238.34	103.28
117.09	184.34	186.95	73.41	995.03	241.07	238.63	92.53
131.43	189.15	208.54	83.79	1077.91	283.27	250.60	77.55
152.50	175.73	246.79	105.15	1109.36	350.07	224.06	45.27
158.92	153.83	274.94	127.60	1200.54	373.49	225.41	66.91
52.05	26.09	105.14	31.01	329.60	175.31	30.34	18.02
5.08	6.81	12.92	3.23	41.56	8.18	14.09	1.47
13.58	13.85	20.12	8.98	121.51	16.67	20.26	10.97
6.96	13.11	7.65	5.61	46.45	18.34	9.85	0.03
9.55	9.09	6.77	5.86	42.64	7.90	8.24	0.68
1.78	16.19	2.54	1.94	20.80	4.27	2.29	0.36
7.15	8.69	8.53	5.26	53.33	12.55	7.68	2.44
4.45	18.67	4.08	4.10	46.88	5.76	4.89	10.62
4.01	5.63	7.29	3.50	27.25	10.20	5.90	0.31
10.30	4.19	11.03	6.09	56.44	16.39	10.44	5.64
4.96	2.12	9.63	3.14	22.65	5.29	5.05	1.64
4.27	2.16	19.67	4.43	39.21	3.44	7.18	9.01
8.59	4.64	12.41	6.03	60.70	8.13	19.24	1.61
6.08	7.53	13.07	5.31	52.87	5.35	13.84	2.29
4.71	2.67	9.39	2.87	35.17	6.82	13.83	0.71
5.19	4.20	11.30	4.09	40.67	7.99	14.29	0.47
6.22	6.00	12.60	4.78	47.10	8.26	17.72	0.65
3.53	2.18	0.84	2.22	12.41	3.06	2.27	0.01
1.62	5.78	3.19	1.71	14.30	3.88	1.10	0.00
1.04	0.59	1.91	0.38	5.95	1.05	2.39	0.00
1.20	5.38	1.01	0.94	7.12	3.13	2.56	0.00
0.34	0.43	0.93	0.39	3.90	0.44	0.88	0.00
1.52	1.02	1.16	0.73	4.38	1.52	0.73	0.00
0.37	0.41	0.50	0.58	6.11	0.46	1.20	0.00
1.68	3.23	0.98	1.77	13.16	1.36	1.52	2.09
0.44	0.76	1.71	0.30	4.41	0.49	1.64	0.00
0.46	0.32	0.93	0.26	4.61	2.20	0.95	0.00
0.24	0.28	0.76	0.19	3.57	0.26	1.68	0.02

8-8 各市一般公共预算支出

单位：亿元

市(县) City(County)	支出合计 Payout	#一般公共服务 General Public Service	#公共安全 Public Security	#教育 Education	#科学技术 Technology	#文化旅游体育与传媒 Culture, Tourism, Sport and Media
2010	3416.14	478.69	189.72	609.37	44.67	54.99
2011	4248.82	559.02	204.80	857.14	56.59	57.54
2012	5006.40	663.07	244.42	1106.51	69.64	69.63
2013	5582.31	733.21	261.22	1171.52	80.00	80.78
2014	6028.69	700.71	274.12	1201.38	81.25	91.16
2015	6799.35	695.32	301.12	1271.00	83.25	105.38
2016	7453.74	750.94	358.41	1343.76	96.10	97.33
2017	8215.52	850.29	417.11	1493.11	137.94	97.52
2018	9217.73	972.55	460.18	1664.67	155.67	103.04
2019	10163.93	1097.40	496.79	1810.71	211.07	127.87
省辖市 City						
郑州市 Zhengzhou	1910.67	151.95	80.90	247.06	63.36	25.76
开封市 Kaifeng	424.60	87.86	19.34	67.15	6.68	4.88
洛阳市 Luoyang	647.57	70.06	34.63	112.85	25.98	11.28
平顶山市 Pingdingshan	404.81	54.02	21.26	77.41	5.83	3.66
安阳市 Anyang	404.52	46.10	22.19	81.05	4.76	6.06
鹤壁市 Hebi	144.49	17.38	7.96	23.93	3.58	2.62
新乡市 Xinxiang	464.70	55.60	23.34	87.40	11.27	8.45
焦作市 Jiaozuo	297.57	34.55	18.73	45.58	4.80	2.93
濮阳市 Puyang	349.95	31.18	17.53	68.18	2.64	4.72
许昌市 Xuchang	362.43	59.47	20.71	69.26	7.34	5.92
漯河市 Luohe	215.15	28.35	11.14	36.47	5.57	2.26
三门峡市 Sanmenxia	267.18	48.37	12.86	44.38	5.15	3.70
南阳市 Nanyang	702.43	73.47	31.27	154.79	12.05	6.38
商丘市 Shangqiu	537.54	54.07	25.70	93.12	9.28	4.51
信阳市 Xinyang	595.82	65.17	25.79	118.57	2.41	6.53
周口市 Zhoukou	656.22	69.39	28.10	120.75	4.36	5.84
驻马店市 Zhumadian	610.00	71.24	26.97	116.55	7.12	5.05
济源市 Jiyuan	77.51	15.41	4.15	14.50	1.18	1.19
省直管县 County Directly Administrated by Province						
巩义市 Gongyi	91.26	7.54	4.04	12.97	2.82	1.57
兰考县 Lankao	78.53	19.02	2.57	12.79	1.00	0.59
汝州市 Ruzhou	70.05	14.52	2.07	15.25	1.72	0.11
滑县 Huaxian	71.28	4.55	2.92	15.48	0.30	0.69
长垣市 Changyuan	61.92	10.29	2.03	12.81	1.66	0.41
邓州市 Dengzhou	82.20	6.67	3.61	16.37	0.11	0.40
永城市 Yongcheng	84.15	5.73	3.43	13.79	1.70	0.70
固始县 Gushi	81.56	7.41	2.73	22.44	0.10	0.68
鹿邑县 Luyi	56.33	2.86	0.99	7.77	0.75	0.57
新蔡县 Xincai	57.53	5.27	1.94	10.87	0.63	0.26

General Public Budget Expenditure of the Local Government by City

(100 million yuan)

#社会保障和就业 Social Security and Employment	#卫生健康支出 Health	#节能保护 Energy Conservation and Environment Protection	#城乡社区事务 Urban and Rural Community Affairs	#农林水事务 Agriculture, Forestry and Water Conservancy	#交通运输 Transportation	#住房保障 Housing Security
461.22	270.21	96.38	165.30	399.19	173.84	77.25
547.96	361.48	95.60	191.30	480.48	281.21	142.64
631.61	425.99	109.45	237.97	551.73	300.43	185.65
731.41	492.48	111.92	309.12	629.85	346.19	191.11
790.87	602.95	119.95	431.74	661.94	364.86	247.57
945.83	717.74	177.77	645.21	791.63	371.01	242.04
1067.40	778.01	195.72	879.33	807.06	347.97	268.58
1160.23	836.66	241.65	1122.67	916.81	296.17	248.12
1298.45	928.95	358.70	1152.43	1001.08	283.19	359.62
1457.14	986.78	352.29	1381.48	1059.70	383.82	284.71
159.90	115.19	122.07	655.05	76.35	52.62	40.42
57.78	47.84	13.63	42.45	46.18	9.55	9.04
76.45	64.46	24.53	129.46	52.94	12.96	9.28
50.47	46.88	10.39	50.09	40.47	11.71	19.22
45.81	47.45	16.50	26.02	44.85	21.25	21.42
15.66	13.11	8.77	16.95	13.77	3.91	6.44
54.78	44.75	17.68	46.21	57.12	27.05	9.31
40.66	31.68	12.11	51.21	24.95	5.95	10.85
41.60	34.77	14.12	18.78	62.04	20.94	19.70
45.37	36.09	12.60	36.01	33.66	13.98	8.00
26.48	19.68	5.07	27.58	21.26	8.50	4.65
26.68	23.86	8.60	25.68	35.28	13.49	5.85
104.30	92.75	15.21	35.86	104.46	32.22	15.43
71.45	73.25	12.09	49.20	78.16	20.88	23.31
73.40	72.20	15.78	43.86	104.12	24.24	15.52
90.41	86.76	8.91	59.29	87.18	32.93	29.74
87.01	81.96	12.13	60.55	90.70	17.58	16.23
8.85	5.87	2.62	6.44	8.34	3.07	1.61
10.65	11.35	6.26	12.16	10.46	1.95	1.40
9.20	7.28	1.62	5.42	12.84	3.16	1.19
10.47	12.45	0.93	6.99	3.16	1.21	0.52
9.63	9.97	2.07	5.01	10.19	6.91	1.27
6.54	6.36	2.70	7.48	8.20	1.27	0.44
11.90	12.78	0.94	4.99	12.71	4.14	4.30
9.25	12.60	1.52	9.00	13.08	3.32	5.81
10.16	11.57	0.44	2.22	17.34	2.85	1.79
7.98	8.59	0.67	11.66	6.72	2.24	3.51
9.03	9.39	1.53	0.88	10.85	1.97	2.56

主要统计指标解释

一般公共预算收入 指国家财政参与社会产品分配所取得的收入，是实现国家职能的财力保证。主要包括税收收入和非税收入。

（1）税收收入：包括国内增值税、国内消费税、进口货物增值税和消费税、出口货物退增值税和消费税、营业税、企业所得税、个人所得税、资源税、城市维护建设税、房产税、印花税、城镇土地使用税、土地增值税、车船税、船舶吨税、车辆购置税、关税、耕地占用税、契税、烟叶税等。

（2）非税收入：包括专项收入、行政事业性收费收入、罚没收入、国有资本经营收入、国有资源（资产）有偿使用收入和其他收入。

一般公共预算支出 指国家财政将筹集起来的资金进行分配使用，以满足经济建设和各项事业的需要。主要包括：

（1）一般公共服务：指政府提供基本公共管理与服务的支出，包括人大事务、政协事务、政府办公厅（室）及相关机构事务、发展与改革事务、统计信息事务、财政事务、税收事务、审计事务、海关事务、人力资源事务、纪检监察事务、人口与计划生育事务、商贸事务、知识产权事务、工商行政管理事务、质量技术监督与检验检疫事务、国土资源事务、海洋管理事务、测绘事务、地震事务、气象事务、民族事务、宗教事务、港澳台侨事务、档案事务、共产党事务、民主党派及工商联事务、群众团体事务、彩票发行事务、国债事务、债券投资、其他一般公共服务支出。

（2）国防：指政府用于国防方面的支出，包括现役部队、预备役部队、民兵、国防科研事业、专项工程、国防动员等方面的支出。

（3）公共安全：指政府维护社会公共安全方面的支出，包括武装警察、公安、国家安全、检察、法院、司法行政、监狱、劳教、国家保密、缉私警察等。

（4）教育：指政府教育事务支出，包括教育管理、学前教育、小学教育、初中教育、普通高中教育、普通高等教育、中专教育、技校教育、职业高中教育、高等职业教育、广播电视教育、留学生教育、特殊教育、干部继续教育、教育机关服务等。

（5）科学技术：指用于科学技术方面的支出，包括科学技术管理事务、基础研究、应用研究、技术研究与开发、科技条件与服务、社会科学、科学技术普及、科技交流与合作等。

（6）文化体育与传媒：指政府在文化、文物、体育、广播影视、新闻出版等方面的支出。

（7）社会保障和就业：指政府在社会保障与就业方面的支出，包括社会保障和就业管理事务、民政管理事务、财政对社会保险基金的补助、补充全国社会保障基金、行政事业单位离退休、企业改革补助、就业补助、抚恤、退役安置、社会福利、残疾人事业、城市居民最低生活保障、其他城镇社会救济、农村社会救济、自然灾害生活救助、红十字事务等。

（8）医疗卫生：指政府在医疗卫生方面的支出，包括医疗卫生管理事务、医疗服务、社区卫生服务、医疗保障、疾病预防控制、卫生监督、妇幼保健、农村卫生、中医药等。

（9）节能环保：指政府节能环保的支出，包括环境保护管理事务、环境监测与监察、污染防治、自然生态保护、天然林保护工程、退耕还林、风沙荒漠治理、退牧还草、已垦草原退耕还草、能源节约利用、污染减排、可再生能源和资源综合利用等支出。

（10）城乡社区事务：指政府城乡社区事务支出，包括城乡社区管理事务、城乡社区规划与管理、城乡社区公共设施、城乡社区住宅、城乡社区环境卫生、建设市场管理与监督等。

（11）农林水事务：指政府农林水事务的支出，包括农业、林业、水利、扶贫、农业综合开发等。

（12）交通运输：指政府交通运输和邮政业方面的支出，包括公路运输、水路运输、铁路运输、民用航空运输、邮政业支出等。

（13）资源勘探电力信息等事务：指政府对资源勘探电力信息等事务支出，包括资源勘探业、制造业、建筑业、电力监管、工业和信息产业监管、安全生产监管、国有资产监管、支持中小企业发展和管理支出等。

（14）商业服务业等事务：指政府对商业服务业等事务的支出，包括商业流通事务、旅游业管理与服务、涉外发展服务支出等。

（15）金融监管等事务：指政府对金融保险业监管等事务方面的支出。

（16）国土资源气象等事务：指政府用于国土资源、海洋、测绘、地震、气象等公益服务事业方面的支出。

（17）住房保障支出：指政府用于住房保障方面的支出。

（18）粮油物资储备事务：指政府用于粮油物资储备事务方面的支出。

（19）国债还本付息支出：指政府在国债还本、付息、发行等方面的支出。

Explanatory Notes on Main Statistical Indicators

General Public Budget Revenue refers to income for the government finance through participating in the distribution of social products. It is the financial guarantee to ensure government functioning. Now it includes Tax Revenue and Non-Tax Revenue:

(1) Tax Revenue: Including Value-added tax, consumption tax, business tax, enterprise income tax, enterprise income tax rebate, personal income tax, resources tax , regulatory taxes on investment in fixed assets, urban maintenance and construction taxes, property taxes, stamp duty, tax on using urban land, land value-added tax, tax on using Vehicles and Ships, tax on using licence, Ship tons of tax, vehicle purchase tax (charges), tax on Slaughtering, banquet tax, customs, agriculture (tobacco) specialty tax, land tax, contract taxes and other tax revenue.

(2) Non-Tax Revenue: Including Special revenue, the Community Chest lottery income, administrative fees income, confiscated income, the state capital operating revenue, compensation income of using state-owned resources (assets), other income.

General Public Budget Expenditure refers to the distribution and use of the funds which the government finance has raised, so as to meet the needs of economic construction and various causes. It includes the following main items:

(1) Commonly Public servings: including affairs of People's Congress, affairs of Committee of People's Political Consultative Conference, the Government Office (room) and related organizations affairs, development and reform Affairs, statistical information Affairs, financial services, revenue Affairs, audit Affairs, customs affairs, personnel affairs, the discipline inspection and supervision Affairs, population and family planning Affairs, commerce and trade Affairs, intellectual property Affairs, administration affairs of industrial and commercial, supervision and administration Affairs of food and drug, quality of technical supervision and inspection and quarantine Affairs, land and natural resources Affairs, marine management Affairs, surveying and mapping Affairs, seismic Affairs, meteorological Affairs, ethical affairs, religion Affairs, Hong Kong, Macao and Taiwan affairs, file Affairs, the Communist Party affairs, other parties and the Federation of Industry and Commerce Services Mass organizations Affairs, Lottery Affairs, Treasury Affairs, bond investment, the other general public Affairs expenditure.

(2) Defense: refers to the government for defense spending, including standing army, the reserve forces and the militia, national defense scientific research career, special engineering, national defense mobilization of expenditure.

(3) National Defense: including Active-duty troops and reserve forces of national defense, national defense mobilization, and other defense expenditure.

(4) Education: including Education and management Affairs, general education, vocational education, adult education, radio and television education, studying abroad education, special education, teacher education and continuing education of cadres, education surcharge and education fund, other educational expenses.

(5) Science and technology: including Science and technology management Affairs, basic research, applied research, technology research and development, conditions and service of science and technology, social science, science and technology popularization , Science and technology exchanges and cooperation, and other science and technology expenditure.

(6) Culture Sport and Medium: including Culture, heritage, sports, radio, television, press, publishing, sports and other cultural and media expenditure.

(7) Social Security and Obtain employment: including Social security and Obtain employment Affairs, civil administration Management Affairs, added the National Social Security Fund, retired from administrative institutions, subsidies for shutdown and bankruptcy enterprises, employment subsidies, pension, placement of retirement, social welfare, handicapped Affairs, the minimum

living guarantee for urban residents, other urban social relief, rural social relief, living relief for natural disaster, the Red Cross Affairs, other social security expenditure and employment expenditure.

(8) Medical Treatment and Public Health: including Medical and health management affairs, medical services, community health services, health ensure, disease prevention and control, sanitation surveillance, health care of female and child, rural sanitation, Chinese traditional medicine, other medical and health expenditure.

(9) Energy conservation and environmental protection: including Environmental management affairs, environmental monitoring and surveillance, pollution control, natural ecological protection, natural forests protection, returning farmland to forests, desertification and sandstorms control, returning farmland to grassland, other environmental protection expenditure.

(10) Urban and Rural Area Community Operating: Including The management of urban and rural communities affairs, planning and management of urban and rural community, public facilities in rural and urban communities, residential of rural and urban communities, sanitation of urban and rural communities, management and supervision of marketable construction, the Government Housing Fund expenditures, expenditures of using land, additional expenditures of urban public utilities, other expenses of urban and rural community affairs.

(11) Farming Forestry and Water Conservancy Operating: including Agriculture, forestry, water conservancy, moving water from north to south, poverty alleviation, agricultural development, and other expenditures of agriculture, forestry, water affairs.

(12) Traffic and Transport: including Highway and waterway transport, rail transport, air transport, and other transport expenses.

(13) Resource exploration of electric power information: Mining, manufacturing, construction, electricity, the information industry, tourism, foreign-related development, grain and oil services, commercial circulation services, material reserves, the financial industry, tobacco affairs, production safety, state-owned assets supervision, the SME affairs, other industrial business Services such as financial expenditures.

(14) Business service and other affairs: refers to the government to business service and other affairs expenses, including commercial distribution affairs, tourism management and service, foreign development service expenditure, etc.

(15) Financial supervision: refers to the government for financial insurance regulatory affairs expenses.

(16) Land and resources weather affairs: refers to the government for land and resources, ocean, surveying and mapping, earthquake, meteorology and so on public service business spending.

(17) Housing security spending: refers to the government for housing safeguard expenses.

(18) Grain and oil materials reserve affairs: refers to the government for cereals and oil materials reserve affairs expenses

(19) National debt repayment of capital and interest expenses: refers to the government in national debt repayment of principal and interest payment and issue of expenditure.

物价
Prices

9

● 资料整理：王晓燕 袁 勇 杨 青 朱娜

简要说明

一、主要内容

本篇包括居民消费价格指数，商品零售价格指数，农业生产资料价格指数，农产品生产价格指数，工业生产者出厂价格指数，工业生产者购进价格指数，固定资产投资价格指数等资料。

二、资料来源

价格指数编制由国家统计局河南调查总队组织实施。由省、市及抽选出的市、县调查队依据国家统计局统一制定的价格统计调查制度向基层采集原始数据汇总后得到。

居民消费、商品零售、农业生产资料价格指数采用抽样调查和重点调查相结合的方法取得，即在全省选择不同经济区域和分布合理的地区，以及有代表性的商品作为样本，对其市场价格进行定期调查，以样本推断总体。由国家统计局河南调查总队消费价格调查处编辑整理。

工业生产者价格调查采用重点调查与典型调查相结合的调查方法。重点调查将全部年主营业务收入2000万元以上的企业列为调查对象，采用主观选样的方法选择调查企业；典型调查是把年主营业务收入2000万元以下的企业作为抽样对象，采用随机抽样的调查方法。由国家统计局河南调查总队生产投资价格调查处编辑整理。

固定资产投资价格指数采用重点调查与典型调查相结合的方法。由国家统计局河南调查总队生产投资价格调查处编辑整理。

Brief Introduction

I. Main Contents

Data on price indices in this chapter including mainly consumer price indices, retail price indices, price indices for means of agricultural production, producer price indices for farm products, Industrial producers ex-factory price index, industrial producers purchase price index, price indices for investment in fixed assets.

II. Sources of Data

Compilation of statistics on price indices is organized by the Department of Henan Survey organizations, NBS. The survey organizations of the provinces, cities directly under the Central Government and of the selected cities and counties collect data from the grassroots units in accordance with the scheme of price survey system, tabulate them and report them to the higher agencies.

Data for compilation of the consumer price indices, the retail price indices and the producer price indices for farm products in Henan province are collected through a combination of sample surveys and surveys of key units. Areas distributed in different economic regions are selected as the sample areas and representative commodities are selected as the sample commodities. Regular surveys are conducted to collect data on their market prices. Population parameters are inferred on the basis of the sample data. Data of this part are provided by the Department of Henan Survey organizations, NBS.

Industrial producer prices are collected through a combined use of the key units' survey and typical units' survey methods. Key units refer to enterprises which annual sale revenue above 20 million yuan, using the method of subjective selection. Typical units refer to the enterprises which annual sale revenue below 20 million yuan, using the method of sampling survey. Data of this part are provided by the Department of Henan Survey organizations, NBS.

Data on prices of investment in fixed assets are collected by a program involving the combined use of surveys on key units and surveys on typical units. Data of this part are provided by the Department of Henan Survey organizations, NBS.

9-1 各种物价总指数

General Price Indices

(上年=100) (preceding year=100)

年 份 Year	居民消费价格总指数 General Consumer Price Index	城 市 Urban Areas	农 村 Rural Areas	商品零售价格总指数 General Retail Price Index	农业生产资料价格总指数 General Price Index for Means of Agricultural Production	工业生产者出厂价格指数 Producer Price Index for Industrial Products	工业生产者购进价格指数 Purchasing Price Index for Industrial Producers	固定资产投资价格指数 Price Index for Investment In Fixed Assets
1978	100.1	100.0	100.1	100.1	97.9			
1980	104.6	106.0	103.8	104.9	100.1			
1985	104.6	106.5	103.6	105.4	103.0			
1990	100.7	100.5	100.9	100.1	98.3	105.5	105.5	
1991	102.3	105.1	100.0	102.0	100.1	104.3	104.4	109.4
1992	105.4	107.7	102.9	105.0	101.2	106.2	110.0	119.8
1993	110.4	110.6	110.3	108.3	109.2	118.1	133.0	126.7
1994	125.2	127.4	123.5	120.6	124.4	124.1	122.0	106.0
1995	116.5	116.9	116.3	114.9	125.8	115.0	114.1	105.9
1996	110.5	109.5	110.9	107.9	107.9	104.1	106.0	103.9
1997	103.5	102.4	103.9	100.6	99.3	100.6	100.6	102.9
1998	97.5	97.9	97.1	96.6	94.2	95.3	94.8	98.7
1999	96.9	96.6	97.1	96.2	95.7	95.4	94.3	98.0
2000	99.2	99.1	99.2	98.5	99.6	104.0	105.1	102.9
2001	100.7	100.7	100.7	99.8	99.1	100.5	101.9	100.4
2002	100.1	99.8	100.6	99.2	100.8	98.6	97.6	98.7
2003	101.6	101.7	101.4	101.3	101.9	105.0	107.8	103.8
2004	105.4	105.4	105.4	105.7	111.4	110.2	115.7	110.1
2005	102.1	102.1	102.1	101.7	107.9	106.1	108.3	101.4
2006	101.3	101.2	101.5	100.9	101.2	104.3	105.3	101.6
2007	105.4	105.4	105.5	104.4	106.1	105.2	106.4	104.6
2008	107.0	106.5	107.9	107.5	120.9	112.1	111.9	109.0
2009	99.4	98.8	100.4	99.4	98.1	94.9	97.1	96.4
2010	103.5	103.4	103.8	103.7	103.1	107.8	110.2	103.5
2011	105.6	105.4	106.1	105.7	111.1	107.2	110.1	107.4
2012	102.5	102.6	102.4	102.3	105.4	99.4	99.2	101.0
2013	102.9	102.9	102.9	101.9	101.3	98.5	99.3	99.9
2014	101.9	102.0	101.6	101.0	97.9	98.1	98.4	100.0
2015	101.3	101.3	101.2	99.8	100.3	95.4	95.4	97.6
2016	101.9	101.9	102.0	100.3	100.8	99.0	99.2	99.2
2017	101.4	101.5	101.2	101.3	99.7	106.8	107.3	107.4
2018	102.3	102.4	102.0	102.9	104.3	103.6	104.0	105.4
2019	103.0	102.9	103.1	102.4	103.8	100.2	101.2	103.2

9-2 各种物价定基指数

Fixed-base Price Indices

(1978年=100) (1978 year =100)

年 份 Year	居民消费价格总指数 General Consumer Price Index	城 市 Urban Areas	农 村 Rural Areas	商品零售价格总指数 General Retail Price Index	农业生产资料价格总指数 General Price Index of Agricultural Means of Production	工业生产者出厂价格指数 Producer Price Index for Industrial Products	工业生产者购进价格指数 Purchasing Price Index for Industrial Producers	固定资产投资价格指数 Price Index for Investment In Fixed Assets
1978	100.0	100.0	100.0	100.0	100.0			
1979	100.4	100.3	100.4	100.4	100.0			
1980	105.0	106.3	104.2	105.3	100.1			
1981	106.5	108.9	105.0	107.0	101.4			
1982	108.0	110.8	106.3	108.6	103.5			
1983	109.7	114.0	107.3	110.5	109.4			
1984	110.6	116.6	107.4	111.5	116.1			
1985	115.7	124.1	111.2	117.5	119.6			
1986	122.0	132.6	116.0	123.3	125.7			
1987	129.7	142.9	122.2	131.1	143.8			
1988	154.9	173.6	144.3	156.9	175.1	100.0	100.0	
1989	183.9	199.5	176.0	186.3	204.6	119.7	130.0	
1990	185.1	200.5	177.6	186.5	201.1	126.3	137.2	100.0
1991	189.4	210.7	177.6	190.2	201.3	131.7	143.2	109.4
1992	199.6	227.0	182.8	199.7	203.7	139.9	157.5	131.1
1993	220.4	251.0	201.6	216.3	222.4	165.2	209.5	166.1
1994	275.9	319.8	249.0	260.8	276.7	205.0	255.6	176.0
1995	321.4	373.8	289.5	299.7	348.1	235.8	291.6	186.4
1996	355.2	409.3	321.1	323.4	375.6	245.4	309.1	193.7
1997	367.6	419.2	333.6	325.0	373.0	246.9	310.9	199.3
1998	358.4	410.4	323.9	314.0	351.3	235.3	294.8	196.7
1999	347.3	396.4	314.6	302.0	336.2	224.5	278.0	192.8
2000	344.6	392.9	312.0	297.5	334.9	233.5	292.2	198.4
2001	347.0	395.6	314.2	296.9	331.9	234.6	297.7	199.1
2002	347.3	394.8	316.1	294.5	334.5	231.4	290.5	196.6
2003	352.9	401.5	320.5	298.4	340.9	243.0	313.0	204.0
2004	371.9	423.2	337.8	315.4	379.7	267.9	362.0	224.6
2005	379.7	432.1	344.9	320.7	409.7	284.1	392.0	227.8
2006	384.7	437.3	350.1	323.6	414.7	296.3	412.7	231.3
2007	405.5	460.9	369.4	337.8	440.0	311.8	439.2	242.0
2008	433.9	490.9	398.6	363.1	532.0	349.6	491.3	263.7
2009	431.3	485.0	400.2	360.9	521.9	331.8	477.2	254.2
2010	446.4	501.5	415.4	374.3	538.1	357.7	525.9	263.1
2011	471.4	528.6	440.7	395.6	597.8	383.4	579.1	282.4
2012	483.2	542.3	451.3	404.7	630.1	381.2	574.2	285.2
2013	497.2	558.0	464.4	412.4	638.3	375.6	570.0	285.0
2014	506.7	569.2	471.8	416.5	624.9	368.2	560.8	284.8
2015	513.3	576.8	477.7	415.5	626.9	351.1	534.9	278.1
2016	523.1	587.5	487.3	416.9	632.2	347.7	530.8	275.7
2017	530.4	596.3	493.2	422.3	630.3	371.4	569.3	296.1
2018	542.6	610.6	503.1	434.5	657.4	384.6	592.3	312.0
2019	558.9	628.6	518.8	445.1	682.3	385.2	599.4	322.0

注：工业生产者出厂价格和工业生产者购进价格指数以1988年=100，固定资产投资价格指数以1990年=100。

a) Producer Price Index for Industrial Products and Purchasing Prices Index for Industrial Products are Calculated as the index on 1988=100, Prices Index for Investment in Fixed Assets is Calculated as the index on 1990=100.

9—3 居民消费价格指数(2019年)
Consumer Price Indices (2019)

(上年=100) (preceding year=100)

项目	Item	全省 The Whole Province	城市 Urban Indices	农村 Rural Indices
总指数	**General Consumer Price Index**	**103.0**	**102.9**	**103.1**
食品烟酒	**Food、Tobacco and Liquor**	**107.4**	**107.1**	**108.0**
食品	Food	110.0	109.6	110.7
粮食	Grain	100.0	100.2	99.7
食用油	Cooking Oil	99.2	98.7	100.0
菜	Vegetables	103.4	104.1	101.7
#鲜菜	Fresh Vegetables	103.4	104.2	101.6
畜肉类	Livestock Meat	133.9	132.4	136.4
#猪肉	Pork	145.9	144.9	147.3
禽肉类	Meal and Poultry	110.4	110.9	109.5
水产品	Aquatic Products	99.3	98.8	100.5
蛋类	Eggs	106.1	106.0	106.3
奶类	Milk	100.6	100.7	100.5
干鲜瓜果类	Dried and Fresh Melons and Fruits	107.0	107.6	105.5
#鲜瓜果	Fresh Fruits	109.1	110.3	106.7
茶及饮料	Tea and Beverages	101.7	101.5	102.0
烟酒	Tobacco and Liquor	101.8	102.0	101.6
在外餐饮	Dining Out	102.7	102.9	102.4
衣着	**Clothing**	**100.7**	**100.8**	**100.5**
服装	Garments	100.7	100.7	100.8
服装材料	Clothing Material	101.2	101.3	100.9
其他衣着及配件	Other Clothing and accessories	100.6	100.0	102.4
衣着加工服务费	Tailoring and Laundering Service	103.0	103.4	102.2
鞋类	Footwear	100.4	100.9	99.6
居住	**Residence**	**100.8**	**100.8**	**100.9**
租赁房房租	Renting	100.0	99.5	102.2
住房保养维修及管理	Maintenance and Management of Housing	101.3	102.1	100.2
水电燃料	Water, Electricity and Fuels	100.7	101.2	100.0
自有住房	Private Housing	100.8	100.4	101.7
生活用品及服务	**Supplies and services**	**100.6**	**100.7**	**100.6**
家具及室内装饰品	Furniture and Decorations	101.5	101.5	101.5
家用器具	Home Appliances	99.2	99.1	99.3
家用纺织品	Home Textile	99.9	99.3	101.3
家庭日用杂品	Daily Use Household Articles	100.9	101.0	100.8
个人护理用品	Personal Article and Service	101.0	101.0	100.7
家庭服务	Household Service	103.6	103.9	102.4
交通和通信	**Transportation and Communication**	**99.0**	**98.4**	**100.0**
交通	Transportation	99.0	98.9	99.1
通信	Communication	99.0	97.5	101.6
教育文化和娱乐	**Education Culture and Recreation**	**102.7**	**103.4**	**101.5**
教育	Education	103.7	105.0	101.8
文化娱乐	Cultural and Recreational Articles	101.1	101.1	100.9
医疗保健	**Health Care**	**101.9**	**101.9**	**101.9**
药品及医疗器具	Medicines and Medical Instrument	103.4	103.3	103.7
医疗服务	Medical Service	100.9	101.0	100.8
其他用品和服务	**Other Articles and Service**	**105.2**	**105.7**	**104.3**
其他用品类	Articles	106.7	107.7	105.3
其他服务类	Service	104.0	104.4	103.0

9-4 分类商品零售价格指数
Retail Price Indices by Category

(上年=100) (preceding year=100)

项 目	Item	2010	2011	2012	2013	2014	2015	2016	2017	2018	2019
商品零售价格总指数	**Retail Price Index of commodities**	**103.7**	**105.7**	**102.3**	**101.9**	**101.0**	**99.8**	**100.3**	**101.3**	**102.9**	**102.4**
食品类	Food	108.7	112.4	103.1	105.6	102.5	101.5	103.4	98.3	101.6	107.2
饮料、烟酒类	Beverage and Tobacco and Alcohol	101.5	104.0	103.8	101.4	99.6	101.0	100.0	101.6	102.6	101.9
服装、鞋帽类	Garments Shoes and Hats	100.9	101.4	103.2	102.7	102.4	102.3	100.6	101.1	101.0	100.8
纺织品类	Textile Product	104.0	109.8	102.4	100.8	100.5	101.0	100.1	100.9	100.8	100.3
家用电器及音像器材	Household Appliance and Audio-video Material	97.8	98.8	99.5	99.8	99.6	98.9	95.6	101.1	100.8	98.3
文化办公用品类	Office Supplies	98.7	98.5	99.3	99.2	100.0	99.0	100.7	103.2	100.5	103.2
日用品类	Articles for Everyday Use	100.1	102.5	102.8	101.3	100.9	100.4	100.2	100.7	101.2	100.9
体育娱乐用品类	Sport and Entertainment Goods	99.8	100.8	100.9	100.3	100.6	100.6	100.1	100.4	101.5	100.8
交通、通信用品类	Transportation and Communication Appliances	96.1	97.1	97.7	97.4	99.3	95.5	95.8	95.7	102.7	102.1
家具类	Furniture	99.6	102.3	101.8	101.4	101.4	100.7	100.9	100.8	102.4	101.9
化妆品类	Cosmetics	100.3	101.1	103.2	102.0	101.0	100.4	101.2	101.3	101.6	101.0
金银珠宝类	Gold and Sliver and Jewellery	111.3	114.3	103.2	91.5	91.6	93.6	106.0	103.1	98.3	107.9
中西药品及医疗保健用品类	Chinese Traditional Medicine and Western Medicine and Health Product	104.0	103.9	102.4	102.2	101.7	103.8	106.1	109.2	105.6	103.9
书报杂志及电子出版物类	Books and Newspapers and Magazines and Electronic Publications	99.4	100.9	103.9	102.5	100.7	102.1	101.8	102.0	104.1	106.4
燃料类	Fuel	110.5	113.6	104.5	98.3	98.5	87.8	96.6	111.4	112.0	96.1
建筑材料及五金电料类	Architectural and Hardware Material	104.3	107.0	101.3	100.0	100.4	99.5	100.5	103.0	102.8	100.9

9-5 农业生产资料价格指数
Price Indices for Means of Agricultural Production

(上年=100) (preceding year=100)

项 目	Item	2010	2011	2012	2013	2014	2015	2016	2017	2018	2019
农业生产资料价格总指数	**Price Indices of Means of Agricultural Production**	**103.1**	**111.1**	**105.4**	**101.3**	**97.9**	**100.3**	**100.8**	**99.7**	**104.3**	**103.8**
农用手工工具	Farm Handtools	101.1	104.9	102.9	105.0	106.1	102.1	104.3	104.3	106.1	101.6
饲料	Forage	109.1	105.5	106.5	106.4	101.0	96.1	98.2	100.4	106.4	99.2
仔畜幼禽及产品畜	Young Poultry and Commodity Animals	101.8	136.4	103.1	98.5	93.6	112.3	151.6	84.3	83.7	161.2
半机械化农具	Semi-mechanized Farm Tools	100.9	105.8	104.6	102.3	102.1	101.6	101.1	102.1	100.8	102.6
机械化农具	Mechanized Farm Machinery	100.1	103.7	100.5	100.3	100.4	99.3	99.5	101.3	100.7	101.5
化学肥料	Chemical Fertilizer	98.5	115.2	106.0	95.4	91.2	101.7	95.7	100.7	109.4	101.1
农药及农药机械	Pesticide and Appliances	100.6	106.0	101.4	102.1	102.6	100.5	99.1	100.4	105.1	104.0
化学农药	Chemical Pesticide	99.4	106.3	101.4	102.4	102.5	100.4	99.1	100.4	105.3	104.0
农药器械	Pesticide Appliances	105.9	102.5	100.8	99.6	103.5	100.5	100.0	100.5	101.6	103.3
农用机油	Oil for Farm Machinery	113.1	114.7	104.2	99.3	97.5	83.8	95.2	114.5	115.2	94.1
其他农用生产资料	Other Means of Agricultural Production	109.5	108.2	107.9	106.0	102.4	101.4	98.3	99.7	100.3	101.4
农用种子	Farm Seed	113.6	108.7	109.2	106.6	102.5	101.8	98.0	99.2	99.4	100.9
未列明的其他农用生产资料	Other Means of Agricultural Production Non-listed	99.5	105.6	100.6	102.0	101.6	98.8	101.1	101.9	103.4	101.1
农业生产服务	Service for Agricultural Production	102.3	106.9	107.1	106.1	103.9	104.8	101.5	100.6	102.5	101.5

9−6 各市(县)居民消费价格指数(2019年)

Consumer Price Indices by City (2019)

各市(县)数据不含所辖市(县)数据(9−7表同)。

Price Indices of every city(county) exclude the data of city(county) under its administration. (the same as table 9-7).

(上年=100) (preceding year=100)

市 City	居民消费价格总指数 Consumer Price Index	食品烟酒 Food, Tobacco, Liquor	衣着 Clothing	居住 Residence	生活用品及服务 Living Supplies and Services	交通和通信 Transportation and Communication	教育文化和娱乐 Education, Culture and Entertainment	医疗保健 Health Care	其他用品和服务 Others
省辖市 City	**102.9**	**107.1**	**100.8**	**100.8**	**100.7**	**98.4**	**103.4**	**101.9**	**105.7**
郑州市 Zhengzhou	103.1	108.1	102.0	99.8	101.2	95.9	105.0	101.6	108.0
开封市 Kaifeng	102.4	105.7	100.5	101.1	99.6	99.9	101.7	101.8	103.6
洛阳市 Luoyang	102.8	106.8	99.1	100.9	100.4	99.0	103.1	103.0	105.8
平顶山市 Pingdingshan	102.9	105.8	101.6	101.9	100.5	99.1	103.5	101.5	104.3
安阳市 Anyang	103.1	107.8	101.2	100.0	100.2	99.5	104.6	99.4	106.7
鹤壁市 Hebi	102.7	107.1	98.8	100.4	99.6	100.4	102.8	102.0	104.1
新乡市 Xinxiang	103.3	106.2	103.2	101.9	101.0	99.3	102.3	103.4	106.6
焦作市 Jiaozuo	103.0	107.3	100.3	101.3	100.7	99.7	101.6	101.7	105.1
濮阳市 Puyang	102.9	105.4	99.0	101.5	100.1	98.2	100.4	113.2	105.3
许昌市 Xuchang	103.0	105.7	98.2	104.1	99.9	99.9	102.7	102.2	105.0
漯河市 Luohe	102.8	105.7	101.4	101.6	101.2	100.1	103.6	100.6	102.4
三门峡市 Sanmenxia	102.2	107.0	94.1	100.7	100.2	100.0	100.8	103.1	105.2
南阳市 Nanyang	103.0	107.0	101.5	100.6	100.9	99.4	103.4	100.8	103.2
商丘市 Shangqiu	102.8	106.7	98.9	102.4	100.2	100.2	101.7	101.5	102.2
信阳市 Xinyang	102.6	105.7	99.5	102.7	100.1	100.2	102.6	100.4	102.7
周口市 Zhoukou	103.1	107.8	101.7	100.6	100.4	100.2	102.3	100.1	106.5
驻马店市 Zhumadian	102.7	106.8	101.0	101.1	99.8	99.1	102.2	100.2	105.4
济源市 Jiyuan									
省直管县 County Directly Administrated by Province									
巩义市 Gongyi									
兰考县 Lankao									
汝州市 Ruzhou									
滑县 Huaxian	103.1	108.1	100.6	99.6	100.6	100.1	100.3	104.8	103.8
长垣市 Changyuan									
邓州市 Dengzhou									
永城市 Yongcheng	102.9	107.9	102.0	100.8	100.9	100.0	100.7	100.2	102.9
固始县 Gushi	103.6	108.6	100.3	100.7	101.3	100.6	103.3	101.8	105.9
鹿邑县 Luyi									
新蔡县 Xincai									

9-7 各市商品零售价格指数(2019年)

(上年=100)

市 City	商品零售价格总指数 General Index	食品类 Food	饮料烟酒类 Beverage and Tabacco, Liquor	服装鞋帽类 Clothing, Shoes and Hats	纺织品类 Textiles	家用电器及音像器材类 Household Appliance and Audio-video Material	文化办公用品类 Cultural and Office Supplies	日用品类 Articles for Daily Use
省辖市 City	**102.5**	**107.1**	**101.9**	**100.8**	**99.8**	**98.2**	**103.0**	**101.0**
郑州市 Zhengzhou	103.0	108.3	101.5	101.9	100.5	97.0	103.4	101.8
开封市 Kaifeng	102.4	105.7	104.5	100.5	98.9	98.5	102.5	101.0
洛阳市 Luoyang	102.0	106.6	103.4	98.9	98.4	98.1	103.2	100.9
平顶山市 Pingdingshan	102.4	105.8	102.0	101.5	101.1	99.1	100.0	100.1
安阳市 Anyang	102.0	108.0	100.4	101.3	100.3	98.5	102.9	100.8
鹤壁市 Hebi	101.8	107.4	100.8	98.7	97.5	98.4	103.3	100.5
新乡市 Xinxiang	103.1	106.4	101.3	103.3	100.6	98.6	103.2	99.8
焦作市 Jiaozuo	102.3	107.3	101.9	100.4	100.0	98.7	103.7	101.0
濮阳市 Puyang	102.0	104.3	102.9	98.8	97.0	98.1	103.2	101.4
许昌市 Xuchang	101.5	105.2	102.8	98.2	100.3	98.2	102.2	100.0
漯河市 Luohe	102.0	105.8	101.0	101.2	99.6	98.6	103.1	101.5
三门峡市 Sanmenxia	102.0	107.4	100.6	94.4	101.0	98.4	103.2	100.2
南阳市 Nanyang	102.3	107.3	100.3	101.5	99.9	98.8	104.5	101.5
商丘市 Shangqiu	101.7	106.8	100.9	98.2	98.3	98.2	104.2	99.7
信阳市 Xinyang	102.0	105.5	101.9	99.3	99.4	98.7	103.0	100.4
周口市 Zhoukou	102.5	108.3	100.5	100.9	100.9	99.0	103.3	100.3
驻马店市 Zhumadian	102.4	106.7	101.6	100.7	99.6	98.5	103.4	99.6
济源市 Jiyuan								

Retail Price Indices by City (2019)

(preceding year=100)

体育娱乐用品类 Sport and Entertainment Goods	交通、通信用品 Traffic and Communi-cation Goods	家具类 Furniture	化妆品类 Cosmetics	金银饰品 Gold、Sliver and Jewellery	中、西药品及医疗保健用品 Chinese Traditional Medicine and Western Medicine and Health Product	书报杂志及电子出版物类 Books& Newspapers、Magazines and E-publication	燃料类 Fuels	建筑材料及五金电料类 Architectural and hardware material
100.9	**102.1**	**101.9**	**101.0**	**108.0**	**103.8**	**106.5**	**96.4**	**101.1**
102.3	102.1	104.8	101.5	110.6	104.1	109.2	96.9	100.8
98.9	101.8	99.3	101.4	100.4	107.3	107.6	96.5	101.3
99.3	101.8	101.5	100.1	106.2	104.3	102.4	96.0	100.6
101.5	104.5	98.8	99.8	108.3	103.2	105.7	96.6	101.4
100.3	102.3	100.5	100.8	110.2	99.1	101.3	96.0	99.2
100.1	101.9	99.5	100.6	108.2	103.9	106.9	95.5	97.9
101.6	101.8	102.7	103.2	108.5	108.9	114.7	96.1	101.8
102.0	101.8	100.2	101.0	109.4	102.9	100.7	96.5	102.4
99.6	101.8	99.9	100.8	109.4	109.0	106.4	97.9	99.0
100.1	101.9	100.7	99.7	109.9	101.2	105.5	96.9	100.1
100.9	101.7	99.3	103.9	105.9	100.9	100.5	98.1	101.5
99.7	101.7	100.0	100.0	108.5	106.2	106.6	96.8	101.6
98.7	101.7	101.9	101.5	108.0	101.8	99.9	95.5	101.3
100.2	102.0	99.3	100.1	102.6	104.1	103.4	95.2	100.6
98.4	101.9	97.9	101.3	105.1	101.5	111.3	96.7	104.1
101.5	101.8	101.7	99.8	109.3	100.3	103.4	96.1	103.0
99.1	102.1	100.1	99.0	109.3	100.5	111.1	96.6	104.2

9-8 各市居民消费价格指数(2019年)

Consumer Price Indices by City (2019)

本表数据为全市口径（9-9表同）。

Price Indices of every city refers to the whole city's caliber (the same as table 9-9).

(上年=100) (preceding year=100)

市(县) City(County)	居民消费价格总指数 Consumer Price Index	食品烟酒 Food, Tobacco, Liquor	衣着 Clothing	居住 Residence	生活用品及服务 Living Supplies and Services	交通和通信 Transportation and Communication	教育文化和娱乐 Education, Culture, Entertainment	医疗保健 Health Care	其他用品和服务 Others
省辖市 City									
郑州市 Zhengzhou	103.1	108.1	102.0	99.8	101.2	95.9	105.0	101.6	108.0
开封市 Kaifeng	102.6	106.0	100.9	100.9	100.8	99.4	103.8	100.5	101.9
洛阳市 Luoyang	102.4	105.1	100.2	100.6	99.5	100.2	102.1	104.7	102.9
平顶山市 Pingdingshan	103.0	106.4	100.5	103.0	100.1	99.0	103.0	101.3	103.9
安阳市 Anyang	103.2	107.3	101.8	100.5	100.5	99.1	103.6	102.0	105.2
鹤壁市 Hebi	103.2	106.6	104.2	102.2	102.3	98.7	102.0	100.1	103.0
新乡市 Xinxiang	102.7	105.5	102.0	101.3	100.9	99.5	101.5	103.4	105.4
焦作市 Jiaozuo	103.0	106.8	103.3	101.6	100.7	98.6	100.4	103.0	104.4
濮阳市 Puyang	102.7	106.0	100.7	101.0	100.5	98.9	102.6	103.1	105.7
许昌市 Xuchang	103.0	107.3	101.1	101.9	100.5	100.2	100.7	101.0	101.8
漯河市 Luohe	102.8	106.7	103.2	100.5	100.0	100.2	99.8	101.1	104.9
三门峡市 Sanmenxia	102.2	106.1	100.7	100.6	100.4	99.3	100.6	100.8	103.4
南阳市 Nanyang	102.8	106.5	101.4	101.4	100.0	99.1	101.9	103.8	102.3
商丘市 Shangqiu	102.8	106.6	100.6	102.4	100.1	99.4	101.4	101.0	103.0
信阳市 Xinyang	102.5	105.1	101.9	102.3	100.6	99.6	100.7	101.7	103.7
周口市 Zhoukou	102.8	106.5	101.2	101.3	100.6	99.7	102.6	100.6	105.1
驻马店市 Zhumadian	102.8	107.0	101.2	102.4	100.3	96.5	101.6	101.7	103.5
济源市 Jiyuan	102.9	108.0	98.2	99.6	104.0	99.1	99.9	102.1	106.7
省直管县 County Directly Administrated by Province									
巩义市 Gongyi	103.7	108.3	104.8	100.3	99.6	98.8	103.8	103.9	106.4
兰考县 Lankao	104.4	114.0	101.7	99.5	99.1	96.2	99.3	103.7	102.5
汝州市 Ruzhou	103.0	107.8	99.2	101.6	100.6	95.6	102.8	101.4	110.6
滑县 Huaxian	103.1	108.1	100.6	99.6	100.6	100.1	100.3	104.8	103.8
长垣市 Changyuan	102.6	104.2	102.6	102.3	102.6	98.8	102.2	102.3	102.4
邓州市 Dengzhou	102.7	105.1	100.6	104.9	100.5	98.8	100.7	103.2	101.7
永城市 Yongcheng	102.5	106.4	100.9	100.1	100.0	102.2	99.8	100.2	101.3
固始县 Gushi	103.6	108.6	100.3	100.7	101.3	100.6	103.3	101.8	105.9
鹿邑县 Luyi	102.2	105.9	100.7	100.7	100.0	99.6	100.4	100.4	102.6
新蔡县 Xincai	103.4	106.0	101.2	100.0	106.3	104.9	97.9	105.7	104.1

9-9 各市商品零售价格指数(2019年)

Retail Price Indices by City (2019)

(上年=100) (preceding year=100)

市(县) City(County)	商品零售价格总指数 General Index	食品类 Food	饮料烟酒 Beverage, Tobacco, Liquor	服装鞋帽类 Clothing, Shoes and Hats	纺织品类 Textiles	家用电器及音像器材类 Household Appliance and Audio-video Material	文化办公用品类 Cultural and Office supplies	日用品 Articles for Daily Use	体育娱乐用品类 Sport and Entertainment Goods
省辖市 City									
郑州市 Zhengzhou	103.0	108.3	101.5	101.9	100.5	97.0	103.4	101.8	102.3
开封市 Kaifeng	102.6	105.3	104.0	100.6	98.9	98.5	103.0	100.1	99.0
洛阳市 Luoyang	102.1	107.0	100.9	100.3	97.9	98.3	97.0	100.2	102.3
平顶山市 Pingdingshan	102.2	107.0	101.3	100.6	101.1	99.2	100.0	100.0	100.7
安阳市 Anyang	102.3	107.8	100.8	101.7	101.1	98.7	102.3	101.0	100.4
鹤壁市 Hebi	103.1	107.3	100.8	103.9	110.7	102.7	101.3	100.5	100.8
新乡市 Xinxiang	103.1	106.5	101.1	102.9	100.5	98.6	103.3	100.1	101.5
焦作市 Jiaozuo	101.7	105.8	100.1	103.1	100.2	100.1	100.0	100.7	100.2
濮阳市 Puyang	102.1	106.9	101.4	100.8	100.0	97.2	100.2	101.7	99.4
许昌市 Xuchang	102.5	106.4	105.1	101.2	100.5	99.4	100.6	100.9	99.6
漯河市 Luohe	103.3	109.5	103.6	103.2	100.1	100.0	100.0	100.0	99.4
三门峡市 Sanmenxia	102.0	107.2	101.8	100.4	100.5	100.0	100.1	100.4	106.2
南阳市 Nanyang	102.5	106.2	100.7	100.9	100.1	98.1	99.5	100.9	99.5
商丘市 Shangqiu	101.9	108.0	100.8	100.9	100.3	99.4	100.4	100.2	100.1
信阳市 Xinyang	101.9	105.6	101.9	101.9	99.9	99.4	99.8	100.2	100.0
周口市 Zhoukou	102.1	106.7	101.6	100.8	100.6	99.3	101.5	100.5	100.8
驻马店市 Zhumadian	102.0	107.8	101.5	101.0	100.6	97.7	99.0	101.6	100.4
济源市 Jiyuan	103.1	108.2	103.3	98.0	110.2	93.3	99.1	108.3	102.7
省直管县 County Directly Administrated by Province									
巩义市 Gongyi	103.0	109.8	99.8	104.7	100.0	96.0	98.9	100.2	100.1
兰考县 Lankao	105.1	118.5	103.6	101.3	100.3	93.5	97.4	100.0	100.0
汝州市 Ruzhou	101.8	108.8	100.9	99.0	105.2	97.5	96.5	103.2	109.8
滑县 Huaxian	102.0	107.5	100.7	100.7	100.3	98.7	103.6	100.4	101.8
长垣市 Changyuan	101.3	104.6	100.6	102.4	101.2	99.7	100.4	101.1	101.6
邓州市 Dengzhou	101.4	104.3	100.3	100.4	100.3	97.8	100.3	100.1	100.3
永城市 Yongcheng	102.6	108.7	100.2	100.6	100.0	99.5	100.0	100.5	100.0
固始县 Gushi	103.0	108.2	102.9	100.2	101.3	98.3	103.8	101.9	100.4
鹿邑县 Luyi	101.8	106.9	100.0	100.8	100.0	100.0	99.9	99.8	100.0
新蔡县 Xincai	104.6	106.4	100.0	101.5	100.0	101.7	100.0	99.9	99.6

9-9 续表 continued

(上年=100) (preceding year=100)

市(县)	City(County)	交通、通信用品 Traffic& Communi-cation Goods	家 具 Furniture	化妆品 Cosmetics	金 银 珠宝类 Gold、Sliver and Jewellery	中、西药品及医疗保健用品 Chinese Traditional Medicine and Western Medicine and Health Product	书报杂志及电子出出版物类 Books& Newspapers、Magazines and E-publication	燃料类 Fuels	建筑材料及五金电料 类 Architectural and Hardware Material
省 辖 市	**City**								
郑 州 市	Zhengzhou	102.1	104.8	101.5	110.6	104.1	109.2	96.9	100.8
开 封 市	Kaifeng	102.5	99.4	101.3	100.5	106.9	107.5	99.2	101.1
洛 阳 市	Luoyang	99.3	98.6	99.9	102.2	110.6	101.4	98.0	101.1
平 顶 山 市	Pingdingshan	101.6	98.6	100.0	108.1	102.7	103.4	97.0	102.4
安 阳 市	Anyang	102.0	100.9	100.6	109.3	101.6	102.2	97.0	99.5
鹤 壁 市	Hebi	97.6	101.2	100.2	107.4	100.0	101.0	98.2	108.2
新 乡 市	Xinxiang	101.8	102.6	102.9	108.6	109.0	113.8	96.0	102.2
焦 作 市	Jiaozuo	100.0	101.7	100.2	107.3	104.0	100.0	95.0	100.6
濮 阳 市	Puyang	98.1	101.1	101.6	111.4	107.3	100.0	96.5	101.2
许 昌 市	Xuchang	100.0	99.8	101.1	107.3	103.8	101.7	96.9	103.3
漯 河 市	Luohe	100.1	99.6	100.6	105.9	103.4	99.9	98.3	100.0
三 门 峡 市	Sanmenxia	99.2	100.3	99.6	108.4	101.3	100.5	97.2	101.6
南 阳 市	Nanyang	97.0	100.1	101.5	103.9	107.2	105.0	101.2	104.0
商 丘 市	Shangqiu	97.8	99.9	101.0	104.6	103.4	99.8	96.5	100.3
信 阳 市	Xinyang	100.0	100.8	100.3	106.8	103.6	101.8	97.4	101.2
周 口 市	Zhoukou	99.6	101.0	100.1	103.9	101.7	101.9	97.4	103.3
驻 马 店 市	Zhumadian	90.2	99.9	100.8	110.2	103.3	110.2	96.3	101.7
济 源 市	Jiyuan	97.5	99.5	101.5	108.6	104.2	100.7	93.5	110.4
省 直 管 县	**County Directly Administrated by Province**								
巩 义 市	Gongyi	97.7	99.9	100.3	115.1	107.4	98.0	97.6	101.0
兰 考 县	Lankao	91.1	101.2	100.0	105.4	111.2	109.2	97.7	101.6
汝 州 市	Ruzhou	92.0	99.7	100.1	104.0	104.1	114.4	96.6	102.2
滑 县	Huaxian	102.2	103.8	100.1	106.2	104.3	100.0	95.2	100.1
长 垣 市	Changyuan	97.3	100.0	105.5	99.5	101.1	100.0	96.1	101.8
邓 州 市	Dengzhou	98.2	100.8	100.3	99.7	105.8	100.2	96.8	102.6
永 城 市	Yongcheng	99.7	100.0	100.2	103.4	100.4	99.3	97.3	100.5
固 始 县	Gushi	102.5	103.3	102.0	110.5	106.1	111.1	95.6	97.7
鹿 邑 县	Luyi	100.0	100.0	100.0	101.0	101.0	100.8	97.6	100.8
新 蔡 县	Xincai	117.1	121.8	97.0	96.5	110.2	99.1	97.7	100.0

9-10 工业生产者出厂价格指数

Producer Price Index for Industrial Products

(上年=100)

类　别	Type	2010	2011	2012	2013	2014	2015	2016	2017	2018	2019
总 指 数	**General Index**	**107.8**	**107.2**	**99.4**	**98.5**	**98.1**	**95.4**	**99.0**	**106.8**	**103.6**	**100.2**
按轻、重工业分	**Grouped by Light & Heavy Industry**										
轻工业	Light Industry	104.3	106.9	100.1	101.8	100.9	99.8	99.1	101.9	101.3	101.0
以农产品为原料	Using Farm Products as Raw Materials	106.0	107.5	100.0	102.1	100.8	99.6	99.2	101.8	101.7	101.5
以非农产品为原料	Using Non-Farm Products as Raw Materials	102.4	104.3	100.5	100.0	101.0	100.5	98.8	102.3	99.9	99.0
重工业	Heavy Industry	110.7	107.3	99.2	97.3	96.9	93.6	99.0	108.9	104.5	99.8
采掘工业	Mining & Quarrying Industry	116.7	112.6	96.8	91.8	91.3	82.1	96.5	116.0	106.7	103.1
原料工业	Raw Materials Industry	112.9	108.4	100.2	96.8	96.9	93.4	99.4	115.7	105.2	98.7
加工工业	Manufacturing Industry	105.0	105.2	99.2	99.1	98.5	96.9	99.1	105.5	103.9	99.8
按部类分	**Grouped by Division**										
生产资料	Means of Production	108.8	107.7	98.6	97.5	97.2	93.9	99.2	109.7	104.9	100.0
采掘工业	Mining & Quarrying Industry	116.8	112.6	96.8	91.8	91.3	82.1	96.5	116.0	106.7	103.1
原料工业	Raw Materials Industry	112.0	108.3	100.1	96.9	97.5	94.1	100.0	116.1	105.1	98.3
加工工业	Manufacturing Industry	104.6	106.1	98.1	99.2	98.5	96.7	99.2	106.5	104.6	100.2
生活资料	Consumer Goods	103.9	105.5	102.5	102.2	100.9	100.4	98.6	99.6	99.9	100.5
食品类	Food	103.7	104.9	102.9	103.5	101.2	100.4	99.6	99.9	100.6	103.8
衣着类	Clothing	105.6	111.4	104.9	100.4	100.9	100.8	99.1	100.3	99.7	99.8
一般日用品类	Articles for Daily Use	103.7	105.0	101.0	100.0	100.3	100.1	97.5	101.4	100.5	99.4
耐用消费品类	Durable Consumer Goods	103.9	105.6	101.5	100.5	99.8	100.0	96.9	96.5	97.8	93.6
按工业部门分	**Grouped by Sector**										
冶金工业	Metallurgical Industry	116.4	108.7	95.2	95.9	95.6	90.5	103.7	117.3	105.0	101.0
电力工业	Power Industry	103.6	104.3	108.0	100.8	99.7	96.9	93.6	101.1	101.4	98.4
煤炭及炼焦工业	Coal and Smelt Industry	113.1	107.8	95.9	89.1	88.5	83.1	100.9	140.9	112.0	98.1
石油工业	Petroleum Industry	127.9	121.7	101.5	96.4	96.9	77.6	91.9	113.4	113.1	96.5
化学工业	Chemical Industry	107.3	111.0	98.8	97.0	97.6	96.8	96.9	107.4	104.7	97.7
机械工业	Machine Buiding Industry	101.4	103.5	100.4	100.1	99.8	99.0	97.8	100.1	100.7	98.9
建筑材料工业	Building Materials Industry	101.1	104.5	101.3	100.5	100.2	98.9	99.0	105.4	104.7	104.2
森林工业	Timber Industry	99.9	106.0	102.2	100.8	101.3	100.7	99.4	101.0	101.7	100.5
食品工业	Food Industry	103.7	104.8	102.4	103.6	101.1	99.9	99.2	99.8	100.5	103.8
纺织工业	Textile Industry	116.4	120.4	88.8	99.5	97.7	95.9	98.3	105.4	104.2	99.2
缝纫工业	Tailoring Industry	105.3	111.4	105.5	99.5	100.7	99.5	97.6	101.0	99.9	99.0
皮革工业	Leather Industry	102.7	106.3	103.0	104.1	108.1	109.3	105.2	102.1	101.5	101.1
造纸工业	Paper Industry	103.4	102.9	99.9	99.1	99.8	98.8	99.3	111.7	107.2	93.5
文教艺术用品工业	Cultural,Educational & Handicrafts Articles	101.8	100.5	102.1	102.5	99.3	98.6	97.8	100.0	102.5	100.2
其他工业	Others	103.5	106.3	100.0	99.1	99.6	99.6	99.3	106.4	107.6	96.9

9-11 工业生产者购进价格指数
Purchasing Price Index for Industrial Producers

(上年=100) (preceding year=100)

类 别	Type	2010	2011	2012	2013	2015	2016	2017	2018	2019
总 指 数	**General Index**	**110.2**	**110.1**	**99.2**	**99.3**	**95.4**	**99.2**	**107.3**	**104.0**	**101.2**
燃料、动力类	Fuels and Motive Power	108.9	106.6	101.6	96.7	91.0	98.1	113.1	106.1	98.2
黑色金属材料类	Ferrous Metals Materials	108.4	108.1	94.1	96.4	85.4	96.7	117.4	107.1	105.0
#钢材	Steel Products	105.9	106.1	95.5	95.9	91.9	96.2	113.1	106.1	98.9
有色金属材料和电线类	Nonferrous Metals Materials and Electric Wire	123.2	109.2	98.2	96.4	95.4	101.2	118.3	104.9	98.1
化工原料类	Chemical Raw Materials	116.8	115.0	91.5	94.6	92.7	99.1	107.2	103.9	96.6
木材及纸浆类	Logging and Paper Pulp	104.7	107.4	102.2	100.8	98.2	98.1	105.4	106.5	98.4
建筑材料及非金属矿类	Building Materials and Nonmetal Minerals	103.9	106.3	101.4	98.8	98.7	97.7	106.6	107.7	111.1
其他工业原材料及半成品类	Others Industry Materials & Semi Finished Articles	107.4	111.5	104.6	104.4	100.5	100.1	101.4	101.9	101.1
农副产品类	Farm Products	108.3	114.2	97.0	101.3	97.0	100.2	99.4	100.0	102.9
纺织原料类	Textile Raw Materials	118.1	111.7	91.6	99.7	93.4	100.0	103.9	99.9	98.3

9-12 固定资产投资价格指数
Price Index for Investment in Fixed Assets

(上年=100) (preceding year=100)

类 别	Type	2010	2011	2012	2013	2015	2016	2017	2018	2019
固定资产投资价格指数	**Price Index for Investment In Fixed Assets**	**103.5**	**107.4**	**101.0**	**99.9**	**97.6**	**99.2**	**107.4**	**105.4**	**103.2**
建筑安装工程	Construction and Installation	104.9	110.1	101.4	99.8	96.5	99.1	110.9	107.4	103.8
设备、工器具购置	Purchase of Equipments and Instruments	100.5	102.3	99.7	99.7	99.0	98.6	100.8	101.5	100.4
其他费用	Other Expenses	101.3	103.0	101.9	101.2	100.5	100.7	100.8	101.0	102.8

主要统计指标解释

商品零售价格指数 是反映一定时期内城乡商品零售价格变动趋势和程度的相对数。商品零售价格的变动与国家的财政收入、市场供需的平衡、消费与积累的比例关系有关。因此，该指数可以从一个侧面对上述经济活动进行观察和分析。

居民消费价格指数 是反映一定时期内城乡居民所购买的生活消费品价格和服务项目价格变动趋势和程度的相对数，是对城市居民消费价格指数和农村居民消费价格指数进行综合汇总计算的结果。利用居民消费价格指数，可以观察和分析消费品的零售价格和服务价格变动对城乡居民实际生活费支出的影响程度。

城市居民消费价格指数 是反映一定时期内城市居民家庭所购买的生活消费品价格和服务项目价格变动趋势和程度的相对数。通过该指数可以观察和分析消费品的零售价格和服务项目价格变动对城镇居民收入和消费支出的影响。

农村居民消费价格指数 是反映一定时期内农村居民家庭所购买的生活消费品价格和服务项目价格变动趋势和程度的相对数。该指数可以观察农村消费品的零售价格和服务项目价格变动对农村居民收入和生活消费支出的影响。

农业生产资料价格指数 指反映一定时期内农业生产资料价格变动趋势和程度的相对数。其编制目的是了解农业生产中投入物质资料价格的变动状况，服务于国民经济核算。1994 年以前，农业生产资料价格指数仅仅是商品零售价格指数的一个类别，此后，从商品零售价格指数中分离出来，单独编制。

农产品生产者价格指数 是反映一定时期内，农产品生产者出售农产品价格水平变动趋势及幅度的相对数。该指数可以客观反映全国农产品生产价格水平和结构变动情况，满足农业与国民经济核算需要。其中某代表品生产价格指数是通过对全部有出售该产品行为的调查单位的个体指数进行几何平均求得的，类价格指数是通过对其所属的类（或代表品）的价格指数进行加权平均求得的。

工业生产者出厂价格指数 是反映一定时期内全部工业产品第一次出售时的出厂价格总水平的变动趋势和变动幅度的相对数。

工业生产者购进价格指数 是反映作为中间投入的原材料、燃料、动力购进价格总水平的变动趋势和变动幅度的相对数。

固定资产投资价格指数 是反映一定时期内固定资产投资品及取费项目的价格变动趋势和变动幅度的相对数。该指数可以准确地反映固定资产投资中涉及的各类投资品和取费项目价格变动趋势和变动幅度，消除按现价计算的固定资产投资指标中的价格变动因素，真实地反映固定资产投资的规模、速度、结构和效益。

Explanatory Notes on Main Statistical Indicators

Retail Price Index reflect the trend and degree of change in retail prices of commodities during a given period. The change in retail prices of commodities is related to government revenue, the equilibrium of market supply and demand, and the ratio of consumption to accumulation. Therefore, the retail price indices are useful from an oblique perspective for observing and analyzing the changes of the above economic activities.

Consumer Price Index reflects the trend and degree of changes in prices of consumer goods and services purchased by urban and rural residents, and is a composite index derived from the urban consumer price index and the rural consumer price index. Consumer price index can be used to analyze the impact of consumer price change on actual expenditure for living cost of urban and rural residents.

Consumer Price Indices of Urban Household reflect the trend and degree of changes in prices of consumer goods and services purchased by urban households during a given period. It can be used to observe and analyze the impact of price changes in consumer goods and services on urban household income and consumption expenditure.

Consumer Price Indices of Rural Household reflect the trend and degree of changes in prices of consumer goods and services purchased by rural households during a given period. It can be used to observe the impact of change in retail prices of consumer goods and service prices on rural household income and consumption expenditure on living.

Price Indices of Means of Agricultural Production reflect the trend and degree of changes in the prices of the means of agricultural production during a given period. Compilation of these indices helps to understand the price changes of material input in agricultural production and facilitate the compilation of national accounts. Before 1994, price indices for means of agricultural production were a sub-category in the retail price indices for commodities, and it has been compiled separately since 1994.

Producer Prices Indices for Farm Products reflect the trend and degree of changes in producers' prices received by farmers when they sell farm products during a given period. These indices depict the change in the level and structure of producer prices for farm products of the country and meet the needs of agricultural statistics and national accounts statistics. The producer price index for a given product is calculated as the geometrical mean of individual indices for all surveyed units which sell such product, and the indices for a product category is obtained as the weighted mean of price indices for all products in the category. Method for calculating accumulative quarterly indices is the same as for calculating the individual quarterly indices.

Producer Price Indices for Industrial Products reflect the trend and degree of changes in general ex-factory prices of all manufactured goods for first sale during a given period.

Purchasing Price Indices for Industrial Producers reflect changes in the level and degree of purchasing prices such as intermediate input such as raw materials, fuels and power.

Price Indices for Investment in Fixed Assets reflect the trend and degree of changes in prices of investment goods and projects in fixed assets during a given period. Removing the factor of price change in the aggregates of investment at current prices, this indicator shows the changes in the prices of commodities and fees involved in the investment of fixed assets, and can be used to observe the actual size, growth, structure, and efficiency of investment in fixed assets.

人民生活

People's Living Conditions

10

● 资料整理：左俊勇

简要说明

一、主要内容

本篇资料反映全省人民生活现状及变化情况，包括居民家庭情况、收入、消费等资料，分为全体居民生活、城镇居民生活和农村居民生活三部分。

二、资料来源

从2013年起，国家统计局开展了城乡一体化住户收支与生活状况调查，全省人民生活状况的数据来源于住户收支生活状况调查，该调查采用抽样调查的方法，国家统计局使用统一的抽样框，以省为总体，在对县级调查网点代表性进行评估的基础上，采用分层、多阶段随机抽样方法抽选调查住宅，确定调查户。采用固定样本户连续记帐的调查方式，调查网点实行样本轮换制度，每五年为一个周期，抽中调查小区五年内保持不变，抽中住宅每年轮换一半。省级数据调查网点分布在18个市、43个县的7200余住宅，2014年以后数据根据城乡一体化调查取得，2014年以前数据为老口径，农民收入为纯收入口径，由国家统计局河南调查总队编辑整理。各省辖市、省直管县数据由河南省地方经济社会调查队编辑整理。

Brief Introduction

I. Main Contents

Data in this chapter show the people's living conditions in Henan province, including basic condition, revenue and expenditure of household, consisting of two parts, on the life of urban and rural households respectively.

II. Sources of Data

Since 2013, the national bureau of statistics (NBS) caries out the integration of urban and rural residents income and expenditure survey and living conditions survey. Data on the living condition of the whole province of people come from the data collected through a sample survey on the rural households conducted. The national bureau of statistics using uniform sampling frame collected the data of living condition through a combination of Regular accounting and One-time accounting .This is on the basis of evaluating representative of the county network. The NBS adopts the survey method of charging to an account continuously for fixed sample. Network survey is set through a sample rotation, which is conducted for every five years. The sample remains unchanged for five years, and the sample rotation is half the year. The provincial sample of provincial data included 7200 households from 18 cities and 43 counties 2014 data cannot do compare with the data of antecedent years. Data in this part are provided by the Department of Henan Survey organizations, NBS. Data of the provincial cities and Provincial-controlled division are provided by Henan provincial survey organizations of social and economy.

10−1 城乡居民家庭人均收支

Per Capita Income, Expenditure in Urban and Rural Areas

指数以上年为100，按可比价格计算。

Indices of preceding year=100, and indices are calculated at comparable prices.

单位：元 (yuan)

年 份 Year	城镇居民家庭人均 Per Capita Income and Expenditure of Urban Household			农村居民家庭人均 Per Capita Income and Expenditure of Rural Household		
	可支配收入 Disposable Income	可支配收入指数 Disposable Income Index	消费支出 Consumption Expenditure	可支配收入 Disposable Income	可支配收入指数 Disposable Income Index	生活消费支出 Household Expenditure
1978	315.00		274.00	104.71		81.70
1979	361.04	114.3	302.98	133.56	127.6	
1980	365.00	108.1	335.02	160.78	120.5	135.51
1981	395.00	103.1	363.23	215.57	133.4	165.57
1982	429.00	103.9	382.47	216.74	99.7	177.90
1983	452.50	101.6	405.00	272.00	124.5	196.35
1984	497.49	108.8	431.68	301.17	110.3	219.64
1985	600.59	114.2	556.72	328.78	107.0	260.19
1986	724.21	113.2	653.83	333.64	99.7	292.48
1987	814.20	104.9	711.27	377.72	110.1	309.90
1988	946.10	87.2	896.55	401.32	98.2	346.73
1989	1111.46	102.2	963.97	457.06	102.5	390.05
1990	1267.73	113.5	1067.67	526.95	105.5	437.73
1991	1384.81	103.9	1199.95	539.29	102.3	454.68
1992	1608.03	107.8	1342.58	588.48	104.9	472.61
1993	1962.75	110.4	1609.26	695.85	109.0	564.93
1994	2618.55	104.7	2155.15	909.81	103.4	731.78
1995	3299.46	107.8	2673.95	1231.97	109.5	929.39
1996	3755.44	103.9	3009.35	1579.19	113.8	1206.43
1997	4093.62	106.4	3378.02	1733.89	107.4	1270.52
1998	4219.42	105.3	3415.65	1864.05	106.5	1240.30
1999	4532.36	111.2	3497.53	1948.36	106.4	1163.98
2000	4766.26	106.1	3830.71	1985.82	103.9	1315.83
2001	5267.42	108.8	4110.17	2097.86	104.9	1375.60
2002	6245.40	114.2	4504.68	2215.74	105.1	1451.51
2003	6926.12	109.0	4941.60	2235.68	99.6	1508.67
2004	7704.90	105.5	5294.19	2553.15	108.1	1664.09
2005	8667.97	110.2	6038.02	2870.58	107.5	1891.57
2006	9810.26	111.9	6685.18	3261.03	112.1	2229.28
2007	11477.05	111.0	7826.72	3851.60	112.2	2676.41
2008	13231.11	108.3	8837.46	4454.24	107.2	3044.21
2009	14371.56	109.9	9566.99	4806.95	107.5	3388.47
2010	15930.26	107.2	10838.49	5523.73	111.0	3682.21
2011	18194.80	108.4	12336.47	6604.03	112.7	4319.95
2012	20442.62	109.5	13732.96	7524.94	111.3	5032.14
2013	22398.03	106.6	14821.98	8475.34	109.5	5627.73
2014	24391.45	106.8	15726.12	9416.10	109.4	6438.12
2014新口径	23672.00	106.8	16184.00	9966.07	109.4	7277.21
2015	25575.61	106.7	17154.30	10852.86	107.6	7887.45
2016	27232.92	104.5	18087.79	11696.74	105.7	8586.59
2017	29557.86	106.9	19422.27	12719.18	107.5	9211.52
2018	31874.19	105.2	20989.15	13830.74	106.5	10392.01
2019	34200.97	104.3	21971.60	15163.74	106.3	11545.99

注：1. 1978年-1991年城镇居民可支配收入根据当年生活费收入测算。

2. 2014年以后为实施城乡一体化调查的数据，2013年以前农村居民人均可支配收入为纯收入口径。(以下相关全省的表格相同)

a) Data on disposable income of urban household on 1978-1991 are calculated on basis of income of living to the corresponding year.

b) Data since 2014 are calculated on the basis of investigation of the integration of urban and rural areas. (the same as the following tables about provincial data)

10-2 家庭平均每人收入、支出及结构(2019年)
Per Capita Income and Expenditure and Structure in Households (2019)

项　　目	Item	绝对数(元) Absolute number (yuan)	结　构(%) Structure (%)
可支配收入	**Disposable Income**	**23902.68**	**100.0**
工资性收入	Laborage	11962.64	50.0
工资	Wages and Salaries	11100.77	46.4
实物福利	Physical Welfare	35.91	0.2
其他	Others	825.96	3.5
经营净收入	Net Business Income	5139.02	21.5
第一产业	Primary Industry	2009.40	8.4
第二产业	Secondary Industry	563.76	2.4
第三产业	Tertiary Industry	2565.86	10.7
财产净收入	Net Income of Properties	1588.67	6.6
转移净收入	Net Income of Transfers	5212.34	21.8
现金可支配收入(未扣除生产费用)	**Cash Disposable Income**	**22344.88**	**100.0**
工资性收入	Laborage	11926.73	53.4
工资	Wages and Salaries	11100.77	49.7
其他	Others	825.96	3.7
经营净收入	Net Business Income	4961.75	22.2
第一产业	Primary Industry	1651.28	7.4
第二产业	Secondary Industry	611.53	2.7
第三产业	Tertiary Industry	2698.94	12.1
财产净收入	Net Income of Properties	630.29	2.8
转移净收入	Net Income of Transfers	4826.10	21.6
消费支出	**Consumption Expenditure**	**16331.79**	**100.0**
食品烟酒	Food,Tobacco and Liquor	4186.81	25.6
衣着	Clothing	1226.52	7.5
居住	Residence	3723.13	22.8
生活用品及服务	Living Supplies and Services	1101.49	6.7
交通通信	Transportation and Communication	1976.01	12.1
教育文化娱乐	Education, Culture and Entertainment	2016.84	12.3
医疗保健	Health Care	1746.08	10.7
其他用品和服务	Others	354.91	2.2
现金消费支出	**Cash Consumption Expenditures**	**13516.46**	**100.0**
食品烟酒	Food,Tobacco and Liquor	4100.14	30.3
衣着	Clothing	1226.45	9.1
居住	Residence	1387.13	10.3
生活用品及服务	Living Supplies and Services	1097.13	8.1
交通通信	Transportation and Communication	1974.57	14.6
教育文化娱乐	Education, Culture and Entertainment	2016.67	14.9
医疗保健	Health Care	1364.88	10.1
其他用品和服务	Others	349.49	2.6

10-3 各市居民家庭人均收支情况(2019年)

Per Capita Income and Expenditure in Urban and Rural Areas by City (2019)

单位：元 (yuan)

市(县) City(County)	居民家庭人均 Per Capita Residents			城镇居民家庭人均 Per Capita (Urban) Residents			农村居民家庭人均 Per Capita (Rural) Residents		
	可支配收入 Disposable Income	消费支出 Consumption Expenditure	#食品 Food	可支配收入 Disposable Income	消费支出 Consumption Expenditure	#食品 Food	可支配收入 Disposable Income	消费支出 Consumption Expenditure	#食品 Food
省辖市 City									
郑州市 Zhengzhou	35942	23765	5590	42087	27183	6339	23536	16864	4079
开封市 Kaifeng	21795	16382	3845	31305	23199	5481	14473	11134	2586
洛阳市 Luoyang	27101	19419	4196	38630	26576	5601	14973	11889	2717
平顶山市 Pingdingshan	24020	14372	2554	34266	18970	4880	14587	10138	2661
安阳市 Anyang	24647	14395	3429	34959	18837	4615	16095	10710	2445
鹤壁市 Hebi	26105	16110	4227	32836	19522	4863	18275	12141	3487
新乡市 Xinxiang	24562	15684	4018	33626	20439	5242	16344	11372	2909
焦作市 Jiaozuo	27116	19659	5503	33956	24285	6779	19374	14424	4058
濮阳市 Puyang	21592	14434	2991	33277	21078	5833	9799	13894	2436
许昌市 Xuchang	25949	16422	2731	34376	21017	3286	18558	12391	2244
漯河市 Luohe	24625	17098	4171	33505	23705	5395	16878	11334	3104
三门峡市 Sanmenxia	23924	16785	2547	32178	22412	3246	15645	11140	1846
南阳市 Nanyang	22638	15681	4138	33442	22625	5744	15167	10879	3028
商丘市 Shangqiu	20175	13587	3924	32336	18262	5072	12668	10701	3216
信阳市 Xinyang	20928	14225	4511	30425	18820	5684	14010	10877	3657
周口市 Zhoukou	18321	14012	4784	28437	18959	6254	12194	11015	3894
驻马店市 Zhumadian	19644	14504	3924	30409	21219	5421	13020	10372	3002
济源市 Jiyuan	29065	20081	4516	36039	24795	5602	20235	14112	3142
省直管县 County Directly Administrated by Province									
巩义市 Gongyi	30467	12444	3574	35577	13507	4172	25076	11323	2943
兰考县 Lankao	18228	15726	3490	27231	20323	3867	13125	13120	3276
汝州市 Ruzhou	23677	13947	2933	30903	19186	3590	18571	10244	2468
滑县 Huaxian	17313	13406	3222	28178	15728	4109	13076	12500	2876
长垣市 Changyuan	25124	15734	3712	29981	18910	3812	21610	13436	3639
邓州市 Dengzhou	22070	17063	4707	31315	24768	6630	16673	12565	3583
永城市 Yongcheng	23755	15994	3319	34400	19066	3416	15880	13722	3248
固始县 Gushi	20495	14150	3923	29505	18088	4900	15048	11769	3333
鹿邑县 Luyi	20118	12001	3614	29292	16360	4761	14454	9309	2960
新蔡县 Xincai	17582	14552	2776	27118	21233	3296	13392	11617	2548

10–4 城镇居民家庭人口及居住情况
Population and Living condition of Urban Households

指　　标	Item	2018	2019
人口及就业情况(人)	**Population and Living condition (person)**		
户均常住人口数	Number of Resident Population During the Period	3.20	3.23
户均就业人数	Average Number of Employee per household	1.75	1.64
#雇主	Employers	0.03	0.02
公职人员	Civil Servants	0.09	0.09
事业单位人员	Staff of Public Institution	0.22	0.21
国有企业雇员	Staff of State-owned Enterprise	0.15	0.13
住房情况	**Housing condition**		
现住房总建筑面积(平方米/人)	Construction area of Present Housing (sq.m/person)	40.89	41.56
期末拥有房屋面积(平方米/人)	Housing Area at year-end (sq.m/person)	44.13	
#自有现住房面积	Area of Private Housing	39.78	40.34
现住房房屋来源结构(%)	Source Structure of Present Housing (%)		
#租赁私房	Leasing Private Housing	2.5	2.0
自建住房	Self-built Housing	32.7	34.3
购买商品房	Purchasing Commercial Housing	44.0	42.8
购买房改住房	Purchasing Housing-reform House	11.0	10.3
购买保障性住房	Purchasing indemnificatory Housing	4.0	4.1
拆迁安置房	Removal Settlement Housing	3.3	3.4
本住户居住空间样式结构(%)	Structure of Residents Living Space Style (%)		
#单栋楼房	Single-span Building	23.7	25.7
单栋平房	Single-span Bungalow	11.3	10.6
四居室及以上单元房	Flat with Four and Over Bedrooms	4.3	4.4
三居室单元房	Flat with Three Bedrooms	35.4	35.1
二居室单元房	Flat with Two Bedrooms	22.2	21.3
住户主要饮用水来源情况结构(%)	Source Structure of Resident Main Drinking Water (%)		
#经过净化处理的自来水	Purificatory Tap water	89.8	90.3
受保护的井水和泉水	Wells and Springs with Protection	8.7	7.8
不受保护的井水和泉水	Wells and Springs without Protection	0.9	1.4
住户厕所类型结构(%)	Structure of Household Toilet Type (%)		
水冲式卫生厕所	Flush Sanitary Toilet	84.7	90.7
水冲式非卫生厕所	Flush Insanitary Toilet	2.8	5.9
卫生旱厕	Sanitary Dry Toilet	5.0	1.7
普通旱厕	General Dry Toilet	6.9	1.4
无厕所	No Toilet	0.6	0.2
住户洗澡设施情况结构(%)	Structure of Resident Shower Facility (%)		
#统一供热水	Unified Hot Water	5.3	4.6
家庭自装热水器	Water Heater Installed by Household	84.6	85.5
无洗澡设施	No Shower Facilities	6.8	6.4
住户主要取暖设备状况结构(%)	Structure of Main Heating Facility (%)		
由市政或小区集中供暖	Unified Heating Supplied by Municipal Administration and Community	28.5	27.8
自行供暖	Self-heating	54.9	55.4
无取暖设备	No Heating Facilities	16.6	16.7

10-5 城镇居民家庭人均收支及结构(2019年)

Per Capita Income, Expenditure and Structure in Urban Areas (2019)

指 标	Item	城镇平均 Average	低收入户 Low Income Households	中低收入户 Lower Middle Income Households
城镇家庭人均可支配收入(元)	**Per Capita Disposable Income of Urban Household (yuan)**	**34201**	**13920**	**22229**
工资性收入	Wage Income	19146	9378	14375
经营净收入	Net Income from Operations	5212	1200	2366
财产净收入	Property Net Income	3188	1330	1939
#出租房屋财产性收入	Income from Renting Room	747	116	354
房屋虚拟租金	Building Virtual Money	2088	1005	1355
转移净收入	Transfer Net Income	6654	2012	3548
城镇家庭人均可支配收入结构(%)	**Structure of Per Capita Disposable Income (%)**			
工资性收入	Wage Income	56.0	67.4	64.7
经营净收入	Net Income from Operations	15.2	8.6	10.6
财产净收入	Net Property Income	9.3	9.6	8.7
转移净收入	Net Transfer Income	19.5	14.5	16.0
家庭人均总支出(元)	**Per Capita Total Expenditure of Households (yuan)**	**28932**	**14886**	**20158**
消费支出	Consumption Expenditure	21972	12015	16238
食品烟酒	Food,Tobacco and Liquor	5550	3266	4382
衣着	Clothing	1706	915	1327
居住	Residence	5190	2749	3556
生活用品及服务	Living Supplies and Services	1529	745	1037
交通通信	Transportation and Communication	2691	1124	2003
教育文化娱乐	Education, Culture and Entertainment	2674	1807	2215
医疗保健	Health Care	2081	1219	1369
其他用品和服务	Others	551	190	348
生产经营费用支出	Production and Operation Costs	923	335	484
财产性支出	Property Expenditure	120	29	50
转移性支出	Transfer Expenditure	1285	618	782
部分商业保险支出	Part of Commercial Insurance	275	56	111
购置资产及非经常性转移支出	Purchase of Assets and Non Regular Payments	3321	1642	1621
购置资产支出	Purchase of Assets	1007	673	161
非经常性转移支出	Non Regular Payments	2313	969	1460
借贷性支出	Debit and Credit	1038	191	871
家庭人均总支出结构(%)	**Structure of Per Capita Expenditure of Households (%)**			
消费支出	Consumption Expenditure	75.9	80.7	80.6
生产经营费用支出	Production and Operation Costs	3.2	2.3	2.4
财产性支出	Property Expenditure	0.4	0.2	0.2
转移性支出	Transfer Expenditure	4.4	4.2	3.9
部分商业保险支出	Part of Commercial Insurance	0.9	0.4	0.6
购置资产及非经常性转移支出	Purchase of Assets and Non Regular Payments	11.5	11.0	8.0
借贷性支出	Debit and Credit	3.6	1.3	4.3

10-5 续表 continued

指 标	Item	中等收入户 Middle Income Households	中高收入户 Upper Middle Income Households	高收入户 High Income Households
城镇家庭人均可支配收入(元)	**Per Capita Disposable Income of Urban Household (yuan)**	**30437**	**42104**	**78152**
工资性收入	Wage Income	18379	22548	37995
经营净收入	Net Income from Operations	3555	4783	17958
财产净收入	Property Net Income	2850	4266	7037
#出租房屋财产性收入	Income from Renting Room	625	1080	2051
房屋虚拟租金	Building Virtual Money	2011	3013	3855
转移净收入	Transfer Net Income	5654	10508	15162
城镇家庭人均可支配收入结构(%)	**Structure of Per Capita Disposable Income (%)**			
工资性收入	Wage Income	60.4	53.6	48.6
经营净收入	Net Income from Operations	11.7	11.4	23.0
财产净收入	Net Property Income	9.4	10.1	9.0
转移净收入	Net Transfer Income	18.6	25.0	19.4
家庭人均总支出(元)	**Per Capita Total Expenditure of Households (yuan)**	**26495**	**34843**	**59370**
消费支出	Consumption Expenditure	21015	27018	40917
食品烟酒	Food,Tobacco and Liquor	5468	7051	9128
衣着	Clothing	1642	2045	3157
居住	Residence	4676	6750	10160
生活用品及服务	Living Supplies and Services	1354	1799	3347
交通通信	Transportation and Communication	2992	3189	5117
教育文化娱乐	Education Culture and Entertainment	2599	3079	4293
医疗保健	Health Care	1865	2448	4278
其他用品和服务	Others	420	656	1438
生产经营费用支出	Production and Operation Costs	879	860	2567
财产性支出	Property Expenditure	111	236	240
转移性支出	Transfer Expenditure	1182	1526	2879
部分商业保险支出	Part of commercial insurance	160	246	1018
购置资产及非经常性转移支出	Purchase of Assets and Non Regular Payments	2437	3937	8751
购置资产支出	Purchase of Assets	676	1312	2818
非经常性转移支出	Non Regular Payments	1761	2625	5933
借贷性支出	Debit and Credit	710	1021	2997
家庭人均总支出结构(%)	**Structure of Per Capita Expenditure of Households (%)**			
消费支出	Consumption Expenditure	79.3	77.5	68.9
生产经营费用支出	Production and Operation Costs	3.3	2.5	4.3
财产性支出	Property Expenditure	0.4	0.7	0.4
转移性支出	Transfer Expenditure	4.5	4.4	4.8
部分商业保险支出	Part of Commercial Insurance	0.6	0.7	1.7
购置资产及非经常性转移支出	Purchase of Assets and Non Regular Payments	9.2	11.3	14.7
借贷性支出	Debit and Credit	2.7	2.9	5.0

10−6 城镇居民家庭人均购买生活消费品及服务现金支出(2019年)
Per Capita Cash Expenditure of Urban Households to Purchase Living Goods and Services (2019)

单位：元 (yuan)

指　标	Index	城镇平均 Average	低收入户 Low Income Households	中低收入户 Lower Middle Income Households	中等收入户 Middle Income Households	中高收入户 Upper Middle Income Households	高收入户 High Income Households
购买生活消费品及服务	**Purchasing Living Goods and Services**	**21971.57**	**12014.61**	**16237.65**	**21015.39**	**27017.86**	**40917.38**
食品烟酒	**Food, Cigarettes and Wine**	**5549.77**	**3265.96**	**4381.83**	**5468.49**	**7051.38**	**9127.58**
食品	Food	3526.01	2324.97	2963.85	3562.98	4427.54	5107.52
谷物	Cereal	517.45	368.32	416.75	447.54	575.13	913.27
薯类	Tubers	62.95	52.34	56.33	66.08	77.19	68.79
豆类	Beans	56.95	44.47	51.32	56.76	72.64	66.85
食用油	Edible Oil	124.59	95.92	109.42	126.94	152.70	155.76
蔬菜和食用菌	Vegetables and Edible Fungus	412.42	291.43	345.29	448.01	529.36	517.35
肉类	Meat	697.97	419.69	583.79	735.37	929.84	979.12
禽类	Poultry	177.24	114.61	157.10	181.52	238.57	227.72
水产品	Aquatic Products	139.85	70.96	96.82	140.90	198.38	239.97
蛋类	Egg	147.07	117.22	134.11	151.78	170.06	179.44
奶类	Milk	348.63	218.15	299.04	356.27	440.60	505.86
干鲜瓜果类	Dried and Fresh Melons and Fruits	471.57	264.64	379.82	475.63	613.67	754.20
糖果糕点类	Sugar and Cake	144.70	87.72	112.60	144.91	182.26	235.26
其他食品	Others	224.62	179.50	221.46	231.29	247.16	263.93
饮料	Beverages	142.58	84.09	116.15	135.73	175.92	240.95
烟	Tobacco	289.06	165.37	221.46	250.89	361.75	541.74
酒类	Liquor	286.58	107.48	170.41	211.73	368.41	729.61
饮食服务	Catering Services	1305.53	584.05	909.96	1307.15	1717.76	2507.76
衣着	**Dress**	**1706.49**	**915.13**	**1327.49**	**1641.51**	**2044.53**	**3157.30**
衣类	Clothing	1346.23	700.05	1010.11	1262.80	1628.08	2601.55
鞋类	Footwear	360.26	215.07	317.37	378.70	416.45	555.75
居住	**Residence**	**5189.51**	**2749.45**	**3556.45**	**4676.06**	**6750.05**	**10159.63**
租赁房房租	Rental Housing Rent	155.92	82.81	99.65	143.75	164.28	353.66
住房维修及管理	Housing Maintenance and Management	824.77	213.91	365.43	510.43	935.47	2687.74
水电燃料及其他	Water, Electricity and Fuels	966.21	630.95	810.61	913.07	1219.15	1485.38
生活用品及服务	**Supplies and Services**	**1528.84**	**744.76**	**1036.76**	**1354.08**	**1798.69**	**3346.78**
家具及室内装饰品	Furniture and Interior Decorations	324.47	134.36	153.74	257.18	313.91	954.85
家用器具	Home Appliances	413.42	195.64	311.71	333.58	500.60	894.50
家用纺织品	Home Textiles	114.70	49.06	69.36	125.87	156.27	219.01
家庭日用杂品	Household Articles for Daily Use	301.11	193.60	252.62	289.57	376.83	464.51
个人用品	Personal Items	307.52	149.20	220.24	291.09	372.94	621.07
家庭服务	Household Services	67.62	22.90	29.09	56.79	78.14	192.84
交通通信	**Transportation and Communication**	**2691.33**	**1123.60**	**2003.04**	**2992.05**	**3189.07**	**5116.70**
交通	Transportation	2025.41	727.71	1471.34	2331.46	2359.43	4023.55
通信	Communication	665.92	395.89	531.70	660.58	829.64	1093.16
教育文化娱乐	**Recreation, Education and Cultural Serveces**	**1806.52**	**2214.71**	**2598.51**	**3079.49**	**4293.46**	**2072.35**
教育	Education	1464.92	1781.79	1862.99	1801.81	2072.35	4293.46
文化娱乐	Recreation Durable Consumer	341.60	432.92	735.52	1277.68	2221.11	2072.35
医疗保健	**Health Care**	**1219.23**	**1369.47**	**1865.03**	**2448.20**	**4277.86**	**2221.11**
医疗器具及药品	Medical Equipment and Drugs	350.71	454.12	529.14	855.43	1221.41	4277.86
医疗服务	Medical Services	868.52	915.35	1335.89	1592.77	3056.45	1221.41
其他用品和服务	**Others**	**189.96**	**347.90**	**419.65**	**656.46**	**1438.06**	**3056.45**

10－7 城镇居民家庭平均每人购买食品数量(2019年)
Food Consumption Per Person of Urban Households (2019)

单位：千克 (kg)

指 标	Indicator	城镇平均 Average	低收入户 Low Income Households	中低收入户 Lower Middle Income Households	中等收入户 Middle Income Households	中高收入户 Upper Middle Income Households	高收入户 High Income Households
面粉	Flour	16.05	15.89	16.11	15.93	18.28	13.93
大米	Rice	16.90	14.74	17.50	16.65	19.75	16.48
食用植物油	Edible Vegetable Oil	7.87	6.88	7.63	8.49	8.78	7.89
鲜菜	Vegetable	97.84	79.42	85.16	105.46	122.36	107.12
猪肉	Pork	20.76	10.48	11.76	14.26	15.85	15.08
牛肉	Beef	13.20	1.03	1.68	2.06	3.19	3.10
羊肉	Mutton	2.09	0.69	1.25	1.92	2.37	2.16
鸡	Chicken	1.59	4.54	5.35	6.05	6.91	5.73
鸭	Duck	5.63	0.47	0.49	0.55	0.61	0.90
鱼类	Fish	0.58	3.14	3.63	4.84	6.17	5.93
虾类	Shrimp	4.56	0.31	0.58	0.81	0.98	1.28
鲜蛋	Fresh Eggs	0.74	13.25	14.13	16.19	17.67	18.06
鲜奶	Fresh Milk	15.58	6.66	9.66	11.31	15.07	16.56
酸奶	Yogurt	11.31	3.02	3.94	5.07	6.57	10.72
奶粉	Milk Powder	5.48	0.50	0.77	0.70	0.74	0.73
鲜瓜果	Fresh Fruit and Melon	67.87	49.02	61.07	69.81	80.49	89.70
坚果类	Nuts	4.26	3.12	3.66	4.12	5.49	5.68
糕点	Cakes	4.93	3.50	3.86	5.69	5.86	6.64
茶叶	Tea	0.20	0.09	0.14	0.21	0.29	0.34
卷烟	Cigarette	19.66	14.59	18.24	19.16	23.74	25.52
啤酒	Beer	3.64	2.94	3.26	3.80	4.39	4.24
白酒	Liquor	2.32	1.27	1.72	2.02	2.85	4.54
果酒	Wine	0.14	0.06	0.05	0.08	0.22	0.37

10-8 城镇居民家庭平均每百户主要消费品年末拥有量(2019年)

Main Consumer Goods Owned Per 100 Urban Households in the year end (2019)

指标	Item	城镇平均 Average	低收入户 Low Income Households	中低收入户 Lower Middle Income Households	中等收入户 Middle Income Households	中高收入户 Upper Middle Income Households	高收入户 High Income Households
家用汽车(辆)	Car (unit)	37.90	25.92	36.08	41.74	40.50	45.22
摩托车(辆)	Motorcycle (unit)	15.42	17.70	18.97	14.06	13.23	13.16
助力车(台)	Electric Bicycle (unit)	114.01	125.72	130.42	119.31	105.16	89.51
洗衣机(台)	Washing Machine (unit)	101.29	100.71	102.63	100.42	101.94	100.75
电冰箱(柜)(台)	Refrigerator (unit)	99.97	99.11	99.21	101.10	99.40	101.05
微波炉(台)	Microware Oven (unit)	44.96	27.70	38.50	45.27	51.24	62.01
彩色电视机(台)	Color TV Set (unit)	116.16	112.93	117.88	116.65	116.00	117.31
#接入有线电视(台)	Cable TV (unit)						
空调(台)	Air Conditioner (unit)	182.70	148.00	172.27	189.53	194.38	209.19
热水器(台)	Water Heater (unit)	94.14	85.41	93.91	95.14	96.59	99.63
#太阳能热水器(台)	Solar Water Heater (unit)						
洗碗机(台)	Dishwasher（unit）	1.74	1.61	2.13	0.71	1.53	2.71
排油烟机(台)	Exhaust Fan (set)	76.25	58.42	72.03	80.43	85.15	85.20
固定电话(线)(部)	Telephone (unit)	15.49	11.44	14.39	14.16	16.98	20.48
移动电话(部)	Mobile Phone (unit)	251.25	256.59	267.66	253.20	239.85	238.99
#接入互联网(部)	Internet Mobile Phones (unit)	182.89	175.20	189.75	190.26	177.43	181.80
计算机(台)	Computers (unit)	64.90	48.38	63.36	63.91	69.97	78.82
#接入互联网(台)	Internet Computers (unit)	47.33	31.60	44.11	46.06	50.47	64.34
照相机(台)	Camera (unit)	12.95	3.51	5.65	11.62	16.81	27.11
中高档乐器(架)	Medium and High-Grade Musical Instrument (unit)	7.40	2.91	4.74	6.76	8.14	14.43
健身器材(台)	Fitness Equipment (unit)	5.81	2.57	3.24	3.75	6.20	13.26
空气净化器(含新风系统)(台)	Air Cleaner (Including Fresh Air System) (unit)	7.34	3.09	3.24	4.62	11.32	14.40
吸尘器(台)	Vacuum Cleaner (unit)	7.19	2.71	3.50	6.89	8.94	13.88

10-9 各市城镇居民家庭人均全年可支配收入情况(2019年)

Per Capita Annual Disposable Income of Urban Households by City (2019)

单位：元 (yuan)

市(县) City(County)	平均可支配收入 Average	低收入户 Low Income Households	中低收入户 Lower Middle Income Households	中等收入户 Middle Income Households	中高收入户 Upper Middle Income Households	高收入户 High Income Households
省 辖 市 City						
郑 州 市 Zhengzhou	42087	19005	28404	37642	49202	90820
开 封 市 Kaifeng	31305	13825	21877	29263	37744	62362
洛 阳 市 Luoyang	38630	16212	27735	37105	47502	79296
平 顶 山 市 Pingdingshan	34266	13425	22896	31497	42689	74950
安 阳 市 Anyang	34959	12566	21330	30030	40506	76182
鹤 壁 市 Hebi	32836	14708	22210	29133	39008	67677
新 乡 市 Xinxiang	33626	12476	20582	28553	40112	67027
焦 作 市 Jiaozuo	33956	15567	25547	33518	41323	62872
濮 阳 市 Puyang	21592	14434	2991	33277	21078	5833
许 昌 市 Xuchang	34376	13079	20903	28387	41218	81581
漯 河 市 Luohe	31169	13230	23208	29525	38928	61803
三 门 峡 市 Sanmenxia	32178	11978	19468	27375	39294	70125
南 阳 市 Nanyang	33442	13196	21970	29431	40363	72778
商 丘 市 Shangqiu	32336	12107	21769	29713	38465	71162
信 阳 市 Xinyang	30425	12914	21337	27857	36417	60427
周 口 市 Zhoukou	28231	11496	19402	25829	35364	57494
驻 马 店 市 Zhumadian	30409	12737	19870	26841	35294	68852
济 源 市 Jiyuan	36039	16289	22632	29331	42053	73344
省 直 管 县 County Directly Administrated by Province						
巩 义 市 Gongyi	35577	15007	19859	29299	40765	90613
兰 考 县 Lankao	27231	8705	17087	23505	32548	79923
汝 州 市 Ruzhou	30903	10797	17174	25175	34411	71018
滑 县 Huaxian	28178	11051	18248	25548	35032	56238
长 垣 市 Changyuan	29981	14464	20272	26328	32758	61322
邓 州 市 Dengzhou	31315	16028	21371	27823	37833	59927
永 城 市 Yongcheng	34400	15963	22420	30319	37375	70378
固 始 县 Gushi	29505	8727	15600	22184	32329	57772
鹿 邑 县 Luyi	29292	10776	19411	28683	40696	5885
新 蔡 县 Xincai	27118	11766	17848	25620	35345	55390

10—10 各市城镇居民家庭消费支出情况(2019年)

Per Capita Consumption Expenditure of Urban Households by City (2019)

单位：元 (yuan)

市(县)	City(County)	消费支出 Consumption Expenditure	食品烟酒 Food, Tobacco, Liquor	衣着 Clothing	居住 Residence	生活用品及服务 Household Appliances and Service	交通、通信及服务 Transport, and Communi-cations	教育及文化娱乐 Education, Culture and Entertainment	医疗、保健及服务 Health Care and Medical Service	其他商品及服务 Other Goods and Services
省辖市	**City**									
郑州市	Zhengzhou	27183	6339	1900	7998	1680	2999	3222	2287	759
开封市	Kaifeng	23199	5481	1837	4823	1894	3783	2175	2502	704
洛阳市	Luoyang	26576	5601	2231	5626	2566	3886	3173	2328	1163
平顶山市	Pingdingshan	18970	4880	1401	4287	1293	2549	1939	2552	370
安阳市	Anyang	18837	4615	1577	4651	1350	2241	2436	1417	552
鹤壁市	Hebi	19522	4863	1828	3895	1672	2636	1987	2071	569
新乡市	Xinxiang	20439	5242	1588	4155	1345	2874	2491	2254	489
焦作市	Jiaozuo	24285	6779	2696	3823	2011	3277	2970	1846	881
濮阳市	Puyang	21078	5833	1233	3896	1363	4720	2060	1607	366
许昌市	Xuchang	21017	5423	1463	4620	1136	2359	2509	2955	553
漯河市	Luohe	23705	5395	2534	4005	2624	4342	2208	1474	1124
三门峡市	Sanmenxia	22412	4978	2207	4401	1431	3517	2637	2733	508
南阳市	Nanyang	22625	5744	2087	5306	1652	2455	2607	2064	710
商丘市	Shangqiu	18262	5072	1661	3621	1287	2147	2459	1642	373
信阳市	Xinyang	18820	5684	1574	4253	1606	2401	1829	1168	304
周口市	Zhoukou	18959	6254	1553	2806	1911	2904	1871	1238	423
驻马店市	Zhumadian	21219	5421	1867	4891	1727	2772	2309	1743	489
济源市	Jiyuan	24795	5602	3431	4044	1992	2555	3904	1248	2019
省直管县	**County Directly Administrated by Province**									
巩义市	Gongyi	13507	4172	1530	2453	1165	1420	1699	803	265
兰考县	Lankao	20323	3867	1477	3440	1388	5304	2007	2485	355
汝州市	Ruzhou	19186	3590	1171	3122	1730	5654	1611	1773	535
滑县	Huaxian	15728	4109	2106	3229	1086	1433	2296	1140	330
长垣市	Changyuan	18910	3812	2247	2562	1824	1976	2489	3676	323
邓州市	Dengzhou	24768	6630	1815	6136	1929	3423	2622	1587	627
永城市	Yongcheng	19066	5265	1868	3539	1497	2351	2860	1190	495
固始县	Gushi	18088	4900	1337	3066	1710	2541	2229	2047	257
鹿邑县	Luyi	16360	4761	1298	3297	2533	1004	1658	1489	321
新蔡县	Xincai	21233	5821	2552	5705	1634	2341	1673	1063	444

10–11 各市按收入等级分的城镇居民家庭人均全年消费支出(2019年)

Per Capita Annual Consumption Expenditure of Urban Households by Level of Income By City (2019)

单位：元 (yuan)

市(县) City(County)	城镇平均 Average	低收入户 Low Income Households	中低收入户 Lower Middle Income Households	中等收入户 Middle Income Households	中高收入户 Upper Middle Income Households	高收入户 High Income Households
省辖市 City						
郑州市 Zhengzhou	27183	17809	21216	26083	33844	43424
开封市 Kaifeng	23199	13458	16376	24084	27595	39067
洛阳市 Luoyang	26576	13449	21363	26888	33408	46075
平顶山市 Pingdingshan	18970	9755	15015	21558	23263	3005
安阳市 Anyang	18837	11877	14107	16994	21025	30669
鹤壁市 Hebi	19522	12310	13685	18048	22491	34904
新乡市 Xinxiang	20439	11111	15425	18246	20569	35148
焦作市 Jiaozuo	24285	14568	20221	23810	29030	38380
濮阳市 Puyang	21078	9280	11220	14761	21074	29357
许昌市 Xuchang	21017	11000	15157	19155	29411	36774
漯河市 Luohe	21359	10914	17082	16848	31003	41877
三门峡市 Sanmenxia	22412	13135	14755	20373	28912	38918
南阳市 Nanyang	22625	8325	11490	13714	17645	31653
商丘市 Shangqiu	18262	9825	12711	22794	23367	26259
信阳市 Xinyang	18820	10843	15999	17204	23708	28095
周口市 Zhoukou	17239	9787	12917	14165	22522	30846
驻马店市 Zhumadian	21219	12975	16603	20588	24704	36062
济源市 Jiyuan	24795	23868	15369	24017	33217	28493
省直管县 County Directly Administrated by Province						
巩义市 Gongyi	13507	7596	8913	15085	19649	20017
兰考县 Lankao	20323	6611	12037	21173	28760	46877
汝州市 Ruzhou	19186	8063	11113	15819	22766	39768
滑县 Huaxian	15728	7551	11948	14981	17012	29135
长垣市 Changyuan	18910	15027	21570	18828	20869	17751
邓州市 Dengzhou	24768	15320	16319	22450	33185	40130
永城市 Yongcheng	19066	10949	11382	21125	23764	31250
固始县 Gushi	18088	12349	16479	16464	23323	23121
鹿邑县 Luyi	16360	10932	14897	17533	17727	24110
新蔡县 Xincai	21233	16633	16851	19391	27439	30546

10-12 各市城镇居民家庭平均每人主要食品消费量(2019年)

Per Capita Consumption of Major Food of Urban Households by City (2019)

单位：千克 (kg)

市(县)	City(County)	粮食 Grain	食用油 Edible Oil	蔬菜及菜制品 Vegetables	猪牛羊肉 Pork, Beef and Mutton	家禽 Poultry	水产品 Aquatic Products	蛋类及其制品 Eggs and Related Products	奶和奶制品 Fresh Milk and Dairy products	干鲜瓜果类 Dry Fresh Fruit	糖果糕点类 Sugar	酒类 Liquor
省辖市	**City**											
郑州市	Zhengzhou	117.7	8.2	107.2	16.0	4.7	7.3	16.0	22.7	87.6	8.7	6.1
开封市	Kaifeng	127.7	7.5	86.5	19.1	5.6	5.4	14.4	15.0	65.1	6.5	14.7
洛阳市	Luoyang	124.6	8.6	96.2	15.1	5.0	5.3	14.3	24.4	63.1	8.1	5.3
平顶山市	Pingdingshan	152.6	7.5	117.7	21.9	8.0	5.4	17.5	17.4	80.3	9.0	5.5
安阳市	Anyang	162.5	11.0	125.5	19.7	4.8	3.8	19.7	20.9	69.4	7.6	6.5
鹤壁市	Hebi	132.0	10.2	89.0	16.9	4.6	3.2	16.5	19.2	60.0	6.0	7.1
新乡市	Xinxiang	144.6	7.3	101.1	17.0	5.8	4.4	18.2	17.9	67.0	8.0	6.3
焦作市	Jiaozuo	110.2	9.6	82.5	17.7	5.7	3.0	15.9	20.0	51.8	5.9	6.8
濮阳市	Puyang	118.0	8.2	100.4	15.7	6.0	4.8	13.2	15.0	60.6	6.7	4.6
许昌市	Xuchang	117.8	6.8	91.3	18.0	5.3	2.9	12.3	15.2	67.7	7.5	4.0
漯河市	Luohe	133.7	8.2	105.7	21.2	6.9	4.9	16.6	11.9	87.5	8.9	6.3
三门峡市	Sanmenxia	136.9	7.2	113.1	16.6	4.2	4.4	14.8	21.6	76.2	7.9	4.2
南阳市	Nanyang	167.1	11.8	110.5	28.7	8.3	4.9	22.0	20.6	52.2	8.0	9.8
商丘市	Shangqiu	149.0	8.7	94.2	19.8	7.4	6.1	15.0	17.0	73.8	5.7	4.4
信阳市	Xinyang	131.7	13.6	104.7	29.7	16.1	13.2	13.7	9.4	54.4	6.5	10.8
周口市	Zhoukou	166.0	10.0	100.0	19.0	11.0	7.0	17.0	14.0	69.0	5.0	7.0
驻马店市	Zhumadian	128.5	8.2	83.1	20.3	11.0	5.8	14.8	14.6	70.4	6.3	6.7
济源市	Jiyuan	100.6	5.6	80.7	12.5	6.1	2.3	15.5	17.8	53.6	5.4	2.0
省直管县	**County Directly Administrated by Province**											
巩义市	Gongyi	126.8	8.7	90.7	11.1	2.2	2.6	13.5	16.0	76.4	6.3	4.3
兰考县	Lankao	136.8	6.1	80.9	11.5	4.5	3.9	14.5	14.8	79.9	5.4	8.5
汝州市	Ruzhou	226.0	9.0	89.0	12.0	5.0	2.0	19.0	18.0	62.0	9.0	4.0
滑县	Huaxian	104.1	6.5	82.0	12.8	6.7	3.1	15.7	10.0	77.7	7.2	3.6
长垣市	Changyuan	145.5	8.1	75.0	12.9	4.7	2.4	13.0	11.0	60.2	4.4	4.5
邓州市	Dengzhou	152.9	10.7	164.8	34.5	13.4	4.4	24.5	17.9	60.7	10.3	13.2
永城市	Yongcheng	84.7	9.0	55.0	20.1	7.6	12.7	22.3	69.2	5.1	3.6	
固始县	Gushi	102.2	8.3	89.3	20.4	17.1	10.3	8.7	4.0	45.1	4.0	5.6
鹿邑县	Luyi	190.8	7.5	135.3	12.3	7.8	4.8	13.7	6.7	48.3	2.9	8.2
新蔡县	Xincai	119.4	8.0	70.0	21.9	11.5	8.0	13.0	5.2	67.4	5.5	10.1

10－13 按收入分组的农民家庭人口，劳动力及居住状况(2019年)

Status of the Peasant Family Population, Labor Force and Housing Conditions by Income Level (2019)

项　目	Item	全省平均 Average	低收入户 Low Income Households	中低收入户 Lower Middle Income Households
平均每户中	Average Number of Permanent			
常住人口	Residents Per Household	3.39	3.72	3.54
整、半劳动力	Average Number of Able-bodied and Semi-abledbodied Laborers Per Household	2.04	1.97	1.99
劳动力占常住人口比重(%)	Percentage of Laborers to Residents Surveyed (%)	60.33	53.05	56.34
平均每个劳动力负担人口	Average Number of Persons Supported by a Laborer	1.66	1.88	1.78
平均每百个常住人口中(人)	Among Per 100 Permanent Residents (person)			
5岁及以下	Age 5 and Below	7.41	8.61	8.13
6－15岁	Age 6-15	20.02	22.92	22.98
16－60岁	Age 16-60	53.18	44.43	48.36
61岁及以上	Age 61 and above	19.39	24.05	20.52
每百个就业劳动力文化程度(人)	Among Per 100 Laborers (person) (by cultur level)			
未上过学	Illiterate or Semiliterate	5.13	7.26	5.88
小学	Primary School	25.49	34.19	28.80
初中	Junior Secondary School	52.80	47.66	51.57
高中	Senior Secondary School	12.18	8.22	11.00
大学专科	Specialty	3.18	2.03	2.11
大学本科	Undergraduate College	1.16	0.63	0.52
研究生	Graduate Degrees	0.05		0.11
每百个就业劳动力从事的主要行业(人)	Among Per 100 Laborers (person)	52.56	66.13	56.67
第一产业	Primary Industry	21.52	17.48	21.04
第二产业	Secondary Industry	25.92	16.39	22.29
第三产业	Tertiary Industry			
居住情况	**Housing condition**			
期末人均住房情况	Per Capita Housing Situation			
现住房面积(平方米)	Living Space (sq.m.)	50.16	42.00	44.17
住房主要建筑材料构成(%)	Construction of Main Building Materials (%)			
#钢筋混凝土	Reinforced Concrete	24.49	22.61	23.27
砖混材料	Brick mixed material	60.44	58.53	59.00
砖瓦砖木	Brick tile and brick wood	14.63	17.99	17.55
住宅外道路路面构成(%)	Construction of the Road Pavement Outside Home (%)			
水泥或柏油路面	Asphalt or Cement Road	74.01	70.97	71.45
沙石或石板等硬质路面	Rigid Pavement	11.91	15.44	12.29
其他	Others	14.08	13.59	16.26
住户主要饮用水来源构成(%)	Construction of Drinking Water for Residents (%)			
#经过净化处理的自来水	After Purification Treatment of Tap Water	59.72	55.78	61.08
受保护的井水和泉水	Protected Well and Spring Water	33.01	34.62	33.09
不受保护的井水和泉水	Unprotected Wells and Springs Water	6.66	9.22	5.06
住户厕所类型构成(%)	Construction of Toilet (%)			
#水冲式卫生厕所	Flush Sanitary Dry Toilet	51.61	49.29	48.56
水冲式非卫生厕所	Flush Insanitary Dry Toilet	31.93	34.02	32.80
卫生旱厕	Sanitary Dry Toilet	7.20	7.25	8.15
普通旱厕	General Dry Toilet	9.17	9.44	10.17
主要炊用能源构成(%)	Construction of Cooking Energy (%)			
柴草	Straw	7.76	12.90	6.17
煤炭	Coal	5.70	4.64	6.01
罐装液化石油气	Canned Liquefied Petroleum Gas	4.58	4.43	3.55
电	Electricity	54.85	49.66	57.60

10−13 续表 continued

项 目	Item	中等收入户 Middle Income Households	中高收入户 Upper Middle Income Households	高收入户 High Income Households
平均每户中	Average Number of Permanent			
常住人口	Residents Per Household	3.47	3.34	2.87
整、半劳动力	Average Number of Able-bodied and Semi-abledbodied Laborers Per Household	2.10	2.09	2.06
劳动力占常住人口比重(%)	Percentage of Laborers to Residents Surveyed (%)	60.5	62.5	71.9
平均每个劳动力负担人口	Average Number of Persons Supported by a Laborer	1.65	1.60	1.39
平均每百个常住人口中(人)	Among Per 100 Permanent Residents (person)			
5岁及以下	Age 5 and Below	7.5	6.9	5.5
6−15岁	Age 6-15	20.3	19.2	13.6
16−60岁	Age 16-60	51.8	58.1	65.8
61岁及以上	Age 61 and above	20.5	15.8	15.1
每百个就业劳动力文化程度(人)	Among Per 100 Laborers (person) (by cultur level)			
未上过学	Illiterate or Semiliterate	6.0	3.8	2.8
小学	Primary School	25.0	20.6	19.4
初中	Junior Secondary School	54.8	56.6	52.9
高中	Senior Secondary School	11.3	13.0	17.2
大学专科	Specialty	1.9	4.5	5.3
大学本科	Undergraduate College	0.9	1.4	2.2
研究生	Graduate Degrees		0.1	0.0
每百个就业劳动力从事的主要行业(人)	Among Per 100 Laborers (person)			
第一产业	Primary Industry	51.9	46.4	43.0
第二产业	Secondary Industry	22.0	23.2	23.6
第三产业	Tertiary Industry	26.1	30.4	33.4
居住情况	**Housing condition**			
期末人均住房情况	Per Capita Housing Situation			
现住房面积(平方米)	Living Space (sq.m.)	49.7	51.7	66.9
住房主要建筑材料构成(%)	Construction of Main Building Materials (%)			
#钢筋混凝土	Reinforced Concrete	22.1	28.0	26.4
砖混材料	Brick mixed material	62.8	58.9	63.0
砖瓦砖木	Brick tile and brick wood	14.9	13.0	9.7
住宅外道路路面构成(%)	Construction of the Road Pavement Outside Home (%)			
水泥或柏油路面	Asphalt or Cement Road	74.5	76.9	76.2
沙石或石板等硬质路面	Rigid Pavement	10.5	9.6	11.7
其他	Others	15.0	13.5	12.0
住户主要饮用水来源构成(%)	Construction of Drinking Water for Residents (%)			
#经过净化处理的自来水	After Purification Treatment of Tap Water	59.0	61.2	61.5
受保护的井水和泉水	Protected Well and Spring Water	34.9	31.8	30.6
不受保护的井水和泉水	Unprotected Wells and Springs Water	5.2	6.4	7.4
住户厕所类型构成(%)	Construction of Toilet (%)			
#水冲式卫生厕所	Flush Sanitary Dry Toilet	53.9	51.0	55.3
水冲式非卫生厕所	Flush Insanitary Dry Toilet	30.5	32.9	29.4
卫生旱厕	Sanitary Dry Toilet	7.4	7.9	5.3
普通旱厕	General Dry Toilet	8.2	8.2	9.9
主要炊用能源构成(%)	Construction of Cooking Energy (%)			
柴草	Straw	6.4	6.3	7.0
煤炭	Coal	5.6	8.3	4.0
罐装液化石油气	Canned Liquefied Petroleum Gas	5.9	4.7	4.3
电	Electricity	55.4	55.5	56.0

10-14 按收入分组的农民家庭人均总收支及结构(2019年)

Per Capita Total Income and Expenditure in Rural Households by Level of Income (2019)

单位：元 (yuan)

项目	Item	全省平均 Average	低收入户 Low Income Households	中低收入户 Lower Middle Income Households
总收入	**Total Cash Income**	**18176**	**8698**	**12150**
工资性收入	Wage Income	5867	2270	3779
经营性收入	Income from Operations	7693	3524	4285
第一产业	Primary Industry	5334	3016	3184
第二产业	Secondary Industry	489	46	281
第三产业	Tertiary Industry	1871	461	820
财产净收入	Property Income	243	128	148
转移净收入	Transfer Income	4372	2776	3937
家庭外出从业人员寄回带回收入	Earning from Migrant Workers	2913	1761	2865
农民家庭平均每人总收入构成(%)	**Structure of Peasant Family Per Capita Income (%)**			
总收入	Total Cash Income	100.0	100.0	100.0
工资性收入	Wage Income	32.3	26.1	31.1
经营性收入	Income from Operations	42.3	40.5	35.3
财产性收入	Property Income	24.1	31.9	32.4
转移性收入	Transfer Income	16.0	20.2	23.6
总支出	**Total Expenditure**	**17077**	**12661**	**13700**
消费支出	Consumption Expenditure	11546	8554	9929
生产经营费用支出	Expenditure of Production Business	2369	2179	1334
第一产业	Primary Industry	1877	1873	1046
第二产业	Secondary Industry	66	31	114
第三产业	Tertiary Industry	426	275	174
财产性支出	Property Expenditure	12	6	9
转移性支出	Transfer Expenditure	383	422	314
部分商业保险支出	Expenditure of Commercial Insurance	82	20	47
购置资产及非经常性转移支出	Expenditure of Purchasing Assets and Non-transfer Expenditur	2271	1350	1851
借贷性支出	Expenditure of Debit and Credit	415	130	216
农民家庭平均每人总支出构成(%)	**Structure of Per Capita Total Expenditure of Rural Households (%)**			
总支出	Total Expenditure	100.0	100.0	100.0
消费支出	Consumption Expenditure	67.6	67.6	72.5
生产经营费用支出	Expenditure of Production Business	13.9	17.2	9.7
财产性支出	Property Expenditure	0.1	0.0	0.1
转移性支出	Transfer Expenditure	2.2	3.3	2.3
部分商业保险支出	Expenditure of Commercial Insurance	0.5	0.2	0.3
购置资产及非经常性转移支出	Expenditure of Purchasing Assets and Non-transfer Expenditur	13.3	10.7	13.5
借贷性支出	Expenditure of Debit and Credit	2.4	1.0	1.6

10-14 续表　continued

单位：元　(yuan)

项　目	Item	中等收入户 Middle Income Households	中高收入户 Upper Middle Income Households	高收入户 High Income Households
总收入	**Total Cash Income**	**16046**	**21121**	**37022**
工资性收入	Wage Income	5789	8064	10633
经营性收入	Income from Operations	5852	7899	19277
第一产业	Primary Industry	4500	6100	11099
第二产业	Secondary Industry	64	204	2162
第三产业	Tertiary Industry	1288	1596	6015
财产性收入	Property Income	171	233	609
转移性收入	Transfer Income	4233	4924	6502
家庭外出从业人员寄回带回收入	Income from Migrant Workers	2875	3375	3971
农民家庭平均每人总收入构成(%)	**Structure of Peasant Family Per Capita Income (%)**			
总收入	Total Cash Income	100.0	100.0	100.0
工资性收入	Wage Income	36.1	38.2	28.7
经营性收入	Income from Operations	36.5	37.4	52.1
财产性收入	Property Income	26.4	23.3	17.6
转移性收入	Transfer Income	17.9	16.0	10.7
总支出	**Total Expenditure**	**15574**	**17989**	**27712**
消费支出	Consumption Expenditure	11001	12416	17058
生产经营费用支出	Expenditure of Production Business	1725	2132	4942
第一产业	Primary Industry	1475	1883	3382
第二产业	Secondary Industry	4	37	163
第三产业	Tertiary Industry	246	212	1398
财产性支出	Property Expenditure	7	10	33
转移性支出	Transfer Expenditure	343	382	468
部分商业保险支出	Expenditure of Commercial Insurance	100	91	171
购置资产及非经常性转移支出	Expenditure of Purchasing Assets and Non-transfer Expenditur	2164	2355	4011
借贷性支出	Expenditure of Debit and Credit	232	603	1028
农民家庭平均每人总支出构成(%)	**Structure of Per Capita Total Expenditure of Rural Households (%)**			
总支出	Total Expenditure	100.0	100.0	100.0
消费支出	Consumption Expenditure	70.6	69.0	61.6
生产经营费用支出	Expenditure of Production Business	11.1	11.9	17.8
财产性支出	Property Expenditure	0.0	0.1	0.1
转移性支出	Transfer Expenditure	2.2	2.1	1.7
部分商业保险支出	Expenditure of Commercial Insurance	0.6	0.5	0.6
购置资产及非经常性转移支出	Expenditure of Purchasing Assets and Non-transfer Expenditur	13.9	13.1	14.5
借贷性支出	Expenditure of Debit and Credit	1.5	3.4	3.7

10-15 按收入分组的农民家庭人均可支配收入及消费性支出(2019年)

Per Capita Disposable Income and Consumption Expenditure of Rural Households by Income Level (2019)

单位：元 (yuan)

项目	Item	全省平均 Average	低收入户 Low Income Households	中低收入户 Lower Middle Income Households
可支配收入	**Disposable Income**	**15164**	**5925**	**10256**
工资性收入	Wages	5867	2270	3779
经营净收入	Net Business Income	5077	1179	2714
第一产业	Primary Industry	3319	1024	2047
第二产业	Secondary Industry	398	10	91
第三产业	Tertiary Industry	1360	145	576
财产净收入	Net Income of Properties	231	122	139
转移净收入	Net Income of Transfers	3989	2354	3623
家庭外出从业人员寄回带回收入	Income from Migrant Workers	2913	1761	2865
生活消费支出	**Living Consumption Expenditure**	**11546**	**8554**	**9929**
食品	Food	3030	2432	2615
衣着	Clothing	819	584	706
居住	Residence	2479	1845	2215
家庭设备、用品及服务	Household Appliances	739	536	574
交通和通讯	Transport and Communications	1369	768	1143
文化、教育、娱乐用品及服务	Culture, Education, Recreation and Service	1459	1203	1330
医疗保健	Health Care	1462	1065	1154
其他商品和服务	Other Goods and Servies	189	122	194

项目	Item	中等收入户 Middle Income Households	中高收入户 Uper Middle Income Households	高收入户 High Income Households
可支配收入	**Disposable Income**	**13800**	**18348**	**31118**
工资性收入	Wages	5789	8064	10633
经营净收入	Net Business Income	3957	5518	13874
第一产业	Primary Industry	2930	4067	7459
第二产业	Secondary Industry	55	154	1977
第三产业	Tertiary Industry	972	1297	4438
财产净收入	Net Income of Properties	164	223	576
转移净收入	Net Income of Transfers	3889	4542	6034
家庭外出从业人员寄回带回收入	Income from Migrant Workers	2875	3375	3971
生活消费支出	**Living Consumption Expenditure**	**11001**	**12416**	**17058**
食品	Food	2801	3287	4295
衣着	Clothing	770	912	1216
居住	Residence	2383	2618	3579
家庭设备、用品及服务	Household Appliances	732	852	1082
交通和通讯	Transport and Communications	1232	1392	2564
文化、教育、娱乐用品及服务	Culture, Education, Recreation and Service	1550	1565	1718
医疗保健	Health Care	1363	1591	2324
其他商品和服务	Other Goods and Servies	170	200	279

10-16 按收入分组的农民家庭人均现金收入及支出(2019年)

Per Capita Cash Income and Expenditure of Rural Households by Income Level (2019)

单位：元 (yuan)

项　目	Item	全省平均 Average	低收入户 Low Income Households	中低收入户 Lower Middle Income Households
现金收入(未扣除生产费用)	**Cash Income (including Product Expenditure)**	**17154**	**8360**	**11412**
现金工资性收入	Cash Income from Wages	5860	2269	3775
现金经营性收入	Cash Income from Business	6942	3300	3702
第一产业	Primary Industry	4582	2793	2601
第二产业	Secondary Industry	489	46	281
第三产业	Tertiary Industry	1871	461	820
现金财产性收入	Cash Income of Properties	243	128	148
现金转移性收入	Cash Income of Transfers	4108	2662	3787
家庭外出从业人员寄回带回收入	Income Taken back by Employees out Home	2913	1761	2865
现金支出	**Cash Expenditure**	**15144**	**11190**	**12093**
现金消费支出	Cash Expenditure on consumption	9628	7092	8340
生产经营现金费用支出	Cash Expenditure on Business	2353	2170	1317
第一产业	Primary Industry	1861	1864	1029
第二产业	Secondary Industry	66	31	114
第三产业	Tertiary Industry	426	275	174
现金财产性支出	Cash Expenditure of Properties	12	6	9
现金转移性支出	Cash Expenditure of Transfers	383	422	314
部分商业保险支出	Expenditure of Commercial Insurance	82	20	47
购置资产及非经常性转移支出	Expenditure of Purchasing Assets and Non-transfer Expenditure	2271	1350	1851
借贷性支出	Expenditure of Debit and Credit	415	130	216

项　目	Item	中等收入户 Middle Income Households	中高收入户 Upper Middle Income Households	高收入户 High Income Households
现金收入(未扣除生产费用)	**Cash Income (including Product Expenditure)**	**15079**	**19731**	**35124**
现金工资性收入	Cash Income from Wages	5784	8054	10620
现金经营性收入	Cash Income from Business	5104	6827	18004
第一产业	Primary Industry	3752	5027	9827
第二产业	Secondary Industry	64	204	2162
第三产业	Tertiary Industry	1288	1596	6015
现金财产性收入	Cash Income of Properties	171	233	609
现金转移性收入	Cash Income of Transfers	4020	4617	5891
家庭外出从业人员寄回带回收入	Income Taken back by Employees out Home	2875	3375	3971
现金支出	**Cash Expenditure**	**13736**	**15982**	**24751**
现金消费支出	Cash Expenditure on Consumption	9180	10423	14118
生产经营现金费用支出	Cash Expenditure on Business	1708	2118	4921
第一产业	Primary Industry	1458	1869	3360
第二产业	Secondary Industry	4	37	163
第三产业	Tertiary Industry	246	212	1398
现金财产性支出	Cash Expenditure of Properties	7	10	33
现金转移性支出	Cash Expenditure of Transfers	343	382	468
部分商业保险支出	Expenditure of Commercial Insurance	100	91	171
购置资产及非经常性转移支出	Expenditure of Purchasing Assets and Non-transfer Expenditure	2164	2355	4011
借贷性支出	Expenditure of Debit and Credit	232	603	1028

10-17 按收入分组的农民家庭主要食品消费量(2019年)
Consumption of Major Food in Rural Households by Income Level (2019)

单位：公斤/人 (kg/person)

项　目	Item	全省平均 Average	低收入户 Low Income Households	中低收入户 Lower Middle Income Households
粮食消费量	Grain Consumption	137.13	117.70	126.09
#小麦	Wheat	92.37	78.58	83.94
稻谷	Rice	22.92	21.60	24.17
玉米	Corn	7.05	4.75	5.37
油脂类消费量	Oil	7.68	6.66	7.03
蔬菜及菜制品消费量	Vegetables	76.34	62.30	68.89
肉类	Meat	14.81	11.42	13.14
禽类	Poultry	5.69	4.11	5.52
水产品	Aquatic Products	3.30	2.55	2.79
蛋类及蛋制品	Eggs and Related Productions	13.04	11.54	12.06
奶和奶制品	Milk and Dairy Products	7.98	6.07	7.87
干鲜瓜果类	Dried and Fresh Melons and Fruits	52.83	40.59	47.52
糖果糕点类	Confectionery	5.46	5.14	5.12
酒	Liquor	5.86	4.21	4.64

项　目	Item	中等收入户 Middle Income Households	中高收入户 Upper Middle Income Households	高收入户 High Income Households
粮食消费量	Grain Consumption	130.23	140.80	179.94
#小麦	Wheat	93.17	95.27	116.25
稻谷	Rice	20.95	22.21	26.28
玉米	Corn	2.52	6.27	18.45
油脂类消费量	Oil	7.53	7.94	9.70
蔬菜及菜制品消费量	Vegetables	74.79	79.65	101.71
肉类	Meat	14.28	16.17	20.30
禽类	Poultry	5.34	6.35	7.62
水产品	Aquatic Products	3.26	3.84	4.32
蛋类及蛋制品	Eggs and Related Productions	12.21	13.12	17.08
奶和奶制品	Milk and Dairy Products	7.10	8.49	11.08
干鲜瓜果类	Dried and Fresh Melons and Fruits	50.42	58.54	71.50
糖果糕点类	Confectionery	4.99	5.80	6.49
酒	Liquor	5.28	6.54	9.40

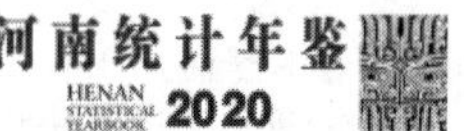

10−18 按收入分组的农民家庭平均每百户主要耐用消费品及生产性固定资产年末拥有量(2019年)

Main Durable Goods and Productive Fixed Assets Owned Per hundred Rural Households at Year-end by Income Level (2019)

项　目	Item	全省平均 Average	低收入户 Low Income Households	中低收入户 Lower Middle Income Households
耐用消费品年末拥有量	**Durable Consumer Goods**			
家用汽车(台)	Car (unit)	24.32	16.30	23.04
摩托车(台)	Motorcycle (unit)	39.60	36.92	36.42
助力车(台)	Electric Bicycle (unit)	121.24	110.08	121.02
洗衣机(台)	Washing Machine (unit)	98.50	92.52	97.78
电冰箱(台)	Refrigerator (unit)	96.23	91.61	94.04
微波炉(台)	Microwave Oven (unit)	13.67	8.68	11.88
彩色电视机(台)	Color TV Set (unit)	114.36	109.72	111.57
空调(台)	Air Conditioner (unit)	103.13	84.76	96.62
热水器(台)	Water Heater (unit)	72.42	61.54	69.53
洗碗机(台)	Dishwasher (unit)	0.88	0.44	0.68
排油烟机(台)	Exhaust Fan (unit)	20.13	13.61	14.62
固定电话(部)	Telephone (unit)	8.07	8.32	7.38
移动电话(部)	Mobile Phone (unit)	269.69	252.26	263.52
#接入互联网	Internet Mobile Phones (unit)	173.24	150.71	161.55
计算机(台)	Computer (unit)	30.07	22.59	21.65
#接入互联网	Internet Computer (unit)	18.61	12.41	13.94
照相机(架)	Camera (unit)	1.64	1.18	1.24
中高档乐器(件)	Medium and High-Grade Musical Instrument (unit)	0.67	0.66	0.17
健身器材(套)	Fitness Equipment (unit)	1.38	0.93	0.91
生产性固定资产数量	**Productive Fixed Assets**			
生产性用房及建筑物(平方米)	Productive Occupancy and Buildings (sq.m.)	1013.29	675.62	419.50
大中型农用拖拉机(台)	Large and Medium Tractors (unit)	2.54	2.43	1.22
小型农用拖拉机(台)	Minitype Tractors (unit)	32.42	29.30	26.88
农用排灌动力机械(台)	Drainage and Irrigation Agricultural Machinery (unit)	14.24	12.35	11.39
插秧机(台)	Transplanter (unit)	0.60	0.28	0.40
收割机(台)	Harvesters (unit)	1.20	0.74	0.64
脱粒机(台)	Thresher (unit)	7.17	6.71	5.33
产品畜(头)	Product Livestock (unit)	146.44	37.49	13.87

10-18 续表 continued

项 目	Item	中等收入户 Middle Income Households	中高收入户 Upper Middle Income Households	高收入户 High Income Households
耐用消费品年末拥有量	**Durable Consumer Goods**			
家用汽车(台)	Car (unit)	24.71	28.22	29.30
摩托车(台)	Motorcycle (unit)	38.34	43.33	42.97
助力车(台)	Electric Bicycle (unit)	122.39	131.03	121.69
洗衣机(台)	Washing Machine (unit)	99.19	100.45	102.56
电冰箱(台)	Refrigerator (unit)	96.34	98.10	101.06
微波炉(台)	Microwave Oven (unit)	11.54	16.27	19.99
彩色电视机(台)	Color TV Set (unit)	115.09	118.64	116.76
空调(台)	Air Conditioner (unit)	98.25	113.42	122.58
热水器(台)	Water Heater (unit)	74.65	77.54	78.83
洗碗机(台)	Dishwasher (unit)	1.27	0.44	1.56
排油烟机(台)	Exhaust Fan (unit)	22.45	23.14	26.84
固定电话(部)	Telephone (unit)	7.93	7.91	8.83
移动电话(部)	Mobile Phone (unit)	270.59	281.40	280.66
#接入互联网	Internet Mobile Phones (unit)	167.94	186.88	199.08
计算机(台)	Computer (unit)	30.53	35.62	39.93
#接入互联网	Internet Computer (unit)	19.01	21.45	26.21
照相机(架)	Camera (unit)	1.29	1.49	2.97
中高档乐器(件)	Medium and High-Grade Musical Instrument (unit)	1.02	0.83	0.69
健身器材(套)	Fitness Equipment (unit)	1.04	1.32	2.71
生产性固定资产数量	**Productive Fixed Assets**			
生产性用房及建筑物(平方米)	Productive Occupancy and Buildings (sq.m.)	680.80	1353.52	1935.47
大中型农用拖拉机(台)	Large and Medium Tractors (unit)	1.73	1.61	5.69
小型农用拖拉机(台)	Minitype Tractors (unit)	35.16	33.94	36.81
农用排灌动力机械(台)	Drainage and Irrigation Agricultural Machinery (unit)	13.89	14.65	18.89
插秧机(台)	Transplanter (unit)	0.45	0.69	1.17
收割机(台)	Harvesters (unit)	0.83	1.51	2.27
脱粒机(台)	Thresher (unit)	7.61	7.74	8.47
产品畜(头)	Product Livestock (unit)	26.86	27.86	625.50

10−19 各市农村居民家庭人均全年可支配收入按收入来源分组情况(2019年)
Per Capita Annual Disposable Income of Rural Household by Source and City (2019)

单位：元 (yuan)

市(县) City(County)	合 计 Total	工资性收入 Net Income from Wages and Salaries	经营净收入 Net Income from Household Operations	财产净收入 Net Income from Properties	转移净收入 Net Income from Transfers
省 辖 市 City					
郑 州 市 Zhengzhou	23536	14880	5124	1555	1977
开 封 市 Kaifeng	14473	6169	5449	136	2718
洛 阳 市 Luoyang	14973	7926	3374	353	3321
平 顶 山 市 Pingdingshan	14587	6580	3887	259	3861
安 阳 市 Anyang	16095	6450	3611	201	5833
鹤 壁 市 Hebi	18275	11817	5175	119	1164
新 乡 市 Xinxiang	16344	8133	5156	127	2928
焦 作 市 Jiaozuo	19374	12588	4328	386	2073
濮 阳 市 Puyang	13894	8131	2369	180	3213
许 昌 市 Xuchang	18558	9978	5062	258	3260
漯 河 市 Luohe	16878	9138	4015	275	3450
三 门 峡 市 Sanmenxia	15645	4967	7466	235	2977
南 阳 市 Nanyang	15167	5105	6090	213	3760
商 丘 市 Shangqiu	12668	5017	4610	152	2889
信 阳 市 Xinyang	14010	5117	5057	205	3631
周 口 市 Zhoukou	12196	3664	4386	163	3984
驻 马 店 市 Zhumadian	13020	4294	4921	113	3692
济 源 市 Jiyuan	20235	16002	2716	712	805
省 直 管 县 County Directly Administrated by Province					
巩 义 市 Gongyi	25076	15103	8083	77	1812
兰 考 县 Lankao	13126	2841	5965	98	4222
汝 州 市 Ruzhou	18571	7703	7968	40	2860
滑 县 Huaxian	13076	3055	5130	93	4798
长 垣 市 Changyuan	21610	7647	8441	211	5312
邓 州 市 Dengzhou	16673	3588	7702	25	5357
永 城 市 Yongcheng	15880	3491	5807	208	6373
固 始 县 Gushi	15048	4248	5836	214	4750
鹿 邑 县 Luyi	14454	5374	6025	20	3035
新 蔡 县 Xincai	13392	3211	3918	11	6252

10-20 各市农村居民家庭人均全年可支配收入分组情况(2019年)

Per Capita Annual Disposable Income of Rural Household by City (2019)

单位：元 (yuan)

市(县)	City(County)	低收入户 Low Income Households	中低收入户 Lower Middle Income Households	中等收入户 Middle Income Households	中高收入户 Upper Middle Income Households	高收入户 High Income Households
省辖市	**City**					
郑州市	Zhengzhou	10755	17206	22112	28636	53616
开封市	Kaifeng	5959	9940	13533	18522	30813
洛阳市	Luoyang	6388	10401	13643	17723	31394
平顶山市	Pingdingshan	6781	9745	12718	16211	33887
安阳市	Anyang	5960	9959	13569	19337	40007
鹤壁市	Hebi	8725	13468	17171	20719	35155
新乡市	Xinxiang	8759	10438	10777	12409	17139
焦作市	Jiaozuo	9107	14314	17903	23307	35714
濮阳市	Puyang	6864	9799	11966	16180	26265
许昌市	Xuchang	7848	12148	16227	22209	41840
漯河市	Luohe	17357	6417	11783	15712	20983
三门峡市	Sanmenxia	5482	9380	12837	17531	37425
南阳市	Nanyang	7500	13201	19395	27446	54746
商丘市	Shangqiu	2267	8002	10870	15621	31455
信阳市	Xinyang	6013	9153	13081	18880	34706
周口市	Zhoukou	10838	4546	6965	10627	13882
驻马店市	Zhumadian	5511	9110	12101	15836	26341
济源市	Jiyuan	9955	15770	19969	23817	31332
省直管县	**County Directly Administrated by Province**					
巩义市	Gongyi	10363	16743	23801	34470	77091
兰考县	Lankao	5773	8485	10823	17311	28661
汝州市	Ruzhou	6806	9809	12678	15282	50568
滑县	Huaxian	6544	9534	13022	19476	41177
长垣市	Changyuan	9185	14134	18837	25769	41865
邓州市	Dengzhou	7742	12670	16462	22271	32188
永城市	Yongcheng	3021	9546	13821	18222	4005
固始县	Gushi	5505	8382	12606	18851	35102
鹿邑县	Luyi	6169	10645	14253	17746	28549
新蔡县	Xincai	6682	9853	12810	16653	24259

10-21 各市农村居民家庭平均每人生活消费总支出(2019年)

Per Capita Consumption Expenditure of Rural Households by City (2019)

单位：元 (yuan)

市(县)	City(County)	生活消费支出合计 Consumption Expenditure	食品烟酒 Food, Tobacco, Liquor	衣着 Clothing	居住 Residence	生活用品及服务 Household Appliances and Services	交通、通信及服务 Transport, and Communi-cations	教育及文化娱乐 Education, Culture and Entertainment	医疗、保健及服务 Health Care and Medical Services	其他商品及服务 Other Goods and Services
省辖市	**City**									
郑州市	Zhengzhou	16864	4079	1200	4351	975	2847	1530	1492	391
开封市	Kaifeng	11134	2586	833	2371	853	1961	1257	1047	226
洛阳市	Luoyang	11889	2717	976	2823	954	1759	1224	1274	161
平顶山市	Pingdingshan	10138	2661	820	2325	687	1044	1147	1300	155
安阳市	Anyang	10710	2445	730	2683	777	1242	1411	1249	172
鹤壁市	Hebi	12141	3487	979	2256	818	1870	1283	1181	266
新乡市	Xinxiang	11372	2909	978	2348	826	1350	1342	1404	217
焦作市	Jiaozuo	14424	4058	1310	2909	1046	1914	1516	1126	545
濮阳市	Puyang	9799	2436	740	1792	809	1454	1256	1088	223
许昌市	Xuchang	12391	3220	937	2103	671	1668	1628	1910	254
漯河市	Luohe	11334	3104	884	2284	1048	1546	1106	1200	164
三门峡市	Sanmenxia	11140	2650	900	1996	715	1990	1271	1422	196
南阳市	Nanyang	10879	3028	814	2639	744	1149	1055	1231	218
商丘市	Shangqiu	10701	3215	781	2221	737	1112	1051	1438	147
信阳市	Xinyang	10877	3657	686	2440	807	918	1223	950	196
周口市	Zhoukou	11015	3894	769	2373	914	1145	974	802	145
驻马店市	Zhumadian	10372	3002	748	2320	672	1118	1216	1124	172
济源市	Jiyuan	14112	3142	943	2389	1288	2770	1668	1651	263
省直管县	**County Directly Administrated by Province**									
巩义市	Gongyi	11323	2943	962	2814	849	1420	1180	995	159
兰考县	Lankao	13120	3276	870	2420	1099	2275	1951	846	383
汝州市	Ruzhou	10244	2468	857	2694	541	1003	1123	1387	171
滑县	Huaxian	12500	2876	781	2879	699	1917	1700	1532	117
长垣市	Changyuan	13436	3639	1162	2939	1123	1364	1751	1273	186
邓州市	Dengzhou	12565	3583	1008	2435	773	1372	1589	1686	118
永城市	Yongcheng	13722	4023	1028	3007	1182	1302	1488	1414	278
固始县	Gushi	11769	3333	528	2634	1211	938	1614	1347	164
鹿邑县	Luyi	9309	2960	706	1998	701	828	1093	882	141
新蔡县	Xincai	11617	3478	581	3051	592	914	1100	1697	204

10-22 各市农村居民家庭平均每人生活消费现金支出(2019年)
Per Capita Cash Consumption Expenditure of Rural Households by City (2019)

单位：元 (yuan)

市(县) City(County)	生活消费支出合计 Consumption Expenditure	食品烟酒 Food, Tobacco, Liquor	衣着 Clothing	居住 Residence	生活用品及服务 Household Appliances and Services	交通、通信及服务 Transport, and Communi-cations	教育及文化娱乐 Education, Culture and Entertainment	医疗、保健及服务 Health Care and Medical Services	其他商品及服务 Other Goods and Services
省辖市 City									
郑州市 Zhengzhou	13675	3992	1200	1504	973	2847	1530	1240	389
开封市 Kaifeng	9647	2555	833	1030	852	1961	1257	934	225
洛阳市 Luoyang	9848	2526	975	1289	948	1757	1223	970	161
平顶山市 Pingdingshan	8455	2573	819	932	686	1044	1146	1101	154
安阳市 Anyang	8647	2358	730	966	765	1242	1411	1014	160
鹤壁市 Hebi	10735	3453	979	1209	818	1870	1283	858	264
新乡市 Xinxiang	9600	2876	978	891	824	1350	1342	1123	216
焦作市 Jiaozuo	12565	4020	1310	1324	1046	1914	1516	892	542
濮阳市 Puyang	9799	2436	740	1792	809	1454	1256	1088	223
许昌市 Xuchang	10595	3055	937	937	670	1668	1628	1447	254
漯河市 Luohe	9646	3064	883	891	1048	1546	1106	944	164
三门峡市 Sanmenxia	9567	2512	900	871	674	1990	1271	1154	195
南阳市 Nanyang	9149	2825	814	1325	744	1149	1055	1019	218
商丘市 Shangqiu	8951	3130	781	843	730	1112	1051	1165	141
信阳市 Xinyang	8867	3325	686	917	794	918	1223	814	190
周口市 Zhoukou	8400	2863	769	885	714	925	1274	826	144
驻马店市 Zhumadian	8626	2889	748	820	672	1118	1216	994	170
济源市 Jiyuan	12331	3049	942	1098	1288	2770	1668	1252	263
省直管县 County Directly Administrated by Province									
巩义市 Gongyi	9984	2880	962	1568	849	1420	1180	965	159
兰考县 Lankao	11419	3272	870	859	1099	2275	1951	716	377
汝州市 Ruzhou	8516	1730	857	1391	540	1003	1123	1006	171
滑县 Huaxian	10152	2789	781	1290	655	1917	1700	905	115
长垣市 Changyuan	11376	3630	1162	1027	1122	1364	1751	1135	184
邓州市 Dengzhou	10624	3507	1008	841	773	1372	1589	1416	117
永城市 Yongcheng	12395	4008	1028	1781	1182	1302	1488	1329	278
固始县 Gushi	9392	2845	528	891	1211	938	1614	1201	164
鹿邑县 Luyi	7867	3284	706	578	701	828	1093	537	141
新蔡县 Xincai	9012	3402	581	697	592	914	1100	1523	203

10-23 各市农村居民家庭平均每人主要食品消费量(2019年)
Per Capita Consumption of Major Food of Rural Households by City (2019)

单位：千克 (kg)

市(县)	City(County)	粮食 Grain	食用油 Edible Oil	蔬菜及食用菌 Vegetables	猪牛羊肉 Pork, Beef and Mutton	家禽 Poultry	水产品 Aquatic Products	蛋类及其制品 Eggs and Related Products	奶和奶制品 Milk and Dairy products	干鲜瓜果 Dry and Fresh Fruits and Melons	糖果糕点 Sugar	酒类 Liquor
省辖市	**City**											
郑州市	Zhengzhou	119.7	8.1	78.2	12.0	3.1	3.6	12.3	13.4	61.7	6.7	5.0
开封市	Kaifeng	113.8	5.9	68.0	10.0	4.1	2.5	10.7	5.4	45.0	4.4	7.1
洛阳市	Luoyang	159.8	10.0	80.4	9.2	1.9	1.2	11.0	11.1	35.2	6.6	4.4
平顶山市	Pingdingshan	145.4	7.7	91.7	15.3	3.8	1.8	13.4	7.2	57.6	7.3	4.1
安阳市	Anyang	163.7	7.6	71.6	10.4	2.5	1.6	14.3	8.6	44.3	5.0	5.8
鹤壁市	Hebi	151.1	10.1	74.7	14.4	3.6	3.2	11.0	12.2	35.9	7.3	8.4
新乡市	Xinxiang	138.6	7.3	77.5	12.1	3.8	2.5	13.5	11.6	60.0	7.0	6.7
焦作市	Jiaozuo	102.5	8.7	53.8	11.5	3.3	1.2	13.4	16.1	42.1	5.1	6.3
濮阳市	Puyang	114.5	8.3	65.2	11.8	4.9	2.1	12.2	8.4	47.3	5.9	5.1
许昌市	Xuchang	152.8	7.9	75.3	16.1	4.1	1.6	9.6	10.0	61.0	7.9	3.3
漯河市	Luohe	144.8	7.3	78.0	14.9	6.2	3.3	12.3	5.3	75.6	6.5	4.0
三门峡市	Sanmenxia	164.9	8.3	83.3	10.3	1.7	1.4	10.4	8.0	48.8	6.4	3.2
南阳市	Nanyang	152.5	7.6	80.3	15.5	4.4	3.1	16.3	9.5	36.4	5.5	7.8
商丘市	Shangqiu	211.0	9.4	82.8	14.6	6.8	3.5	13.8	8.2	61.3	4.7	6.3
信阳市	Xinyang	152.2	10.9	92.6	25.1	14.2	10.9	11.9	4.5	42.8	5.2	13.9
周口市	Zhoukou	135.0	9.0	70.0	14.0	8.0	5.0	14.0	8.0	55.0	4.0	5.0
驻马店市	Zhumadian	126.9	7.9	69.9	15.6	8.2	3.9	11.7	4.9	53.8	5.3	7.9
济源市	Jiyuan	104.1	6.3	54.3	9.0	3.4	0.9	11.8	12.3	38.7	5.1	4.4
省直管县	**County Directly Administrated by Province**											
巩义市	Gongyi	141.5	7.5	84.0	8.4	1.4	1.4	9.8	11.1	63.0	7.3	2.7
兰考县	Lankao	115.9	8.6	100.0	11.1	5.1	3.1	14.2	8.1	91.5	5.2	11.1
汝州市	Ruzhou	167.0	9.0	81.0	12.0	2.0	1.0	12.0	8.0	62.0	7.0	4.0
滑县	Huaxian	148.2	9.3	77.3	13.1	3.6	2.3	15.1	4.2	64.3	5.9	8.1
长垣市	Changyuan	158.3	7.2	89.8	14.2	5.6	3.0	16.5	11.2	89.8	6.0	5.7
邓州市	Dengzhou	157.1	6.6	85.3	19.8	6.6	4.8	20.7	12.9	52.6	8.7	9.1
永城市	Yongcheng	177.8	13.4	79.3	15.5	11.5	5.8	14.0	9.9	65.0	4.2	9.7
固始县	Gushi	142.4	9.5	68.9	20.5	16.0	7.4	11.3	1.8	31.5	3.3	12.1
鹿邑县	Luyi	177.1	10.4	90.3	16.9	8.3	6.7	17.1	6.1	46.8	3.1	8.0
新蔡县	Xincai	169.0	5.4	83.4	19.2	7.4	5.6	13.6	2.4	59.4	7.1	9.3

10−24 各市农村居民家庭住房情况(2019年)

Housing Conditions of Rural Households by City (2019)

市(县) City(County)	实际住房按主要建筑材料分的户数占比重(%) Proportion of Real Houses by Main Building Materials			
	#钢筋混凝土 Reinforced Concrete Structure	砖混材料 Brick Mixed Structure	砖瓦砖木 Brick Tile and Wood	竹草土坯 Bamboo Grass Adobe
省辖市 City				
郑州市 Zhengzhou	39.7	57.7	2.5	
开封市 Kaifeng	14.6	70.8	14.3	
洛阳市 Luoyang	13.8	81.9	3.8	0.1
平顶山市 Pingdingshan	22.7	65.6	10.0	1.7
安阳市 Anyang	14.6	64.7	20.7	
鹤壁市 Hebi	16.7	66.3	14.0	0.3
新乡市 Xinxiang	16.4	69.6	14.0	
焦作市 Jiaozuo	22.5	65.7	11.6	
濮阳市 Puyang	9.5	51.9	38.4	0.2
许昌市 Xuchang	19.6	75.6	4.8	
漯河市 Luohe	16.9	76.9	6.2	
三门峡市 Sanmenxia	0.2	0.7	0.1	0.0
南阳市 Nanyang	34.5	58.8	6.4	
商丘市 Shangqiu	12.2	65.5	22.3	
信阳市 Xinyang	51.9	31.3	16.0	0.8
周口市 Zhoukou	29.0	42.0	28.9	
驻马店市 Zhumadian	26.6	64.5	8.8	
济源市 Jiyuan	62.9	35.7	1.4	
省直管县 County Directly Administrated by Province				
巩义市 Gongyi	20.8	79.2	4.2	
兰考县 Lankao	16.6	61.9	21.5	
汝州市 Ruzhou	23.0	70.0	7.0	
滑县 Huaxian	5.0	38.0	57.0	
长垣市 Changyuan	19.4	64.5	16.1	
邓州市 Dengzhou	63.4	31.3	5.4	
永城市 Yongcheng	32.2	46.1	20.4	
固始县 Gushi	58.7	41.6	68.7	
鹿邑县 Luyi	37.0	52.0	11.0	
新蔡县 Xincai	41.6	45.5	12.9	

注：拥有住房，包括出租的住房面积和价值，但不包括租住的面积。实际住房，包括租住的面积。
a) Owned houses include leasing housing area and value, but exclude the area of rental area.The actual housing including the rental area.

主要统计指标解释

期内常住人口数　指居住在一个住宅内，共同分享生活开支或收入的一群人。凡计算为家庭常住人口的成员其全部收支都包括在本家庭中。

户均就业人数　指家庭人口与就业人口之比。

可支配收入　指调查户在调查期内获得的、可用于最终消费支出和储蓄的综合，即调查户可以用来自由支配的收入。可支配收入既包括现金，也包括实物收入。按照收入的来源，可支配收入包含四项，分别为：工资性收入、经营净收入、财产净收入和转移净收入。计算公式为：

可支配收入=工资性收入+经营净收入+财产净收入+转移净收入

总支出　指全部家庭支出。包括消费支出、生产经营费用支出、财产性支出、转移性支出、部分商业保险支出、购置资产及非经常性转移支出、借贷性支出。

消费性支出　指用户用于满足家庭日常生活消费需要的全部支出，包括用于消费品的支出和用于服务性消费的支出。根据用途不同，消费支出可以划分为食品烟酒、衣着、居住、生活用品及服务、交通通讯、教育文化娱乐、医疗保健、其他用品及服务八大类。根据来源不同，消费支出可以划分为现金消费支出、实物消费支出（含自产自用、来自单位、来自政务和其他社会组织）。

收入分组方法　是将所有调查户分别按照全体居民、城镇居民、农村居民，将户人均可支配收入由低到高排队，按20%，20%，20%，20%，20%的比例依次分成：低收入户、中低收入户、中等收入户、中高收入户、高收入户等五组。

Explanatory Notes on Main Statistical Indicators

Number of Usual Population refers to members of households living and sharing living cost and income together. All the income and expenditure of all the members of such households are included in the income and expenditure of the household.

Number of Employee per Household refers to the ratio between number of persons in an urban household and the number of employed persons.

Disposal Income refers to the total income at the disposal of investigation residents which can be used for final consumption and savings in the investigation period. It includes income both in cash and in kind from four categories: income from wages and salaries, net income from household operations, net income from transfers and net income from properties. The following formula is used:

Disposal income = income from wages and salaries+ net income from household operations+ net income from transfers+ net income from properties

Total Expenditure refers to all expenditure of households. It includes consumption expenditure, production and operation expenditure, property expenditure, transfer expenditure, expenditure on commercial insurance, expenditure on purchase of assets and non regular transfer expenditure and expenditure on debit and credit.

Consumption Expenditure refers to total expenditure of households for consumption in daily life, including expenditure on consumer goods and on services. It is classified by usage into eight categories of food; clothing; housing; household appliances and services; health care and medical services; transport and communications; recreation, education and cultural services; and miscellaneous goods and services. It is classified by source of expenditure into expenditure in cash and reality consumption expenditure (including it from produce on their own, from the unit, from government and other social groups).

Methods of Income Group All households in the sample are grouped according to all the residents, urban residents and rural residents, by per capita disposal income of the household, into groups of low income, lower middle income, middle income, upper middle income and high income, each group consisting of 20%, 20%, 20%, 20% and 20% of all households respectively.

城市概况
General Survey of Cities

◉ 资料整理：靳伟莉　贾梁　陈琛

简要说明

一、主要内容

本篇反映河南省城市社会经济发展和城市建设的规模及综合水平的资料。城市公用事业概况主要包括：城市建设、供水、供气、供热、市政设施、公共交通、城市绿化、环境卫生等资料。

二、统计范围

包括全省所有设市城市在建成区范围内的城市规划管理、投资、建设或经营管理相关设施的单位。

三、资料来源

省辖市主要经济指标由河南省统计局地方经济社会调查队编辑整理。省辖市和县级市城市公用事业基本情况资料由省住房城乡建设厅和省交通厅提供，由河南省统计局社会与科技处和服务业统计处编辑整理。

Brief Introduction

I. Main Contents

Data in this chapter present the scale and the comprehensive level of Social economic development and urban construction of Henan provincial cities, main include supply of water, gas and heating; municipal infrastructure; public transportation; urban greenery; public transportation and environmental, sanitation.

II. Scope of Statistics

Data in this chapter cover all units under the jurisdiction of cities which are engaged in urban planning and management, investment, construction and operation of relevant facilities.

III. Sources of Data

Data on Districts are provided by Henan provincial survey organizations of social and economy. Data on basic conditions and overall level of urban public facilities in provincial and county city are collected by the Henan provincial bureau of Housing and Urban-Rural development. Data on this chapter are provided by Department of social and scientific and technological of Henan provincial bureau of statistics and Department of Service industry statistical of Henan provincial bureau of statistics.

11-1 城市社会经济主要指标

Major Social and Economic Indicators of Cities

本表价值量指标均按当年价格计算。
Data in value terms in this table are calculated at current prices.

指 标	Item	2018	2019
生产总值(亿元)	Gross Domestic Product (100 million yuan)	16835.87	21092.05
第一产业	Primary Industry	493.14	547.83
第二产业	Secondary Industry	7062.68	8659.77
第三产业	Tertiary Industry	9280.05	11884.45
一般公共预算收入(亿元)	Total Revenue of Local Governments (100 million yuan)	2002.13	2141.45
一般公共预算支出(亿元)	Total Expenditures of Local Governments (100 million yuan)	3441.20	3851.12
限额以上批发零售业商品销售总额(亿元)	Total Sales of Enterprise above Designated Size in Wholesale and Retail Sale Trades (100 million yuan)	10096.84	12082.05
当年实际使用外资金额(万美元)	Amount of Foreign Capital Actually Vtilized This Year (USD 10 000)	1145730.00	967396.00
金融机构住户存款余额(亿元)	Outstanding Amount of Savings Deposit in Urban and Rural Areas (year-end) (100 million yuan)	15498.32	17450.12
在校学生数(万人)	Student Enrollment (10 000 persons)		
普通中学	Number of Regular Secondary Schools	168.56	174.90
普通小学	Number of Primary Schools	243.63	254.54

11-2 省辖市市区社会经济主要指标(2019年)

本表价值量指标均按当年价格计算。
Data in value terms in this table are calculated at current prices.

指标	Item	郑州 Zhengzhou	开封 Kaifeng	洛阳 Luoyang	平顶山 Pingdingshan	安阳 Anyang
年底(末)户籍人口(万人)	Total Population (year-end) (10 000 persons)	397.20	171.80	209.20	111.06	119.29
城镇单位从业人员期末人数(万人)	Number of Employed Persons in Urban Area (year-end) (10 000 persons)	154.95	21.77	38.32	27.49	20.93
行政区域土地面积(平方公里)	Land Area of Administrative Area(sq.km)	1010	1816	879	443	637
#建成区面积	Developed Areas	581	177	218	73	88
生产总值(亿元)	Gross Domestic Product (100 million yuan)	7973.00	895.00	2184.00	868.00	898.00
#第二产业	Secondary Industry	2892.54	319.41	924.30	460.58	463.69
第三产业	Tertiary Industry	5060.70	506.59	1241.47	401.84	418.79
一般公共收入(亿元)	Public Financial Revenue of Local Governments (100 million yuan)	929.72	76.32	207.78	85.98	86.07
一般公共支出(亿元)	Public Financial Expenditures of Local Governments (100 million yuan)	1442.01	181.66	306.74	148.51	162.37
当年实际使用外资金额(万美元)	Amount of Foreign Capital Actually Vtilized This Year (USD 10 000)	329013	44194	176913	17693	27083
金融机构住户存款余额(亿元)	Outstanding Amount of Savings Deposit (100 million yuan)	5860.61	829.59	1875.00	899.48	693.87
在岗职工工资总额(亿元)	Total Wages of Staff and Workers (100 million yuan)	1343.22	113.43	278.27	183.87	131.00
在校学生数(万人)	Student Enrollment (10 000 persons)					
中等职业学校	Number of Vocational Secondary Schools	23.38	2.37	6.15	3.36	2.07
普通中学	Number of Regular Secondary Schools	31.84	12.06	12.47	6.88	11.37
小学	Number of Primary Schools	51.94	15.85	18.89	10.20	18.27

Major Social and Economic Indicators of Districts in Cities Directly Under the Province (2019)

鹤　壁 Hebi	新　乡 Xinxiang	焦　作 Jiaozuo	濮　阳 Puyang	许　昌 Xuchang	漯　河 Luohe	三门峡 Sanmenxia	南　阳 Nanyang	商　丘 Shangqiu	信　阳 Xinyang	周　口 Zhoukou	驻马店 Zhumadian
65.46	110.01	98.28	74.72	134.57	134.94	63.05	203.78	189.10	157.60	64.21	85.69
12.17	18.39	18.71	21.51	17.24	17.13	9.88	25.49	16.33	17.78	11.29	19.05
679	432	578	330	1099	1020	1948	2135	1797	3604	-	1365
64	126	117	64	124	-	61	160	145	103	78	95
457.00	962.00	743.00	624.00	806.00	965.00	531.00	981.00	646.00	706.00	317.00	536.00
270.15	446.97	314.69	254.66	437.75	432.19	235.63	300.71	256.29	270.92	145.98	233.33
173.50	508.80	420.56	344.80	344.65	469.40	265.87	622.46	316.03	353.84	163.74	271.42
50.52	69.59	72.76	55.86	91.23	66.64	54.01	76.56	69.69	51.84	37.76	59.15
85.71	146.46	133.11	112.80	158.43	135.33	111.56	173.60	162.67	148.31	108.53	133.32
61645	48319	21479	23072	29674	68321	51514	16747	13655	9798	17445	10831
288.15	716.54	573.97	603.80	662.92	568.02	381.77	1025.78	763.10	778.49	384.15	544.87
65.82	114.66	109.90	136.38	117.37	98.80	68.56	159.75	95.46	96.51	76.29	115.02
1.68	3.59	1.39	2.29	1.39	2.40	0.77	4.25	2.30	1.75	2.59	2.04
5.45	7.85	5.32	11.32	8.07	8.42	3.38	17.71	10.91	10.00	4.30	7.55
6.70	11.23	7.51	11.00	12.01	11.81	4.80	25.22	18.22	14.25	6.40	10.24

11–3 城市建设基本情况

Basic Statistics on City Construction

指　　标	Item	2005	2010	2015	2018	2019
城市个数(个)	Number of Cities (unit)	38	38	38	38	39
城区面积(平方公里)	Urban Area (sq.km)		4101	4810	5132	5364
建成区面积(平方公里)	Area of Built-up Districts (sq.km)	1572	2014	2503	2797	2944
年底供水综合生产能力(万立方米/日)	General Production Capacity of Tap Water Supply (year-end) (10 000 cu.m/day)	1027	1010	1121	1167	1281
全年供水总量(万立方米)	Total Annual Volume of Water Supply (10 000 cu.m)	183436	179122	196709	216305	221104
#生活用水量	Consumption of Tap Water for Residential Use		76986	87545	118543	123427
平均每人每天生活用水量(升)	Per Capita Daily Consumption of Tap Water for Residential Use (liter)	147.1	109.1	111.0	134.8	133.9
用水普及率(%)	Percentage of Population with Access to Tap Water (%)	91.9	91.0	93.1	96.7	97.4
公共交通标准运营车辆(标台)	Standard Public Vehicles Under Operation (Standard unit)	12514	18912	27355	37833	39149
出租汽车数(辆)	Taxi (unit)			61555	63398	62552
煤气家庭用量(万立方米)	Consumption of Coal Gas for Residential Use (10 000cu.m)	12735	15420	1553	23	27
天然气家庭用量(万立方米)	Consumption of Natural Gas for Residential Use (10 000cu.m)	18649	48243	109376	157916	216812
液化石油气家庭用量(吨)	Consumption of Liquefied Petroleum Gas for Residential Use (ton)	198629	201931	179752	174613	151749
燃气普及率(%)	Percentage of Population with Access to Gas (%)		73.4	86.0	96.3	97.1
集中供热面积(万平方米)	Heated Area (10 000 sq.m)	5361	10737	22375	43421	51600
道路长度(千米)	Length of Roads (km)	7090	9413	12318	14538	15766
道路面积(万平方米)	Area of Roads (10 000sq.m)	15653	21767	29915	36673	39506
排水管道长度(千米)	Length of Sewage Pipelines (km)	10201	14733	20467	25027	27932
建成区绿化覆盖面积(公顷)	Coverage Space of Green Areas Developed (hectare)	50822	73652	94345	121864	120799
建成区绿化覆盖率(%)	Coverage Rate of Green Areas Developed (%)	32.3	36.5	37.7	40.0	41.0
公园个数(个)	Number of Parks (unit)	272	262	327	443	523
公园绿地面积(公顷)	Public Green Areas (hectare)		18361	25201	31934	35361
人均公园绿地面积(平方米)	Per Capita Public Green Area (sq.m)		8.7	10.2	12.7	13.6
生活垃圾清运量(万吨)	Collection,Transport and Disposal of Consumption Wastes (10 000 tons)	754	694	892	1019	1134
生活垃圾无害化处理率(%)	Harmless Treatment Rate of Consumption Wastes (%)	58.1	82.5	96.0	99.7	99.7
城市污水排放量(亿吨)	Volume of Consumption Waste Water in Cities (100 million tons)		14.74	19.47	20.04	20.73
城市污水处理量(亿吨)	Processing Volume of Consumption Waste Water in Cities (100 million tons)		12.91	18.22	19.49	20.25
城市污水处理厂集中处理率(%)	Concentration Treatment Rate of Consumption Waste Water in Cities (%)			93.1	97.3	97.7

11-4 城市市政公用设施水平情况(2019年)

Statistics on Level of Public Facilities by City (2019)

市 City	人口密度(人/平方公里) Population Density (person/sq.km)	人均日生活用水量(升) Daily Water Consumption Per Capita (liter)	用水普及率(%) Water Coverage Rate (%)	燃气普及率(%) Gas Coverage Rate (%)	建成区供水管道密度(公里/平方公里) Built-up Areas Density of Water Pipes (km/sq.km)	人均城市道路面积(平方米) Road Surface Area Per Capita (sq.m)	建成区排水管道密度(公里/平方公里) Density of sewers in Built District (km/sq.km)	污水处理率(%) Wastewater Treatment Rate (%)
全　省 Total	**4850**	**133.88**	**97.4**	**97.1**	**8.76**	**15.19**	**8.73**	**97.7**
郑州市 Zhengzhou	8793	147.91	100.0	95.5	8.94	9.39	7.97	98.1
巩义市 Gongyi	10283	97.54	89.4	97.8	5.39	11.20	7.25	100.0
荥阳市 Xingyang	2176	170.9	96.7	95.0	8.89	19.35	8.71	96.6
新密市 Xinmi	2723	112.96	99.7	98.3	8.63	16.75	4.99	99.8
新郑市 Xinzheng	7904	165.21	90.7	100.0	10.57	16.15	7.43	96.9
登封市 Dengfeng	3296	112.5	85.0	96.2	4.93	19.47	5.16	98.8
开封市 Kaifeng	5332	144.88	97.1	99.4	14.29	20.63	8.07	95.9
洛阳市 Luoyang	7206	135.61	94.1	99.9	7.91	13.01	6.80	99.6
偃师市 Yanshi	9057	135.89	97.0	81.1	9.81	14.57	8.67	98.0
平顶山市 Pingdingshan	3495	136.27	98.8	98.4	14.60	16.47	8.37	98.3
舞钢市 Wugang	1817	116.85	98.9	97.3	6.52	20.22	13.52	91.3
汝州市 Ruzhou	3004	126.64	62.3	72.2	8.13	15.31	8.21	99.8
安阳市 Anyang	5000	206.54	100.0	99.3	9.75	19.49	14.88	98.0
林州市 Linzhou	5689	141.93	100.0	99.0	10.48	15.34	9.74	95.2
鹤壁市 Hebi	3760	84.26	98.3	98.8	9.45	20.69	8.75	96.1
新乡市 Xinxiang	5647	148.2	100.0	99.4	7.20	15.39	6.81	96.3
长垣市 Changyuan	7447	75.75	98.4	97.1	10.96	21.15	13.98	99.7
卫辉市 Weihui	3593	192.86	99.3	90.0	7.42	12.11	5.82	89.9
辉县市 Huixian	1947	187.93	99.1	99.3	17.81	12.89	12.60	93.0
焦作市 Jiaozuo	5779	132.04	99.8	98.2	8.99	17.48	9.92	99.0
沁阳市 Qinyang	4112	75.03	85.4	93.1	8.86	28.34	11.92	95.0
孟州市 Mengzhou	1353	91.32	97.3	94.5	12.80	26.97	19.05	96.1
濮阳市 Puyang	4014	186.15	98.4	98.6	14.38	16.08	11.43	96.2
许昌市 Xuchang	3046	129.99	96.8	98.9	5.10	34.09	7.59	98.0
禹州市 Yuzhou	8312	108.35	94.2	100.0	6.82	16.13	8.73	99.7
长葛市 Changge	2631	116.96	95.0	98.6	4.35	21.58	10.54	96.0
漯河市 Luohe	5799	128.42	99.8	100.0	9.92	18.30	14.43	98.1
三门峡市 Sanmenxia	6699	108.5	98.2	98.3	4.89	13.62	4.80	97.6
义马市 Yima	1515	69.55	99.6	92.9	7.50	18.38	7.25	94.5
灵宝市 Lingbao	6428	109.13	99.8	90.7	4.74	16.04	7.53	94.0
南阳市 Nanyang	2504	89.73	98.2	100.0	2.98	14.29	9.29	99.7
邓州市 Dengzhou	9813	95.42	93.5	91.2	17.99	17.51	15.10	97.5
商丘市 Shangqiu	9367	98.49	99.3	98.8	8.76	13.50	7.25	98.6
永城市 Yongcheng	5868	117.78	99.6	96.0	7.21	17.77	11.54	96.4
信阳市 Xinyang	2441	94.85	98.0	96.3	12.60	14.83	3.41	97.1
周口市 Zhoukou	4463	163.92	99.2	98.6	5.26	21.97	9.87	96.8
项城市 Xiangcheng	5117	97.87	96.7	93.5	10.22	17.76	13.01	93.5
驻马店市 Zhumadian	2786	178.63	94.1	98.0	6.27	23.39	10.06	98.8
济源市 Jiyuan	3974	149.05	100.0	100.0	9.53	19.76	8.81	98.9

11-4 续表 continued

市 City	人均公园绿地面积(平方米) Public Recreational Green Space Per Capita (sq.m)	建成区绿化覆盖率(%) Green Coverage Rate of Built-up District (%)	建成区绿地率(%) Green Space Rate of Built-up District (%)	生活垃圾无害化处理率(%) Consumption Wastes Harmless Treatment Rate (%)	建成区面积(平方公里) Built-up District Area (sq.km)
全　省 Total	**13.6**	**41.0**	**36.2**	**99.7**	2944
郑州市 Zhengzhou	14.5	41.1	36.1	100.0	581
巩义市 Gongyi	15.0	40.2	36.6	100.0	36
荥阳市 Xingyang	12.8	31.7	28.5	100.0	38
新密市 Xinmi	11.2	36.9	33.0	100.0	32
新郑市 Xinzheng	13.9	37.1	32.1	100.0	34
登封市 Dengfeng	13.7	41.6	37.1	100.0	30
开封市 Kaifeng	12.2	40.9	36.1	100.0	138
洛阳市 Luoyang	11.9	40.2	33.4	96.7	256
偃师市 Yanshi	10.6	40.2	37.1	100.0	21
平顶山市 Pingdingshan	13.1	41.6	38.0	100.0	73
舞钢市 Wugang	12.4	41.4	36.9	100.0	17
汝州市 Ruzhou	14.2	41.9	36.0	100.0	42
安阳市 Anyang	12.1	41.9	36.5	100.0	88
林州市 Linzhou	11.8	40.0	35.7	100.0	25
鹤壁市 Hebi	14.8	43.2	37.3	100.0	64
新乡市 Xinxiang	12.0	40.1	38.0	100.0	126
长垣市 Changyuan	12.1	41.0	37.1	100.0	42
卫辉市 Weihui	9.5	35.9	30.4	100.0	23
辉县市 Huixian	9.6	37.5	33.2	100.0	22
焦作市 Jiaozuo	15.1	42.0	36.6	100.0	113
沁阳市 Qinyang	9.5	36.4	31.1	100.0	21
孟州市 Mengzhou	11.2	39.5	34.7	100.0	17
濮阳市 Puyang	14.8	40.6	36.2	100.0	64
许昌市 Xuchang	15.8	41.5	36.4	100.0	112
禹州市 Yuzhou	10.9	39.8	34.4	100.0	47
长葛市 Changge	15.0	39.7	34.2	100.0	28
漯河市 Luohe	15.6	42.3	37.5	100.0	68
三门峡市 Sanmenxia	13.1	36.8	33.5	99.1	61
义马市 Yima	20.0	41.0	35.7	100.0	19
灵宝市 Lingbao	11.6	39.4	35.0	100.0	23
南阳市 Nanyang	14.3	42.3	38.1	98.6	160
邓州市 Dengzhou	10.2	40.5	38.6	100.0	38
商丘市 Shangqiu	14.4	47.1	42.1	98.5	69
永城市 Yongcheng	14.8	42.0	36.9	100.0	49
信阳市 Xinyang	14.1	44.6	38.0	100.0	103
周口市 Zhoukou	13.9	39.0	34.0	100.0	78
项城市 Xiangcheng	12.0	38.4	34.7	100.0	37
驻马店市 Zhumadian	15.3	45.1	39.3	100.0	95
济源市 Jiyuan	13.0	42.1	37.8	100.0	55

11-5 城市供、排水情况(2019年)

Basic Statistics on Tap Water Supply and Drainage in Cities (2019)

市 City	综合生产能力(万立方米/日) Production Capacity of Tap Water Supply (10 000 cu.m/day)	供水管道长度(公里) Length of Water Supply Pipelines (km)	供水总量(万立方米) Total Volume of Water Supply (10 000 cu.m)	居民家庭用水 Water for use	用水人口(万人) Number of Residents with Access to Tap Water (10000person)	污水排放量(万立方米) Volume of Sewage Drainage (10 000 cu.m)
全省 Total	**1282**	**27811**	**221104**	**95183**	**2533.4**	**207300**
郑州市 Zhengzhou	207	5258	45647	24195	670.4	44310
巩义市 Gongyi	7	192	1936	731	33.1	1363
荥阳市 Xingyang	4	379	2252	1012	19.4	2236
新密市 Xinmi	7	274	1475	876	21.2	1340
新郑市 Xinzheng	16	401	1768	1073	24.6	1506
登封市 Dengfeng	4	241	1169	475	16.5	980
开封市 Kaifeng	64	1974	11862	4046	99.5	11198
洛阳市 Luoyang	103	2021	17450	7135	224.7	17401
偃师市 Yanshi	4	208	1292	815	18.5	1136
平顶山市 Pingdingshan	70	1245	10919	4449	89.8	14029
舞钢市 Wugang	7	148	1393	447	12.2	975
汝州市 Ruzhou	19	339	1978	1088	25.6	1799
安阳市 Anyang	90	858	10585	4376	76.5	8236
林州市 Linzhou	12	283	1470	1002	21.6	1202
鹤壁市 Hebi	33	606	5085	1482	48.2	4184
新乡市 Xinxiang	51	924	10242	4277	79.1	9013
长垣市 Changyuan	7	463	1929	715	31.5	1524
卫辉市 Weihui	15	192	2111	914	16.1	1515
辉县市 Huixian	15	464	2466	976	22.5	2283
焦作市 Jiaozuo	90	1160	8397	3272	80.8	8359
沁阳市 Qinyang	8	191	602	267	11.9	600
孟州市 Mengzhou	5	238	885	394	14.9	797
濮阳市 Puyang	49	920	7579	3201	60.6	6316
许昌市 Xuchang	34	571	5111	2653	56.0	4542
禹州市 Yuzhou	14	353	2472	1549	40.9	1860
长葛市 Changge	16	218	1872	549	18.9	1685
漯河市 Luohe	42	679	6523	2029	61.8	6500
三门峡市 Sanmenxia	20	314	3254	1582	48.0	3580
义马市 Yima	15	156	1748	297	16.9	1442
灵宝市 Lingbao	11	163	2364	597	18.6	2105
南阳市 Nanyang	68	1394	10477	3838	157.6	9711
邓州市 Dengzhou	15	684	2379	1080	36.7	2141
商丘市 Shangqiu	41	672	6773	3310	95.8	6150
永城市 Yongcheng	13	351	3257	1656	47.5	2755
信阳市 Xinyang	26	1301	4678	2149	62.1	4218
周口市 Zhoukou	24	408	5599	1875	44.3	5346
项城市 Xiangcheng	9	411	2865	925	29.7	2260
驻马店市 Zhumadian	24	608	7454	2386	48.5	7302
济源市 Jiyuan	26	550	3785	1489	31.0	3402

11-6 城市天然气、石油液化气供应情况(2019年)
Basic Statistics on Supply of Natural Gas and Liquefied Gas in Cities (2019)

市	City	天然气 Natural Gas 供气管道长度(公里) Length of Gas Supply Pipelines (km)	供气总量合计(万立方米) Volume of Gas Supply (10 000 cu.m)	#居民家庭 Households	用气人口(万人) Population with Access to Gas (10 000person)	天然气汽车加气站(座) Natural Gas Station (unite)	液化气 Liquefied Gas 供气总量合计(吨) Volume of Gas Supply (ton)	#居民家庭 Households	用气人口(万人) Population with Access to Gas (10 000person)
全省	**Total**	**29203.85**	**601761**	**216813**	**2106.66**	**196**	**176726**	**151749**	**417.98**
郑州市	Zhengzhou	6182.92	163175	43206	559.69	14	12552	7012	80.55
巩义市	Gongyi	779.60	20653	1800	30.20	2	5850	3100	6.00
荥阳市	Xingyang	240.62	3489	2977	15.00	2	3100	2600	4.10
新密市	Xinmi	424.39	6752	2528	19.00	2	650	646	1.94
新郑市	Xinzheng	259.84	10680	2822	21.11	3	3742	2000	6.00
登封市	Dengfeng	454.00	8214	672	12.64	3	5005	5000	6.00
开封市	Kaifeng	1662.94	18516	6148	90.88	20	26650	25600	10.95
洛阳市	Luoyang	637.36	62395	34971	216.50	15	14892	14880	22.10
偃师市	Yanshi	42.73	1486	1292	11.42	1	1021	1016	4.00
平顶山市	Pingdingshan	520.99	14928	7897	89.43	10			
舞钢市	Wugang	93.78	961	681	12.02	2			
汝州市	Ruzhou	384.95	3418	1483	27.60		2000	1200	2.00
安阳市	Anyang	1950.10	48569	12306	71.64	3	5710	2504	4.32
林州市	Linzhou	581.19	3489	2921	19.51	1	811	808	1.89
鹤壁市	Hebi	548.44	7800	5500	46.00	7	1000	995	2.47
新乡市	Xinxiang	2182.38	25784	12664	76.56	7	1280	1180	2.03
长垣市	Changyuan	317.00	3134	2592	26.38	3	2560	2555	4.70
卫辉市	Weihui	198.67	2928	1390	13.30	4	1065	1060	1.25
辉县市	Huixian	207.25	7120	3220	17.43	3	1020	1010	5.10
焦作市	Jiaozuo	1786.64	27395	6895	79.46				
沁阳市	Qinyang	470.00	3548	993	10.87	1	1440	550	2.15
孟州市	Mengzhou	190.00	2160	1646	14.50	1			
濮阳市	Puyang	465.18	8452	5087	60.79	21			
许昌市	Xuchang	531.26	14131	7973	55.23	9	8470	3832	2.00
禹州市	Yuzhou	184.10	12600	3082	22.96	2	5055	5015	20.48
长葛市	Changge	350.00	20801	1205	8.10	1	6800	6200	11.50
漯河市	Luohe	379.70	3855	2623	36.00	4	7765	7751	25.95
三门峡市	Sanmenxia	286.29	12892	1052	29.37	2	3449	3161	18.70
义马市	Yima	126.50	876	350	11.98		1240	1228	3.78
灵宝市	Lingbao	259.24	2662	571	13.80		680	650	3.10
南阳市	Nanyang	2226.50	12761	8725	127.44	17	10873	10848	32.96
邓州市	Dengzhou	104.53	605	524	8.24	4	5029	4920	27.54
商丘市	Shangqiu	860.89	12089	6038	57.55	2	13005	13000	37.73
永城市	Yongcheng	285.99	3339	1346	28.40	8	4030	3810	17.37
信阳市	Xinyang	817.19	16752	5791	43.19	15	8680	6780	17.82
周口市	Zhoukou	848.19	8333	5896	29.97	3	4600	4600	14.05
项城市	Xiangcheng	270.35	2080	1450	19.70	1	2310	2280	9.00
驻马店市	Zhumadian	735.50	7510	4572	42.08		3959	3959	8.45
济源市	Jiyuan	356.65	15430	3924	30.72	3	433		

11-7 城市道路、园林和绿化情况(2019年)

Basic Statistics on Road, Botanical Garden and Green Coverage Area in Cities (2019)

市 City	道路长度(公里) Length of Road (km)	道路面积(万平方米) Road Area (10000sq.m)	道路照明灯盏数(盏) Number of Road Lamp (unit)	绿化覆盖面积(公顷) Green Coverage Area (hectare)	#建成区 Built-up Areas	园林绿地面积(公顷) Botanical Garden Areas (hectare)	公园绿地面积(公顷) Public Green Areas (hectare)	公园个数(个) Number of Parks (unit)
全省 Total	**15766.52**	**39506**	**1038579**	**131448**	**120800**	**115269**	**35362**	**523**
郑州市 Zhengzhou	2273.77	6297	110977	26795	23839	23194	9704	181
巩义市 Gongyi	144.00	414	17287	1468	1433	1337	554	3
荥阳市 Xingyang	171.59	389	11800	1226	1220	1095	257	4
新密市 Xinmi	131.15	357	14871	1172	1171	1055	238	5
新郑市 Xinzheng	139.93	438	9103	1266	1265	1104	377	13
登封市 Dengfeng	179.54	377	11109	1435	1257	1200	265	9
开封市 Kaifeng	755.97	2115	42666	6790	5653	5709	1251	14
洛阳市 Luoyang	952.00	3107	82595	10269	10261	8534	2836	20
偃师市 Yanshi	141.43	277	16052	846	843	786	201	5
平顶山市 Pingdingshan	408.21	1497	65866	3307	3055	2993	1186	16
舞钢市 Wugang	129.16	250	3351	738	696	655	154	2
汝州市 Ruzhou	273.70	628	9548	1759	1744	1501	583	12
安阳市 Anyang	597.21	1491	39265	3752	3687	3238	925	12
林州市 Linzhou	173.11	332	28710	1088	1008	941	255	2
鹤壁市 Hebi	462.80	1015	22254	2845	2771	2507	727	10
新乡市 Xinxiang	562.88	1217	33983	5069	5067	4803	950	17
长垣市 Changyuan	350.42	677	17149	1798	1727	1573	387	9
卫辉市 Weihui	97.50	196	8095	833	823	707	154	2
辉县市 Huixian	128.55	292	9254	851	840	752	217	10
焦作市 Jiaozuo	593.56	1415	26363	4763	4759	4144	1218	16
沁阳市 Qinyang	185.18	396	8654	781	765	668	133	5
孟州市 Mengzhou	119.00	414	12140	665	664	587	172	2
濮阳市 Puyang	430.54	991	34400	2689	2598	2522	913	10
许昌市 Xuchang	592.01	1973	47505	4753	4652	4233	911	9
禹州市 Yuzhou	366.42	701	25194	2099	1849	1711	472	4
长葛市 Changge	198.58	429	10377	1112	1096	956	298	3
漯河市 Luohe	543.20	1134	29568	3123	2894	2589	965	13
三门峡市 Sanmenxia	321.27	666	32089	2316	2252	2106	640	7
义马市 Yima	142.70	312	4770	796	765	685	339	4
灵宝市 Lingbao	102.37	299	6443	921	905	813	217	1
南阳市 Nanyang	1320.19	2293	38359	9100	6758	8423	2289	16
邓州市 Dengzhou	262.32	687	22368	1820	1540	1648	400	6
商丘市 Shangqiu	502.06	1302	49966	3300	3250	2921	1393	42
永城市 Yongcheng	355.73	848	15099	2169	2043	1889	708	10
信阳市 Xinyang	433.72	939	28681	5893	4607	5111	896	6
周口市 Zhoukou	311.45	981	36991	3631	3025	3418	620	8
项城市 Xiangcheng	287.37	545	8388	1484	1405	1294	367	3
驻马店市 Zhumadian	381.13	1206	24512	4300	4288	3740	786	4
济源市 Jiyuan	244.80	613	22777	2429	2329	2126	402	8

11-8 城市市容环境卫生情况(2019年)
Basic Statistics on Urban Sanitation in Cities (2019)

市 City	排水管道长度(公里) Length of Drainage Pipelines (km)	污水处理总量(万立方米) Volume of Sewage Treatment (10 000 cu.m)	道路清扫保洁面积(万平方米) Road Area Under Cleaning Program (10 000 sq.m)	生活垃圾 Living Garbage 清运量(万吨) Volume of Disposal (10 000 tons)	无害化处理量(万吨) Volume of Harmless Treatment (10 000 tons)	公共厕所(座) Number of Public Lavatories (unit)	市容环卫专用车辆设备总数(辆) Number of Special Vehicles for Enviromental Sanitation (unit)
全 省 Total	**27933**	**202547**	**42347**	**1134.58**	**1130.65**	**10675**	**18258**
郑 州 市 Zhengzhou	4790	43447	6297	268.90	268.90	1903	7694
巩 义 市 Gongyi	270	1363	568	10.26	10.26	52	122
荥 阳 市 Xingyang	403	2159	489	16.26	16.26	60	134
新 密 市 Xinmi	162	1338	498	12.84	12.84	125	150
新 郑 市 Xinzheng	270	1459	603	8.11	8.11	158	219
登 封 市 Dengfeng	252	968	438	17.20	17.20	79	61
开 封 市 Kaifeng	1152	10739	1949	43.52	43.52	932	599
洛 阳 市 Luoyang	2436	17322	3124	70.06	67.71	884	1073
偃 师 市 Yanshi	182	1112	402	8.14	8.14	60	44
平 顶 山 市 Pingdingshan	710	13794	1186	36.42	36.42	400	555
舞 钢 市 Wugang	227	890	195	5.37	5.37	78	58
汝 州 市 Ruzhou	366	1796	725	13.80	13.80	82	177
安 阳 市 Anyang	1310	8074	1491	32.88	32.88	466	654
林 州 市 Linzhou	267	1145	464	14.08	14.08	97	75
鹤 壁 市 Hebi	621	4018	959	21.58	21.58	168	308
新 乡 市 Xinxiang	1061	8679	1741	51.81	51.81	542	702
长 垣 市 Changyuan	600	1518	1008	21.02	21.02	55	100
卫 辉 市 Weihui	143	1362	279	7.28	7.28	6	157
辉 县 市 Huixian	282	2123	419	25.89	25.89	54	97
焦 作 市 Jiaozuo	1124	8275	1671	28.97	28.97	175	286
沁 阳 市 Qinyang	250	570	383	6.93	6.93	43	96
孟 州 市 Mengzhou	339	766	367	5.46	5.46	34	36
濮 阳 市 Puyang	761	6076	1387	33.08	33.08	154	259
许 昌 市 Xuchang	1015	4453	1784	36.12	36.12	447	464
禹 州 市 Yuzhou	517	1855	630	12.97	12.97	80	114
长 葛 市 Changge	291	1617	475	7.95	7.95	57	50
漯 河 市 Luohe	1017	6375	1400	27.23	27.23	387	158
三 门 峡 市 Sanmenxia	293	3494	462	16.16	16.01	212	99
义 马 市 Yima	135	1363	249	5.66	5.66	54	63
灵 宝 市 Lingbao	181	1979	441	8.76	8.76	65	64
南 阳 市 Nanyang	1571	9650	2256	56.63	55.85	652	716
邓 州 市 Dengzhou	574	2086	641	12.78	12.78	148	151
商 丘 市 Shangqiu	579	6063	1950	43.02	42.37	610	1393
永 城 市 Yongcheng	627	2655	799	17.02	17.02	131	89
信 阳 市 Xinyang	357	4095	895	42.39	42.39	367	252
周 口 市 Zhoukou	778	5175	779	21.28	21.28	228	264
项 城 市 Xiangcheng	532	2114	549	11.25	11.25	92	60
驻 马 店 市 Zhumadian	957	7214	1805	36.67	36.67	427	510
济 源 市 Jiyuan	529	3365	589	18.83	18.83	111	155

主要统计指标解释

城区面积 包括：市本级（1）街道办事处所辖地域；（2）城市公共设施、居住设施和市政公用设施等连接到的其他镇（乡）地域；（3）常住人口在3000人以上独立的工矿区、开发区、科研单位、大专院校等特殊区域。

建成区面积 城市行政区内实际已成片开发建设、市政公用设施和公共设施基本具备的区域。对核心城市，它包括集中连片的部分以及分散的若干个已经成片建设起来，市政公用设施和公共设施基本具备的地区；对一城多镇来说，它包括由几个连片开发建设起来的，市政公用设施和公共设施基本具备的地区组成。因此建成区范围，一般是指建成区外轮廓线所能包括的地区，也就是这个城市实际建设用地所达到的范围。

供水总量 指报告期供水企业（单位）供出的全部水量。包括有效供水量和漏损水量。

有效供水量指水厂将水供出厂外后，各类用户实际使用到的水量。包括售水量和免费供水量。

城市燃气 指符合《城镇燃气设计规范》的规定，供城市生产和生活作燃料使用的天然气、人工煤气和液化石油气等气体能源的统称。

供气总量 指报告期燃气企业（单位）向用户供应的燃气数量。包括销售量和损失量

集中供热面积 指从一个或多个热源通过热网向城市的热用户供给生产和生活热能，供热企业（单位）向城市各类房屋建筑物、构筑物及其附属设施供热的全部建筑面积。

道路长度 指道路长度和与道路相通的桥梁、隧道的长度，按车行道中心线计算。

道路面积 指道路实际铺装面积和与道路相通的广场、桥梁、隧道的铺装面积（统计时，将人行道面积单独统计）。

人行道面积按道路两侧面积相加计算，包括步行街和广场，不含人车混行的道路。

排水管道长度 指所有排水总管、干管、支管、检查井及连接井进出口等长度之和。计算时应按单管计算，即在同一条街道上如有两条或两条以上并排的排水管道时，应按每条排水管道的长度相加计算。

污水排放总量 指生活污水、工业废水的排放总量，包括从排水管道和排水沟（渠）排出的污水量。

污水处理量 指污水处理厂（或污水处理装置）实际处理的污水量。包括物理处理量、生物处理量和化学处理量。

其中处理本市（县）外，指污水处理厂作为区域设施，不仅处理本市（县）的污水，还处理本市（县）以外其他市、县或乡镇等的污水。这部分污水处理量单独统计，并在计算本市（县）的污水处理率时扣除。

公园绿地面积 城市中向公众开放的、以游憩为主要功能，有一定的游憩设施和服务设施，同时兼有健全生态、美化景观、防灾减灾等综合作用的绿化用地。它是城市建设用地、城市绿地系统和城市市政公用设施的重要组成部分。

生活垃圾清运量 指报告期内收集和运送到各生活垃圾处理厂(场)和生活垃圾最终消纳点的生活垃圾数量。生活垃圾指城市日常生活或为城市日常生活提供服务的活动中产生的固体废物以及法律行政规定的视为城市生活垃圾的固体废物。包括：居民生活垃圾、商业垃圾、集市贸易市场垃圾、街道清扫垃圾、公共场所垃圾和机关、学校、厂矿等单位的生活垃圾。

生活垃圾处理量 指报告期内简易处理场和各种生活垃圾无害化处理场（厂）处理生活垃圾总量。生活垃圾简易处理量指生活垃圾简易处理场所处理的生活垃圾总量。生活垃圾无害化处理量指生活垃圾无害化处理场（厂）所处理的生活垃圾总量。

Explanatory Notes on Main Statistical Indicators

City Area include three parts:(1), area under the jurisdiction of the street agency;(2), urban public facilities, residential facilities and municipal public facilities connected to other towns area, (3) Independent industrial and mining district, development area, scientific research units, colleges and other special areas with over 3000 resident population.

Area of Built Districts refers to the Urban area that already development and construction and have public facilities. Core cities include focused even dispersion of parts, as well as several have film build up, the urban areas of basic public infrastructure and public facilities; on more than one city, town, it included several continuous development and construction, municipal and public facilities and public areas with basic facilities. Scope of the built-up area, generally refer to the built-up areas can include outer contour line, which is achieved by the actual construction of the city's range.

Volume of Water Supply refers to the total volume of water supplied by water-works (units) during the reference period, including both the effective water supply and loss during the water supply.

Available water supply refers to all kinds of users actually use water volume after water plant form water factory. Includes water sale and free water.

City gas refers to supply to urban for production and daily life, such as natural gas, manufactured gas and LPG gas energy collectively.

Volume of gas supply refers to Volume of gas supply for household by gas enterprises in reference period. Including sales and the amount of loss.

Central heating Area refers to supply to user Production and life heat energy us heat net from one or more Means from one or more sources of heat, all heat area of urban housing buildings, structures and their ancillary equipment by Heating enterprise (units).

Road length refers to the length of roads with paved surface including bridges and tunnels connected with roads. Length of the roads is measured by the central lines for vehicles for paved roads.

Road area refers to actual pavement area and with a road paving of squares, bridges, tunnels area (statistics, sidewalk area separate statistics). The sidewalk area are calculated on add of both sides area, including walking Street and square, does not contain mixed line of road vehicles and pedestrians.

Length of Urban Sewage Pipes refers to the total length of general drainage, trunks, branch and inspection wells, connection wells, inlets and outlets, etc. if there are two or more than two side-by-side in a street pipes, length of pipes should be Calculated by adding length.

Volume of waste water discharge refers to Sewage and industrial waste water, include sewer and drain (drainage) discharge of waste water.

Treatment capacity Sewage treatment plant (or sewage treatment plant) the actual amount of sewage treatment. Including physical treatment, biological treatment and chemical treatment. Which deal with the city (County), sewage treatment plants as a regional facility, not only dealing with the city (County) of sewage, also deals with the city (County), such as cities, counties or towns other than water. This portion of the amount of sewage to individual statistics and in the calculation of the city (County) when the sewage treatment rate of deduction.

Park Green Area refers to green areas open to the public for amusement and rest with the facilities of amusement, rest and services. Its function includes perfecting ecology, beautifying landscape, and preventing and reducing disaster. Park green areas include comprehensive park, community park, topic park, belt-shaped park and green area nearby street. Total areas of comprehensive park, topic park and belt-shaped is the area of park.

Consumption Wastes Transported refers to volume of consumption wastes collected and transported to disposal factories or sites. Consumption wastes are solid wastes produced from urban households or from service activities for urban households, and solid wastes regarded by laws and regulations as urban consumption wastes, including those from households, commercial activities, markets, cleaning of streets, public sites, offices, schools, factories, mining units and other sources.

Volume of consumption Wastes treatment refers to Volume of consumption Wastes Simple processing and consumption wastes treated in the reporting period.

农业
Agriculture

12

● 资料整理：郑宝卫　郑　洁　樊福顺　金民伟　王　思

简要说明

一、主要内容

本篇包括我省农业生产和农村经济的基本情况，内容主要包括耕地、农业机械拥有量、农林牧渔业增加值、农作物播种面积、主要农产品及畜禽产品产量、水利设施与除涝治水等方面的统计资料。

二、统计范围

统计范围包括农村各种经济组织和农户经营的农林牧渔业生产活动；各种专业性农、林、牧、渔场的农业生产活动；国家各级机关、团体、学校、部队进行的农业生产活动；集体所有制的乡、镇、村办农场的农业生产活动；以及工矿企业经营的农、林、牧、渔业生产活动。

根据第三次全国农业普查结果，按照国际惯例，对2007年以后农业、畜牧业及农林牧渔业总产值增加值等数据进行了修订。具体修订情况见相关表的标注。2010年以后的农业、林业增加值数据是按照国家统计局制定的新《统计用产品分类目录》进行了调整。

三、资料来源

全省粮食作物播种面积及产量由国家统计局河南调查总队农业调查处编辑整理；市级粮食作物播种面积及产量由河南省地方经济社会调查队产量处编辑整理；农村基本情况、农林牧渔业增加值、经济作物播种面积及产量等由河南省统计局农业农村处编辑整理；畜牧业生产情况由国家统计局河南调查总队农村调查处和河南省统计局农业农村处编辑整理；林业生产情况、渔业生产情况、耕地面积、灌溉、水库和除涝、治水资料，农业机械拥有情况及农机化作业情况、农村基层组织情况等由河南省统计局农业农村处根据河南省林业局、河南省农业农村厅水产局、河南省自然资源厅、河南省水利厅、河南省农业机械技术中心等部门提供的资料整理编辑。

Brief Introduction

I. Main Contents

The data in this chapter show the basic conditions of agricultural production and rural economy, including mainly cultivated number of rural employed persons, land, quantity of agricultural machinery, value-added of agriculture, forestry, animal husbandry and fishery, sown areas of farm crops, output of major products and livestock, facilities of water conservancy and efforts to eliminate water-logging and combat alkalinity, productive fixed assets owned by rural households.

II. Scope of Statistics

Statistics on agriculture cover in agriculture statistics are production activities in agriculture, forestry, animal husbandry and fishery undertaken by rural economic units of various types and by rural households; production activities of farms specializing in agriculture, forestry, animal husbandry and fishery; production activities in agriculture undertaken by government agencies, institutions, schools and military units; production activities in agriculture undertaken by collective farms run by townships and villages; and production activities in agriculture, forestry, animal husbandry and fishery undertaken by manufacturing and mining enterprises.

Data on value-added of agriculture, forestry, animal husbandry and fishery and production of agriculture and animal husbandry in 2006 have been reflected basis on the second agricultural census. Data on value-added of agriculture and forestry since 2010 are adjusted according to the new classified catalogue of statistics product which formulated by NBS.

III. Sources of Data

The sown area and yield of grain crops in the whole province are edited and sorted out by the agricultural investigation department of Henan survey team of National Bureau of statistics; the sown area and output of municipal grain crops are edited and sorted out by the production department of Henan local economic and social investigation team; the basic rural information, added value of agriculture, forestry, animal husbandry and fishery, planting area and yield of economic crops are edited and sorted out by agricultural and rural Department of Henan Provincial Bureau of statistics; animal husbandry The situation of agricultural production is compiled and arranged by the rural investigation department of Henan investigation team of National Bureau of statistics and the agricultural and rural Department of Henan Provincial Bureau of statistics; the data of forestry production, fishery production, cultivated land area, irrigation, reservoir and waterlogging control, agricultural machinery ownership and agricultural mechanization, rural grass-roots organizations, etc. are compiled and sorted out by the agricultural and rural Department of Henan Provincial Bureau of statistics according to the forestry of Henan Province Materials provided by Industry Bureau, Fishery Bureau of Henan agricultural and rural department, natural resources department of Henan Province, water resources department of Henan Province, agricultural machinery technology center of Henan Province.

12-1 农林牧渔业总产值

Gross Output Value of Agriculture, Forestry, Animal Husbandry and Fishery

本表数据为当年价。
Data in this table are calculated at current prices.

单位：亿元 (100 million yuan)

年 份 Year	农林牧渔业 Agriculture, Forestry, Animal Husbandry and Fishery	农 业 Agriculture	林 业 Forestry	牧 业 Animal Husbandry	渔 业 Fishery	农林牧渔专业及辅助性活动 Service for Agriculture, Forestry, Animal Husbandry and Fishery and Auxiliary
1978	95.38	81.74	2.58	10.87	0.19	
1980	134.62	113.17	3.88	17.28	0.29	
1985	241.54	188.79	10.29	41.19	1.27	
1990	502.01	372.19	20.77	105.17	3.88	
1995	1304.25	865.82	38.32	391.08	9.03	
2000	1981.54	1264.29	56.18	641.56	19.51	
2005	3309.70	1790.37	83.92	1251.65	35.26	148.50
2010	5619.70	3504.07	115.29	1733.07	66.30	200.96
2011	6055.54	3553.25	127.32	2088.14	66.33	220.50
2012	6473.70	3897.46	140.85	2120.56	77.59	237.23
2013	6938.24	4126.25	152.35	2313.49	82.50	263.65
2014	7244.34	4399.17	152.40	2307.23	91.07	294.47
2015	7299.58	4503.71	134.28	2229.01	105.20	327.38
2016	7405.42	4459.29	121.28	2355.99	107.27	361.59
2017	7562.53	4552.68	128.88	2368.92	107.79	404.26
2018	7757.94	4825.97	136.98	2210.88	119.28	464.83
2019	8541.77	5408.59	140.76	2316.50	118.16	557.76
省辖市 City						
郑州市 Zhengzhou	234.56	152.86	4.48	54.83	10.67	11.71
开封市 Kaifeng	601.95	381.13	5.20	165.87	6.50	43.26
洛阳市 Luoyang	466.81	285.25	17.11	114.77	5.28	44.40
平顶山市 Pingdingshan	330.12	180.44	5.36	120.88	3.46	19.98
安阳市 Anyang	367.39	255.64	4.00	85.29	0.73	21.72
鹤壁市 Hebi	121.00	45.27	1.72	63.88	0.90	9.23
新乡市 Xinxiang	428.76	263.23	3.70	135.78	4.54	21.52
焦作市 Jiaozuo	280.84	187.81	2.92	60.93	0.85	28.34
濮阳市 Puyang	364.71	212.17	3.55	105.43	2.33	41.24
许昌市 Xuchang	295.72	154.29	2.91	112.56	1.53	24.43
漯河市 Luohe	240.93	123.91	1.63	105.60	1.69	8.10
三门峡市 Sanmenxia	245.67	188.00	16.65	35.90	1.38	3.74
南阳市 Nanyang	1012.15	692.69	27.10	246.83	11.14	34.39
商丘市 Shangqiu	771.37	531.82	10.53	187.89	5.24	35.89
信阳市 Xinyang	945.51	630.23	20.80	178.14	41.86	74.48
周口市 Zhoukou	926.16	612.36	4.17	235.18	4.15	70.30
驻马店市 Zhumadian	867.14	493.51	7.27	288.86	13.52	63.98
济源市 Jiyuan	40.98	18.00	1.66	17.89	2.38	1.05
省直管县 County Directly Administrated by Province						
巩义市 Gongyi	24.58	9.35	1.17	9.33	0.63	4.11
兰考县 Lankao	101.56	53.41	1.99	37.85	1.41	6.90
汝州市 Ruzhou	72.91	28.19	1.31	37.91	0.30	5.20
滑县 Huaxian	130.69	97.71	0.27	24.37	0.04	8.29
长垣市 Changyuan	75.04	53.29	0.81	17.20	0.62	3.13
邓州市 Dengzhou	183.31	110.95	0.52	59.19	1.03	11.63
永城市 Yongcheng	147.37	100.32	2.32	37.00	1.08	6.66
固始县 Gushi	141.58	81.73	2.12	49.44	5.79	2.50
鹿邑县 Luyi	118.08	82.47	0.52	25.34	0.63	9.12
新蔡县 Xincai	98.39	59.10	1.03	31.31	1.70	5.26

12-2 农林牧渔业总产值指数(上年=100)

Gross Output Value and Related Indices of Agriculture, Forestry, Animal Husbandry and Fishery (Preceding year=100)

本表数据按可比价格计算。
Data in this table are calculated at comparable prices.

年 份 Year	农林牧渔业 Agriculture, Forestry, Animal Husbandry and Fishery	农 业 Agriculture	林 业 Forestry	牧 业 Animal Husbandry	渔 业 Fishery	农林牧渔专业及辅助性活动 Service for Agriculture, Forestry, Animal Husbandry and Fishery and Auxiliary
1978	109.6	110.2	109.7	105.3	100.7	
1980	105.0	106.4	117.9	93.7	114.0	
1985	104.3	98.8	119.3	143.6	130.5	
1990	107.8	107.0	105.0	111.9	119.8	
1995	117.6	113.3	106.1	128.5	115.3	
2000	105.4	104.2	105.6	107.2	112.1	
2005	107.5	107.7	104.7	107.6	122.5	104.0
2010	104.6	104.3	104.5	105.0	107.5	105.0
2011	103.8	104.3	107.1	102.2	107.2	105.5
2012	104.5	104.2	104.9	104.6	105.8	106.0
2013	104.4	104.1	107.0	104.1	106.5	108.9
2014	104.2	103.9	104.8	104.1	107.8	109.5
2015	104.6	105.6	101.7	102.2	110.5	109.7
2016	104.5	105.3	105.1	102.2	106.1	109.7
2017	104.5	105.0	106.3	102.5	106.4	109.9
2018	103.9	103.6	107.4	102.4	106.0	115.0
2019	103.0	105.2	105.9	94.8	109.9	111.7
省 辖 市 City						
郑 州 市 Zhengzhou	95.8	100.0	76.7	83.1	96.1	114.8
开 封 市 Kaifeng	103.6	117.3	89.0	77.0	79.3	103.9
洛 阳 市 Luoyang	104.0	104.9	105.0	100.5	105.7	107.1
平 顶 山 市 Pingdingshan	102.5	102.9	77.8	103.4	102.9	107.7
安 阳 市 Anyang	98.1	98.9	100.6	93.8	98.1	106.2
鹤 壁 市 Hebi	103.7	104.1	107.0	102.3	105.0	114.0
新 乡 市 Xinxiang	103.4	107.3	78.7	96.4	89.7	112.8
焦 作 市 Jiaozuo	104.2	107.8	56.9	101.8	97.6	103.0
濮 阳 市 Puyang	103.8	115.6	90.5	82.8	103.8	106.5
许 昌 市 Xuchang	102.5	105.9	108.9	94.9	110.2	113.0
漯 河 市 Luohe	102.7	108.5	116.9	93.9	118.5	108.0
三 门 峡 市 Sanmenxia	104.0	104.4	199.7	90.8	80.3	116.6
南 阳 市 Nanyang	103.5	104.0	107.6	99.9	107.1	117.7
商 丘 市 Shangqiu	102.7	106.2	106.2	92.7	76.1	114.6
信 阳 市 Xinyang	103.2	105.4	104.1	93.2	105.4	119.0
周 口 市 Zhoukou	103.1	107.1	40.5	94.5	84.7	113.6
驻 马 店 市 Zhumadian	103.0	108.7	123.5	91.5	102.6	116.5
济 源 市 Jiyuan	104.2	103.8	120.7	101.7	105.6	118.7
省 直 管 县 County Directly Administrated by Province						
巩 义 市 Gongyi	98.3	103.5	116.3	87.9	110.7	109.0
兰 考 县 Lankao	103.0	102.6	102.2	102.4	102.1	108.1
汝 州 市 Ruzhou	102.5	105.8	36.6	106.8	108.7	106.9
滑 县 Huaxian	102.5	101.1	65.2	108.9	81.7	104.5
长 垣 市 Changyuan	103.4	104.7	43.7	105.3	104.6	113.0
邓 州 市 Dengzhou	102.1	105.2	111.9	92.3	109.4	118.9
永 城 市 Yongcheng	104.1	103.8	107.8	103.0	109.3	114.5
固 始 县 Gushi	103.2	105.4	102.4	98.4	106.5	108.0
鹿 邑 县 Luyi	103.9	103.4	101.2	102.1	103.4	114.6
新 蔡 县 Xincai	103.8	103.2	105.0	103.2	105.2	114.1

12-3 农林牧渔业增加值

Value-Added of Agriculture, Forestry, Animal Husbandry and Fishery

本表数据为当年价。
Data in this table are calculated at current prices.

单位：亿元 (100 million yuan)

年份 Year	农林牧渔业 Agriculture, Forestry, Animal Husbandry and Fishery	农业 Agriculture	林业 Forestry	牧业 Animal Husbandry	渔业 Fishery	农林牧渔专业及辅助性活动 Service for Agriculture, Forestry, Animal Husbandry and Fishery and Auxiliary
1985	173.43	139.96	9.19	23.07	1.21	
1990	325.77	251.82	16.61	54.08	3.26	
1995	762.99	512.10	28.55	215.85	6.49	
2000	1160.22	751.03	41.72	353.77	13.70	
2005	1892.01	1068.85	51.19	699.67	24.33	47.96
2010	3192.82	2053.47	69.49	958.84	45.34	65.68
2011	3421.09	2074.29	76.50	1153.18	45.29	71.84
2012	3654.20	2270.35	84.93	1168.97	52.90	77.05
2013	3913.47	2401.96	91.86	1277.03	56.35	86.27
2014	4089.88	2558.88	91.89	1275.14	62.32	101.66
2015	4154.41	2625.48	84.40	1233.56	72.12	138.85
2016	4217.40	2606.00	79.11	1305.65	72.89	153.75
2017	4310.55	2665.72	84.39	1316.03	73.14	171.26
2018	4500.54	2858.94	88.13	1282.12	81.26	190.08
2019	4860.38	3101.69	68.46	1382.96	82.29	224.98
省辖市 City						
郑州市 Zhengzhou	147.88	92.92	1.60	40.91	5.45	7.00
开封市 Kaifeng	329.35	212.36	2.39	100.62	2.87	11.11
洛阳市 Luoyang	269.72	166.13	7.89	67.50	3.62	24.59
平顶山市 Pingdingshan	181.43	94.08	2.73	74.71	2.15	7.77
安阳市 Anyang	207.99	142.49	1.46	53.64	0.41	9.99
鹤壁市 Hebi	67.62	25.51	0.70	37.00	0.62	3.79
新乡市 Xinxiang	259.89	159.86	1.72	88.90	3.13	6.27
焦作市 Jiaozuo	155.34	106.91	1.37	41.01	0.49	5.56
濮阳市 Puyang	207.03	121.60	1.61	68.33	1.58	13.91
许昌市 Xuchang	170.92	93.77	1.43	65.95	1.13	8.64
漯河市 Luohe	140.23	68.00	0.76	68.02	1.02	2.43
三门峡市 Sanmenxia	137.88	107.84	8.13	19.19	1.02	1.70
南阳市 Nanyang	580.93	413.89	13.77	134.35	7.45	11.46
商丘市 Shangqiu	441.01	322.87	5.49	96.66	3.91	12.09
信阳市 Xinyang	540.00	354.30	11.72	97.76	33.93	42.29
周口市 Zhoukou	507.28	329.43	1.72	140.37	3.00	32.75
驻马店市 Zhumadian	491.05	279.85	3.19	175.93	8.95	23.14
济源市 Jiyuan	24.84	9.89	0.77	12.12	1.58	0.48
省直管县 County Directly Administrated by Province						
巩义市 Gongyi	13.89	4.75	0.41	6.36	0.39	1.98
兰考县 Lankao	59.64	30.77	0.92	26.00	0.51	1.43
汝州市 Ruzhou	41.78	17.00	0.65	21.98	0.17	1.98
滑县 Huaxian	72.54	52.83	0.14	14.41	0.03	5.14
长垣市 Changyuan	50.49	33.78	0.30	14.66	0.41	1.35
邓州市 Dengzhou	99.13	63.38	0.28	30.37	0.59	4.51
永城市 Yongcheng	80.07	57.56	1.30	18.22	0.88	2.12
固始县 Gushi	86.64	49.95	1.11	30.30	4.45	0.84
鹿邑县 Luyi	62.23	43.31	0.24	13.31	0.51	4.87
新蔡县 Xincai	52.30	30.93	0.34	18.04	1.50	1.49

12-4 农林牧渔业增加值指数(上年=100)

Value-Added Related Indices of Agriculture, Forestry, Animal Husbandry and Fishery (Preceding year=100)

本表数据按可比价格计算。
Data in this table are calculated at comparable prices.

年份 Year	农林牧渔业 Agriculture, Forestry, Animal Husbandry and Fishery	农业 Agriculture	林业 Forestry	牧业 Animal Husbandry	渔业 Fishery	农林牧渔专业及辅助性活动 Service for Agriculture, Forestry, Animal Husbandry and Fishery and Auxiliary
1985	100.8					
1990	105.4					
1995	111.9					
2000	104.5	103.2	105.2	106.6	110.2	
2005	107.6	107.7	104.7	107.6	119.0	104.0
2010	104.5	104.2	104.3	104.9	107.4	104.8
2011	103.7	104.2	107.0	102.0	106.9	105.3
2012	104.5	104.2	104.9	104.6	105.7	105.9
2013	104.3	104.1	107.0	104.1	106.5	108.9
2014	104.2	103.9	104.8	104.1	107.8	109.6
2015	104.5	105.5	101.7	102.2	110.5	109.7
2016	104.4	105.2	105.0	102.2	106.1	109.6
2017	104.5	105.0	106.3	102.5	106.4	109.9
2018	103.8	103.6	107.4	102.4	105.9	115.0
2019	102.7	105.1	106.2	94.7	109.9	111.3
省辖市 City						
郑州市 Zhengzhou	95.7	100.2	76.3	83.3	96.3	115.0
开封市 Kaifeng	103.6	113.9	78.7	82.3	78.0	103.7
洛阳市 Luoyang	104.0	104.9	105.0	100.5	105.7	107.1
平顶山市 Pingdingshan	102.5	103.2	79.0	103.5	102.9	107.7
安阳市 Anyang	98.1	99.0	97.8	94.1	97.9	105.8
鹤壁市 Hebi	103.7	104.1	107.0	102.5	105.0	114.0
新乡市 Xinxiang	103.4	107.3	82.7	96.6	89.6	112.8
焦作市 Jiaozuo	104.2	107.8	56.9	101.8	97.6	103.0
濮阳市 Puyang	103.8	115.4	90.5	83.0	103.8	106.5
许昌市 Xuchang	102.5	106.1	108.9	94.9	110.2	113.0
漯河市 Luohe	102.7	108.8	116.9	94.2	118.5	108.0
三门峡市 Sanmenxia	104.0	104.4	171.9	90.8	80.3	116.6
南阳市 Nanyang	103.5	104.1	107.6	100.3	107.3	117.2
商丘市 Shangqiu	102.7	105.7	106.2	93.1	77.0	113.7
信阳市 Xinyang	103.2	104.8	104.1	93.3	105.4	118.2
周口市 Zhoukou	103.1	107.5	41.5	94.5	84.9	112.8
驻马店市 Zhumadian	103.0	108.8	123.6	93.2	102.7	115.7
济源市 Jiyuan	104.2	103.8	120.7	101.7	105.6	118.7
省直管县 County Directly Administrated by Province						
巩义市 Gongyi	98.3	103.5	116.4	89.6	110.7	109.0
兰考县 Lankao	103.0	102.9	102.6	102.6	102.3	108.1
汝州市 Ruzhou	102.5	106.6	38.5	107.6	108.9	106.9
滑县 Huaxian	102.5	101.1	65.3	108.9	81.6	104.5
长垣市 Changyuan	103.4	104.4	43.7	104.7	104.6	113.0
邓州市 Dengzhou	102.1	105.2	107.8	92.3	112.3	118.9
永城市 Yongcheng	104.1	103.8	107.8	103.2	109.4	114.5
固始县 Gushi	103.2	105.3	102.4	98.4	106.5	108.0
鹿邑县 Luyi	103.9	103.4	101.2	102.1	103.4	114.6
新蔡县 Xincai	103.8	103.4	104.9	103.5	105.2	114.1

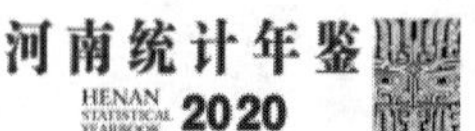

12-5 河南省十大优势特色农业产值

Output Value of Ten Dominant Characteristic Agriculture in Henan Province

本表按当年价格计算。
Data in this table are calculated at current prices.

品种	Kind	产值（亿元）Output Value (100 million yuan)				占农林牧渔业的比重（%）Proportion (%)			
		2016	2017	2018	2019	2016	2017	2018	2019
优势特色农业	Dominant Characteristic Agriculture	3837.52	3978.56	4343.37	4994.14	51.8	52.6	56.0	58.5
小麦	Wheat	786.13	838.25	789.02	827.13	10.6	11.1	10.2	9.7
花生	Peanut	279.76	224.64	259.31	331.06	3.8	3.0	3.3	3.9
草畜	Grass Livestocks	394.42	450.42	468.88	650.98	5.3	6.0	6.0	7.6
牛的饲养	Cattles	228.41	227.50	236.53	341.59	3.1	3.0	3.0	4.0
羊的饲养	Sheep and Goats	92.16	153.34	163.30	232.06	1.2	2.0	2.1	2.7
奶产品	Milk Product	73.85	69.58	69.06	77.33	1.0	0.9	0.9	0.9
林果	Timber and Fruit	345.63	400.69	465.78	423.67	4.7	5.3	6.0	5.0
食用坚果	Edible Nuts	44.05	42.57	41.15	52.02	0.6	0.6	0.5	0.6
园林水果	Garden Fruit	301.58	358.12	424.62	371.65	4.1	4.7	5.5	4.4
蔬菜	Vegetables	1424.28	1388.37	1378.21	1600.02	19.2	18.4	17.8	18.7
花卉	Flowers and Plants	30.67	30.69	19.25	158.85	0.4	0.4	0.2	1.9
茶叶	Tea	155.68	94.01	196.62	220.62	2.1	1.2	2.5	2.6
食用菌	Edible Fungi	215.59	330.59	353.19	349.61	2.9	4.4	4.6	4.1
中草药材	Chinese Herbs	98.10	113.11	290.39	314.04	1.3	1.5	3.7	3.7
水产	Aquatic Products	107.27	107.79	122.71	118.16	1.4	1.4	1.6	1.4

12-6 农业生产条件

Conditions of Agriculture

年 份 Year	耕地面积 (千公顷) Area of Cultivated land (1 000 hectares)	农用机械总动力 (万千瓦) Total Power of Agricultural Machinery (10 000 kw)	灌溉面积 (千公顷) Irrigated Area (1 000 hectares)	化肥施用折纯量 (万吨) Consumption of Chemical Fertilizer by 100% Effective Component (10 000 tons)	农村用电量 (亿千瓦小时) Electricity Consumption in Rural Areas (100 million kwh)	农用柴油使用量 (万吨) Diesel Oil Use for Agriculture (10 000 tons)	农药施用实物量 (万吨) Consumption of Chemical Pesticides (10 000 tons)	农用塑料薄膜使用量 (万吨) Plastic Film Use for Agriculture (10 000 tons)	地膜覆盖面积 (千公顷) Mulch Area (1 000hectare)
1978	7157.30	974.40	3722.67	52.54	13.25				
1979	7138.70	1079.30	3636.00	60.05	14.59				
1980	7128.10	1178.00	3536.23	72.52	17.23				
1981	7121.30	1262.10	3388.00	81.90	20.85				
1982	7109.30	1356.30	3265.33	105.50	22.76				
1983	7100.70	1405.90	3210.00	130.67	23.50				
1984	7079.30	1507.00	3278.67	140.16	25.83				
1985	7033.20	1590.00	3189.97	143.58	28.33				
1986	6998.90	1737.90	3212.71	148.73	33.30				
1987	6972.60	1865.90	3250.07	135.58	37.29				
1988	6956.40	2004.20	3358.76	150.57	40.81				
1989	6944.40	2153.40	3438.00	184.25	45.20				
1990	6933.20	2264.00	3550.09	213.18	46.93		3.31	2.75	
1991	6920.00	2330.40	3676.59	239.74	52.06		3.88	3.15	
1992	6887.80	2424.40	3779.72	251.13	59.58		4.76	3.45	
1993	6871.00	2624.00	3868.33	288.21	61.10		5.44	3.84	
1994	6830.00	2780.50	3931.30	292.47	70.54		6.53	4.87	
1995	6805.80	3115.40	4044.19	322.21	85.07		7.56	5.32	
1996	6786.30	4256.40	4191.05	345.33	103.66		8.33	6.17	
1997	6773.40	4337.90	4333.06	355.31	118.27		8.49	6.95	
1998	6834.00	4764.40	4513.86	382.80	121.21		9.10	7.49	
1999	6825.90	5342.90	4648.78	399.85	122.54		9.61	7.94	
2000	6875.25	5780.60	4725.31	420.71	125.80	79.56	9.55	9.19	651.10
2001	6907.30	6078.70	4766.00	441.73	134.61	83.51	9.85	9.41	738.22
2002	7262.80	6548.20	4802.36	468.83	141.36	85.10	10.20	9.86	797.30
2003	7187.20	6953.20	4792.22	467.89	144.59	84.58	9.87	9.88	823.38
2004	7177.50	7521.10	4829.10	493.16	157.69	86.86	10.12	10.16	871.71
2005	7201.20	7934.20	4864.12	518.14	172.15	89.79	10.51	10.84	887.01
2006	7202.40	8309.10	4918.80	540.43	188.82	93.04	11.16	11.84	923.91
2007	7201.90	8718.70	4955.84	569.68	223.43	96.40	11.80	12.66	957.71
2008	7202.20	9429.30	4989.20	601.68	237.36	99.20	11.91	13.07	960.38
2009	8192.01	9817.90	5033.03	628.67	257.76	104.20	12.14	14.14	1002.25
2010	8177.45	10195.88	5080.96	655.15	269.41	107.90	12.49	14.70	1032.13
2011	8161.90	10515.79	5150.44	673.71	281.82	107.92	12.87	15.16	1028.34
2012	8156.76	10872.73	5205.63	684.43	290.03	111.07	12.83	15.52	1050.86
2013	8140.71	11149.96	4969.11	696.37	305.42	113.40	13.01	16.78	1072.89
2014	8126.06	11476.81	5101.74	705.75	313.23	116.00	12.99	16.35	1076.68
2015	8105.93	11710.08	5333.90	716.09	321.01	114.70	12.87	16.20	1032.10
2016	8111.01	9858.82	5360.30	715.03	317.23	112.40	12.71	16.31	1019.29
2017	8112.28	10038.32	5389.79	706.70	328.82	108.80	12.07	15.73	984.36
2018	8158.29	10204.46	5408.31	692.79	330.59	103.92	11.36	15.28	1005.12
2019	-	10356.97	5452.93	666.72	353.83	100.08	10.72	15.08	995.34

注：1. 2008年及以前年份耕地面积为年底常用耕地面积，2009年数据为第二次全省土地调查数据，2010年以后数据已按2009年数据口径进行了调整。
2. 2013年及以前年份的数据为农田有效灌溉面积。(下表同)
3. 2016年以后数据不再包含农用运输车和三轮运输车。
4.因第三次全省土地调查，2019年耕地面积数据尚未确定。

a) Data on area of cultivated land of 2008and before were cultivated land area at year-end, data in 2009 are from the second provincial land survey, and data since 2010 were adjusted by 2009's caliber.
b) The irrigated area before 2013 refer to the effective irrigation area of farmland. (The same as following tables)
c) Data on total power of agricultural machinery exclude the number of agricultural vehicles and three wheeled transport vehicles since 2016.
d) Due to the third provincial land survey, the cultivated land area data in 2019 has not been determined.

12-7 各市耕地面积

Arable Land Area by City

单位：千公顷 (1 000 hectares)

市(县) City(County)	2017				2018			
	耕地面积 Cultivated land Area	水田 Paddy Field	水浇地 Irrigated land	旱地 Dry Land	耕地面积 Cultivated land Area	水田 Paddy Field	水浇地 Irrigated land	旱地 Dry Land
省辖市 City								
郑州市 Zhengzhou	314.92	1.08	192.05	121.80	314.14	1.07	190.95	122.12
开封市 Kaifeng	416.03	6.30	391.61	18.12	418.04	6.18	393.80	18.06
洛阳市 Luoyang	433.86	1.68	82.09	350.09	434.44	1.74	81.80	350.90
平顶山市 Pingdingshan	320.11	1.10	217.62	101.39	322.47	1.10	218.39	102.98
安阳市 Anyang	407.12	0.04	330.28	76.80	408.74	0.04	332.02	76.69
鹤壁市 Hebi	119.25		109.38	9.87	119.67		109.86	9.81
新乡市 Xinxiang	472.19	39.52	413.71	18.95	475.66	39.25	417.48	18.92
焦作市 Jiaozuo	195.75	2.90	178.80	14.06	196.69	2.89	179.77	14.03
濮阳市 Puyang	281.10	25.09	253.67	2.35	281.22	24.99	253.88	2.34
许昌市 Xuchang	336.22	0.00	248.87	87.35	337.89	0.00	250.23	87.65
漯河市 Luohe	190.09		189.52	0.57	190.24		189.67	0.57
三门峡市 Sanmenxia	175.57	0.07	29.18	146.32	179.72	0.07	32.36	147.30
南阳市 Nanyang	1052.19	26.74	305.44	720.01	1055.84	26.72	308.66	720.46
商丘市 Shangqiu	707.74	0.00	569.74	138.00	716.30	0.00	576.46	139.83
信阳市 Xinyang	841.67	626.37	7.54	207.76	850.16	629.39	12.61	208.17
周口市 Zhoukou	857.34	0.28	810.42	46.64	858.86	0.28	812.01	46.57
驻马店市 Zhumadian	945.40	21.00	205.19	719.21	952.16	21.33	208.73	722.10
济源市 Jiyuan	45.72		16.35	29.37	46.05		16.72	29.34
省直管县 County Directly Administrated by Province								
巩义市 Gongyi	39.66		12.82	26.83	40.03		13.23	26.80
兰考县 Lankao	68.06	2.66	65.39	0.02	68.46	2.61	65.83	0.02
汝州市 Ruzhou	62.36	0.00	43.62	18.74	63.37	0.00	43.77	19.60
滑县 Huaxian	133.31		133.17	0.13	135.36		135.23	0.13
长垣市 Changyuan	68.82	4.35	64.38	0.08	70.41	4.34	65.98	0.08
邓州市 Dengzhou	168.69	0.01	63.94	104.74	168.94	0.01	63.85	105.07
永城市 Yongcheng	137.50		1.42	136.08	139.35		1.42	137.93
固始县 Gushi	156.16	143.60	0.27	12.29	156.25	143.70	0.27	12.28
鹿邑县 Luyi	84.92	0.00	84.91	0.01	85.19	0.00	85.18	0.01
新蔡县 Xincai	100.17		0.64	99.53	100.27		1.19	99.08

12-8 各市农业机械和农产品加工机械年末拥有量(2019年)

市(县) City(County)	农业机械总动力(万千瓦) Total Power of Agricultural Machinery (10 000 kw)	农用大中型拖拉机(混合台)(台) Large and Medium-sized Tractors (unit)	大中型拖拉机配套农具(部) Number of Large and Medium-sized Tractor Towing Farm Machinery (unit)
1980	1178	59666	74100
1990	2264	49288	65700
2000	5781	66200	118700
2010	10196	274400	642600
2011	10516	310700	732000
2012	10873	338500	802200
2013	11150	357800	849900
2014	11477	378100	896100
2015	11710	402300	948300
2016	9859	432700	1007400
2017	10038	458549	1051961
2018	10204	347150	631862
2019	10357	373074	654206
省辖市 City			
郑州市 Zhengzhou	440	16495	23567
开封市 Kaifeng	591	21597	43008
洛阳市 Luoyang	528	10893	13167
平顶山市 Pingdingshan	406	19183	26059
安阳市 Anyang	507	17687	25561
鹤壁市 Hebi	234	5928	7594
新乡市 Xinxiang	778	21207	45693
焦作市 Jiaozuo	254	15598	20664
濮阳市 Puyang	376	11665	23372
许昌市 Xuchang	388	12862	19620
漯河市 Luohe	256	9235	20251
三门峡市 Sanmenxia	121	3170	4973
南阳市 Nanyang	1462	54480	76480
商丘市 Shangqiu	866	33898	72679
信阳市 Xinyang	679	33749	34984
周口市 Zhoukou	980	38221	43115
驻马店市 Zhumadian	1418	44062	151181
济源市 Jiyuan	72	3144	2238
省直管县 County Directly Administrated by Province			
巩义市 Gongyi	50	1292	1785
兰考县 Lankao	76	3710	4505
汝州市 Ruzhou	153	3622	8300
滑县 Huaxian	223	4894	10395
长垣市 Changyuan	103	3046	9404
邓州市 Dengzhou	201	12083	11361
永城市 Yongcheng	137	4396	12820
固始县 Gushi	138	5778	6770
鹿邑县 Luyi	103	5200	5220
新蔡县 Xincai	145	5459	8600

注：1. 农业机械总动力：2015年及以前数据中包含农用运输车和三轮运输车，从2016年开始，不再包含在内。
2. 从2018年开始，农用大中型拖拉机统计标准由14.7千瓦及以上提高到22.1千瓦及以上。

Number of Agricultural Machinery and Machinery for Processing Farm Products at Year-end by City (2019)

节水灌溉机械(万套) Water-saving Irrigation Machinery (10 000 units)	饲草料加工机械(台(套)) Composite Feed Processing Machinery (units)	农产品初加工动力机械 Agricultural Products Primary Processing Power Machinery (万台) (10 000 units)	(万千瓦) (10 000 kw)	农产品初加工作业机械(万台) Agricultural Products Primary Processing Machine (10 000 units)
	113800	32.86	223.80	
	99200	53.09	355.10	
	115300	67.76	466.80	43.18
17.37	169200	80.24	582.70	50.82
17.98	180700	81.63	582.91	52.14
19.73	182500	82.71	594.05	54.47
20.81	184400	83.19	598.77	55.72
21.30	186400	84.36	605.37	56.95
21.56	187100	85.57	611.00	57.59
21.83	187400	85.45	609.41	57.68
21.91	188383	85.54	610.06	57.86
22.71	183010	85.21	608.67	56.97
23.04	185829	85.48	609.58	57.12
1.18	7661	4.47	36.16	2.80
3.22	12421	5.57	38.12	3.08
1.71	9750	7.57	54.91	4.54
0.63	11193	3.79	25.05	2.68
0.07	4896	3.48	22.84	2.35
0.15	1376	1.02	6.50	0.60
0.38	17095	5.68	41.77	2.63
0.04	5276	1.73	11.24	1.09
0.51	5098	2.29	19.67	1.85
0.02	16130	4.74	29.52	2.17
0.30	573	1.38	10.40	0.74
0.46	5182	1.92	12.70	0.95
2.19	14615	10.34	74.03	5.75
2.62	21983	9.07	68.36	4.57
0.41	6044	8.54	54.82	9.18
1.57	17242	6.71	49.15	7.04
7.57	26704	6.82	51.67	4.79
0.01	2590	0.34	2.68	0.32
0.01	1479	1.05	6.07	0.50
0.28	1213	0.90	5.96	0.33
0.00	6340	1.82	13.66	0.62
0.00	2373	1.03	6.58	0.54
0.12	660	0.49	4.05	0.36
0.29	1658	1.35	13.47	0.54
0.85	5602	1.32	9.34	0.69
0.01	1255	0.72	7.32	0.73
0.23	1300	0.42	3.18	2.67
1.28	6052	0.79	6.90	0.51

a) Total power of agricultural machinery : Data on 2015 and before include the power of agricultural vehicles and three wheeled transport vehicles, while since 2016, the data do not include that.

b) In the annual report from the Provincial Agricultural Machinery Bureau in 2018, the standard of medium-sized agricultural tractors has been adjusted from ⩾ 14.7kw to ⩾ 22.1kw.

12-9 各市农田水利情况

Condition of Irrigation and Conservancy Project by City

单位：千公顷 (1 000 hectares)

市(县) City(County)	农村用电量(亿千瓦小时) Electricity Consumption in Rural Areas (100 million kwh)	灌溉面积 Irrigated Area	#耕地灌溉面积 Irrigated Area of Cultivated Land	节水灌溉面积 Water Water Saving Irrigated Area	节水灌溉面积占灌溉面积比重(%) Proportion of Water Saving Irrigation Area to Irrigation Area (%)	农业灌溉供水量(亿立方米) Irrigated Water Supply (100million cu.m)
2000	125.80	4785.59	4725.31	949.61	19.8	135.59
2005	172.15	4941.21	4864.12	1309.14	26.5	103.41
2010	269.41	5172.01	5080.96	1536.64	29.7	116.21
2011	281.82					
2012	290.03	5026.93	4922.72	1174.31	23.4	138.26
2013	305.42	5088.50	4969.11	1295.84	25.5	142.62
2014	313.23	5521.62	5101.74	1476.53	26.7	117.49
2015	321.01	5333.90	5210.64	1672.16	31.4	110.63
2016	317.23	5360.28	5244.49	1806.61	33.7	111.14
2017	328.82	5389.79	5273.63	1893.27	35.1	123.58
2018	330.59	5408.31	5288.69	1997.86	36.9	118.25
2019	353.83	5452.93	5328.94	2190.19	40.2	107.59
省辖市 City						
郑州市 Zhengzhou	43.06	206.57	194.15	126.33	61.2	3.91
开封市 Kaifeng	12.47	356.42	336.18	65.30	18.3	9.16
洛阳市 Luoyang	25.83	154.76	146.62	84.66	54.7	4.26
平顶山市 Pingdingshan	12.98	217.75	214.15	121.80	55.9	2.50
安阳市 Anyang	27.04	306.40	301.63	130.18	42.5	4.96
鹤壁市 Hebi	2.88	92.96	89.65	73.70	79.3	2.04
新乡市 Xinxiang	67.08	365.37	363.76	208.73	57.1	15.93
焦作市 Jiaozuo	15.49	182.48	172.20	139.32	76.3	8.60
濮阳市 Puyang	10.20	237.77	227.32	161.69	68.0	7.63
许昌市 Xuchang	10.93	246.58	246.24	191.84	77.8	2.48
漯河市 Luohe	6.45	147.67	147.67	28.55	19.3	1.48
三门峡市 Sanmenxia	3.67	61.56	57.25	27.43	44.6	1.16
南阳市 Nanyang	24.60	497.13	489.23	202.23	40.7	8.79
商丘市 Shangqiu	27.71	619.36	602.20	165.19	26.7	7.72
信阳市 Xinyang	18.49	535.51	521.64	103.39	19.3	8.56
周口市 Zhoukou	22.19	575.72	575.05	156.80	27.2	12.42
驻马店市 Zhumadian	20.91	623.76	621.30	193.57	31.0	4.70
济源市 Jiyuan	1.83	25.16	22.70	9.46	37.6	1.15
省直管县 County Directly Administrated by Province						
巩义市 Gongyi	20.33	18.54	16.51	7.27	39.2	0.38
兰考县 Lankao	2.71	58.47	57.77	8.15	13.9	1.41
汝州市 Ruzhou	3.26	50.89	50.89	25.87	50.8	0.76
滑县 Huaxian	5.71	111.93	108.68	48.42	43.3	2.15
长垣市 Changyuan	5.50	45.76	45.09	22.10	48.3	1.35
邓州市 Dengzhou	2.83	114.44	112.80	40.94	35.8	1.83
永城市 Yongcheng	3.52	88.74	88.74	32.79	37.0	0.58
固始县 Gushi	3.83	105.47	105.26	38.54	36.5	2.79
鹿邑县 Luyi	1.27	66.30	66.30	18.25	27.5	0.40
新蔡县 Xincai	0.97	70.29	70.17	20.60	29.3	0.65

注：2011年以后的水利建设情况数据根据第一次全国水利普查数据调整。

a) Data on the construction of water conservancy are calculated from The first national water resources census since 2011.

12-10 各市农用物资消耗情况(2019年)
Consumption of Agricultural Materials by City (2019)

单位：吨 (ton)

市(县)	City(County)	农用化肥使用折纯量 Consumption of Chemical Fertilizer by 100% Effective Component	#氮肥 Nitrogenous Fertilizer	#磷肥 Phosphate Fertilizer	#钾肥 Potash Fertilizer	农用塑料薄膜使用量 Plastic Film Use for Agriculture	农用柴油使用量 Diesel Oil Use for Agriculture	农药使用量 Consumption of Chemical Pesticides
省辖市	**City**							
郑州市	Zhengzhou	187830	49925	26651	14327	5346	42108	2910
开封市	Kaifeng	321938	112230	57702	33670	12551	49019	4329
洛阳市	Luoyang	233351	65879	31624	22656	4693	42971	4139
平顶山市	Pingdingshan	341057	91386	34062	21284	3241	54789	3378
安阳市	Anyang	432097	120868	40729	26199	18160	42386	5633
鹤壁市	Hebi	73996	24382	9988	3686	1005	11500	980
新乡市	Xinxiang	519743	159870	61511	23982	3295	76546	8309
焦作市	Jiaozuo	194741	50208	20786	6285	2121	34426	3694
濮阳市	Puyang	291586	86864	36689	27078	7253	36737	3233
许昌市	Xuchang	202923	50634	23663	13131	3313	26789	3147
漯河市	Luohe	172830	34225	11660	8925	2736	23658	2205
三门峡市	Sanmenxia	86279	22264	9750	10381	3261	18720	2510
南阳市	Nanyang	762346	228061	124758	81229	25293	140303	14620
商丘市	Shangqiu	778648	176299	108989	82103	12094	65555	11476
信阳市	Xinyang	448822	205267	79221	32312	13967	69036	10371
周口市	Zhoukou	860678	270073	133861	81349	19347	156693	18192
驻马店市	Zhumadian	733984	143909	80470	61291	12586	99452	7613
济源市	Jiyuan	24366	7876	4816	2683	504	10120	495
省直管县	**County Directly Administrated by Province**							
巩义市	Gongyi	23693	6599	2653	1213	106	3667	138
兰考县	Lankao	72210	27895	12427	6397	1710	10525	592
汝州市	Ruzhou	92057	18325	10771	5373	673	14996	664
滑县	Huaxian	206557	55207	8142	11455	4199	12097	2066
长垣市	Changyuan	65272	17497	7988	5737	747	11035	994
邓州市	Dengzhou	172081	42608	27188	15763	3135	24655	2637
永城市	Yongcheng	170865	21607	9191	6757	1853	10703	1751
固始县	Gushi	113842	47318	14699	6206	4534	11637	3823
鹿邑县	Luyi	96926	53476	12233	7782	679	38384	991
新蔡县	Xincai	79277	16052	12228	10822	1182	7842	2421

12-11 水库、灌区和除涝治水情况

Reservoirs， Irrigation, Flood Prevention, Water and Soil Conservation

指 标	Item	2000	2010	2015	2016	2017	2018	2019
年底水库数(座)	**Number of Reservoirs at Year-end (unit)**	**2396**	**2350**	**2653**	**2650**	**2655**	**2654**	**2510**
大型水库(1亿立方米以上)	Large Reservoirs (100 million and over cu.m)	21	21	25	25	26	26	27
中型水库(1千万至1亿立方米)	Medium-sized Reservoirs (10 million - 100 million cu.m)	102	108	121	122	124	124	121
小型水库(10万至1千万立方米)	Small Reservoirs (100 thousand -10 million cu.m)	2273	2221	2507	2503	2505	2504	2362
塘坝数量(座)	Small Reservoirs (in a hilly area, unit)		277838	160097	160168	162769	163655	164680
窖池数量(座)	Pits(unit)			277873	278185	277843	274274	274406
年底灌区数(处)	Number of Irrigation Areas at Year-end (unit)	171	191	664	666	660	668	668
规模以上灌区渠道长度(公里)	Irrigation Channel Length Above Designated Size (km)		2075	2454	2665	2679	2686	2686
除涝面积(千公顷)	Flooded or Waterlogged Area Under Control (1 000 hectares)	1848.11	1973.30	2074.64	2108.10	2106.00	2136.92	2149.32
堤防长度(公里)	Total Length of Dikes (km)	15758	16313	19531	19591	19743	20023	20075
达标堤防长度(公里)	Standards Length of Dikes (km)		6440	10617	10692	10805	11071	11162
堤防保护耕地面积(千公顷)	Area of Protected Land by Dikes (1 000 hectares)	3260	3388	3524	3512	3532	3538	3548

12-12 各市水库和除涝治水情况(2019年)

Reservoirs, Flood Prevention, Water and Soil Conservation by City (2019)

市(县) City(County)	水库数量(座) Reservoir (unit)	塘坝数量(座) Spoilage (unit)	机电井数量(眼) Motor-pumped Well (unit)	年底灌区数(处) Number of Irrigation Areas at Year-end (unit)	除涝面积(千公顷) Flooded or Waterlogged Area Under Control (1 000 hectares)
省 辖 市 City					
郑 州 市 Zhengzhou	134	628	51916	43	35
开 封 市 Kaifeng	1		130840	5	119
洛 阳 市 Luoyang	153	696	17644	60	6
平 顶 山 市 Pingdingshan	163	1198	46992	31	63
安 阳 市 Anyang	55	1006	72117	10	73
鹤 壁 市 Hebi	14	220	25607	41	33
新 乡 市 Xinxiang	30	711	95537	26	183
焦 作 市 Jiaozuo	28	153	51727	18	74
濮 阳 市 Puyang			61776	23	89
许 昌 市 Xuchang	24	98	72274	11	88
漯 河 市 Luohe			50725	3	102
三 门 峡 市 Sanmenxia	91	147	4889	40	
南 阳 市 Nanyang	508	19807	96666	80	221
商 丘 市 Shangqiu	15		178296	8	206
信 阳 市 Xinyang	1115	131194	16485	170	106
周 口 市 Zhoukou			168084	18	387
驻 马 店 市 Zhumadian	160	8357	143418	74	355
济 源 市 Jiyuan	19	465	3817	7	8
省 直 管 县 County Directly Administrated by Province					
巩 义 市 Gongyi	17	74	1687	4	
兰 考 县 Lankao			14688	2	19
汝 州 市 Ruzhou	25	323	13627	14	5
滑 县 Huaxian			39409		47
长 垣 市 Changyuan			12980	3	32
邓 州 市 Dengzhou	16	2715	27385	8	44
永 城 市 Yongcheng			27505	1	63
固 始 县 Gushi	97	18131	624	20	29
鹿 邑 县 Luyi			21332		56
新 蔡 县 Xincai		275	18270	25	31

12-13 农业生产情况
Agriculture Production

年份 Year	播种面积(千公顷) Total Sown Area (1 000hectares)	#粮食 Grain	#棉花 Cotton	#油料 Oil- bearing Crops	粮食产量(万吨) Grain Output (10 000tons)	#小麦 Wheat	棉花产量(万吨) Cotton (10 000tons)	油料产量(万吨) Oil- bearing Crops (10 000tons)	园林水果产量(万吨) Garden Fruits (10 000tons)
1978	10966.70	9123.30	612.00	465.33	2097.40	868.18	22.42	24.16	47.11
1979	10917.00	9066.70	555.33	632.67	2134.50	969.00	19.84	36.87	52.37
1980	10788.20	8858.90	626.67	710.00	2148.68	890.37	40.62	46.20	43.55
1981	11013.00	9029.30	641.33	744.67	2314.50	1083.50	35.50	55.99	52.30
1982	11076.00	8923.30	754.00	709.33	2217.10	1220.10	32.04	44.16	46.63
1983	11326.70	9286.70	794.00	607.33	2904.00	1455.75	63.24	51.52	58.67
1984	11432.70	8996.70	1162.00	579.33	2893.50	1653.00	86.89	52.50	41.01
1985	11685.30	9029.30	814.30	793.70	2710.53	1528.23	54.73	96.18	53.33
1986	11819.50	9372.20	619.33	921.33	2545.67	1567.90	39.86	98.99	61.23
1987	11952.90	9365.20	717.33	977.33	2948.41	1626.00	57.00	136.57	77.84
1988	11930.20	9053.80	916.03	952.84	2663.00	1520.95	63.71	96.17	74.81
1989	11999.40	9262.00	836.15	915.43	3149.44	1695.13	52.72	118.48	76.75
1990	11889.70	9316.10	823.00	876.40	3303.66	1639.86	67.61	152.29	63.92
1991	12001.90	9040.40	1193.20	896.00	3010.30	1554.28	94.77	127.62	63.67
1992	11936.30	8804.70	1247.90	908.60	3109.61	1650.67	65.85	133.63	87.79
1993	12068.00	8969.00	974.00	1075.00	3639.21	1922.13	66.01	204.50	125.12
1994	12087.70	8810.90	966.70	1242.00	3253.80	1798.42	62.81	225.00	170.54
1995	12136.80	8810.00	1000.10	1271.50	3466.50	1754.18	77.00	298.00	211.66
1996	12257.40	8965.30	933.30	1181.10	3839.90	2026.76	73.57	278.46	247.26
1997	12276.74	8879.90	868.30	1208.50	3894.66	2372.35	79.00	276.66	269.26
1998	12567.05	9101.98	800.00	1235.90	4009.61	2073.53	72.84	312.13	312.60
1999	12659.90	9032.30	733.30	1316.10	4253.25	2291.46	70.73	349.25	349.42
2000	13136.91	9029.60	779.33	1492.54	4101.50	2235.95	70.38	392.55	364.73
2001	13127.70	8822.79	858.20	1443.97	4119.88	2299.71	82.77	362.49	399.12
2002	13359.80	8975.10	793.10	1537.00	4209.98	2248.39	76.49	420.68	427.01
2003	13684.40	8923.30	926.67	1569.90	3569.47	2292.50	37.67	309.91	430.38
2004	13805.69	8970.07	951.80	1554.96	4260.00	2480.93	66.67	408.75	507.07
2005	13922.60	9153.40	781.47	1605.80	4582.00	2577.69	67.70	449.60	555.69
2006	13995.39	9455.80	748.20	1489.10	5112.30	2936.50	81.00	460.07	591.78
2007	14381.42	9528.52	653.16	1464.65	5252.92	2958.31	69.98	478.27	663.80
2008	14473.45	9746.87	527.62	1452.62	5405.80	3036.20	56.66	493.48	714.77
2009	14322.07	9890.62	436.53	1442.27	5506.87	3092.20	42.03	514.34	756.98
2010	14320.79	10027.00	354.23	1431.68	5581.82	3121.00	33.89	515.66	797.50
2011	14373.33	10244.43	280.57	1413.60	5733.92	3144.90	27.04	501.69	835.56
2012	14386.89	10434.56	169.40	1378.05	5898.38	3223.07	16.95	530.38	872.91
2013	14586.50	10697.43	114.96	1361.87	6023.80	3266.33	11.68	542.13	891.25
2014	14731.54	10944.97	88.11	1339.01	6133.60	3385.20	8.44	531.41	899.36
2015	14879.73	11126.30	64.34	1311.84	6470.22	3526.90	6.77	538.99	919.68
2016	14902.72	11219.55	50.03	1302.35	6498.01	3618.62	4.88	549.82	927.12
2017	14732.53	10915.13	40.00	1397.49	6524.25	3705.21	4.40	586.95	931.98
2018	14769.06	10906.08	36.68	1461.40	6648.91	3602.85	3.79	631.03	907.39
2019	14676.43	10734.54	33.80	1533.93	6695.36	3741.77	2.71	645.45	950.74

注：依据第三次全国农业普查结果，对2007-2016年农业生产数据进行了修订（以下相关表格同）。

a) According to the results of the Third National Agricultural Census, the data of production from 2007 to 2016 were revised (the same as other tables).

12-14 农作物播种面积

单位：千公顷

市(县) City(County)	播种面积总计 Total	粮食作物 Grain	夏粮 Summer Harvest	秋粮 Autumn Harvest	谷物 Cereal	#稻谷 Rice	#小麦 Wheat	#玉米 Corn	豆类 Beans	大豆 Soybean
2012	14386.89	10434.56	5494.66	4939.90	9717.68	621.77	5468.80	3564.70	487.79	448.04
2013	14586.50	10697.43	5543.70	5153.72	10014.77	610.97	5517.98	3823.60	460.80	424.01
2014	14731.54	10944.97	5606.83	5338.14	10270.37	614.65	5581.24	4009.42	413.25	381.90
2015	14879.73	11126.30	5648.60	5477.70	10498.94	616.35	5623.14	4189.91	370.35	343.56
2016	14902.72	11219.55	5730.24	5489.31	10608.13	614.09	5704.91	4210.46	366.40	341.06
2017	14732.53	10915.13	5741.31	5173.82	10412.61	615.03	5714.64	3998.94	389.85	345.17
2018	14769.06	10906.08	5770.11	5135.97	10367.18	620.41	5739.85	3918.96	424.00	385.55
2019	14676.43	10734.54	5718.65	5015.89	10193.87	616.60	5706.65	3801.33	428.00	394.67
省辖市 City										
郑州市 Zhengzhou	402.86	307.34	156.74	150.60	292.75	0.16	156.74	135.48	6.22	5.22
开封市 Kaifeng	864.28	525.69	304.33	221.36	498.73	6.69	304.33	186.94	13.36	12.81
洛阳市 Luoyang	661.70	497.11	239.11	258.00	433.76	1.64	239.10	176.26	30.16	21.62
平顶山市 Pingdingshan	551.55	444.48	219.93	224.55	416.65	1.35	219.93	194.81	14.93	13.93
安阳市 Anyang	729.82	565.90	304.54	261.36	546.40	0.12	304.54	241.62	4.43	3.97
鹤壁市 Hebi	196.52	169.60	89.74	79.87	166.83		89.74	77.09	0.51	0.31
新乡市 Xinxiang	870.79	716.85	385.84	331.01	696.08	20.16	385.83	289.36	14.41	14.33
焦作市 Jiaozuo	353.07	279.93	150.00	129.93	273.62	4.22	150.00	119.41	4.11	4.06
濮阳市 Puyang	520.32	427.47	232.80	194.67	396.13	22.94	232.80	139.88	23.57	23.28
许昌市 Xuchang	578.90	448.53	230.67	217.86	380.75		230.67	149.34	42.10	41.97
漯河市 Luohe	365.63	271.08	146.00	125.08	226.29		146.00	80.29	39.53	39.53
三门峡市 Sanmenxia	253.85	162.21	76.67	85.54	134.67		76.67	56.85	20.89	16.29
南阳市 Nanyang	2010.39	1300.27	727.73	572.53	1220.82	37.28	725.22	449.35	52.47	40.29
商丘市 Shangqiu	1440.70	1088.20	602.13	486.07	1027.04	0.28	599.96	426.80	51.86	49.49
信阳市 Xinyang	1176.56	822.87	310.67	512.20	808.37	477.55	310.67	20.15	6.69	5.53
周口市 Zhoukou	1833.83	1372.13	733.53	638.60	1229.90	0.15	733.53	496.14	112.14	105.32
驻马店市 Zhumadian	1806.83	1292.45	786.80	505.65	1247.49	27.17	786.47	433.27	26.75	24.49
济源市 Jiyuan	53.00	42.94	21.40	21.54	40.87	0.07	21.40	19.33	1.59	1.55
省直管县 County Directly Administrated by Province										
巩义市 Gongyi	48.24	43.13	22.67	20.47	41.72	0.16	22.67	18.59	0.53	0.37
兰考县 Lankao	131.41	100.73	59.33	41.40	96.83	0.16	59.33	37.31	1.57	1.40
汝州市 Ruzhou	110.45	94.81	47.93	46.88	91.96		47.93	43.48	0.95	0.67
滑县 Huaxian	271.69	206.53	120.80	85.73	205.17	0.09	120.80	84.16	0.52	0.49
长垣市 Changyuan	129.19	106.67	56.00	50.67	103.69	2.05	56.00	45.46	2.60	2.57
邓州市 Dengzhou	328.17	217.07	138.87	78.20	205.02	1.93	138.18	58.55	9.94	7.86
永城市 Yongcheng	249.04	209.20	112.00	97.20	170.67		112.00	58.33	38.87	38.67
固始县 Gushi	216.97	152.00	37.33	114.67	151.57	110.93	37.33	3.31	0.15	0.15
鹿邑县 Luyi	187.97	143.07	72.87	70.20	127.27		72.87	54.41	14.75	14.00
新蔡县 Xincai	200.84	152.27	86.80	65.47	148.75	2.49	86.80	59.46	2.29	1.31

Total Sown Areas of Farm Crops

(1 000 hectares)

经济作物 Cash Crops	油料 Oilbearing Crops	#花生 Peanuts	#油菜籽 Rapeseeds	棉花 Cotton	麻类 Fiber Crops	糖料 Sugar Crops	烟叶 Fluecured Tobacco	中草药材 Chinese Herbs	蔬菜及食用菌 Vegetables and Edible Fungus	瓜果 Melon and Fruit	其他 Others	花卉 Flowers and Plants
3952.33	1378.05	999.67	250.98	169.40	6.61	3.23	125.42	122.73	1676.77	308.05	162.07	106.01
3889.08	1361.87	1016.70	228.58	114.96	6.54	3.11	137.15	121.20	1682.96	309.75	151.55	105.59
3786.58	1339.01	1023.57	207.70	88.11	4.68	2.94	123.80	118.80	1654.84	297.05	157.36	115.06
3753.43	1311.84	1023.96	186.58	64.34	4.56	2.60	114.27	113.58	1671.03	292.69	178.51	71.11
3683.17	1302.35	1051.03	162.19	50.03	4.11	2.42	109.21	99.81	1682.12	312.36	120.77	86.35
3817.40	1397.49	1151.93	155.69	40.00	3.29	2.31	103.95	112.19	1736.14	318.24	103.80	147.56
3862.98	1461.40	1203.18	145.02	36.68	3.00	2.03	94.88	132.44	1721.09	307.69	103.77	92.18
3941.88	1533.93	1223.11	171.51	33.80	2.82	1.62	86.50	153.59	1732.94	308.60	88.09	123.56
95.53	31.08	25.59	4.55	1.16		0.00	0.25	0.56	55.32	6.72	0.44	3.03
338.58	110.16	107.74	2.02	6.44		0.04		0.59	170.87	47.46	3.03	1.42
164.59	39.82	26.52	9.09	2.74			18.41	27.20	67.60	7.26	1.56	9.61
107.07	38.39	26.15	9.93	0.62		0.01	10.80	2.74	48.36	5.84	0.31	1.68
163.92	55.75	50.53	3.78	1.97		0.00	0. 00	2.08	89.96	12.95	1.22	0.65
26.92	14.37	13.53	0.60	0.50				0.62	11.21	0.22		1.74
153.94	78.27	75.90	2.17	1.06				6.17	63.76	4.43	0.25	1.49
73.13	25.84	24.76	0.41	0.14				10.41	33.59	3.15		0.52
92.85	23.46	23.12	0.30	0.97		0.00		3.14	59.12	5.59	0.59	0.76
130.37	18.97	12.56	5.85	0.80			9.33	13.16	41.62	3.04	43.46	43.30
94.55	15.00	11.89	2.20	0.24			5.65	0.12	62.75	10.81		1.12
91.64	13.04	4.49	4.46	1.18		0.00	16.03	24.51	32.63	3.42	0.83	0.07
710.13	378.21	302.68	27.40	1.66	0.00	0.07	17.39	25.92	249.00	25.98	11.89	15.28
352.50	78.59	72.61	5.44	3.73		0.09	0.71	5.36	213.24	45.22	5.55	1.31
353.69	163.33	66.96	71.66	0.77	2.79	0.71	0.35	5.50	142.47	27.08	10.69	32.97
461.70	92.87	66.85	5.07	2.71	0.03	0.39	2.46	17.45	265.22	77.87	2.70	2.31
514.38	356.06	310.65	16.52	0.45		0.31	4.66	7.25	121.28	21.49	2.88	5.89
10.05	0.73	0.54	0.07	0.33			0.47	0.81	4.96	0.09	2.67	0.41
5.10	2.57	1.29	1.00	0.33				0.05	1.63	0.16	0.36	0.02
30.68	16.68	16.37	0.31	1.05				0.05	9.07	2.67	1.15	0.08
15.64	6.24	3.71	2.12	0.27			1.13	0.19	7.24	0.51	0.06	0.04
65.15	25.14	25.00	0.10	0.43		0.00	0.00	0.34	33.11	5.42	0.71	0.22
22.52	9.41	8.44	0.96	0.30				0.14	10.49	2.03	0.17	0.08
111.10	61.72	55.17	2.36	0.51		0.00	1.18	1.85	39.97	4.58	1.29	0.61
39.84	1.88	1.44	0.40	0.12				2.77	29.10	5.97		0.28
64.97	19.43	8.50	9.52	0.07	1.70	0.09		0.12	36.73	6.84		0.66
44.91	5.80	3.95	1.09	0.09	0.03	0.00	0.91	5.34	30.76	1.98		0.03
48.57	27.36	21.77	2.05	0.24		0.11		0.99	13.29	6.59		0.06

12-15 主要农产品产量

单位：万吨

市(县) City(County)	粮食 Grain	夏粮 Summer Harvest	秋粮 Autumn Harvest	谷物 Cereal	#稻谷 Rice	#小麦 Wheat	#玉米 Corn	豆类 Beans	#大豆 Soybean
2012	5898.38	3231.72	2666.65	5720.95	472.80	3223.07	2011.38	78.97	74.81
2013	6023.80	3275.08	2748.72	5859.83	463.16	3266.33	2116.47	72.87	69.34
2014	6133.60	3395.20	2738.39	5989.56	500.53	3385.20	2088.89	54.00	51.52
2015	6470.22	3537.70	2932.52	6331.75	499.88	3526.90	2288.50	48.84	46.75
2016	6498.01	3628.32	2869.69	6360.41	508.29	3618.62	2216.29	49.00	46.90
2017	6524.25	3715.98	2808.27	6382.89	485.25	3705.21	2170.14	53.36	50.36
2018	6648.91	3613.70	3035.21	6483.41	501.41	3602.85	2351.38	101.70	95.57
2019	6695.36	3745.40	2949.96	6528.85	512.50	3741.77	2247.37	102.00	98.21
省辖市 City									
郑州市 Zhengzhou	149.67	76.03	73.64	141.87	0.06	75.72	65.98	1.16	1.03
开封市 Kaifeng	307.38	190.87	116.51	296.79	5.31	190.87	100.09	2.72	2.61
洛阳市 Luoyang	237.80	110.48	127.32	209.26	0.92	110.48	91.56	7.04	5.31
平顶山市 Pingdingshan	229.66	119.16	110.50	218.25	0.68	119.16	98.30	4.15	3.95
安阳市 Anyang	376.06	206.41	169.64	367.51	0.10	206.41	160.95	1.06	0.98
鹤壁市 Hebi	121.78	65.29	56.49	120.05		65.29	54.76	0.10	0.07
新乡市 Xinxiang	476.02	272.99	203.03	465.08	13.00	272.99	178.84	4.89	4.87
焦作市 Jiaozuo	207.66	115.22	92.44	204.73	3.66	115.22	85.85	1.27	1.27
濮阳市 Puyang	291.51	166.92	124.59	278.56	18.29	166.92	93.35	6.43	6.37
许昌市 Xuchang	297.69	168.80	128.89	270.54		168.80	101.32	11.82	11.79
漯河市 Luohe	187.38	110.60	76.78	172.98		110.60	62.38	10.86	10.86
三门峡市 Sanmenxia	69.08	32.78	36.30	60.01		32.78	26.85	4.68	3.87
南阳市 Nanyang	710.59	425.81	284.78	679.05	28.02	425.10	221.42	8.57	6.58
商丘市 Shangqiu	730.84	441.94	288.90	710.72	0.26	440.97	269.50	14.03	13.18
信阳市 Xinyang	560.38	147.62	412.76	555.37	395.09	147.62	12.67	0.65	0.55
周口市 Zhoukou	911.50	550.49	361.01	866.32	0.14	550.49	314.46	28.16	27.11
驻马店市 Zhumadian	808.89	530.69	278.20	793.75	18.19	530.54	244.73	4.71	4.34
济源市 Jiyuan	23.35	12.21	11.14	22.63	0.03	12.21	10.36	0.45	0.44
省直管县 County Directly Administrated by Province									
巩义市 Gongyi	16.98	8.68	8.30	16.37	0.06	8.37	7.86	0.11	0.08
兰考县 Lankao	57.60	35.42	22.18	55.28	0.18	35.42	19.65	0.48	0.45
汝州市 Ruzhou	46.17	24.68	21.49	44.83		24.68	20.03	0.28	0.21
滑县 Huaxian	161.52	93.42	68.10	160.57	0.09	93.42	67.02	0.13	0.12
长垣市 Changyuan	75.86	43.18	32.68	74.75	1.00	43.18	30.50	0.81	0.80
邓州市 Dengzhou	122.48	83.09	39.39	118.41	1.24	82.85	30.62	2.66	2.10
永城市 Yongcheng	134.46	83.16	51.30	124.51		83.16	41.35	9.95	9.92
固始县 Gushi	111.67	17.11	94.56	111.45	92.33	17.11	2.01	0.03	0.03
鹿邑县 Luyi	96.30	54.00	42.30	92.50		54.00	37.30	3.90	3.82
新蔡县 Xincai	94.08	57.98	36.10	93.28	1.40	57.98	33.90	0.25	0.15

Output of Major Farm Products

(10 000 tons)

油 料 Oil-bearing Crops	#花生 Peanuts	#油菜籽 Rapeseeds	棉 花 Cotton	麻类 Fiber Crops	糖料 Sugar Crops	烟 叶（未加工） Flue-cured Tobacco	中草药材 Chinese Herbs	蔬菜及食用菌 Vegetables and Edible Fungus	瓜 果 Melon and Fruit
530.38	453.73	57.86	16.95	3.67	21.89	30.68		6839.94	1515.71
542.13	469.19	55.35	11.68	3.65	22.28	34.65		6745.29	1534.13
531.41	466.09	49.69	8.44	2.87	20.74	29.99		6848.11	1468.76
538.99	477.12	46.21	6.77	2.87	17.88	28.85		6970.99	1519.94
549.82	494.27	40.90	4.88	2.71	16.67	28.26	122.63	7238.18	1613.93
586.95	529.81	42.08	4.40	2.24	16.24	26.70	144.01	7530.22	1670.46
631.03	572.44	38.97	3.79	2.12	15.39	25.31	155.31	7260.67	1585.37
645.45	576.72	44.25	2.71	1.94	11.93	22.76	164.74	7368.74	1638.92
11.79	10.89	0.76	0.12		0.00	0.06	0.14	213.17	26.04
51.46	50.82	0.56	0.94		0.29		0.18	809.93	253.69
13.28	10.13	2.31	0.34			4.74	6.69	281.82	20.84
12.58	9.82	2.36	0.07		0.07	2.80	0.62	232.87	23.55
23.79	23.01	0.55	0.24		0.00	0.00	0.77	480.52	79.67
4.48	4.37	0.08	0.05				0.97	42.90	0.88
34.13	33.56	0.54	0.11				1.53	308.00	23.30
13.52	13.22	0.08	0.02				39.22	194.14	17.34
9.88	9.80	0.08	0.13		0.00		0.65	253.44	24.10
6.42	4.79	1.55	0.08			2.82	8.55	150.55	12.06
5.74	5.07	0.55	0.03			1.18	0.06	192.48	43.70
3.23	1.33	0.98	0.12		0.00	3.82	5.66	123.44	9.11
168.13	151.78	7.77	0.23	0.00	0.61	4.96	62.35	1127.21	131.36
39.65	37.88	1.66	0.50		0.82	0.28	1.95	981.16	297.66
54.19	31.72	18.64	0.08	1.94	5.02	0.12	3.07	437.21	121.18
41.21	35.43	1.36	0.41	0.01	2.82	0.78	25.91	1048.71	434.03
151.71	142.90	4.42	0.05		2.29	1.09	6.11	469.97	120.14
0.24	0.21	0.01	0.04			0.10	0.29	21.22	0.27
0.54	0.36	0.15	0.03				0.03	5.18	0.53
7.93	7.85	0.08	0.20				0.00	32.47	11.90
2.00	1.52	0.43	0.03			0.30	0.09	33.44	1.64
11.60	11.57	0.02	0.06		0.00	0.00	0.15	194.52	34.02
3.80	3.55	0.25	0.04				0.03	58.32	13.79
28.89	27.57	0.69	0.05		0.00	0.44	3.94	203.19	22.95
0.79	0.66	0.12	0.03				0.07	202.32	72.66
6.25	3.45	2.47	0.01	1.22	0.64		0.02	131.99	36.44
2.07	1.64	0.30	0.01	0.01	0.01	0.28	14.36	118.98	7.49
9.70	8.43	0.48	0.02		0.87		0.04	49.60	32.65

12-16 蔬菜瓜果播种面积

单位：千公顷

市(县)	City(County)	蔬菜及食用菌 Vegetables and Edible fungus	叶菜类 Leaf Vegetables	白菜类 Chinese Cabbage	甘蓝类 Cabbages	块根、块茎类 Root and Stem Tuber for Vegetable	瓜菜类 Melons for Vegetable
	2012	1676.77	190.67	188.28	51.70	218.62	175.49
	2013	1682.96	192.98	185.59	52.01	225.45	175.36
	2014	1654.84	192.68	185.36	48.41	226.78	175.44
	2015	1671.03	208.00	198.79	42.75	190.65	212.17
	2016	1682.12	225.90	150.10	42.17	175.49	208.66
	2017	1736.14	237.67	150.58	42.90	174.26	208.14
	2018	1721.09	239.03	157.11	41.24	184.57	200.61
	2019	1732.94	255.43	160.33	44.73	192.13	203.21
省辖市	**City**						
郑州市	Zhengzhou	55.32	8.82	3.47	1.03	4.00	4.40
开封市	Kaifeng	170.87	16.53	17.58	6.49	27.76	11.65
洛阳市	Luoyang	67.60	9.72	4.72	1.30	9.58	7.88
平顶山市	Pingdingshan	48.36	9.19	4.84	1.26	6.13	4.91
安阳市	Anyang	89.96	11.23	8.82	1.65	5.81	12.81
鹤壁市	Hebi	11.21	2.23	1.56	0.39	0.94	1.62
新乡市	Xinxiang	63.76	11.40	12.36	0.55	4.81	8.02
焦作市	Jiaozuo	33.59	4.98	4.92	1.11	4.26	5.64
濮阳市	Puyang	59.12	7.32	5.93	1.32	3.59	8.82
许昌市	Xuchang	41.62	7.43	5.44	0.34	5.78	3.08
漯河市	Luohe	62.75	12.43	4.47	0.71	4.71	7.16
三门峡市	Sanmenxia	32.63	4.20	2.75	1.69	5.41	3.18
南阳市	Nanyang	249.00	32.59	22.16	11.24	36.79	21.74
商丘市	Shangqiu	213.24	27.34	21.01	2.82	16.03	22.82
信阳市	Xinyang	142.47	25.48	13.23	5.46	20.25	16.89
周口市	Zhoukou	265.22	43.45	16.62	4.52	21.59	42.80
驻马店市	Zhumadian	121.28	20.77	9.83	2.77	14.24	19.06
济源市	Jiyuan	4.96	0.33	0.62	0.07	0.45	0.74
省直管县	**County Directly Administrated by Province**						
巩义市	Gongyi	1.63	0.43	0.15	0.01	0.35	0.21
兰考县	Lankao	9.07	1.21	0.71	0.20	0.61	1.09
汝州市	Ruzhou	7.24	1.49	1.10	0.23	0.90	0.79
滑县	Huaxian	33.11	7.84	3.23	0.65	2.06	4.44
长垣市	Changyuan	10.49	1.89	1.45	0.02	0.95	1.95
邓州市	Dengzhou	39.97	3.97	2.96	1.82	5.04	5.69
永城市	Yongcheng	29.10	1.48	3.04	0.35	4.06	5.57
固始县	Gushi	36.73	6.98	3.45	1.33	3.98	3.57
鹿邑县	Luyi	30.76	7.45	2.79	0.93	2.12	4.30
新蔡县	Xincai	13.29	1.94	1.33	0.44	2.65	1.84

Total Sown Areas of Vegetables and Fruits

(1000 hectare)

菜用豆类 Legume for Vegetable	茄果菜类 Eggplant and Fruit for Vegetable	葱蒜类 Shallot and Garlic for Vegetable	水生菜类 Aquicolous Vegetable	其他蔬菜 Other Vegetables	瓜果类 Melon and Fruit	西瓜 Watermelon	甜瓜 Honey-dew Melon	草莓 Strawberry
126.87	273.52	222.91	31.50	197.21	308.05	256.67	46.28	4.94
124.69	327.35	224.06	30.94	144.52	309.75	258.45	45.88	5.23
126.39	321.08	213.85	30.24	134.61	297.05	248.15	43.51	5.20
135.38	346.40	208.32	24.55	104.01	292.69	241.45	44.78	6.40
143.65	387.74	217.45	25.58	105.38	312.36	257.03	47.63	7.71
145.08	398.50	235.63	26.54	116.82	318.24	260.86	48.12	9.25
139.49	385.75	232.65	25.41	115.24	307.69	251.08	46.49	9.76
127.09	388.58	241.15	23.72	96.57	308.60	250.11	45.97	10.34
3.79	6.02	19.83	0.57	3.38	6.72	5.03	0.18	1.24
7.86	23.67	52.99	2.43	3.91	47.46	43.75	3.57	0.09
6.72	17.33	8.46	0.36	1.53	7.26	5.18	1.07	0.89
4.00	9.17	5.01	0.29	3.56	5.84	4.76	0.87	0.18
6.24	33.18	6.10	0.14	3.98	12.95	5.37	7.41	0.06
0.73	2.17	0.55	0.00	1.02	0.22	0.14	0.03	0.03
4.23	13.28	5.09	0.24	3.78	4.43	3.74	0.61	0.05
3.22	4.71	3.50	0.28	0.97	3.15	2.70	0.19	0.07
6.16	12.76	6.14	1.79	5.27	5.59	3.54	1.40	0.40
2.63	12.88	2.18	0.49	1.37	3.04	2.42	0.50	0.07
2.69	19.18	5.49	0.05	5.86	10.81	7.03	2.48	0.97
2.24	9.05	2.44	0.35	1.32	3.42	2.90	0.38	0.13
18.21	41.72	30.90	8.11	25.54	25.98	20.20	5.24	0.50
9.54	69.59	35.31	0.76	8.03	45.22	40.58	2.74	1.62
15.40	18.40	14.05	4.38	8.93	27.08	20.63	4.23	1.93
24.10	72.09	25.94	2.61	11.49	77.87	64.81	11.83	1.16
8.88	21.55	16.91	0.84	6.43	21.49	17.30	3.22	0.92
0.46	1.81	0.26	0.01	0.21	0.09	0.05	0.00	0.03
0.12	0.17	0.17	0.00	0.02	0.16	0.15	0.00	0.01
0.77	2.34	1.91	0.14	0.09	2.67	1.72	0.91	0.02
0.48	0.90	0.73	0.00	0.62	0.51	0.35	0.09	0.04
2.07	6.79	3.08	0.05	2.89	5.42	1.52	3.87	0.02
0.67	2.46	0.96	0.10	0.04	2.03	1.50	0.51	0.01
3.23	9.26	4.83	2.10	1.07	4.58	3.57	0.94	0.06
2.81	7.89	2.61	0.32	0.97	5.97	5.58	0.21	0.17
4.01	4.34	6.06	1.31	1.71	6.84	4.82	1.18	0.84
2.82	4.57	2.85	0.08	2.86	1.98	0.99	0.65	0.30
0.63	2.07	2.09	0.10	0.20	6.59	4.84	1.35	0.34

12-17 蔬菜及食用菌、瓜果产量

单位：万吨

市(县) City(County)	蔬菜及食用菌 Vegetables and Edible fungus	叶菜类 Leaf Vegetables	白菜类 Chinese Cabbage	甘蓝类 Cabbages	块根、块茎类 Root and Stem Tuber for Vegetable	瓜菜类 Melons for Vegetable
2012	6839.94	778.42	888.40	233.85	1019.10	824.08
2013	6745.29	782.09	932.95	241.10	1065.19	821.63
2014	6848.11	784.62	975.49	228.56	1096.56	855.04
2015	6970.99	795.78	983.75	205.66	925.79	989.86
2016	7238.18	924.53	828.76	205.96	906.71	1040.30
2017	7530.22	961.76	842.08	212.09	901.12	1059.34
2018	7260.67	944.40	812.72	198.26	900.80	996.04
2019	7368.74	971.76	833.93	211.50	907.23	1021.79
省辖市 City						
郑州市 Zhengzhou	213.17	28.91	20.73	4.84	19.44	21.52
开封市 Kaifeng	809.93	78.71	96.69	28.27	144.94	65.85
洛阳市 Luoyang	281.82	38.18	26.01	5.59	35.68	34.86
平顶山市 Pingdingshan	232.87	35.22	26.54	6.97	35.14	26.89
安阳市 Anyang	480.52	51.75	52.14	9.86	34.91	99.25
鹤壁市 Hebi	42.90	5.53	10.70	1.22	4.09	5.81
新乡市 Xinxiang	308.00	41.22	65.61	2.32	24.48	44.59
焦作市 Jiaozuo	194.14	22.98	31.01	6.49	26.17	38.95
濮阳市 Puyang	253.44	27.52	28.56	7.44	16.62	38.86
许昌市 Xuchang	150.55	20.93	25.76	1.45	27.17	15.31
漯河市 Luohe	192.48	37.65	22.70	1.77	23.09	27.30
三门峡市 Sanmenxia	123.44	10.89	11.21	7.97	20.89	15.33
南阳市 Nanyang	1127.21	130.25	117.36	62.49	182.58	119.09
商丘市 Shangqiu	981.16	109.72	119.57	15.09	81.98	118.51
信阳市 Xinyang	437.21	71.72	52.23	19.17	71.99	61.86
周口市 Zhoukou	1048.71	188.99	78.42	18.84	89.71	213.61
驻马店市 Zhumadian	469.97	70.28	44.91	11.43	65.89	70.84
济源市 Jiyuan	21.22	1.31	3.77	0.29	2.44	3.38
省直管县 County Directly Administrated by Province						
巩义市 Gongyi	5.18	0.74	0.58	0.04	1.33	1.03
兰考县 Lankao	32.47	4.84	2.98	0.78	2.92	4.42
汝州市 Ruzhou	33.44	5.42	6.98	1.21	4.42	3.37
滑县 Huaxian	194.52	36.32	20.98	4.60	13.58	36.08
长垣市 Changyuan	58.32	9.34	8.81	0.08	6.00	12.61
邓州市 Dengzhou	203.19	18.35	21.72	10.90	27.69	31.40
永城市 Yongcheng	202.32	5.66	21.17	4.07	25.52	42.39
固始县 Gushi	131.99	25.62	16.40	4.79	25.42	17.32
鹿邑县 Luyi	118.98	29.50	12.56	2.43	9.36	18.75
新蔡县 Xincai	49.60	4.63	8.67	1.18	10.00	8.00

Output of Vegetables, Edible Fungis and Fruits

(10 000tons)

菜用豆类 Legume for Vegetable	茄果菜类 Eggplant and Fruit for Vegetable	葱蒜类 Shallot and Garlic for Vegetable	水生菜类 Aquicolous Vegetable	其他蔬菜 Others	食用菌 Edible Fungus	瓜果类 Melon and Fruit	西瓜 Watermelon	甜瓜 Honey-dew Melon	草莓 Strawberry
477.60	1018.63	863.76	134.91	460.53	140.66	1515.71	1328.94	172.12	14.64
468.03	1039.70	841.00	129.39	267.33	156.86	1534.13	1342.89	176.67	14.58
480.37	1063.11	810.84	123.69	263.11	166.71	1468.76	1285.42	169.34	14.00
515.61	1235.79	751.66	100.38	288.95	177.76	1519.94	1349.91	152.37	17.66
540.75	1386.27	815.87	105.96	304.27	178.79	1613.93	1402.18	191.70	20.05
560.80	1461.41	914.54	107.86	328.35	180.86	1670.46	1447.01	201.38	22.08
519.05	1406.77	888.41	103.27	325.70	165.26	1585.37	1364.32	196.99	22.68
464.67	1427.54	925.95	96.06	334.40	173.91	1638.92	1417.17	187.29	25.70
13.58	28.08	57.31	2.96	15.52	0.27	26.04	21.75	0.45	3.60
35.76	106.59	214.05	13.37	19.30	6.41	253.69	239.01	14.26	0.20
22.14	69.09	32.10	1.10	7.56	9.50	20.84	16.72	2.87	1.04
15.27	39.31	18.12	1.27	15.58	12.55	23.55	20.34	2.62	0.42
26.33	142.50	37.35	0.67	19.15	6.61	79.67	35.08	44.07	0.18
2.34	8.06	1.73	0.00	2.53	0.90	0.88	0.71	0.08	0.04
13.28	68.18	19.61	0.73	12.57	15.39	23.30	20.28	2.82	0.11
13.60	27.49	18.31	1.10	6.65	1.39	17.34	14.94	0.82	0.17
22.24	50.63	19.63	5.47	20.57	15.89	24.10	17.75	4.67	1.06
9.41	36.30	7.53	1.93	4.30	0.45	12.06	9.90	1.87	0.20
8.00	41.36	16.70	0.26	12.39	1.27	43.70	31.83	6.83	3.48
6.34	26.45	8.42	1.83	4.61	9.51	9.11	8.05	0.78	0.26
88.09	150.80	146.87	37.57	65.14	26.97	131.36	115.98	14.29	1.00
42.17	276.48	142.48	3.44	48.96	22.77	297.66	279.35	11.01	5.04
43.26	50.41	30.84	9.99	18.85	6.89	121.18	98.84	17.22	4.37
75.81	219.58	103.89	11.13	38.93	9.79	434.03	381.61	50.35	1.70
25.84	79.66	50.31	3.19	21.55	26.08	120.14	104.83	12.26	2.78
1.21	6.56	0.71	0.04	0.23	1.27	0.27	0.20	0.00	0.07
0.27	0.67	0.41	0.00	0.10	0.01	0.53	0.51	0.00	0.02
2.35	6.69	6.21	0.51	0.21	0.57	11.90	7.99	3.79	0.05
1.56	3.46	3.04	0.02	3.02	0.93	1.64	1.04	0.39	0.06
9.38	41.25	17.65	0.31	14.10	0.28	34.02	9.72	24.22	0.06
3.32	12.02	4.91	0.37	0.62	0.23	13.79	11.25	2.48	0.03
15.81	42.17	17.66	11.26	5.49	0.73	22.95	19.77	3.00	0.15
18.74	50.68	24.93	1.95	7.16	0.05	72.66	71.93	0.40	0.33
9.96	12.17	12.95	3.27	4.07	0.03	36.44	28.98	5.82	1.64
7.13	19.53	8.28	0.25	11.05	0.15	7.49	4.60	2.35	0.48
1.84	9.59	4.58	0.31	0.47	0.34	32.65	25.34	5.62	1.41

12-18 各市茶园、果园面积
Area of Tea Garden and Orchard

单位：千公顷 (1 000 hectares)

市(县)	City(County)	茶园面积 Tea Garden	果园面积 Orchard	#苹果园 Apple Orchards	#梨园 Pears Orchards	#葡萄园 Grapes Orchards	#柑橘园 Orange Orchards	#猕猴桃园 Chinese Goosebeery Orchards	#桃园 Peach Orchards
	2012	87.63	467.96	179.73	52.12	29.69	10.99	10.24	76.42
	2013	97.69	477.19	177.67	52.48	32.50	11.54	10.30	76.57
	2014	105.47	460.05	173.09	53.15	34.07	11.75	10.82	70.20
	2015	114.00	457.47	171.48	54.94	36.41	11.60	10.99	74.04
	2016	118.29	449.55	157.84	54.81	38.05	11.60	11.16	78.87
	2017	115.76	442.67	147.39	55.49	36.94	11.74	11.34	82.42
	2018	115.67	434.07	129.06	63.36	39.04	8.53	12.00	88.23
	2019	114.64	432.28	119.29	65.53	41.99	4.47	13.33	90.34
省辖市	**City**								
郑州市	Zhengzhou	0.03	20.03	2.01	1.24	3.66	0.00	0.07	2.37
开封市	Kaifeng	0.00	17.76	8.32	1.41	1.50		0.01	5.13
洛阳市	Luoyang		42.80	15.21	2.64	4.62		0.31	4.28
平顶山市	Pingdingshan	0.03	15.66	0.87	3.10	2.50	0.02	0.12	4.07
安阳市	Anyang		24.12	6.36	2.33	1.02		0.01	4.85
鹤壁市	Hebi		1.86	0.32	0.23	0.10		0.00	0.66
新乡市	Xinxiang		16.63	3.38	2.00	1.59	0.00	0.02	6.66
焦作市	Jiaozuo		6.73	1.03	0.85	0.67		0.12	2.68
濮阳市	Puyang		10.77	3.88	2.04	0.56			2.09
许昌市	Xuchang		4.38	1.10	0.42	0.71		0.01	0.77
漯河市	Luohe		3.11	0.09	0.62	1.35		0.13	0.65
三门峡市	Sanmenxia		64.68	46.65	1.63	2.65		0.08	5.02
南阳市	Nanyang	4.97	85.72	4.48	14.95	3.95	4.19	11.80	21.71
商丘市	Shangqiu		53.44	21.55	14.30	6.42		0.14	9.12
信阳市	Xinyang	106.46	19.71	0.13	3.97	4.95	0.26	0.45	7.20
周口市	Zhoukou		22.14	3.09	5.94	2.70		0.01	5.01
驻马店市	Zhumadian	3.14	20.69	0.43	7.61	2.94		0.04	7.62
济源市	Jiyuan	0.02	2.05	0.38	0.26	0.10		0.01	0.45
省直管县	**County Directly Administrated by Province**								
巩义市	Gongyi		1.60	0.22	0.15	0.29		0.00	0.11
兰考县	Lankao	0.00	5.00	2.93	0.58	0.37			0.90
汝州市	Ruzhou		4.19	0.43	0.27	0.45	0.01	0.02	0.92
滑县	Huaxian		4.49	1.49	0.82	0.52		0.00	1.04
长垣市	Changyuan		1.48	0.10	0.16	0.33			0.16
邓州市	Dengzhou	0.02	4.57	0.24	1.28	0.45	0.31	0.14	1.53
永城市	Yongcheng		5.42	1.18	1.72	0.84		0.00	1.06
固始县	Gushi	6.73	0.95	0.00	0.14	0.19	0.02	0.22	0.14
鹿邑县	Luyi		0.57	0.24	0.05	0.16			0.12
新蔡县	Xincai		2.90	0.42	1.43	0.34		0.01	0.65

12-19 茶叶、园林水果及食用坚果产量
Output of Tea, Garden Fruit and Edible Nuts

单位：万吨 (10 000tons)

市(县)	City(County)	茶叶 Tea	园林水果 Garden Fruit	#苹果 Apple	#梨 Pear	#葡萄 Grape	#枣 Jujube	#柿 Persimmon	#桃 Peach	柑橘 Orange	食用坚果 Edible Nuts	核桃 Walnut	板栗 Chinese Chiestnut
2012		5.14	872.91	438.99	104.82	55.33	40.78	54.41	110.33	4.04	33.06	10.97	22.09
2013		5.59	891.25	445.86	108.24	55.83	41.77	54.81	109.79	4.81	37.45	8.30	12.23
2014		6.11	899.36	444.83	113.52	58.57	35.85	54.53	112.83	4.67	38.40	10.70	17.70
2015		6.49	919.68	453.19	115.53	64.00	32.63	52.19	118.89	4.94	46.50	16.59	28.36
2016		6.86	927.12	442.42	118.27	68.54	33.00	51.14	127.26	4.79	47.82	18.04	28.10
2017		6.40	931.98	434.53	121.84	70.29	29.91	50.87	133.58	4.91	49.95	19.10	29.56
2018		6.34	907.39	402.74	122.86	76.96	25.23	48.39	141.42	3.91	48.59	20.34	28.22
2019		6.53	950.74	408.79	137.43	83.22	18.30	46.39	154.60	4.63	49.49	21.51	27.88
省辖市	**City**												
郑州市	Zhengzhou	0.00	25.59	3.45	2.16	4.30	3.96	1.01	2.96		3.67	3.67	0.00
开封市	Kaifeng	0.00	48.31	22.99	3.96	3.99	0.41	1.35	14.93		0.10	0.10	
洛阳市	Luoyang		85.32	44.73	5.58	10.12	0.95	7.27	7.92		5.21	4.64	0.55
平顶山市	Pingdingshan	0.00	23.64	0.98	3.46	9.14	0.14	1.44	5.89		2.42	1.83	0.60
安阳市	Anyang		48.83	17.91	7.23	2.60	5.87	1.70	11.82		0.67	0.66	0.01
鹤壁市	Hebi		3.79	1.03	1.06	0.47	0.17	0.31	0.74		0.08	0.08	
新乡市	Xinxiang		31.81	7.55	3.81	2.35	0.34	0.72	16.57	0.00	0.21	0.20	
焦作市	Jiaozuo		14.59	2.61	2.20	1.54	0.13	1.02	6.21		0.76	0.76	0.00
濮阳市	Puyang		28.39	14.48	5.24	1.45	0.61	0.16	3.37		0.35	0.35	
许昌市	Xuchang		6.73	1.79	1.08	1.76	0.16	0.09	1.54		0.54	0.54	
漯河市	Luohe		9.50	0.26	1.62	5.16	0.02	0.10	2.12		0.02	0.02	
三门峡市	Sanmenxia		250.66	196.90	6.18	7.92	2.48	15.83	15.11		5.45	4.82	0.62
南阳市	Nanyang	0.26	107.25	2.01	15.10	2.82	0.45	3.77	19.13	4.49	6.97	3.08	3.87
商丘市	Shangqiu		179.57	82.38	58.96	17.84	0.21	2.68	14.94		0.06	0.06	
信阳市	Xinyang	6.15	14.18	0.05	3.56	2.80	0.20	0.79	6.06	0.14	16.36	0.02	16.30
周口市	Zhoukou		50.73	8.18	9.64	6.07	1.94	7.50	16.67		0.02	0.02	
驻马店市	Zhumadian	0.12	18.10	0.45	5.71	2.75	0.27	0.27	8.01	0.00	6.01	0.08	5.93
济源市	Jiyuan		3.73	1.05	0.88	0.15	0.00	0.40	0.63		0.58	0.58	
省直管县	**County Directly Administrated by Province**												
巩义市	Gongyi		2.91	0.58	0.34	0.74	0.01	0.14	0.23		0.40	0.40	0.00
兰考县	Lankao	0.00	13.75	7.77	1.96	1.14	0.06	0.03	2.33		0.07	0.07	
汝州市	Ruzhou		4.36	0.41	0.29	0.66	0.08	0.93	1.29		0.17	0.16	0.00
滑县	Huaxian		16.10	5.68	3.46	1.55	0.34	1.00	3.76		0.23	0.23	
长垣市	Changyuan		1.58	0.19	0.17	0.65	0.27	0.00	0.29		0.07	0.07	
邓州市	Dengzhou	0.00	3.92	0.09	0.78	0.32	0.01	0.07	2.21	0.22	0.06	0.05	0.00
永城市	Yongcheng		27.26	5.26	17.57	1.79	0.04	0.29	2.06				
固始县	Gushi	0.30	1.49		0.21	0.35	0.03	0.21	0.39	0.00	0.34	0.01	0.34
鹿邑县	Luyi		1.24	0.49	0.09	0.25	0.01	0.01	0.39		0.01	0.01	
新蔡县	Xincai		2.05	0.44	1.00	0.28		0.02	0.30		0.00		0.00

12-20 各市林业生产情况(2019年)

单位：千公顷

市(县)	City(County)	当年造林面积 CurrentNew Forest Area	#人工造林 By Manpower	飞播造林 Afforestation by Aerial Seeding	封山育林 Closing Hillsides for Afforestation	其中：无林地和疏林地封山育林 without Forest Land and Sparse Forest Land
全　　省	**Total**	**196.49**	**164.77**	**13.34**	**18.29**	**18.29**
省 辖 市	**City**					
郑 州 市	Zhengzhou	6.67	6.33		0.34	0.34
开 封 市	Kaifeng	8.16	8.16			
洛 阳 市	Luoyang	12.62	7.72	2.33	2.57	2.57
平顶山市	Pingdingshan	8.98	8.98			
安 阳 市	Anyang	5.06	4.33		0.66	0.66
鹤 壁 市	Hebi	6.66	5.96	0.67		
新 乡 市	Xinxiang	7.06	4.78	2.00	0.28	0.28
焦 作 市	Jiaozuo	4.29	2.69	1.33	0.26	0.26
濮 阳 市	Puyang	4.76	4.76			
许 昌 市	Xuchang	7.49	6.82	0.67		
漯 河 市	Luohe	4.82	4.82			
三门峡市	Sanmenxia	20.40	15.12	2.33	2.95	2.95
南 阳 市	Nanyang	43.78	34.89	3.00	5.89	5.89
商 丘 市	Shangqiu	6.65	6.65			
信 阳 市	Xinyang	26.86	22.28		4.57	4.57
周 口 市	Zhoukou	6.40	6.40			
驻马店市	Zhumadian	11.02	10.63		0.40	0.40
济 源 市	Jiyuan	4.80	3.45	1.00	0.36	0.36
省直管县	**County Directly Administrated by Province**					
巩 义 市	Gongyi	2.32	2.32			
兰 考 县	Lankao	1.33	1.33			
汝 州 市	Ruzhou	2.92	2.92			
滑　　县	Huaxian	1.48	1.48			
长 垣 市	Changyuan	1.45	1.45			
邓 州 市	Dengzhou	2.27	1.93		0.35	0.35
永 城 市	Yongcheng	0.75	0.75			
固 始 县	Gushi	2.28	2.28			
鹿 邑 县	Luyi	1.54	1.54			
新 蔡 县	Xincai	1.61	1.61			

Conditions of Forestry Production by City (2019)

(1 000 hectares)

				森林抚育面积	木材产量(万立方米)	大径竹产量(万根)
退化林修复 Restoration of Degraded Forest	用材林 Timber Forest	经济林 Economic Forest	防护林 Shelter Forest	Area of Tending Woods	Wood (10 000 Cubic metres)	Bamboo Wood (10 000 pieces)
0.10	**46.45**	**27.58**	**122.37**	**303.04**	**256.03**	**120.44**
	0.37	2.69	3.62	4.07	7.64	
	3.47	0.48	4.21	4.87	16.52	
		4.28	8.35	50.41	9.08	
		2.00	6.98	21.46	5.75	
0.07	2.62	0.48	1.90	5.20	8.64	
0.03		3.39	3.24	4.32	1.21	
	0.85	0.39	5.82	5.15	17.40	
	0.53	0.37	3.40	6.74	9.59	
	2.29	0.19	2.28	3.48	2.22	
	1.00	2.60	3.89	4.93	9.83	
	1.07	0.21	3.53	0.44	9.65	
	0.15	1.68	18.58	37.02	6.44	
	5.57	2.08	36.14	81.94	23.20	
	1.88	0.31	4.46	7.67	21.53	
	11.15	5.36	10.34	46.55	50.21	120.44
	5.86		0.54	8.55	19.78	
	9.64	0.54	0.84	7.94	34.49	
		0.55	4.25	2.30	2.85	
		0.74	1.58	0.73	0.88	
		0.33	1.00	0.40	5.14	
		0.58	2.33	2.83	0.78	
	1.34	0.15		0.80		
		0.07	1.38		3.67	
		0.14	2.14		2.69	
		0.13	0.62	0.80	6.80	
	0.26		1.78	0.86	8.45	30.00
	1.54			0.73		
	1.61			0.73		

12-21 牧渔业产量

Output of Animal Husbandry and Fishery

年 份 Year	肉类产量(万吨) Total Output of Meat (10 000 tons)	#猪肉 Pork	#牛肉 Beef	#羊肉 Mutton	#禽肉 Poultry	大牲畜年底头数(万头) Large Animals at Year-end (10 000 heads)	#役畜 Draught Animals	猪年底头数(万头) Hogs (10 000 heads)	禽蛋产量(万吨) Poultry Eggs (10 000 tons)	奶类产量(万吨) Output of Milk (10 000 tons)	水产品产量(万吨) Total Aquatic Products (10 000 tons)
1978	45.64	42.20				515.03	401.70	1724.90			2.47
1979	55.14	50.00				521.50	400.40	1592.30			2.30
1980	55.03	49.45	0.69	2.88	1.90	541.99	423.75	1474.24	15.86	2.20	2.91
1981	51.58	44.30	0.60	3.36		607.00	498.90	1386.50	16.31		3.00
1982	54.26	47.60	0.52	3.46		671.50	542.10	1310.70	16.75		3.25
1983	51.33	43.70	0.88	3.41		704.70	562.20	1195.70	21.41		3.78
1984	58.59	49.60	1.83	3.31		794.70	615.70	1327.00	31.38		4.89
1985	71.83	61.08	3.01	3.38	4.10	886.35	664.55	1621.74	37.15	4.50	6.37
1986	79.42	65.00	5.50	3.70		957.44	708.10	1539.41	37.32		6.61
1987	86.63	66.10	8.90	5.00		1000.82	738.44	1404.72	43.55		7.62
1988	103.75	76.87	12.24	6.48		1069.20	779.57	1586.18	50.43		9.39
1989	121.53	88.11	15.26	7.89		1111.56	794.04	1680.22	53.62		9.83
1990	134.86	97.45	18.16	8.05	9.40	1116.33	798.30	1750.32	59.58	7.40	10.48
1991	157.95	108.73	24.82	7.76		1102.10	782.25	1820.80	73.81		10.77
1992	171.66	119.23	25.67	7.96		1135.50	794.90	1959.70	79.29		11.55
1993	203.51	137.60	32.64	9.90	19.30	1211.00	843.00	2085.00	95.58	7.50	13.83
1994	253.31	165.81	44.00	12.57	25.70	1329.18	919.79	2325.17	125.28	8.90	15.84
1995	333.00	210.37	64.39	21.10	31.00	1420.45	985.76	2667.72	140.01	9.80	18.09
1996	347.72	225.63	59.45	21.72	34.10	1089.14	783.00	2229.67	154.54	9.70	20.51
1997	403.00	256.12	64.88	25.23	49.30	1420.87	857.03	2931.91	201.40	10.60	23.88
1998	461.63	297.86	76.71	28.00	50.76	1416.84	803.70	3439.66	229.34	12.30	27.02
1999	485.11	313.95	82.21	29.96	51.47	1448.42	530.60	3556.43	251.82	15.90	28.83
2000	517.00	337.88	83.00	32.00	55.00	1445.73	482.84	3787.69	270.00	20.20	32.17
2001	540.65	343.77	89.23	34.51	63.90	1435.93	479.53	3672.07	286.00	30.00	31.46
2002	570.01	366.49	89.20	37.85	66.40	1409.78	437.03	3800.00	302.00	39.00	36.22
2003	603.55	386.00	93.00	42.00	74.00	1469.45	430.00	3917.80	326.20	52.60	38.95
2004	643.00	412.37	98.33	44.06	79.55	1491.19	427.00	4152.87	347.40	78.90	42.70
2005	689.00	441.20	102.75	47.38	87.51	1508.80	412.90	4439.00	375.30	108.50	51.68
2006	584.60	391.30	82.00	23.80	76.60	1114.26	410.12	3953.30	329.50	142.26	40.98
2007	545.87	338.88	75.28	24.82	84.58	985.75	387.21	4184.00	333.14	149.82	45.68
2008	573.35	366.84	70.70	25.51	91.52	910.09	337.42	4458.81	363.82	201.86	50.58
2009	591.61	389.18	64.75	24.46	96.88	814.97	369.30	4524.05	370.74	203.56	53.77
2010	608.96	407.72	58.67	23.35	101.32	719.19	296.16	4540.55	372.29	207.04	57.86
2011	604.28	405.67	53.14	22.54	105.59	619.07	243.38	4560.84	370.13	214.85	65.47
2012	632.84	431.57	47.80	22.07	114.60	537.56	211.21	4577.45	379.00	220.85	71.72
2013	648.97	452.99	43.89	21.66	113.48	487.16	200.09	4415.68	380.58	219.07	85.01
2014	662.02	476.63	41.02	21.80	108.34	447.59	192.82	4407.38	370.81	227.28	91.76
2015	647.22	466.45	37.84	21.81	108.97	411.70	183.71	4361.95	372.30	233.66	102.37
2016	625.94	449.04	34.87	21.85	110.05	353.67	167.47	4268.82	379.56	223.30	94.76
2017	655.84	466.90	35.04	26.10	118.97	376.09	108.50	4390.00	401.18	212.87	94.67
2018	669.41	479.04	34.80	26.90	121.94	377.01	107.96	4337.15	413.61	208.90	98.38
2019	560.06	344.43	36.22	28.11	145.24	388.27	92.21	3170.46	442.42	208.55	99.08

12-22 畜禽产品年末存栏数量及产量
Number of Livestock and Output of Livestock Products at Year-end

单位：万头、万只 (10 000 heads)

指标	Item	1980	1990	2000	2005	2010	2015	2017	2018	2019
年底存栏总头数	**Number of Livestock at Year-end**									
#大牲畜	Large Livestock	541.99	1116.33	1445.73	1508.80	719.19	411.70	376.09	377.01	388.27
#从事农事劳役	Draught Animals	423.75	798.30	482.84	412.90	296.16	183.71	108.50	107.96	92.21
牛	Cow	339.60	892.50	1340.20	1447.00	695.05	402.68	372.67	373.41	385.13
#肉牛	Cattle	177.70		282.80	514.06	346.53	181.76	230.51	231.12	257.32
#乳牛	Dairy	0.90	1.90	6.70	31.22	52.35	37.22	33.66	34.33	35.60
马	Horse	52.20	39.20	29.30	17.29	8.05	2.80	0.97	0.91	0.72
驴	Donkey	94.30	120.90	49.50	29.60	12.34	5.13	2.18	2.33	2.11
骡	Mule	55.90	63.70	26.80	14.91	3.76	1.09	0.28	0.35	0.30
猪	Pig	1474.24	1750.32	3787.69	4439.00	4540.55	4361.95	4390.00	4337.15	3170.46
羊	Sheep	1147.80	1279.50	2961.40	3988.00	1895.40	1926.00	1682.02	1734.07	1898.81
山羊	Goat	764.80	1129.50	2730.10	3509.00	1662.88	1552.77	1412.88	1473.96	1896.09
绵羊	Sheep	383.00	150.00	231.30	479.00	232.52	373.23	269.14	260.11	405.02
家禽	Poultry		19849.90	42529.00	61958.00	56708.51	57070.49	65019.50	65799.73	69601.71
猪牛羊出栏头(只)数	**Slaughtered Fattened Hogs, Cattle and Sheep**									
肉猪	Hogs	684.70	1182.40	4180.00	5568.00	5382.80	6151.36	6220.00	6402.38	4502.10
肉用牛	Cattle	9.00	167.90	578.00	702.64	390.08	251.29	232.95	231.16	238.43
肉用羊	Sheep and Goats	289.10	834.00	2903.80	4225.00	1959.16	1790.23	2145.00	2208.19	2301.11
肉用禽	Poultry					81530.72	83132.35	90681.61	92767.28	108816.02
肉类总产量(万吨)	**Total Output of Meat (10 000 tons)**	**55.03**	**134.86**	**517.00**	**689.00**	**608.96**	**647.22**	**655.84**	**669.41**	**560.06**
#猪肉	Pork	49.40	97.40	337.90	441.20	407.72	466.45	466.90	479.04	344.43
牛肉	Beef	0.70	18.20	83.00	102.75	58.67	37.84	35.04	34.80	36.22
羊肉	Mutton	2.90	8.10	32.00	47.38	23.35	21.81	26.10	26.90	28.11
禽肉	Meat of Poultry	1.90	9.40	55.00	87.51	101.32	108.97	118.97	121.94	145.24
兔肉	Rabbit	0.10	0.30	4.20	5.66	9.46	6.23	4.85	4.41	4.20
其他畜产品产量	**Others Output of Livestock Products**									
奶类总产量(万吨)	Output of Milk (10 000 tons)	**2.20**	**7.40**	**20.20**	**108.50**	**207.04**	**233.66**	**212.87**	**208.90**	**208.55**
牛奶	Cow Milk	0.80	2.70	16.10	104.00	190.06	223.57	202.86	202.65	204.07
羊奶	Sheep Milk	1.40	4.70	4.10	5.00	16.98	10.10	10.01	6.24	4.47
羊毛总产量(吨)	Output of Wool (ton)	10708	6745	10844	14335	11984	7246	9214	6849	6447
山羊粗毛	Goat Wool	771	1372	2858	2873	4297	2245	3450	2719	2467
绵羊毛	Sheep Wool	9937	5373	7986	11462	7687	5000	5765	4130	3649
羊绒产量(吨)	Cashmere (ton)	52	102	277	7135	181	311	581	313	331
蜂蜜产量(吨)	Honey (ton)	5287	11908	23105	27441	61820	27907	71487	61393	61093
禽蛋产量(万吨)	Poultry Eggs (10 000 tons)	16	60	270	375	372	372	401	414	442
蚕茧产量(吨)	Output of Silkworm Cocoons (ton)			15190	20366	16751	7715	21563	11865	11543
#桑蚕茧	Mulberry Silkworm Cocoons			12560	14803	13287	7256	15415	6012	6006
柞蚕茧	Tussore Silkworm Cocoons			2630	5563	3464	459	6148	5852	5537

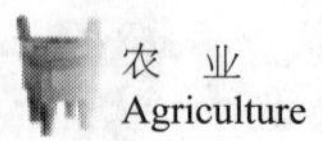

12−23 各市牲畜饲养情况(2019年底)
Number of Livestock by City (End of 2019)

市(县) City(County)	牛 (万头) Cattles (10 000 heads)	马 (头) Horses (head)	驴 (头) Donkeys (head)	骡 (头) Mules (head)	猪年底头数 (万头) Hogs (year-end) (10 000 heads)	羊年底只数 (万只) Sheep and Goats (year-end) (10 000 heads)	家 禽 (万只) Poultry (10 000 heads)	兔 (万只) Rabbits (10 000 heads)
省 辖 市 City								
郑 州 市 Zhengzhou	4.12	15	697	12	47.53	25.07	1041.91	19.99
开 封 市 Kaifeng	31.57	31	3682	1	203.52	163.01	3601.64	45.25
洛 阳 市 Luoyang	27.45	132	733	322	108.08	73.03	2145.99	119.73
平 顶 山 市 Pingdingshan	16.04	1214	2086	609	171.22	108.39	1821.46	21.80
安 阳 市 Anyang	4.42	216	431	94	102.37	52.11	3153.45	13.17
鹤 壁 市 Hebi	1.86	80	74	106	61.69	28.09	2084.55	1.96
新 乡 市 Xinxiang	16.38	24	966	21	127.01	58.81	3390.67	26.89
焦 作 市 Jiaozuo	6.23	53	61		49.72	27.12	1251.01	49.23
濮 阳 市 Puyang	4.23	614	3285	656	81.11	60.69	6852.92	20.33
许 昌 市 Xuchang	8.96	591	476	4	167.89	53.61	1647.75	29.07
漯 河 市 Luohe	2.83				154.08	19.55	2412.54	5.37
三 门 峡 市 Sanmenxia	16.58				71.46	36.77	627.47	0.53
南 阳 市 Nanyang	75.92	448	1161	20	436.72	251.02	4960.57	28.97
商 丘 市 Shangqiu	33.68	152	280		248.88	259.92	7794.95	67.96
信 阳 市 Xinyang	12.72				209.07	71.70	5487.01	53.62
周 口 市 Zhoukou	26.48	1680	1698	1165	446.02	290.03	8020.77	144.72
驻 马 店 市 Zhumadian	66.39	1979	5481		470.74	156.03	4473.28	373.03
济 源 市 Jiyuan	2.63				17.96	10.46	203.41	13.86
省 直 管 县 County Directly Administrated by Province								
巩 义 市 Gongyi	0.48	8	208	8	13.40	3.39	78.26	1.65
兰 考 县 Lankao	2.46	18	3635		14.70	27.99	829.70	3.98
汝 州 市 Ruzhou	5.37	737	521	430	53.01	33.10	661.02	4.03
滑 县 Huaxian	1.89	32	5		30.24	14.34	1350.71	2.06
长 垣 市 Changyuan	0.90		570		14.76	5.48	438.16	18.71
邓 州 市 Dengzhou	15.98				91.92	40.49	892.58	5.90
永 城 市 Yongcheng	2.04				36.25	44.26	2091.08	13.54
固 始 县 Gushi	1.01				42.04	28.53	1689.10	8.50
鹿 邑 县 Luyi	0.98				51.59	16.39	849.68	
新 蔡 县 Xincai	3.58		1260		50.79	17.91	501.63	50.61

12-24 各市畜产品产量(2019年)

Output of Livestock Products by City (2019)

市(县) City(County)	猪牛羊出栏头(只)数 Slaughtered Fattened Hogs, Cattle, Sheep and Goats			猪肉产量 (万吨) Output of Pork (10 000 tons)	蜂蜜 (吨) Honey (ton)	禽蛋 (万吨) Poultry Eggs (10 000 ton)	绵羊毛 (吨) Sheep Wool (ton)		山羊粗毛 (吨) Goat Wool (ton)
	猪(万头) Hogs (10 000 heads)	牛(万头) Cattle (10 000 heads)	羊(万只) Sheep and Goats (10 000 units)					#细羊毛 Fine Wool	
省辖市 City									
郑州市 Zhengzhou	87.78	5.14	28.32	6.50	170.60	10.78	16.92	11.14	1.20
开封市 Kaifeng	302.44	15.87	192.35	22.84	1766.27	30.30	465.20	10.04	6.68
洛阳市 Luoyang	129.76	17.12	78.36	9.92	1720.21	14.62	329.86	121.59	348.30
平顶山市 Pingdingshan	243.24	13.67	139.59	18.26	1544.84	14.50	470.91	25.18	81.62
安阳市 Anyang	170.11	2.86	70.10	14.11	80.96	17.12	207.20	1.85	3.27
鹤壁市 Hebi	106.23	1.16	26.09	8.13	5.54	12.52	57.56	28.41	45.63
新乡市 Xinxiang	292.90	8.41	85.31	21.68	92.42	28.74	210.38	52.78	52.93
焦作市 Jiaozuo	104.42	6.26	31.68	7.68	111.30	11.83	353.43	0.46	0.00
濮阳市 Puyang	101.10	4.21	109.19	7.58	0.37	26.48	698.12	4.09	1.35
许昌市 Xuchang	248.90	7.43	78.64	18.65	998.60	14.45	23.43		11.82
漯河市 Luohe	238.68	2.13	24.19	17.49	14.03	15.70			
三门峡市 Sanmenxia	77.80	7.08	40.29	6.06	2537.85	4.86	351.70	35.04	308.32
南阳市 Nanyang	511.14	50.97	328.84	38.35	24800.56	33.30	321.82	12.90	1054.63
商丘市 Shangqiu	317.27	22.64	342.30	24.00	198.76	51.09			
信阳市 Xinyang	277.09	8.81	82.37	20.71	6159.46	38.03			
周口市 Zhoukou	525.85	17.28	360.98	38.93	60.60	48.82	25.83	14.81	
驻马店市 Zhumadian	669.26	46.01	214.48	50.80	20769.83	30.71	113.16	103.01	545.98
济源市 Jiyuan	38.15	1.49	6.61	2.86	60.43	2.57	3.85	0.10	5.30
省直管县 County Directly Administrated by Province									
巩义市 Gongyi	24.00	0.30	4.53	1.72	76.83	0.77			0.01
兰考县 Lankao	24.68	1.74	37.92	1.85		8.39	41.95	10.04	6.68
汝州市 Ruzhou	62.60	3.70	20.12	4.72	201.39	5.31	23.81		
滑县 Huaxian	35.98	0.96	23.13	2.70	8.22	5.60	99.30		
长垣市 Changyuan	21.53	0.79	10.39	1.64		2.96	0.02		0.22
邓州市 Dengzhou	93.99	10.38	62.53	7.07	29.14	6.28			9.39
永城市 Yongcheng	40.28	2.14	74.66	3.02		12.52			
固始县 Gushi	69.04	1.65	37.85	5.27	13.60	12.50			
鹿邑县 Luyi	63.83	0.86	21.22	4.82		4.27			
新蔡县 Xincai	60.04	3.85	28.30	4.56	2.94	3.15			

主要统计指标解释

农林牧渔业总产值 指以货币表现的农、林、牧、渔业全部产品和对农林牧渔业生产活动进行的各种支持性服务活动的价值总量，它反映一定时期内农林牧渔业生产总规模和总成果。1957 年以前的农林牧渔业总产值中包括了厩肥和农民自给性手工业（如农民自制衣服、鞋、袜，自己从事粮食初步加工等）。1958 年及以后，林业中增加了村及村以下竹木采伐产值；牧业中取消了厩肥产值；副业中取消了农民自给性手工业产值，增加了村及村以下办的工业产值； 渔业中增加了海洋捕捞水产品产值。1980 年及以后，在副业中增加了农民家庭兼营工业商品部分的产值。从 1984 年起村及村以下工业产值划归工业。从 1993 年起取消副业，将野生动物的捕猎划入牧业，野生植物采集和农民家庭兼营商品性工业划归农业。从 2003 年起，执行新的国民经济行业分类标准，农林牧渔业总产值中包括了农林牧渔服务业产值，2018 年以后农林牧渔服务业产值改称农林牧渔专业及辅助性活动产值。林业中增加了森林采运业产值。农业中取消了家庭兼营商品性工业产值，将野生林产品的采集划归林业。第一、二、三次农业普查以后，根据农业普查结果，对农业、畜牧业、渔业年报数据和农业、畜牧业、渔业产值进行了修订。2010 年执行《统计用产品分类目录》， 对 2009 年的农业、林业产值做了相应调整。

农林牧渔业总产值的计算方法通常是按农、林、牧、渔业产品及其副产品的产量分别乘以各自单位产品价格求得；少数生产周期较长，当年没有产品或产品产量不易统计的，则采用间接方法匡算其产值；然后将四业产品产值及农林牧渔专业及辅助性活动产值相加即为农林牧渔业总产值。

粮食产量 指农业生产经营者日历年度内生产的全部粮食数量。按收获季节包括夏收粮食、早稻和秋收粮食，按作物品种包括谷物、薯类和豆类。其产量计算方法：谷物按脱粒后的原粮计算，豆类按去豆荚后的干豆计算；薯类（包括甘薯和马铃薯，不包括芋头和木薯）1963 年以前按每 4 公斤鲜薯折 1 公斤粮食计算，从 1964 年开始改为按 5 公斤鲜薯折 1 公斤粮食计算。城市郊区作为蔬菜的薯类（如马铃薯等）按鲜品计算，并且不作粮食统计。1989 年以前全国粮食产量数据主要靠全面报表取得，1989 年开始使用抽样调查数据。

棉花产量 指全社会的产量。包括春播棉和夏播棉。产量按皮棉计算。不包括木棉。

油料产量 指全部油料作物的生产量。包括花生、油菜籽、芝麻、向日葵籽、胡麻籽（亚麻籽）和其他油料。不包括大豆、木本油料和野生油料。花生以带壳干花生计算。

水产品产量 指渔业（捕捞和养殖）生产活动的最终有效成果，包括全部海水和淡水鱼类、甲壳类（虾、蟹）、贝类、头足类、藻类和其他类渔业产品的最终产量。水产品产量是通过各级水产和统计部门逐级上报取得数据。1995 年及以前，贝类中牡蛎按鲜肉计算；蚶、蛤、蛏按 5 斤鲜品折 1 斤计算。1996 年以后则统一按鲜品计算。

猪、牛、羊肉产量 指当年出栏并已屠宰、除去头蹄下水后带骨肉（即胴体重）的重量。

期初(末)畜禽存栏头(只)数 指报告期初（末）农村各种合作经济组织和国营农场、农民个人、机关、团体、学校、工矿企业、部队等单位以及城镇居民饲养的大牲畜、猪、羊、家禽等畜禽的存栏数。

常用耕地 是指耕地总资源中专门种植农作物并经常进行耕种、能够正常收获的土地。包括当年实际耕种的熟地；弃耕、休闲不满三年，随时可以复耕的地；开荒利用三年以上的地。不包括临时种植农作物的坡度在 25 度以上的陡坡地；在河套、湖畔、库区临时开发的成片或零星土地；也不包括已列为国家和省（区、市）退耕计划但临时耕种的土地。

农作物播种面积 指农业生产经营者应在日历年度内收获农作物在全部土地（耕地或非耕地）上的播种或移植面积。凡是本年内收获的农作物，无论是本年还是上年播种，都算为播种面积，但不包括本年播种，下年收获的农作物面积。

有效灌溉面积 指具有一定的水源，地块比较平整，灌溉工程或设备已经配套，在一般年景下当年能够进行正常灌溉的耕地面积。

农用化肥施用量 指本年内实际用于农业生产的化肥数量，包括氮肥、磷肥、钾肥和复合肥。化肥施用量要求按折纯量计算数量。折纯量是指把氮肥、磷肥、钾肥分别按含氮、含五氧化二磷、含氧化钾的百分之一百成份进行折算后的数量。复合肥按其所含主要成分折算。

农业机械总动力 指全部农业机械动力的额定功率之和。农业机械是指用于种植业、畜牧业、渔业、农产品初加工、农用运输和农田基本建设等活动的机械及设备。农机总动力按使用能源不同分为以下四部分：

柴油发动机动力：指全部柴油发动机额定功率之和；

汽油发动机动力：指全部汽油发动机额定功率之和；

电动机动力：指全部电动机（含潜水电泵的电动机）额定功率之和；

其他机械动力：指采用柴油、汽油、电力之外的其他能源，如水力、风力、煤炭、太阳能等动力机械功率之和。

Explanatory Notes on Main Statistical Indicators

Gross Output Value of Agriculture, Forestry, Animal Husbandry and Fishery refers to the total value of products of agriculture, forestry, animal husbandry and fishery, and total value of services in support of agriculture, forestry, animal husbandry and fishery activities. It reflects the total scale and results of agricultural production during a given period. Prior to 1957, China' s gross agricultural output value included barnyard manure and handicraft products for self-consumption (clothes, shoes, stockings, and initial grain processing undertaken by peasants). Since 1958, cutting and felling of bamboo and trees by villages and other cooperative organizations under villages have been included in forestry; value of barnyard manure has been excluded from animal husbandry; self consumed handicrafts have not been included from sideline occupations, while the output value of industries run by villages and cooperative organizations under village has been included in sideline occupations; and the output value of fish catches by motor fishing boats has been added to fishery. Since 1980, the value of handicraft products made for sale by individuals in households has been added to sideline occupations. Since 1984, industries run by villages and under villages have been included in the sector of industry. Since 1993, the subdivision of sideline occupations has been cancelled, and the hunting of wild animals has been classified into animal husbandry, and the gathering of wild plants and commodity industry run by rural household have been included in farming. A new industrial classification of economic activities was introduced in 2003. Under the new classification, value of services to agriculture, forestry, animal husbandry and fishery is included in the gross output value of agriculture. In 2018, the output value of agriculture, forestry, animal husbandry and fishery services was renamed the output value of professional and auxiliary activities in support of agriculture, forestry, animal husbandry and fishery, value of wood felling and transport is included in forestry, value of industrial output by rural households is not included in agriculture. According to the result of the first, second, third Agriculture Census, efforts were made to adjust the annual reports of animal husbandry and fishery output and the output value of agriculture, animal husbandry and fishery output to make the figures from the annual reports consistent with the census data. "The Classification of Products for Statistical Purposes" implemented in 2010 made relevant revision on the output value of agriculture and forestry in 2009.

Gross output value of agriculture is obtained by multiplying the output of each product or by-product by its price, resulting in the output value of each single item. For a small number of products, annual output of which is not available or difficult to get due to the long production (growing) process involved, the output value is estimated through an indirect approach. The sum of output values of all products of agriculture, forestry, animal husbandry and fishery and professional and auxiliary activities in support of agriculture, forestry, animal husbandry and fishery is then equal to the gross output value of agriculture.

Grain Output refers to the total output of grains produced by agricultural producers within a calendar year. It includes summer grain, early rice and autumn grain if classified by harvest seasons; it covers cereal, tubers and beans if classified by type of crops. Output of cereal should be limited to husked grain only. Output of beans refers to dry beans without pods. The output of tubers (sweet potatoes and potatoes, not including taros and cassava) are converted into that of grain at the ratio 4:1, i.e. 4 kilograms of fresh tubers were equivalent to 1 kilogram of grain up to 1963. Since 1964 the ratio for conversion has been 5:1. Tubers supplied as vegetables (such as potatoes) in cities and suburbs are calculated as fresh vegetables and their output is not included in the output of grain. Data on grain production before 1989 were obtained through the Comprehensive Statistical Reporting System. Since 1989, data from sample surveys are used.

Cotton Output refers to cotton production in the whole country including cotton planted in spring and in autumn. Output is measured as the weight of ginned cotton. Ceiba is not included.

Output of Oil-bearing Crops refers to the total production of oil-bearing crops of various kinds, including peanuts (dry, in shell), rapeseeds, sesame, sunflower seeds, flax seeds, and other oil-bearing crops. Soybeans, oil-bearing woody plants, and wild oil-bearing crops are not included.

Output of Aquatic Products refers to final output actually yielded from fishing production (fishery and breeding), including all output of marine and freshwater fish, crustaceans (shrimps, crabs), shellfish, cephalopod, seaweed and other fishery products. Data on output of aquatic products are reported by aquatic product and statistical agencies level by level. Before 1995, among the shellfish, oyster was counted as fresh meat; 5 kilograms of ark shell, clams and frogs are equivalent to 1 kilogram of fresh aquatic products; they have all been counted as fresh aquatic products since 1996.

Output of Pork, Beef, and Mutton refers to the meat of slaughtered hogs, cattle, sheep and goats with head, feet, and offal taken away.

Number of Livestock or Poultry in Stock at Beginning (or End) refers to the total number of large animals, pigs, sheep, fowls, etc. raised by rural cooperative organizations, state farms, rural individuals, government agencies, schools, industrial and mining enterprises, army, and urban residents at the beginning (or end) of the reference period.

Regularly Cultivated Land refers to farmland among the total land resources which is exclusively used for farming and is under regular cultivation with harvest in normal years. Included are currently cultivated land, land that has been abandoned or put in idle for less than 3 years and could be re-used for cultivation at any time, and new-claimed land that has been put into cultivation for more than 3 years. Excluded under this category are steep slope land over 25 degrees under temporary cultivation, land (large or small plots) that is claimed along river bends, lake sides or banks of reservoirs, as well as land that has been designated under the "Green for Grain" programs of the state and provincial governments but is still temporarily under cultivation.

Sown Area of Crops refers to area of all land (cultivated or non-cultivated area) sown or transplanted with crops that are harvested within the calendar year by agricultural producers. All crops harvested within the year are counted as sown area, regardless of being sown in this year or the previous year. Crops sown this year but will be harvested in the coming year are excluded.

Irrigated Area refers to areas that are effectively irrigated, i.e. level land, which has water source and complete sets of irrigation facilities to lift and move adequate water for irrigation purpose under normal conditions.

Consumption of Chemical Fertilizers in Agriculture refers to the quantity of chemical fertilizers applied in agriculture in the year, including nitrogenous fertilizer, phosphate fertilizer, potash fertilizer, and compound fertilizer. The consumption of chemical fertilizers is required in calculation to convert the gross weight into weight containing 100% effective component (e.g. 100% nitrogen content in nitrogenous fertilizer, 100% phosphorous-pent oxide contents in phosphate fertilizer, 100% potassium oxide contents in potash fertilizer). Compound fertilizer is converted with its major component.

Total Power of Agricultural Machinery refers to the total rated capacity of all agricultural machinery. Agricultural machinery refers to the machineries and equipments which are used for activities of planting, animal husbandry, fishery, primary processing of agricultural products, agricultural transport and infrastructure construction of farmland. Total power of agricultural machinery is grouped into four parts according to the energy used:

Diesel engine power refers to the total rated capacity of all diesel engines.

Gasoline engine power refers to the total rated capacity of all gasoline engines.

Motor power refers to the total rated capacity of all motors (include submersible pump motors).

Other mechanical powers refer to the total mechanical capacity of the sources of energy besides diesel, gasoline and motor power, such as hydro power, wind power, coal and solar energy.

工业
Industry

13

● 资料整理：张 静　冀寒阳　刘 佳　王姣慧

简要说明

一、主要内容

本篇包括河南省规模以上工业企业单位数，工业增加值指数，工业主要产品产量和主要经济效益指标；规模以下工业单位数、工业增加值指数及从业人员情况。

二、统计范围

工业统计调查范围为河南省全部工业法人企业和个体工业单位。1997年以前，我国工业的统计范围按隶属关系划分，分为乡及乡以上独立核算工业企业和非独立核算生产单位、村办工业、城镇合作工业、农村合作工业、城镇个体工业、农村个体工业六大部分，（其中，1984年以前不包括农村的村及村以下办工业）。1998年起，年起，工业统计调查对象范围的界定由按隶属关系划分，改变为按企业规模划分，分为“规模以上工业”和“规模以下工业”。规模以上工业是指全部国有及年主营业务收入在500万元及以上非国有工业企业，规模以下工业是指年主营业务收入在500万元及以上非国有工业企业及个体工业。2006年年报起，规模以上工业统计范围由全部国有及年主营业务收入在500万元以上非国有工业企业改为年主营业务收入在500万元及以上的工业法人企业，相应改变规模以下工业的调查范围为年主营业务收入在500万元以下的工业企业及个体工业。从2011年定报起，规模以上工业统计范围调整为年主营业务收入在2000万元及以上的工业法人企业，相应改变规模以下工业的调查范围为年主营业务收入在2000万元以下的工业企业及个体工业。

三、资料来源

年主营业务收入2000万元及以上的工业法人企业实行全数调查，由河南省统计局工业处整理提供；年主营业务收入2000万元及以上的工业企业实行目录抽样调查，个体工业经营户实行整群抽样调查，省级数据由国家统计局河南调查总队整理提供，省级以下数据由河南省统计局工业处提供；能源类产品产量由河南省统计局能源统计处提供。

四、数据使用注意事项

2018年规模以上工业企业利润总额、营业收入等财务指标和工业产品产量数据与上年公布的数据存在不可比因素，其主要原因是：（一）根据统计制度，每年定期对规模以上工业企业调查范围进行调整。每年有部分企业达到规模标准纳入调查范围，也有部分企业因规模变小而退出调查范围，还有新建投产企业、破产、注（吊）销企业等变化。（二）加强统计执法，对统计执法检查中发现的不符合规模以上工业统计要求的企业进行了清理，对相关基数依规进行了修正。（三）加强数据质量管理，剔除跨地区、跨行业重复统计数据。根据国家统计局最新开展的企业组织结构调查情况，对企业集团（公司）跨地区、跨行业重复计算进行了剔重。（四）“营改增”政策实施后，服务业企业改交增值税且税率较低，工业企业逐步将内部非工业生产经营活动剥离，转向服务业，使工业企业财务数据有所减小。

Brief Introduction

I. Main Contents

Data on this chapter including number of industrial enterprises, value-added of industrial enterprises, output, beneficial indicators of industrial enterprises above designated size , unit, value-added and employed persons of industrial enterprises below designated size and individual.

II. Scope of Statistics

The scopes of industrial statistics are all corporate and individual industrial enterprises. Before 1997, the scopes of industrial statistics include six parts, as enterprises above township, Village-run enterprises, cooperative industry in cities and towns, rural cooperative industry, urban individual industrial, individual industries in rural areas. From 1998 to 2005, the scope of the industrial statistical investigation was divided into " industrial enterprises above designated size " and "below designated size ". Industrial enterprises above designated size refers to all State-owned industrial enterprises and non-State-owned industrial enterprises with revenue from principal business over 5 million yuan, and industrial enterprises above designated size refers to non-State-owned industrial enterprises with revenue from principal business below 5 million yuan and individual enterprises. From 2006 to 2010, the industrial enterprises above designated size refers to all industrial enterprises with revenue from principal business over 5 million yuan, and the industrial enterprises below designated size refers to all industrial enterprises with revenue from principal business below 5 million yuan and individual. Since 2011, the industrial enterprises above designated size refers to all industrial enterprises with revenue from principal business over 20 million yuan, and the industrial enterprises below designated size refers to all industrial enterprises with revenue from principal business below 20 million yuan and individual industry.

III. Sources of Data

Data on industrial enterprises with principal business revenue above 5 million yuan are collected through a combination of full survey, which are provided by the Department of Industrial of the Henan provincial bureau of Statistics. Data on industrial enterprises with principal business revenue below 5 million yuan are collected through a combination of sample survey directory, data on individual household are collected through a combination of cluster sample survey. Provincial data are provided by the Department of Henan Survey organizations. The following data at the provincial levelare provided by the Department of Industrial of the Henan provincial bureau of Statistics. Data on output of energy product are provided by the Department of Energy of the Henan provincial bureau of Statistics.

IV. Data Usage Notes

Data of 2018 of main indicators of industrial enterprises above designated size nationwide are not comparable with the data of previous year, the reasons are as following: (1) According to the statistical system, the investigation scope of industrial enterprises above designated size should be adjusted regularly every year. Every year, some enterprises meet the scale criteria to be included in the scope of investigation, some enterprises withdraw from the scope of investigation because of the smaller scale, and there are other changes: new enterprises, bankruptcy, annotation (cancellation) enterprises, etc. (2)Strengthening of statistical law enforcement, cleaning up enterprises found in the inspection of statistical law enforcement that do not meet the standard of industrial statistics above designated size, and amending the relevant cardinality in accordance with regulations. (3) Strengthening data quality management and eliminating duplicated statistical data across regions and across industries. According to the latest survey of organizational structure of enterprises carried out by the National Bureau of Statistics, the repeated calculation of enterprise groups (companies) across regions and industries is weighed.(4)After the implementation of the program to replace the business tax with a value-added tax, the value-added tax was paid by the service enterprises and the tax rate was lower. The industrial enterprises gradually stripped off the internal non-industrial production and operation activities and turned to the service industry, which reduced the financial data of the industrial enterprises.

13-1 各种分组的规模以上工业增加值指数

Indices of Value-added

上年=100 (Preceding year=100)

项 目	Item	2000	2005	2010	2012	2013	2014	2015	2016	2017	2018	2019
指 数	**Indices**	**111.6**	**123.3**	**119.0**	**114.6**	**111.8**	**111.2**	**108.6**	**108.0**	**108.0**	**107.2**	**107.8**
按注册类型分	**By Registration status**											
内资企业	Domestic Funded	111.6	124.0	119.8	113.4	111.3	111.0	108.5	108.2	108.0	107.2	108.1
国有	State-owned	114.6	109.5	115.5	105.5	106.6	103.1	98.6	99.9	101.8	114.8	109.9
集体	Collective-owned	106.7	128.8	115.9	109.6	109.9	107.5	105.4	106.7	107.3	83.0	80.9
股份合作	Cooperative	111.1	130.3	122.2	107.5	109.7	105.3	111.1	104.8	102.4	89.4	111.7
联营	Joint Ownership	93.6	120.7	101.9	95.3	103.3	83.9	73.5	113.4	103.9	105.7	103.8
有限责任公司	Limited Liability Corporations	108.3	119.9	120.5	114.2	114.0	112.9	110.6	109.5	110.3	107.5	103.4
股份有限公司	Share-holding Corporation Ltd	112.8	115.8	116.7	109.9	105.3	103.8	102.2	109.4	106.0	108.4	108.7
私营	Private	122.2	148.5	121.6	116.3	111.7	111.9	108.6	106.9	106.0	105.5	110.3
其他	Others	102.0	164.1	129.0	117.3	120.5	113.2	108.4	114.0	111.6	109.5	107.7
港澳台商投资	Enterprises with Funds from Hong Kong, Macao and Taiwan	113.9	110.8	117.4	173.6	127.3	117.4	116.0	103.6	108.9	106.5	109.9
外商投资	Foreign Funded	106.4	115.2	118.0	104.1	108.5	109.0	100.8	108.4	103.0	108.2	98.4
按控股类型分	**By Controlling Type**											
#国有控股	State-holding			113.6	104.3	105.3	100.4	97.9	98.3	105.6	108.2	104.7
集体控股	Collective-holding			117.9	109.0	110.3	104.5	101.2	106.9	105.1	101.0	92.3
私人控股	Private-holding			121.5	117.0	113.2	114.1	110.9	109.6	108.0	106.4	109.1
港澳台控股	Hong Kong, Macao and Taiwan-holding			117.4	182.1	130.0	117.7	116.4	104.6	108.6	106.6	110.9
外商控股	Foreign-holding			110.7	103.5	106.6	105.0	100.5	108.0	106.1	102.2	100.3
按所有制分	**By Proprietorial System**											
公有制	Public-owned		114.0	115.3	105.2	106.1	101.2	98.6	100.0	106.2	107.6	104.2
非公有制	Non-Public-owned		137.0	121.8	118.4	113.9	114.2	111.0	109.7	108.5	107.1	109.0
按轻重工业分	**Grouped by Light & Heavy Industry**											
轻工业	Enterprises of Light Industry	106.2	128.8	120.0	116.2	111.5	110.4	108.1	108.2	109.4	106.0	107.3
重工业	Enterprises of Heavy Industry	114.2	121.0	118.8	113.9	111.9	111.7	108.9	107.9	107.2	108.5	108.1
按企业规模分	**Grouped by Size of Enterprises**											
大型企业	Large Enterprises	116.0	114.3	116.3	111.8	110.3	107.5	106.7	104.8	107.6	109.0	107.5
中型企业	Medium-sized Enterprises	103.0	112.5	118.7	112.2	111.6	110.5	108.6	107.4	107.3	106.4	101.1
小型企业	Small Enterprises	110.4	138.0	122.4	118.4	113.6	116.4	111.6	112.9	108.7	104.0	109.3
微型企业	Micro-enterprises							68.9	82.7	96.4	123.3	115.8

13–2 规模以上工业企业主要指标(2019年)

单位：亿元

行 业	Sector	单位数(个) Number of Enterprises (unit)	平均从业人员(万人) Average Employees (10 000 persons)
总 计	**Total**	**19524**	**489.14**
按轻重工业分	**Grouped by Light & Heavy Industry**		
轻工业	Enterprises of Light Industry	7513	180.24
重工业	Heavy Industry	12011	308.91
按企业规模分	**Grouped by Size of Enterprises**		
大型企业	Large Enterprises	529	194.12
中型企业	Medium-sized Enterprises	2654	143.82
小型企业	Small Enterprises	13979	140.04
微型企业	Micro-enterprises	2362	11.17
按所有制分	**By Proprietorial System**		
公有制	Public-owned	1006	100.43
非公有制	Non-Public-owned	18518	388.72
按行业分	**By Sector**		
煤炭开采和洗选业	Mining and Washing of Coal	190	29.23
石油和天然气开采业	Extraction of Petroleum and Natural Gas	3	3.20
黑色金属矿采选业	Mining of Ferrous Metal Ores	20	0.33
有色金属矿采选业	Mining of Non-ferrous Metal Ores	137	2.58
非金属矿采选业	Mining and Processing of Nonmetal Ores	183	1.44
开采辅助活动	Support Activities for Mining	8	1.11
其他采矿业	Mining of Other Ores		
农副食品加工业	Processing of Food from Agricultural Products	1474	32.00
食品制造业	Manufacture of Foods	708	21.38
酒、饮料和精制茶制造业	Manufacture of Liquor, Beverages and Refined Tea	360	8.65
烟草制品业	Manufacture of Tobacco	13	1.38
纺织业	Manufacture of Textile	727	19.64
纺织服装服饰业	Manufacture of Textile,Wearing Apparel and Accessories	609	18.14
皮革、毛皮、羽毛及其制品和制鞋业	Manufacture of Leather, Fur, Feather and Its Products, Footwear	451	11.79
木材加工及木、竹、藤、棕、草制品业	Processing of Timbers, Manufacture of Wood, Bamboo, Rattan, Palm, and Straw Products	587	8.76
家具制造业	Manufacture of Furniture	360	5.46
造纸及纸制品业	Manufacture of Paper and Paper Products	301	6.62
印刷和记录媒介的复制业	Printing,Reproduction of Recording Media	240	4.27
文教、工美、体育和娱乐用品制造业	Manufacture of Articles for Culture, Education, Arts and Crafts, Sport and Entertainment Activities	508	10.27
石油加工、炼焦及核燃料加工业	Processing of Petroleum ,Coking, Processing of Nucleus Fuel	104	3.32
化学原料及化学制品制造业	Manufacture of Raw Chemical Material and Chemical Products	1063	21.39
医药制造业	Manufacture of Medicines	435	11.75
化学纤维制造业	Manufacture of Chemical Fiber	39	2.01
橡胶和塑料制品业	Manufacture of Rubber and Plastic	661	11.65
非金属矿物制品业	Manufacture of Non-metallic Mineral Products	3417	44.22
黑色金属冶炼及压延加工业	Smelting and Pressing of Ferrous Metals	225	11.72
有色金属冶炼及压延加工业	Smelting and Pressing of Non-ferrous Metals	542	20.41
金属制品业	Manufacture of Metal Products	1024	16.82
通用设备制造业	Manufacture of General Purpose Machinery	1157	23.41
专用设备制造业	Manufacture of Special Purpose Machinery	1072	20.85
汽车制造业	Manufacture of Automobile	621	16.20
铁路、船舶、航空航天和其他运输设备制造业	Manufacture of Railway, Ship, Aerospace, and other Transport Equipments	201	8.37
电气机械及器材制造业	Manufacture of Electrical Machinery and Apparatus	850	22.24
计算机、通信和其他电子设备制造业	Manufacture of Computer , Communication and Other Electronic Equipment	303	40.78
仪器仪表制造业	Manufacture of Measuring Instrument and Machinery	200	4.67
其他制造业	Manufacture of Others	59	2.16
废弃资源综合利用业	Utilization of Waste Resources	73	0.94
金属制品、机械和设备修理业	Repair Service of Metal Products, Machinery and Equipment	21	0.63
电力、热力的生产和供应业	Production and Supply of Electric Power and Heat Power	323	13.89
燃气生产和供应业	Production and Supply of Gas	136	2.47
水的生产和供应业	Production and Supply of Water	119	3.01

Main Indicators of Industrial Enterprises above Designated Size by Sector (2019)

(100 million yuan)

增加值指数 (%) Indices (%)	资产总计 Total Assets	流动资产合计 Total Current Assets	负债合计 Total Liabilities	营业收入 Business Revenue	营业成本 Business Cost	利润总额 Total Profits
107.8	**52698.04**	**24349.12**	**29388.86**	**50076.58**	**42377.55**	**3547.88**
107.3	12172.40	5344.82	4996.02	14537.97	11839.27	1293.81
108.1	40525.63	19004.30	24392.84	35538.61	30538.28	2254.07
107.5	26964.42	13273.51	16723.92	23806.59	20462.41	1355.24
101.1	11460.05	4622.83	5831.14	11374.74	9376.45	988.55
109.3	12947.61	5912.26	6113.82	13840.57	11647.93	1108.54
115.8	1325.96	540.52	719.97	1054.69	890.75	95.54
104.2	17845.79	7001.21	12153.36	11607.78	9875.81	331.47
109.0	34852.25	17347.91	17235.50	38468.80	32501.75	3216.41
110.2	2941.28	1192.22	1968.41	1525.67	1276.95	71.50
102.6	334.53	46.72	338.65	114.98	127.53	-41.51
78.1	107.72	57.48	52.25	49.31	39.69	4.61
121.3	391.14	140.17	253.09	173.89	127.38	14.95
111.1	152.06	57.50	57.60	154.00	113.29	19.88
123.6	122.66	67.09	118.55	132.11	116.54	4.64
94.5	2427.51	952.16	1013.64	3748.44	3297.78	262.95
111.2	1819.46	777.83	772.44	1675.90	1360.29	193.36
97.0	720.99	323.36	388.16	725.55	564.71	58.57
100.9	391.96	292.07	121.26	500.06	158.64	20.15
111.9	1016.08	424.54	445.31	1255.04	1076.54	111.84
116.8	599.34	207.65	159.74	826.20	682.55	84.61
118.3	557.98	209.02	173.74	719.14	594.65	81.71
102.8	332.70	137.00	92.14	476.90	399.91	45.53
116.2	283.93	103.20	71.13	334.61	261.88	42.30
100.0	490.05	247.03	316.24	521.11	445.49	28.93
123.8	259.87	122.74	99.34	272.66	228.37	23.27
110.5	566.02	286.47	186.79	619.55	511.36	67.33
98.6	797.27	365.11	599.74	1011.59	865.25	17.86
106.8	3387.97	1325.17	2090.92	2973.38	2491.38	183.96
115.0	1117.64	497.32	463.04	1048.55	723.15	136.58
104.8	260.27	109.57	157.10	236.90	217.50	9.77
107.0	728.90	303.46	291.03	833.81	687.02	74.61
104.1	4114.60	1986.03	1882.99	4141.94	3346.36	414.91
114.7	1837.36	953.00	1216.91	2543.46	2280.29	114.43
113.0	5142.81	2232.62	3048.37	4758.42	4242.61	286.89
122.5	1190.48	562.72	442.11	1441.73	1181.08	151.70
119.4	1894.30	982.06	766.54	2029.88	1659.61	172.09
110.9	1989.47	1143.35	1011.16	1889.61	1545.07	152.45
106.9	1785.77	955.69	1004.82	2315.24	1949.75	185.08
85.9	680.71	372.92	288.78	553.29	436.54	52.30
119.1	2566.43	1491.77	1436.20	2530.61	2132.96	161.84
111.4	4231.38	3588.27	3140.26	3966.01	3752.11	121.25
112.1	366.34	207.11	138.62	388.58	310.14	42.44
106.1	165.90	93.57	53.68	104.23	84.52	7.23
94.1	108.80	54.09	50.40	161.07	133.07	18.73
88.0	48.90	36.04	34.52	42.28	35.89	2.53
102.5	5517.06	945.90	3950.75	2663.80	2441.89	72.64
96.8	725.79	339.86	436.31	492.35	390.23	58.42
87.8	524.58	159.24	256.11	124.72	87.58	15.58

13-3 规模以上国有控股工业企业主要指标(2019年)

单位：亿元

行 业	Sector	单位数 (个) Number of Enterprises (unit)	平均从业人员 (万人) Average Employees (10 000 persons)
总 计	**Total**	**784**	**92.07**
按轻重工业分	**Grouped by Light & Heavy Industry**		
轻工业	Enterprises of Light Industry	114	7.96
重工业	Heavy Industry	670	84.12
按企业规模分	**Grouped by Size of Enterprises**		
大型企业	Large Enterprises	144	71.35
中型企业	Medium-sized Enterprises	248	15.38
小型企业	Small Enterprises	343	4.93
微型企业	Micro-enterprises	49	0.42
按行业分	**By Sector**		
煤炭开采和洗选业	Mining and Washing of Coal	60	25.67
石油和天然气开采业	Extraction of Petroleum and Natural Gas	2	3.17
黑色金属矿采选业	Mining of Ferrous Metal Ores	2	0.12
有色金属矿采选业	Mining of Non-ferrous Metal Ores	21	0.97
非金属矿采选业	Mining and Processing of Nonmetal Ores	14	0.25
开采辅助活动	Support Activities for Mining	2	1.03
其他采矿业	Mining of Other Ores		
农副食品加工业	Processing of Food from Agricultural Products	27	1.32
食品制造业	Manufacture of Foods	12	1.12
酒、饮料和精制茶制造业	Manufacture of Liquor, Beverages and Refined Tea	8	0.58
烟草制品业	Manufacture of Tobacco	11	1.33
纺织业	Manufacture of Textile	5	1.00
纺织服装服饰业	Manufacture of Textile,Wearing Apparel and Accessories	11	0.23
皮革、毛皮、羽毛及其制品和制鞋业	Manufacture of Leather, Fur, Feather and Its Products, Footwear	3	0.22
木材加工及木、竹、藤、棕、草制品业	Processing of Timbers, Manufacture of Wood, Bamboo, Rattan, Palm, and Straw Products	3	0.04
家具制造业	Manufacture of Furniture		
造纸及纸制品业	Manufacture of Paper and Paper Products	4	0.29
印刷和记录媒介的复制业	Printing,Reproduction of Recording Media	7	0.27
文教、工美、体育和娱乐用品制造业	Manufacture of Articles for Culture, Education, Arts and Crafts, Sport and Entertainment Activities	2	0.04
石油加工、炼焦及核燃料加工业	Processing of Petroleum ,Coking, Processing of Nucleus Fuel	9	0.96
化学原料及化学制品制造业	Manufacture of Raw Chemical Material and Chemical Products	52	4.15
医药制造业	Manufacture of Medicines	8	0.68
化学纤维制造业	Manufacture of Chemical Fiber	4	0.51
橡胶和塑料制品业	Manufacture of Rubber and Plastic	8	0.77
非金属矿物制品业	Manufacture of Non-metallic Mineral Products	78	3.14
黑色金属冶炼及压延加工业	Smelting and Pressing of Ferrous Metals	7	3.51
有色金属冶炼及压延加工业	Smelting and Pressing of Non-ferrous Metals	37	7.43
金属制品业	Manufacture of Metal Products	19	0.52
通用设备制造业	Manufacture of General Purpose Machinery	30	2.65
专用设备制造业	Manufacture of Special Purpose Machinery	37	4.18
汽车制造业	Manufacture of Automobile	22	1.41
铁路、船舶、航空航天和其他运输设备制造业	Manufacture of Railway, Ship, Aerospace, and other Transport Equipments	11	3.73
电气机械及器材制造业	Manufacture of Electrical Machinery and Apparatws	25	2.09
计算机、通信和其他电子设备制造业	Manufacture of Computer , Communication and Other Electronic Equipment	12	1.51
仪器仪表制造业	Manufacture of Measuring Instrument and Machinery	13	0.98
其他制造业	Manufacture of Others	2	1.24
废弃资源综合利用业	Utilization of Waste Resources	2	0.05
金属制品、机械和设备修理业	Repair Service of Metal Products, Machinery and Equipment	4	0.41
电力、热力的生产和供应业	Production and Supply of Electric Power and Heat Power	136	11.90
燃气生产和供应业	Production and Supply of Gas	22	0.55
水的生产和供应业	Production and Supply of Water	52	2.06

Main Indicators of State-holding Industrial Enterprises above Designated Size (2019)

(100 million yuan)

增加值指数 (%) Indices (%)	资产总计 Total Assets	流动资产合计 Total Current Assets	负债合计 Total Liabilities	营业收入 Business Revenue	营业成本 Business Cost	利润总额 Total Profits
104.7	**17162.25**	**6660.37**	**11753.48**	**10917.01**	**9276.03**	**301.94**
101.8	1211.33	695.65	687.34	1210.29	786.07	44.37
105.4	15950.92	5964.72	11066.14	9706.72	8489.96	257.58
103.9	12040.85	4880.54	8253.38	8332.57	7122.20	212.18
105.6	3157.98	1147.50	2277.81	1661.76	1366.66	48.84
111.8	1789.90	582.06	1094.72	885.67	759.02	36.25
105.6	173.52	50.27	127.56	37.01	28.15	4.67
108.8	2694.76	1078.53	1821.06	1258.77	1054.02	58.42
101.9	331.14	43.83	337.44	113.14	125.79	-41.53
90.9	39.73	12.64	6.81	18.14	13.93	1.42
167.1	115.00	32.88	78.53	53.19	37.06	4.33
228.4	32.37	19.65	22.85	17.37	12.92	2.01
114.7	115.85	62.95	114.31	124.34	110.41	3.88
122.2	123.40	66.80	77.34	181.80	167.18	10.08
99.5	67.56	33.87	47.72	57.91	49.10	1.06
111.1	139.56	56.43	140.59	34.52	32.81	-4.05
100.8	388.67	289.65	119.66	496.68	156.36	19.96
106.6	114.07	58.19	64.03	94.98	84.66	3.02
109.1	10.32	5.70	2.85	7.00	4.29	0.75
56.6	12.94	9.40	5.06	12.88	10.32	1.12
116.0	4.22	1.30	5.52	3.20	2.68	0.01
100.0						
99.5	42.40	14.18	37.91	43.44	34.12	2.39
98.2	21.33	15.27	7.71	13.58	10.66	1.11
83.0	2.95	1.82	2.03	3.59	3.15	0.18
89.7	332.94	131.82	285.37	498.81	402.91	-2.22
98.6	1306.95	464.85	1053.35	853.00	744.50	7.29
114.0	79.02	31.73	35.37	72.94	55.46	4.19
104.3	133.96	69.87	99.69	151.71	145.29	3.34
106.3	91.37	52.84	63.14	66.83	53.35	3.18
97.5	667.61	271.70	336.52	298.05	211.00	38.88
101.7	719.68	349.31	505.94	520.13	463.99	5.52
103.5	1789.76	889.81	1259.88	1685.52	1549.13	51.06
105.7	64.49	37.33	47.66	69.48	59.76	2.47
98.7	394.35	234.50	256.27	181.07	148.52	5.66
119.7	925.03	569.18	562.84	598.66	508.51	27.35
102.2	171.71	96.19	138.59	161.37	140.02	2.77
112.1	354.70	234.43	199.08	249.37	189.65	18.91
111.8	802.74	462.67	532.96	286.03	245.82	8.53
86.4	164.83	92.00	94.58	86.16	68.98	2.34
129.6	85.09	64.40	48.52	72.26	59.56	3.39
196.6	134.48	83.42	46.15	61.45	48.38	3.22
81.7	10.55	7.72	4.40	3.73	2.36	0.75
118.9	28.44	19.75	24.10	18.99	16.16	0.15
106.8	4149.24	543.85	3002.37	2271.16	2111.47	40.40
100.8	121.96	37.25	88.47	99.23	88.54	4.39
102.5	377.09	112.63	176.80	76.53	53.20	6.19

13-4 规模以上公有制工业企业主要指标(2019年)

单位：亿元

行 业	Sector	单位数(个) Number of Enterprises (unit)	平均从业人员(万人) Average Employees (10 000 persons)
总 计	**Total**	**1006**	**100.43**
按轻重工业分	**Grouped by Light & Heavy Industry**		
轻工业	Enterprises of Light Industry	193	12.33
重工业	Heavy Industry	813	88.10
按企业规模分	**Grouped by Size of Enterprises**		
大型企业	Large Enterprises	160	75.79
中型企业	Medium-sized Enterprises	289	17.61
小型企业	Small Enterprises	476	6.44
微型企业	Micro-enterprises	81	0.58
按行业分	**By Sector**		
煤炭开采和洗选业	Mining and Washing of Coal	68	26.44
石油和天然气开采业	Extraction of Petroleum and Natural Gas	3	3.20
黑色金属矿采选业	Mining of Ferrous Metal Ores	2	0.12
有色金属矿采选业	Mining of Non-ferrous Metal Ores	23	1.04
非金属矿采选业	Mining and Processing of Nonmetal Ores	16	0.27
开采辅助活动	Support Activities for Mining	2	1.03
其他采矿业	Mining of Other Ores		
农副食品加工业	Processing of Food from Agricultural Products	36	1.79
食品制造业	Manufacture of Foods	16	2.06
酒、饮料和精制茶制造业	Manufacture of Liguor, Beverages and refined tea	15	0.82
烟草制品业	Manufacture of Tobacco	12	1.35
纺织业	Manufacture of Textile	10	1.16
纺织服装服饰业	Manufacture of Textile,Wearing Apparel and Accessories	12	0.24
皮革、毛皮、羽毛及其制品和制鞋业	Manufacture of Leather, Fur, Feather and Its Products, Footwear	7	0.29
木材加工及木、竹、藤、棕、草制品业	Processing of Timbers, Manufacture of Wood, Bamboo, Rattan, Palm, and Straw Products	4	0.06
家具制造业	Manufacture of Furniture		
造纸及纸制品业	Manufacture of Paper and Paper Products	12	0.70
印刷和记录媒介的复制业	Printing,Reproduction of Recording Media	17	0.48
文教、工美、体育和娱乐用品制造业	Manufacture of Articles for Culture, Education, Arts and Crafts, Sport and Entertainment Activities	3	0.04
石油加工、炼焦及核燃料加工业	Processing of Petroleum ,Coking, Processing of Nucleus Fuel	9	0.96
化学原料及化学制品制造业	Manufacture of Raw Chemical Material and Chemical Products	71	4.43
医药制造业	Manufacture of Medicines	19	1.06
化学纤维制造业	Manufacture of Chemical Fiber	5	1.50
橡胶和塑料制品业	Manufacture of Rubber and Plastic	22	1.17
非金属矿物制品业	Manufacture of Non-metallic Mineral Products	104	3.41
黑色金属冶炼及压延加工业	Smelting and Pressing of Ferrous Metals	8	3.57
有色金属冶炼及压延加工业	Smelting and Pressing of Non-ferrous Metals	41	7.46
金属制品业	Manufacture of Metal Products	38	0.90
通用设备制造业	Manufacture of General Purpose Machinery	42	2.87
专用设备制造业	Manufacture of Special Purpose Machinery	56	4.63
汽车制造业	Manufacture of Automobile	27	1.92
铁路、船舶、航空航天和其他运输设备制造业	Manufacture of Railway, Ship, Aerospace, and other Transport Equipments	12	3.74
电气机械及器材制造业	Manufacture of Electrical Machinery and Apparatus	34	2.25
计算机、通信和其他电子设备制造业	Manufacture of Computer , Communication and Other Electronic Equipment	14	1.77
仪器仪表制造业	Manufacture of Measuring Instrument and Machinery	13	0.98
其他制造业	Manufacture of Others	4	1.26
废弃资源综合利用业	Utilization of Waste Resources	3	0.23
金属制品、机械和设备修理业	Repair Service of Metal Products, Machinery and Equipment	5	0.41
电力、热力的生产和供应业	Production and Supply of Electric Power and Heat Power	140	11.93
燃气生产和供应业	Production and Supply of Gas	23	0.55
水的生产和供应业	Production and Supply of Water	58	2.31

Main Indicators of Public-owned Industrial Enterprises above Designated Size (2019)

(100 million yuan)

增加值指数 (%) Indices (%)	资产总计 Total Assets	流动资产合计 Total Current Assets	负债合计 Total Liabilities	营业收入 Business Revenue	营业成本 Business Cost	利润总额 Total Profits
104.2	**17845.79**	**7001.21**	**12153.36**	**11607.78**	**9875.81**	**331.47**
100.9	1516.20	820.96	854.42	1500.75	1031.18	65.26
105.1	16329.59	6180.25	11298.94	10107.03	8844.63	266.21
103.8	12438.57	5059.61	8496.75	8712.64	7455.40	222.66
103.5	3287.66	1217.26	2345.10	1808.52	1493.71	55.96
108.8	1927.71	668.62	1174.61	1034.98	885.54	47.47
106.6	191.86	55.72	136.90	51.64	41.15	5.38
109.4	2753.45	1110.94	1854.96	1292.55	1081.62	50.56
101.9	334.53	46.72	338.65	114.98	127.53	-41.51
114.7	39.73	12.64	6.81	18.14	13.93	1.42
137.9	116.64	33.77	79.65	54.53	37.94	4.60
159.1	33.67	20.39	23.33	28.82	22.47	2.33
114.7	115.85	62.95	114.31	124.34	110.41	3.88
114.2	148.34	76.99	87.74	244.91	221.87	16.13
104.1	113.77	61.48	81.82	90.66	74.75	3.36
105.8	159.83	62.82	149.17	50.67	46.18	-2.01
100.9	390.39	291.03	120.34	499.01	158.17	19.97
105.9	124.86	61.39	68.56	109.19	97.71	3.58
108.9	10.65	5.96	3.15	7.35	4.60	0.75
44.2	15.30	10.13	5.63	16.69	13.48	1.50
89.7	4.49	1.54	5.55	3.92	3.27	0.13
100.7	66.37	22.20	57.98	72.40	60.24	3.00
110.0	34.91	25.17	15.20	28.78	23.16	1.91
77.5	3.03	1.86	2.03	3.61	3.17	0.18
89.7	332.94	131.82	285.37	498.81	402.91	-2.22
97.8	1375.34	501.30	1103.11	980.37	865.08	9.47
111.8	105.24	46.31	52.65	93.08	72.68	4.24
100.4	233.57	97.82	148.15	200.09	185.89	6.60
101.6	123.74	66.05	77.51	102.35	81.93	7.35
97.5	684.20	279.92	345.08	321.62	231.68	39.76
103.0	744.20	362.49	515.87	552.26	494.12	6.41
101.5	1793.46	892.55	1262.01	1693.80	1557.23	51.09
106.7	83.64	52.31	59.66	90.75	77.89	3.22
99.7	406.89	239.53	260.09	206.36	169.71	8.31
118.3	952.75	588.41	579.45	635.06	538.44	30.95
97.7	202.15	110.97	153.88	189.99	164.51	3.56
114.2	354.88	234.49	199.11	250.20	190.31	18.94
109.0	833.53	490.45	557.72	306.79	263.57	9.74
85.6	191.97	108.54	109.02	100.69	80.17	4.56
129.1	85.09	64.40	48.52	72.26	59.56	3.39
136.3	135.25	83.64	46.23	64.93	51.30	3.72
84.7	13.91	9.07	8.08	7.66	5.68	0.77
118.9	28.80	20.09	24.25	19.65	16.77	0.15
106.8	4172.01	554.36	3021.10	2277.85	2118.63	40.71
101.9	122.86	37.31	89.12	99.93	89.12	4.40
102.8	403.56	121.37	192.49	82.73	58.11	6.57

13-5 分行业规模以上私营工业企业主要指标(2019年)

单位：亿元

行业	Sector	单位数(个) Number of Enterprises (unit)	平均从业人员(万人) Average Employees (10 000 persons)
总计	**Total**	**11979**	**191.95**
按轻重工业分	**Grouped by Light & Heavy Industry**		
轻工业	Enterprises of Light Industry	4674	88.55
重工业	Heavy Industry	7305	103.40
按企业规模分	**Grouped by Size of Enterprises**		
大型企业	Large Enterprises	153	33.74
中型企业	Medium-sized Enterprises	1298	67.96
小型企业	Small Enterprises	8946	84.18
微型企业	Micro-enterprises	1582	6.06
按行业分	**By Sector**		
煤炭开采和洗选业	Mining and Washing of Coal	76	0.77
石油和天然气开采业	Extraction of Petroleum and Natural Gas		
黑色金属矿采选业	Mining of Ferrous Metal Ores	15	0.19
有色金属矿采选业	Mining of Non-ferrous Metal Ores	71	0.91
非金属矿采选业	Mining and Processing of Nonmetal Ores	134	0.98
开采辅助活动	Support Activities for Mining	3	0.03
其他采矿业	Mining of Other Ores		
农副食品加工业	Processing of Food from Agricultural Products	932	14.17
食品制造业	Manufacture of Foods	418	7.58
酒、饮料和精制茶制造业	Manufacture of Liquor, Beverages and refined tea	213	2.93
烟草制品业	Manufacture of Tobacco		
纺织业	Manufacture of Textile	494	11.62
纺织服装服饰业	Manufacture of Textile,Wearing Apparel and Accessories	387	10.40
皮革、毛皮、羽毛及其制品和制鞋业	Manufacture of Leather, Fur, Feather and Its Products, Footwear	299	7.50
木材加工及木、竹、藤、棕、草制品业	Processing of Timbers, Manufacture of Wood, Bamboo, Rattan, Palm, and Straw Products	461	6.02
家具制造业	Manufacture of Furniture	249	4.03
造纸及纸制品业	Manufacture of Paper and Paper Products	177	3.41
印刷和记录媒介的复制业	Printing,Reproduction of Recording Media	144	2.28
文教、工美、体育和娱乐用品制造业	Manufacture of Articles for Culture, Education, Arts and Crafts, Sport and Entertainment Activities	325	5.82
石油加工、炼焦及核燃料加工业	Processing of Petroleum ,Coking, Processing of Nucleus Fuel	62	1.52
化学原料及化学制品制造业	Manufacture of Raw Chemical Material and Chemical Products	611	8.65
医药制造业	Manufacture of Medicines	219	4.48
化学纤维制造业	Manufacture of Chemical Fiber	20	0.31
橡胶和塑料制品业	Manufacture of Rubber and Plastic	428	7.01
非金属矿物制品业	Manufacture of Non-metallic Mineral Products	2320	24.62
黑色金属冶炼及压延加工业	Smelting and Pressing of Ferrous Metals	136	4.15
有色金属冶炼及压延加工业	Smelting and Pressing of Non-ferrous Metals	321	5.40
金属制品业	Manufacture of Metal Products	695	9.42
通用设备制造业	Manufacture of General Purpose Machinery	730	12.21
专用设备制造业	Manufacture of Special Purpose Machinery	630	9.05
汽车制造业	Manufacture of Automobile	343	5.42
铁路、船舶、航空航天和其他运输设备制造业	Manufacture of Railway, Ship, Aerospace, and other Transport Equipments	116	2.01
电气机械及器材制造业	Manufacture of Electrical Machinery and Apparatws	489	8.64
计算机、通信和其他电子设备制造业	Manufacture of Computer, Communication and Other Electronic Equipment	150	6.29
仪器仪表制造业	Manufacture of Measuring Instrument and Machinery	107	2.18
其他制造业	Manufacture of Others	32	0.51
废弃资源综合利用业	Utilization of Waste Resources	45	0.35
金属制品、机械和设备修理业	Repair Service of Metal Products, Machinery and Equipment	7	0.06
电力、热力的生产和供应业	Production and Supply of Electric Power and Heat Power	60	0.37
燃气生产和供应业	Production and Supply of Gas	33	0.32
水的生产和供应业	Production and Supply of Water	27	0.32

Main Indicators of Private Industrial Enterprises above Designated Size (2019)

(100 million yuan)

增加值指数 (%) Indices (%)	资产总计 Total Assets	流动资产合计 Total Current Assets	负债合计 Total Liabilities	营业收入 Business Revenue	营业成本 Business Cost	利润总额 Total Profits
110.3	**12814.69**	**5820.65**	**5131.38**	**17676.13**	**14788.31**	**1666.91**
102.7	4816.86	1930.21	1622.84	6441.08	5373.60	643.24
115.2	7997.83	3890.45	3508.54	11235.05	9414.72	1023.68
108.4	2659.69	1447.96	1278.26	4202.98	3562.39	371.08
96.0	3335.22	1218.08	1086.11	4849.50	4029.00	502.51
115.2	6179.88	2885.43	2433.56	7922.12	6604.30	726.72
239.9	639.90	269.18	333.45	701.53	592.63	66.60
118.3	78.47	43.24	40.55	163.26	137.40	15.94
100.0						
66.1	60.70	43.48	39.43	29.81	24.70	2.95
88.5	89.04	32.58	40.28	37.87	29.69	3.31
100.5	97.33	28.40	22.87	108.51	79.45	16.11
267.3	1.36	0.86	0.64	5.60	4.49	0.51
107.5	924.60	334.77	302.61	1527.84	1342.99	114.44
98.0	431.26	169.14	145.65	585.78	487.14	59.96
96.7	175.50	72.36	59.81	218.73	180.27	19.85
100.0						
103.1	538.86	204.90	209.63	742.62	630.97	76.81
99.8	370.41	118.05	100.41	494.61	402.54	55.26
88.4	348.78	143.32	125.72	488.99	404.41	54.51
101.7	224.76	93.34	56.15	363.55	306.39	34.96
106.8	202.50	72.93	40.19	269.92	206.84	37.84
104.7	208.75	99.08	111.03	274.40	229.72	26.52
126.2	118.64	49.65	45.84	135.40	114.29	10.81
110.7	337.00	155.04	95.69	339.48	270.15	42.94
98.7	179.91	93.61	122.00	241.97	223.53	3.86
113.5	816.95	336.33	400.49	907.33	759.65	74.68
107.5	330.62	129.87	124.21	379.81	298.43	40.11
105.3	13.27	5.78	3.94	18.85	16.54	1.23
118.9	375.21	146.79	128.36	539.98	443.17	52.21
107.6	1715.42	803.24	669.29	2278.60	1875.67	228.55
122.2	576.14	295.96	314.60	1139.33	1005.62	76.17
124.6	646.30	392.11	391.50	1372.99	1205.01	116.65
116.0	615.80	285.12	203.12	912.28	737.47	109.37
121.0	818.95	415.51	290.08	1102.32	908.14	93.38
118.3	526.32	274.99	198.64	702.08	556.24	78.94
113.2	340.80	139.88	141.13	568.12	477.44	48.39
84.0	131.83	50.48	34.00	139.57	110.67	17.57
119.5	591.08	347.55	222.24	766.81	638.05	68.71
128.7	381.61	236.69	151.97	375.25	322.94	29.58
99.2	110.60	52.91	33.66	177.74	142.61	22.01
121.0	21.35	8.19	4.77	29.13	24.90	2.32
130.7	40.76	18.80	19.51	92.31	76.67	13.51
129.5	2.67	2.12	1.39	3.85	3.44	0.09
131.6	263.89	71.85	175.90	62.93	47.60	7.55
126.6	70.71	42.38	48.55	56.14	47.55	3.99
104.3	36.56	9.34	15.55	22.36	15.57	5.29

13-6 规模以上工业主要产业单位数及增加值(2019年)

Main indicators of Industrial Enterprises above Designated Size (2019)

行 业	Sector	单位数 (个) Number of Enterprises (unit)	增加值占规模以上工业比重(%) Proportion of Added Value on Industry (%)	增加值指数 (上年=100) Indices of Value-Added of Industry (Preceding year=100)
五大主导产业	**High-growth industries**	**8624**	**45.5**	**108.1**
装备制造	Electronic Information Industry	313	14.6	117.4
食品制造	Equipment Manufacturing Industry	3999	14.7	101.0
新型材料制造	Automobile and Parts Industry	629	5.6	115.1
电子制造	Food Industry	2883	5.5	111.4
汽车制造	Modern Furniture Industry	800	5.0	106.9
传统产业	**Traditional Pillar Industries**	**8766**	**46.7**	**106.6**
冶金工业	Metallurgical Industry	810	9.9	114.5
建材工业	Building Materials Industry	3445	8.7	103.9
化学工业	Chemical Industry	1369	8.3	103.2
轻纺工业	Textile Industry	2556	7.9	107.8
能源工业	Energy Industry	586	11.8	108.6
战略性新兴产业	**Strategic Emerging Industries**	**2855**	**19.0**	**113.7**
高耗能行业	**Carrying Energy Industries**	**5961**	**35.3**	**105.9**
煤炭开采和洗选业	Mining and Washing of Coal	189	5.0	110.2
化学原料及化学制品制造业	Manufacture of Chemical Raw Material and Chemical Products	1127	5.5	106.8
非金属矿物制品业	Manufacture of Non-metallic Mineral Products	3556	9.1	104.1
黑色金属冶炼及压延加工业	Manufacture and Processing of Ferrous Metals	253	4.4	114.7
有色金属冶炼及压延加工业	Manufacture and Processing of Non-ferrous Metals	557	5.5	113.0
电力、热力的生产和供应业	Production and Supply of Electric Power and Heat Power	279	5.7	102.5
高技术产业	**High Technology Industries**	**1056**	**9.9**	**109.2**
医药制造业	Manufacture of Medicines	431	2.7	115.0
航空、航天器及设备制造业	Manufacture of Aviation, Spacecraft, and Equipment	10		140.4
电子及通信设备制造业	Manufacture of Electronic and Communication Equipment	321	5.7	110.8
计算机及办公设备制造业	Manufacture of Computer and Office Equipment	36	0.2	101.0
医疗仪器设备及仪器仪表制造业	Manufacture of Medical Equipment and Instruments	251	1.2	114.0
信息化学品制造业	Manufacture of Information Chemicals	7	0.1	119.3

13-7 规模以上能源原材料工业增加值结构

Struction of Added value on Raw Energy Material Industries Above Designated Size

行　业	sector	2010	2012	2015	2016	2017	2018	2019
能源原材料工业占规模以上	**Proportion in Value-added of Industry Enterprises**							
工业增加值比重(%)	**Above Designated Size(%)**	**51.5**	**48.7**	**39.1**	**38.0**	**38.5**	**41.0**	**41.9**
煤炭开采和洗选业	Mining and Washing of Coal	9.9	8.0	3.4	2.6	3.2	4.9	5.0
石油和天然气开采业	Extraction of Petroleum and Natural Gas	1.1	1.0	0.4	0.1	0.1	0.6	0.3
黑色金属矿采选业	Mining of Ferrous Metal Ores	0.6	0.5	0.3	0.2	0.4	0.2	0.1
有色金属矿采选业	Mining of Non-ferrous Metal Ores	3.4	3.3	2.1	2.0	1.9	0.7	1.1
非金属矿采选业	Mining and Processing of Nonmetal Ores	0.9	0.9	0.8	0.8	0.7	0.5	0.5
石油加工、炼焦和	Processing of Petroleum ,Coking,							
核燃料加工业	Processing of Nucleus Fuel	2.8	1.9	1.1	1.1	1.3	2.8	2.3
化学原料和化学制品制造业	Manufacture of Raw Chemical Material							
	and Chemical Products	5.1	5.1	4.9	5.3	5.4	5.7	5.5
橡胶制品业	Manufacture of Rubber	0.9	0.7	0.6	0.7	0.7	0.4	2.1
非金属矿物制品业	Manufacture of Non-metallic Mineral Products	12.7	12.9	13.4	13.0	12.4	8.6	9.1
黑色金属冶炼和压延加工业	Manufacture and Processing of Ferrous Metals	5.1	5.5	4.5	4.0	3.7	4.1	4.4
有色金属冶炼和压延加工业	Manufacture and Processing of Non-ferrous Metals	5.4	4.5	3.5	3.7	4.1	5.2	5.5
废弃资源综合利用业	Utilization of waste Resources	0.1	0.2	0.2	0.1	0.1	0.3	0.4
电力、热力生产和供应业	Production and Supply of Electric							
	Power and Heat Power	3.0	3.9	3.5	3.6	3.9	6.1	5.7
燃气生产和供应业	Production and Supply of Gas	0.3	0.3	0.3	0.4	0.4	0.6	0.9
水的生产和供应业	Production and Supply of Water	0.1	0.1	0.2	0.2	0.2	0.4	0.5

13-8 各市规模以上工业企业主要财务指标(2019年)

单位：亿元

年份 市(县)	year City(County)	单位数 (个) Number of Enterprises (unit)	平均从业人员 (万人) Average Employees (10 000 persons)	资产总计 Total Assets	流动资产合计 Total Current Assets
全　　省	**Total**	**19524**	**489.14**	**52698.04**	**24349.12**
省辖市	**City**				
郑州市	Zhengzhou	2425	70.60	11063.65	7032.88
开封市	Kaifeng	1038	23.66	1711.86	687.67
洛阳市	Luoyang	1799	42.11	6616.24	2690.92
平顶山市	Pingdingshan	823	27.69	3406.03	1518.83
安阳市	Anyang	757	14.40	2131.61	950.62
鹤壁市	Hebi	387	12.68	1327.36	459.36
新乡市	Xinxiang	1341	26.28	2629.98	1335.75
焦作市	Jiaozuo	1102	30.42	3120.81	1243.13
濮阳市	Puyang	687	10.78	1274.08	490.39
许昌市	Xuchang	1530	37.38	3485.17	1627.12
漯河市	Luohe	572	18.15	1305.43	565.23
三门峡市	Sanmenxia	369	9.41	1748.35	809.38
南阳市	Nanyang	1551	28.11	3297.13	1503.28
商丘市	Shangqiu	1400	40.27	2464.42	879.58
信阳市	Xinyang	1136	22.46	1432.39	480.76
周口市	Zhoukou	1334	45.49	2577.33	876.72
驻马店市	Zhumadian	1052	22.12	1852.14	526.84
济源市	Jiyuan	221	7.13	1254.07	670.65
省直管县	**County Directly Administrated by Province**				
巩义市	Gongyi	487	5.98	920.45	468.73
兰考县	Lankao	224	4.17	225.32	107.36
汝州市	Ruzhou	191	3.40	450.16	210.86
滑县	Huaxian	232	1.86	104.89	42.01
长垣市	Changyuan	232	3.91	349.79	221.06
邓州市	Dengzhou	143	2.46	161.58	54.07
永城市	Yongcheng	271	6.35	786.35	348.58
固始县	Gushi	199	3.10	90.27	34.98
鹿邑县	Luyi	236	3.87	262.11	124.75
新蔡县	Xincai	137	1.83	106.02	27.68

Main Financial Indicators of Industrial Enterprises above Designated Size by City (2019)

(100 million yuan)

负债合计 Total Liabilities	营业收入 Business Revenue	营业成本 Business Cost	利润总额 Total Profits	增加值指数 (上年=100) Indices of Value-Added (Preceding year=100)
29388.86	**50076.58**	**42377.55**	**3547.88**	**107.8**
7470.60	8960.06	7708.89	516.12	106.1
839.65	1496.86	1263.44	115.90	108.8
3584.23	4978.56	4157.35	320.15	108.6
2169.62	2420.70	2118.34	109.76	108.7
1539.70	1888.45	1642.54	37.52	100.8
814.58	1215.63	1071.04	52.57	108.4
1555.52	2412.77	2066.71	119.56	108.5
1507.53	3410.12	2814.23	281.95	108.7
943.74	1050.17	951.63	20.34	108.3
1601.34	4790.09	3908.95	470.68	108.4
599.33	1927.67	1669.00	117.54	108.4
1138.66	1331.06	1137.43	72.46	108.0
1723.73	2294.41	1875.22	164.96	108.1
1114.83	3440.50	2948.35	303.13	108.8
637.16	1787.48	1537.33	124.65	108.5
779.70	3513.68	2798.53	510.22	108.5
691.91	1641.15	1331.90	140.91	108.1
677.02	1517.23	1376.66	69.44	108.8
610.14	1005.29	825.24	109.12	106.5
98.13	223.01	180.01	19.05	109.8
281.21	322.14	271.75	25.00	108.0
43.90	141.56	106.78	11.95	109.7
159.37	436.72	367.23	27.94	109.9
59.28	226.90	184.90	24.02	107.3
490.79	745.77	613.54	91.39	109.4
17.69	233.95	202.23	18.45	109.0
128.06	197.26	127.88	48.41	108.9
22.79	118.50	100.21	6.05	109.2

13-9 各市规模以上国有控股工业企业主要财务指标(2019年)

单位：亿元

市(县) City(County)	平均从业人员(万人) Average Employees (10 000 persons)	资产总计 Total Assets	流动资产合计 Total Current Assets
全 省 Total	**92.07**	**17162.25**	**6660.37**
省 辖 市 City			
郑 州 市 Zhengzhou	10.52	2977.89	1252.56
开 封 市 Kaifeng	1.51	510.65	144.50
洛 阳 市 Luoyang	14.75	2576.36	1090.28
平 顶 山 市 Pingdingshan	15.41	2280.67	995.70
安 阳 市 Anyang	4.85	995.26	375.84
鹤 壁 市 Hebi	3.12	548.62	170.71
新 乡 市 Xinxiang	4.88	834.10	315.38
焦 作 市 Jiaozuo	5.08	877.39	282.07
濮 阳 市 Puyang	5.05	640.13	165.46
许 昌 市 Xuchang	4.22	767.16	362.75
漯 河 市 Luohe	0.59	132.53	41.39
三 门 峡 市 Sanmenxia	5.02	997.62	417.16
南 阳 市 Nanyang	6.18	882.84	343.02
商 丘 市 Shangqiu	4.78	809.68	296.31
信 阳 市 Xinyang	1.97	245.92	77.36
周 口 市 Zhoukou	1.19	96.28	11.11
驻 马 店 市 Zhumadian	1.62	458.22	113.96
济 源 市 Jiyuan	1.32	530.93	204.80
省 直 管 县 County Directly Administrated by Province			
巩 义 市 Gongyi	0.25	13.27	4.36
兰 考 县 Lankao	0.04	1.87	1.09
汝 州 市 Ruzhou	1.18	128.89	70.60
滑 县 Huaxian	0.03	3.66	0.65
长 垣 市 Changyuan	0.08	42.48	4.77
邓 州 市 Dengzhou	0.24	27.74	10.15
永 城 市 Yongcheng	3.62	607.99	265.45
固 始 县 Gushi	0.06	0.54	0.12
鹿 邑 县 Luyi			
新 蔡 县 Xincai	0.03	0.38	0.11

Main Financial Indicators of State-holding Industrial Enterprises above Designated Size by City (2019)

(100 million yuan)

负债合计 Total Liabilities	营业收入 Business Revenue	营业成本 Business Cost	利润总额 Total Profits	增加值指数(上年=100) Indices of Value-Added (Preceding year=100)
11753.48	**10917.01**	**9276.03**	**301.94**	**104.7**
1868.63	1385.40	1049.98	61.35	105.2
343.90	241.83	201.83	13.19	98.1
1671.16	1909.41	1614.28	46.42	102.0
1580.83	1479.71	1309.26	45.91	111.5
713.56	689.47	578.19	14.26	98.4
485.47	318.25	291.12	-2.55	104.9
596.96	509.47	442.59	17.42	101.9
532.43	612.52	540.66	22.87	93.0
610.52	443.18	423.69	-11.10	104.1
507.79	445.81	328.85	14.96	105.4
98.57	103.67	74.49	0.46	101.8
705.13	765.79	677.70	16.91	102.1
584.01	501.31	423.17	-3.46	105.4
595.50	392.33	330.70	32.13	105.7
176.93	249.18	228.54	10.09	102.8
75.45	83.57	77.08	0.39	105.6
311.03	317.56	250.17	10.20	118.1
295.61	468.55	433.73	12.49	110.7
10.48	5.03	3.75	0.28	70.3
1.02	2.01	1.85	-0.02	84.2
113.55	68.71	54.10	4.66	111.4
2.13	1.99	1.41	0.14	123.4
31.92	17.67	14.81	0.80	93.7
14.24	10.89	7.34	2.43	92.5
429.59	228.96	179.42	31.88	105.8
0.30	0.23	0.16	-0.02	336.1
0.05	1.21	1.06	0.02	130.0

13-10 各市规模以上公有制工业企业主要财务指标(2019年)

Main Financial Indicators of Public-owned Industrial Enterprises above Designated Size by City (2019)

单位：亿元 (100 million yuan)

市(县) City(County)	平均从业人员(万人) Average Employees (10 000 persons)	资产总计 Total Assets	流动资产合计 Total Current Assets	负债合计 Total Liabilities	营业收入 Business Revenue	营业成本 Business Cost	利润总额 Total Profits	增加值指数(上年=100) Indices of Value-Added (Preceding year=100)
全 省 Total	**100.43**	**17845.79**	**7001.21**	**12153.36**	**11607.78**	**9875.81**	**331.47**	**104.2**
省 辖 市 City								
郑 州 市 Zhengzhou	11.40	3053.74	1293.80	1924.12	1467.19	1117.94	57.64	105.1
开 封 市 Kaifeng	1.76	520.95	148.75	345.67	266.18	224.35	14.37	96.5
洛 阳 市 Luoyang	15.32	2661.14	1131.31	1726.95	2046.37	1743.32	48.67	101.6
平 顶 山 市 Pingdingshan	16.02	2310.87	1012.40	1605.07	1505.80	1332.94	46.38	111.5
安 阳 市 Anyang	4.90	998.39	378.55	715.87	692.97	581.23	14.19	98.5
鹤 壁 市 Hebi	3.54	593.44	199.96	508.89	363.79	327.79	4.57	102.9
新 乡 市 Xinxiang	6.52	978.08	362.48	678.58	605.41	525.48	21.24	101.6
焦 作 市 Jiaozuo	5.68	906.77	300.26	549.13	645.70	567.63	23.80	91.9
濮 阳 市 Puyang	5.11	645.67	169.11	614.42	446.47	426.83	-11.26	103.7
许 昌 市 Xuchang	4.46	805.93	383.53	523.43	497.22	375.51	17.77	106.3
漯 河 市 Luohe	1.53	184.00	74.70	137.96	139.08	103.73	3.08	103.9
三 门 峡 市 Sanmenxia	5.15	1006.17	420.71	711.39	771.98	682.61	17.53	98.2
南 阳 市 Nanyang	6.77	923.56	363.12	601.99	537.26	451.92	-1.45	104.8
商 丘 市 Shangqiu	4.93	814.03	298.01	597.70	400.99	338.42	32.56	102.4
信 阳 市 Xinyang	2.07	250.55	79.38	178.88	257.78	236.22	10.56	101.0
周 口 市 Zhoukou	1.75	155.88	38.86	105.89	145.34	127.66	8.68	105.5
驻 马 店 市 Zhumadian	1.76	468.87	121.16	316.54	327.52	258.82	10.49	120.0
济 源 市 Jiyuan	1.75	567.76	225.10	310.89	490.73	453.40	12.67	112.6
省 直 管 县 County Directly Administrated by Province								
巩 义 市 Gongyi	0.55	30.78	12.33	32.23	12.35	9.36	-9.90	97.3
兰 考 县 Lankao	0.04	1.87	1.09	1.02	2.01	1.85	-0.02	84.2
汝 州 市 Ruzhou	1.18	128.89	70.60	113.55	68.71	54.10	4.66	111.4
滑 县 Huaxian	0.03	3.66	0.65	2.13	1.99	1.41	0.14	81.3
长 垣 市 Changyuan	0.13	45.42	6.97	34.61	18.95	15.90	0.92	93.7
邓 州 市 Dengzhou	0.26	28.64	10.72	14.78	11.67	7.63	2.53	93.2
永 城 市 Yongcheng	3.64	608.02	265.46	429.61	229.29	179.73	31.88	105.8
固 始 县 Gushi	0.07	0.88	0.27	0.36	1.67	1.38	0.03	131.9
鹿 邑 县 Luyi	0.01	0.16	0.10	0.04	0.49	0.38	0.09	202.8
新 蔡 县 Xincai	0.04	1.05	0.22	0.14	1.68	1.42	0.04	79.0

13-11 各市规模以上私营工业企业主要财务指标(2019年)

Main Financial Indicators of Private Industrial Enterprises above Designated Size by City (2019)

单位：亿元 (100 million yuan)

市(县) City(County)	平均从业人员(万人) Average Employees (10 000persons)	资产总计 Total Assets	流动资产合计 Total Current Assets	负债合计 Total Liabilities	营业收入 Business Revenue	营业成本 Business Cost	利润总额 Total Profits	增加值指数(上年=100) Indices of Value-Added (Preceding year=100)
全省 Total	**191.95**	**12814.69**	**5820.65**	**5131.38**	**17676.13**	**14788.31**	**1666.91**	**110.3**
省辖市 City								
郑州市 Zhengzhou	11.31	1123.85	786.72	652.53	1378.81	1124.68	144.15	102.9
开封市 Kaifeng	12.47	578.22	240.48	197.93	720.35	611.30	64.33	109.7
洛阳市 Luoyang	13.87	1097.60	534.64	444.58	1340.97	1076.72	147.37	119.0
平顶山市 Pingdingshan	5.66	438.06	199.55	200.60	449.33	390.49	29.21	107.7
安阳市 Anyang	5.76	628.56	334.95	466.70	715.05	638.06	20.62	107.3
鹤壁市 Hebi	4.72	318.81	105.50	129.61	434.78	388.65	20.65	125.1
新乡市 Xinxiang	12.53	977.64	579.50	525.34	1156.67	999.69	59.59	109.6
焦作市 Jiaozuo	12.64	813.49	377.92	316.87	1531.70	1251.98	149.04	119.0
濮阳市 Puyang	2.64	192.20	93.91	81.62	205.88	185.53	8.15	107.4
许昌市 Xuchang	16.28	1165.52	414.50	214.52	2221.53	1785.70	285.14	108.7
漯河市 Luohe	6.28	341.83	118.54	108.97	455.77	391.24	40.44	101.4
三门峡市 Sanmenxia	2.14	194.01	95.51	106.76	152.67	128.68	10.27	103.4
南阳市 Nanyang	10.73	944.45	469.66	466.76	799.64	682.86	43.17	109.3
商丘市 Shangqiu	21.85	907.79	349.85	291.35	1931.49	1653.32	175.22	109.0
信阳市 Xinyang	13.42	725.04	212.71	225.61	918.02	783.87	76.42	108.7
周口市 Zhoukou	25.99	1439.13	484.97	403.45	2139.37	1716.35	312.33	105.1
驻马店市 Zhumadian	10.44	591.10	155.25	116.18	583.21	480.26	60.27	101.0
济源市 Jiyuan	3.22	337.37	266.52	181.98	540.90	498.93	20.55	114.9
省直管县 County Directly Administrated by Province								
巩义市 Gongyi	3.55	350.48	225.79	194.49	582.56	471.51	84.40	108.0
兰考县 Lankao	2.03	85.72	43.96	35.10	120.18	96.16	11.78	115.5
汝州市 Ruzhou	0.83	81.97	26.79	38.69	104.77	94.90	4.69	106.5
滑县 Huaxian	1.26	62.13	27.84	25.65	91.85	68.99	6.87	115.5
长垣市 Changyuan	2.83	236.94	172.25	92.08	337.15	284.82	19.85	111.8
邓州市 Dengzhou	1.06	89.42	27.51	28.83	105.81	83.78	10.96	103.7
永城市 Yongcheng	2.52	161.28	73.38	54.75	495.80	416.94	58.09	112.3
固始县 Gushi	2.27	71.62	26.94	12.02	181.46	158.40	14.73	105.4
鹿邑县 Luyi	1.98	45.38	23.02	15.43	54.35	41.73	9.66	99.4
新蔡县 Xincai	0.81	35.27	11.35	9.12	51.71	43.23	2.14	94.8

13-12 分行业规模以上工业企业主要经济效益指标(2019年)

行 业	Sector	总资产贡献率(%) Ratio of Total Assets to Industrial Output Value (%)
总 计	**Total**	**11.0**
按轻重工业分	**Grouped by Light & Heavy Industry**	
轻工业	Light Industry	16.3
重工业	Heavy Industry	9.4
按企业规模分	**Grouped by Size of Enterprises**	
大型企业	Large Enterprises	9.9
中型企业	Medium-sized Enterprises	12.7
小型企业	Small Enterprises	12.0
微型企业	Micro-enterprises	9.6
按所有制分	**By Proprietorial System**	
公有制	Public-owned	7.4
非公有制	Non-Public-owned	12.9
按行业分	**Grouped by Sectors**	
煤炭开采和洗选业	Mining and Washing of Coal	7.0
石油和天然气开采业	Extraction of Petroleum and Natural Gas	-6.3
黑色金属矿采选业	Mining of Ferrous Metal Ores	8.9
有色金属矿采选业	Mining of Non-ferrous Metal Ores	8.5
非金属矿采选业	Mining and Processing of Nonmetal Ores	19.0
开采辅助活动	Support Activities for Mining	6.2
其他采矿业	Mining of Other Ores	
农副食品加工业	Processing of Food from Agricultural Products	13.5
食品制造业	Manufacture of Foods	12.9
酒、饮料和精制茶制造业	Manufacture of Liquor, Beverages and Refined Tea	13.3
烟草制品业	Manufacture of Tobacco	83.2
纺织业	Manufacture of Textile	13.8
纺织服装服饰业	Manufacture of Textile,Wearing Apparel and Accessories	17.8
皮革、毛皮、羽毛及其制品和制鞋业	Manufacture of Leather, Fur, Feather and Its Products, Footwear	18.5
木材加工及木、竹、藤、棕、草制品业	Processing of Timbers, Manufacture of Wood, Bamboo, Rattan, Palm, and Straw Products	17.5
家具制造业	Manufacture of Furniture	18.4
造纸及纸制品业	Manufacture of Paper and Paper Products	10.6
印刷和记录媒介的复制业	Printing, Reproduction of Recording Media	12.2
文教、工美、体育和娱乐用品制造业	Manufacture of Articles for Culture, Education, Arts and Crafts, Sport and Entertainment Activities	15.2
石油加工、炼焦及核燃料加工业	Processing of Petroleum ,Coking, Processing of Nucleus Fuel	15.6
化学原料及化学制品制造业	Manufacture of Raw Chemical Material and Chemical Products	9.3
医药制造业	Manufacture of Medicines	16.4
化学纤维制造业	Manufacture of Chemical Fiber	5.6
橡胶和塑料制品业	Manufacture of Rubber and Plastic	13.8
非金属矿物制品业	Manufacture of Non-metallic Mineral Products	14.4
黑色金属冶炼及压延加工业	Smelting and Pressing of Ferrous Metals	9.7
有色金属冶炼及压延加工业	Smelting and Pressing of Non-ferrous Metals	9.1
金属制品业	Manufacture of Metal Products	16.5
通用设备制造业	Manufacture of General Purpose Machinery	12.8
专用设备制造业	Manufacture of Special Purpose Machinery	11.0
汽车制造业	Manufacture of Automobile	14.9
铁路、船舶、航空航天和其他运输设备制造业	Manufacture of Railway, Ship, Aerospace, and other Transport Equipments	9.3
电气机械及器材制造业	Manufacture of Electrical Machinery and Apparatus	9.4
计算机、通信和其他电子设备制造业	Manufacture of Computer , Communication and Other Electronic Equipment	6.9
仪器仪表制造业	Manufacture of Measuring Instrument and Machinery	14.4
其他制造业	Manufacture of Others	6.0
废弃资源综合利用业	Utilization of Waste Resources	27.8
金属制品、机械和设备修理业	Repair Service of Metal Products, Machinery and Equipment	8.9
电力、热力的生产和供应业	Production and Supply of Electric Power and Heat Power	4.4
燃气生产和供应业	Production and Supply of Gas	9.3
水的生产和供应业	Production and Supply of Water	5.2

Main Economic Efficiency Indicators of Industrial Enterprises above Designated Size by Sector (2019)

成本费用利润率 (%) Ratio of Profits to Industrial Cost (%)	资产负债率 (%) Assets-Liability Ratio (%)	产品销售率 (%) Products Sales Rate (%)
7.7	**55.8**	**98.2**
10.0	41.0	98.7
6.8	60.2	97.9
6.1	62.0	98.1
9.6	50.9	98.4
8.8	47.2	98.1
10.1	54.3	98.2
3.0	68.1	97.8
9.2	49.5	98.3
5.0	66.9	95.6
-24.0	101.2	100.5
10.4	48.5	94.9
10.1	64.7	92.3
15.5	37.9	98.3
3.6	96.7	99.9
7.6	41.8	99.2
13.0	42.5	98.5
9.0	53.8	97.9
10.1	30.9	104.4
9.8	43.8	97.8
11.5	26.7	98.9
12.9	31.1	98.6
10.6	27.7	97.6
14.6	25.1	97.3
5.9	64.5	104.8
9.4	38.2	99.2
12.3	33.0	96.3
1.9	75.2	99.0
6.7	61.7	97.0
15.0	41.4	96.5
4.2	60.4	94.9
9.9	39.9	99.6
11.2	45.8	98.3
4.8	66.2	98.4
6.4	59.3	97.8
11.8	37.1	98.6
9.3	40.5	98.1
8.8	50.8	94.8
8.7	56.3	98.8
10.4	42.4	97.9
6.9	56.0	97.7
3.2	74.2	98.9
12.2	37.8	96.7
7.5	32.4	98.1
13.1	46.3	97.7
6.3	70.6	101.5
2.8	71.6	99.4
13.7	60.1	99.5
14.6	48.8	98.0

13-13 分行业规模以上国有控股工业企业主要经济效益指标(2019年)

Main Economic Efficiency Indicators of State-holding Industrial Enterprises above Designated Size by Sector (2019)

行业	Sector	总资产贡献率 (%) Ratio of Total Assets to Industrial Output Value (%)	成本费用利润率 (%) Ratio of Profits to Industrial Cost (%)	资产负债率 (%) Assets-Liability Ratio (%)
总 计	**Total**	**7.4**	**2.9**	**68.5**
按轻重工业分	**Grouped by Light & Heavy Industry**			
轻工业	Enterprises of Light Industry	30.7	5.0	56.7
重工业	Heavy Industry	5.6	2.7	69.4
按企业规模分	**Grouped by Size of Enterprises**			
大型企业	Large Enterprises	8.0	2.7	68.5
中型企业	Medium-sized Enterprises	6.7	3.2	72.1
小型企业	Small Enterprises	4.8	4.3	61.2
微型企业	Micro-enterprises	3.7	14.5	73.5
按行业分	**By Sector**			
煤炭开采和洗选业	Mining and Washing of Coal	6.7	4.9	67.6
石油和天然气开采业	Extraction of Petroleum and Natural Gas	-6.3	-24.2	101.9
黑色金属矿采选业	Mining of Ferrous Metal Ores	8.2	8.8	17.1
有色金属矿采选业	Mining of Non-ferrous Metal Ores	8.8	9.6	68.3
非金属矿采选业	Mining and Processing of Nonmetal Ores	10.1	13.4	70.6
开采辅助活动	Support Activities for Mining	5.6	3.2	98.7
其他采矿业	Mining of Other Ores			
农副食品加工业	Processing of Food from Agricultural Products	9.9	5.9	62.7
食品制造业	Manufacture of Foods	5.0	1.9	70.6
酒、饮料和精制茶制造业	Manufacture of Liquor, Beverages and refined tea	-0.6	-10.6	100.7
烟草制品业	Manufacture of Tobacco	83.8	10.1	30.8
纺织业	Manufacture of Textile	5.4	3.3	56.1
纺织服装服饰业	Manufacture of Textile,Wearing Apparel and Accessories	12.1	12.4	27.6
皮革、毛皮、羽毛及其制品和制鞋业	Manufacture of Leather, Fur, Feather and Its Products, Footwear	10.8	9.7	39.1
木材加工及木、竹、藤、棕、草制品业	Processing of Timbers, Manufacture of Wood, Bamboo, Rattan, Palm, and Straw Products	3.8	0.3	130.8
家具制造业	Manufacture of Furniture			
造纸及纸制品业	Manufacture of Paper and Paper Products	12.4	5.9	89.4
印刷和记录媒介的复制业	Printing, Reproduction of Recording Media	9.4	8.8	36.1
文教、工美、体育和娱乐用品制造业	Manufacture of Articles for Culture, Education, Arts and Crafts, Sport and Entertainment Activities	9.3	5.2	68.6
石油加工、炼焦及核燃料加工业	Processing of Petroleum, Coking, Processing of Nucleus Fuel	25.4	-0.5	85.7
化学原料及化学制品制造业	Manufacture of Raw Chemical Material and Chemical Products	3.8	0.9	80.6
医药制造业	Manufacture of Medicines	9.0	6.1	44.8
化学纤维制造业	Manufacture of Chemical Fiber	3.6	2.2	74.4
橡胶和塑料制品业	Manufacture of Rubber and Plastic	6.1	5.0	69.1
非金属矿物制品业	Manufacture of Non-metallic Mineral Products	8.9	15.0	50.4
黑色金属冶炼及压延加工业	Smelting and Pressing of Ferrous Metals	3.9	1.1	70.3
有色金属冶炼及压延加工业	Smelting and Pressing of Non-ferrous Metals	8.1	3.1	70.4
金属制品业	Manufacture of Metal Products	7.5	3.7	73.9
通用设备制造业	Manufacture of General Purpose Machinery	4.3	3.2	65.0
专用设备制造业	Manufacture of Special Purpose Machinery	5.5	4.7	60.9
汽车制造业	Manufacture of Automobile	4.6	1.8	80.7
铁路、船舶、航空航天和其他运输设备制造业	Manufacture of Railway, Ship, Aerospace, and other Transport Equipments	6.9	8.2	56.1
电气机械及器材制造业	Manufacture of Electrical Machinery and Apparatus	2.4	3.1	66.4
计算机、通信和其他电子设备制造业	Manufacture of Computer, Communication and Other Electronic Equipment	2.9	2.9	57.4
仪器仪表制造业	Manufacture of Measuring Instrument and Machinery	6.2	4.9	57.0
其他制造业	Manufacture of Others	3.6	5.6	34.3
废弃资源综合利用业	Utilization of Waste Resources	9.8	26.8	41.7
金属制品、机械和设备修理业	Repair Service of Metal Products, Machinery and Equipment	3.2	0.8	84.7
电力、热力的生产和供应业	Production and Supply of Electric Power and Heat Power	4.4	1.8	72.4
燃气生产和供应业	Production and Supply of Gas	5.1	4.6	72.5
水的生产和供应业	Production and Supply of Water	3.9	9.1	46.9

13-14 分行业规模以上公有制工业企业主要经济效益指标(2019年)

Main Economic Efficiency Indicators of Public-owned Industrial Enterprises above Designated Size by Sector (2019)

行业	Sector	总资产贡献率 (%) Ratio of Total Assets to Industrial Output Value (%)	成本费用利润率 (%) Ratio of Profits to Industrial Cost (%)	资产负债率 (%) Assets-Liability Ratio (%)
总计	**Total**	**7.4**	**3.0**	**68.1**
按轻重工业分	**Grouped by Light & Heavy Industry**			
轻工业	Enterprises of Light Industry	26.6	5.6	56.4
重工业	Heavy Industry	5.6	2.7	69.2
按企业规模分	**Grouped by Size of Enterprises**			
大型企业	Large Enterprises	7.9	2.7	68.3
中型企业	Medium-sized Enterprises	6.8	3.3	71.3
小型企业	Small Enterprises	5.3	4.9	60.9
微型企业	Micro-enterprises	3.9	11.7	71.4
按行业分	**By Sector**			
煤炭开采和洗选业	Mining and Washing of Coal	6.4	4.2	67.4
石油和天然气开采业	Extraction of Petroleum and Natural Gas	-6.3	-24.0	101.2
黑色金属矿采选业	Mining of Ferrous Metal Ores	8.2	8.8	17.1
有色金属矿采选业	Mining of Non-ferrous Metal Ores	9.0	10.0	68.3
非金属矿采选业	Mining and Processing of Nonmetal Ores	13.9	9.3	69.3
开采辅助活动	Support Activities for Mining	5.6	3.2	98.7
其他采矿业	Mining of Other Ores			
农副食品加工业	Processing of Food from Agricultural Products	13.1	7.1	59.2
食品制造业	Manufacture of Foods	5.8	3.9	71.9
酒、饮料和精制茶制造业	Manufacture of Liquor, Beverages and Refined Tea	1.2	-3.9	93.3
烟草制品业	Manufacture of Tobacco	83.5	10.0	30.8
纺织业	Manufacture of Textile	5.8	3.4	54.9
纺织服装服饰业	Manufacture of Textile,Wearing Apparel and Accessories	11.8	11.7	29.5
皮革、毛皮、羽毛及其制品和制鞋业	Manufacture of Leather, Fur, Feather and Its Products, Footwear	12.2	10.0	36.8
木材加工及木、竹、藤、棕、草制品业	Processing of Timbers, Manufacture of Wood, Bamboo, Rattan, Palm, and Straw Products	6.5	3.3	123.7
家具制造业	Manufacture of Furniture			
造纸及纸制品业	Manufacture of Paper and Paper Products	10.3	4.3	87.4
印刷和记录媒介的复制业	Printing, Reproduction of Recording Media	9.7	7.1	43.5
文教、工美、体育和娱乐用品制造业	Manufacture of Articles for Culture, Education, Arts and Crafts, Sport and Entertainment Activities	9.2	5.2	66.8
石油加工、炼焦及核燃料加工业	Processing of Petroleum, Coking, Processing of Nucleus Fuel	25.4	-0.5	85.7
化学原料及化学制品制造业	Manufacture of Raw Chemical Material and Chemical Products	3.8	1.0	80.2
医药制造业	Manufacture of Medicines	8.8	4.8	50.0
化学纤维制造业	Manufacture of Chemical Fiber	4.7	3.3	63.4
橡胶和塑料制品业	Manufacture of Rubber and Plastic	8.7	7.8	62.6
非金属矿物制品业	Manufacture of Non-metallic Mineral Products	8.9	14.1	50.4
黑色金属冶炼及压延加工业	Smelting and Pressing of Ferrous Metals	3.9	1.2	69.3
有色金属冶炼及压延加工业	Smelting and Pressing of Non-ferrous Metals	8.1	3.1	70.4
金属制品业	Manufacture of Metal Products	7.8	3.7	71.3
通用设备制造业	Manufacture of General Purpose Machinery	5.0	4.2	63.9
专用设备制造业	Manufacture of Special Purpose Machinery	5.8	5.1	60.8
汽车制造业	Manufacture of Automobile	4.7	1.9	76.1
铁路、船舶、航空航天和其他运输设备制造业	Manufacture of Railway, Ship, Aerospace, and other Transport Equipments	6.9	8.2	56.1
电气机械及器材制造业	Manufacture of Electrical Machinery and Apparatus	2.5	3.3	66.9
计算机、通信和其他电子设备制造业	Manufacture of Computer, Communication and Other Electronic Equipment	3.9	4.8	56.8
仪器仪表制造业	Manufacture of Measuring Instrument and Machinery	6.2	4.9	57.0
其他制造业	Manufacture of others	4.0	6.1	34.2
废弃资源综合利用业	Utilization of Waste Resources	8.9	11.4	58.1
金属制品、机械和设备修理业	Repair Service of Metal Products, Machinery and Equipment	3.4	0.8	84.2
电力、热力的生产和供应业	Production and Supply of Electric Power and Heat Power	4.4	1.8	72.4
燃气生产和供应业	Production and Supply of Gas	5.1	4.5	72.5
水的生产和供应业	Production and Supply of Water	3.8	8.9	47.7

13-15 分行业规模以上私营工业企业主要经济效益指标(2019年)

Main Economic Efficiency Indicators of Private Industrial Enterprises above Designated Size by Sector (2019)

行业	Sector	总资产贡献率(%) Ratio of Total Assets to Industrial Output Value (%)	成本费用利润率(%) Ratio of Profits to Industrial Cost (%)	资产负债率(%) Assets-Liability Ratio (%)
总计	**Total**	16.9	10.5	40.0
按轻重工业分	**Grouped by Light & Heavy Industry**			
轻工业	Enterprises of Light Industry	16.8	11.2	33.7
重工业	Heavy Industry	16.9	10.1	43.9
按企业规模分	**Grouped by Size of Enterprises**			
大型企业	Large Enterprises	17.9	9.7	48.1
中型企业	Medium-sized Enterprises	18.9	11.6	32.6
小型企业	Small Enterprises	15.7	10.2	39.4
微型企业	Micro-enterprises	13.2	10.6	52.1
按行业分	**By Sector**			
煤炭开采和洗选业	Mining and Washing of Coal	27.3	10.9	51.7
石油和天然气开采业	Extraction of Petroleum and Natural Gas			
黑色金属矿采选业	Mining of Ferrous Metal Ores	10.0	10.9	65.0
有色金属矿采选业	Mining of Non-ferrous Metal Ores	7.2	9.9	45.2
非金属矿采选业	Mining and Processing of Nonmetal Ores	21.8	18.0	23.5
开采辅助活动	Support Activities for Mining	51.6	10.5	47.1
其他采矿业	Mining of Other Ores			
农副食品加工业	Processing of Food from Agricultural Products	15.2	8.2	32.7
食品制造业	Manufacture of Foods	17.4	11.5	33.8
酒、饮料和精制茶制造业	Manufacture of Liquor, Beverages and Refined Tea	14.9	10.1	34.1
烟草制品业	Manufacture of Tobacco			
纺织业	Manufacture of Textile	17.2	11.6	38.9
纺织服装服饰业	Manufacture of Textile,Wearing Apparel and Accessories	18.6	12.7	27.1
皮革、毛皮、羽毛及其制品和制鞋业	Manufacture of Leather, Fur, Feather and Its Products, Footwear	20.3	12.7	36.1
木材加工及木、竹、藤、棕、草制品业	Processing of Timbers, Manufacture of Wood, Bamboo, Rattan, Palm, and Straw Products	19.9	10.7	25.0
家具制造业	Manufacture of Furniture	22.7	16.5	19.9
造纸及纸制品业	Manufacture of Paper and Paper Products	16.2	10.8	53.2
印刷和记录媒介的复制业	Printing, Reproduction of Recording Media	13.0	8.8	38.6
文教、工美、体育和娱乐用品制造业	Manufacture of Articles for Culture, Education, Arts and Crafts, Sport and Entertainment Activities	16.2	14.7	28.4
石油加工、炼焦及核燃料加工业	Processing of Petroleum, Coking, Processing of Nucleus Fuel	7.6	1.6	67.8
化学原料及化学制品制造业	Manufacture of Raw Chemical Material and Chemical Products	12.9	9.0	49.0
医药制造业	Manufacture of Medicines	15.6	11.9	37.6
化学纤维制造业	Manufacture of Chemical Fiber	11.6	7.0	29.7
橡胶和塑料制品业	Manufacture of Rubber and Plastic	18.4	10.9	34.2
非金属矿物制品业	Manufacture of Non-metallic Mineral Products	18.0	11.3	39.0
黑色金属冶炼及压延加工业	Smelting and Pressing of Ferrous Metals	17.2	7.2	54.6
有色金属冶炼及压延加工业	Smelting and Pressing of Non-ferrous Metals	22.4	9.3	60.6
金属制品业	Manufacture of Metal Products	22.2	13.8	33.0
通用设备制造业	Manufacture of General Purpose Machinery	15.3	9.3	35.4
专用设备制造业	Manufacture of Special Purpose Machinery	19.7	12.8	37.7
汽车制造业	Manufacture of Automobile	18.7	9.4	41.4
铁路、船舶、航空航天和其他运输设备制造业	Manufacture of Railway, Ship, Aerospace, and other Transport Equipments	15.1	14.5	25.8
电气机械及器材制造业	Manufacture of Electrical Machinery and Apparatus	14.6	9.9	37.6
计算机、通信和其他电子设备制造业	Manufacture of Computer, Communication and Other Electronic Equipment	9.7	8.6	39.8
仪器仪表制造业	Manufacture of Measuring Instrument and Machinery	23.9	14.2	30.4
其他制造业	Manufacture of Others	14.3	8.7	22.3
废弃资源综合利用业	Utilization of Waste Resources	48.2	16.9	47.9
金属制品、机械和设备修理业	Repair Service of Metal products, Machinery and Equipment	10.3	2.4	52.3
电力、热力的生产和供应业	Production and Supply of Electric Power and Heat Power	4.0	13.5	66.7
燃气生产和供应业	Production and Supply of Gas	7.6	7.7	68.7
水的生产和供应业	Production and Supply of Water	17.8	31.5	42.5

13-16 各市规模以上工业企业主要经济效益指标(2019年)

Main Economic Efficiency Indicators of Industrial Enterprises above Designated Size by City (2019)

年份 市(县)	Year City(County)	总资产贡献率(%) Ratio of Total Assets to Industrial Output Value (%)	成本费用利润率(%) Ratio of Profits to Industrial Cost (%)	资产负债率(%) Assets-Liability Ratio (%)	产品销售率(%) Products Sales Rate (%)
全省	**Total**	**11.0**	**7.7**	**55.8**	**98.2**
省辖市	**City**				
郑州市	Zhengzhou	9.7	6.2	67.5	98.3
开封市	Kaifeng	9.8	8.4	49.1	103.6
洛阳市	Luoyang	9.1	7.1	54.2	97.9
平顶山市	Pingdingshan	6.7	4.8	63.7	97.8
安阳市	Anyang	6.5	2.1	72.2	99.3
鹤壁市	Hebi	7.5	4.6	61.4	97.5
新乡市	Xinxiang	7.9	5.2	59.2	97.9
焦作市	Jiaozuo	13.6	9.1	48.3	98.1
濮阳市	Puyang	5.8	1.9	74.1	98.8
许昌市	Xuchang	20.5	11.1	46.0	98.1
漯河市	Luohe	14.2	6.6	45.9	99.0
三门峡市	Sanmenxia	8.7	5.8	65.1	94.6
南阳市	Nanyang	8.1	7.8	52.3	97.2
商丘市	Shangqiu	16.4	9.7	45.2	98.3
信阳市	Xinyang	12.3	7.6	44.5	98.1
周口市	Zhoukou	23.1	17.1	30.3	98.4
驻马店市	Zhumadian	10.4	9.7	37.4	98.7
济源市	Jiyuan	9.7	4.8	54.0	98.1
省直管县	**County Directly Administrated by Province**				
巩义市	Gongyi	15.4	12.4	66.3	96.0
兰考县	Lankao	10.5	9.4	43.6	99.6
汝州市	Ruzhou	9.0	8.4	62.5	98.6
滑县	Huaxian	15.3	9.3	41.9	99.6
长垣市	Changyuan	11.4	6.9	45.6	99.2
邓州市	Dengzhou	17.5	11.9	36.7	98.2
永城市	Yongcheng	18.0	13.7	62.4	98.6
固始县	Gushi	27.9	8.6	19.6	99.9
鹿邑县	Luyi	21.5	32.8	48.9	98.6
新蔡县	Xincai	7.3	5.4	21.5	101.1

13－17 各市规模以上国有控股工业企业主要经济效益指标(2019年)

Main Economic Efficiency Indicators of State-holding Industrial Enterprises above Designated Size by City (2019)

市(县) City(County)	总资产贡献率 (%) Ratio of Total Assets to Industrial Output Value (%)	成本费用利润率 (%) Ratio of Profits to Industrial Cost (%)	资产负债率 (%) Assets-Liability Ratio (%)
全　　省 Total	**7.4**	**2.9**	**68.5**
省 辖 市 City			
郑　州　市 Zhengzhou	9.7	5.2	62.8
开　封　市 Kaifeng	6.0	5.8	67.4
洛　阳　市 Luoyang	8.0	2.6	64.9
平 顶 山 市 Pingdingshan	5.8	3.2	69.3
安　阳　市 Anyang	7.5	2.2	71.7
鹤　壁　市 Hebi	4.2	-0.8	88.5
新　乡　市 Xinxiang	4.5	3.5	71.6
焦　作　市 Jiaozuo	5.9	3.9	60.7
濮　阳　市 Puyang	3.0	-2.3	95.4
许　昌　市 Xuchang	12.9	4.0	66.2
漯　河　市 Luohe	19.6	0.6	74.4
三 门 峡 市 Sanmenxia	7.7	2.3	70.7
南　阳　市 Nanyang	4.5	-0.7	66.2
商　丘　市 Shangqiu	9.3	8.5	73.6
信　阳　市 Xinyang	7.5	4.3	71.9
周　口　市 Zhoukou	4.3	0.5	78.4
驻 马 店 市 Zhumadian	7.5	3.7	67.9
济　源　市 Jiyuan	6.5	2.8	55.7
省 直 管 县 County Directly Administrated by Province			
巩　义　市 Gongyi	5.4	6.1	79.0
兰　考　县 Lankao	0.6	-0.8	54.4
汝　州　市 Ruzhou	9.2	7.4	88.1
滑　　　县 Huaxian	4.9	7.8	58.2
长　垣　市 Changyuan	1.7	4.8	75.1
邓　州　市 Dengzhou	11.1	27.0	51.3
永　城　市 Yongcheng	11.1	15.0	70.7
固　始　县 Gushi	-3.1	-8.4	55.7
鹿　邑　县 Luyi			
新　蔡　县 Xincai	6.7	1.7	13.4

13-18 各市规模以上公有制工业企业主要经济效益指标(2019年)
Main Economic Efficiency Indicators of Public-owned Industrial Enterprises above Designated Size by City (2019)

市(县) City(County)	总资产贡献率 (%) Ratio of Total Assets to Industrial Output Value (%)	成本费用利润率 (%) Ratio of Profits to Industrial Cost (%)	资产负债率 (%) Assets-Liability Ratio (%)
全 省 Total	**7.4**	**3.0**	**68.1**
省 辖 市 City			
郑 州 市 Zhengzhou	9.4	4.6	63.0
开 封 市 Kaifeng	6.1	5.7	66.4
洛 阳 市 Luoyang	7.8	2.5	64.9
平 顶 山 市 Pingdingshan	5.7	3.2	69.5
安 阳 市 Anyang	7.5	2.2	71.7
鹤 壁 市 Hebi	5.2	1.3	85.8
新 乡 市 Xinxiang	4.7	3.6	69.4
焦 作 市 Jiaozuo	5.9	3.8	60.6
濮 阳 市 Puyang	3.0	-2.3	95.2
许 昌 市 Xuchang	12.7	4.2	65.0
漯 河 市 Luohe	16.9	2.7	75.0
三 门 峡 市 Sanmenxia	7.7	2.4	70.7
南 阳 市 Nanyang	4.7	-0.3	65.2
商 丘 市 Shangqiu	9.3	8.5	73.4
信 阳 市 Xinyang	7.5	4.3	71.4
周 口 市 Zhoukou	9.1	6.4	67.9
驻 马 店 市 Zhumadian	7.4	3.7	67.5
济 源 市 Jiyuan	6.4	2.7	54.8
省 直 管 县 County Directly Administrated by Province			
巩 义 市 Gongyi	-25.3	-79.6	104.7
兰 考 县 Lankao	0.6	-0.8	54.4
汝 州 市 Ruzhou	9.2	7.4	88.1
滑 县 Huaxian	4.9	7.8	58.2
长 垣 市 Changyuan	1.9	5.2	76.2
邓 州 市 Dengzhou	11.4	26.2	51.6
永 城 市 Yongcheng	11.1	15.0	70.7
固 始 县 Gushi	6.2	1.9	41.3
鹿 邑 县 Luyi	59.0	22.3	26.9
新 蔡 县 Xincai	5.2	2.3	13.7

13-19 各市规模以上私营工业企业主要经济效益指标(2019年)

Main Economic Efficiency Indicators of Private Industrial Enterprises above Designated Size by City (2019)

市(县)	City(County)	总资产贡献率 (%) Ratio of Total Assets to Industrial Output Value (%)	成本费用利润率 (%) Ratio of Profits to Industrial Cost (%)	资产负债率 (%) Assets-Liability Ratio (%)
全省	**Total**	**16.9**	**10.5**	**40.0**
省辖市	**City**			
郑州市	Zhengzhou	17.1	11.7	58.1
开封市	Kaifeng	14.2	9.8	34.2
洛阳市	Luoyang	17.2	12.5	40.5
平顶山市	Pingdingshan	9.6	7.0	45.8
安阳市	Anyang	6.9	3.0	74.3
鹤壁市	Hebi	9.3	5.0	40.7
新乡市	Xinxiang	9.7	5.4	53.7
焦作市	Jiaozuo	26.0	11.0	39.0
濮阳市	Puyang	7.4	4.1	42.5
许昌市	Xuchang	30.0	15.0	18.4
漯河市	Luohe	14.4	9.8	31.9
三门峡市	Sanmenxia	7.7	7.3	55.0
南阳市	Nanyang	7.1	5.7	49.4
商丘市	Shangqiu	23.6	10.0	32.1
信阳市	Xinyang	14.0	9.2	31.1
周口市	Zhoukou	25.0	17.2	28.0
驻马店市	Zhumadian	12.4	11.7	19.7
济源市	Jiyuan	10.5	3.9	53.9
省直管县	**County Directly Administrated by Province**			
巩义市	Gongyi	28.9	16.9	55.5
兰考县	Lankao	16.7	10.9	41.0
汝州市	Ruzhou	7.6	4.7	47.2
滑县	Huaxian	15.5	8.2	41.3
长垣市	Changyuan	12.6	6.3	38.9
邓州市	Dengzhou	14.6	11.7	32.2
永城市	Yongcheng	44.0	13.4	33.9
固始县	Gushi	28.1	8.9	16.8
鹿邑县	Luyi	22.8	21.9	34.0
新蔡县	Xincai	8.4	4.4	25.9

13-20 各市主要工业产品产量(2019年)

Output of Major Industrial Products by City (2019)

市(县) City(County)	化学纤维 (吨) Chemical Fiber (ton)	纱 (万吨) Yarn (10 000tons)	布 (万米) Cloth (10 000m)	服装 (万件) Garments (10 000sets)	卷烟 (亿支) Cigarettes (100millinrolls)	饮料酒 (千升) Alcoholic Beverages (1 000 litre)
全省 Total	**557725.16**	**322.89**	**131996.57**	**110803.96**	**1541.07**	**2998669**
省辖市 City						
郑州市 Zhengzhou		0.37	3215.61	2125.57		664546
开封市 Kaifeng		52.55	835.00	2058.15		31489
洛阳市 Luoyang	92267.52	1.47	3333.00	97.19		250845
平顶山市 Pingdingshan	125953.35	13.70	2174.78	355.18		34414
安阳市 Anyang		7.65	4498.27	1878.24		22619
鹤壁市 Hebi	4652.00	3.73	1835.50	3406.90		15843
新乡市 Xinxiang	179600.00	22.98	1718.62	1632.85		349812
焦作市 Jiaozuo	9579.14	4.70	1929.53	743.21		79117
濮阳市 Puyang	4796.00	1.35		1205.48		158
许昌市 Xuchang	981.45	16.95	23201.04	1073.39		4412
漯河市 Luohe	4485.00	0.53		184.45		17461
三门峡市 Sanmenxia		0.33	32136.00	177.89		28555
南阳市 Nanyang		60.69	13649.49	3056.49		173806
商丘市 Shangqiu	54183.70	64.41		34304.63		370971
信阳市 Xinyang	71239.00	1.52		3048.36		162392
周口市 Zhoukou	9988.00	61.92	43121.73	51408.14		644022
驻马店市 Zhumadian		8.03	348.00	4047.84		148207
济源市 Jiyuan						
省直管县 County Directly Administrated by Province						
巩义市 Gongyi				17.24		
兰考县 Lankao		1.58		91.76		36
汝州市 Ruzhou						
滑县 Huaxian		6.61	1229.00	412.23		1113
长垣市 Changyuan						
邓州市 Dengzhou		15.09	2087.00	713.92		106985
永城市 Yongcheng		0.15		3860.17		3370
固始县 Gushi				22.21		9028
鹿邑县 Luyi		0.74		2396.84		23354
新蔡县 Xincai		4.00	348.00	1939.50		1511

13-20 续表 1 continued

市(县) City(County)	液体乳 (吨) Liquid Milk (ton)	熟肉制品 (吨) Raise Meat Products (ton)	速冻米面食品 (吨) Quick-frozen Rice and Wheat Flour foods (ton)	机制纸及纸板 (万吨) Machinemade Paper and Paperboard (10 000 tons)	塑料制品 (万吨) Plastic Products (10 000 tons)	原煤 (万吨) Coal (10 000 tons)	焦炭 (万吨) Synthetic Detergents (10 000 tons)	十种有色金属 (万吨) Ten Kinds of Nonferrous Metals (10 000 tons)
全　　省 Total	**1988923**	**1193997**	**1909824**	**386.83**	**424.42**	**10873.27**	**2029.53**	**435.55**
省 辖 市 City								
郑 州 市 Zhengzhou	313944	163865	1170980	33.12	10.11	2085.92		24.26
开 封 市 Kaifeng	15660	20222	16936	6.28	9.26			4.78
洛 阳 市 Luoyang	16870			1.37	19.24	773.97	66.96	128.22
平顶山市 Pingdingshan	49461	2469		19.83	2.18	3094.27	495.67	0.15
安 阳 市 Anyang		50492		1.93	5.33	259.58	958.10	12.56
鹤 壁 市 Hebi		51256	120011	1.75	2.92	519.90		0.29
新 乡 市 Xinxiang	39942	17019	69874	101.75	38.74	413.65		8.25
焦 作 市 Jiaozuo	368875	11742		48.32	69.28	268.72		38.50
濮 阳 市 Puyang		13135	3590	31.26	3.39			
许 昌 市 Xuchang				12.81	8.05	763.85	277.76	
漯 河 市 Luohe	17358	664740	2437	53.16	11.80			
三门峡市 Sanmenxia	34759				1.05	1149.44		50.76
南 阳 市 Nanyang	907943	12548	3801	21.02	12.89			0.42
商 丘 市 Shangqiu		11144	419548	16.13	8.33	1422.39		8.24
信 阳 市 Xinyang		25290		0.06	0.57		49.59	
周 口 市 Zhoukou	15363	82502	77094	7.29	211.76			0.86
驻马店市 Zhumadian	76099	67571	22940	30.75	9.23	34.07		
济 源 市 Jiyuan	132649		2613		0.28	87.49	181.46	158.27
省直管县 County Directly Administrated by Province								
巩 义 市 Gongyi					0.54	256.31		21.77
兰 考 县 Lankao			13192	0.24	3.28			
汝 州 市 Ruzhou						381.82	159.85	
滑 县 Huaxian		3095		1.93	2.02			
长 垣 市 Changyuan			3989		0.45			
邓 州 市 Dengzhou		9701	293	4.58	6.48			
永 城 市 Yongcheng				2.10	0.13	1422.39		8.24
固 始 县 Gushi								
鹿 邑 县 Luyi					0.57			
新 蔡 县 Xincai								

13-20 续表 2　　contiuned

市(县)　City(County)	发电量(亿千瓦小时) Electricity (100 million kwh)	生铁(万吨) Pig Iron (10 000 tons)	粗钢(万吨) Steel (10 000 tons)	钢材(万吨) Steel Products (10 000 tons)	硫酸(万吨) Sulfuric Acid (10 000 tons)	烧碱(万吨) Caustic Soda (10 000 tons)	原铝(万吨) Aluminum (10 000 tons)
全　省 Total	**2765.83**	**2573.76**	**3299.09**	**3837.97**	**418.57**	**173.91**	**185.75**
省 辖 市 City							
郑 州 市 Zhengzhou	372.12	36.55	116.54	161.99			22.30
开 封 市 Kaifeng	44.75			9.09		12.32	
洛 阳 市 Luoyang	449.59		34.06	36.44	32.80		117.00
平顶山市 Pingdingshan	208.90	172.77	363.63	355.62		45.55	
安 阳 市 Anyang	124.16	1469.42	1486.02	1508.63	11.31		
鹤 壁 市 Hebi	128.24				9.14		
新 乡 市 Xinxiang	197.96			13.41			
焦 作 市 Jiaozuo	202.44			46.78	52.17	61.73	38.21
濮 阳 市 Puyang	59.05			34.86			
许 昌 市 Xuchang	91.76			344.36			
漯 河 市 Luohe	31.83					10.32	
三门峡市 Sanmenxia	188.61			0.66	157.66	3.82	
南 阳 市 Nanyang	115.32	224.37	274.87	275.60			
商 丘 市 Shangqiu	126.88		289.36	329.01			8.24
信 阳 市 Xinyang	80.25	301.04	337.15	340.35			
周 口 市 Zhoukou	51.25			0.03			
驻马店市 Zhumadian	68.03			5.55			
济 源 市 Jiyuan	224.69	369.61	397.47	375.59	155.50	40.16	
省直管县 County Directly Administrated by Province							
巩 义 市 Gongyi	71.62	36.55	60.81	19.83			21.77
兰 考 县 Lankao	1.62						
汝 州 市 Ruzhou	23.91						
滑 县 Huaxian	0.52						
长 垣 市 Changyuan	49.43			0.25			
邓 州 市 Dengzhou	2.78						
永 城 市 Yongcheng	52.23		289.36	301.74			8.24
固 始 县 Gushi							
鹿 邑 县 Luyi	2.34						
新 蔡 县 Xincai				3.54			

13-20 续表 3 contiuned

市(县) City(County)	合成氨 (万吨) Synthetic Ammonia (10 000 tons)	农用化肥(折纯量) (万吨) Synthetic Ammonia (10 000 tons)	化学农药(原药) (吨) Chemical Pesticide (ton)	人造板 (万立方米) Artificial Board (10 000 cu.m)	水 泥 (万吨) Cement (10 000 tons)	平板玻璃 (万重量箱) Plate Glass (10 000 weight cases)	小型拖拉机 (台) Small Tractors (unit)
全 省 Total	**525.57**	**406.50**	**78133**	**1355.30**	**10465.59**	**1973.25**	**134247**
省 辖 市 City							
郑 州 市 Zhengzhou		0.77	2848	1.00	1437.89		
开 封 市 Kaifeng	103.55	40.88	19896	250.04	43.02		117593
洛 阳 市 Luoyang	13.48	10.81	181	3.97	545.08	1003.27	8679
平 顶 山 市 Pingdingshan				0.24	1068.57		
安 阳 市 Anyang	13.10	48.71	1552	3.95	529.48		
鹤 壁 市 Hebi			164	1.49	195.33		
新 乡 市 Xinxiang	159.47	91.64	3639	45.49	1970.25	38.56	
焦 作 市 Jiaozuo	57.11	44.39	2074	13.65	588.36		
濮 阳 市 Puyang	30.34	23.25	16468	60.04	79.54	0.26	
许 昌 市 Xuchang		4.10		176.40	873.49		7975
漯 河 市 Luohe		11.10	241	138.26	55.12	62.44	
三 门 峡 市 Sanmenxia	2.48	0.34			673.36		
南 阳 市 Nanyang		1.01		30.36	1039.98		
商 丘 市 Shangqiu		7.71	2081	179.66	200.67	866.60	
信 阳 市 Xinyang				207.56	546.75		
周 口 市 Zhoukou			28990	71.55	83.87		
驻 马 店 市 Zhumadian	146.05	81.10		171.64	391.17	2.12	
济 源 市 Jiyuan		40.71			143.64		
省 直 管 县 County Directly Administrated by Province							
巩 义 市 Gongyi					137.68		
兰 考 县 Lankao				198.41	0.00		
汝 州 市 Ruzhou					438.22		
滑 县 Huaxian		40.48	38				
长 垣 市 Changyuan					25.25	38.56	
邓 州 市 Dengzhou				7.51	99.77		
永 城 市 Yongcheng				7.20	28.32		
固 始 县 Gushi				57.17	66.69		
鹿 邑 县 Luyi					8.96		
新 蔡 县 Xincai		0.97		56.24	35.19		

主要统计指标解释

工业 指从事自然资源的开采，对采掘品和农产品进行加工和再加工的物质生产部门。具体包括：(1)对自然资源的开采，如采矿、晒盐等(但不包括禽兽捕猎和水产捕捞)；(2)对农副产品的加工、再加工，如粮油加工、食品加工、缫丝、纺织、制革等；(3)对采掘品的加工、再加工，如炼铁、炼钢、化工生产、石油加工、机器制造、木材加工等，以及电力、自来水、煤气的生产和供应等；(4)对工业品的修理、翻新，如机器设备的修理、交通运输工具(如汽车)的修理等。

工业统计调查单位为工业法人单位。

工业法人单位指从事工业生产经营活动的法人单位。工业法人单位应同时具备以下条件：①依法成立，有自己的名称、组织机构和场所，能够独立承担民事责任；②独立拥有（或授权）使用资产，承担负债，有权与其他单位签订合同；③具有包括资产负债表在内的帐户，或者能够根据需要编制帐户。

国有及国有控股企业 指国有企业加上国有控股企业。国有企业(即原全民所有制工业或国营工业)指企业全部资产归国家所有，并按《中华人民共和国企业法人登记管理条例》规定登记注册的非公司制的经济组织。包括国有企业、国有独资公司和国有联营企业。1957 年以前的公私合营和私营工业，后均改造为国营工业，1992 年改为国有工业，这部分工业的资料不单独分列时，均包括在国有企业内。国有控股企业是对混合所有制经济的企业进行的“国有控股”分类。它是指这些企业的全部资产中国有资产(股份)相对其他所有者中的任何一个所有者占资(股)最多的企业。该分组反映了国有经济控股情况。

本篇涉及的其他企业登记注册类型的解释详见综合篇。

轻工业 指主要提供生活消费品和制作手工工具的工业。按其所使用的原料不同，可分为两大类：(1)以农产品为原料的轻工业，是指直接或间接以农产品为基本原料的轻工业。主要包括食品制造、饮料制造、烟草加工、纺织、缝纫、皮革和毛皮制作、造纸以及印刷等工业；(2)以非农产品为原料的轻工业，是指以工业品为原料的轻工业。主要包括文教体育用品、化学药品制造、合成纤维制造、日用化学制品、日用玻璃制品、日用金属制品、手工工具制造、医疗器械制造、文化和办公用机械制造等工业。

重工业 指为国民经济各部门提供物质技术基础的主要生产资料的工业。按其生产性质和产品用途，可以分为下列三类：(1)采掘(伐)工业，是指对自然资源的开采，包括石油开采、煤炭开采、金属矿开采、非金属矿开采等工业；(2)原材料工业，指向国民经济各部门提供基本材料、动力和燃料的工业。包括金属冶炼及加工、炼焦及焦炭、化学、化工原料、水泥、人造板以及电力、石油和煤炭加工等工业；(3)加工工业，是指对工业原材料进行再加工制造的工业。包括装备国民经济各部门的机械设备制造工业、金属结构、水泥制品等工业，以及为农业提供的生产资料如化肥、农药等工业。

根据上述划分原则，修理业中以重工业产品为修理作业对象的划为重工业，反之划为轻工业。

资产总计 指企业过去的交易或者事项形成的、由企业拥有或者控制的、预期会给企业带来经济利益的资源。资产一般按流动性分为流动资产和非流动资产。其中流动资产可分为货币资金、交易性金融资产、应收票据、应收账款、预付款项、其他应收款、存货等；非流动资产可分为长期股权投资、固定资产、无形资产及其他非流动资产等。根据会计“资产负债表”中“资产总计”项目的期末余额数填报。

流动资产合计 资产满足以下条件之一应归为流动资产：(1) 预计在一个正常营业周期中变现、出售或耗用，主要包括存货、应收账款等；(2) 主要为交易目的而持有；(3) 预计在资产负债表日起一年内（含一年）变现；(4) 自资产负债日起一年内，交换其他资产或清偿负债的能力不受限制的现金或现金等价物。包括货币资金、应收票据、应收账款、存货等项目。根据会计“资产负债表”中“流动资产合计”项目的期末余额数填报。

固定资产原价 指固定资产的成本，包括企业在购置、自行建造、安装、改建、扩建、技术改造某项固定资产时所发生的全部支出总额。根据会计“固定资产”科目的期末借方余额填报。

累计折旧 指企业在报告期末提取的历年固定资产折旧累计数。根据会计“累计折旧”科目的期末贷方余额填报。

负债合计 指企业过去的交易或者事项形成的，预期会导致经济利益流出企业的现时义务。负债一般按偿还期长短分为流动负债和非流动负债。根据会计“资产负债表”中“负债合计”项目的期末余额数填报。

流动负债合计 负债满足下列条件之一的应归为流动负债：(1) 预计在一个正常营业周期中清偿；(2) 主要为交易目的而持有；(3) 自资产负债表日起一年内到期应予清偿；(4) 企业无权自主地将清偿推迟至资产负债表日后一年以上。包括短期借款、应付票据、应付账款、应付职工薪酬、应交税费等项目。根据会计“资产负债表”中“流动负债合计”项目的期末余额数填报。

所有者权益合计 指企业资产扣除负债后由所有者享有的剩余权益。公司的所有者权益又称股东权益。包括实收资本、资本公积、盈余公积、未分配利润等。根据会计“资产负债表”中“所有者权益合计”项目的期末余额数填报。

应收账款 指企业因销售商品、提供劳务等经营活动所形成的债权，包括应向客户收取的货款、增值税款和为客户代垫的运杂费等。来源于会计“资产负债表”中“应收账款”项目的期末余额数。

存货 指企业在日常活动中持有以备出售的产成品或商品、处在生产过程中的在产品、在生产过程或提供劳务过程中耗用的材料或物料等，通常包括原材料、在产品、半成品、产成品、商品以及周转材料等。来源于会计“资产负债表”中“存货”项目的期末余额数。

产成品 指企业已经完成全部生产过程并验收入库，可以按照合同规定的条件送交订货单位，或者可以作为商品对外销售的产品。来源于会计“产成品”科目的借方余额。

营业收入 指企业经营主要业务和其他业务所确认的收入总额。营业收入包括“主营业务收入”和“其他业务收入”。来源于会计“利润表”中“营业收入”项目的本年累计数。

营业成本 指企业经营主要业务和其他业务所发生的成本总额。包括企业（单位）在报告期内从事销售商品、提供劳务等日常活动发生的各种耗费。包括“主营业务成本”和“其他业务成本”。来源于会计“利润表”中“营业成本”项目的本年累计数。

主营业务税金及附加 指企业经营主要业务应负担的营业税、消费税、城市维护建设税、教育费附加等。根据会计“主营业务税金及附加”科目的期末借方余额填报。

利润总额 指企业在一定会计期间的经营成果，是生产经营过程中各种收入扣除各种耗费后的盈余，反映企业在报告期内实现的盈亏总额。根据会计“利润表”中“利润总额”项目的本期金额数填报。

应交增值税 指企业按税法规定，从事货物销售或提供加工、修理修配劳务等增加货物价值的活动本期应交纳的税金。计算公式为：

应交增值税=销项税额−（进项税额−进项税额转出）−出口抵减内销产品应纳税额−减免税款+出口退税

进项税额指企业在报告期内购入货物或接受应税劳务而支付的、准予从销项税额中抵扣的增值税额。

销项税额指企业在报告期内销售货物或提供应税劳务应收取的增值税额。

总资产贡献率 反映企业全部资产的获利能力，是企业经营业绩和管理水平的集中体现，是评价和考核企业盈利能力的核心指标。计算公式为：

$$\text{总资产贡献率}(\%)=\frac{\text{利润总额}+\text{税金总额}+\text{利息支出}}{\text{平均资产总额}}\times 100\%$$

公式中：税金总额为主营业务税金及附加与应交增值税之和；平均资产总额为期初期末资产之和的算术平均值。

资产负债率 该指标既反映企业经营风险的大小，也反映企业利用债权人提供的资金从事经营活动的能力。计算公式为：

$$\text{资产负债率}(\%)=\frac{\text{负债总额}}{\text{资产总额}}\times 100\%$$

资产与负债均为报告期期末数。

流动资产周转次数 指一定时期内流动资产完成的周转次数，反映投入工业企业流动资金的周转速度。计算公式为：

$$\text{流动资产周转次数}=\frac{\text{主营业务收入}}{\text{全部流动资产平均余额}}$$

公式中：全部流动资产平均余额为期初和期末的流动资产之和的算术平均值。

成本费用利润率 反映企业投入的生产成本及费用的经济效益，同时也反映企业降低成本所取得的经济效益。计算公式为：

$$成本费用利润率(\%)=\frac{利润总额}{成本费用总额}\times100\%$$

公式中：成本费用总额为主营业务成本、销售费用、管理费用、财务费用之和。

产品销售率 该指标反映工业产品已实现销售的程度，是分析工业产销衔接情况，研究工业产品满足社会需求的指标。计算公式为：

$$产品销售率(\%)=\frac{工业销售产值}{工业总产值}\times100\%$$

Explanatory Notes on Main Statistical Indicators

Industry refers to the material production sector which is engaged in the extraction of natural resources and processing and reprocessing of minerals and agricultural products, including (1) extraction of natural resources, such as mining, salt production (but not including hunting and fishing); (2) processing and reprocessing of farm and sideline produces, such as rice husking, flour milling, wine making, oil pressing, silk reeling, spinning and weaving, and leather making; (3) manufacture of industrial products, such as steel making, iron smelting, chemicals manufacturing, petroleum processing, machine building, timber processing; water and gas production and electricity generation and supply; (4)repairing of industrial products such as the repairing of machinery and means of transport (including cars).

In industrial surveys, the units of enquiry are industrial corporate units.

Industrial corporate units refer to corporate units engaging in industrial production and operation activities, which meet the following requirements: (1) They are established legally, having their own names, organizations, location, and are able to take civil liability independently; (2) They possess (or are authorized to use) assets independently, assume liabilities and are entitled to sign contracts with other units; (3) They have accounts including the balance sheets or can compile the accounts according to the need.

State-owned and State-holding Enterprises refer to state-owned enterprises plus State-holding enterprises. State-owned enterprises (originally known as State-run enterprises with ownership by the whole society) are non-corporate economic entities registered in accordance with the Regulation of the People's Republic of China on the Management of Registration of Legal Enterprises, where all assets are owned by the State. Included in this category are State-owned enterprises, State-funded corporations and State-owned joint-operation enterprises. Joint State-private industries and private industries, which existed before 1957, were transformed into state-run industries since 1957, and into State-owned industries after 1992. Statistics on those enterprises are included in the State-owned industries instead of being grouped them separately. State-holding enterprises are a sub-classification of enterprises with mixed ownership, referring to enterprises where the percentage of State assets (or shares by the State) is larger than any other single share holder of the same enterprise. This sub-classification illustrates the control of the State over a particular industry.

For explanation of enterprises of other types of registration covered in this chapter, please refer to General Survey.

Light Industry refers to the industry that produces consumer goods and hand tools. It consists of two categories, depending on the materials used:

(1) Industries using farm products as raw materials. These are the branches of light industry which directly or indirectly use farm products as basic raw materials, including the manufacture of food and beverages, tobacco processing, textile, clothing, fur and leather manufacturing, paper making, printing, etc.

(2) Industries using non-farm products as raw materials. These are the branches of light industry which use manufactured goods as raw materials, including the manufacture of cultural, educational articles and sports goods, chemicals, synthetic fibre, chemical products for daily use, glass products for daily use, metal products for daily use, hand tools, medical apparatus and instruments, and the manufacture of cultural and office machinery.

Heavy Industry refers to the industry which produces capital goods, and provides various sectors of the national economy with necessary material and technical basis for production. It consists of the following three branches according to the purpose of production or the use of products:

(1) Mining, quarrying and logging industry, which refers to the industry that extracts natural resources, including extraction of

petroleum, coal, metal and non-metal ores.

(2) Raw materials industry refers to the industry that provides various sectors of the national economy with raw materials, fuels and power. It includes smelting and processing of metals, coking and coke chemistry, chemical materials and building materials such as cement, plywood, and power, petroleum refining and coal dressing.

(3) Manufacturing industry which refers to the industry that processes raw materials. It includes machine-building industries which equip sectors of the national economy; industries producing metal structure and cement products; and industries producing means of agricultural production, such as chemical fertilizers and pesticides.

In accordance with the above principles of classification, the repairing trades, which are engaged primarily in repairing products of heavy industry, are classified as heavy industry while those which are engaged in repairing products of light industry are classified as light industry.

Total Assets refer to all resources that are owned or controlled by enterprises through previous trades or transactions with expectation of making economic profits. Classified by the degree of liquidity, total assets include current assets, and non-current assets. Current assets can be classified into monetary assets, trading financial assets, notes receivable, accounts receivable, advanced payments, other prepaid money and inventories. Non-current assets can be divided into long-term equity investment, fixed assets, intangible assets and other non-current assets. Data on this indicator can be obtained by the year-end figures of total assets in the Assets and Liability Table of accounting records of enterprises.

Total Current Assets refer to the assets that meet one of the following requirements: (1) expected to be cashed, sold or used in a normal operation cycle, mainly including inventory and accounts receivable; (2) be owned for trading purpose mainly; (3) expected to be cashed in one year (including one year) from the day of the Assets and Liability Table; (4) unlimited cash or cash equivalents that can be exchanged with other assets or being capable of settling debts during one year since the day of Assets and Liability Table. Included are monetary assets, notes receivable, accounts receivable and inventories. Data on this indicator can be obtained by the year-end figures of total current assets in the Assets and Liability Table of the accounting records of enterprises.

Original Value of Fixed Assets refers to the cost of fixed assets, or the total expenditure of an enterprise spent on certain fixed assets, through purchase, construction, installation, transformation, expansion or technical upgrading. It is reported according to the year-end debit balance of fixed assets of accounting records.

Accumulated Depreciation refers to the accumulated figure of fixed assets depreciation over the past years that are extracted by the enterprise at the end of the reference period. It is reported according to the year-end credit balance of accumulated depreciation of accounting records.

Total Liabilities refer to payable liabilities of enterprises that accumulated from previous trades or transactions with expectation of economic profits leaking out. In terms of payment, it can be divided into liquid liabilities and long-term liabilities. Data on this item is obtained from the year-end figures on total liabilities from the Assets and Liability Table of the accounting record of the enterprises.

Total Liquid Liabilities refer to the liabilities that meet one of the following requirements: (1) expected to be repaid in a normal operation cycle; (2) be owned for trading purpose mainly; (3) expected to be repaid in one year from the day of the Assets and Liability Table; (4) enterprise has no right to postpone the settlement of which over a year from the day of the Assets and Liability Table. Included are short-term loans, notes payable, accounts payable, employee compensations, taxes and expenses due. Data on this indicator can be obtained by the year-end figures of total liquid liabilities in the Assets and Liability Table of the accounting records of enterprises.

Total Equity refers to the residual ownership of enterprise investors by deducting total liabilities from the total assets, including the paid-in capital, accumulation of capital, operating surplus and non-distributed profits. Data are obtained from the year-end figures on "total equity" from the Assets and Liability Table of the accounting record of enterprise.

Accounts Receivable refers to creditor's rights formed by business activities such as selling goods, providing labor, which include payment for goods that should be charged to the customer, value-added tax and advance freight for the clients. It comes from the ending balance of accounts receivable in balance sheet.

Inventories refers to finished goods or commodities held in preparation for sale in enterprises' daily activities, goods in the production process, material or the physical materials consumed in the production process or in the process of providing labor, usually include raw materials, goods in the production process, semi-finished products, finished products, goods and materials in flow. It comes from the ending balance of inventory in balance sheet.

Finished Goods refers to the products that the enterprises have completed all of the production process and accepted and put in storage, and can be sent to the ordering units in accordance with the contract stipulations, or can be on sale. It come from the debit balance of Finished Products of accounting.

Business Revenue refers to the total revenue recognized by an enterprise in its principal business and other business operations. Business revenue includes " revenue from principal Business" and " revenue from other business". It comes from this year' s cumulative report of "business revenue" items from the "income statement".

Business Cost refers to the total cost incurred by an enterprise in its principal business and other business operations. It includes various expenditures incurred by enterprises (units) in their daily activities of selling goods and providing labour services during the reporting period. It includes "Cost of principal business" and "Cost of other business". It comes from this year' s cumulative report of "operating cost" items from the "income statement".

Tax and Extra Charges from Principal Business refer to the sales tax, consumption tax, urban maintenance and construction tax and education expenses shouldered by the enterprise from its principal business. Data are obtained from the year-end debit balance of "tax and extra charges from principal business" in the accounting record of enterprise.

Total Profits refers to the operation results in a certain accounting period, and it is the balance of various incomes minus various spendings in the course of operation, reflecting the total profits and losses of enterprises in reference period. Data are obtained from the amount of "total profits" in the "profit table" of the accounting record of enterprise.

Value-added Tax Payable refers to the payable tax of enterprises which engaged in selling of goods or providing services that bring added value to the goods, such as processing, repairing, fitting and other activities should be paid according to Tax Law. The formula is as follows:

Value-added Tax Payable = tax on sales-(tax on purchase-transferred tax on purchase)-exports deduct tax payable on domestic sales-tax relief+the export tax rebate.

Tax on Purchase refers to the value-added tax payable by enterprises that purchase goods or receiving taxable services during the reference period and this part of the tax is allowed to be deducted from the tax on sales.

Tax on Sales refers to the value-added tax chargeable by enterprises that sell goods or provide taxable services during the reference period.

Ratio of Profits, Taxes and Interests to Average Assets reflects the profit-making capability of all assets of the enterprise and is a key indicator manifesting the performance and management and evaluating the profit-making potential of the enterprise. It is calculated as follows:

$$\begin{array}{c}\text{Ratio of Profits,}\\ \text{Taxes and Interests}\\ \text{to Average Assets (\%)}\end{array} = \frac{\begin{array}{c}\text{total profits +}\\ \text{total taxes +}\\ \text{interest payment}\end{array}}{\text{average assets}} \times 100\%$$

In the above formula, total taxes is the sum of tax and extra charges on the principal business and value-added tax payable; and average assets is the arithmetic mean of the sum of beginning assets and ending assets.

Ratio of Debts to Assets reflects both the operation risk and the capability of the enterprise in making use of the capital from the creditors. It is calculated as follows:

$$\text{Ratio of Debts to Assets (\%)} = \frac{\text{total debts}}{\text{total assets}} \times 100\%$$

Both assets and debts are figures at the end of the reference period.

Turnover of Current Assets refers to the number of times of turnover of current assets in a given period of time, which reflects the speed of the turnover of current assets of industrial enterprises, and is calculated as follows:

$$\text{Turnover of Current Assets} = \frac{\text{sales revenue of products}}{\text{average balance of total current assets}}$$

In the above formula, average balance of total current assets refers to the arithmetic mean of the sum of current assets at the beginning and at the end of the reference period.

Ratio of Profits to Total Industrial Costs refers to the ratio of profits realized in a given period to the total costs in the same period, which reflects the economic efficiency of input cost and is calculated as follows:

$$\text{Ratio of Profits to Total Industrial Cost (\%)} = \frac{\text{total profits}}{\text{total costs}} \times 100\%$$

Total costs in the above formula are the sum of cost of principal business, marketing cost, management cost and financial cost.

Sales Ratio of Products is an indicator reflecting the actual sale of industrial products, analyzing the production-selling and supply-demand relations. It is calculated as:

$$\text{Sales Ratio of Products (\%)} = \frac{\text{value of industrial sales}}{\text{gross industrial output value (current prices)}} \times 100\%$$

建筑业

Construction

14

⊙ 资料整理：高 彦

简要说明

一、主要内容

本篇反映河南省建筑业企业的基本情况和经营情况。包括企业个数、从业人员数、建筑业总产值、房屋建筑面积、资产、利润、税金、劳动生产率等资料。

二、统计范围

从2002年起，由原具有建筑业业资质等级四级及四级以上的独立核算建筑业企业，调整为具有建筑业资质的总承包和专业承包、劳务分包建筑业企业。

三、资料来源

建筑业资料采取全面调查的方法，由河南省统计局固定资产投资处编辑整理。

Brief Introduction

I. Main Contents

Data in this chapter show the general and operation situation of the construction industry in Henan provincial. They cover the situation of production and management of the construction enterprises, including the number of enterprises; number of employed persons; gross output value of the construction industry; floor space of buildings under construction; profits and taxes ; and labour productivity etc.

II. Scope of Statistics

Starting from 2002 the scope of construction statistics has been adjusted to include all the construction enterprises of various types of ownership with qualification certificates and independent accounting systems, replacing the previous criteria that required construction enterprises of various types of ownership to have qualification certificates at or above Class 4 with independent accounting systems.

III. Sources of Data

Data on construction enterprises are collected in accordance with the Reporting Form System of Construction Statistics, which are provided by Department of investment in fixed assets of the Henan provincial Bureau of Statistics.

14-1 建筑业企业主要统计指标

Main Indicators on Construction Enterprises

年份 Year	单位数 (个) Number of Enterprise (unit)	建筑业总产值 (亿元) Gross Output Value of Construction (100 million yuan)	从业人员 (万人) Number of Employed Person (10 000persons)	房屋建筑面积(万平方米) Floor Spece of Buildings (10 000 sq.m) 施工 Under Construction	竣工 Completed	资产 (亿元) Asset (100 million yuan)	利润 (亿元) Profit (100 million yuan)	税金 (亿元) Tax (100 million yuan)	劳动生产率(按总产值计算) (元/人.年) Overall Labor Productivity by Total Output (yuan/person.year)
1978									
1979									
1980									
1981									
1982									
1983	249	13.30		1050.00	608.40		0.90	0.26	4749
1984	264	19.53		1177.00	647.10		1.10	0.38	5762
1985	375	26.09		1287.70	607.90		1.39	0.58	7435
1986	383	29.20		1324.70	659.70		1.09	0.45	7991
1987	412	31.56		1482.90	731.30		1.16	0.68	8429
1988	442	36.81		1829.20	674.90		1.10	0.91	9720
1989	403	39.26		1355.50	594.60		0.64	0.95	10759
1990	393	41.05		1264.50	609.70		1.02	1.14	11985
1991	493	53.91		1614.72	701.61		0.98	1.67	13098
1992	511	70.33		1934.10	878.60		1.27	2.04	16060
1993	979	101.26		2476.25	1015.03	108.10	1.10	2.74	19549
1994	1332	145.52		2966.28	1322.53	147.44	1.47	3.99	24100
1995	1384	182.07		3386.46	1533.55	186.59	2.07	5.18	27121
1996	2278	271.56		5335.91	2726.45	255.43	4.02	8.32	27910
1997	1975	294.69		4984.41	2447.91	274.48	2.60	8.63	31485
1998	2027	304.96	93.79	5061.35	2418.40	305.48	2.11	9.23	35619
1999	1936	316.99	79.77	5016.55	2584.82	324.54	3.72	9.51	40279
2000	1983	357.34	79.90	5308.29	2629.33	356.53	3.09	11.76	45237
2001	1824	452.49	84.01	6295.47	3146.07	437.70	5.86	14.40	52002
2002	1926	536.73	92.65	7118.44	3630.82	562.05	7.53	16.93	57930
2003	1905	634.52	93.44	8026.07	3433.59	656.32	9.40	20.36	65943
2004	2556	817.13	107.66	9086.52	4186.89	828.57	19.05	27.65	83239
2005	2842	1066.15	125.03	10813.15	4787.12	926.11	25.55	37.01	83308
2006	2834	1530.95	141.37	14472.92	6530.01	1130.11	37.10	50.78	108464
2007	3110	2151.72	176.43	19015.67	9177.80	1484.90	57.43	74.30	123272
2008	3894	2824.06	197.86	21966.53	10289.20	1898.06	92.92	98.71	140560
2009	4146	3596.49	224.34	24596.04	11994.23	2386.99	118.67	129.09	162702
2010	4341	4400.61	235.00	28677.13	13156.03	2856.03	161.65	162.31	183639
2011	4511	5279.36	228.91	33282.01	15146.83	3562.79	200.09	185.44	224132
2012	4738	6009.08	227.12	38328.73	16397.59	4159.13	232.86	210.94	287736
2013	5149	7003.20	237.19	43408.63	18179.14	4981.35	312.47	257.48	277186
2014	5129	7911.89	240.89	48825.35	19818.32	5812.88	321.89	275.37	307264
2015	5142	8047.65	238.83	53132.48	18026.91	5759.66	322.38	273.37	287604
2016	5710	8807.99	261.06	55784.03	19425.80	7135.13	440.61	347.82	322917
2017	6358	10086.58	276.01	55694.68	20226.02	8111.68	477.13	404.68	354856
2018	6732	11360.52	292.08	63789.69	20624.12	9876.33	535.71	505.50	373130
2019	7304	12701.68	296.92	64256.07	20736.33	10238.79	589.14	484.42	403962

注：本表不包括劳务分包企业(下同)。
a) Construction Enterprises in this table exclude work subcontractors enterprises (the same as following tables).

14-2 建筑业企业主要经济指标
Main Economic Indicators on Construction Enterprises

指 标	Item	2014	2015	2016	2017	2018	2019
企业单位数（个）	Number of Construction Enterprises (unit)	5129	5142	5710	6358	6732	7304
从业人员（万人）	Number of Employed Persons (10 000 persons)	240.89	238.83	261.06	276.01	292.08	296.92
固定资产原价（亿元）	Original Value of Fixed Assets (100 million yuan)	1037.24	1031.21	1146.22	1064.87	1125.01	1241.21
自有施工机械设备年末总台数（万台）	Total Number of Machinery and Equipment Owned (10 000 sets)	78.93	64.77	64.59	68.24	65.60	65.75
自有施工机械设备年末净值（亿元）	Net Value of Machinery and Equipment Owned (100 million yuan)	310.59	317.51	330.29	344.86	347.40	306.66
自有施工机械设备年末总功率（万千瓦）	Total Power of Machinery and Equipment Owned (10 000 kw)	1650.01	1651.00	2264.27	1700.70	1695.31	1430.49
建筑业总产值（亿元）	Gross Output Value of Construction (100 million yuan)	7911.89	8047.65	8807.99	10086.58	11360.52	12700.97
全员劳动生产率	Overall Labor Productivity						
按总产值计算（元/人）	In Terms of Gross Output Value (yuan/person)	307264	287604	322917	354856	373130	403962
房屋建筑施工面积（万平方米）	Floor Space of Buildings under Construction (10 000 sq.m)	48825	53132	55784	55695	63790	64256
房屋建筑竣工面积（万平方米）	Floor Space of Buildings Completed (10 000 sq.m)	19818	18027	19426	20226	20624	20736
技术装备率（元/期末人数）	Value of Machines per Laborer (yuan/person)	12893	13294	12652	12494	11894	10328
动力装备率（千瓦/期末人数）	Power of Machines per Laborer (kw/person)	6.85	6.91	8.67	6.16	5.80	4.82
主营业务收入（亿元）	Revenue from Principal Business (100 million yuan)	7435.36	7398.20	8332.02	7989.55	10131.43	10923.33
主营业务成本（亿元）	Costs of Principal Business (100 million yuan)	6437.53	6401.10	7182.65	6873.05	7765.87	9682.63
主营业务税金及附加（亿元）	Taxes and Extra Charges on Pincipal Business Accounts (100 million yuan)	253.62	251.89	236.68	208.64	203.22	172.1
本年固定资产折旧（亿元）	Depreciation of Fixed Assets (100 million yuan)	66.18	65.90	66.57	73.96	70.44	105.10
应付职工薪酬（亿元）	Wages Payable (100 million yuan)	857.81	849.73	1297.95	1245.68	1181.67	2080.89
利润总额（亿元）	Total Profits (100 million yuan)	321.89	322.38	440.61	477.13	535.71	589.14
税金总额（亿元）	Total Tax (100 million yuan)	275.37	273.37	347.82	404.68	505.50	484.42
产值利润率（%）	Ratio of Profit to Gross Output Value (%)	4.1	4.0	3.9	4.3	4.1	4.6
产值利税率（%）	Ratio of Pre-tax Profit to Gross Output Value (%)	7.6	7.4	7.8	7.8	7.6	8.5

14–3 建筑业企业房屋建筑竣工面积及竣工价值(2019年)

Floor space and Value of Building completed of Construction Enterprises (2019)

指 标	Item	竣工面积(万平方米) Floor space Completed (10 000 sq.m)	竣工价值(亿元) Value of Floor Space Completed (10 million yuan)
竣工房屋	**Buildings Completed**	**20736.33**	**5128.28**
住宅房屋	Residential Building	14217.50	2382.67
商业及服务用房屋	Buildings for Commercial and Service	1596.04	1594.97
商厦房屋(批发和零售用房)	Malls Housing	380.61	187.07
宾馆用房屋(住宿用房)	Hotel	182.30	23.77
餐饮用房屋(餐饮用房)	Dining	50.22	5.96
商务会展用房屋	Commercial Exhibition	87.57	20.64
其他商业及服务用房屋(居民服务业用房)	Others (Residents Service)	895.34	1357.52
办公用房屋	Official Building	1160.93	179.47
科研、教育、医疗用房屋	Buildings for Scientific Research, Education and Public Health and Medical	1282.33	529.05
科学研究用房屋	Buildings for Scientific Research	72.62	7.70
教育用房屋	Buildings for Education	957.80	476.41
医疗用房屋(卫生医疗用房)	Buildings for Public Health and Medical	251.91	44.94
文化、体育、娱乐用房屋	Buildings for Culture and Sports and Amusement	233.09	51.87
厂房及建筑物	Workshop and Buildings	1676.42	310.79
#厂房	Workshop	950.49	143.43
仓库	Buildings for Other Uses	159.68	20.57
其他未列明的房屋建筑物	Others	410.34	58.90

14-4 建筑业企业生产情况(2019年)

指标	Item	合计 Total	内资 Domestic Funded	港澳台商投资 Funded from Hong Kong, Macao and Taiwan
企业个数(个)	Number of Enterprises (unit)	7304	7294	2
签订的合同额(亿元)	Contract Value Signed (100 million yuan)	24408.86	24394.61	4.80
上年结转合同额	Value from Contracts Signed in Last Year	9930.40	9926.53	3.35
本年新签合同额	Value from New Contracts Signed in this Year	14478.46	14468.08	1.45
承包工程完成情况(亿元)	Conditions Finished of Contracted Projects (100 million yuan)			
直接从建设单位承揽	Contracted Directly from Investors			
工程完成的产值	Output Value of Finished Projects	12466.39	12457.54	0.45
自行完成施工产值	Output Value of Own-completed Buildings	12284.58	12275.74	0.45
分包出去工程的产值	Output Value of Projects Subcontracted	181.82	181.80	
从建设单位以外承揽	Contracted From Non-investors			
工程完成的产值	Output Value of Finished Projects	416.39	416.38	
建筑业总产值(亿元)	Gross Output Value of Construction (100 million yuan)	12700.97	12692.12	0.45
建筑工程	Construction	11009.57	11005.93	0.40
安装工程	Installation	1209.11	1203.91	0.05
其他	Others	482.29	482.29	
#装配式建筑工程产值	Output Value of Prefabricated Construction Project	655.37	655.37	
#装修装饰	Building Decoration	437.28	437.03	
#在外省完成的产值	Output Value Completed in other Provinces	2744.76	2744.00	
建筑业竣工产值(亿元)	Output Value of Buildings Completed (100 million yuan)	7455.85	7448.31	0.05
从业人员(万人)	Number of Persons Engaged (10 000 persons)	296.92	296.74	0.01
#工程技术人员	Engineering	38.35	38.33	
直接从事生产经营活动的平均人数(万人)	Annual Average people Directly Engaged in Production and Business Operation Activities (10 000 persons)	314.41	314.23	0.02
全员劳动生产率	Overall Labor Productivity			
按总产值计算(元/人)	In Terms of Gross Output Value (yuan/person)	403962	403916	265260
房屋建筑施工面积(万平方米)	Floor Space of Buildings Under Construction (10 000 sq.m)	64256.07	64255.22	
#本年新开工	Beginning Projects This Year	25870.70	25870.70	
房屋建筑竣工面积(万平方米)	Floor Space of Buildings Completed (10 000 sq.m)	20736.33	20736.33	
房屋竣工率(%)	Rate of Floor Space of Buildings Completed (%)	32.27	32.27	
自有施工机械设备年末总台数(台)	Number of Machinery and Equipment Owned (set)	657528	657489	1

Main Indicators on Construction Enterprises (2019)

外商投资 Foreign Funded	#国有控股 State-holding	#集体控股 Collective-holding	#私人控股 Private-holding	房屋建筑业 Floor Space Construction	土木工程建筑业 Civil Engineering Construction	建筑安装业 Building Installation	建筑装饰和其他建筑业 Building Decoration and Others	公有制 Public-owned	非公有制 Non-public owned
8	340	252	6416	2901	1972	800	1631	592	6712
9.45	12030.72	715.70	11130.18	15062.70	7069.43	1243.93	1032.80	12746.42	11662.44
0.52	5872.12	165.41	3724.46	6695.98	2654.26	340.45	239.71	6037.53	3892.87
8.93	6158.60	550.29	7405.72	8366.72	4415.16	903.48	793.09	6708.89	7769.57
8.40	3735.78	648.71	7676.96	7008.90	3845.51	821.49	790.50	4384.49	8081.91
8.39	3724.32	638.43	7521.01	6954.09	3812.28	798.48	719.73	4362.75	7921.82
0.02	11.46	10.28	155.96	54.81	33.23	23.02	70.77	21.73	160.08
0.02	128.17	5.43	252.84	128.00	180.26	64.81	43.32	133.60	282.79
8.40	3852.50	643.86	7773.85	7082.09	3992.54	863.29	763.05	4496.35	8204.62
3.24	3493.55	495.61	6671.30	6452.87	3488.94	508.32	559.44	3989.16	7020.42
5.16	294.84	106.37	739.20	399.98	374.30	285.25	149.57	401.21	807.90
	64.11	41.88	363.36	229.24	129.30	69.72	54.03	105.99	376.30
	551.62	2.27	96.82	123.01	517.12	7.92	7.32	553.88	101.49
0.25	56.45	8.27	360.10	227.19	24.38	20.14	165.58	64.72	372.56
0.76	1867.76	5.56	829.61	1174.07	1148.70	277.70	144.29	1873.32	871.44
7.49	1225.21	335.52	5649.29	5213.54	1491.99	347.27	403.05	1560.73	5895.11
0.17	53.76	16.50	214.11	183.70	76.22	17.35	19.65	70.26	226.66
0.02	7.47	2.03	27.43	22.57	10.46	2.72	2.61	9.49	28.86
0.17	59.71	17.14	224.68	192.63	82.96	16.97	21.85	76.85	237.56
506182	645234	375613	345992	367644	481267	508755	349261	585093	345369
0.85	17783.74	2789.35	42185.84	59668.80	2798.34	1183.71	605.22	20573.09	43682.98
	4061.56	1543.92	19564.92	23341.91	1438.88	652.50	437.41	5605.48	20265.22
	2221.57	1297.06	16645.98	18693.19	1168.05	480.36	394.74	3518.63	17217.70
	12.49	46.50	39.46	31.33	41.74	40.58	65.22	17.10	39.42
38	98434	33581	498815	394404	158241	39171	65712	132015	525513

14-5 建筑业企业主要财务指标(2019年)

单位：万元

指 标	Item	合 计 Total	内 资 Domestic Funded	港澳台商投资 Funded from Hong Kong, Macao and Taiwan	外商投资 Foreign Funded
资产总计	Total Assets	102387896	102035776	186502	165618
流动资产合计	Total Circulating Funds	81069205	80777213	184967	107024
#应收工程款	Accounts Receivable	23491354	23442923	153	48278
存货	Stock	12948448	12882268	51805	14375
固定资产原价	Original Value of Fixed Assets	12418965	12368410	1313	49242
累计折旧	Total Depreciation Drawn Accumulated	5180282	5170891	42	9348
#本年折旧	Draw Depreciation This Year	1052396	1052223	7	166
在建工程	Under Construction Project	1576812	1573261		3552
流动负债合计	Liquid Liabilities	58737587	58490239	175508	71841
#应付账款	Accounts payable	22340727	22277121	50444	13162
非流动负债合计	Non-current liabilities	3437587	3383641	90	53856
负债合计	Total Liabilities	65214511	64913217	175598	125697
所有者权益合计	Owners, Equity	37173385	37122559	10905	39921
#实收资本	Paid-in Capitals	21774527	21755068	3041	16418
个人资本	Individual	7002059	7001206	853	
营业收入	Business Revenue	111575417	111485949	4890	84578
#主营业务收入	Revenue from Principal Business	109305161	109226675	4890	73596
营业成本	Operating costs	99162955	99092726	4030	66200
#主营业务成本	Cost of Principle Business	96886690	96821108	4030	61553
营业税金及附加	Business tax and extra	1796070	1794206	3	1861
#主营业务税金及附加	Main business taxes and add	1721397	1719625	3	1769
其他业务利润	Other Profit from Business	95740	95697		43
销售费用	Sales expenses	500561	499465	0	1096
管理费用	Management Expenses	3492726	3485058	293	7375
研发费用	R&D Expenses	583585	583050		536
财务费用	Financial Expenses	724098	724675	-4	-572
#利息收入	Income of Interest	378231	378236	-4	-1
营业利润	Profits of Business	5602509	5592001	568	9940
利润总额	Total Profits	5895409	5884926	452	10031
利税总额	Total Pre-tax Profits	10742440	10728370	596	13474
应付职工薪酬	Wages Payable	20812232	20798429	563	13240
亏损企业个数(个)	Number of Loss-Making Enterprises (unit)	914	913		1
应交增值税	VAT Payable	3125634	3123820	141	1673

Main Financial Indicators on Construction Enterprises by Registration Status (2019)

(10 000 yuan)

#国有控股 State-holding	#集体控股 Collective-holding	#私人控股 Private-holding	房屋建筑业 Floor Space Construction	土木工程建筑业 Civil Engineering Construction	建筑安装业 Building Installation	建筑装饰和其他建筑业 Building Decoration and Others	公有制 Public-owned	非公有制 Non-public owned
40040466	3397506	55111115	50733125	37201176	8023023	6430574	43437972	58949924
30931864	2523337	44472845	40320315	28816619	6721159	5211112	33455202	47614004
7016773	863228	14779689	10912927	8287597	2463587	1827243	7880001	15611353
4073505	294704	7874387	6883904	4608765	753643	702136	4368209	8580239
4171359	763426	6989058	4921753	5685690	940209	871313	4934785	7484181
2043906	328321	2597864	1788449	2549844	507330	334659	2372227	2808054
345527	64527	598156	376928	477573	128311	69585	410054	642342
663612	61274	824842	683240	705872	81460	106241	724886	851926
28597621	1710179	26038622	29190581	21841822	4781692	2923492	30307800	28429787
12802755	696266	8146577	11218463	7986326	2179311	956627	13499021	8841707
2007984	78806	1228099	1655893	1605353	82659	93682	2086790	1350797
31281063	2144605	29156638	31984422	24729888	5325246	3174955	33425668	31788843
8759403	1252901	25954478	18748703	12471288	2697777	3255618	10012304	27161081
4499780	681321	15823143	10456400	7381272	1655617	2281238	5181101	16593426
76391	47772	6673792	3805300	1888644	489985	818130	124162	6877897
36078357	5176172	65958947	59882727	36421303	8131131	7140257	41254529	70320889
35362927	5117128	64582232	58985998	35543169	7908146	6867848	40480056	68825106
33117991	4313479	57851796	53646095	32095057	7263777	6158026	37431470	61731486
32385147	4226807	56546686	52766187	31170082	7038421	5912000	36611954	60274736
305091	274784	1145317	1027662	563399	68593	136417	579875	1216195
281344	272813	1099997	996175	537792	61363	126067	554157	1167240
34613	2758	58135	42647	47400	2843	2850	37371	58369
53192	35360	393312	230720	172216	45134	52490	88552	412009
1027400	283864	2076026	1574505	1182661	389499	346062	1311264	2181463
370474	1801	182821	166130	350662	35529	31264	372275	211311
215575	30878	451357	385272	248966	38127	51734	246453	477645
76533	894	300696	340060	35225	3328	-382	77427	300804
1012023	292570	4043317	3018801	1877509	315507	390692	1304593	4297916
1025254	295437	4319945	3276439	1901796	325665	391508	1320691	4574718
1843762	812637	7615188	6083272	3340209	588801	730158	2656399	8086041
7161054	930009	12106466	12404537	5473969	1910102	1023624	8091064	12721168
40	22	819	273	228	128	285	62	852
537163	244387	2195247	1810658	900621	201772	212583	781551	2344083

14-6 各市建筑业企业总产值

Total Output Value of Construction by City

单位：亿元 (100 million yuan)

市(县) City(County)	2000	2005	2010	2011	2012	2013	2014	2015	2016	2017	2018	2019
全 省 Total	**357.34**	**1066.15**	**4400.61**	**5279.36**	**6009.08**	**7003.20**	**7911.89**	**8047.65**	**8807.99**	**10086.58**	**11360.52**	**12700.97**
省辖市 City												
郑州市 Zhengzhou	105.93	299.39	1352.33	1549.16	1816.99	2264.38	2715.24	2715.91	2891.14	3495.60	4225.26	4729.49
开封市 Kaifeng	10.77	35.16	105.80	132.88	164.04	198.46	216.34	212.85	241.99	352.37	377.53	428.35
洛阳市 Luoyang	50.18	168.54	877.67	1110.90	1214.38	1202.35	1263.52	1255.70	1323.31	1119.41	958.06	1123.28
平顶山市 Pingdingshan	15.48	31.18	88.66	102.88	121.59	130.40	137.92	120.66	126.99	156.80	180.89	203.96
安阳市 Anyang	28.68	71.78	319.14	359.22	410.82	532.27	601.64	678.74	771.07	895.15	991.99	1017.36
鹤壁市 Hebi	3.65	6.34	34.25	43.37	42.37	50.61	58.24	61.08	67.67	84.77	76.22	89.70
新乡市 Xinxiang	26.84	79.44	238.71	294.56	344.56	418.86	449.31	443.91	490.11	592.95	698.78	809.08
焦作市 Jiaozuo	9.31	36.26	87.51	99.18	108.09	121.99	114.34	96.70	110.60	89.17	92.01	106.86
濮阳市 Puyang	23.45	46.84	138.98	168.44	192.39	224.91	235.04	228.38	251.82	282.19	288.79	298.51
许昌市 Xuchang	9.69	21.28	85.04	95.32	106.11	120.28	159.95	127.98	138.15	161.67	186.00	200.00
漯河市 Luohe	3.73	10.10	35.29	41.72	42.86	51.45	55.09	49.93	54.56	65.78	69.09	82.31
三门峡市 Sanmenxia	7.55	26.25	82.44	104.68	112.55	126.56	133.64	117.05	133.98	165.72	198.90	232.64
南阳市 Nanyang	21.29	75.70	197.79	242.66	260.52	292.65	310.00	328.76	376.47	421.98	470.63	530.64
商丘市 Shangqiu	9.42	43.76	170.41	214.74	228.96	272.16	322.59	362.93	424.81	530.89	610.80	658.38
信阳市 Xinyang	14.78	43.34	207.15	247.60	278.23	321.66	372.18	428.70	482.71	561.48	625.03	650.95
周口市 Zhoukou	9.73	40.60	184.06	216.63	250.73	298.99	352.64	361.95	403.14	473.90	545.92	624.77
驻马店市 Zhumadian	6.09	23.14	175.48	233.82	284.85	342.04	377.51	425.19	480.42	590.79	709.21	853.27
济源市 Jiyuan	0.78	7.08	19.88	21.61	29.04	33.17	36.72	31.23	39.04	45.97	55.42	61.42
省直管县 County Directly Administrated by Province												
巩义市 Gongyi	0.52	3.50	9.24	11.68	11.47	16.94	18.70	15.35	16.36	19.30	23.14	27.09
兰考县 Lankao	0.08	0.31	4.80	5.93	7.62	8.51	10.12	11.20	14.64	88.69	106.53	124.10
汝州市 Ruzhou	0.16	0.52	1.01	1.43	2.03	2.78	3.82	4.17	5.37	10.59	13.13	14.99
滑县 Huaxian	0.22	6.07	18.72	22.07	24.08	26.18	29.02	33.08	38.22	55.56	68.89	34.31
长垣市 Changyuan	4.24	7.78	61.53	78.67	104.86	141.61	151.71	161.07	177.06	219.42	263.69	313.48
邓州市 Dengzhou	0.58	3.81	18.69	25.56	34.76	31.49	38.83	41.05	51.47	70.58	85.55	97.81
永城市 Yongcheng	1.44	5.86	22.04	26.92	34.78	49.05	49.11	48.66	54.10	64.19	77.22	93.08
固始县 Gushi	2.72	5.10	21.69	25.01	27.32	34.50	34.53	32.71	38.50	43.56	50.15	59.48
鹿邑县 Luyi	0.82	4.87	10.66	13.63	15.51	20.82	26.85	34.69	40.94	52.54	64.89	79.12
新蔡县 Xincai	0.18	0.26	10.58	14.74	16.13	17.54	19.69	22.57	26.04	40.80	50.56	61.78

14-7 各市建筑业企业利税总额
Total Pre-Tax Profits of Construction Enterprises by City

单位：万元 (10 000 yuan)

市(县)	City(County)	2000	2005	2010	2015	2016	2017	2018	2019
全省	**Total**	**148547**	**625512**	**3239587**	**5957558**	**7112063**	**8818132**	**10412100**	**10742440**
省辖市	**City**								
郑州市	Zhengzhou	35374	136720	981163	1801655	1649242	2162155	2450922	2412211
开封市	Kaifeng	3581	18134	69580	172487	204672	311480	355869	392610
洛阳市	Luoyang	6407	96068	435593	582412	468388	584433	574803	558782
平顶山市	Pingdingshan	5962	19443	60208	108088	114257	119752	211344	147825
安阳市	Anyang	15184	29358	168267	417861	552928	779472	979025	893923
鹤壁市	Hebi	1296	1649	20348	36227	55054	73203	86553	100898
新乡市	Xinxiang	15297	56331	282720	308212	500240	542119	1017920	1011505
焦作市	Jiaozuo	2673	17570	59892	74608	67261	61056	73435	340570
濮阳市	Puyang	11834	24647	94763	153925	141639	184502	258357	244190
许昌市	Xuchang	6812	8436	54114	161803	159745	153383	116407	134147
漯河市	Luohe	2363	5093	30699	52793	48549	55112	52268	47888
三门峡市	Sanmenxia	2626	12422	71644	144220	103844	173873	188239	189940
南阳市	Nanyang	10156	45817	216463	232857	438718	532994	584444	556459
商丘市	Shangqiu	8610	33083	136697	265895	412639	514473	818234	763358
信阳市	Xinyang	7246	44549	197830	320301	567853	761340	560205	679226
周口市	Zhoukou	9263	38970	196239	362657	604498	662238	762419	834410
驻马店市	Zhumadian	3624	30310	149536	317404	995229	1108665	1278032	1388709
济源市	Jiyuan	241	6915	13832	30530	27308	37884	43624	45789
省直管县	**County Directly Administrated by Province**								
巩义市	Gongyi	420	3594	8948	25323	19396	21129	37399	31965
兰考县	Lankao	106	428	2955	18270	24376	78826	116658	120268
汝州市	Ruzhou	26	344	999	4450	7576	5060	11574	10005
滑县	Huaxian	64	4085	12871	23162	50021	103778	104844	36554
长垣市	Changyuan	5342	13344	98909	165938	195916	210716	347521	364364
邓州市	Dengzhou	207	1188	20956	44021	68228	111966	118304	120315
永城市	Yongcheng	444	4915	18550	47592	76403	70177	148693	153486
固始县	Gushi	1835	3208	11541	35168	41668	52110	55704	69359
鹿邑县	Luyi	1301	8136	11652	22798	80320	68132	132047	137006
新蔡县	Xincai	134	291	16246	26904	37889	77740	93435	93514

14-8 各市建筑业企业利润总额
Total Profits of Construction Enterprises by City

单位：万元 (10 000 yuan)

市(县)	City(County)	2000	2005	2010	2015	2016	2017	2018	2019
全省	**Total**	**30936**	**255460**	**1616515**	**3223825**	**4406111**	**4771302**	**5357104**	**5895409**
省辖市	**City**								
郑州市	Zhengzhou	3508	40921	490101	931924	1050648	1184087	1305018	1369829
开封市	Kaifeng	418	6952	33919	100232	135931	199642	212208	230664
洛阳市	Luoyang	-8040	39499	159910	215929	297777	302184	265714	314445
平顶山市	Pingdingshan	528	7813	29104	61959	85332	74219	125928	75295
安阳市	Anyang	1411	6107	73664	215140	320296	424472	490526	392283
鹤壁市	Hebi	-57	-388	8743	18128	32372	37782	44264	58938
新乡市	Xinxiang	4511	23368	179761	193916	347238	365905	685157	684267
焦作市	Jiaozuo	88	6175	28387	39761	40787	34255	29582	299643
濮阳市	Puyang	5261	11735	46593	78639	71004	53126	121829	119728
许昌市	Xuchang	4307	2563	27695	95679	96632	96607	61475	87032
漯河市	Luohe	1454	2394	12734	28815	26492	31695	21794	25167
三门峡市	Sanmenxia	710	2950	40519	89537	78765	92390	111635	111717
南阳市	Nanyang	3271	20315	95397	120430	273503	276229	252977	262538
商丘市	Shangqiu	5148	17363	82915	160289	262070	253255	372323	378472
信阳市	Xinyang	2725	24434	101907	174082	329944	373279	297842	377633
周口市	Zhoukou	4782	23148	119227	218278	396044	423282	405462	496431
驻马店市	Zhumadian	895	15027	78544	182584	547094	527731	532337	588911
济源市	Jiyuan	17	5086	7395	17015	14184	21162	21036	22415
省直管县	**County Directly Administrated by Province**								
巩义市	Gongyi	222	1843	4933	17354	12268	14878	21517	18231
兰考县	Lankao	88	348	1219	12967	18777	64446	68680	74202
汝州市	Ruzhou	15	109	516	2877	5492	2533	5591	4100
滑县	Huaxian	0	1792	5772	12774	29162	64269	55117	15856
长垣市	Changyuan	1591	9713	68503	118362	137638	145964	214018	216714
邓州市	Dengzhou	45	209	13386	27175	44060	45559	48353	44696
永城市	Yongcheng	201	3389	10576	31765	53551	39923	73650	80313
固始县	Gushi	801	1348	4836	23085	30384	34013	28363	39111
鹿邑县	Luyi	833	6648	7331	14607	48089	38210	67817	78577
新蔡县	Xincai	70	23	13456	20525	32306	66577	73232	73823

14-9 各市建筑业企业主要指标(2019年)

市(县) City(County)	企业个数 (个) Number of Enterprises (unit)	从业人员 (万人) Number of Employed Persons (10 000 person)	直接从事生产经营活动的平均人数 (万人) Annual Average People Directly Engaged in Production and Business Operation Activities(10 000 person)	签定的合同额 (亿元) Value of Signed Contract (100 million yuan)
全　　省 Total	**7304**	**296.92**	**314.41**	**24408.86**
省　辖　市 City				
郑　州　市 Zhengzhou	1860	82.46	87.17	13273.70
开　封　市 Kaifeng	349	12.74	13.65	638.99
洛　阳　市 Luoyang	565	22.47	24.84	1909.09
平 顶 山 市 Pingdingshan	361	6.03	6.12	337.83
安　阳　市 Anyang	385	35.57	36.01	1513.98
鹤　壁　市 Hebi	156	2.94	3.29	142.76
新　乡　市 Xinxiang	680	23.07	25.17	1026.09
焦　作　市 Jiaozuo	263	4.37	4.42	198.79
濮　阳　市 Puyang	271	9.31	11.17	422.11
许　昌　市 Xuchang	185	4.31	4.92	375.94
漯　河　市 Luohe	104	2.65	2.90	106.13
三 门 峡 市 Sanmenxia	178	3.91	4.18	563.55
南　阳　市 Nanyang	441	15.16	16.52	657.34
商　丘　市 Shangqiu	251	15.50	14.60	996.01
信　阳　市 Xinyang	301	19.64	20.87	676.77
周　口　市 Zhoukou	399	15.98	16.14	684.42
驻 马 店 市 Zhumadian	463	19.16	20.72	811.89
济　源　市 Jiyuan	92	1.65	1.70	73.48
省 直 管 县 County Directly Administrated by Province				
巩　义　市 Gongyi	36	0.69	0.83	36.30
兰　考　县 Lankao	71	2.72	3.10	138.01
汝　州　市 Ruzhou	36	0.55	0.56	17.51
滑　　县 Huaxian	67	1.79	1.87	46.96
长　垣　市 Changyuan	291	9.91	11.02	391.71
邓　州　市 Dengzhou	57	1.73	2.08	109.16
永　城　市 Yongcheng	46	1.98	2.22	104.71
固　始　县 Gushi	27	2.40	2.38	75.53
鹿　邑　县 Luyi	35	1.79	1.77	84.22
新　蔡　县 Xincai	48	1.16	1.21	43.36

Main Indicators of Construction Enterprises by City (2019)

总产值 (亿元) Gross Output Value (100 million yuan)	竣工产值 (亿元) Output Value of Buildings Completed (100 million yuan)	房屋建筑施工面积 (万平方米) Floor Space of Buildings Under Construction (10 000 sq.m)	房屋建筑竣工面积 (万平方米) Floor Space of Buildings Completed (10 000 sq.m)	自有施工机械设备年末净值 (亿元) Net Value of Machinery and Equipment Owned (100 million yuan)
12700.97	**7455.85**	**64256.07**	**20736.33**	**1430.49**
4729.49	1778.61	32015.15	5724.44	522.25
428.35	246.73	2081.09	840.81	24.91
1123.28	324.70	5090.79	1091.89	95.39
203.96	1581.92	917.44	294.26	66.93
1017.36	601.93	5486.59	3021.64	134.37
89.70	41.11	692.01	202.01	17.52
809.08	453.02	2457.51	1626.02	130.60
106.86	47.36	619.57	185.88	11.85
298.51	183.39	702.53	282.46	60.98
200.00	83.01	1079.84	331.51	18.18
82.31	49.84	485.90	249.33	11.93
232.64	124.21	920.34	232.37	77.83
530.64	298.06	2154.72	969.44	50.01
658.38	428.19	2285.01	1398.47	38.24
650.95	404.01	2847.34	1685.14	66.38
624.77	483.80	2060.16	1421.98	59.15
853.27	299.77	2140.19	1109.84	40.07
61.42	26.18	219.90	68.86	3.93
27.09	13.21	145.60	48.67	1.89
124.10	99.42	460.07	299.39	1.84
14.99	8.52	85.27	34.77	5.33
34.31	24.66	180.57	118.65	3.58
313.48	174.35	393.65	179.36	74.16
97.81	54.90	153.95	60.85	4.78
93.08	55.63	453.76	317.71	13.69
59.48	46.54	343.04	232.17	9.68
79.12	72.15	762.94	641.32	1.46
61.78	24.58	139.03	112.71	0.87

14-10 各市建筑业企业个数(2019年)

单位：个

市(县) City(County)	企业个数 Number of Enterprises	内资 Domestic Funded	港澳台商投资 Funded from Hong Kong, Macao and Taiwan	外商投资 Foreign Funded	公有制 Public-owned	非公有制 Non-public owned
全省 Total	**7304**	**7294**	**2**	**8**	**592**	**6712**
省辖市 City						
郑州市 Zhengzhou	1860	1856	2	2	127	1733
开封市 Kaifeng	349	348		1	27	322
洛阳市 Luoyang	565	565			55	510
平顶山市 Pingdingshan	361	361			32	329
安阳市 Anyang	385	384		1	23	362
鹤壁市 Hebi	156	156			10	146
新乡市 Xinxiang	680	678		2	31	649
焦作市 Jiaozuo	263	262		1	15	248
濮阳市 Puyang	271	271			14	257
许昌市 Xuchang	185	185			12	173
漯河市 Luohe	104	104			11	93
三门峡市 Sanmenxia	178	178			21	157
南阳市 Nanyang	441	441			50	391
商丘市 Shangqiu	251	250		1	34	217
信阳市 Xinyang	301	301			54	247
周口市 Zhoukou	399	399			23	376
驻马店市 Zhumadian	463	463			45	418
济源市 Jiyuan	92	92			8	84
省直管县 County Directly Administrated by Province						
巩义市 Gongyi	36	36			3	33
兰考县 Lankao	71	71			1	70
汝州市 Ruzhou	36	36			2	34
滑县 Huaxian	67	67			1	66
长垣市 Changyuan	291	291			5	286
邓州市 Dengzhou	57	57			7	50
永城市 Yongcheng	46	46			7	39
固始县 Gushi	27	27			2	25
鹿邑县 Luyi	35	35				35
新蔡县 Xincai	48	48			4	44

Number of Construction Enterprises by City (2019)

(unit)

#国有控股 State-holding	#集体控股 Collective-holding	#私人控股 Private-holding	房屋建筑业 Floor Space Construction	土木工程建筑业 Civil Engineering Construction	建筑安装业 Building Installation	建筑装饰和其他建筑业 Building Decoration and Others
340	**252**	**6416**	**2901**	**1972**	**800**	**1631**
97	30	1725	472	480	342	566
13	14	308	175	82	49	43
24	31	491	204	110	64	187
17	15	318	148	114	30	69
11	12	340	272	63	30	20
7	3	123	92	41	10	13
15	16	612	239	170	65	206
8	7	219	100	62	25	76
10	4	242	92	96	30	53
2	10	162	85	46	19	35
4	7	85	50	22	8	24
16	5	150	54	90	7	27
33	17	370	154	145	39	103
21	13	200	131	65	10	45
27	27	237	135	93	24	49
8	15	360	183	130	22	64
22	23	394	279	135	16	33
5	3	80	36	28	10	18
	3	28	23	11	2	
1		69	43	26	1	1
1	1	33	22	11	1	2
1		64	45	13	6	3
4	1	276	70	50	16	155
6	1	50	27	21	7	2
5	2	38	30	8	3	5
1	1	24	17	7	2	1
		35	20	12	1	2
3	1	43	39	7	1	1

14-11 各市建筑业企业总产值(2019年)

单位：亿元

市(县) City(County)	总产值 Gross Output Value	内 资 Domestic Funded	港澳台商投资 Funded from Hong Kong, Macao and Taiwan	外商投资 Foreign Funded	公有制 Public-owned	非公有制 Non-public owned
全　　省 Total	**12700.97**	**12692.12**	**0.45**	**8.40**	**4496.35**	**8204.62**
省 辖 市 City						
郑 州 市 Zhengzhou	4729.49	4728.79	0.45	0.25	2512.02	2217.46
开 封 市 Kaifeng	428.35	428.26		0.09	88.52	339.83
洛 阳 市 Luoyang	1123.28	1123.28			492.12	631.16
平 顶 山 市 Pingdingshan	203.96	203.96			68.21	135.75
安 阳 市 Anyang	1017.36	1016.46		0.89	32.10	985.26
鹤 壁 市 Hebi	89.70	89.70			13.97	75.73
新 乡 市 Xinxiang	809.08	807.07		2.01	54.82	754.26
焦 作 市 Jiaozuo	106.86	102.60		4.26	33.53	73.32
濮 阳 市 Puyang	298.51	298.51			59.89	238.62
许 昌 市 Xuchang	200.00	200.00			23.79	176.21
漯 河 市 Luohe	82.31	82.31			18.90	63.41
三 门 峡 市 Sanmenxia	232.64	232.64			158.83	73.81
南 阳 市 Nanyang	530.64	530.64			180.94	349.70
商 丘 市 Shangqiu	658.38	657.47		0.90	214.81	443.57
信 阳 市 Xinyang	650.95	650.95			176.71	474.24
周 口 市 Zhoukou	624.77	624.77			74.28	550.49
驻 马 店 市 Zhumadian	853.27	853.27			287.32	565.95
济 源 市 Jiyuan	61.42	61.42			5.58	55.84
省 直 管 县 County Directly Administrated by Province						
巩 义 市 Gongyi	27.09	27.09			2.17	24.92
兰 考 县 Lankao	124.10	124.10				124.10
汝 州 市 Ruzhou	14.99	14.99			2.84	12.15
滑 县 Huaxian	34.31	34.31			1.69	32.62
长 垣 市 Changyuan	313.48	313.48			2.96	310.52
邓 州 市 Dengzhou	97.81	97.81			45.70	52.11
永 城 市 Yongcheng	93.08	93.08			42.71	50.37
固 始 县 Gushi	59.48	59.48			3.13	56.35
鹿 邑 县 Luyi	79.12	79.12				79.12
新 蔡 县 Xincai	61.78	61.78			15.34	46.44

Total Output Value of Construction Enterprises by City (2019)

(100 million yuan)

#国有控股 State-holding	#集体控股 Collective-holding	#私人控股 Private-holding	房屋建筑业 Floor Space Construction	土木工程建筑业 Civil Engineering Construction	建筑安装业 Building Installation	建筑装饰和其他建筑业 Building Decoration and Others
3852.50	**643.86**	**7773.85**	**7082.09**	**3992.54**	**863.29**	**763.05**
2463.63	48.39	2213.69	2607.37	1604.35	326.18	191.59
58.57	29.96	329.49	285.82	57.11	12.89	72.55
446.76	45.35	619.68	430.50	393.81	273.39	25.58
56.45	11.76	118.22	133.92	60.48	5.88	3.68
21.84	10.25	927.00	956.04	43.01	15.07	3.23
12.62	1.35	67.69	63.77	20.40	3.35	2.19
29.65	25.17	713.11	344.25	198.03	62.48	204.32
13.95	19.58	62.90	50.59	32.60	9.45	14.21
59.51	0.38	213.49	81.49	154.57	37.19	25.26
14.61	9.18	168.59	105.59	83.67	7.45	3.29
5.25	13.65	56.74	54.66	17.19	4.79	5.67
153.06	5.77	72.33	38.14	188.87	1.63	4.01
115.65	65.29	304.25	296.29	193.15	31.00	10.19
171.38	43.42	405.22	421.16	165.30	20.34	51.58
74.60	102.11	444.62	412.31	178.80	22.12	37.71
13.53	60.75	506.76	313.50	266.66	22.25	22.37
139.03	148.29	495.51	453.78	311.66	4.76	83.07
2.40	3.19	54.58	32.91	22.89	3.06	2.55
	2.17	23.20	21.00	6.02	0.07	
		123.75	100.24	21.98	1.40	0.47
1.19	1.65	12.15	10.38	4.33		0.29
1.69		29.57	21.21	7.80	4.63	0.67
0.43	2.53	284.56	57.98	34.41	22.44	198.64
42.60	3.11	52.11	36.66	49.32	11.71	0.12
39.30	3.41	47.44	56.36	36.25	0.26	0.21
1.60	1.53	52.33	36.44	13.14	0.50	9.40
		79.12	43.71	29.50	1.48	4.43
11.83	3.51	45.57	47.23	13.89	0.51	0.15

14-12 各市建筑业企业资产总计(2019年)

单位：亿元

市(县) City(County)	资产合计 Total Assets	内资 Domestic Funded	港澳台商投资 Funded from Hong Kong, Macao and Taiwan	外商投资 Foreign Funded	公有制 Public-owned	非公有制 Non-public owned
全　省 Total	**10238.79**	**10203.58**	**18.65**	**16.56**	**4343.80**	**5894.99**
省辖市 City						
郑州市 Zhengzhou	4742.09	4723.40	18.65	0.04	2594.24	2147.86
开封市 Kaifeng	291.57	291.24		0.33	85.06	206.51
洛阳市 Luoyang	916.19	916.19			443.56	472.63
平顶山市 Pingdingshan	295.80	295.80			135.90	159.90
安阳市 Anyang	591.85	590.76		1.09	42.04	549.81
鹤壁市 Hebi	164.87	164.87			44.40	120.47
新乡市 Xinxiang	576.41	569.31		7.11	88.13	488.29
焦作市 Jiaozuo	113.00	106.71		6.29	43.80	69.20
濮阳市 Puyang	320.38	320.38			65.62	254.76
许昌市 Xuchang	285.34	285.34			13.44	271.90
漯河市 Luohe	110.71	110.71			5.06	105.65
三门峡市 Sanmenxia	356.65	356.65			280.68	75.97
南阳市 Nanyang	359.15	359.15			85.75	273.40
商丘市 Shangqiu	377.83	376.12		1.71	241.85	135.97
信阳市 Xinyang	201.48	201.48			58.28	143.20
周口市 Zhoukou	219.14	219.14			26.81	192.32
驻马店市 Zhumadian	259.36	259.36			75.07	184.29
济源市 Jiyuan	56.99	56.99			14.13	42.86
省直管县 County Directly Administrated by Province						
巩义市 Gongyi	22.80	22.80			7.37	15.43
兰考县 Lankao	44.67	44.67				44.67
汝州市 Ruzhou	10.50	10.50			1.68	8.82
滑县 Huaxian	33.25	33.25			0.91	32.35
长垣市 Changyuan	235.50	235.50			2.25	233.25
邓州市 Dengzhou	26.18	26.18			11.30	14.88
永城市 Yongcheng	43.25	43.25			27.09	16.17
固始县 Gushi	20.19	20.19			0.92	19.26
鹿邑县 Luyi	20.05	20.05				20.05
新蔡县 Xincai	7.91	7.91			1.91	6.00

Total Assets of Construction Enterprises by City (2019)

(100 million yuan)

#国有控股 State-holding	#集体控股 Collective-holding	#私人控股 Private-holding	房屋建筑业 Floor Space Construction	土木工程建筑业 Civil Engineering Construction	建筑安装业 Building Installation	建筑装饰和其他建筑业 Building Decoration and Others
4004.05	**339.75**	**5511.11**	**5073.31**	**3720.12**	**802.30**	**643.06**
2521.71	72.53	2053.58	2591.47	1553.60	339.02	258.00
63.98	21.07	198.28	156.29	57.40	24.96	52.92
404.03	39.52	460.15	292.45	356.41	234.98	32.35
125.58	10.32	124.76	201.32	77.15	6.25	11.07
24.18	17.86	500.78	512.64	55.62	14.75	8.84
41.23	3.17	106.08	87.17	72.08	2.91	2.71
67.37	20.76	452.12	204.02	195.69	49.71	126.99
19.43	24.37	56.80	49.23	41.55	12.85	9.36
64.42	1.20	225.51	110.43	151.50	38.55	19.90
5.04	8.40	265.84	93.43	173.41	13.45	5.05
3.06	2.00	98.52	54.71	28.59	6.43	20.99
275.03	5.65	72.79	43.88	307.53	1.77	3.47
59.99	25.76	252.62	211.57	111.78	26.59	9.20
232.55	9.30	120.14	107.67	222.57	1.72	45.87
27.55	30.74	135.51	106.03	66.21	15.30	13.94
9.57	17.24	180.55	93.21	111.86	5.69	8.37
47.82	27.25	167.02	134.46	109.64	3.69	11.57
11.53	2.60	40.05	23.32	27.53	3.69	2.44
	7.37	13.63	17.65	5.03	0.12	
		44.67	32.27	10.64	1.71	0.05
0.86	0.82	8.82	5.95	3.80		0.76
0.91		30.76	23.45	5.97	3.03	0.81
2.25		220.23	62.14	31.00	20.64	121.72
10.46	0.84	14.88	8.71	14.63	2.73	0.10
26.64	0.45	15.46	19.05	23.39	0.23	0.59
0.65	0.27	17.44	8.62	5.04	0.74	5.79
		20.05	8.79	10.58	0.20	0.47
1.26	0.65	5.98	5.74	2.04	0.07	0.06

14-13 各市建筑业企业负债合计(2019年)

单位：亿元

市(县) City(County)	负债合计 Total Liabilities	内资 Domestic Funded	港澳台商投资 Funded from Hong Kong, Macao and Taiwan	外商投资 Foreign Funded	公有制 Public-owned	非公有制 Non-public owned
全省 Total	**6521.45**	**6491.32**	**17.56**	**12.57**	**3342.57**	**3178.88**
省辖市 City						
郑州市 Zhengzhou	3395.56	3377.94	17.56	0.06	2088.29	1307.27
开封市 Kaifeng	152.31	152.28		0.03	57.36	94.95
洛阳市 Luoyang	645.31	645.31			357.02	288.29
平顶山市 Pingdingshan	183.90	183.90			95.74	88.17
安阳市 Anyang	272.46	271.65		0.82	24.14	248.32
鹤壁市 Hebi	119.07	119.07			32.14	86.93
新乡市 Xinxiang	248.85	242.79		6.06	53.98	194.87
焦作市 Jiaozuo	57.44	52.53		4.91	26.41	31.03
濮阳市 Puyang	194.06	194.06			54.55	139.51
许昌市 Xuchang	207.90	207.90			9.14	198.76
漯河市 Luohe	61.22	61.22			3.08	58.13
三门峡市 Sanmenxia	241.83	241.83			201.49	40.34
南阳市 Nanyang	203.84	203.84			58.96	144.88
商丘市 Shangqiu	228.09	227.40		0.70	169.75	58.35
信阳市 Xinyang	95.35	95.35			35.13	60.22
周口市 Zhoukou	63.47	63.47			13.83	49.64
驻马店市 Zhumadian	118.59	118.59			52.21	66.38
济源市 Jiyuan	32.21	32.21			9.35	22.86
省直管县 County Directly Administrated by Province						
巩义市 Gongyi	9.99	9.99			4.39	5.60
兰考县 Lankao	19.98	19.98				19.98
汝州市 Ruzhou	4.99	4.99			0.79	4.19
滑县 Huaxian	11.60	11.60			0.60	11.00
长垣市 Changyuan	82.69	82.69			1.43	81.26
邓州市 Dengzhou	9.86	9.86			4.39	5.47
永城市 Yongcheng	25.01	25.01			21.32	3.70
固始县 Gushi	10.06	10.06			0.22	9.85
鹿邑县 Luyi	1.66	1.66				1.66
新蔡县 Xincai	1.92	1.92			0.46	1.46

Total Liabilities of Construction Enterprises by City (2019)

(100 million yuan)

#国有控股 State-holding	#集体控股 Collective-holding	#私人控股 Private-holding	房屋建筑业 Floor Space Construction	土木工程建筑业 Civil Engineering Construction	建筑安装业 Building Installation	建筑装饰和其他建筑业 Building Decoration and Others
3128.11	**214.46**	**2915.66**	**3198.44**	**2472.99**	**532.52**	**317.50**
2035.96	52.33	1229.01	1886.06	1141.26	218.76	149.48
45.21	12.15	89.16	76.96	27.78	14.14	33.43
332.49	24.53	280.03	187.07	241.30	197.68	19.26
88.44	7.29	62.23	129.28	47.14	2.97	4.51
14.18	9.96	213.48	226.46	30.51	8.94	6.54
31.66	0.47	78.96	55.28	62.60	0.76	0.43
45.04	8.94	171.88	105.48	96.89	20.03	26.45
10.00	16.41	23.27	27.64	20.97	6.43	2.40
53.73	0.81	121.48	77.09	88.07	21.71	7.19
4.77	4.37	196.08	60.42	139.10	6.75	1.63
2.63	0.46	54.54	29.30	8.93	3.07	19.92
197.75	3.74	38.62	28.40	211.27	0.66	1.51
40.28	18.68	131.79	123.32	63.06	14.21	3.25
165.01	4.73	49.15	48.59	149.97	0.90	28.63
15.93	19.20	54.84	48.70	30.47	10.11	6.06
2.72	11.11	43.46	21.32	37.08	2.23	2.85
34.46	17.75	56.46	55.22	58.96	1.49	2.91
7.82	1.52	21.23	11.85	17.64	1.68	1.04
	4.39	4.31	7.84	2.12	0.03	
		19.98	14.66	4.16	1.15	
0.78	0.01	4.19	2.47	2.29		0.22
0.60		10.26	8.62	1.80	1.11	0.07
1.43		72.04	36.87	13.37	7.29	25.16
4.31	0.08	5.47	3.07	6.05	0.75	-0.01
21.28	0.04	3.44	6.29	18.46	0.14	0.12
0.08	0.14	8.33	4.78	2.06	0.09	3.14
		1.66	0.73	0.75	0.10	0.08
0.27	0.18	1.46	1.31	0.55	0.04	0.03

14-14 各市建筑业企业主营业务收入(2019年)

单位：亿元

市(县) City(County)	工程结算收入 Revenue of Project Settlement Accounts	内资 Domestic Funded	港澳台商投资 Funded from Hong Kong, Macao and Taiwan	外商投资 Foreign Funded	公有制 Public-owned	非公有制 Non-public owned
全　　省 Total	**10930.52**	**10922.67**	**0.49**	**7.36**	**4048.01**	**6882.51**
省　辖　市 City						
郑　州　市 Zhengzhou	4131.91	4131.42	0.49		2274.19	1857.73
开　封　市 Kaifeng	358.77	358.67		0.10	82.10	276.68
洛　阳　市 Luoyang	912.39	912.39			448.30	464.09
平 顶 山 市 Pingdingshan	164.86	164.86			59.34	105.52
安　阳　市 Anyang	985.81	984.20		1.61	31.58	954.23
鹤　壁　市 Hebi	80.20	80.20			14.54	65.66
新　乡　市 Xinxiang	693.36	691.97		1.40	50.89	642.48
焦　作　市 Jiaozuo	91.77	87.52		4.25	32.27	59.50
濮　阳　市 Puyang	266.75	266.75			49.90	216.85
许　昌　市 Xuchang	151.76	151.76			24.72	127.04
漯　河　市 Luohe	57.27	57.27			8.94	48.33
三 门 峡 市 Sanmenxia	322.48	322.48			259.45	63.03
南　阳　市 Nanyang	426.31	426.31			126.47	299.84
商　丘　市 Shangqiu	551.15	551.15			170.69	380.46
信　阳　市 Xinyang	476.85	476.85			138.98	337.87
周　口　市 Zhoukou	520.19	520.19			73.39	446.80
驻 马 店 市 Zhumadian	689.64	689.64			195.52	494.12
济　源　市 Jiyuan	49.04	49.04			6.74	42.30
省 直 管 县 County Directly Administrated by Province						
巩　义　市 Gongyi	24.25	24.25			2.18	22.07
兰　考　县 Lankao	94.12	94.12				94.12
汝　州　市 Ruzhou	7.28	7.28			2.42	4.86
滑　　县 Huaxian	28.93	28.93			1.53	27.40
长　垣　市 Changyuan	292.34	292.34			0.69	291.65
邓　州　市 Dengzhou	64.75	64.75			33.41	31.34
永　城　市 Yongcheng	82.15	82.15			36.84	45.31
固　始　县 Gushi	52.83	52.83			3.05	49.78
鹿　邑　县 Luyi	76.79	76.79				76.79
新　蔡　县 Xincai	44.66	44.66			9.57	35.09

Revenue from Principal Business of Construction Enterprises by City (2019)

(100 million yuan)

#国有控股 State-holding	#集体控股 Collective-holding	#私人控股 Private-holding	房屋建筑业 Floor Space Construction	土木工程建筑业 Civil Engineering Construction	建筑安装业 Building Installation	建筑装饰和其他建筑业 Building Decoration and Others
3536.29	**511.71**	**6458.22**	**5898.60**	**3554.32**	**790.81**	**686.78**
2223.71	50.48	1780.49	2179.59	1486.07	275.86	190.39
57.28	24.82	272.14	224.02	52.53	14.80	67.43
412.03	36.27	452.27	301.33	300.84	286.06	24.16
51.06	8.29	88.93	102.81	53.83	4.51	3.70
21.56	10.01	890.99	924.49	39.61	17.80	3.91
13.37	1.18	55.94	52.78	23.40	2.81	1.22
28.72	22.17	626.60	286.61	163.51	56.17	187.07
14.42	17.85	48.97	43.51	29.43	10.60	8.23
48.74	1.17	199.86	83.43	134.51	29.86	18.95
16.61	8.11	119.44	73.96	65.50	8.24	4.05
1.56	7.38	42.16	36.42	13.47	1.93	5.45
251.81	7.64	61.84	30.33	287.52	2.10	2.52
77.03	49.44	263.30	241.72	149.50	28.67	6.42
133.93	36.75	349.95	358.76	154.33	5.42	32.65
69.85	69.12	325.62	302.08	130.28	17.18	27.31
13.62	59.77	408.51	260.26	219.45	21.47	19.01
97.42	98.10	430.90	372.60	230.39	4.11	82.54
3.59	3.16	40.32	23.89	20.17	3.22	1.77
	2.18	20.61	18.88	5.22	0.15	
		94.12	75.23	17.06	1.83	
1.19	1.23	4.86	4.50	2.77		0.01
1.53		24.51	20.34	4.87	3.04	0.67
0.69		288.53	47.61	38.91	23.99	181.82
30.56	2.85	31.34	21.32	34.95	8.36	0.12
33.44	3.40	42.38	51.48	29.61	0.16	0.89
2.30	0.75	45.76	33.45	13.16	0.35	5.86
		76.79	42.46	28.42	1.48	4.43
6.88	2.69	34.64	33.51	10.65	0.38	0.11

14-15 各市建筑业企业利润总额(2019年)

单位：万元

市(县) City(County)	利润总额 Total Profits	内资 Domestic Funded	港澳台商投资 Funded from Hong Kong, Macao and Taiwan	外商投资 Foreign Funded	公有制 Public-owned	非公有制 Non-public Owned
全　省 Total	**5895409**	**5884926**	**452**	**10031**	**1320691**	**4574718**
省辖市 City						
郑州市 Zhengzhou	1369829	1369491	452	-113	507584	862246
开封市 Kaifeng	230664	230586		78	25521	205143
洛阳市 Luoyang	314445	314445			83831	230615
平顶山市 Pingdingshan	75295	75295			5524	69771
安阳市 Anyang	392283	392006		276	8574	383709
鹤壁市 Hebi	58938	58938			2957	55981
新乡市 Xinxiang	684267	680685		3581	85608	598658
焦作市 Jiaozuo	299643	298354		1289	8049	291594
濮阳市 Puyang	119728	119728			14927	104802
许昌市 Xuchang	87032	87032			8783	78250
漯河市 Luohe	25167	25167			2398	22769
三门峡市 Sanmenxia	111717	111717			77969	33748
南阳市 Nanyang	262538	262538			79086	183451
商丘市 Shangqiu	378472	373553		4920	119020	259453
信阳市 Xinyang	377633	377633			104633	273000
周口市 Zhoukou	496431	496431			55837	440594
驻马店市 Zhumadian	588911	588911			127240	461671
济源市 Jiyuan	22415	22415			3152	19264
省直管县 County Directly Administrated by Province						
巩义市 Gongyi	18231	18231			1428	16804
兰考县 Lankao	74202	74202				74202
汝州市 Ruzhou	4100	4100			635	3465
滑县 Huaxian	15856	15856			155	15701
长垣市 Changyuan	216714	216714			546	216168
邓州市 Dengzhou	44696	44696			22910	21786
永城市 Yongcheng	80313	80313			49920	30394
固始县 Gushi	39111	39111			2980	36131
鹿邑县 Luyi	78577	78577				78577
新蔡县 Xincai	73823	73823			15419	58404

Total Profits of Construction Enterprises by City (2019)

(10 000 yuan)

#国有控股 State-holding	#集体控股 Collective-holding	#私人控股 Private-holding	房屋建筑业 Floor Space Construction	土木工程建筑业 Civil Engineering Construction	建筑安装业 Building Installation	建筑装饰和其他建筑业 Building Decoration and Others
1025254	**295437**	**4319945**	**3276439**	**1901796**	**325665**	**391508**
483662	23922	828124	727122	442493	120657	79558
10692	14829	205259	154776	42737	8572	24580
60216	23615	224259	145836	125546	27375	15689
4495	1029	61421	38581	31899	1687	3128
3264	5310	395819	398716	12789	6233	-25455
1435	1522	50558	46393	10812	657	1077
61110	24498	570813	235447	216274	73266	159279
3400	4650	289443	276608	13092	6390	3553
14551	375	93929	32173	66464	14405	6687
5600	3183	72551	44772	36398	2556	3307
880	1519	20816	19456	4477	249	985
76915	1054	32368	14387	92698	701	3931
52696	26390	152681	112099	117161	26766	6511
94849	24171	234604	224614	127282	5234	21343
65800	38833	256409	213245	128600	6165	29625
8340	47496	391427	277151	191001	18680	9599
75633	51607	421760	306659	231677	4024	46551
1717	1434	17705	8407	10398	2051	1560
	1428	16240	13299	4871	61	
		74202	47473	23584	2667	477
363	273	3465	2082	1556		462
155		14850	12447	1838	1271	300
546		209362	33868	16630	10941	155276
21209	1701	21786	11218	25132	7886	460
47321	2599	29802	33440	45233	84	1557
2320	660	34499	26054	7941	413	4703
		78577	44668	27383	1878	4649
10790	4630	58173	55888	17554	225	156

14-16 各市建筑业企业利税总额(2019年)

单位：万元

市(县) City(County)	利税总额 Total Pre-tax Profits	内资 Domestic Funded	港澳台商投资 Funded from Hong Kong, Macao and Taiwan	外商投资 Foreign Funded	公有制 Public-owned	非公有制 Non-public owned
全省 Total	**10742440**	**10742440**	**596**	**13474**	**2656399**	**8086041**
省辖市 City						
郑州市 Zhengzhou	2412211	2412211	596	-113	868705	1543506
开封市 Kaifeng	392610	392610		279	40329	352281
洛阳市 Luoyang	558782	558782			139720	419062
平顶山市 Pingdingshan	147825	147825			29731	118095
安阳市 Anyang	893923	893923		713	21150	872773
鹤壁市 Hebi	100898	100898			14377	86521
新乡市 Xinxiang	1011505	1011505		3913	114384	897122
焦作市 Jiaozuo	340570	340570		3762	19466	321104
濮阳市 Puyang	244190	244190			26580	217610
许昌市 Xuchang	134147	134147			12837	121310
漯河市 Luohe	47888	47888			6737	41151
三门峡市 Sanmenxia	189940	189940			122349	67591
南阳市 Nanyang	556459	556459			194511	361948
商丘市 Shangqiu	763358	763358		4920	218542	544816
信阳市 Xinyang	679226	679226			187824	491402
周口市 Zhoukou	834410	834410			130032	704378
驻马店市 Zhumadian	1388709	1388709			502191	886518
济源市 Jiyuan	45789	45789			6936	38854
省直管县 County Directly Administrated by Province						
巩义市 Gongyi	31965	31965			2263	29702
兰考县 Lankao	120268	120268				120268
汝州市 Ruzhou	10005	10005			4432	5573
滑县 Huaxian	36554	36554			1895	34659
长垣市 Changyuan	364364	364364			773	363591
邓州市 Dengzhou	120315	120315			73991	46324
永城市 Yongcheng	153486	153486			78145	75341
固始县 Gushi	69359	69359			4395	64964
鹿邑县 Luyi	137006	137006				137006
新蔡县 Xincai	93514	93514			18830	74683

Total Pre-tax Profits of Construction Enterprises by City (2019)

(10 000 yuan)

#国有控股 State-holding	#集体控股 Collective-holding	#私人控股 Private-holding	房屋建筑业 Floor Space Construction	土木工程建筑业 Civil Engineering Construction	建筑安装业 Building Installation	建筑装饰和其他建筑业 Building Decoration and Others
1843762	**812637**	**7615188**	**6083272**	**3340209**	**588801**	**730158**
782078	86628	1490916	1284490	793568	201114	133040
18728	21600	350881	270273	70403	12103	39831
101843	37877	408124	254410	197315	81857	25200
22784	6946	109023	80151	60080	3015	4579
12313	8837	853756	874855	28968	14940	-24840
11875	2502	74941	73697	22747	2610	1843
76792	37592	859643	358542	294180	95768	263016
7640	11827	313026	295719	23406	13850	7595
25930	650	197689	80190	120921	29261	13819
6263	6574	113035	74047	49780	5571	4749
1728	5009	36024	34457	8844	1143	3444
117936	4413	65658	34932	149235	1100	4674
139556	54955	305787	252501	246133	48063	9762
163997	54546	489263	490028	223318	9708	40304
101052	86772	468360	415915	196314	22013	44984
33671	96361	637806	449200	329844	36053	19312
216534	285657	805061	740018	505588	6982	136120
3043	3893	36195	19848	19565	3650	2726
	2263	28834	24336	7520	109	
		120268	81135	35480	2875	778
1628	2804	5573	5911	3585		509
1895		28635	28520	5513	2084	437
773		353903	53139	35573	18385	257266
67165	6827	46324	30817	73852	15180	465
71273	6872	69073	79826	71572	195	1894
2970	1425	61612	48029	13705	570	7054
		137006	76156	49628	3214	8008
13331	5500	74350	71566	21393	351	204

主要统计指标解释

建筑业统计单位　指从事房屋、构筑物建造和设备安装活动的法人企业。建筑业法人企业应同时具备的条件是：① 依法成立，有自己的名称、组织机构和场所，能够承担民事责任；②独立拥有和使用资产，承担负债，有权与其他单位签订合同；③独立核算盈亏，能够编制资产负债表。

建筑业总产值　是以货币形式表现的建筑业企业在一定时期内生产的建筑业产品和提供的服务的总和。建筑业总产值包括：

（1）建筑工程产值：指列入建筑工程预算内的各种工程价值。

（2）安装工程产值：指设备安装工程价值，不包括被安装设备本身的价值。

（3）其他产值：建筑业总产值中除建筑工程、安装工程以外的产值。包括房屋构筑物修理产值、非标准设备制造产值、总包企业向分包企业收取的管理费以及不能明确划分的施工活动所完成的产值。

a. 房屋构筑物修理产值：指房屋和构筑物修理所完成的产值，但不包括被修理房屋、构筑物本身价值和生产设备的修理产值。

b. 非标准设备制造产值：指加工制造没有定型的非标准生产设备的加工费和原材料价值（如化工厂、炼油厂用的各种罐、槽，矿井生产统一使用的各种漏斗、三角槽、阀门等）以及附属加工厂为本企业承建工程制作的非标准设备的价值。

房屋建筑施工面积　指在报告期内施工的全部房屋建筑面积，包括本期新开工的房屋面积、上期施工跨入本期继续施工的房屋面积、上期停缓建在本期恢复施工的房屋面积、本期竣工的房屋面积及本期施工后又停缓建的房屋面积。

房屋建筑竣工面积　指在报告期内房屋建筑按照设计要求全部完工，达到了住人和使用条件，经验收鉴定合格，正式移交使用单位的房屋建筑面积。

自有机械设备年末总台数　指归本企业所有，属于本企业固定资产的生产性机械设备年末总台数。包括施工机械、生产设备、运输设备以及其他设备。

自有机械设备年末总功率　指本企业自有施工机械、生产设备、运输设备以及其他设备等列为在册固定资产的生产性机械设备年末总功率，按设定能力或查定能力计算。包括机械本身的动力和为该机械服务的单独动力设备，如电动机等。计算单位用千瓦，动力换算可按 1 马力＝0.735 千瓦折合成千瓦数。电焊机、变压器、锅炉不计算动力。

工程结算收入　指企业承包工程实现的工程价款结算收入，以及向发包单位收取的除工程价款以外的按规定列作营业收入的各种款项，如临时设施费、劳动保险费、施工机械调迁费等以及向发包单位收取的各种索赔款。

工程结算利润　指已结算工程实现的利润，如亏损以“－”号表示。计算公式为：

工程结算利润＝工程结算收入－工程结算成本－工程结算税金及附加－经营费用

Explanatory Notes on Main Statistical Indicators

Statistical Unit in Construction refers to corporate enterprise engaged in the construction of buildings and structures and in the installation of equipment. A corporate construction enterprise should meet the following 3 requirements: ①being set up in line with relevant legal basis, having its full name, organization and location, and capable of taking civil liabilities; ②independently possessing and using its assets and assuming its liabilities, and entitled to sign contracts with other institutions; and ③ making independent accounts of its profits and losses, and capable of compiling its own balance sheet

Gross Output Value of Construction refers to total of construction products and services, expressed in money terms, produced or rendered by construction and installation enterprises during a given period of time. It includes:

(1) Output value of construction projects: the value of projects covered by the project budgets;

(2) Output value of installation projects: the value of the installation of equipment, (excluding the value of the equipment to be installed);

(3) Other output values: the output value of construction industry apart from that of construction projects and installation projects. It includes: output value of repair of buildings and structures; output value of non-standard equipment manufacturing; overhead expenses received by contracted enterprises from the sub-contracted enterprises and the completed output value of construction activities for which there is no clear definition.

a. Output value of repair of buildings and structures: the value created through the repairs of buildings or structures. It does not include the value of buildings or structures being repaired and the value of the repair of production equipment;

b. Output value of manufactured non-standard equipment: the value of non-standard production equipment, including raw materials and manufacturing cost, made for the construction project (i.e., chemical plant; kettles or tanks used by refineries; various fillers, triangle tanks, valves used by mines). It also includes the output value of equipment manufactured by subsidiary workshops.

Floor Space of Buildings Under Construction refers to floor space of buildings under construction during the reference period, including newly started buildings, buildings started earlier and continued during the reference period, and buildings suspended earlier but restarted during the reference period, buildings completed during the reference period, and buildings under construction and then suspended during the reference period.

Floor Space of Buildings Completed refers to the floor space of buildings that are completed in the reference period in accordance with the requirements of the design, up to the standard for putting them into use, and have been checked and accepted by concerned departments as qualified ones.

Total Number of Machinery and Equipment Owned by the End of Year refers to the number of machines and equipment owned by the enterprises, and listed as the fixed assets of the enterprises by the end of the year, including machinery and equipment for construction, production and transportation.

Total Power of Machinery and Equipment Owned by the End of Year refers to the total power of machinery and equipment owned by the enterprises, and listed as the fixed assets of the enterprises by the end of the year, including machinery and equipment for construction, production and transportation. The power of the machinery is calculated on basis of the designed or verified capacity, covering the power of the machinery/equipment and the separate power equipment serving the machinery/equipment (such as electric motors), but excluding welders, transformers and boilers. The unit used for the calculation of power is kilowatt, with horsepower converted to kilowatt by 1 horsepower=0.735 kilowatt.

Income from Settlement of Projects refers to the income received by the construction enterprise from the contracted project through settlement procedures, and other charges of Operating income in addition to the value of the project, such as temporary facility fee, labour insurance premium, moving cost of construction equipment, as well as various types of claims to the contract.

Profit from Settlement of Projects refers to profit realized through settled projects. It is calculated with the following formula:

Profit from Settlement of Projects＝Income from Settlement of Projects－Settled Cost－Settled Taxes and Other Cost －Operating expenses

房地产业

Real Estate

15

● 资料整理：贾云静

简要说明

一、本篇资料的主要内容及统计范围

本篇资料通过对一定时期内房地产开发企业开发经营活动的数量方面的描述，反映报告期内房地产开发企业土地开发和购置情况、投资总规模及完成情况、实际到位资金情况、房屋建筑面积和造价情况、房屋新开工面积情况、商品房销售情况以及资产负债和经营情况。

本篇资料的统计范围包括全部有开发经营活动的房地产开发经营业法人单位。

二、本篇的资料来源及统计调查方法

本篇统计资料是根据《房地产开发统计报表制度》进行搜集和加工整理而得，全部数据采用全面调查的统计方法。本篇资料由河南省统计局固定资产投资统计处编辑整理。

Brief Introduction

I. Main Contents and Scope

Statistics in this chapter describe activities made by real estate development companies during a given period of time, and reflect the development and purchase of land, size of investment and its progressing, funds actually available, floor space and cost of housing constructed, floor space of new housing starts, sales of commercial housing, assets and liabilities, and operation status of real estate developers during the reference period.

Data in this chapter covers all legal entities with development and operating activities engaged in real estate development.

II. Sources of Data

Data in this chapter are collected and compiled with the Statistical Reports Program on Real Estate Development, which has a full coverage of all companies.Data in this chapter are provided by the Department of investment in fixed assets of Henan provincial Bureau of Statistics.

15-1 房地产开发企业主要指标
Main Indicators of Enterprises for Real Estate Development

年份 Year	企业个数 (个) Number of Enterprises (unit)	本年完成投资额 (亿元) Investment Completed This Year (100 million yuan)	#住宅 Residential Buildings	房屋建筑面积竣工率 (%) Rate of Floor Space of Buildings Completed (%)	商品房销售面积 (万平方米) Floor Space of Commercialized Buildings Sold (10 000 sq.m)	#住宅 Residential Buildings	商品房销售额 (亿元) Total Sale of Commercialized Buildings (100 million yuan)	#住宅 Residential Buildings
1990		3.43						
1991		4.07		42.2	83.16		2.99	
1992		8.78		35.1	103.36		4.83	
1993		25.27		31.2	100.20		6.41	
1994	896	49.61	35.22	39.3	225.04	198.19	16.43	9.58
1995	880	62.56	39.38	64.0	660.29	484.53	26.14	20.86
1996	731	54.84	30.49	37.1	255.82	215.27	22.75	18.55
1997	509	51.75	27.15	35.5	220.49	201.65	20.26	17.69
1998	655	58.10	32.09	33.3	279.61	262.94	27.32	24.70
1999	677	70.41	42.94	33.2	297.10	275.28	30.37	26.41
2000	1020	77.87	50.37	36.0	509.21	438.41	64.18	50.51
2001	938	102.84	75.87	32.6	529.21	483.77	65.59	56.55
2002	1108	138.36	101.31	35.9	639.94	584.74	88.29	75.50
2003	1430	185.56	135.10	31.3	862.71	795.78	120.75	103.60
2004	1774	258.82	174.81	28.8	1055.37	948.61	165.91	136.76
2005	1906	388.52	271.62	28.0	1724.82	1539.60	322.01	255.37
2006	2100	581.95	432.64	24.0	2409.33	2190.99	484.72	403.72
2007	2586	837.11	639.08	26.4	3928.04	3569.18	885.16	742.83
2008	4146	1206.71	970.86	21.8	3191.98	2943.36	746.46	629.40
2009	3798	1553.76	1235.21	21.2	4336.90	4019.26	1156.22	1005.21
2010	4176	2114.08	1685.21	21.7	5452.23	5092.49	1658.79	1454.57
2011	4963	2626.54	2021.19	21.8	6275.16	5725.12	2196.81	1788.04
2012	5316	3035.29	2203.06	19.9	5968.49	5455.50	2286.67	1915.57
2013	5438	3843.76	2827.09	16.6	7310.21	6561.41	3074.14	2516.26
2014	5662	4375.71	3289.20	18.8	7879.67	7009.09	3440.58	2739.71
2015	6158	4818.93	3529.15	13.1	8556.34	7645.84	3945.55	3300.33
2016	6687	6179.13	4558.07	13.3	11306.27	10137.13	5612.90	4839.03
2017	7205	7090.25	5330.80	12.4	13313.89	11707.26	7129.40	5897.68
2018	7536	7015.47	5387.62	12.2	13990.50	12482.88	8055.30	6903.79
2019	7930	7464.59	6055.37	11.4	14277.55	12981.63	9009.98	8016.93

注：商品房销售面积、销售额2005年开始采用新口径，与以前不可比，新口径包括期房销售和现房销售(下同)。

a) Figures on Floor Space and Sales of selling House are Accounted in New Caliber in 2005, So they are different from former years. New Caliber Include marketable housing and futures marketable housing (the same as following tables).

15-2 房地产开发企业(单位)个数和从业人员数

Number of Employed Persons and Enterprises for Real Estate Development

指 标	Item	2010	2011	2012	2013	2014	2015	2016	2017	2018	2019
企业个数（个）	**Number of Enterprises (unit)**	**4176**	**4963**	**5316**	**5438**	**5662**	**6158**	**6687**	**7205**	**7536**	**7930**
#国有控股	State-holding	209	237	251	234	233	249	266	298	321	338
集体控股	Collective-holding	167	172	167	148	133	123	117	112	95	81
私人控股	Private-holding	3511	4104	4407	4498	4670	5125	5565	6000	6263	6737
港澳台控股	Hong Kong, Macao and Taiwan-holding	63	68	66	63	56	50	50	51	54	57
外资控股	Foreign-holding	61	58	49	44	37	29	23	20	19	21
从业人数（人）	**number of Employed Persons (person)**	**100350**	**138716**	**144708**	**158600**	**173215**	**192193**	**211588**	**222085**	**249944**	**276088**
#国有控股	State-holding	6352	6227	6600	6636	7254	8026	8679	10542	11582	11683
集体控股	Collective-holding	4257	9225	13720	9945	5602	5476	4990	4759	3664	3041
私人控股	Private-holding	81719	108264	108426	123771	138896	154686	171281	179848	204471	232770
港澳台控股	Hong Kong, Macao and Taiwan-holding	1694	1900	1573	1507	1685	1590	1810	1988	2043	1877
外资控股	Foreign-holding	2491	2461	1700	1918	1710	1300	762	636	664	671

15-3 各市房地产开发企业(单位)个数(2019年)

Number of Enterprises for Real Estate Development by City (2019)

单位：个 (unit)

市(县) City(County)	企业(单位)个数 Enterprises Number	一级 First Class	二级 Second Class	三级 Third Class	四级 Fourth Class	暂定 Provisional	其他 Others
全 省 Total	**7930**	**111**	**613**	**943**	**663**	**4256**	**1344**
省 辖 市 City							
郑 州 市 Zhengzhou	1438	40	151	160	13	891	183
开 封 市 Kaifeng	292	3	24	21	8	194	42
洛 阳 市 Luoyang	602	16	74	144	81	261	26
平 顶 山 市 Pingdingshan	517	10	33	64	34	264	112
安 阳 市 Anyang	304	2	44	40	9	175	34
鹤 壁 市 Hebi	136	1	2	22	19	68	24
新 乡 市 Xinxiang	550	2	54	69	15	303	107
焦 作 市 Jiaozuo	283	4	18	38	19	176	28
濮 阳 市 Puyang	185	1	18	14	4	121	27
许 昌 市 Xuchang	445	4	46	72	42	173	108
漯 河 市 Luohe	202	2	10	24	55	105	6
三 门 峡 市 Sanmenxia	208	1	10	32	23	109	33
南 阳 市 Nanyang	536	10	51	85	117	230	43
商 丘 市 Shangqiu	584	3	15	30	6	321	209
信 阳 市 Xinyang	594	7	17	57	157	296	60
周 口 市 Zhoukou	468	2	15	28	9	275	139
驻 马 店 市 Zhumadian	511	3	17	30	50	249	162
济 源 市 Jiyuan	75		14	13	2	45	1
省 直 管 县 County Directly Administrated by Province							
巩 义 市 Gongyi	58	2	2	7	2	38	7
兰 考 县 Lankao	37		1			20	16
汝 州 市 Ruzhou	43	1	3	1		38	
滑 县 Huaxian	37		7	5	1	15	9
长 垣 市 Changyuan	40		8	2		9	21
邓 州 市 Dengzhou	60		4	5	5	18	28
永 城 市 Yongcheng	60		2	8	1	46	3
固 始 县 Gushi	51	3	1	6	16	24	1
鹿 邑 县 Luyi	41		1	4		17	19
新 蔡 县 Xincai	68			3		28	37

15-4 各市房地产开发企业从业人员(2019年)
Number of Employed Persons in Enterprises for Real Estate Development (2019)

单位：人 (person)

市(县) City(County)	从业人员 Number of Employed Persons	一级 First Class	二级 Second Class	三级 Third Class	四级 Fourth Class	暂定 Provisional	其他 Others
全省 Total	**276088**	**9185**	**26444**	**27185**	**16350**	**151831**	**45093**
省辖市 City							
郑州市 Zhengzhou	49980	3532	6546	4800	411	30566	4125
开封市 Kaifeng	13479	281	1558	527	190	8890	2033
洛阳市 Luoyang	15068	1001	2769	3171	1090	6723	314
平顶山市 Pingdingshan	11376	588	1185	1712	419	5562	1910
安阳市 Anyang	7362	133	1624	946	126	3832	701
鹤壁市 Hebi	3365	18		497	522	1858	470
新乡市 Xinxiang	12076	29	1897	1110	211	6751	2078
焦作市 Jiaozuo	8570	262	857	1003	479	5195	774
濮阳市 Puyang	6269	189	642	503	54	4041	840
许昌市 Xuchang	9971	578	1812	1218	649	3886	1828
漯河市 Luohe	7865	225	664	919	1716	4168	173
三门峡市 Sanmenxia	4928	7	379	699	487	2526	830
南阳市 Nanyang	13812	699	1788	2376	1916	6180	853
商丘市 Shangqiu	51343	180	2294	2900	365	30416	15188
信阳市 Xinyang	18649	1080	537	2100	5159	8382	1391
周口市 Zhoukou	17970	88	657	865	397	11185	4778
驻马店市 Zhumadian	22621	295	838	1570	2143	10972	6803
济源市 Jiyuan	1384		397	269	16	698	4
省直管县 County Directly Administrated by Province							
巩义市 Gongyi	1295	60	54	104	28	890	159
兰考县 Lankao	2420		98			1210	1112
汝州市 Ruzhou	1360	131	121	45		1063	
滑县 Huaxian	1192		305	170	10	432	275
长垣市 Changyuan	1650		558	65		292	735
邓州市 Dengzhou	1541		140	143	130	585	543
永城市 Yongcheng	2747		195	550	38	1857	107
固始县 Gushi	2304	927	60	159	389	745	24
鹿邑县 Luyi	1410		42	105		557	706
新蔡县 Xincai	1519			75		700	744

15-5 房地产开发投资额

Completed Investment in Real Estate Development

单位：亿元 (100 million yuan)

项　　目	Item	2005	2010	2012	2013	2014	2015	2016	2017	2018	2019
投资总额	**Total Investment**	**388.52**	**2114.08**	**3035.29**	**3843.76**	**4375.71**	**4818.93**	**6179.13**	**7090.25**	**7015.47**	**7464.59**
#国有控股	State-holding		100.87	193.56	292.53	359.98	404.77	663.17	807.65	793.90	775.66
集体控股	Collective-holding		153.07	119.33	114.01	113.43	89.93	72.58	73.69	63.13	91.60
私人控股	Private-holding		1618.75	2279.02	2809.27	3138.71	3361.14	4334.01	4957.02	4961.06	5346.82
港澳台控股	Hong Kong, Macao and Taiwan-holding		46.97	55.08	59.10	56.26	81.75	55.97	90.88	59.95	90.48
外资控股	Foreign-holding		59.62	58.39	47.67	32.80	27.68	17.36	11.66	16.54	26.18
按构成分	**By Composition**										
建筑、安装工程	Construction and Installation	283.87	1657.06	2397.41	3132.97	3704.57	4125.78	4974.04	5511.54	5331.81	5434.31
设备、工器具购置	Purchase of Equipment and Instruments	2.84	25.34	44.27	57.26	87.05	117.27	170.72	158.61	185.13	104.21
其他费用	Others	101.81	431.68	593.61	653.53	584.10	575.88	1034.37	1420.10	1498.53	1926.07
#土地购置费	Total Value of Land Purchased	74.81	293.23	307.36	391.70	352.80	362.68	681.51	951.90	1137.61	1626.67
按工程用途分	**By Use of Projects**										
住宅	Residential Buildings	271.62	1685.21	2203.06	2827.09	3289.20	3529.15	4558.07	5330.80	5387.62	6055.37
#144平方米以上	Over 144 sq.m		253.23	302.78	352.01	375.65	429.98	690.76	905.69	902.09	989.10
90平方米以下	Under 90 sq.m		422.33	676.46	857.86	1028.50	1272.26	1530.62	1704.78	1682.93	1538.31
办公楼	Office Buildings	14.05	56.74	136.35	175.40	198.84	218.54	230.86	226.38	251.17	256.39
商业营业用房	Houses for Bussiness Use	67.79	192.77	319.39	442.10	531.22	694.23	789.84	882.70	781.11	658.63
其他	Others	35.06	179.36	376.49	399.17	356.46	377.00	600.36	650.38	595.58	494.20
新增固定资产	**Newly Increased Fixed Assets**	**189.47**	**861.63**	**1602.45**	**1572.90**	**2008.37**	**1717.29**	**1780.82**	**1625.20**	**1689.15**	**2020.29**
本年实际到位资金	**Actual Funds for Investment**	**388.52**	**2114.08**	**3455.04**	**4402.70**	**4688.97**	**5076.92**	**6558.25**	**7090.57**	**7128.38**	**7918.28**
国内贷款	Domestic Loans	60.75	209.37	321.09	387.13	527.01	475.69	698.56	897.12	665.70	659.20
利用外资	Foreign Investment	2.10	1.51	1.13	5.40	0.67	3.22	1.76	0.99		0.72
自筹资金	Self-raising Funds	180.91	1144.53	1920.72	2472.67	2601.55	2956.20	3671.81	4171.17	4418.06	4635.67
其他资金	Others	144.76	758.67	1212.10	1537.51	1559.74	1641.82	2186.12	2021.29	2044.62	2622.69

15-6 房地产开发企业(单位)建设房屋建筑面积和造价
Floor Space and Cost of Buildings Developed by Enterprises for Real Estate Development

市(县) City(County)	施工房屋面积(万平方米) Floor Space Under Construction (10 000 sq.m)	竣工房屋面积(万平方米) Floor Space Completed (10 000 sq.m)	房屋建筑面积竣工率(%) Rate of Floor Space of Buildings Completed (%)	竣工房屋价值(亿元) Value of Buildings Completed (100 million yuan)	竣工房屋造价(元/平方米) Cost of Buildings Completed (yuan/sq.m)
1997	1042.19	370.26	35.5	32.10	867
1998	1175.96	392.03	33.3	28.41	725
1999	1339.60	444.87	33.2	34.05	765
2000	1657.53	597.21	36.0	40.49	678
2001	1976.84	644.40	32.6	45.74	710
2002	2484.01	892.32	35.9	67.83	760
2003	3210.26	1005.52	31.3	86.33	859
2004	3940.64	1135.32	28.8	100.94	889
2005	4902.98	1370.94	28.0	144.72	1056
2006	7017.17	1681.42	24.0	184.87	1099
2007	10550.90	2785.48	26.4	326.78	1173
2008	13906.18	3026.04	21.8	403.95	1335
2009	16074.35	3400.98	21.2	434.30	1277
2010	20393.98	4426.94	21.7	630.25	1424
2011	25343.32	5527.42	21.8	923.85	1671
2012	29559.36	5870.54	19.9	1059.08	1804
2013	35979.33	5965.87	16.6	1117.83	1874
2014	38857.60	7324.34	18.8	1417.52	1935
2015	40994.40	5390.32	13.1	1079.75	2003
2016	47359.55	6299.44	13.3	1260.41	2001
2017	49942.29	6201.71	12.4	1270.17	2048
2018	54685.56	6655.23	12.2	1413.25	2124
2019	57567.10	6571.21	11.4	1583.17	2409
省辖市 City					
郑州市 Zhengzhou	19583.60	2107.40	10.8	620.82	2946
开封市 Kaifeng	2153.27	133.53	6.2	32.54	2437
洛阳市 Luoyang	4725.14	499.98	10.6	130.96	2619
平顶山市 Pingdingshan	2622.36	91.44	3.5	21.82	2386
安阳市 Anyang	2223.16	141.52	6.4	31.81	2248
鹤壁市 Hebi	1089.75	72.24	6.6	15.16	2098
新乡市 Xinxiang	2635.89	359.78	13.6	80.66	2242
焦作市 Jiaozuo	923.65	84.41	9.1	17.71	2098
濮阳市 Puyang	1775.74	119.69	6.7	28.20	2356
许昌市 Xuchang	2902.08	174.73	6.0	52.83	3024
漯河市 Luohe	1315.31	75.56	5.7	13.50	1787
三门峡市 Sanmenxia	1372.30	134.30	9.8	32.67	2433
南阳市 Nanyang	3019.70	197.95	6.6	39.42	1991
商丘市 Shangqiu	3274.01	470.39	14.4	95.43	2029
信阳市 Xinyang	2314.58	584.51	25.3	119.51	2045
周口市 Zhoukou	2034.13	620.48	30.5	114.80	1850
驻马店市 Zhumadian	3289.07	699.31	21.3	134.33	1921
济源市 Jiyuan	313.37	3.98	1.3	1.01	2547
省直管县 County Directly Administrated by Province					
巩义市 Gongyi	332.79	72.84	21.9	17.31	2377
兰考县 Lankao	377.34	49.48	13.1	8.49	1717
汝州市 Ruzhou	287.98	30.87	10.7	7.88	2553
滑县 Huaxian	346.80	31.38	9.0	6.04	1926
长垣市 Changyuan	221.39	31.58	14.3	7.50	2374
邓州市 Dengzhou	348.57	8.83	2.5	1.68	1907
永城市 Yongcheng	594.71				
固始县 Gushi	269.38	134.45	49.9	24.34	1810
鹿邑县 Luyi	227.84	15.76	6.9	1.49	944
新蔡县 Xincai	462.38	55.15	11.9	9.22	1671

15-7 房地产开发企业开发情况
Operating Statistics of Enterprises for Real Estate Development

项　目	Item	2005	2010	2012	2013	2014	2015	2016	2017	2018	2019
本年购置土地面积（万平方米）	Land Space Purchased This year (10 000sq.m)	2016	2864	1743	1502	1116	951	1108	1015	1018	858
本年待开发的土地面积（万平方米）	Land Space Pending Development This year(10 000sq.m)	764	1209	1319	1310	1344	1628	2476	2307	2594	2731
房屋建筑面积（万平方米）	Floor Space of Building Construction (10 000 sq.m)										
施工面积	Floor Space Under Construction	4903	20394	29559	35979	38858	40994	47360	49942	54686	57567
#住宅	Residential Buildings	3895	16902	23467	28114	29831	31211	35579	37518	41350	43971
竣工面积	Floor Space Completed	1371	4427	5871	5966	7324	5390	6299	6202	6655	6571
#住宅	Residential Buildings	1151	3853	4888	4916	5767	4238	5015	4702	5074	5163
房屋竣工价值(亿元)	Value of Buildings Completed (100 million yuan)	145	630	1059	1118	1418	1080	1260	1270	1413	1583
房屋竣工造价（元/平方米）	Cost of Buildings Completed (yuan/sq.m)	1056	1424	1804	1874	1935	2003	2001	2048	2124	2409
商品房销售面积（万平方米）	Floor Space of Commercialized Buildings Sold (10 000 sq.m)	1725	5452	5968	7310	7880	8556	11306	13314	13991	14278
现房销售面积	Sale Space of marketable housing	791	1911	2179	2548	2891	2812	3236	3468	3295	2896
期房销售面积	Sale Space of futures marketable housing	934	3541	3789	4762	4989	5744	8070	9846	10696	11381
商品房销售额(亿元)	Total Sales of Commercialized Buildings Sold (100 million yuan)	322	1659	2287	3074	3441	3946	5613	7129	8055	9010
现房销售额	Sale of marketable housing	129	439	646	838	1072	1039	1233	1371	1407	1330
期房销售额	Sale of futures marketable housing	193	1220	1641	2236	2369	2907	4380	5759	6648	7680
商品住宅销售套数（万套）	Total Number of Flats of Residential Buildings Sold (10 000 sets)		46	49	58	62	69	91	104	111	113
现房销售套数	Sale of marketable housing		15	16	19	22	21	24	26	25	22
期房销售套数	Sale of futures marketable housing		31	32	39	41	48	67	78	86	91
商品房待售面积（万平方米）	Area of commercialized Buildings for Sale (10 000 sq.m)	307	1161	2453	2717	3694	3607	3395	2847	2801	2529

15-8　房地产开发企业施工、销售和待售情况(2019年)

项　　目	Item	合　计 Total	住　宅 Commercially Residential Buildings
房屋施工面积(万平方米)	Floor Space of Buildings under Construction (10 000 sq.m)	57567.10	43971.26
#新开工	Started This Year	15836.53	12607.65
房屋竣工面积(万平方米)	Floor Space of Buildings Completed (10 000 sq.m)	6571.21	5162.69
#不可销售面积	Floor Space Cannot be Solded	176.23	83.12
住宅竣工套数(万套)	Total Number of Flats of Residential Buildings Completed (10 000 sets)	45.20	45.20
竣工房屋价值(亿元)	Value of Buildings Completed (100 million yuan)	1583.17	1226.26
商品房销售面积(万平方米)	Sold Area of Commercialized Buildings (10 000 sq.m)	14277.55	12981.63
现房销售	Sale of marketable housing	2896.42	2476.79
期房销售	Sale of futures marketable housing	11381.13	10504.84
商品房销售额(亿元)	Total Sale of Commercialized Buildings (100 million yuan)	9009.98	8016.93
现房销售	Sale of marketable housing	1329.85	1062.37
期房销售	Sale of futures marketable housing	7680.13	6954.56
商品住宅销售套数(万套)	Total Number of Flats of Residential Buildings Sold (10 000 sets)	113.02	113.02
现房销售	Sale of marketable housing	21.72	21.72
期房销售	Sale of futures marketable housing	91.31	91.31
商品房待售面积(万平方米)	Floor Number of Space of Buildings Emptied Sold (10 000 sq.m)	2529.37	1694.00
#待售1-3年	On Sale for 1-3Years	598.57	381.67
待售3年以上	On Sale Over 3 Years	491.44	317.46

Situation of Construction, Sale and for Sale of Real Estate Enterprises (2019)

#90平方米以下 Under 90 sq.m	#144平方米以上 Over 144sq.m	办公楼 Office Buildings	商业营用房 House for Business Use	其 他 Others
8956.27	6268.37	1856.95	6130.07	5608.82
1874.17	1747.78	428.14	1298.68	1502.07
1115.35	690.85	240.06	694.09	474.37
12.85	5.90	1.20	11.77	80.15
14.01	3.98	-	-	-
280.74	177.03	65.24	175.17	116.50
2168.05	1533.06	217.12	881.89	196.92
440.09	234.10	41.63	296.01	81.98
1727.96	1298.96	175.48	585.87	114.93
1511.00	1197.22	226.77	663.59	102.69
175.74	120.40	33.34	199.81	34.33
1335.26	1076.82	193.43	463.78	68.37
26.95	9.40	-	-	-
5.43	1.47	-	-	-
21.53	7.93	-	-	-
374.38	277.62	128.42	492.36	214.59
63.35	71.07	37.57	126.28	53.05
43.04	48.40	35.65	101.49	36.84

15-9 各市房地产开发投资情况(2019年)

Development and Investment Completed for Real Estate by City (2019)

市(县) City(County)	投资总额(亿元) Total Investment (100 million yuan)	住宅 Residential Buildings	#90平方米以下 Under 90 sq.m	#144平方米以上 Over 144sq.m	办公楼 Office Buildings	商业营业用房 Houses for Business Use	其他 Other
全省 Total	**7464.59**	**6055.37**	**1538.31**	**989.10**	**256.39**	**658.63**	**494.20**
省辖市 City							
郑州市 Zhengzhou	3349.86	2555.02	1012.39	511.91	206.68	257.63	330.53
开封市 Kaifeng	310.77	255.45	34.18	33.28	3.09	40.43	11.80
洛阳市 Luoyang	366.49	280.51	57.44	48.83	12.51	38.45	35.02
平顶山市 Pingdingshan	146.75	117.41	14.48	14.99	2.09	14.14	13.11
安阳市 Anyang	173.48	147.77	5.86	27.56	2.42	11.41	11.88
鹤壁市 Hebi	93.66	77.85	12.40	7.84	1.34	12.24	2.23
新乡市 Xinxiang	331.42	302.49	43.51	56.60	3.94	17.35	7.64
焦作市 Jiaozuo	105.40	94.69	9.89	15.11	0.58	8.51	1.62
濮阳市 Puyang	240.63	204.28	10.24	29.38	4.72	19.67	11.96
许昌市 Xuchang	396.80	358.16	42.90	48.17	4.79	21.10	12.75
漯河市 Luohe	146.13	128.25	14.88	10.95	1.29	14.62	1.96
三门峡市 Sanmenxia	152.24	128.80	27.12	25.68	2.82	13.62	7.00
南阳市 Nanyang	236.41	195.67	36.60	33.11	2.99	30.25	7.50
商丘市 Shangqiu	334.32	284.09	54.38	36.96	0.02	39.01	11.20
信阳市 Xinyang	390.21	335.33	65.81	48.73	1.78	38.49	14.61
周口市 Zhoukou	293.96	254.81	47.82	12.57	1.70	34.54	2.92
驻马店市 Zhumadian	380.29	320.31	47.06	24.59	3.59	46.42	9.98
济源市 Jiyuan	15.76	14.46	1.34	2.83	0.04	0.76	0.50
省直管县 County Directly Administrated by Province							
巩义市 Gongyi	53.48	44.84	5.94	12.65	2.88	2.25	3.53
兰考县 Lankao	33.63	29.10	0.34	5.31	0.18	2.39	1.95
汝州市 Ruzhou	18.60	15.73	1.55	1.86	0.23	1.67	0.98
滑县 Huaxian	20.83	17.54	0.32	2.07		1.44	1.86
长垣市 Changyuan	26.93	24.85	1.01	16.67	0.62	0.86	0.60
邓州市 Dengzhou	26.77	20.90	0.34	0.35		4.75	1.12
永城市 Yongcheng	30.03	27.78	0.54	0.45		2.20	0.05
固始县 Gushi	39.55	35.79	0.66	1.15	0.01	2.20	1.55
鹿邑县 Luyi	26.84	21.35		0.01		5.41	0.08
新蔡县 Xincai	34.55	32.02	3.09	3.04		2.39	0.14

15-10 各市房地产开发企业实际到位资金(2019年)

Actual Funds in Place of Enterprises for Real Estate Development (2019)

单位：亿元 (100 million yuan)

市(县) City(County)	合计 Total	国内贷款 Domestic Loans	利用外资 Foreign Investment	自筹资金 Self-raising Funds	其他资金来源 Others
全省 Total	**7918.28**	**659.20**	**0.72**	**4635.67**	**2622.69**
省辖市 City					
郑州市 Zhengzhou	3564.90	454.08		1785.48	1325.33
开封市 Kaifeng	307.69	13.81		252.02	41.86
洛阳市 Luoyang	465.03	14.06		194.17	256.80
平顶山市 Pingdingshan	160.63	12.28		72.48	75.86
安阳市 Anyang	202.03	6.11		129.68	66.25
鹤壁市 Hebi	93.99	1.65		64.97	27.37
新乡市 Xinxiang	342.04	19.28		230.93	91.83
焦作市 Jiaozuo	114.58	5.21		81.08	28.28
濮阳市 Puyang	251.32	2.34	0.72	137.23	111.03
许昌市 Xuchang	441.63	21.48		263.31	156.84
漯河市 Luohe	151.55	2.83		96.24	52.47
三门峡市 Sanmenxia	145.32	8.12		91.55	45.66
南阳市 Nanyang	254.90	13.16		141.18	100.55
商丘市 Shangqiu	359.96	7.78		306.59	45.59
信阳市 Xinyang	359.08	30.36		263.50	65.22
周口市 Zhoukou	295.40	19.40		243.77	32.24
驻马店市 Zhumadian	375.82	25.99		274.49	75.34
济源市 Jiyuan	32.44	1.28		7.01	24.14
省直管县 County Directly Administrated by Province					
巩义市 Gongyi	34.76	0.50		32.97	1.29
兰考县 Lankao	33.50			31.27	2.23
汝州市 Ruzhou	16.96	1.64		7.12	8.21
滑县 Huaxian	31.05	0.28		17.00	13.77
长垣市 Changyuan	26.71	0.18		24.76	1.77
邓州市 Dengzhou	30.89	3.42		15.03	12.44
永城市 Yongcheng	27.25			27.25	
固始县 Gushi	40.92	3.27		19.98	17.67
鹿邑县 Luyi	28.92			20.67	8.25
新蔡县 Xincai	23.34	0.67		22.67	

15-11 各市房地产开发施工房屋面积(2019年)

Floor Space of Buildings under Construction by City (2019)

单位：万平方米 (10 000 sq.m)

市(县)	City(County)	施工房屋面积 Floor Space of Buildings under Construction	住宅 Residential Buildings	#90平方米以下 Under 90 sq.m	#144平方米以上 Over 144 sq.m	办公楼 Office Buildings	商业营业用房 Houses for Business Use	其他 Others
全省	**Total**	**57567.10**	**43971.26**	**8956.27**	**6268.37**	**1856.95**	**6130.07**	**5608.82**
省辖市	**City**							
郑州市	Zhengzhou	19583.60	13298.54	4563.44	2126.74	1383.45	1856.19	3045.41
开封市	Kaifeng	2153.27	1700.03	239.87	212.35	23.53	308.15	121.56
洛阳市	Luoyang	4725.14	3489.12	622.22	476.96	119.58	483.62	632.81
平顶山市	Pingdingshan	2622.36	2025.60	446.37	264.24	35.30	324.68	236.77
安阳市	Anyang	2223.16	1821.16	100.54	298.41	42.58	157.31	202.10
鹤壁市	Hebi	1089.75	900.97	135.00	53.33	25.66	111.01	52.10
新乡市	Xinxiang	2635.89	2276.39	461.13	406.66	32.99	231.61	94.90
焦作市	Jiaozuo	923.65	792.79	53.07	126.14	5.76	88.94	36.16
濮阳市	Puyang	1775.74	1504.81	58.07	151.39	19.39	141.01	110.53
许昌市	Xuchang	2902.08	2439.91	262.85	376.74	19.82	214.47	227.88
漯河市	Luohe	1315.31	1184.41	173.02	186.80	10.88	94.36	25.66
三门峡市	Sanmenxia	1372.30	1033.60	154.00	195.03	27.56	184.66	126.48
南阳市	Nanyang	3019.70	2435.52	364.29	340.11	46.87	397.68	139.63
商丘市	Shangqiu	3274.01	2695.08	458.04	362.25	0.74	507.10	71.09
信阳市	Xinyang	2314.58	1813.81	220.80	236.27	8.00	297.19	195.58
周口市	Zhoukou	2034.13	1756.32	190.45	143.29	14.86	201.71	61.24
驻马店市	Zhumadian	3289.07	2556.59	439.51	246.28	35.52	492.23	204.73
济源市	Jiyuan	313.37	246.60	13.61	65.37	4.44	38.13	24.19
省直管县	**County Directly Administrated by Province**							
巩义市	Gongyi	332.79	294.75	57.40	83.65	22.37	12.81	2.86
兰考县	Lankao	377.34	322.15	2.05	44.85	1.32	33.35	20.52
汝州市	Ruzhou	287.98	209.58	20.74	27.18	2.42	56.22	19.76
滑县	Huaxian	346.80	302.99	2.73	51.09		13.64	30.17
长垣市	Changyuan	221.39	195.80	5.60	134.29	4.52	7.78	13.29
邓州市	Dengzhou	348.57	290.92	7.06	5.03		39.39	18.25
永城市	Yongcheng	594.71	468.00	23.44	25.29	0.04	103.65	23.02
固始县	Gushi	269.38	221.73	3.86	12.92	0.47	17.14	30.04
鹿邑县	Luyi	227.84	177.04		4.10		41.55	9.25
新蔡县	Xincai	462.38	380.59	21.76	50.17		74.58	7.20

15-12 各市房地产开发竣工房屋面积(2019年)
Floor Space of Buildings Completed by City (2019)

单位：万平方米 (10 000 sq.m)

市(县) City(County)	竣工房屋面积 Floor Space of Buildings Completed	住宅 Residential Buildings	#90平方米以下 Under 90 sq.m	#144平方米以上 Over 144 sq.m	办公楼 Office Buildings	商业营业用房 Houses for Business Use	其他 Others
全省 Total	**6571.21**	**5162.69**	**1115.35**	**690.85**	**240.06**	**694.09**	**474.37**
省辖市 City							
郑州市 Zhengzhou	2107.40	1478.08	487.27	253.62	196.66	166.32	266.33
开封市 Kaifeng	133.53	109.59	2.39	17.47	0.10	23.11	0.72
洛阳市 Luoyang	499.98	344.45	70.91	50.74	31.97	55.21	68.35
平顶山市 Pingdingshan	91.44	68.83	10.77	6.42	1.15	13.82	7.64
安阳市 Anyang	141.52	109.48	10.21	8.68		15.41	16.63
鹤壁市 Hebi	72.24	56.33	14.01	1.33	1.59	10.37	3.96
新乡市 Xinxiang	359.78	325.45	60.49	67.03	1.44	22.38	10.51
焦作市 Jiaozuo	84.41	67.98	4.88	1.97		14.41	2.02
濮阳市 Puyang	119.69	108.26	1.24	5.07		11.04	0.39
许昌市 Xuchang	174.73	162.38	23.35	37.14	1.32	6.51	4.51
漯河市 Luohe	75.56	55.14	2.26	0.17		20.20	0.22
三门峡市 Sanmenxia	134.30	100.66	14.39	19.24		12.40	21.24
南阳市 Nanyang	197.95	165.51	38.35	39.44	2.37	27.02	3.05
商丘市 Shangqiu	470.39	368.80	51.01	41.73	0.31	95.57	5.70
信阳市 Xinyang	584.51	506.04	69.27	63.10	0.02	49.41	29.04
周口市 Zhoukou	620.48	565.56	149.73	23.94	2.40	45.52	7.00
驻马店市 Zhumadian	699.31	569.01	104.84	53.36	0.73	103.44	26.13
济源市 Jiyuan	3.98	1.12		0.39		1.94	0.92
省直管县 County Directly Administrated by Province							
巩义市 Gongyi	72.84	51.00	23.12	27.88	9.35	12.49	
兰考县 Lankao	49.48	46.40		2.99	0.10	2.82	0.17
汝州市 Ruzhou	30.87	19.85	5.79		1.15	9.86	0.02
滑县 Huaxian	31.38	28.17	0.71	3.33		1.21	2.00
长垣市 Changyuan	31.58	31.58		31.58			
邓州市 Dengzhou	8.83	7.78	0.40	0.51		1.03	0.03
永城市 Yongcheng							
固始县 Gushi	134.45	122.01	2.88	9.85	0.02	5.91	6.51
鹿邑县 Luyi	15.76	12.42				3.34	
新蔡县 Xincai	55.15	50.75	11.45	1.05		4.40	

15-13 各市房地产开发竣工房屋价值(2019年)
Value of Buildings Completed by City (2019)

单位：亿元 (100 million yuan)

市(县)	City(County)	竣工房屋价值 Value of Buildings Completed	住宅 Residential Buildings	#90平方米以下 Under 90 sq.m	#144平方米以上 Over 144 sq.m	办公楼 Office Buildings	商业营业用房 Houses for Business Use	其他 Others
全省	**Total**	**1583.17**	**1226.26**	**280.74**	**177.03**	**65.24**	**175.17**	**116.50**
省辖市	**City**							
郑州市	Zhengzhou	620.82	438.43	152.39	73.47	51.36	57.24	73.79
开封市	Kaifeng	32.54	26.20	0.55	4.51	0.02	6.04	0.28
洛阳市	Luoyang	130.96	87.28	17.53	16.42	11.50	14.72	17.46
平顶山市	Pingdingshan	21.82	16.12	2.41	1.71	0.29	4.03	1.37
安阳市	Anyang	31.81	24.21	2.08	1.53		5.02	2.59
鹤壁市	Hebi	15.16	11.62	2.51	0.38	0.25	2.28	1.00
新乡市	Xinxiang	80.66	72.75	14.24	16.02	0.45	5.41	2.05
焦作市	Jiaozuo	17.71	14.02	1.56	0.43		3.19	0.51
濮阳市	Puyang	28.20	25.82	0.22	0.50		2.35	0.03
许昌市	Xuchang	52.83	49.91	8.55	13.21	0.39	1.72	0.81
漯河市	Luohe	13.50	9.49	0.34	0.04		3.96	0.05
三门峡市	Sanmenxia	32.67	24.76	3.50	4.55		3.16	4.75
南阳市	Nanyang	39.42	34.43	9.02	8.55	0.38	4.05	0.56
商丘市	Shangqiu	95.43	73.10	8.34	8.57	0.05	21.29	0.99
信阳市	Xinyang	119.51	104.29	13.13	10.22		10.90	4.32
周口市	Zhoukou	114.80	103.39	26.11	5.08	0.35	9.66	1.39
驻马店市	Zhumadian	134.33	110.14	18.27	11.74	0.18	19.68	4.33
济源市	Jiyuan	1.01	0.30		0.11		0.49	0.23
省直管县	**County Directly Administrated by Province**							
巩义市	Gongyi	17.31	12.94	5.87	7.07	2.27	2.09	
兰考县	Lankao	8.49	7.94		0.56	0.02	0.51	0.03
汝州市	Ruzhou	7.88	4.67	1.18		0.29	2.91	0.01
滑县	Huaxian	6.04	5.70	0.08	0.48		0.26	0.09
长垣市	Changyuan	7.50	7.50		7.50			
邓州市	Dengzhou	1.68	1.42	0.06	0.10		0.26	0.01
永城市	Yongcheng							
固始县	Gushi	24.34	22.28	0.46	1.31		1.09	0.97
鹿邑县	Luyi	1.49	1.11				0.37	
新蔡县	Xincai	9.22	8.53	1.75	0.19		0.69	

15−14 房地产开发企业房屋销售情况
Selling of Enterprises for Real Estate Development

指标	Item	2005	2010	2012	2013	2014	2015	2016	2017	2018	2019
商品房销售额（亿元）	**Total Sales of Commercialized Buildings Sold (100 million yuan)**	**322.01**	**1658.79**	**2286.67**	**3074.14**	**3440.58**	**3945.55**	**5612.90**	**7129.40**	**8055.30**	**9009.98**
商品住宅	Commercially Residential Buildings	255.37	1454.57	1915.57	2516.26	2739.71	3300.33	4839.03	5897.68	6903.79	8016.93
#90平方米以下	Under 90 sq.m		400.76	530.66	620.02	664.51	850.73	1309.88	1370.75	1521.53	1511.00
144平方米以上	Over 144 sq.m		301.59	294.95	407.11	454.02	551.39	879.32	1034.99	1211.13	1197.22
#别墅、高档公寓	Villas and Good Apartments	24.19	20.55	22.18	32.38	29.58	45.48	74.20	95.80	67.41	54.83
办公楼	Office Buildings	7.60	50.31	111.57	187.16	164.40	123.18	141.16	226.34	225.26	226.77
商业营业用房	Houses for Bussiness Use	58.32	137.09	228.15	334.53	437.64	457.80	552.52	879.31	801.74	663.59
其他房屋	Others	0.72	16.82	31.38	36.19	98.83	64.24	80.20	126.06	124.51	102.69
商品房销售面积（万平方米）	**Sold Area of Commercialized Buildings Sold (10 000 sq.m)**	**1724.82**	**5452.23**	**5968.49**	**7310.21**	**7879.67**	**8556.34**	**11306.27**	**13313.89**	**13990.50**	**14277.55**
商品住宅	Commercially Residential Buildings	1539.60	5092.49	5455.50	6561.41	7009.09	7645.84	10137.13	11707.26	12482.88	12981.63
#90平方米以下	Under 90 sq.m		1106.32	1251.73	1374.32	1492.55	1811.42	2449.92	2479.46	2665.76	2168.05
144平方米以上	Over 144 sq.m		941.14	898.24	1001.95	1016.57	1084.55	1473.11	1765.99	1666.92	1533.06
#别墅、高档公寓	Villas and Good Apartments	94.85	41.14	33.69	41.23	32.72	58.64	90.56	94.34	64.50	53.43
办公楼	Office Buildings	24.86	60.79	126.49	205.44	181.67	149.50	173.35	236.90	224.00	217.12
商业营业用房	Houses for Bussiness Use	154.91	246.44	297.96	444.99	554.60	639.18	816.65	1148.24	1042.89	881.89
其他房屋	Others	5.45	52.51	88.54	98.37	134.30	121.82	179.14	221.49	240.74	196.92

15-15 各市房地产开发商品房屋销售面积(2019年)

Floor Space of Commercialized Buildings Sold by City (2019)

单位：万平方米 (10 000sq.m)

市(县) City(County)	商品房屋销售面积 Floor Space of Commercialized Buildings Sold	现房 Marketable Housing	期房 Futures Marketable Housing	住宅 Residential Buildings	#90平方米以下 Under 90 sq.m	#144平方米以上 Over 144sq.m	办公楼 Office Buildings	商业营业用房 Houses for Business Use	其他 Others
全　　省 Total	**14277.55**	**2896.42**	**11381.13**	**12981.63**	**2168.05**	**1533.06**	**217.12**	**881.89**	**196.92**
省辖市 City									
郑州市 Zhengzhou	3593.27	612.34	2980.93	3241.97	1104.88	392.41	141.07	184.20	26.03
开封市 Kaifeng	542.88	84.54	458.34	498.80	33.93	51.09	1.37	37.95	4.75
洛阳市 Luoyang	934.77	75.41	859.35	805.64	91.75	103.37	31.61	48.85	48.67
平顶山市 Pingdingshan	531.01	38.64	492.36	505.05	52.91	58.03	4.29	19.42	2.24
安阳市 Anyang	483.30	46.91	436.39	454.75	17.18	77.58	1.61	16.97	9.97
鹤壁市 Hebi	238.49	16.05	222.44	215.21	21.26	11.85	6.82	13.83	2.63
新乡市 Xinxiang	752.67	101.13	651.54	713.47	78.25	118.83	0.82	24.26	14.11
焦作市 Jiaozuo	239.13	27.22	211.91	225.76	16.32	30.78	0.45	11.53	1.39
濮阳市 Puyang	449.97	14.89	435.08	437.44	6.96	35.82		11.68	0.85
许昌市 Xuchang	638.29	14.76	623.53	622.13	27.07	90.27	0.17	11.98	4.02
漯河市 Luohe	334.28	10.59	323.69	321.99	6.41	17.43	2.92	9.20	0.17
三门峡市 Sanmenxia	285.47	50.45	235.02	270.12	35.88	63.00	0.83	9.48	5.04
南阳市 Nanyang	698.24	109.30	588.95	596.11	87.20	93.56	9.33	82.47	10.34
商丘市 Shangqiu	1276.11	272.72	1003.39	1160.02	217.60	142.99	8.67	102.72	4.70
信阳市 Xinyang	935.02	464.58	470.44	844.84	127.90	103.72	0.44	72.14	17.60
周口市 Zhoukou	823.23	510.35	312.87	723.86	47.60	51.81	3.67	89.38	6.31
驻马店市 Zhumadian	1435.72	437.00	998.72	1266.04	192.91	76.38	3.03	130.39	36.26
济源市 Jiyuan	85.70	9.55	76.15	78.43	2.07	14.12		5.44	1.84
省直管县 County Directly Administrated by Province									
巩义市 Gongyi	71.82	4.70	67.11	66.30	13.11	26.31	4.58	0.94	
兰考县 Lankao	127.11	44.35	82.77	116.88	1.47	13.16		8.53	1.70
汝州市 Ruzhou	104.06	10.00	94.06	98.50	6.11	11.61	0.36	5.21	
滑县 Huaxian	70.69	0.09	70.59	69.68	0.47	7.99		1.01	
长垣市 Changyuan	73.64	5.33	68.31	73.64	2.53	48.34			
邓州市 Dengzhou	108.62	0.34	108.28	88.51	0.16			19.85	0.26
永城市 Yongcheng	189.80		189.80	170.92		1.30		18.88	
固始县 Gushi	143.63	111.86	31.76	124.74	1.11	7.13		9.92	8.97
鹿邑县 Luyi	103.65	8.40	95.25	91.93	1.03	2.04		11.66	0.06
新蔡县 Xincai	182.34	18.06	164.28	176.59	9.39	12.36		5.75	

15-16 各市房地产开发商品房屋销售额(2019年)

Total Sales of Commercialized Buildings Commercial Houses by City (2019)

单位：亿元 (100 million yuan)

市(县) City(County)	商品房屋销售额 Total Sales of Commercialized Buildings	现房 Marketable Housing	期房 Futures Marketable Housing	住宅 Residential Buildings	#90平方米以下 Under 90 sq.m	#144平方米以上 Over 144sq.m	办公楼 Office Buildings	商业营业用房 Houses for Business Use	其他 Others
全省 Total	**9009.98**	**1329.85**	**7680.13**	**8016.93**	**1511.00**	**1197.22**	**226.77**	**663.59**	**102.69**
省辖市 City									
郑州市 Zhengzhou	3403.56	261.16	3142.40	3025.45	979.84	556.18	177.12	177.98	23.02
开封市 Kaifeng	308.10	43.28	264.82	272.29	15.10	27.18	1.14	30.58	4.08
洛阳市 Luoyang	604.00	38.87	565.13	515.59	51.41	79.62	23.03	40.28	25.10
平顶山市 Pingdingshan	254.25	17.31	236.94	239.11	25.69	28.81	1.80	12.01	1.33
安阳市 Anyang	254.18	22.77	231.41	234.48	8.49	41.70	1.01	14.50	4.18
鹤壁市 Hebi	110.25	8.66	101.60	94.31	9.69	7.10	4.16	11.34	0.44
新乡市 Xinxiang	421.44	43.21	378.23	398.79	39.67	68.93	0.50	17.06	5.08
焦作市 Jiaozuo	121.98	15.27	106.71	114.69	8.66	15.81	0.35	6.49	0.45
濮阳市 Puyang	240.47	7.32	233.15	230.95	4.38	24.56		9.30	0.22
许昌市 Xuchang	373.46	5.59	367.87	362.42	15.52	55.94	0.10	9.75	1.19
漯河市 Luohe	183.06	7.77	175.29	172.01	3.81	11.95	1.62	9.33	0.11
三门峡市 Sanmenxia	116.52	17.96	98.56	108.88	13.87	29.25	0.37	5.85	1.43
南阳市 Nanyang	330.62	47.18	283.44	271.33	39.10	41.08	5.78	48.10	5.41
商丘市 Shangqiu	681.86	131.63	550.23	602.07	127.06	88.90	5.72	71.67	2.41
信阳市 Xinyang	473.23	214.51	258.73	419.51	59.82	51.88	0.25	46.28	7.20
周口市 Zhoukou	393.21	238.44	154.77	326.17	23.78	25.91	2.07	61.71	3.26
驻马店市 Zhumadian	690.92	204.77	486.15	584.38	84.37	34.30	1.76	87.86	16.92
济源市 Jiyuan	48.86	4.17	44.70	44.50	0.75	8.13		3.49	0.87
省直管县 County Directly Administrated by Province									
巩义市 Gongyi	43.81	0.56	43.25	39.60	8.38	15.42	3.37	0.84	
兰考县 Lankao	57.07	19.69	37.38	50.03	0.60	5.54		6.06	0.98
汝州市 Ruzhou	45.23	4.42	40.81	42.58	2.56	5.42	0.13	2.52	
滑县 Huaxian	28.52	0.05	28.46	27.91	0.15	3.06		0.61	
长垣市 Changyuan	34.60	2.06	32.54	34.60	1.09	22.82			
邓州市 Dengzhou	58.70	0.12	58.59	45.63	0.06			12.98	0.09
永城市 Yongcheng	86.50		86.50	76.87		0.75		9.62	
固始县 Gushi	63.97	49.77	14.20	54.99	0.45	2.95		5.69	3.29
鹿邑县 Luyi	44.69	3.01	41.68	37.26	0.31	0.66		7.42	0.01
新蔡县 Xincai	72.89	7.45	65.44	69.71	3.79	3.66		3.18	

15-17 房地产开发企业(单位)财务状况

Financial Conditions of Enterprises for Real Estate Development

单位：万元 (10 000 yuan)

年份 Year	实收资本合计 Total Capital Hold	资产总计 Total Assets	累计折旧 Total Depreciation	#本年折旧 Depriciation This Year	负债总计 Total Liabilities	所有者权益 Owners' Equity	资产负债率(%) Ratio of Liabilities to Assets (%)
1995		1764785	14267	5342	1279978	484807	72.5
1996	551806	1807658	26520	7591	1387989	419669	76.8
1997	406745	1740105	19949	7588	1447544	292561	83.2
1998	505463	2280437	30805	8592	1910905	369532	83.8
1999	510523	2173758	36403	10014	1753236	420520	80.7
2000	817805	3018825	56674	12183	2338003	680822	77.4
2001	945883	3442486	63638	15519	2604287	838199	75.7
2002	1150354	4595641	85859	17913	3481164	1114477	75.7
2003	1455042	5510446	102740	19951	4038378	1472068	73.3
2004	2202011	8276947	129627	29240	5938250	2338698	71.7
2005	2318891	9784926	143625	29277	6816474	2968452	69.7
2006	3014227	12757587	186086	48428	8971739	3785848	70.3
2007	4432599	19659483	230093	45495	13732874	5926609	69.9
2008	6637409	26964335	304507	73239	17873731	9090604	66.3
2009	7364502	33620940	378972	80626	22812498	10808442	67.9
2010	8508683	45243820	493246	114146	32685619	12558201	72.2
2011	11222136	65168658	585018	136696	48594182	16574476	74.6
2012	13021039	86412935	688028	144209	66347192	20065743	76.8
2013	17606463	118597788	946125	228537	92631519	25966268	78.1
2014	18176192	149779271	998051	250516	119599889	30179382	79.8
2015	21513722	182626392	1135933	315165	145839268	36787123	79.9
2016	22900193	225366766	1366514	333911	184403598	40963168	81.8
2017	26183913	275919831	1483932	320358	230676820	45243011	83.6
2018	29954843	337085759	1880308	441240	279404629	57681129	82.9
2019	32316944	385908471	2025147	437070	325472376	60436095	84.3
省辖市 City							
郑州市 Zhengzhou	14682198	212254962	765467	117607	180948170	31306791	85.3
开封市 Kaifeng	1048170	10554549	46872	13870	9242411	1312138	87.6
洛阳市 Luoyang	2307969	31402718	220859	41825	26491241	4911477	84.4
平顶山市 Pingdingshan	1503377	11877211	109293	16455	10034053	1843158	84.5
安阳市 Anyang	927984	11695534	50292	6170	10216625	1478908	87.4
鹤壁市 Hebi	445975	4002946	16374	4902	3556210	446736	88.8
新乡市 Xinxiang	1477317	14922955	97900	26976	12318835	2604120	82.5
焦作市 Jiaozuo	512245	5988936	33713	10229	5173339	815597	86.4
濮阳市 Puyang	588281	7358889	20609	5689	6576221	782668	89.4
许昌市 Xuchang	1402730	16796330	85320	21554	14535888	2260442	86.5
漯河市 Luohe	503221	6672424	15278	5261	6031301	641123	90.4
三门峡市 Sanmenxia	410808	4636535	19540	3765	4172983	463552	90.0
南阳市 Nanyang	1334000	11749397	79534	17637	9534218	2215179	81.1
商丘市 Shangqiu	1434883	11819467	150524	67467	8721867	3097600	73.8
信阳市 Xinyang	1076838	9439449	101519	20520	7529618	1909831	79.8
周口市 Zhoukou	1288236	6105549	114019	34499	3961388	2144160	64.9
驻马店市 Zhumadian	1143146	7054095	79287	19487	5113551	1940544	72.5
济源市 Jiyuan	229568	1576529	18748	3159	1314456	262073	83.4
省直管县 County Directly Administrated by Province							
巩义市 Gongyi	103594	1384770	8342	3179	1248054	136716	90.1
兰考县 Lankao	110295	525655	1778	703	373275	152381	71.0
汝州市 Ruzhou	161888	1275450	10122	1584	1092900	182550	85.7
滑县 Huaxian	84188	1084619	2322	578	938439	146180	86.5
长垣市 Changyuan	108318	1425533	12933	2478	1255703	169830	88.1
邓州市 Dengzhou	95089	748349	3298	719	588034	160316	78.6
永城市 Yongcheng	64435	1050412	4845	970	883086	167326	84.1
固始县 Gushi	169963	1688385	7069	2521	1459734	228651	86.5
鹿邑县 Luyi	51182	552541	2263	777	443876	108665	80.3
新蔡县 Xincai	125615	1432269	28266	4115	1215635	216633	84.9

15-18 房地产开发企业(单位)经营状况

Operating Statistics on Enterprises for Real Estate Development

单位：万元 (10 000 yuan)

年份 Year	主营业务总收入 Revenue from Principal Business	土地转让收入 Land Transferred	商品房屋销售收入 Commercialized Buildings Sold	房屋出租收入 Houses Leased	其他收入 Others	税金及附加 Taxes and other Charges	利润总额 Total Profits
1995	296217	12144	261429	6646	15998		
1996	255167	5452	233920	3017	12778	11632	-25046
1997	253688	5168	219637	15007	13876	10766	-25754
1998	351299	13176	281049	12390	44684	14994	-24228
1999	372131	5429	305042	8766	52894	13786	-32030
2000	589976	5061	540151	2006	42758	25236	-31592
2001	795263	9742	667394	28533	89594	38027	-37939
2002	1076871	5910	922688	23136	125137	54990	-24806
2003	1456160	21772	1368253	18096	48039	76469	-33501
2004	2020881	15111	1918110	38611	49049	115015	26208
2005	2811080	61734	2675030	11543	62773	160582	176260
2006	3979391	24054	3887229	23325	44783	258454	273585
2007	6090315	45874	5939029	14200	91212	438474	632245
2008	7046582	53621	6772130	29211	191620	481789	694067
2009	8933162	63141	8721890	13006	135125	645284	1015016
2010	12005594	37385	11676405	137383	154421	895513	1328860
2011	13865231	45658	13400414	203150	216009	1080415	1583907
2012	15709431	77198	15133586	209955	288692	1378609	1817922
2013	26254232	175336	25111237	529686	437973	2173958	3930904
2014	25292238	67897	24247358	736829	240155	2133701	3056275
2015	28395941	83725	27499841	480320	332056	2536014	3322897
2016	36784420	321760	35468060	374437	620163	2539248	3480551
2017	38948846	227613	36845532	303183	1572518	2300725	4265452
2018	50433460	411162	47712645	327319	1982334	2348577	7805689
2019	54581933	331337	51814049	335237	2101310	2588286	7700565
省辖市 City							
郑州市 Zhengzhou	20345252	153484	18669627	161019	1361122	1096067	2976464
开封市 Kaifeng	1733591	9763	1600079	10375	113375	101448	283918
洛阳市 Luoyang	2831494	6750	2749954	46242	28548	161588	328100
平顶山市 Pingdingshan	1046763	4782	973704	7822	60455	78022	29824
安阳市 Anyang	1466062		1446051	656	19355	68522	105582
鹤壁市 Hebi	595764	5000	589310	14	1441	34841	41459
新乡市 Xinxiang	2795208	86428	2611502	13063	84216	117298	442373
焦作市 Jiaozuo	1083599	7283	1056268	1543	18504	44757	81042
濮阳市 Puyang	1394165		1384729	394	9042	57313	64939
许昌市 Xuchang	1772646	7381	1736073	3218	25974	73344	180078
漯河市 Luohe	957677	81	930142	408	27046	39162	93999
三门峡市 Sanmenxia	558655		544886	1747	12022	19077	48687
南阳市 Nanyang	1790792	5344	1671111	6483	107854	89438	310354
商丘市 Shangqiu	4830408	36567	4602371	69489	121981	163532	783224
信阳市 Xinyang	3457249	986	3403667	7550	45048	152374	610887
周口市 Zhoukou	3553083	5626	3510715	2118	34624	70770	600105
驻马店市 Zhumadian	4207281	1764	4173033	2171	30313	207977	711733
济源市 Jiyuan	162245	99	160829	925	391	12758	7795
省直管县 County Directly Administrated by Province							
巩义市 Gongyi	622483		617228	3461	1795	19968	176575
兰考县 Lankao	340476	100	324737	11	15628	19333	68967
汝州市 Ruzhou	188492	1000	186043	600	849	14078	-2919
滑县 Huaxian	175732		175432		301	6505	2144
长垣市 Changyuan	241250	121	222124	40	18966	14948	9499
邓州市 Dengzhou	164157	1055	159667		3436	9247	29264
永城市 Yongcheng	811420		811420			14083	185738
固始县 Gushi	439995		437388	1148	1458	21035	91163
鹿邑县 Luyi	481098	771	477003		3324	4919	81646
新蔡县 Xincai	506845	1639	498429	1182	5595	38478	64086

注：税金及附加2010年及以前为主营业务税金及附加口径，2011年以来为税金及附加口径。

a) Taxes and other charges are taxes and other charges on principal business in 2010 and before. Since 2011, the caliber were taxes and other charges.

主要统计指标解释

本年土地购置面积 指房地产开发企业本年通过各种方式获得土地使用权的土地面积。

待开发土地面积 指房地产开发企业经有关部门批准，通过各种方式获得土地使用权，但尚未开工建设的土地面积。

计划总投资 指房地产开发企业在建的建设工程按照总体设计（或按设计概算或预算）规定的内容全部建成计划需要的总投资。

自开始建设累计完成投资 指房地产开发企业在建的房屋建设工程或正在开发的土地开发工程从开始建设到本年末止累计完成的全部投资。

房地产开发投资 指房地产开发企业本年完成的全部用于房屋建设工程、土地开发工程的投资额以及公益性建筑和土地购置费等的投资。

土地购置费 指房地产开发企业通过各种方式取得土地使用权而支付的费用。土地购置费按本年实际发生额计入投资。土地购置费为分期付款的，分期计入房地产开发投资。

本年实际到位资金小计 指房地产开发企业本年实际到位，可用于房地产开发的各种货币资金。包括国内贷款、利用外资、自筹资金和其他资金。

房屋施工面积 指房地产开发企业本年施工的全部房屋建筑面积。包括本年新开工的房屋建筑面积、上年跨入本年继续施工的房屋建筑面积、上年停缓建在本年恢复施工的房屋建筑面积、本年竣工的房屋建筑面积以及本年施工后又停缓建的房屋建筑面积。多层建筑应填各层建筑面积之和。

房屋新开工面积 指房地产开发企业本年新开工建设的房屋建筑面积，以单位工程为核算对象。不包括在上年开工跨入本年继续施工的房屋建筑面积和上年停缓建而在本年恢复施工的房屋建筑面积。房屋的开工应以房屋正式开始破土刨槽（地基处理或打永久桩）的日期为准。房屋新开工面积指整栋房屋的全部建筑面积，不能分割计算。

房屋竣工面积 指房地产开发企业本年按照设计要求已全部完工，达到住人和使用条件，经验收鉴定合格或达到竣工验收标准，可正式移交使用的各栋房屋建筑面积的总和。

商品房销售面积 指房地产开发企业本年出售商品房屋的合同总面积（即双方签署的正式买卖合同中所确定的建筑面积）。

商品房销售额 指房地产开发企业本年出售商品房屋的合同总价款（即双方签署的正式买卖合同中所确定的合同总价）。该指标与商品房销售面积同口径。

Explanatory Notes on Main Statistical Indicators

Land Space Purchased in the Year refers to the area of land with its use rights already obtained in this year by real estate development companies.

Land Space Pending Development refers to the area of land with its use rights already approved by authorities and obtained by real estate development companies but the land development not yet starts.

Total Investment Planned refers to the total amount required for the completion of the activities according to the planned design or budget for the project under construction by real estate development companies.

Accumulative Investment Actually Completed Since Starting of Construction refers to all the investment accomplished by real estate development companies in the construction of building or the development of land from the beginning to the end of the year.

Investment in Real Estate Development refers to the investment made by real estate development companies in the construction of housing, development of land, nonprofit buildings and value of land purchased.

Value of Land Purchased refers to the payment made by real estate development companies for land use rights. The actual payment incurred in the year is included in the investment. The payment by installment when occurring is included in the investment.

Total Actual Funds in Place This Year refers to the total amount available for real estate development regardless of kinds of currencies. It includes domestic loans, foreign investment, self-raising funds and others.

Floor Space of Buildings under Construction refers to the total space area of the buildings under construction in the year by real estate development companies. It includes buildings started in the year, continued from the previous year, suspended in earlier years but restarted in the year, completed in the year, and started in the year but suspended in the year as well. The floor space of a multi-storied building should be the sum of floor space of all the stories.

Floor Space of Buildings Started This Year refers to the total floor space area of the buildings started in the year by real estate development companies. It excludes the buildings started in previous years and continued in the year, and the buildings suspended in previous years but restarted in the year. The start of a construction is defined by the date of ground breaking or pile driving. The floor space of the building includes that of the entire building.

Floor Space of Buildings Completed refers to the total floor space area of the buildings completed in the year by real estate development companies, which meet the requirements as designed, reach the criteria set for people to live in or use, have passed the acceptance checks, and are ready for delivery or use.

Area of Commercialized Housing Sold refers to total contracted area of commercialized housing (i.e. area of floor space as designated in the formal contracts signed by both sides) sold by real estate development companies during the reference time.

Value of Commercialized Housing Sold refers to the total contracted value (i.e. value of sales/purchase for selling/purchase of commercialized housing as designated in the contract signed by both sides) received from the sales of the buildings by real estate development companies during the reference time. This indicator has the same coverage as the area of commercialized housing sold.

批发和零售业、住宿和餐饮业

Wholesale and Retail Sale trades,Hotels and Catering Services

16

资料整理：赵文献　宋谊晴

简要说明

一、主要内容

本篇包括河南省商品市场状况和批发零售业、住宿餐饮业经营情况以及主要财务状况。

二、统计范围

辖区内批发零售业和住宿餐饮业企业（单位）、个体经营户、连锁经营企业和亿元商品交易市场。

社会消费品零售总额不包括农业生产资料、居民购买住房；不包括各种经济类型的制造业法人企业、产业活动单位和个体工业直接售给城乡居民（包括本企业职工）和社会集团的商品；不包括农民在田间地头出售的农产品。

限额以上批发和零售业、住宿和餐饮业企业统计限额标准：批发业，年主营业务收入2000万元及以上;零售业，年主营业务收入500万元及以上;住宿业，年主营业务收入200万元及以上;餐饮业，年主营业务收入200万元及以上。

三、资料来源

达到限额以上标准的批发和零售业、住宿和餐饮业企业、个体经营户和其他行业附营的产业活动单位经营性指标和财务指标以及连锁经营企业、亿元商品交易市场采用全面调查的方法取得资料；限额以下批发零售企业采用抽样调查方法取得资料，限额以下住宿和餐饮业企业采用全面调查方法取得资料；批发零售和住宿餐饮业个体经营户资料采用抽样调查方法取得。由省统计局贸易外经处编辑整理。

Brief Introduction

I. Main Contents

Data in this chapter include the conditions of commodity market and wholesale and retail trades, hotels and catering services in Henan province.

II. Scope of Statistics

Wholesale and retail , accommodation catering enterprises (units), individual, chain business enterprises and one hundred million yuan commodity trading market.

Total retail sales of consumer goods do not include means of agricultural production; purchase of housing by residents; and do not include commodities that various types of corporate enterprise, industrial activity units and individual industrial directly sale to residents and social groups; and do not include agricultural products that sold by farmers in the fields.

Criteria for wholesale and retail sale trades, hotels and catering services above designated size are as follows: wholesale trade, having main business income over 20 million yuan; retail trade, having main business income over 5 million yuan; hotels, having main business income over 2 million yuan; catering services, having main business income over 2 million yuan.

III. Sources of Data

Data on business index and financial indicators of wholesale and retail trades, hotels and catering services enterprises, individual, Industrial activity unit above designated size, Chain group, trading market above one hundred million yuan are collected through comprehensive reporting form system. Data on enterprises and individual enterprises below the designated size are collected by sample surveys. Data in this chapter are provided by the Department of Trade and External Economic Relations of the Henan provincial bureau of Statistics.

16–1 社会消费品零售总额

Total Retail Sale of Consumer Goods

单位：亿元 (100 million yuan)

年 份 Year	社会消费品零售总额 Total Retail Sales of Consumer Goods	#批发和零售业 Wholesale and Retail Trades	住宿和餐饮业 Hotels and Catering Services	城 镇 Urban	乡 村 Rural
1978	71.79				
1980	96.04				
1985	180.59				
1990	314.31	300.50	13.81	244.31	70.00
1991	368.92	352.39	16.53	290.23	78.69
1992	470.30	447.23	23.07	373.33	96.97
1993	577.52	548.95	28.57	462.82	114.70
1994	788.97	739.65	49.32	629.42	159.55
1995	955.58	884.95	70.63	755.93	199.64
1996	1191.13	1098.33	92.80	933.55	257.58
1997	1422.11	1284.41	137.71	1126.35	295.77
1998	1558.75	1418.50	140.26	1231.71	327.04
1999	1682.22	1532.29	149.93	1329.38	352.85
2000	1858.46	1687.86	170.61	1468.33	390.14
2001	2057.80	1858.34	199.47	1628.17	429.63
2002	2275.39	2036.23	239.16	1808.58	466.81
2003	2518.19	2245.95	272.24	2010.11	508.07
2004	2923.73	2621.52	302.21	2363.63	560.11
2005	3362.58	3011.77	350.80	2738.23	624.35
2006	3908.68	3467.77	440.91	3203.99	704.69
2007	4658.58	4086.67	571.90	3842.56	816.01
2008	5772.92	5050.87	722.05	4783.79	989.13
2009	6689.09	5884.81	804.28	5551.18	1137.91
2010	7922.66	6972.81	949.86	6602.68	1319.98
2011	9337.22	8223.04	1114.18	7786.36	1550.87
2012	10767.69	9484.15	1283.54	8971.78	1795.91
2013	12243.51	10806.41	1437.09	10172.35	2071.16
2014	13777.41	12172.61	1604.80	11412.70	2364.72
2015	15475.80	13670.39	1805.40	12784.75	2691.05
2016	17274.50	15261.47	2013.03	14247.07	3027.43
2017	19289.11	17040.56	2248.55	15892.34	3396.77
2018	21267.96	18778.81	2489.14	17500.93	3767.02
2019	23476.13	20699.86	2776.26	19297.91	4178.21

注：1993年以后数据已根据河南省第四次全国经济普查结果修订。

a) The data since 1993 have been revised according to the results of the fourth national economic census in Henan Province.

16−2 各市社会消费品零售总额(2019年)

Total Retail Sale of Consumer Goods by City (2019)

单位：亿元 (100 million yuan)

市(县)	City(County)	社会消费品零售总额 Total Retail Sales of Consumer Goods	城镇 Urban Area	乡村 Urual Area	批发和零售业 Wholesale and Retail Sale Trade	住宿和餐饮业 Hotels and Catering Services
全省	**Total**	**23476.13**	**19297.91**	**4178.21**	**20699.86**	**2776.26**
省辖市	**City**					
郑州市	Zhengzhou	5324.44	4811.62	512.82	4382.67	941.77
开封市	Kaifeng	1030.60	824.90	205.70	892.21	138.39
洛阳市	Luoyang	2170.79	1881.53	289.26	1772.10	398.69
平顶山市	Pingdingshan	1033.25	843.80	189.44	845.94	187.31
安阳市	Anyang	900.09	723.95	176.14	782.25	117.84
鹤壁市	Hebi	299.25	282.37	16.88	246.21	53.04
新乡市	Xinxiang	996.14	896.85	99.29	878.78	117.37
焦作市	Jiaozuo	920.23	753.88	166.34	768.56	151.67
濮阳市	Puyang	689.09	480.97	208.12	566.27	122.81
许昌市	Xuchang	1271.65	991.82	279.82	1019.86	251.78
漯河市	Luohe	673.32	539.33	134.00	568.00	105.32
三门峡市	Sanmenxia	501.82	416.43	85.39	434.18	67.64
南阳市	Nanyang	2077.16	1596.67	480.49	1726.17	351.00
商丘市	Shangqiu	1480.74	1106.86	373.88	1215.58	265.16
信阳市	Xinyang	1214.21	986.04	228.17	849.39	364.82
周口市	Zhoukou	1679.62	1375.66	303.96	1316.99	362.63
驻马店市	Zhumadian	1022.37	731.25	291.12	870.34	152.03
济源市	Jiyuan	191.36	185.02	6.34	152.19	39.17
省直管县	**County Directly Administrated by Province**					
巩义市	Gongyi	287.37	263.33	24.04	214.15	73.22
兰考县	Lankao	200.47	145.08	55.39	167.46	33.01
汝州市	Ruzhou	258.88	176.32	82.56	228.90	29.98
滑县	Huaxian	172.12	129.28	42.83	152.27	19.84
长垣市	Changyuan	180.65	170.76	9.89	154.67	25.98
邓州市	Dengzhou	197.82	152.46	45.36	154.46	43.36
永城市	Yongcheng	223.52	176.75	46.77	161.52	61.99
固始县	Gushi	203.87	167.15	36.72	151.82	52.04
鹿邑县	Luyi	236.09	201.50	34.59	176.70	59.39
新蔡县	Xincai	148.25	104.82	43.43	122.87	25.39

16-3 限额以上批发和零售业法人基本情况(2019年)

Basic Conditions of Corporation in Wholesale and Retail Trades above Designated Size (2019)

指标名称	Item	法人企业 (个) Corporate Enterprises (unit)	从业人员期末人数 (人) Persons Employed (person)	法人属产业活动单位数 (个) Establish_ments Units (unit)	#批发和零售业 Wholesale and Retail Trades
总　计	**Total**	**11897**	**570591**	**17196**	**16964**
批发业	**Wholesale Trades**	**4885**	**195154**	**3197**	**3085**
按国民经济行业分	By Sector				
农、林、牧产品	Agricalturel, Forestry and Livestock Products	416	11697	156	134
食品、饮料及烟草制品	Food, Beverages, Tobaccos	525	44601	421	395
纺织、服装及家庭用品	Textiles, Wearing Apparel and Household Articles	276	13373	63	43
文化、体育用品及器材	Culture, Sports Supplies and Equipment	139	6517	79	78
医药及医疗器材	Medicine and the Medical Equipment	503	37474	1274	1272
矿产品、建材及化工产品	Mineral Products, Building Materials and Chemical Products	2122	53361	1089	1056
机械设备、五金产品及电子产品	Machinery Hardware and Electronic Products	696	22204	100	93
贸易经纪与代理	Trade Brokers and Agents	21	828		
其他	Others	187	5099	15	14
按登记注册类型分	By Registration				
内资企业	Domestic-Funded Enterprises	4873	194604	3195	3085
港澳台商投资企业	Enterprises With Investment from Hong Kong, Macao and Taiwan	7	362	2	
外商投资企业	Enterprises With Foreign Investment	5	188		
按控股情况分	By Controlling Type				
国有控股	State-holding	324	49871	1834	1785
集体控股	Collective-holding	44	1909	78	78
私人控股	Private-holding	4259	128848	1012	954
港澳台商控股	Hong Kong, Macao and Taiwan-holding	8	362	2	
外商控股	Foreign-holding	6	313		
其他	Others	218	13598	271	268
按经营形式分	By Management Style				
独立门店	Independent Store	3003	126998	2286	2212
连锁总店	Head Office of Chain Store	15	3137	356	351
连锁直营店	Chain Direct-sale Store	6	608	45	45
连锁加盟店	Chain Franchisee Store				
其他	Others	1399	64411	510	477

16−3 续表 continued

指标名称	Item	法人企业（个）Corporate Enterprises (unit)	从业人员期末人数（人）Persons Employed (person)	法人属产业活动单位数（个）Establish_ments Units (unit)	#批发和零售业 Wholesale and Retail Trades
零售业	**Retail trades**	**7012**	**375437**	**13999**	**13879**
按国民经济行业分	By Sector				
综合	Comprehensive	1006	118139	1576	1557
食品、饮料及烟草制品	Food, Beverages, Tobaccos	508	21314	605	585
纺织、服装及日用品	Textiles, Wearing Apparel and Household Articles	312	19438	382	379
文化、体育用品及器材	Culture, Sports supplies and Equipment	378	20191	629	616
医药及医疗器材	Medicine and Medical Equipment	331	36879	7608	7602
汽车、摩托车、燃料及零配件	Automobile, Motorcycle, Fuel and Spare Parts	2649	101646	2128	2112
家用电器及电子产品	Household Appliances and Electronic Products	988	27724	823	806
五金、家具及室内装饰材料	Hardware, Furniture and Indoor Decoration Materials	442	12108	11	10
货摊、无店铺及其他	Non-store and Others	398	17998	237	212
按登记注册类型分	By Registration				
内资企业	Domestic-Funded Enterprises	6972	357140	13627	13510
港澳台商投资企业	Enterprises With Investment from Hong Kong, Macao and Taiwan	22	16189	266	264
外商投资企业	Enterprises With Foreign Investment	18	2108	106	105
按控股情况分	By Controlling Type				
国有控股	State-holding	247	28782	3070	3040
集体控股	Collective-holding	73	4121	59	56
私人控股	Private-holding	6319	294867	9340	9264
港澳台商控股	Hong Kong, Macao and Taiwan-holding	19	16325	267	265
外商控股	Foreign-holding	20	2455	6	5
其他	Others	330	28887	1257	1249
按经营形式分	By Management Style				
独立门店	Independent Store	5907	275166	6054	5967
连锁总店	Head Office of Chain Store	162	60153	6415	6398
连锁直营店	Chain Direct-sale Store	40	4950	461	457
连锁加盟店	Chain Franchisee Store	6	208	21	21
其他	Others	559	34960	1048	1036
按零售业态分	By Retail Formats				
有店铺零售	Store Retailing	6570	355734	13879	13764
无店铺零售	Non-store Retailing	439	19703	120	115

16-4 限额以上住宿和餐饮业法人基本情况(2019年)

Basic Conditions of Corporation of Hotels and Catering Services above Designated Size (2019)

指标名称	Item	法人企业(个) Corporate Enterprises (unit)	从业人员期末人数(人) Persons Employed (person)	法人属产业活动单位数(个) Establish_ments Units (unit)	#住宿和餐饮业 Wholesale and Retail Trades
总　计	**Total**	**2565**	**140277**	**639**	**612**
住宿业	**Hotels**	**1432**	**87749**	**156**	**141**
按国民经济行业分	By sector				
旅游饭店	Tourist hotel	577	49455	68	61
一般旅馆	Fonda	781	34765	78	72
其他住宿业	Others	69	3238	10	8
按登记注册类型分	By Registration				
内资企业	Domestic-Funded Enterprises	1416	84918	149	135
国有企业	State-owned	73	9282	20	13
集体企业	Collective-owned	22	1289	2	1
股份合作企业	Cooperative	1	120		
联营企业	Joint Ownership	1	41		
有限责任公司	Limited Liability Corporations	486	34242	62	60
股份有限公司	Share-holding Corporation Ltd	33	2667	5	4
私营企业	Private	800	37277	60	57
其他企业	Other				
港澳台商投资企业	Enterprises With Investment from Hong Kong, Macao and Taiwan	11	2159	4	4
外商投资企业	Enterprises With Foreign Investment	5	672	3	2
按控股情况分	By Controlling Type				
国有控股	State-holding	116	14990	33	25
集体控股	Collective-holding	43	3159	10	9
私人控股	Private-holding	1153	58087	100	96
港澳台商控股	Hong Kong, Macao and Taiwan-holding	7	1455		
外商控股	Foreign-holding	4	357	3	2
其他	Others	108	9597	10	9
按经营形式分	By Management Style				
独立门店	Independent Store	1287	80349	130	116
连锁总店	Head Office of Chain Store	7	226	11	11
连锁直营店	Chain Direct-sale Store	11	763		
连锁加盟店	Chain Franchisee Store	49	1484	4	4
其他	Others	78	4927	11	10
按星级分	By Star Level				
五星	Five-star	33	7456	10	9
四星	Four-star	120	15047	17	17
三星	Three-star	209	15466	30	25
二星	Two-star	47	2924	7	6
一星	One-star	4	218		
其他	Others	1019	46638	92	84

16-4 续表 continued

指标名称	Item	法人企业（个）Corporate Enterprises (unit)	从业人员期末人数（人）Persons Employed (person)	法人属产业活动单位数（个）Establish_ments Units (unit)	#住宿和餐饮业 Wholesale and Retail Trades
餐饮业	**Catering Services**	**1133**	**52528**	**483**	**471**
按国民经济行业分	By sector				
正餐服务	Dinner	1040	43673	282	273
快餐服务	Snack	58	7168	178	176
饮料及冷饮服务	Drinks and Cold drinks	4	245	19	18
其他餐饮业	Others	16	656		
按登记注册类型分	By Registration				
内资企业	Domestic-Funded Enterprises	1128	46824	339	329
国有企业	State-owned	5	375		
集体企业	Collective-owned	4	48	3	3
股份合作企业	Cooperative	1	38		
联营企业	Joint Ownership				
有限责任公司	Limited Liability Corporations	306	16006	178	171
股份有限公司	Share-holding Corporation Ltd	20	886	2	2
私营企业	Private	792	29471	156	153
其他企业	Other				
港澳台商投资企业	Enterprises With Investment from Hong Kong, Macao and Taiwan	3	212	4	4
外商投资企业	Enterprises With Foreign Investment	2	5492	140	138
按控股情况分	By Controlling Type				
国有控股	State-holding	17	1690		
集体控股	Collective-holding	8	240	5	5
私人控股	Private-holding	1051	41369	245	237
港澳台商控股	Hong Kong, Macao and Taiwan-holding	3	212	4	4
外商控股	Foreign-holding	2	5492	140	138
其他	Others	52	3525	89	87
按经营形式分	By Management Style				
独立门店	Independent Store	1038	39859	159	152
连锁总店	Head Office of Chain Store	14	7354	254	252
连锁直营店	Chain Direct-sale Store	9	277	18	18
连锁加盟店	Chain Franchisee Store	4	639	14	14
其他	Others	68	4399	38	35

16-5 各市批发和零售、住宿和餐饮业法人企业单位数(2019年)

Number of Corporations in Wholesale and Retail Sale, Hotels and Catering Services by City (2019)

单位：个 (unit)

市(县)	City(County)	批发业 Wholesale Trade	#限额以上 Above Designated Size	零售业 Retail Sale	#限额以上 Above Designated Size	住宿业 Hotels	#限额以上 Above Designated Size	餐饮业 Catering Services	#限额以上 Above Designated Size
省辖市	**City**								
郑州市	Zhengzhou	82002	1411	59354	1100	1915	317	4259	243
开封市	Kaifeng	7075	194	11335	356	400	71	939	57
洛阳市	Luoyang	10763	506	15074	501	657	139	957	79
平顶山市	Pingdingshan	9406	158	9377	340	303	72	693	49
安阳市	Anyang	7261	126	7738	232	242	49	429	19
鹤壁市	Hebi	1992	44	3505	93	91	14	245	6
新乡市	Xinxiang	10445	261	10712	361	240	48	545	48
焦作市	Jiaozuo	5170	240	5841	272	168	40	318	19
濮阳市	Puyang	3939	107	5840	167	86	27	279	21
许昌市	Xuchang	8563	200	11326	277	272	79	665	59
漯河市	Luohe	2337	99	3543	185	103	40	311	25
三门峡市	Sanmenxia	3800	228	4378	224	191	55	263	18
南阳市	Nanyang	13057	424	24477	684	493	117	1527	120
商丘市	Shangqiu	6797	282	10749	542	303	61	700	78
信阳市	Xinyang	3318	157	8709	608	305	106	738	102
周口市	Zhoukou	5275	220	10640	579	274	94	922	103
驻马店市	Zhumadian	6967	147	10958	446	307	93	968	86
济源市	Jiyuan	1869	81	1418	45	31	10	83	1
省直管县	**County Directly Administrated by Province**								
巩义市	Gongyi	2864	70	1093	30	36	9	73	7
兰考县	Lankao	1174	37	1873	123	45	16	139	15
汝州市	Ruzhou	1612	39	2521	99	49	5	197	2
滑县	Huaxian	1479	21	2000	52	17	6	87	6
长垣市	Changyuan	2590	66	1699	69	21	4	88	24
邓州市	Dengzhou	610	30	1282	125	22	8	181	26
永城市	Yongcheng	961	9	1635	71	27	8	113	21
固始县	Gushi	490	26	1372	165	37	22	111	23
鹿邑县	Luyi	538	31	956	58	44	24	84	19
新蔡县	Xincai	541	30	1062	134	34	21	126	21

16-6 各市批发和零售、住宿和餐饮业法人企业从业人员(2019年)

Number of Persons Employed in Wholesale and Retail Sale, Hotels and Catering Services by City (2019)

单位：人 (person)

市(县)	City(County)	批发业 Wholesale Trade	#限额以上 Above Designated Size	零售业 Retail Sale	#限额以上 Above Designated Size	住宿业 Hotels	#限额以上 Above Designated Size	餐饮业 Catering Services	#限额以上 Above Designated Size
省辖市	**City**								
郑州市	Zhengzhou	398868	50138	305400	80665	35088	22069	43389	18808
开封市	Kaifeng	52166	6520	68273	12314	7112	3748	9043	1729
洛阳市	Luoyang	73416	14066	110304	30643	13571	7795	11801	4018
平顶山市	Pingdingshan	64620	5741	66796	12878	6741	3691	7119	1665
安阳市	Anyang	42820	3797	43195	8136	5548	3236	3824	496
鹤壁市	Hebi	15176	1741	20162	4509	1441	642	1999	234
新乡市	Xinxiang	70212	9465	69504	16763	5454	3014	6470	2076
焦作市	Jiaozuo	42465	4803	52433	11891	4088	2485	4853	1004
濮阳市	Puyang	27022	3005	36812	7962	1895	1325	3038	984
许昌市	Xuchang	72602	7209	88891	17204	7680	5541	7524	1828
漯河市	Luohe	27950	2417	39567	16036	2708	1795	4375	1024
三门峡市	Sanmenxia	29044	6140	28697	7006	5674	4079	2557	632
南阳市	Nanyang	121830	17024	182611	24219	10695	6389	17760	4105
商丘市	Shangqiu	92834	26445	136965	53107	7111	4458	11471	4939
信阳市	Xinyang	29681	7494	73244	28650	8820	6488	8733	3131
周口市	Zhoukou	68711	20569	98424	22613	8108	5438	11742	2904
驻马店市	Zhumadian	52519	7144	86239	19025	7483	4730	10922	2936
济源市	Jiyuan	9338	1436	7376	1816	1098	826	592	15
省直管县	**County Directly Administrated by Province**								
巩义市	Gongyi	21762	976	8405	1193	972	600	895	158
兰考县	Lankao	8148	1097	14469	3644	837	587	1433	349
汝州市	Ruzhou	18941	699	19728	3170	884	449	1476	21
滑县	Huaxian	11571	549	12958	1108	390	293	658	124
长垣市	Changyuan	24609	3599	13714	2142	567	263	2142	967
邓州市	Dengzhou	5141	463	10431	2662	332	186	2134	589
永城市	Yongcheng	10656	997	19257	5911	630	401	1710	676
固始县	Gushi	3611	980	8913	4107	915	820	979	375
鹿邑县	Luyi	10921	3789	9286	1579	1091	922	978	428
新蔡县	Xincai	7622	669	12694	2711	845	594	1879	446

16-7 各市批发和零售、住宿和餐饮业限额以上企业(单位)单位数(2019年)

Number of Corporation in Wholesale and Retail Sale, Hotels and Catering Services Above Designated Size by City (2019)

单位：个 (unit)

市(县) City(County)	批发业 Wholesale Trade	限额以上法人 Corporations Above Designated Size	产业活动单位、个体经营户 Establishment and Individual	零售业 Retail Sale	限额以上法人 Corporations Above Designated Size	产业活动单位、个体经营户 Establishment and Individual
省辖市 City						
郑州市 Zhengzhou	1413	1411	2	1314	1100	214
开封市 Kaifeng	205	194	11	529	356	173
洛阳市 Luoyang	514	506	8	918	501	417
平顶山市 Pingdingshan	169	158	11	879	340	539
安阳市 Anyang	132	126	6	325	232	93
鹤壁市 Hebi	47	44	3	114	93	21
新乡市 Xinxiang	266	261	5	499	361	138
焦作市 Jiaozuo	240	240		420	272	148
濮阳市 Puyang	108	107	1	337	167	170
许昌市 Xuchang	218	200	18	576	277	299
漯河市 Luohe	101	99	2	274	185	89
三门峡市 Sanmenxia	241	228	13	397	224	173
南阳市 Nanyang	438	424	14	878	684	194
商丘市 Shangqiu	292	282	10	769	542	227
信阳市 Xinyang	168	157	11	866	608	258
周口市 Zhoukou	225	220	5	729	579	150
驻马店市 Zhumadian	149	147	2	585	446	139
济源市 Jiyuan	82	81	1	53	45	8
省直管县 County Directly Administrated by Province						
巩义市 Gongyi	70	70		90	30	60
兰考县 Lankao	37	37		179	123	56
汝州市 Ruzhou	42	39	3	198	99	99
滑县 Huaxian	24	21	3	79	52	27
长垣市 Changyuan	66	66		85	69	16
邓州市 Dengzhou	30	30		142	125	17
永城市 Yongcheng	9	9		106	71	35
固始县 Gushi	28	26	2	188	165	23
鹿邑县 Luyi	32	31	1	64	58	6
新蔡县 Xincai	30	30		134	134	

16-7 续表 continued

单位：个 (unit)

市(县) City(County)	住宿业 Hotels	限额以上法人 Corporations Above Designated Size	产业活动单位、个体经营户 Establishment, Individual	餐饮业 Catering Services	限额以上法人 Corporations Above Designated Size	产业活动单位、个体经营户 Establishment, Individual
省辖市 City						
郑州市 Zhengzhou	365	317	48	622	243	379
开封市 Kaifeng	125	71	54	219	57	162
洛阳市 Luoyang	222	139	83	704	79	625
平顶山市 Pingdingshan	122	72	50	433	49	384
安阳市 Anyang	72	49	23	154	19	135
鹤壁市 Hebi	21	14	7	43	6	37
新乡市 Xinxiang	77	48	29	173	48	125
焦作市 Jiaozuo	76	40	36	127	19	108
濮阳市 Puyang	43	27	16	110	21	89
许昌市 Xuchang	118	79	39	384	59	325
漯河市 Luohe	60	40	20	116	25	91
三门峡市 Sanmenxia	88	55	33	262	18	244
南阳市 Nanyang	145	117	28	255	120	135
商丘市 Shangqiu	89	61	28	197	78	119
信阳市 Xinyang	152	106	46	284	102	182
周口市 Zhoukou	114	94	20	166	103	63
驻马店市 Zhumadian	116	93	23	135	86	49
济源市 Jiyuan	13	10	3	22	1	21
省直管县 County Directly Administrated by Province						
巩义市 Gongyi	16	9	7	88	7	81
兰考县 Lankao	21	16	5	48	15	33
汝州市 Ruzhou	13	5	8	58	2	56
滑县 Huaxian	12	6	6	21	6	15
长垣市 Changyuan	4	4		37	24	13
邓州市 Dengzhou	9	8	1	43	26	17
永城市 Yongcheng	12	8	4	40	21	19
固始县 Gushi	31	22	9	41	23	18
鹿邑县 Luyi	25	24	1	20	19	1
新蔡县 Xincai	21	21		21	21	

16-8 各市批发和零售、住宿和餐饮业限上企业(单位)从业人员(2019年)

Number of Persons Employed in Wholesale and Retail Sale, Hotels and Catering Services Above Designated Size by City (2019)

单位：人 (Person)

市(县)	City(County)	批发业 Wholesale Trade	限额以上法人 Corporations Above Designated Size	产业活动单位、个体经营户 Establishment, Individual	零售业 Retail Sale	限额以上法人 Corporations Above Designated Size	产业活动单位、个体经营户 Establishment, Individual
省辖市	**City**						
郑州市	Zhengzhou	50174	50138	36	84065	80665	3400
开封市	Kaifeng	6597	6520	77	15313	12314	2999
洛阳市	Luoyang	14227	14066	161	36513	30643	5870
平顶山市	Pingdingshan	5876	5741	135	19149	12878	6271
安阳市	Anyang	3933	3797	136	10326	8136	2190
鹤壁市	Hebi	1978	1741	237	5009	4509	500
新乡市	Xinxiang	9611	9465	146	19667	16763	2904
焦作市	Jiaozuo	4803	4803		14182	11891	2291
濮阳市	Puyang	3013	3005	8	10259	7962	2297
许昌市	Xuchang	7409	7209	200	21576	17204	4372
漯河市	Luohe	3076	2417	659	17686	16036	1650
三门峡市	Sanmenxia	6275	6140	135	8605	7006	1599
南阳市	Nanyang	17158	17024	134	27653	24219	3434
商丘市	Shangqiu	26553	26445	108	56309	53107	3202
信阳市	Xinyang	8071	7494	577	32373	28650	3723
周口市	Zhoukou	20608	20569	39	24582	22613	1969
驻马店市	Zhumadian	7198	7144	54	21264	19025	2239
济源市	Jiyuan	1456	1436	20	1905	1816	89
省直管县	**County Directly Administrated by Province**						
巩义市	Gongyi	976	976		2512	1193	1319
兰考县	Lankao	1097	1097		4355	3644	711
汝州市	Ruzhou	746	699	47	4567	3170	1397
滑县	Huaxian	660	549	111	2136	1108	1028
长垣市	Changyuan	3599	3599		2741	2142	599
邓州市	Dengzhou	463	463		3047	2662	385
永城市	Yongcheng	997	997		6341	5911	430
固始县	Gushi	1085	980	105	4533	4107	426
鹿邑县	Luyi	3792	3789	3	1652	1579	73
新蔡县	Xincai	669	669		2711	2711	

16-8 续表 continued

单位：人 (Person)

市(县) City(County)	住宿业 Hotels	限额以上法人 Corporations Above Designated Size	产业活动单位、个体经营户 Establishment, Individual	餐饮业 Catering Services	限额以上法人 Corporations Above Designated Size	产业活动单位、个体经营户 Establishment, Individual
省辖市 City						
郑州市 Zhengzhou	24613	22069	2544	27444	18808	8636
开封市 Kaifeng	4511	3748	763	4839	1729	3110
洛阳市 Luoyang	9704	7795	1909	14000	4018	9982
平顶山市 Pingdingshan	4739	3691	1048	6196	1665	4531
安阳市 Anyang	4219	3236	983	3236	496	2740
鹤壁市 Hebi	1027	642	385	1025	234	791
新乡市 Xinxiang	3456	3014	442	4613	2076	2537
焦作市 Jiaozuo	3079	2485	594	3372	1004	2368
濮阳市 Puyang	1753	1325	428	2337	984	1353
许昌市 Xuchang	6335	5541	794	8242	1828	6414
漯河市 Luohe	2125	1795	330	2659	1024	1635
三门峡市 Sanmenxia	4817	4079	738	3737	632	3105
南阳市 Nanyang	6855	6389	466	6495	4105	2390
商丘市 Shangqiu	4831	4458	373	6689	4939	1750
信阳市 Xinyang	7248	6488	760	6064	3131	2933
周口市 Zhoukou	5950	5438	512	4155	2904	1251
驻马店市 Zhumadian	5193	4730	463	3904	2936	968
济源市 Jiyuan	954	826	128	459	15	444
省直管县 County Directly Administrated by Province						
巩义市 Gongyi	709	600	109	1523	158	1365
兰考县 Lankao	674	587	87	899	349	550
汝州市 Ruzhou	566	449	117	694	21	673
滑县 Huaxian	531	293	238	522	124	398
长垣市 Changyuan	263	263		1375	967	408
邓州市 Dengzhou	212	186	26	898	589	309
永城市 Yongcheng	450	401	49	934	676	258
固始县 Gushi	1010	820	190	673	375	298
鹿邑县 Luyi	927	922	5	438	428	10
新蔡县 Xincai	594	594		446	446	

16-9 限额以上批发和零售企业(单位)商品分类销售总额(2019年)

Total Sales of Enterprises above Designated Size of Wholesale and Retail Trade by Category of Main Commodities (2019)

单位：亿元 (100 million yuan)

指标	Item	合计 Total	批发业 Wholesale Trade	零售业 Retail Trade
粮油、食品类	Food	959.36	476.06	483.30
#粮油类	Grain and oils	333.42	212.32	121.10
肉禽蛋类	Meat, Poultry and Eggs	164.19	92.24	71.95
水产品类	Aquatic products	17.89	3.67	14.23
蔬菜类	Vegetables	61.60	18.44	43.16
干鲜果品类	Nuts	63.77	12.36	51.41
饮料类	Beverages	151.00	42.46	108.54
烟酒类	Tobacco and Liquor	1262.80	1104.98	157.82
服装、鞋帽、针纺织品类	Clothing, Shoes, Hats and Textiles	509.66	78.24	431.42
服装类	Clothing	363.37	42.31	321.07
鞋帽类	Shoes and Hats	88.75	16.61	72.14
针纺织品类	Knitwear and Textiles	57.54	19.32	38.21
化妆品类	Cosmetics	115.56	6.25	109.32
金银珠宝类	Gold, Silver and Jewelry	95.70	11.98	83.72
日用品类	Articles for Daily Use	232.04	27.81	204.23
儿童玩具类	Children Toys			
五金、电料类	Hardware and Electrical Materials	79.68	32.96	46.72
体育、娱乐用品类	Sports and Recreation Articles	20.43	3.70	16.73
照相器材类	Photographic equipment class	2.74	0.60	2.14
书报杂志类	Newspapers and Magazines	127.50	59.28	68.22
电子出版物及音像制品类	E-journal and Video Products	4.31	1.35	2.96
家用电器和音像器材类	Household Appliances and Video Appliances	604.69	296.18	308.52
中西药品类	Traditional Chinese and Western Medicines	1501.69	1272.45	229.25
#西药类	Western Medicines	988.00	859.76	128.23
中草药及中成药类	Traditional Chinese Medicines	174.92	141.15	33.77
文化办公用品类	Cultural and Official Goods	161.84	57.25	104.60
计算机及其配套产品	Computer and its supporting products	75.55	14.36	61.18
家具类	Furniture	83.29	9.44	73.85
通讯器材类	Communication Appliances	348.63	262.07	86.56
煤炭及制品类	Coal and Related Products	1545.28	1526.44	18.83
木材及制品类	Wood and Wooden Products	5.39	5.34	0.05
石油及制品类	Petroleum and Related Products	1480.50	839.90	640.59
化工材料及制品类	Raw Chemical Materials	511.83	506.03	5.80
#化肥类	Fertilizer	147.13	144.76	2.37
金属材料类	Metal Materials	1905.82	1902.93	2.89
建筑及装潢材料类	Building and Decoration Materials	379.44	328.80	50.64
机电产品及设备类	Mechanical and Electrical Products	238.93	209.03	29.90
#农机类	Agricultural Machinery	63.88	62.71	1.17
汽车类	Automobile	2160.42	178.54	1981.88
种子饲料类	Seed and Feedstuff	43.23	42.60	0.63
棉麻类	Cotton, Hemp	52.59	52.45	0.14
其他类	Others	652.95	537.65	115.30

16－10 各市限额以上批发和零售企业(单位)商品分类批发总额(2019年)

Total Wholesale Value of Enterprises above Designated Size of Wholesales and Retail Trades by City and Sort (2019)

单位：万元 (10 000 yuan)

市(县) City(County)	粮油食品类 Grain and Oil, Food	日用品类 Articles for Daily Use	服装、鞋帽针纺织品类 Clothing,Shoes and Hats, Knitwear and Textiles	文化办公用品类 Cultural and Office Supplies	家用电器和音像器材类 Household and Video Appliances	中西药品类 Traditional Chinese and Western Medicines	书报杂志类 Newspapers and Magazines
省辖市 City							
郑州市 Zhengzhou	844212	83391	290106	484768	2170082	7016331	486161
开封市 Kaifeng	176272	6605	4804	16799	45707	158643	1379
洛阳市 Luoyang	113712	1054	6100	4540	253199	888864	13175
平顶山市 Pingdingshan	38898	1149	302			251734	
安阳市 Anyang	44714	57			10501	478065	7519
鹤壁市 Hebi	41704					23923	
新乡市 Xinxiang	255255	679	47424	12043	61612	643714	58
焦作市 Jiaozuo	44806	2388	1183	513	23268	117890	
濮阳市 Puyang	44699	5804	1827	5020	29210	193889	173
许昌市 Xuchang	41435	50637	6328	323	245	365291	924
漯河市 Luohe	925041	5514	7731	12	6824	140566	
三门峡市 Sanmenxia	69618	11	2625	8	842	118757	
南阳市 Nanyang	619316	8350	64241	13784	249666	795972	26986
商丘市 Shangqiu	224401	55276	312206	51388	77435	716773	
信阳市 Xinyang	415642	7847	21635	1533	63639	131741	6737
周口市 Zhoukou	336597	5512	25323	22009	41074	369633	5294
驻马店市 Zhumadian	296811	26610	72	3577	19158	417462	11782
济源市 Jiyuan	4037	1480					
省直管县 County Directly Administrated by Province							
巩义市 Gongyi	1161	14	16	10		6339	
兰考县 Lankao	37354				307	1494	1379
汝州市 Ruzhou	15504	18	82				
滑县 Huaxian	31927	52			1281	16499	7519
长垣市 Changyuan	8		1			116881	
邓州市 Dengzhou	43113	34	1	4	74	41033	
永城市 Yongcheng	5	3	6			3294	
固始县 Gushi	25900		5			8	
鹿邑县 Luyi	30137	822	1143	5747	3989	1712	
新蔡县 Xincai	12626	189	35	227	3450	3716	363

16–11 各市限额以上批发和零售企业(单位)商品分类零售总额(2019年)

Retail Trades Value of Enterprises above Designated Size in Wholesales and Retail Trades by City and Sort (2019)

单位：万元 (10 000 yuan)

市(县)	City(County)	粮油食品类 Grain and Oil, Food	日用品类 Articles for Daily Use	服装、鞋帽针纺织类 Clothing,Shoes and Hats, Knitwear and Textiles	文化办公用品类 Cultural and Office Supplies	家用电器和音像器材类 Household and Video Appliances	中西药品类 Traditional Chinese and Western Medicines	书报杂志类 Newspapers and Magazines
省辖市	**City**							
郑州市	Zhengzhou	1333976	894150	1628119	622385	975904	802987	123086
开封市	Kaifeng	177004	52988	304009	16453	185540	51455	24006
洛阳市	Luoyang	578675	190906	360866	39399	291119	136328	53429
平顶山市	Pingdingshan	267332	111231	132320	71775	108931	133103	35516
安阳市	Anyang	84418	18555	40182	6690	75354	#VALUE!	32136
鹤壁市	Hebi	39062	7553	19809	1445	29506	14727	8574
新乡市	Xinxiang	190786	61520	132988	14077	112454	122461	46366
焦作市	Jiaozuo	99596	24936	74706	8130	80817	43859	24962
濮阳市	Puyang	114829	42473	83874	5342	87974	35969	31241
许昌市	Xuchang	216654	50440	155381	5545	138410	62296	39073
漯河市	Luohe	145325	33224	128946	18192	112353	67790	18772
三门峡市	Sanmenxia	101434	23077	82295	7788	40637	94839	13312
南阳市	Nanyang	234863	78283	209767	32145	167439	78224	65457
商丘市	Shangqiu	322855	98624	257815	70361	176861	146970	47375
信阳市	Xinyang	496954	159533	246036	37338	130586	107057	43402
周口市	Zhoukou	436006	55938	241403	17897	190245	150242	50724
驻马店市	Zhumadian	208355	152059	199839	24779	90355	60016	53726
济源市	Jiyuan	8305	2515	6363	2386	1	6673	3677
省直管县	**County Directly Administrated by Province**							
巩义市	Gongyi	36947	35472	43256	2135	11397	10764	4452
兰考县	Lankao	52763	17472	50985	5308	31195	10509	3374
汝州市	Ruzhou	46037	34776	36276	8369	16398	24482	7138
滑县	Huaxian	30566	7602	20369	776	17112		423
长垣市	Changyuan	13691	7627	16976	2790	26104	11133	4669
邓州市	Dengzhou	25595	6950	13242	5629	12136	8919	9168
永城市	Yongcheng	61380	11156	49697	1727	13488	14333	7571
固始县	Gushi	42211	10654	24885	2919	9416	6029	9531
鹿邑县	Luyi	20213	4011	11254	2944	17431	17038	5281
新蔡县	Xincai	32297	25653	18586	12755	10874	15675	5046

16−12 限额以上批发和零售企业(单位)商品购销存总额(2019年)

Total Purchases, Sales and Inventory above Designated Size of Wholesale and Retail Trades (2019)

单位：万元 (10 000yuan)

指 标	Iterm	商品购进额 purchases	#进口 Imports	商品销售额 Total Sales
总 计	**Total**	**141688356**	**2093506**	**163444997**
批发业	**Wholesale Trades**	**101977281**	**1290498**	**113603566**
按国民经济行业分	By sector			
农、林、牧产品	Farming, forestry, animal husbandry products	2837776	548	3014321
食品、饮料及烟草制品	Food, drinks and tobacco products	11120321	53742	15349183
纺织、服装及家庭用品	Textile, clothing and household items	4492673	40527	4892066
文化、体育用品及器材	Cultural and sports supplies and equipment	2187985	6729	2500307
医药及医疗器材	Pharmaceutical and medical equipment	13227655	158456	15311020
矿产品、建材及化工产品	Minerals, building materials and chemical products	53420079	857899	56423633
机械设备、五金产品及电子产品	Mechanical equipment, metal products and electronic products	12518996	161887	13687481
贸易经纪与代理	Trade brokers and agents	312687	10668	325181
其他批发业	Others	1859108	41	2100374
按登记注册类型分	By Registration status			
内资企业	Domestic Funded Enterprises	101809285	1282193	113390296
国有企业	State-owned	7347816	1217	10467653
集体企业	Collective-owned	1553046		1572071
股份合作企业	Cooperative	6354		6339
联营企业	Joint Ownership			5955
有限责任公司	Limited Liability Corporations	55020896	1059929	60403914
股份有限公司	Share-holding Corporation Ltd	8848162		8290687
私营企业	Private	28981827	221048	32587201
其他企业	Other	51185		56474
港澳台商投资企业	Enterprises with Funds from Hong Kong, Macao and Taiwan	46324	1856	70170
外商投资企业	Foreign Funded	121671	6448	143101
个体经营	Individual			
按控股情况分	By Controlling Type			
#国有控股	State-ownedand State-holding	44296813	607776	48713025
零售业	**Retail Trades**	**39711075**	**803009**	**49841431**
按国民经济行业分	By sector			
综合零售	Comprehensive retail	5534829	7662	8345950
食品、饮料及烟草制品	Food, drinks and tobacco products	1109246	3270	1461112
纺织、服装及日用品	Textile, clothing and household items	811607	1233	1301290
文化、体育用品及器材	Cultural and sports supplies and equipment	1165844		1351321
医药及医疗器材	Pharmaceutical and medical equipment	1881093	6209	2446868
汽车、摩托车、燃料及零配件	Automobiles, motorcycles, fuel and spare parts	23186760	625755	27551857
家用电器及电子产品	Household appliances and electronic products	3467536	4046	3895749
五金、家具及室内装饰材料	Hardware, furniture and interior decoration materials	705453	901	901010
货摊、无店铺及其他	Booth and others	1848708	153931	2586275
按登记注册类型分	By Registration status			
内资企业	Domestic Funded Enterprises	37512059	792482	46478087
国有企业	State-owned	263471		869754
集体企业	Collective-owned	56691		62200
股份合作企业	Cooperative			
联营企业	Joint Ownership	548		836
有限责任公司	Limited Liability Corporations	17894512	604982	21431420
股份有限公司	Share-holding Corporation Ltd	3730468	5356	5508672
私营企业	Private	15565850	182145	18604582
其他企业	Other	519		623
港澳台商投资企业	Enterprises with Funds from Hong Kong, Macao and Taiwan	1594620	10527	2644593
外商投资企业	Foreign Funded	604396		718752
个体经营	Individual			
按控股情况分	By Controlling Type			
#国有控股	State-ownedand State-holding	5164502	124138	7228268

16-12 续表 continued

单位：万元 (10 000yuan)

指标	Iterm	批发额 Wholesale trade	#出口 Imports	零售额 Retail Trade	年末商品库存额 Inventory (year-end)
总计	**Total**	**110367284**	**2535404**	**52301000**	**12627108**
批发业	**Wholesale Trades**	**106730206**	**2404111**	**6113118**	**8087322**
按国民经济行业分	By sector				
农、林、牧产品	Farming, forestry, animal husbandry products	2816049	46064	102260	1668118
食品、饮料及烟草制品	Food, drinks and tobacco products	14407437	76038	867256	890214
纺织、服装及家庭用品	Textile, clothing and household items	4650989	259750	198984	493064
文化、体育用品及器材	Cultural and sports supplies and equipment	2338931	28710	154344	194450
医药及医疗器材	Pharmaceutical and medical equipment	14887608	1135	418841	938246
矿产品、建材及化工产品	Minerals, building materials and chemical products	52586196	1171601	3515826	3392643
机械设备、五金产品及电子产品	Mechanical equipment, metal products and electronic products	12806155	736664	834724	466086
贸易经纪与代理	Trade brokers and agents	325181	45165		4286
其他批发业	Others	1911661	38985	20884	40215
按登记注册类型分	By Registration status				
内资企业	Domestic Funded Enterprises	106520349	2378175	6109705	8085243
国有企业	State-owned	10438343		29311	1801112
集体企业	Collective-owned	1571991		80	6235
股份合作企业	Cooperative	6339			129
联营企业	Joint Ownership	5955			594
有限责任公司	Limited Liability Corporations	57231233	1082906	2895539	2825422
股份有限公司	Share-holding Corporation Ltd	6631008	7506	1645793	1857991
私营企业	Private	30585169	1287763	1532818	1593059
其他企业	Other	50310		6164	702
港澳台商投资企业	Enterprises with Funds from Hong Kong, Macao and Taiwan	66757	15320	3413	
外商投资企业	Foreign Funded	143101	10616		848
个体经营	Individual				
按控股情况分	By Controlling Type				
#国有控股	State-ownedand State-holding	45980779	650629	2700468	4781000
零售业	**Retail Trades**	**3637079**	**131294**	**46187881**	**4539786**
按国民经济行业分	By sector				
综合零售	Comprehensive retail	124868		8219111	702793
食品、饮料及烟草制品	Food, drinks and tobacco products	196144	4460	1262681	146839
纺织、服装及日用品	Textile, clothing and household items	127283	2050	1170909	100055
文化、体育用品及器材	Cultural and sports supplies and equipment	107061	1995	1244260	153512
医药及医疗器材	Pharmaceutical and medical equipment	434164		2008529	268847
汽车、摩托车、燃料及零配件	Automobiles, motorcycles, fuel and spare parts	1587857	1847	25961518	2472976
家用电器及电子产品	Household appliances and electronic products	561082	36	3333624	405079
五金、家具及室内装饰材料	Hardware, furniture and interior decoration materials	200154	1835	699798	66501
货摊、无店铺及其他	Booth and others	298467	119072	2287451	223184
按登记注册类型分	By Registration status				
内资企业	Domestic Funded Enterprises	3517157	131294	42944458	4383307
国有企业	State-owned	145998		723756	27996
集体企业	Collective-owned	8320		53879	8984
股份合作企业	Cooperative				
联营企业	Joint Ownership			836	10
有限责任公司	Limited Liability Corporations	1253928	126381	20173456	2029301
股份有限公司	Share-holding Corporation Ltd	954843		4553830	356352
私营企业	Private	1154069	4913	17438078	1960612
其他企业	Other			623	51
港澳台商投资企业	Enterprises with Funds from Hong Kong, Macao and Taiwan	2400		2642193	120939
外商投资企业	Foreign Funded	117521		601230	35540
个体经营	Individual				
按控股情况分	By Controlling Type				
#国有控股	State-ownedand State-holding	1391614	118996	5836653	338564

16-13 各市限额以上批发和零售企业(单位)商品购、销、存总额(2019年)

Total Purchases, Sales and Inventory of Enterprises above Designated Size of Wholesale and Retail Trades by City (2019)

单位：亿元 (100 million yuan)

市(县)	City(County)	商品购进额 purchases	商品销售额 Total Sales	批发额 Wholesale trade	零售额 Retail Trade	年末商品库存额 Inventory (year-end)
全省	**Total**	**14168.84**	**16344.50**	**11036.73**	**5230.10**	**1262.71**
省辖市	**City**					
郑州市	Zhengzhou	6488.12	7106.03	5116.08	1969.17	615.63
开封市	Kaifeng	277.42	366.50	196.76	168.94	25.20
洛阳市	Luoyang	1147.55	1386.79	897.62	474.72	81.10
平顶山市	Pingdingshan	712.73	781.83	611.55	168.85	31.74
安阳市	Anyang	464.74	510.62	381.89	127.51	45.65
鹤壁市	Hebi	307.59	344.88	297.68	43.99	6.65
新乡市	Xinxiang	458.55	548.09	319.90	228.19	37.59
焦作市	Jiaozuo	299.98	347.46	219.68	127.02	17.61
濮阳市	Puyang	289.20	345.37	223.64	120.83	13.77
许昌市	Xuchang	276.30	375.35	196.34	178.66	29.93
漯河市	Luohe	325.80	403.38	203.18	198.49	12.04
三门峡市	Sanmenxia	391.32	550.10	459.59	87.78	15.69
南阳市	Nanyang	612.40	725.75	461.76	260.80	51.80
商丘市	Shangqiu	728.13	861.87	532.23	326.66	41.35
信阳市	Xinyang	372.62	447.03	178.09	265.04	41.21
周口市	Zhoukou	442.19	568.32	288.08	261.48	161.03
驻马店市	Zhumadian	309.90	382.87	183.82	198.56	28.20
济源市	Jiyuan	264.30	292.25	268.83	23.42	6.52
省直管县	**County Directly Administrated by Province**					
巩义市	Gongyi	154.35	160.10	126.17	30.76	6.45
兰考县	Lankao	31.45	42.18	17.39	24.24	1.55
汝州市	Ruzhou	120.87	134.03	109.03	23.82	2.73
滑县	Huaxian	14.75	17.23	8.63	8.60	1.56
长垣市	Changyuan	35.55	47.83	24.65	23.18	2.62
邓州市	Dengzhou	28.03	32.52	13.17	19.20	1.69
永城市	Yongcheng	205.52	213.86	182.77	31.08	2.27
固始县	Gushi	32.57	38.37	14.02	24.35	1.94
鹿邑县	Luyi	33.15	36.69	27.00	9.69	0.99
新蔡县	Xincai	17.55	23.69	4.73	18.46	1.41

16-14 限额以上住宿和餐饮业企业(单位)经营情况(2019年)

Management of Enterprises above Designated Size of Star-rated Hotels and Catering Services (2019)

单位：万元 (10 000 yuan)

指标名称	Item	营业额 Total Business Revenue	客房收入 Guest room Revenue	餐费收入 Meal Revenue	商品销售额 Total Retail Sales of Consumer Goods	其他收入 Other Revenue
总 计	**Total**	**2390210**	**815324**	**1383105**	**67172**	**124609**
住宿业	**Hotels**	**1388308**	**741396**	**512816**	**36425**	**97670**
按国民经济行业分	By sector					
旅游饭店	Tourist hotel	763946	375804	308689	17548	61905
一般旅馆	General hotel	576972	338247	188069	17909	32747
其他住宿业	Others	43502	25032	14654	920	2895
按登记注册类型分	By Registration					
内资企业	Domestic-Funded Enterprises	1331354	718463	487231	34091	91569
国有企业	State-owned	126823	49883	55543	3953	17444
集体企业	Collective-owned	17972	8143	6496	276	3057
股份合作企业	Cooperative	1396	569	712	91	23
联营企业	Joint Ownership	598	598			
有限责任公司	Limited Liability Corporations	588455	302414	218738	16918	50385
股份有限公司	Share-holding Corporation Ltd	37528	18600	15150	1956	1823
私营企业	Private	558583	338256	190593	10896	18838
其他企业	Other					
港澳台商投资企业	Enterprises With Investment from Hong Kong, Macao and Taiwan	45670	17297	21068	1676	5628
外商投资企业	Enterprises With Foreign Investment	11284	5636	4517	658	473
个体经营	Individual					
按控股情况分	By Controlling Type					
#国有控股	State-holding	232165	97042	94034	6245	34844
按经营形式分	By Management Style					
独立门店	Independent store	1220509	636299	466333	29091	88786
连锁总店	Head office of Chain Store	11450	6245	4233	36	936
连锁直营店	Chain Direct-sale Store	12507	8628	3318	88	474
连锁加盟店	Chain Franchisee Store	32577	29287	2416	401	474
其他	Others	111265	60938	36517	6809	7000
按星级分	By Star Level					
五星	Five-star	145740	62205	64299	3450	15786
四星	Four-star	221734	98988	97406	5251	20089
三星	Three-star	217996	104331	89867	7648	16150
二星	Two-star	28484	13029	13569	578	1308
一星	One-star	1512	1315	185	13	
其他	Others	772842	461528	247491	19486	44338

16-14 续表 continued

单位：万元 (10 000 yuan)

指标名称	Item	营业额 Total Business Revenue	客房收入 Guest room Revenue	餐费收入 Meal Revenue	商品销售额 Total Retail Sales of Consumer Goods	其他收入 Other Revenue
餐饮业	**Catering Services**	**1001902**	**73928**	**870289**	**30747**	**26939**
按国民经济行业分	By sector					
正餐服务	Dinner	809256	73432	696277	25288	14259
快餐服务	Snack	151266	258	137421	2742	10845
饮料及冷饮服务	Drinks and cold drinks	6371		6167	52	152
其他餐饮业	Others	19552		18092	35	1426
按登记注册类型分	By Registration					
内资企业	Domestic-Funded Enterprises	880492	73928	759342	30640	16582
国有企业	State-owned	5805	1774	3646	118	268
集体企业	Collective-owned	1113		1109	4	
股份合作企业	Cooperative	367		367		
联营企业	Joint Ownership					
有限责任公司	Limited Liability Corporations	301760	24735	260871	10717	5438
股份有限公司	Share-holding Corporation Ltd	16902	2584	12015	2222	82
私营企业	Private	554545	44835	481335	17580	10794
其他企业	Other					
港澳台商投资企业	Enterprises With Investment from Hong Kong, Macao and Taiwan	6869		6820	48	1
外商投资企业	Enterprises With Foreign Investment	114541		104126	59	10356
个体经营	Individual					
按控股情况分	By Controlling Type					
#国有控股	State-holding	40013	4202	31074	2783	1955
按经营形式分	By Management Style					
独立门店	Independent store	729540	69592	624736	22315	12896
连锁总店	Head office of Chain Store	163439		150196	2887	10356
连锁直营店	Chain Direct-sale Store	8900	421	8407	50	22
连锁加盟店	Chain Franchisee Store	9252		9235		18
其他	Others	90771	3916	77715	5494	3647

16−15 各市限额以上住宿和餐饮企业(单位)经营情况(2019年)

Operation Conditions of Enterprises above Designated Size of Star-rated Hotels and Catering Services by City (2019)

单位：万元 (10 000 yuan)

市(县)	City(County)	营业额 Total Business Revenue	客房收入 Guest Room Revenue	餐费收入 From Meals	商品销售额 Total Retail Sales of Consumer Goods	其他收入 Other Revenue
省辖市	**City**					
郑州市	Zhengzhou	879656	274515	502085	25881	77175
开封市	Kaifeng	94081	35238	53463	2256	3125
洛阳市	Luoyang	196993	68351	114032	4846	9764
平顶山市	Pingdingshan	80232	25071	50441	2993	1728
安阳市	Anyang	39345	19365	17599	434	1947
鹤壁市	Hebi	10725	4996	5128	152	449
新乡市	Xinxiang	62883	24713	34364	1349	2456
焦作市	Jiaozuo	36217	14602	20433	416	765
濮阳市	Puyang	30312	11474	17173	176	1488
许昌市	Xuchang	109957	39284	63337	1826	5510
漯河市	Luohe	53562	21735	29553	304	1970
三门峡市	Sanmenxia	57530	22109	29740	2395	3286
南阳市	Nanyang	170206	59769	100884	4962	4591
商丘市	Shangqiu	136928	40620	85749	8296	2264
信阳市	Xinyang	142666	51834	83219	2714	4899
周口市	Zhoukou	153283	52396	92988	6657	1241
驻马店市	Zhumadian	123540	43890	76569	1363	1719
济源市	Jiyuan	12095	5363	6348	152	232
省直管县	**County Directly Administrated by Province**					
巩义市	Gongyi	11068	4082	5974	734	278
兰考县	Lankao	34021	11455	20617	1690	258
汝州市	Ruzhou	5268	1994	3154	15	105
滑县	Huaxian	5742	1927	3734	38	43
长垣市	Changyuan	11660	1678	9924	52	6
邓州市	Dengzhou	15356	3193	11660	329	174
永城市	Yongcheng	11636	3778	7384	102	373
固始县	Gushi	20946	6540	13833	446	127
鹿邑县	Luyi	21923	10391	10454	762	316
新蔡县	Xincai	23088	10240	12838		10

16-16　各市限额以上住宿企业(单位)经营情况(2019年)

Operation Conditions of Star-rated Hotels above Designated Sized by City (2019)

单位：万元　(10 000 yuan)

市(县)	City(County)	营业额 Total Business Revenue	客房收入 Guest Room Revenue	餐费收入 From Meals	商品销售额 Total Retail Sales of Consumer Goods	其他收入 other Revenue
省辖市	**City**					
郑州市	Zhengzhou	466693	256314	137928	15044	57407
开封市	Kaifeng	63113	32997	25789	1305	3022
洛阳市	Luoyang	128799	64315	52836	2047	9601
平顶山市	Pingdingshan	44176	24626	16106	1802	1643
安阳市	Anyang	31888	18831	10793	355	1909
鹤壁市	Hebi	8454	4690	3179	152	433
新乡市	Xinxiang	38343	21227	14631	503	1983
焦作市	Jiaozuo	21990	11643	9286	313	748
濮阳市	Puyang	18568	9581	7520	29	1438
许昌市	Xuchang	78231	37688	34253	1005	5285
漯河市	Luohe	28897	17230	10932	218	517
三门峡市	Sanmenxia	44042	21184	18226	1581	3050
南阳市	Nanyang	96346	48903	41576	2684	3182
商丘市	Shangqiu	62516	35717	21510	4053	1236
信阳市	Xinyang	90545	45048	39907	1125	4465
周口市	Zhoukou	87676	47563	35712	3367	1035
驻马店市	Zhumadian	66213	38476	26561	691	486
济源市	Jiyuan	11818	5363	6071	152	232
省直管县	**County Directly Administrated by Province**					
巩义市	Gongyi	9097	3868	4246	705	278
兰考县	Lankao	19994	10060	8896	824	214
汝州市	Ruzhou	3984	1994	1870	15	105
滑县	Huaxian	3732	1927	1745	38	23
长垣市	Changyuan	2369	1456	913		
邓州市	Dengzhou	4958	2510	2279	121	49
永城市	Yongcheng	4203	2798	935	99	371
固始县	Gushi	13575	6076	7268	127	104
鹿邑县	Luyi	12463	10095	1956	175	237
新蔡县	Xincai	10891	8666	2215		10

16－17 各市限额以上餐饮企业(单位)经营情况(2019年)

Operation Conditions of Catering Services above Designated Size by City (2019)

单位：万元 (10 000 yuan)

市(县) City(County)	营业额 Total Business Revenue	客房收入 Guest Room Revenue	餐费收入 From Meals	商品销售额 Total Retail Sales of Consumer Goods	其他收入 other Revenue
省辖市 City					
郑州市 Zhengzhou	412963	18201	364156	10838	19768
开封市 Kaifeng	30968	2241	27674	951	103
洛阳市 Luoyang	68194	4036	61196	2799	164
平顶山市 Pingdingshan	36056	445	34335	1191	85
安阳市 Anyang	7458	535	6806	79	38
鹤壁市 Hebi	2271	306	1949		16
新乡市 Xinxiang	24539	3486	19733	846	474
焦作市 Jiaozuo	14227	2960	11147	103	17
濮阳市 Puyang	11744	1893	9653	147	51
许昌市 Xuchang	31726	1596	29084	821	225
漯河市 Luohe	24666	4504	18622	86	1454
三门峡市 Sanmenxia	13488	925	11513	813	236
南阳市 Nanyang	73860	10866	59307	2278	1409
商丘市 Shangqiu	74412	4902	64239	4243	1028
信阳市 Xinyang	52121	6786	43312	1589	433
周口市 Zhoukou	65607	4833	57277	3291	206
驻马店市 Zhumadian	57327	5414	50009	672	1233
济源市 Jiyuan	277		277		
省直管县 County Directly Administrated by Province					
巩义市 Gongyi	1971	214	1728	29	
兰考县 Lankao	14027	1396	11721	866	44
汝州市 Ruzhou	1284		1284		
滑县 Huaxian	2010		1990		20
长垣市 Changyuan	9291	222	9011	52	6
邓州市 Dengzhou	10398	684	9381	208	126
永城市 Yongcheng	7433	980	6449	3	2
固始县 Gushi	7370	464	6565	319	23
鹿邑县 Luyi	9460	296	8497	587	79
新蔡县 Xincai	12197	1574	10623		

16-18 限额以上批发和零售、住宿和餐饮法人企业主要财务指标(2019年)

Main Financial Indicators of Enterprises in Wholesale and Retail Trades, Hotels and Catering Services above Designated Size (2019)

单位：万元 (10 000 yuan)

指　标	Item	批发业 Wholesale	零售业 Retail Sale	住宿业 Hotels	餐饮业 Catering Services
期末资产负债	**Assets and Liability (year-end)**				
流动资产合计	Current Assets	44698443	17445680	1762302	542747
应收帐款	Accounts Receivable	10277494	1881556	164202	78297
存货	Inventory	5901433	3892120	71286	39252
固定资产原价	Original Value of Fixed Assets	4430931	4967894	2298814	547213
累计折旧	Accumulated Depreciation	1456189	1523257	859154	163783
本年折旧	Depreciation of Deducted This Year	248367	308380	104385	23289
固定资产净额	Net Fixed Assets	9077917	2112773	977314	212058
在建工程	Project under Construction	335812	271732	183097	35711
无形资产	Intangible Assets	784192	1000662	160011	25097
土地使用权	Land Use Right	275637	510494	59675	12592
资产总计	Total Assets	54689186	24330680	4225887	1177131
流动负债合计	Total Flow liabilities	36632017	14091960	2126163	504296
应付账款	Accounts Payable	7373544	2540544	217207	66144
负债合计	Total Liabilities	40783088	17351515	2965367	649286
所有者权益合计	Total Creditors'Equity	14477143	6916860	1225557	500368
实收资本	Actual Capital	7298709	6643700	1336036	358210
损益及分配	**Profit and Loss Apportionment**				
营业收入	Business Income	103545481	44437892	1350345	977273
主营业务收入	Revenue from Principle Busintss	102991457	43597289	1325748	959560
营业成本	Operating Costs	94979671	38601521	611628	545430
营业税金及附加	Sales Tax and Extra Changes	1409347	204819	25427	13771
其他业务利润	Other Profits	153458	494702	13002	7466
销售费用	Selling Expenses	2279341	2514503	332596	202726
管理费用	Management Expenses	1581166	1353629	349624	129885
研发费用	R&D Expenses	19892	5559	529	927
财务费用	Financial Expenses	550415	356144	67866	16097
利息收入	Interest Income	159634	8545	1979	801
利息费用	Intrest Expenses	462386	133906	34812	6686
投资收益	Investment Income	115303	6348	34155	203
营业利润	Operating Profit	2709866	1350611	-12900	65458
营业外收入	Non-operating Income	149012	60865	6983	3308
营业外支出	Non-business Expenses	67886	36681	3733	1508
利润总额	Total Profit	2796488	1379094	-10006	67254
应交所得税	Payable Income Tax	518987	174406	11589	7831
人工成本及增值税	**Labor cost and value added tax**				
应付职工薪酬	Wages Payable	1412209	1591394	351558	201842
应交增值税	VAT payable	1122858	517607	29988	17822

16-19 各市限额以上批发和零售法人企业主要财务指标(2019年)

Main Financial Indicators of Enterprises in Wholesale and Retail Trades above Designated Size by City (2019)

单位：万元 (10 000 yuan)

市(县) City(County)	流动资产合计 Circulating Funds	#存货 Inventory	固定资产原价 Fixed Asset	资产总计 Original Values of Fixed Asset	所有者权益 Owners' Equity	营业收入 Business Income	营业成本 Operating Costs
省辖市 City							
郑州市 Zhengzhou	28990450	3648072	2375529	34520482	7854241	62186391	57416832
开封市 Kaifeng	921627	199596	342953	1348139	611499	3201034	2720235
洛阳市 Luoyang	6226105	809937	703693	7133731	1424052	12757675	11692594
平顶山市 Pingdingshan	2027176	233137	390052	2597379	690318	7254624	6759707
安阳市 Anyang	1936055	253549	242591	2307039	610819	4655530	4266947
鹤壁市 Hebi	746874	97771	101788	1000788	236299	3022564	2902552
新乡市 Xinxiang	1774583	304919	434519	2236113	679335	5072003	4474774
焦作市 Jiaozuo	1147996	145546	265041	1490764	360643	3105514	2776374
濮阳市 Puyang	1410568	171552	206301	1707429	411540	3228272	2992116
许昌市 Xuchang	1407739	282210	394594	2082524	773692	3447192	2940717
漯河市 Luohe	893875	156382	165273	1330708	410628	3701977	3229423
三门峡市 Sanmenxia	3809289	201413	396046	5598303	766004	5565078	5184036
南阳市 Nanyang	2727529	519108	701417	3812688	1445625	6667322	5745009
商丘市 Shangqiu	1829588	371656	585123	2851190	1592922	7936656	6651201
信阳市 Xinyang	1195588	295303	653960	1969759	979371	4201538	3503565
周口市 Zhoukou	2865539	1767953	735614	3644172	1077697	5344295	4357064
驻马店市 Zhumadian	1778972	274547	599371	2622474	1167560	3908515	3378894
济源市 Jiyuan	454570	60903	104961	766183	301761	2727192	2589152
省直管县 County Directly Administrated by Province							
巩义市 Gongyi	178326	26898	15899	325939	66482	1517445	1383713
兰考县 Lankao	80403	17545	79528	173091	114546	375865	274303
汝州市 Ruzhou	728338	29447	46579	790144	134458	1235786	1127694
滑县 Huaxian	54663	12428	30377	88512	50705	163510	142600
长垣市 Changyuan	240248	26834	24598	292134	108145	473740	363566
邓州市 Dengzhou	138646	26896	63533	276804	135272	301200	245357
永城市 Yongcheng	268301	28364	47909	318733	131489	1906839	1800465
固始县 Gushi	127662	16259	93024	233369	134496	369224	313211
鹿邑县 Luyi	157770	81369	93628	262226	163587	348560	267857
新蔡县 Xincai	58019	11815	49273	108861	65029	230769	167273

16-19 续表 continued

单位：万元 (10 000 yuan)

市(县) City(County)	营业税金及附加 Sales Tax and Extra Changes	销售费用 Selling Expenses	管理费用 Management Expenses	财务费用 Financial Expenses	营业利润 Operating Profits	利润总额 Total Profits	本年应缴增值税 VAT Payable
省辖市 City							
郑州市 Zhengzhou	294564	1923458	979722	403997	1225951	1258809	462602
开封市 Kaifeng	66111	117901	84815	20479	182005	185335	42957
洛阳市 Luoyang	109416	415781	246657	69695	213787	215583	91659
平顶山市 Pingdingshan	73091	171089	111039	27456	116176	129019	72772
安阳市 Anyang	66981	111353	71392	24968	114196	116560	52927
鹤壁市 Hebi	23106	33876	26575	11970	20920	21306	12154
新乡市 Xinxiang	72633	229282	111831	24232	135787	141052	60043
焦作市 Jiaozuo	45349	128354	69520	13032	66327	67021	33853
濮阳市 Puyang	45979	78499	59622	11487	41587	42793	33770
许昌市 Xuchang	73808	151509	129011	30522	130806	131723	57943
漯河市 Luohe	47827	153386	69132	19161	179601	183736	92725
三门峡市 Sanmenxia	57291	110557	74582	16957	71506	89649	86807
南阳市 Nanyang	142260	293261	192861	39614	226690	233544	105729
商丘市 Shangqiu	144017	280756	256651	61233	552503	552892	162888
信阳市 Xinyang	101809	220892	132461	34457	198726	199720	96557
周口市 Zhoukou	139030	193672	179834	62865	368230	376606	82464
驻马店市 Zhumadian	93841	142362	115932	19518	153705	162211	49784
济源市 Jiyuan	17055	37855	23159	14918	61976	68026	42830
省直管县 County Directly Administrated by Province							
巩义市 Gongyi	1095	17134	9333	1645	76732	72767	3457
兰考县 Lankao	3255	32007	17857	7243	41037	41051	7007
汝州市 Ruzhou	3386	24183	11614	12144	45176	45342	10222
滑县 Huaxian	690	7989	5743	864	5967	6013	975
长垣市 Changyuan	2847	64287	16076	2580	23163	23243	4236
邓州市 Dengzhou	2616	12447	9537	4985	25526	25497	2853
永城市 Yongcheng	3331	68682	15049	4747	13532	13583	11006
固始县 Gushi	3106	15453	11101	2989	22339	22318	2508
鹿邑县 Luyi	4647	16563	11585	7807	39915	39908	3870
新蔡县 Xincai	8278	18859	10095	2737	24042	24094	4036

16-20 各市限额以上住宿和餐饮法人企业主要财务指标(2019年)

Main Economic Indicators of Enterprises in Hotels and Catering Services above Designated Size by City (2019)

单位：万元 (10 000 yuan)

市(县) City(County)	流动资产合计 Circulating Funds	#存货 Inventory	固定资产原价 Original Values of Fixed Asset	资产总计 Total Assets	所有者权益 Owners' Equity	#实收资本 Paid-in Capital	营业收入 Business Income
省辖市 City							
郑州市 Zhengzhou	883563	33953	864340	1744721	308949	544207	858101
开封市 Kaifeng	152091	4221	195559	330880	164901	147020	94713
洛阳市 Luoyang	293853	10380	291851	689502	261229	186404	196050
平顶山市 Pingdingshan	67991	3456	131679	212155	134765	136336	76998
安阳市 Anyang	35541	1882	66218	102511	36035	20566	38300
鹤壁市 Hebi	8216	562	9775	17570	2229	7239	10147
新乡市 Xinxiang	79594	2754	62676	163303	27884	35455	61342
焦作市 Jiaozuo	54458	2214	61519	106785	-4308	20185	35066
濮阳市 Puyang	34683	1901	72762	121341	46780	24806	30776
许昌市 Xuchang	130555	6573	162619	315998	49783	85431	107855
漯河市 Luohe	29957	1573	32589	63647	16934	15349	51909
三门峡市 Sanmenxia	36549	4020	90830	155244	22865	14169	53702
南阳市 Nanyang	120105	8340	174043	359343	135038	80684	160886
商丘市 Shangqiu	53013	4367	65837	115824	50090	34481	123749
信阳市 Xinyang	135461	8787	258348	383909	216447	165181	139311
周口市 Zhoukou	87686	6667	114946	215928	122715	81739	159145
驻马店市 Zhumadian	82365	7840	171840	255645	137855	89096	117804
济源市 Jiyuan	19369	1048	18597	48714	-4265	5898	11764
省直管县 County Directly Administrated by Province							
巩义市 Gongyi	14086	647	18233	33945	1336	6912	11159
兰考县 Lankao	10172	2053	47880	54009	29592	21352	32020
汝州市 Ruzhou	8138	337	3378	13759	8546	8969	4633
滑县 Huaxian	1894	191	2680	5478	2372	1352	5701
长垣市 Changyuan	2918	397	3529	12573	8354	10809	11723
邓州市 Dengzhou	5461	812	17495	32555	28536	10099	14521
永城市 Yongcheng	3794	325	4091	9425	3277	2542	11475
固始县 Gushi	11494	1768	24579	39899	27836	15071	20129
鹿邑县 Luyi	6672	1370	13298	22127	9605	5516	20264
新蔡县 Xincai	8278	1134	10942	17095	10949	5759	21665

16−20 续表 continued

单位：万元 (10 000 yuan)

市(县) City(County)	营业成本 Operating Costs	营业税金及附加 Sales Tax and Extra Changes	销售费用 Selling Expenses	管理费用 Management Expenses	财务费用 Financial Expenses	营业利润 Operating Profits	利润总额 Total Profits
省辖市 City							
郑州市 Zhengzhou	334370	8695	288987	221557	25332	-19788	-18184
开封市 Kaifeng	42963	1390	17058	18954	7774	6918	6979
洛阳市 Luoyang	106963	4655	47172	43073	9862	-5411	-5469
平顶山市 Pingdingshan	47023	1549	14123	12277	1065	-1598	-1400
安阳市 Anyang	17263	492	9064	12451	962	-2780	-2685
鹤壁市 Hebi	4637	191	2721	2245	95	249	252
新乡市 Xinxiang	29937	1813	12672	13524	2511	1565	1794
焦作市 Jiaozuo	16026	254	9482	8102	1978	-1071	-654
濮阳市 Puyang	16668	299	9627	6504	3287	-5325	-5000
许昌市 Xuchang	58593	2293	15061	25657	8517	10551	10894
漯河市 Luohe	36167	467	5636	4623	816	3715	4162
三门峡市 Sanmenxia	25458	1380	14287	12904	3520	-4331	-3741
南阳市 Nanyang	94084	4371	23212	21260	6063	12578	12686
商丘市 Shangqiu	73937	2715	13181	17386	3123	13126	13092
信阳市 Xinyang	75952	2758	19815	22881	3735	14129	13936
周口市 Zhoukou	98936	3339	17720	16820	2546	19745	20085
驻马店市 Zhumadian	72642	2378	13544	15343	2333	11450	11646
济源市 Jiyuan	5439	161	1960	3950	442	-1165	-1145
省直管县 County Directly Administrated by Province							
巩义市 Gongyi	4977	257	2708	1978	66	1036	1044
兰考县 Lankao	13301	217	1693	1177	397	15392	15423
汝州市 Ruzhou	2884	83	827	1146	226	-531	-528
滑县 Huaxian	3573	108	1102	843	111	-47	-28
长垣市 Changyuan	6976	723	2013	1437	143	646	650
邓州市 Dengzhou	7879	645	877	1219	388	3237	3232
永城市 Yongcheng	6584	160	2326	1112	101	1195	1162
固始县 Gushi	11729	335	2729	2344	937	2476	1849
鹿邑县 Luyi	12322	199	1469	2280	571	3470	3470
新蔡县 Xincai	13455	684	1321	1246	368	4585	4585

16-21 各种分组的连锁企业单位数(2019年)

Number of Chain Enterprise By variety of Group (2019)

单位：个 (unit)

指标名称	Item	连锁总店 Head Offices of Chain Store	连锁门店数 Number of Chain Stores	直营店 Under Direct Management	加盟店 Through License Arrangement
批发和零售业	**Wholesale and Retail**	**108**	**6151**	**5670**	**481**
按登记注册类型分	By Status of Registration				
内资企业	Domestic Funded Enterprises	106	5841	5360	481
国有企业	State-owned	7	81	81	
集体企业	Collective-owned				
有限责任公司	Limited Liability Corporations	52	3262	3037	225
股份有限公司	Share-holding Corporation Ltd	19	1450	1327	123
私营企业	Private	28	1048	915	133
私营独资企业	Proprietorship	1	3	3	
私营合伙企业	Partnership				
私营有限责任公司	Limited Liability Corporations	26	980	847	133
私营股份有限公司	Share-holding Corporation Ltd	1	65	65	
其他企业	Others				
港、澳、台商投资企业	Enterprises with Funds from Hong Kong, Macao and Taiwan	2	310	310	
外商投资企业	Foreign Funded				
按国民经济行业分	By Sector				
批发业	Wholesale Trades	13	894	894	
食品、饮料及烟草制品批发	Food, drink and tobacco products wholesale				
矿产品、建材及化工产品批发	Minerals, building materials and chemical products wholesale	12	892	892	
机械设备、五金产品及电子产品批发	Mechanical equipment, metal products and electronic products wholesale	1	2	2	
零售业	Retail Trades	95	5257	4776	481
综合零售	Comprehensive retail	37	1151	1141	10
食品、饮料及烟草制品专门零售	Food, drink and tobacco retail	2	75	75	
纺织、服装及日用品专门零售	Special retail textile, clothing and daily necessities	1	20	20	
文化、体育用品及器材专门零售	Cultural and sports supplies and equipment retail	5	28	28	
医药及医疗器材专门零售	Pharmaceutical and medical equipment	32	3143	2806	337
汽车、摩托车、燃料及零配件专门零售	Automobiles, motorcycles, fuel and spare parts	7	670	547	123
家用电器及电子产品专门零售	Household appliances and electronic products retail	11	170	159	11
按业态分	By Format				
便利店	Neighbourhood Market	2	133	133	
超市	Supermarker	20	490	480	10
大型超市	large supermarket	10	419	419	
百货店	Department Store	4	47	47	
专业店	Professional Shop	61	4801	4349	452
#加油站	Gas station	19	1562	1439	123
专卖店	Regie Shop	7	157	138	19
住宿和餐饮业	**Hotels and Catering**	**16**	**282**	**281**	**1**
按登记注册类型分	By Status of Registration				
内资企业	Domestic Funded Enterprises	14	143	142	1
有限责任公司	Limited Liability Corporations	6	97	97	
私营企业	Private	8	46	45	1
私营独资企业	proprietorship	1	3	3	
私营有限责任公司	Limited Liability Corporations	7	43	42	1
港、澳、台商投资企业	Enterprises with Funds from Hong Kong, Macao and Taiwan				
外商投资企业	Foreign Funded	2	139	139	
按国民经济行业分	By Sector				
住宿业	Hotels	2	9	9	
旅游饭店	Tourist hotel				
一般旅馆	General hotel				
其他住宿业	Others	1	2	2	
餐饮业	Catering Services	14	273	272	1
正餐服务	Restaurant	10	58	57	1
快餐服务	Fast food	3	211	211	
小吃服务	Snack	1	4	4	

16-22 各种分组的连锁企业基本情况(2019年)

Basic Conditions of Chain Enterprise By variety of Group (2019)

指标名称	Item	营业面积(平方米) Operational Area(sq.m)	从业人数(人) Employed Persons(person)	商品销售总额(万元) Total Sale Value (10 000yuan)	零售额(万元) Retail Sale (10 000yuan)
批发和零售业	**Wholesale and Retail**	**5877456**	**65504**	**9033754**	**7442069**
按登记注册类型分	By Status of Registration				
内资企业	Domestic Funded Enterprises	4903938	56696	7439715	5848031
国有企业	State-owned	58424	1128	163667	163667
集体企业	Collective-owned				
有限责任公司	Limited Liability Corporations	2017685	37785	2766492	2259237
股份有限公司	Share-holding Corporation Ltd	2478780	9040	3999189	2999508
私营企业	Private	349049	8743	510368	425618
私营独资企业	Proprietorship	8500	210	6533	6533
私营合伙企业	Partnership				
私营有限责任公司	Limited Liability Corporations	332688	8181	487466	402716
私营股份有限公司	Share-holding Corporation Ltd	7861	352	16369	16369
其他企业	Others				
港、澳、台商投资企业	Enterprises with Funds from Hong Kong, Macao and Taiwan	973518	8808	1594039	1594039
外商投资企业	Foreign Funded				
按国民经济行业分	By Sector				
批发业	Wholesale Trades	1578381	4255	2461254	1412060
食品、饮料及烟草制品批发	Food, drink and tobacco products wholesale				
矿产品、建材及化工产品批发	Minerals, building materials and chemical wholesale products	1576881	4194	2442393	1398012
机械设备、五金产品及电子产品批发	Mechanical equipment, metal products and electronic products wholesale	1500	61	18861	14047
零售业	Retail Trades	4299075	61249	6572500	6030010
综合零售	Comprehensive retail	2482986	38712	3235758	3107169
食品、饮料及烟草制品专门零售	Food, drink and tobacco retail	8718	399	18574	18574
纺织、服装及日用品专门零售	Special retail textile, clothing and daily necessities	5500	30	8805	8805
文化、体育用品及器材专门零售	Cultural and sports supplies and equipment retail	18543	728	32658	32658
医药及医疗器材专门零售	Pharmaceutical and medical equipment	464292	14831	694156	677227
汽车、摩托车、燃料及零配件专门零售	Automobiles, motorcycles, fuel and spare parts	903531	3318	1921080	1791814
家用电器及电子产品专门零售	Household appliances and electronic products retail	415505	3231	661469	393762
按业态分	By Format				
便利店	Neighbourhood Market	35743	880	39277	39277
超市	Supermarker	511688	9089	591746	469018
大型超市	large supermarket	1603684	24380	2437393	2431534
百货店	Department Store	323501	3981	154799	154799
专业店	Professional Shop	3290452	25663	5658224	4195460
#加油站	Gas station	2480412	7512	4363472	3189827
专卖店	Regie Shop	37828	783	64893	64893
住宿和餐饮业	**Hotels and Catering**	**87262**	**7433**		
按登记注册类型分	By Status of Registration				
内资企业	Domestic Funded Enterprises	53824	2224		
有限责任公司	Limited Liability Corporations	29254	1252		
私营企业	Private	24570	972		
私营独资企业	proprietorship	720	70		
私营有限责任公司	Limited Liability Corporations	23850	902		
港、澳、台商投资企业	Enterprises with Funds from Hong Kong, Macao and Taiwan				
外商投资企业	Foreign Funded	33438	5209		
按国民经济行业分	By Sector				
住宿业	Hotels	180	100		
旅游饭店	Tourist hotel				
一般旅馆	General hotel				
其他住宿业	Others		18		
餐饮业	Catering Services	87082	7333		
正餐服务	Restaurant	30204	1052		
快餐服务	Fast food	53078	6216		
小吃服务	Snack	3800	65		

16−23 连锁企业商品购进和配送情况(2019年)

Conditions of Purchase and Delivery of Chain Enterprise (2019)

单位：万元 (10 000 yuan)

指标名称	Item	商品购进总额 Total Purchases	统一配送商品购进额 Centralized Pruchase and	自有配送中心配送商品购进额 Self Centralized Purchase and Delivery	非自有配送中心配送商品购进额 Non-self Centralized Purchase and Delivery
批发和零售业	**Wholesale and Retail**	**7469016**	**4208842**	**2482151**	**354387**
按登记注册类型分	By Status of Registration				
内资企业	Domestic Funded Enterprises	6505873	4070551	2482151	216096
国有企业	State-owned	151312	109290	15597	178
集体企业	Collective-owned				
有限责任公司	Limited Liability Corporations	2346491	2016150	1327358	215124
股份有限公司	Share-holding Corporation Ltd	3572250	1582237	1035522	
私营企业	Private	435820	362874	103674	794
私营独资企业	Proprietorship	5553			
私营合伙企业	Partnership				
私营有限责任公司	Limited Liability Corporations	417260	349868	103674	794
私营股份有限公司	Share-holding Corporation Ltd	13007	13007		
其他企业	Others				
港、澳、台商投资企业	Enterprises with Funds from Hong Kong, Macao and Taiwan	963144	138291		138291
外商投资企业	Foreign Funded				
按国民经济行业分	By Sector				
批发业	Wholesale Trades	1904897	716555	520664	
食品、饮料及烟草制品批发	Food, drink and tobacco products wholesale				
矿产品、建材及化工产品批发	Minerals, building materials and chemical products wholesale	1889987	701646	520664	
机械设备、五金产品及电子产品批发	Mechanical equipment, metal products and electronic products wholesale	14909	14909		
零售业	Retail Trades	5564120	3492287	1961487	354387
综合零售	Comprehensive retail	2407429	1325291	767026	143470
食品、饮料及烟草制品专门零售	Food, drink and tobacco retail	14789	13007		
纺织、服装及日用品专门零售	Special retail textile, clothing and daily necessities	5281	5281		
文化、体育用品及器材专门零售	Cultural and sports supplies and equipment retail	26008	18319	10226	
医药及医疗器材专门零售	Pharmaceutical and medical equipment	537327	535099	101994	210917
汽车、摩托车、燃料及零配件专门零售	Automobiles, motorcycles, fuel and spare parts	1916697	1124213	673059	
家用电器及电子产品专门零售	Household appliances and electronic products retail	656589	471078	409183	
按业态分	By Format				
便利店	Neighbourhood Market	44549	44549	13254	
超市	Supermarker	521652	353216	5634	5001
大型超市	large supermarket	1730829	857671	679857	138469
百货店	Department Store	100091	59546	57972	
专业店	Professional Shop	4950987	2774301	1652967	210917
其中：加油站	Gas station	3806685	1825859	1193723	
专卖店	Regie Shop	46449	45478		
住宿和餐饮业	**Hotels and Catering**	**46654**	**33356**		**13**
按登记注册类型分	By Status of Registration				
内资企业	Domestic Funded Enterprises	19091	5793		13
有限责任公司	Limited Liability Corporations	12586	169		
私营企业	Private	6506	5625		13
私营独资企业	proprietorship	406			
私营有限责任公司	Limited Liability Corporations	6100	5625		13
港、澳、台商投资企业	Enterprises with Funds from Hong Kong, Macao and Taiwan				
外商投资企业	Foreign Funded	27562	27562		
按国民经济行业分	By Sector				
住宿业	Hotels	22	21		13
旅游饭店	Tourist hotel				
一般旅馆	General hotel				
其他住宿业	Others	13	13		13
餐饮业	Catering Services	46632	33335		
正餐服务	Restaurant	7238	5773		
快餐服务	Fast food	38725	27562		
小吃服务	Snack	670			

16-24 各种分组的住宿餐饮业连锁企业主要指标(2019年)

Main Indicators of Chain Hotels and Catering Services Enterprise By variety of Group (2019)

指标名称	Item	客房数(间) Number of Rooms (unit)	床位数(个) Number of Beds (unit)	餐位数(位) Numbers of Seats in Restaurant (unit)	营业额(万元) Bussiness revinue (10 000yuan)	餐费收入(万元) From Meals (10 000yuan)
总　计	**Total**	**1230**	**2880**	**46674**	**142466**	**135041**
按登记注册类型分	By Status of Registration					
内资企业	Domestic Funded Enterprises	1230	2880	27664	54302	46878
有限责任公司	Limited Liability Corporations	1000	2500	21862	41840	34737
私营企业	Private	230	380	5802	12462	12141
私营独资企业	proprietorship			102	876	876
私营有限责任公司	Limited Liability Corporations	230	380	5700	11586	11265
港、澳、台商投资企业	Enterprises with Funds from Hong Kong, Macao and Taiwan					
外商投资企业	Foreign Funded			19010	88163	88163
按国民经济行业分	By Sector					
住宿业	Hotels	1230	2880	250	4598	2
旅游饭店	Tourist hotel					
一般旅馆	General hotel					
其他住宿业	Others	230	380		321	
餐饮业	Catering Services			46424	137868	135039
正餐服务	Restaurant			7554	13486	13486
快餐服务	Fast food			38170	123517	120688
小吃服务	Snack			700	865	865

16−25 亿元以上商品交易市场情况

Statistics on Commodity Exchange Market of Turnover above 100 million yuan

类别	Type	2018		2019	
		摊位数量（个）Number of Booths (unit)	成交额（亿元）Total Turnover (100 million yuan)	摊位数量（个）Number of Booths (unit)	成交额（亿元）Total Turnover (100 million yuan)
总计	**Total**	**105144**	**2680.75**	**105670**	**3231.57**
粮油、食品类	Food	31564	1625.21	31607	1875.56
#粮油类	Grain,Edible Oil, Fruits, Vegetables	3383	257.78	3588	323.02
肉禽蛋类	Meat, Poultry and Eggs	2619	160.27	2393	119.80
水产品类	Aquatic Products	4229	348.92	4522	422.46
蔬菜类	Vegetables	9087	326.45	8570	365.62
干鲜果品类	Dried and Fresh Melons and Fruits	4842	294.03	5211	376.13
饮料类	Beverages	2844	108.67	2801	107.26
烟酒类	Tobacco and Liquor	1664	26.49	1807	30.29
服装、鞋帽、针纺织品类	Garments,Footwears, Hats, Kintwear and Textiles	30657	265.31	29805	268.45
服装类	Clothing	18905	169.94	18045	166.99
鞋帽类	Shoes and Hats	6566	67.60	6701	81.12
针纺织品类	Knitwear and Textiles	5186	27.77	5059	20.33
化妆品类	Cosmetics	1006	11.66	985	11.92
金银珠宝类	Gold,Silver and Fewelry	350	9.71	335	6.55
日用品类	Articles for Daily Use	6558	21.19	6651	21.97
其中：可穿戴智能设备	Childern toys	584	2.54	556	2.23
五金、电料类	Hardware and Electrical Materials	4347	31.05	5177	34.42
体育、娱乐用品类	Sports & Recreation Articles	1026	5.09	658	2.06
书报杂志类	Newspapers and Magazines	465	1.99	45	0.16
电子出版物及音像制品类	E-journals and Video Products	436	2.41	55	0.70
家用电器和音像器材类	Household Appliances and Video Appliances	2137	50.22	1879	27.80
中西药品类	Traditional Chinese and Western Medicines	968	43.28	584	27.11
#西药类	Western Medicines	61	0.43	64	0.48
中草药及中成药类	Traditional Chinese l Medicines	892	42.72	492	26.45
文化办公用品类	Cultural and Official Appliances	3949	39.65	3972	39.89
家具类	Furniture	2105	57.96	1776	29.22
通讯器材类	Communication Appliances	367	34.54	257	1.70
煤炭及制品类	Coal and Related Products	9	0.01		
木材及制品类	Wood and Wooden Products	538	19.59	6	0.02
石油及制品类	Petroleum and Related Products	920	14.36		
化工材料及制品类	Chemical Materials and Related Products	356	1.89	532	2.32
#化肥类	Fertilizers	60	0.81	60	0.96
金属材料类	Metals Materials	3856	500.91	2161	443.32
建筑及装潢材料类	Building and Decoration Materials	8276	199.11	8757	147.14
机电产品及设备类	Mechanical & Electrical Products	1391	10.80	1529	11.38
#农机类	Agricultural Machineries	22	0.27	23	0.28
汽车类	Automobiles	1627	126.82	690	103.29
种子饲料类	Seeds and Feedstuff	92	0.24	70	0.28
棉麻类	Cotton and Hemp	11	0.01	142	0.06
其他类	Others	4709	72.61	3389	38.71

16-26 各市亿元以上商品交易市场情况

Statistics on Commodity Exchange Market of Turnover above 100 million yuan by City

市(县)	City(County)	2018 摊位数量(个) Number of Booths (unit)	2018 成交额(亿元) Total Turnover (100 million yuan)	2019 摊位数量(个) Number of Booths (unit)	2019 成交额(亿元) Total Turnover (100 million yuan)
省辖市	**City**				
郑州市	Zhengzhou	33065	1118.77	32470	1288.42
开封市	Kaifeng	1215	10.43	1561	12.47
洛阳市	Luoyang	12050	381.06	8500	313.94
平顶山市	Pingdingshan	1601	17.92	1694	26.79
安阳市	Anyang	468	13.76	530	9.82
鹤壁市	Hebi	336	19.70	349	19.99
新乡市	Xinxiang	3520	47.90	5178	66.66
焦作市	Jiaozuo	1919	20.95	1794	19.01
濮阳市	Puyang				
许昌市	Xuchang	1769	93.88	3357	323.43
漯河市	Luohe	4509	28.38	4509	28.64
三门峡市	Sanmenxia	253	7.52	70	6.53
南阳市	Nanyang	10663	120.49	11222	267.81
商丘市	Shangqiu	14467	518.58	14116	525.16
信阳市	Xinyang	6091	39.11	6416	43.87
周口市	Zhoukou	4347	115.10	4555	137.70
驻马店市	Zhumadian	6082	113.19	6437	123.41
济源市	Jiyuan	2789	14.01	2912	17.92
省直管县	**County Directly Administrated by Province**				
巩义市	Gongyi				
兰考县	Lankao				
汝州市	Ruzhou			43	7.63
滑县	Huaxian				
长垣市	Changyuan				
邓州市	Dengzhou	2478	32.53	2483	32.86
永城市	Yongcheng	1004	11.62	1004	10.58
固始县	Gushi	3940	6.96	4265	7.78
鹿邑县	Luyi				
新蔡县	Xincai	484	5.66	484	5.95

16-27 按行业分企业信息化及电子商务情况（2019）
Informationization and E-commerce Situation by Sector (2019)

行业	Sector	企业个数（个）Number of Enterprises (unit)	期末使用计算机数（台）Number of Computers in Use at Year-end (set)	每百人使用计算机数（台）Number of Computers in Use Per 100 People (unit)	企业拥有网站数（个）Number of Websites Owned by Enterprises (unit)
总计	**Total**	**54474**	**1721642**	**19**	**24458**
采矿业	Mining	490	76316	21	169
制造业	Manufacturing	17376	521878	13	10824
电力、热力、燃气及水生产和供应业	Production and Supply of Electricity, Gas and Water	565	91721	40	270
建筑业	Construction	7836	203448	10	2976
批发和零售业	Wholesale and Retail Trade	10588	196163	36	3444
交通运输、仓储和邮政业	Transport, Storage and Post	2031	63973	18	594
住宿和餐饮业	Hotels and Catering Services	2437	31326	23	823
信息传输、软件和信息技术	Information Transmission, Software and	629	175622	110	516
房地产业	Real Estate	7741	122365	34	2627
租赁和商务服务业	Leasing and Business Services	1359	39170	14	559
科学研究和技术服务业	Scientific Research and Technical Services	925	82253	69	549
水利、环境和公共设施管理业	Management of Water Conservancy, Environment and Public Facilities	375	7825	9	176
居民服务、修理和其他服务业	Services to Households, Repair and Other Services	439	3322	7	124
教育	Education	716	50958	61	310
卫生和社会工作	Health and Social Service	469	39229	48	309
文化、体育和娱乐业	Culture, Sports and Entertainment	498	16073	43	188

注：有电子商务交易活动的企业是指通过互联网开展电子商务销售或电子商务采购的企业(下表同)。

a) Enterprises with e-commerce transaction activities refer to enterprises that carry out e-commerce sales or e-commerce procurement through the Internet (the same as the table below).

16-27 续表 continued

行业	Sector	每百家企业拥有网站数(个) Number of Websites Owned Per 100 Enterprises (unit)	有电子商务交易活动 E-commerce Transactions		电子商务销售额(亿元) Sales of E-commerce (100 million yuan)	电子商务采购额(亿元) Purchase Amount of E-commerce (100 million yuan)
			企业数(个) Number of Enterprises (unit)	比重(%) Proportion (%)		
总计	**Total**	**45**	**3831**	**7.0**	**4262.26**	**2460.14**
采矿业	Mining	34	16	3.3	16.23	34.10
制造业	Manufacturing	62	1142	6.6	2161.90	1156.73
电力、热力、燃气及水生产和供应业	Production and Supply of Electricity, Gas and Water	48	34	6.0	2.09	21.03
建筑业	Construction	38	334	4.3	2.57	150.78
批发和零售业	Wholesale and Retail Trade	33	1047	9.9	1702.32	946.08
交通运输、仓储和邮政业	Transport, Storage and Post	29	81	4.0	25.80	7.33
住宿和餐饮业	Hotels and Catering Services	34	498	20.4	14.44	0.42
信息传输、软件和信息技术	Information Transmission, Software and	82	156	24.8	316.09	13.63
房地产业	Real Estate	34	173	2.2	0.51	0.75
租赁和商务服务业	Leasing and Business Services	41	94	6.9	3.19	92.40
科学研究和技术服务业	Scientific Research and Technical Services	59	74	8.0	6.32	36.33
水利、环境和公共设施管理业	Management of Water Conservancy, Environment and Public Facilities	47	46	12.3	2.70	0.08
居民服务、修理和其他服务业	Services to Households, Repair and Other Services	28	22	5.0	0.19	0.08
教育	Education	43	17	2.4	3.42	0.05
卫生和社会工作	Health and Social Service	66	21	4.5	0.10	0.11
文化、体育和娱乐业	Culture, Sports and Entertainment	38	76	15.3	4.39	0.23

注：有电子商务交易活动的企业是指通过互联网开展电子商务销售或电子商务采购的企业（下表同）。

a) Enterprises with e-commerce transaction activities refer to enterprises that carry out e-commerce sales or e-commerce procurement through the Internet (the same as the table below).

16-28 按地区分企业信息化及电子商务情况(2019)

Informationization and E-commerce Situation by Region (2019)

地区 Region	企业个数(个) Number of Enterprises (unit)	期末使用计算机数(台) Number of Computers in Use at Year-end (set)	每百人使用计算机数(台) Number of Computers in Use Per 100 People (unit)	企业拥有网站数(个) Number of Websites Owned by Enterprises (unit)	每百家企业拥有网站数(个) Number of Websites Owned Per 100 Enterprises (unit)	有电子商务交易活动 E-commerce Transactions 企业数(个) Number of Enterprises (unit)	比重(%) Proportion (%)	电子商务销售额(亿元) Sales of E-commerce (100 million yuan)	电子商务采购额(亿元) Purchase Amount of E-commerce (100 million yuan)
全　省 Total	**54474**	**1721638**	**18.4**	**24457**	**45**	**3831**	**7.0**	**4262.26**	**2460.14**
省辖市 City									
郑州市 Zhengzhou	10484	636176	30.8	6969	66	1385	13.2	1703.36	811.47
开封市 Kaifeng	2421	47948	12.5	994	41	135	5.6	65.87	30.61
洛阳市 Luoyang	4471	187143	28.9	2024	45	281	6.3	367.19	280.86
平顶山市 Pingdingshan	2576	77576	18.6	851	33	135	5.2	90.00	53.58
安阳市 Anyang	1987	60370	12.7	981	49	117	5.9	81.25	53.16
鹤壁市 Hebi	892	32815	19.0	452	51	43	4.8	60.96	48.38
新乡市 Xinxiang	3497	96010	18.7	1945	56	228	6.5	111.35	51.01
焦作市 Jiaozuo	2367	59740	14.1	952	40	136	5.7	187.06	142.33
濮阳市 Puyang	1587	62050	24.2	754	48	88	5.5	58.85	49.62
许昌市 Xuchang	3093	66698	13.7	998	32	181	5.9	55.85	41.25
漯河市 Luohe	1254	29384	11.9	520	41	80	6.4	656.41	447.24
三门峡市 Sanmenxia	1292	40558	22.9	421	33	119	9.2	242.15	85.58
南阳市 Nanyang	4114	91146	17.3	1546	38	225	5.5	131.41	97.66
商丘市 Shangqiu	3532	59792	8.1	1288	36	190	5.4	121.44	68.91
信阳市 Xinyang	3441	56759	11.1	1206	35	221	6.4	96.39	51.08
周口市 Zhoukou	3751	52212	7.2	1237	33	121	3.2	100.06	53.72
驻马店市 Zhumadian	3116	45681	9.5	1054	34	108	3.5	120.80	44.46
济源市 Jiyuan	599	19580	20.2	265	44	38	6.3	11.86	49.22
省直管县 County Directly Administrated by Province									
巩义市 Gongyi	727	16242	17.4	433	59	52	7.1	7.29	0.48
兰考县 Lankao	569	6179	8.5	226	40	61	10.7	1.65	0.23
汝州市 Ruzhou	511	7053	12.5	171	33	30	5.9	14.93	0.11
滑县 Huaxian	456	5787	11.0	201	44	21	4.6	0.29	0.02
长垣市 Changyuan	781	21447	16.2	485	62	39	5.0	2.41	0.14
邓州市 Dengzhou	486	5441	12.1	125	26	23	4.7	0.27	0.15
永城市 Yongcheng	534	11973	11.9	164	31	39	7.3	0.49	15.96
固始县 Gushi	622	7479	10.1	187	30	29	4.6	0.63	0.49
鹿邑县 Luyi	627	5772	8.2	153	24	16	2.6	0.61	0.05
新蔡县 Xincai	498	3164	8.1	142	29	10	2.0	0.89	0.00

主要统计指标解释

社会消费品零售总额 指企业（单位、个体户）通过交易直接售给个人、社会集团非生产、非经营用的实物商品金额，以及提供餐饮服务所取得的收入金额。个人包括城乡居民和入境人员，社会集团包括机关、社会团体、部队、学校、企事业单位、居委会或村委会等。

批发业 指向其他批发或零售单位（含个体经营者）及其他企事业单位、机关团体等批量销售生活用品、生产资料的活动，以及从事进出口贸易和贸易经纪与代理的活动，包括拥有货物所有权，并以本单位(公司)的名义进行交易活动,也包括不拥有货物的所有权，收取佣金的商品代理、商品代售活动；还包括各类商品批发市场中固定摊位的批发活动，以及以销售为目的的收购活动。

零售业 指百货商店、超级市场、专门零售商店、品牌专卖店、售货摊等主要面向最终消费者（如居民等）的销售活动，以互联网、邮政、电话、售货机等方式的销售活动，还包括在同一地点，后面加工生产，前面销售的店铺（如面包房）；谷物、种子、饲料、牲畜、矿产品、生产用原料、化工原料、农用化工产品、机械设备（乘用车、计算机及通信设备除外）等生产资料的销售不作为零售活动；多数零售商对其销售的货物拥有所有权，但有些则是充当委托人的代理人，进行委托销售或以收取佣金的方式进行销售。

批发和零售业商品购进、销售、库存额 指各种登记注册类型的批发和零售业企业(单位)以本企业（单位）为总体的，从国内、国外市场购进的商品总价，销售和出口的商品总价，库存的商品总价等情况。该指标可以反映商品流转过程中商品的购进、销售、库存之间的比例关系和存在的问题。

商品购进额 指从本企业以外的单位和个人购进（包括从国外直接进口）作为转卖或加工后转卖的商品金额（含增值税）。商品购进包括：(1）从工农业生产者、批发和零售业、住宿和餐饮业、出版社或报社的出版发行部门和其他服务业等企事业单位和个体经营户购进的商品；(2）从机关、社会团体购进的商品；(3）从海关、市场管理部门购进的缉私和没收的商品；(4）从居民收购的废旧商品等。不包括：(1）企业为本单位自身经营用，不是作为转卖而购进的商品，如材料物资、包装物、低值易耗品、办公用品等；(2）未通过买卖行为而收入的商品，如接受其他部门移交的商品、借入的商品、收入代其他单位保管的商品、其他单位赠送的样品、加工回收的成品等；(3）经本单位介绍，由买卖双方直接结算，本单位只收取手续费的业务；(4）销售退回和买方拒付货款的商品；(5）商品溢余；(6）期货交易商品。

商品销售额 指对本单位以外的单位和个人出售的商品金额（包括售给本单位消费用的商品，含增值税）。商品销售包括（1）售给城乡居民和社会集团消费用的商品；(2）售给农业、工业、建筑业、服务业等国民经济各行业用于生产、经营用的商品，包括售予批发和零售业作为转卖或加工后转卖的商品；(3）对国（境）外直接出口的商品。不包括：(1）未通过买卖行为付出的商品，如随机构变动移交给其他企业单位的商品、借出的商品、归还受其他单位委托代保管的商品、付出的加工原料和赠送给其他单位的样品等；(2）经本单位介绍，由买卖双方直接结算，本单位只收取手续费的业务；(3）购货退回的商品；(4）商品损耗和损失；(5）出售本单位自用的废旧物资。

商品库存额 对于批发和零售业法人单位和个体经营户，是指报告期末取得所有权的全部商品金额（含增值税）；对于批发和零售业产业活动单位，是指报告期末实际在库且归属法人具有所有权的全部商品金额（含增值税）。库存商品包括：(1)存放在本单位（如门市部、批发站、采购站、经营处）的仓库、货场、货柜和货架中的商品；(2)挑选、整理、包装中的商品；(3)已记入购进而尚未运到本单位的商品，即发货单或银行承兑凭证已到而货未到的商品；(4)寄放他处的商品，如因购货方拒绝付款而暂时存在购货方的商品；(5)委托其他单位代销（未作销售或调出）尚未售出的商品；(6)代其他单位购进尚未交付的商品。不包括：所有权不属于本单位的商品；委托外单位加工的商品；外贸企业代理其他单位从国外进口，尚未付给订货单位的商品；代国家储备部门保管的商品。

连锁总店（总部） 指负责连锁企业资源（商号、商誉、经营模式、服务标准、管理模式等等）的开发、配置、控制或使用等功能的企业核心管理机构。连锁经营是指经营同类商品或服务，使用统一商号的若干店铺，在同一总店（总部）的管理下，采取统一采购或特许经营等方式，实现规模效益的组织形式，包括直营连锁、特许连锁和自愿连锁三种形式。其中，直营连锁是指连锁店铺由连锁公司全资或控股开设，在总部的直接控制下，开展统一经营的连锁经营形式；特许连锁是指拥有注册商标、企业标志、专利、专有技术等经营资源的企业（特许人），以合同形式将其拥有的经营资源许可其他经营者（被特许人）使用，被特许人按合同约定在统一的经营模式下开展经营，并向特许人支付特许经营费用的连锁经营形式；自愿连锁是指若干个店铺或企业自愿组合起来，在不改变各自资产所有权关系的情况下，以同一个品牌形象面对消费者，以共同进货为纽带开展的连锁经营形式。

亿元以上商品交易市场 指年成交额在亿元及以上的商品交易市场。商品交易市场是指经有关部门和组织批准设立，有固定场所、设施，有经营管理部门和监管人员，若干市场经营者入内，常年或实际开业三个月以上，集中、公开、独立地进行生活消费品、生产资料等现货商品交易以及提供相关服务的交易场所，包括各类消费品市场、生产资料市场等。

住宿业 指为旅行者提供短期留宿场所的活动，有些单位只提供住宿，也有些单位提供住宿、饮食、商务、娱乐一体的服务，不包括主要按月或按年长期出租房屋住所的活动。

餐饮业 指通过即时制作加工、商业销售和服务性劳动等，向消费者提供食品和消费场所及设施的服务。

营业额 指住宿和餐饮业单位在经营活动中因提供服务或销售商品等取得的收入。包括：客房收入、餐费收入、商品销售额（含增值税）和其他收入。其中，客房收入指住宿和餐饮业单位在经营活动中因提供住宿服务取得的收入。餐费收入指本单位为顾客提供就餐服务取得的收入，包括：经烹饪、调制加工后出售的各种食品，如主食、炒菜、凉拌菜等的收入。

Explanatory Notes on Main Statistical Indicators

Total Retail Sales of Consumer Goods refer to the amount obtained by enterprises (units, self-employed individuals) through direct sales of non-production and non-business physical commodity to individuals, social institutions, and revenue from providing catering services. Individuals include rural and urban households, population from abroad, social institutions include government agencies, social organizations, military units, schools, institutions, neighbourhood (village) committees.

Wholesale Trade refers to the activities of selling wholesale commodities for daily use and capital goods to enterprises of wholesale and retail trades (including self-employed individuals) and other enterprises, institutions and government organs and organizations, and the activities of engaging in import and export and acting as a trade agent. The wholesaler may have the ownership of the commodities for wholesale and trade in the name of its own (a company), and the wholesaler can act as commission agent or commodity broker without the ownership of commodities. Also included are the wholesale activities at the fixed stalls in wholesale market and the acquisition for sales purpose.

Retail Trade refers to the activities of department store, supermarket, franchised store, brand store, retail stall and on-the-spot-making-selling store selling commodities to the final consumers (residents) by any means including internet, post, telephone, sales machine. It also includes shops with sales and production localted in the same places (such as bakeries). Retail trade excludes the activities of sales of capital goods such as grain, seed, feed, livestock, mineral products, raw material for production, industrial chemicals, chemical products for agricultural use, machine and equipment (excluding vehicles, computers and communication equipment). Most retailers have the ownership of commodities to sell, but some are acting as agents or brokers to make transactions for a commission.

Purchase, Sales and Stock of Commodities by Wholesale and Retail Trades refer to the total volume of commodities purchased, total volume of sales and exports, and the stock of commodities by wholesale and retail enterprises (establishments) of different status of registration from domestic and overseas markets. This indicator reflects the relationship among purchase, sales and stock of commodities in the circulation of goods and reveals the existing problems.

Total Purchases of Commodities refer to the total value of purchases of commodities by enterprises (establishments) from other establishments or individuals (including direct import from abroad) for the purpose of re-selling, either with or without further processing of the commodities purchased. The commodities include: (1) commodities purchased from agricultural and industrial producer, wholesaler, retailer, publishing house and other enterprises, institutions and individual operators of service business; (2) commodities purchased from institutions and government departments; (3) confiscated goods purchased from the customs authorities or market management agencies; (4) second-hand goods and wastes purchased from residents; The commodities exclude (1) commodities purchased by enterprises (establishments) for use in their own business operation, commodities obtained without buying or selling procedures such as materials, consumable goods of low value, office appliance, etc. (2) received goods without trading, such as goods handed over from others, borrowed goods, preserved goods for others, donated goods from others, processed and retrieved goods, etc. (3) goods of direct settlement between buyer and seller with handling fees introduced by others, (4) goods returned or refused to pay by the buyer, (5) excessive goods, (6) futures trading commodities.

Total Sales of Commodities refer to value of commodities sold by the establishments to other establishments and individuals (including goods sold for self consumption, including the value-added tax). The commodities include: (1) commodities sold to urban and rural residents and social groups for their consumption; (2) commodities sold to establishments in all industries for their production and operation, including agriculture, industry, construction, and catering services including commodities sold to wholesale and retail establishments for re-selling, with or without further processing; and (3) commodities for direct export to abroad. Excluded are (1) extended commodities without trading, such as goods handed over to other enterprises and institutions because of the change of organizations, lent goods, returned goods preserved for others, extended processing materials and samples donated to others, (2) goods of direct settlement between buyer and seller with handling fees introduced by others, (3) goods returned after purchase, (4) damaged and spoiled goods, (5) waste and used goods of self use,

Total Stock of Commodities For the legal entities and self-employed individuals engaged in wholesale and retail trade, it refers to total value (including VAT) of commodities possessed at the end of the reference period; and for wholesale and retail establishments, it refers to the value (including VAT) of all commodities actually in stock and owned by their legal persons at the end of reference period. The commodities in stock includes: (1) commodities located in storage, garages, counters, and shelves of operating places of wholesale and retail trades (such as sale stores, wholesale centres, procurement stations and operating offices); (2) commodities in the process of being selected, sorted, and packed; (3) commodities not arrived but recorded as purchase in the account, i.e. commodities not arrived but payment receipts for the commodities from the sellers or the banks arrived; (4) commodities deposited in other places rather than places mentioned above, for instance: commodities in the hold of purchasers temporarily due to the refusal of payment; (5) commodities entrusted to other units to sell but not sold yet; (6) commodities purchased for other units but not delivered yet. Commodities not included as stock are those not owned by the enterprises (units), commodities on commission for processing, imported commodities of agency of foreign trade enterprise but not yet delivered to ordering units and finally those put in stock on behalf of the state reserves units.

Chain Head Stores (headquarter) refer to the core leading stores responsible for development, allocation, administration and utilization of resources (name of stores, brand of stores, operation model, service standard, management way, etc.) of chain stores. Chain stores refers to the stores engaged in providing homogeneous commodities or services, with the central leadership of head store (headquarters) and guided by common policies, conduct centralized purchase and distributed selling of commodities, in order to gain better efficiency through standardized operation. The chain stores include regular chain stores, franchise chain stores and voluntary chain stores.

Regular Chain store refers to chain stores that are invested or controlled by the headquarters. They operate under direct and unified management from the headquarters.

Franchise chain store refers to the chain stores (franchisees) which are franchised with operation resources such as trade marks, names, patent and operation know-how by the franchisors in form of contract and pay the operation fees to the franchisors.

Voluntary chain store refers to the stores operate jointly on the voluntary bases while maintaining their status of independent legal entities with full ownership of their assets. They sell goods of same brand from same channel of resource to the consumers.

Large Commodity Markets with Transaction Value over 100 Million Yuan refers to the commodity markets with an annual transaction at and above 100 million. The commodity market refers to the markets approved and managed by related departments, where there are fixed sites, facilities, managers and administration offices, where there are a certain number of traders to operate for three month and above or all the year, where the commodities including the articles for daily consumption and capital goods and services are traded in a centralized, independent and open way. Such market includes markets of daily goods and market of capital goods, etc.

Hotel Services refer to the accommodation services provided to visitors. Some units may provide only accommodation while others provide a combination of accommodation, meals, business services and/or recreational facilities. It excludes activities related to the provision of long-term primary residences in facilities such as apartments typically leased on a monthly or annual basis.

Catering Services refer to the activities of providing foods, serving locations and facilities to customers through instant processing, commercial sales and service-type labor.

Business Revenue refers to revenue of hotels and catering services received from providing services or selling commodities through business activities, including income from hotels, from catering services, from selling of commodities (including VAT) and from other services. Income from hotels refers to income of hotels and catering services by providing lodging services through business activities. Income from catering services refers to income from providing catering services, including selling of cooked or prepared foods, such as staple food, cooked dishes, or cold dishes.

金融业
Financial Intermediation

17

◉ 资料整理：赵国顺

简要说明

一、主要内容

本篇包括金融机构、证券业、保险业和国债发行情况资料。

二、资料来源

金融机构和国债发行情况资料来源于中国人民银行郑州中心支行。证券业资料来源于河南证监局。保险业资料来源于河南保监局。本篇资料由河南省统计局国民经济核算处编辑整理。

Brief Introduction

I. Main Contents

Data in this chapter including four aspects: the financial activities of the financial institutions; the situations of the securities industry; the situation regarding the insurance business and the situation regarding the issuance of treasury bonds.

II. Sources of Data

Data on financial institutions and issuance of treasury bonds are calculated from The People's Bank of China and Zhengzhou Central Sub-branch. Data on securities industry are calculated from Henan provincial Securities Regulatory Commission. Data on insurance business are calculated from Henan provincial Insurance Regulatory. Data on this chapter are provided of Department of National Accounts of the Henan provincial Bureau of Statistics.

17-1 金融机构和保险业主要指标

Main Indicators of Financial Institutions and Insurance

单位：亿元 (100 million yuan)

Year	金融机构人民币存款年底余额 Total Saving Deposit Balance	金融机构人民币贷款年底余额 Total Loan Balance	#短期 Short-term	#中长期 Medium-term & Long-term	保险公司保费收入 Premium Income of Insarance Companies	保险公司赔款及给付 Claim & Payment of Insarance Companies
1978	45.71	99.99				
1979	52.00	108.14				
1980	57.77	125.01				
1981	68.45	146.42				
1982	74.08	153.73				
1983	88.10	174.83				
1984	136.84	229.88				
1985	146.42	284.91				
1986	184.66	350.21				
1987	231.71	392.32				
1988	270.67	447.99				
1989	329.01	511.90				
1990	593.96	773.04			6.57	3.18
1991	754.03	945.90			8.47	4.49
1992	936.04	1127.26			13.65	5.46
1993	1143.66	1366.98			18.48	7.55
1994	1602.95	1704.82			21.03	11.89
1995	2131.69	2170.17			25.57	11.47
1996	2707.65	2665.41			26.87	15.23
1997	3271.76	3320.89			34.84	16.02
1998	3772.51	3878.53			44.92	17.78
1999	4198.10	4179.51			47.89	15.83
2000	4753.41	4356.94	3114.58	1057.50	55.77	17.30
2001	5530.16	4885.73	3336.16	1447.99	69.57	21.85
2002	6451.59	5553.58	3673.39	1702.63	126.22	22.68
2003	7618.03	6422.66	4025.08	2138.16	162.98	27.53
2004	8631.79	7092.31	4200.53	2487.19	202.05	33.84
2005	10003.96	7434.53	4088.16	2736.63	213.55	38.16
2006	11492.55	8567.33	4731.54	3259.90	252.31	50.98
2007	12576.42	9545.48	5213.08	3800.96	323.56	100.88
2008	15255.42	10368.05	5180.84	4302.41	518.92	128.77
2009	19175.06	13437.43	6016.17	6066.05	565.39	148.23
2010	23148.83	15871.32	6995.81	7806.31	793.28	153.91
2011	26646.15	17506.24	8273.66	8690.17	839.82	171.14
2012	31970.43	20301.72	9977.52	9608.35	841.13	199.55
2013	37591.70	23511.41	11823.35	11029.60	916.52	279.75
2014	41374.91	27228.27	12801.98	13625.90	1036.08	324.03
2015	47629.91	31432.62	13763.71	16416.30	1248.76	447.71
2016	53977.62	36501.17	14253.21	20570.22	1555.15	548.03
2017	59068.66	41743.31	14528.69	25748.37	2020.07	625.86
2018	63867.63	47834.76	15267.62	30454.25	2262.85	654.75
2019	69508.66	55659.00	16672.11	36230.33	2430.84	668.59

注：各项存款、贷款年底余额1989年及以前为国家银行口径，1990年以后为金融机构口径。

a) The balance of Deposits and loans before 1998 are measured by statistics of state-owned banks, otherwise, after 1990, they are evaluated by data from financial institutions.

17-2 金融机构人民币存贷款情况
Deposits and Loans of Financial Institutions

单位：亿元 (100 million yuan)

项目	Item	2018	2019
各项存款	**Deposits**	**63867.63**	**69508.66**
境内存款	Domestic Savings	63854.56	69493.36
住户存款	Household Savings	36092.63	40513.55
非金融企业存款	Non-financial Corporate Deposits	16188.78	16904.34
广义政府存款	General Government Deposits	9084.53	9365.10
非银行业金融机构存款	Non-banking Financial Institutions Deposits	2488.62	2710.37
境外存款	Overseas Deposits	13.07	15.30
各项贷款	**Loans**	**47834.76**	**55659.00**
境内贷款	Domestic Loans	47829.40	55654.44
住户贷款	Households Loans	18145.41	22156.90
短期贷款	Short-term Loans	3726.12	4355.19
中长期贷款	Medium and Long-term Loans	14419.28	17801.71
非金融企业及机关团体贷款	Non-financial Companies and Organizations Loans	29684.00	33495.54
境外贷款	Foreign Loans	5.36	4.56

17-3 各类银行人民币存贷款情况（2019年）
Deposits and Loans of Financial Institutions (2019)

单位：亿元 (100 million yuan)

项目	Item	大型银行 Large Banks	中小型银行 Small and Medium Banks	区域性中小型银行 Urban Commercial Banks	农村信用社 Rural Credit Cooperatives
各项存款	**Deposits**	**33436.81**	**8826.33**	**22895.53**	**3288.10**
境内存款	Domestic Savings	33424.36	8823.66	22895.36	3288.10
个人存款	Individual Deposit	22117.11	1807.44	13692.91	2894.53
单位存款	Unit Deposit	10782.70	6445.17	7510.10	393.58
国库定期存款	Treasury deposit	0.03			
非存款类金融机构存款	Financial Institutions Deposits	524.51	571.05	1692.35	
境外存款	Overseas Deposits	12.45	2.67	0.16	
各项贷款	**Loans**	**26099.07**	**11627.81**	**15240.09**	**1953.95**
境内贷款	Domestic Loans	26098.61	11624.55	15239.26	1953.95
短期贷款	Short-term Loans	4357.20	4859.48	6822.57	637.64
#个人贷款及透支	Personal Loans and Overdrafts	1471.73	628.84	1975.53	278.94
#个人消费贷款	Personal Consumption Loans	1143.82	404.87	426.11	41.07
单位贷款及透支	Unit Loans and Overdrafts	2885.47	4230.64	4594.42	358.70
中长期贷款	Medium-term & Long-term Loans	20899.95	6182.03	7502.40	1304.88
个人贷款	Personal Loan	10584.50	3019.59	3626.45	569.18
#个人消费贷款	Personal Consumption Loans	10065.96	2599.53	2299.55	267.15
单位贷款	Unit Loans	10315.45	3162.44	3868.54	735.70
票据融资	Bill Financing	836.77	575.37	876.70	11.42
融资租赁	Financing Lease				
各项垫款	Advance Payment	4.70	7.67	37.58	
境外贷款	Foreign Loans	0.46	3.27	0.83	

17-4 各市金融机构贷款年底余额
Loans of Financial Institutions by City

单位：亿元 (100 million yuan)

市(县)	City(County)	2018	#短期 Short-term	#中长期 Medium-term & Long-term	2019	#短期 Short-term	#中长期 Medium-term & Long-term
省辖市	**City**						
郑州市	Zhengzhou	21202.24	4599.79	15820.67	25364.33	5372.89	18809.25
开封市	Kaifeng	1498.76	479.61	991.31	1704.45	502.20	1176.77
洛阳市	Luoyang	4072.46	1648.91	1916.00	4852.50	1889.10	2359.38
平顶山市	Pingdingshan	1868.66	852.07	811.60	2070.33	904.32	922.08
安阳市	Anyang	1463.66	511.50	845.15	1672.01	521.65	1021.64
鹤壁市	Hebi	610.01	258.90	347.89	649.48	287.78	357.97
新乡市	Xinxiang	1726.90	590.47	1102.58	2027.78	655.99	1321.12
焦作市	Jiaozuo	1353.45	539.90	744.82	1515.27	511.18	900.26
濮阳市	Puyang	862.88	258.90	586.19	1022.43	278.58	716.22
许昌市	Xuchang	1748.15	806.13	913.99	1992.90	834.27	1111.55
漯河市	Luohe	795.35	375.18	396.32	908.89	362.78	519.38
三门峡市	Sanmenxia	808.35	361.88	393.78	840.17	373.96	443.54
南阳市	Nanyang	2344.21	1112.28	1159.45	2643.84	1104.51	1434.60
商丘市	Shangqiu	1620.31	674.44	913.51	1980.67	805.19	1138.75
信阳市	Xinyang	1722.34	701.27	1009.93	1908.58	696.03	1193.74
周口市	Zhoukou	1237.49	527.00	687.98	1502.06	512.96	976.22
驻马店市	Zhumadian	1635.17	633.81	994.13	1716.02	620.76	1090.18
济源市	Jiyuan	285.80	139.71	109.37	327.27	161.31	126.47
省直管县	**County Directly Administrated by Province**						
巩义市	Gongyi	267.20	102.89	148.59	278.94	96.27	161.87
兰考县	Lankao	180.52	52.61	127.19	210.70	54.43	151.41
汝州市	Ruzhou	237.52	122.75	114.76	261.84	118.80	141.82
滑县	Huaxian	139.83	37.32	99.61	169.59	37.32	120.92
长垣县	Changyuan	219.14	75.49	143.59	241.52	71.31	170.21
邓州市	Dengzhou	211.37	119.70	90.61	257.32	132.13	113.74
永城市	Yongcheng	292.01	177.53	110.81	339.52	212.11	122.37
固始县	Gushi	187.54	98.78	88.76	208.97	97.39	111.58
鹿邑县	Luyi	133.74	47.20	86.54	151.07	36.38	114.49
新蔡县	Xincai	119.27	66.03	53.24	157.86	83.16	74.70

17-5 个人贷款总额
Total Amount of Personal Loans

单位：亿元 (100 million yuan)

指标	Indicators	2005	2010	2015	2017	2018	2019
个人贷款总额	**Total Amount of Personal Loans**	**377.79**	**1898.14**	**5961.59**	**11021.18**	**13582.83**	**17248.46**
个人消费贷款	Personal Consumption Loan	347.30	1623.94	5961.59	11021.18	13582.83	17248.46
#个人住房贷款	Housing Mortgage Loan	269.71	1257.00	4719.70	9054.72	11320.64	14192.79
汽车消费贷款	Car Consumption Loan	41.02	68.09	71.49	79.65	65.35	46.79
个人住房贷款占个人消费贷款额比重(%)	**Percentage of Housing Mortgage Loan in Personal Consumption Loan (%)**	**77.7**	**77.4**	**79.2**	**82.2**	**83.3**	**82.3**

注：2015年以后数据不含公积金贷款。
a) Data since 2015 do not include provident fund loans.

17-6 各市证券交易额

Stock Turnover by City

单位：亿元 (100 million yuan)

市 City	2010	2011	2012	2013	2014	2015	2016	2017	2018	2019
全　省 Total	**25066**	**19874**	**15987**	**18586**	**36533**	**100578**	**51654**	**72738**	**60364**	**76910**
郑州市 Zhengzhou	13929	11177	9242	10132	21409	54869	27571	41782	32768	41734
开封市 Kaifeng	578	446	316	441	731	2296	1271	1371	1143	1399
洛阳市 Luoyang	2387	1886	1434	1830	3414	10204	5450	7248	6599	8660
平顶山市 Pingdingshan	939	741	538	718	1177	3637	1323	2204	1924	2405
安阳市 Anyang	645	574	406	494	841	2272	1242	1513	1319	1820
鹤壁市 Hebi	250	204	162	153	317	780	378	616	520	533
新乡市 Xinxiang	931	788	705	759	1466	3898	2032	2987	2825	2967
焦作市 Jiaozuo	641	463	363	449	878	2669	1522	2434	1915	2063
濮阳市 Puyang	454	337	312	341	662	2561	1001	1105	850	1166
许昌市 Xuchang	860	629	454	585	1021	3217	979	2074	1870	2368
漯河市 Luohe	312	240	181	282	367	1187	620	744	703	1143
三门峡市 Sanmenxia	438	283	213	276	458	1312	627	917	840	1063
南阳市 Nanyang	828	618	492	638	1128	3317	2007	2498	2087	3023
商丘市 Shangqiu	290	371	278	337	544	1803	1081	1262	1214	1516
信阳市 Xinyang	525	380	311	386	881	2537	1403	1702	1527	1967
周口市 Zhoukou	416	296	230	306	453	1536	1013	830	827	1220
驻马店市 Zhumadian	488	362	294	383	627	2016	1406	1130	1134	1545
济源市 Jiyuan	154	80	58	73	159	468	272	319	301	319

17-7 各市国债发行情况
Issuance of National Debt by City

单位：万元 (10 000 yuan)

市 City	2000	2005	2010	2012	2013	2014	2015	2016	2017	2018	2019
全 省 Total	**485000**	**460969**	**618676**	**406549**	**617544**	**226256**	**575315**	**721789**	**589887**	**533493**	**684105**
郑州市 Zhengzhou	160330	190559	140710	127292	197459	64297	147775	165744	136224	139142	210419
开封市 Kaifeng	23266	18625	31839	16598	18066	6091	15767	16918	16466	15668	16348
洛阳市 Luoyang	79250	68155	55497	58884	66022	25102	70383	78712	65938	62623	84808
平顶山市 Pingdingshan	21000	13410	24190	9140	15522	5218	16030	45033	18070	18703	19742
安阳市 Anyang	30500	16682	13050	9350	30300	8173	26826	34782	27841	22637	23738
鹤壁市 Hebi	2880	3360	10755	3711	7714	1575	4789	13230	7138	4271	4451
新乡市 Xinxiang	30737	24089	45620	17054	25976	10575	41586	38782	32377	31157	43141
焦作市 Jiaozuo	25021	11699	31401	33237	49336	20966	51015	58950	53549	40999	42739
濮阳市 Puyang	35300	35975	45013	24604	41366	22477	45038	40376	60364	43455	62184
许昌市 Xuchang	14600	10770	10737	9384	13934	5379	16112	20667	20067	14146	15971
漯河市 Luohe	3296	6080	8191	8902	15142	3899	8551	24661	6953	6304	7606
三门峡市 Sanmenxia	11710	9690	18821	16683	22276	8843	26949	39412	29081	28630	29237
南阳市 Nanyang	8000	17220	25086	14152	24980	8106	21534	31067	28693	33448	32900
商丘市 Shangqiu	6515	4505	22454	12951	23326	4550	16529	32036	13728	10639	14184
信阳市 Xinyang	8275	9900	37562	9077	14013	3752	7666	11653	7059	4967	9717
周口市 Zhoukou	8800	5575	28285	15044	25154	11164	23988	31010	29139	24014	30301
驻马店市 Zhumadian	11600	9125	59963	16847	18472	9817	19278	15393	21664	17280	22271
济源市 Jiyuan	3920	5550	9502	3640	8486	6272	15499	23363	15536	15410	14348

17-8　证券市场情况

Basic Statistics on Securities Market

指　标	Item	2013	2014	2015	2016	2017	2018	2019
年末河南上市公司数量(家)	Number of Listed Companies in Henan at the Year-end(unit)	95	99	101	108	116	120	124
年末发行股票(只)	Number of Listed Stocks at the Year-end (unit)	97	99	105	110	118	122	124
发行A股	A Shares	65	67	73	74	78	79	81
#新发行	Issued in this Year		1	6	1	4	1	2
发行境外股票	Overseas stock	32	32	32	36	40	41	43
#新发行	Issued in this Year	3	3	1	3	3	3	2
截止年末募集资金总额(亿元)	Capital Avaliable at the end year (100 million yuan)	1831.32	2249.21	2631.60	2984.70	3085.44	3731.95	-
本年首次发行、再融资募集资金(亿元)	Capital Avaliable from First Issued and Refinancing (100 million yuan)	226.63	417.89	377.35	442.85	521.78	225	776
#A股	A Shares	210.38	256.32	226.71	436.73	431.73	100.80	772.80
年末A股上市公司流通股市价总值(亿元)	Total Market Value of Circulation Stock of Companies Listed in A Share Market at the Year-end(100 million yuan)	2992.47	2278.90	6581.30	3617.80	7307.38	5418.56	7211.21
股票成交量(亿元)	Total Stock Turnover (100 million yuan)	18586.20	29757.37	100578.31	51234.66	47297.17	35604.08	51237.08
债券成交量金额(亿元)	Bonds Turnover (100 million yuan)	582.35	407.29	590.61	594.44	830.07	377.09	475.25
投资者开户数(万户)	Total Investors (10 000 households)	421.51	447.07	579.00	687.00	778.45	861.00	971.77
#机构	Institutions	0.42	0.50	0.28	0.62	0.70	0.74	0.84
个人	Individuals	421.09	446.57	578.42	686.38	777.75	860.50	970.94
证券营业部个数(个)	Number of Business Departments of Security Companies (unit)	208	219	301	287	335	409	414
#外省证券公司设本省营业部	Number of Local Business Departments of Security Companies from Other Provinces	159	156	234	221	268	323	325

17-9 河南A股股票发行情况(1993-2019年)

Issuance of A Shares (1993-2019)

股票名称 Name of Stocks	证券代码 Code of Stocks	发行(上市)日期 Issue or the Listing date	发行数量(万股) Total Issued Volume (10 000 shares)	发行价格(元/股) Issued Prices (yuan/share)	发行总市值(万元) Issued Aggregate Market Value (10 000yuan)	募集资金净额(万元) Net Capitalization Collected (10 000yuan)
中原环保	000544.SZ	1993/12/08	4500	3.50	15750	15075
神马股份	600810.SH	1994/01/06	4950	4.68	23166	23166
洛阳玻璃	600876.SH	1995/10/31	5000	5.03	25150	23900
焦作万方	000612.SZ	1996/09/26	3201	6.80	21767	21127
东方银星	600753.SH	1996/09/27	2000	5.18	10360	9760
*ST思 达	000676.SZ	1996/12/24	1250	5.20	6500	6000
大地传媒	000719.SZ	1997/03/31	1478			
许继电气	000400.SZ	1997/04/18	5000	9.24	46200	44700
银鸽投资	600069.SH	1997/04/30	4000	4.62	18480	17810
宇通客车	600066.SH	1997/05/08	3500	9.75	34125	33075
郑州煤电	600121.SH	1998/01/07	8000	5.50	44000	42520
豫能控股	001896.SZ	1998/01/22	8000	3.36	26880	25920
莲花味精	600186.SH	1998/08/25	10000	7.01	70100	68000
黄河旋风	600172.SH	1998/11/26	4000	6.40	25600	24721
双汇发展	000895.SZ	1998/12/10	5000	6.24	31200	30046
同力水泥	000885.SZ	1999/03/19	6000	7.08	42480	40980
安彩高科	600207.SH	1999/07/14	18000	7.20	129600	127623
神火股份	000933.SZ	1999/08/31	7000	7.50	52500	51170
新乡化纤	000949.SZ	1999/10/21	7500	7.80	58500	56752
太龙药业	600222.SH	1999/11/05	3500	6.52	22820	21823
羚锐制药	600285.SH	2000/10/18	4000	8.30	33200	32030
天方药业	600253.SH	2000/12/27	6000	7.75	46500	44820
平高电气	600312.SH	2001/02/21	6000	12.45	74700	72787
安阳钢铁	600569.SH	2001/08/20	27500	6.80	187000	182925
中孚实业	600595.SH	2002/06/26	5000	8.30	41500	39939
豫光金铅	600531.SH	2002/07/30	4500	7.34	33030	31502
瑞 贝 卡	600439.SH	2003/07/10	2400	10.40	24960	23956
中原高速	600020.SH	2003/08/08	28000	6.36	178080	172754
大有能源	600403.SH	2003/10/09	3000	6.67	20010	19078
风神股份	600469.SH	2003/10/21	7500	4.30	32250	30533
华兰生物	002007.SZ	2004/06/25	2200	15.74	34628	32985
轴研科技	002046.SZ	2005/05/26	2500	6.39	15975	14784
平煤股份	601666.SH	2006/11/23	37000	8.16	301920	294892
新野纺织	002087.SZ	2006/11/30	8000	5.19	41520	38821
恒星科技	002132.SZ	2007/04/27	4100	8.00	32800	30200
中航光电	002179.SZ	2007/11/01	3000	16.19	48570	46231
利达光电	002189.SZ	2007/12/03	5000	5.1	25500	23512

17-9 续表 continued

股票名称 Name of Stocks	证券代码 Code of Stocks	发行(上市)日期 Issue or the Listing date	发行数量(万股) Total Issued Volume (10 000 shares)	发行价格(元/股) Issued Prices (yuan/share)	发行总市值(万元) Issued Aggregate Market Value (10 000yuan)	募集资金净额(万元) Net Capitalization Collected (10 000yuan)
三全食品	002216.SZ	2008/02/20	2350	21.59	50737	48864
濮耐股份	002225.SZ	2008/04/25	6000	4.79	28740	27012
辉煌科技	002296.SZ	2009/09/29	1550	25.00	38750	37004
汉威电子	300007.SZ	2009/10/30	1500	27.00	40500	37364
华英农业	002321.SZ	2009/12/16	3700	16.98	62826	58884
森源电气	002358.SZ	2010/02/10	2200	26.00	57200	54715
豫金刚石	300064.SZ	2010/03/26	3800	21.32	81016	74502
远东传动	002406.SZ	2010/05/18	4700	26.60	125020	121490
多 氟 多	002407.SZ	2010/05/18	2700	39.39	106353	99085
中原特钢	002423.SZ	2010/06/03	7900	9.00	71100	67383
新大新材	300080.SZ	2010/06/25	3500	43.40	151900	148008
中原内配	002448.SZ	2010/07/16	2350	21.80	51230	47275
郑 煤 机	601717.SH	2010/08/03	14000	20.00	280000	270040
新 开 源	300109.SZ	2010/08/25	900	30.00	27000	24805
雏鹰农牧	002477.SZ	2010/09/15	3350	35.00	117250	108623
林州重机	002535.SZ	2011/01/11	5120	25.00	128000	120520
西泵股份	002536.SZ	2011/01/11	2400	36.00	86400	81749
四 方 达	300179.SZ	2011/02/15	2000	24.75	49500	46312
通达股份	002560.SZ	2011/03/03	2000	28.80	57600	53389
好 想 你	002582.SZ	2011/05/20	1860	46.00	85560	81478
佰 利 联	002601.SZ	2011/07/15	2400	55.00	132000	125818
新 开 普	300248.SZ	2011/07/29	1120	30.00	33600	29903
北玻股份	002613.SZ	2011/08/30	6700	13.50	90450	82145
新天科技	300259.SZ	2011/08/31	1900	21.90	41610	38732
隆华节能	300263.SZ	2011/09/16	2000	33.00	66000	61074
明泰铝业	601677.SH	2011/09/19	6000	20.00	120000	113549
中信重工	601608.SH	2012/07/06	68500	4.67	319895	308557
一拖股份	601038.SH	2012/08/08	15000	5.40	81000	77373
洛阳钼业	603993.SH	2012/10/09	20000	3.00	60000	55815
牧原股份	002714.SZ	2014/01/17	6050	24.07	72210	66782
清 水 源	300437.SZ	2015/04/23	1670	10.53	17585	15230
普 莱 柯	603566.SH	2015/05/18	4000	15.52	62080	55988
科迪乳业	002770.SZ	2015/06/30	6840	6.85	46854	40698
濮阳惠成	300481.SZ	2015/06/30	2000	9.13	18260	14599
光力科技	300480.SZ	2015/07/02	2300	7.28	16744	13938
思维列控	603508.SH	2015/12/24	4000	33.56	134240	127427
安图生物	603658.SH	2016/09/01	4200	14.58	61236	57453
中原证券	601375.SH	2017/01/03	70000	4.00	280000	266981
三晖电气	002857.SZ	2017/03/23	2000	10.26	20520	17647
森霸股份	300701.SZ	2017/09/15	2000	13.14	26280	23617
设 研 院	300732.SZ	2017/12/12	1800	41.42	74556	68872
建龙微纳	688357.SH	2019/12/04	1446	43.28	62583	56992
天迈科技	300807.SZ	2019/12/19	1700	17.68	30056	26069

注：2007年及以前为发行日期，2008年起为上市日期。
a) Data before 2007 is issue date, and Since 2008 is listing date.

17－10 保险业务情况

Main Indicators of Insurance Business

单位：亿元 (100 million yuan)

项 目	Item	2010	2011	2012	2013	2014	2015	2016	2017	2018	2019
保费收入	**Premium Income**	**793.28**	**839.82**	**841.13**	**916.52**	**1036.08**	**1248.76**	**1555.15**	**2020.07**	**2262.85**	**2430.84**
财产保险	Property Insurance	134.72	163.33	195.77	238.83	278.38	320.16	372.95	443.59	521.08	566.55
#机动车辆险	Motor Vehicle Insurance	119.34	139.95	162.66	197.36	237.73	271.09	308.70	364.40	386.92	404.40
企业财产险	Enterprise Property Insurance	6.63	8.94	8.67	8.14	7.90	7.34	6.95	7.65	7.79	8.34
家庭财产险	Family Property Insurance	0.20	0.24	0.22	0.23	0.41	0.41	0.60	1.04	1.63	2.92
人身保险	Personal Insurance	658.56	676.49	645.36	677.69	757.70	928.60	1182.19	1576.47	1741.77	1864.29
寿险	Life Insurance	618.34	637.16	595.49	613.40	659.88	794.72	1003.37	1297.95	1348.87	1378.85
健康险	Health Insurance	31.03	28.31	37.10	49.49	79.05	111.44	151.10	240.54	357.68	449.95
意外伤害险	Accident Insurance	9.19	11.02	12.78	14.81	18.77	22.44	27.73	37.99	35.22	35.48
赔款及给付	**Claim and Payment**	**153.91**	**171.14**	**199.55**	**279.75**	**324.03**	**447.71**	**548.03**	**625.86**	**654.75**	**668.59**
财产保险	Property Insurance	70.72	80.54	102.50	122.08	141.02	156.14	184.32	217.56	272.65	309.96
#机动车辆险	Motor Vehicle Insurance	58.66	68.59	88.85	105.82	122.65	134.92	154.16	175.80	202.83	226.54
企业财产险	Enterprise Property Insurance	5.27	3.57	3.70	3.55	4.72	3.15	4.34	5.27	4.09	3.59
家庭财产险	Family Property Insurance	0.08	0.06	0.06	0.04	0.06	0.11	0.15	0.29	0.57	0.89
人身保险	Personal Insurance	83.19	90.60	97.05	157.67	183.01	291.57	363.72	408.30	382.10	358.63
寿险	Life Insurance	68.64	76.14	83.72	141.09	161.27	251.99	316.69	327.36	267.33	198.22
健康险	Health Insurance	11.58	11.61	9.79	12.83	17.18	34.97	40.70	72.94	108.82	152.95
意外伤害险	Accident Insurance	2.97	2.85	3.54	3.75	4.57	4.61	6.33	8.00	5.95	7.46

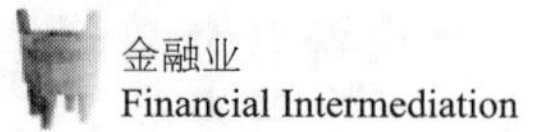

17-11 各市国内保险业务主要指标(2019年)

Main Indicators of Domestic Insurance Business by City (2019)

单位：亿元 (100 million yuan)

市 City	保费收入 Premium Income	财产保险 Property Insurance	#机动车辆险 Motor Vehicle Insurance	#企业财产险 Enterprise Property Insurance	#家庭财产险 Family Property Insurance	人身保险 Personal Insurance	寿险 Life Insurance	健康险 Health Insurance	意外伤害险 Accident Insurance
全省 Total	**2430.84**	**566.55**	**404.40**	**8.34**	**2.92**	**1864.29**	**1378.85**	**449.95**	**35.48**
省辖市 City	36.50	0.07	0.06			36.43	1.51	34.86	0.06
郑州市 Zhengzhou	758.05	194.51	133.49	5.13	1.00	563.54	413.21	136.02	14.31
开封市 Kaifeng	89.37	18.16	12.40	0.13	0.17	71.21	49.30	20.29	1.62
洛阳市 Luoyang	160.43	34.22	26.18	0.30	0.11	126.21	100.35	24.12	1.75
平顶山市 Pingdingshan	89.15	21.58	15.65	0.23	0.13	67.57	52.77	13.84	0.97
安阳市 Anyang	99.51	24.97	19.67	0.25	0.22	74.54	60.00	13.56	0.98
鹤壁市 Hebi	25.53	7.56	5.63	0.10	0.06	17.97	13.70	3.97	0.30
新乡市 Xinxiang	128.88	25.33	19.27	0.34	0.12	103.56	80.04	21.45	2.08
焦作市 Jiaozuo	106.15	20.82	16.56	0.22	0.05	85.33	62.64	21.14	1.55
濮阳市 Puyang	87.48	18.17	13.84	0.26	0.06	69.31	53.90	14.04	1.37
许昌市 Xuchang	93.61	20.44	16.31	0.21	0.09	73.17	56.76	15.00	1.42
漯河市 Luohe	55.60	10.32	7.69	0.07	0.04	45.28	34.66	9.87	0.75
三门峡市 Sanmenxia	43.39	9.41	6.69	0.05	0.05	33.97	27.75	5.82	0.41
南阳市 Nanyang	184.36	39.36	26.72	0.35	0.17	145.00	107.53	35.27	2.20
商丘市 Shangqiu	122.94	32.71	23.22	0.19	0.24	90.22	65.36	23.50	1.36
信阳市 Xinyang	116.77	24.64	16.78	0.09	0.07	92.12	76.32	14.58	1.22
周口市 Zhoukou	112.60	31.35	22.54	0.08	0.16	81.25	58.88	20.95	1.43
驻马店市 Zhumadian	102.56	27.55	17.70	0.16	0.17	75.00	55.56	17.95	1.50
济源市 Jiyuan	17.97	5.37	4.00	0.17	0.01	12.60	8.63	3.75	0.22

市 City	赔款及给付 Claim and Payment	财产保险 Property Insurance	#机动车辆险 Motor Vehicle Insurance	#企业财产险 Enterprise Property Insurance	#家庭财产险 Family Property Insurance	人身保险 Personal Insurance	寿险 Life Insurance	健康险 Health Insurance	意外伤害险 Accident Insurance
全省 Total	**668.59**	**309.96**	**226.54**	**3.59**	**0.89**	**358.63**	**198.22**	**152.95**	**7.46**
省辖市 City	35.47	1.42	1.24	0.01	0.01	34.05	0.03	34.02	
郑州市 Zhengzhou	209.09	106.19	79.80	1.76	0.23	102.90	44.42	56.18	2.30
开封市 Kaifeng	24.56	9.71	7.00	0.06	0.04	14.84	7.53	7.04	0.27
洛阳市 Luoyang	40.44	19.01	13.46	0.09	0.02	21.43	17.18	3.88	0.37
平顶山市 Pingdingshan	23.84	11.16	8.22	0.16	0.04	12.68	9.25	3.26	0.17
安阳市 Anyang	30.60	14.01	11.23	0.08	0.19	16.59	13.00	2.77	0.82
鹤壁市 Hebi	8.91	5.40	3.35	0.03	0.02	3.51	2.61	0.80	0.11
新乡市 Xinxiang	30.36	13.19	9.79	0.07	0.03	17.18	11.06	5.75	0.37
焦作市 Jiaozuo	28.41	12.91	8.96	0.10	0.01	15.50	9.18	5.78	0.54
濮阳市 Puyang	21.65	8.24	6.81	0.21	0.02	13.41	10.35	2.77	0.29
许昌市 Xuchang	23.48	11.48	9.45	0.06	0.01	12.00	8.41	3.27	0.32
漯河市 Luohe	13.73	5.93	4.63	0.09	0.01	7.80	5.72	1.95	0.13
三门峡市 Sanmenxia	12.68	5.75	4.01	0.03	0.05	6.93	5.74	1.05	0.14
南阳市 Nanyang	44.74	20.65	13.46	0.19	0.02	24.09	16.87	6.65	0.57
商丘市 Shangqiu	31.79	15.80	12.05	0.35	0.09	15.99	7.37	8.32	0.30
信阳市 Xinyang	25.48	14.30	9.43	0.07	0.02	11.18	8.89	2.12	0.17
周口市 Zhoukou	30.91	16.97	12.36	0.05	0.04	13.94	10.30	3.40	0.24
驻马店市 Zhumadian	26.93	14.48	9.00	0.07	0.05	12.45	9.02	3.16	0.27
济源市 Jiyuan	5.55	3.36	2.29	0.10		2.19	1.33	0.79	0.07

主要统计指标解释

信贷资金 指金融机构以信用方式积聚和分配的货币资金。金融机构信贷资金的来源有各项存款、金融债券、对国际金融机构负债、流通中现金、其他项目等；信贷资金的运用有各项贷款、有价证券及投资、黄金占款、外汇买卖、财政借款及在国际金融机构中的资产等。

存款 指企业、机关、团体或居民把货币资金存入银行或其他信贷机构保管，可随时或按约定时间支取款项，并取得一定利息的一种信用活动形式。根据存款对象或性质的不同可划分为住户存款、非金融企业存款、政府存款、非银行业金融机构存款等科目。它是银行信贷资金的主要来源。

贷款 指银行或其他信贷机构根据资金必须归还的原则，按一定利率，为企业、个人等提供资金的一种信用活动形式。我国银行贷款分为短期贷款、中长期贷款、融资租赁、票据融资、各项垫款、境外贷款等。

保险公司 在中国境内的、经过保险监督管理部门批准设立，并依法登记注册的各类商业保险公司。

保险金额 指保险人承担赔偿或者给付保险金责任的最高限额。

证券 由债券购买者承购的或因销售产品而拥有的，可在金融市场上交易并代表一定债权的书面证明。包括政府债券、金融债券、企业债券、商业票据、股票、支付固定收入但不提供法人企业残余价值分享权的优先股等。

股票 指股票购买者及直接投资者对其投资企业净资产所拥有的权益。股票是股份公司签发的证明股东投资并按其所持股份享有权益和承担义务的权益性证券。

保费 指投保人为取得保险人在约定范围内所承担赔偿责任而支付给保险人的费用。

赔款 指保险人根据保险合同的规定，向被保险人支付的赔偿保险责任损失的金额。

给付 包括死伤医疗给付和满期给付。死伤医疗给付是指保险人根据人寿保险及长期健康保险合同的规定，因被保险人在保险期内发生保险责任范围内的保险事故支付给被保险人(或受益人)的金额。满期给付是指被保险人生存期满，保险人按人寿保险合同规定支付给被保险人的满期保险金额。

Explanatory Notes on Main Statistical Indicators

Credit Funds refer to the monetary funds accumulated and distributed in the means of credit by the financial institutions. The sources of credit funds include various deposits, financial bonds, liabilities to international financial institutions, currency in circulation, other items. The uses of credit funds include loans, securities and investment, position for bullion purchase, foreign exchange trading, advances to treasury, and assets with international financial institutions.

Deposit is a form of credit by which enterprises, institutions, organizations or households can put money into banks and other credit institutions for safekeeping and interest earning and can withdraw anytime or at appointed time.l. According to different depositors, deposits are divided into household deposits, non financial enterprise deposits, government deposits, non banking financial institutions deposits. Deposits are major sources of the credit funds of banks.

Loan is a form of credit by which banks and other credit institutions provide funds at certain interest rate to enterprises and individuals in the light of the principle of unconditional repayment. Loans from Chinese banks include short-term loan, medium-term and long-term loans, financial lease, bill financing, various money advanced, foreign loans.

Insurance Companies refer to commercial insurance companies of various forms registered by law and established in China with the approval of insurance regulatory agencies.

Amount Insured refers to the maximum that the insurant will get for the claim of the case insured.

Securities refer to written certificates representing creditors' rights, purchased by bond holders or owned by selling products, which can be transacted at the financial markets. They include government bonds, financial bonds, corporation bonds, commercial drafts, stocks, preferential stocks that provide fixed income without the right to share the residual value of corporations, etc.

Stocks refer to the rights by stockholders and direct investors on the net assets of corporations they invested in. Stocks refer to negotiable securities on creditor's rights, issued by stock companies certifying the investment by stockholders and their rights and duties depending on their stocks.

Premium is the fee paid by the insurant to the insurer to obtain the obligation of compensation from the insurance within the agreed terms.

Settled Claim is the compensation paid by the insurer to the insurant in accordance with the insurance contract.

Payment includes payment for death, injury or medical treatment and payment at maturity. Payment for death, injury or medical treatment refers to the money paid to the insurant (or the beneficiary) in accordance with the life or health insurance contract when the insurant encounters accidents within the insured period covered in the contract. Payment at maturity refers to the payment to the insurant in accordance with the life insurance contract at the end of the insured period.

其他服务业

Other Services

18

● 资料整理：陈 哲

简要说明

一、主要内容

本篇主要包括河南省规模以上服务业企业单位数、从业人数、营业收入、营业利润、应付职工薪酬等主要财务指标。

二、统计范围

辖区内年营业收入1000万元及以上，或年末从业人员50人及以上服务业法人单位。包括交通运输、仓储和邮政业，信息传输、软件和信息技术服务业，租赁和商务服务业，科学研究和技术服务业，水利、环境和公共设施管理业，教育，卫生和社会工作；以及物业管理、房地产中介服务等自有房地产经营活动、其他房地产业行业。

辖区内年营业收入500万元及以上，或年末从业人员50人及以上服务业法人单位。主要包括居民服务、修理和其他服务业，文化、体育和娱乐业。

三、资料来源

规模以上服务业法人企业实行全数调查，由河南省统计局服务业统计处整理提供。

Brief Introduction

I. Main Contents

Data on this chapter including number of Services enterprises above designated size, employment, main financial indicators of operating income, operating profit, employee compensation and so on in Henan.

II. Scope of Statistics

The Services enterprises with revenue from principal business over 10 million yuan or employee at the end of year over 50 persons includes: transportation, storage and post, Information transfer, software and Information technology services, leasing and business services, management of water conservancy, environment and public facilities, education, sanitation and social work, property management, real estate intermediary and so on.

The Services enterprises with revenue from principal business over 5 million yuan or employee over 50 person at the end of year includes: resident services, repairing and other services, culture, sports and entertainment.

III. Sources of Data

Data on services enterprises above designated size are collected through a combination of full survey, which are provided by the Department of Services industry of the Henan provincial bureau of Statistics.

18-1 规模以上服务业企业主要财务指标(2019年)
Main indictors of Enterprises Above Designated size in Service Industry (2019)

单位：亿元 (100 million yuan)

指标	indictor	单位数(个) Number of Enterprises (unit)	资产总计 Total Assets	所有者权益 Owner's Equity	营业收入 Revenue	营业成本 Cost of Operation
总计	**Total**	**8733**	**29094.82**	**12857.96**	**6706.99**	**4942.73**
交通运输、仓储和邮政业	Traffic, Transport, Storage and Post	2191	14360.58	6575.79	2814.92	2200.77
信息传输、软件和信息技术服务业	Information Transfer, Software and Information Technology Services	682	1824.91	728.47	1125.62	764.19
房地产业(不含房地产开发经营)	Realty Industry	660	770.46	183.69	203.57	126.55
租赁和商务服务业	Tenancy and Business Services	1493	7107.19	2978.82	891.70	665.29
科学研究和技术服务业	Scientific Research and Technical Service	1022	925.48	422.01	722.79	539.47
水利、环境和公共设施管理业	Management of Water Conservancy, Environment and Public Facilities	409	2832.32	1393.53	232.22	154.98
居民服务、修理和其他服务业	Resident Services, Repair and other Services	505	72.76	35.54	100.98	67.42
教育	Education	741	280.64	152.14	189.18	120.97
卫生和社会工作	Health and Social Work	490	421.96	158.75	264.55	202.45
文化、体育和娱乐业	Culture, Sports and Entertainment	540	498.52	229.22	161.46	100.64

指标	indictor	营业税金及附加 Business tax and Extra Charges	营业利润 Total Profits	应付职工薪酬 Wages Payable	应交增值税 Value Added Tax Payable	从业人员平均人数(人) Average Employees (person)
总计	**Total**	**62.02**	**790.98**	**1216.55**	**137.79**	**1432403**
交通运输、仓储和邮政业	Traffic, Transport, Storage and Post	18.56	300.29	452.15	37.67	464763
信息传输、软件和信息技术服务业	Information Transfer, Software and Information Technology Services	5.22	165.51	158.11	36.91	145807
房地产业(不含房地产开发经营)	Realty Industry	5.18	23.29	51.20	8.45	109106
租赁和商务服务业	Tenancy and Business Services	11.47	117.37	252.68	20.88	252948
科学研究和技术服务业	Scientific Research and Technical Service	7.22	62.33	123.63	18.62	116321
水利、环境和公共设施管理业	Management of Water Conservancy, Environment and Public Facilities	3.51	32.97	31.37	5.12	86832
居民服务、修理和其他服务业	Resident Services, Repair and other Services	1.76	16.39	18.62	2.15	48386
教育	Education	3.48	34.88	41.60	3.18	86475
卫生和社会工作	Health and Social Work	0.96	15.89	57.23	1.34	83101
文化、体育和娱乐业	Culture, Sports and Entertainment	4.66	22.06	29.96	3.47	38664

18-2 各市规模以上服务业企业单位数(2019年)

Number of Enterprises Above Designated size in Service Industry by Sector and City (2019)

单位：个 (unit)

市(县) City(County)	合　计 Total	交通运输、仓储及邮政业 Transport, Storage and Post	信息传输、软件和信息技术服务业 Information Tansmission, Software and Information Technology Services	房地产业(不含房地产开发经营) Realty Industry	租赁和商务服务业 Leasing and Business Services
全　　省 Total	**8733**	**2191**	**682**	**660**	**1493**
省 辖 市 City					
郑州市 Zhengzhou	2116	314	345	247	477
开封市 Kaifeng	357	89	22	23	64
洛阳市 Luoyang	554	126	35	65	90
平顶山市 Pingdingshan	436	103	14	43	67
安阳市 Anyang	156	58	10	5	22
鹤壁市 Hebi	100	31	13	6	19
新乡市 Xinxiang	303	78	15	19	68
焦作市 Jiaozuo	319	172	11	22	29
濮阳市 Puyang	252	85	10	17	44
许昌市 Xuchang	649	124	32	40	90
漯河市 Luohe	111	67	10	3	12
三门峡市 Sanmenxia	166	52	8	6	26
南阳市 Nanyang	521	162	13	45	82
商丘市 Shangqiu	593	180	60	36	153
信阳市 Xinyang	623	140	21	33	94
周口市 Zhoukou	798	180	41	17	69
驻马店市 Zhumadian	577	186	16	29	76
济源市 Jiyuan	102	44	6	4	11
省直管县 County Directly Administrated by Province					
巩义市 Gongyi	112	38	1	15	12
兰考县 Lankao	91	14	3	7	10
汝州市 Ruzhou	150	36	4	5	27
滑县 Huaxian	45	8	1	2	8
长垣市 Changyuan	65	10	1	7	9
邓州市 Dengzhou	57	18	1	5	8
永城市 Yongcheng	93	30	6	5	26
固始县 Gushi	121	56	1	9	18
鹿邑县 Luyi	192	27	4	4	17
新蔡县 Xincai	75	16		5	21

18-2 续表 continued

单位：个 (unit)

市(县) City(County)	科学研究和技术服务业 Scientific Research, and Technical Service	水利、环境和公共设施管理业 Management of Water Conservancy, Environment and Public Facilities	居民服务、修理和其他服务业 Resident Services, Repair and other services	教育 Education	卫生和社会工作 Health and Social Work	文化、体育和娱乐业 Culture, Sports and Entertainment
全 省 Total	**1022**	**409**	**505**	**741**	**490**	**540**
省 辖 市 City						
郑 州 市 Zhengzhou	416	57	50	44	68	98
开 封 市 Kaifeng	32	18	36	36	7	30
洛 阳 市 Luoyang	71	33	25	13	31	65
平 顶 山 市 Pingdingshan	60	30	27	38	19	35
安 阳 市 Anyang	12	13	4	18	12	2
鹤 壁 市 Hebi	7	4	1	8	9	2
新 乡 市 Xinxiang	24	15	14	35	15	20
焦 作 市 Jiaozuo	24	14	15	16	9	7
濮 阳 市 Puyang	20	11	22	25	12	6
许 昌 市 Xuchang	100	47	58	70	33	55
漯 河 市 Luohe	6	5	2	3		3
三 门 峡 市 Sanmenxia	11	12	9	3	20	19
南 阳 市 Nanyang	34	32	44	42	35	32
商 丘 市 Shangqiu	46	15	33	35	10	25
信 阳 市 Xinyang	59	62	45	48	59	62
周 口 市 Zhoukou	70	10	54	226	91	40
驻 马 店 市 Zhumadian	27	19	60	77	55	32
济 源 市 Jiyuan	3	12	6	4	5	7
省 直 管 县 County Directly Administrated by Province						
巩 义 市 Gongyi	3	4	6	23	7	3
兰 考 县 Lankao	5	3	21	13	4	11
汝 州 市 Ruzhou	19	17	10	17	6	9
滑 县 Huaxian	3	3	3	9	8	
长 垣 市 Changyuan	5	7	3	14	3	6
邓 州 市 Dengzhou	3	1	3	10	5	3
永 城 市 Yongcheng	4	3	3	7	4	5
固 始 县 Gushi	3	5	9	8	4	8
鹿 邑 县 Luyi	12	3	12	85	17	11
新 蔡 县 Xincai	3	2	10	6	4	8

18-3 各市规模以上服务业企业营业收入(2019年)

Operating income of Everage Employed Persons of Enterprises Above Designated size in Service Industry by Sector and City (2019)

单位：亿元　　(100 million yuan)

市(县) City(County)	合计 Total	交通运输、仓储及邮政业 Transport, Storage and Post	信息传输、软件和信息技术服务业 Information Transmission, Software and Information Technology Services	房地产业(不含房地产开发经营) Realty Industry	租赁和商务服务业 Leasing and Business Services
全　省 Total	**6706.99**	**2814.92**	**1125.62**	**203.57**	**891.70**
省辖市 City					
郑州市 Zhengzhou	3398.51	1691.69	453.22	132.06	501.66
开封市 Kaifeng	171.94	51.63	36.21	3.36	24.81
洛阳市 Luoyang	426.53	64.84	104.05	14.18	23.55
平顶山市 Pingdingshan	158.34	54.25	32.69	3.39	20.95
安阳市 Anyang	113.04	46.35	37.55	0.84	11.43
鹤壁市 Hebi	39.48	11.96	11.69	0.20	6.32
新乡市 Xinxiang	168.71	55.21	45.58	2.25	32.51
焦作市 Jiaozuo	134.16	77.42	22.11	1.44	11.42
濮阳市 Puyang	142.96	42.54	27.44	1.02	29.99
许昌市 Xuchang	341.78	79.16	45.89	8.33	63.22
漯河市 Luohe	65.40	36.29	18.24	0.71	4.59
三门峡市 Sanmenxia	72.92	23.50	16.48	0.84	12.10
南阳市 Nanyang	226.26	103.95	52.48	5.38	15.71
商丘市 Shangqiu	277.46	106.82	60.38	12.23	46.50
信阳市 Xinyang	246.79	89.51	43.24	5.43	23.92
周口市 Zhoukou	455.46	162.94	67.65	6.06	40.39
驻马店市 Zhumadian	220.91	85.44	44.70	4.12	20.19
济源市 Jiyuan	46.34	31.43	6.03	1.73	2.40
省直管县 County Directly Administrated by Province					
巩义市 Gongyi	20.71	8.98	0.03	0.47	2.31
兰考县 Lankao	24.35	4.27	0.40	0.55	3.05
汝州市 Ruzhou	46.80	22.89	0.69	0.75	9.32
滑县 Huaxian	10.13	1.52	0.74	0.05	1.71
长垣市 Changyuan	30.78	0.91	0.25	0.18	17.54
邓州市 Dengzhou	9.32	2.17	0.03	0.24	0.85
永城市 Yongcheng	26.23	14.16	0.66	0.81	4.33
固始县 Gushi	43.56	28.04		1.09	2.98
鹿邑县 Luyi	36.06	4.34	0.98	0.94	4.93
新蔡县 Xincai	13.78	6.85		0.63	2.44

18-3 续表　continued

单位：亿元　(100 million yuan)

市(县) City(County)	科学研究和技术服务业 Scientific Research, and Technical Service	水利、环境和公共设施管理业 Management of Water Conservancy, Environment and Public Facilities	居民服务、修理和其他服务业 Resident Services, Repair and other Services	教育 Education	卫生和社会工作 Health and Social Work	文化、体育和娱乐业 Culture, Sports and Entertainment
全　省 Total	**722.79**	**232.22**	**100.98**	**189.18**	**264.55**	**161.46**
省辖市 City						
郑州市 Zhengzhou	392.97	86.53	20.08	16.91	40.19	63.20
开封市 Kaifeng	9.49	11.69	9.75	11.09	5.62	8.29
洛阳市 Luoyang	175.64	9.52	2.71	4.76	17.58	9.70
平顶山市 Pingdingshan	11.20	14.50	3.06	6.57	5.73	6.00
安阳市 Anyang	3.70	7.13	0.18	3.01	2.65	0.20
鹤壁市 Hebi	1.05	4.21	0.07	0.92	2.88	0.18
新乡市 Xinxiang	4.43	9.52	1.53	6.55	9.09	2.04
焦作市 Jiaozuo	4.00	8.06	1.04	3.71	4.53	0.43
濮阳市 Puyang	14.87	1.46	1.95	3.38	19.79	0.52
许昌市 Xuchang	33.47	16.23	15.82	22.90	34.18	22.58
漯河市 Luohe	1.20	1.22	2.51	0.39		0.25
三门峡市 Sanmenxia	2.65	2.39	0.65	0.40	12.08	1.83
南阳市 Nanyang	7.31	9.01	4.94	6.71	15.77	5.00
商丘市 Shangqiu	9.94	14.36	7.64	9.20	5.33	5.06
信阳市 Xinyang	11.21	22.84	6.11	13.42	24.32	6.79
周口市 Zhoukou	32.69	3.96	12.03	61.11	48.93	19.70
驻马店市 Zhumadian	6.77	7.17	10.38	17.82	15.05	9.27
济源市 Jiyuan	0.21	2.41	0.55	0.31	0.83	0.44
省直管县 County Directly Administrated by Province						
巩义市 Gongyi	0.32	0.72	0.21	3.85	3.67	0.15
兰考县 Lankao	0.62	0.75	4.33	2.86	4.53	2.99
汝州市 Ruzhou	3.08	2.85	1.74	2.83	1.63	1.02
滑县 Huaxian	1.02	0.91	0.18	1.68	2.32	
长垣市 Changyuan	0.26	1.83	0.67	3.08	5.87	0.19
邓州市 Dengzhou	0.30	0.99	0.18	3.87	0.31	0.38
永城市 Yongcheng	0.60	0.55	0.41	0.64	3.27	0.80
固始县 Gushi	0.20	1.98	1.61	1.88	4.52	1.26
鹿邑县 Luyi	3.07	0.89	1.82	11.16	5.88	2.05
新蔡县 Xincai	0.37	0.31	0.88	0.89	0.64	0.77

18-4 各市规模以上服务业企业营业利润(2019年)

Profit of Enterprises Above Designated size in Service Industry by Sector and City (2019)

单位：亿元 (100 million yuan)

市(县) City(County)	合计 Total	交通运输、仓储及邮政业 Transport, Storage and Post	信息传输、软件和信息技术服务业 Information Transmission, Software and Information Technology Services	房地产业(不含房地产开发经营) Realty Industry	租赁和商务服务业 Leasing and Business Services
全 省 Total	**790.98**	**300.29**	**165.51**	**23.29**	**117.37**
省 辖 市 City					
郑 州 市 Zhengzhou	343.58	194.84	39.68	13.35	58.73
开 封 市 Kaifeng	33.22	8.08	8.14	0.48	5.12
洛 阳 市 Luoyang	18.51	-1.29	3.51	1.05	0.34
平 顶 山 市 Pingdingshan	18.31	2.63	6.85	0.08	2.29
安 阳 市 Anyang	9.51	0.94	7.10	-0.01	0.25
鹤 壁 市 Hebi	-2.27	-0.75	-0.12		0.22
新 乡 市 Xinxiang	16.97	2.67	8.92	-0.26	2.86
焦 作 市 Jiaozuo	10.96	5.37	3.73	0.13	-0.05
濮 阳 市 Puyang	8.67	1.74	5.40	0.01	0.14
许 昌 市 Xuchang	66.18	10.05	9.74	1.39	18.91
漯 河 市 Luohe	5.26	0.89	3.38	-0.01	0.79
三 门 峡 市 Sanmenxia	3.36	1.17	0.71		0.37
南 阳 市 Nanyang	28.33	5.36	13.81	0.64	2.47
商 丘 市 Shangqiu	61.40	20.19	14.25	3.28	11.09
信 阳 市 Xinyang	36.68	9.48	10.67	0.98	3.66
周 口 市 Zhoukou	90.01	25.90	19.49	0.97	7.06
驻 马 店 市 Zhumadian	39.15	10.66	9.96	1.12	2.93
济 源 市 Jiyuan	3.14	2.35	0.30	0.10	0.19
省 直 管 县 County Directly Administrated by Province					
巩 义 市 Gongyi	0.16	0.09	-0.01	0.07	0.07
兰 考 县 Lankao	7.08	1.38	0.15	0.13	1.27
汝 州 市 Ruzhou	4.37	0.50	0.22	0.11	1.36
滑 县 Huaxian	-0.33	-0.07	-0.04	-0.02	-0.33
长 垣 市 Changyuan	2.82	0.14	0.01	-0.04	1.26
邓 州 市 Dengzhou	1.73	0.07			0.05
永 城 市 Yongcheng	3.30	1.48	0.12	0.18	0.64
固 始 县 Gushi	6.87	4.88		0.22	0.37
鹿 邑 县 Luyi	8.35	0.90	0.25	0.18	1.08
新 蔡 县 Xincai	3.79	1.24		0.21	0.98

18-4 续表 continued

单位：亿元 (100 million yuan)

市(县) City(County)	科学研究和技术服务业 Scientific Research, and Technical Service	水利、环境和公共设施管理业 Management of Water Conservancy, Environment and Public Facilities	居民服务、修理和其他服务业 Resident Services, Repair and other Services	教育 Education	卫生和社会工作 Health and Social Work	文化、体育和娱乐业 Culture, Sports and Entertainment
全省 Total	**62.33**	**32.97**	**16.39**	**34.88**	**15.89**	**22.06**
省辖市 City						
郑州市 Zhengzhou	23.70	7.30	0.26	0.22	-0.13	5.63
开封市 Kaifeng	1.66	3.14	2.66	2.76	0.26	0.92
洛阳市 Luoyang	12.69	1.21	0.32	0.50	0.03	0.15
平顶山市 Pingdingshan	1.43	3.02	0.41	0.60	0.42	0.58
安阳市 Anyang	0.09	0.97	0.02	0.31	-0.09	-0.07
鹤壁市 Hebi	-0.05	-1.40	0.01	-0.28	0.12	-0.02
新乡市 Xinxiang	0.18	0.73	0.05	0.62	1.02	0.18
焦作市 Jiaozuo	0.17	1.23	0.01	0.51	-0.09	-0.05
濮阳市 Puyang	0.82	0.18	0.06	0.45	0.25	-0.38
许昌市 Xuchang	7.81	3.11	3.60	4.34	3.36	3.87
漯河市 Luohe	0.08	0.05	0.05	0.04		-0.01
三门峡市 Sanmenxia	0.23	0.11	0.05	0.09	0.08	0.55
南阳市 Nanyang	1.48	1.02	0.80	1.70	0.33	0.72
商丘市 Shangqiu	1.98	6.24	1.76	1.13	0.42	1.06
信阳市 Xinyang	1.93	3.82	1.17	2.44	1.42	1.11
周口市 Zhoukou	7.13	0.89	2.78	15.06	6.37	4.36
驻马店市 Zhumadian	0.99	1.31	2.37	4.33	2.04	3.44
济源市 Jiyuan	0.03	0.04	0.03	0.04	0.07	-0.01
省直管县 County Directly Administrated by Province						
巩义市 Gongyi	0.06	0.03	0.04	0.06	-0.23	-0.02
兰考县 Lankao	0.29	0.15	1.44	0.93	0.08	1.26
汝州市 Ruzhou	0.48	0.63	0.28	0.36	0.23	0.20
滑县 Huaxian	-0.04	0.05	0.02	0.17	-0.07	
长垣市 Changyuan	-0.13	0.46	0.02	0.33	0.76	0.01
邓州市 Dengzhou	0.04	0.04	0.05	1.33	0.03	0.12
永城市 Yongcheng	0.12	0.17	0.08	0.11	0.25	0.15
固始县 Gushi	0.04	0.25	0.35	0.23	0.36	0.17
鹿邑县 Luyi	0.57	0.45	0.23	2.89	1.40	0.40
新蔡县 Xincai	0.09	0.10	0.35	0.26	0.24	0.32

18-5 各市规模以上服务业企业应付职工薪酬(2019年)
Wages Payable of Enterprises Above Designated size in Service Industry by Sector and City (2019)

单位：亿元 (100 million yuan)

市(县) City(County)	合 计 Total	交通运输、仓储及邮政业 Transport, storage and post	信息传输、软件和信息技术服务业 Information Transmission, Software and Information Technology Services	房地产业(不含房地产开发经营) Realty Industry	租赁和商务服务业 Leasing and Business Services
全 省 Total	**1216.55**	**452.15**	**158.11**	**51.20**	**252.68**
省 辖 市 City					
郑 州 市 Zhengzhou	731.03	304.36	70.19	34.03	183.94
开 封 市 Kaifeng	16.42	4.67	2.58	0.62	1.71
洛 阳 市 Luoyang	74.17	12.13	21.35	5.40	5.27
平 顶 山 市 Pingdingshan	25.65	7.08	4.24	1.31	5.49
安 阳 市 Anyang	17.94	6.73	4.66	0.57	1.94
鹤 壁 市 Hebi	5.82	1.53	1.21	0.10	1.42
新 乡 市 Xinxiang	25.06	6.86	6.25	0.39	3.97
焦 作 市 Jiaozuo	22.39	12.79	2.47	0.71	1.76
濮 阳 市 Puyang	30.99	5.33	2.59	0.47	15.86
许 昌 市 Xuchang	39.72	7.66	7.48	1.63	4.11
漯 河 市 Luohe	9.24	3.38	2.22	0.25	2.38
三 门 峡 市 Sanmenxia	13.06	3.00	2.44	0.22	1.16
南 阳 市 Nanyang	35.30	14.56	7.05	1.28	3.84
商 丘 市 Shangqiu	46.13	19.69	6.62	1.82	7.08
信 阳 市 Xinyang	34.65	11.20	5.57	1.00	3.70
周 口 市 Zhoukou	54.76	17.79	6.33	0.61	4.91
驻 马 店 市 Zhumadian	28.61	10.12	4.29	0.73	3.51
济 源 市 Jiyuan	5.53	3.26	0.57	0.04	0.63
省 直 管 县 County Directly Administrated by Province					
巩 义 市 Gongyi	4.46	1.15	0.03	0.26	1.20
兰 考 县 Lankao	2.78	0.33	0.02	0.13	0.18
汝 州 市 Ruzhou	4.15	1.24	0.10	0.10	0.91
滑 县 Huaxian	1.93	0.19	0.21	0.05	0.07
长 垣 市 Changyuan	4.17	0.20	0.01	0.13	0.54
邓 州 市 Dengzhou	2.61	0.82	0.03	0.07	0.15
永 城 市 Yongcheng	3.93	1.48	0.10	0.11	0.35
固 始 县 Gushi	5.17	2.41		0.39	0.72
鹿 邑 县 Luyi	4.70	0.44	0.04	0.12	0.50
新 蔡 县 Xincai	1.70	0.57		0.10	0.31

18-5 续表 continued

单位：亿元 (100 million yuan)

市(县) City(County)	科学研究和技术服务业 Scientific Research, and Technical Service	水利、环境和公共设施管理业 Management of Water Conservancy, Environment and Public Facilities	居民服务、修理和其他服务业 Resident Services, Repair and other Services	教育 Education	卫生和社会工作 Health and Social Work	文化、体育和娱乐业 Culture, Sports and Entertainment
全　　省 Total	**123.63**	**31.37**	**18.62**	**41.60**	**57.23**	**29.96**
省　辖　市 City						
郑　州　市 Zhengzhou	85.34	9.63	9.06	4.82	11.40	18.26
开　封　市 Kaifeng	0.90	2.11	0.50	1.31	1.12	0.90
洛　阳　市 Luoyang	18.87	1.57	0.47	1.73	4.98	2.40
平顶山市 Pingdingshan	1.83	1.34	0.52	1.86	1.28	0.70
安　阳　市 Anyang	0.50	1.84	0.05	1.10	0.50	0.05
鹤　壁　市 Hebi	0.18	0.14		0.51	0.72	0.01
新　乡　市 Xinxiang	0.61	1.15	0.49	2.68	2.29	0.37
焦　作　市 Jiaozuo	0.69	1.18	0.37	1.20	1.14	0.08
濮　阳　市 Puyang	1.74	0.68	0.33	1.24	2.51	0.24
许　昌　市 Xuchang	3.43	1.97	1.18	2.50	8.48	1.28
漯　河　市 Luohe	0.25	0.52	0.13	0.09		0.02
三门峡市 Sanmenxia	1.13	0.61	0.18	0.18	3.83	0.31
南　阳　市 Nanyang	1.42	1.59	0.74	1.74	2.56	0.52
商　丘　市 Shangqiu	1.59	2.04	1.43	2.64	2.39	0.83
信　阳　市 Xinyang	1.33	2.80	0.96	2.83	4.16	1.10
周　口　市 Zhoukou	2.78	1.13	1.02	11.32	6.93	1.94
驻马店市 Zhumadian	0.94	0.69	1.07	3.72	2.69	0.85
济　源　市 Jiyuan	0.09	0.38	0.12	0.11	0.23	0.10
省直管县 County Directly Administrated by Province						
巩　义　市 Gongyi	0.05	0.07	0.07	0.59	1.01	0.03
兰　考　县 Lankao	0.08	0.27	0.23	0.26	1.07	0.21
汝　州　市 Ruzhou	0.29	0.45	0.31	0.46	0.18	0.11
滑　　县 Huaxian	0.04	0.38	0.05	0.58	0.36	
长　垣　市 Changyuan	0.07	0.19	0.20	1.26	1.52	0.05
邓　州　市 Dengzhou	0.05	0.36	0.04	0.91	0.10	0.08
永　城　市 Yongcheng	0.04	0.06	0.04	0.21	1.43	0.11
固　始　县 Gushi	0.02	0.23	0.25	0.33	0.54	0.28
鹿　邑　县 Luyi	0.34	0.07	0.13	2.12	0.77	0.17
新　蔡　县 Xincai	0.07	0.04	0.14	0.18	0.17	0.12

18-6 各市规模以上服务业企业平均从业人员人数(2019年)

Number of Everage Employed Persons of Enterprises Above Designated size in Service Industry by Sector and City (2019)

单位：人 (person)

市(县) City(County)	合计 Total	交通运输、仓储及邮政业 Transport, Storage and Post	信息传输、软件和信息技术服务业 Information Transmission, Software and Information Technology Services	房地产业(不含房地产开发经营) Realty Industry	租赁和商务服务业 Leasing and Business Services
全　省 Total	**1432403**	**464763**	**145807**	**109106**	**252948**
省辖市 City					
郑州市 Zhengzhou	574194	210911	62000	61779	96135
开封市 Kaifeng	35368	9359	3154	1295	4252
洛阳市 Luoyang	93680	19207	15585	13922	9573
平顶山市 Pingdingshan	53698	17982	2816	5056	12854
安阳市 Anyang	30464	8577	3266	1516	5481
鹤壁市 Hebi	15048	2776	1265	382	7450
新乡市 Xinxiang	43060	10100	5508	1182	9650
焦作市 Jiaozuo	46179	25049	3323	1584	5985
濮阳市 Puyang	48240	8093	2478	1413	21926
许昌市 Xuchang	70467	12973	13069	3897	6945
漯河市 Luohe	18258	5607	1850	612	6943
三门峡市 Sanmenxia	20348	5519	2358	764	2966
南阳市 Nanyang	63227	23001	4294	4361	11386
商丘市 Shangqiu	79826	32889	6331	4510	15330
信阳市 Xinyang	65301	18778	5155	2842	10466
周口市 Zhoukou	104367	25816	8883	1601	14110
驻马店市 Zhumadian	61377	23686	4033	2229	9494
济源市 Jiyuan	9301	4440	439	161	2002
省直管县 County Directly Administrated by Province					
巩义市 Gongyi	8047	2392	85	651	631
兰考县 Lankao	6860	666	40	249	348
汝州市 Ruzhou	10810	2682	181	209	2613
滑县 Huaxian	6469	394	368	166	325
长垣市 Changyuan	7828	348	12	522	817
邓州市 Dengzhou	6044	2130	145	254	529
永城市 Yongcheng	7528	2717	275	385	906
固始县 Gushi	12009	4499		1273	1980
鹿邑县 Luyi	11310	1043	75	334	1307
新蔡县 Xincai	4940	1494		340	996

18-6 续表 continued

单位：人 (person)

市(县) City(County)	科学研究和技术服务业 Scientific Research, and Technical Service	水利、环境和公共设施管理业 Management of Water Conservancy, Environment and Public Facilities	居民服务、修理和其他服务业 Resident Services, Repair and other Services	教育 Education	卫生和社会工作 Health and Social Work	文化、体育和娱乐业 Culture, Sports and Entertainment
全省 Total	**116321**	**86832**	**48386**	**86475**	**83101**	**38664**
省辖市 City						
郑州市 Zhengzhou	67046	21683	22541	6796	12872	12431
开封市 Kaifeng	1696	8525	1096	2522	1788	1681
洛阳市 Luoyang	16368	3085	912	2734	7791	4503
平顶山市 Pingdingshan	2841	3174	1613	3864	2064	1434
安阳市 Anyang	860	6331	169	2716	1397	151
鹤壁市 Hebi	435	160	2	1135	1419	24
新乡市 Xinxiang	1111	3043	1728	6724	3037	977
焦作市 Jiaozuo	1231	1791	1869	3104	2011	232
濮阳市 Puyang	1641	4087	765	3030	4323	484
许昌市 Xuchang	6449	7852	2387	5144	9463	2288
漯河市 Luohe	412	1767	821	201		45
三门峡市 Sanmenxia	1319	1997	681	371	3497	876
南阳市 Nanyang	2337	5765	1623	3873	5220	1367
商丘市 Shangqiu	3470	3608	3415	5451	3295	1527
信阳市 Xinyang	2800	6148	2846	5495	7333	3438
周口市 Zhoukou	4205	5109	2853	25029	11832	4929
驻马店市 Zhumadian	1920	1952	2687	8068	5297	2011
济源市 Jiyuan	180	755	378	218	462	266
省直管县 County Directly Administrated by Province						
巩义市 Gongyi	173	205	106	1911	1853	40
兰考县 Lankao	179	2401	473	454	1621	429
汝州市 Ruzhou	758	1491	970	1140	494	272
滑县 Huaxian	161	2394	169	1389	1103	
长垣市 Changyuan	217	897	619	2648	1606	142
邓州市 Dengzhou	151	860	130	1367	273	205
永城市 Yongcheng	145	205	130	697	1756	312
固始县 Gushi	65	578	667	947	1177	823
鹿邑县 Luyi	617	214	354	5425	1525	416
新蔡县 Xincai	186	183	472	508	426	335

运输和邮电

Transport, Postal and Telecommunication Services

19

● 资料整理：陈 琛

简要说明

一、主要内容

本篇反映河南省交通运输业和邮政、通信、软件业发展的基本情况。交通运输业资料主要包括：主要运输方式的线路里程、运输设备拥有量、货物运输量和旅客运输量。邮政、通信业资料主要包括：全省邮政局(所)及邮路情况，邮政设备拥有量，邮政业务完成情况，邮政通信业发展水平等资料。

二、统计范围

铁路包括国家铁路、合资铁路、地方铁路。公路里程包括全省范围内所有国道、省道、县道、乡道(含村道)、专用公路。民用车辆拥有量包括辖区内全部登记注册民用车辆。公路、水路运输量统计范围是在全省交通运输主管部门办理营运证的从事公路、水路客、货运输的营业性的车辆和船舶所完成的运输量。邮电通信包括省邮政管理局、省邮政公司、省通信管理局及所有从事邮电通信运营的企业。

三、资料来源

铁路资料由郑州铁路局、武汉铁路局、登封铁路公司提供；公路资料由省交通运输厅提供；民用车辆资料由省公安厅、省农机局和各省辖市统计局提供。民航资料由郑州新郑国际机场、南方航空公司河南分公司提供；邮政业资料由河南省邮政管理局、省邮政公司和省通信管理局提供。由河南省统计局服务业统计处编辑整理。

Brief Introduction

I. Main Contents

Data in this chapter present the development of transportation, post, telecommunication and software in Henan province. Data on traffic and transport include the length of the routes of main transportation, the possession of transport equipment, the condition of technological quality, freight traffic and passenger traffic accomplished. Data on post and telecommunication cover mainly the situation of post offices and postal routes; telephone lines, telegraph lines and the possession of post facilities; business volume of postal services achieved; and the level of development of postal services.

II. Scope of Statistics

Data on railway transportation including National railway, joint-venture and local railways. The length of highways refer to the road of the national, provincial, county, town and dedicated lanes. Data on the possession of civil motor vehicles include all registered vehicles. Data on passenger traffic and freight traffic by highways, the statistical scope encompasses all the enterprises, institutional units and individuals (including joint-households) engaged in highway freight or passenger transport business. The data on civil aviation transport cover the civil enterprises that set up base in Henan. The data on post cover the Henan provincial bureau of post, Henan provincial postal company, Henan provincial bureau of communications authority and all enterprises for post.

III. Sources of Data

Data on railway transportation are calculated from Henan provincial operation bureau of local railways, Zhengzhou Railway Administration, Wuhan Railway Administration. Data on highway transportation are calculated from Henan provincial bureau of transportation. Data on civilian vehicles are calculated from Henan provincial bureau of public safety, Henan provincial bureau of agricultural machinery and municipal Henan provincial bureau of statistics. Data on civil aviation are calculated from Xinzheng international airport and Henan Branch of China Southern airlines. Data on postal services come from the Henan provincial bureau of post, Henan provincial post company and Henan provincial communications authority. Data in this chapter are provided by the Department of Services industry of the Henan provincial bureau of Statistics.

19-1 交通运输基本情况
Basic Conditions of Transport

年份 Year	铁路营业里程(公里) Length of Railways in Operation (km)	公路里程(公里) Length of Highways (km)	#高速公路 Expressway	通航里程(公里) Length of Navigable Inland Waterways (km)	民用汽车拥有量(万辆) Possession of Civil Motor Vehicles (10 000 units)	#私人汽车 Private Vehicles
1949	1224	3909		2312	0.04	
1952	1225	5766		2916	0.11	
1957	1318	14945		3837	0.33	
1962	1690	17876		2537	1.05	
1965	1823	19907		3389	1.10	
1970	2792	22320		2072	1.71	
1975	3113	26934		2268	3.80	
1978	3212	31549		2202	6.30	
1979	3216	36155		1352	7.35	
1980	3192	36423		1361	8.51	
1981	3460	36478		1419	10.13	
1982	3401	36912		1110	11.28	
1983	3305	37196		1110	12.21	
1984	3342	37704		1110	14.10	
1985	3248	38840		1110	17.82	
1986	3344	39286		1110	18.42	3.29
1987	3409	39713		1110	21.60	3.72
1988	3358	40622		1110	24.92	5.87
1989	3546	41170		1110	28.61	6.97
1990	3536	43150		1110	30.79	7.65
1991	3384	44199		1110	33.38	8.12
1992	3486	45049		1105	34.32	8.46
1993	3456	46487		1105	38.40	7.04
1994	3350	47704	81	1104	45.23	12.45
1995	3382	49707	230	1104	46.93	12.18
1996	3426	50907	294	1104	51.41	14.98
1997	3428	55016	416	1104	60.35	19.41
1998	3461	57172	465	1104	68.09	22.01
1999	3354	60330	465	1104	76.59	29.93
2000	3354	64453	505	1104	84.73	34.93
2001	3319	69041	1077	1587	92.46	39.24
2002	3347	71741	1231	1587	105.82	50.41
2003	3410	73831	1418	1208	119.75	57.20
2004	3752	75718	1759	1381	130.97	64.10
2005	4000	79506	2678	1439	206.01	132.16
2006	3988	236351	3439	1439	252.94	169.91
2007	3989	238676	4556	1439	292.69	209.22
2008	3989	240645	4841	1439	338.44	248.77
2009	3898	242314	4861	1439	404.53	305.49
2010	4224	245089	5016	1439	484.89	377.32
2011	4203	247587	5196	1439	582.14	463.08
2012	4822	249649	5830	1439	645.92	529.67
2013	4822	249831	5859	1439	746.90	628.22
2014	5108	249857	5859	1439	896.02	774.37
2015	5205	250584	6305	1589	1342.13	866.76
2016	5466	267441	6448	1589	1481.66	1010.01
2017	5470	267805	6523	1589	1286.02	1166.82
2018	5460	268589	6600	1589	1459.24	1327.36
2019	6080	269832	6967	1675	1620.60	1480.08

注：2006年起，公路里程包括村道(以下相关表同)。
a) Length of ways include county ways since 2006 (the same as following tables).

19–2 旅客和货物运输量
Passenger and Freight Traffic

年份 Year	客运量 (万人) Passenger Traffic (10000 persons)	#铁路 Railway	#公路 Highway	#水运 Waterway	货运量 (万吨) Freight Traffic (10000 tons)	#铁路 Railway	#公路 Highway	#水运 Waterway
1978	11145	4319	6781	45	18176	6722	11321	133
1979	12784	4513	8218	53	17533	6693	10728	112
1980	15092	4860	10151	81	17047	6758	10183	106
1981	17559	4752	12724	83	16403	6614	9705	84
1982	20129	4680	15373	76	19847	6934	12794	119
1983	23050	5060	17907	82	21579	7142	14308	129
1984	25985	5474	20412	97	23908	7456	16296	155
1985	36576	5723	30729	121	35642	8101	27340	201
1986	43590	5659	37822	105	36436	8420	27799	217
1987	46140	5524	40510	100	39539	8632	30670	237
1988	54667	6073	48421	168	38357	8772	29282	303
1989	52328	5476	46634	211	38245	9089	28811	345
1990	53567	4429	48977	150	38111	9038	28818	255
1991	53846	4223	49494	119	39923	9193	30486	244
1992	58096	4271	53703	106	44018	9343	34404	271
1993	61285	4602	56511	146	47347	9811	37182	354
1994	62686	4563	57996	81	50988	9974	40428	395
1995	61964	4288	57522	82	53582	10373	42692	324
1996	66490	3818	62464	129	55920	10594	44800	382
1997	69863	3843	65786	152	56113	9996	45542	433
1998	74182	4133	69917	55	58150	9416	48250	342
1999	78009	4366	73493	76	59218	9657	49208	352
2000	83912	4727	79017	91	60678	10172	50133	372
2001	85412	4980	80259	95	65191	11196	53596	398
2002	90334	5085	85078	86	68397	12148	55743	505
2003	81323	4864	76301	63	69689	12925	56100	663
2004	91013	5695	85016	84	73796	14732	58147	915
2005	98099	5842	91920	97	78827	14806	62684	1334
2006	108060	6313	101345	105	86608	15190	69898	1516
2007	122557	6585	115460	160	101410	16010	83537	1858
2008	(139290)	7476	(131291)	(167)	(116889)	16226	(98433)	(2226)
	130436	7476	122414	190	138392	16226	118198	3964
2009	144666	7724	136278	206	169643	13856	151343	4439
2010	167804	8399	158630	255	202470	14224	183291	4950
2011	193882	8952	184213	268	240965	14312	220122	6527
2012	208094	9628	197785	250	272240	12779	251772	7685
2013	(225738)	11160	(213900)	(261)	(304369)	12762	(282970)	(8632)
	137571	11160	125450	255	184669	12762	162040	9854
2014	141780	12400	128279	254	200626	11577	179680	9350
2015	(146066)	13068	(131788)	280	(211854)	9802	(191572)	10459
	126812	13068	112535	280	192715	9802	172431	10459
2016	122342	14525	106415	288	205385	9562	184255	11545
2017	116574	16178	98753	347	229458	9406	207066	12879
2018	112611	17095	93707	331	259461	10012	235183	14240
2019	111458	18278	91281	306	(281221)	10502	(253457)	17236
	111458	18278	91281	306	218647	10502	190883	17236

注：2008年客货运输量为公路水路运输量专项调查数据，2013年、2015年客货运输量按交通部新统计方法测算，2019年货运量按交通部道路货物运输量专项调查数据测算，括号内均为原口径数据。

a) Data on passenger and freight traffic in 2008 are calculated on basis of Highway and waterway traffic special investigation,Data on passenger and freight traffic in 2013 and 2015 are calculated on new statistical methods of the Ministry of Communications, Data on freight traffic in 2019 are calculated on basis of freight traffic special investigation of the Ministry of Communications,and data in the brackets are original data.

19−3 旅客和货物周转量
Passenger-Kilometers and Freight Ton-Kilometers

年份 Year	旅客周转量(亿人公里) Passenger-Kilometers (100 million passenger-km)	#铁路 Railways	#公路 Highways	货物周转量(亿吨公里) Freight Ton-Kilometers (100 million ton-km)	#铁路 Railways	#公路 Highways
1949	6.46	6.45	0.01	16.53	16.00	0.21
1952	15.62	15.26	0.36	39.12	36.56	0.88
1957	33.23	30.85	2.33	112.68	106.68	3.13
1962	90.02	82.01	7.98	131.21	125.02	4.08
1965	46.46	37.79	8.65	227.88	219.56	6.07
1970	80.54	64.74	15.66	332.55	322.03	8.74
1975	105.23	82.18	22.90	390.77	372.64	16.29
1978	123.22	92.62	30.47	508.41	484.79	21.57
1979	140.25	105.73	34.37	529.00	507.56	19.77
1980	163.98	122.40	41.35	547.65	525.31	21.01
1981	176.99	126.76	49.98	563.45	537.75	24.45
1982	195.70	135.60	59.87	617.77	578.55	37.41
1983	226.31	155.09	70.96	674.22	624.37	47.86
1984	253.11	171.10	81.71	702.70	643.53	55.88
1985	323.50	209.77	113.36	838.22	728.25	105.72
1986	358.20	228.54	129.34	881.90	777.12	99.73
1987	400.06	249.01	150.75	1020.81	880.94	133.83
1988	484.77	290.16	194.24	1079.26	932.37	139.64
1989	488.56	280.00	208.16	1157.63	1007.00	142.70
1990	423.46	229.90	193.10	1169.44	1001.79	160.66
1991	459.53	249.52	209.64	1199.31	1022.17	170.03
1992	511.40	275.46	235.56	1302.34	1085.18	209.03
1993	538.45	295.85	242.15	1337.03	1099.61	227.37
1994	566.29	305.35	260.74	1432.97	1164.43	258.41
1995	573.85	304.66	262.11	1538.82	1233.74	295.18
1996	584.25	285.72	289.65	1603.52	1263.13	326.16
1997	620.28	296.80	314.26	1547.18	1179.62	352.74
1998	640.16	310.79	320.93	1452.74	1083.35	355.48
1999	689.89	339.15	342.56	1432.08	1058.12	363.56
2000	740.98	378.80	353.78	1476.51	1101.74	363.94
2001	779.93	401.77	369.41	1573.28	1185.36	375.78
2002	820.83	421.00	390.00	1649.22	1234.77	398.87
2003	822.92	462.10	350.02	1891.73	1463.20	405.20
2004	963.09	542.00	395.40	2107.26	1650.00	422.02
2005	1000.70	535.43	437.84	2282.60	1759.77	467.00
2006	1113.77	586.88	492.72	2415.89	1810.80	538.76
2007	1264.10	620.68	601.81	2729.30	1962.93	681.85
2008	(1444.29)	667.32	(734.96)	(2969.81)	1985.84	(848.22)
	1517.33	667.32	808.32	5215.84	1985.84	2995.15
2009	1645.18	675.48	914.80	6146.09	1955.36	3927.08
2010	1840.64	747.20	1031.18	7141.82	1980.23	4860.63
2011	2033.68	766.45	1211.28	8471.07	2120.10	5949.04
2012	2144.50	779.57	1309.58	9436.42	2088.97	6863.01
2013	(2328.12)	853.38	(1417.54)	(10357.41)	2096.81	(7702.95)
	1661.89	853.38	712.39	7205.05	2096.81	4488.01
2014	1858.89	895.65	844.86	7367.09	1926.50	4822.37
2015	(1941.88)	910.24	(898.08)	(7582.38)	1666.02	(5208.16)
	1787.70	910.24	743.91	6916.89	1666.02	4542.67
2016	1857.17	938.30	760.57	7336.28	1685.89	4838.53
2017	1945.20	1029.09	736.62	8165.54	1899.81	5341.67
2018	1979.25	1061.11	711.19	8934.35	2014.91	5893.92
2019	2012.66	1091.34	699.03	(9742.43)	2079.80	(6446.46)
	2012.66	1091.34	699.03	8595.74	2079.80	5299.76

注：2008年客货周转量为公路水路运输量专项调查数据，2013年、2015年客货周转量按交通部新统计方法测算，2019年货物周转量按交通部道路货物运输量专项调查数据测算,括号内均为原口径数据。

a) Data on passenger-kilometers and freight ton-kilometers in 2008 are calculated on basis of Highway and waterway traffic special investigation, and data in 2013 and 2015 are calculated on new statistical methods of the Ministry of Communications, Data on freight ton-kilometers in 2019 are calculated on basis of freight traffic special investigation of the Ministry of Communicationsand data in the brackets are original data.

19-4 铁路、公路、内河通车通航里程(年底数)

Length of Railways, Highways and Navigable Inland Waterways (Year-end)

单位：公里 (km)

指 标	Item	2000	2005	2010	2015	2016	2017	2018	2019
铁 路	**Length of Railways**	**3354**	**4000**	**4224**	**5205**	**5466**	**5470**	**5460**	**6080**
#电气化	Electrified Railways		1309	2109	2291	2302	2301	2299	2299
#高铁	High-speed Rail					1308	1308	1308	1915
中央铁路	National Railways	2043	2788	3395	4397	4659	4663	4653	5273
地方铁路	Local Railways	1311	1212	829	808	807	807	807	807
公 路	**Length of Highways**	**64453**	**79506**	**245089**	**250584**	**267441**	**267805**	**268589**	**269832**
#高级、次高级路面	Senior and Second-senior	46917	63474	165944	188020	220248	223406	237604	243121
#高速公路	Expressways	505	2678	5016	6305	6448	6523	6600	6967
内 河	**Length of Navigable Inland Waterways**	**1104**	**1439**	**1439**	**1589**	**1589**	**1589**	**1589**	**1675**

注：铁路通车里程为正线里程；铁路电气化里程为郑州铁路局全局数据。

a) Length of railways refers to trunk lines.Length of electrified railways refers to data of Zhengzhou Railway Administration.

19-5 交通运输工具拥有量(年底数)

Possession of Means of Transportation (Year-end)

指 标	Item	2000	2005	2010	2015	2016	2017	2018	2019
铁路	**Railways**								
国家铁路	National Railways								
内燃机车(台)	Diesel Locomotives(unit)	951	446	297	220	215	212	219	221
电力机车(台)	Electric Locomotives(unit)	981	570	837	1053	1048	1043	1113	1241
客车(辆)	Passenger Coaches(unit)	4981	1860	2400	2699	2985	2868	2071	1996
地方铁路	Local Railways								
内燃机车(台)	Diesel Locomotives(unit)	85	106	64	5	6	6	5	5
货车(辆)	Freight Cars(unit)	1476	1219	622	20	20	20	20	20
公路	**Highways**								
载货汽车(辆)	Trucks(unit)	363723	491669	907504	1297191	1329070	1446283	1622244	1768531
#重型	Heavy	212965	136946	307187	426097	432688	485683	547636	577577
中型	Middle			144914	69610	50867	42177	41727	39725
轻型	Light	150758	199410	443372	797052	842608	916549	1031574	1150378
载客汽车(辆)	Buses and Cars(unit)	456068	988796	3049045	8170640	9665820	11246977	12816534	14284766
#大型	Large	32771	46187	61940	69068	72016	75192	78307	79243
中型	Middle			80896	38589	38389	37898	37516	36459
小型	Small	423297	672144	2660344	7834810	9390964	11005065	12570471	14040709
内河	**Inland Rivers**								
机动船(艘)	Motor Vessels (unit)	3314	4687	4916	5202	5296	5302	5153	5153
驳船(艘)	Barges (unit)	418	431	127	308	306	303	316	314

注：国家铁路为郑州铁路局数据。由于郑州铁路局调整，2005年以后的数据与以前年份不可比。2015年起，受地方铁路改制影响，地方铁路交通运输工具拥有量数据仅包含登封铁路公司。

a) Data on national railways are calculated by ZhengZhou Railways Administration. Because of The Change of ZhengZhou Railways Administration, data since 2005 could not be Compared with former Years.Data of Locomotives only refers to DengFeng railway company since 2015.

19-6 各市公路线路里程(2019年底)

Length of Highways by City (End of 2019)

单位：公里 (km)

市(县) City(County)	总计 Total	等级公路 Expressway and Class Ⅰ to Ⅳ Highways	高速 Expressway	一级 First Class	二级 Second Class	三级 Third Class	四级 Four Class
全省 Total	**269832**	**248155**	**6967**	**4007**	**27813**	**21474**	**187895**
郑州市 Zhengzhou	13827	12986	631	629	1926	1603	8197
开封市 Kaifeng	9512	8491	461	101	1216	271	6443
洛阳市 Luoyang	19756	18791	520	164	2189	1941	13976
平顶山市 Pingdingshan	14762	14665	452	187	1886	1262	10880
安阳市 Anyang	12994	11911	291	301	1580	1197	8542
鹤壁市 Hebi	4582	4147	77	129	342	327	3272
新乡市 Xinxiang	13540	12993	269	205	2300	1215	9004
焦作市 Jiaozuo	8107	7612	240	234	1612	946	4581
濮阳市 Puyang	6979	6826	218	294	1030	691	4593
许昌市 Xuchang	10019	8948	281	275	1178	793	6421
漯河市 Luohe	5430	5205	126	80	547	519	3934
三门峡市 Sanmenxia	10134	9459	315	71	1094	973	7007
南阳市 Nanyang	40149	37304	792	352	3334	3317	29506
商丘市 Shangqiu	24884	20244	511	243	1792	1344	16356
信阳市 Xinyang	26824	24127	592	147	1968	2080	19340
周口市 Zhoukou	24038	22685	513	264	1638	1280	18991
驻马店市 Zhumadian	21769	19312	584	239	1630	1329	15530
济源市 Jiyuan	2527	2449	96	94	552	382	1325
省直管县 County Directly Administrated by Province							
巩义市 Gongyi	2180	2035	57	69	170	418	1321
兰考县 Lankao	1822	1749	50	23	236	102	1339
汝州市 Ruzhou	2954	2863	100	19	424	331	1990
滑县 Huaxian	3723	3213	56	64	406	92	2595
长垣市 Changyuan	2099	2010	55		453	109	1393
邓州市 Dengzhou	4521	4065	80	45	369	282	3286
永城市 Yongcheng	3556	3325	115	2	315	268	2627
固始县 Gushi	3260	3073	74	10	262	267	2459
鹿邑县 Luyi	3198	2682	46	73	139	182	2243
新蔡县 Xincai	2327	2282	71		231	72	1907

19-6 续表 continued

单位：公里 (km)

市(县)	City(County)	等外公路 Highways Below Class Ⅳ	有铺装路面里程 paved Highway	沥青混凝土 Bitumen	水泥混凝土 concrete	简易铺装路面里程 Simply Paved Highway	未铺装路面里程 Unpaved Highway
全　　省	**Total**	**21677**	**229152**	**52149**	**177003**	**13969**	**26711**
郑　州　市	Zhengzhou	841	12152	4694	7458	722	954
开　封　市	Kaifeng	1020	8395	4133	4263	84	1032
洛　阳　市	Luoyang	965	18357	3395	14962	57	1342
平顶山市	Pingdingshan	96	13162	2299	10863	8	1592
安　阳　市	Anyang	1084	11128	2385	8742	282	1584
鹤　壁　市	Hebi	435	3673	765	2908	362	546
新　乡　市	Xinxiang	546	12232	3371	8861	752	557
焦　作　市	Jiaozuo	495	6999	2006	4993	583	525
濮　阳　市	Puyang	154	6780	2060	4721	45	154
许　昌　市	Xuchang	1071	8126	2139	5987	708	1185
漯　河　市	Luohe	225	4800	594	4206	405	225
三门峡市	Sanmenxia	674	9310	2119	7191	40	783
南　阳　市	Nanyang	2845	35236	6846	28390	924	3988
商　丘　市	Shangqiu	4640	17780	3979	13801	3453	3651
信　阳　市	Xinyang	2699	21726	2372	19354	456	4643
周　口　市	Zhoukou	1352	18659	4376	14284	4025	1354
驻马店市	Zhumadian	2457	18303	3712	14590	928	2539
济　源　市	Jiyuan	79	2332	904	1428	136	59
省直管县	**County Directly Administrated by Province**						
巩　义　市	Gongyi	145	1945	428	1517	90	145
兰　考　县	Lankao	72	1744	918	827	2	76
汝　州　市	Ruzhou	91	2328	394	1934		626
滑　　县	Huaxian	511	3106	538	2568	106	511
长　垣　市	Changyuan	89	1963	600	1363	47	90
邓　州　市	Dengzhou	456	4050	774	3276	15	456
永　城　市	Yongcheng	231	2925	483	2442	181	450
固　始　县	Gushi	188	2891	491	2400	181	188
鹿　邑　县	Luyi	515	2374	614	1761	308	515
新　蔡　县	Xincai	45	1781	471	1310	501	45

19−7 各种民用车辆拥有量(2019年底)

Possession of Civil Vehicles (End of 2019)

单位：辆 (unit)

指标	Item	总计 Total	营运 Commerial	非营运 Non-commerial	#进口 Imports	#私人 Private-owned	#新注册 Newly-registered	报废 Abandoned
合计	**Total**	**21843427**	**1672700**	**16637622**	**409688**	**16640488**	**1920582**	**113339**
汽车	Vehicles	16205986	1300385	14905601	404321	14800767	1756828	91051
载客汽车	Passenger Vehicles	14284766	234725	14050041	402803	13564300	1497789	47313
大型	Large	79243	61545	17698	386	481	7117	5267
中型	Medium	36459	11944	24515	683	3883	2424	2691
小型	Small	14040709	161024	13879685	398695	13435531	1482660	36939
微型	Minicar	128355	212	128143	3039	124405	5588	2416
#轿车	Saloon Cars	8707686	156035	8551651	144013	8333896	910601	19841
载货汽车	Trucks	1768531	1027526	741005	1403	1123755	240563	42400
重型	Heavy	577577	563482	14095	295	104618	86289	34536
中型	Medium	39725	33378	6347	9	26200	2250	3070
轻型	Light	1150378	430526	719852	1096	992166	152015	4700
微型	Mini	851	140	711	3	771	9	94
#普通载货	Cargo Vehicle	813059	235045	578014	1073	724473	95874	6342
其他汽车	Others	152689	38134	114555	115	112712	18476	1338
#三轮	Tricycle	47320	15429	31891		46353	5947	96
低速货车	Low-speed truck	37799	17906	19893		34868		143
电车	Buses	139	139				50	
摩托车	Motorcycle	1832531	81241	1751290	5330	1817719	113274	7133
普通	Standard	1825889	81236	1744653	5330	1811088	112845	7048
轻便	Light	6642	5	6637		6631	429	85
拖拉机	Tractors	3512749						
#大中型	Large and Medium	373074						
小型	Small	3139675						
挂车	Trailer	291831	290796	1035	37	22002	50380	15154
其他类型车	Others	191	139	52			50	1

注：1.拖拉机数据来源于农机管理局，其他数据来源于公安厅。

2.全省“营运”、“非营运”、“进口”、“私人”、“新注册”和“报废”车辆分类中不包括“拖拉机”分类数据。

a) Data of Tractor was calculated from the Administration of agricultural machinery,data of cars and other vehicles was calculated from Provincial public security department.

b) In addition to the total, other index data in Penn column does not include the tractor.

19-8 各市民用车辆拥有量(2019年底)

Possession of Civil Vehicles by City (End of 2019)

单位：辆 (unit)

市 City	民用汽车 Civil Vehicles	载客汽车 Passenger Vehicles	#大型 Large	#轿车 Sedan	载货汽车 Trucks	#重型 Heavy	#普通载货 Ordinary Trucks
全省 Total	**16205986**	**14284766**	**79243**	**8707686**	**1768531**	**577577**	**813059**
郑州市 Zhengzhou	3814832	3554534	18866	2169635	240218	82023	78719
开封市 Kaifeng	649222	573091	3077	341642	71257	13987	41023
洛阳市 Luoyang	1206336	1079645	6774	649895	118639	31040	64862
平顶山市 Pingdingshan	725094	637149	3964	337710	76323	20672	38225
安阳市 Anyang	870190	780330	3870	522774	83754	34287	33673
鹤壁市 Hebi	282331	249792	1829	167143	27788	11341	12039
新乡市 Xinxiang	1057602	931220	4325	600156	119045	37951	60773
焦作市 Jiaozuo	598662	504127	2420	332667	86301	51487	21878
濮阳市 Puyang	691534	601736	2894	395060	84695	28822	36259
许昌市 Xuchang	711729	631515	3152	378138	75116	21338	33683
漯河市 Luohe	367005	317146	1697	202520	48224	20503	17626
三门峡市 Sanmenxia	327512	290553	1784	176897	33972	11528	16896
南阳市 Nanyang	1154225	996374	5515	575590	147480	39208	77047
商丘市 Shangqiu	1124758	943868	7164	603658	166472	49233	83332
信阳市 Xinyang	685994	585077	3392	332971	80050	13510	46676
周口市 Zhoukou	994199	800234	4515	439882	184121	74923	80518
驻马店市 Zhumadian	752622	634378	2808	358153	109367	28533	63018
济源市 Jiyuan	169618	152191	756	112137	15441	7191	6588

市 City	其他汽车 Other	#新注册 Newly-registered	摩托车 Motors	挂车 Trailer	拖拉机 Tractors	机动车驾驶员(万人) Number of Motor Drivers (10 000 Person)	#汽车 Automobile Drivers
全省 Total	**152689**	**1756828**	**1832531**	**291831**	**3512749**	**2964**	**2847**
郑州市 Zhengzhou	20080	430011	64492	24325	114892	452	450
开封市 Kaifeng	4874	64482	44802	6983	208056	131	130
洛阳市 Luoyang	8052	114760	141264	13570	183695	220	210
平顶山市 Pingdingshan	11622	74659	153708	10180	123476	145	139
安阳市 Anyang	6106	82664	62688	22929	136910	146	141
鹤壁市 Hebi	4751	24856	19060	6822	84864	51	50
新乡市 Xinxiang	7337	106580	76593	18497	180520	208	205
焦作市 Jiaozuo	8234	58525	78596	41772	57490	125	121
濮阳市 Puyang	5103	62340	33454	15695	68246	117	116
许昌市 Xuchang	5098	68039	27255	7244	50995	117	113
漯河市 Luohe	1635	41817	34328	9866	89540	69	68
三门峡市 Sanmenxia	2987	28411	159629	5890	48935	69	63
南阳市 Nanyang	10371	129500	264902	20018	807778	290	260
商丘市 Shangqiu	14418	131951	81530	26937	189629	230	226
信阳市 Xinyang	20867	93496	263694	2654	231405	152	138
周口市 Zhoukou	9844	129321	114682	40177	321558	252	242
驻马店市 Zhumadian	8877	100572	201714	12412	606811	162	149
济源市 Jiyuan	1986	12670	10140	5860	7949	27	26

19-9 各市私人车辆拥有量(2019年底)

Possession of Private Vehicles by City (End of 2019)

单位：辆 (unit)

市 City	民用汽车 Civil Vehicles	载客汽车 Passenger Vehicles	载货汽车 Trucks	其他汽车 Other Special Vehicles	摩托车 Motors	#普通 Bicycle Motor
全　　省 Total	**14800767**	**13564300**	**1123755**	**112712**	**1817719**	**1811088**
郑　州　市 Zhengzhou	3448339	3315090	123282	9967	61807	61692
开　封　市 Kaifeng	604124	548686	52117	3321	44047	43913
洛　阳　市 Luoyang	1106100	1019351	80874	5875	139305	136524
平顶山市 Pingdingshan	670304	607394	52968	9942	152874	152023
安　阳　市 Anyang	800353	747464	48676	4200	61841	61686
鹤　壁　市 Hebi	261111	238031	19035	4045	18891	18763
新　乡　市 Xinxiang	986228	893501	87426	5301	75668	75566
焦　作　市 Jiaozuo	522753	481143	34811	6799	77522	76930
濮　阳　市 Puyang	633700	577759	53164	2777	33049	33022
许　昌　市 Xuchang	660506	605297	51750	3459	26917	26873
漯　河　市 Luohe	329646	303871	24835	940	34181	34134
三门峡市 Sanmenxia	299936	276861	21254	1821	158868	157936
南　阳　市 Nanyang	1057925	958329	91946	7650	263666	263578
商　丘　市 Shangqiu	1038591	911084	114520	12987	80551	80475
信　阳　市 Xinyang	643247	556496	67789	18962	263240	262998
周　口　市 Zhoukou	892367	770440	114606	7321	114252	114180
驻马店市 Zhumadian	689808	608002	75979	5827	201100	201004
济　源　市 Jiyuan	155723	145495	8710	1518	9940	9791

19－10 客货运量及周转量

Passenger and Freight Traffic, Turnover Volume

指 标	Item	2005	2010	2012	2013	2014	2015	2016	2017	2018	2019
运输量	**Traffic Volume**										
客运量	Passenger Traffic										
（万人）	(10 000 persons)	98099	167804	208094	225738	141777	146066	122342	116574	112611	111458
#铁路	Railways	5842	8399	9628	11160	12400	13068	14525	16178	17095	18278
国家铁路	National Railways	5758	8392	9628	11160	12400	13068	14525	16178	17095	18278
地方铁路	Local Railways	84	7								
公路	Highways	91920	158630	197785	125450	128279	112535	106415	98753	93707	91281
水运	Waterways	97	255	250	255	254	280	288	345	331	306
货运量	Freight Traffic										
（万吨）	(10 000 tons)	78827	202470	272240	304369	200628	211854	205385	229458	259461	218647
#铁路	Railways	14806	14224	12779	12762	11577	9802	9562	9406	10012	10502
国家铁路	National Railways	12697	13292	11772	11685	10540	9482	9257	9095	9623	10231
地方铁路	Local Railways	2109	931	1007	1077	1037	321	305	311	389	270
公路	Highways	62684	183291	251772	162040	179680	172431	184255	207066	235183	190883
水运	Waterways	1334	4950	7685	9854	9350	10459	11545	12961	14240	17236
周转量	**Turnover Volume**										
旅客周转量	Passenger-Kilometers										
（百万人公里）	(million person-km)	100070	184064	214450	232812	185889	194188	185717	194520	197925	201266
#铁路	Railways	53543	74720	77957	85337	89565	91024	93830	102909	106111	109134
国家铁路	National Railways	53468	74715	77957	85337	89565	91024	93830	102909	106111	109134
地方铁路	Local Railways	75	5								
公路	Highways	43784	103118	130958	71239	84486	74391	76057	73662	71119	69903
水运	Waterways	53	60	60	63	54	54	57	63	61	66
货物周转量	Freight Ton-Kilometers										
（百万吨公里）	(million ton-km)	228260	714182	943642	1035741	736709	758238	733628	816554	893435	859574
#铁路	Railways	175977	198023	208897	209681	192650	166602	168589	189981	201491	207980
国家铁路	National Railways	173606	197118	207904	208607	191593	166447	168444	189854	201333	207857
地方铁路	Local Railways	2371	905	992	1074	1057	156	145	127	157	123
公路	Highways	46700	486063	686301	448801	482237	454267	483853	534167	589392	529976
水运	Waterways	5549	30028	48390	55719	61559	70529	80861	92046	102175	121233

注：2009年3月起国家铁路运输量包含漯阜公司，地方铁路数据不包括漯阜公司;2015年起，受地方铁路改制影响，地方铁路数据仅包含登封铁路公司。

a) Data of LuoFu company was adjusted from local railways to national railways since March 2009.Data of Locomotives only refers to DengFeng railway company since 2015.

19-11 各市公路客货运输量(2019年)

Passenger and Freight Traffic of Highway by City (2019)

市(县)	City(County)	客运量 (万人) Passenger Traffic (10 000 persons)	旅客周转量 (亿人公里) Passenger-Kilometers (100 million person-km)	货运量 (万吨) Freight Traffic (10 000 tons)	货物周转量 (亿吨公里) Freight Ton-Kilometers (100 million ton-km)
全省	**Total**	**91281**	**699.03**	**190883**	**5299.76**
省辖市	**City**				
郑州市	Zhengzhou	7095	90.85	21660	500.00
开封市	Kaifeng	3298	25.18	4169	116.63
洛阳市	Luoyang	10502	55.23	12865	345.23
平顶山市	Pingdingshan	6336	33.11	7724	187.13
安阳市	Anyang	3981	20.66	13823	498.72
鹤壁市	Hebi	633	3.45	4913	181.66
新乡市	Xinxiang	5598	29.20	13576	343.99
焦作市	Jiaozuo	1534	6.97	15270	483.60
濮阳市	Puyang	3121	27.69	6794	202.86
许昌市	Xuchang	4549	16.38	8830	168.59
漯河市	Luohe	1852	10.06	5873	216.20
三门峡市	Sanmenxia	2293	12.58	4702	165.60
南阳市	Nanyang	9962	107.08	13981	504.50
商丘市	Shangqiu	7493	55.31	13564	417.01
信阳市	Xinyang	4374	39.01	7473	86.31
周口市	Zhoukou	5437	59.47	16968	598.31
驻马店市	Zhumadian	12547	101.98	13928	206.17
济源市	Jiyuan	676	4.81	4771	77.24
省直管县	**County Directly Administrated by Province**				
巩义市	Gongyi	856	2.41	3839	91.70
兰考县	Lankao	517	3.65	1891	56.80
汝州市	Ruzhou	1012	8.83	1935	40.01
滑县	Huaxian	1104	7.16	1729	14.04
长垣市	Changyuan	1622	9.94	1537	19.72
邓州市	Dengzhou	1137	9.84	1327	14.09
永城市	Yongcheng	1166	6.93	2321	53.58
固始县	Gushi	739	4.50	2545	22.79
鹿邑县	Luyi	1000	15.34	1658	25.00
新蔡县	Xincai	1259	11.75	2214	20.65

19-12 铁路主要站客货发送量(2019年)

Number of Passengers and Volume of Freight Dispatched from Principal Railway Stations (2019)

车站名称	Name	旅客发送量(万人) Number of Passengers Dispatched (10 000 persons)	车站名称	Name	货物发送量(万吨) Volume of Freight Dispatched (10 000 tons)
郑　　州	Zhengzhou	3518.22	郑 州 北	Northern zhengzhou	26.89
郑 州 东	Eastern zhengzhou	3154.90	新　　密	Xinmi	29.19
巩　　义	Gongyi	99.02	上　　街	Shangjie	78.16
开　　封	Kaifeng	365.51	新　　郑	Xinzheng	215.25
兰　　考	Lankao	135.38	开　　封	Kaifeng	71.51
洛　　阳	Luoyang	624.00	洛 阳 东	Eastern luoyang	35.29
洛阳龙门	Luoyang Longmen	635.61	巩　　义	Gongyi	48.75
偃　　师	Yanshi	36.23	平顶山西	Western pingdingshan	235.42
安　　阳	Anyang	371.22	安　　阳	Anyang	55.38
新　　乡	Xinxiang	436.25	鹤 壁 北	Northern hebi	213.54
焦　　作	Jiaozuo	316.60	新　　乡	Xinxiang	92.76
许　　昌	Xuchang	215.97	焦 作 北	Northern jiaozuo	50.67
三 门 峡	Sanmenxia	126.46	许　　昌	Xuchang	8.52
三门峡南	Southern sanmenxia	171.89	三 门 峡	Sanmenxia	129.75
灵　　宝	Lingbao	57.59	三门峡西	Western sanmenxia	141.78
南　　阳	Nanyang	361.61	南　　阳	Nanyang	6.08
商　　丘	Shangqiu	916.86	商　　丘	Shangqiu	44.59
商 丘 南	Southern shangqiu	117.68	商 丘 北	Northern shangqiu	23.36
民　　权	Minquan	141.66	济　　源	Jiyuan	207.22

注：本表为郑州铁路局辖区内主要站数据。

a) Data in this table are from Principal stations of zhengzhou Railways Administration.

19—13　铁路分货类运输量
Freight Traffic of Railway by Category

货　类	Type of Freight	2018		2019	
		运输量（万吨）Traffic Volume (10 000 tons)	货物周转量（万吨公里）Freight Ton-Kilometers (10 000 ton-km)	运输量（万吨）Traffic Volume (10 000 tons)	货物周转量（万吨公里）Freight Ton-Kilometers (10 000 ton-km)
煤	Coal	1474	340492	32296	9245757
石油	Petroleum	3689	1133591	1520	320864
焦炭	Coke	7661	2229523	3842	1122255
金属矿石	Metal Ores	3099	1075089	7153	1926809
钢铁及有色金属	Steel and Iron,	771	222194	3398	1083481
非金属矿石	Nonmetal Ores	97	34146	1484	400361
磷矿石	Phosphorus Ores	571	148815	122	46796
矿建材料	Mineral Building Materials	11	4004	955	248671
水泥	Cement	271	106570	28	5458
木材	Timber	3699	1210366	309	92622
粮食	Grain	165	70188	3641	1026025
棉花	Cotton	2115	796131	222	97435
化肥和农药	Chemical Fertilizers and Pesticides	16	7659	2276	778825
盐	Salt	1442	543338	7	3056
化工品	Chemical Products	83	28582	1603	595389
工业机械	Industry Machinery	15	6172	603	177875
电子电气	Electronic and Electric	0	7	16	6436
金属制品	Metal Products	610	189482	79	24201
农业机具	Agriculture Implements	32	9067	0	8
鲜活易腐货物	Fresh, Live and Perishable Goods	28	10690	29	8119
农副土特产品	Agriculture Products	261	94665	30	9199
饮食烟草	Diet and Tobaccos	31	12746	305	95465
纺织品	Textile Products	132	54344	53	23970
文教用品	Cultural and Educational Products	19	5957	143	60735
医药品	Medicine Products	637	215528	21	5049
零担	Fragmentary Freight	5064	1913947	1	312
集装箱	Container	60281	18877584	5905	2058187

注：铁路为郑州铁路局全局数。
a) Freight Traffic of railway refers to data of Zhengzhou Railways Administration, highway refers to data of transportation department.

19-14 铁路运输主要技术经济指标

Major Economic and Technical Indicators of Railway Transport

指　　标	Item	2010	2015	2016	2017	2018	2019
货运机车日产量	Average Daily Ton-kilometers of Freight						
（万吨公里）	Locomotives (10 000 ton-kms)	133	115	113	115	117	114
内燃机车	Diesel Locomotives	125	20	21	22	23	21
电力机车	Electric Locomotives	135	118	116	117	119	115
货运机车平均牵引总重量（吨）	Average Total Tonnage of Freight Locomotives (ton)	3667	3460	3390	3430	3431	3398
内燃机车	Diesel Locomotives	3634	1873	1811	1827	1850	1881
电力机车	Electric Locomotives	3674	3475	3404	3418	3443	3408
客运机车日车公里（公里）	Daily Distance per Passenger Locomotive (km)	823	814	788	808	783	805
货运机车日车公里（公里）	Daily Distance per Freight Locomotive (km)	443	448	445	452	457	463
内燃机车万吨公里耗油	Oil Consumption of Diesel Locomotive						
（公斤）	Per 10 000 tons.km (kg)	23.0	129.9	138.0	131.3	135.1	134.1
电力机车万吨公里耗电	Electricity Consumption of Electric						
（千瓦小时）	Locomotive Per 10 000 tons.km (kwh)	107.4	107.1	107.8	106.5	105.3	105.8
旅客列车技术速度（公里/小时）	Technical Speed of Passenger Trains (km/hr)	85.6	88.4	87.5	85.6	87.8	88.6
旅客列车旅行速度（公里/小时）	Traveling Speed of Passenger Trains (km/hr)	73.9	77.1	76.7	77.3	77.0	78.5
货物列车技术速度（公里/小时）	Technical Speed of Freight Trains (km/hr)	46.5	48.9	48.8	48.0	48.7	49.4
货物列车旅行速度（公里/小时）	Running Speed of Freight Trains (km/hr)	33.6	33.7	34.3	35.4	36.0	38.1
货物列车运行正点率（%）	Punctuality Rate of Freight Trains in Running (%)	85.9	93.8	94.3	94.6	95.2	95.1
货物列车出发正点率（%）	Punctuality Rate of Freight Trains at Departure (%)	88.0	93.5	94.0	94.9	95.0	95.4
货车周转时间　　（天）	Trunning Around Time of Freight Cars (day)	1.6	1.8	1.6	1.5	1.5	1.4
货车一次作业时间（小时）	Handling Time of Freight Cars (hour)	24.5	29.5	26.1	25.3	25.8	24.5
货车中转停留时间（小时）	Transfer Waiting Time Per Freight Car (hour)	4.2	4.9	4.8	4.3	4.3	4.0

注：本表数据来源于郑州铁路局。

a) Data in this chapter are from ZhengZhou Railways Administration.

19－15 民航基本情况
Main Indicators of Civil Aviation

指　　标	Item	2012	2015	2016	2017	2018	2019
航线条数(条)	Number of Civil Aviation Routes (unit)	49	61	63	66	70	77
#国际	International Routes	2	11	8	9	9	7
国内	Domestic Routes	45	47	52	56	60	69
地区	Regional Routes	2	3	3	1	1	1
航线里程(公里)	Length of Civil Aviation Routs (km)	60804	71597	76951	82951	91575	127636
#国际	International Routes	2838	10777	9580	13223	13223	21991
国内	Domestic Routes	54756	55781	62332	68115	76739	103929
地区	Regional Routes	3210	5039	5039	1613	1613	1716
飞行架次	Number of Flight	37363	41782	42271	44037	48144	47509
#国际	International Routes	916	2786	3047	2663	2414	2654
国内	Domestic Routes	35277	37345	38223	40886	45046	44141
地区	Regional Routes	1170	1651	1001	488	684	714
民用机场数(个)	Number of Civil Airports (unit)	3	3	3	3	4	4
#可降737以上机型	Airports Serving Boeing 737 and above	3	3	3	3	3	4
民用飞机架数(架)	Number of Civil Aircraft (unit)	20	26	28	31	31	30
通航国家和地区(个)	Navigable Country and Region (unit)	4	5	5	4	5	6
#通航城市	Navigable City	4	10	9	7	7	7
客货吞吐量	Passenger and Cargo throughput						
旅客吞吐量(万人)	Passenger throughput (10 000 persons)	1268.87	1860.69	2229.09	2596.58	2955.74	3184.70
货邮吞吐量(万吨)	Cargo throughput (10 000 tons)	15.31	40.58	45.90	50.51	51.73	52.42

注：民用机场数和客货吞吐量为全省数据，其他指标数据为中国南方航空河南航空有限公司数据修正后数据，2017年和2018年航线里程（国际）为修正后数据。

a) Data of Civil Airports and Passenger and Cargo throughput refer to the whole province,and other data come from China southern airlines co., henan branch.

19－16 邮政行业基本情况及邮政水平(年底数)
Basic Conditions and Level of Post Services (Year-end)

指　　标	Item	2012	2015	2016	2017	2018	2019
局所网络	Offices and Network						
邮政局所(处)	Number of Post Offices (unit)	2531	2595	2595	2603	2626	2625
邮路总长度(公里)	Length of Postal Routes (km)	63846	74234	77488	425176	412682	591371
#汽车邮路总长度	Length of Postal Routes and Rural	55415	70167	73460	132459	112308	120572
铁路邮路总长度	Delivery Routes	7621	3508	3508	3499	3499	4301
农村投递线路总长度(公里)	Rural Delivery Routes(km)	197726	194476	190288	192167	191463	182441
邮政行业业务总量(万元)	Business Volume of Post (10 000 yuan)	691594	1637756	2332232	3327145	4367143	5904545
函件(万件)	Number of Letters (10 000 pcs)	17517	12011	9496	11865	10722	9533
包裹(万件)	Number of Parcels (10 000 pcs)	284	198	160	153	120	111
快递(万件)	Pieces of Express Mail Services (10 000 pcs)	12503	51450	83875	107378	152632	211093
报刊期发数(万份)	Issue of Newspapers and Magazines (10 000 copies)	1010	980	1032	883	870	836
集邮业务(万枚)	Collecting Stamps (10 000 units)	7595	6766	7129	6758	6648	3883
邮政水平	Level of Post Services						
平均每一邮电局所服务面积(平方公里)	Average Area Served by Every Post Office (sq.km)	66	64	64	61	64	64
平均每一邮电局所服务人口(万人)	Average People Served by Every Post Office (10 000 persons)	4.1	3.6	3.6	3.7	3.6	3.8
平均每人发函件数(件)	Average Number of Letters Mailed per Capita (piece)	1.7	1.2	1.0	1.2	1.1	1.0
平均每百人订有报刊数(份)	Average Number of Newspaper and Magazine Subscribed per 100 Persons (piece)	9.6	10.4	10.7	9.0	9.2	8.0

注：1.2010年起快递为全社会快递业务量；邮政业务总量也做同口径调整。

2.2017年起邮路总长度为全社会总长度，包含邮政公司和EMS的邮路长度，同时减去租用或无偿使用的邮路长度。

a) The caliber of Business Volume of Express Mail is the whole volume of the society since 2010, same as the Post.

b) Length of Postal Route refiers to the whole social length, incuding the length of China Post's and EMS's route, excluding the length of rented or free postal route.

19-17 邮电通信行业基本情况

年份 Year	邮电业务总量（万元）Business Volume of Postal and Telecommunications Services (10 000 yuan)	#邮政行业业务总量 Business Volume of Postal Services	函件（万件）Number of Letters (10 000 pcs)	包裹（万件）Package (10 000 pcs)	快递业务量（万件）Pieces of Express Mail Services (10 000 pcs)	订销报刊期发数（万份）Subscription and Issue of Newspapers and Magazines (10 000 pcs)
1978	(5450)7120		11629			
1979	7540		12783			
1980	8062		14230			
1981	8390		14823			
1982	8666		14726			
1983	9024		15144			
1984	9647		16974			
1985	11057		20304			
1986	11977		21055			
1987	14675		24020			
1988	19182		25368			
1989	22805		23345			
1990	(27872)48983		22032			
1991	59324		17335			
1992	80685		17795			
1993	122245		20260			
1994	188902		21963			
1995	302583		21958	648		
1996	461609		22470	648	225	
1997	643107		19164	489	173	
1998	1035556		18799	489	197	
1999	1384139		19452	509	296	
2000	(1869359)1300586	117999	21408	499	423	
2001	1740235	210508	29260	492	539	
2002	2201977	236549	29532	482	761	
2003	3035707	264200	35938	486	945	880
2004	4359263	282726	26470	433	1105	768
2005	5565060	318093	24471	415	1163	686
2006	7214687	365236	23030	405	1136	707
2007	9331635	412016	21515	367	1248	759
2008	11241309	470421	22147	315	1497	846
2009	12968686	548800	19786	271	1788	809
2010	(15077061)5359762	(897962)607027	24704	253	(1793)5765	803
2011	5958822	627996	32396	264	8378	1062
2012	6613588	691594	17516	283	12503	1010
2013	7949251	924593	17570	295	19444	951
2014	10110624	1165358	15828	264	29484	1029
2015	13172754	1637756	12011	198	51450	980
2016	(20658962)9860822	2332232	9496	160	83875	1032
2017	18160442	3327145	11865	153	107378	883
2018	43837204	4367143	10722	120	152632	870
2019	65892361	5904545	9533	111	211093	836

注：1.邮电业务总量2010-2016年按2010年不变价计算，2000-2009年按2000年不变价格计算，1990-1999年按1990年不变价格计算，1978-1989年按1980年不变价格计算。括号内为上个时期不变价数据。
2.2007年起，局用交换机容量包含接入网设备容量。
3.2010年起快递为全社会快递业务量，括号内为原口径数据。
4.2010年起，国际互联网用户含手机上网用户。
5.邮电业务总量2017年按2015年不变价计算，同时对2016年数据进行了调整，2016年括号内为上个时期不变价数据。邮政行业业务总量仍为2010年不变价格，邮电业务总量采取简单相加方法处理。

Basic Conditions of Postal and Telecommunication Services

集 邮 业 务 (万枚) Stamps for Collection (10 000 units)	固定电话 用 户 (万户) Subscribers of Fixed Telephone (10 000 subscribers)	移动电话 用 户 (万户) Subscribers of Mobile Telephone (10 000 subscribers)	本地电话 局用交换 机容量 (万门) Capacity of Local Telephone Exchanges (10 000 line)	长途光缆 线路长度 (公里) Length of Optical Cable Lines (km)	电话普及率 (含移动) (部/百人) Populariza-tion Rate of Telephone (sets/100 persons)	国际互联 网用户 (万户) Number of Subscribers of Internet Services (10 000 subscribers)
	12.05		21.15		0.17	
	12.40		22.01		0.17	
	12.96		22.58		0.18	
	13.12		22.92		0.18	
	13.37		23.77		0.18	
	13.25		24.45		0.17	
	14.33		25.23		0.19	
	15.67		26.91		0.20	
	16.75		27.39		0.21	
	14.00		29.47		0.17	
	16.10		32.50		0.20	
	18.92		35.31		0.23	
	22.76		40.79		0.27	
	27.31		54.45		0.31	
	36.65		66.04		0.42	
	55.70		103.31		0.63	
	89.31		171.76		0.99	
	135.74		238.36		1.50	
	205.71	23.87	349.34		2.51	
2295	292.55	48.02	479.17		3.70	
1045	442.76	118.64	723.20		6.05	
13581	773.51	173.04	837.21		8.68	
13614	912.10	310.30	969.87		12.95	67.52
12352	1096.09	503.03	1049.71	18029	16.79	185.66
10441	1180.31	531.00	1095.47	20658	17.86	208.42
9159	1370.86	1072.57	1159.70	26650	25.72	245.81
10500	1625.03	1392.31	1296.62	32644	31.14	269.17
8769	1863.48	1814.81	1349.56	33093	37.90	274.28
7038	2027.50	2351.20	1376.00	33536	44.90	326.87
6883	1940.47	2914.54	2548.50	34927	49.50	403.26
7100	1562.44	3498.89	2382.21	35718	51.20	494.38
6064	1463.89	4016.84	2304.06	36127	55.10	625.49
8158	1432.00	4449.72	1996.00	36446	59.00	3043.42
7090	1340.39	5061.69	1855.45	30519	68.07	3857.20
7585	1288.90	5787.70	1804.26	30271	75.38	5098.00
6138	1224.38	7200.22	1843.36	30296	89.60	5657.14
5338	1143.04	7712.93	1298.35	31430	94.10	5672.06
6766	1009.66	7975.06	1043.95	33578	95.22	6626.93
7129	798.60	7889.01	901.07	32533	91.14	8145.49
6758	735.04	8553.36	879.63	34589	97.40	9670.83
6648	689.57	9354.14	1540.45	37905	111.27	11199.61
3883	757.84	9841.08	1212.32	35017	121.27	11016.79

a) The Business Volume of Postal and Telecommunication Services since 2000 are calculated at 2000 constant prices.1990~1999 are calculated at 1990 constant prices.1978~1989 are calculated at 1980 constant prices. Data in bracket are calculated at last period constant prices.

b) Data on capacity of local telephone exchanges include network equipment since 2007.

c) Data of pieces of express mail refer to the whole social since 2010, data in the brakfets are original data.

d) Data on Subscribers of Internet Services include Mobile Internet since 2010.

e)The Business Volume of Postal and Telecommunication Services on 2017 was calculated at 2015 constant price, and the data on 2016 was adjusted, the data in brackets of 2016 was calculated the constant price of the last period. The Business Volume of Pos.

19-18 通信行业基本情况及通信水平(年底数)

Basic Conditions and Level of Telecommunication Services (Year-end)

指　　标	Item	2015	2016	2017	2018	2019
通信网络	**Network of Telecommunication**					
电信业务总量(亿元)	Business Volume of Telecommunication Services (100 million yuan)	1153.50	(1832.67) 752.86	1483.33	3947.01	5998.78
移动电话用户期末数(万户)	Number of Mobile Telephones Subscribers at Year-end (10 000 subscribers)	7975	7889	8553	9354	9841
4G移动电话用户（万户）	4G Mobile Phone Users (10 000 subscribers)	2075.90	4403.50	6045.70	7232.20	8067.40
5G移动电话用户（万户）	5G Mobile Phone Users (10 000 subscribers)					19.28
固定电话用户(万户)	Number of Local Telephone Subscribers of at Year-end (10 000 subscribers)	1010	799	735	690	758
住宅电话用户(万户)	Number of Household Telephone Subscribers (10 000 subscribers)	556.11	427.20	350.69	334.40	204.54
国际互联网用户(万户)	Number of Subscribers of Internet Service (10 000 Subscribers)	6626.93	8145.49	9670.83	11199.61	11016.79
IPTV（网络电视）用户(万户)	IPTV Users(10 000 Subscribers)	45.10	315.00	529.40	1645.68	1775.25
物联网终端用户(万户)	Internet of Things End Users (10 000 Subscribers)	311.80	491.30	1151.00	3778.50	7043.21
电信主要通信能力	**Major Capacity of Telecommunication Services**					
局用电话交换机容量(万门)	Capacity of Office Telephone Exchanges (10 000 units)	1044	901	880	1540	1212
移动电话交换机容量(万户)	Capacity of Mobile Telephone Exchanges (10 000 subscribers)	11713	12357	12239	12116	14005
长途光缆线路长度(公里)	Length of Optical Cable Lines(km)	33578	32533	34589	37905	35017
移动电话基站数（万个）	Number of Mobile Phone Base Stations (10 000 units)	25	30	33	34	43
固定互联网宽带接入端口（万个）	Fixed Internet Broadband Access Terminal (10 000 units)	2403	4346	4476	4781	4753
通信水平	**Level of Telecommunication**					
固定电话普及率(部/百人)	Popularization Rate of Telephone (sets/100 persons)	10.7	8.4	7.7	7.2	7.9
移动电话普及率(部/百人)	Popularization Rate of Mobile Telephone (sets/100 persons)	84.5	82.8	89.7	104.1	113.4
已通固定电话的乡(镇)比重(%)	Percentage of Townships with Telephone (%)	100	100	100	100	100
移动电话(GSM)网络覆盖县(市)	Number of County(city) Covered by GSM (unit)	109	109	109	109	109
移动电话(CDMA)网络覆盖县(市)	Number of County(city) Covered by CDMA (unit)	109	109	109	109	109
移动电话漫游国家和地区(个)	Number of country (Territory) Roamed through Mobile Telephone (unit)	245	245	245	245	245
数据通信网覆盖地(市)	Number of Region(city) Covered by Data Traffic (unit)	18	18	18	18	18

注：1.从2012年起，长途电话业务电路包含固定电话网、移动电话网和各类数据通信网内为疏通长话业务开放使用的长途电路。
2.电信业务总量2017年按2015年不变价计算，同时对2016年数据进行了调整，2016年括号内为上个时期不变价数据。

a) since 2012, Long-distance Call Lines include Fixed Telephone, Mobile Telephones and other Communication network.

b) The Business Volume of Telecommunication Serviceson 2017 was calculated at 2015 constant price, and the data on 2016 was adjusted, the data in brackets of 2016 was calculated the constant price of the last period.

19－19　各市邮政网和业务量(2019年)

Network and Business Volume of Post by City (2019)

市(县) City(County)	邮政局所 (处) Number of Post Offices (unit)	邮路总长度 (公里) Length of Postal Routes (km)	农村投递线路总长度 (公里) Rural Delivery Routes (km)	邮政行业业务总量 (亿元) Business Volume of Post (100 million yuan)	函件 (万件) Number of Letters (10 000 pcs)
全　　省 Total	**2625**	**591371**	**182441**	**590.45**	**9532.85**
郑　州　市 Zhengzhou	245	502042	13290	201.72	4506.85
开　封　市 Kaifeng	116	4098	9105	15.12	79.51
洛　阳　市 Luoyang	202	5846	12460	42.34	427.45
平顶山市 Pingdingshan	137	2662	8334	11.18	1123.76
安　阳　市 Anyang	121	5997	11172	23.16	168.79
鹤　壁　市 Hebi	31	606	2795	5.97	47.79
新　乡　市 Xinxiang	171	4621	14105	29.54	608.19
焦　作　市 Jiaozuo	115	1612	7679	33.69	75.29
濮　阳　市 Puyang	99	2056	6183	12.95	95.57
许　昌　市 Xuchang	104	2478	7677	20.27	667.53
漯　河　市 Luohe	62	1355	3647	22.33	159.66
三门峡市 Sanmenxia	84	1640	6573	6.50	106.29
南　阳　市 Nanyang	274	14759	21504	34.54	270.85
商　丘　市 Shangqiu	209	20922	12062	58.51	389.69
信　阳　市 Xinyang	227	9221	16150	16.68	418.75
周　口　市 Zhoukou	200	4501	16418	24.35	172.77
驻马店市 Zhumadian	203	6220	12061	28.60	181.32
济　源　市 Jiyuan	25	735	1226	3.01	32.79

市(县) City(County)	包裹 (万件) Package (10 000 pcs)	快递业务量 (万件) Business Volume of Express Delivery (10 000 pcs)	快递业务收入 (亿元) Pieces of Express Mail Services (100 million yuan)	订销报刊期发数 (万份) Subscription and Issue of Newspapers and Magazines (10 000 pcs)	集邮业务 (万枚) Collecting Stamps (10 000 units)
全　　省 Total	**111.34**	**211093**	**188.64**	**836**	**3883**
郑　州　市 Zhengzhou	21.07	82329	89.27	82	861
开　封　市 Kaifeng	5.62	4876	4.53	42	179
洛　阳　市 Luoyang	12.80	15899	11.83	63	579
平顶山市 Pingdingshan	1.79	2951	3.15	52	148
安　阳　市 Anyang	3.01	6652	4.42	48	140
鹤　壁　市 Hebi	0.37	2110	1.54	16	61
新　乡　市 Xinxiang	7.61	8646	9.32	69	261
焦　作　市 Jiaozuo	4.88	13507	7.90	50	361
濮　阳　市 Puyang	6.43	3299	3.05	35	87
许　昌　市 Xuchang	6.89	7299	6.34	36	92
漯　河　市 Luohe	2.44	8920	6.55	19	51
三门峡市 Sanmenxia	1.14	1886	1.82	31	82
南　阳　市 Nanyang	6.80	10620	8.52	93	247
商　丘　市 Shangqiu	14.31	21623	12.75	47	93
信　阳　市 Xinyang	1.51	4191	4.42	56	147
周　口　市 Zhoukou	3.48	6685	6.07	47	196
驻马店市 Zhumadian	10.64	8783	6.47	41	264
济　源　市 Jiyuan	0.55	816	0.68	10	34

注：本表全省合计包括郑州邮区中心局数据。
a) Data of Total include Data of Center situation in zhengzhou postal district.EMS only refers to postal.

19-20 各市电信网和业务量(2019年)

市 City	局用电话交换机容量(万门) Capacity of Office Telephone Exchanges (10 000 lines)	移动电话交换机容量(万户) Capacity of Mobile Telephone Exchanges (10 000 subscribers)	电信业务总量(亿元) Business Volume of Telecommunications (100 million yuan)	(固定)互联网宽带接入端口数(万个) Fixed Internet Broadband Access Terminal (10 000 units)
全省 Total	**1212**	**14005**	**5998.78**	**4753**
郑州市 Zhengzhou	232	2881	1268.42	716
开封市 Kaifeng	50	468	255.32	213
洛阳市 Luoyang	153	1326	474.97	432
平顶山市 Pingdingshan	50	600	255.88	222
安阳市 Anyang	47	607	319.16	342
鹤壁市 Hebi	14	143	98.76	84
新乡市 Xinxiang	112	942	381.80	332
焦作市 Jiaozuo	64	651	210.93	216
濮阳市 Puyang	33	375	218.19	152
许昌市 Xuchang	50	707	222.21	223
漯河市 Luohe	33	234	139.55	109
三门峡市 Sanmenxia	27	340	126.89	116
南阳市 Nanyang	73	1109	449.68	372
商丘市 Shangqiu	78	864	431.45	376
信阳市 Xinyang	57	625	310.69	265
周口市 Zhoukou	64	1253	431.59	296
驻马店市 Zhumadian	62	801	358.27	238
济源市 Jiyuan	15	78	44.68	50

Network of Telecommunications and Business Volume by City (2019)

移动电话通话时长 (万分钟) Length of Calls of Mobile Telephone (10 000 minutes)	移动电话用户 (万户) Number of Mobile Telephone Subscribers (10 000 subscribers)	4G电话用户 (万户) Fourth Generation Telephone Subscribers (10 000 subscribers)	移动短信业务量 (亿条) SMS Business (100 million piece)	固定电话用户 (万户) Fixed Telephone Subscribers (10 000 subscribers)	家庭宽带接入用户 (万户) Household Broadband Subscribers (10 000 subscribers)	国际互联网用户 (万户) International Internet Service Subscribers (10 000 subscribers)
3204101	**9841.08**	**8067.40**	**1028.90**	**757.84**	**2437.87**	**11016.79**
614201	1665.71	1468.02	235.65	173.72	412.06	1976.77
136938	438.12	354.25	40.89	33.06	100.97	446.89
252225	730.37	616.38	92.00	75.19	197.77	957.12
146188	472.84	390.13	54.91	30.63	116.59	505.43
179683	554.28	452.10	51.45	51.04	140.64	672.05
52638	164.13	132.52	15.59	12.09	39.88	195.30
212032	626.90	516.58	67.83	52.56	164.16	786.00
136074	364.48	308.02	41.53	26.26	103.75	522.13
125355	373.03	295.95	32.39	24.41	98.81	457.57
131077	429.67	346.08	45.77	38.27	100.84	495.90
75660	243.90	196.14	21.46	15.67	58.00	266.78
82061	222.42	181.54	29.16	18.06	60.73	294.17
253071	857.54	688.60	73.74	61.76	192.09	804.04
227103	729.05	565.84	55.80	44.18	171.88	737.91
153477	545.95	430.89	53.47	40.16	133.85	536.41
217633	714.55	563.15	56.84	21.91	177.46	664.89
176898	628.24	495.72	52.81	31.38	147.03	584.18
31786	79.87	65.48	7.65	7.50	21.36	113.26

主要统计指标解释

铁路营业里程 又称营业长度，指投入客货运输营业或临时营业的线路长度。

铁路电气化里程 指具备了电力机车牵引条件，并已交付运营的线路里程。

公路里程 指报告期末公路的实际长度。统计范围：包括城间、城乡间、乡（村）间能行驶汽车的公共道路，公路通过城镇街道的里程，公路桥梁长度、隧道长度、渡口宽度。不包括城市街道里程，断头路里程，农（林）业生产用道路里程，工（矿）企业等内部道路里程。统计原则：按已竣工验收或交付使用的实际里程计算；两条或多条公路共同经由同一路段的重复里程，只计算一次。

内河航道里程 指在一定时期内，能通航运输船舶及排筏的天然河流、湖泊水库、运河及通航渠道的长度。包括全年季节性通航累计三个月以上的航道，不包括仅供零散流放竹、木排的河道。两省以河为界的航道里程，双方均按一半计算，以免重复。该指标可以反映内河水运网的规模、水平和发展情况。

民用航空航线里程 指统计期间内全部民用航空航线的航线总长度。航线长度指民用航空航线的计费距离。计算航线里程可按重复和不重复两种方法，前者是指各航线长度相加的总和；后者则要扣除各航线之间相同航段重复计算的部分。

货（客）运量 指在一定时期内，各种运输工具实际运送的货物（旅客）数量。它是反映运输业为国民经济和人民生活服务的数量指标，也是制定和检查运输生产计划、研究运输发展规模和速度的重要指标。货运按吨计算，客运按人计算。货物不论运输距离长短、货物类别，均按实际重量统计。旅客不论行程远近或票价多少，均按一人一次客运量统计；半价票、小孩票也按一人统计。

货物（旅客）周转量 指在一定时期内，由各种运输工具运送的货物（旅客）数量与其相应运输距离的乘积之总和。它是反映运输业生产总成果的重要指标，也是编制和检查运输生产计划，计算运输效率、劳动生产率以及核算运输单位成本的主要基础资料。计算货物周转量通常按发出站与到达站之间的最短距离，也就是计费距离计算。计算公式为：

货物（旅客）周转量＝∑货物（旅客）运输量×运输距离

民用汽车拥有量 指报告期末，在公安交通管理部门按照《机动车注册登记工作规范》，已注册登记领有民用车辆牌照的全部汽车数量。汽车拥有量统计的主要分类：根据汽车结构分为载客汽车、载货汽车以及其他汽车；根据汽车所有者的不同分为个人（私人）汽车、单位汽车；根据汽车的使用性质分为营运汽车、非营运汽车和特种汽车；根据汽车大小规格不同载客汽车分为大型、中型、小型和微型，载客汽车分为重型、中型、轻型和微型。

电信 指利用有线、无线的电磁系统或者光电系统，传送、发射或者接受语音、文字、数据图像以及其他任何形式信息的活动。主要包括固定电信服务、移动电信服务和其他电信服务。

移动电话用户 指在电信运营企业营业网点办理开户登记手续，通过移动电话交换机进入移动电话网，占用移动电话号码的各类电话用户。包括各类签约用户、智能网预付费用户、无线上网卡用户。

互联网上网人数 指过去半年内使用过互联网的6周岁及以上中国居民人数。

固定电话用户 指在电信运营企业营业网点办理开户登记手续并已接入固定电话网上的全部电话用户。包括普通电话用户、公用电话用户、窄带综合业务数字网（N—ISDN）用户、智能网专用接入终端用户等。按行政区划分为城市电话用户和农村电话用户。

城市电话用户 指直辖市、省辖市、地级市、县级市的市区、市郊区及县城(包括县人民政府所在地的县城关区或行政建制相当于县人民政府所在地的镇)范围内接入局用交换机的电话用户数，包括分布在农村地区的独立工矿区、林区、驻军等接入局用交换机的电话用户数。

农村电话用户 指县城关区以下的集镇和农村接入局用交换机的电话用户数。

住宅电话用户 指私人付费或安装在居民住宅并按照私人或住宅电话用户登记注册和收费的各类电话用户。

固定长途电话交换机容量 指用于接入长途电话网的电话交换机的设备额定容量，包括国际电话交换机容量。

局用交换机容量 指安装在电信企业内用于接续本地固定电话的电话交换机容量，包括接入网设备容量（安装在电信运营企业用于连接语音用户的远端节点的设备容量）。

移动电话交换机容量 指移动电话交换机根据一定话务模型和交换机处理能力计算出来的最大同时服务用户的数量。按报告期末已割接入网正式投入使用的设备实际容量统计。

Explanatory Notes on Main Statistical Indicators

Length of Railways in Operation refers to the total length of the trunk line for passenger and freight transportation in full operation or temporary operation.

Length of Electrified Railways refers to the length of the section of railways in operation in which the power supply lines and other equipment are installed for the running of electrified locomotives. The proportion of the length of electrified railways to the total length of railways in operation is an important indicator to show the modernization of railways.

Length of Highways refers to the actual length of highways at the end of reference period. It covers public roads running vehicles among cities, city and rural areas, township (villages), highways passing through streets at small cities and towns, length of bridges and tunnels, width of ferry piers. It does not include the length of streets in cities, dead end highways, the length of streets built for agricultural (forest) production and inside factories (mines). It can only be calculated with the actual mileage having been completed, checked and accepted or put into operation. If two or more highways go the same section of the way, the length of the section is only calculated for once.

Length of Navigable Inland Waterways an indicator reflecting the size and development of inland water network, it refers to the length of the natural rivers, lakes, reservoirs, canals, and ditches open to navigation during a given period, which enables the transport by ships and rafts. It includes the channels open to navigation for over an accumulative 3 months in a year, yet this does not include the river courses which are only used to float odd logs and bamboo rafts.

Length of Civil Aviation Routes refers to the length of all routes for civil aviation flights, which is used to account the freight, during the period of statistics.. There are usually two ways to calculate the route length: duplicated calculation and non-duplicated calculateion, the former is the sum of length of all civil aviation routes, and the latter should deduct the duplication length of same route among all routes.

Freight (Passenger) Traffic refers to the volume of freight (passenger) transported with various means. Freight transport is calculated in tons and passenger traffic is calculated in the number of persons. Despite the type of freight and travelling distance, the freight transport is calculated in the actual weight of the goods: and despite the travelling distance and ticket price, the passenger traffic is calculated by the principle that one person can be counted only once in one travel. The passenger who travel with a half price ticket or a child ticket is also calculated as one person. The freight (passenger) traffic provides a quantitative measure to show how the transport industry serves the national economy and people, and is also an important indicator for planning the transport industry and for studying the development scale and speed of the transport industry.

Freight Ton-kilometers (Passenger-kilometers) refer to the sum of the products of the volume of transported cargo (passengers) multiplying by the transport distance, usually using ton-kilometer and passenger-kilometer as units for measurement. Normally, the shortest distance between the departure station and the destination station (i.e., the payable distance) is the basis to calculate the freight ton-kilometers. This is an important indicator to show the total results of the transport industry, to prepare and examine the transport plan and to measure the efficiency, the labour productivity and the unit cost of transport.

The formula is as follows:

Freight Ton-kilometers (Passenger-kilometers) =∑{Freight (Passenger) Traffic x Distance of Transportation}

Measuring unit: ton-kilometer (person-kilometer)

Possession of civil Motor Vehicles refer to the total numbers of vehicles that are registered and received vehicles' license tags according to the Work Standard for Motor Vehicles Registration formulated by transport management office under department of public security at the end of reference period. They are divided into following categories according to the structure of motor vehicles: passenger vehicles, trucks and others; and private vehicles and vehicles for units use according to ownerships; working vehicles, non-working vehicles and special motor vehicles according to kind of usage; large passenger vehicles; medium passenger vehicles and small passenger vehicles, heavy trucks, light-heavy trucks and light trucks according to sizes of vehicles.

Telecom refers to fixed telecom service, mobile telecom service and other telecommunications services.

Mobile Telephone Subscribers refer to persons who have gone through registration procedures in the operation points of enterprises engaged in telecommunications and are hence connected with the mobile telephone communication network through the mobile telephone switchboards and occupy mobile phone numbers. Included are various types of subscriber, prepaid users for intelligent network and wireless network card users.

Internet Users refer to the number of Chinese citizens aged 6 and over who use the Internet in the past six months.

Local Telephone Subscribers refer to all subscribers who have gone through registration procedures in the operation points of enterprises engaged in telecommunications and are hence connected to the local telecommunications service provider through fixed line network. Included are general subscribers, public telephones subscribers, N-ISDN subscribers and intelligent network terminal subscribers. They are also classified in terms of administrative districts as urban telephone subscribers and rural telephone subscribers according to location.

Urban Telephone Subscribers refer to the number of telephone subscribers, located at the different administrative districts of municipalities directly under the Central Government, cities under the jurisdiction of province, cities at prefecture level, downtown and suburb of city at county level town and county towns, that are connected to the public line telephone network, including rural mineral area, forest area, military area.

Rural Telephone Subscribers refer to telephone subscribers, located at the towns below the level of county town and villages, that are connected to the public line telephone network.

Household Telephone Subscribers refer to all kinds of subscribers with telephone sets paid privately or installed in the dwelling units of residents, and registered as private subscribers or residence subscribers for payment.

Capacity of Long Distance Telephone Exchanges refers to the rated capacity of telephone exchanges to connect long distance telephone network, including capacity of international telephone exchanges.

Capacity of Office Telephone Exchanges refers to the capacity (measured in gate) of telephone exchanges installed in the offices of telecommunication service providers for communication between fixed telephones. It includes the capacity of access network equipment (capacity of equipment installed in the offices of telecommunication service providers for connecting distant nodes of voice users).

Capacity of Mobile Telephone Exchanges refers to the capacity of the maximum services provided to subscribers at any one time as computed based on a certain model of calls distribution and transacting capacity of the mobile telephone exchanges. It is calculated based on the actual capacity of equipments connected to network through cutover and put into operation officially at the end of the reference period.

资源和环境

Resources and Environment

20

● 资料整理：秦红涛

简要说明

一、主要内容

本篇包括自然状况，自然资源，水环境，大气环境，固体废物，生态环境，自然灾害和环境污染治理投资等资料。

二、资料来源

自然状况包括土地、山脉、河流等数据资料，根据有关历史资料整理。气象资料由河南省气象局提供；矿产资源数据由河南省国土资源厅提供；环境污染与治理、污染物排放及处理、工业污染治理投资情况为省环境保护厅提供；水资源、城市生活垃圾清运及处理、耕地变动、森林资源、自然灾害等情况分别为省水利厅、省住房和城乡建设厅、省国土资源厅、省林业厅、省民政厅提供。由省统计局能源处、社会与科技统计处和固定资产投资处编辑整理。

2020年年鉴刊载的2017年环境污染与治理、污染物排放及处理相关数据，出自第二次全国污染源普查数据。由省生态环境厅按照生态环境部统一要求提供。

Brief Introduction

I. Main Contents

Data in this chapter mainly reflect administrative areas, Natural Conditions and Natural Resources. the Water Environment, Atmospheric environment, solid waste, ecological environment, natural disasters and investment in environmental pollution treatment.

II. Sources of Data

Data on environmental pollution and reatment, pollutants from consumption, investment in the Data on natural conditions cover land area, mountain ranges, rivers and so on. Data on natural conditions are compiled by the Department of Comprehensive Statistics using relevant historical data. Data on meteorological phenomena and mineral are provided respectively by Henan Provincial Bureau of Meteorological and Henan Provincial Bureau of Land and Resources. treatment of industrial pollution are provided by the Henan provincial bureau of environmental protection. Data on water resource, city life garbage removed and disposed, change of cultivated land, forest resources, natural disaster are provided from the Henan provincial bureau of Land and Resources, Henan provincial bureau of Water Resources, Henan provincial bureau of Housing and Urban-Rural Development, Henan provincial bureau of Forestry Administration and Henan provincial bureau of civil affairs. Data in this chapter are provided by Department of Energy , social and scientific and technological, and investment in fixed assets of the Henan provincial Bureau of Statistics.

The data on environmental pollution and treatment, pollutant discharge and treatment in 2017 published in the 2020 Yearbook are from the data of the second national pollution source census. Provided by the Provincial Department of ecological environment in accordance with the unified requirements of the Ministry of ecological environment.

20-1 生态环境保护情况
Basic Conditions of Environmental Protection

指标名称	Item	2005	2010	2015	2017	2018	2019
森林面积(万公顷)	Forest Area (10 000 hectares)	270.30	336.59	394.50	409.65	416.50	
森林覆盖率(%)	Forest-coverage Rate (%)	16.2	20.2	23.6	24.5	24.9	
活立木蓄积量(万立方米)	Total Standing Stock Volume (10 000cu.m)	13371	18051	22881	22881	26564	
森林蓄积量(万立方米)	Stock Volume of the Forest (10 000cu.m)	8405	12936	17095	17895	20719	
当年造林面积(万公顷)	Area of Afforestation for This Year (10 000 hectares)	26.35	27.71	20.00	15.99	17.36	19.65
人工造林面积	Artificial afforestation	18.67	21.23	15.47	12.63	13.73	16.48
无林地和疏林地本年新封	Closure in non-stocked Land and Scattered Wood Land	7.68	5.15	3.19	1.98	1.89	1.83
湿地面积(万公顷)	Area of Wetlands (10 000 hectares)	110.87	110.87	62.79	62.79	62.79	62.79
自然保护区数(个)	Number of Nature Reserves (unit)	32	35	30	30	30	30
#国家级自然保护区	National-level Nature Reserves	10	11	12	13	13	13
自然保护区面积(万公顷)	Area of Nature Reserves (10 000 hectares)	73.77	73.48	75.90	76.24	74.32	74.32
自然保护区面积占国土面积比重(%)	Percentage of Nature Reserves in the Region (%)	4.3	4.4	4.5	4.6	4.5	4.5

20-2 自然资源
Natural Resources

项目	Item	2005	2010	2018	2019
地理位置	**Geographical Position**				
东经	East Longitude	110°21′～116°39′	110°21′～116°39′	110°21′～116°39′	110°21′～116°39′
北纬	North Latitude	31°23′～36°23′	31°23′～36°23′	31°23′～36°23′	31°23′～36°23′
矿产资源(保有储量)	**Mineral Resources (Ensured Reserves)**				
煤炭(亿吨)	Coal (100 million tons)	260.00	279.74	388.41	389.07
铁矿(矿石,亿吨)	Iron Ore (100 million tons)	10.60	16.35	20.55	20.53
铝矿(铝土矿矿石,亿吨)	Aluminium (100 million tons)	4.59	7.84	11.84	12.80
钼矿(钼,万吨)	Molybdenum (10 000 tons)	374.60	365.05	601.24	750.72
金矿(金,吨)	Gold mine (ton)	353.58	379.15	716.96	748.85
冶金用白云岩(矿石,亿吨)	Metallurgical Dolomite (100 million tons)	0.32	1.45	3.31	2.98
钨矿(VO3 万吨)	Tungsten (VO3,10 000 tons)	56.63	43.86	24.87	60.23
蓝晶石(万吨)	kyanite (10 000 tons)	416.60	355.26	375.98	375.98
红柱石(万吨)	Andalusite (10 000 tons)	1016.89	995.38	854.30	854.30
天然碱(矿物,万吨)	Trona (10 000 tons)	8384.90	8830.11	14621.01	14608.76

20-3 水资源情况

Water Resources

指标名称	Item	2005	2010	2015	2017	2018	2019
降水量(毫米)	Precipitation(mm)	905.8	841.7	704.1	827.8	755.0	875.9
水资源总量(亿立方米)	Total Amount of Water Resources (100 million cu.m)	558.56	534.89	287.17	423.06	339.83	168.56
#地表水资源量	Surface Water Resources	435.92	415.70	186.74	311.24	241.67	105.79
地下水资源量	Ground Water Resources	219.74	214.66	173.07	206.54	187.97	119.12
地表水与地下水资源重复量	Duplicated Measurement Between Surface Water and Ground Water		95.47	72.64	94.73	89.81	56.34
用水总量(亿立方米)	Water Use (100 million cu.m)	197.81	224.61	222.83	233.77	234.63	237.85
农业用水	Agriculture	114.59	125.59	120.09	122.84	119.92	121.80
工业用水	Industry	45.71	55.57	52.51	50.97	50.38	45.19
生活用水	Consumption	37.51	36.11	41.17	40.16	40.70	41.63
生态环境补水	Ecological Protection		7.34	9.07	19.80	23.62	29.23

20-4 废水中主要污染物排放情况

Main Pollutant Emission in Waste Water

指标名称	Item	2017
废水排放总量(亿吨)	Total Waste Water Discharge (100 millin tons)	27.44
工业废水排放量	Industrial Waste Water Discharge	5.11
城镇生活污水排放量	Urban Living Waste Water Discharge	17.80
农村生活污水排放量	Rural Living Waste Water Discharge	4.51
集中式治理设施污水排放量	Waste Water Discharged from Centralized Treatment Facilities	0.01
化学需氧量(COD)排放量(万吨)	COD Emission (10 000 tons)	143.55
工业废水中COD排放量	COD Emission from Industrial Waste Water	2.39
农业COD排放量	COD Emission from Agricultur	79.26
城镇生活污水中COD排放量	COD Emission from Urban Living Waste Water Discharge	25.74
农村生活污水中COD排放量	COD Emission from Rural Living Waste Water Discharge	36.11
集中式治理设施污水中COD排放量	COD Emission from Waste Water Discharged from Centralized Treatment Facilities	0.05
氨氮排放量(万吨)	Ammonia Nitrogen Emission (10 000 tons)	4.56
工业废水中氨氮排放量	Ammonia Nitrogen Emission from Industrial Waste Wate	0.11
农业氨氮排放量	Ammonia Nitrogen Emission from Agriculture	1.23
城镇生活污水中氨氮排放量	Ammonia Nitrogen Emission from Urban Living Waste Water Discharge	2.42
农村生活污水中氨氮排放量	Ammonia Nitrogen Emission from Rural Living Waste Water Discharge	0.79
集中式治理设施污水中氨氮排放量	Ammonia Nitrogen Emission from Waste Water Discharged from Centralized Treatment Facilities	0.00

注：本表数据为第二次全国污染源普查数据。

a) Data in this table are from the results of the second national pollution source census.

20-5 各市年平均气温和平均年降水量(2019年)

Annual Average Temperature and Average Annual Precipitation by City (2019)

市 City	年平均气温(摄氏度) Annual Average Temperature (degree centigrade)	平均年降水量(毫米) Average Annual Precipitation (mm)
全省 Total	**15.7**	**512.6**
郑州市 Zhengzhou	16.1	509.5
开封市 Kaifeng	15.8	454.7
洛阳市 Luoyang	15.1	611.3
平顶山市 Pingdingshan	15.8	533.2
安阳市 Anyang	15.1	414.5
鹤壁市 Hebi	15.2	398.1
新乡市 Xinxiang	15.6	380.8
焦作市 Jiaozuo	16.0	341.3
濮阳市 Puyang	14.8	467.8
许昌市 Xuchang	15.6	530.6
漯河市 Luohe	15.5	557.2
三门峡市 Sanmenxia	14.0	577.9
南阳市 Nanyang	16.2	547.1
商丘市 Shangqiu	15.2	563.5
信阳市 Xinyang	16.6	689.0
周口市 Zhoukou	16.1	469.7
驻马店市 Zhumadian	16.0	508.3
济源市 Jiyuan	15.9	546.6

20-6 大气环境情况
Basic Conditions of Atmosphere Environment

指标名称	Item	2017
二氧化硫(SO2)排放量(万吨)	Sulphur Dioxide Emission (10 000 tons)	16.44
工业SO2排放量	Sulphur Dioxide Emission From Industry	13.07
城镇生活SO2排放量	Sulphur Dioxide Emission From Urban Living	0.81
农村生活SO2排放量	Sulphur Dioxide Emission From Rural Living	2.54
非工业企业锅炉SO2排放量	Sulphur Dioxide Emission From Boilers of Non-Industrial Enterprises	0.02
集中式治理设施SO2排放量	Sulphur Dioxide Emission from Centralized Treatment Facilities	0.00
氮氧化物排放量(万吨)	Nitrogen Oxides Emission (10 000tons)	100.39
工业氮氧化物排放量	Nitrogen Oxides Emission From Industry	21.44
城镇生活氮氧化物排放量	Nitrogen Oxides Emission From Urban Living	0.44
农村生活氮氧化物排放量	Nitrogen Oxides Emission From Rural Living	1.86
非工业企业锅炉氮氧化物排放量	Nitrogen Oxides Emission From Boilers of Non-Industrial Enterprises	0.06
机动车氮氧化物排放量	Nitrogen Oxides Emission From Motor Vehicle	41.92
非道路移动源氮氧化物排放量	Nitrogen Oxides Emission From Non-road Mobile Sources	34.66
集中式治理设施氮氧化物排放量	Nitrogen Oxides Emission From Centralized Treatment Facilities	0.01
烟(粉)尘排放量(万吨)	Smoke and Dust Emission ((10 000 tons)	37.99
工业烟(粉)尘排放量	Smoke and Dust Emission From Industry	22.92
城镇生活烟尘排放量	Smoke and Dust Emission From Urban Living	1.17
农村生活烟尘排放量	Smoke and Dust Emission From Rural Living	11.99
非工业企业锅炉烟(粉)尘排放量	Smoke and Dust Emission From Boilers of Non-Industrial Enterprises	0.00
机动车烟尘排放量	Smoke and Dust Emission From Motor Vehicle	0.65
非道路移动源烟尘排放量	Smoke and Dust Emission From Non-road Mobile Sources	1.25
集中式治理设施烟尘排放量	Smoke and Dust Emission From Centralized Treatment Facilities	0.00

20-7 固体废物的产生及利用情况
Production and Utilization of Industrial Solid Wastes

指标名称	Item	2017
一般工业固体废物产生量(万吨)	Volume of General Industrial Solid Wastes Produced (10 000tons)	17581.61
一般工业固体废物综合利用量(万吨)	Volume of General Industrial Solid Wastes Utilized (10 000tons)	10205.80
#综合利用往年贮存量(万吨)	Volume of Storage of Former Years Utilized	28.98
一般工业固体废物综合利用率(%)	Proportion of General Industrial Solid Wastes Utilized (%)	58.0
一般工业固体废物处置量(万吨)	Volume of General Industrial Solid Wastes Disposed (10 000tons)	4961.08
#处置往年贮存量(万吨)	Accumulated in Previous Years	65.34
一般工业固体废物处置率(%)	Proportion of General Industrial Solid Wastes Disposed (%)	28.1
一般工业固体废物贮存量(万吨)	Storage capacity of General Industrial Solid Wastes(10 000tons)	2509.03
一般工业固体废物倾倒丢弃量(吨)	Dump quantity of General Industrial Solid Wastes(ton)	80.68
危险废物产生量(吨)	Volume of Hazardous waste (ton)	1846084.14
危险废物自行综合利用量(吨)	Volume of Hazardous waste Utilized (ton)	1267824.82
#综合利用处置往年贮存量	Volume of Storage of Former Years Utilized	53362.36
危险废物综合利用率(%)	Proportion of Hazardous waste Utilized (%)	66.75
危险废物自行处置量(吨)	Volume of Hazardous wastes Treated (ton)	198060.52
危险废物贮存量(吨)	Storage capacity of Hazardous wastes(ton)	498574.94

20−8　农村环境基本情况
Basic Condition of Rural Enviroment

指　　标	Item	2016	2017	2018	2019
农村自来水普及率(%)	Popularizing rate of rural Tap water (%)	78.4	85.3	87.0	91.0
农村卫生厕所普及率(%)	Popularizing rate of rural Sanitation toilets (%)	80.3	75.2	81.2	84.7
农村太阳能热水器面积(万平方米)	Area of Rural Solar water heater (10 000 cu.m)	603	396	639	612

20−9　自然灾害情况
Conditions of Natural Disasters

指标名称	Item	2016	2017	2018	2019
地质灾害次数(次)	Number of Geological disasters (time)	89	20	7	6
地质灾害直接经济损失(万元)	Direct Economic Losses in Geological disasters (10 000 yuan)	2437	279	894	335
森林火灾次数(次)	Number of Forest fires (time)	191	81	41	156
森林火灾受害森林面积（火场总面积，公顷）	Destructed Forest area in Forest fires (ha)	382	237	126	596
突发环境事件次数(次)	Number of Environmental Emergencies (time)	4	5	12	6

20-10 各市农村改厕情况(2019年)
Condition of Rural Compost toilets by City (2019)

市	City	累计卫生厕所户数(万户) Sanitary toilet number (10 000 household)	卫生厕所普及率(%) Popularizing Rate of Sanitary toilets (%)	无害化卫生厕所普及率(%) Popularizing Rate of Harmless Sanitary toilets (%)	农村改厕投资合计(万元) Investment in Compost toilets (10 000 yuan)
全　　省	**Total**	**1389.03**	**84.70**	**59.17**	**624108**
郑州市	Zhengzhou	72.36	91.52	79.00	37949
开封市	Kaifeng	63.75	82.00	55.68	42748
洛阳市	Luoyang	89.38	86.32	68.50	66466
平顶山市	Pingdingshan	66.14	75.85	45.56	15067
安阳市	Anyang	76.77	84.52	61.71	61368
鹤壁市	Hebi	16.54	85.60	61.11	8046
新乡市	Xinxiang	90.48	84.60	53.37	27836
焦作市	Jiaozuo	45.94	91.31	52.98	64068
濮阳市	Puyang	67.00	85.20	57.60	22407
许昌市	Xuchang	63.05	87.05	71.75	14244
漯河市	Luohe	29.25	82.13	52.43	11663
三门峡市	Sanmenxia	29.83	84.00	46.00	18155
南阳市	Nanyang	143.66	83.40	71.20	55037
商丘市	Shangqiu	141.47	84.50	53.20	43459
信阳市	Xinyang	90.06	79.00	76.00	35414
周口市	Zhoukou	188.69	82.06	38.75	73326
驻马店市	Zhumadian	102.46	83.30	50.47	24574
济源市	Jiyuan	12.20	92.30	69.80	2281
省直管县	**County Directly Administrated by Province**				
巩义市	Gongyi	13.35	93.43	85.44	9484
兰考县	Lankao	12.04	86.42	80.36	13800
汝州市	Ruzhou	14.25	82.64	61.00	807
滑县	Huaxian	22.35	81.21	50.61	12290
长垣市	Changyuan	15.18	95.04	91.25	6497
邓州市	Dengzhou	21.95	87.10	73.90	9577
永城市	Yongcheng	30.37	97.30	78.01	10170
固始县	Gushi	32.37	86.00	75.40	3328
鹿邑县	Luyi	24.23	87.00	65.00	10175
新蔡县	Xincai	15.65	83.50	47.81	1964

20-11　各市农村可再生能源利用情况(2019年)

Condition of Rural Renewable energy utilization by City (2019)

地　区　City	户用沼气池（万户） Household biogas digester (10 000 households)	沼气工程（个） Biogas project （unit）	太阳能热水器（万平方米） Solar water heater (10 000 cu m)
全　省 Total	**368.51**	**5497**	**611.99**
省辖市 City			
郑州市 Zhengzhou	18.08	312	7.60
开封市 Kaifeng	9.30	30	42.65
洛阳市 Luoyang	23.21	57	29.01
平顶山市 Pingdingshan	21.17	144	54.93
安阳市 Anyang	17.97	1171	36.97
鹤壁市 Hebi	6.03	95	9.34
新乡市 Xinxiang	40.26	685	44.16
焦作市 Jiaozuo	12.78	387	29.84
濮阳市 Puyang	9.59	159	26.57
许昌市 Xuchang	13.67	66	31.96
漯河市 Luohe	16.92	93	21.15
三门峡市 Sanmenxia	10.47	60	13.20
南阳市 Nanyang	37.22	621	94.52
商丘市 Shangqiu	48.07	64	23.44
信阳市 Xinyang	19.95	812	33.61
周口市 Zhoukou	35.68	369	70.73
驻马店市 Zhumadian	25.58	221	38.94
济源市 Jiyuan	2.56	151	3.37
省直管县 County Directly Administrated by Province			
巩义市 Gongyi	1.77	70	0.21
兰考县 Lankao	1.72	5	7.76
汝州市 Ruzhou	3.86	26	10.02
滑县 Huaxian	5.58	21	1.01
长垣市 Changyuan	5.90	18	6.75
邓州市 Dengzhou	3.41	68	9.60
永城市 Yongcheng	5.43	14	4.19
固始县 Gushi	3.13	87	8.47
鹿邑县 Luyi	5.77	33	14.06
新蔡县 Xincai	2.77	41	8.20

20-12 工业重点调查单位分行业工业废水排放及处理利用情况(2017年)

Industrial waste water discharge, treatment and utilization in Key research Industrial unit by Sector (2017)

行业	Sector	汇总工业企业数(个) Number of Enterprises (unit)	工业废水排放量(万吨) Volume of Industrial Waste Water (10 000tons)	废水治理设施数(套) Number of Wastewater treatment facilities (set)
总计	**Total**	**86821**	**51133.81**	**14696**
农、林、牧、渔专业及辅助性活动	Agriculture, Forestry, Animal husbandry, Fishery and Auxiliary Activities	131	4.49	12
煤炭开采和洗选业	Mining and Washing of Coal	455	9872.81	555
石油和天然气开采业	Extraction of Petroleum and Natural Gas	12	0.96	20
黑色金属矿采选业	Mining of Ferrous Metal Ores	130	1.80	22
有色金属矿采选业	Mining of Non-ferrous Metal Ores	450	36.79	168
非金属矿采选业	Mining and Processing of Nonmetal Ores	640	4.91	84
开采辅助活动	Support Activities for Mining	55	268.32	22
其他采矿业	Mining of Other Ores	9		
农副食品加工业	Processing of Food from Agricultural Products	6058	3674.69	1848
食品制造业	Manufacture of Foods	2819	1815.17	860
酒、饮料和精制茶制造业	Manufacture of Liquor,Beverages and refined tea	1673	1972.08	555
烟草制品业	Manufacture of Tobacco	20	53.50	8
纺织业	Manufacture of Textile	2166	907.57	148
纺织服装、服饰业	Manufacture of Textile, Wearing Apparel and Accessories	2942	218.82	42
皮革、毛皮、羽毛及其制品和制鞋业	Manufacture of Leather, Fur, Feather and Its Products and Footwear	2068	1574.80	193
木材加工和木、竹、藤、棕、草制品业	Processing of Timbers, Manufacture of Wood, Bamboo, Rattan, Palm, and Straw Products	5297	17.73	76
家具制造业	Manufacture of Furniture	2614	1.79	105
造纸和纸制品业	Manufacture of Paper and Paper Products	1782	7710.95	276
印刷和记录媒介复制业	Printing,Reproduction of Recording Media	1364	12.28	82
文教、工美、体育和娱乐用品制造业	Manufacture of Articles for Culture, Education, Arts and Crafts, Sport and Entertainment Activities	1437	129.89	152
石油加工、炼焦和核燃料加工业	Processing of Petroleum ,Coking, Processing of Nucleus Fuel	608	1617.00	96
化学原料和化学制品制造业	Manufacture of Raw Chemical Material and Chemical Products	2991	8250.13	796
医药制造业	Manufacture of Medicines	920	2233.13	339
化学纤维制造业	Manufacture of Chemical Fiber	63	1793.52	27
橡胶和塑料制品业	Manufacture of Rubber and Plastic Prodncts	4163	39.67	288
非金属矿物制品业	Manufacture of Non-metallic Mineral Products	16525	328.83	4673
黑色金属冶炼和压延加工业	Smelting and Pressing of Ferrous Metals	474	625.33	550
有色金属冶炼和压延加工业	Smelting and Pressing of Non-ferrous Metals	692	345.89	240
金属制品业	Manufacture of Metal Products	7956	124.05	557
通用设备制造业	Manufacture of General Purpose Machinery	7621	251.17	149
专用设备制造业	Manufacture of Special Purpose Machinery	4844	99.21	134
汽车制造业	Manufacture of Automobile	1496	386.85	188
铁路、船舶、航空航天和其他运输设备制造业	Manufacture of Railway, ship, aerospace, and other transport equipment	506	42.49	93
电气机械和器材制造业	Manufacture of Electrical Machinery and Apparatus	2386	580.05	361
计算机、通信和其他电子设备制造业	Manufacture of Computer, Communication and Other Electronic Equipment	566	710.47	66
仪器仪表制造业	Manufacture of Measuring Instruments and Machinery	509	21.06	15
其他制造业	Manufacture of others	476	9.66	25
废弃资源综合利用业	Utilization of waste Resources	591	142.66	119
金属制品、机械和设备修理业	Repairing of Metal products, machinery and equipment	263	10.09	13
电力、热力生产和供应业	Production and Supply of Electric Power and Heat Power	355	2817.12	670
燃气生产和供应业	Production and Supply of Gas	142	0.38	2
水生产和供应业	Production and Supply of Water	552	2425.69	67

20-13 工业重点调查单位分行业工业废气排放及处理情况(2017年)

Industrial Wastes gas discharge and treatment and utilization in Key research Industrial unit by Sector (2017)

行业	Sector	废气治理设施数(套) Number of Wastegas treatment facilities (set)	工业废气排放量(亿标立方米) Volume of Industrial Waste Gas (100 million cu.m)	工业二氧化硫排放量(吨) Volume of Industrial so2 (ton)
总计	**Total**	**87083**	**54550.23**	**130650.39**
农、林、牧、渔专业及辅助性活动	Agriculture, Forestry, Animal husbandry, Fishery and Auxiliary Activities	41	0.05	3.11
煤炭开采和洗选业	Mining and Washing of Coal	541	9.63	148.75
石油和天然气开采业	Extraction of Petroleum and Natural Gas	9	0.01	354.25
黑色金属矿采选业	Mining of Ferrous Metal Ores	70	4.54	68.78
有色金属矿采选业	Mining of Non-ferrous Metal Ores	274	0.76	12.15
非金属矿采选业	Mining and Processing of Nonmetal Ores	603	34.45	161.05
开采辅助活动	Support Activities for Mining	22		1.44
其他采矿业	Mining of Other Ores n.e.c			
农副食品加工业	Processing of Food from Agricultural Products	7129	195.07	991.14
食品制造业	Manufacture of Foods	386	111.14	660.72
酒、饮料和精制茶制造业	Manufacture of Liquor, Beverages and refined tea	212	70.16	645.85
烟草制品业	Manufacture of Tobacco	62	2.92	13.25
纺织业	Manufacture of Textile	385	1688.59	203.43
纺织服装、服饰业	Manufacture of Textile, Wearing and Accessories	8	0.06	23.19
皮革、毛皮、羽毛及其制品和制鞋业	Manufacture of Leather, Fur, Feather and Its Products and Footwear	446	612.63	81.54
木材加工和木、竹、藤、棕、草制品业	Processing of Timbers, Manufacture of Wood, Bamboo, Rattan, Palm, and Straw Products	3403	7.29	862.41
家具制造业	Manufacture of Furniture	3044	1.61	2.70
造纸和纸制品业	Manufacture of Paper and Paper Products	313	1850.89	1361.15
印刷和记录媒介复制业	Printing,Reproduction of Recording Media	84	0.17	2.46
文教、工美、体育和娱乐用品制造业	Manufacture Articles for Culture, Education, Arts and Crafts, Sport and Entertainment Activities	517	0.12	75.64
石油加工、炼焦和核燃料加工业	Processing of Petroleum, Coking, Processing of Nucleus Fuel	700	707.02	3474.08
化学原料和化学制品制造业	Manufacture of Raw Chemical Material and Chemical Products	2987	3669.22	7148.32
医药制造业	Manufacture of Medicines	560	45.48	374.48
化学纤维制造业	Manufacture of Chemical Fiber	81	13727.51	76.66
橡胶和塑料制品业	Manufacture of Rubber and Plastic Products	1495	42.75	125.79
非金属矿物制品业	Manufacture of Non-metallic Mineral Products	31432	9932.49	42304.23
黑色金属冶炼和压延加工业	Smelting and Pressing of Ferrous Metals	905	2791.78	15361.86
有色金属冶炼和压延加工业	Smelting and Pressing of Non-ferrous Metals	1491	2409.35	28031.51
金属制品业	Manufacture of Metal Products	8175	62.67	297.82
通用设备制造业	Manufacture of General Purpose Machinery	7205	91.65	197.13
专用设备制造业	Manufacture of Special Purpose Machinery	8706	54.87	24.59
汽车制造业	Manufacture of Automobile	1793	19.08	2.64
铁路、船舶、航空航天和其他运输设备制造业	Manufacture of Railway, ship, aerospace, and other transport equipment	773	4.90	104.34
电气机械和器材制造业	Manufacture of Electrical Machinery and Apparatus	1059	88.28	2.67
计算机、通信和其他电子设备制造业	Manufacture of Computer Communication and Other Electronic Equipment	219	51.77	2.74
仪器仪表制造业	Manufacture of Measuring Instruments and Machinery	124		0.04
其他制造业	Manufacture of others	55	0.36	9.60
废弃资源综合利用业	Utilization of waste Resources	479	14.31	191.26
金属制品、机械和设备修理业	Repairing of Metal products, machinery and equipment	57		0.23
电力、热力生产和供应业	Production and Supply of Electric Power and Heat Power	1205	16246.65	27224.55
燃气生产和供应业	Production and Supply of Gas	32		22.86
水生产和供应业	Production and Supply of Water	1		0.00

20-14 工业重点调查单位分行业工业固体废物产生及处理利用情况(2017年)

Industrial Solid Wastes Produced discharge and treatment and utilization in Key research Industrial unit by Sector (2017)

单位：万吨 (10 000tons)

行业	Sector	一般工业固体废物产生量 Volume of General Industrial Solid Wastes Produced	一般工业固体废物综合利用量 Volume of General Industrial Solid Wastes Utilized	一般工业固体废物贮存量 Storage capacity of General Industrial Solid Wastes	一般工业固体废物处置量 Volume of General Industrial Solid Wastes Treated
总计	**Total**	**17581.61**	**10205.80**	**2509.03**	**4961.08**
农、林、牧、渔专业及辅助性	Agriculture, Forestry, Animal husbandry, Fishery and Auxiliary Activities	1.16	0.51		0.65
煤炭开采和洗选业	Mining and Washing of Coal	2588.80	1933.93	463.31	269.33
石油和天然气开采业	Extraction of Petroleum and Natural Gas	3.34	3.34		
黑色金属矿采选业	Mining of Ferrous Metal Ores	321.26	104.53	70.12	147.56
有色金属矿采选业	Mining of Non-ferrous Metal Ores	4031.44	93.28	499.78	3440.45
非金属矿采选业	Mining and Processing of Nonmetal Ores	203.68	111.74	38.01	53.97
开采辅助活动	Support Activities for Mining	29.13	16.53	3.00	9.60
其他采矿业	Mining of Other Ores				
农副食品加工业	Processing of Food from Agricultural Products	228.75	224.47	1.09	3.19
食品制造业	Manufacture of Foods	24.65	18.05		6.59
酒、饮料和精制茶制造业	Manufacture of Liquor, Beverages and refined tea	39.90	35.12	0.17	4.62
烟草制品业	Manufacture of Tobacco	1.24	1.24		
纺织业	Manufacture of Textile	15.71	14.61	0.03	1.17
纺织服装、服饰业	Manufacture of Textile, Wearing Apparel and Accessories	0.89	0.69	0.02	0.18
皮革、毛皮、羽毛及其制品和制鞋业	Manufacture of Leather, Fur, Feather and Its Products and Footwear	6.65	6.22		0.43
木材加工和木、竹、藤、棕、草制品业	Processing of Timbers, Manufacture of Wood, Bamboo, Rattan, Palm, and Straw Products	93.36	93.18		0.19
家具制造业	Manufacture of Furniture	2.00	1.98	0.01	0.01
造纸和纸制品业	Manufacture of Paper and Paper Products	83.38	78.57	0.21	4.60
印刷和记录媒介复制业	Printing, Reproduction of Recording Media	4.99	4.95		0.04
文教、工美、体育和娱乐用品制造业	Manufacture of Articles for Culture, Education, Arts and Crafts,Sport and Entertainment Activities	0.81	0.78		0.03
石油加工、炼焦和核燃料加工业	Processing of Petroleum, Coking, Processing of Nucleus Fuel	136.96	129.97	1.56	5.44
化学原料和化学制品制造业	Manufacture of Raw Chemical Material and Chemical Products	1141.56	818.85	121.95	207.02
医药制造业	Manufacture of Medicines	23.33	21.66		1.68
化学纤维制造业	Manufacture of Chemical Fiber	41.88	41.87		0.02
橡胶和塑料制品业	Manufacture of Rubber and Plastic Products	11.28	11.23	0.04	0.02
非金属矿物制品业	Manufacture of Non-metallic Mineral Products	442.60	417.40	2.50	25.27
黑色金属冶炼和压延加工业	Smelting and Pressing of Ferrous Metals	1371.80	1353.43	1.65	16.73
有色金属冶炼和压延加工业	Smelting and Pressing of Non-ferrous Metals	2312.20	476.51	1228.57	611.42
金属制品业	Manufacture of Metal Products	43.33	42.74	0.02	0.58
通用设备制造业	Manufacture of General Purpose Machinery	150.43	146.71	0.12	3.61
专用设备制造业	Manufacture of Special Purpose Machinery	22.93	22.48	0.04	0.41
汽车制造业	Manufacture of Automobile	29.40	28.11	0.01	1.28
铁路、船舶、航空航天和其他运输设备制造业	Manufacture of Railway, ship, aerospace, and other transport equipment	5.11	5.03		0.07
电气机械和器材制造业	Manufacture of Electrical Machinery and Apparatus	6.66	5.20	0.01	1.46
计算机、通信和其他电子设备制造业	Manufacture of Computer, Communication and Other Electronic Equipment	7.06	6.45		0.60
仪器仪表制造业	Manufacture of Measuring Instruments and Machinery	0.09	0.09		
其他制造业	Manufacture of others	0.12	0.12		
废弃资源综合利用业	Utilization of waste Resources	27.20	25.06	0.10	2.20
金属制品、机械和设备修理业	Repairing of Metal products, machinery and equipment	1.01	0.94		0.07
电力、热力生产和供应业	Production and Supply of Electric Power and Heat Power	4120.72	3904.52	76.67	139.53
燃气生产和供应业	Production and Supply of Gas	0.83	0.82		
水生产和供应业	Production and Supply of Water	3.94	2.90		1.04

主要统计指标解释

森林覆盖率 以行政区域为单位的森林面积占区域土地总面积的百分比。计算公式为：

森林覆盖率= 森林面积/土地总面积×100%

湿地 指天然或人工、长久或暂时性的沼泽地、泥炭地或水域地带，包括静止或流动、淡水、半咸水、咸水体，低潮时水深不超过 6 米的水域以及海岸地带地区的珊瑚滩和海草床、滩涂、红树林、河口、河流、淡水沼泽、沼泽森林、湖泊、盐沼及盐湖。

自然保护区 指为了保护自然环境和自然资源，促进国民经济的持续发展，将一定面积的陆地和水体划分出来，并经各级人民政府批准而进行特殊保护和管理的区域个数。根据保护对象，自然保护区分为自然生态系统类、野生生物类、自然遗迹类。风景名胜区、文物保护区不计在内。

水资源总量 指当地降水形成的地表和地下产水总量，即地表径流量与降水入渗补给量之和。

地表水资源量 指河流、湖泊以及冰川等地表水体中可以逐年更新的动态水量，即天然河川径流量。

地下水资源量 指地下饱和含水层逐年更新的动态水量，即降水和地表水入渗对地下水的补给量。

用水总量 指各类用水户取用的包括输水损失在内的毛水量。

农业用水 包括农田灌溉用水、林果地灌溉用水、草地灌溉用水、鱼塘补水和畜禽用水。

工业用水 指工矿企业在生产过程中用于制造、加工、冷却、空调、净化、洗涤等方面的用水，按新水取用量计，不包括企业内部的重复利用水量。

生活用水 包括城镇生活用水和农村生活用水。城镇生活用水由居民用水和公共用水（含第三产业及建筑业等用水）组成；农村生活用水指居民生活用水。

生态环境补水 仅包括人为措施供给的城镇环境用水和部分河湖、湿地补水，而不包括降水、径流自然满足的水量。

废水排放总量 为工业废水排放量、城镇生活污水排放量和集中式治理设施污水排放量之和。

工业废水排放量 指报告期内经过企业厂区所有排放口排到企业外部的工业废水量。包括生产废水、外排的直接冷却水、超标排放的矿井地下水和与工业废水混排的厂区生活污水，不包括外排的间接冷却水(清污不分流的间接冷却水应计算在废水排放量内)。

城镇生活污水排放量 指报告期内城镇居民排放生活污水的量。城镇生活包括"住宿业与餐饮业、居民服务和其他服务业、医院和独立燃烧设施以及城镇生活污染源"。

集中式治理设施污水排放量 指报告期内集中式治理设施的渗滤液排放量。集中式治理设施包括垃圾处理场（厂）和危险废物（医疗废物）集中处置厂。

化学需氧量（COD）排放量 为工业、农业、城镇生活和集中式治理设施排放的废水中 COD 排放量之和。

氨氮排放量 为工业、农业、城镇生活和集中式治理设施排放的废水中氨氮排放量之和。

二氧化硫排放量 指报告期内工业、城镇生活和集中式治理设施 SO_2 排放量之和。

工业 SO_2 排放量 指报告期内企业在燃料燃烧和生产工艺过程中排入大气的 SO_2 总量。

烟（粉）尘排放量 指报告期内工业、城镇生活、机动车和集中式治理设施烟（粉）尘排放量之和。

工业烟（粉）尘排放量 指报告期内企业在燃料燃烧和生产工艺过程中排入大气的烟尘及工业粉尘的总质量之和。烟尘或工业粉尘排放量可以通过除尘系统的排风量和除尘设备出口烟尘浓度相乘求得。

一般工业固体废物产生量 指未被列入《国家危险废物名录》或者根据国家规定的危险废物鉴别标准（GB5085）、固体废物浸出毒性浸出方法（GB5086）及固体废物浸出毒性测定方法（GB／T 15555）鉴别方法判定不具有危险特性的工业固体废物。计算公式是：

一般工业固体废物产生量=（一般工业固体废物综合利用量-其中：综合利用往年贮存量）+一般工业固体废物贮存量+（一般工业固体废物处置量-其中：处置往年贮存量）+一般工业固体废物倾倒丢弃量

一般工业固体废物综合利用量 指报告期内企业通过回收、加工、循环、交换等方式，从固体废物中提取或者使其转化为可以利用的资源、能源和其他原材料的固体废物量（包括当年利用的往年工业固体废物累计贮存量）。如用作农业肥料、生产建筑材料、筑路等。

一般工业固体废物综合利用率 指一般工业固体废物综合利用量占一般工业固体废物产生量与综合利用往年贮存量之和的百分率。计算公式为：

一般工业固体废物综合利用率= 一般工业固体废物综合利用量/一般工业固体废物产生量+综合利用往年贮存量×100%

一般工业固体废物处置量 指报告期内企业将工业固体废物焚烧和用其他改变工业固体废物的物理、化学、生物特性的方法，达到减少或者消除其危险成分的活动，或者将工业固体废物最终置于符合环境保护规定要求的填埋场的活动中，所消纳固体废物的量。

一般工业固体废物处置率 指一般工业固体废物处置量占一般工业固体废物产生量与处置往年贮存量之和的百分率。计算公式为：

一般工业固体废物处置率= 一般工业固体废物处置量/一般工业固体废物产生量+处置往年贮存量×100%

环境污染治理投资 指城市环境基础设施投资、工业企业污染防治投资和完成环保验收项目环保投资之和。

Explanatory Notes on Main Statistical Indicators

Forest Coverage Rate Taking the administrative jurisdiction as the unit, the percentage of area of afforested land to the area of total land. The formula for calculating forest coverage rate is as follows:

Forest coverage rate = area of afforested land/area of total land ×100%

Wetlands refer to marshland and peat bog, whether natural or man-made, permanent or temporary; water covered areas, whether stagnant or flowing, with fresh or semi-fresh or salty water that is less than 6 meters deep at low tide; as well as coral beach, weed beach, mud beach, mangrove, river outlet, rivers, fresh-water marshland, marshland forests, lakes, salty bog and salt lakes along the coastal areas.

Natural Reserves refer to number of certain areas of land, or waters that have been set aside and put under special protection and management in order to protect natural environment and natural resources, and promote the sustainable development of national economy. They are subject to formal approval from governments of various levels. According to the protected targets, natural reserves can be divided into three categories: reserves of natural ecological system, natural reserves of wildlife species, and natural heritage of historical significance.Scenic spots and cultural preservation zones are not included.

Total Water Resources refers to total volume of surface water and groundwater and is measured as run-off for surface water and replenishment of groundwater with rainfall in local area.

Surface Water Resources refers to total volume of year by year renewable dynamic resources which exist in rivers, lakes, glaciers and other surface water and are the natural run-off of rivers.

Groundwater Resources refers to total volume of year by year renewable dynamic resources which exist in saturation acquifers of groundwater and are measured as replenishment of groundwater with rainfall and surface water.

Water Use refers to gross water used by various water users, including losses during distribution.

Water Use by Agriculture includes uses of water by irrigation of farming fields, forestry and orchards, irrigation of grassland, replenishment of fishing farms and water used by animal husbandry.

Water Use by Industry refers to new withdrawals of water, excluding reuse of water within enterprises.

Water Use by Living Consumption includes use of water for living consumption in both urban and rural areas. Urban water use by living consumption is composed of household use and public use (including tertiary industry and construction). Rural water use by living consumption includes water used by households.

Water Use by Ecological and Environmental Protection includes replenishment of rivers and lakes and use for urban environment.

Waste water discharge Resources for industrial wastewater emissions, urban sewage emissions and centralized treatment facilities of wastewater.

Waste Water Discharged by Industry refers to the volume of waste water discharged by industrial enterprises through all their outlets, including waste water from production process, directly cooled water, groundwater from mining wells which does not meet discharge standards and sewage from households mixed with waste water produced by industrial activities, but excluding indirectly cooled water discharged (It should be included if the discharge is not separated from waste water).

Urban Waste Water Discharge refers to annual discharge of non-industrial waste water by urban households. Include accommodations industry and food industry, residents service and other services, hospitals and independent combustion facilities and urban life pollution sources.

Centralized treatment facilities wastewater refers to report period of centralized treatment facilities leachate emissions. Centralized management facilities including landfill (factory) and hazardous waste (medical waste) disposal factory.

Volume of Chemical Oxygen Demand (COD) refers to volume of COD in wastewater discharge form Industry, agriculture, urban life and centralized management facilities emissions.

Volume of Ammonia nitrogen refers to volume of ammonia nitrogen in wastewater discharge form Industry, agriculture, urban life and centralized management facilities emissions.

Volume of Sulfur dioxide refers to volume of SO_2 form Industry, urban life and centralized management facilities emissions.

Volume of Industrial Sulfur Dioxide Discharged refers to the volume of sulfur dioxide discharged to the air in the process of fuel burning or in the production process.

Volume of Industrial Soot Discharged refers to the volume of solid soot in the smoke discharged in the process of fuel burning in the area of the factory.

Industrial Dust Discharged refers to the total weight of solid dust discharged by industrial enterprises in the production process, such as dust of refractory materials from iron plants, dust from coke-screening system or from sintering machines of coking plants, dust from lime kilns, cement dust from building material enterprises, etc., but excluding smoke and dust discharged by power plants.

Common Industrial Solid Wastes Produced refers to the industrial solid wastes that are not listed in the 《National Catalogue of Hazardous Wastes》, or not regarded as hazardous according to the national hazardous waste identification standards (GB5085), solid waste-Extraction procedure for leaching toxicity (GB5086) and solid waste-Extraction procedure for leaching toxicity (GB/T 15555). The calculation formula is as followed:

Common Industrial Solid Wastes Produced = (common industrial solid wastes utilized − the proportion of utilized stock of previous years) + common industrial solid waste stock + (common industrial solid wastes disposed − the proportion of disposed stock of previous years) + common industrial solid wastes discharged.

Common Industrial Solid Wastes Utilized refers to volume of solid wastes from which useful materials can be extracted or which can be converted into usable resources, energy or other materials by means of reclamation, processing, recycling and exchange (including utilizing in the year the stocks of industrial solid wastes of the previous year). Examples of such utilizations include fertilizers, building materials and road materials.

Rate of Common Utilization of Industrial Solid Wastes refers to the percentage of industrial solid wastes utilized over industrial solid wastes produced.

Rate of General Utilization of Industrial Solid Wastes= General Industrial Solid Wastes Utilized / (General Industrial Solid Wastes Produced+ Solid Wastes Utilized of ever reserves)×100%

Common Industrial Solid Waste Disposal refers to enterprises during the reporting period the industrial solid waste incineration and other changes of industrial solid waste methods of physical, chemical, biological characteristics, activities to reduce or eliminate its dangerous substances, or the final placing of industrial solid waste landfill activities comply with the environmental protection requirements, the Council is satisfied that the amount of solid waste.

Rate of Common Industrial Solid Waste Disposal refer to general industrial solid waste disposal accounted for general industrial solid waste generation and disposal of storage volume and percentage in previous years. Calculation formula is:

Rate of General industrial solid waste disposal= General industrial solid waste disposal / (General Industrial Solid Wastes Produced+ Disposal of ever reserves) ×100%

Investment in Environment Pollution Harnessing Projects refers to the proportion of investment in fixed assets in the total investment in harnessing industrial pollution and in the construction of urban environment infrastructure facilities.

科学技术
Science and Technology

21

● 资料整理：郑文革　贾梁

简要说明

一、主要内容

本篇包括全社会以及大中型工业企业、政府部门属研究机构、高校的研究与试验发展（R&D)活动及规模以上工业企业的研究与试验发展（R&D)人员、经费支出情况；全省专利申请和授权情况；科研成果及科研项目，技术市场技术合同成交资料；测绘、质量监督、气象、地震等综合技术服务部门业务机构及业务活动情况。

二、统计范围

科技活动统计资料范围为全社会有研究与试验发展（R&D)活动的企事业单位，具体包括工业企业、政府部门属研究机构、普通高等学校以及研究与试验发展（R&D)活动相对密集行业（包括农、林、牧、渔业，建筑业，交通运输、仓储和邮政业，信息传输、计算机服务和软件业，金融业，租赁和商务服务业，科学研究、技术服务和地质勘查业，水利、环境和公共设施管理业，卫生、社会保障和社会福利业，文化、体育和娱乐业等）中从事研究与试验发展（R&D)活动的企事业单位。

三、资料来源

全省综合资料、企业及有关行业企事业单位的研究与试验发展（R&D)活动情况资料由省统计局调查提供；政府部门属研究机构资料由省科技厅和国防科技工业局调查提供；科学研究、技术服务和地址勘查业企事业的研究与试验发展（R&D)活动情况资料，以及科技论文资料、技术市场资料由省科技厅调查提供；高校资料由省教育厅调查提供；测绘、产品质量监督抽查、专利、气象、地震等资料，分别由省自然资源厅、省市场监督管理局、省气象局、省地震局等部门调查提供。

四、统计调查方法

研究与试验发展(R&D)活动情况采用全面调查取得；测绘、产品质量监督抽查、专利资料采用抽样等多种调查方法取得。

科技活动统计资料口径变动说明：2005年以前科技活动统计资料只包括大中型工业企业、政府部门属研究机构、普通高等学校，2005年及以后年份扩大到了全社会范围。本篇资料由河南省统计局社会与科技统计处编辑整理。

Brief Introduction

I. Main Contents

Data on this chapter include the R&D personnel, the expenditure funds of R&D activities under whole society, large and medium-sized industrial enterprise, government departments, universities and colleges, data on patents application accepted and granted; data on technological markets; data on activities of the surveying and mapping, product quality supervision., Weather and earthquake, etc.

II. Scope of Statistics

Data on research and development (R&D) activities of enterprises and institutions all over the country, mainly including industrial enterprises, scientific and technological institutions under government departments, universities and colleges and R&D-intensive enterprises of different industries (such as agriculture, forestry, animal husbandry, fisher, construction, transport, storage and post, information transmission, computer services and software, financial intermediation, leasing and business services, scientific research, technical service and geologic prospecting, management of water conservancy, environment and public facilities , health, social security and social welfare, culture, sports and entertainment).

III. Sources of Data

Data on national aggregates and R&D activities of various enterprises and institutions are from Henan provincial bureau of statistics; data on scientific and technological institutions under government departments are from Henan provincial bureau of scientific and technological and Henan provincial bureau of defense science, technology industry; data on scientific research, technical service and geologic prospecting, scientific and technological papers; technological markets and high and new-tech industrial enterprises in development zones are from Henan provincial bureau of scientific and technological; data on scientific and technological activities in universities and colleges are from Henan provincial bureau of Education; Data on the development of surveying and mapping, product quality supervision and patents, Weather and earthquake are respectively provided by the provincial natural resources department, the provincial market supervision and Administration Bureau, the Provincial Meteorological Bureau, and the Provincial Seismological Bureau.

IV. Statistical methodology

Data on R&D activities of industrial enterprises, scientific and technological institutions under government departments, universities and colleges are collected through complete surveys. Data on surveying and mapping, product quality supervision and patent applications are through sample surveys and other surveys.

Changes of the statistical coverage of data on scientific and technological activities: Data only included large and medium-sized industrial enterprises, scientific research institutions under government departments, and universities and colleges before 2005. Since 2005 (inclusive) data have covered all industries. Data on this chapter are provided by Department of social and technological of Henan provincial bureau of statistics.

21-1 研究与试验发展(R&D)主要指标

Basic Statistics on R&D Activities

年 份 Year	有(R&D)活动的单位数 (个) Number of Institutions for R&D (unit)	(R&D)人员 (人) R&D Personnel (person)	(R&D)人员折合全时当量 (人年) Full-time Equivalent of R&D Personnel (person-year)	(R&D)经费内部支出 (万元) Internal Expenditures on R&D (10 000 yuan)	(R&D)经费外部支出 (万元) External Expenditures on R&D (10 000 yuan)	(R&D)项目数 (项) R&D Projects (item)	(R&D)机构数 (个) Number of R&D Institutions (unit)
2000	1017		34629	248024	15050	7904	1331
2001	985		36138	283091	24064	8100	1122
2002	982		41492	293151	31148	8470	1151
2003	989		40742	341910	24664	9293	1173
2004	1090		38250	423560	24573	12105	1423
2005	1107		50888	556090	39913	16069	1498
2006	1109		58716	798414	47729	18904	1432
2007	1169		64888	1011302	59761	24395	1531
2008	1286		72830	1240890	55061	27349	1727
2009	1636		92571	1747599	96107	22347	1821
2010	1555	144408	101668	2113773	89253	24050	1798
2011	1585	167386	118266	2644922	109950	28422	1817
2012	1720	185116	128323	3107803	124399	30319	1870
2013	2051	216269	152541	3553486	109470	33015	2064
2014	2473	232105	161441	4000099	91021	36449	2203
2015	2850	241171	158855	4350430	92040	39956	2543
2016	3112	249876	173265	4941880	117270	41513	2953
2017	4112	266427	162504	5820538	146023	49904	3327
2018	3956	256175	166807	6715193	171764	53480	2781
2019	5393	296349	191570	7930369	229987	65835	3408

21-2 研究与试验发展(R&D)活动概况
Basic Statistics on R&D Activities

指　标	Item	2018	2019
有研究与试验发展(R&D)活动的单位数(个)	Number of Institutions for R&D (unit)	3956	5393
研究与试验发展(R&D)人员(人)	Number of Persons for R&D (person)	256175	296349
#女性	Female	64258	73988
#研究人员	Researchers	101471	121472
#全时人员	Full-time Personnel	161616	194829
非全时人员	Part-time Personnel	94559	101520
#博士毕业	Graduated from Doctor	10161	12985
硕士毕业	Graduated from Master	32440	35778
本科毕业	Graduated from Bachelor	103616	124731
其他学历	Other Degree	109958	122855
研究与试验发展(R&D人)员折合全时当量(人年)	Full-time Equivalent of R&D Personnel (person-year)	166807	191570
#研究人员	Researchers	63461	76108
#基础研究	Basic Research	5147	7421
应用研究	Applied Research	17877	22196
试验发展	Experimental Development	143790	161967
研究与试验发展(R&D)经费内部支出(万元)	Internal Expenditures on R&D (10 000 yuan)	6715193	7930369
#基础研究	Basic Research	128167	191391
应用研究	Applied Research	711029	722441
试验发展	Experimental Development	5875998	7016537
#日常性支出	Daily spending	5924115	7397272
#人员劳务费	Labour Cost	1894935	2212465
#资产性支出	Assets spending	791078	505937
#仪器和设备	Instruments and Equipment	732870	417314
#政府资金	Government Funds	604031	780117
企业资金	Self-raised Funds by Enterpirses	5763715	6867595
境外资金	Foreign Funds	23608	4884
其他资金	Other Funds	323839	277773
研究与试验发展(R&D)经费外部支出(万元)	External Expenditures on R&D (10 000 yuan)	171764	229987
#对境内研究机构支出	Expenses on Domestic R&D Institutions	50807	45467
对境内高等学校支出	Expenses on Domestic Colleges and Universities	27421	30448
对境内企业支出	Expenses on Domestic Enterprises	78418	147866
对境外支出	Expenses on Overseas	14988	5976
研究与试验发展(R&D)产出情况	Statistics on R&D Outputs		
专利申请数(件)	Number of Patent Applications (piece)	44586	51033
#发明专利申请数	Inventions	17128	18008
专利授权数数(件)	Number of Patents Applications Granted (piece)	9743	11200
#发明专利	Inventions	3236	3397
有效发明专利数(件)	Number of Effective Invention Patent (piece)	38719	49042
专利所有权转让及许可数(件)	Assignment and Permit of Patent Ownership (piece)	102	1741
专利所有权转让及许可收入(万元)	Income from Assignment and Permit of Patent Ownership (10 000 yuan)	2554	14618
植物新品种权授予数(项)	Number of New Varieties of Plants Applications Granted (item)	84	125
形成国家或行业标准数(项)	Become National or Trade standards (item)	884	1206
发表科技论文(篇)	Scientific and Technological Treatise Published (paper)	63350	65819
出版科技著作(种)	Scientific and Technological Books Publiced (type)	2921	2857
研究与试验发展(R&D)项目(课题)情况	Statistics on R&D Topics		
项目(课题)数(项)	Projects of R&D (item)	53480	65835
项目(课题)参加人员(人)	Number of R&D Personnel (person)	155469	182064
#研究人员	Researchers	51286	60393
项目(课题)经费内部支出(万元)	Internal Expenditures on R&D (10 000 yuan)	5978533	7747700
研究与试验发展(R&D)机构情况	Statistics on R&D Institutions		
机构数(个)	Number of R&D Institutions (unit)	2781	3408
从事研究与试验发展(R&D)人员(人)	Number of R&D Personnel (person)	95315	106204
#博士毕业	Graduated from Doctor	3930	4673
#硕士毕业	Graduated from Master	16299	17465
研究与试验发展(R&D)经费支出(万元)	Expenditures on R&D (10 000 yuan)	2952991	3833074
科研用仪器设备原价(万元)	Original price of Equipment for S&T (10 000yuan)	3386480	4037730
#进口	Import	647974	505787

21-3 研究与试验发展(R&D)活动概况(2019年)

Basic Statistics on R&D Activities (2019)

指标	Item	总计 Total	#科学研究与技术开发机构 Institution for Scientific Research and Technological Empolder	#全日制普通高等学校 Full-time Regular Institutions of Higher Edcation	#企业 Enterprises
有研究与试验发展(R&D)活动的单位数(个)	Number of Institutions for R&D (unit)	5393	67	197	5003
研究与试验发展(R&D)人员(人)	Number of Persons for R&D (person)	296349	14754	37743	235582
#女性	Female	73988	4248	17808	48727
#研究人员	Researchers	121472	9360	30968	76406
#全时人员	Full-time Personnel	194829	10251	11669	169768
非全时人员	Timing Personnel	101520	4503	26074	65814
研究与试验发展(R&D人)员折合全时当量	Full-time Equivalent of R&D Personnel				
(人年)	(person-year)	191570	11175	13783	162041
#研究人员	Researchers	76108	9068	11459	53004
#基础研究	Basic Research	7421	1151	5472	444
应用研究	Applied Research	22196	3655	6696	11110
试验发展	Experimental Development	161967	6369	1616	150494
研究与试验发展(R&D)经费内部支出(万元)	Internal Expenditures on R&D (10 000 yuan)	7930369	525982	412169	6927817
#基础研究	Basic Research	191391	35396	143723	6744
应用研究	Applied Research	722441	135495	204743	366976
试验发展	Experimental Development	7016537	355091	63704	6554098
#日常性支出	Daily spending	7397272	435148	287088	6626728
#人员劳务费	Labour Fee	2212465	147423	63343	1970834
#资产性支出	Assets spending	505937	90834	125081	273930
#仪器和设备	Instruments and Equipment	417314	49299	105735	250106
#政府资金	Government Funds	780117	353494	214801	172143
企业资金	Self-raised Funds by Enterpirses	6867595	5645	104266	6738515
境外资金	Foreign Funds	4884	3	9	4860
其他资金	Other Funds	277773	166840	93093	12298
研究与试验发展(R&D)经费外部支出(万元)	External Expenditures on R&D (10 000 yuan)	229987	736	8373	220623
#对国内研究机构支出	Expenses on Domestic R&D Institutions	45467	203	1901	43363
对国内高等学校支出	Expenses on Domestic Colleges and Universities	30448	164	2048	28200
对国内企业支出	Expenses on Domestic Enterprises	147866	370	1556	145941
对境外支出	Expenses on Overseas	5976		2857	3119

21-3 续表 continued

指标	Item	总计 Total	#科学研究与技术开发机构 Institution for Scientific Research and Technological Empolder	#全日制普通高等学校 Full-time Regular Institutions of Higher Edcation	#企业 Enterprises
研究与试验发展(R&D)产出情况	Statistics on R&D Outputs				
专利申请数(件)	Number of Patent Applications (piece)	51033	1888	12824	35980
#发明专利申请数	Inventions	18008	1445	5524	10815
专利授权数(件)	Number of Patents Applications Granted (piece)	11200	923	10135	
#发明专利	Inventions	3397	566	2788	
有效发明专利数(件)	Number of Effective Invention Patent (piece)	49042	3935	9975	34865
专利所有权转让及许可数(件)	Assignment and Permit of Patent Ownership (piece)	1741	15	323	1399
专利所有权转让及许可收入(万元)	Income from Assignment and Permit of Patent Ownership (10 000 yuan)	14618	172	2142	12264
植物新品种权授予数(项)	Number of New Varieties of Plants Applications Granted (item)	125	83	37	
形成国家或行业标准数(项)	Become National or Trade standards(item)	1206	110	45	1025
发表科技论文(篇)	Scientific and Technological Treatise Published (paper)	65819	3457	50235	10245
出版科技著作(种)	Scientific and Technological Books Publiced (type)	2857	149	2567	
研究与试验发展(R&D)项目(课题)情况	Statistics on R&D Topics				
项目(课题)数(项)	Projects of R&D (item)	65835	1485	34570	28888
项目(课题)参加人员折合全时当量(人年)	Number of R&D Personnel (person-year)	182064	10356	13784	154443
#研究人员	Researchers	60393	7128	11460	40922
项目(课题)经费内部支出(万元)	Internal Expenditures on R&D (10 000 yuan)	7747700	381429	233259	7098803
研究与试验发展(R&D)机构情况	Statistics on R&D Institutions				
机构数(个)	Number of R&D Institutions (unit)	3408	115	687	2514
从事研究与试验发展(R&D)人员(人)	Number of R&D Personnel (person)	106204	14754	3923	86071
#博士毕业	Graduated from Doctor	4673	1020	2070	1396
#硕士毕业	Graduated from Master	17465	5957	1029	10015
研究与试验发展(R&D)经费支出(万元)	Expenditures on R&D (10 000 yuan)	3833074	525982	58183	3225823
科研用仪器设备原价(万元)	Original price of Equipment for S&T (10 000yuan)	4037730	594473	682629	2734507
#进口	Import	505787	140777	353828	3166

21-4 研究与试验发展(R&D)经费支出情况(2019年)

Statistics on Appropriation Expenditure for R&D (2019)

单位：万元 (10 000 yuan)

指 标	Item	(R&D)经费内部支出 Internal Expenditures on R&D	政府资金 Government Funds	企业资金 Self-raised Funds by Enterpirses	境外资金 Foreign Funds	其他资金 Other Funds	(R&D)经费外部支出 External Expenditures on R&D
总 计	**Total**	**7930369**	**780117**	**6867595**	**4884**	**277773**	**229987**
按数据来源分组	**Grouped by Data Source**						
科研单位	Scientific and Technological Sector	568702	382139	14377	15	172171	991
#科研机构	Scientific and Technological Institutions	525982	353494	5645	3	166840	736
事业单位	Public Institution	42720	28646	8732	12	5331	255
高等院校	Institutions of Higer Education	412169	214801	104266	9	93093	8373
#理工农医院校	Schools of Science, Engineering, Agriculture and Medicine	338852	172862	79031	9	86949	8355
人文社科院校	Schools of humanities and Social Science	73318	41939	25235		6144	19
工业企业	Industrial Enterprises	6087153	135195	5946405	4860	693	173172
大中型工业企业	Large and Medium-sized Industrial Enterprises	3242448	91743	3145534	4653	517	110394
规上小型工业企业	Small-sized Industrial Enterprises above Designated Size	1388065	12738	1375327			35581
规上微型工业企业	Miniature industrial enterprises above Designated Size	1456640	30714	1425544	207	176	27198
重点建筑业和服务业企业	Key services	808208	36508	760145		11555	47336
非工业企业	Non-industrial Enterprises	5297	441	4805		51	114
事业单位	Public Institution	21681	11033	10437		211	
按执行部门分组	**Grouped by Executive Departments**						
企业	Enterprises	6927817	172143	6738515	4860	12298	220623
#大中型	Large and Medium-sized Enterprises	5379518	138623	5224170	4653	12072	188226
科研机构	Scientific and Technological Institutions	525982	353494	5645	3	166840	736
高等院校	Institutions of Higer Education	412169	214801	104266	9	93093	8373
其他	Others	64401	39679	19169	12	5541	255
按隶属关系分组	**Grouped by Administrative Relationship**						
中央	Central	1790031	341757	1277043	219	171012	60440
地方	Local	6140338	438360	5590552	4664	106762	169547

21-5 研究与试验发展(R&D)活动机构情况(2019年)

Basic Statistics on Institutions Having R&D Activities (2019)

指标	Item	机构数(个) Number of Institutions (unit)	机构从事(R&D)活动人员(人) Number of R&D Personnel (person)	#博士毕业 Graduated from Doctor	#硕士毕业 Graduated from Master	机构(R&D)经费内部支出(万元) Expenditures on R&D (10 000 yuan)	机构科研用仪器设备原价(万元) Original price of Equipment for S&T (10 000yuan)	#进口 Import
总计	**Total**	**3408**	**106204**	**4673**	**17465**	**3833074**	**4037730**	**505787**
按数据来源分组	**Grouped by Data Source**							
科研单位	Scientific and Technological Sector	133	15297	1149	6138	546324	610156	144260
#科研机构	Scientific and Technological Institutions	115	14754	1020	5957	525982	594473	140777
事业单位	Public Institution	18	543	129	181	20342	15683	3483
高等院校	Institutions of Higer Education	687	3923	2070	1029	58183	682629	353828
#理工农医院校	Schools of Science, Engineering, Agriculture and Medicine	615	2416	998	681	52151	680686	353755
人文社科院校	Schools of humanities and Social Science	72	1507	1072	348	6032	1943	74
企业	Enterprises	2514	86071	1396	10015	3225823	2734507	3166
事业单位	Public Institution	74	913	58	283	2744	10438	4532
按执行部门分组	**Grouped by Executive Departments**							
企业	Enterprises	2514	86071	1396	10015	3225823	2734507	3166
科研机构	Scientific and Technological Institutions	115	14754	1020	5957	525982	594473	140777
高等院校	Institutions of Higer Education	687	3923	2070	1029	58183	682629	353828
其他	Others	92	1456	187	464	23086	26121	8015

21-6 研究与试验发展(R&D)人员情况(2019年)

Basic Statistics on Personnel Engaged in R&D Activities (2019)

指　标	Item	单位数 (个) Number of Institutions (unit)	#有(R&D)活动的单位数 Number of Institutions for R&D	(R&D)人员 (人) Number of Persons for R&D (person)	#研究人员 Researchers	(R&D)人员折合全时当量(人年) Number of Persons for R&D Anounted to Full-time (person-year)	#研究人员 Researchers
总　计	**Total**	**27772**	**5393**	**296349**	**121472**	**191570**	**76108**
按数据来源分组	**Grouped by Data Source**						
科研单位	Scientific and Technological Sector	238	110	16512	10322	12536	9890
#科研机构	Scientific and Technological Institutions	115	67	14754	9360	11175	9068
事业单位	Public Institution	123	43	1758	962	1361	822
高等院校	Institutions of Higer Education	255	197	37743	30968	13783	11459
#理工农医院校	Schools of Science, Engineering, Agriculture and Medicine	157	115	14594	12131	9723	8079
人文社科院校	Schools of humanities and Social Science	98	83	23149	18837	4061	3381
工业企业	Industrial Enterprises	19512	4458	206775	63968	140361	43513
大中型工业企业	Large and Medium-sized Industrial Enterprises	501	319	100594	31472	71058	22054
规上小型工业企业	Small-sized Industrial Enterprises above Designated Size	2641	958	47437	14856	30848	9749
规上微型工业企业	Miniature industrial enterprises above Designated Size	16370	3181	58744	17640	38454	11710
重点建筑业和服务业企业	Key services	7399	523	28290	12303	21281	9378
非工业企业	Non-industrial Enterprises	165	22	517	135	399	113
事业单位	Public Institution	203	83	6512	3776	3210	1754
按执行部门分组	**Grouped by Executive Departments**						
企业	Enterprises	27076	5003	235582	76406	162041	53004
#大中型	Large and Medium-sized Enterprises	4650	1543	172329	57069	120493	40115
科研机构	Scientific and Technological Institutions	115	67	14754	9360	11175	9068
高等院校	Institutions of Higer Education	255	197	37743	30968	13783	11459
其他	Others	326	126	8270	4738	4571	2576
按隶属关系分组	**Grouped by Administrative Relationship**						
中央	Central	437	188	51879	24883	39846	20738
地方	Local	27335	5206	244470	96589	151725	55371

21-7 研究与试验发展(R&D)产出情况(2019年)

指　标	Item	专　利申请数(件) Number of Patent Applications (piece)	#发明专利申请数 Inventions	专　利授权数(件) Number of Patents Applications Granted (piece)	#发明专利授权数 Inventions
总　计	**Total**	**51033**	**18008**	**11200**	**3397**
按数据来源分组	**Grouped by Data Source**				
科研单位	Scientific and Technological Sector	2197	1657	1065	609
#科研机构	Scientific and Technological Institutions	1888	1445	923	566
事业单位	Public Institution	309	212	142	43
高等院校	Institutions of Higer Education	12824	5524	10135	2788
#理工农医院校	Schools of Science, Engineering, Agriculture and Medicine	12048	5383	9578	2741
人文社科院校	Schools of humanities and Social Science	776	141	557	47
工业企业	Industrial Enterprises	30397	8734		
大中型工业企业	Large and Medium-sized Industrial Enterprises	9988	3692		
规上小型工业企业	Small-sized Industrial Enterprises above Designated Size	6671	1914		
规上微型工业企业	Miniature industrial enterprises above Designated Size	13738	3128		
重点建筑业和服务业企业	Key services	5541	2066		
非工业企业	Non-industrial Enterprises	42	15		
事业单位	Public Institution	32	12		
按执行部门分组	**Grouped by Executive Departments**				
企业	Enterprises	35980	10815		
#大中型	Large and Medium-sized Enterprises	21109	7346		
科研机构	Scientific and Technological Institutions	1888	1445	923	566
高等院校	Institutions of Higer Education	12824	5524	10135	2788
其他	Others	341	224	142	43
按隶属关系分组	**Grouped by Administrative Relationship**				
中央	Central	9222	4596	717	487
地方	Local	41811	13412	10483	2910

Statistics on Achievements for R&D (2019)

有效发明专利数(件) Number of Effective Invention Patent (piece)	专利所有权转让及许可数(件) Assignment and Permit of Patent Ownership (piece)	专利所有权转让及许可收入(万元) Income from Assignment and Permit of Patent Ownership (10 000 yuan)	植物新品种权授予数(项) Number of New Varieties of Plants Applications Granted (item)	形成国家或行业标准数(项) Become National or Trade Standards (item)	发表科技论文(篇) Scientific Papers Published (paper)	出版科技著作(种) Science and Technology Workers Published (type)
49042	**1741**	**14618**	**125**	**1206**	**65819**	**2857**
4202	19	212	88	136	4151	185
3935	15	172	83	110	3457	149
267	4	40.0	5	26	694	36
9975	323	2142	37	45	50235	2567
9865	320	2136	37	45	35198	1099
110	3	6			15037	1468
30245	1232	9212		822	6308	
9365	170	265		408	4574	
8075	528	2400		210	1142	
12805	534	6547		204	592	
4612	166	3047			3912	
8	1	5			25	
					1188	105
34865	1399	12264		1025	10245	
21090	840	51284		797	9480	
3935	15	172	83	110	3457	149
9975	323	2142	37	45	50235	2567
267	4	40	5	26	1882	141
11370	116	2675	21	322	7896	37
37672	1625	11943	104	884	57923	2820

21-8 规模以上工业企业研究与试验发展(R&D)人员活动情况(2019年)

单位：人

类别	Item	(R&D)人员合计(人) R&D Personnel	参加项目人员 Participating in project Personnel	管理和服务人员 Management and Service Personnel
总计	**Total**	**222218**	**206802**	**15416**
按企业规模分组	**By Size**			
大型企业	Large-sized	108852	102310	6542
中型企业	Medium-sized	51062	47450	3612
小型企业	Small-sized	56053	51470	4583
微型企业	Miniature	6251	5572	679
按工业行业大类分组	**By Sector**			
#煤炭开采和洗选业	Mining and Washing of Coal	13379	12363	1016
石油和天然气开采业	Extraction of Petroleum and Natural Gas	1959	1790	169
黑色金属矿采选业	Mining of Ferrous Metal Ores			
有色金属矿采选业	Mining of Non-ferrous Metal Ores	1228	1144	84
非金属矿采选业	Mining and Processing of Nonmetal Ores	35	30	5
农副食品加工业	Processing of Food from Agricultural Products	7487	7045	442
食品制造业	Manufacture of Foods	6519	6134	385
酒、饮料和精制茶制造业	Manufacture of Liquor,Bevevages and refined tea	2597	2435	162
烟草制品业	Manufacture of Tobacco	812	732	80
纺织业	Manufacture of Textile	4731	4477	254
纺织服装服饰业	Manufacture of Textile, Wearing Apparel and Accessories	1538	1426	112
皮革、毛皮、羽毛及其制品和制鞋业	Manufacture of Leather, Fur, Featherand Its Products, Footwear	1929	1844	85
木材加工及木、竹、藤、棕、草制品业	Processing of Timbers, Manufacture of Wood, Bamboo, Rattan, Palm, and Straw Products	1065	996	69
家具制造业	Manufacture of Furniture	601	559	42
造纸及纸制品业	Manufacture of Paper and Paper Products	1856	1720	136
印刷和记录媒介的复制业	Printing,Reproduction of Recording Media	1741	1659	82
文教、工美、体育和娱乐用品制造业	Manufacture of Articles for Culture, Education, Arts and Crafts, Sport and Entertainment Activities	2415	2278	137
石油加工、炼焦及核燃料加工业	Processing of Petroleum, Coking, Processing of Nucleus Fuel	1022	929	93
化学原料及化学制品制造业	Manufacture of Raw Chemical Material and Chemical Products	13067	12171	896
医药制造业	Manufacture of Medicines	10622	9865	757
化学纤维制造业	Manufacture of Chemical Fiber	1815	1632	183
橡胶和塑料制品业	Manufacture of Rubber and Plastic Products	3898	3639	259
非金属矿物制品业	Manufacture of Non-metallic Mineral Products	18172	16737	1435
黑色金属冶炼及压延加工业	Smelting and Pressing of Ferrous Metals	7670	7245	425
有色金属冶炼及压延加工业	Smelting and Pressing of Non-ferrous Metals	10520	9804	716
金属制品业	Manufacture of Metal Products	5884	5457	427
通用设备制造业	Manufacture of General Purpose Machinery	15560	14629	931
专用设备制造业	Manufacture of Special Purpose Machinery	17119	15910	1209
汽车制造业	Manufacture of Automobile	14918	13527	1391
铁路、船舶、航空航天和其他运输设备制造业	Manufacture of Railway, ship, aerospace, and other transport equipment	5134	4771	363
电气机械及器材制造业	Manufacture of Electrical Machinery and Apparatus	15854	14295	1559
计算机、通信和其他电子设备制造业	Manufacture of Computer, Communication and Other Electronic Equipment	17673	16945	728
仪器仪表制造业	Manufacture of Measuring Instruments and Machinery	5339	4968	371
其他制造业	Manufacture of others	1358	1192	166
废弃资源综合利用业	Utilization of waste Resources	176	162	14
金属制品、机械和设备修理业	Repairing of Metal products, machinery and equipment	627	560	67
电力、热力的生产和供应业	Production and Supply of Electric Power and Heat Power	3506	3397	109
燃气生产和供应业	Production and Supply of Gas	435	404	31
水的生产和供应业	Production and Supply of Water	281	262	19

Basic Statistics on R&D Activities in Enterprises above Designated Size (2019)

(person)

#女性 Female	#研究人员 Researchers	#全时人员 Full-time Personnel	非全时人员 Part-time Personnel	(R&D)人员折合全时当量合计(人年) Full-time Equivalent of R&D Personnel (person-year)	#研究人员 Researchers	#基础研究人员 Basic Research	应用研究人员 Applied Research	试验发展人员 Experimental Development
45963	**101365**	**158948**	**63270**	**149057**	**66981**	**202**	**5569**	**143286**
20585	45669	76551	32301	75706	31274	170	4080	71456
11616	25132	35816	15246	32946	16073	3	522	32422
12036	28890	41311	14742	35686	18423	29	926	34731
1726	1674	5270	981	4720	1211		42	4678
457	6419	6717	6662	6935	3638	4	814	6117
651	723	1486	473	1703	666		705	998
166	702	765	463	813	464	21	129	663
8	11	24	11	20	7		3	18
2032	3796	3697	3790	5080	2607	3	600	4477
2001	3247	4115	2404	4019	2000		299	3720
683	871	1828	769	1762	550		18	1744
107	463	480	332	755	430			755
1834	2443	3300	1431	2618	1332		101	2517
690	836	1000	538	986	530		7	980
700	568	1556	373	1469	405		18	1451
190	511	799	266	594	288		42	552
141	323	447	154	367	196		11	356
365	901	1214	642	1372	659		1	1372
386	964	1252	489	1217	677		1	1216
700	1095	1691	724	1821	798		24	1798
181	581	623	399	553	313			553
2920	6160	8544	4523	8314	3832	4	153	8156
4253	4434	7543	3079	6348	2677	3	67	6278
428	820	1399	416	646	186		22	624
723	2043	2734	1164	2513	1307	4	20	2489
3595	8632	12582	5590	11834	5510	25	208	11602
920	3831	6089	1581	5401	2653		6	5395
1715	4759	6843	3677	6441	2884	13	703	5725
1120	2873	4294	1590	4036	1934		90	3946
2833	6662	11225	4335	10478	4415	102	661	9715
3083	6901	12931	4188	11407	4556		168	11240
2569	6060	12193	2725	10214	3843		340	9874
1170	1072	4293	841	4332	787		17	4314
3706	6821	12601	3253	11448	4771	18	138	11292
3289	8994	14976	2697	13252	6845		42	13209
1147	2364	4362	977	3689	1496		101	3588
307	774	1190	168	1197	682			1197
27	98	109	67	94	51		6	88
128	358	560	67	522	298			522
317	1902	1693	1813	2777	1538	6	13	2758
124	249	209	226	254	145		30	224
87	149	246	35	223	124		12	211

21-9 规模以上工业企业研究与试验发展(R&D)经费支出活动情况(2019年)

单位：万元

类别	Item	(R&D)经费内部支出 Internal Expenditures on R&D	#基础研究支出 Basic Research	应用研究支出 Applied Research	试验发展支出 Experimental Development
总计	**Total**	**6087153**	**3674**	**223271**	**5860208**
按企业规模分组	**By Size**				
大型企业	Large-sized	3242448	2351	161431	3078665
中型企业	Medium-sized	1388065	31	23601	1364433
小型企业	Small-sized	1312347	1292	36775	1274281
微型企业	Miniature	144293		1464	142829
按工业行业大类分组	**By Sector**				
#煤炭开采和洗选业	Mining and Washing of Coal	172855		22265	150590
石油和天然气开采业	Extraction of Petroleum and Natural Gas	29329		10055	19274
黑色金属矿采选业	Mining of Ferrous Metal Ores				
有色金属矿采选业	Mining of Non-ferrous Metal Ores	28958	319	2916	25722
非金属矿采选业	Mining and Processing of Nonmetal Ores	183		29	154
农副食品加工业	Processing of Food from Agricultural Products	188592	31	11418	177143
食品制造业	Manufacture of Foods	130904		7535	123368
酒、饮料和精制茶制造业	Manufacture of Liquor,Beverages and refined tea	69652		1825	67827
烟草制品业	Manufacture of Tobacco	24026			24026
纺织业	Manufacture of Textile	101540		7126	94414
纺织服装服饰业	Manufacture of Textile, Wearing Apparel,Accessories	33273		421	32852
皮革、毛皮、羽毛及其制品和制鞋业	Manufacture of Leather, Fur, Featherand Its Products, Footwear	66447		826	65621
木材加工及木、竹、藤、棕、草制品业	Processing of Timbers, Manufacture of Wood, Bamboo, Rattan, Palm, and Straw Products	30582		1999	28582
家具制造业	Manufacture of Furniture	15790		393	15397
造纸及纸制品业	Manufacture of Paper and Paper Products	54057		1	54057
印刷和记录媒介的复制业	Printing,Reproduction of Recording Media	31398		85	31313
文教、工美、体育和娱乐用品制造业	Manufacture of Articles for Culture, Education, Arts and Crafts, Sport and Entertainment Activities	47605		315	47290
石油加工、炼焦及核燃料加工业	Processing of Petroleum, Coking, Processing of Nucleus Fuel	48649			48649
化学原料及化学制品制造业	Manufacture of Raw Chemical Material and Chemical Products	397040	466	3485	393089
医药制造业	Manufacture of Medicines	242845	15	7360	235470
化学纤维制造业	Manufacture of Chemical Fiber	26738		202	26536
橡胶和塑料制品业	Manufacture of Rubber and Plastic Products	82028	289	976	80763
非金属矿物制品业	Manufacture of Non-metallic Mineral Products	515584	1060	10398	504126
黑色金属冶炼及压延加工业	Smelting and Pressing of Ferrous Metals	412383		398	411985
有色金属冶炼及压延加工业	Smelting and Pressing of Non-ferrous Metals	470700	117	54448	416135
金属制品业	Manufacture of Metal Products	143432		4492	138940
通用设备制造业	Manufacture of General Purpose Machinery	427068	1021	31460	394586
专用设备制造业	Manufacture of Special Purpose Machinery	443142		3148	439995
汽车制造业	Manufacture of Automobile	560613		24245	536368
铁路、船舶、航空航天和其他运输设备制造业	Manufacture of Railway, ship, aerospace, and other transport equipment	155449		917	154532
电气机械及器材制造业	Manufacture of Electrical Machinery and Equipment	558337	296	6846	551196
计算机、通信和其他电子设备制造业	Manufacture of Computer, Communication, and Other Electronic Equipment	318882		3783	315099
仪器仪表制造业	Manufacture of Measuring Instrument	103725		2773	100952
其他制造业	Manufacture of others	36893			36893
废弃资源综合利用业	Utilization of waste Resourles	6047		308	5739
金属制品、机械和设备修理业	Repairing of Metal products, machinery and equipment	7917			7917
电力、热力的生产和供应业	Production and Supply of Electric Power and Heat Power	39083	60	100	38923
燃气生产和供应业	Production and Supply of Gas	11324		623	10701
水的生产和供应业	Production and Supply of Water	7970		102	7868

Basic Statistics on R&D Activities in Enterprises above Designated Size (2019)

(10 000 yuan)

政府资金 Government Funds	企业资金 Self-raised Funds by Enterpirses	境外资金 Foreign Funds	其他资金 Other Funds	(R&D)经费外部支出 External Expenditures on R&D	对境内研究机构支出 Expenses on Domestic R&D Institutions	对境内高等学校支出 Expenses on Domestic Universities	对境外支出 Expenses on Overseas
135195	**5950779**	**486**	**693**	**173172**	**38190**	**24856**	**107027**
91743	3149722	465	517	110394	23893	15025	70359
12738	1375327			35581	7867	3853	22121
14590	1297582		176	22523	6073	5146	11061
16124	128149	21		4675	357	832	3486
368	172156		332	11641	1811	6630	3200
284	29023		22	3120	38	1758	1324
	28958			630	238	42	350
48	122		13				
2041	186093	458		2195	658	1219	178
1142	129761			658	93	216	323
1911	67741			305	165	84	56
	24026			2727	1303	596	827
1955	99585			244		198	46
60	33213			223	129	13	82
1115	65333			104			104
51	30531			292	36		257
76	15715			51	25	22	3
225	53832			808	30	294	484
563	30835			19			19
1307	46298			121		62	59
200	48449			2291	171	675	1425
2544	394333		163	6718	1826	1047	3839
8278	234567			22059	17014	2396	2464
463	26275			1843	640	500	703
1299	80729			197	135	62	
3675	511909			2417	1093	994	328
1030	411352			529	237	206	86
3420	467272	7		2698	513	325	1454
1623	141809			762	137	119	473
17247	409800	21		6428	1040	2222	2971
8494	434648		1	6726	447	753	5527
55283	505330			65852	281	791	64228
9196	146253			3014	35		2979
6017	552158		162	8995	4058	1454	2999
2016	316865			3880	639	503	2738
2828	100897			4357	596	507	2206
	36893			1950		39	1911
50	5997			944	900	44	
	7917						
358	38724			8376	3904	1088	3384
2	11322						
26	7944						

21-10 规模以上工业企业研究与试验发展(R&D)活动情况(2019年)

Basic Statistics on R&D Activities in Enterprises above Designated Size (2019)

类　别	Item	新产品销售收入（万元）Sales Revenue of New Products (10 000 yuan)	专利申请数（项）Total Patent Applications (item)	有效发明专利数（项）Number of Inverntions In Force (item)
总 计	**Total**	**67883527**	**30397**	**30245**
按企业规模分组	**By Size**			
大型企业	Large-sized	50350030	9988	9365
中型企业	Medium-sized	9228332	6671	8075
小型企业	Small-sized	7463933	12702	11697
微型企业	Miniature	841233	1036	1108
按工业行业大类分组	**By Sector**			
#煤炭开采和洗选业	Mining and Washing of Coal	398506	309	137
石油和天然气开采业	Extraction of Petroleum and Natural Gas	232	248	67
黑色金属矿采选业	Mining of Ferrous Metal Ores			
有色金属矿采选业	Mining of Non-ferrous Metal Ores	178815	131	77
非金属矿采选业	Mining and Processing of Nonmetal Ores		5	7
农副食品加工业	Processing of Food from Agricultural Products	1323760	637	400
食品制造业	Manufacture of Foods	996071	558	677
酒、饮料和精制茶制造业	Manufacture of Liquor,Beverages and refined tea	267364	188	173
烟草制品业	Manufacture of Tobacco	28977	853	360
纺织业	Manufacture of Textile	765108	348	181
纺织服装服饰业	Manufacture of Textile, Wearing Apparel and Accessories	134673	182	250
皮革、毛皮、羽毛及其制品和制鞋业	Manufacture of Leather, Fur, Featherand Its Products, Footwear	399857	246	109
木材加工及木、竹、藤、棕、草制品业	Processing of Timbers, Manufacture of Wood, Bamboo, Rattan, Palm, and Straw Products	80061	117	53
家具制造业	Manufacture of Furniture	36424	121	25
造纸及纸制品业	Manufacture of Paper and Paper Products	422609	269	246
印刷和记录媒介的复制业	Printing,Reproduction of Recording Media	432673	259	207
文教、工美、体育和娱乐用品制造业	Manufacture of Articles for Culture, Education, Arts and Crafts, Sport and Enterntainment Activities	205690	176	130
石油加工、炼焦及核燃料加工业	Processing of Petroleum, Coking, Processing of Nucleus Fuel	94014	136	295
化学原料及化学制品制造业	Manufacture of Raw Chemical Material and Chemical Products	2915173	1563	1942
医药制造业	Manufacture of Medicines	1979576	1209	1464
化学纤维制造业	Manufacture of Chemical Fiber	307326	33	104
橡胶和塑料制品业	Manufacture of Rubber and Plastic Products	680862	529	347
非金属矿物制品业	Manufacture of Non-metallic Mineral Products	3234003	2763	2421
黑色金属冶炼及压延加工业	Smelting and Pressing of Ferrous Metals	4914851	429	414
有色金属冶炼及压延加工业	Smelting and Pressing of Non-ferrous Metals	4931892	783	976
金属制品业	Manufacture of Metal Products	1088122	1066	1019
通用设备制造业	Manufacture of General Purpose Machinery	4097032	3041	3052
专用设备制造业	Manufacture of Special Purpose Machinery	4738301	3753	4937
汽车制造业	Manufacture of Automobile	4552317	2180	1679
铁路、船舶、航空航天和其他运输设备制造业	Manufacture of Railway, ship, aerospace, and other transport equipment	895237	942	1489
电气机械及器材制造业	Manufacture of Electrical Machinery and Equipment	7550347	3105	3803
计算机、通信和其他电子设备制造业	Manufacture of Computer, Communication and Other Electronic Equipment	19246092	1414	1030
仪器仪表制造业	Manufacture of Measuring Instrument	637703	1097	1214
其他制造业	Manufacture of others	146040	173	194
废弃资源综合利用业	Utilization of waste Resources	30355	48	4
金属制品、机械和设备修理业	Repairing of Metal products, machinery and equipment	110459	65	67
电力、热力的生产和供应业	Production and Supply of Electric Power and Heat Power	681	1223	404
燃气生产和供应业	Production and Supply of Gas	28467	33	36
水的生产和供应业	Production and Supply of Water	29958	48	64

21-11 研究与试验发展(R&D)项目(课题)情况(2019年)

Statistics on R&D Projects (Topics) (2019)

指 标	Item	项目(课题)数(项) Projects of R&D (item)	项目(课题)参加人员折合全时当量(人年) Full-time Equivalent of R&D Personnel (person-year)	#研究人员 Researchers	项目(课题)经费内部支出支出(万元) Internal Expenditures on R&D (10 000 yuan)
总　计	**Total**	**65835**	**182064**	**60393**	**7747700**
按数据来源分组	**Grouped by Data Source**				
科研单位	Scientific and Technological Sector	1756	11451	7829	404478
#科研机构	Scientific and Technological Institutions	1485	10356	7128	381429
事业单位	Public Institution	271	1095	701	23048
高等院校	Institutions of Higer Education	34570	13784	11460	233259
#理工农医院校	Schools of Science, Engineering, Agriculture and Medicine	13774	9723	8079	201441
人文社科院校	Schools of humanities and Social Science	20966	4133	3441	31957
企业	Enterprises	28888	154443	40922	7098803
事业单位	Public Institution	621	2387	182	11161
按执行部门分组	**Grouped by Executive Departments**				
企业	Enterprises	28888	154443	40922	7098803
科研机构	Scientific and Technological Institutions	1485	10356	7128	381429
高等院校	Institutions of Higer Education	34570	13784	11460	233259
其他	Others	892	3482	884	34210

21−12 各市研究与试验发展(R&D)人员情况(2019年)
Basic Statistics on Personnel Engaged in R&D Activities by City (2019)

市(县) City(County)	单位数 (个) Number of Institutions (unit)	#有(R&D)活动 Number of Institutions for R&D	(R&D)活动人员 (人) Number of Persons for R&D (person)	#研究人员 Researchers	(R&D)活动人员折合全时当量 (人年) Full-time Equivalent of R&D Personnel (person-year)	#研究人员 Researchers
全　省 **Total**	**27772**	**5394**	**296349**	**121472**	**191570**	**76107**
省辖市 City						
郑州市 Zhengzhou	4924	1509	99028	45713	66771	29143
开封市 Kaifeng	1363	238	9872	4641	5922	2556
洛阳市 Luoyang	2361	691	36925	16737	25674	12299
平顶山市 Pingdingshan	1165	242	14919	4702	10435	3084
安阳市 Anyang	978	88	8799	4138	5323	2394
鹤壁市 Hebi	483	90	4716	1321	2325	600
新乡市 Xinxiang	1778	430	23934	10071	14138	5896
焦作市 Jiaozuo	1397	298	17039	5560	10074	3351
濮阳市 Puyang	919	125	5821	2381	4278	1727
许昌市 Xuchang	2013	250	12098	4518	8264	3035
漯河市 Luohe	706	129	5356	1250	3855	804
三门峡市 Sanmenxia	537	92	5564	1797	3540	1078
南阳市 Nanyang	1991	426	18596	7111	11526	4192
商丘市 Shangqiu	1925	203	10157	3594	4989	1641
信阳市 Xinyang	1631	210	7103	2566	4256	1338
周口市 Zhoukou	1781	141	6575	2466	3482	1254
驻马店市 Zhumadian	1508	193	6112	2062	3980	1139
济源市 Jiyuan	312	39	3735	844	2739	576
省直管县 County Directly Administrated by Province						
巩义市 Gongyi	549	90	2761	2581	1823	912
兰考县 Lankao	275	65	1223	1129	808	460
汝州市 Ruzhou	300	86	1691	1583	1054	532
滑县 Huaxian	257	6	294	284	245	140
长垣市 Changyuan	398	80	3927	3647	2351	941
邓州市 Dengzhou	177	8	352	298	218	125
永城市 Yongcheng	346	24	3843	3653	1584	902
固始县 Gushi	293	15	329	318	242	73
鹿邑县 Luyi	313	11	826	753	290	127
新蔡县 Xincai	189	8	170	164	122	54

21-13 各市研究与试验发展(R&D)经费支出情况(2019年)

Statistics on Appropriation Expenditure for R&D by City (2019)

单位：万元 (10 000 yuan)

市(县)	City(County)	(R&D)经费内部支出 Intramural Expenditures on R&D	政府资金 Government Funds	企业资金 Self-raised Funds by Enterpirses	境外资金 Foreign Funds	其他资金 Other Funds	(R&D)经费外部支出 External Expenditures on R&D
全　　省	**Total**	**7930369**	**780117**	**6867595**	**4884**	**277773**	**229987**
省 辖 市	**City**						
郑州市	Zhengzhou	2367410	338271	1929108	216	99815	69465
开封市	Kaifeng	241332	40651	194211		6469	39277
洛阳市	Luoyang	1192325	188541	896385		107399	45301
平顶山市	Pingdingshan	382818	10351	368100		4367	9125
安阳市	Anyang	295297	40127	248405		6765	1563
鹤壁市	Hebi	76144	1488	74613		43	13265
新乡市	Xinxiang	625568	93607	496404	12	35545	10816
焦作市	Jiaozuo	461348	13754	443720	3	3872	8195
濮阳市	Puyang	160773	3776	156673		324	3422
许昌市	Xuchang	529900	6291	523439		170	3533
漯河市	Luohe	133934	1059	127984	4580	311	1015
三门峡市	Sanmenxia	198419	2348	186292	73	9706	1742
南阳市	Nanyang	410756	6619	403097		1040	10379
商丘市	Shangqiu	273944	6552	266594		798	2259
信阳市	Xinyang	157488	6223	150624		641	4658
周口市	Zhoukou	147391	7251	140075		65	2978
驻马店市	Zhumadian	139545	9503	129621		422	1922
济源市	Jiyuan	135977	3704	132252		21	1072
省直管县	**County Directly Administrated by Province**						
巩义市	Gongyi	131593	595	130998			247
兰考县	Lankao	29513	35	29478			43
汝州市	Ruzhou	73791	2144	71380			1141
滑县	Huaxian	8878		8878			17
长垣市	Changyuan	144921	1572	143350			45
邓州市	Dengzhou	7956		7956			
永城市	Yongcheng	74240	115	73793		332	1156
固始县	Gushi	6044	90	5954			156
鹿邑县	Luyi	25451	51	25400			4
新蔡县	Xincai	2822	174	2648			101

21-14 各市研究与试验发展(R&D)产出情况(2019年)

Statistics on Achievements for R&D by City (2019)

市(县) City(County)	专利申请数(件) Total Patens Applications (piece)	#发明专利申请数 Inventions	专利授权数(件) Number of Patents Applications Granted (piece)	#发明专利授权数 Number of Patent Applicatons Granted	有效发明专利数(件) Number of Inventions In Force (piece)
全 省 Total	**51033**	**18008**	**11200**	**3397**	**49042**
省 辖 市 City					
郑 州 市 Zhengzhou	20602	7715	5706	1525	16613
开 封 市 Kaifeng	966	341	342	120	995
洛 阳 市 Luoyang	6131	2409	880	569	8829
平 顶 山 市 Pingdingshan	1481	686	176	58	2027
安 阳 市 Anyang	1337	486	283	101	1700
鹤 壁 市 Hebi	387	83	30	4	502
新 乡 市 Xinxiang	5417	1802	1230	460	4500
焦 作 市 Jiaozuo	3153	1092	808	293	2855
濮 阳 市 Puyang	780	254	27	2	1026
许 昌 市 Xuchang	2186	869	78	10	2776
漯 河 市 Luohe	1031	175	246	9	560
三 门 峡 市 Sanmenxia	511	133	27	2	536
南 阳 市 Nanyang	2594	768	473	134	2874
商 丘 市 Shangqiu	1421	421	351	30	1092
信 阳 市 Xinyang	958	272	386	59	640
周 口 市 Zhoukou	688	192	36	4	622
驻 马 店 市 Zhumadian	749	213	78	11	586
济 源 市 Jiyuan	641	97	43	6	309
省 直 管 县 County Directly Administrated by Province					
巩 义 市 Gongyi	556	77			489
兰 考 县 Lankao	58	9			55
汝 州 市 Ruzhou	137	62			187
滑 县 Huaxian	50	15			67
长 垣 市 Changyuan	882	229			601
邓 州 市 Dengzhou	31	13			36
永 城 市 Yongcheng	166	13			72
固 始 县 Gushi	47	5			49
鹿 邑 县 Luyi	28	5			16
新 蔡 县 Xincai	41	4			38

21-14 续表 continued

市(县) City(County)	专利所有权转让及许可数(件) Assignment and Permit of Patent Ownership (piece)	专利所有权转让及许可收入(万元) Income from Assignment and Permit of Patent Ownership (10 000 yuan)	植物新品种权授予数(项) Number of New Varieties of Plants Applications Granted (item)	形成国家或行业标准数(项) Become National or Trade Standards (item)	发表科技论文(篇) Scientific Papers Published (paper)	出版科技著作(种) Science and Technology Workers Published (type)
全 省 Total	**1741**	**14618**	**125**	**1206**	**65819**	**2857**
省 辖 市 City						
郑 州 市 Zhengzhou	715	2821	73	392	32961	1407
开 封 市 Kaifeng	38	722	5	38	3645	226
洛 阳 市 Luoyang	353	3001	7	180	5662	137
平 顶 山 市 Pingdingshan	4	4605		22	2082	127
安 阳 市 Anyang	57	2	5	27	1875	61
鹤 壁 市 Hebi	1		1	9	373	13
新 乡 市 Xinxiang	51	217	4	72	5720	288
焦 作 市 Jiaozuo	82	92	6	137	3107	83
濮 阳 市 Puyang	19	430		21	328	10
许 昌 市 Xuchang	158	1	2	63	774	37
漯 河 市 Luohe	36	0	7	10	920	50
三 门 峡 市 Sanmenxia	56		4	9	954	13
南 阳 市 Nanyang	71			78	1885	124
商 丘 市 Shangqiu	58	2400		23	1781	81
信 阳 市 Xinyang		70	6	19	1700	55
周 口 市 Zhoukou	1	2	1	17	579	54
驻 马 店 市 Zhumadian	40	225	3	12	1000	61
济 源 市 Jiyuan	1	30	1	77	473	29
省 直 管 县 County Directly Administrated by Province						
巩 义 市 Gongyi	11	1000		3	4	
兰 考 县 Lankao	1	200				
汝 州 市 Ruzhou	3	4600		2	10	
滑 县 Huaxian	3					
长 垣 市 Changyuan				7	44	
邓 州 市 Dengzhou				1	1	
永 城 市 Yongcheng				2	408	
固 始 县 Gushi						
鹿 邑 县 Luyi					7	
新 蔡 县 Xincai					1	

21-15 各市规模以上工业企业研究与试验发展(R&D)活动情况(2019年)

Basic Statistics on R&D Activities in Enterprises above Designated Size by City (2019)

市(县) City(County)	(R&D)人员合计(人) R&D Personnel (person)	参加项目人员 Participating in project Personnel	管理和服务人员 Management and Service Personnel	#女性 Female	#研究人员 Researchers	全时人员 Full-time Personnel	非全时人员 Part-time Personnel
全省 Total	**222218**	**206802**	**15416**	**45963**	**101365**	**158948**	**63270**
省辖市 City							
郑州市 Zhengzhou	53513	49909	3604	10467	25114	39770	13743
开封市 Kaifeng	6495	5928	567	1348	3302	4928	1567
洛阳市 Luoyang	27039	25222	1817	5307	9850	20680	6359
平顶山市 Pingdingshan	13470	12579	891	1710	6431	9500	3970
安阳市 Anyang	6522	6075	447	929	3509	4926	1596
鹤壁市 Hebi	4767	4510	257	1209	2147	3765	1002
新乡市 Xinxiang	18886	17409	1477	4624	8295	14613	4273
焦作市 Jiaozuo	16945	15951	994	3456	6600	11955	4990
濮阳市 Puyang	5316	5023	293	1220	2718	4109	1207
许昌市 Xuchang	11705	10498	1207	2422	5233	7736	3969
漯河市 Luohe	5294	5059	235	1258	2969	2370	2924
三门峡市 Sanmenxia	4179	3801	378	729	2081	2441	1738
南阳市 Nanyang	17826	16351	1475	4527	9020	12715	5111
商丘市 Shangqiu	9471	8886	585	1424	5037	5450	4021
信阳市 Xinyang	5866	5439	427	1713	3046	3710	2156
周口市 Zhoukou	6240	5939	301	1763	2854	3714	2526
驻马店市 Zhumadian	5105	4815	290	1155	2196	3517	1588
济源市 Jiyuan	3579	3408	171	702	963	3049	530
省直管县 County Directly Administrated by Province							
巩义市 Gongyi	2761	2581	180	414	1359	1819	942
兰考县 Lankao	1211	1122	89	202	690	915	296
汝州市 Ruzhou	1679	1572	107	258	862	1199	480
滑县 Huaxian	294	284	10	20	168	262	32
长垣市 Changyuan	3916	3637	279	1106	1639	3064	852
邓州市 Dengzhou	352	298	54	90	201	288	64
永城市 Yongcheng	3713	3557	156	180	2109	1674	2039
固始县 Gushi	329	318	11	89	101	240	89
鹿邑县 Luyi	826	753	73	127	402	612	214
新蔡县 Xincai	170	164	6	81	76	133	37

21−15 续表 1 continued

市(县)	City(County)	(R&D)人员折合全时当量合计(人年) Full-time Equivalent of R&D Persnnel (person-year)	#研究人员 Researchers	#基础研究人员 Basic Research	应用研究人员 Applied Research	试验发展人员 Experimental Development
全　省	**Total**	**149057**	**66981**	**202**	**5569**	**143286**
省辖市	**City**					
郑州市	Zhengzhou	39311	18402	5	769	38537
开封市	Kaifeng	4453	2268		59	4394
洛阳市	Luoyang	19130	6706	125	747	18259
平顶山市	Pingdingshan	9605	4527		298	9307
安阳市	Anyang	4205	2258	18	44	4144
鹤壁市	Hebi	2360	965		377	1982
新乡市	Xinxiang	11431	4694	11	380	11040
焦作市	Jiaozuo	10271	4227		571	9699
濮阳市	Puyang	4025	2087		331	3695
许昌市	Xuchang	8113	3539	16	78	8020
漯河市	Luohe	3819	2140	4	216	3598
三门峡市	Sanmenxia	2678	1308	13	566	2098
南阳市	Nanyang	11533	5777	6	671	10855
商丘市	Shangqiu	4639	2434		163	4476
信阳市	Xinyang	3788	1939		161	3627
周口市	Zhoukou	3352	1425	5	86	3261
驻马店市	Zhumadian	3650	1513		25	3625
济源市	Jiyuan	2697	772		28	2669
省直管县	**County Directly Administrated by Province**					
巩义市	Gongyi	1823	912		18	1804
兰考县	Lankao	800	455		11	789
汝州市	Ruzhou	1042	525		7	1035
滑县	Huaxian	245	140			245
长垣市	Changyuan	2350	940	7	353	1990
邓州市	Dengzhou	218	125		6	212
永城市	Yongcheng	1455	829		36	1418
固始县	Gushi	242	73			242
鹿邑县	Luyi	290	127			290
新蔡县	Xincai	122	54			122

21-15 续表 2 continued

单位：万元 (10 000 yuan)

市(县) City(County)	(R&D)经费内部支出合计 Internal Expenditures on R&D	基础研究支出 Basic Research	应用研究支出 Applied Research	#试验发展支出 Experimental Development	政府资金 Government Funds	企业资金 Self-raised Funds by Enterpirses	境外资金 Foreign Funds	其他资金 Other Funds
全　　省 Total	**6087153**	**3674**	**223271**	**5860208**	**135195**	**5950779**	**486**	**693**
省辖市 City								
郑州市 Zhengzhou	1358003	740	34849	1322414	56696	1301286	21	
开封市 Kaifeng	170991		2521	168470	845	170145		
洛阳市 Luoyang	793083	1358	19652	772074	29280	763802		1
平顶山市 Pingdingshan	345177		5954	339222	3316	341699		162
安阳市 Anyang	239289	688	812	237789	518	238771		
鹤壁市 Hebi	75182		6897	68285	839	74343		
新乡市 Xinxiang	495886	95	25167	470623	15544	480341		
焦作市 Jiaozuo	435220		20744	414476	6034	429186		
濮阳市 Puyang	151749		3531	148218	792	150935		22
许昌市 Xuchang	512953	264	7953	504736	2812	510142		
漯河市 Luohe	132471	289	5359	126823	293	131720	458	
三门峡市 Sanmenxia	165284	117	46239	118928	439	164838	7	
南阳市 Nanyang	396139	60	13106	382973	3007	392969		163
商丘市 Shangqiu	260781		16248	244533	3224	257226		332
信阳市 Xinyang	148862		6323	142539	487	148362		13
周口市 Zhoukou	140808	63	5198	135548	3189	137619		
驻马店市 Zhumadian	131666		1947	129720	5455	126212		
济源市 Jiyuan	133610		772	132838	2427	131183		
省直管县 County Directly Administrated by Province								
巩义市 Gongyi	127793	105	1660	126029	595	127199		
兰考县 Lankao	27004		867	26138	35	26970		
汝州市 Ruzhou	70137		219	69918	2144	67993		
滑县 Huaxian	8878			8878		8878		
长垣市 Changyuan	144817	95	23394	121327	1572	143245		
邓州市 Dengzhou	7956		678	7278		7956		
永城市 Yongcheng	73341		5306	68036	115	72894		332
固始县 Gushi	6044			6044	90	5954		
鹿邑县 Luyi	25451			25451	51	25400		
新蔡县 Xincai	2822			2822	174	2648		

21-15 续表 3 continued

单位：万元 (10 000 yuan)

市(县)	City(County)	(R&D)经费外部支出合计 External Expenditures on R&D	#对境内研究机构支出 Expenses on Domestic R&D Institutions	对境内高等学校支出 Expenses on Domestic Universities	对境外支出 Expenses on Overseas
全省	**Total**	**173172**	**38190**	**24856**	**107027**
省辖市	**City**				
郑州市	Zhengzhou	44270	10328	4159	28492
开封市	Kaifeng	38631	825	302	37504
洛阳市	Luoyang	16277	6172	1540	8498
平顶山市	Pingdingshan	9116	1191	4044	3729
安阳市	Anyang	1521	90	483	948
鹤壁市	Hebi	13252	290	335	12628
新乡市	Xinxiang	10223	1446	4568	4182
焦作市	Jiaozuo	7685	4390	1679	1312
濮阳市	Puyang	3410	206	1203	2000
许昌市	Xuchang	2846	721	863	909
漯河市	Luohe	1007	214	349	305
三门峡市	Sanmenxia	1731	1167	169	378
南阳市	Nanyang	10379	3661	2221	4341
商丘市	Shangqiu	2259	448	257	1149
信阳市	Xinyang	4640	3804	551	100
周口市	Zhoukou	2973	1665	1134	174
驻马店市	Zhumadian	1916	1423	244	249
济源市	Jiyuan	1038	151	756	130
省直管县	**County Directly Administrated by Province**				
巩义市	Gongyi	247	142	33	72
兰考县	Lankao	43	13	30	0
汝州市	Ruzhou	1131	366	645	120
滑县	Huaxian	17		17	
长垣市	Changyuan	45			45
邓州市	Dengzhou				
永城市	Yongcheng	1156	311	227	212
固始县	Gushi	156	105	51	
鹿邑县	Luyi	4	2	1	1
新蔡县	Xincai	101	64		37

21-15 续表 4 continued

市(县) City(County)	新产品销售收入(万元) Sales Revenue of New Products (10 000 yuan)	企业办科技机构(个) Number of Institutions of S&T in Enterprises (unit)	专利申请数(项) Total Patent Applications (item)	有效发明专利数(项) Number of Inventions In Force (item)
全 省 Total	**67883527**	**2141**	**30397**	**30245**
省 辖 市 City				
郑 州 市 Zhengzhou	28774944	499	9579	7144
开 封 市 Kaifeng	1251241	69	449	405
洛 阳 市 Luoyang	7876871	247	4221	5833
平 顶 山 市 Pingdingshan	1820874	70	1168	1726
安 阳 市 Anyang	2221628	40	831	1257
鹤 壁 市 Hebi	783720	37	368	483
新 乡 市 Xinxiang	4395330	152	3423	2440
焦 作 市 Jiaozuo	3556818	170	1693	1736
濮 阳 市 Puyang	627860	50	684	983
许 昌 市 Xuchang	3971568	90	1868	2293
漯 河 市 Luohe	1483628	70	798	525
三 门 峡 市 Sanmenxia	288521	22	372	445
南 阳 市 Nanyang	3566798	152	1876	2141
商 丘 市 Shangqiu	1392805	98	898	1020
信 阳 市 Xinyang	807839	78	368	425
周 口 市 Zhoukou	963372	82	641	579
驻 马 店 市 Zhumadian	1463912	153	595	512
济 源 市 Jiyuan	2635801	62	565	298
省 直 管 县 County Directly Administrated by Province				
巩 义 市 Gongyi	1480014	64	556	489
兰 考 县 Lankao	52183	6	58	55
汝 州 市 Ruzhou	87243	27	136	186
滑 县 Huaxian	80450	2	50	67
长 垣 市 Changyuan	1538640	19	881	600
邓 州 市 Dengzhou	35029	8	31	36
永 城 市 Yongcheng	278959	21	162	71
固 始 县 Gushi	15339	3	47	49
鹿 邑 县 Luyi	445456	5	28	16
新 蔡 县 Xincai	24147	5	41	38

21－16 大中型工业企业研究与试验发展(R&D)活动情况

Basic Statistics on R&D Activities in Large and Medium-Sized Industrial Enterprises

单位：亿元 (100 million yuan)

指　标	Item	2015	2016	2017	2018	2019
企业(R&D)活动人员（人）	Number of Persons for R&D (person)	159964	160343	158624	135284	148031
企业办科技机构（个）	Number of R&D Institutions Operated by Enterprises (unit)	1290	1386	1387	865	903
企业办科技机构人员（人）	Personner of R&D Institutions Operated by Enterprises (person)	95264	95514	95870	72686	70957
当年(R&D)经费内部支出	External Expenditures on R&D	326.49	358.41	401.58	405.71	463.05
新产品销售收入	Sales Revenue of New Products	5584.41	5861.62	6749.98	7005.10	5957.84
#出口	Export	2857.05	2790.01	3159.26	3365.38	2090.54
仪器和设备原价	Original price of Equipment for S&T	144.43	162.22	209.48	179.53	195.03
引进技术经费支出	Expenditures on Imported Technology	3.61	0.73	1.79	0.57	1.13
消化吸收经费支出	Expenditures on Digestion and Absorption	1.42	0.82	0.68	0.05	0.09
购买国内技术支出	Expenditures on Domestic Technology	1.78	1.87	4.74	13.15	7.30
技术改造经费支出	Expenditures on Technical Reform	98.21	102.19	93.87	102.69	97.46

21－17 三种专利申请受理量及授权量

Three Types of Patent Application Accepted and Granted

单位：项 (item)

项　目	Item	2005	2010	2012	2013	2014	2015	2016	2017	2018	2019
申请量合计	**Total Applications Examined**	**8981**	**25149**	**43442**	**55920**	**62434**	**74373**	**94669**	**119243**	**154381**	**144010**
#发明	Inventions	1703	6408	10910	15580	19646	21338	28582	35626	46868	30260
实用新型	Utility Models	4594	13856	23594	29420	30716	40778	51358	66805	89620	96203
外观设计	Designs	2684	4885	8938	10920	12072	12257	14729	16812	17893	17547
#个人	Individuals	5955	9528	14468	18500	18689	22399	27859	33092	36345	38499
大专院校	Universities and Colleges	311	1387	2470	4254	6336	9980	14438	16528	18543	19397
科研单位	Research Institutions	166	578	1122	983	1062	1418	1668	1731	2220	2235
工矿企业	Industrial and Mineral Enterprises	2534	13449	24670	30887	34695	39047	48822	65182	93911	77731
机关团体	Government Agencies and Organizations	15	207	712	1296	1652	1529	1882	2710	3362	6148
授权量合计	**Total Applications Granted**	**3748**	**16539**	**26833**	**29482**	**33366**	**47766**	**49145**	**55407**	**82318**	**86247**
#发明	Inventions	356	1498	3168	3173	3493	5384	6811	7914	8339	6991
实用新型	Utility Models	2304	11048	18739	21153	23539	32592	32197	35822	59417	65341
外观设计	Designs	1088	3993	4926	5156	6334	9790	10137	11671	14562	13915
#个人	Individuals	2535	6395	7742	8529	8405	12395	13369	15565	19667	18192
大专院校	Universities and Colleges	65	630	1708	2108	3412	6135	8105	8732	9205	10012
科研单位	Research Institutions	60	410	534	398	454	571	529	636	864	1159
工矿企业	Industrial and Mineral Enterprises	1076	9043	16469	18057	20509	27806	26312	29606	51314	54123
机关团体	Government Agencies and Organizations	12	61	380	390	586	859	830	868	1268	2761
发明专利拥有量	**Patent ownership**		**4501**	**8683**	**11249**	**13535**	**17571**	**22601**	**28615**	**33524**	**37311**

21−18 规模(限额)以上企业创新活动情况

Innovative Activities in Enterprises above Designated size

行　　业	Sector	调　查企业数(个) Number of Enterprises Surveyed (unit)	开展创新活动企业数(个) Number of Enterprises Engaged in Innovative Activities (unit)	实现创新企业数(个) Number of Enterprises Achieved Innovation (unit)
	2013-2014	31864	11983	11709
	2016	42750	13103	12615
	2017	43326	13609	12843
	2018	39615	13481	12862
	2019	40049	15150	14503
按规模分	**by Size**			
大型	Large	966	674	647
中型	Medium	7154	3396	3287
小型	Small	25289	9744	9300
微型	Micro	6640	1336	1269
按登记注册类型分	**by Status of Registration**			
内资企业	Domestic Funded	39526	14873	14236
港、澳、台商投资企业	Funded from Hong Kong, Macao and Taiwan	249	125	119
外商投资企业	Foreign Funded	274	152	148
按行业分	**by Sector**			
采矿业	Mining	541	184	174
制造业	Manufacturing	18394	8395	7900
电力、热力、燃气及水生产和供应业	Production and Supply of Electricity, Heat, Gas and Water	577	193	179
建筑业	Construction	3746	1227	1202
批发和零售业	Wholesale and Retail Trades	11088	3314	3293
交通运输、仓储和邮政业	Transport, Storage and Post	2189	495	484
信息传输、软件和信息技术服务业	Information Transmission, Software and Information Technology	682	416	396
租赁和商务服务业	Leasing and Business Services	1463	395	383
科学研究和技术服务业	Scientific Research and Technical Services	963	413	377
水利、环境和公共设施管理业	Management of Water Conservancy, Environment and Public Facilities	406	118	115

21-18 续表 continued

行 业	Sector	实现各种创新类型的企业数 Number of Enterprises Achieved Various Types of Innovation				
		实现产品创新 Achieved Product Innovation	实现工艺创新 Achieved Technique Innovation	实现组织创新 Achieved Organization Innovation	实现营销创新 Achieved Marketing Innovation	同时实现四种创新 Achieved Four Types of Innovation
	2013-2014	4907	4360		10512	2834
	2016	4059	5156	9013	8794	2264
	2017	4007	5145	9131	9042	2122
	2018	4584	5412	9075	8399	2296
	2019	5106	6198	10285	9878	2658
按规模分	**by Size**					
大型	Large	392	452	478	395	214
中型	Medium	1236	1477	2403	2243	660
小型	Small	3253	3915	6474	6346	1662
微型	Micro	225	354	930	894	122
按登记注册类型分	**by Status of Registration**					
内资企业	Domestic Funded	4968	6045	10117	9724	2606
港、澳、台商投资企业	Funded from Hong Kong, Macao and Taiwan	57	63	73	67	23
外商投资企业	Foreign Funded	81	90	95	87	29
按行业分	**by Sector**					
采矿业	Mining	17	66	125	69	3
制造业	Manufacturing	3645	4216	5248	5382	1784
电力、热力、燃气及水生产和供应业	Production and Supply of Electricity, Heat, Gas and Water	15	66	134	83	7
建筑业	Construction	276	438	1040	584	155
批发和零售业	Wholesale and Retail Trades	565	765	2343	2695	385
交通运输、仓储和邮政业	Transport, Storage and Post	81	123	390	283	50
信息传输、软件和信息技术服务业	Information Transmission, Software and Information Technology	239	214	316	269	137
租赁和商务服务业	Leasing and Business Services	65	91	309	236	32
科学研究和技术服务业	Scientific Research and Technical Services	175	187	293	201	91
水利、环境和公共设施管理业	Management of Water Conservancy, Environment and Public Facilities	28	32	87	76	14

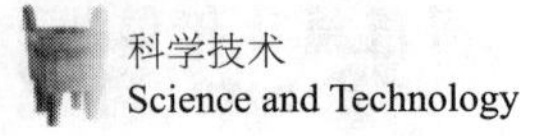

21-19 各市规模(限额)以上企业创新活动情况(2019年)
Innovative Activities in Enterprises above Designated size by City (2019)

地 区 City	调查企业数(个) Number of Enterprises Surveyed (unit)	开展创新活动企业数(个) Number of Enterprises Engaged in Innovative Activities (unit)	实现创新企业数(个) Number of Enterprises Achieved Innovation (unit)	实现各种创新类型的企业数 Number of Enterprises Achieved Various Types of Innovation				
				实现产品创新 Achieved Product Innovation	实现工艺创新 Achieved Technique Innovation	实现组织创新 Achieved Organization Innovation	实现营销创新 Achieved Marketing Innovation	同时实现四种创新 Achieved Four Types of Innovation
全 省 Total	**40049**	**15150**	**14503**	**5106**	**6198**	**10285**	**9878**	**2658**
省 辖 市 City								
郑 州 市 Zhengzhou	7802	3567	3416	1447	1761	2641	2245	832
开 封 市 Kaifeng	1905	641	618	209	276	401	412	95
洛 阳 市 Luoyang	3361	1474	1394	573	651	973	850	281
平顶山市 Pingdingshan	1654	621	590	182	269	444	380	93
安 阳 市 Anyang	1414	467	449	123	163	320	275	60
鹤 壁 市 Hebi	654	179	170	83	94	125	119	54
新 乡 市 Xinxiang	2491	927	872	375	396	630	604	202
焦 作 市 Jiaozuo	1908	743	694	281	314	510	464	143
濮 阳 市 Puyang	1270	455	439	112	140	315	287	45
许 昌 市 Xuchang	2441	724	711	230	281	484	407	96
漯 河 市 Luohe	999	315	300	118	139	201	205	54
三门峡市 Sanmenxia	895	284	269	84	121	199	166	42
南 阳 市 Nanyang	3012	1168	1087	378	447	802	779	215
商 丘 市 Shangqiu	2766	1111	1089	247	309	740	876	142
信 阳 市 Xinyang	2370	582	562	192	226	339	380	90
周 口 市 Zhoukou	2587	959	925	144	274	580	759	65
驻马店市 Zhumadian	2069	784	771	264	253	480	582	118
济 源 市 Jiyuan	451	149	147	64	84	101	88	31
省直管县 County Directly Administrated by Province								
巩 义 市 Gongyi	654	241	230	125	146	155	161	76
兰 考 县 Lankao	442	160	150	61	59	104	108	31
汝 州 市 Ruzhou	425	210	198	57	79	151	125	25
滑 县 Huaxian	336	103	100	19	28	74	68	13
长 垣 市 Changyuan	591	241	236	82	102	190	171	49
邓 州 市 Dengzhou	328	83	79	15	19	50	51	5
永 城 市 Yongcheng	430	110	107	43	56	80	88	28
固 始 县 Gushi	478	108	108	27	29	70	87	18
鹿 邑 县 Luyi	390	130	122	9	77	101	110	6
新 蔡 县 Xincai	342	133	132	41	38	63	100	7

21-20 技术市场成交合同情况(2019年)
Statistics on Transaction of Technology (2019)

指标	Item	合同数(个) Number of Contracts (unit)	成交额(万元) Transaction Value (10 000 yuan)
总计	**Total**	**9310**	**2340686**
按合同类别分	**Grouped by Contract Type**		
技术开发	Technological Development	3413	493182
技术转让	Technological Transfer	675	178964
技术咨询	Technological Consultation	929	156690
技术服务	Technological Services	4293	1511850
按知识产权分	**Grouped by Intellectual Property**		
技术秘密	Technology Secret	1642	258522
专利	Patent	846	382564
计算机软件著作权	Computer Software	755	79219
植物新品种权	New varieties of Plants	96	9253
集成电路布图设计专有权	Exclusive right of integrated circuit layout design	17	2458
生物、医药新品种权	New varieties of Biology and Medicine	82	46126
设计著作权	Design and copyright	67	3620
未涉及知识产权	Others	5805	1558925
按技术领域分	**Grouped by Technology**		
电子信息	Electronic Information Technology	2854	316513
航空航天	Aeronautic and Astronautic Technology	175	45288
先进制造	Advanced manufacturing technology	1669	469898
生物、医药和医疗器械	Biological ,Medical and Medical Device Technology	616	138471
新材料及其应用	New Materials and Their Application	423	250078
新能源与高效节能	New Energy, High Efficiency and Energy Saving	1013	189017
环境保护与资源综合利用	Environmental Protetion and Resources comprehensive utilization Technology	748	87736
核应用	Nuclear application	6	1559
农业	Agriculture Technology	643	107948
现代交通	Modern Communication	136	34024
城市建设与社会发展	City Construction and Social Development	1027	700155
按社会经济目标分	**Grouped by Social and Economic Service Objection**		
环境保护、生态建设及污染防治	Environmental protection, ecological construction and pollution control	687	117277
能源生产、分配和合理利用	Energy production, distribution and rational utilization	1012	227054
卫生事业发展	Health	382	78665
教育事业发展	Education	240	39320
基础设施以及城市和农村规划	Infrastructure and urban and rural planning	291	59394
社会发展和社会服务	Social development and social services	3035	970072
地球和大气层的探索与利用	Exploration and utilization of the earth and atmosphere	3	377
民用空间探测及开发	Detection and development of Civilian space	32	2762
农林牧渔业发展	Animal husbandry fishery development	685	126721
工商业发展	Industrial and commercial development	1022	235255
非定向研究	The directional research	277	36566
其他民用目标	Others Civilian space	1484	399259
国防	National defense	160	47965

21-21 各市技术市场成交合同情况
Statistics on Transaction of Technology by City

市 City	合同数(个) Number of Contracts (unit)			成交额(万元) Transaction Value (10 000 yuan)		
	2017	2018	2019	2017	2018	2019
全省 Total	**5877**	**7298**	**9310**	**769285**	**1497380**	**2340686**
郑州市 Zhengzhou	3779	4399	4953	347830	823485	1275411
开封市 Kaifeng	75	82	103	4931	10290	15284
洛阳市 Luoyang	1075	1308	1629	299742	368234	482667
平顶山市 Pingdingshan	16	14	54	8538	4901	57093
安阳市 Anyang	2	50	90	60	15443	20445
鹤壁市 Hebi	16	17	48	568	1354	5250
新乡市 Xinxiang	230	291	670	34974	83162	179638
焦作市 Jiaozuo	416	551	823	30035	113696	149691
濮阳市 Puyang		2	35		150	6526
许昌市 Xuchang	26	28	55	3476	3258	3002
漯河市 Luohe		11	13		2214	4543
三门峡市 Sanmenxia	9	14	5	3154	2286	5771
南阳市 Nanyang	99	284	497	9925	34672	82110
商丘市 Shangqiu	12	4	6	2418	490	963
信阳市 Xinyang	25	49	82	2392	8699	11118
周口市 Zhoukou	5	10	10	4131	5774	11857
驻马店市 Zhumadian	36	44	116	10885	12099	19569
济源市 Jiyuan	52	140	121	6225	7173	9749

21－22　软科学基本情况

Statistics on Soft science

项　目	Item	2015	2016	2017	2018	2019
完成软科学课题(项)	Completed soft science subject (item)	791	1054	665	500	560
正在进行的软科学课题(项)	Underway soft science subject (item)	1160	720	597	848	799
投入软科学研究经费(万元)	Investment funds(10 000yuan)	600	600	600	600	600
投入软科学研究人力(人.年)	Person Engaged in Soft Science(person.year)	7200	5000	4430	5880	5590
发表科学论文(篇)	Published scientific paper (paper)	960	980	602	485	505
#国外发表	Published abroad	24	29	6	9	16
获奖成果(项)	Award-winning achievements(item)	8	7	47	39	18

21－23　产品质量监督抽查情况(2019年)

Results of Sampling Check under State Supervision on the Quality of Products (2019)

项　目	Item	抽查产品(种) Production Supervised (kinds)	抽查企业(家) Number of Enterprises Supervised (unit)	抽查产品(批) Production Supervised (batch-time)	不合格产品(批) Production Unqualified (batch-time)
合　计	**Total**	**171**	**6813**	**7555**	**493**
食品相关产品	Food	9	381	445	14
日用消费品	Consumer Goods	47	1586	1827	141
建筑与装饰装修材料	Building & Decoration Material	34	2032	2292	124
农业生产资料	Agricultural Means of Production	7	206	208	14
工业生产资料	Industrial Means of Production	74	2608	2783	200

21-24 国家和地方标准、计量基本情况
National and local standards, measuring basic situation

指标名称	Item	2017	2018	2019
国家情况	**National conditions**			
计量基准和社会公用计量	Standards of measurement and public standards			
标准建立项目（项）	of measurement set up projects (item)	277	266	286
计量仪器检定按类别分(台、件)	Measurement instrument calibration (set)	761425	386804	375785
长度	length	41999	36693	40640
温度	Temperature	31947	36358	37233
力学	Mechanics	454139	230318	32817
电磁	Electromagnetism	14384	34511	92601
光学	Photology	782	2602	1904
声学	Acoustics	6871	7188	7600
化学	Chemistry	14646	15122	14116
放射性	Radioaction	2822	2656	3638
无线电	Radio	707	1235	935
时间频率	Temporal frequency	2680	2772	2691
其他	Others	190448	17349	141610
地方情况	**Local conditions**			
本年末标准累计(个)	Criterion Accumulative (unit)	1013	1268	1445
本年度制、修订标准合计(个)	Total (unit)	169	255	197
制定	Formulation	158	243	183
修订	Amendment	11	12	14

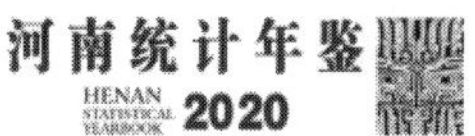

21−25 测绘行业单位、人员及测绘成果提供情况

Statistics on Unit,Persons Engaged and Output in Certificated Units in Surveying and Mapping Industry

指标	Item	2015	2016	2017	2018	2019
持证单位数（个）	**Number of Certificated Units (units)**	**925**	**980**	**1013**	**1043**	**1063**
甲级	First	36	37	39	52	65
乙级	Second	263	302	315	326	331
丙级	Third	294	311	335	359	375
丁级	Fourth	332	330	324	306	292
测绘从业人员年末人数(人)	**Number of Staff and Workers (person)**	**22847**	**24163**	**24789**	**25992**	**25637**
#测绘专业技术人员	Number of Professional	13190	13778	14405	15479	14351
#高级	Senior	1281	1317	1361	1449	1665
中级	Medium	4164	4159	4285	4648	5210
初级	Jumior	5278	5442	5589	6147	6803
地形图（张）	**Topographic Map(unit)**	**2956**	**1286**	**903**	**752**	**250**
1:10000	scale	2676	1081	635	505	118
1:50000	scale	276	201	266	233	128
测绘基准成果（点）	**Surveying and Mapping Datum Product (point)**	**329**	**211**	**160**	**1789**	**2606**
航摄成果（平方千米）	**Aerial Photograph(sq.km)**	**18582**	**5078**		**122**	**20071**
卫星影像（平方千米）	**Satellite Imagery(sq.km)**	**1477838**	**977933**	**1622706**	**2827755**	**3256051**

21−26 气象部门基本情况

Basic Statistics on Meteorological Department

项　　目	Item	2014	2015	2016	2017	2018	2019
气象观测业务台站(个)	**Meteorological observation station (unit)**						
地面观测	Surface Observation	121	121	121	121	121	121
高空探测	Aerological Sounding	3	3	3	3	3	3
区域气象观测站	Regional Meteorological Observation Station	2404	2431	2512	2598	2657	2541
天气雷达观测	Weather Radar Observation	18	18	18	18	18	18
大气成分观测	Atmospheric Composition Observation	1	1	6	26	26	26
辐射观测	Radiation Observation	3	3	3	4	25	26
农业气象观测	Agricultural Meteorological Observation	35	35	35	35	35	35
农业气象试验站	Agrometeorological Experimental Station	4	4	4	4	4	4
中国气象局卫星数据	China Meteorological Administration of Satellite						
广播系统	Data Broadcast System	122	122	122	122	122	122
闪电定位监测	Lightning Positioning Monitoring	19	19	19	32	32	32
紫外线观测	Ultraviolet Observations	18	18	18	18	18	26
风廓线雷达观测	Wind Profile Radar Observations	2	2	2	2	2	2
导航卫星气象观测	Navigation Satellite Meteorological Observation	39	39	39	39	38	37
酸雨观测	Acid Rain Observation	18	18	18	18	18	18
装备	**Equipment**						
高性能计算机	High Performance Computer		1	1	1	1	
服务器(套)	Server (unit)	392	559	306	320	410	379
个人计算机(含个人工作站)	Personal Computer (Including personal workstation)	3932	3936	3843	3921	3641	3785
远程会商系统设备(多点控	Remote Consultation System Equipment (Multipoint						
制单元和会议终端)(套)	control unit and conference terminals) (unit)	19	19	19	19	20	20
人工影响天气地面作业(次)	Weather Modification Ground Operations (time)	2481	1282	1572	814	1042	1140
设备高炮(门)	Equipment Anti-aircraft Gun (unit)	272	271	267	271	268	260
火箭发射系统(部)	Rocket-firing System (unit)	398	401	418	379	415	396
全省气象部门职工总数(人)	Total Number of Employees of Provincial Meteorological	2128	2111	2080	2034	1985	1972

21-27 各市地震台(网)基本情况(2019年)

Basic Statistics on Earthquake Station (Net) by City (2019)

市 City	国家地震观测台（网） National Earthquake Observation Station (Set)			市、县地震台 City、County Earthquake Observation Station		
	国家级台 National Station	省级台 Provincial Station	强震观测点 Strong Motion Observation Spots	市、县级台 City、County Station	企业台 Enterprise Station	宏观观测点 Macro-Observation Spots
总计 **Total**	**3**	**10**	**20**	**91**	**17**	**2002**
郑州市 Zhengzhou		2	1	6	1	76
开封市 Kaifeng			1	4		120
洛阳市 Luoyang	1		4	9	8	292
平顶山市 Pingdingshan				6		6
安阳市 Anyang			3	6		83
鹤壁市 Hebi		4	2	1	1	83
新乡市 Xinxiang			5	10		90
焦作市 Jiaozuo			1	8		266
濮阳市 Puyang			2	5		81
许昌市 Xuchang				2		63
漯河市 Luohe						56
三门峡市 Sanmenxia		1	1	3	1	74
南阳市 Nanyang	1			11	6	158
商丘市 Shangqiu				2		44
信阳市 Xinyang	1	2		1		206
周口市 Zhoukou		1		9		161
驻马店市 Zhumadian				7		127
济源市 Jiyuan				1		16

主要统计指标解释

研究与试验发展(R&D) 指在科学技术领域，为增加知识总量，以及运用这些知识去创造新的应用进行的系统的创造性的活动，包括基础研究、应用研究、试验发展三类活动。国际上通常采用 R&D 活动的规模和强度指标反映一国的科技实力和核心竞争力。

基础研究 指为了获得关于现象和可观察事实的基本原理的新知识(揭示客观事物的本质、运动规律，获得新发现、新学说)而进行的实验性或理论性研究，它不以任何专门或特定的应用或使用为目的。其成果以科学论文和科学著作为主要形式。用来反映知识的原始创新能力。

应用研究 指为获得新知识而进行的创造性研究，主要针对某一特定的目的或目标。应用研究是为了确定基础研究成果可能的用途，或是为达到预定的目标探索应采取的新方法(原理性)或新途径。其成果形式以科学论文、专著、原理性模型或发明专利为主。用来反映对基础研究成果应用途径的探索。

试验发展 指利用从基础研究、应用研究和实际经验所获得的现有知识，为产生新的产品、材料和装置，建立新的工艺、系统和服务，以及对已产生和建立的上述各项作实质性的改进而进行的系统性工作。其成果形式主要是专利、专有技术、具有新产品基本特征的产品原型或具有新装置基本特征的原始样机等。在社会科学领域，试验发展是指把通过基础研究、应用研究获得的知识转变成可以实施的计划（包括为进行检验和评估实施示范项目）的过程。人文科学领域没有对应的试验发展活动。主要反映将科研成果转化为技术和产品的能力，是科技推动经济社会发展的物化成果。

R&D 人员 指参与研究与试验发展项目研究、管理和辅助工作的人员， 包括项目（课题）组人员，企业科技行政管理人员和直接为项目（课题）活动提供服务的辅助人员。反映投入从事拥有自主知识产权的研究开发活动的人力规模。

R&D 人员全时当量 指全时人员数加非全时人员按工作量折算为全时人员数的总和。例如：有两个全时人员和三个非全时人员（工作时间分别为 20%、30%和 70%），则全时当量为 2+0.2+0.3+0.7=3.2 人年。为国际上比较科技人力投入而制定的可比指标。

R&D 经费内部支出合计 指调查单位用于内部开展 R&D 活动（基础研究、应用研究和试验发展）的实际支出。包括用于 R&D 项目（课题）活动的直接支出，以及间接用于 R&D 活动的管理费、服务费、与 R&D 有关的基本建设支出以及外协加工费等。不包括生产性活动支出、归还贷款支出以及与外单位合作或委托外单位进行 R&D 活动而转拨给对方的经费支出。

R&D 经费内部支出中政府资金 指 R&D 经费内部支出中来自各级政府部门的各类资金，包括财政科学技术拨款、科学基金、教育等部门事业费以及政府部门预算外资金的实际支出。

R&D 经费内部支出中企业资金 指 R&D 经费内部支出中来自本企业的自有资金和接受其他企业委托而获得的经费，以及科研院所、高校等事业单位从企业获得的资金的实际支出。

R&D 项目（课题）数 指在当年立项并开展研究工作、以前年份立项仍继续进行研究的研发项目（课题）数，包括当年完成和年内研究工作已告失败的研发项目（课题），但不包括委托外单位进行的研发项目（课题）数。

R&D 项目（课题）经费内部支出 指调查单位内部在报告年度进行研发项目（课题）研究和试制等的实际支出。包括劳务费、其他日常支出、固定资产购建费、外协加工费等，不包括委托或与外单位合作进行项目（课题）研究而拨付给对方使用的经费。

专利 是专利权的简称，是对发明人的发明创造经审查合格后，由专利局依据专利法授予发明人和设计人对该项发明创造享有的专有权。包括发明、实用新型和外观设计。反映拥有自主知识产权的科技和设计成果情况。

Explanatory Notes on Main Statistical Indicators

Research and Development (R&D) refers to systematic and creative activities in the field of science and technology aiming at increasing the knowledge and using the knowledge for new application. R&D includes 3 categories of activities: basic research, applied research and experimentation for development. The scale and intensity of R&D are widely used internationally to reflect the strength of S&T and the core competitiveness of a country in the world.

Basic Research refers to empirical or theoretical research aiming at obtaining new knowledge on the fundamental principles regarding phenomena or observable facts to reveal the intrinsic nature and underlying laws and to acquire new discoveries or new theories. Basic research takes no specific or designated application as the aim of the research. Results of basic research are mainly released or disseminated in the form of scientific papers or monographs. This indicator reflects the innovation capacity for original knowledge.

Applied Research refers to creative research aiming at obtaining new knowledge on a specific objective or target. Purpose of the applied research is to identify the possible uses of results from basic research, or to explore new (fundamental) methods or new approaches. Results of applied research are expressed in the form of scientific papers, monographs, fundamental models or invention patents. This indicator reflects the exploration of ways to apply the results of basic research.

Experiments and Development refer to systematic activities aiming at using the knowledge from basic and applied researches or from practical experience to develop new products, materials and equipment, to establish new production process, systems and services, or to make substantial improvement on the existing products, process or services. Results of experiment and development activities are embodied in patents, exclusive technology, and monotype of new products or equipment. In social sciences, experiment and development activities refer to the process of converting the knowledge from basic or applied researches into feasible programmes (including conduct of demonstration projects for assessment and evaluation). There are no experiment and development activities in the science of humanities. This indicator reflects the capability of transferring the results of S&T into technique and products, and measures the realization of S&T in spearheading the economic and social development.

R & D Personnel refer to persons engaged in research, management and supporting activities of R & D, including persons in the project teams, persons engaged in the management of S&T activities of enterprises and supporting staff providing direct service to the research projects. This indicator reflects the size of personnel engaged in R&D activities with independent intellectual property.

Full-time Equivalent of R&D Personnel refers to the sum of the full-time persons and the full-time equivalent of part-time persons converted by workload. For instance, if there are 2 full-time persons and 3 part-time workers (20%, 30% and 70% of working hours respectively on R&D activities), the full-time equivalent are 2+0.2+0.3+0.7=3.2 person-years. This is an internationally comparable indicator of S&T manpower input.

Total Internal Expenditure of Funds on R&D refers to the real expenditure of surveyed units on their own R&D activities (basic research, application study, test and development) including direct expenditure on R&D activities, indirect expendure of management and services on R&D activities, expenditure on capital construction and material processing by others. Excluding the expenditure on production activities, return of loan, and fees transferred to cooperated and entrusted agencies on R&D activities.

Internal Expenditure of Government Funds refer to the expenditure of funds on R&D activities from government agencies at different levels, including appropriate funds on science and technology from financial departments, scientific funds, operating expenses from education departments and the real expenditure of extrabudgetary funds from government agencies.

Internal Expenditure of Funds of Enterprises refer to the expenditure of funds on R&D activities from self-raised funds of enterprises and funds from other enterprises through entrustment, and the expenditure of funds of institutions, such a institution of scientific research and universityies, from enterprises.

Number of R&D Projects (subjects) refers to the number of R&D projects (subjects) set up and implemented at the reference year, and the number of R&D projects (subjects) set up in former years and under implementation, including the projects (subjects) finished and failed at the reference year, excluding the projects (subjects) implemented by others throught entrustment.

Internal Expenditure of Funds on R&D Projects (subjects) refers to the real expenditure of internal funds of the surveyed units on research and test of R&D projects (subjects) at the reference year, including service fee, other daily expenditure, cost for captital goods, cost of external process; excluding expenditure of funds transferred to other cooperated and entrusted units of the projects.

Patent is an abbreviation for the patent right and refers to the exclusive right of ownership by the inventors or designers for the creation or inventions, given from the patent offices after due process of assessment and approval in accordance with the Patent Law. Patents are granted for inventions, utility models and designs. This indicator reflects the achievements of S&T and design with independent intellectual property.

教育

Education

22

◉ 资料整理：赵 霞

简要说明

一、主要内容

本篇包括公办教育和民办教育、学历教育和非学历教育。具体有高等教育（研究生教育、普通高等教育和成人教育）、中等教育（高中阶段教育和初中阶段教育）、初等教育（小学）、学前教育、特殊教育（盲聋哑和弱智学校等）以及教育经费等资料。主要指标包括学校数、在校生数、招生数、毕业生数、教职工数和专任教师数、教育经费总投入及财政性教育经费等。

二、资料来源

教育事业统计资料由省教育厅提供；技工学校的资料由省人力资源和社会保障厅提供。由省统计局社会与科技处编辑整理。

Brief Introduction

I. Main Contents

Data on education cover the situations on education funded by government and non-government agencies, and the education with and without academic credentials including higher education (education of postgraduates, general higher education and adult education), secondary education(senior and junior high schools), elementary education (primary schools),preschool education, special education (schools for the blind, deaf-mutes and mentally retarded) and their expenditure. The main indicators include the number of schools, the number of students enrolled, the number of new students enrolled, the number of graduates, the number of stuff and workers, the number of full-time teachers, sources and outlay of education funding and education expenditure.

II. Sources of Data

Data on education undertakings are calculated from Henan Provincial bureau of Education. Data on technical training schools are calculated from Henan provincial bureau of Henan Resources and Social Security. Data in this chapter are provided by Department of social and technology of Henan provincial bureau of statistics.

22-1 各级各类学校数

Number of Schools by Level and Type

单位：所 (unit)

年份 year	小学 Primary Schools	普通中学 Regular Secondary Schools	高中 Senior Secondary Schools	初中 Junior Secondary Schools	职业中学 Vocational Secondary Schools	普通高等学校 Regular Institutions of Higher Education
1978	48772	26586	3705	22881		24
1979	34983	25826	2976	22850		24
1980	46672	12672	2431	10241	1	25
1981	45939	10304	1703	8601	6	26
1982	46542	10510	1279	9231	8	26
1983	46265	10324	1177	9147	21	32
1984	46232	9969	1102	8867	41	38
1985	41935	9459	1069	8390	390	43
1986	45250	9730	1058	8672	370	47
1987	44865	9632	1027	8605	336	47
1988	44379	9406	1003	8403	378	47
1989	43951	8961	958	8003	466	47
1990	43286	8249	920	7329	480	47
1991	42455	7369	854	6515	539	49
1992	42370	6893	789	6104	636	47
1993	42071	6644	719	5925	685	48
1994	41899	6476	661	5815	785	50
1995	41698	6367	641	5726	785	50
1996	41466	6282	635	5647	761	50
1997	41526	6142	645	5497	742	50
1998	41238	6069	643	5426	722	51
1999	41404	6120	688	5432	696	56
2000	41269	6217	761	5456	609	52
2001	39825	6384	819	5565	520	64
2002	37729	6399	854	5545	484	66
2003	36379	6363	888	5475	462	71
2004	34164	6229	909	5320	442	82
2005	33026	6207	945	5262	455	83
2006	31410	6045	955	5090	515	84
2007	30677	5864	920	4944	552	82
2008	30214	5718	908	4810	584	84
2009	29420	5571	868	4703	589	89
2010	28603	5441	825	4616	563	107
2011	27793	5388	792	4596	452	117
2012	27452	5336	785	4551	409	120
2013	26086	5326	776	4550	381	127
2014	25578	5340	774	4566	367	129
2015	24673	5335	770	4565	356	129
2016	22822	5349	792	4557	324	129
2017	20372	5328	813	4515	314	134
2018	18622	5371	852	4519	289	140
2019	18117	5492	889	4603	270	141

22-2　各级各类学校专任教师数

Number of Full-time Teachers by Level and Type of school

单位：万人　　(10 000 persons)

年份 year	小　学 Primary Schools	普通中学 Regular Secondary Schools	高　中 Senior Secondary Schools	初　中 Junior Secondary Schools	职业中学 Vocational Secondary Schools	普通高等学校 Regular Institutions of Higher Education
1978	42.88	29.34	4.98	24.36		0.54
1979	43.66	30.01	5.09	24.92		0.62
1980	44.72	30.13	4.48	25.65	0.00	0.68
1981	47.20	26.99	3.91	23.08	0.01	0.71
1982	41.95	22.58	3.52	19.05	0.01	0.84
1983	42.52	22.17	3.46	18.71	0.04	0.91
1984	42.81	21.86	3.41	18.45	0.02	0.97
1985	43.09	22.21	3.41	18.80	0.68	1.10
1986	43.62	22.93	3.54	19.39	0.77	1.27
1987	43.52	23.69	3.73	19.96	0.81	1.33
1988	43.79	24.01	3.79	20.22	0.88	1.38
1989	43.76	23.84	3.77	20.07	1.13	1.38
1990	44.34	24.05	3.79	20.25	1.27	1.40
1991	37.93	23.54	3.83	19.71	1.34	1.42
1992	37.55	23.49	3.76	19.73	1.51	1.45
1993	38.19	23.60	3.62	19.98	1.72	1.47
1994	38.87	23.94	3.48	20.46	2.08	1.55
1995	39.23	24.68	3.45	21.23	2.28	1.55
1996	40.02	25.48	3.51	21.97	2.44	1.64
1997	41.12	26.38	3.61	22.77	2.67	1.65
1998	42.55	27.60	3.75	23.85	2.76	1.70
1999	44.66	29.09	4.09	25.00	2.67	1.88
2000	45.93	30.86	4.57	26.29	2.49	2.02
2001	47.56	32.90	5.13	27.77	2.35	2.46
2002	49.62	35.06	6.03	29.03	2.39	2.85
2003	48.85	35.88	6.72	29.16	2.21	3.33
2004	47.85	36.55	7.60	28.95	2.23	4.18
2005	47.55	37.30	8.40	28.90	2.29	4.63
2006	47.82	37.64	9.19	28.45	2.68	5.29
2007	48.30	37.88	9.79	28.09	2.76	5.88
2008	48.53	37.89	10.27	27.62	2.91	6.49
2009	48.91	38.30	10.49	27.81	3.16	7.15
2010	49.04	38.10	10.43	27.67	3.25	7.75
2011	49.58	38.65	10.43	28.22	3.20	8.20
2012	49.69	38.97	10.73	28.24	3.08	8.60
2013	49.45	38.80	10.81	27.99	2.76	9.09
2014	46.99	41.83	12.67	29.16	2.66	9.51
2015	47.21	42.87	13.01	29.86	2.66	9.80
2016	47.42	43.63	13.55	30.08	2.58	10.27
2017	48.86	46.21	14.45	31.76	2.50	10.84
2018	50.02	49.24	15.33	33.90	2.43	11.54
2019	51.03	52.04	16.30	35.74	2.37	12.40

22-3 各级各类学校在校学生数

Student Enrollment by Level and Type of school

单位：万人 (10 000 persons)

年份 year	小学 Primary Schools	普通中学 Regular Secondary Schools	高中 Senior Secondary Schools	初中 Junior Secondary Schools	职业中学 Vocational Secondary Schools	普通高等学校 Regular Institutions of Higher Education
1978	1140.26	521.62	116.38	405.24		2.73
1979	1147.88	504.04	106.42	397.62		3.38
1980	1133.75	487.27	83.75	403.52	0.02	4.59
1981	1110.65	412.31	60.66	351.65	0.27	4.93
1982	1098.47	361.41	49.25	312.16	0.51	4.63
1983	1054.04	341.32	47.82	293.50	1.11	4.80
1984	1055.08	354.20	50.87	303.33	2.28	5.33
1985	1034.97	357.46	52.27	305.19	10.89	6.85
1986	1015.67	366.96	54.66	312.30	11.92	7.50
1987	997.75	373.51	54.41	319.10	11.63	7.57
1988	980.05	362.64	52.51	310.13	11.94	7.99
1989	969.82	349.05	49.54	299.51	14.50	8.01
1990	961.15	352.56	49.26	303.30	15.61	8.04
1991	944.02	357.66	48.80	308.86	17.77	8.18
1992	936.71	359.78	46.21	313.57	20.40	8.95
1993	951.50	362.96	43.52	319.44	25.86	10.44
1994	991.06	384.80	42.51	342.29	35.74	11.71
1995	1039.56	417.86	42.91	374.95	45.86	12.24
1996	1105.58	454.48	44.02	410.46	51.18	12.79
1997	1169.96	480.21	46.68	433.53	56.84	13.60
1998	1200.06	512.51	51.13	461.38	60.10	14.64
1999	1186.97	568.86	61.06	507.80	53.75	18.55
2000	1130.63	638.14	75.15	562.99	48.27	26.24
2001	1070.73	683.38	94.73	588.65	38.71	36.91
2002	1104.59	733.35	125.55	607.80	41.52	46.80
2003	1058.61	750.51	146.42	604.09	42.32	55.72
2004	1014.06	759.42	168.75	590.67	45.93	70.28
2005	986.84	758.22	188.39	569.83	49.31	85.19
2006	997.09	742.22	201.58	540.64	59.90	97.41
2007	1018.71	719.83	212.63	507.20	66.22	109.52
2008	1036.60	691.46	207.26	484.20	72.76	125.02
2009	1052.03	675.45	201.20	474.25	80.88	136.88
2010	1070.53	661.56	192.16	469.40	79.47	145.67
2011	1092.90	657.48	189.50	467.98	75.78	150.01
2012	1079.20	646.42	192.63	453.78	73.15	155.90
2013	939.98	574.28	189.23	385.05	54.92	161.83
2014	928.60	588.91	189.55	399.36	46.74	167.97
2015	937.05	599.12	194.31	404.81	39.80	176.69
2016	965.59	615.43	199.60	415.83	38.96	187.48
2017	982.06	634.65	205.49	429.16	42.50	200.47
2018	994.60	661.94	210.06	451.88	43.47	214.08
2019	1012.48	684.36	215.88	468.48	43.55	231.97

注：本表普通高等学校在校生是指全省普通本专科在校生总数。

a) The number of students in regular institutions of higher education in this table refer to the total number of students in Colleges and universities in the whole province.

22-4 各级各类学校招生数

New Student Enrollment by Level and Type of school

单位：万人 (10 000 persons)

年份 year	小学 Primary Schools	普通中学 Regular Secondary Schools	高中 Senior Secondary Schools	初中 Junior Secondary Schools	职业中学 Vocational Secondary Schools	普通高等学校 Regular Institutions of Higher Education
1978	254.37	234.71	53.79	180.92		1.39
1979	249.91	215.50	48.55	166.95		1.07
1980	239.12	169.65	28.69	140.96	0.02	1.25
1981	226.50	146.95	24.44	122.51	0.24	1.25
1982	219.17	124.70	18.17	106.53	0.27	1.36
1983	198.48	119.04	17.04	102.00	0.88	1.65
1984	197.99	119.69	17.40	102.29	1.36	1.89
1985	174.24	118.93	17.22	101.71	5.42	2.67
1986	190.38	123.72	17.77	105.95	5.00	2.42
1987	184.06	124.03	17.84	106.19	4.56	2.64
1988	181.53	121.80	17.09	104.71	4.95	2.72
1989	179.88	118.08	16.27	101.81	6.34	2.61
1990	172.46	122.53	16.92	105.61	6.37	2.66
1991	164.72	125.47	16.49	108.98	8.28	2.76
1992	169.53	125.38	15.28	110.10	9.53	3.38
1993	190.31	130.28	14.86	115.42	12.71	4.05
1994	220.01	144.20	13.98	130.23	16.96	4.17
1995	232.52	158.34	14.58	143.76	20.75	4.32
1996	239.94	164.89	15.12	149.77	20.48	4.49
1997	239.79	171.79	16.41	155.38	23.61	4.66
1998	217.82	189.67	18.72	170.95	23.56	5.02
1999	193.65	220.12	24.42	195.70	16.95	7.88
2000	171.11	246.46	31.48	214.98	16.83	11.69
2001	163.32	246.96	37.63	209.33	14.63	14.01
2002	185.77	253.93	50.93	203.00	17.05	16.61
2003	164.35	253.19	53.77	199.42	16.85	19.02
2004	162.49	257.45	61.33	196.12	17.40	25.74
2005	169.44	259.58	69.99	189.59	20.30	27.76
2006	176.86	233.85	67.75	166.10	28.51	33.77
2007	183.22	231.49	70.57	160.92	28.83	35.52
2008	186.92	233.55	68.42	165.13	28.90	44.51
2009	184.51	225.18	64.50	160.68	33.03	45.74
2010	187.76	221.66	62.85	158.81	30.40	47.83
2011	193.44	226.25	64.63	161.62	27.18	47.14
2012	190.97	224.73	66.57	158.16	24.06	49.82
2013	181.06	203.82	66.11	137.71	18.34	50.84
2014	159.44	202.99	64.49	138.50	15.23	51.43
2015	169.30	206.21	67.98	138.23	13.49	55.92
2016	173.16	213.66	69.53	144.13	14.17	60.60
2017	172.38	220.42	70.97	149.45	17.28	63.57
2018	173.56	232.52	72.65	159.86	15.47	70.87
2019	173.76	232.85	74.98	157.87	17.16	78.89

22-5 各级各类学校毕业生数

Graduates by Level and Type of school

单位：万人 (10 000 persons)

年份 year	小 学 Primary Schools	普通中学 Regular Secondary Schools	高 中 Senior Secondary Schools	初 中 Junior Secondary Schools	职业中学 Vocational Secondary Schools	普通高等学校 Regular Institutions of Higher Education
1978	185.03	213.34	44.37	168.97		0.96
1979	179.69	204.86	50.44	154.42		0.41
1980	173.62	109.74	45.66	64.08	0.01	
1981	173.52	131.24	43.45	87.79	0.01	0.90
1982	165.80	104.44	27.36	77.08	0.02	1.65
1983	168.90	87.90	15.85	72.05	0.28	1.47
1984	166.90	86.78	14.74	72.04	0.28	1.35
1985	158.48	88.92	15.44	73.48	2.08	1.17
1986	172.97	91.60	16.70	74.90	2.52	1.75
1987	172.82	97.24	17.78	79.46	3.11	2.53
1988	167.45	99.44	18.03	81.40	3.62	2.29
1989	162.51	100.39	17.27	83.12	3.64	2.56
1990	162.60	99.36	16.70	82.66	4.17	2.61
1991	161.86	98.77	15.96	82.81	5.26	2.72
1992	162.39	99.90	15.01	84.89	4.86	2.59
1993	163.26	102.34	14.45	87.89	5.35	2.66
1994	166.48	103.90	13.98	89.92	6.16	2.93
1995	168.96	109.35	13.51	95.84	9.22	3.76
1996	165.13	115.90	13.82	102.08	12.41	3.91
1997	168.57	133.16	13.78	119.38	15.18	3.89
1998	180.67	145.88	14.93	130.95	17.23	3.96
1999	205.01	153.97	15.50	138.47	17.95	3.99
2000	225.57	162.16	17.47	144.69	18.65	4.17
2001	220.41	176.44	19.84	156.60	15.32	4.61
2002	202.55	203.04	25.78	177.26	12.57	7.12
2003	204.18	225.16	36.38	188.78	11.68	10.90
2004	203.54	240.69	42.48	198.21	11.97	13.43
2005	191.90	252.02	53.66	198.36	13.97	16.52
2006	166.71	245.24	57.36	187.88	15.40	20.21
2007	160.19	254.20	65.10	189.10	17.21	26.72
2008	168.90	258.05	74.98	183.07	17.93	30.25
2009	165.75	233.36	70.17	163.18	22.31	33.41
2010	165.35	225.35	70.43	154.92	24.93	38.25
2011	167.61	222.00	66.55	155.45	25.05	43.30
2012	170.44	213.82	64.01	149.81	24.84	43.53
2013	164.48	203.46	63.13	140.34	24.41	45.02
2014	140.81	174.94	60.28	114.66	18.93	44.53
2015	140.55	184.67	61.05	123.62	17.28	46.58
2016	144.16	192.81	63.31	129.50	13.42	48.69
2017	150.31	195.43	63.14	132.29	12.56	50.41
2018	160.70	199.71	66.08	133.63	12.04	55.99
2019	158.13	209.17	67.99	141.19	13.52	59.34

22-6　各级各类学校、教职工和专任教师情况(2019年)

Basic Statistics on Schools, Teachers and Staff and Full-time Teachers (2019)

项　目	Item	学校数(所) Number of Schools (unit)	教职工数(人) Educational Personnel (person)	# 女性 Female	专任教师(人) Full-time Teachers (person)	# 女性 Female
高等教育	**Higher Education**	**209**	**164222**	**82837**	**125330**	**65007**
研究生培养机构	Institutions Providing Postgraduate Programs	8	248	30	248	30
普通高校	Regular Higher Education Institutions	(19)	(17264)	(5650)	(17264)	(5650)
科研机构	Research Institutions	8	248	30	248	30
普通高等学校	Regular Higher Education Institutions	141	162050	81776	123977	64324
本科院校	HEIs Offering Degree Programs	57	102357	49916	77089	38917
#独立学院	Independent Institutions	5	5754	3019	4744	2521
高职(专科)院校	Higher Vocational Colleges	84	59693	31860	46888	25407
其他机构(教学点)	Other Institutions	(1)				
成人高等学校	Adult HEIs	10	895	477	570	337
民办的其他高等教育机构	Other Non-government HEIs	50	1029	554	535	316
中等教育	**Secondary Education**	**6262**	**652367**	**400761**	**568801**	**362135**
高中阶段教育	Senior Secondary Education	1559	257271	143729	210727	123045
高中	Senior Secondary Schools	890	185750	107484	163017	96842
普通高中	Regular Senior Secondary Schools	889	185744	107483	163013	96841
完全中学	Combined Secondary Schools	169	37084	22269	32170	19935
高级中学	Regular High Schools	601	124005	67852	111954	63224
十二年一贯制学校	12-Year Schools	119	24655	17362	18889	13682
成人高中	Adult High Schools	1	6	1	4	1
中等职业教育	Secondary Vocational Education	669	71521	36245	47710	26203
普通中专	Regular Specialized Secondary Schools	145	19427	10120	15044	8335
成人中专	Adult Specialized Secondary Schools	159	11081	5606	7983	4333
职业高中	Vocational High Schools	270	27243	14149	23683	12913
其他机构(不计校数)	Other Institutions	(21)	1244	730	1000	622
技工学校	Skilled Workers Schools	95	12526	5640		
初中阶段教育	Junior Secondary Education	4703	395096	257032	358074	239090
初中	Junior Secondary Schools	4603	394337	256535	357366	238609
初级中学	Regular Junior Secondary Schools	3486	275316	171251	260952	166464
九年一贯制学校	9-Year Schools	1117	119021	85284	96414	72145
成人初中	Adult Junior Secondary Schools	100	759	497	708	481
初等教育	**Primary Education**	**18981**	**540981**	**390425**	**511554**	**375402**
普通小学	Regular Primary Schools	18117	539350	389539	510350	374747
小学	Primary Schools	18117	467382	349921	439936	335485
小学教学点	Primary Schools Teaching Point	(13726)	71968	39618	70414	39262
成人小学	Adult Primary Schools	864	1631	886	1204	655
#扫盲班	Literacy Courses	20	78	43	73	39
工读学校	**Correctional Work-Study Schools**	**3**	**67**	**27**	**60**	**25**
特殊教育	**Special Education Schools**	**150**	**4505**	**3237**	**4158**	**3102**
学前教育	**Pre-school Education Institutions**	**23181**	**390652**	**361214**	**226163**	**223811**
#城区公办幼儿园	City Public Kindergarten	682	27742	25764	17474	17133
镇区公办幼儿园	Town Public Kindergarten	1693	27528	25554	18854	18293
乡村公办幼儿园	Country Public Kindergarten	2745	18709	16574	11770	11338

注：括号内数据不计入总计。
a) Data of total is not include data in the brackets.

22-7 各级各类学校专任教师分学历的人数与构成(2019年)

Number and Composition of Full-time Teachers in Schools by Educational Level (2019)

单位：人 (person)

学　　历	Educational Level	专任教师 Full-time Teacher	构成(%) Composition (%)
普通高等学校教师	**Regular Higher Educational Institutions**	**123977**	**100.0**
博士研究生	Doctor	19947	16.1
硕士研究生	Master	49946	40.3
本科毕业	Undergraduate	52631	42.5
专科及以下	Specialized Courses and Below	1453	1.2
普通中等专业学校教师	**Specialized Secondary Schools**	**15044**	**100.0**
博士研究生	Doctor	19	0.1
硕士研究生	Master	1857	12.3
本科毕业	Undergraduate	12362	82.2
专科及以下	Specialized Courses and Below	806	5.4
高中教师	**Teachers of Senior Secondary School**	**138269**	**100.0**
大学本科毕业及以上	Undergraduates and over	135751	98.2
大学专科毕业	Specilized Courses	2509	1.8
高中阶段毕业及以下	Senior Secondary and below	9	0.0
初中教师	**Teachers of Junior Secondary School**	**327211**	**100.0**
大学本科毕业及以上	Undergraduates and over	265511	81.1
大学专科毕业	Specilized Courses	60463	18.5
高中阶段毕业	Senior Secondary	1236	0.4
高中阶段毕业以下	Below Senior	1	0.0
小学教师	**Teachers of Primary School**	**565248**	**100.0**
大学专科毕业及以上	Specialized secondary of Higher Education and over	546565	96.7
高中阶段毕业	Senior Secondary	18682	3.3
高中阶段毕业以下	Below Senior	1	0.0
幼儿园教师	**Teachers of Kindergartens**	**226163**	**100.0**
大学专科毕业及以上	Specialized Secondary of Higher Education and Over	169611	75.0
高中阶段毕业	Senior Secondary	50747	22.4
高中阶段毕业以下	Below Senior	5805	2.6

注：本表专任教师按照授课对象进行分类。

a) Data in this table according to the classification of teaching object.

22-8 各级各类学历教育学生情况(2019年)

Basic Statistics on Students by Level and Type of Education (2019)

单位：人 (person)

项 目	Item	招生数 Entrants	在校生数 Enrolment	# 女生 Female Students	毕业生数 Graduates
高等教育	**Higher Education**	**1053040**	**2922327**	**1593236**	**774845**
研究生	Postgraduates	20962	55395	32858	16107
博 士	Doctor's Degree	937	3271	1645	335
硕 士	Master's Degree	20025	52124	31213	15772
普通本专科	Undergraduate in Regular HEIs	788900	2319653	1227146	593363
本 科	Normal Courses	337741	1197185	668831	276666
专 科	Short-cycle Courses	451159	1122468	558315	316697
成人本专科	Undergraduate in Adult HEIs	212846	420347	269407	124199
本 科	Normal Courses	111510	227679	144791	64308
专 科	Short-cycle Courses	101336	192668	124616	59891
网络本专科生	Web-based Undergraduates	30332	126932	63825	41176
本 科	Normal Courses	30332	65831	36222	16668
专 科	Short-cycle Courses		61101	27603	24508
中等教育	**Secondary Education**	**2865291**	**8296898**	**3822233**	**2581867**
高中阶段教育	Senior Secondary Education	1286605	3559508	1670531	1110474
高中	Senior Secondary Schools	749785	2161177	1093246	682240
普通高中	Regular Senior Secondary Schools	749785	2158790	1091719	679853
完全中学	Combined Secondary Schools	103994	301723	149780	93844
高级中学	Regular High Schools	593153	1726852	881533	555713
十二年一贯制学校	12-Year Schools	45965	110623	51147	24639
附设普通高中班	Attached Ordinary High School Class	6673	19592	9259	5657
成人高中	Adult High Schools		2387	1527	2387
中等职业教育	Secondary Vocational Education	536820	1398331	577285	428234
普通中专	Regular Specialized Secondary Schools	290185	795994	365688	231604
成人中专	Adult Specialized Secondary Schools	45673	86076	32969	41498
职业高中	Vocational High Schools	85004	228567	95939	70773
技工学校	Skilled Workers Schools	115958	287694	82689	84359
初中阶段教育	Junior Secondary Education	1578686	4737390	2151702	1471393
初中	Junior Secondary Schools	1578686	4684765	2120991	1411868
初级中学	Regular Junior Secondary Schools	1189613	3581873	1659444	1107894
九年一贯制学校	9-Year Schools	278044	775599	320310	203629
十二年一贯制学校	12-Year Schools	40683	115019	47421	29254
完全中学	Combined Secondary Schools	67967	203807	90425	67008
附设普通初中班	Supporting Regular Junior Secondary Schools	2379	8467	3391	4083
成人初中	Adult Junior Secondary Schools		52625	30711	59525
初等教育	**Primary Education**	**1737602**	**10249155**	**4750232**	**1718296**
普通小学	Regular Primary Schools	1737602	10124818	4684355	1581313
小学	Primary Schools	1409340	8275324	3856681	1288632
小学教学点	Primary Schools Teaching Point	160167	685787	334818	56744
附设小学班	Attached Primary Schools Classes	2851	59395	28162	45386
九年一贯制学校	9-Year Schools	149943	1002541	424211	173184
十二年一贯制学校	12-Year Schools	15301	101771	40483	17367
成人小学	Adult Primary Schools		124337	65877	136983
#扫盲班	Literacy Courses		2846	1623	
工读学校	**Correctional Work-Study Schools**	**84**	**216**		**56**
特殊教育	**Special Education Schools**	**10472**	**54849**	**19998**	**3007**
学前教育	**Pre-school Education Institutions**	**1253449**	**4308701**	**2045317**	**1646408**

22-9 各级教育入学率及升学率情况
Enrolment Ratio and Promotion Rate by Levels

单位：% (%)

指标名称	Item	2017	2018	2019
学前教育毛入园率	Pre-school Eduacation Gross Enrollment Rate	86.5	88.1	89.5
小学学龄儿童净入学率	Net Enrollment Rate of Primary Schools	100.0	100.0	100.0
#男生	Male	100.0	100.0	100.0
女生	Female	100.0	100.0	100.0
小学升学率	Promotion Rate from Primary Schools to Junior Secondary Schools	99.4	99.5	99.8
初中阶段毛入学率	Gross Enrollment Rate of Junior Middle School Stage	109.7	109.4	108.1
#男生	Male	110.2	109.8	107.4
女生	Female	109.1	109.0	108.6
初中升学率	Promotion Rate from Junior Secondary Schools to Senior Secondary Schools	88.8	80.6	79.3
九年义务教育巩固率	Percentage of Student Enrollment Consolidated of Nine-year Compulsory Education	94.3	94.6	95.5
#男生	Male	94.2	94.6	95.2
女生	Female	94.3	94.7	95.8
高中阶段毛入学率	The Gross Enrollment Rate of Senior Secondary School	90.6	91.2	91.6
高等教育毛入学率	The Gross Enrollment Rate of Higher Education	41.8	45.6	49.3

22-10 成人学校基本情况(2019年)
Basic Statistics on Adult Schools (2019)

单位：人 (person)

各类学校	Various Schools	学校数(所) Number of Schools (unit)	教职工数 Teachers and Staff	#专任教师 Full-time Teachers	在校学生数 Student Enrollment	招生数 New Student Enrollment	毕业生数 Graduates
成人高等学校	**Adult Institutions of Higher Eduation**	**10**	**895**	**570**	**420347**	**212846**	**124199**
广播电视大学	Radio and TV Universities	1	236	151	18	12	12
职工、农民学院	Schools of Higher Eduation for Staff, Workers and Peasants	8	495	319	4312	2283	2750
教育学院	Pedagogical Colleges	1			10		35
其他机构	Others	(4)	164	100			
高校函授部、夜大学	Correspondence Departments or Evening Universities Run by Institutions of Higher Education	(83)			416007	210551	121402
成人中等专业学校	**Specialized Secondary Schools for Adults**	159	11081	7983	127574	54167	43873
成人中学	**Secondary Schools for Adults**	101	765	712	55012		61912
职工中学	Secondary Schools for Staff and Workers	8	17	12	12713		13658
农民中学	Secondary Schools for Peasants	93	748	700	42299		48254
技术培训学校	**Techinical Training Schools**	4602	11883	7001	982688		987540
职工技术培训学校	Techinical Training Schools for Staff and Workers	72	1592	1261	41821		46994
农民技术培训学校	Techinical Training Schools for Peasants	4074	6671	4090	857058		870111
其他培训机构	Other Training Organizations	456	3620	1650	83809		70435
成人初等学校	**Primary Schools for Adults**	**864**	**1631**	**1204**	**124337**		**136983**
职工初等学校	Primary Schools for Staff and Workers	24	24		12845		16439
农民初等学校	Primary Schools for peasants	840	1607	1204	111492		120544
#扫盲班	Literacy Courses	20	78	73	2846		

注：其他机构、高校函授部、夜大学不计入成人高等学校总校数。

a) Number of Adult Institutions of Higher Eduation excludes those of Other Institutions , Correspondence Departments or Evening Universities Run by Institutions of Higher Education.

22-11 分学科研究生情况(2019年)

Number of Postgraduate Students by Academic Field (2019)

单位：人 (person)

项目	Item	招生数 Entrants	硕士 Master's Degree	博士 Doctor's Degree	在校学生数 Enrolment	硕士 Master's Degree	博士 Doctor's Degree	毕业生数 Graduates	硕士 Master's Degree	博士 Doctor's Degree
分学科研究生数(总计)	**Total**	**20962**	**20025**	**937**	**55395**	**52124**	**3271**	**16107**	**15772**	**335**
#女生	Female	12640	12162	478	32858	31213	1645	9532	9377	155
学术型学位	Academic Degree	8361	7512	849	24427	21286	3141	7985	7650	335
专业学位	Professional Degree	12601	12513	88	30968	30838	130	8122	8122	
哲学	Philosophy	85	85		266	266		146	146	
经济学	Economics	451	443	8	1074	1045	29	385	381	4
法学	Law	1149	1107	42	3088	2939	149	1115	1098	17
教育学	Education	2272	2251	21	5698	5646	52	1739	1735	4
文学	Literature	812	789	23	2068	1981	87	845	831	14
历史学	History	291	269	22	860	749	111	221	210	11
理学	Science	1691	1488	203	4700	4028	672	1699	1595	104
工学	Engineering	5588	5293	295	14842	13751	1091	3681	3585	96
农学	Agriculture	1460	1385	75	3497	3213	284	936	897	39
医学	Medicine	3692	3478	214	9695	9050	645	2432	2387	45
军事学	Military Science									
管理学	Administrators	2968	2936	32	8209	8060	149	2504	2503	1
艺术学	Art	503	501	2	1398	1396	2	404	404	
分学科研究生数(普通高校)	**Regular HEIs**	**20889**	**19955**	**934**	**55204**	**51944**	**3260**	**16054**	**15722**	**332**
#女生	Female	12624	12146	478	32813	31169	1644	9519	9364	155
学术型学位	Academic Degree	8288	7442	846	24236	21106	3130	7932	7600	332
专业学位	Professional Degree	12601	12513	88	30968	30838	130	8122	8122	
哲学	Philosophy	85	85		266	266		146	146	
经济学	Economics	451	443	8	1074	1045	29	385	381	4
法学	Law	1149	1107	42	3088	2939	149	1115	1098	17
教育学	Education	2272	2251	21	5698	5646	52	1739	1735	4
文学	Literature	812	789	23	2068	1981	87	845	831	14
历史学	History	291	269	22	860	749	111	221	210	11
理学	Science	1689	1486	203	4697	4025	672	1698	1594	104
工学	Engineering	5518	5226	292	14655	13575	1080	3630	3537	93
农学	Agriculture	1460	1385	75	3497	3213	284	936	897	39
医学	Medicine	3692	3478	214	9695	9050	645	2432	2387	45
军事学	Military Science									
管理学	Administrators	2967	2935	32	8208	8059	149	2503	2502	1
艺术学	Art	503	501	2	1398	1396	2	404	404	

22-12 分学科本科学生情况(2019年)

Number of Undergraduate Students by Academic Field (2019)

单位：人 (person)

项 目	Item	普通本科 Ordinary Undergraduates			成人本科 Adult Undergraduates			网络本科 Web-based Undergraduates		
		招生数 Entrants	在校学生数 Enrolment	毕业生数 Graduates	招生数 Entrants	在校学生数 Enrolment	毕业生数 Graduates	招生数 Entrants	在校学生数 Enrolment	毕业生数 Graduates
总 计	**Total**	**337741**	**1197185**	**276666**	**111510**	**227679**	**64308**	**30332**	**65831**	**16668**
#女生	Female	186749	668831	158276	71874	144791	40284	8119	36222	9642
#师范	Teacher Training	39514	141374	36327	22704	41677	10830			
哲 学	Philosophy	62	226	47						
经济学	Economics	16565	63141	13628	1624	3087	890	1076	2603	865
法 学	Law	11341	41471	9226	4453	8210	2197	1644	3309	981
教育学	Education	19086	58323	12635	13297	23248	5404	1717	3158	606
文 学	Literature	27855	101676	22638	8312	16312	5241	1228	2753	819
#外语	Foreign Language	15179	54484	11167	1767	3718	1257	350	725	174
历史学	History	1595	5891	1350	102	191	61			
理 学	Science	18985	72104	16904	2997	6255	2161		177	205
工 学	Engineering	115278	401350	86067	21107	43224	12070	10201	19431	4311
农 学	Agriculture	7365	26273	5908	865	2035	841			
医 学	Medicine	20371	85913	20263	34764	79728	23477	5884	17574	4701
管理学	Administrators	63609	218352	57953	23206	43991	11545	8582	16826	4180
艺术学	Art	33863	120699	30047	783	1398	421			
职业本科	Professional Undergraduate	1766	1766							

22-13 分学科专科学生情况(2019年)

Number of Students in Junior College by Field (2019)

单位：人 (person)

项　目	Item	普通专科 Normal College			成人专科 Adult College			网络专科 Web-based College		
		招生数 Entrants	在校学生数 Enrolment	毕业生数 Graduates	招生数 Entrants	在校学生数 Enrolment	毕业生数 Graduates	招生数 Entrants	在校学生数 Enrolment	毕业生数 Graduates
总　计	**Total**	**451159**	**1122468**	**316697**	**101336**	**192668**	**59891**		**61101**	**24508**
#女生	Female	214755	558315	163395	64406	124616	36604		27603	11879
#师范生	Teacher Training Students	36487	95370	31578	24331	48691	14445			
农林牧渔大类	Agriculture, Forestry, Husbandry and Fishing	4844	12400	3538	1286	2130	620			
资源环境与安全大类	Resources and Environment	5268	11987	2245	874	1424	450			
能源动力与材料大类	Energy and Material	2926	8373	2753	408	1067	652		1193	503
土木建筑大类	Civil Engineering	31602	76877	22687	8526	15230	4418		7597	3355
水利大类	Water Resources	1242	3178	1051	194	483	197			
装备制造大类	Manufacturing	47161	119006	34848	6320	12303	3695		5364	1438
生物与化工大类	Biology and Chemstry	1665	4302	1329	155	384	61			
轻工纺织大类	Light Industry and Textile	1404	2973	885						
食品药品与粮食大类	Medicine, Food and Grain	5245	13660	4107	306	485	62			
交通运输大类	Transportation and Communication	21617	53727	14758	965	2732	2091			
电子信息大类	Electronic Information	74867	170800	39597	6951	12626	3374		6107	1571
医药卫生大类	Medicine and Health	71414	183928	52600	9226	20025	8411		7266	2836
财经商贸大类	Finance and Business	78456	199106	62049	30527	55944	16051		22714	9533
旅游大类	Tourism	14163	36406	10210	555	1011	306		964	242
文化艺术大类	Culture and Arts	27064	66022	15101	174	312	192		103	126
新闻传播大类	Journalistic Communication	3308	9029	2202	6	6	6			
教育与体育大类	Education and Sport	48168	126055	39853	26748	52658	15598		2820	1664
公安与司法大类	Public Security and Law	4279	13487	5031	1209	2066	999		1823	1242
公共管理与服务大类	Public Adminlstration and Service	6466	11152	1853	6906	11782	2708		5150	1998

注：2019年网络专科停止招生。

a) The web-based junior colleges stop the enrollmen in 2019.

22-14 中等职业学校分学科学生情况(2019年)
Number of Students in Secondary Vocational Schools by Field (2019)

单位：人 (person)

项 目	Item	招生数 Entrants	在校学生数 Enrolment	毕业生数 Graduates	#获得职业资格证书 Recitpents of Vocational Qualifications
总 计	**Total**	**420862**	**1110637**	**343875**	**219728**
#女生	Female	181581	494596	164369	101841
农林牧渔类	Agriculture,Forestry,Husbandry & Fisheries	32150	79285	28819	21435
资源环境类	Resources and Environment	1010	5112	4161	3826
能源与新能源类	Energy and New Energy	582	1470	346	320
土木水利类	Civil Engineering and Water Resources	17304	43793	13229	8119
加工制造类	Manufacturing	29663	81367	24661	17707
石油化工类	Petroleum and Chemical	282	1135	501	440
轻纺食品类	Light Industry,Textile,and Food	1464	5188	3356	823
交通运输类	Transport and Communication	47437	130794	43004	29794
信息技术类	Information Technologies	85270	206960	56126	34184
医药卫生类	Medicine and Health	24415	77066	28200	12760
休闲保健类	Leisure and Health	5630	13340	3480	2568
财经商贸类	Finance and Business	47244	129813	40252	25093
旅游服务类	Tourism Services	20003	46770	11647	8609
文化艺术类	Culture and Arts	34705	97597	27376	15454
体育与健身	Sports and Fitness	15157	33335	7352	5214
教育类	Education	49464	140693	49535	32441
司法服务类	Justice Services	1	315	95	
公共管理与服务类	Public Administration and Services	8780	15105	1104	739
其他	Others	301	1499	631	202

注：本表数据不含技工学校有关数据。
a) Data in this table unclude data of technical school.

22-15 网络教育学生情况(2019年)

Statistics on Web-based Education Students (2019)

单位：人 (person)

类　别	Types	毕业生人数本科 Graduates (normal courses)	招生人数本科 New Students Enrollment (normal courses)	在校学生人数本科 Students Enrollment (normal courses)
总　计	**Total**	**16668**	**30332**	**65831**
#女	Female	9642	8119	36222
经济学	Economics	865	1076	2603
法　学	Law	981	1644	3309
教育学	Education	606	1717	3158
文　学	Literature	819	1228	2753
理　学	Science	205		177
工　学	Engineering	4311	10201	19431
医　学	Medicine	4701	5884	17574
管理学	Administration	4180	8582	16826

22-16 网络教育学生情况(2019年)

Statistics on Web-based Education Students (2019)

单位：人 (person)

类　别	Types	毕业生人数专科 Graduates (short-cycle courses)	在校学生人数专科 Enrolment (short-cycle courses)
总　计	**Total**	**24508**	**61101**
#女	Female	11879	27603
能源动力与材料大类	Energy Power and Materials	503	1193
土木建筑大类	Civil Engineering	3355	7597
装备制造大类	Manufacturing	1438	5364
电子信息大类	Electronic Information	1571	6107
医药卫生大类	Medicine and Health	2836	7266
财经商贸大类	Finance and Business	9533	22714
旅游大类	Tourism	242	964
文化艺术大类	Culture and Arts	126	103
教育与体育大类	Education and Sport	1664	2820
公安与司法大类	Public Security	1242	1823
公共管理与服务大类	Public Adminlstration and Service	1998	5150

22-17 进城务工子女和农村留守儿童在校情况(2019年)
Statistics on Children of Migrant Workers and Rural Left-behind Children in Schools (2019)

单位：人 (person)

项目	Item	普通小学 Regular Primary School					初中 Junior Middle School			
		毕业生数 Graduates	招生数 Entrants	#受过学前教育 Trained in preschool education	在校生数 Enrolment	#女生 Female	毕业生数 Graduates	招生数 Entrants	在校生数 Enrolment	#女生 Female
进城务工人员随迁子女	Children Living with the Rural Migrant Workers in Cities	58549	81635	81564	477432	212929	49568	66425	196408	87820
#外省迁入	Move from Other Provinces	5215	6861	6845	40626	18239	3708	4807	14566	6170
本省外县迁入	Move from Other Counties	53334	74774	74719	436806	194690	45860	61618	181842	81650
农村留守儿童	Rural Left-behind Children	105	420	370	3288	1040	39	287	724	253

22-18 普通高等学校办学条件
Running Conditions of Regular Institutions of Higher Education

指标	Item	2017	2018	2019
学校产权占地面积(万平方米)	Occupying Space of School Property Rights (10 000 sq.m)	11079.40	11575.85	11925.44
学校产权校舍建筑面积(万平方米)	Schoolhouse Building Space of School Property Rights (10 000 sq.m)	5977.66	6162.42	6294.80
学校产权一般图书(万册)	Common Books of School Property Rights (10 000 volumes)	16444.31	17561.66	18373.46
学校产权固定资产总值(亿元)	Fixed Assets of School Property Rights (100 million yuan)	924.48	1102.99	1099.23
#教学、科研仪器设备值	Value of Equipment for Teaching and Scientific Research	219.03	248.07	275.92

22-19 各市普通高等学校情况(2019年)

Basic Statistics on Regular Institutions of Higher Education by City (2019)

单位：人 (person)

市 City	学校数(所) Schools (unit)	教职工数 Educational Personnel	招生数 Entrants	专科 Junior College Student	本科 Undergraduate	在校学生数 Enrolment	专科 Junior College Student	本科 Undergraduate
全省 Total	**141**	**162050**	**788773**	**451032**	**337741**	**2319376**	**1122191**	**1197185**
郑州市 Zhengzhou	62	70607	361435	200610	160825	1078675	515782	562893
开封市 Kaifeng	5	8319	32683	18993	13690	104044	48993	55051
洛阳市 Luoyang	7	9735	42490	19410	23080	133575	46654	86921
平顶山市 Pingdingshan	6	5305	23998	13566	10432	74109	36470	37639
安阳市 Anyang	6	6765	35594	19402	16192	99373	42813	56560
鹤壁市 Hebi	3	1431	8619	8619		20388	20388	
新乡市 Xinxiang	10	12723	55004	20545	34459	175060	48771	126289
焦作市 Jiaozuo	6	6890	35057	20643	14414	100142	51135	49007
濮阳市 Puyang	2	1631	9090	9090		20883	20883	
许昌市 Xuchang	4	3513	20827	14876	5951	55051	33785	21266
漯河市 Luohe	3	5806	15815	15815		40925	40925	
三门峡市 Sanmenxia	2	1166	8575	8575		20312	20312	
南阳市 Nanyang	6	7708	36570	23659	12911	99185	53515	45670
商丘市 Shangqiu	6	8031	40190	22807	17383	113208	56141	57067
信阳市 Xinyang	6	6141	26041	10604	15437	86990	30883	56107
周口市 Zhoukou	3	3204	19253	10941	8312	50179	25742	24437
驻马店市 Zhumadian	3	2147	10872	6217	4655	32108	13830	18278
济源市 Jiyuan	1	928	6660	6660		15169	15169	

22-19 续表 continued

单位：人 (person)

市 City	预计毕业生数 Estimated for Next Year	专科 Junior College Student	本科 Undergraduate	毕业生数 Graduates	专科 Junior College Student	本科 Undergraduate	授予学位数 Degrecs Conferred
全 省 Total	**650335**	**341947**	**308388**	**593235**	**316569**	**276666**	**273111**
郑 州 市 Zhengzhou	303015	158859	144156	270378	146422	123956	122743
开 封 市 Kaifeng	29258	15484	13774	27259	14173	13086	13072
洛 阳 市 Luoyang	37336	14549	22787	33692	11484	22208	22091
平顶山市 Pingdingshan	21847	12039	9808	21051	11056	9995	9568
安 阳 市 Anyang	28261	11642	16619	26259	10294	15965	15806
鹤 壁 市 Hebi	6424	6424		5270	5270		
新 乡 市 Xinxiang	46922	14414	32508	42539	13456	29083	28190
焦 作 市 Jiaozuo	26366	15000	11366	23170	14983	8187	8010
濮 阳 市 Puyang	6082	6082		5690	5690		
许 昌 市 Xuchang	15075	9540	5535	13332	7841	5491	5453
漯 河 市 Luohe	12816	12816		11700	11700		
三门峡市 Sanmenxia	5997	5997		5639	5639		
南 阳 市 Nanyang	27923	15815	12108	27501	15435	12066	12017
商 丘 市 Shangqiu	33037	18383	14654	30410	17035	13375	13294
信 阳 市 Xinyang	24643	10247	14396	22896	10634	12262	12171
周 口 市 Zhoukou	12576	6685	5891	13348	7360	5988	5782
驻马店市 Zhumadian	8482	3696	4786	8426	3422	5004	4914
济 源 市 Jiyuan	4275	4275		4675	4675		

22-20 各市普通高中情况(2019年)

Statistics on Regular Senior Secondary Schools by City (2019)

单位：人 (person)

市(县)	City(county)	学校数(所) Number of Schools (unit)	教职工数 Teachers and Staff	#专任教师 Full-time Teachers	招生数 Entrants	在校学生数 Enrolment	#女生 Female	毕业生数 Graduates
全省	**Total**	**889**	**185744**	**163013**	**749785**	**2158790**	**1091719**	**677814**
省辖市	**City**							
郑州市	Zhengzhou	127	22259	19156	71365	204189	101872	62174
开封市	Kaifeng	50	8767	7392	39943	117122	59114	33860
洛阳市	Luoyang	81	14917	13280	49034	143427	77411	46184
平顶山市	Pingdingshan	42	7623	6787	36537	99304	50603	29110
安阳市	Anyang	56	9717	8143	40938	112959	58764	32188
鹤壁市	Hebi	16	3412	2545	12318	35064	17543	9827
新乡市	Xinxiang	67	12788	10565	45302	123981	63491	34835
焦作市	Jiaozuo	32	6702	5916	24424	74386	38250	26072
濮阳市	Puyang	38	8070	6701	30058	83306	42855	26484
许昌市	Xuchang	35	7874	7122	29329	79584	40415	23968
漯河市	Luohe	20	3800	3285	15616	46390	23521	16228
三门峡市	Sanmenxia	20	4284	3961	13049	39839	21511	14609
南阳市	Nanyang	92	18154	16351	86089	235888	118360	65849
商丘市	Shangqiu	39	12023	10410	53575	155611	78768	51366
信阳市	Xinyang	69	14680	13544	64005	187812	88687	63850
周口市	Zhoukou	57	17040	15332	75016	231163	116245	78889
驻马店市	Zhumadian	41	12346	11336	57918	173058	86456	57053
济源市	Jiyuan	7	1288	1187	5269	15707	7853	5268
省直管县	**County Directly Administrated by Province**							
巩义市	Gongyi	8	1342	1296	4763	14604	7796	5049
兰考县	Lankao	5	1471	1272	7064	21413	10956	5578
汝州市	Ruzhou	9	1537	1472	8055	21216	10684	5395
滑县	Huaxian	11	2352	1938	9328	24448	12839	6536
长垣市	Changyuan	9	2715	1693	7451	20966	10210	6066
邓州市	Dengzhou	9	1753	1570	11422	29737	15331	8334
永城市	Yongcheng	6	1396	1237	8167	23128	12393	7216
固始县	Gushi	14	3133	2948	13658	38841	17500	11482
鹿邑县	Luyi	6	2062	1835	8039	23796	12098	7615
新蔡县	Xincai	5	1241	1137	6920	21074	10828	6964

注：本表专任教师是指普通高中学校的专任教师。

a) Data of full-time teachers in this table refer to the full-time teachers in regular senior secondary schools.

22-21　各市中等职业学校情况(2019年)
Statistics on Secondary Vocational Schools by City (2019)

单位：人　　(person)

市(县) City(county)	学校数(所) Number of Schools (unit)	教职工数 Teachers and Staff	#专任教师 Full-time Teachers	#双师型教师 Double-qualified teachers	招生数 Entrants	在校学生数 Enrolment	毕业生数 Graduates	#获得职业资格证书 With Professional Qualification Certificates	预计毕业生数 Estimated Graduates for Next Year
全　省 Total	**574**	**58995**	**47710**	**11629**	**420862**	**1110637**	**343875**	**219728**	**335370**
省辖市 City									
郑州市 Zhengzhou	117	15392	11375	3116	123829	330373	97933	65727	97827
开封市 Kaifeng	27	2267	1780	426	13848	36321	12791	10311	11685
洛阳市 Luoyang	55	4033	3450	647	37364	95967	28454	19944	28172
平顶山市 Pingdingshan	22	2039	1617	344	16894	48814	10621	6663	19526
安阳市 Anyang	16	2393	2067	603	15345	40680	12179	5880	12082
鹤壁市 Hebi	5	860	747	347	8448	21810	7335	6236	6109
新乡市 Xinxiang	27	3167	2542	718	20893	57428	15891	11701	18047
焦作市 Jiaozuo	24	2131	1760	476	10583	31188	11460	4346	10719
濮阳市 Puyang	22	2183	1775	483	14111	42710	12076	7204	14214
许昌市 Xuchang	25	2472	1941	500	12325	32246	7914	7174	9135
漯河市 Luohe	20	1849	1608	531	12303	27151	9524	7172	7039
三门峡市 Sanmenxia	18	1324	1071	280	4119	12696	4972	1839	4465
南阳市 Nanyang	80	5417	4555	804	35419	94624	26802	12619	25718
商丘市 Shangqiu	30	2980	2519	516	18656	50096	12921	9939	14090
信阳市 Xinyang	28	3559	3104	521	28043	75679	23095	20981	26009
周口市 Zhoukou	28	3850	3268	700	19223	53274	13578	12948	15504
驻马店市 Zhumadian	27	2584	2149	498	27726	54595	34406	7702	13310
济源市 Jiyuan	3	495	382	119	1733	4985	1923	1342	1719
省直管县 County Directly Administrated by Province									
巩义市 Gongyi	3	298	281	112	1336	3764	1012	775	1200
兰考县 Lankao	2	150	128	22	126	384	383	383	119
汝州市 Ruzhou	5	407	357	84	6202	23257	1271	513	11258
滑县 Huaxian	3	481	456	53	2700	7713	1590	1590	1927
长垣市 Changyuan	2	589	458	125	4198	12689	2555	2307	4728
邓州市 Dengzhou	2	535	499	58	5185	13037	3461	823	3095
永城市 Yongcheng	4	328	314	77	2616	6587	1111	1105	1543
固始县 Gushi	7	845	748	62	5104	13872	4448	4101	5217
鹿邑县 Luyi	4	293	259	61	446	1637	191	181	362
新蔡县 Xincai	4	201	160	36	13152	15370	23617	93	753

注：本表数据不含技工学校有关数据。
a) Data in this table unclude data of technical school.

22-22 各市普通初中教育情况(2019年)

Statistics on Regular Junior Secondary Schools by City (2019)

市(县)	City(county)	学校数(所) Schools (unit)	专任教师(人) Full-time Teachers (person)	#女性 Female	#城镇 Urban	乡村 Rural Area	#学历合格高一级教师 The Degree Higher Qualified Teachers
全省	**Total**	**4603**	**327211**	**211044**	**259354**	**67857**	**7938**
省辖市	**City**						
郑州市	Zhengzhou	359	30391	21507	26846	3545	3395
开封市	Kaifeng	226	14708	9879	11055	3653	248
洛阳市	Luoyang	322	21527	13917	18928	2599	807
平顶山市	Pingdingshan	230	16154	10813	11898	4256	212
安阳市	Anyang	267	16795	11360	12495	4300	231
鹤壁市	Hebi	64	4933	3166	4495	438	100
新乡市	Xinxiang	335	20235	13680	14777	5458	602
焦作市	Jiaozuo	182	10178	6881	8356	1822	139
濮阳市	Puyang	154	13726	9617	11069	2657	294
许昌市	Xuchang	205	14453	9403	11062	3391	258
漯河市	Luohe	104	7183	4691	5714	1469	79
三门峡市	Sanmenxia	115	6962	4324	5657	1305	75
南阳市	Nanyang	459	37933	24526	32302	5631	337
商丘市	Shangqiu	417	25846	15410	18761	7085	264
信阳市	Xinyang	329	25796	14026	18745	7051	330
周口市	Zhoukou	486	32036	20564	24910	7126	246
驻马店市	Zhumadian	317	26425	16019	20501	5924	261
济源市	Jiyuan	32	1930	1261	1783	147	60
省直管县	**County Directly Administrated by Province**						
巩义市	Gongyi	28	2289	1642	2097	192	29
兰考县	Lankao	53	2759	1920	1930	829	22
汝州市	Ruzhou	58	3404	2323	2081	1323	47
滑县	Huaxian	51	3677	2594	2475	1202	24
长垣市	Changyuan	37	2936	2323	2362	574	59
邓州市	Dengzhou	65	5554	3701	4670	884	60
永城市	Yongcheng	59	4076	2471	3516	560	58
固始县	Gushi	55	5046	2554	3824	1222	14
鹿邑县	Luyi	55	3284	2047	2787	497	18
新蔡县	Xincai	48	2733	1315	1857	876	13

注：本表专任教师按照授课对象进行分类。
a) Data in this table according to the classification of teaching object.

22-22 续表 continued

市(县) City(county)	在校学生数(人) Enrolment (person)	#女性 Female	#城镇 Urban	乡村 Rural Area	校舍建筑面积(平方米) Architectural Area of the Building (Square meters)	教学及辅助用房面积(平方米) Teaching and Auxiliary Area (Square meters)	城镇 Urban	乡村 Rural Area
全 省 Total	**4684765**	**2120991**	**3826237**	**858528**	**58341806**	**20802652**	**16343043**	**4459609**
省 辖 市 City								
郑 州 市 Zhengzhou	430416	181256	380806	49610	6021060	2034307	1739015	295292
开 封 市 Kaifeng	219096	96640	174348	44748	2551350	937507	717147	220360
洛 阳 市 Luoyang	283579	135097	251730	31849	4084240	1477452	1277985	199467
平 顶 山 市 Pingdingshan	259881	120328	187925	71956	2852323	923861	672481	251380
安 阳 市 Anyang	280400	124884	217378	63022	2778175	1103954	824201	279754
鹤 壁 市 Hebi	71331	31101	65977	5354	984919	353473	302734	50740
新 乡 市 Xinxiang	312046	138445	236112	75934	3605692	1493964	1056182	437782
焦 作 市 Jiaozuo	116252	52551	101495	14757	1891013	678690	537823	140867
濮 阳 市 Puyang	195433	87845	165075	30358	2069536	813664	664374	149290
许 昌 市 Xuchang	205526	92258	161137	44389	2707371	944860	752026	192834
漯 河 市 Luohe	100642	45474	84984	15658	1355742	448783	368114	80669
三 门 峡 市 Sanmenxia	70949	34093	61062	9887	1369284	473972	381909	92064
南 阳 市 Nanyang	590226	274327	510073	80153	6642606	2224330	1881069	343261
商 丘 市 Shangqiu	358799	162129	281481	77318	4186813	1714862	1220292	494570
信 阳 市 Xinyang	354816	160858	269006	85810	4113084	1492527	1065646	426881
周 口 市 Zhoukou	442493	205843	358494	83999	6218779	1993978	1550677	443302
驻 马 店 市 Zhumadian	368554	166551	296137	72417	4426920	1557403	1205205	352198
济 源 市 Jiyuan	24326	11311	23017	1309	482897	135064	126163	8901
省 直 管 县 County Directly Administrated by Province								
巩 义 市 Gongyi	24177	11264	22093	2084	464438	141741	134809	6932
兰 考 县 Lankao	35469	15883	25938	9531	600864	251296	172121	79175
汝 州 市 Ruzhou	52605	24165	31573	21032	674472	192996	116952	76044
滑 县 Huaxian	59788	26484	42898	16890	551942	196641	129520	67120
长 垣 市 Changyuan	49117	20886	40334	8783	636250	179404	147084	32320
邓 州 市 Dengzhou	82400	38097	70149	12251	928212	329845	280564	49281
永 城 市 Yongcheng	77891	34925	67162	10729	606903	261827	220647	41180
固 始 县 Gushi	66850	29404	53432	13418	737848	302346	199978	102368
鹿 邑 县 Luyi	40941	19318	35494	5447	688346	241493	189446	52047
新 蔡 县 Xincai	46355	22398	37468	8887	691170	196966	132337	64629

22-23 各市普通小学教育情况(2019年)

Statistics on Regular Junior Secondary Schools by City (2019)

市(县)	City(county)	学校数(所) Schools (unit)	专任教师(人) Full-time Teachers (person)	#女性 Female	#城镇 Urban	乡 村 Rural Area	#学历合格高一级教师 The Degree Higher Qualified Teachers
全　　省	**Total**	**18117**	**565248**	**420233**	**337663**	**227585**	**318116**
省 辖 市	**City**						
郑 州 市	Zhengzhou	958	48883	40073	39922	8961	37316
开 封 市	Kaifeng	920	27438	20763	15498	11940	12116
洛 阳 市	Luoyang	843	32647	24070	23635	9012	21168
平顶山市	Pingdingshan	1170	28730	21684	16866	11864	14288
安 阳 市	Anyang	1245	28866	22344	16908	11958	19654
鹤 壁 市	Hebi	306	7878	6086	5497	2381	4791
新 乡 市	Xinxiang	1269	32196	25834	18988	13208	19081
焦 作 市	Jiaozuo	514	17658	13773	12377	5281	10489
濮 阳 市	Puyang	781	24144	18843	13922	10222	14416
许 昌 市	Xuchang	819	25702	19397	15671	10031	12462
漯 河 市	Luohe	495	11261	8575	6794	4467	6280
三门峡市	Sanmenxia	239	10496	7703	7739	2757	6900
南 阳 市	Nanyang	1772	63577	45848	39227	24350	32225
商 丘 市	Shangqiu	1865	49237	34265	26324	22913	22577
信 阳 市	Xinyang	1050	42160	29868	22230	19930	25863
周 口 市	Zhoukou	1858	63357	44414	30879	32478	31781
驻马店市	Zhumadian	1922	48240	34678	22932	25308	24584
济 源 市	Jiyuan	91	2778	2015	2254	524	2125
省直管县	**County Directly Administrated by Province**						
巩 义 市	Gongyi	70	3524	2802	3058	466	2630
兰 考 县	Lankao	202	4709	3706	2471	2238	2686
汝 州 市	Ruzhou	385	5277	3881	2809	2468	2575
滑 县	Huaxian	292	6969	5278	3034	3935	3756
长 垣 市	Changyuan	227	5209	4614	3194	2015	3099
邓 州 市	Dengzhou	298	8322	5755	4744	3578	3845
永 城 市	Yongcheng	308	7050	5073	4475	2575	4821
固 始 县	Gushi	179	7864	5492	4374	3490	4967
鹿 邑 县	Luyi	200	7289	5019	3695	3594	3136
新 蔡 县	Xincai	247	5914	3789	1939	3975	2281

注：本表专任教师按照授课对象进行分类。

a) Data in this table according to the classification of teaching object.

22-23 续表 continued

市(县) City(county)	在校学生数(人) Enrolment (person)	#女性 Female	#城镇 Urban	乡村 Rural Area	校舍建筑面积(平方米) Architectural Area of the Building (Square meters)	教学及辅助用房面积(平方米) Teaching and Auxiliary Area (Square meters)	城镇 Urban	乡村 Rural Area
全 省 Total	**10124818**	**4684355**	**6728164**	**3396654**	**72547537**	**39253672**	**19955966**	**19297706**
省 辖 市 City								
郑 州 市 Zhengzhou	967943	438962	807542	160401	6603962	2932913	2307837	625076
开 封 市 Kaifeng	504499	230122	313309	191190	3162646	1727158	842441	884717
洛 阳 市 Luoyang	610623	292523	477117	133506	4737298	2417283	1429213	988071
平 顶 山 市 Pingdingshan	546823	255369	335793	211030	3543093	1881299	935842	945457
安 阳 市 Anyang	632553	288940	393173	239380	3728210	2236721	1034975	1201747
鹤 壁 市 Hebi	155801	71508	121440	34361	1186983	629515	387715	241801
新 乡 市 Xinxiang	639534	290534	411190	228344	4142693	2513785	1280813	1232972
焦 作 市 Jiaozuo	276030	129762	215044	60986	2010147	997037	658267	338770
濮 阳 市 Puyang	434083	198932	272874	161209	2759802	1652394	835072	817321
许 昌 市 Xuchang	428144	197032	284700	143444	3026361	1628613	863389	765223
漯 河 市 Luohe	209449	97059	143670	65779	1478858	771011	395971	375041
三 门 峡 市 Sanmenxia	158587	76393	128687	29900	1522473	669610	428810	240801
南 阳 市 Nanyang	1223454	564679	837186	386268	9120110	4780331	2384802	2395529
商 丘 市 Shangqiu	844263	389273	503341	340922	5853171	3722252	1796724	1925528
信 阳 市 Xinyang	669164	307256	426742	242422	5070588	2858791	1326630	1532161
周 口 市 Zhoukou	957795	452339	550732	407063	7854466	3879486	1463978	2415508
驻 马 店 市 Zhumadian	809233	376710	454293	354940	6298069	3775217	1443456	2331761
济 源 市 Jiyuan	56840	26962	51331	5509	448605	180256	140033	40223
省 直 管 县 County Directly Administrated by Province								
巩 义 市 Gongyi	55385	26080	49459	5926	491347	238116	198597	39518
兰 考 县 Lankao	87325	40211	50028	37297	643254	363021	173369	189652
汝 州 市 Ruzhou	125601	58563	68247	57354	875815	507647	234926	272720
滑 县 Huaxian	160772	72594	74149	86623	1031014	598903	187475	411428
长 垣 市 Changyuan	99986	44201	69678	30308	638985	352859	201279	151580
邓 州 市 Dengzhou	172489	80751	95523	76966	1213500	646657	273031	373626
永 城 市 Yongcheng	155427	71948	105371	50056	1003151	652130	378024	274106
固 始 县 Gushi	121422	54920	78349	43073	891482	575134	306455	268679
鹿 邑 县 Luyi	99919	47383	58621	41298	779793	403756	153185	250571
新 蔡 县 Xincai	101670	49258	47105	54565	742932	411072	115510	295562

22-24 各市特殊教育情况(2019年)

Statistics on Special Education by City (2019)

单位：人 (person)

市(县) City(county)	学校数(所) Number of Schools (unit)	专任教师 Full-time Teachers	#女性 Female	招生数 Entrants	在校学生数 Enrolment	#女生 Female	毕业生数 Graduates
全省 Total	**150**	**4156**	**3102**	**10472**	**54849**	**19998**	**3007**
省辖市 City							
郑州市 Zhengzhou	13	447	374	594	3278	1164	287
开封市 Kaifeng	9	180	148	696	2490	908	95
洛阳市 Luoyang	14	330	245	914	3843	1470	299
平顶山市 Pingdingshan	9	225	170	817	3756	1444	201
安阳市 Anyang	8	187	141	561	3290	1214	255
鹤壁市 Hebi	2	45	33	157	910	324	56
新乡市 Xinxiang	8	224	174	763	4274	1593	250
焦作市 Jiaozuo	8	177	113	301	2023	771	147
濮阳市 Puyang	7	176	138	433	2239	851	84
许昌市 Xuchang	5	101	67	215	1594	512	68
漯河市 Luohe	7	120	96	282	1470	556	84
三门峡市 Sanmenxia	5	114	89	202	1256	491	94
南阳市 Nanyang	14	369	275	1434	6659	2534	293
商丘市 Shangqiu	10	373	283	611	4112	1519	191
信阳市 Xinyang	10	265	179	585	3000	1098	151
周口市 Zhoukou	10	431	288	1017	4941	1732	126
驻马店市 Zhumadian	10	336	247	825	5310	1670	262
济源市 Jiyuan	1	56	42	65	404	147	64
省直管县 County Directly Administrated by Province							
巩义市 Gongyi	1	22	20	66	311	131	25
兰考县 Lankao	1	21	20	363	675	258	10
汝州市 Ruzhou	1	16	12	183	928	333	60
滑县 Huaxian	1	25	22	204	1098	413	124
长垣市 Changyuan	1	53	42	141	823	279	61
邓州市 Dengzhou	1	28	22	237	1206	461	42
永城市 Yongcheng	1	38	31	18	162	65	1
固始县 Gushi	1	21	16	64	273	102	25
鹿邑县 Luyi	1	41	32	101	395	133	11
新蔡县 Xincai	1	22	17	59	1063	125	

22-25 各市技工学校基本情况(2019年)

Basic Statistics on Technical Schools by City (2019)

单位：人 (person)

市 City	学校数(所) Number of Schools (unit)	在职教职工数 Teachers and Staff	在校学生数 Student Enrollment	招生数 New Student Enrollment	毕业生数 Graduates
全 省 Total	**95**	**12526**	**287694**	**115958**	**84359**
郑 州 市 Zhengzhou	21	3140	104780	35111	31702
开 封 市 Kaifeng	8	1056	36254	15057	9261
洛 阳 市 Luoyang	9	643	16713	7260	2964
平 顶 山 市 Pingdingshan	8	928	18670	12951	3535
安 阳 市 Anyang	4	292	3079	1320	968
鹤 壁 市 Hebi	2	496	5132	1666	1279
新 乡 市 Xinxiang	4	977	17155	4752	5274
焦 作 市 Jiaozuo	4	653	9920	3862	2686
濮 阳 市 Puyang	4	368	4789	1889	1895
许 昌 市 Xuchang	2	665	5097	2855	1466
漯 河 市 Luohe	3	591	13856	3539	4993
三 门 峡 市 Sanmenxia	4	580	13628	4750	6075
南 阳 市 Nanyang	11	545	6846	3386	1803
商 丘 市 Shangqiu	3	201	4410	2276	1419
信 阳 市 Xinyang	2	138	1303	518	333
周 口 市 Zhoukou	1	285	7302	4181	1351
驻 马 店 市 Zhumadian	3	656	10997	4748	5001
济 源 市 Jiyuan	2	312	7763	5837	2354

22-26 各市成人高等教育基本情况(2019年)

Basic Statistics on Adult Education Schools by City (2019)

单位：人 (person)

市 City	学校数(所) Number of Schools (unit)	教职工数 Teachers and Staff	#专任教师 Full-time Teachers	在校学生数 Student Enrollment	招生数 New Student Enrollment	毕业生数 Graduates
全　省 Total	**10**	**895**	**570**	**420347**	**212846**	**124199**
郑州市 Zhengzhou	4	487	293	123578	67185	36593
开封市 Kaifeng	1			28264	15480	8705
洛阳市 Luoyang	3	148	88	46195	24069	11907
平顶山市 Pingdingshan				26310	13225	8745
安阳市 Anyang				16460	9308	3670
鹤壁市 Hebi						1
新乡市 Xinxiang				66375	25891	21439
焦作市 Jiaozuo	1	260	189	21664	12370	3308
濮阳市 Puyang				5		14
许昌市 Xuchang				11649	6758	4464
漯河市 Luohe				2879	1406	427
三门峡市 Sanmenxia				517	404	271
南阳市 Nanyang				38104	17643	13581
商丘市 Shangqiu				8332	4273	3016
信阳市 Xinyang				16096	8597	2492
周口市 Zhoukou				11573	6033	2577
驻马店市 Zhumadian	1			2306	204	2961
济源市 Jiyuan				40		28

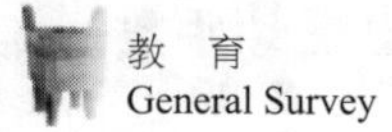

22-27 各市学前教育情况(2019年)
Statistics on Pre-school Education by City (2019)

市(县) City(county)	幼儿园数(所) Number of Kindergartens (unit)	专任教师数(人) Full-time Teachers	#女性 Female	在园幼儿数(人) Student Enrollment (person)	#女童 Girl	#公办幼儿园 Public Kindergartens
全 省 Total	**23181**	**226163**	**223811**	**4308701**	**2045317**	**1330190**
省 辖 市 City						
郑 州 市 Zhengzhou	1729	29922	29497	414477	195490	139202
开 封 市 Kaifeng	1285	11704	11631	216757	102073	56324
洛 阳 市 Luoyang	1305	14599	14530	264679	127968	58836
平 顶 山 市 Pingdingshan	1676	13245	13103	233937	110981	65259
安 阳 市 Anyang	1867	12426	12304	230164	108757	52464
鹤 壁 市 Hebi	436	3693	3659	60428	28581	8936
新 乡 市 Xinxiang	1946	15566	15463	267981	125666	65332
焦 作 市 Jiaozuo	786	8466	8387	147915	70949	39952
濮 阳 市 Puyang	1032	9587	9533	176751	82314	53311
许 昌 市 Xuchang	1266	11760	11700	201260	95745	31577
漯 河 市 Luohe	567	5473	5409	101211	48613	38148
三 门 峡 市 Sanmenxia	432	5388	5340	78217	37826	25615
南 阳 市 Nanyang	2132	18607	18394	411495	193950	149743
商 丘 市 Shangqiu	1616	19523	19308	403109	191329	133697
信 阳 市 Xinyang	1506	12313	12081	305622	143170	114980
周 口 市 Zhoukou	2306	20098	19857	430392	208049	160628
驻 马 店 市 Zhumadian	1093	11912	11779	332183	158293	120744
济 源 市 Jiyuan	201	1881	1836	32123	15563	15442
省 直 管 县 County Directly Administrated by Province						
巩 义 市 Gongyi	124	2148	2130	34599	16629	15326
兰 考 县 Lankao	247	1908	1902	41364	19437	10942
汝 州 市 Ruzhou	448	3040	3019	55810	26496	12542
滑 县 Huaxian	378	2379	2365	58775	27811	17989
长 垣 市 Changyuan	263	2509	2499	42349	19768	12594
邓 州 市 Dengzhou	388	2408	2371	67817	32283	36019
永 城 市 Yongcheng	232	4020	4018	72442	34221	15541
固 始 县 Gushi	306	2267	2229	61287	27588	12068
鹿 邑 县 Luyi	140	1307	1251	40824	19830	21329
新 蔡 县 Xincai	59	778	773	42682	21204	11570

22－28　各市各级普通学校生师比(2019年)

Student-Teacher Ratio by Level of Regular Schools by City (2019)

(教师人数=1)　　(Number of Teachers =1)

市(县) City(county)	普通小学 Primary School	初中 Junior Secondary School	普通高中 Regular Senior Secondary School	中等职业学校 Secondary Vocational School
全省 Total	**17.84**	**14.28**	**15.52**	**20.02**
省辖市 City				
郑州市 Zhengzhou	19.80	14.14	13.04	24.80
开封市 Kaifeng	18.12	14.88	18.27	19.44
洛阳市 Luoyang	18.69	13.16	13.53	20.70
平顶山市 Pingdingshan	19.01	16.08	15.42	28.92
安阳市 Anyang	21.80	16.70	16.14	14.61
鹤壁市 Hebi	19.73	14.46	17.58	22.79
新乡市 Xinxiang	19.81	15.18	15.48	21.03
焦作市 Jiaozuo	15.63	11.38	14.60	14.35
濮阳市 Puyang	17.80	14.08	15.68	21.30
许昌市 Xuchang	16.62	14.18	13.56	15.20
漯河市 Luohe	18.20	13.85	14.98	11.89
三门峡市 Sanmenxia	15.03	10.19	10.27	11.08
南阳市 Nanyang	19.20	15.55	16.28	17.99
商丘市 Shangqiu	17.06	13.88	17.59	17.33
信阳市 Xinyang	15.82	13.75	15.61	22.47
周口市 Zhoukou	15.01	13.78	16.88	15.85
驻马店市 Zhumadian	16.76	13.91	18.22	22.99
济源市 Jiyuan	20.46	12.60	13.23	10.05
省直管县 County Directly Administrated by Province				
巩义市 Gongyi	15.72	10.56	11.27	11.73
兰考县 Lankao	17.78	12.86	18.36	3.00
汝州市 Ruzhou	23.73	15.45	15.00	65.15
滑县 Huaxian	23.07	16.26	15.43	16.91
长垣市 Changyuan	18.95	16.73	19.52	20.40
邓州市 Dengzhou	20.73	14.84	20.16	26.13
永城市 Yongcheng	21.46	19.11	18.90	18.30
固始县 Gushi	15.44	13.25	16.76	18.55
鹿邑县 Luyi	13.61	12.47	17.21	6.32
新蔡县 Xincai	17.19	16.96	25.36	96.06

22-29 各市每十万人口各级学校平均在校生数(2019年)

Number of Average Students Enrollment by Level of school per 10 0000 Population by City (2019)

单位：人 (person)

市(县) City(county)	学前教育 Pre-school Education	小 学 Primary School	初中阶段 Junior Secondary School	高中阶段 Senior Secondary School
全 省 Total	**4469.72**	**10503.19**	**4859.84**	**3690.05**
省 辖 市 City				
郑 州 市 Zhengzhou	4003.99	9350.66	4157.97	6176.26
开 封 市 Kaifeng	4737.96	11027.54	4789.09	4146.47
洛 阳 市 Luoyang	3823.63	8821.23	4096.66	3699.79
平 顶 山 市 Pingdingshan	4654.81	10880.53	5171.04	3318.70
安 阳 市 Anyang	4432.88	12182.75	5400.41	3018.34
鹤 壁 市 Hebi	3703.83	9549.56	4372.11	3800.55
新 乡 市 Xinxiang	4609.00	10999.33	5366.87	3415.10
焦 作 市 Jiaozuo	4112.01	7673.59	3231.79	3210.71
濮 阳 市 Puyang	4895.61	12023.13	5413.06	3623.01
许 昌 市 Xuchang	4510.43	9595.12	4606.04	2620.45
漯 河 市 Luohe	3793.23	7849.82	3771.91	3275.50
三 门 峡 市 Sanmenxia	3435.80	6966.17	3116.54	2906.31
南 阳 市 Nanyang	4101.99	12196.00	5883.67	3362.95
商 丘 市 Shangqiu	5496.74	11512.26	4892.54	2865.13
信 阳 市 Xinyang	4728.14	10352.33	5489.19	4096.51
周 口 市 Zhoukou	4968.62	11057.18	5108.32	3367.96
驻 马 店 市 Zhumadian	4714.62	11485.32	5230.83	3387.12
济 源 市 Jiyuan	4378.22	7747.04	3315.52	3878.29
省 直 管 县 County Directly Administrated by Province				
巩 义 市 Gongyi	4100.12	6563.34	2865.07	2176.68
兰 考 县 Lankao	6335.43	13374.94	5432.53	3338.49
汝 州 市 Ruzhou	5751.83	12944.55	5421.52	4583.43
滑 县 Huaxian	5452.23	14913.91	5546.20	2983.40
长 垣 市 Changyuan	5365.39	12667.68	6222.86	4263.90
邓 州 市 Dengzhou	4965.00	12628.23	6032.65	3131.56
永 城 市 Yongcheng	5835.04	12519.29	6273.94	2393.48
固 始 县 Gushi	5558.91	11013.33	6063.49	4781.22
鹿 邑 县 Luyi	4619.67	11306.89	4632.91	2878.01
新 蔡 县 Xincai	5018.46	11954.14	5450.32	4285.01

22−30 各市教育经费情况(2019年)

Basic Statistics on Educational Funds by City (2019)

单位：万元 (10 000 yuan)

市(县) City(County)	合计 Total	国家财政性教育经费 Government Appropriation for Education	#一般公共预算教育经费 General Public Budget Expenditure on Education	民办学校中举办者投入 Funds from Runners of Private Schools	社会捐赠经费 Donations and Fund Raising for Running Schools	事业收入 Income from Teahing Research and other Auxiliary Activity	学费 Tuition	其他教育经费 Other Educational Funds
全　　省 Total	**26685217**	**20678150**	**17733939**	**305184**	**13403**	**5349332**	**4538394**	**339149**
省 本 级 Provincial Level	4606675	2711423	2309179	2950	9932	1594317	1258466	288054
郑 州 市 Zhengzhou	3473333	2749521	2319726	72467	263	643078	590501	8004
开 封 市 Kaifeng	986193	760390	657934	12331	418	211520	186644	1533
洛 阳 市 Luoyang	1480472	1236576	1127048	14737	914	225729	195930	2515
平 顶 山 市 Pingdingshan	1060406	846847	739416	39909	57	170906	152148	2688
安 阳 市 Anyang	1157916	947779	779758	10687	83	196901	182178	2467
鹤 壁 市 Hebi	347953	281238	237630	5280	43	60136	52404	1255
新 乡 市 Xinxiang	1244488	975617	851191	5231	72	259576	233934	3992
焦 作 市 Jiaozuo	691853	521335	453800	4392	41	164065	145894	2020
濮 阳 市 Puyang	898935	770612	656230	2001	232	121000	111791	5090
许 昌 市 Xuchang	965539	771333	680860	5373	42	188346	168407	446
漯 河 市 Luohe	548371	431899	352995	18640	120	94162	79274	3549
三 门 峡 市 Sanmenxia	576885	507924	434937	9533	106	56361	50072	2961
南 阳 市 Nanyang	2054316	1760068	1523764	9386	514	283530	245919	818
商 丘 市 Shangqiu	1437686	1112317	926404	7860	212	315534	250286	1762
信 阳 市 Xinyang	1549701	1332264	1130148	13203	19	202158	169606	2057
周 口 市 Zhoukou	1770645	1398367	1239185	24071	184	345828	295012	2194
驻 马 店 市 Zhumadian	1638018	1396965	1169557	46078	51	193378	149610	1546
济 源 市 Jiyuan	195832	165675	144179	1053	101	22805	20318	6198
省 直 管 县 County Directly Administrated by Province								
巩 义 市 Gongyi	169054	146583	128336			22471	20517	
兰 考 县 Lankao	187580	155951	127863	273		31350	26840	6
汝 州 市 Ruzhou	202583	160389	152477	9357	36	32792	29344	9
滑 县 Huaxian	212221	172702	152000	286	20	38783	35931	430
长 垣 市 Changyuan	184648	135973	124152	352		48323	42976	
邓 州 市 Dengzhou	228313	199226	163955	437	24	28539	25007	88
永 城 市 Yongcheng	197959	156564	137883	1189		40077	30736	128
固 始 县 Gushi	306343	253513	224449	10782		42048	32936	
鹿 邑 县 Luyi	144351	109026	99308	205		35121	31463	
新 蔡 县 Xincai	193817	130796	112840	35911		27111	9896	

22−31　外国留学生情况(2019年)

Basic condition of International student (2019)

单位：人、人次　　(person, person-time)

项　　目	Item	招生数 Entrants	在校生数 Enrolment	毕(结)业生数 Graduates
外国留学生数	**Number of International Student**	**2751**	**5528**	**1694**
#女性	Female	1118	2217	768
按层次分	**by Level**			
博士研究生	Doctor's Degree	177	302	5
硕士研究生	Master's Degree	254	594	61
本科	Undergraduate	850	2894	257
专科	College	62	118	10
培训(非学历)	Training (Non-academic)	1408	1620	1361
按大洲分	**by Continents**			
亚洲	Asia	1707	4007	1077
非洲	Africa	779	1156	392
欧洲	Europe	182	233	131
北美洲	North America	49	80	68
南美洲	South America	25	36	23
大洋洲	Oceania	9	16	3

主要统计指标解释

教育　指国家、社会、私人依照国家有关法规开办的各类教育机构的活动，以及其他与教育相关的活动。主要包括学前教育、初等教育、中等教育、高等教育和其他教育等类别。学前教育指按照国家幼儿教育规定对学龄前幼儿进行保育和教育活动；初等教育指义务教育法规定的初等教育和成人扫盲教育活动；中等教育指小学毕业到大学专科教育以前的教育；高等教育指经教育行政部门批准、由国家、地方、社会办的获取学历的高等教育活动和经教育主管部门批准举办的成人高等教育活动；其他教育主要指职业技能培训、特殊教育以及其他未列明的教育活动。

国家财政性教育经费　包括一般公共预算安排的教育经费，政府性基金预算安排的教育经费，企业办学中的企业拨款，校办产业和社会服务收入用于教育的经费，其他属于国家财政性教育经费。

财政预算内教育经费　指中央、地方各级财政或上级主管部门在年度内安排，并计划拨到教育部门和其他部门主办的各级各类学校、教育事业单位，列入国家预算支出科目的教育经费，包括教育事业拨款、科研经费拨款、基建拨款和其他经费拨款。

在园幼儿数　指在单独设立的、小学附设的学前班、幼儿班及托儿所附设的幼儿班的幼儿数。托幼混合班仅统计三至周六岁的幼儿数。不包括季节性的农忙时临时组织的幼儿园。

学前教育毛入园率　指学前教育在学人数占国家规定的年龄组人口数的比重。计算公式为：

$$学前教育毛入园率=\frac{在园儿童数}{学前教育学龄人口总数}\times100\%$$

小学学龄儿童净入学率　指小学学龄人口中正在接受小学教育人数所占比重。计算公式为：

$$学龄儿童净入学率=\frac{小学学龄人口中已经进入小学学习的在校学生总数}{小学学龄人口数}\times100\%$$

小学五年巩固率　指小学五年级在校学生中，能够从一年级连续学习五年的学生数占入学时本年级学生数比重。计算公式为：

$$小学五年的巩固率=\frac{在校学生数}{该年级入小学一年级时的学生数}\times100\%$$

初中阶段毛入学率　指初中阶段在校学生总数与12-14岁学龄组人口数的比重。计算公式为：

$$初中阶段毛入学率=\frac{初中阶段在校学生数}{12至14学龄组人口数}\times100\%$$

初中三年巩固率　指初中三年级在校学生中，能够从一年级连续学习三年的学生占入学时本年级学生数比重。计算公式为：

$$初中三年巩固率=\frac{三年级在校学生数}{该年级入初中一年级时的学生数}\times100\%$$

高中阶段毛入学率　指高中阶段(包括普通高中、职业高中、中等专业学校、技工学校、成人中等专业学校、成人高中)在校学生总数与15—17岁学龄组人口数的比重。计算公式为：

$$高中阶段毛入学率=\frac{高中阶段在校学生数}{15-17岁学龄组人口数}\times100\%$$

特殊教育　指独立设置的招收盲聋哑和残疾儿童，以及其他特殊需要的儿童，青少年进行普通或职业初中，中等教育的教学。

普通高等学校　指通过国家普通高等教育招生考试，招收高中毕业生为主要培养对象，实施高等学历教育的全日制大学、独立设置的学院、独立学院和高等专科学校、高等职业学校及其他普通高教机构。

大学、独立设置的学院主要实施本科及本科层次以上的教育。独立学院主要实施本科层次的教育。高等专科学校、高等职业学校实施专科层次的教育。其他普通高教机构是指承担国家普通招生计划任务不计校数的机构，包括普通高等学校分校、大专班等。

成人高等学校 指通过国家成人高等教育招生考试，招收具有高中毕业或同等学力的人员为主要培养对象，利用函授、业余、脱产等多种形式，对其实施高等学历教育的学校。包括：职工高等学校、农民高等学校、管理干部学院、教育学院、独立函授学院、广播电视大学、其他成人高教机构等。其他成人高教机构是指承担国家成人招生计划任务不计校数的机构。

初中毕业生升学率 计算初中毕业生升学率所用分子数为高级中学招生数，包括：普通高中招生数、职业高中招生数、技工学校招生数、普通中专招收初中毕业生数、普通中专举办的成人中专招收应届初中毕业生数及成人中专招收应届初中毕业生数，分母是初中毕业生人数。

Explanatory Notes on Main Statistical Indicators

Education refers to education institutions offered activities in the state, society, private in according to the relevant regulations of the state of all kinds of, as well as other and education related activities. Mainly include preschool education, elementary mainly include education, secondary education, higher education and other education classes.

Government Appropriation for Education refers to the general public budget appropriation fund for education, educational funds budgeted by government funds, enterprise appropriation for enterprise-run schools, income from school-run enterprises and social services that are used for education purpose and other national appropriations for education.

Budgetary Fund for Education refers to education funding that is planned to be allocated to various schools and education institutions by central and local financial departments at various levels within the reference year, which is within the State budgetary expenditure, including: appropriated funds for education, for science and research, for capital construction and others.

The number of infant refers infant in all kinds of kindergarten. nursery and education establishment, enrolling children in 3-6 years old.

Pre-school education entrance rate refers proportion of number of Pre-school education persons in Pre-school education school-age population×100%.

Pre-school education entrance rate= number of Pre-school education persons/ Pre-school education school-age population.

Net Enrolment Ratio of Primary Schools refers to the proportion of school age children enrolled at schools to the total number of school age children both in and outside schools (including retarded children, but excluding blind, deaf and mute children). The formula is:

$$\text{Net Enrolment Ratio of Primary Schools} = \frac{\text{Total Primary School - age Children at Schools}}{\text{Total Primary School - age Children Whether or Not Attending School}} \times 100\%$$

Elementary school five years Consolidate rate refers to the proportion of Primary school pupils to the A primary school grade.

Elementary school five years Consolidate rate= Primary school pupils/ the A primary school grade×100%.

The junior middle school stage gross enrollment rate refers to the proportion of number of middle school students in school to 12-14 years old population.

The junior middle school stage gross enrollment rate= number of middle school students/12-14 years old population×100%

Junior school three years Consolidate rate refers to the proportion of Junior school students to the Junior school grade.

Junior school three years Consolidate rate= Junior school students / the Junior school grade×100%.

The senior middle school stage gross enrollment rate refers to the proportion of number of senior middle school students in school to 15-17 years old population.

The senior middle school stage gross enrollment rate= number of senior middle school students/15-17 years old population×100%

Higher Education gross enrollment rate refers to the proportion of number of Higher Education students in school to 18-22 years old population.

Special Education Schools refer to educational establishments set up independently, enrolling blind, deaf, dumb, amentia or other special children, and educational establishment, providing regular or vocational junior and senior secondary education for hobbledehoy.

Regular Institutions of Higher Education refer to educational establishments recruiting graduates from senior secondary schools as the main target through National Matriculation TEST. They include full-time universities, independently established colleges, colleges, and institutions of higher professional education, institutions of higher vocational education and other institutions of higher education.

Universities and independently established colleges primarily provide undergraduate and above courses; colleges mainly impart undergraduate courses, institutions of higher professional education and institutions of higher vocational education primarily provide professional trainings; and other institutions of higher education refer to educational establishments, which are responsible for enrolling higher education students under the State Plan but not enumerated in the total number of schools, including: branch schools of universities and colleges and junior colleges.

Institutions of Higher Education for Adults refer to educational establishments, enrolling personnel with senior secondary school or equivalent education through National Matriculation TEST for Adult, and providing higher education courses in forms of correspondence, spare time, or full time for adults. Institutions of higher learning for adults include schools of higher education for staff and workers, schools of higher education for peasants, colleges for management cadres, pedagogical colleges, independent correspondence colleges, radio and television universities and other educational establishments of higher education for adult. Other educational establishments of higher education for adult refer undertakings to enrol adult students but not enumerated in the number of schools under the State Plan.

Junior high school graduates entering middle schools rate refers to ordinary high school include, professional high school include, technicians schools include average technical secondary school, junior middle school graduate recruit average technical secondary school, the number of the adult technical secondary school recruit fresh held the junior middle school graduates number and adult secondary recruit fresh junior high school graduates number, the molecules is Senior middle schools recruit students, the denominator is junior high school graduates.

卫生和社会工作

Public Health and Social Work

23

◉ 资料整理：孔令惠　赵 霞

简要说明

一、主要内容

本篇主要反映卫生、社会服务、残疾人事业的发展情况。

卫生统计资料主要包括医疗卫生机构、卫生人员、卫生设施、卫生经费、基层医疗卫生服务、妇幼保健、疾病控制、居民病伤死亡原因、医疗保障制度等情况。

社会服务统计资料主要包括社会服务企事业机构、社会组织、人员、床位情况，优抚和社会救济情况，社会服务机构情况，婚姻服务情况，殡葬服务情况，社会捐赠和福利彩票销售情况等。

残疾人统计资料主要包括残疾人康复、教育、就业、社会保障、扶贫和残联组织建设情况。

二、资料来源

卫生部分的资料由省卫生健康委员会提供，社会服务资料由省民政厅提供，由省统计局社会与科技处编辑整理。

Brief Introduction

I. Main Contents

Data in this chapter mainly reflect the development of public health, civil affairs, and work for person with disabilities.

Data on public health include mainly the number of medical and health institutions, health personnel, health facility, health expenses, medical and health services at grass-root level, maternal and child health, disease control, major diseases as the causes of death, and health security system.

Data on civil affairs include: institutions, social organizations, personnel and beds of social services, social welfare relief, community service facilities and marriage registration service, funeral and interment services, social donations and welfare lottery.

Data on disabled persons cover information on the rehabilitation, education, employment and poverty alleviation of disabled persons and institutions serving the needs of disabled persons.

II. Sources of Data

Data on public health are calculated from Health commission of Henan Province. Data on social services are calculated from Henan provincial civil bureau of civil affairs. Data on this chapter are provided by department of social and technology of the Henan province Bureau of Statistics.

23-1 卫生事业基本情况
Basic Statistics on Public Health

年份 Year	卫生机构数(个) Number of Health Institutions (unit)	#医院、卫生院 Hospitals & Health Centers	卫生机构床位数(万张) Number of Beds in Health Institutions (10 000 units)	#医院、卫生院 Hospitals & Health Centers	卫生技术人员数(万人) Medical Technical Personnel (10 000 persons)	#执业(助理)医师 Licensed (Assistant) Doctors	每万人口拥有 per 10 000 Population 卫生机构床位数(张) Number of Beds in Health Institutions (unit)	每万人口拥有 per 10 000 Population 执业(助理)医师数(人) Licensed (Assistant) Doctors (person)
1978	7356	2476	10.20	9.73	11.44	4.38	14.4	6.2
1979	7702	2501	11.23	10.63	12.89	4.79	15.6	6.7
1980	7831	2530	11.92	11.17	14.48	5.41	16.4	7.4
1981	8483	2563	12.49	11.65	16.31	6.81	16.9	9.2
1982	8513	2578	13.08	12.11	17.34	7.31	17.4	9.7
1983	8504	2611	13.77	12.74	18.38	7.82	18.0	10.2
1984	8583	2665	14.24	13.13	19.12	8.10	18.4	10.5
1985	9207	2688	14.91	13.77	19.49	8.36	19.0	10.7
1986	8933	2713	15.31	13.99	20.15	8.50	19.2	10.6
1987	8833	2730	16.90	15.42	20.44	8.49	20.7	10.4
1988	8865	2756	17.55	15.95	21.36	8.85	21.1	10.6
1989	8721	2810	17.96	16.25	21.85	9.61	21.2	11.3
1990	8676	2824	18.21	16.36	22.28	9.94	21.1	11.5
1991	8639	2834	18.49	16.56	23.03	9.93	21.1	11.3
1992	8375	2857	18.91	16.97	23.91	10.14	21.3	11.4
1993	7669	2892	18.91	17.22	24.39	10.16	21.1	11.4
1994	7656	2944	19.14	17.45	25.13	10.55	21.2	11.7
1995	7661	2965	19.23	17.54	25.50	10.57	21.1	11.6
1996	7253	2987	18.95	17.54	25.77	10.57	20.7	11.5
1997	7194	3001	18.92	17.58	26.20	10.67	20.5	11.5
1998	11774	2999	19.42	17.99	26.32	10.68	20.8	11.5
1999	11643	3014	19.71	18.26	26.66	10.89	21.0	11.6
2000	10764	3027	19.86	18.34	26.84	11.11	20.9	11.7
2001	10719	3024	19.99	18.50	27.18	11.12	20.9	11.6
2002	13291	3094	19.73	18.75	26.48	10.17	20.5	10.6
2003	13621	3149	20.37	19.28	27.87	10.64	21.1	11.0
2004	13821	3182	20.90	19.72	28.42	10.94	21.5	11.3
2005	14554	3260	21.40	20.23	28.92	11.11	21.9	11.4
2006	14629	3292	22.52	21.23	30.07	11.55	22.9	11.8
2007	11888	3281	23.95	22.61	29.79	11.59	24.3	11.7
2008	11683	3263	26.83	25.22	30.99	11.93	27.1	12.0
2009	12157	3282	30.24	28.30	34.64	13.96	30.3	14.0
2010	75741	3282	32.76	30.44	37.28	15.48	34.8	16.5
2011	76201	3304	34.92	32.49	39.52	15.58	37.2	16.6
2012	69222	3356	39.39	36.57	42.88	16.77	41.9	17.8
2013	71464	3471	42.98	40.03	46.91	18.06	45.7	19.2
2014	71157	3470	45.93	42.83	49.45	18.93	48.7	20.1
2015	71397	3585	48.96	45.65	51.96	19.86	51.6	21.0
2016	71273	3662	52.16	48.74	54.67	20.68	54.7	21.7
2017	71089	3693	55.90	52.21	58.05	22.03	58.5	23.0
2018	71352	3873	60.85	57.04	62.13	23.55	63.4	24.5
2019	70735	4023	64.00	60.05	65.39	25.14	66.4	26.1

注：从2010年起村卫生室、2013年起计划生育技术服务机构，其机构、人员分别计入卫生机构总数、卫生人员总数（下表同）。

a) Data on Number of Health Institutions and Personnel include Village Hospital & Health Center since 2010, and include family planning fertility technical service institution since 2013 (the same as the following table).

23−2　卫生事业发展情况

Basic Statistics on Public Health Development

项　　目	Item	1990	1995	2000	2005	2010	2018	2019
卫生机构数(个)	**Number of Health Institutions (unit)**	**8676**	**7661**	**10764**	**14554**	**75741**	**71352**	**70735**
#村卫生室	Village Clinics					64140	56173	56079
医院	Hospitals	789	896	966	1172	1198	1825	1974
疗养院、所	Sanatoriums	12	8	7	5	6	2	2
门诊部、所	Outpatient Department	5142	3942	196	68	86	396	502
诊所、卫生所、医务室	Clinics, Health clinic, Infirmary					6694	7615	7408
乡镇街道卫生院	Township Health Centers			2084	2084	2084	2048	2049
社区卫生服务中心(站)	Community Health Service Station			861	1017	861	1498	1523
专科防治所、站	Specialized Prevention & Treatment Centers (Stations，Institutions)	45	44	45	32	20	21	21
妇幼保健所、站	Maternity and Child Care Centers (Institutions, Stations)	138	142	135	167	167	163	163
卫生机构床位数(万张)	**Number of Beds in Health Institutions (10 000 units)**	**18.21**	**19.23**	**19.86**	**21.40**	**32.76**	**60.85**	**64.00**
#医院、卫生院	Hospital & Health Center	16.36	17.54	18.34	20.23	30.44	57.04	60.05
#医院	Hospitals	10.80	12.10	13.26	14.97	22.10	45.57	48.11
疗养院、所	Sanatoriums	0.22	0.15	0.15	0.06	0.09	0.01	0.01
门诊部	Outpatient Department	1.10	0.84	0.51	0.11	0.11	0.04	0.03
平均每千人口卫生机构床位数(张)	Beds of Health Institutions per 1 000 Population (unit)	2.11	2.11	2.09	2.19	3.48	6.34	6.64
#医院、卫生院	Hospitals & Health Centers	1.89	1.93	1.93	2.07	3.24	5.94	6.23
医院病床使用率(%)	Utilization Rate of Beds (%)	75.71	68.08	59.60	67.01	85.36	87.62	88.07
卫生机构人员数(万人)	**Number of Persons in Health Institutions (10 000 persons)**	**27.06**	**31.31**	**33.50**	**36.23**	**59.11**	**86.30**	**88.78**
#卫生技术人员	Medical Technical Personnel	22.28	25.50	26.84	28.92	37.28	62.13	65.39
#执业(助理)医师	Licensed (Assistant) Doctors	9.94	10.57	11.11	11.11	15.48	23.55	25.14
护士	Nurses	2.16	3.19	3.84	7.71	12.14	26.31	27.89

注：1.1996年及以后年度门诊部、所不含诊所、卫生保健所和医务室,与以前年度不可比(下同)。
2.1998年及以后年度卫生机构包括个体开业(下同)。
3.2002年以来医生、护士人员数为“执业医师、执业助理医师与注册护士人员数”。
4.2007年起，诊所、卫生室、医务室与社区卫生服务中心(站)分开统计。

a) The numbers of Outpatient Department since 1996 exclude cliniques, hygiene places and infirmaries. It cannot be compared with former years (the same as in following tables).

b) The number of health institutions include the number of clinics run by private since 1998 (the same as the following tables).

c) Number of doctors and nurses since 2002 is the Number of registered doctors, deputy doctors and junior nurses.

d) Number of clinics, hedth clinic, infirmary and community sanitation service station are calculated by separate statistics system since 2007.

23-3 卫生机构、床位、人员数(2019年)

Number of Health Institutions, Beds and Persons (2019)

机构类别	Type of Institutions	机构数(个) Institutions (unit)	床位数(张) Beds (unit)	人员合计(人) Total of Persons (Person)	#卫生技术人员 Medical Technical Personnel	#其他技术人员 Other Technical Personnel	#管理人员 Administrative Personnel	#工勤人员 Logistics Workers
总计	**Total**	**70735**	**640008**	**887784**	**653894**	**36851**	**36045**	**64966**
医院合计	**Total Number of Hospitals**	**1974**	**481111**	**516587**	**432725**	**21706**	**23852**	**38304**
综合医院	General Hospitals	1209	340328	371214	313691	14225	16647	26651
中医医院	Hospitals Specialized in Traditional Chinese Medicine	317	75536	84808	70550	4296	3442	6520
中西医结合医院	Hospitals Combining Chinese and Western Medicine	46	5173	5100	4211	215	261	413
专科医院	Specialized Hospital	388	59254	54928	43864	2953	3462	4649
口腔医院	Hospitals for Mouth Cavity Diseases Care	17	1214	2980	2418	103	164	295
眼科医院	Hospital for Eye Care	41	3004	3519	2616	280	384	239
耳鼻喉科医院	ENT Hospital	8	461	499	396	35	38	30
肿瘤医院	Tumor Hospitals	11	7202	7617	6511	322	327	457
心血管病医院	Heart and Blood Vessel Trouble Hospital	9	3209	4484	3804	210	342	128
胸科医院	Chest Hospital	2	1244	1400	1217	92	41	50
血液病医院	Hematonosis Hospital	3	144	84	77	1	3	3
妇产(科)医院	Maternity Hospitals	37	2419	3454	2633	142	184	495
儿童医院	Hospitals for Children	3	2867	4086	3488	101	262	235
精神病医院	Mental Hospitals	69	17748	8237	6357	570	394	916
传染病医院	Hospitals of Infectious Diseases	11	3852	3265	2676	121	225	243
皮肤病医院	Dermatosis Hospital	8	422	405	301	28	34	42
结核病医院	Tuberculosis Hospitals							
麻风病医院	Leprosy hospital	1	40	36	22	1	4	9
职业病医院	Diseases hospital	1	99	185	133	4	18	30
骨科医院	Orthopaedics Hospitals	51	4838	5733	4714	260	386	373
康复医院	Rehabilitation Hospitals	30	5609	3156	2316	278	201	361
整形外科医院	Plastic Surgery Hospital	1	34	422	126	68	35	193
美容医院	Cosmetic Hospital	10	216	854	441	209	78	126
其他专科医院	Other Specialized Hospitals	75	4632	4512	3618	128	342	424
护理院	Nursing Homes	14	820	537	409	17	40	71
基层医疗卫生机构	**Primary-level Medical and Health Care Institutions**	**67561**	**132205**	**293042**	**167775**	**8545**	**5740**	**14954**
社区卫生服务中心(站)	Community Health Service Stations	1523	12504	26472	22233	1078	1333	1828
卫生院	Heath Center	2049	119395	109310	85865	7134	3865	12446
村卫生室	Village clinics	56079		130227	34195			
门诊部	Clinics	502	306	7559	6679	139	340	401
诊所、卫生室、医务室	Clics,Individual-Run Medical Units and	7408		19474	18803	194	202	279
专业公共卫生机构	**Specialized Public Health Agency**	**1014**	**26547**	**72959**	**50794**	**5915**	**5787**	**10463**
疾病预防控制中心	Center for Disease Prevention and Control	180		16454	9336	1882	1526	3710
专科疾病防治院(所、站)	Specialized Prevention & Treatment Centers or Stations	22	1568	1744	1213	166	118	247
健康教育所(站、中心)	Health Education Center	5		56	9	10	26	11
妇幼保健院(所、站)	Maternity and Child Care Centers	163	24954	38204	30775	2158	1677	3594
急救中心(站)	First-aid Center	43	25	592	328	66	98	100
采供血机构	Collectting and Supply Institutions for Blood	23		2380	1636	214	122	408
卫生监督所(中心)	Health Inspection Institution (center)	179		7750	5105	493	1070	1082
计划生育技术服务机构	Family Planning Fertility Technical Service Institution	399		5779	2392	926	1150	1311
其他卫生机构	**Other Health Agencies**	**186**	**145**	**5196**	**2600**	**685**	**666**	**1245**

23−4 卫生机构各类人员

Employed Persons In Health Institutions by Types of Occupation

单位：人 (person)

人员类别	Type of Personnel	1990	2000	2005	2010	2015	2016	2017	2018	2019
各类人员总计	**Total**	**270573**	**335031**	**362263**	**591059**	**771319**	**796744**	**827671**	**862996**	**887784**
卫生技术人员	Medical Technical Personnel	222771	268427	289157	372818	519638	546732	580497	621316	653894
其他技术人员	Other Technical Personnel	2256	12428	23409	24100	35457	36610	37581	37712	36851
管理人员	Adminlstrative Personnel	19856	23554	20060	25348	35181	34791	36158	36387	36045
工勤人员	Logistics Workers	25690	30622	29637	40013	64531	64755	63826	64275	64966
乡村医生和卫生员	Village Doctors & Assistants				128780	116512	113856	109457	103306	96032
卫生技术人员	**Medical Technical Personnel**	**222771**	**268427**	**289157**	**372818**	**519638**	**546732**	**580497**	**621316**	**653894**
执业(助理)医师	Practice (assistant) Physicians	99354	111113	111134	154801	198616	206766	220337	235474	251429
注册护士	Registered Nurses	46391	63032	77132	121384	205366	222121	241605	263100	278898
药剂人员	Pharmacists	25812	28094	22432	20488	24950	25902	26790	27765	28308
技师(士)	Technicians	10244	13982	13987	23343	30631	32729	34328	36324	38827
#检验人员	Laboratory Technicians	10244	13982	13987	14445	18254	19547	20433	21527	22994
其他	Others	40970	52206	64472	52802	60075	59214	57437	58653	56432
平均每千人口	**Personnel per 1 000 Population**									
卫生技术人员	Medical Technical Personnel	2.58	2.82	2.96	3.96	5.48	5.74	6.07	6.47	6.78
#执业(助理)医师	Licensed (Assistant) Doctors	1.15	1.17	1.14	1.65	2.10	2.17	2.30	2.45	2.61

23−5 卫生总费用

Total Health Expenditure

指标名称	Index	2012	2013	2014	2015	2016	2017	2018
卫生总费用(亿元)	Total Health Expenditure (100 million yuan)	1517.63	1701.35	1878.78	2258.50	2472.63	2747.67	3100.17
#政府卫生支出	Government Health Expenditure	489.46	561.33	612.55	729.70	794.42	844.81	935.60
社会卫生支出	Social Health Expenditure	381.86	437.19	533.89	734.65	859.06	1015.67	1170.29
居民个人现金卫生支出	Out-of-pocket Health Expenditure	646.31	702.84	732.35	794.14	819.15	887.19	994.28
人均卫生总费用(元)	Per Capita Health Expenditure (yuan)	1613.47	1807.45	1997.07	2382.38	2594.03	2874.43	3215.94
卫生总费用占GDP比重(%)	Health Expenditure as Percentage of GDP (%)	5.13	5.29	5.38	6.10	6.11	6.11	6.45
门诊病人次均医药费用(元)	Outpatient Average expenses per time (yuan)	86.9	95.3	103.9	110.7	116.6	126.1	151.3

23-6 卫生部门医院住院病人前十位疾病构成(ICD-10)(2019年)
Percentage of 10 Main Diseases of Inpatients in Hospitals of Health Sector (ICD-10) (2019)

顺序 No.	市	City	疾病构成(%) As % of Total
	十种疾病构成	**Total**	
1	呼吸系统疾病	Diseases of the Respiratory System	11.02
2	消化系统疾病	Diseases of the Digestive System	9.02
3	脑血管病	Cerebrovascular Disease	7.19
4	缺血性心脏病	Ischaemic Heart Disease	6.86
5	损伤、中毒和外因	External Causes of Injury and Poison	5.63
6	妊娠、分娩和产褥期病	Pregnancy,childbirth and the Puerperium	5.61
7	泌尿生殖系统疾病	Disease of the Genitourinary System	5.51
8	恶性肿瘤	Malignant Tumour	4.98
9	神经系统疾病	Diseases of the Nervous System	4.94
10	肌肉骨骼系统和结缔组织疾病	Diseases of Musculoskeletal System and Connective Tissue	3.24

顺序 No.	县	County	疾病构成(%) As % of Total
	十种疾病构成	**Total**	
1	呼吸系统疾病	Diseases of the Respiratory System	18.42
2	脑血管病	Cerebrovascular Disease	10.98
3	消化系统疾病	Diseases of the Digestive System	9.24
4	妊娠、分娩和产褥期病	Pregnancy, childbirth and the Puerperium	8.17
5	损伤、中毒和外因	External Causes of Injury and Poison	7.87
6	缺血性心脏病	Ischaemic Heart Disease	7.01
7	神经系统疾病	Diseases of the Nervous System	4.72
8	泌尿生殖系统疾病	Disease of the Genitourinary System	4.46
9	恶性肿瘤	Malignant Tumour	3.53
10	内分泌、营养和代谢疾病	Endocrine, Nutritional and Metabolic Diseases	2.87

23-7 部分市、县前十位主要疾病死亡率(2019年)

Death Rate of Ten Major Diseases in Partial Cities and Counties (2019)

单位：1/10万 (1/100 000)

死亡原因	Cause of Death	死亡率 Death Rate
市 县	**City and County**	
心脏病	Cerebrovascular Disease	160.88
脑血管病	Heart Diseases	157.38
恶性肿瘤	Malignant Tumour	139.88
伤害	Injury and Poison	38.92
呼吸系统疾病	Diseases of the Respiratory System	38.24
内分泌，营养和代谢疾病	Endocrine, Nutritional & Metabolic Diseases	14.45
消化系统疾病	Diseases of the Digestive System	5.39
泌尿生殖系统疾病	Disease of the Genitourinary System	4.16
传染病和寄生虫病	Infestious and Parasitic Diseases	3.94
神经系统疾病	Diseases of the Nervous System	3.30
城 市	**City**	
心脏病	Heart Diseases	163.21
恶性肿瘤	Malignant Neoplasms	139.50
脑血管病	Cerebrovascular Disease	137.49
呼吸系统疾病	Diseases of the Respiratory System	46.34
伤害	Injury and Poison	33.83
内分泌，营养和代谢疾病	Endocrine, Nutritional & Metabolic Diseases	18.72
消化系统疾病	Diseases of the Digestive System	8.60
神经系统疾病	Diseases of the Nervous System	4.59
传染病和寄生虫病	Infestious and Parasitic Diseases	3.96
泌尿生殖系统疾病	Disease of the Genitourinary System	3.46
县	**County**	
脑血管病	Cerebrovascular Disease	163.29
心脏病	Heart Diseases	160.19
恶性肿瘤	Malignant Neoplasms	139.99
伤害	Injury and Poison	40.44
呼吸系统疾病	Diseases of the Respiratory System	35.83
内分泌，营养和代谢疾病	Endocrine, Nutritional & Metabolic Diseases	13.18
消化系统疾病	Diseases of the Digestive System	4.44
泌尿生殖系统疾病	Disease of the Genitourinary System	4.37
传染病和寄生虫病	Infestious and Parasitic Diseases	3.93
神经系统疾病	Diseases of the Nervous System	2.92

23-8 甲乙类法定报告传染病发病及死亡情况(2019年)

Incidence and Death from Class A and B Infectious Diseases (2019)

病名 Name	发病率(1/10万) Incidence Rate (per100 000 persons)	病名 Diseases	死亡率(1/10万) Death Rate (1/100000)	病名 Diseases	病死率(%) Mortality Rate (%)
肝　炎 Hepatitis	86.406	艾滋病 AIDS	1.286	狂犬病 Hydrophobia	86.487
肺结核 Pulmonary Tuberculosis	51.799	肺结核 Pulmonary Tuberculosis	0.118	艾滋病 AIDs	37.447
梅　毒 Syphilis	19.031	肝　炎 Hepatitis	0.058	出血热 Hemorrhage Fever	1.747
痢　疾 Dysentery	8.181	狂犬病 Hydrophobia	0.033	疟　疾 Malaria	0.431
淋　病 Gonorrhea	3.570	梅　毒 Syphilis	0.004	肺结核 Pulmonary Tuberculosis	0.227
艾滋病 AIDs	3.434	出血热 Hemorrhage Fever	0.004	肝　炎 Hepatitis	0.306
猩红热 Scarlet Fever	2.510	疟　疾 Malaria	0.001	梅　毒 Syphilis	0.022
布　病 Brucellosis	2.303	痢　疾 Dysentery		痢　疾 Dysentery	
百日咳 Pertussis	0.555	淋　病 Gonorrhea		淋　病 Gonorrhea	
新生儿破伤风 Newborn Tetanus	0.004	麻　疹 Measles		麻　疹 Measles	
登革热 Dengue Fever	0.297	百日咳 Pertussis		百日咳 Pertussis	
疟　疾 Malaria	0.242	流　脑 Epidemic Encephalitis		流　脑 Epidemic Encephalitis	
出血热 Hemorrhage Fever	0.238	猩红热 Scarlet Fever		猩红热 Scarlet Fever	
伤寒+副伤寒 Typhoid and Paratyphoid Fever	0.112	布　病 Brucellosis		布　病 Brucellosis	
麻　疹 Measles	0.078	炭　疽 Anthrax		炭　疽 Anthrax	
狂犬病 Hydrophobia	0.039	新生儿破伤风 Newborn Tetanus		新生儿破伤风 Newborn Tetanus	
炭　疽 Anthrax	0.018	乙　脑 Encephaliois B		乙　脑 Encephaliois B	
乙　脑 Encephaliois B	0.010	登革热 Dengue Fever		登革热 Dengue Fever	
流　脑 Epidemic Encephalitis	0.008	伤寒+副伤寒 Typhoid and Paratyphoid Fever		伤寒+副伤寒 Typhoid and Paratyphoid Fever	

23-9 防病工作情况

Basic Condition of Disease Prevention and Cure

指　标	Item	2012	2013	2017	2018	2019
传染病发病总例数（甲、乙）(万例)	**Number of Incidence from infectious disease(A、B) (10 000 persons)**	**29.5**	**22.8**	**18.3**	**18.5**	**17.2**
发病率(1/10万)	Incidence Disease Rate (1/100 000)	314.2	399.0	192.4	193.9	178.8
传染病死亡总人数(人)	Number of Death from infectious disease (person)	1869	1438	1420	1568	1445
死亡率(1/10万)	Death Rate (1/100 000)	2.0	1.5	1.5	1.6	1.5
结核病登记病人数(千例)	Number of register of Tuberculosis (1000 persons)	70.6	65.2	56.7	54.2	47.9
登记患病率(‰)	Register sicken Rate (‰)	0.67	0.75	0.60	0.57	0.50
结核病新发病人数(千例)	Number of New Incidence from Tuberculosis (1000 persons)	24.2	18.8	13.0	15.5	17.8
登记新发病率(1/万)	Register New Incidence Disease Rate (1/10 000)	2.30	2.00	1.36	1.62	1.85
结核病死亡人数(人)	Number of Death from Tuberculosis (person)	126	141	88	97	113
死亡率(1/10万)	Death Rate (1/100 000)	0.12	0.15	0.09	0.10	0.12
“五苗”接种率(%)	Five Type of bacterins inoculability Rate (%)	99.7	99.7	97.5	98.2	98.4
乙肝疫苗全程接种率(%)	Hepatitis B Bacterins Quite inoculability Rate (%)	99.7	99.7	98.3	98.4	98.4

23-10 各市医疗卫生机构情况(2019年)
Conditions of Health Institutions by City (2019)

单位：个 (unit)

地区 City (County)	合计 Total	城市 Urban Area	农村 Rural Area	#医院 Hospital	#公立医院 Public Hospitals	#基层医疗卫生机构 Health Care Institutions at Grass-root Level	#社区卫生服务中心(站) Community health sevice centers	乡镇街道卫生院 Township Health Centers	村卫生室 Village Clinics	#专业公共卫生机构 Specialized Public Health Institutions	#疾病预防控制中心 Center for Disease Control and Prevention	#妇幼保健院(所/站) Women and Children Care Agencies
全　　省 Total	**70735**	**6857**	**63878**	**1974**	**691**	**67561**	**1523**	**2049**	**56079**	**1014**	**180**	**163**
省辖市 City												
郑　州　市 Zhengzhou	4999	1618	3381	255	74	4649	287	103	2537	80	15	14
开　封　市 Kaifeng	3431	568	2863	93	34	3215	87	92	2557	94	11	8
洛　阳　市 Luoyang	4570	759	3811	158	55	4291	204	153	3258	112	16	15
平顶山市 Pingdingshan	3715	426	3289	89	59	3551	130	97	2865	59	11	10
安　阳　市 Anyang	5765	779	4986	100	32	5596	50	91	4078	59	10	10
鹤　壁　市 Hebi	1340	182	1158	53	19	1264	13	25	1048	19	6	5
新　乡　市 Xinxiang	4959	310	4649	128	58	4763	109	148	4122	62	13	13
焦　作　市 Jiaozuo	2671	212	2459	91	37	2509	72	77	2046	66	12	11
濮　阳　市 Puyang	4086	461	3625	65	33	3967	66	77	3388	40	8	6
许　昌　市 Xuchang	3703	240	3463	103	22	3547	62	78	3194	50	7	6
漯　河　市 Luohe	1824	280	1544	63	20	1723	41	51	1358	36	6	4
三门峡市 Sanmenxia	1802	143	1659	53	34	1718	58	73	1445	25	7	6
南　阳　市 Nanyang	6336	105	6231	164	53	6081	20	216	5725	78	14	14
商　丘　市 Shangqiu	6084	138	5946	89	36	5916	55	192	5567	57	10	9
信　阳　市 Xinyang	4182	381	3801	118	37	3983	190	193	3223	71	11	10
周　口　市 Zhoukou	7357	187	7170	205	48	7095	15	179	6383	45	11	11
驻马店市 Zhumadian	3330	68	3262	138	34	3129	14	192	2813	55	11	10
济　源　市 Jiyuan	581		581	9	6	564	50	12	472	6	1	1
省直管县 County Directly Administrated by Province												
巩　义　市 Gongyi	649		649	15	1	628	27	18	489	4	1	1
兰　考　县 Lankao	645		645	12	3	629		16	609	3	1	1
汝　州　市 Ruzhou	507		507	9	6	492	5	15	460	5	1	1
滑　　　县 Huaxian	1201		1201	21	3	1175	3	20	1113	5	1	1
长　垣　市 Changyuan	732		732	16	3	712		19	603	4	1	1
邓　州　市 Dengzhou	905		905	30	4	868	3	25	840	7	1	1
永　城　市 Yongcheng	797		797	12	6	776	2	28	726	6	1	1
固　始　县 Gushi	772		772	17	3	751	13	30	658	3	1	1
鹿　邑　县 Luyi	866		866	20	4	841	1	22	729	4	1	1
新　蔡　县 Xincai	457		457	25	5	424		23	401	6	1	1

23-11　各市医疗卫生机构床位情况(2019年)

Number of Beds in Health Institutions by City (2019)

单位：张　　　　　　　　　　　　　　　　　　　　　　　　　　　(unit)

地　区　City(County)	合计 Total	城市 Urban Area	农村 Rural Area	#医院 Hospital	#公立医院 Public Hospitals	#基层医疗卫生机构 Health Care Institutions at Grass-root Level	#社区卫生服务中心(站) Community health sevice centers	#乡镇卫生院 Township Health Centers	#专业公共卫生机构 Specialized Public Health Institutions	#妇幼保健院(所、站) Women and Children Care Agencies	#专科疾病防治院(所、站) Specialized Disease Prevention & Treatment Institution
全　省 Total	**640008**	**242110**	**397898**	**481111**	**353119**	**132205**	**12504**	**119395**	**26547**	**24954**	**1568**
省　辖　市 City											
郑　州　市 Zhengzhou	100492	71930	28562	87910	67312	8548	2412	5965	4034	3914	120
开　封　市 Kaifeng	31171	12780	18391	24098	15869	5548	472	5076	1525	1417	108
洛　阳　市 Luoyang	52979	24113	28866	40061	29824	10690	961	9680	2128	2048	60
平顶山市 Pingdingshan	31464	9900	21564	23904	21373	6135	574	5524	1380	1202	178
安　阳　市 Anyang	33323	14167	19156	23702	19910	7880	821	7034	1741	1661	80
鹤　壁　市 Hebi	10049	5018	5031	8124	5925	1671	155	1516	254	254	
新　乡　市 Xinxiang	39035	11942	27093	29147	23474	8669	881	7788	1219	1084	130
焦　作　市 Jiaozuo	25638	12045	13593	18815	14628	5414	1781	3633	1409	1409	
濮　阳　市 Puyang	24249	8213	16036	16378	10092	6853	156	6697	1018	1018	
许　昌　市 Xuchang	23888	8432	15456	18362	9634	4547	395	4152	979	909	70
漯　河　市 Luohe	16056	8694	7362	11603	8774	3547	548	2995	906	906	
三门峡市 Sanmenxia	15354	6066	9288	12315	11124	2527	190	2337	512	512	
南　阳　市 Nanyang	61730	17482	44248	43788	30741	15778	1101	14677	2164	1904	260
商　丘　市 Shangqiu	41717	8535	33182	27999	23344	11585	550	11035	2133	1881	252
信　阳　市 Xinyang	36360	8419	27941	24066	17141	10413	684	9709	1881	1881	
周　口　市 Zhoukou	49746	6653	43093	35858	18272	12146	629	11517	1742	1582	160
驻马店市 Zhumadian	43609	7721	35888	32703	23634	9684	184	9500	1222	1222	
济　源　市 Jiyuan	3148		3148	2278	2048	570	10	560	300	150	150
省直管县 County Directly Administrated by Province											
巩　义　市 Gongyi	3989		3989	3090		800	20	780	99	99	
兰　考　县 Lankao	6003		6003	4219		1404		1404	380	380	
汝　州　市 Ruzhou	6743		6743	4828		1655	248	1407	260	220	40
滑　县 Huaxian	6717		6717	4318		2141	170	1971	258	258	
长　垣　市 Changyuan	4419		4419	3380		960		960	79	79	
邓　州　市 Dengzhou	8249		8249	5599		2125	400	1725	525	265	260
永　城　市 Yongcheng	7472		7472	4899		2125	70	2055	448	350	98
固　始　县 Gushi	7246		7246	4376		1880	207	1673	990	990	
鹿　邑　县 Luyi	5563		5563	4177		1306	90	1216	80	80	
新　蔡　县 Xincai	4081		4081	2871		1030		1030	180	180	

23-12 各市卫生人员情况(2019年)

Employed Persons in Health Care Institutions by City (2019)

单位：人 (person)

地区 City(County)	卫生人员 Medical Personnel	#卫生技术人员 Medical Technical Personnel	#执业(助理)医师 Licensed (Assistant) Doctors	#执业医师 Licensed Doctor	#注册护士 Registered Nurse	#药师(士) Pharmacist	乡村医生和卫生员 Village Doctors and Assistants	其他技术人员 Other Technical Personnel
全 省 Total	**887784**	**653894**	**251429**	**191821**	**278898**	**28308**	**96032**	**36851**
省辖市 City								
郑州市 Zhengzhou	147557	121189	44608	40197	59273	4713	4091	5919
开封市 Kaifeng	45978	33983	13322	9954	14166	1393	4758	2026
洛阳市 Luoyang	68491	53589	20866	16685	24087	2081	5148	2702
平顶山市 Pingdingshan	44674	33184	12256	9173	13806	1542	4474	1821
安阳市 Anyang	46992	34739	14926	10538	14319	1167	5527	1809
鹤壁市 Hebi	14366	10331	4215	3228	4289	426	1764	498
新乡市 Xinxiang	54437	39403	16073	12254	16719	1815	5997	2649
焦作市 Jiaozuo	31692	23440	9434	7317	9693	1028	2661	1578
濮阳市 Puyang	32907	22748	9200	6596	9244	916	5681	1498
许昌市 Xuchang	36789	26070	10303	7619	10793	1101	4786	1415
漯河市 Luohe	22220	16183	5956	4746	6860	724	2598	1100
三门峡市 Sanmenxia	20048	15816	6061	4752	6687	625	1428	852
南阳市 Nanyang	78536	55680	20182	14925	23118	2928	10693	3142
商丘市 Shangqiu	63250	43631	16212	10530	16265	2210	8389	3325
信阳市 Xinyang	50836	34062	13176	9743	13778	1392	8098	2113
周口市 Zhoukou	69387	47215	18574	12004	18013	2299	11682	2477
驻马店市 Zhumadian	53920	38263	14287	10121	16024	1775	7680	1838
济源市 Jiyuan	5704	4368	1778	1439	1764	173	577	89
省直管县 County Directly Administrated by Province								
巩义市 Gongyi	6746	5402	2120	1682	2336	216	572	187
兰考县 Lankao	8136	6023	2187	1510	2185	223	798	383
汝州市 Ruzhou	8956	6158	2277	1622	2262	281	930	631
滑县 Huaxian	8851	6302	2703	1673	2575	213	1383	311
长垣市 Changyuan	7164	5160	2302	1557	2060	297	878	128
邓州市 Dengzhou	9071	5766	1991	1408	2386	292	1363	492
永城市 Yongcheng	9415	6840	2361	1568	2535	262	1209	497
固始县 Gushi	9241	5784	2178	1547	2232	196	1625	345
鹿邑县 Luyi	7218	4804	2075	1106	1748	244	1502	171
新蔡县 Xincai	6118	4149	1680	1007	1444	155	1069	237

23-13 农村乡镇卫生院医疗服务情况
Situations of Medical Services in Township Health Centers

年份 Year / 市 City	诊疗人次(万次) Visits (10 000 times)	病床使用率(%) Utilization Rate of Beds (%)	出院者平均住院日(日) Average Duration of Hospitalization (day)
1990	4679	41.00	5.90
1995	5660	43.60	4.80
1996	5390	39.29	4.73
1997	5073	40.60	4.72
1998	4713	39.09	4.51
1999	4098	37.21	5.22
2000	4130	36.94	4.97
2001	4398	36.33	4.52
2002	4150	36.69	4.26
2003	4054	37.64	5.09
2004	4165	36.51	5.06
2005	4205	38.38	5.01
2006	4616	42.11	4.86
2007	5357	54.53	7.39
2008	6077	64.94	4.63
2009	6230	63.44	5.19
2010	6473	64.13	5.37
2011	6914	62.58	6.04
2012	8130	65.06	6.30
2013	8935	61.74	6.86
2014	9649	62.08	7.01
2015	10471	62.59	7.14
2016	11244	62.14	7.21
2017	10636	63.26	6.80
2018	10559	63.08	7.00
2019	11626	63.26	6.80
郑州市 Zhengzhou	896	68.62	7.20
开封市 Kaifeng	728	54.37	7.60
洛阳市 Luoyang	663	67.48	7.90
平顶山市 Pingdingshan	528	57.47	8.80
安阳市 Anyang	438	66.12	8.20
鹤壁市 Hebi	125	51.90	7.20
新乡市 Xinxiang	627	62.59	7.20
焦作市 Jiaozuo	309	50.82	7.50
濮阳市 Puyang	316	68.87	6.30
许昌市 Xuchang	593	46.68	7.50
漯河市 Luohe	250	68.40	7.30
三门峡市 Sanmenxia	217	49.85	9.10
南阳市 Nanyang	1241	71.13	5.80
商丘市 Shangqiu	1604	64.66	6.80
信阳市 Xinyang	853	71.46	5.80
周口市 Zhoukou	1057	61.58	6.60
驻马店市 Zhumadian	1116	57.65	6.50
济源市 Jiyuan	63	55.06	8.50

23-14 妇女儿童卫生保健状况

Basic Statistics on Health Care of Women and Children

指　　标	Item	2005	2010	2015	2017	2018	2019
婚前医学检查率(%)	Rate of Medical Examination before Marriage (%)	1.1	4.9	70.6	74.2	76.5	77.8
城市	Urban Areas	1.9	6.4	54.5	61.7	67.0	67.4
农村	Rural Areas	0.5	4.1	77.7	80.5	81.1	83.2
婴儿死亡率（‰）	Infant Mortality (‰)	10.8	7.1	4.4	4.0	3.8	3.6
城市	Urban Areas	10.0	5.5	3.5	2.7	2.1	3.0
农村	Rural Areas	11.1	8.0	4.6	4.3	4.1	3.7
5岁以下儿童死亡率(‰)	Mortality of Child under 5 Years Old (‰)	13.8	8.7	5.9	5.3	5.3	4.8
城市	Urban Areas	10.7	6.4	4.4	3.4	2.5	3.7
农村	Rural Areas	15.3	10.0	6.3	5.8	5.8	5.0
孕产妇死亡率(1/10万)	Mortality Rate of Pregnant and Lying-in Women (1/100 000)	44.8	15.2	10.5	10.4	10.9	9.7
城市	Urban Areas	33.3	20.2	11.0	12.1	11.6	5.1
农村	Rural Areas	49.3	13.2	10.2	9.5	10.0	11.7
全省住院分娩率(%)	Hospitalization Rate of Parturition in Province (%)	87.8	98.9	100.0	100.0	99.9	100.0
农村孕产妇住院分娩率(%)	Hospital Parturition Rate of Rural Pregnant Women (%)	85.0	98.7	100.0	100.0	99.8	100.0
产前检查率（%）	Medical Prenatal Examination Rate (%)	85.0	91.2	94.9	93.4	94.2	93.7
孕产妇系统管理率（%）	Systematic Management Rate of Pregnant and Lying-in Women (%)	67.2	76.4	86.0	84.9	85.3	83.8
城市	Urban Areas	67.6	80.0	86.0	86.5	85.3	85.0
农村	Rural Areas	67.0	75.0	86.0	84.0	85.4	83.1
5岁以下儿童中、重度营养不良患病率(%)	moderate and Serious malnutrition Rate of Children under 5 Years old (%)	3.4	2.0	1.6	1.5	1.8	1.5
城市	Urban Areas	2.4	1.5	1.6	1.5	1.7	1.4
农村	Rural Areas	4.0	2.2	1.6	1.4	1.9	1.6
7岁以下儿童保健管理率（%）	Health Care Rate of Children under 7 Years Old (%)	70.2	76.7	86.6	87.7	88.2	89.7
城市	Urban Areas		83.6	88.8	88.9	89.6	91.5
农村	Rural Areas		74.0	85.6	87.0	87.5	88.6
卡介苗疫苗接种率(%)	BCG (%)	99.4	99.8	99.6	99.4	99.3	99.6
脊髓灰质炎疫苗接种率(%)	Poliomyelitis (%)	99.2	99.3	98.3	93.7	98.8	98.6
百白破疫苗接种率(%)	DPT(%)	99.2	99.5	98.7	96.9	97.1	98.5
麻疹疫苗接种率(%)	Measles (%)	98.7	99.3	98.3	97.5	98.0	98.2
乙肝疫苗接种率（%）	Inoculation Rate of Hepatitis B Vaccine (%)	99.1	99.8	98.1	98.3	98.4	98.4

23-15 社会服务机构基本情况(2019年)

Statistics on Social Service Institutions (2019)

指标名称	Item	单位数(个) Number of Institutions (unit)	职工人数(人) Number of Staff and Workers (persons)
社会工作	**Social Work**	**42089**	**218725**
提供住宿的社会服务机构	Social Welfare Institutions with Accommodations	2686	29004
养老机构	Pension Institutions	2549	26147
#社会福利院	Social Welfare Homes	60	1199
精神疾病服务机构	Social Welfare Institutions for Mental Diseases	6	845
儿童福利和救助保护机构	Social Welfare and Protection Institutions for Children	24	734
#儿童福利机构	Welfare Institutions for Children	21	674
未成年人救助保护中心	Juvenile Rescue and Protection Centers	3	60
其他提供住宿的服务机构	Other Social Welfare Institutions with Accommodations	107	1278
#生活无着人员救助管理站	Salvation Stations	97	1151
不提供住宿的社会服务机构和设施	Social Welfare Institutions without Accommodations	39403	189721
#低保服务机构	Service Institutions for People under Minimum Living Standard	49	422
福利彩票发行机构	Welfare Lottery Issuing Institutions	40	653
社区服务机构和设施	Community Service Institutions and Facilities	39313	188567
其他社会服务机构	**Other Social Service Institutions**	**281**	**5582**
婚姻服务机构	Marriage Registration Institutions	43	345
殡葬服务机构	Funeral Service Institutions	238	5237
殡仪馆	Funeral Home	110	3261
公墓	Cemetery	46	918
殡葬管理单位	Funeral and Interment Management Institutions	82	1058

注：1.民政厅组织各地民政部门对养老机构进行规范性整顿，调整了"社区服务机构和设施"和养老机构台账，数据与以前年份不可比。
2.社区服务机构和设施数据为2020年4月省民政厅组织各地民政部门对全省社区服务机构和设施的全面摸底结果，数据与以前年份不可比。
3.儿童福利和救助保护机构不包含承担儿童福利和救助保护职能的综合性社会福利机构，数据与以前年份不可比。

a) The Department of civil affairs carry out standardized rectification of pension institutions, and adjusted the accounts of community service institutions and facilities, and the pension institutions. The data are not comparable with those of previous years.

b) The data of the number of community service institutions and facilities are the results of a comprehensive survey of community service institutions and facilities organized by the provincial Civil Affairs Department in April 2020. The data are not comparable with those of previous years.

c) The number of social welfare and protection institutions for children do not include comprehensive social welfare institutions that undertake the functions of children welfare and protection, and the data are not comparable with those in previous years.

23-16 各市孤儿和家庭收养基本情况(2019年)

Statistics on Orphans and Children Adopted by Families by City (2019)

单位：人 (Person)

市（县） City(County)	孤儿数 Number of orphans	集中供养 Centralized support	社会散居 Live scattered	家庭收养儿童数 Number of Children Adopted by Families
全省 Total	**18284**	**3932**	**14172**	**397**
省本级 Privincial Level				109
郑州市 Zhengzhou	1216	742	443	61
开封市 Kaifeng	849	230	614	10
洛阳市 Luoyang	883	350	533	1
平顶山市 Pingdingshan	1020	278	731	86
安阳市 Anyang	513	77	434	17
鹤壁市 Hebi	235	95	140	
新乡市 Xinxiang	608	142	460	5
焦作市 Jiaozuo	408	172	229	4
濮阳市 Puyang	509	85	416	10
许昌市 Xuchang	774	152	618	16
漯河市 Luohe	436	137	275	
三门峡市 Sanmenxia	237	125	112	19
南阳市 Nanyang	3761	433	3279	13
商丘市 Shangqiu	1452	223	1224	11
信阳市 Xinyang	1033	163	870	1
周口市 Zhoukou	2344	141	2191	4
驻马店市 Zhumadian	1943	365	1565	11
济源市 Jiyuan	63	22	38	19
省直管县 County Directly Administrated by Province				
巩义市 Gongyi	53	18	35	
兰考县 Lankao	173		173	
汝州市 Ruzhou	205	87	118	
滑县 Huaxian	124		124	7
长垣市 Changyuan	81		81	
邓州市 Dengzhou	804	26	778	11
永城市 Yongcheng	217	70	147	5
固始县 Gushi	220		220	
鹿邑县 Luyi	413		413	
新蔡县 Xincai	148	15	133	

23-17 各市社会救助情况(2019年)

Statistics on Social Relief by City (2019)

单位：人 (person)

市(县) City(County)	城市居民最低生活保障人数 Number of Urban Residents Receiving Minimum Living Allowance	农村最低生活保障人数 Number of Rural Residents Receiving Minimum Living Allowance	农村特困人员集中供养人数 Number of Rural Residents in Exceptional Poverty with Centralized Livelihood Guaranteed	农村特困人员分散供养人数 Number of Rural Residents in Exceptional Poverty with Decentralized Livelihood Guaranteed
全　省 Total	**440656**	**2725942**	**73373**	**418781**
省辖市 City				
郑州市 Zhengzhou	14414	39873	2511	9331
开封市 Kaifeng	19142	132667	3320	13785
洛阳市 Luoyang	24081	157171	5302	18902
平顶山市 Pingdingshan	31790	121445	3677	23072
安阳市 Anyang	12381	89847	1818	14377
鹤壁市 Hebi	10909	25745	222	4073
新乡市 Xinxiang	17649	132264	1763	15211
焦作市 Jiaozuo	15011	65555	1926	3025
濮阳市 Puyang	8840	128837	1672	16522
许昌市 Xuchang	23173	57433	4528	15354
漯河市 Luohe	3120	41484	2823	10985
三门峡市 Sanmenxia	13477	58001	2176	4767
南阳市 Nanyang	33293	428280	8419	77077
商丘市 Shangqiu	23786	288068	6186	42116
信阳市 Xinyang	81173	325641	5875	54029
周口市 Zhoukou	43459	353197	11862	48736
驻马店市 Zhumadian	54485	280434	8748	46780
济源市 Jiyuan	10473		545	639
省直管县 County Directly Administrated by Province				
巩义市 Gongyi	706	11199	385	1750
兰考县 Lankao	2454	22518	641	2396
汝州市 Ruzhou	3733	37720	639	3409
滑县 Huaxian	1274	37853	711	6253
长垣市 Changyuan	5518	23475	362	3247
邓州市 Dengzhou	1840	46151	356	9503
永城市 Yongcheng	3548	44954	2161	5842
固始县 Gushi	18200	63152	1713	13967
鹿邑县 Luyi	4422	51728	1520	5973
新蔡县 Xincai	11066	42727	510	4569

23–18 各市医疗救助基本情况(2019年)
Basic Statistics on Medical Aid by City (2019)

市(县) City(County)	资助参加基本医疗保险人数(人) Civil Affairs Aid for Medical Insurance (persons)	门诊和住院医疗救助人数(人次) Direct Medical Aid (persons-time)	资助参加基本医疗保险资金数(万元) Civil Affairs Expenses of Medical Insurance (10 000 yuan)	门诊和住院医疗救助资金数(万元) Expenses for Direct Medical Aid (10 000 yuan)
全　省 Total	**4303661**	**2255526**	**34230**	**150924**
省辖市 City				
郑州市 Zhengzhou	62344	36431	445	3856
开封市 Kaifeng	324746	88992	1997	6522
洛阳市 Luoyang	236074	101294	5097	8525
平顶山市 Pingdingshan	281186	87610	1398	4714
安阳市 Anyang	204401	104667	1272	6599
鹤壁市 Hebi	48231	11869	189	1748
新乡市 Xinxiang	129392	42505	1994	3903
焦作市 Jiaozuo	133782	55978	820	4392
濮阳市 Puyang	260940	157706	1119	9519
许昌市 Xuchang	91115	50297	1545	3243
漯河市 Luohe	36983	72075	823	3131
三门峡市 Sanmenxia	163752	62508	949	5831
南阳市 Nanyang	475180	347057	2748	17533
商丘市 Shangqiu	440870	135815	4059	13490
信阳市 Xinyang	566781	383870	2617	20666
周口市 Zhoukou	566108	200437	4045	20322
驻马店市 Zhumadian	260602	302446	2900	15629
济源市 Jiyuan	21174	13969	211	1300
省直管县 County Directly Administrated by Province				
巩义市 Gongyi	11912	9437	294	570
兰考县 Lankao	87002	26155	831	616
汝州市 Ruzhou	39594	30641	208	1184
滑县 Huaxian	38097	43615	379	3089
长垣市 Changyuan	32245	10070	806	771
邓州市 Dengzhou	52769	30222	163	1497
永城市 Yongcheng	51546	37027	723	3219
固始县 Gushi	99343	88817	601	3677
鹿邑县 Luyi	34109	56021	750	1666
新蔡县 Xincai	70251	8640	778	1980

23-19 各市社区服务基本情况(2019年)

Statistics on Community Service Facilities by City (2019)

市 City	社区服务机构和设施(个) Number of Community Service Institutions and Facilities (unit)	年末职工人数(人) Number of Staffs at the End of the Year (person)	#女性 Female	床位数(张) Number of Beds (unit)	年末收养人数(人) Number of Adopted Person at the End of the Year (person)
全省 Total	**39313**	**188567**	**55581**	**116938**	**70882**
郑州市 Zhengzhou	1732	11759	5992	7981	4973
开封市 Kaifeng	2960	11258	2487	1662	930
洛阳市 Luoyang	1265	12130	5369	10294	7707
平顶山市 Pingdingshan	3059	19762	4626	5089	1911
安阳市 Anyang	3464	17592	3637	4548	2710
鹤壁市 Hebi	815	2384	936	6812	2657
新乡市 Xinxiang	1548	7447	3045	4848	3624
焦作市 Jiaozuo	1476	6224	1850	4391	1558
濮阳市 Puyang	1581	8414	2116	1569	714
许昌市 Xuchang	3257	12623	4153	13226	7455
漯河市 Luohe	1769	6215	5136	5226	4135
三门峡市 Sanmenxia	1279	4941	1472	526	402
南阳市 Nanyang	5315	26426	5769	24399	17632
商丘市 Shangqiu	2234	10430	2205	1592	760
信阳市 Xinyang	2848	7566	1071	6065	3148
周口市 Zhoukou	1161	5733	1849	7756	5695
驻马店市 Zhumadian	3068	16058	3277	10862	4825
济源市 Jiyuan	482	1605	591	92	46

23−20 各市婚姻服务基本情况(2019年)

Statistics on Marriages and Divorces by City (2019)

地　区 City	结婚登记(对) Total Number of Registered Marriages (couples)	初　婚(人) First Marriages (persons)	再　婚(人) Re-marriages (persons)	离　婚(对) Divorces (couples)	#民　政 Civil Affairs
全　省 Total	**764451**	**1204458**	**324444**	**353677**	**312724**
省本级 Provincisl Level	1654	2674	634	86	86
郑州市 Zhengzhou	71984	91203	52765	49619	46506
开封市 Kaifeng	34482	55476	13488	17030	15490
洛阳市 Luoyang	48191	76293	20089	23434	21204
平顶山市 Pingdingshan	32650	48255	17045	17159	15080
安阳市 Anyang	39205	61108	17302	18029	15720
鹤壁市 Hebi	10981	18886	3076	4950	4328
新乡市 Xinxiang	38830	57425	20235	21125	18876
焦作市 Jiaozuo	23405	36083	10727	11802	10394
濮阳市 Puyang	26553	42435	10671	11540	9883
许昌市 Xuchang	32683	49252	16114	17132	15354
漯河市 Luohe	16223	24360	8086	8187	7075
三门峡市 Sanmenxia	14361	22033	6689	7240	5921
南阳市 Nanyang	65500	104040	26960	32588	26736
商丘市 Shangqiu	78570	128630	28510	29735	26360
信阳市 Xinyang	56338	95244	17432	23357	20487
周口市 Zhoukou	102059	179322	24796	28927	25405
驻马店市 Zhumadian	66046	104678	27414	29257	25654
济源市 Jiyuan	4736	7061	2411	2480	2165

23–21 残疾人事业基本情况(2019年)

Basic Information of Person with Disabilities (2019)

单位：人 (Person)

项　目	Item	2019
康复	**Rehabilitation**	
总体康复服务情况	**General Rehabilitation**	
得到基本康复服务的残疾人	People Receiving Basic Rehabilitation	480164
#得到辅助器具适配服务	Receiving Adaption and Services with Assistive Devices	182145
服务建档立卡贫困残疾人	Poor Disabled People in File	66717
服务因病致（返）贫残疾人	Poor Disabled People Due to Illness	17575
按残疾类别接受服务情况	**According to the Disability**	
视力残疾人	Visual Disability	43313
听力残疾人	Hearing Disability	27425
言语残疾人	Speech Disability	2195
肢体残疾人	Physical Disability	297482
智力残疾人	Intellectual Disability	37828
精神残疾人	Mental Disability	43393
多重残疾人	Multiple Disability	17409
0–17岁未持证残疾儿童	0-17 year-old Children without Certificate	11119
分年龄接受服务情况	**According to the Age**	
0–6岁残疾儿童	0-6 year-old Disabled Children	19123
7–17岁残疾儿童	7-17 year-old Disabled Children	21222
18–59岁残疾人	18-59 year-old Disabled People	211172
60岁及以上残疾人	60 years old and above	228647
接受康复服务内容情况	**According to the Rehabilitation Service Content**	
康复医疗	Medical Rehabilitation	24132
功能训练	Functional Training	60591
辅助器具	Auxiliary Appliance	182145
支持性服务	Supporting Services	229329
接受康复服务项目情况	**According to the Rehabilitation Service Category**	
视力残疾	Visual Disability	
康复医疗	Medical Rehabilitation	864
功能训练	Functional Training	1975
辅助器具	Auxiliary Appliance	21962
支持性服务	Supporting Services	20886
听力、言语残疾	Hearing, Speech Disability	
康复医疗	Medical Rehabilitation	1092
功能训练	Functional Training	2747
辅助器具	Auxiliary Appliance	16737
支持性服务	Supporting Services	17871
肢体残疾	Physical Disablity	
康复医疗	Medical Rehabilitation	5540
功能训练	Functional Training	41286
辅助器具	Auxiliary Appliance	138349
支持性服务	Supporting Services	136095
智力残疾	Intellectual Disability	
康复医疗	Medical Rehabilitation	1428
功能训练	Functional Training	10477
支持性服务	Supporting Services	29612
其他	Others	3171
精神残疾	Mental Disability	
康复医疗	Medical Rehabilitation	15224
功能训练	Functional Training	4253
支持性服务	Supporting Services	25665
其他	Others	2018
按辅助器具项目情况	**According to the Assistive Devices**	
盲杖及助视器	White Cane and Vison-aids	21962
人工耳蜗及助听器	Cochlear and Hearing-aid	15799
假肢、矫形器、轮椅等主要肢体残疾辅助器具	Prosthesis, Orthosis, Wheelchair and other Main Assistive Devices for Physical Disability	138349
其他各类辅助器具	Other Assistive Devices	6151

23-21 续表 continued

项 目	Item	2019
教育	**Education**	
学前教育阶段	Pre-school Education	
接受残疾人事业专项彩票公益金助学项目资助	Accept Aid from Welfare Lottery Funds for Disabled Persons	1228
高等教育阶段	Higher Education	
高等特殊教育机构录取残疾考生	Disabled Students at Special Higher Education Institutions	346
普通高等院校录取残疾考生	Disabled Students at Regular Higher Education Institutions	928
就业	**Employment**	
残疾人就业人数	Eemployed PWDS	431831
按比例就业	Employed on Percentage	25221
集中就业	Centralized Employment	12389
个体就业	Self-employed	87121
公益性岗位就业	Employment at Public Welfare	3784
辅助性就业	Supporting Employment	15470
从事农业种养加	Engaged in Planting, Breeding and Processing	226475
灵活就业	Fixable Employment	61371
盲人按摩	**Massage by Persons with Visual Disability**	
保健按摩人员培训	Massage Therapists Training	1200
医疗按摩人员培训	Medical Massage Training	750
维权	**Rights Protection**	
执法检查	Law Enforcement Inspection	
人大执法检查或专题调研(次)	Law enforcement inspection of National People's Congress and Special investigation (time)	5
政协视察或专题调研(次)	Inspection of CPPCC and Special investigation (time)	4
法律救助	Legal Aid and Assistance	
残疾人法律救助工作站(个)	Legal aid Workstations for disabled People (unit)	123
残疾人法律救助工作站办理案件(件)	Cases of Legal aid workstations for disabled People (case)	21
无障碍设施建设	Construction of Barrier-free Facilities	
贫困残疾人家庭无障碍改造(户)	Barrier-free Reconstruction for Poor Family with Disabled People (household)	63201
无障碍环境建设检查(次)	Barrier-free Check (time)	46
无障碍培训(人次)	Barrier-free Training (person-time)	646
残疾人信访	Letters and Calls from Disabled Persons	
残疾人来信(件)	Letters from Disabled Persons (case)	510
残疾人来访(人次)	Visit from Disabled Persons (person-time)	1328
残疾人来电(通)	Calls from Disabled Persons (person-time)	1800
网上投诉（件）	Online Complaints	12
残联组织建设	**Organization of the Disabled Persons' Federation**	
残疾人工作者数(人)	Disabled Worker (person)	8071

主要统计指标解释

医疗卫生机构 指从卫生（卫生计生）行政部门取得《医疗机构执业许可证》、《中医诊所备案证》、《计划生育技术服务许可证》，或从民政、工商行政、机构编制管理部门取得法人单位登记证书，为社会提供医疗服务、公共卫生服务或从事医学科研和医学在职培训等工作的单位。医疗卫生机构包括医院、基层医疗卫生机构、专业公共卫生机构、其他医疗卫生机构。

基层医疗卫生机构 包括社区卫生服务中心、社区卫生服务站、街道卫生院、乡镇卫生院、村卫生室、门诊部、诊所（医务室）。

专业公共卫生机构 包括疾病预防控制中心、专科疾病防治机构、妇幼保健机构（含妇幼保健计划生育服务中心）、健康教育机构、急救中心（站）、采供血机构、卫生监督机构、取得《医疗机构执业许可证》或《计划生育技术服务许可证》的计划生育技术服务机构。

其他医疗卫生机构 包括疗养院、临床检验中心、医学科研机构、医学在职教育机构、医学考试中心、农村改水中心、人才交流中心、统计信息中心等卫生事业单位。

医院 指设有固定床位，能收容病人住院并能为病人提供医疗、护理服务的医疗机构。包括综合医院、中医医院、中西医结合医院、民族医院、各类专科医院和护理院，不包括专科疾病防治院、妇幼保健院和疗养院。

卫生技术人员 包括执业医师、执业助理医师、注册护士、药师（士）、检验技师（士）、影像技师（士）、卫生监督员和见习医（药、护、技）师（士）等卫生专业人员。不包括从事管理工作的卫生技术人员（如院长、副院长、党委书记等）。

执业医师 指《医师执业证》"级别"为"执业医师"且实际从事医疗、预防保健工作的人员，不包括实际从事管理工作的执业医师。执业医师类别分为临床、中医、口腔和公共卫生四类。

执业助理医师 指《医师执业证》"级别"为"执业助理医师"且实际从事医疗、预防保健工作的人员，不包括实际从事管理工作的执业医师。执业助理医师类别分为临床、中医、口腔和公共卫生四类。

注册护士 指具有注册护士证书且实际从事护理工作的人员，不包括从事管理工作的护士。

收养性单位（提供食宿的社会福利单位） 指提供食宿的、不以盈利为目的的革命伤残人休养院、复退军人慢性病疗养院、复退军人精神病院、光荣院、社会福利院、儿童福利院、精神病人福利院、老年收养性机构（敬老院、养老院、老年公寓）等收养性的社会福利企业单位的总称。

收养性单位年末在院人数（收养人数） 指收养单位报告期末实际收养的优抚对象、社会"三无"对象和自费人员的总人数。

社会福利企业单位 指以集中安置有一定劳动能力的残疾人就业为目的（残疾职工占生产人员10%以上）、带有社会福利性质的企业总称。社会福利企业分类为：社会福利工厂、假肢厂、其他福利企业。

Explanatory Notes on Main Statistical Indicators

Medical and Health Care Institutions refer to the units which have been qualified the Certification of Health Care Institution, filing certificate of traditional Chinese medicine clinic, certification of family planning technical service by the administration of public health (family planning), or qualified the Certification of Corporate Unit by the civil affairs, administration for industry and commerce, commission office for public sector reform, and engaging in medical health care services, public health services, or medicine research and on-job training, etc., including: hospitals, health care institutions at grass-root level, specialized public health institutions, and other medical and health care institutions.

Health Care Institutions at Grass-root Level include community health service centers, community health service stations, urban health centers, township health centers, village clinics, outpatient departments and clinics (health centers).

Specialized Public Health Institutions include centers for disease control and prevention, specialized disease prevention and treatment institutions, women and children care agencies(including women and children health care family planning service center), health education institutions, first aid centers, blood gathering and supplying institutions, health supervision and inspection agencies, and family planning technical service centers that obtained the Certification of Health Care Institution or certification of family planning technical service centers.

Other Medical and Health Care Institutions include sanatoriums, clinical laboratory centers, medicinal scientific research institutions, on-job training institutions, medical examination centers, rural water improvement centers, talent exchange centers, and statistical information centers, etc.

Hospitals refer to medical institutions with permanent hospital beds, which are able to take in patients and provide them with medical and nursing services. Include general hospital, hospital of traditional Chinese medicine, hospital of combining traditional Chinese and western medicine, national hospital, all kinds of specialized subject hospital and nursing homes, not including specialized subject hospital, maternity and child care centers, and convalescent hospital.

Medical Technical Personnel include Licensed Doctors, Licensed Assistant Doctors, Pharmacists, inspection technician, image technicians, hygiene supervisors and apprentice physicians and other health professionals. Not including engaged in the management of the health technical personnel.

Licensed Doctors refer to the medical workers who have obtained the licenses of qualified doctors and are employed in medical treatment, disease prevention or healthcare institutions, excluding the licensed doctors engaged in management job. The licensed doctors are divided into 4 categories: clinician, Chinese medicine physicians, dentist and public health physicians.

Licensed Assistant Doctors refer to the medical workers who have obtained the licenses of qualified assistant doctors and are employed in medical treatment, disease prevention or healthcare institutions, excluding the licensed assistant doctors engaged in management job. The classification of licensed assistant doctors is clinician, Chinese medicine, dentist and public health.

Registered nurse refers to has registered nurse certificate and actually engaged in nursing work of the staff, not including engaged in the management of the nurse.

Social Welfare Enterprises refers to those welfare-oriented enterprises employing a significant number of handicapped people with certain labour ability (handicapped employees shall exceed 10% of the production staff), including welfare factories, artificial limb plants as well as other welfare enterprises.

文化和体育

Culture and Sports

24

● 资料整理：孔令惠

简要说明

一、主要内容

本篇包括文化、文物机构、档案、广播、电视、新闻出版、文化及相关产业增加值、规模以上企业等方面的活动情况。

二、资料来源

文化机构人员，艺术表演团体，艺术表演场馆，公共图书馆，博物馆，群众艺术馆，文化馆等资料由河南省文化和旅游厅提供；档案资料由省档案局（馆）提供；文物机构资料由省文物局提供；广播、电视资料由省广播电视局提供；新闻出版资料由省新闻出版局提供；体育资料由省体育局提供。由省统计局社会与科技处编辑整理。

Brief Introduction

I. Main Contents

Data in this chapter mainly reflect the situations on culture, relics institutions, archives, broadcasting, television; news and publication.

II. Sources of Data

Data on the number of the staff and workers in cultural situations, art performing groups and performance venues, public libraries, museums, art venues, cultural venues are provided by Henan Provincial Department of culture and tourism; the archives are provided by the Provincial Archives Bureau (Museum); the information of cultural relics institutions is provided by the Provincial Bureau of cultural relics; the radio and television materials are provided by the provincial radio and Television Bureau; the press and publication materials are provided by the provincial press and Publication Bureau; and the sports materials are provided by the provincial sports and Education Bureau. It is edited by the social and science and Technology Department of the Provincial Bureau of statistics.

24-1 文化及相关产业增加值
Value-Added of Cultural and Related Industry

年份	增加值 Value-Added (100 million)	文化制造业 Culture Manufacturing	文化批发和零售业 Wholesaleand Retail of Culture	文化服务业 Services of Culture	构成(%) Composition (%) 文化制造业 Culture Manufacturing	文化批发和零售业 Wholesaleand Retail of Culture	文化服务业 Services of Culture	占GDP比重(%) Percentage to GDP (%)
2004	101.40							1.21
2008	249.70							1.41
2009	293.62							1.53
2010	367.13							1.62
2011	454.37							1.73
2012	670.00	363.30	34.30	271.90	54.2	5.1	40.6	2.31
2013	815.69	435.89	56.61	323.19	53.4	6.9	39.6	2.58
2014	984.66	528.16	117.83	338.67	53.6	12.0	34.4	2.85
2015	1111.87	588.47	128.71	394.70	52.9	11.6	35.5	3.00
2016	1212.80	608.62	157.23	446.95	50.2	13.0	36.9	3.01
2017	1349.23	588.26	167.30	593.66	43.6	12.4	44.0	3.01
2018	2142.51	569.58	298.96	1273.97	26.6	14.0	59.5	4.29

注：2013年以前增加值数据为法人单位口径。

a) The data on value-added before 2013 were on the caliber of establishment.

24－2 文化及相关产业规模以上企业分类主要指标(2018年)

Main Indicators of Culture and Related Industry above Designated Size by Type (2018)

项目	Item	法人单位数(个) Number of Institutional Unit (unit)	从业人员期末人数(人) Number of Employed Persons at yearend (person)	资产总计(万元) Total Assets (10 000 yuan)	营业收入(万元) Business Revenue (10 000 yuan)	利润总额(万元) Total Profits (10 000 yuan)	税金合计(万元) Tax and Expenses (10 000 yuan)	应付职工薪酬(万元) Wages Payable (10 000 yuan)
全省	**Total**	**3026**	**397922**	**31739130**	**22770583**	**2113652**	**688009**	**2633730**
文化核心领域	**Core Area**	**2018**	**267241**	**23768290**	**13817235**	**1423190**	**418631**	**1732266**
新闻信息服务	News and Information Service	67	20964	1726500	968759	27562	23150	213608
内容创作生产	Content Authoring	588	118577	7759899	6147425	695046	154652	688781
创意设计服务	Creative Design Service	531	44227	3718583	3076267	351700	131165	424183
文化传播渠道	Channels of Cultural Transmission	431	39991	2987809	2319630	111869	46847	216730
文化投资运营	Cultural Investment and Operation	11	1794	1023329	107164	5293	3447	10877
文化娱乐休闲服务	Cultural Entertainment and Service	390	41688	6552171	1197990	231720	59371	178087
文化相关领域	**Related Area**	**1008**	**130681**	**7970840**	**8953347**	**690463**	**269378**	**901464**
文化辅助生产和中介服务	Subsidiary Production and Intermediary Services	517	89698	6178293	5746846	470505	183158	656288
文化装备生产	Production of Cultural Equipment	105	12907	566163	790794	67545	16102	73314
文化消费终端生产	Terminal Production of Cultural Consumption	386	28076	1226384	2415708	152413	70118	171861

24－3 文化及相关产业规模以上企业分类主要指标(2019年)

Main Indicators of Culture and Related Industry above Designated Size by Type (2019)

项目	Item	法人单位数(个) Number of Institutional Unit (unit)	从业人员期末人数(人) Number of Employed Persons at yearend (person)	资产总计(万元) Total Assets (10 000 yuan)	营业收入(万元) Business Revenue (10 000 yuan)	利润总额(万元) Total Profits (10 000 yuan)	税金合计(万元) Tax and Expenses (10 000 yuan)	应付职工薪酬(万元) Wages Payable (10 000 yuan)
全省	**Total**	**2866**	**345543**	**30529765**	**23574629**	**2075060**	**624774**	**2320321**
文化核心领域	**Core Area**	1967	238655	23280876	14600959	1403247	411775	**1591897**
新闻信息服务	News and Information Service	64	22193	1401059	1140526	-17048	27487	220911
内容创作生产	Content Authoring	607	104112	8408874	6490514	793276	178291	621127
创意设计服务	Creative Design Service	474	35970	3450843	2931806	278213	110222	352817
文化传播渠道	Channels of Cultural Transmission	442	38076	3117658	2629485	106666	30091	211868
文化投资运营	Cultural Investment and Operation	12	3344	475042	190113	14193	9568	19018
文化娱乐休闲服务	Cultural Entertainment and Service	368	34960	6427400	1218515	227947	56117	166156
文化相关领域	**Related Area**	**899**	**106888**	**7248889**	**8973670**	**671814**	**212999**	**728424**
文化辅助生产和中介服务	Subsidiary Production and Intermediary Services	461	75116	5615536	5956965	487717	151535	566231
文化装备生产	Production of Cultural Equipment	95	9231	572502	676734	53896	13142	51305
文化消费终端生产	Terminal Production of Cultural Consumption	343	22541	1060851	2339972	130201	48322	110888

24-4 文化及相关产业规模以上企业主要经济指标(2018年)

Main Economic Indicators of Culture and Related Industry Enterprises above Designated Size (2018)

单位：亿元 (100 million yuan)

指标	Item	合计 Total	文化制造业 Cultural Manufacturing Industry	文化批零业 Cultural wholesale and Retail Industry	文化服务业 Cultural Service Industry	#内资 Domestic Funded	公有制 Public-owned	非公有制 Non-public owned
企业单位数（个）	Number of Enterprises (unit)	3026	909	650	1467	2996	354	2672
期末从业人员（人）	Employed Persons (person)	397922	198294	36256	163372	386680	78063	319859
资产总计	Total Assets	3173.91	1093.65	216.21	1864.05	3103.30	1166.21	2007.70
固定资产原价	Fixed Assets Price	1233.20	602.22	35.36	595.63	1191.05	329.17	904.03
本年折旧	Depreciation in This Year	92.90	52.00	2.03	38.87	88.57	18.35	74.54
负债合计	Total Liabilities	1551.39	505.99	120.89	924.52	1509.67	643.90	907.49
所有者权益合计	Total Owner's Equity	1622.49	587.66	95.32	939.51	1593.60	522.28	1100.21
营业收入	Business Revenue	2277.06	1190.25	352.49	734.32	2174.72	574.32	1702.73
营业成本	Operating Cost	1787.19	1006.75	292.79	487.65	1701.38	433.74	1353.45
营业税金及附加	Business Tax and Add	22.25	8.93	2.71	10.61	21.78	3.85	18.41
销售费用	Sales Expenses	96.71	25.75	19.70	51.26	94.13	34.71	61.99
管理费用	Management Fee	130.18	35.25	12.62	82.31	127.16	53.67	76.50
财务费用	Financial Expenses	33.69	17.01	2.17	14.51	32.95	7.12	26.57
#利息收入	Income of Interest	5.31	1.60	0.02	3.70	5.30	3.37	1.95
#利息支出	Interest Expense	23.45	12.91	0.77	9.76	22.85	6.13	17.32
投资收益	Income from Investment	10.16	0.19	0.57	9.39	10.12	8.26	1.90
营业利润	Operating Profits	214.70	98.90	18.86	96.95	205.29	49.16	165.54
应付职工薪酬	Value Added Tax Payable	263.37	128.85	16.70	117.82	249.45	82.92	180.45
应交增值税	Total Profits	46.55	21.64	5.82	19.09	45.60	13.59	32.96
利润总额	Wages Payable	211.37	101.30	19.82	90.24	201.62	41.30	170.07

24-5 文化及相关产业规模以上企业主要经济指标(2019年)

Main Economic Indicators of Culture and Related Industry Enterprises above Designated Size (2019)

单位：亿元 (100 million yuan)

指　标	Item	合计 Total	文化制造业 Cultural Manufacturing Industry	文化批零业 Cultural wholesale and Retail Industry	文化服务业 Cultural Service Industry	#内资 Domestic Funded	公有制 Public-owned	非公有制 Non-public owned
企业单位数（个）	Number of Enterprises (unit)	2866	883	607	1376	2839	328	2538
期末从业人员（人）	Employed Persons (person)	345543	175225	31289	139029	335412	71934	273609
资产总计	Total Assets	3052.98	1142.93	220.67	1689.38	2992.95	1076.83	1976.14
固定资产原价	Fixed Assets Price	1159.77	654.18	34.99	470.60	1137.51	296.83	862.95
本年折旧	Depreciation in This Year	81.46	52.64	1.97	26.85	80.23	14.50	66.96
负债合计	Total Liabilities	1458.65	484.33	123.63	850.70	1428.07	590.30	868.36
所有者权益合计	Total Owner's Equity	1591.39	656.17	96.54	838.68	1561.95	486.54	1104.85
营业收入	Business Revenue	2357.46	1248.54	392.81	716.11	2284.06	601.57	1755.89
营业成本	Operating Cost	1887.29	1036.96	339.10	511.23	1823.14	495.18	1392.10
税金及附加	Business Tax and Add	26.27	12.78	2.27	11.23	25.99	4.84	21.44
销售费用	Sales Expenses	90.16	28.02	19.52	42.62	88.48	28.05	62.11
管理费用	Management Fee	105.78	32.11	12.60	61.07	103.78	35.68	70.10
财务费用	Financial Expenses	31.69	15.59	2.00	14.11	31.20	6.41	25.28
#利息收入	Income of Interest	4.44	1.22	0.00	3.21	4.42	2.91	1.53
#利息支出	Interest Expense	23.26	11.47	0.64	11.15	22.92	8.23	15.03
投资收益	Income from Investment	9.67	0.25	0.96	8.47	9.66	8.59	1.09
营业利润	Operating Profits	199.03	112.27	16.52	70.24	194.95	27.69	171.34
应付职工薪酬	Wages Payable	232.03	111.96	15.69	104.38	226.55	75.82	156.22
应交增值税	Value Added Tax Payable	36.21	16.93	3.16	16.11	35.71	10.00	26.21
利润总额	Total Profits	207.51	117.95	16.99	72.57	203.32	30.79	176.72

24-6 各市文化及相关产业规模以上企业主要指标(2018年)

Main Indicators of Enterprises in Culture and Related Industry above Designated Size by City (2018)

市(县)	City(county)	法人单位数(个) Number of Institutional Unit (unit)	从业人员期末人数(人) Number of Employed Persons at year-end (person)	资产总计(亿元) Total Assets (100 million yuan)	营业收入(亿元) Business Revenue (100 million yuan)	利润总额(亿元) Total Profits (100 million yuan)	税金合计(亿元) Tax and Expenses (100 million yuan)	应付职工薪酬(亿元) Wages Payable (100 million yuan)
总计	**Total**	**3026**	**397922**	**3173.91**	**2277.06**	**211.37**	**68.80**	**263.37**
省辖市	**City**							
郑州市	Zhengzhou	505	71245	861.88	470.45	32.52	11.74	65.94
开封市	Kaifeng	242	25275	148.07	183.04	26.16	4.59	22.27
洛阳市	Luoyang	269	33984	427.68	248.96	19.85	7.95	31.53
平顶山市	Pingdingshan	166	22528	300.55	94.76	9.56	1.97	9.34
安阳市	Anyang	37	4658	66.95	25.73	1.04	0.80	2.84
鹤壁市	Hebi	32	2367	15.20	8.12	0.62	0.17	1.22
新乡市	Xinxiang	91	13538	137.71	74.19	2.32	2.01	9.76
焦作市	Jiaozuo	83	12340	105.48	75.89	5.97	2.06	8.62
濮阳市	Puyang	57	4918	50.01	43.04	5.75	1.28	5.05
许昌市	Xuchang	322	62692	340.96	384.99	33.92	11.60	36.63
漯河市	Luohe	73	13350	155.02	121.94	4.18	4.18	8.34
三门峡市	Sanmenxia	62	3086	48.75	21.39	1.38	0.89	1.50
南阳市	Nanyang	278	33406	171.94	129.57	7.70	2.61	18.75
商丘市	Shangqiu	255	32061	76.30	121.26	17.45	7.71	12.30
信阳市	Xinyang	227	22806	88.76	76.49	12.39	2.24	10.96
周口市	Zhoukou	134	18825	82.66	103.70	16.67	3.63	10.44
驻马店市	Zhumadian	165	19122	80.93	87.48	13.37	3.25	7.10
济源市	Jiyuan	28	1721	15.07	6.05	0.53	0.13	0.77
省直管县	**County Directly Administrated by Province**							
巩义市	Gongyi	24	2796	12.71	5.38	0.59	0.24	0.72
兰考县	Lankao	67	5318	22.73	33.59	5.08	1.02	2.72
汝州市	Ruzhou	59	5035	21.00	53.08	6.25	0.17	2.94
滑县	Huaxian	13	1852	25.88	5.99	0.54	0.20	1.08
长垣市	Changyuan	16	541	1.47	2.63	0.18	0.05	0.19
邓州市	Dengzhou	11	1632	6.65	3.80	0.23	0.09	0.59
永城市	Yongcheng	50	5620	26.05	27.74	3.36	2.21	1.90
固始县	Gushi	28	5633	6.05	13.45	1.12	0.19	1.79
鹿邑县	Luyi	38	3788	7.06	10.53	1.61	0.48	1.82
新蔡县	Xincai	42	1117	3.80	7.06	1.94	0.16	0.45

24-7 各市文化及相关产业规模以上企业主要指标(2019年)

Main Indicators of Enterprises in Culture and Related Industry above Designated Size by City (2019)

市(县)	City(county)	法人单位数(个) Number of Institutional Unit (unit)	从业人员期末人数(人) Number of Employed Persons at year-end (person)	资产总计(亿元) Total Assets (100 million yuan)	营业收入(亿元) Business Revenue (100 million yuan)	利润总额(亿元) Total Profits (100 million yuan)	税金合计(亿元) Tax and Expenses (100 million yuan)	应付职工薪酬(亿元) Wages Payable (100 million yuan)
总计	**Total**	**2866**	**345543**	**3052.98**	**2357.46**	**207.51**	**62.48**	**232.03**
省辖市	**City**							
郑州市	Zhengzhou	515	63524	825.47	471.44	25.30	10.37	57.53
开封市	Kaifeng	207	22502	153.90	159.21	19.87	2.92	12.44
洛阳市	Luoyang	268	36142	438.59	302.12	15.54	8.99	36.08
平顶山市	Pingdingshan	133	13595	294.52	93.10	10.50	1.34	8.56
安阳市	Anyang	32	4546	51.56	19.06	0.70	0.39	2.94
鹤壁市	Hebi	31	2784	24.16	13.29	1.01	0.24	1.04
新乡市	Xinxiang	82	10393	69.47	76.02	1.79	1.16	7.75
焦作市	Jiaozuo	62	11685	111.95	72.16	3.51	3.15	10.01
濮阳市	Puyang	45	3355	42.26	37.91	1.70	0.62	3.19
许昌市	Xuchang	317	51102	417.50	419.95	45.98	14.62	28.46
漯河市	Luohe	68	10945	74.38	115.32	7.58	1.14	8.69
三门峡市	Sanmenxia	61	3472	46.00	17.59	1.04	0.26	1.89
南阳市	Nanyang	227	24442	172.34	143.61	10.03	4.36	12.75
商丘市	Shangqiu	238	28756	80.99	156.35	25.10	5.67	13.41
信阳市	Xinyang	209	16593	66.01	61.03	7.95	1.60	6.60
周口市	Zhoukou	205	26243	92.59	124.09	20.29	3.47	13.77
驻马店市	Zhumadian	142	14122	74.20	69.47	9.53	2.10	6.35
济源市	Jiyuan	24	1342	17.08	5.74	0.09	0.09	0.56
省直管县	**County Directly Administrated by Province**							
巩义市	Gongyi	18	2227	12.25	4.91	0.18	0.13	0.91
兰考县	Lankao	68	5647	38.85	38.90	5.23	1.08	3.32
汝州市	Ruzhou	47	5124	19.25	62.17	7.08	0.19	4.74
滑县	Huaxian	13	2181	25.35	7.23	0.66	0.14	1.26
长垣市	Changyuan	11	312	1.39	2.03	0.11	0.02	0.09
邓州市	Dengzhou	11	1388	7.82	4.26	0.49	0.12	0.57
永城市	Yongcheng	46	5855	17.18	64.28	9.23	0.92	2.01
固始县	Gushi	25	3551	4.36	7.68	0.82	0.17	1.11
鹿邑县	Luyi	95	10334	20.36	34.13	6.04	0.70	5.91
新蔡县	Xincai	31	1461	2.68	5.56	1.37	0.16	0.52

24-8 各市文化及相关产业规模以上文化制造业企业主要指标(2018年)

Main Indicators of Cultural Manufacturing Enterprises above Designated Size by City (2018)

市(县)	City(county)	法人单位数(个) Number of Institutional Unit (unit)	从业人员期末人数(人) Number of Employed Persons at year-end (person)	资产总计(亿元) Total Assets (100 million yuan)	营业收入(亿元) Business Revenue (100 million yuan)	利润总额(亿元) Total Profits (100 million yuan)	税金合计(亿元) Tax and Expenses (100 million yuan)	应付职工薪酬(亿元) Wages Payable (100 million yuan)
总计	**Total**	**909**	**198294**	**1093.65**	**1190.25**	**101.30**	**30.58**	**128.85**
省辖市	**City**							
郑州市	Zhengzhou	103	12917	60.56	68.75	11.74	2.61	7.60
开封市	Kaifeng	54	12694	54.86	98.83	8.44	1.93	15.29
洛阳市	Luoyang	63	8655	31.40	57.19	10.24	1.22	4.80
平顶山市	Pingdingshan	47	8639	30.89	55.73	6.17	0.54	4.86
安阳市	Anyang	13	2343	9.33	9.06	0.57	0.37	1.52
鹤壁市	Hebi	10	1547	9.83	4.39	0.27	0.07	0.85
新乡市	Xinxiang	30	8293	51.30	57.17	1.16	1.52	7.47
焦作市	Jiaozuo	42	8748	65.74	64.67	5.19	1.76	6.75
濮阳市	Puyang	31	3257	25.03	24.82	1.28	1.16	3.90
许昌市	Xuchang	170	55342	312.22	340.29	27.07	8.50	33.28
漯河市	Luohe	53	12132	144.83	111.66	3.99	3.87	7.82
三门峡市	Sanmenxia	5	744	7.27	6.16	0.58	0.53	0.53
南阳市	Nanyang	107	23680	122.36	91.56	2.83	1.52	15.42
商丘市	Shangqiu	51	8408	42.71	53.33	4.86	1.52	3.40
信阳市	Xinyang	49	10070	34.39	37.73	3.85	0.58	5.19
周口市	Zhoukou	41	8322	48.24	53.03	6.77	0.73	5.76
驻马店市	Zhumadian	35	12208	41.15	54.73	6.27	2.14	4.32
济源市	Jiyuan	5	295	1.52	1.15	0.02	0.01	0.09
省直管县	**County Directly Administrated by Province**							
巩义市	Gongyi	7	2317	3.91	3.32	0.27	0.10	0.54
兰考县	Lankao	23	3400	18.76	24.82	1.82	0.43	1.98
汝州市	Ruzhou	22	3785	17.61	46.72	5.56	0.07	2.44
滑县	Huaxian	7	1281	3.13	3.37	0.42	0.20	0.79
长垣市	Changyuan							
邓州市	Dengzhou	3	1047	5.67	2.42	0.10	0.07	0.38
永城市	Yongcheng	16	2237	15.38	14.08	2.08	0.58	0.81
固始县	Gushi	10	3849	3.78	9.70	0.71	0.07	1.14
鹿邑县	Luyi	11	2520	3.21	3.81	0.33	0.02	1.23
新蔡县	Xincai	5	415	2.29	2.57	0.47	0.05	0.20

24-9 各市文化及相关产业规模以上文化制造业企业主要指标(2019年)

Main Indicators of Cultural Manufacturing Enterprises above Designated Size by City (2019)

市(县)	City(county)	法人单位数(个) Number of Institutional Unit (unit)	从业人员期末人数(人) Number of Employed Persons at year-end (person)	资产总计(亿元) Total Assets (100 million yuan)	营业收入(亿元) Business Revenue (100 million yuan)	利润总额(亿元) Total Profits (100 million yuan)	税金合计(亿元) Tax and Expenses (100 million yuan)	应付职工薪酬(亿元) Wages Payable (100 million yuan)
总计	**Total**	**883**	**175225**	**1142.93**	**1248.54**	**117.95**	**29.71**	**111.96**
省辖市	**City**							
郑州市	Zhengzhou	78	9047	51.86	48.10	5.07	1.82	6.75
开封市	Kaifeng	70	15786	80.24	108.45	12.98	1.43	9.03
洛阳市	Luoyang	63	8612	41.78	74.19	10.49	3.09	7.05
平顶山市	Pingdingshan	41	8346	29.99	66.48	7.23	0.48	6.14
安阳市	Anyang	12	2463	9.16	10.17	0.60	0.19	1.71
鹤壁市	Hebi	10	1972	16.40	9.48	0.84	0.18	0.68
新乡市	Xinxiang	26	6749	43.50	43.14	0.58	0.93	6.35
焦作市	Jiaozuo	30	9269	78.67	62.97	3.40	2.36	8.63
濮阳市	Puyang	21	1752	22.48	21.34	1.00	0.36	1.56
许昌市	Xuchang	171	45209	387.68	368.57	37.86	11.04	25.15
漯河市	Luohe	55	10246	71.61	112.61	7.50	1.10	8.41
三门峡市	Sanmenxia	6	1587	5.01	3.77	-0.07	0.08	0.80
南阳市	Nanyang	82	15728	128.52	101.29	4.68	2.58	9.47
商丘市	Shangqiu	48	8370	47.90	79.35	10.43	1.34	4.97
信阳市	Xinyang	41	7799	29.84	28.42	2.77	0.55	2.70
周口市	Zhoukou	94	14681	58.58	71.67	10.06	0.89	8.74
驻马店市	Zhumadian	31	7407	38.41	37.45	2.49	1.28	3.78
济源市	Jiyuan	4	202	1.30	1.07	0.03	0.01	0.05
省直管县	**County Directly Administrated by Province**							
巩义市	Gongyi	5	1819	3.51	3.26	0.07	0.08	0.70
兰考县	Lankao	29	4464	35.86	30.24	2.31	0.61	2.75
汝州市	Ruzhou	21	4186	16.23	56.75	6.36	0.07	4.23
滑县	Huaxian	8	1615	3.13	4.31	0.64	0.12	0.96
长垣市	Changyuan							
邓州市	Dengzhou	2	756	6.70	2.63	0.28	0.09	0.34
永城市	Yongcheng	15	2461	8.35	48.77	8.10	0.41	0.90
固始县	Gushi	6	1804	2.06	3.43	0.28	0.06	0.45
鹿邑县	Luyi	64	8982	16.85	27.04	4.58	0.26	5.29
新蔡县	Xincai	4	367	1.37	2.14	0.27	0.03	0.17

24-10 各市文化及相关产业限额以上文化批零业企业主要指标(2018年)

Main Indicators of Cultural wholesale and Retail Enterprises above Designated Size by City (2018)

市(县)	City(county)	法人单位数(个) Number of Institutional Unit (unit)	从业人员期末人数(人) Number of Employed Persons year-end (person)	资产总计(亿元) Total Assets (100 million yuan)	营业收入(亿元) Business Revenue (100 million yuan)	利润总额(亿元) Total Profits (100 million yuan)	税金合计(亿元) Tax and Expenses (100 million yuan)	应付职工薪酬(亿元) Wages Payable (100 million yuan)
总计	**Total**	**650**	**36256**	**216.21**	**352.49**	**19.82**	**8.53**	**16.70**
省辖市	**City**							
郑州市	Zhengzhou	99	4083	96.23	143.06	3.64	0.94	3.51
开封市	Kaifeng	88	4825	18.71	29.91	3.01	0.86	1.80
洛阳市	Luoyang	65	3012	15.31	22.67	2.55	0.30	1.44
平顶山市	Pingdingshan	40	2047	4.81	13.41	0.32	0.68	0.82
安阳市	Anyang	13	829	8.51	12.93	0.78	0.38	0.54
鹤壁市	Hebi	13	505	2.41	2.26	0.04	0.06	0.20
新乡市	Xinxiang	28	1110	5.03	9.28	0.35	0.17	0.55
焦作市	Jiaozuo	21	630	3.48	4.52	0.21	0.06	0.36
濮阳市	Puyang	11	486	3.46	3.84	0.22	0.03	0.30
许昌市	Xuchang	31	1189	7.16	13.40	0.26	0.71	0.57
漯河市	Luohe	11	877	4.24	6.57	0.22	0.14	0.41
三门峡市	Sanmenxia	26	661	2.85	6.97	0.10	0.10	0.30
南阳市	Nanyang	70	3809	11.70	21.30	2.09	0.48	1.39
商丘市	Shangqiu	64	7968	12.63	34.25	3.61	2.74	2.45
信阳市	Xinyang	24	1468	4.49	6.96	0.58	0.15	0.74
周口市	Zhoukou	22	1552	7.12	11.26	1.04	0.32	0.65
驻马店市	Zhumadian	22	1124	7.61	9.34	0.78	0.41	0.62
济源市	Jiyuan	2	81	0.45	0.56	0.02	0.00	0.05
省直管县	**County Directly Administrated by Province**							
巩义市	Gongyi	2	47	0.36	0.40	0.03	0.00	0.06
兰考县	Lankao	14	434	1.40	2.31	0.25	0.08	0.19
汝州市	Ruzhou	7	256	1.11	2.56	0.11	0.02	0.14
滑县	Huaxian	3	91	0.45	0.90	0.05	0.00	0.06
长垣市	Changyuan	10	256	0.97	2.22	0.11	0.04	0.08
邓州市	Dengzhou	3	204	0.77	1.01	0.12	0.01	0.08
永城市	Yongcheng	4	2086	4.65	9.70	0.62	1.28	0.64
固始县	Gushi	2	194	0.24	0.77	0.04	0.01	0.10
鹿邑县	Luyi	6	237	1.25	1.77	0.13	0.09	0.09
新蔡县	Xincai	6	113	0.64	1.50	0.19	0.08	0.04

24-11 各市文化及相关产业限额以上文化批零业企业主要指标(2019年)

Main Indicators of Cultural wholesale and Retail Enterprises above Designated Size by City (2019)

市(县)	City(county)	法人单位数(个) Number of Institutional Unit (unit)	从业人员期末人数(人) Number of Employed Persons year-end (person)	资产总计(亿元) Total Assets (100 million yuan)	营业收入(亿元) Business Revenue (100 million yuan)	利润总额(亿元) Total Profits (100 million yuan)	税金合计(亿元) Tax and Expenses (100 million yuan)	应付职工薪酬(亿元) Wages Payable (100 million yuan)
总计	**Total**	**607**	**31289**	**220.67**	**392.81**	**16.99**	**5.43**	**15.69**
省辖市	**City**							
郑州市	Zhengzhou	136	4385	109.48	183.57	3.33	0.71	3.92
开封市	Kaifeng	53	2447	12.74	20.05	1.13	0.28	1.03
洛阳市	Luoyang	65	2941	18.13	25.87	1.17	0.29	1.40
平顶山市	Pingdingshan	24	1669	4.72	11.44	0.41	0.20	0.74
安阳市	Anyang	12	610	2.30	5.08	0.25	0.12	0.46
鹤壁市	Hebi	11	399	2.41	2.11	0.07	0.02	0.17
新乡市	Xinxiang	27	1069	7.58	26.36	0.35	0.12	0.50
焦作市	Jiaozuo	19	607	3.55	4.35	0.21	0.04	0.33
濮阳市	Puyang	11	578	5.30	5.14	0.29	0.03	0.33
许昌市	Xuchang	28	1004	7.57	11.22	0.42	0.38	0.58
漯河市	Luohe	9	413	1.38	2.17	0.10	0.02	0.18
三门峡市	Sanmenxia	21	415	2.43	3.30	0.07	0.06	0.29
南阳市	Nanyang	62	3793	12.55	27.17	2.87	1.37	1.55
商丘市	Shangqiu	56	7307	12.95	39.83	4.26	1.37	2.29
信阳市	Xinyang	25	1395	4.48	7.39	0.58	0.14	0.72
周口市	Zhoukou	26	1210	5.38	9.65	0.77	0.17	0.62
驻马店市	Zhumadian	20	966	7.28	7.47	0.67	0.12	0.58
济源市	Jiyuan	2	81	0.44	0.62	0.03	0.00	0.02
省直管县	**County Directly Administrated by Province**							
巩义市	Gongyi	1	50	0.36	0.46	0.03	0.00	0.06
兰考县	Lankao	14	387	1.55	2.40	0.30	0.07	0.16
汝州市	Ruzhou	3	131	0.64	1.94	0.07	0.02	0.12
滑县	Huaxian	2	72	0.37	0.94	0.04	0.00	0.06
长垣市	Changyuan	5	164	0.92	1.84	0.10	0.02	0.04
邓州市	Dengzhou	3	201	0.77	1.15	0.09	0.02	0.09
永城市	Yongcheng	4	2218	4.55	11.30	0.34	0.21	0.67
固始县	Gushi	2	182	0.25	0.88	0.04	0.00	0.10
鹿邑县	Luyi	5	161	0.46	1.27	0.14	0.05	0.07
新蔡县	Xincai	6	104	0.62	1.04	0.10	0.03	0.04

24-12 各市文化及相关产业规模以上文化服务业企业主要指标(2018年)

Main Indicators of Culture Service Enterprises above Designated Size by City (2018)

市(县) City(county)	法人单位数(个) Number of Institutional Unit (unit)	从业人员期末人数(人) Number of Employed Persons year-end (person)	资产总计(亿元) Total Assets (100 million yuan)	营业收入(亿元) Business Revenue (100 million yuan)	利润总额(亿元) Total Profits (100 million yuan)	税金合计(亿元) Tax and Expenses (100 million yuan)	应付职工薪酬(亿元) wages Payable (100 million yuan)
总计 Total	**1467**	**163372**	**1864.05**	**734.32**	**90.24**	**29.70**	**117.82**
省辖市 City							
郑州市 Zhengzhou	303	54245	705.09	258.64	17.14	8.19	54.83
开封市 Kaifeng	100	7756	74.50	54.31	14.71	1.81	5.18
洛阳市 Luoyang	141	22317	380.96	169.11	7.06	6.43	25.30
平顶山市 Pingdingshan	79	11842	264.86	25.61	3.07	0.75	3.66
安阳市 Anyang	11	1486	49.11	3.73	-0.31	0.05	0.77
鹤壁市 Hebi	9	315	2.96	1.47	0.30	0.05	0.17
新乡市 Xinxiang	33	4135	81.37	7.74	0.81	0.31	1.74
焦作市 Jiaozuo	20	2962	36.25	6.70	0.57	0.24	1.51
濮阳市 Puyang	15	1175	21.52	14.38	4.25	0.09	0.86
许昌市 Xuchang	121	6161	21.58	31.31	6.59	2.39	2.78
漯河市 Luohe	9	341	5.94	3.71	-0.03	0.18	0.11
三门峡市 Sanmenxia	31	1681	38.64	8.26	0.70	0.25	0.67
南阳市 Nanyang	101	5917	37.88	16.71	2.77	0.60	1.94
商丘市 Shangqiu	140	15685	20.95	33.69	8.98	3.45	6.45
信阳市 Xinyang	154	11268	49.87	31.79	7.96	1.51	5.03
周口市 Zhoukou	71	8951	27.29	39.41	8.86	2.58	4.03
驻马店市 Zhumadian	108	5790	32.17	23.42	6.32	0.70	2.17
济源市 Jiyuan	21	1345	13.10	4.34	0.50	0.11	0.63
省直管县 County Directly Administrated by Province							
巩义市 Gongyi	15	432	8.45	1.66	0.29	0.14	0.13
兰考县 Lankao	30	1484	2.57	6.47	3.01	0.50	0.54
汝州市 Ruzhou	30	994	2.28	3.80	0.58	0.07	0.36
滑县 Huaxian	3	480	22.30	1.72	0.07	0.00	0.23
长垣市 Changyuan	6	285	0.50	0.41	0.07	0.02	0.11
邓州市 Dengzhou	5	381	0.21	0.37	0.01	0.01	0.13
永城市 Yongcheng	30	1297	6.02	3.96	0.66	0.34	0.45
固始县 Gushi	16	1590	2.03	2.98	0.37	0.11	0.55
鹿邑县 Luyi	21	1031	2.61	4.95	1.15	0.36	0.50
新蔡县 Xincai	31	589	0.86	2.99	1.28	0.04	0.21

24-13 各市文化及相关产业规模以上文化服务业企业主要指标(2019年)

Main Indicators of Culture Service Enterprises above Designated Size by City (2019)

市(县) City(county)	法人单位数(个) Number of Institutional Unit (unit)	从业人员期末人数(人) Number of Employed Persons year-end (person)	资产总计(亿元) Total Assets (100 million yuan)	营业收入(亿元) Business Revenue (100 million yuan)	利润总额(亿元) Total Profits (100 million yuan)	税金合计(亿元) Tax and Expenses (100 million yuan)	应付职工薪酬(亿元) wages Payable (100 million yuan)
总计 Total	**1376**	**139029**	**1689.38**	**716.11**	**72.57**	**27.34**	**104.38**
省辖市 City							
郑州市 Zhengzhou	301	50092	664.13	239.77	16.89	7.84	46.86
开封市 Kaifeng	84	4269	60.92	30.70	5.77	1.21	2.39
洛阳市 Luoyang	140	24589	378.68	202.06	3.88	5.61	27.62
平顶山市 Pingdingshan	68	3580	259.81	15.18	2.86	0.66	1.68
安阳市 Anyang	8	1473	40.10	3.81	-0.15	0.08	0.77
鹤壁市 Hebi	10	413	5.36	1.70	0.10	0.04	0.20
新乡市 Xinxiang	29	2575	18.39	6.52	0.86	0.11	0.90
焦作市 Jiaozuo	13	1809	29.72	4.83	-0.10	0.75	1.05
濮阳市 Puyang	13	1025	14.48	11.43	0.40	0.23	1.31
许昌市 Xuchang	118	4889	22.24	40.16	7.70	3.20	2.74
漯河市 Luohe	4	286	1.39	0.54	-0.02	0.01	0.10
三门峡市 Sanmenxia	34	1470	38.56	10.51	1.04	0.12	0.80
南阳市 Nanyang	83	4921	31.28	15.15	2.47	0.41	1.74
商丘市 Shangqiu	134	13079	20.14	37.17	10.41	2.96	6.16
信阳市 Xinyang	143	7399	31.69	25.21	4.59	0.92	3.18
周口市 Zhoukou	85	10352	28.63	42.77	9.46	2.40	4.41
驻马店市 Zhumadian	91	5749	28.51	24.54	6.37	0.71	1.99
济源市 Jiyuan	18	1059	15.34	4.05	0.03	0.08	0.49
省直管县 County Directly Administrated by Province							
巩义市 Gongyi	12	358	8.38	1.18	0.08	0.05	0.16
兰考县 Lankao	25	796	1.44	6.26	2.62	0.39	0.40
汝州市 Ruzhou	23	807	2.38	3.48	0.66	0.10	0.38
滑县 Huaxian	3	494	21.85	1.97	-0.02	0.02	0.24
长垣市 Changyuan	6	148	0.48	0.19	0.01	0.00	0.05
邓州市 Dengzhou	6	431	0.35	0.49	0.13	0.01	0.14
永城市 Yongcheng	27	1176	4.28	4.21	0.78	0.30	0.44
固始县 Gushi	17	1565	2.05	3.37	0.50	0.10	0.56
鹿邑县 Luyi	26	1191	3.05	5.82	1.32	0.39	0.55
新蔡县 Xincai	21	990	0.70	2.38	1.00	0.09	0.31

24-14 文化文物机构和人员情况(2019年)

Number of Institutions and Employed persons in Cultural Industry (2019)

指标名称	Item	机构(个) Number of Institutions (unit)	文化部门 Culture Department	其他部门 Other Department	从业人员(人) Number of Employed Persons (person)	文化部门 Culture Department	其他部门 Other Department
总 计	**Total**	**19215**	**4003**	**15212**	**136701**	**43794**	**92907**
文化合计	**Cultural**	**18574**	**3498**	**15076**	**124324**	**32904**	**91420**
艺术表演团体	Arts Performance Troupes	2221	170	2051	51542	8310	43232
艺术表演场馆	Arts Performance Places	191	135	56	4483	2389	2094
公共图书馆	Public Libraries	164	164		2910	2910	
文化馆	Cultural Centers	205	205		3194	3194	
文化站	Cultural Stations	2458	2458		8031	8031	
艺术展览创作机构	Art Exhibition and Creative Institutions	9	9		100	100	
艺术教育业	Culture and Education	9	9		280	280	
文化科研机构	Art Research Institutions	17	17		175	175	
文化市场经营机构(不含非公有制艺术表演团体)	Institutions of Business of Culture (Excluding non-public Art Performance Troupes)	12968		12968	46014		46014
文化行政主管部门	Admisistrative Department of Culture	172	172		4734	4734	
其他文化机构	Other Cultural Institutions	160	159	1	2861	2781	80
文物合计	**Cultural Relics**	**641**	**505**	**136**	**12377**	**10890**	**1487**
博物馆	Museums	340	209	131	7400	5949	1451
文物保护管理机构	Agencies of Cultural Relics Preservation	126	124	2	2408	2398	10
文物科研机构	Scientific and Research Agencies	15	15		706	706	
文物商店	Cultural Relics Shops	5	2	3	66	40	26
其他文物机构	Other Cultural Relics Agencies	155	155		1797	1797	

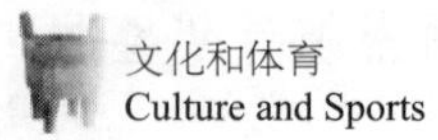

24-15 艺术表演场馆基本情况(2019年)

Basic Statistics of Arts Performance Places (2019)

指标名称	Item	机构数(个) Number of Institutions (unit)	从业人员(人) Number of Employed Persons (person)	座席数(个) Number of Seats (unit)	演(映)出场次(场次) Number of Performances (10 000 shows)	#艺术演出 Art Performance
总　计	**Total**	**191**	**4483**	**137925**	**20700**	**8820**
按登记注册类型分	By Status of Registration					
国　有	State-owned	129	2313	72856	3690	2500
其　他	Others	62	2170	65069	17010	6320
按管理部门分	By Management Department					
文化部门	Culture Department	135	2389	73876	4060	2500
其他部门	Others	56	2094	64049	16640	6320
按机构类型分	By Type					
剧场	Theatres	56	929	33767	2860	2430
影剧院	Music Halls and Cinemas	85	1511	42917	2430	1370
书场、曲艺场	Storytelling, Recitation and Ballad Places	6	110	38790	1220	1560
杂技、马戏场	Acrobatics and Circus Places	1	16	500	330	330
音乐厅	Concert Halls	7	249	540	500	510
综合性	General Performance Theartres	11	487	8913	1080	620
其他艺术表演场馆	Others	25	1181	12498	12280	2000
按隶属关系分	By Jurisdiction of Management					
省、区、市	Province, Autonomous Regions and Municipalities	2	195	3205	980	90
地、市	Prefectures, cities	28	664	6793	900	650
县、市及以下	Counties and Below	161	3624	127927	18820	8080

指标名称	Item	观众人次(万人次) Number of Audiences (10 000 person-times)	#艺术演出 Art Performances	收入合计(万元) Total Income (10 000 yuan)	#财政拨款 Government	#演出收入 Performance Income	支出合计(万元) Total Expenses (1000 yuan)
总　计	**Total**	**721.11**	**347.88**	**82459.60**	**7075.60**	**23746.30**	**61877.80**
按登记注册类型分	By Status of Registration						
国　有	State-owned	220.87	115.05	14488.90	5920.60	1263.10	16654.50
其　他	Others	500.24	232.84	67970.70	1155.00	22483.20	45223.30
按管理部门分	By Management Department						
文化部门	Culture Department	226.37	115.05	15086.30	5955.10	1263.10	17233.90
其他部门	Others	494.74	232.84	67373.30	1120.50	22483.20	44643.90
按机构类型分	By Type						
剧场	Theatres	144.43	107.60	7554.00	2336.00	2422.60	8914.80
影剧院	Music Halls and Cinemas	90.65	45.64	5662.30	1169.90	272.20	6041.00
书场、曲艺场	Storytelling, Recitation and Ballad Places	79.70	43.90	84.80	1.20	37.60	84.00
杂技、马戏场	Acrobatics and Circus Places	9.00	9.00	109.00		109.00	95.00
音乐厅	Concert Halls	4.58	3.64	1000.50		72.40	508.70
综合性	General Performance Theartres	85.40	41.52	9316.00	3147.00	793.30	9436.90
其他艺术表演场馆	Others	307.35	96.59	58733.00	421.50	20039.20	36797.40
按隶属关系分	By Jurisdiction of Management						
省、区、市	Province, Autonomous Regions and Municipalities	56.90	15.00	6379.80	2576.60		8084.70
地、市	Prefectures, cities	44.93	35.05	3935.60	473.50	1044.70	4113.00
县、市及以下	Counties and Below	619.27	297.83	72144.20	4025.50	22701.60	49680.10

24-16 艺术表演团体基本情况(2019年)

Basic Statistics of Arts Performance Troupes (2019)

指标名称	Item	剧团数(个) Number of Performance Troupes (unit)	从业人员(人) Number of Employed Persons (person)	演出场次(万场次) Number of Performances (10000 times)	#国内演出 Domestic performance	#农村 Rural Areas
总　计	**Total**	**2221**	**51542**	**38.98**	**38.95**	**27.08**
按登记注册类型分	**By Registration Status**					
国有	State-owned	168	8159	4.84	4.82	4.18
集体	Collective-owned	1	16	0.03	0.01	0.01
其他	Others	2052	43367	34.12	34.12	22.89
按隶属关系分	**By Jurisdiction of Management**					
省、区、市	Province, Autonomous Regions and Municipalities	6	1146	0.21	0.2	0.13
地、市	Prefectures, cities	26	2134	0.84	0.83	0.52
县、市及以下	Counties and Below	2189	48262	37.93	37.92	26.43
按管理部门分	**By Management Department**					
文化部门	Culture Department	170	8310	4.90	4.88	4.22
其他部门	Other Department	2051	43232	34.07	34.07	22.86
按剧种分	**Grouped by Type of Drama**					
话剧、儿童剧、滑稽剧团	Drama, Children's Play and Comedy Troupes	176	3534	2.89	2.89	1.90
歌舞、音乐类	Song and Dance,Musicals	138	2864	0.97	0.97	1.09
京剧、昆曲类	Beijing Opera and Kunqu Opera	5	200	0.08	0.08	0.04
地方戏曲类	Local Opera	962	28827	18.13	18.13	17.02
杂技、魔术、马戏类	Acrobatics,Magic, Circus	87	2524	6.05	6.03	1.51
曲艺类	Folk Arts	229	4442	3.27	3.27	2.76
综合性艺术表演团体	Comprehensive Art Performing Troupes	624	9151	7.58	7.58	2.76

指标名称	Item	国内演出观众人次(万人次) Number of Audience (10 000 persontimes)	#农村 Rural Areas	收入合计(万元) Total Income (10 000 yuan)	支出合计(万元) Total EXpenses (1000 yuan)	政府采购的公益演出活动 Public performance by government procurement: 演出场次(万场次) Number of Performances (10 000 times)	观众人次(万人次) Number of Audience (10 000 persontimes)
总　计	**Total**	**20174**	**12987**	**357160**	**189749**	**2.49**	**2506.81**
按登记注册类型分	**By Registration Status**						
国有	State-owned	4926	4254	85244	76985	2.44	2430.11
集体	Collective-owned	17	7	18	18	0.00	9.00
其他	Others	15231	8726	271898	112746	0.04	67.70
按隶属关系分	**By Jurisdiction of Management**						
省、区、市	Province, Autonomous Regions and Municipalities	273	205	30816	22586	0.14	220.83
地、市	Prefectures, cities	1068	733	29522	29571	0.48	597.01
县、市及以下	Counties and Below	18832	12049	296823	137592	1.86	1688.97
按管理部门分	**By Management Department**						
文化部门	Culture Department	5025	4319	86946	78694	2.49	2506.81
其他部门	Other Department	15149	8668	270214	111055		
按剧种分	**Grouped by Type of Drama**						
话剧、儿童剧、滑稽剧团	Drama, Children's Play and Comedy Troupes	818	618	12537	14244	0.01	11.52
歌舞、音乐类	Song and Dance,Musicals	340	223	12645	12147	0.10	81.90
京剧、昆曲类	Beijing Opera and Kunqu Opera	14	8	1745	1802	0.01	5.08
地方戏曲类	Local Opera	11965	9714	198810	88147	2.17	2220.83
杂技、魔术、马戏类	Acrobatics,Magic, Circus	3380	248	16710	12038	0.05	38.70
曲艺类	Folk Arts	1076	863	7085	4968	0.03	13.60
综合性艺术表演团体	Comprehensive Art Performing Troupes	2581	1314	107628	56404	0.11	135.18

24-17 娱乐场所基本情况

Basic Statistics on Entertainment

指标名称	Item	2016	2017	2018	2019
机构数(个)	Number of Institutions (unit)	1857	2198	2230	2281
游艺	Carnival	408	439	433	388
歌舞	Musical	1441	1748	1785	1885
其他	Others	8	11	12	8
从业人员(人)	Number of Employed Persons (person)	16651	18653	15458	16640
资产总计(万元)	Total assets (10 000yuan)	254419	239790	230509	235484
营业收入(万元)	Operating Revenue (10 000yuan)	107244	126723	99069	111016
营业成本(万元)	Operating Cost (10 000yuan)	75956	89060	68145	91417
养老、医疗、事业等保险费	Insurance expenses of Pension, Medical and Business	2719	3044	2670	2033
工资总额	Total Wages	31827	39261	35819	38446
税金总额	Total Taxes	3339	6521	3133	3701
营业利润(万元)	Operating Profit (10 000yuan)	31288	37663	30925	19598

24−18 公共图书馆基本情况(2019年)

Basic Statistics on Libraries (2019)

指标名称	Item	总计 Total	#少儿图书馆 Chilren Libraries	#省、区、直辖市(级) Provincial Level	地市级 prefecture-level	县市级 County-level	#县图书馆 county Libraries
机构数(个)	Number of Institutions (unit)	164	9	2	20	142	87
从业人员(人)	Number of Employed Persons (person)	2910	123	202	777	1931	1166
总藏量(万册)	Total Collections (10 000 volumes)	3409.42	191.32	413.63	1245.15	1750.64	850.58
#图书	Books	2855.01	167.39	323.85	1053.91	1477.25	713.36
报刊	Newspapers and periodicals	360.61	17.27	36.03	133.04	191.54	87.94
本年收入(万元)	Income of this Year (10 000yuan)	56249.70	4060.00	6439.30	27679.10	22131.30	10695.80
本年支出(万元)	Expenditures of this Year (10 000yuan)	57976.10	3711.30	7058.70	29383.30	21534.10	10520.00
公共图书馆少儿文献(万册)	Children's Literature in Public Libraries (10 000 volumes)	479.94	134.90	56.16	212.69	211.10	83.59
电子图书(万册)	Electronic Books (10 000 volumes)	2629.28	270.46	332.68	1172.74	1123.86	565.85
本年新购图书(万册)	Number of Books Purchased this Year (10 000 volumes)	375.64	46.98	10.03	199	166.61	88.75
当年购买的报刊种类(万种)	Category of Newspapers and Periodicals Bought this Year (10 000 items)	3.68	0.34	0.25	1.52	1.91	0.84
累计发放有效借书证数(万个)	Number of Effective Library card Totally Distributed (10 000 seats)	209.52	21.94	19.40	93.59	96.54	42.04
总流通人次(万人次)	Number of Circulation (10 000person-times)	4295.2	294.27	211.42	1793.02	2290.76	1013.49
#书刊文献外借人次	Borrowing from Libraries	1531.24	118.91	86.18	443.24	1001.81	496.19
书刊文献外借册次(万册次)	Number of Books and Periodicals Lent (10 000volume-times)	2465.40	298.24	169.52	804.66	1491.22	678.75
为读者服务举办各种活动次数(次)	Activities Provided for Readers (times)	10920	3140	443	5146	5331	2853
参加人数(万人次)	Number of Readers Involved (10 000 person-times)	310.40	61.26	16.08	145.64	148.68	86.68
组织各类讲座次数(次)	Number of Lectures (times)	6750	2485	138	3635	2977	1632
举办展览(个)	Exhibitions Held (unit)	1708	178	129	578	1001	597
举办培训班(个)	Training Courses Held (unit)	2462	477	176	933	1353	624
计算机(台)	Computers (set)	10445	333	265	3055	7125	4226
#电子阅览室终端数(台)	Terminals in Electronic Media Reading Rooms (set)	7190	193	126	1996	5068	3108
阅览室坐席数(万个)	Seats Capacity of Reading Rooms (10 000 seats)	6.3	0.6	0.2	2.3	3.7	2.0
实际使用公共用房建筑面积(万平方米)	Floor Space of Public Buildings (10 000 sq.m)	72.63	2.99	3.89	31.80	36.94	21.61
#书库	Storeroom for Books	16.29	0.46	1.04	7.06	8.19	4.06

24－19 分地区公共图书馆基本情况(2019年)
Basic Statistics on Public Libraries by City (2019)

市(县)	City(County)	机构数 (个) Number of Institutions (unit)	从业人员 (人) Number of Employed Persons (person)	总藏量 (万册) Total Collections (10 000 volumes)	#图书 Books	少儿文献 (万册) Children's Literature (10 000 volumes)
全　　省	**Total**	**164**	**2910**	**3409.42**	**2855.01**	**479.94**
省　本　级	**Provincial Level**	**2**	**202**	**413.63**	**323.85**	**56.16**
省　辖　市	**City**					
郑　州　市	Zhengzhou	15	371	430.58	369.84	64.33
开　封　市	Kaifeng	8	115	134.94	111.59	24.96
洛　阳　市	Luoyang	17	318	465.16	416.11	105.81
平 顶 山 市	Pingdingshan	10	129	195.20	161.40	7.35
安　阳　市	Anyang	7	109	167.11	129.40	36.70
鹤　壁　市	Hebi	6	67	75.78	68.02	14.57
新　乡　市	Xinxiang	11	151	163.69	122.55	12.44
焦　作　市	Jiaozuo	8	75	152.46	135.98	12.01
濮　阳　市	Puyang	7	113	115.12	107.03	22.00
许　昌　市	Xuchang	7	158	142.82	121.83	20.90
漯　河　市	Luohe	5	74	68.74	60.90	6.18
三 门 峡 市	Sanmenxia	7	93	162.17	130.83	13.76
南　阳　市	Nanyang	12	190	207.57	163.29	19.90
商　丘　市	Shangqiu	9	193	106.49	86.20	18.02
信　阳　市	Xinyang	11	213	143.67	122.62	19.86
周　口　市	Zhoukou	11	174	103.09	90.70	16.43
驻 马 店 市	Zhumadian	10	138	92.26	73.38	6.24
济　源　市	Jiyuan	1	27	68.96	59.53	2.33
省 直 管 县	**County Directly Administrated by Province**					
巩　义　市	Gongyi	1	7	24.02	19.30	3.00
兰　考　县	Lankao	1	18	16.80	16.77	5.21
汝　州　市	Ruzhou	1	8	14.36	11.34	
滑　　　县	Huaxian	1	9	8.81	8.45	2.50
长　垣　市	Changyuan	1	5	9.90	9.33	2.49
邓　州　市	Dengzhou	1	21	17.00	14.94	
永　城　市	Yongcheng	1	23	26.42	22.10	11.85
固　始　县	Gushi	1	37	14.07	13.41	4.89
鹿　邑　县	Luyi	1	22	4.90	4.20	0.50
新　蔡　县	Xincai	1	10	8.17	8.10	2.00

24-20 文物业、博物馆和文物管理机构基本情况

Statistics on Cultural Relics, Museums and Agencies of cultural relics Preservation

指标名称	Item	2017	2018	2019
文物业	**Cultural Relics**			
机构(个)	Number of Institutions (unit)	632	632	641
从业人员(人)	Number of Employed Persons (person)	12267	12186	12377
本年收入合计(万元)	Total Revenue this Year (1000yuan)	251727	246360	286290
本年支出合计(万元)	Total Expenditure this Year (1000yuan)	213729	262594	281955
资产总计(万元)	Total Assets (1000yuan)	683303	757028	723775
实际使用房屋建筑面积(万平方米)	Floor Space of Buildings Actually Used (10 000 sq.m)	147.13	149.55	153.40
藏品数（件/套）	Number of Collections (piece/set)	1987274	2065508	2102575
#一级品	Grade One	2620	2712	2888
本年新增藏品数（件/套）	Number of Newly Increased Collections this Year (piece/set)	21651	34654	62035
举办陈列展览(个)	Exhibition & Displays (unit)	1312	1447	1608
参观人次(万人次)	Spectators (10 000 person-times)	6738.26	7222.54	7480.59
博物馆	**Museums**			
机构数(个)	Number of Institutions (unit)	335	335	340
#免费开放馆数	Number of Free Museums	289	290	295
从业人员(人)	Number of Employed Persons (person)	6782	6959	7400
#专业技术人员	Professional Skilled Person	1924	1948	2046
藏品数（件/套）	Number of Collections (pieces)	966764	1019373	1148305
#一级品	Grade One	2064	2155	2318
陈列展览（个）	Exhibition & Displays (unit)	1277	1402	1574
参观人次(万人次)	Spectators (10 000 person-times)	5542.75	6040.11	6429.16
#未成年人	Minors	1647.88	1841.00	2074.90
门票销售总额(万元)	Income from Tickets (1000yuan)	7214	7784	7242
收入合计(万元)	Total Revenue (1000yuan)	83700	91537	106389
支出合计(万元)	Total Expenditure (1000yuan)	95176	116854	113719
资产总计(万元)	Total Assets (1000yuan)	327410	420774	379324
实际使用房屋建筑面积(万平方米)	Floor Space of Buildings Actually Used (10 000 sq.m)	111.35	113.31	121.42
#展览用房	Room for Exhibition	61.37	62.92	66.40
#库房	Storeroom	12.09	11.94	12.69
文物管理机构	**Agencies of Cultural Relics Preservation**			
机构数(个)	Number of Institutions (unit)	125	125	126
从业人员(人)	Number of Employed persons (person)	2831	2583	2408
#专业技术人员	Professional Skilled Person	543	530	482
藏品数(件/套)	Number of Collections (pieces)	217635	211876	106353
#一级品	Grade One	303	303	307
陈列展览（个）	Exhibition & Displays (unit)	27	36	27
参观人次(万人次)	Spectators (10 000 person-times)	1192.63	1181.83	1049.43
门票销售总额(万元)	Income from Tickets	35418	37500	37416
收入合计(万元)	Total Revenue (1000yuan)	46560	51429	49638
支出合计(万元)	Total Expenditure (1000yuan)	38915	44587	44480
资产总计(万元)	Total Assets (1000yuan)	224297	223240	226651
实际使用房屋建筑面积(万平方米)	Floor Space of Buildings Actually Used (10 000 sq.m)	22.20	22.03	18.81
#展览用房	Room for Exhibition	8.49	8.34	7.16
#文物库房	Storeroom For Relics	1.67	1.71	1.65

24-21 国家综合档案馆基本情况(2019年底)

Basic Statistics on the National comprehensive Archives (End of 2019)

分 类	Item	机构数（个）Number of Institutions (unit)	馆藏档案（卷）Number of Archives (volume)	开放档案（卷）Arcives open to Public (volume)
总 计	**Total**	**177**	**16655524**	**4019969**
省 级	Province Level	1	406847	204758
市 级	City Level	18	4762141	1424738
县 级	County Level	158	11486536	2390473

分 类	Item	利用档案（卷次）Utilized Archives (volume-time)	馆藏资料（册）Number of Material Stored (volume)	库房面积（平方米）Areas of Storerooms (sq.m)
总 计	**Total**	**681983**	**3077362**	**406723**
省 级	Province Level	6142	91472	13823
市 级	City Level	189254	588634	124289
县 级	County Level	486587	2397256	268611

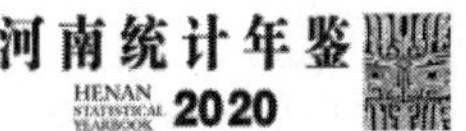

24-22 新闻出版业主要指标

Main Indicators of Press and Publication Industry

指标名称	Item	2017	2018	2019
机构和人员情况	**Agencies and Employed Persons**			
机构数(个)	Agencies (unit)	9892	10680	12002
从业人员(人)	Employed Persons (penson)	124986	125078	118371
出版情况	**Publishing**			
图书出版	Publishing of Books			
图书种数(种)	Sort of Books (sort)	9497	8868	8950
图书总印数(万册)	Total Printed Copies of Books (10 000volumes)	27498	31068	37473
图书总印张(千印张)	Total Printed Sheets of Books (1 000 sheets)	2143038	2381192	2811022
图书定价总金额(万元)	Total Priced Value of Books (10 000 yuan)	326836	361560	429072
期刊出版	Magazine			
期刊种数(种)	Sort of Magazine (sort)	241	241	240
期刊总印数(万册)	Total Printed Copies of Magazine (10 000 volumes)	8517	8351	7752
期刊总印张(千印张)	Total Printed Sheets of Magazine (1 000 sheets)	410058	399511	365962
期刊定价总金额(万元)	Total Priced Value of Magazine (10 000 yuan)	54315	54995	58053
报纸出版	Publishing of Newspaper			
报纸种数(种)	Sort of Newspaper (sort)	120	120	77
报纸总印数(万份)	Total Printed Copies of Newspaper (10 000 volumes)	178615	167782	157481
报纸总印张(千印张)	Total Printed Sheets of Newspaper (1 000 sheets)	4433090	3881373	3217861
报纸定价总金额(万元)	Total Priced Value of Newspaper (10 000 yuan)	220194	226148	229930
音像及电子出版物出版	Audio Products and Electronic Publications			
音像及电子出版物出版种数(种)	Category of Audio Products and Electronic Publications (kind)	200	186	291
音像及电子出版物出版数量(万盒)	Number of Audio Products and Electronic Publications (10 000 cases)	218	307.32	18.27
音像及电子出版物发行数量(万盒)	Total Issuance of Audio and Electronic Publications (10 000 cases)	225	306	16
印刷企业单位数(个)	Number of Enterprises of Printing (unit)	3135	3113	2932
出版物发行情况	**Issuance of Publication**			
出版物购进数量(万册/张/份/盒)	Number of Publication Bought (10 000 volumes/paper/cases)	161334	172638	183589
出版物购进金额(万元)	Total Bought Value (10 000yuan)	1334435	1423339	1538938
出版物销售数量(万册/张/份/盒)	Volume of Saling Printing (10 000 volumes/paper/cases)	161025	170365	184966
出版物销售金额(万元)	Total Sales Amount of Publication (10 000 yuan)	1322491	1409289	1531478
出版物库存数量(万册/张/份/盒)	Storage of Publication (10 000 volumes/paper/cases)	16015	18391	16987
出版物库存金额(万元)	Publication Inventory (10 000 yuan)	211797	229149	238854

24-23 课本出版情况(2019年)

Basic Statistics of Publication of Textbook (2019)

项　　目	Item	种　数(种) Number of Items (number)	新出版(种) New Publication (number)	总印数(万册) Printed Copies (10 000)	总印张(千印张) Printed Sheets (1000)	定价总金额(万元) Total Priced Value (10 000 yuan)
总　　计	**Total**	**1150**	**389**	**19642.47**	**1326296.43**	**145081.50**
#大专及以上课本	Textbooks for Colleges and Universities	781	305	193.09	31333.83	7611.78
中专、技校课本	Textbooks for Secondary Technical Schools	29	17	7.55	922.85	247.81
中学课本	Textbooks for Secondary Schools	98	16	9665.87	761633.63	72993.40
小学课本	Textbooks for Primary Schools	142	22	9740.93	528077.99	62272.51
教学用书	Teaching Materials	42	8	4.22	590.58	744.26

24-24 音像制品及电子出版物情况

Basic Statistics of Audio-video Products and Electronic Publications

指标名称	Item	2017	2018	2019
录像制品出版品种(种)	Number of Publication of video Products	63	35	21
#新出版	Newly Published	63	35	21
录像制品出版数量(万盒、万张)	Volume of Publication of Video Products (10 000 cases)	6.56	3.41	3.03
#新出版	Newly Published	6.56	3.41	3.03
录像制品发行数量(万盒、万张)	Total Issuance of Video Products (10 000 cases)	8.91	2.79	2.11
录音制品出版品种(种)	Number of Publication of Andio Products	4	6	8
#新出版	Newly Published	4	6	8
录音制品出版数量(万盒、万张)	Volume of Publication of Audio Products (10 000 cases)	1.66	1.40	0.95
#新出版	Newly Published	1.66	1.40	0.95
录音制品发行数量(万盒、万张)	Total Issuance of Audio Products (10 000 cases)	1.10	1.40	0.45
电子出版物出版品种(种)	Electronic Publications (kind)	133	145	262
#新出版	Newly Published	133	145	262
电子出版物出版数量(万张)	Number of Electronic Publications (10 000 cases)	210.13	302.51	14.29
#新出版	Newly Published	210.13	302.23	14.29

24−25 各市出版物发行网点数和从业人数(2019年)

Issuing Institutions and Spots of Publication by City (2019)

市（县）	City(County)	发行机构合计（处）Issuing Institutions (unit)	#国有书店及国有发行点 State-owned Book Store and Issuing Spots	集体个体零售 Collective and Private Retail	国有书店及国有发行点从业人数（人）Employed Persons of State-owned Bookstores and Issuing Spots (person)
合计	**Total**	**8611**	**1620**	**6361**	**12542**
省直	**Directly Administated by Province**	**23**	**11**		**1067**
省辖市	**City**				
郑州市	Zhengzhou	2165	214	1439	773
开封市	Kaifeng	309	115	187	749
洛阳市	Luoyang	696	163	481	728
平顶山市	Pingdingshan	366	83	280	665
安阳市	Anyang	480	49	430	468
鹤壁市	Hebi	142	33	109	153
新乡市	Xinxiang	493	94	385	730
焦作市	Jiaozuo	253	27	225	463
濮阳市	Puyang	396	20	374	443
许昌市	Xuchang	207	73	134	513
漯河市	Luohe	194	34	160	258
三门峡市	Sanmenxia	174	34	140	245
南阳市	Nanyang	888	201	682	1372
商丘市	Shangqiu	678	135	535	1106
信阳市	Xinyang	402	91	304	1107
周口市	Zhoukou	289	112	171	924
驻马店市	Zhumadian	392	127	265	712
济源市	Jiyuan	64	4	60	66
省直管县	**County Directly Administrated by Province**				
巩义市	Gongyi	93	52	41	53
兰考县	Lankao	29	10	19	76
汝州市	Ruzhou	43	4	39	100
滑县	Huaxian	47	5	42	62
长垣市	Changyuan	75	6	69	75
邓州市	Dengzhou	25	4	21	161
永城市	Yongcheng	25	11	14	145
固始县	Gushi	36	2	34	207
鹿邑县	Luyi	20	3	17	70
新蔡县	Xincai	30	13	17	43

24-26 广播电视业基本情况
Basic Statistics on Radio and Television Industry

指标名称	Index	2017	2018	2019
广播电台情况	**Broadcasting stations**			
广播电台(座)	Number of broadcasting stations (set)	18	18	18
中、短波转播发射台(座)	Transmission and Relaying Stations of Medium and Short Wave Broadcast (unit)	30	30	30
公共广播节目套数（套）	Number of Public Radio Programs (set)	157	158	159
广播综合人口覆盖率(%)	Population Coverage Rate of Radio Programs (%)	98.62	99.05	99.44
公共广播节目播出时间(时：分)	Annual Broadcasting Hours of Radio Programs (hour:minute)	682541:42	693501:29	696540:56
制作广播节目时间(时：分)	Annual Production Hours of Radio Programs (hour:minute)	314471:33	303968:19	299863:35
被中央台采用新闻类节目(条)	Number of News Programs Adopted by CCTV (item)	4285	3888	3125
电视台情况	**TV stations**			
电视台(座)	Number of TV stations (set)	18	18	18
调频、电视转播发射台(座)	Frequency Modulation, Television Transmission and Relaying Stations (set)	161	161	161
公共电视节目套数(套)	Number of Public Programs (set)	174	174	174
电视综合人口覆盖率(%)	Population Coverage Rate of TV Programs (%)	98.84	99.04	99.47
公共电视节目播出时间(时：分)	Broadcasting Hours of Public TV Programs (hour:minute)	958750:10	958862:40	954844:06
制作电视节目时间(时：分)	Preduction Hours of Public TV Programs (hour:minute)	135879:57	149881:23	137491:44
被中央台采用新闻类节目数(条)	Number of News Programs Adopted by CCTV (item)	2752	2988	2816
有线广播电视覆盖用户数(万户)	Users of Cable Radios and TVs (10 000 households)	1011.59	974.89	903.09
#数字电视覆盖用户数	Digital TV	804.42	811.70	784.90
#付费数字电视实际用户数	Pay TV	59.82	44.71	37.52
有线电视入户率(%)	Popularization Rate of Cable TV	30.7	29.9	27.5

24-27 广播电视业经营情况
Basic Statistics on Radio and Television Operation

单位：万元 (10 000yuan)

指标名称	Index	2017	2018	2019
单位数	Number of Work Units	556	599	614
从业人员(人)	Number of Employed Persons (person)	58391	48966	46761
总收入	Total Income	916350.94	765468.97	838245.96
行政事业单位	Income of Agencies and Institutions	398181.24	447703.09	461510.22
企业单位	Revenue form Principal Business of Enterprises	518169.70	317765.88	376735.74
实际创收收入	Actual Income of Institutions and Enterprises	524697.11	514340.39	544431.49
#广告收入	From Advertisement	202523.56	193467.23	147069.71
#网络收入	From Internet	169288.25	146966.56	143369.22
#新媒体业务收入	From New Media Business Income		30102.97	78712.01
资产总额	Total Assets	2611716.71	2469679.31	2534579.58

24-28 分市广播电视覆盖率

Coverage Rate of Radio and TV

单位：% (%)

市(县)	City(County)	2018 广播覆盖率 Radio Coverage Rate	2018 电视覆盖率 TV Coverage Rate	2019 广播覆盖率 Radio Coverage Rate	2019 电视覆盖率 TV Coverage Rate
合计	**Total**	**99.05**	**99.04**	**99.44**	**99.47**
省辖市	**City**				
郑州市	Zhengzhou	99.59	99.85	99.60	99.85
开封市	Kaifeng	100.00	100.00	100.00	100.00
洛阳市	Luoyang	97.76	98.10	96.79	98.42
平顶山市	Pingdingshan	98.92	97.87	98.95	97.96
安阳市	Anyang	100.00	99.69	100.00	99.70
鹤壁市	Hebi	100.00	100.00	100.00	100.00
新乡市	Xinxiang	99.95	99.80	99.95	99.80
焦作市	Jiaozuo	99.91	99.38	99.92	99.49
濮阳市	Puyang	96.76	97.47	100.00	100.00
许昌市	Xuchang	100.00	100.00	100.00	100.00
漯河市	Luohe	100.00	100.00	100.00	100.00
三门峡市	Sanmenxia	97.61	98.16	100.00	100.00
南阳市	Nanyang	97.99	97.02	98.85	98.56
商丘市	Shangqiu	100.00	100.00	100.00	100.00
信阳市	Xinyang	97.67	99.08	99.68	99.78
周口市	Zhoukou	98.92	99.60	99.33	100.00
驻马店市	Zhumadian	99.63	98.90	99.51	99.01
济源市	Jiyuan	100.00	100.00	100.00	100.00
省直管县	**County Directly Administrated by Province**				
巩义市	Gongyi	97.02	100.00	97.32	100.00
兰考县	Lankao	100.00	100.00	100.00	100.00
汝州市	Ruzhou	100.00	98.80	100.00	99.83
滑县	Huaxian	100.00	100.00	100.00	100.00
长垣市	Changyuan	100.00	100.00	100.00	100.00
邓州市	Dengzhou	100.00	100.00	100.00	100.00
永城市	Yongcheng	100.00	100.00	100.00	100.00
固始县	Gushi	93.50	98.98	100.00	100.00
鹿邑县	Luyi	100.00	100.00	100.00	100.00
新蔡县	Xincai	100.00	100.00	100.00	100.00

24-29 运动员人数
Number of Athletes

单位：人 (person)

人员分类	Category of Personnel	2018	#女 Female	2019	#女 Female
等级运动员人数	**Number of Athletes in Grades**	**2300**	**829**	**2618**	**915**
运动健将	Master of Sports	153	81	72	25
一级运动员	First Grades	799	299	1320	514
二级运动员	Second Grades	1348	449	1226	376

24-30 体育彩票发行情况
Issue of Sports Lottery Ticket

单位：万元 (10 000 yuan)

项　目	Item	2013	2014	2015	2016	2017	2018	2019
体育彩票销售点(个)	Sale Place of Sports Lottery (unit)	7947	8555	9153	9474	10221	10608	11209
体育彩票销售收入	Sale Revenue of Sports Lottery	616824	826226	1020710	1199500	1336539	1828002	1624323
用于兑奖金额	Bonus	363325	495070	658521	761000	847096	1237079	1250417

主要统计指标解释

文化 主要包括新闻出版业、广播电视电影和影像业、文化艺术业等类别。新闻业指新华通讯社、各新闻单位及派驻的记者站、境外驻我国的新闻机构、中心、办事处联络站等的活动；出版业指国家批准的出版社的活动；广播电视电影和影像业指对广播、电视、电影、录音、录像内容的制作、编导、播出、放映等活动；文化艺术业主要包括文艺创作与表演、艺术表演场馆、图书与档案馆、文物及文化保护、博物馆、烈士陵园、纪念馆、文化艺术经纪代理等活动。

体育 主要包括体育组织、体育场馆、以及其他体育活动。

娱乐业 主要包括室内娱乐活动、游乐园、休闲健身娱乐活动、以及其他娱乐活动。

艺术表演团体 指由文化部门主办或实行行业管理（经文化行政部门审批或已申报登记并领取相关许可证），专门从事表演艺术等活动的各类专业艺术表演团体，含民间职业剧团。不包括群众业余文艺表演团队。

艺术表演场馆 指由文化部门主办或实行行业管理（经文化市场行政部门审批或已申报登记并领取相关许可证），有观众席、舞台、灯光设备，公开售票、专供文艺团体演出的文化活动场所。附属于文化部门机构内非独立核算的剧场、排演场，公开营业的也应单独统计。

文化市场经营机构 指经文化市场行政部门审批或已申报登记并领取相关许可证的、从事文化经营和文化服务活动的机构。

公共图书馆 指文化部门主办的面向社会服务的图书馆。

广播节目综合人口覆盖率 是指根据国家广电总局制定的《广播电视人口覆盖率统计技术标准和方法》，在对象区内采用无线、有线、卫星等技术手段能够收听到包括中央、省、地市、县广播节目其中任意一套的人口数与总人口的比。

电视节目综合人口覆盖率 是指根据国家广电总局制定的《广播电视人口覆盖率统计技术标准和方法》，在对象区内采用无线、有线、卫星等技术手段能够收看到包括中央、省、地市、县级电视节目中任意一套的人口数与总人口的比。

有线电视入户率 指能接收到有线广播电视台、有线广播电视站(系统内和系统外)和共享天线系统播放的有线电视节目的家庭户数与总户数的比率。计算公式：

有线电视入户率= 年末有线电视总用户数/年末总户数×100%

等级运动员 是指经考核正式批准授予技术等级的运动员，分为国际级运动健将、运动健将、一级、二级运动员。

Explanatory Notes on Main Statistical Indicators

Culture mainly includes Journalism, radio, television and film and video industry, culture art industry etc. Journalism refers to The Xinhua news agency, the press agencies and their reporter station. In our country overseas news agency, center, office activities; The publishing refers to the activities approved by the state; Radio, television and film and video refers to broadcasting, television, films, sound recording, video content production, broadcast playwright-director, showing activities; Culture and art owner to should include the creation of literature and art and performance, artistic performance venues, books and archives, cultural relics and culture protection, museums, martyr cemetery, memorial, arts and culture, as an agent and other activities.

Sports include sports organizations, sports venues, and other physical activities.

Entertainment include entertainment activities interior, amusement park, the leisure fitness entertainment activities, and other recreational activities.

Arts Performance Troupes refer to the various professional performing arts groups, which sponsored by the cultural sectors or guided by the cultural society (approved by the cultural market administration, or registered and permitted with the relative certificate), including non-governmental troupes, such as drama troupes, dialect troupes, comedy troupes, children troupes, Opera troupes, puppetry troupes, Shadowgraph troupes, etc., comprehensive professional arts performance troupes. The mass amateur arts performance troupes are not included.

Arts Performance Places refer to the various sites for cultural activities, which sponsored by the cultural sectors or guided by the cultural society (approved by the cultural market administration, or registered and permitted with the relative certificate), with the facility of auditorium, stage, and lighting, and selling tickets in public. The theaters and rehearse sites which are affiliated to the cultural sectors without independent financial accounts which are open to the public should be covered independently.

Cultural Market Operating Units refer to the units dealing in culture and cultural services, which registered and permitted with the relative certificate by cultural market administration.

Public library refers to the library service set up by the social cultural departments.

Radio Coverage of Population refers to the percentage of population, which can listen to one of central, provincial, city, prefecture, and county radio programs by wireless, cable, satellite and other technical means, in the surveying area, to national total population, according to Statistical Standard and Method on Television and Radio Coverage of Population established by the State Administration of Broadcasting, Film and Television.

Television Coverage of Population refers to the percentage of population, which can watch one of central, provincial, city, prefecture, and county television programs by wireless, cable, satellite and other technical means, in the surveying area, to national total population, according to Statistical Standard and Method on Television and Radio Coverage of Population established by the State Administration of Broadcasting, Film and Television.

Cable Television Coverage of Household refers to the percentage of households, which can watch television by cable of radio and television network, to national total household.

Class athletes refers to formally approved by the examination on the level of the athletes awarded technology, divided into international sports, master of sports, level 1, level 2 player.

公共管理、社会保障和社会组织

Public Management , Social Security and Social Organizations

25

● 资料整理：赵 霞

简要说明

一、主要内容

本篇包括公检法司、安全生产、工会组织、劳动保障情况等。公检法司的资料主要包括公安机关的刑事案件立案情况和治安案件查处情况，交通、火灾事故情况，省应急管理厅的火灾事故情况，检察机关的办案情况，人民法院审理案件和收结案情况，以及司法部门律师、公证、调解工作等资料。

二、资料来源

公检法司统计资料分别由河南省公安厅、河南省高级人民法院、河南省人民检察院和河南省司法厅提供。劳动争议仲裁由河南省人力资源和社会保障厅提供。工会组织情况由河南省总工会提供。安全生产由河南省应急管理厅提供。参加社会保险人数、社会保险基金收支资料由省人力资源和社会保障厅提供。由省统计局社会与科技处编辑整理。

Brief Introduction

I. Main Contents

Data in this chapter include This article includes the public prosecution law department, safety production, trade union organization, labor security, etc. The information of the public prosecution and law division mainly includes the criminal case filing of public security organs, the investigation and treatment of public security cases, traffic and fire accidents, the fire accidents of provincial emergency management department, the handling of cases by the procuratorial organs, the trial and closing of cases by the people's court, and the lawyers, notarization and mediation of the judicial department.

II. Sources of Data

The statistics of the public prosecution and law department are provided by Henan Provincial Public Security Department, Henan Provincial High People's court, Henan people's Procuratorate and Henan Provincial Judicial Department. Labor dispute arbitration shall be provided by the Department of human resources and social security of Henan Province. The organization of trade unions shall be provided by the Henan Federation of trade unions. The safety production is provided by Henan emergency management department. The number of participants in social insurance and income and expenditure information of social insurance funds shall be provided by the Provincial Department of human resources and social security. Edited and organized by the social and scientific and Technological Department of the Provincial Bureau of statistics.

25-1 公安机关立案的刑事案件情况

Criminal Case of Register in Public Security Organs

案件类别	Category of Cases	立案(起) Number of Cases Registered (case)		构成(%) Composition (%)	
		2018	2019	2018	2019
总 计	**Total**	**414645**	**380261**	**100.0**	**100.0**
杀人	Homicide	471	523	0.1	0.1
伤害	Injury	7158	6458	1.7	1.7
抢劫	Robbery	1193	766	0.3	0.2
强奸	Rape	2387	2724	0.6	0.7
拐卖妇女、儿童	Abducting Women or Children	302	218	0.1	0.1
盗窃	Larceny	249021	196958	60.1	51.8
诈骗	Fraud	84946	97138	20.5	25.5
走私	Smuggling		3		0.0
伪造、变造货币,出售、购买、运输、持有、使用假币	Forging Currency, Selling, Buying, Transporting, Holding and Using Counterfeit Currency	61	74	0.0	0.0
其他	Others	69106	75399	16.7	19.8

25-2 公安机关受理和查处治安案件情况(2019年)

Cases of Offence Against Public Order Handled by Public Security Organs (2019)

案件类别	Category of Cases	受理(起) Number of cases Accepted to be Treated (case)	查处(起) Number of cases Investigated and Treated (case)	每万人口受理案件数(起) Number of Cases Accepted per 10 000 Population (case)
合 计	**Total**	**594482**	**553646**	**61.67**
扰乱单位秩序	Disturbing Business Orders	2866	2744	0.30
扰乱公共场所秩序	Disturbing the Orders in Public Places	1866	1736	0.19
寻衅滋事	Causing Quarrels and Making Troubles	10564	9886	1.10
阻碍执行职务	Obstructing Government Workers in Performing Their Duties	2336	2259	0.24
非法携带枪支、弹药、管制刀具	Violation of Firearms Control Regulations	590	565	0.06
违反危险物质管理规定	Violation of Explosives Control Regulations	7812	7571	0.81
殴打他人	Battering Other Persons	161830	150881	16.79
故意伤害	Willfully Injuring Others	25864	24856	2.68
盗窃	Stealing Property	103244	90979	10.71
敲诈勒索	Extortion and Blackmail	544	505	0.06
抢夺	Robbery and Snatch	151	131	0.02
伪造、变造、倒卖有价票证、凭证	Forge/alter/scalp Valuable Coupons or Certificates	94	89	0.01
违反旅馆业管理	Violating the Hotel Management Regulations	4635	4413	0.48
违反房屋出租管理	Violating the Rent Control Regulations	2097	2039	0.22
诈骗	Swindling, Seizing and Extorting Property	12116	10481	1.26
卖淫、嫖娼	Prostitution or Soliciting Prostitutes	4783	4697	0.50
赌博或赌博提供条件	Gambling	15894	15675	1.65
毒品违法活动	Illegal Drug Related Action	8529	8463	0.88
其他	Others	228667	215676	23.72

25-3　交通事故情况(2019年)

Basic Statistics on Traffic Accidents (2019)

项　目	Item	发生数 (起) Number of Traffic Accidents (case)	死亡人数 (人) Number of Deaths (person)	受伤人数 (人) Number of Injuries (person)	直接财产损失 (万元) Direct Property Losses (10 000 yuan)
总　计	**Total**	**18277**	**2757**	**16180**	**10828.00**
机动车	Vehicles	15286	2504	12496	10154.30
#汽车	Motor Vehicles	12521	2086	10944	9244.75
摩托车	Motorcycles	1687	262	1080	435.55
拖拉机	Tractors	62	21	58	20.71
非机动车	Non-motor-driven Vehicles	2863	202	3603	559.96
#自行车	Bicycles	2073	125	2618	407.09
行人乘车人	Pedestrians and Passengers	128	51	81	113.74
其他	Others				

注：2018年5月公安部在原有统计系统基础上全国推广应用道路交通事故执法办案系统，2019年统计口径作出相应调整，统计范围扩大，与以前年份公布的数据不可比。

a) In May 2018, the Ministry of public security applied the law enforcement and case handling system for road traffic accidents across the country on the basis of the original statistical system. In 2019, the statistical caliber was adjusted accordingly, and the statistical scope was expanded, and the data are not comparable with those of previous years.

25-4　各市火灾事故情况(2019年)

Basic Statistics on Fires by City (2019)

市	City	发　生 (起) Number of Accidents (case)	死　亡 (人) Number of Deaths (person)	受　伤 (人) Number of Injuries (person)	直接经济损失 (万元) Direct economic loss (10 000 yuan)	人口火灾发生率 (1/10万人) The population incidence of fire (1/100000 person)	平均每起事故损失 (元) Average losses per accident (yuan)
合　计	**Total**	**10122**	**21**	**25**	**13854.78**	**10.50**	**13687.79**
郑州市	Zhengzhou	2371	2	5	1435.96	22.90	6056.35
开封市	Kaifeng	424	1	1	534.37	9.27	12603.10
洛阳市	Luoyang	662	4	11	2818.48	9.56	42575.24
平顶山市	Pingdingshan	686			351.00	13.65	5116.56
安阳市	Anyang	417	2		2042.90	8.03	48990.47
鹤壁市	Hebi	105	4	1	126.03	6.44	12002.78
新乡市	Xinxiang	759		1	486.18	13.05	6405.59
焦作市	Jiaozuo	482			283.65	13.40	5884.93
濮阳市	Puyang	713		2	495.19	19.75	6945.20
许昌市	Xuchang	427			471.52	9.57	11042.58
漯河市	Luohe	334		3	1013.02	12.52	30329.79
三门峡市	Sanmenxia	228			388.80	10.02	17052.66
南阳市	Nanyang	708			707.93	7.06	9999.00
商丘市	Shangqiu	265			455.70	3.61	17196.41
信阳市	Xinyang	434	1		530.93	6.71	12233.48
周口市	Zhoukou	531			370.81	6.13	6983.19
驻马店市	Zhumadian	463	6	1	292.50	6.57	6317.57
济源市	Jiyuan	113	1		1049.80	15.40	92902.37

25−5 人民检察院审查逮捕、审查起诉情况(2019年)
Arrests and Prosecution Approved by People's Procuratorate (2019)

案件分类	Category of Cases	批捕、决定逮捕合计 Total of Arrests		决定起诉合计 Total of Public Prosecutions	
		(件) (case)	(人) (person)	(件) (case)	(人) (person)
合　计	**Total**	**46789**	**67531**	**92771**	**128017**
危害公共安全案	Offences Against Public Security	4129	4476	37477	38195
破坏社会主义市场经济秩序案	Offences Against Socialist Market Economic Order	4040	6544	4885	9256
侵犯公民人身、民主权利案	Offences Against Citizens' Personal and Democratic Rights	8568	10160	10664	13659
侵犯财产案	Offences Against Properties	17225	25345	21383	32193
妨害社会管理秩序案	Offences Against Social Management of Order	12549	20684	17606	33728
危害国防利益案	Offences Against National Defense	29	52	19	50
军人违反职责案	Offences on Dereliction of Duty by Servicemen				
贪污贿赂案	Offences on Corruption and Bribery	200	217	625	787
渎职侵权案	Offences on Abuse and Dereliction of Duty	38	44	109	146
其他	Others	11	9	3	3

25−6 人民检察院处理申诉案件情况(2019年)
Appeals Handled by People's Procuratorate (2019)

单位：件　　(case)

案件分类	Category of Cases	受　案 Cases Accepted	立案复查 Cases Registered for-Reinvestigation	结　案 Cases Settled	#改变原决定 Original Decision Changed
合　计	**Total**	**1920**	**223**	**110**	**5**
不服检察机关处理决定	Appeals Against Decision of Procuratorate's Offices	209	70	40	5
不服不批捕	Appeals Against Rejection of Arrest	25	2	3	
不服不起诉	Appeals Against Rejection of Prosecuting	153	62	33	5
不服撤案	Appeals Against Withdrawal of the Case				
不服原免予起诉	Appeals Against Original Exemption of Lawsuit				
其他	Others	31	6	4	
不服法院刑事判决裁定	Appeals Against Judgment of Criminal Case	1711	153	70	
刑罚执行中被害人申诉	Appeals of the Victim at the Punishment	205	24	18	
刑罚执行中被告人申诉	Appeals of the Defendant at the Punishment	383	31	15	
刑罚执行完毕后被害人申诉	Appeals of the Victim after the Punishment	137	12	3	
刑罚执行完毕后被告人申诉	Appeals of the Defendant after the Punishment	884	79	29	
其他	Others	102	7	5	

25-7 人民检察院出庭公诉情况(2019年)
Public Prosecutions Appearing in Court by People's Procuratorate (2019)

单位：件 (case)

案件类别	Category of Cases	适用简易程序 Summary Procedure Applied	出庭公诉 Public Prose-cutions Appearing in Court	一审 First Trial	二审 Second Trial	上诉案 Appeal Cases	抗诉案 Procu-ratoral Appeal Cases	再审 Retrial
合计	**Total**	**39402**	**92346**	**91162**	**1160**	**753**	**407**	**24**
贪污贿赂	Corruption and Bribery	91	726	646	74	51	23	6
渎职侵权	Dereliction of Duty and Infringement of Citizens' Right	12	114	93	21	11	10	
刑事案件	Criminal Cases	39299	91506	90423	1065	691	374	18

25-8 人民检察院办理刑事抗诉案件情况(2019年)
Criminal Appeals Handled by People's Procuratorate (2019)

案件类别	Category of Cases	提出抗诉(件) Presenting Procuratoral Appeal (case)	审判结果 合计(件) Total Result of Judgement (case)	改判 Revising Judgment (件) (case)	改判 Revising Judgment (人) (person)	维持原判(件) Affirming Original Judgment (case)	发回重审(件) Remanding for Retrial (case)
合计	**Total**	**522**	**438**	**227**	**330**	**126**	**85**
二审小计	Sub-total of Second Trial	492	414	208	300	123	83
贪污贿赂案件	Corruption and Bribery Cases	19	21	13	19	7	2
渎职侵权案件	Dereliction of Duty and Infingement of Citizens' Right Cases	10	16	2	1	11	4
刑事案件	Criminal Cases	463	377	193	280	105	77
再审小计	Sub-total of Retrial	30	24	19	30	3	2
贪污贿赂案件	Corruption and Bribery Cases	7	6	5	7	1	
渎职侵权案件	Dereliction of Duty and Infingement of Citizens' Right Cases						
刑事案件	Criminal Cases	23	18	14	23	2	2

25-9 人民检察院办理民事、行政抗诉案件情况(2019年)

Civil and Administrative Appeals Handled by People's Procuratorate (2019)

单位：件 (case)

案件类别	Category of Cases	合计 Total	民事案件 Civil Cases	行政案件 Administrative Cases
受理	Cases Accepted	7211	6292	919
提请抗诉	Submitting Procuratoral Appeal	472	439	33
抗诉	Procuratoral Appeal	305	288	17
提出再审检察建议	Giving Retrial Procuratorate Suggestion	396	392	4
抗诉案件再审	Retrial of Procuratoral Appeal	233	225	8
改判	Revising Judgment	118	114	4
发回重审	Remanding for Retrial	25	24	1
调解	Mediation	8	8	
维持原判	Affirming Original Judgment	59	56	3
其他	Others	23	23	

25-10 人民检察院办理公益诉讼案件情况(2019年)

Information on Public Interest Litigation Cases Handled by the people's procuratorate (2019)

单位：件 (case)

案件类别	Category of Cases	线索 Clue	立案 Register	诉前程序 Pre Litigation Procedure	起诉 Prosecute
合计	**Total**	7304	4584	3265	179
民事公益诉讼	Civil Public Interest Litigation	416	318	167	168
环境资源领域	Environmental Resources Field	276	222	122	124
食品药品领域	Food and Drug Field	102	86	44	41
英烈保护领域	Heroic Protection Field	2	2		
其他领域	Others	36	8	1	3
行政公益诉讼	Administrative Public Interest Litigation	6888	4266	3098	11
环境资源领域	Environmental Resources Field	5357	3036	2151	6
食品药品领域	Food and Drug Field	711	581	457	2
国土出让领域	Territorial Transfer Field	208	141	89	
国有财产保护领域	State-owned Property Field	188	164	126	2
其他领域	Others	424	344	275	1

25-11 人民检察院受理举报、控告和申诉案件情况(2019年)

Case of Reporting, Accusation and Petition Handled by People's Procuratorate (2019)

单位：件 (cases)

案件类别	Category of Cases	受理 Cases Accepted	处理 Cases Handled	#分送检察机关 Handled by General Office of People's Procuratorate	#转其他机关 Transfering to Other Organs
合计	**Total**	**19192**	**18895**	**15779**	**1024**
首次举报	First Report of an Offence	1725	1678	687	627
首次控告	First Accusation	1200	1178	860	172
首次申诉	First Petition	16267	16039	14232	225

25-12 人民检察院纠正违法情况

Law-breaking Cases Rectified by People's Procuratorate

项目	Item	2017	2018	2019
书面提出纠正	Written Rectification			
件次合计（件次）	Total of Written Rectification (Case-times)	2757	2113	2419
立案监督小计	Sub-total of Supervision of Cases Filing	2517	1754	1946
监督立案	Supervision of Cases Filing	1418	1052	840
监督撤案	Supervision of Cases Withdrawed	1099	702	1106
侦查监督小计	Sub-total of Supervision of Investigation	166	278	394
审查批捕环节	Supervision of Investigation in the Process of Arrests Approved	107	112	97
审查起诉环节	Supervision of Investigation in the Process of Prosecution	59	166	297
刑事审判监督	Supervision of Criminal Trial	74	81	79
刑罚执行监督人次小计(人次)	Sub-total of Supervision of Punishment Execution (person-times)	10859	6072	3209
监管活动	Administration of Prison and Custody	5940	2330	1098
超期羁押	Excessive Custody	581	326	224
减刑、假释、暂予监外执行	Commutation of Sentence, Parole and Released,Temporary execution outside prison	4338	3416	1887
已纠正件次合计（件次）	Rectified Total of Rectified (Case-times)	2214	1573	1583
立案监督小计	Sub-total of Supervision of Cases Filing	2056	1348	1341
监督立案	Supervision of Cases Filing	1168	812	611
监督撤案	Supervision of Cases Withdrawed	888	536	730
侦查监督小计	Sub-total of Supervision of Investigation	89	163	208
审查批捕环节	Supervision of Investigation in the Processof Arrests Approved	72	72	65
审查起诉环节	Supervision of Investigation in the Processof Prosecution	17	91	143
刑事审判监督	Supervision of Criminal Trial	69	62	34
刑罚执行监督人次小计(人次)	Sub-total of Supervision of Punishment Execution (person-times)	10605	5718	2548
监管活动	Administration of Prison and Custody	5843	2306	1059
超期羁押	Excessive Custody	545	279	221
减刑、假释、暂予监外执行	Commutation of Sentence, Parole and Released,Temporary execution outside prison	4217	3133	1268

25-13 人民检察院检察官基本情况

Basic Statistics on Procurator

单位：人 (person)

指　标	Item	2017	2018	2019
检察长人数	Number of Chief Procurators	184	174	179
#女性	Female	24	23	22
副检察长人数	Number of Deputy Chief Procurators	709	546	537
#女性	Female	76	71	70
检察官人数	Number of Procurators	3991	3874	4091
#女性	Female	1186	1181	1348
司法辅助人员数	ancillary judicial personel	4736	4578	3879
#女性	Female	1521	1581	1486

25-14 人民法院审理刑事一审案件收结案情况

Basic Statistics on Criminal Case at First Trial by People's Court

单位：件 (case)

项　目	Item	2018		2019	
		收案 Cases Accepted	结案 Cases Settled	收案 Cases Accepted	结案 Cases Settled
合　计	**Total**	**92472**	**91981**	**97052**	**96128**
危害公共安全罪	Offences Against Public Security	35592	35468	38075	37982
破坏社会主义经济秩序罪	Offences Against Socialist Economic Order	4642	4699	5195	5032
侵犯公民人身权利、民主权利罪	Offences Against Citizens' Personal and Democratic Rights	10969	10862	11121	10949
侵犯财产罪	Offences Against Properties	20507	20232	22005	21522
妨害社会管理秩序罪	Offences Against Social Management of Order	19636	19349	19729	19671
危害国防利益罪	Offences Against National Defense	28	30	34	31
贪污贿赂罪	Offences on Corruption and Bribery	890	1051	729	752
渎职罪	Offences on Dereliction of Duty	205	287	158	185
其他	Others	3	3	6	4

25-15 各市人民法院审理刑事案件罪犯情况(2019年)

Criminal Offenders Heard by Courts by City (2019)

市（县） City(County)	刑事罪犯总数（人） Number of Offenders (person)	#青少年犯罪 Young Offenders	不满18岁 Less Than 18 Years	18-25岁 Between 18 and 25 Years	青少年罪犯占刑事罪犯比重(%) Proportion of Young Offenders in the Total (%)
全省 Total	**118134**	**19328**	**3464**	**15864**	16.4
省辖市 City					
郑州市 Zhengzhou	16159	2951	449	2502	18.3
开封市 Kaifeng	4909	940	197	743	19.1
洛阳市 Luoyang	6727	1207	246	961	17.9
平顶山市 Pingdingshan	5471	858	125	733	15.7
安阳市 Anyang	6625	1082	223	859	16.3
鹤壁市 Hebi	1953	430	85	345	22.0
新乡市 Xinxiang	7037	1063	153	910	15.1
焦作市 Jiaozuo	6193	1186	194	992	19.2
濮阳市 Puyang	4929	788	110	678	16.0
许昌市 Xuchang	5101	823	120	703	16.1
漯河市 Luohe	2440	302	48	254	12.4
三门峡市 Sanmenxia	3586	581	66	515	16.2
南阳市 Nanyang	14197	1669	335	1334	11.8
商丘市 Shangqiu	8693	1496	208	1288	17.2
信阳市 Xinyang	5936	942	201	741	15.9
周口市 Zhoukou	8876	1402	236	1166	15.8
驻马店市 Zhumadian	8276	1456	434	1022	17.6
济源市 Jiyuan	1026	152	34	118	14.8
省直管县 County Directly Administrated by Province					
巩义市 Gongyi	1257	138	13	125	11.0
兰考县 Lankao	630	117	30	87	18.6
汝州市 Ruzhou	902	117	23	94	13.0
滑县 Huaxian	965	181	35	146	18.8
长垣市 Changyuan	481	80	11	69	16.6
邓州市 Dengzhou	1454	132	27	105	9.1
永城市 Yongcheng	1186	185	43	142	15.6
固始县 Gushi	892	138	42	96	15.5
鹿邑县 Luyi	174	96	29	67	55.2
新蔡县 Xincai	1022	163	63	100	15.9

25-16 人民法院审理婚姻家庭、继承一审案件收结案情况(2019年)

First Trial Civil Cases of Marriage, Family Affairs and Inheritance Accepted and Settled by Courts (2019)

单位：件 (case)

项 目	Item	收案 Cases Accepted	结案 Cases Settled	调解 Mediate	判决 Judgment	不予受理 Dismiss	驳回起诉 Reject	撤诉 With-drawal	其他 Other
合　计	**Total**	**143492**	**140638**	**43323**	**58186**	**47**	**2969**	**35478**	**635**
婚姻家庭纠纷	Marriage and Family Affairs Disputes	136619	133873	39387	56643	41	2700	34493	609
离婚纠纷	Divorce Disputes	109602	107636	30962	46527	20	1882	27859	386
抚养纠纷	Foster Disputes	8479	8253	2960	2886	6	268	2071	62
扶养纠纷	Upbringing Disputes	325	310	79	116		17	94	4
赡养纠纷	Support Disputes	2726	2665	653	1032		55	888	37
收养关系纠纷	Adoption Disputes	153	152	36	64		9	40	3
监护权纠纷	Custody Disputes	63	63	12	18		5	27	1
探望权纠纷	Visting Right Disputes	470	466	171	185	1	5	101	3
其他	Others	14801	14328	4514	5815	14	459	3413	113
继承纠纷	Inheritance Disputes	6758	6657	3884	1511	6	268	962	26
法定继承纠纷	Legal Inheritance Disputes	6122	6050	3784	1206	4	241	793	22
遗嘱继承纠纷	Testament Inheritance Disputes	138	133	35	50	1	7	40	
其他	Others	498	474	65	255	1	20	129	4
其他	Others	115	108	52	32		1	23	

25-17 人民法院审理合同纠纷一审案件收结案情况(2019年)

First Trial Cases of Contract Disputes Accepted and Settled by Courts (2019)

单位：件 (case)

项 目	Item	收案 Cases Accepted	结案 Cases Settled	判决 Judgment	不予受理 Dismiss	驳回起诉 Reject	撤诉 With-drawal	调解 Mediate	其他 Other
合　计	**Total**	**642977**	**629090**	**289597**	**822**	**36362**	**145451**	**151841**	**5017**
借款合同	Loan Contracts	293329	289147	141484	203	18181	54812	73465	1002
买卖合同	Trade Contracts	84290	81449	33337	150	4483	20884	22015	580
电信合同	Telecom Contracts	310	291	185		3	87	16	
租赁合同	Lease Contracts	25262	24774	11233	52	1360	6434	5573	122
劳动争议	Work Disputes	27547	26577	11354	23	1230	6080	7691	199
房地产合同	Real Estate Contracts	178	179	102		16	39	19	3
供用动力合同	Power Supply Contracts	453	394	138		24	115	117	
建设工程合同	Construction Contracts	22632	20958	9488	60	1568	5156	4372	314
农村承包合同	Rural Contracts	1859	1828	789	6	200	562	257	14
承揽合同	Contracts for Work	6453	6116	2520	24	261	1453	1805	53
其他	Others	180664	177377	78967	304	9036	49829	36511	2730

25-18 人民法院审理民事一审案件收结案情况(2019年)

First Trial Civil Affairs Cases Accepted and Settled by Courts (2019)

单位：件 (case)

项 目	Item	收案 Cases Accepted	结案 Cases Settled	判决 Judgment	不予受理 Dismiss
合 计	**Total**	**1010278**	**987517**	**458518**	**1221**
人格权纠纷	Disputes of Personal Rights	15467	14829	7832	16
婚姻家庭、继承纠纷	Disputes of Marriage, Family Affairs and Inheritance	143492	140638	58186	47
物权纠纷	Disputes of Ownership and Related Rights	22057	20937	9099	113
合同、无因管理、不当得利纠纷	Disputes of Contract, No Cause Management, Improper Profit	652088	637724	293032	852
知识产权与竞争纠纷	Disputes of Intellectual Property Rights	9754	10736	2631	2
劳动争议、人事争议	Disputes of Labor and Personnel	27880	27261	12876	70
海事海商纠纷	Disputes of Maritime	5	5	2	
与公司、证券、保险、票据等有关的民事纠纷	Disputes of Bill, Securities and Stocks	30064	28715	15091	33
侵权责任纠纷	Disputes of Infringement of Right	102203	99664	55015	62
其他	Others	7268	7008	4754	26

项 目	Item	驳回起诉 Reject	撤诉 With-drawal	调解 Mediate	其他 Other
合 计	**Total**	**49184**	**224960**	**246242**	**7392**
人格权纠纷	Disputes of Personal Rights	450	3316	3168	47
婚姻家庭、继承纠纷	Disputes of Marriage, Family Affairs and Inheritance	2969	35478	43323	635
物权纠纷	Disputes of Ownership and Related Rights	2403	6561	2611	150
合同、无因管理、不当得利纠纷	Disputes of Contract, No Cause Management, Improper Profit	37276	148038	153376	5150
知识产权与竞争纠纷	Disputes of Intellectual Property Rights	76	4485	3488	54
劳动争议、人事争议	Disputes of Labor and Personnel	2189	4879	6572	675
海事海商纠纷	Disputes of Maritime		1	1	1
与公司、证券、保险、票据等有关的民事纠纷	Disputes of Bill, Securities and Stocks	1002	5290	6910	389
侵权责任纠纷	Disputes of Infringement of Right	2201	15451	26749	186
其他	Others	618	1461	44	105

25－19　人民法院审理行政一审案件收结案情况(2019年)
First Trial Administrative Cases Accepted and Settled by Courts (2019)

单位：件 (case)

项　目	Item	收案 Cases Accepted	结案 Cases Settled	判决 Judgment	不予立案 Dismiss	驳回起诉 Reject	撤诉 With-drawal	调解 Mediate	其他 Other
合　计	**Total**	**20467**	**19475**	**9288**	**374**	**4364**	**4728**	**29**	**692**
公安	Public Security	1734	1637	718	33	180	644		62
资源	Natural Resources	1879	1822	807	34	544	323	2	112
城乡建设	Urban and Rural Construction	2700	2769	1467	43	598	581	7	73
计划生育	Family Planning	3	6	2		1	3		
工商	Industry and Commerce	498	476	248	7	61	147		13
商标	Trademark								
质量监督检验检疫	Quality Supervision, Inspection and Quarantine	18	17	7		2	5		3
卫生	Health	36	37	10	2	16	8	1	
食品药品安全	Food and Drug Safety	276	275	67	5	81	117		5
农业	Agriculture	27	28	6	3	8	9		2
物价	Prices	3	3	1		1	1		
环境保护	Environment Protection	72	70	39		5	19	1	6
交通运输	Traffic and Transport	75	74	20		20	32		2
信息电讯	Information Telecommunication	3	4	1		2	1		
邮政	Postal Service	4	2	1		1			
专利	Patent	3	4	1			3		
新闻出版	Press and Publications								
税务	Taxes	24	24	8	2	7	7		
金融	Finance	4	8	5		1			2
外汇	Foreign Exchange								
海关	Customs								
财政	Government Finance	31	24	5	5	2	12		
劳动和社会保障	Labour and Social Security	535	540	349	6	58	114	1	12
审计	Audit	3	5	3	1	1			
经贸	Economy and Trade								
水利	Water Conservancy	52	52	40		8	3		1
旅游	Tourism	1	1	1					
烟草专卖	Tobacco Monopoly	3	3	1			2		
司法	Justice	29	26	11	2	7	5		1
民政	Civil Administration	154	153	70	4	30	43		6
教育	Education	29	29	8	10	8	3		
文化	Culture								
广播电视电影	Broadcasting, Television and Film								
统计	Statistics	1	1				1		
电力	Electric Power	7	7	4		2	1		
国有资产	State Assets	21	26	8		9	8		1
外资	Foreign Capital								
盐业	Salt Industry	37	40	12		2	22		4
体育	Sports	2	2				2		
行政监察	Administrative Supervision	5	5	2	1	1	1		
乡政府	Townships Government	547	525	277	13	114	76	2	43
其他	Others	11651	10780	5089	203	2594	2535	15	344

25－20　全省法官及建立少年法庭情况
Statistics on Judges and Juvenile Courts

指　标	Item	2017	2018	2019
法官及陪审员情况(人)	Juudges and juror (person)			
法院员额法官人数	Specified Number of Judges in court	6790	7592	7304
#女法官	Female	1896	2261	2245
高级法院员额法官人数	Specified Number of Judges in Superior Court	186	222	210
#女法官	Female	52	91	70
人民陪审员人数	Number of juror	32215	33511	23984
#女陪审员	Female	9718	10325	7390
建立少年法庭数(个)	Number of Juvenile Courts (unit)	97	99	99

25-21 律师、公证和调解工作基本情况

Basic Statistics on Lawyers, Notarization and Mediation

项　目	Item	2015	2016	2017	2018	2019
律师工作	Lawyers					
律师事务所（个）	Number of Law Offices (unit)	1124	1174	1222	1334	1436
律师人数（人）	Number of Lawyers (person)	14775	16396	18681	21760	23964
#女性	Female	3852	4597	4733	6843	7673
#专职律师	Full-time Lawyers	14233	15459	16846	20361	21476
#女性	Female	3508	4334	4701	6579	6886
兼职律师	Part-time Lawyers	558	601	658	703	716
#中共党员	Member of Communist Party of China	3815	4779	4816	6008	6524
律师人员学历构成（人）	Education Composition of Lawer (person)					
#博士	Doctor's Degree	123	150	188	158	172
硕士、双学士	Master's Degree, Double Bachelor's Degree	1442	2975	2173	2881	3384
法律专业本科	Bachelor Degree in Law	11938	11607	11949	16066	15826
其他专业本科	Bachelor Degree In Other Specialities	1234	1664	2398	2655	1958
担任法律顾问（家）	Number of Units with Permanent Legal Advisors (unit)	20577	20989	23043	26787	28070
民事案件代理（件）	Agent of Civil Cases (case)	112421	133805	193667	247359	249694
刑事案件辩护及代理（件）	Agent and Defender of Criminal Cases (case)	23389	24936	51417	63722	65186
行政案件代理（件）	Agent of Administrative Action (case)	5777	7415	9232	11128	10848
非诉讼法律事务（件）	Agent of Non-Litigious Legal Affairs (case)	33757	33753	66741	49443	35221
咨询和代书（件）	Advisory Services and Legal Documents Written on Behalf of Clients (case)	389347	385969	377519	521297	444264
公证工作	Notarization					
公证处（个）	Number of Notary Offices (unit)	178	178	161	164	164
#涉外公证处	Foreign-related Notary offices	36	37	36	37	38
公证人员（人）	Notarial Personnel (person)	1221	1265	1210	1336	1758
#公证员	Notaries	713	684	675	711	679
公证员助理	Assistant Notaries	508	581	535	625	655
办理公证文书（万件）	Number of Notarized Documents (10 000 cases)	49.5	48.7	47.0	48.7	57.2
人民调解工作	Number of People's Mediation					
人民调解委员会（万个）	Number of People's Mediation Committees (10 000 units)	5.57	5.58	5.52	5.49	5.41
人民调解员（万人）	Number of Mediators (10 000 persons)	20.68	20.78	21.51	14.90	15.54
调解民间纠纷（万件）	Number of Civil Disputes Mediated (10 000 cases)	101.80	100.71	101.75	80.79	81.82

25-22 法律援助工作情况

Statistics on legal aid

项　目	Item	2015	2016	2017	2018	2019
法律援助机构（个）	Number of Institutions (unit)	211	213	234	207	252
工作人员（人）	Staffs(person)	1023	1061	998	1054	955
#法律专业	Major in Law	838	846	755	757	665
受理案件　（件）	Aid Case Received (case)	88402	97390	105648	112041	141509
民事法律援助	Civil	67342	72572	70681	55280	44797
刑事法律援助	Criminal	20350	24027	34187	56179	96316
行政法律援助	Administrative	710	791	780	582	396
咨询（人次）	Consultation Persons (person-time)	688791	719332	785623	795174	803267

注：根据值班律师法律帮助工作的开展及司法部统计口径的变更，2019年起值班律师法律帮助案件纳入刑事法律援助案件中。
a) According to the development of legal aid work for duty lawyers and the change of statistical caliber of the Ministry of justice, legal aid cases of lawyers on duty will be included in criminal legal aid cases since 2019.

25-23 法律服务基本情况(2019年)

Basic Statistics on Legal Services (2019)

地　区 Region	律师人数(人) Number of Lawer (person)	#女性 Female	专职律师人数(人) Number of full-time lawyer (person)	#女性 Female	公证员(人) Notary personnel (person)	#女性 Female	获得法律援助的受援人数(人) Number of Persons Received legal aid (person)
全　省 Total	**23964**	**7673**	**21476**	**6886**	**679**	**359**	**146428**
省辖市 City							
郑州市 Zhengzhou	11591	4280	10143	3828	120	77	28857
开封市 Kaifeng	560	139	510	111	29	15	7427
洛阳市 Luoyang	1667	527	1564	507	53	32	9077
平顶山市 Pingdingshan	738	169	677	157	31	17	6677
安阳市 Anyang	1163	335	1047	302	39	20	8488
鹤壁市 Hebi	157	40	135	34	13	6	2452
新乡市 Xinxiang	1070	387	1008	321	39	17	8399
焦作市 Jiaozuo	572	160	515	151	43	24	6692
濮阳市 Puyang	552	155	494	149	33	16	6853
许昌市 Xuchang	587	162	503	149	22	10	6188
漯河市 Luohe	321	100	315	89	20	13	4224
三门峡市 Sanmenxia	417	105	365	97	23	15	2897
南阳市 Nanyang	1280	280	1174	247	64	32	11110
商丘市 Shangqiu	931	234	860	223	39	18	9818
信阳市 Xinyang	746	156	687	152	38	17	7276
周口市 Zhoukou	846	230	766	195	38	13	8726
驻马店市 Zhumadian	621	164	570	126	31	15	9399
济源市 Jiyuan	145	50	143	48	4	2	1308
省直管县 County Directly Administrated by Province							
巩义市 Gongyi	68	26	58	21	4	2	1605
兰考县 Lankao	95	24	89	22	3	2	1072
汝州市 Ruzhou	108	16	84	14	5	3	1124
滑县 Huaxian	198	51	186	46	3	1	1753
长垣市 Changyuan	49	18	41	18	3		1916
邓州市 Dengzhou	50	4	50	4	4	3	1313
永城市 Yongcheng	97	19	89	19	9	2	1053
固始县 Gushi	95	10	87	10	5	2	1209
鹿邑县 Luyi	65	16	63	15	4		831
新蔡县 Xincai	32	12	30	12	2		531

注：全省获得法律援助的受援人数包含省本级560人。

a) The total number of persons received legal includes 560 people at the provincial level.

25−24 劳动人事仲裁委员会受理及处理案件情况(2019年)

单位：件

项　目	Item	合　计 Total
上期未结争议案件数	**Number of Cases Left Over from Last Period**	**621**
当期立案受理情况	**Cases Accepted**	
立案受理案件总数	Number of Cases	26629
#十人以上劳动(人事)争议	Number of Collective Labour Disputes	186
#劳动者申请	Number of Cases Appealed by Laborers	23473
立案受理案件涉及劳动者人数(人)	Number of Persons Involoved in Collective Disputes (person)	31556
#十人以上劳动(人事)争议	Number of Collective Labor Disputes	3766
按争议类型分	Grouped by Dispute type	
劳动报酬	Labor Remuneration	9777
社会保险	Social Insurances	5931
#工伤保险	Work Injury Insurance	2058
确认劳动关系	Confirm Labor (personnel) Relations	4145
工作时间及休假	Working Hours and Holidays	904
解除、终止劳动合同	Relieve or End the Labor Contract	3751
履行聘用合同	Fulfill the Labor (Recruit) Contract	115
解除人事关系	Remove the Labor (recruit) Contract	85
其他	Others	1921
案件处理情况	**Cases settled**	
当期审结案件数	Number of Cases Settled	26632
涉案金额(万元)	Involving Amount (10 000 yuan)	93083
按处理方式分	by Manners of Settlement	
仲裁调解	by Mediation	14038
仲裁裁决	by Arbitration Lawsuit	11093
#终局裁决	Final Arbitration	2662
其他	Others	1501
按处理结果分	by Result of Settlement	
用人单位胜诉	Lawsuits Won by Units	2503
劳动者胜诉	Lawsuit Won by Laborers	12299
双方部分胜诉	Lawsuit Partly Won by Both Parties	9535
其他	Others	2295
期末累计未结案数	**Number of Cases Unsettled**	**618**

Cases Accepted and Heard by Board of Labor Arbitration (2019)

(case)

劳动争议 Labor Dispute				劳动人事争议 Personnel Disputes	
国有企业 State-owned Enterprises	集体企业 Collective-owned Enterprises	港澳台及外资企业 Foreign Funded and Hong Kong, Macao and Taiwan Funded Enterprises	私营企业 Private Enterprises	机　关 Administrative Authority	事业单位 Public Institution
56	**44**	**6**	**475**	**1**	**25**
2247	756	240	22183	137	955
56	6		122		1
2136	585	225	19416	126	877
3957	911	257	25150	154	995
1254	71		2401		29
543	159	38	8887	22	94
508	259	28	4519	47	549
141	55	11	1822	6	20
555	111	19	3403	20	28
88	55	12	739	1	9
471	125	57	2845	36	205
35			48	7	25
4		1	61		19
43	47	85	1681	4	26
2251	772	240	22163	126	959
4443	1722	418	72765	493	13076
974	422	128	11925	83	440
1216	301	84	8926	38	498
391	182	26	1714	12	336
61	49	28	1312	5	21
254	72	23	2088	19	40
1305	332	65	9867	60	613
564	287	143	8197	43	256
128	81	9	2011	4	50
52	**28**	**6**	**495**	**12**	**21**

25-25 工会组织情况

Basic Statistics on Trade Unions

单位：万人 (10 000 persons)

年份 Year	工会基层组织数（万个） Number of Grassroot Trade Unions (10 000 units)	工会组织基层单位的职工与会员人数 Membership and Staff and Workers in Grassroot Trade Unions				工会专职工作人员人数 Number of Full-time Personnel of Trade Unions
		职工人数 Staff and Workers	#女职工 Female	会员人数 Membership	#女会员 Female	
2000	3.61	672.80		611.60		2.38
2001	4.86	757.84		700.10		
2002	5.68	811.02	298.59	749.51	270.99	3.28
2003	5.23	777.38	291.23	717.47	263.68	3.55
2004	5.38	785.64	297.21	734.64	266.71	3.20
2005	6.14	841.38	303.38	803.68	281.73	3.06
2006	6.94	905.50	325.51	866.43	306.15	3.36
2007	8.15	1070.20	380.30	1016.70	360.10	4.10
2008	9.13	1164.40	404.10	1125.00	392.10	4.50
2009	10.30	1291.31	443.76	1208.81	419.37	5.09
2010	11.43	1396.41	499.99	1324.06	480.69	6.45
2011	14.89	1517.46	548.67	1441.09	526.66	10.35
2012	19.42	1698.29	625.82	1616.72	602.21	13.02
2013	20.43	1734.41	642.58	1653.14	620.27	13.52
2014	21.12	1789.89	662.51	1707.29	642.37	13.67
2015	21.44	1852.19	685.95	1780.90	667.73	13.13
2016	21.61	1905.14	701.74	1832.35	682.88	13.70
2017	21.49	1900.16	700.19	1825.72	681.25	13.72
2018	20.50	1859.45	686.55	1778.42	665.94	13.06
2019	18.44	1716.66	637.34	1634.81	615.07	11.55

25-26 全省工会组织基本情况

Basic Statistics on Trade Unions

指标名称	Item	2016	2017	2018	2019
工会基层组织数（万人）	Number of Grassroot Trade Unions (10 000 persons)	21.61	21.49	20.50	18.44
基层工会专职工作人员人数	Number of Full-time Personnel of Grassroot Trade Unions				
（万人）	(10 000 persons)	13.70	13.72	13.06	11.55
已建工会组织的基层单位职工人数	Staff and Workers in Grassroot Trade Unions				
（万人）	(10 000 persons)	1905.14	1900.16	1859.45	1716.66
#女职工	Female Staff and Workers	701.74	700.19	686.55	637.34
#农民工	Migrant workers	851.56	855.49	837.84	759.27
#女性	Female	292.44	295.93	287.90	261.58
已建工会组织的基层单位工会	Membership in Grassroot Trade Unions				
会员人数（万人）	(10 000 persons)	1832.35	1825.72	1778.42	1634.81
#女会员	Female Membership	682.88	681.25	665.94	615.07
职工代表数	Number of worker representative	130.20	140.09	105.17	97.60
#女性	Female	52.50	56.62	32.96	28.36
企业职工代表大会中女性代表比重	Proportion of Female Representatives in Enterprise				
(%)	Staff and Workers'Congress (%)	40.32	40.42	31.34	29.06

25-27 各市基层工会劳动法律监督工作情况(2019年)

Statistics on Labor Law Supervision Work of Primary Trade Union by City (2019)

单位：个、件 (units, case)

市 City	基层工会劳动法律监督组织 Labor Law Supervision Organizations of Grassroot Trade Union		基层以上工会劳动法律监督组织 Labor Law Supervision Organizations of Trade Union Above Grassroot	
	组织个数 Number of Organizations	本年度工会劳动法律监督组织受理违法、违规案件 Accepted Cases of Violation of Laws and Regulations	组织个数 Number of Organizations	本年度工会劳动法律监督组织受理违法、违规案件 Accepted Cases of Violation of Laws and Regulations
全　省 Total	**15944**	**822**	**307**	**436**
郑　州　市 Zhengzhou	1175	32	29	43
开　封　市 Kaifeng	93	1	4	1
洛　阳　市 Luoyang	2861	11	31	13
平顶山市 Pingdingshan	238	24	5	
安　阳　市 Anyang	179	5	5	2
鹤　壁　市 Hebi	106		3	
新　乡　市 Xinxiang	1982	53	12	37
焦　作　市 Jiaozuo	812	52	36	50
濮　阳　市 Puyang	935	2	14	45
许　昌　市 Xuchang	157		3	23
漯　河　市 Luohe	1256		17	11
三门峡市 Sanmenxia	675	10	10	24
南　阳　市 Nanyang	3461	596	87	138
商　丘　市 Shangqiu	266	10	3	8
信　阳　市 Xinyang	586	20	12	16
周　口　市 Zhoukou	97		4	23
驻马店市 Zhumadian	911	1	13	2
济　源　市 Jiyuan	154	5	19	

25-28 参加各类保险人数

Persons Covered of Insurans

单位：万人 (10 000 persons)

年份 Year	基本养老保险 Basic Pension Insurance	城镇职工基本养老保险 Basic Pension Insurance for Urban Employee	失业保险 Unemployment Insurance	医疗保险 Basic Medical Insurance	工伤保险 Work Injury Insurance	生育保险 Maternity Insurance
2000		662.68	671.00	287.00	198.00	172.00
2001		639.05	676.00	456.40	245.00	207.00
2002		645.53	670.00	537.28	218.79	204.54
2003		659.25	679.97	567.93	210.61	199.29
2004		688.70	681.60	590.19	324.72	200.66
2005		716.17	681.90	640.70	404.00	228.30
2006		762.60	682.80	704.00	432.90	238.40
2007		804.68	684.65	726.03	452.32	254.02
2008		948.57	689.00	840.87	501.20	313.35
2009		1019.09	694.82	1970.13	521.02	379.76
2010		1079.33	696.46	2043.75	551.74	412.87
2011	4474.29	1168.38	701.19	2122.26	655.54	460.69
2012	5990.31	1270.63	735.50	2222.20	720.56	520.29
2013	6192.74	1349.99	741.29	2297.20	773.09	569.60
2014	6275.34	1431.55	773.30	2340.03	805.71	590.17
2015	6362.64	1508.71	783.34	2344.90	856.68	609.46
2016	6643.76	1750.02	788.07	2360.75	876.97	646.80
2017	6907.80	1897.59	805.57	10410.70	900.88	692.73
2018	7089.00	2006.54	819.91	10435.74	926.26	755.35
2019	7333.04	2133.84	837.26	10289.78	966.24	765.30

注：1.基本养老保险参保人数为城镇职工基本养老保险参保人数与城乡居民基本养老保险参保人数之和。

2.2009年-2016年医疗保险参保人数为城镇职工基本医疗保险人数与城镇居民基本医疗保险参保人数之和。

3.2017年起医疗保险参保人数为城镇职工基本医疗保险参保人数与城乡居民基本医疗保险参保人数之和。

a) Number of persons covered of basic pension insurance refers to the number of persons covered of basic pension insurance for urban employee and number of persons covered of basic pension insurance for urban and rural residents.

b) Number of persons covered of basic medical insurance refers to the number of persons covered of basic medical insurance for urban employee and number of persons covered of basic medical insurance for urban and rural residents in 2009-2016.

c) Number of persons covered of basic medical insurance refers to the number of persons covered of basic medical insurance for urban employee and number of persons covered of basic medical insurance for urban and rural residents since 2017.

25-29 社会保险基金
Social Insurance Fund

单位：亿元 (100 million yuan)

年　份 Year	基金收入 Revenue	基金支出 Expenses	累计结余 Balance at theYear-end
2003	187.50	151.10	145.20
2004	216.10	166.90	195.80
2005	257.10	203.20	244.20
2006	298.50	239.20	303.30
2007	365.20	289.60	363.80
2008	540.61	445.51	496.21
2009	558.14	462.74	595.57
2010	609.40	484.90	664.70
2011	723.60	581.25	806.68
2012	872.46	702.51	977.21
2013	1304.45	1043.23	1505.51
2014	1440.14	1210.84	1734.19
2015	1515.98	1310.66	1828.51
2016	1738.63	1473.87	2093.26
2017	2636.55	2365.21	2586.76
2018	3181.20	2939.47	2831.89
2019	3341.76	3177.85	2976.55

注：1.2015年社保基金收入、支出、累计结余数据不含机关事业单位养老保险数据。
2.2017年起社会保险基金数据包含已整合的原新型农村合作医疗保险数据。
a) Data on 2015 exclude Agencies and institutions Endowment insurance.
b) Since 2017 the data include the data of the new rural cooperative medical insurance.

25−30 各市城镇职工参加基本养老保险人数

Number of People Participated in Basic Pension Insurance by City

单位：万人 (10 000 persons)

市(县) City(County)	2007	2008	2009	2010	2011	2012	2013	2014	2015	2016	2017	2018	2019
省辖市 City													
郑州市 Zhengzhou	119.00	127.74	141.12	158.14	198.28	251.76	290.69	331.98	370.70	379.61	449.94	490.98	534.76
开封市 Kaifeng	52.67	55.43	60.22	62.48	59.25	62.14	64.54	67.91	70.84	62.45	82.93	88.09	93.74
洛阳市 Luoyang	76.86	80.26	85.98	90.60	95.65	100.34	105.98	110.91	114.98	110.85	136.78	141.63	145.31
平顶山市 Pingdingshan	35.60	36.80	40.01	42.28	44.72	47.63	49.77	50.91	53.03	49.27	70.79	74.67	79.00
安阳市 Anyang	52.48	55.10	58.78	61.58	65.22	67.63	69.79	71.78	74.42	71.61	93.16	98.44	104.86
鹤壁市 Hebi	13.24	13.88	14.57	15.37	16.40	17.33	18.09	19.20	20.29	21.13	27.85	29.76	32.02
新乡市 Xinxiang	53.69	57.75	61.26	65.74	71.49	76.11	80.43	84.31	88.31	93.24	118.34	125.04	131.58
焦作市 Jiaozuo	41.82	42.08	45.99	48.20	50.70	52.70	53.97	55.70	57.16	54.00	70.58	74.49	78.24
濮阳市 Puyang	21.01	21.38	24.35	25.86	27.41	28.73	29.95	31.26	32.07	25.24	39.84	42.05	44.65
许昌市 Xuchang	33.08	34.21	37.07	38.76	40.70	42.50	45.09	48.53	52.31	51.49	70.70	74.43	79.10
漯河市 Luohe	20.58	20.94	23.10	24.33	25.72	27.69	29.82	31.36	32.39	29.90	41.47	43.88	46.08
三门峡市 Sanmenxia	21.99	23.58	25.08	26.39	27.51	28.80	29.94	30.92	31.98	30.49	42.07	43.85	46.02
南阳市 Nanyang	68.27	65.21	72.62	75.38	80.02	83.88	86.72	89.36	91.58	70.98	112.77	116.74	124.31
商丘市 Shangqiu	34.66	37.45	41.13	43.57	47.52	50.58	53.10	55.25	57.73	50.35	81.70	85.79	91.33
信阳市 Xinyang	41.97	42.96	48.12	50.60	54.10	58.48	60.49	62.88	65.40	59.24	89.04	92.60	96.71
周口市 Zhoukou	37.29	40.61	44.15	47.03	51.95	55.48	57.41	60.13	62.20	57.40	92.02	97.88	105.99
驻马店市 Zhumadian	25.59	26.40	28.68	30.74	34.94	37.22	39.12	40.69	41.83	38.77	67.53	69.74	72.87
济源市 Jiyuan	9.71	10.25	10.98	11.64	12.49	14.15	15.27	16.63	17.43	17.50	21.54	22.62	28.45
省直管县 County Directly Administrated by Province													
巩义市 Gongyi					8.95	9.95	10.47	10.61	11.13	8.65	11.20	12.08	12.91
兰考县 Lankao					3.65	4.79	4.85	5.28	5.60	3.88	7.12	8.80	10.69
汝州市 Ruzhou					4.46	4.67	4.93	5.24	5.58	4.95	7.59	8.14	8.70
滑县 Huaxian					5.31	5.49	5.69	5.90	6.11	5.55	8.72	9.39	10.09
长垣市 Changyuan					3.30	3.56	3.91	4.24	4.51	4.81	7.60	8.32	9.39
邓州市 Dengzhou					7.53	7.80	8.05	8.29	8.53	5.19	9.59	9.77	10.19
永城市 Yongcheng					7.07	7.53	7.72	7.84	8.40	7.46	11.75	12.34	13.07
固始县 Gushi					8.93	11.87	12.44	12.88	13.53	10.80	15.40	16.09	16.53
鹿邑县 Luyi					4.29	4.49	4.55	4.67	4.88	4.21	7.46	7.80	8.13
新蔡县 Xincai					1.70	2.63	2.75	2.82	3.01	2.85	5.34	5.52	5.80

注：2016年城镇职工基本养老保险参保人数为企业职工基本养老保险参保人数，不包括机关事业单位养老保险参保人数。

a) Date on 2016 only include the number of people work in enterprises, exclude the number of people work in government agencies and institutions.

25-31 各市参加基本医疗保险人数

Number of People Participated in Basic Medical Insurance by City

单位：万人 (10 000 persons)

市(县)	City(County)	2007	2008	2009	2010	2011	2012	2013	2014	2015	2016	2017	2018	2019
省辖市	**City**													
郑州市	Zhengzhou	64.96	74.76	208.80	230.83	261.64	296.53	315.40	329.47	344.52	360.70	821.56	826.11	848.52
开封市	Kaifeng	31.68	36.13	86.21	89.95	92.83	99.23	101.66	104.52	105.01	97.41	503.93	504.59	469.38
洛阳市	Luoyang	74.64	82.99	183.30	189.44	195.91	202.24	197.75	210.39	214.41	215.98	668.81	688.91	694.20
平顶山市	Pingdingshan	55.55	60.23	120.08	122.88	126.62	128.22	127.54	127.85	127.98	128.35	515.53	515.62	510.29
安阳市	Anyang	52.51	55.87	116.13	119.94	121.48	122.19	121.91	124.13	124.62	124.91	575.77	576.69	570.49
鹤壁市	Hebi	18.66	20.39	46.92	38.70	38.80	39.24	39.21	39.60	41.39	41.44	147.73	148.38	148.06
新乡市	Xinxiang	53.23	55.59	129.51	135.09	141.57	142.18	142.12	143.17	144.15	144.70	582.46	585.25	579.25
焦作市	Jiaozuo	41.65	43.52	95.45	91.83	93.20	93.97	94.64	95.02	95.20	95.55	348.61	348.97	348.09
濮阳市	Puyang	39.48	46.68	79.74	79.78	80.30	80.50	69.50	64.50	60.00	60.00	375.00	375.60	375.60
许昌市	Xuchang	31.01	34.22	85.93	88.61	89.91	90.79	92.40	93.10	95.07	95.14	458.30	457.23	448.54
漯河市	Luohe	21.42	24.62	64.33	67.84	73.20	78.12	76.48	76.89	74.69	74.82	256.42	256.89	234.85
三门峡市	Sanmenxia	27.37	28.56	59.11	62.21	64.04	64.93	66.73	59.78	59.84	59.96	219.95	220.10	218.05
南阳市	Nanyang	63.00	65.60	143.09	154.10	158.33	160.50	161.92	163.14	164.02	164.35	1114.71	1115.26	1082.48
商丘市	Shangqiu	37.61	39.51	124.87	128.11	135.34	142.24	153.82	154.96	140.30	139.11	870.08	880.23	877.41
信阳市	Xinyang	47.80	51.30	124.28	128.61	132.62	134.02	134.62	134.73	133.34	137.50	832.30	832,12	803.00
周口市	Zhoukou	36.65	39.83	112.92	121.12	129.34	137.76	140.41	140.88	140.52	141.59	1113.85	1094.78	1099.53
驻马店市	Zhumadian	36.01	38.00	106.49	109.13	116.02	121.44	122.06	125.47	127.25	127.68	840.20	841.83	814.78
济源市	Jiyuan	6.80	8.04	18.58	19.11	19.80	20.88	23.73	24.43	24.46	25.63	70.15	70.50	69.53
省直管县	**County Directly Administrated by Province**													
巩义市	Gongyi					13.90	12.93	12.93	11.17	11.23	10.24	74.06	74.21	73.82
兰考县	Lankao					6.90	7.19	7.46	7.27	7.17	7.08	82.58	82.00	82.11
汝州市	Ruzhou					11.00	11.53	11.63	11.09	11.17	11.12	105.44	103.96	102.61
滑县	Huaxian					12.80	13.01	13.74	13.96	14.01	13.99	138.74	138.60	135.46
长垣市	Changyuan					8.70	8.76	8.85	9.47	10.19	10.57	87.78	87.81	86.64
邓州市	Dengzhou					16.40	16.19	16.62	16.84	16.54	15.36	168.20	167.95	163.34
永城市	Yongcheng					18.20	17.22	18.49	17.76	16.72	15.53	149.35	149.90	149.72
固始县	Gushi					14.30	14.31	14.50	14.51	10.61	12.21	159.63	158.78	158.50
鹿邑县	Luyi					10.30	10.62	10.67	10.50	8.60	8.62	120.80	120.73	119.75
新蔡县	Xincai					7.40	9.57	10.10	10.98	11.02	11.04	111.08	111.32	111.79

注：2017年以后医疗保险参保人数为职工基本医疗保险参保人数与城乡居民基本医疗保险参保人数之和。

a) The number of people participated in basic medical insurance the sum of the number of employees and urban and rural residents articipating in basic medical insurance.

25-32 各市参加失业保险人数

Number of People Participated in Unemployment Insurance by City

单位：万人 (10 000 persons)

市(县) City(County)	2007	2008	2009	2010	2011	2012	2013	2014	2015	2016	2017	2018	2019
省辖市 City													
郑州市 Zhengzhou	86.22	87.08	87.74	89.75	92.71	131.24	133.13	154.94	172.62	187.63	195.24	196.19	211.71
开封市 Kaifeng	36.20	36.20	35.78	34.10	33.96	34.23	34.27	34.61	35.08	23.82	25.02	25.60	27.32
洛阳市 Luoyang	59.71	59.10	59.78	59.99	60.23	60.83	61.07	63.46	63.64	63.59	63.78	64.01	64.21
平顶山市 Pingdingshan	45.55	46.60	46.60	46.98	46.98	47.44	45.93	46.41	45.56	45.79	46.48	47.15	47.73
安阳市 Anyang	39.66	39.90	40.00	40.06	40.28	40.51	40.54	41.89	41.72	41.89	42.76	42.81	42.26
鹤壁市 Hebi	15.22	15.22	15.20	15.45	15.47	15.75	14.69	14.66	14.20	14.21	14.65	14.81	14.05
新乡市 Xinxiang	45.38	45.10	44.95	44.90	44.84	45.15	44.92	45.34	44.39	44.26	46.49	46.41	46.41
焦作市 Jiaozuo	34.44	34.19	34.18	35.40	35.20	35.45	35.06	35.86	34.69	34.86	35.32	36.08	36.71
濮阳市 Puyang	29.51	29.87	31.26	30.84	31.21	31.04	29.40	30.09	29.71	30.12	31.68	31.84	31.95
许昌市 Xuchang	27.64	27.01	27.00	27.00	27.00	27.50	27.50	27.50	27.50	27.50	28.01	28.50	28.50
漯河市 Luohe	14.95	16.86	16.98	17.02	17.10	17.64	17.10	17.54	17.54	17.56	18.03	18.20	18.32
三门峡市 Sanmenxia	22.35	22.65	22.71	22.70	22.79	23.24	22.23	22.32	23.07	23.06	23.18	23.59	23.76
南阳市 Nanyang	61.49	61.26	62.61	62.66	63.19	65.01	62.15	63.15	61.45	62.07	63.53	64.92	64.75
商丘市 Shangqiu	34.86	35.00	35.48	34.91	35.03	35.25	34.20	34.76	34.33	34.42	36.95	36.80	37.14
信阳市 Xinyang	39.11	39.17	39.29	39.23	39.41	39.70	38.88	38.92	37.81	37.68	38.73	39.04	38.05
周口市 Zhoukou	38.60	38.63	38.10	38.00	38.12	39.54	38.41	38.92	38.01	38.01	39.86	40.51	40.62
驻马店市 Zhumadian	31.80	34.03	35.37	36.61	37.04	38.92	38.83	38.21	37.80	37.92	39.95	40.39	40.94
济源市 Jiyuan	7.05	6.86	6.85	6.86	6.83	7.06	9.57	11.47	11.22	11.01	11.45	11.51	11.30
省直管县 County Directly Administrated by Province													
巩义市 Gongyi					5.90	6.00	6.00	5.86	5.82	5.70	5.92	5.90	5.70
兰考县 Lankao					2.90	2.90	2.90	2.90	3.26	2.94	3.01	3.07	3.61
汝州市 Ruzhou					3.30	3.40	3.30	3.41	3.41	3.41	3.73	4.08	3.80
滑县 Huaxian					4.33	4.33	4.33	4.33	4.08	4.08	4.20	3.85	3.01
长垣市 Changyuan					2.82	2.88	2.80	3.03	2.71	3.01	4.00	3.61	3.61
邓州市 Dengzhou					5.60	5.61	5.61	5.61	5.21	5.21	5.21	5.21	4.87
永城市 Yongcheng					4.80	4.80	4.80	4.80	4.80	4.80	5.00	4.24	4.38
固始县 Gushi					5.27	5.30	5.22	5.30	5.09	5.06	5.11	5.11	4.87
鹿邑县 Luyi					3.39	3.60	3.60	3.60	3.60	3.42	3.50	3.51	3.52
新蔡县 Xincai					3.11	3.20	3.13	3.13	3.13	3.15	3.30	3.30	3.31

25-33 各市参加工伤保险人数

Number of People Participated in Work Injury Insurance by City

单位：万人 (10 000 persons)

市(县) City (County)	2007	2008	2009	2010	2011	2012	2013	2014	2015	2016	2017	2018	2019
省辖市 City													
郑州市 Zhengzhou	47.30	52.53	55.71	57.84	84.57	134.95	147.29	154.47	164.97	173.77	178.58	186.03	193.77
开封市 Kaifeng	22.66	25.10	25.93	27.09	32.24	33.00	33.61	34.33	34.96	24.87	28.60	29.95	33.51
洛阳市 Luoyang	41.52	45.72	47.90	49.50	55.13	60.02	61.56	64.10	66.51	68.13	69.16	72.48	77.06
平顶山市 Pingdingshan	19.74	21.71	23.09	23.72	29.00	32.13	33.20	35.05	36.83	38.45	39.20	40.35	41.43
安阳市 Anyang	28.11	31.39	32.59	34.11	40.30	42.77	43.88	45.79	48.04	49.46	50.25	51.48	53.07
鹤壁市 Hebi	6.42	6.67	7.03	7.44	9.16	11.01	11.56	12.03	12.51	12.75	13.39	13.67	14.65
新乡市 Xinxiang	36.57	43.21	44.80	48.55	50.93	51.30	52.92	55.20	57.41	58.65	59.69	61.14	63.20
焦作市 Jiaozuo	20.96	23.11	24.12	25.10	27.48	30.11	31.33	32.82	34.45	35.08	35.78	36.54	35.38
濮阳市 Puyang	11.91	16.89	17.87	19.04	21.87	22.20	22.70	23.50	24.50	25.01	22.75	22.80	24.14
许昌市 Xuchang	14.98	16.12	16.73	17.50	21.76	22.23	23.03	24.13	25.42	26.11	26.74	27.34	29.08
漯河市 Luohe	10.91	13.40	14.15	14.56	17.81	19.56	20.28	21.17	22.39	22.91	22.75	23.80	24.95
三门峡市 Sanmenxia	12.55	14.01	14.46	15.13	18.13	20.05	20.58	21.01	21.56	21.94	22.38	22.90	23.53
南阳市 Nanyang	28.77	33.19	34.27	35.65	47.07	49.22	50.46	52.41	54.64	56.33	57.92	59.75	61.75
商丘市 Shangqiu	11.36	15.23	16.06	16.60	25.71	30.40	31.01	31.64	32.13	32.43	29.23	29.73	31.14
信阳市 Xinyang	16.20	19.34	20.01	20.95	29.82	32.93	33.68	31.85	33.32	35.48	36.79	38.50	41.23
周口市 Zhoukou	14.44	16.00	17.00	18.00	28.93	36.78	40.00	41.82	43.10	47.76	48.54	48.78	51.25
驻马店市 Zhumadian	11.88	14.14	14.60	15.16	24.06	27.19	28.20	29.53	30.73	31.32	33.51	35.64	37.66
济源市 Jiyuan	5.21	5.44	5.69	5.91	7.28	7.77	8.34	9.36	11.21	11.61	11.80	11.92	12.21
省直管县 County Directly Administrated by Province													
巩义市 Gongyi					4.68	7.43	7.86	7.86	8.10	7.96	8.10	8.13	8.30
兰考县 Lankao					1.67	1.67	1.76	2.23	2.44	2.59	2.74	2.94	4.39
汝州市 Ruzhou					2.40	2.64	3.03	3.04	3.29	3.41	3.55	3.63	3.82
滑县 Huaxian					3.03	3.50	3.68	3.71	3.81	3.92	4.03	4.14	4.71
长垣市 Changyuan					3.03	3.03	3.03	3.12	3.30	3.54	3.76	4.00	4.90
邓州市 Dengzhou					4.12	4.12	4.35	4.40	4.50	4.60	4.90	4.99	5.09
永城市 Yongcheng					12.12	12.35	9.63	9.63	9.63	9.63	6.13	6.33	6.45
固始县 Gushi					3.72	4.38	4.40	1.84	2.29	2.40	2.56	3.04	4.53
鹿邑县 Luyi					1.90	2.70	3.01	3.01	3.01	3.01	3.10	3.10	3.29
新蔡县 Xincai					1.44	1.83	1.92	1.92	2.00	2.00	2.01	2.10	2.16

25-34 各市参加生育保险人数

Number of People Participated in Maternity Insurance by City

单位：万人 (10 000 persons)

市(县) City(County)	2007	2008	2009	2010	2011	2012	2013	2014	2015	2016	2017	2018	2019
省辖市 City													
郑州市 Zhengzhou	20.79	28.70	37.98	39.95	58.57	75.84	85.04	94.73	101.45	117.77	143.71	176.32	193.26
开封市 Kaifeng	20.02	21.00	22.01	22.50	23.00	23.61	24.60	24.90	20.14	21.73	25.76	29.10	30.26
洛阳市 Luoyang	35.52	40.00	43.68	44.70	48.94	52.52	54.11	54.96	56.41	57.26	59.92	63.92	66.29
平顶山市 Pingdingshan	15.46	20.50	22.31	26.92	28.42	31.47	32.83	33.66	34.31	34.68	42.57	43.85	44.11
安阳市 Anyang	22.07	23.60	24.73	25.04	25.53	26.37	27.60	29.03	29.99	30.54	31.10	31.73	32.20
鹤壁市 Hebi	7.51	8.10	9.02	9.51	10.01	10.62	10.81	10.91	11.12	11.22	14.38	14.91	14.80
新乡市 Xinxiang	22.74	23.70	24.89	26.04	26.84	28.73	29.90	30.37	31.47	32.33	32.77	35.05	37.32
焦作市 Jiaozuo	20.22	22.00	23.30	24.24	25.59	26.97	28.18	28.49	29.18	29.59	30.54	33.55	34.34
濮阳市 Puyang	10.51	14.40	17.66	21.72	22.17	22.80	14.30	14.40	14.80	15.00	15.10	15.20	15.20
许昌市 Xuchang	15.69	16.10	18.01	18.51	19.02	19.63	20.47	20.80	21.66	22.17	22.41	23.34	23.80
漯河市 Luohe	3.45	5.50	8.35	9.51	11.06	12.43	13.06	13.30	13.89	14.32	16.79	17.49	17.65
三门峡市 Sanmenxia	8.36	9.60	10.04	11.53	12.62	13.97	14.82	14.93	15.12	15.58	20.99	22.00	20.87
南阳市 Nanyang	19.22	23.00	25.30	28.80	31.42	34.20	36.33	37.31	40.06	42.94	44.53	47.72	49.41
商丘市 Shangqiu	4.43	4.80	6.59	6.60	13.52	17.08	19.25	19.60	19.62	20.60	22.82	25.51	28.69
信阳市 Xinyang	12.01	17.30	20.13	21.87	23.73	26.05	28.46	29.59	33.55	35.97	40.83	43.83	31.79
周口市 Zhoukou	1.90	11.00	16.93	20.98	24.91	30.27	33.07	34.86	35.96	37.89	38.89	39.93	31.96
驻马店市 Zhumadian	11.43	17.00	19.11	20.02	21.52	23.56	25.15	26.49	28.51	30.10	30.35	31.25	32.24
济源市 Jiyuan	2.70	3.00	4.07	4.53	4.84	5.36	7.21	8.84	9.50	10.12	11.02	11.44	11.61
省直管县 County Directly Administrated by Province													
巩义市 Gongyi					4.50	5.19	5.19	5.25	5.07	4.74	5.12	5.31	5.24
兰考县 Lankao					0.60	0.60	0.90	0.90	0.90	1.38	1.38	2.37	2.48
汝州市 Ruzhou					2.80	3.06	3.25	3.35	3.40	3.42	3.43	3.74	3.90
滑县 Huaxian					2.60	2.69	2.91	2.96	3.13	3.15	3.21	3.33	2.71
长垣市 Changyuan					1.00	1.08	1.31	1.55	1.75	1.91	1.96	2.11	2.44
邓州市 Dengzhou					2.40	4.41	4.57	4.65	4.70	4.72	4.72	4.75	4.75
永城市 Yongcheng					2.70	2.27	2.56	2.57	2.59	2.59	4.62	6.40	6.80
固始县 Gushi					3.70	3.85	4.02	4.00	3.67	3.72	3.04	3.30	3.77
鹿邑县 Luyi					1.50	1.60	1.20	2.16	2.16	2.30	2.32	2.48	2.84
新蔡县 Xincai					1.10	1.19	1.19	1.39	1.50	2.15	2.13	2.14	2.21

25-35 安全生产基本情况

Basic Statistics on safetyin production

指　标	Indicate	2017	2018	2019
发生伤亡事故总数(起)	Casuatlty Accidents (case)	1324	1077	823
农林牧渔业	Agriculture, Forestry, Animal Husbandry and Fishery	13	5	6
采矿业	Mining	11	7	6
商贸制造业	Trade Manufacturing	71	41	43
建筑业	Construction	55	63	48
交通运输仓储业	Transport and Storage	1151	946	712
其它行业	Others	23	15	8
造成死亡总人数(人)	Death (person)	891	756	568
农林牧渔业	Agriculture, Forestry, Animal Husbandry and Fishery	3		6
采矿业	Mining	39	14	11
商贸制造业	Trade Manufacturing	85	69	67
建筑业	Construction	79	81	63
交通运输仓储业	Transport and Storage	655	572	409
其它行业	Others	30	20	12
一次死亡3-9人较大事故(起)	Major Accidents with 3-9 People Dead (case)	26	24	15
农林牧渔业	Agriculture, Forestry, Animal Husbandry and Fishery			1
采矿业	Mining	4	1	1
商贸制造业	Trade Manufacturing	6	4	3
建筑业	Construction	3	4	4
交通运输仓储业	Transport and Storage	11	14	5
其它行业	Others	2	1	1
一次死亡3-9人较大事故中死亡人数(人)	Number of People Dead in Major Accidents (person)	97	103	59
农林牧渔业	Agriculture, Forestry, Animal Husbandry and Fishery			4
采矿业	Mining	18	4	5
商贸制造业	Trade Manufacturing	20	18	14
建筑业	Construction	12	18	12
交通运输仓储业	Transport and Storage	41	60	21
其它行业	Others	6	3	3
一次死亡10人以上重特大事故(起)	Extra Serious Accident with more than 10 People Dead (case)	2	1	1
农林牧渔业	Agriculture, Forestry, Animal Husbandry and Fishery			
采矿业	Mining	1		
商贸制造业	Trade Manufacturing		1	1
建筑业	Construction			
交通运输仓储业	Transport and Storage	1		
其它行业	Others			
一次死亡10人以上重特大事故中死亡人数(人)	Number of People Dead in Extra Serious Accidents	24	11	15
农林牧渔业	Agriculture, Forestry, Animal Husbandry and Fishery			
采矿业	Mining	12		
商贸制造业	Trade Manufacturing		11	15
建筑业	Construction			
交通运输仓储业	Transport and Storage	12		
其它行业	Others			
煤矿死亡人数(人)	Death Toll from Coal Mine Accidents (person)	19	11	5
骨干煤矿企业	Key Coal Mine Enterprises	5	11	4
地方煤矿	Local Coal Mine	14		1
煤矿百万吨死亡率	Death Rate in Million tons Coal Production	0.179	0.102	0.047
骨干煤矿企业	Key Coal Mine Enterprises	0.049	0.110	0.041
地方煤矿	Local Coal Mine	2.997		0.135

主要统计指标解释

受理劳动争议案件数 指劳动争议仲裁委员会根据国家有关规定，对劳动争议当事人的申请予以审查，符合受理条件而正式立案、准备处理的劳动争议案件数。

要案 指县、处级以上干部的犯罪案件。该指标主要反映职务犯罪案件中县、处级以上干部被人民检察院依法立案侦查的情况。

批准逮捕 指人民检察院对公安机关、国家安全机关、监狱管理机关提出逮捕的犯罪嫌疑人进行审查，根据事实，依法做出逮捕决定。该指标主要反映人民检察院对提请逮捕犯罪嫌疑人进行审查后依法做出批准逮捕决定的情况。

决定逮捕 指人民检察院对直接立案侦查的案件，认为需要逮捕犯罪嫌疑人时，依据法律做出的逮捕决定。该指标主要反映人民检察院对直接受理的案件行使决定逮捕权的情况。

提起公诉 指人民检察院对公安机关、国家安全机关、监狱管理机关和检察机关侦查部门等移送起诉的案件进行审查，根据事实，做出提起公诉的案件。该指标主要反映人民检察院对各种刑事案件向人民法院提起公诉的情况。

适用简易程序 指人民法院对依法可能判处三年以下有期徒刑、拘役、管制、单处罚金的公诉案件，事实清楚，证据充分，人民检察院建议或者同意适用简易程序的案件 ；告诉才处理的案件；被害人起诉的有证据证明的轻微刑事案件。

提出抗诉 指人民检察院对人民法院的判决、裁定认为确有错误，向人民法院提出对案件重新进行审理的诉讼活动。包括按照第二审程序提出的抗诉和按照审判监督程序（再审程序）提出的抗诉。

撤回抗诉 指上级人民检察院对下级人民检察院按照第二审程序提出的抗诉，经审查，认为抗诉不当时向同级人民法院撤回抗诉，同时通知提出抗诉的下级人民检察院。

立案监督 指人民检察院对侦查机关刑事立案活动的监督。包括对应当立案而不立案的监督和不应立案而立案的监督。

监督立案 包括侦查机关接到要求说明不立案理由后主动立案和执行通知立案两个内容。

监管活动 指人民检察院对监狱等监管改造场所的管理活动进行的监督。

青少年罪犯 指人民法院在报告期内判决发生法律效力的有罪判决中 14 周岁以上不满 25 周岁的罪犯。其中 14 周岁以上不满 18 周岁的罪犯为未成年罪犯。

行政案件 指公民、法人和其他组织不服行政机关作出的具体行政行为，向人民法院提起行政诉讼，人民法院依法审理的案件。

单独赔偿 指单独提起行政赔偿的案件。当事人对行政行为的合法性没有争议，就行政侵权造成的损害赔偿单独提起赔偿诉讼。

公证人员 指在公证处工作的人员总称，包括公证处主任、副主任、公证员、公证员助理（助理公证员）和其他从事辅助性工作的人员。

公证文书 指公证处根据当事人申请，依照事实和法律，按照法定程序制作的，具有法律效力的司法证明文书。

受理劳动争议案件数 指劳动争议仲裁委员会根据国家有关规定，对劳动争议当事人的申请予以审查，符合受理条件而正式立案、准备处理的劳动争议案件数。

城镇职工基本养老保险

1.（参保）职工人数 指报告期末按照国家法律、法规和有关政策规定参加基本养老保险并在社保经办机构已建立缴费记录档案的职工人数，包括中断缴费但未终止养老保险关系的职工人数，不包括只登记未建立缴费记录档案的人数。

2.（参保）离退休人员人数 指报告期末参加基本养老保险的离休、退休和退职人员的人数。

3.基金收入 指根据国家有关规定，由纳入基本养老保险范围的缴费单位和个人按国家规定的缴费基数和缴费比例缴纳的养老保险基金，以及通过其他方式取得的形成基金来源的收入。包括单位和职工个人缴纳的基本养老保险费、基本养老保险基金利息收入、上级补助收入、下级上解收入、转移收入、财政补贴和其他收入。

4.基金支出 指按照国家政策规定的开支范围和开支标准从养老保险基金中支付给参加基本养老保险的个人的养老金、丧葬抚恤补助，以及由于保险关系转移、上下级之间调剂资金等原因而发生的支出。包括离休金、退休金、退职金、各种补贴、医疗费、死亡丧葬补助费、抚恤救济费、社会保险经办机构管理费、补助下级支出、上解上级支出、转移支出、其他支出等。

5.基金累计结余 指截止报告期末基本养老保险基金收支相抵后的累计余额。

基本医疗保险

1.参保人数 指报告期末按国家有关规定参加相应基本医疗保险的人数。

2.基金收入 指由用人单位和个人按照国家规定的缴费基数、缴费比例或缴费标准缴纳的基本医疗保险基金，财政补助资金以及通过其他方式取得的形成基金来源的款项，包括：单位缴纳收入、个人缴纳收入、财政补助收入（含医疗救助补助个人收入）、财政补贴收入、利息收入和其他收入。

3.基金支出 指按照国家政策规定的开支范围和开支标准，从基本医疗保险基金中支付给参保人员的医疗保险待遇支出，以及其他支出。包括住院医疗费用支出、门急诊医疗费用支出、个人账户基金支出、其他支出。

4.基金累计结余 指截止报告期末基本医疗保险基金累计结余金额。

失业保险

1.参保人数 指报告期末按照国家法律、法规和有关政策规定参加了失业保险的城镇企业、事业单位的职工及地方政府规定参加失业保险的其他人员的人数。

2.基金收入 指报告期内筹集的失业保险基金的总额，包括失业保险费收入、利息收入、财政补贴收入、其他收入、转移收入、上级补助收入、下级上解收入。

3.基金支出 指报告期内为保障失业人员基本生活、促进其再就业等支出的基金总额，包括失业保险金支出、医疗补助金支出、丧葬补助金和抚恤金支出、职业培训和职业介绍补贴支出、农民合同制工人一次性生活补助支出、其他支出、转移支出、上级补助支出、下级上解支出。

4.基金累计结余 指截止报告期末失业保险基金收支相抵后的累计余额。

工伤保险

1.参加保险人数 指报告期末依据国家有关规定参加工伤保险的职工人数和有雇工的个体工商户的雇工数。

2.享受保险待遇人数 指年初至报告期末因工伤或职业病而享受工伤保险待遇的人数。为享受工伤医疗待遇中未评定等级的人数、享受伤残待遇人数以及享受因工死亡待遇人数之和。

3.基金收入 指根据国家有关规定，由参加工伤保险的单位按国家规定的缴费基数和缴费比例缴纳的工伤保险基金，以及通过其他形式取得的形成基金来源的款项。包括：单位缴纳的社会统筹基金收入、财政补贴收入、利息收入、其他收入。

4.基金支出 指按照国家政策规定的开支范围和开支标准从工伤保险基金中支付给参加工伤保险的人员及供养直系亲属工伤保险待遇支出及其他支出。包括工伤医疗费、伤残补助金、工亡补助金、护理费、丧葬补助费、工伤预防费用、职业康复费用和其他支出。

5.基金累计结余 指截止报告期末工伤保险基金累计结余金额。

生育保险

1.参保人数 指报告期末依据有关规定参加生育保险的人数。

2.基金收入 指根据国家有关规定，由参加生育保险的单位按照国家规定的缴费基数和缴费比例缴纳的生育保险基金，以及通过其他方式取得的形成基金来源的款项，包括：单位缴纳的基金收入、利息收入和其他收入。

3.基金支出 指按照国家政策规定的开支范围和开支标准，从生育保险基金中支付给参加生育保险的职工，因妊娠、分娩和计划生育手术而享受的待遇及其他支出。包括：生育津贴、医疗费用支出及其他支出。

4.基金累计结余 指截止报告期末生育保险基金累计结余金额。

Explanatory Notes on Main Statistical Indicators

Number of Labour Dispute Cases Accepted refers to the number of cases of labour dispute submitted that, after being reviewed by the labour dispute arbitration committees in line with the relevant state regulations, are accepted and registered for treatment.

Key Cases refer to crimes committed by county and director-level officials. This indicator reflects the situation of those county and director-level officials involved in criminal cases registered and handled by People's Procuratorate offices.

Approval for Arrest refers to the decision made by people's procuratorate office, in accordance with the law and relevant facts, to approve the arrest of the suspect(s) as proposed by the public security departments, state security departments or prisons authority. This indicator reflects approved arrests made by people's procuratorate offices that are proposed by related departments.

Decision on Arrest refers to decision made by the people's procuratorate office, in accordance with laws, to arrest the suspect(s) in the cases that are accepted and to be investigated by procurators office. This indicator mainly reflects the implementation of the decision on arrest by people's procuratorate office.

Cases by Public Prosecution refer to those ones that are instituted by People's Procuratorate offices after their examination of such cases transferred by public security organs, national security organs, jail management organs and prosecutorial organs on the bases of the facts found. This indicator reflects the situation of public prosecutions instituted to the people's courts by People's Procuratorate Offices.

Application of Summary Procedure refers to those cases of public prosecution where the suspects might be, according to law, sentenced to fixed-term imprisonment of not more than three years, criminal detention, public surveillance or punishment with fines exclusively by People's Court ;, those cases where the facts are clear and the evidence is sufficient, and for which the People's Procuratorate suggests or agrees to the application of summary procedure; those cases to be handled only upon complaints; and those minor criminal cases prosecuted by the victims with evidence.

Protests Presented refers to those protests presented by local People's Procuratorate at any level who considers that there exists some definite error in a judgment or order of first instance made by a People's Court at the same level to the People's Court at the next higher level, including the protests raised in accordance with the second instance and protests raised in accordance with procedure for trial supervision.

Withdrawal of Protests refers to the actions made by the People's Procuratorate at the next higher level when it considers the protests inappropriate by withdrawing the protests from the People's Court at the same level and notifying the People's Procuratorate at the next lower level.

Case Registration Supervision refers to the actions made by the People's Procuratorate to supervise the registration of criminal cases initiated by investigative authorities, including supervision of the cases which have wrongly not been registered and have wrongly been registered.

Supervision of Case Registration includes both the supervision of those registrations initiated by investigatory authorities and the supervision of those registrations according to notifications after hearing declined reasons for registration.

Supervisory Activities refers to the supervision of the People's Procuratorate over the management of prisons as well as other places of criminal reformation under supervision.

Juvenile Criminals refers to the offenders within the age range of 14 to 25 convicted guilty by the court during the reporting period while those between 14 and 18 are defined as minor offenders.

Administrative Cases refers to the cases filed by citizens, corporations and other organizations against the specific administrative conducts of administrative authorities and handled by the court.

Separate Compensation refers to cases that are separately filed for administrative compensation by the party who has no dispute on the legality of administrative conducts but brings proceedings separately to claim for damages caused by administrative tort.

Notary Personnel refers to people working for notary offices including: directors, deputy directors, notaries, assistant notaries and other people providing assistance.

Notary Documents refer to legally binding judicial notary documents developed at the request of the interested party based on facts and the law following certain legal proceedings.

Number of Labour Disputes Cases Accepted refers to the number of cases of labour disputes submitted that, after being reviewed by the labour dispute arbitration committees in line with the relevant national regulations, are accepted and registered for treatment.

Basic Pension Insurance

1. Number of staff and workers covered refer to staff and workers participating in the basic pension insurance programme according to national laws, regulations and related policies at the end of the reference period, who have already had payment records in social security management agencies, including those who have interrupt payment without terminating the insurance programme. Those who have registered in the programme but with no payment records are not included.

2. Number of retirees participating in the basic pension insurance programme refer to the number of retirees participating in basic pension insurance programmes by the end of the reference period.

3. Revenue of the basic pension insurance programme refers to payments made by employers and individuals participating in the pension insurance programme in accordance with the basis and proportion stipulated in State regulations, and income from other sources that become source of pension insurance fund, including the premium paid by employers and staff and workers, interest income, subsidies from higher level agencies, income as transfer from subordinate agencies, transferred income, government financial subsidies and other income.

4. Expenditure of basic pension insurance programme refer to payment made on pensions and funeral subsidies to those retired and resigned people covered in pension insurance programmes according to related national policies on scope and standard of expenditure. Also included are expenditure which arises due to shift of the insurance relationship or adjustment of funds among agencies. More specifically, included are pensions for resigned people, pensions for retired people, pension for people quitting jobs, various subsidies, medical fees, funeral subsidies, compensation payments, management fees for social security agencies, expenses on subsidies to lower subordinates, expenses as transfer to agencies at higher level, transferred expenditure and other expenditure.

5. Balance of basic pension insurance programme refers to the balance of basic pension insurance funds at the end of the reference period after deducting expenses from revenue.

Basic Medical Care Insurance

1. Number of people participating in the insurance programme refers to people participating in the basic medical care insurance programme according to related regulations at the end of the reference period.

2. Revenue of the insurance programme refers to payments made by employers and individuals participating in the medical care insurance programme in accordance with the basis and proportion stipulated in State regulations, and income from other sources that become source of medical insurance fund, including income paid by units, individual paid income, financial assistance's income (including individual income from medicaid) , financial subsidies' income, interest income and other income.

3. Expenditure of the insurance programme refers to payment made to people covered in basic medical care insurance programme within the scope and standards of expenditure according to related national policies, and medical care payment and other expenses, including medical expenses of hospital inpatients, medical expenses for outpatients and emergency patients, payment from individual accounts and other expenditure.

4. Balance of the basic medical care insurance programme refers to the balance of medical care insurance funds at the end of the reference period.

Unemployment Insurance

1. Number of people covered refers to staff and workers in urban enterprises or institutions who have participated in the unemployment insurance programme according to relevant policies and regulations, and other people who have participated according to local government regulations at the end of the reference period.

2. Revenue of the unemployment insurance programme refers to the total unemployment insurance funds raised in the reference period, including unemployment insurance premium, interest income, financial subsidies, other income, transferred income, subsidies from higher level agencies and income as transfer from subordinate agencies.

3. Expenditure of the unemployment insurance programme refers to total expenses during the reference period to guarantee the basic livelihood of unemployed people, and to encourage their re-employment. Included are unemployment relief, medical fees, funeral subsidies, compensation payments, training expenses, management fees for unemployment insurance agencies, subsidies to lower level agencies, expenses as transfer to higher level agencies, transferred expenditure and other expenditure.

4. Balance of the unemployment insurance programme refers to the balance of revenue of the programme after deducting expenses at the end of the reference period.

Work Injury Insurance

1. Number of people covered refers to staff and workers who have participated in the work injury insurance programme and number of employees in private business according to relevant national regulations at the end of the reference period.

2. Number of beneficiaries refers to number of people benefited from work injury insurance, as a result of work injury or occupational disease. It is the sum of beneficiaries from the work injury medical treatment without rating, disabilities and deaths at work places.

3. Revenue of the work injury insurance programme refers to payments made by employers participating in the work injury insurance programme in accordance with the basis and proportion stipulated in State regulations, and income from other sources that become source of work injury insurance fund, including income of social comprehensive funds paid by employers, government financial subsidies, interest income and other income.

4. Expenditure of the work injury insurance programme refers to payments made from work injury insurance funds to those who participated in the work injury insurance programme and their direct dependents within the scope and standards of expenditure according to related national policies, and other expenditure, including medical fees for work injury, injury and disability subsidies, death subsidies, nursing fees, funeral subsidies, injury prevention fees, occupational rehabilitation fees and other expenditure.

5. Balance of the work injury insurance programme refers to the balance of the work injury funds at the end of the reference period.

Maternity Insurance

1. Number of people covered refers to people who have participated in the maternity insurance programme according to relevant regulation at the end of the reference period.

2. Revenue of maternity insurance refers to payments made by employers participating in the maternity insurance programme in accordance with the basis and proportion stipulated in State regulations, and income from other sources that become source of maternity insurance fund, including income of funds paid by employers, interest income and other income.

3. Expenditure of the maternity insurance programme refers to payments made from maternity insurance funds to staff and workers who participate in the maternity insurance programme within the scope and standards of expenditure in accordance with related national policies, expenses paid for pregnancy, child delivery or surgeries related to family planning, and other expenditure, including allowance for child bearing, medical fees and other expenditure.

4. Balance of the maternity programme refers to the balance of the maternity insurance funds at the end of the reference period.

各县（市、区）主要统计指标

Main Indicators of County (City, Municipal Districts)

26–1 各县(市、区)人口及就业人员(2019年)

Population and Employed Person by County and District (2019)

县市区	County and District	年末总户数(万户) Total Households (year-end) (10 000 household)	年末总人口(万人) Population (year-end) (10 000 persons)	常住人口(万人) Resident Population (10 000 persons)	#城镇 Urban	城镇化率(%) Urban Proportion (%)	就业人员(万人) Employment (10 000 persons)	第一产业 Primary Industry	第二、三产业 Secondary and Tertiary Industry
郑州市	**Zhengzhou**								
中原区	Zhongyuan	26.73	111.39	111.39	101.99	91.56	48.40	0.44	47.96
二七区	Erqi	21.02	84.76	84.76	77.18	91.05	28.20	0.32	27.88
管城区	Guancheng	18.87	85.11	85.11	74.55	87.60	52.90	1.38	51.52
金水区	Jinshui	42.25	178.92	178.92	164.89	92.16	105.00	1.07	103.93
上街区	Shangjie	3.96	16.25	16.25	14.97	92.16	5.80	0.34	5.46
惠济区	Huiji	7.44	31.10	31.10	23.94	76.98	21.00	3.27	17.73
中牟县	Zhongmu	18.13	120.63	120.63	67.17	55.68	88.20	22.81	65.39
巩义市	Gongyi	21.09	85.55	84.39	50.47	59.81	51.80	12.10	39.70
荥阳市	Xingyang	17.62	67.00	67.00	39.37	58.77	42.80	8.64	34.16
新密市	Xinmi	20.96	81.70	81.70	50.34	61.62	50.10	9.60	40.50
新郑市	Xinzheng	19.52	101.27	101.27	62.66	61.87	74.50	16.44	58.06
登封市	Dengfeng	17.41	72.65	72.65	42.31	58.24	41.60	14.65	26.95
开封市	**Kaifeng**								
龙亭区	Longting	12.80	32.04	44.23	35.99	81.36	26.20	3.73	22.47
顺河区	Shunhe	8.49	23.08	25.06	21.88	87.29	10.35	1.26	9.09
鼓楼区	Gulou	5.41	15.71	15.76	15.05	95.50	7.71	1.41	6.30
禹王台区	Yuwangtai	4.69	13.73	14.37	11.33	78.81	5.16	1.52	3.64
祥符区	Xiangfu	22.30	77.87	67.27	27.03	40.19	47.68	22.06	25.62
杞县	Qixian	38.51	114.57	89.13	35.66	40.01	70.61	29.35	41.26
通许县	Tongxu	17.96	65.49	51.57	20.58	39.90	38.91	19.26	19.65
尉氏县	Weishi	27.10	98.27	84.81	34.02	40.12	53.78	29.16	24.62
兰考县	Lankao	29.39	87.01	65.29	28.46	43.59	62.31	22.75	39.56
洛阳市	**Luoyang**								
老城区	Laocheng	6.36	17.31	20.37	19.23	94.40	5.10	0.42	4.68
西工区	Xigong	10.76	33.14	37.67	35.81	95.06	19.12	0.51	18.60
瀍河区	Chanhe	6.35	17.91	20.01	18.96	94.75	6.21	0.98	5.23
涧西区	Jianxi	19.68	60.50	71.55	64.08	89.56	24.43	0.79	23.64
吉利区	Jili	2.18	6.87	7.23	5.26	72.86	4.65	0.84	3.81
洛龙区	Luolong	22.08	68.43	74.14	51.69	69.72	43.86	6.04	37.82
孟津县	Mengjin	15.91	47.01	43.67	22.62	51.80	27.90	9.31	18.60
新安县	Xinan	15.66	53.65	49.41	24.60	49.78	35.88	10.66	25.22
栾川县	Luanchuan	10.56	34.77	35.42	18.33	51.75	25.19	5.71	19.48
嵩县	Songxian	17.14	61.11	52.40	20.04	38.24	32.18	14.27	17.91
汝阳县	Ruyang	12.91	49.36	42.33	16.44	38.84	27.31	12.33	14.98
宜阳县	Yiyang	19.85	70.67	60.83	24.23	39.84	39.13	15.30	23.83
洛宁县	Luoning	13.87	49.71	42.92	16.00	37.29	25.87	12.52	13.35
伊川县	Yichuan	25.79	85.19	77.85	36.76	47.22	51.47	17.00	34.47
偃师市	Yanshi	18.27	61.38	56.43	35.05	62.12	39.34	10.15	29.19

26-1 续表 1 continued

县市区 County and District	年末总户数（万户） Total Households (year-end) (10 000 household)	年末总人口（万人） Population (year-end) (10 000 persons)	常住人口（万人） Resident population (10 000 persons)	#城镇 Urban	城镇化率（%） Urbanization Rate (%)	就业人员（万人） Employment (10 000 persons)	第一产业 Primary Industry	第二、三产业 Secondary Industry and Tertiary Industry
平顶山市 Pingdingshan								
新华区 Xinhua	12.70	39.96	40.95	39.26	95.88	21.22	0.89	20.34
卫东区 Weidong	10.92	30.04	32.15	31.62	98.36	10.20	1.06	9.14
石龙区 Shilong	1.97	6.24	5.13	4.61	89.83	2.87	0.77	2.10
湛河区 Zhanhe	8.16	25.65	30.16	24.78	82.16	13.24	2.75	10.49
宝丰县 Baofeng	16.89	54.35	50.07	22.61	45.16	34.14	13.89	20.26
叶县 Yexian	23.07	92.43	78.41	31.73	40.47	48.61	26.86	21.75
鲁山县 Lushan	24.55	96.41	78.68	31.69	40.28	50.87	22.42	28.45
郏县 Jiaxian	21.16	64.86	57.82	25.48	44.06	37.64	17.77	19.87
舞钢市 Wugang	10.39	35.11	32.17	19.31	60.04	20.23	8.55	11.68
汝州市 Ruzhou	31.39	110.13	97.03	47.70	49.16	69.56	30.20	39.35
安阳市 Anyang								
文峰区 Wenfeng	15.62	34.67	45.10	40.23	89.20	16.37	0.80	15.57
北关区 Beiguan	8.23	28.26	31.03	26.91	86.73	19.32	1.73	17.59
殷都区 Yindu	7.48	26.43	28.70	25.24	87.96	34.72	9.07	25.65
龙安区 Longan	7.38	27.12	29.26	16.84	57.55	17.62	7.28	10.34
安阳县 Anyang	32.94	98.42	84.56	38.25	45.23	34.84	17.16	17.68
汤阴县 Tangyin	14.50	51.35	44.31	22.24	50.20	32.26	11.86	20.40
滑县 Huaxian	46.89	139.68	107.80	37.76	35.03	77.24	30.03	47.21
内黄县 Neihuang	19.80	79.52	66.89	22.83	34.13	52.08	17.32	34.76
林州市 Linzhou	32.56	109.34	81.57	46.16	56.59	68.05	18.62	49.43
鹤壁市 Hebi								
鹤山区 Heshan	3.27	13.06	12.90	11.04	85.62	4.02	1.05	2.97
山城区 Shancheng	5.87	24.56	24.31	21.24	87.38	4.18	1.04	3.14
淇滨区 Qibin	12.00	26.76	29.87	23.93	80.13	22.94	2.76	20.18
浚县 Xunxian	19.55	72.28	68.12	27.51	40.38	45.70	16.74	28.96
淇县 Qixian	8.77	29.86	27.96	16.31	58.32	20.58	5.76	14.82
新乡市 Xinxiang								
红旗区 Hongqi	12.30	33.00	45.74	43.80	95.75	21.43	0.98	20.45
卫滨区 Weibin	7.58	22.40	22.57	22.57	100.00	8.14	0.95	7.19
凤泉区 Fengquan	3.62	14.56	15.86	9.47	59.72	7.30	2.44	4.86
牧野区 Muye	11.01	31.26	34.09	33.01	96.82	14.06	1.45	12.61
新乡县 Xinxiang	8.60	35.20	34.86	19.93	57.18	27.90	0.97	26.93
获嘉县 Huojia	11.87	44.74	41.48	19.87	47.91	26.92	12.41	14.51
原阳县 Yuanyang	18.86	75.78	65.12	24.14	37.07	42.53	21.54	20.99
延津县 Yanjin	14.71	51.12	45.79	18.12	39.57	28.18	13.50	14.68
封丘县 Fengqiu	23.95	83.72	71.86	28.04	39.02	39.78	16.62	23.16
长垣市 Changyuan	25.84	88.18	78.93	39.32	49.81	53.25	8.70	44.55
卫辉市 Weihui	15.90	53.08	49.14	23.18	47.17	25.71	12.30	13.41
辉县市 Huixian	26.37	86.77	75.99	37.81	49.75	46.95	17.30	29.65

26-1 续表 2 continued

县市区	County and District	年末总户数(万户) Total Households (year-end) (10 000 household)	年末总人口(万人) Population (year-end) (10 000 persons)	常住人口(万人) Resident population (10 000 persons)	#城镇 Urban	城镇化率(%) Urbanization Rate (%)	就业人员(万人) Employment (10 000 persons)	第一产业 Primary Industry	第二、三产业 Secondary Industry and Tertiary Industry
焦作市	**Jiaozuo**								
解放区	Jiefang	9.01	30.07	30.61	30.12	98.43	9.82	0.05	9.77
中站区	Zhongzhan	3.08	11.89	10.82	7.18	66.35	6.30	1.57	4.73
马村区	Macun	3.56	14.39	14.21	9.22	64.91	4.70	0.89	3.81
山阳区	Shanyang	11.77	45.44	49.29	37.01	75.08	12.79	0.81	11.98
修武县	Xiuwu	7.02	27.44	25.65	13.60	53.01	18.24	4.34	13.90
博爱县	Boai	10.34	40.23	37.43	20.92	55.90	24.24	7.51	16.73
武陟县	Wuzhi	19.21	73.68	67.33	31.47	46.74	44.57	19.07	25.50
温县	Wenxian	14.11	46.06	42.21	21.85	51.75	32.32	12.43	19.89
沁阳市	Qinyang	12.48	49.44	44.52	28.02	62.94	32.78	10.36	22.42
孟州市	Mengzhou	11.37	39.24	37.64	19.81	52.64	30.35	5.43	24.92
濮阳市	**Puyang**								
华龙区	Hualong	23.30	62.92	74.20	59.80	80.59	55.43	9.73	45.70
清丰县	Qingfeng	22.35	72.85	63.94	21.10	33.00	42.11	16.09	26.02
南乐县	Nanle	14.94	54.84	45.82	16.40	35.80	29.98	12.09	17.89
范县	Fanxian	17.29	56.60	45.57	16.67	36.59	29.17	12.24	16.93
台前县	Taiqian	11.02	38.88	32.64	11.68	35.78	22.27	9.34	12.93
濮阳县	Puyang	31.44	114.80	98.87	42.28	42.76	63.57	25.03	38.54
许昌市	**Xuchang**								
魏都区	Weidu	15.99	45.55	52.53	50.70	96.52	15.64	0.05	15.59
建安区	Jianan	29.01	91.46	79.75	35.49	44.50	45.91	19.15	26.76
鄢陵县	Yanling	20.48	68.39	57.41	25.55	44.50	30.07	10.54	19.53
襄城县	Xiangcheng	26.76	89.03	69.55	30.47	43.81	43.50	24.65	18.85
禹州市	Yuzhou	43.76	126.98	116.70	59.02	50.57	73.48	31.27	42.22
长葛市	Changge	21.08	79.07	70.27	40.32	57.38	54.07	11.37	42.70
漯河市	**Luohe**								
源汇区	Yuanhui	9.72	34.59	34.46	24.03	69.74	26.51	5.90	20.61
郾城区	Yancheng	14.45	53.53	51.73	29.99	57.98	34.40	13.87	20.53
召陵区	Zhaoling	13.45	55.95	50.43	27.07	53.68	31.11	14.10	17.01
舞阳县	Wuyang	16.94	62.69	56.44	26.53	47.00	36.71	16.19	20.52
临颍县	Linying	20.38	78.57	73.76	36.38	49.32	47.56	18.33	29.23

26-1 续表 3 continued

县市区 County and District	年末总户数（万户）Total Households (year-end) (10 000 household)	年末总人口（万人）Population (year-end) (10 000 persons)	常住人口（万人）Resident population (10 000 persons)	#城镇 Urban	城镇化率(%) Urbanization Rate (%)	就业人员（万人）Employment (10 000 persons)	第一产业 Primary Industry	第二、三产业 Secondary Industry and Tertiary Industry
三门峡市 Sanmenxia								
湖滨区 Hubin	9.89	30.42	32.62	30.37	93.11	18.38	3.10	15.28
陕州区 Shanzhou	11.81	35.06	35.13	17.63	50.18	19.00	9.49	9.51
渑池县 Mianchi	12.67	35.93	35.38	18.41	52.04	21.58	7.13	14.45
卢氏县 Lushi	12.94	37.08	36.02	15.24	42.31	20.10	11.49	8.61
义马市 Yima	5.07	16.81	14.81	14.30	96.56	8.73	0.70	8.03
灵宝市 Lingbao	21.11	75.55	73.69	35.42	48.07	48.30	22.07	26.23
南阳市 Nanyang								
宛城区 Wancheng	30.56	90.28	94.19	61.43	65.22	55.43	23.63	31.80
卧龙区 Wolong	33.39	101.30	96.22	62.95	65.42	57.59	15.65	41.94
南召县 Nanzhao	22.39	66.41	54.36	22.69	41.74	35.35	18.60	16.75
方城县 Fangcheng	35.73	110.78	85.46	34.73	40.64	64.27	37.11	27.16
西峡县 Xixia	15.18	47.76	43.18	22.14	51.28	38.55	5.20	33.35
镇平县 Zhenping	28.34	104.94	86.94	37.35	42.96	49.46	21.03	28.43
内乡县 Neixiang	23.20	72.76	56.71	24.21	42.69	33.24	14.25	18.99
淅川县 Xichuan	21.09	72.66	62.55	27.90	44.61	47.15	18.90	28.25
社旗县 Sheqi	22.03	75.05	63.45	26.71	42.09	43.25	24.35	18.89
唐河县 Tanghe	42.91	146.79	120.31	52.56	43.69	66.10	36.94	29.17
新野县 Xinye	23.64	84.59	63.08	26.90	42.65	48.80	21.99	26.81
桐柏县 Tongbai	15.91	48.55	40.12	19.15	47.72	26.89	8.79	18.09
邓州市 Dengzhou	49.84	180.01	136.59	60.09	43.99	88.04	49.09	38.95
商丘市 Shangqiu								
梁园区 Liangyuan	27.01	95.15	98.13	53.16	54.17	61.13	18.88	42.25
睢阳区 Suiyang	29.74	86.87	87.63	43.25	49.36	54.10	11.05	43.05
民权县 Minquan	29.41	93.70	70.07	27.54	39.30	58.78	22.67	36.11
睢县 Suixian	25.18	89.54	66.92	26.78	40.02	58.67	23.98	34.69
宁陵县 Ningling	23.56	66.98	50.78	19.09	37.59	43.15	22.74	20.41
柘城县 Zhecheng	33.70	104.90	68.22	26.86	39.37	51.70	20.20	31.50
虞城县 Yucheng	45.50	112.09	82.15	33.31	40.55	65.56	26.09	39.47
夏邑县 Xiayi	44.51	123.06	85.31	36.03	42.23	62.76	22.78	39.98
永城市 Yongcheng	46.52	158.11	124.15	62.70	50.50	93.75	22.45	71.30

26-1 续表 4 continued

县市区 County and District	年末总户数(万户) Total Households (year-end) (10 000 household)	年末总人口(万人) Population (year-end) (10 000 persons)	常住人口(万人) Resident population (10 000 persons)	#城镇 Urban	城镇化率(%) Urbanization Rate (%)	就业人员(万人) Employment (10 000 persons)	第一产业 Primary Industry	第二、三产业 Secondary Industry and Tertiary Industry
信阳市 Xinyang								
浉河区 Shihe	21.84	67.11	67.49	47.38	70.20	37.20	14.35	22.85
平桥区 Pingqiao	29.10	87.26	74.76	43.96	58.80	46.98	19.25	27.73
罗山县 Luoshan	22.47	77.56	54.93	24.27	44.19	39.83	19.27	20.56
光山县 Guangshan	29.01	86.31	59.57	24.87	41.75	44.20	21.83	22.37
新县 Xinxian	13.04	37.37	29.05	14.61	50.28	22.39	7.90	14.49
商城县 Shangcheng	24.46	80.07	52.97	22.07	41.66	38.52	15.25	23.27
固始县 Gushi	55.63	179.16	110.25	49.45	44.85	101.83	30.48	71.35
潢川县 Huangchuan	28.27	88.53	67.96	35.89	52.81	44.71	28.84	15.87
淮滨县 Huaibin	24.54	78.47	56.95	24.06	42.25	43.71	21.41	22.31
息县 Xixian	32.38	106.08	72.46	30.05	41.47	60.58	32.36	28.22
周口市 Zhoukou								
川汇区 Chuanhui	19.64	54.90	72.26	47.11	65.19	23.32	3.96	19.36
淮阳区 Huaiyang	38.62	133.64	97.36	40.26	41.35	85.44	35.44	50.00
扶沟县 Fugou	21.32	77.63	58.76	24.37	41.48	46.08	16.44	29.64
西华县 Xihua	27.50	98.56	73.45	30.43	41.43	57.71	19.08	38.63
商水县 Shangshui	32.36	126.36	87.73	33.94	38.69	76.84	28.52	48.32
沈丘县 Shenqiu	34.49	133.18	93.08	38.93	41.82	76.56	29.67	46.89
郸城县 Dancheng	42.74	137.23	95.34	39.46	41.39	84.05	31.02	53.03
太康县 Taikang	43.91	153.24	102.82	41.15	40.02	86.82	38.32	48.50
鹿邑县 Luyi	40.30	124.49	88.37	40.29	45.59	76.90	31.41	45.49
项城市 Xiangcheng	37.33	126.92	97.05	48.65	50.13	73.39	20.67	52.72
驻马店市 Zhumadian								
驿城区 Yicheng	23.94	83.07	104.36	72.89	69.84	62.25	18.80	43.45
西平县 Xiping	25.82	91.02	68.10	27.66	40.62	64.86	12.64	52.22
上蔡县 Shangcai	40.31	154.54	97.38	39.15	40.20	82.08	39.06	43.02
平舆县 Pingyu	34.98	102.63	71.11	30.75	43.24	64.47	29.56	34.91
正阳县 Zhengyang	25.95	84.47	62.27	22.31	35.83	54.63	27.03	27.60
确山县 Queshan	17.02	53.81	40.27	17.96	44.59	33.08	14.01	19.07
泌阳县 Biyang	27.63	93.77	67.44	29.08	43.12	57.75	13.65	44.10
汝南县 Runan	23.09	87.07	65.53	26.60	40.59	54.86	30.41	24.45
遂平县 Suiping	16.44	57.35	43.07	19.37	44.96	33.41	15.01	18.40
新蔡县 Xincai	33.09	115.03	85.05	32.07	37.71	68.91	18.92	49.99

26-2 各县(市、区)生产总值和指数(2019年)

县市区	County and District	生产总值(亿元) Gross Domestic Products (100 million yuan)	第一产业 Primary Industry	第二产业 Secondary Industry	第三产业 Tertiary Industry
郑州市	**Zhengzhou**				
中原区	Zhongyuan	1184.86	0.11	496.85	687.90
二七区	Erqi	754.76	0.05	177.82	576.89
管城区	Guancheng	1625.72	1.06	799.35	825.30
金水区	Jinshui	2620.17	0.46	363.79	2255.91
上街区	Shangjie	158.52	0.03	74.16	84.33
惠济区	Huiji	278.16	3.78	94.77	179.61
中牟县	Zhongmu	1216.39	35.24	623.88	557.27
巩义市	Gongyi	801.21	11.91	470.98	318.32
荥阳市	Xingyang	535.52	27.01	264.73	243.78
新密市	Xinmi	683.10	19.97	356.25	306.87
新郑市	Xinzheng	1273.66	25.02	662.79	585.86
登封市	Dengfeng	448.06	16.23	230.17	201.66
开封市	**Kaifeng**				
龙亭区	Longting	292.41	5.65	79.59	207.16
顺河区	Shunhe	139.86	2.50	71.28	66.08
鼓楼区	Gulou	98.23	2.15	16.29	79.78
禹王台区	Yuwangtai	95.18	3.33	38.44	53.41
祥符区	Xiangfu	269.04	55.08	113.81	100.15
杞县	Qixian	356.20	83.89	125.03	147.29
通许县	Tongxu	286.39	53.71	113.40	119.27
尉氏县	Weishi	436.98	53.73	214.95	168.30
兰考县	Lankao	389.87	58.21	176.43	155.23
洛阳市	**Luoyang**				
老城区	Laocheng	217.61	1.46	145.33	70.81
西工区	Xigong	458.46	0.29	151.02	307.15
瀍河区	Chanhe	119.15	0.59	32.97	85.60
涧西区	Jianxi	601.43	2.03	268.28	331.13
吉利区	Jili	180.55	1.48	124.71	54.37
洛龙区	Luolong	613.66	12.26	202.73	398.67
孟津县	Mengjin	328.14	24.50	192.73	110.92
新安县	Xinan	501.89	23.65	287.91	190.33
栾川县	Luanchuan	267.55	14.44	142.55	110.56
嵩县	Songxian	198.37	29.93	67.62	100.83
汝阳县	Ruyang	180.49	14.14	79.10	87.24
宜阳县	Yiyang	306.16	38.03	124.33	143.81
洛宁县	Luoning	205.11	31.24	75.96	97.91
伊川县	Yichuan	419.55	29.26	191.71	198.59
偃师市	Yanshi	443.57	21.70	245.51	176.36
平顶山市	**Pingdingshan**				
新华区	Xinhua	320.99	1.65	179.00	140.33
卫东区	Weidong	290.46	1.10	167.07	122.28
石龙区	Shilong	38.02	0.41	22.83	14.78
湛河区	Zhanhe	218.48	2.36	91.67	124.44
宝丰县	Baofeng	324.08	17.58	166.78	139.72
叶县	Yexian	207.02	48.12	61.43	97.47
鲁山县	Lushan	160.63	26.81	47.68	86.15
郏县	Jiaxian	196.80	23.76	89.32	83.72
舞钢市	Wugang	136.07	12.08	72.43	51.56
汝州市	Ruzhou	475.73	39.80	194.37	241.57

Gross Domestic Product and Its indices by County and District (2019)

人均生产总值 (元) (按常住人口计算) Per Capita GDP (yuan) (calculated atresidents)	生产总值指数 (%) (上年=100) Indices of Gross Domestic Products (%) (preced-ing year=100)	第一产业 Primary Industry	第二产业 Secondary Industry	第三产业 Tertiary Industry	人均生产总值指数 (%) Indices of Per Capita GDP (%)
107973	107.0	87.8	107.3	106.8	103.8
89546	107.4	49.8	107.2	107.5	104.5
192758	106.2	94.4	105.6	107.0	104.3
147452	106.6	102.3	107.2	106.5	104.3
103444	105.6	12.0	104.0	107.4	98.0
90525	106.5	101.8	108.1	105.7	104.3
102741	106.9	93.3	107.0	108.2	103.7
95260	105.8	96.8	107.0	104.1	105.1
81216	104.1	96.4	104.6	104.7	100.7
83810	105.6	97.0	105.7	106.3	105.1
127199	108.0	96.9	108.3	108.4	104.5
62065	101.6	96.1	100.2	104.5	100.2
66585	106.8	100.4	107.5	106.7	104.8
55881	106.0	102.6	106.2	105.9	105.0
62451	107.2	100.0	108.7	107.0	105.6
66790	107.2	102.6	110.1	105.1	105.1
40141	106.8	103.4	108.2	107.4	106.2
39867	106.8	104.2	108.2	107.3	107.3
55387	107.2	103.6	109.0	107.1	107.8
51438	107.6	104.4	108.7	107.2	108.1
59942	108.0	102.8	109.8	107.6	107.1
108342	110.6	100.6	111.5	109.2	107.9
123122	108.9	102.3	111.5	107.5	106.7
60462	109.3	102.2	114.5	107.5	106.7
84599	107.6	102.7	107.3	107.9	105.4
252074	97.0	102.6	92.8	109.8	95.1
84295	107.7	102.1	108.3	107.7	103.9
75548	108.7	103.9	110.3	107.1	107.9
102000	108.4	104.0	110.8	105.0	107.8
75883	108.5	103.6	111.0	105.9	108.0
37965	108.1	103.7	109.9	108.4	107.8
42352	108.3	103.7	109.9	107.7	109.0
49974	108.2	103.9	109.7	108.0	108.8
47413	107.7	103.7	108.7	108.4	108.3
53499	108.2	103.8	109.4	107.7	108.9
78004	108.0	103.6	109.8	106.0	108.7
78357	107.0	101.3	107.7	106.1	106.9
90316	108.8	101.1	109.1	108.5	108.8
73969	107.3	100.5	108.2	105.9	107.4
72224	107.3	102.1	106.9	107.9	107.4
64744	108.0	102.3	108.4	108.6	107.9
26393	107.2	102.4	109.4	108.6	107.2
20406	106.6	102.3	108.6	106.8	106.6
34030	108.1	102.3	109.6	108.5	108.1
42292	108.0	102.3	109.6	106.7	107.9
49077	107.6	102.2	108.2	108.1	106.2

26-2 续表 1

县 市	County and city	生产总值（亿元）Gross Domestic Products (100 million yuan)	第一产业 Primary Industry	第二产业 Secondary Industry	第三产业 Tertiary Industry
安阳市	**Anyang**				
文峰区	Wenfeng	245.70	1.04	70.24	174.41
北关区	Beiguan	155.98	1.37	49.13	105.47
殷都区	Yindu	324.86	10.06	216.29	98.51
龙安区	Longan	171.51	3.10	128.02	40.39
安阳县	Anyang	92.05	13.25	22.88	55.91
汤阴县	Tangyin	162.49	25.77	63.61	73.12
滑县	Huaxian	372.60	67.40	143.78	161.42
内黄县	Neihuang	168.07	64.41	35.29	68.37
林州市	Linzhou	535.87	11.59	269.15	255.13
鹤壁市	**Hebi**				
鹤山区	Heshan	77.45	3.07	58.06	16.31
山城区	Shancheng	133.44	4.03	91.05	38.36
淇滨区	Qibin	246.24	6.38	121.03	118.83
浚县	Xunxian	286.70	29.33	164.20	93.17
淇县	Qixian	234.96	21.02	149.28	64.66
新乡市	**Xinxiang**				
红旗区	Hongqi	541.80	2.04	257.70	282.06
卫滨区	Weibin	128.87	0.97	43.48	84.42
凤泉区	Fengquan	79.29	1.77	40.48	37.04
牧野区	Muye	215.20	1.54	106.85	106.80
新乡县	Xinxiang	211.27	8.71	124.43	78.13
获嘉县	Huojia	153.48	17.40	67.41	68.68
原阳县	Yuanyang	232.03	33.66	88.71	109.66
延津县	Yanjin	147.51	24.17	51.36	71.98
封丘县	Fengqiu	233.03	48.60	84.48	99.96
长垣市	Changyuan	469.32	49.14	252.57	167.62
卫辉市	Weihui	170.63	24.86	65.70	80.07
辉县市	Huixian	338.81	40.77	156.94	141.10
焦作市	**Jiaozuo**				
解放区	Jiefang	176.78	0.22	30.36	146.19
中站区	Zhongzhan	118.20	0.62	82.18	35.40
马村区	Macun	63.60	1.42	35.31	26.88
山阳区	Shanyang	383.97	5.05	166.86	212.06
修武县	Xiuwu	150.65	9.95	69.39	71.31
博爱县	Boai	292.94	18.68	181.20	93.05
武陟县	Wuzhi	463.26	38.92	259.45	164.89
温县	Wenxian	290.96	30.41	140.17	120.37
沁阳市	Qinyang	447.28	21.61	264.90	160.76
孟州市	Mengzhou	373.47	22.90	250.39	100.19

continued

人均生产总值（元）（按常住人口计算）Per Capita GDP (yuan) (calculated atresidents)	生产总值指数（%）（上年=100）Indices of Gross Domestic Products (%) (preced-ing year=100)	第一产业 Primary Industry	第二产业 Secondary Industry	第三产业 Tertiary Industry	人均生产总值指数（%）Indices of Per Capita GDP (%)
54588	98.2	89.9	97.3	98.7	96.7
50388	102.8	95.9	96.2	106.1	104.3
47401	98.6	97.0	96.5	105.1	97.0
58726	99.7	96.8	97.9	108.3	97.5
20624	105.1	99.8	99.5	109.7	104.9
36688	108.8	100.0	115.0	107.1	108.1
34677	105.8	102.3	107.4	106.3	105.6
25160	98.9	98.2	95.7	101.8	98.6
65723	106.2	76.6	106.4	108.9	105.7
59853	105.7	103.1	106.8	102.0	105.6
54925	106.0	103.0	106.3	105.4	106.3
82951	107.3	102.9	109.5	105.1	108.2
42103	107.9	103.1	110.0	105.7	108.1
87669	107.0	103.3	108.8	103.1	107.3
118582	110.3	101.8	112.3	108.2	109.3
57197	104.0	101.9	109.8	100.8	102.8
50025	107.1	98.3	109.6	103.0	106.3
63238	106.8	97.4	108.6	104.9	106.2
60665	107.7	100.9	108.0	108.7	107.3
37037	107.8	103.8	110.0	106.6	107.6
35663	108.3	104.0	111.6	106.8	108.4
32251	107.1	102.8	108.8	107.7	107.3
32462	107.7	104.2	112.4	105.5	107.7
59847	108.1	103.1	110.3	105.8	106.6
34748	107.8	104.0	111.2	106.7	107.9
44613	100.4	102.4	97.7	103.4	100.1
57858	106.5	104.2	102.5	107.4	106.1
109718	109.9	104.0	109.8	110.2	109.0
44800	104.9	104.2	104.5	105.7	104.5
78104	108.3	104.3	109.0	107.6	107.0
58850	106.2	104.5	106.8	105.9	105.5
77657	108.6	104.1	108.8	109.3	109.0
68956	107.9	104.2	109.2	106.6	107.1
69022	108.1	104.3	109.3	107.8	107.9
100575	108.1	104.0	108.6	107.9	107.5
99383	108.2	104.2	109.0	106.9	107.6

26-2 续表 2

县 市 County and city	生产总值（亿元）Gross Domestic Products (100 million yuan)	第一产业 Primary Industry	第二产业 Secondary Industry	第三产业 Tertiary Industry
濮 阳 市 Puyang				
华 龙 区 Hualong	623.57	24.11	254.66	344.80
清 丰 县 Qingfeng	195.79	47.44	63.16	85.19
南 乐 县 Nanle	168.96	38.45	48.41	82.10
范 县 Fanxian	213.64	21.17	97.78	94.68
台 前 县 Taiqian	115.69	11.82	42.62	61.25
濮 阳 县 Puyang	263.85	50.13	64.26	149.46
许 昌 市 Xuchang				
魏 都 区 Weidu	416.94	0.17	155.43	261.34
建 安 区 Jianan	546.65	27.34	298.65	220.67
鄢 陵 县 Yanling	370.27	37.17	156.67	176.43
襄 城 县 Xiangcheng	452.49	38.29	193.99	220.21
禹 州 市 Yuzhou	833.20	31.01	471.77	330.43
长 葛 市 Changge	776.12	28.30	557.90	189.92
漯 河 市 Luohe				
源 汇 区 Yuanhui	231.92	9.67	74.30	147.95
郾 城 区 Yancheng	271.48	22.90	101.50	147.07
召 陵 区 Zhaoling	461.62	30.82	256.39	174.40
舞 阳 县 Wuyang	253.46	31.97	122.32	99.17
临 颍 县 Linying	359.99	42.43	175.42	142.14
三 门 峡 市 Sanmenxia				
湖 滨 区 Hubin	288.02	6.05	119.52	162.46
陕 州 区 Shanzhou	243.36	23.84	116.11	103.41
渑 池 县 Mianchi	218.99	19.86	113.79	85.34
卢 氏 县 Lushi	115.65	26.63	34.33	54.69
义 马 市 Yima	140.99	1.62	92.69	46.69
灵 宝 市 Lingbao	436.54	58.18	228.28	150.08
南 阳 市 Nanyang				
宛 城 区 Wancheng	430.28	32.58	142.74	254.96
卧 龙 区 Wolong	550.76	25.37	158.05	367.34
南 召 县 Nanzhao	169.41	21.74	68.86	78.80
方 城 县 Fangcheng	252.48	44.02	82.92	125.53
西 峡 县 Xixia	251.15	32.94	101.73	116.48
镇 平 县 Zhenping	256.93	35.58	81.14	140.20
内 乡 县 Neixiang	245.39	41.69	109.39	94.31
淅 川 县 Xichuan	233.37	41.39	84.01	107.98
社 旗 县 Sheqi	172.50	40.68	45.71	86.10
唐 河 县 Tanghe	360.64	82.72	98.62	179.30
新 野 县 Xinye	263.38	51.44	74.92	137.03
桐 柏 县 Tongbai	178.58	24.69	73.58	80.31
邓 州 市 Dengzhou	450.04	94.62	146.19	209.23

continued

人均生产总值(元)(按常住人口计算) Per Capita GDP (yuan) (calculated atresidents)	生产总值指数(%)(上年=100) Indices of Gross Domestic Products (%) (preced-ing year=100)	第一产业 Primary Industry	第二产业 Secondary Industry	第三产业 Tertiary Industry	人均生产总值指数(%) Indices of Per Capita GDP (%)
78862	106.9	103.4	103.8	110.2	106.3
31075	107.2	103.2	112.5	105.6	107.5
36926	107.2	103.6	109.0	107.8	109.1
47815	107.0	104.1	109.3	105.0	109.1
35498	107.7	104.2	105.4	110.3	109.6
27516	105.1	103.5	100.7	108.1	104.5
79744	106.3	51.5	106.6	106.2	105.4
68735	106.9	102.3	107.0	107.6	106.3
64643	105.5	102.1	104.5	107.6	104.9
65210	107.0	102.0	108.6	106.6	106.4
71566	107.8	102.2	108.4	107.7	107.3
110771	107.7	102.1	108.6	105.7	107.0
67341	107.2	102.5	108.9	106.5	107.2
52511	107.3	102.2	109.0	106.6	107.2
91581	107.7	102.6	108.7	106.9	107.7
44932	107.5	102.5	109.1	106.9	107.5
48832	107.7	102.6	109.1	107.1	107.7
88428	107.7	103.3	109.6	106.5	107.4
69330	108.0	104.1	109.0	107.5	107.8
61952	107.1	104.2	108.2	106.1	106.9
32133	108.2	105.3	111.4	107.6	108.0
95295	105.0	103.3	104.5	106.1	104.8
59261	107.9	103.2	109.1	107.8	107.8
45770	106.1	103.2	104.3	108.0	105.6
57192	108.2	103.1	107.8	108.9	108.1
31027	107.2	103.9	109.0	106.3	106.7
29658	107.4	103.5	109.3	107.5	108.9
58313	107.0	103.8	108.7	106.1	106.7
29613	107.1	103.7	109.0	106.8	106.1
43179	107.0	103.6	108.5	106.5	107.1
37292	107.9	103.7	109.4	108.3	110.4
27135	107.1	103.9	109.0	107.8	105.4
30006	106.9	103.9	107.8	107.9	106.9
41661	107.2	103.7	109.2	107.2	106.4
44303	106.8	103.7	107.5	107.2	104.3
33160	105.6	101.3	107.7	106.5	107.5

26-2 续表 3

县 市 County and city	生产总值（亿元）Gross Domestic Products (100 million yuan)	第一产业 Primary Industry	第二产业 Secondary Industry	第三产业 Tertiary Industry
商 丘 市 Shangqiu				
梁 园 区 Liangyuan	333.17	32.15	144.76	156.26
睢 阳 区 Suiyang	313.11	41.81	111.53	159.77
民 权 县 Minquan	323.99	50.04	123.73	150.22
睢 县 Suixian	222.88	46.05	85.90	90.92
宁 陵 县 Ningling	181.71	28.80	70.34	82.58
柘 城 县 Zhecheng	271.87	48.28	112.74	110.85
虞 城 县 Yucheng	338.38	51.81	152.19	134.39
夏 邑 县 Xiayi	317.77	52.03	132.16	133.58
永 城 市 Yongcheng	615.79	77.95	265.80	272.04
信 阳 市 Xinyang				
浉 河 区 Shihe	330.73	37.68	99.54	193.50
平 桥 区 Pingqiao	389.68	44.00	167.70	177.98
罗 山 县 Luoshan	232.36	51.05	84.24	97.08
光 山 县 Guangshan	230.52	53.69	73.97	102.85
新 县 Xinxian	163.05	28.74	64.88	69.42
商 城 县 Shangcheng	235.19	45.54	96.68	92.98
固 始 县 Gushi	409.55	85.80	126.69	197.07
潢 川 县 Huangchuan	301.53	56.84	112.77	131.92
淮 滨 县 Huaibin	225.92	41.26	91.70	92.97
息 县 Xixian	253.91	53.10	87.06	113.75
周 口 市 Zhoukou				
川 汇 区 Chuanhui	317.16	7.44	145.98	163.74
淮 阳 区 Huaiyang	270.81	52.01	118.17	100.63
扶 沟 县 Fugou	225.50	41.05	103.11	81.35
西 华 县 Xihua	279.47	52.53	124.42	102.52
商 水 县 Shangshui	300.53	54.66	128.99	116.88
沈 丘 县 Shenqiu	332.04	51.48	139.89	140.67
郸 城 县 Dancheng	327.84	52.19	154.18	121.46
太 康 县 Taikang	372.71	62.14	154.13	156.44
鹿 邑 县 Luyi	398.88	57.36	169.05	172.46
项 城 市 Xiangcheng	374.18	43.67	168.41	162.10
驻 马 店 市 Zhumadian				
驿 城 区 Yicheng	536.11	31.36	233.33	271.42
西 平 县 Xiping	240.21	54.82	80.50	104.89
上 蔡 县 Shangcai	260.76	47.80	106.64	106.32
平 舆 县 Pingyu	254.60	44.06	106.43	104.11
正 阳 县 Zhengyang	242.40	57.73	92.29	92.39
确 山 县 Queshan	182.85	36.76	69.61	76.49
泌 阳 县 Biyang	285.76	56.57	118.96	110.23
汝 南 县 Runan	243.27	53.90	102.85	86.52
遂 平 县 Suiping	226.42	34.10	106.03	86.29
新 蔡 县 Xincai	272.25	50.81	85.49	135.95

continued

人均生产总值 (元) (按常住人口计算) Per Capita GDP (yuan) (calculated atresidents)	生产总值指数 (%) (上年=100) Indices of Gross Domestic Products (%) (preced-ing year=100)	第一产业 Primary Industry	第二产业 Secondary Industry	第三产业 Tertiary Industry	人均生产总值指数 (%) Indices of Per Capita GDP (%)
34194	105.3	102.2	103.5	107.9	103.7
36059	106.5	102.2	107.1	107.6	105.9
46106	107.5	102.2	108.8	108.6	107.6
33323	107.5	102.5	109.5	109.0	107.1
35749	107.8	102.2	108.7	109.5	107.4
39768	107.2	102.3	108.4	108.6	107.3
41066	107.2	102.4	108.1	108.2	107.7
36989	107.5	102.6	108.7	108.8	108.3
49655	108.4	103.8	109.8	108.1	108.0
49091	105.8	102.5	106.3	106.4	105.3
52240	107.4	102.5	108.4	107.7	107.3
43094	106.3	102.5	106.5	108.9	103.5
38273	106.4	102.7	107.1	108.5	107.2
56252	106.0	102.6	106.3	107.5	104.7
44502	105.3	102.5	108.0	103.8	104.8
37249	107.7	103.1	109.6	108.8	107.1
44470	106.2	100.7	106.7	109.5	104.8
39294	107.9	101.8	108.9	110.7	108.1
34452	103.3	102.0	95.7	112.6	107.3
43931	105.6	102.2	104.7	106.9	105.0
34321	107.9	102.4	108.8	110.4	107.1
27774	107.2	102.5	107.8	109.6	108.8
38315	107.1	102.5	108.7	108.3	108.0
37984	107.1	102.6	107.9	109.6	108.2
34204	107.6	102.4	108.1	109.5	108.0
35630	107.8	102.4	108.4	110.2	109.0
36180	108.5	102.7	109.3	110.8	109.8
45278	108.5	103.0	109.7	109.3	107.8
38502	107.6	102.3	105.6	112.2	109.0
51766	107.6	102.0	108.4	107.7	105.0
35242	107.2	102.4	108.9	108.8	107.1
26760	107.8	102.2	110.2	108.4	107.7
35729	107.3	102.5	109.8	107.0	108.1
38893	107.2	102.1	110.3	107.8	107.7
45357	106.6	102.3	107.5	108.2	106.4
42338	106.7	102.6	108.0	107.8	106.6
37090	107.9	102.4	110.6	108.7	108.2
52508	106.6	101.9	109.3	105.1	106.1
32088	108.2	103.4	110.7	108.9	107.9

26-3 各县(市、区)固定资产投资、建筑业及规模以上工业主要指标(2019年)

Main Indicators on Investment in Fixed Assets、Construction and Enterprises above Designated Size Industry by County and District (2019)

县市区 County and District	工业增加值增速(%) Growth Rate of Value Added of Industry (%)	营业收入(亿元) Business Revenue (100 million yuan)	利润总额(亿元) Profits (100 million yuan)	固定资产投资增速(%) Growth Rate of Investment in Fixed Assets (%)	#房地产开发 Growth Rate of Real Estate (%)	建筑业总产值(亿元) Gross Output Value of Construction (100 million yuan)
郑州市 Zhengzhou						
中原区 Zhongyuan	6.2	953.84	76.71	8.5	11.7	539.18
二七区 Erqi	18.6	203.49	12.48	0.8	-3.1	340.32
管城区 Guancheng	4.5	1648.80	172.13	-3.6	17.8	219.07
金水区 Jinshui	6.6	100.22	7.98	3.5	7.8	1802.70
上街区 Shangjie	4.7	111.10	1.03	10.1	31.3	33.21
惠济区 Huiji	7.1	144.44	1.97	7.8	17.1	184.21
中牟县 Zhongmu	12.2	555.71	50.32	-0.9	-12.2	112.27
巩义市 Gongyi	6.5	981.72	109.12	9.1	-3.6	27.09
荥阳市 Xingyang	5.3	237.10	12.91	11.4	-24.8	96.35
新密市 Xinmi	5.0	257.22	36.33	-38.2	-11.6	49.58
新郑市 Xinzheng	1.9	3314.81	26.84	16.2	-0.7	32.22
登封市 Dengfeng	-1.2	245.94	8.30	4.8	-24.0	15.57
开封市 Kaifeng						
龙亭区 Longting	15.7	292.77	7.96	15.0	29.7	17.36
顺河区 Shunhe	3.7	74.51	15.24	-20.6	-7.8	124.20
鼓楼区 Gulou	8.4	52.41	1.03	11.8	-44.8	10.34
禹王台区 Yuwangtai	8.3	91.39	2.20	11.6	-47.1	36.67
祥符区 Xiangfu	7.3	176.88	18.19	11.4	151.4	17.73
杞县 Qixian	8.6	141.72	13.71	11.3	35.6	8.14
通许县 Tongxu	8.3	74.56	4.82	11.4	46.5	21.69
尉氏县 Weishi	8.7	341.96	33.70	11.5	-6.2	22.59
兰考县 Lankao	9.8	222.57	19.05	10.0	41.3	124.10
洛阳市 Luoyang						
老城区 Laocheng	9.5	7.88	0.32	16.0	12.3	28.37
西工区 Xigong	9.3	254.49	10.55	16.8	-6.4	151.87
瀍河区 Chanhe	9.0	211.89	0.82	9.1	16.7	173.90
涧西区 Jianxi	9.9	789.80	36.78	8.2	-3.7	57.40
吉利区 Jili	9.6	456.44	2.94	15.7	-53.9	23.75
洛龙区 Luolong	10.2	498.29	41.92	32.0	75.2	82.93
孟津县 Mengjin	9.7	467.83	66.04	15.8	70.4	17.80
新安县 Xinan	9.8	736.97	38.49	-8.7	2.4	26.22
栾川县 Luanchuan	10.1	328.98	21.55	16.5	24.9	50.83
嵩县 Songxian	9.7	55.99	3.75	13.2	130.2	6.74
汝阳县 Ruyang	9.4	49.67	5.31	13.3	56.4	7.13
宜阳县 Yiyang	9.3	158.98	16.11	12.6	-1.1	13.80
洛宁县 Luoning	9.3	174.22	20.47	15.6	-11.1	11.68
伊川县 Yichuan	9.2	275.47	3.05	-9.6	71.2	4.19
偃师市 Yanshi	7.5	437.63	52.05	10.1	21.4	16.39
平顶山市 Pingdingshan						
新华区 Xinhua	8.2	305.34	16.21	27.2	-11.6	22.79
卫东区 Weidong	11.1	331.80	14.92	10.2	-20.9	56.18
石龙区 Shilong	5.6	66.31	3.31	17.4		8.82
湛河区 Zhanhe	6.4	176.94	1.86	19.6	-24.2	57.22
宝丰县 Baofeng	10.0	248.92	21.57	0.3	-17.9	4.18
叶县 Yexian	8.1	160.91	6.25	13.6	-48.2	11.59
鲁山县 Lushan	9.4	128.04	3.64	19.9	69.4	11.86
郏县 Jiaxian	9.5	129.24	10.50	19.9	-4.9	8.72
舞钢市 Wugang	9.6	275.69	6.48	23.0	-30.3	3.53
汝州市 Ruzhou	8.0	313.50	25.00	-14.5	1.4	14.99

26-3 续表 1　　continued

县市区	County and District	工业增加值增速(%) Growth Rate of Value Added of Industry (%)	营业收入(亿元) Business Revenue (100 million yuan)	利润总额(亿元) Profits (100 million yuan)	固定资产投资增速(%) Growth Rate of Investment in Fixed Assets (%)	#房地产开发 Growth Rate of Real Estate (%)	建筑业总产值(亿元) Gross Output Value of Construction (100 million yuan)
安阳市	**Anyang**						
文峰区	Wenfeng	-4.1	127.31	5.60	3.9	-5.8	23.88
北关区	Beiguan	-11.2	16.65	0.29	2.2	42.3	117.04
殷都区	Yindu	-4.3	418.65	5.32	24.1	76.7	88.93
龙安区	Longan	-1.8	286.30	1.12	-32.6	-0.3	10.21
安阳县	Anyang	0.2	426.46	7.99	11.3	50.0	45.89
汤阴县	Tangyin	17.0	164.88	13.39	-7.2	-13.0	23.58
滑县	Huaxian	9.7	141.21	11.95	-33.5	30.1	34.31
内黄县	Neihuang	-4.6	53.76	3.86	7.1	81.4	4.05
林州市	Linzhou	8.8	208.64	-12.00	-17.7	-30.9	652.16
鹤壁市	**Hebi**						
鹤山区	Heshan	7.4	83.53	9.00	12.4		2.72
山城区	Shancheng	5.1	68.58	1.70	10.4	5.0	5.90
淇滨区	Qibin	8.8	497.94	14.32	11.5	-0.3	47.87
浚县	Xunxian	8.5	272.11	17.57	10.9	16.0	14.47
淇县	Qixian	9.2	287.75	9.98	12.1	10.1	3.20
新乡市	**Xinxiang**						
红旗区	Hongqi	12.7	564.58	37.26	18.9	3.1	62.71
卫滨区	Weibin	12.2	83.80	-0.21	12.5	-27.5	17.84
凤泉区	Fengquan	9.4	78.87	-0.51	26.1	66.7	10.98
牧野区	Muye	10.3	186.46	4.95	-43.4	-58.3	108.40
新乡县	Xinxiang	8.3	291.63	16.04	15.3	124.9	30.67
获嘉县	Huojia	11.5	78.46	2.62	31.5	83.2	25.19
原阳县	Yuanyang	12.4	129.54	5.80	31.4	15.3	13.65
延津县	Yanjin	9.4	85.02	3.09	31.5	20.1	10.14
封丘县	Fengqiu	11.5	47.77	2.34	10.8	-27.6	147.66
长垣市	Changyuan	9.9	435.77	27.94	10.0	-10.7	313.48
卫辉市	Weihui	11.5	121.65	6.28	25.3	76.5	17.27
辉县市	Huixian	-5.0	264.56	13.96	10.0	-4.4	19.89
焦作市	**Jiaozuo**						
解放区	Jiefang	0.1	18.97	1.11	12.9	6.3	21.47
中站区	Zhongzhan	9.0	259.91	29.51	12.9		11.15
马村区	Macun	2.1	99.32	3.93	12.5	-23.3	12.64
山阳区	Shanyang	8.0	729.95	55.10	13.1	11.0	15.38
修武县	Xiuwu	8.5	218.20	6.00	10.1	2.8	3.53
博爱县	Boai	8.6	416.90	29.04	10.0	30.2	3.41
武陟县	Wuzhi	9.0	470.82	35.85	12.4	4.1	4.84
温县	Wenxian	9.3	231.56	19.07	12.0	-8.7	3.58
沁阳市	Qinyang	8.7	452.57	48.57	12.2	-21.1	6.37
孟州市	Mengzhou	8.7	465.92	53.77	12.2	-59.7	5.24

26-3 续表 2 continued

县市区 County and District	工业增加值增速(%) Growth Rate of Value Added of Industry (%)	营业收入(亿元) Business Revenue (100 million yuan)	利润总额(亿元) Profits (100 million yuan)	固定资产投资增速(%) Growth Rate of Investment in Fixed Assets (%)	#房地产开发 Growth Rate of Real Estate (%)	建筑业总产值(亿元) Gross Output Value of Construction (100 million yuan)
濮阳市 Puyang						
华龙区 Hualong	9.5	558.37	0.84	21.6	29.4	84.09
清丰县 Qingfeng	7.7	39.69	2.13	22.5	44.1	8.74
南乐县 Nanle	7.3	70.40	4.00	4.3	51.8	3.01
范县 Fanxian	9.1	185.06	5.88	-21.1	4.3	2.74
台前县 Taiqian	7.9	52.56	2.53	20.7	-13.2	3.87
濮阳县 Puyang	3.3	94.17	4.96	-5.8	9.4	16.38
许昌市 Xuchang						
魏都区 Weidu	8.2	359.37	9.86	5.2	29.5	86.61
建安区 Jianan	7.2	585.00	43.95	4.5	23.9	22.54
鄢陵县 Yanling	8.0	53.41	4.72	8.4	32.0	30.44
襄城县 Xiangcheng	8.7	385.40	35.29	5.2	34.6	13.65
禹州市 Yuzhou	8.7	1369.37	184.18	8.6	27.4	7.15
长葛市 Changge	8.9	2002.80	192.68	0.1	61.1	8.68
漯河市 Luohe						
源汇区 Yuanhui	8.3	159.29	7.25	8.1	-20.6	16.01
郾城区 Yancheng	8.3	99.91	2.48	15.5	95.6	24.89
召陵区 Zhaoling	8.4	1197.23	73.37	13.9	18.7	13.70
舞阳县 Wuyang	8.4	92.74	-0.07	5.5	19.6	4.18
临颍县 Linying	8.6	372.00	34.51	11.3	87.0	18.45
三门峡市 Sanmenxia						
湖滨区 Hubin	10.0	98.65	3.22	10.5	3.3	166.36
陕州区 Shanzhou	9.1	518.56	22.81	10.3	46.7	5.19
渑池县 Mianchi	8.7	146.38	9.28	10.1	185.5	13.20
卢氏县 Lushi	9.0	21.03	4.45	10.3	-5.7	11.97
义马市 Yima	3.7	126.58	-7.61	10.0	-36.3	8.56
灵宝市 Lingbao	8.7	339.97	40.30	10.1	8.4	12.97
南阳市 Nanyang						
宛城区 Wancheng	5.6	158.50	-5.22	15.1	-6.6	42.96
卧龙区 Wolong	8.3	393.18	16.31	17.6	-2.0	88.37
南召县 Nanzhao	9.7	55.85	5.88	-9.8	29.5	19.25
方城县 Fangcheng	8.1	68.85	8.64	16.8	11.6	21.98
西峡县 Xixia	9.4	443.81	12.76	20.8	0.9	16.25
镇平县 Zhenping	9.2	113.64	7.73	15.5	79.1	9.47
内乡县 Neixiang	8.6	311.88	66.72	20.8	42.4	32.63
淅川县 Xichuan	8.5	111.67	8.10	22.1	136.7	49.32
社旗县 Sheqi	7.8	22.89	2.09	-32.9	167.3	27.71
唐河县 Tanghe	8.3	122.84	3.99	15.0	19.4	38.14
新野县 Xinye	8.5	119.03	5.41	20.8	40.5	16.12
桐柏县 Tongbai	6.9	87.47	8.54	21.9	3.0	25.63
邓州市 Dengzhou	7.3	223.22	24.02	5.3	-16.9	97.81

26-3 续表 3 continued

县市区	County and District	工业增加值增速(%) Growth Rate of Value Added of Industry (%)	营业收入(亿元) Business Revenue (100 million yuan)	利润总额(亿元) Profits (100 million yuan)	固定资产投资增速(%) Growth Rate of Investment in Fixed Assets (%)	#房地产开发 Growth Rate of Real Estate (%)	建筑业总产值(亿元) Gross Output Value of Construction (100 million yuan)
商丘市	**Shangqiu**						
梁园区	Liangyuan	8.3	291.93	13.81	7.6	7.4	216.68
睢阳区	Suiyang	8.3	273.62	12.79	9.6	16.8	71.43
民权县	Minquan	9.0	497.43	36.08	12.6	13.4	72.33
睢县	Suixian	8.6	226.50	23.58	12.0	-20.4	20.30
宁陵县	Ningling	8.9	229.49	18.00	13.0	24.2	21.77
柘城县	Zhecheng	9.1	265.13	35.42	11.7	-34.8	30.06
虞城县	Yucheng	8.5	450.21	34.57	12.6	-15.1	17.16
夏邑县	Xiayi	9.0	449.24	37.49	13.2	12.1	50.11
永城市	Yongcheng	9.4	742.05	91.38	10.0	-20.7	93.08
信阳市	**Xinyang**						
浉河区	Shihe	10.8	89.81	2.38	6.1	-6.2	110.09
平桥区	Pingqiao	9.1	539.20	17.09	16.2	2.4	39.20
罗山县	Luoshan	9.3	141.24	16.14	-7.9	-41.0	93.02
光山县	Guangshan	9.3	62.18	5.59	12.5	-13.2	45.82
新县	Xinxian	6.1	81.76	10.48	13.8	-47.7	56.98
商城县	Shangcheng	9.1	151.18	12.69	13.0	29.9	59.12
固始县	Gushi	9.0	233.89	18.45	10.0	8.2	59.48
潢川县	Huangchuan	8.3	203.44	16.38	11.5	-27.4	66.95
淮滨县	Huaibin	9.5	228.80	21.25	14.0	7.2	53.95
息县	Xixian	-3.2	42.81	4.21	13.9	2.7	51.00
周口市	**Zhoukou**						
川汇区	Chuanhui	5.4	518.01	45.08	18.0	2.5	177.14
淮阳区	Huaiyang	8.8	238.30	29.84	9.9	1.5	27.49
扶沟县	Fugou	8.5	305.33	65.72	9.4	7.4	19.00
西华县	Xihua	8.6	400.60	55.19	1.5	-24.0	36.26
商水县	Shangshui	8.4	263.19	53.15	4.3	50.7	48.03
沈丘县	Shenqiu	8.6	408.31	50.27	9.5	12.3	17.13
郸城县	Dancheng	8.3	317.13	48.72	9.5	395.8	47.98
太康县	Taikang	8.7	456.44	66.85	9.7	-11.8	132.06
鹿邑县	Luyi	8.9	197.11	48.41	10.0	25.0	79.12
项城市	Xiangcheng	8.4	407.22	46.99	10.1	40.7	32.13
驻马店市	**Zhumadian**						
驿城区	Yicheng	8.2	556.74	24.91	12.2	3.2	253.11
西平县	Xiping	8.6	57.29	4.40	12.1	17.6	66.17
上蔡县	Shangcai	8.9	104.17	13.07	12.4	20.0	40.59
平舆县	Pingyu	8.7	147.16	19.21	12.1	21.3	92.59
正阳县	Zhengyang	8.2	159.35	16.12	11.8	15.8	53.96
确山县	Queshan	8.5	91.39	20.22	10.6	-9.3	150.61
泌阳县	Biyang	8.1	129.85	14.56	12.3	13.1	54.65
汝南县	Runan	8.4	150.80	13.22	12.1	17.6	22.19
遂平县	Suiping	8.5	114.60	9.15	12.1	3.7	41.92
新蔡县	Xincai	9.2	118.49	6.05	10.0	18.9	61.78

26-4 各县(市、区)城镇单位就业人员和工资(2019年)

Number and Wages of Employed Person in Urban Units by County and District (2019)

县市区	County and District	城镇单位年末就业人员（人）Number of Employed Person in Urban Area (person)	城镇单位年平均就业人员（人）Average Number of Employed Person in Urban Area (person)	城镇单位就业人员平均工资（元）Average Wage of Employed Persons in Urban Area (yuan)	#在岗职工平均工资 Average Wage of Working Staff and Workers
郑州市	**Zhengzhou**				
中原区	Zhongyuan	141191	141554	91236	93251
二七区	Erqi	142931	139899	83347	84835
管城区	Guancheng	100915	99271	85175	87119
金水区	Jinshui	368641	347465	87966	93888
上街区	Shangjie	23674	23423	74684	76836
惠济区	Huiji	44894	44061	79607	80085
中牟县	Zhongmu	45201	44626	81903	87997
巩义市	Gongyi	55455	55608	62399	63291
荥阳市	Xingyang	42603	44793	77847	78887
新密市	Xinmi	61175	59797	68261	69834
新郑市	Xinzheng	81719	79784	78352	80985
登封市	Dengfeng	56757	56132	56674	57837
开封市	**Kaifeng**				
龙亭区	Longting	81460	80584	60154	61243
顺河区	Shunhe	42989	42393	64996	66097
鼓楼区	Gulou	32437	32190	60061	63863
禹王台区	Yuwangtai	12146	12255	57043	57345
祥符区	Xiangfu	48705	48482	54469	54564
杞县	Qixian	40182	39345	54045	54011
通许县	Tongxu	30189	28592	54870	55112
尉氏县	Weishi	29799	29646	59254	59187
兰考县	Lankao	57281	55491	59289	59877
洛阳市	**Luoyang**				
老城区	Laocheng	13927	14025	76293	79887
西工区	Xigong	75581	76023	91997	101193
瀍河区	Chanhe	17077	17213	91329	98288
涧西区	Jianxi	97586	97581	77457	85408
吉利区	Jili	17645	17592	62599	63949
洛龙区	Luolong	90857	88887	87310	94067
孟津县	Mengjin	38107	37619	58539	61148
新安县	Xinan	75365	74900	55127	56147
栾川县	Luanchuan	27621	26908	60883	69736
嵩县	Songxian	20516	20228	56555	62426
汝阳县	Ruyang	18861	18038	59590	62785
宜阳县	Yiyang	30962	30167	53342	56132
洛宁县	Luoning	20091	20035	51238	53337
伊川县	Yichuan	39795	39211	52433	54060
偃师市	Yanshi	28758	28951	60442	61850
平顶山市	**Pingdingshan**				
新华区	Xinhua	140702	140881	71596	71911
卫东区	Weidong	44267	43730	62418	62982
石龙区	Shilong	6293	6323	48103	49012
湛河区	Zhanhe	47544	48051	66658	74636
宝丰县	Baofeng	27775	26619	47667	48160
叶县	Yexian	30413	28815	50017	50788
鲁山县	Lushan	32055	31364	54294	54426
郏县	Jiaxian	32210	31214	50688	51085
舞钢市	Wugang	34955	34710	52449	53498
汝州市	Ruzhou	63390	61111	51250	51816

26-4 续表 1 continued

县市区	County and District	城镇单位年末就业人员(人) Number of Employed Person in Urban Area (person)	城镇单位年平均就业人员(人) Everage Number of Employed Person in Urban Area (person)	城镇单位就业人员平均工资(元) Average Wage of Employed Persons in Urban Area (yuan)	#在岗职工平均工资 Average Wage of Working Staff and Workers
安阳市	**Anyang**				
文峰区	Wenfeng	67887	68410	75967	81780
北关区	Beiguan	51114	48515	56959	58191
殷都区	Yindu	47093	46824	65232	65628
龙安区	Longan	10794	10427	56064	57647
安阳县	Anyang	22722	21408	62627	71708
汤阴县	Tangyin	30498	29599	52495	54888
滑县	Huaxian	63574	63816	57925	60187
内黄县	Neihuang	23883	23508	57515	59836
林州市	Linzhou	142494	140424	55724	58339
鹤壁市	**Hebi**				
鹤山区	Heshan	10042	9951	61359	62168
山城区	Shancheng	14244	14294	56216	56965
淇滨区	Qibin	97425	97340	59395	63773
浚县	Xunxian	29882	29197	49169	50422
淇县	Qixian	25299	25480	48977	50945
新乡市	**Xinxiang**				
红旗区	Hongqi	95115	95159	71379	71625
卫滨区	Weibin	24392	24456	61928	62550
凤泉区	Fengquan	7630	7502	49902	50075
牧野区	Muye	52401	47942	73688	76246
新乡县	Xinxiang	41582	41103	52732	53304
获嘉县	Huojia	19529	18946	49933	50661
原阳县	Yuanyang	26988	26724	55817	56190
延津县	Yanjin	24891	24177	56674	57668
封丘县	Fengqiu	34381	33918	58176	57973
长垣市	Changyuan	84471	79681	56875	57082
卫辉市	Weihui	23176	22705	54761	56124
辉县市	Huixian	41920	41558	51251	54789
焦作市	**Jiaozuo**				
解放区	Jiefang	40066	37932	67848	69484
中站区	Zhongzhan	26114	23104	59180	59287
马村区	Macun	10585	10614	61715	61904
山阳区	Shanyang	48747	44745	62496	64704
修武县	Xiuwu	32865	32506	60204	60128
博爱县	Boai	19563	18606	51804	51908
武陟县	Wuzhi	36038	34587	53567	54057
温县	Wenxian	30658	30458	53113	53500
沁阳市	Qinyang	35134	32851	58087	58603
孟州市	Mengzhou	43485	43407	62096	63794

26-4 续表 2 continued

县市区 County and District	城镇单位年末就业人员（人）Number of Employed Person in Urban Area (person)	城镇单位年平均就业人员（人）Everage Number of Employed Person in Urban Area (person)	城镇单位就业人员平均工资（元）Average Wage of Employed Persons in Urban Area (yuan)	#在岗职工平均工资 Average Wage of Working Staff and Workers
濮阳市 Puyang				
华龙区 Hualong	215188	213589	71759	75578
清丰县 Qingfeng	25177	24525	61636	66838
南乐县 Nanle	19004	18952	61426	64784
范县 Fanxian	19345	19329	63203	67015
台前县 Taiqian	15987	15905	51068	52438
濮阳县 Puyang	44984	43831	56551	57800
许昌市 Xuchang				
魏都区 Weidu	74895	69307	71972	74493
建安区 Jianan	44315	44963	64710	64758
鄢陵县 Yanling	32943	32744	58531	59635
襄城县 Xiangcheng	49446	49322	64964	66901
禹州市 Yuzhou	57821	58046	58573	59704
长葛市 Changge	111047	109753	56241	56527
漯河市 Luohe				
源汇区 Yuanhui	53163	52319	56749	57379
郾城区 Yancheng	47616	47497	70558	69819
召陵区 Zhaoling	70473	69096	63916	64104
舞阳县 Wuyang	46271	46543	53781	53825
临颍县 Linying	51367	51542	58278	58617
三门峡市 Sanmenxia				
湖滨区 Hubin	55166	55628	77173	83074
陕州区 Shanzhou	16933	16736	74771	75481
渑池县 Mianchi	17561	17024	71360	72163
卢氏县 Lushi	13793	13603	57521	61212
义马市 Yima	35876	37460	55926	56002
灵宝市 Lingbao	43425	41636	51036	52782
南阳市 Nanyang				
宛城区 Wancheng	66021	65856	78485	80317
卧龙区 Wolong	102971	101419	59917	60048
南召县 Nanzhao	28419	27836	52713	53768
方城县 Fangcheng	42354	41826	58361	59009
西峡县 Xixia	37086	36773	52820	53366
镇平县 Zhenping	55753	55211	51571	51865
内乡县 Neixiang	42834	41377	50215	51108
淅川县 Xichuan	47344	46131	55993	56464
社旗县 Sheqi	27665	27335	43287	44456
唐河县 Tanghe	45167	44419	53722	54154
新野县 Xinye	34115	33836	44530	44820
桐柏县 Tongbai	29021	28510	46478	46541
邓州市 Dengzhou	64171	62078	53134	54199

26-4 续表 3 continued

县市区 County and District	城镇单位年末就业人员(人) Number of Employed Person in Urban Area (person)	城镇单位年平均就业人员(人) Everage Number of Employed Person in Urban Area (person)	城镇单位就业人员平均工资(元) Average Wage of Employed Persons in Urban Area (yuan)	#在岗职工平均工资 Average Wage of Working Staff and Workers
商丘市 Shangqiu				
梁园区 Liangyuan	102468	96806	53138	53185
睢阳区 Suiyang	60860	59573	84556	84785
民权县 Minquan	95126	93955	62369	62469
睢县 Suixian	65711	64021	58676	58764
宁陵县 Ningling	43034	42660	56224	56442
柘城县 Zhecheng	50993	49189	53522	53492
虞城县 Yucheng	82592	74823	54910	55296
夏邑县 Xiayi	89527	87107	56210	56421
永城市 Yongcheng	91988	91002	57520	57942
信阳市 Xinyang				
浉河区 Shihe	79747	79219	63881	65169
平桥区 Pingqiao	108662	108160	63464	64227
罗山县 Luoshan	26814	26514	59188	60911
光山县 Guangshan	30964	30599	58099	58667
新县 Xinxian	27550	27143	59529	59914
商城县 Shangcheng	31297	31008	57628	57980
固始县 Gushi	80207	77831	64332	64708
潢川县 Huangchuan	48746	47290	50747	50787
淮滨县 Huaibin	44960	45684	57104	57221
息县 Xixian	46874	45532	51191	51191
周口市 Zhoukou				
川汇区 Chuanhui	112856	112224	70104	70772
淮阳区 Huaiyang	37853	36646	45756	45902
扶沟县 Fugou	55471	54220	46380	46473
西华县 Xihua	37666	36827	55846	55947
商水县 Shangshui	87452	85873	50841	50861
沈丘县 Shenqiu	71550	69662	50155	50312
郸城县 Dancheng	38704	38506	53478	53439
太康县 Taikang	70321	69895	64697	64741
鹿邑县 Luyi	58330	57608	55003	54997
项城市 Xiangcheng	65682	61722	57087	57236
驻马店市 Zhumadian				
驿城区 Yicheng	190521	184009	66227	67563
西平县 Xiping	43573	42686	53966	54123
上蔡县 Shangcai	45193	43939	54137	54395
平舆县 Pingyu	54763	50732	58407	58530
正阳县 Zhengyang	36381	35726	58770	58751
确山县 Queshan	34127	33401	56519	57943
泌阳县 Biyang	55699	54991	54144	54175
汝南县 Runan	37741	36155	46730	46747
遂平县 Suiping	42683	42223	56390	56702
新蔡县 Xincai	49901	47168	53183	53240

26-5 各县(市、区)城乡居民收入和社会消费品零售总额(2019年)

Per Capita Net Income of Rural and Urban Residents, Total Retail Sales of Consumer Goods by County and District (2019)

县市区 County and District	居民人均可支配收入(元) Per Capita Disposable Income of Residents (yuan)	农村居民人均可支配收入(元) Disposable Income of Rural Household (yuan)	城镇居民人均可支配收入(元) Per Capita Net Income of Urban Residents (yuan)	社会消费品零售总额(亿元) Total Retail Sales of Consumer Goods (100 million yuan)
郑州市 Zhengzhou				
中原区 Zhongyuan	41203	25056	43747	455.13
二七区 Erqi	42353	26531	45133	523.50
管城区 Guancheng	40113	28322	42756	1128.31
金水区 Jinshui	46839	28224	49601	1411.18
上街区 Shangjie	45178	24091	48608	40.74
惠济区 Huiji	33638	27597	36479	233.65
中牟县 Zhongmu	26474	21310	33135	349.95
巩义市 Gongyi	30467	25076	35577	287.37
荥阳市 Xingyang	28997	22360	35757	166.98
新密市 Xinmi	29192	22434	35680	197.87
新郑市 Xinzheng	29910	23503	35991	365.66
登封市 Dengfeng	27422	20217	34750	164.10
开封市 Kaifeng				
龙亭区 Longting	28519	16641	33922	159.85
顺河区 Shunhe	29117	15726	32465	67.09
鼓楼区 Gulou	32997	16807	34836	138.02
禹王台区 Yuwangtai	27489	15987	31833	58.07
祥符区 Xiangfu	18483	14265	27037	82.73
杞县 Qixian	18485	14995	25657	115.12
通许县 Tongxu	19056	15537	26678	88.46
尉氏县 Weishi	19900	15355	28973	120.81
兰考县 Lankao	18228	13126	27231	200.47
洛阳市 Luoyang				
老城区 Laocheng	35982	16562	38934	68.94
西工区 Xigong	41843	18847	44999	300.95
瀍河区 Chanhe	37649	18737	40194	107.86
涧西区 Jianxi	39009	22229	40558	311.32
吉利区 Jili	35191	18082	44518	18.22
洛龙区 Luolong	31218	16841	39801	289.54
孟津县 Mengjin	22904	15120	32732	98.04
新安县 Xinan	26048	17543	37561	114.94
栾川县 Luanchuan	22468	13116	34230	105.91
嵩县 Songxian	19122	13113	31963	124.03
汝阳县 Ruyang	17876	12229	29620	105.48
宜阳县 Yiyang	18849	12440	31668	142.90
洛宁县 Luoning	17952	12150	31023	78.95
伊川县 Yichuan	23101	15941	33761	153.35
偃师市 Yanshi	28315	21299	34586	150.37
平顶山市 Pingdingshan				
新华区 Xinhua	37401	18948	38252	139.83
卫东区 Weidong	37659	19977	38178	166.04
石龙区 Shilong	25451	16950	27839	5.39
湛河区 Zhanhe	34254	19709	38213	87.07
宝丰县 Baofeng	23691	17323	34205	81.34
叶县 Yexian	19913	13477	33148	92.04
鲁山县 Lushan	17280	10409	31600	73.85
郏县 Jiaxian	20022	13151	31861	78.13
舞钢市 Wugang	25904	15901	34635	50.69
汝州市 Ruzhou	23677	18571	30903	258.88

26-5 续表 1　　continued

县市区	County and District	居民人均可支配收入(元) Per Capita Disposable Income of Residents (yuan)	农村居民人均可支配收入(元) Disposable Income of Rural Household (yuan)	城镇居民人均可支配收入(元) Per Capita Net Income of Urban Residents (yuan)	社会消费品零售总额(亿元) Total Retail Sales of Consumer Goods (100 million yuan)
安阳市	**Anyang**				
文峰区	Wenfeng	34741	21029	39709	157.79
北关区	Beiguan	32131	21389	35452	99.54
殷都区	Yindu	31639	20876	38837	89.89
龙安区	Longan	26723	18243	34319	48.79
安阳县	Anyang	22304	18052	30851	65.39
汤阴县	Tangyin	21734	16054	29738	43.31
滑县	Huaxian	17313	13076	28178	172.12
内黄县	Neihuang	16193	13384	24432	61.19
林州市	Linzhou	27122	21845	33117	162.09
鹤壁市	**Hebi**				
鹤山区	Heshan	28986	16994	31323	18.13
山城区	Shancheng	31036	18012	33191	49.68
淇滨区	Qibin	31541	16668	37985	91.95
浚县	Xunxian	21228	18781	27112	98.48
淇县	Qixian	24630	18710	30714	41.03
新乡市	**Xinxiang**				
红旗区	Hongqi	34769	18633	36458	167.75
卫滨区	Weibin	36168		36168	129.37
凤泉区	Fengquan	25122	16778	32238	11.37
牧野区	Muye	35644	20060	37131	71.53
新乡县	Xinxiang	26455	20145	32927	51.50
获嘉县	Huojia	19963	16349	25220	66.73
原阳县	Yuanyang	17972	14277	26271	77.43
延津县	Yanjin	20137	16743	26970	55.04
封丘县	Fengqiu	17212	12575	26813	56.17
长垣市	Changyuan	25124	21610	29981	32.93
卫辉市	Weihui	20732	16607	26879	95.68
辉县市	Huixian	24209	17605	33146	180.65
焦作市	**Jiaozuo**				
解放区	Jiefang	36594		36594	114.03
中站区	Zhongzhan	25671	18114	30752	32.65
马村区	Macun	25363	18049	30438	27.62
山阳区	Shanyang	36505		36505	136.97
修武县	Xiuwu	25110	18491	32985	62.73
博爱县	Boai	25611	18571	33008	86.93
武陟县	Wuzhi	24643	19289	33107	135.28
温县	Wenxian	25264	19414	32645	98.46
沁阳市	Qinyang	27786	20506	33612	126.30
孟州市	Mengzhou	26287	20359	33510	99.24

26-5 续表 2 continued

县市区 County and District	居民人均可支配收入（元）Per Capita Disposable Income of Residents (yuan)	农村居民人均可支配收入（元）Disposable Income of Rural Household (yuan)	城镇居民人均可支配收入（元）Per Capita Net Income of Urban Residents (yuan)	社会消费品零售总额（亿元）Total Retail Sales of Consumer Goods (100 million yuan)
濮阳市 Puyang				
华龙区 Hualong	34475	16916	36647	313.74
清丰县 Qingfeng	18551	15764	26972	64.17
南乐县 Nanle	18329	14772	27228	61.24
范县 Fanxian	14966	11277	24399	75.63
台前县 Taiqian	14213	10677	23420	46.80
濮阳县 Puyang	20296	14576	30289	127.50
许昌市 Xuchang				
魏都区 Weidu	36392		36392	362.96
建安区 Jianan	23731	18662	32448	154.07
鄢陵县 Yanling	23588	18712	31986	118.10
襄城县 Xiangcheng	22142	17482	30391	121.37
禹州市 Yuzhou	25780	19220	34757	287.42
长葛市 Changge	25573	18916	32647	227.72
漯河市 Luohe				
源汇区 Yuanhui	30878	20539	37483	180.99
郾城区 Yancheng	27992	19901	36002	169.38
召陵区 Zhaoling	26104	19289	33945	114.11
舞阳县 Wuyang	17213	11427	25477	96.28
临颍县 Linying	22496	17667	29075	112.56
三门峡市 Sanmenxia				
湖滨区 Hubin	31634	16944	33509	121.24
陕州区 Shanzhou	21003	14197	30715	57.57
渑池县 Mianchi	24707	17605	34083	59.25
卢氏县 Lushi	16503	10719	28696	47.32
义马市 Yima	30946	19556	31349	44.58
灵宝市 Lingbao	23732	18007	32536	171.86
南阳市 Nanyang				
宛城区 Wancheng	28808	17170	37380	254.36
卧龙区 Wolong	28982	17024	37706	507.59
南召县 Nanzhao	18528	12774	29491	93.94
方城县 Fangcheng	19837	14314	31045	156.59
西峡县 Xixia	25367	17876	34919	64.84
镇平县 Zhenping	21181	15778	31124	194.86
内乡县 Neixiang	21127	15119	31783	94.67
淅川县 Xichuan	20630	13338	33230	115.68
社旗县 Sheqi	18321	13006	28300	78.41
唐河县 Tanghe	21165	15239	31324	160.21
新野县 Xinye	22743	17590	32095	96.47
桐柏县 Tongbai	19780	12811	30159	61.74
邓州市 Dengzhou	22070	16673	31315	197.82

26-5 续表 3 continued

县市区	County and District	居民人均可支配收入(元) Per Capita Disposable Income of Residents (yuan)	农村居民人均可支配收入(元) Disposable Income of Rural Household (yuan)	城镇居民人均可支配收入(元) Per Capita Net Income of Urban Residents (yuan)	社会消费品零售总额(亿元) Total Retail Sales of Consumer Goods (100 million yuan)
商丘市	**Shangqiu**				
梁园区	Liangyuan	23430	13028	33727	380.87
睢阳区	Suiyang	21285	12896	32932	228.22
民权县	Minquan	17929	12120	29536	106.05
睢县	Suixian	17950	12115	29794	106.32
宁陵县	Ningling	16417	12043	26088	72.55
柘城县	Zhecheng	17622	12410	28215	117.59
虞城县	Yucheng	18637	12648	30442	122.29
夏邑县	Xiayi	19425	12594	31919	123.34
永城市	Yongcheng	23755	15880	34400	223.52
信阳市	**Xinyang**				
浉河区	Shihe	26964	17056	32640	210.01
平桥区	Pingqiao	24080	15035	32443	166.49
罗山县	Luoshan	19765	13811	29531	85.48
光山县	Guangshan	19560	14134	29333	105.26
新县	Xinxian	20669	14077	29267	59.89
商城县	Shangcheng	19165	13577	29344	78.51
固始县	Gushi	20495	15048	29505	203.87
潢川县	Huangchuan	21917	15223	29837	120.11
淮滨县	Huaibin	18400	12803	28754	81.13
息县	Xixian	18502	12863	29157	103.46
周口市	**Zhoukou**				
川汇区	Chuanhui	24547	16446	30344	238.22
淮阳区	Huaiyang	17095	11425	27616	157.25
扶沟县	Fugou	17444	12452	26553	89.11
西华县	Xihua	17155	11732	27169	139.70
商水县	Shangshui	16846	11777	27425	104.27
沈丘县	Shenqiu	17626	11999	27950	142.13
郸城县	Dancheng	17884	12432	28098	141.15
太康县	Taikang	17323	12479	26967	237.78
鹿邑县	Luyi	20118	14454	29292	236.09
项城市	Xiangcheng	20280	13655	29050	193.92
驻马店市	**Zhumadian**				
驿城区	Yicheng	26103	13316	33807	282.41
西平县	Xiping	18510	13954	27556	64.51
上蔡县	Shangcai	17856	12690	28718	112.45
平舆县	Pingyu	18929	13224	29503	72.39
正阳县	Zhengyang	16478	12728	25831	72.80
确山县	Queshan	18702	12786	28674	46.02
泌阳县	Biyang	18767	13031	29436	89.57
汝南县	Runan	17460	13157	26242	61.87
遂平县	Suiping	19503	13712	29174	72.10
新蔡县	Xincai	17582	13392	27118	148.25

26-6 各县(市)农业生产条件(2019年)
Agricultural Conditions by County and City (2019)

县 市	County and city	农用机械总动力(万千瓦) Total Agricultural Machinery Power (10 000kw)	农村用电量(万千瓦时) Electricity Consumed in Rural Areas (10 000 kwh)	化肥施用折纯量(吨) Consumption of Chemical Fertilizers (ton)	农药使用量(吨) Consump tion of Agricultural Pesticides (ton)	农用塑料薄膜使用量(吨) Consumption of Plastic Film (ton)
郑州市	**Zhengzhou**					
中牟县	Zhongmu	67.53	30047.29	34241	901	2704
巩义市	Gongyi	50.29	203338.66	23693	138	106
荥阳市	Xingyang	45.77	31634.90	26218	553	453
新密市	Xinmi	93.88	46210.26	25908	265	685
新郑市	Xinzheng	63.35	42098.14	29395	399	386
登封市	Dengfeng	68.78	47562.59	23607	244	135
开封市	**Kaifeng**					
杞县	Qixian	160.09	21751.82	69399	954	3566
通许县	Tongxu	77.39	4876.74	35810	1034	2083
尉氏县	Weishi	122.01	35756.43	48825	842	2270
兰考县	Lankao	75.79	27111.29	72210	592	1710
洛阳市	**Luoyang**					
孟津县	Mengjin	45.44	22242.88	19592	390	376
新安县	Xinan	49.33	6944.64	21025	480	551
栾川县	Luanchuan	33.34	33453.26	5631	69	78
嵩县	Songxian	60.46	13536.88	23100	396	251
汝阳县	Ruyang	48.22	19316.83	16206	472	527
宜阳县	Yiyang	65.57	22577.21	46022	904	827
洛宁县	Luoning	39.47	8354.85	22319	436	476
伊川县	Yichuan	77.30	36008.85	24516	299	489
偃师市	Yanshi	91.49	28840.24	33111	388	159
平顶山市	**Pingdingshan**					
宝丰县	Baofeng	46.05	17534.29	48202	387	279
叶县	Yexian	79.81	20612.64	90100	616	1006
鲁山县	Lushan	39.37	30516.08	42307	425	355
郏县	Jiaxian	40.05	13252.46	40159	588	589
舞钢市	Wugang	28.71	5458.85	14443	551	253
汝州市	Ruzhou	152.83	32604.77	92057	664	673
安阳市	**Anyang**					
安阳县	Anyang	56.79	19926.67	38666	809	24
汤阴县	Tangyin	56.85	23496.46	41245	502	202
滑县	Huaxian	222.61	57077.46	206557	2066	4199
内黄县	Neihuang	76.56	41520.63	77023	1418	13567
林州市	Linzhou	44.24	66829.59	34393	264	48
鹤壁市	**Hebi**					
浚县	Xunxian	150.89	7924.05	44869	585	866
淇县	Qixian	33.53	7214.37	6435	225	34

26-6 续表 1 continued

县 市	County and city	农用机械总动力(万千瓦) Total Agricultural Machinery Power (10 000kw)	农村用电量(万千瓦时) Electricity Consumed in Rural Areas (10 000 kwh)	化肥施用折纯量(吨) Consumption of Chemical Fertilizers (ton)	农药使用量(吨) Consumption of Agricultural Pesticides (ton)	农用塑料薄膜使用量(吨) Consumption of Plastic Film (ton)
新乡市	**Xinxiang**					
新乡县	Xinxiang	51.72	190968.15	26270	538	35
获嘉县	Huojia	57.37	19711.38	35315	434	94
原阳县	Yuanyang	137.60	38086.54	39958	721	737
延津县	Yanjin	102.99	23366.36	123963	885	158
封丘县	Fengqiu	128.58	12609.05	73708	2276	237
长垣市	Changyuan	102.91	54979.23	65272	994	747
卫辉市	Weihui	72.00	25401.16	45465	680	303
辉县市	Huixian	86.54	261950.45	79380	928	370
焦作市	**Jiaozuo**					
修武县	Xiuwu	24.38	8503.38	13073	341	49
博爱县	Boai	21.31	11696.01	28000	423	607
武陟县	Wuzhi	65.26	20280.63	52185	1268	329
温县	Wenxian	39.64	31164.16	22836	406	199
沁阳市	Qinyang	40.16	34502.10	29056	669	248
孟州市	Mengzhou	35.66	34357.47	26657	439	658
濮阳市	**Puyang**					
清丰县	Qingfeng	77.99	17444.25	65442	590	394
南乐县	Nanle	69.29	34366.86	54635	470	3094
范县	Fanxian	50.39	12949.66	29403	419	443
台前县	Taiqian	28.14	9728.86	11518	188	248
濮阳县	Puyang	127.65	16792.53	99324	1272	579
许昌市	**Xuchang**					
鄢陵县	Yanling	82.28	6823.07	26814	863	940
襄城县	Xiangcheng	69.07	14914.48	39689	476	667
禹州市	Yuzhou	88.08	29007.05	44498	407	827
长葛市	Changge	57.95	29991.59	37529	605	472
漯河市	**Luohe**					
舞阳县	Wuyang	60.77	13079.13	36375	657	384
临颍县	Linying	91.03	21330.86	47649	736	1156
三门峡市	**Sanmenxia**					
渑池县	Mianchi	32.80	5904.60	18150	271	824
卢氏县	Lushi	18.11	3176.57	13396	205	841
义马市	Yima	1.20	2243.74	1006	21	80
灵宝市	Lingbao	39.38	12133.84	33611	1222	875
南阳市	**Nanyang**					
南召县	Nanzhao	43.65	6644.99	13026	397	596
方城县	Fangcheng	144.80	22604.39	61089	1375	3279
西峡县	Xixia	15.53	26583.42	23718	309	1997

26-6 续表 2 continued

县 市	County and city	农用机械总动力（万千瓦）Total Agricultural Machinery Power (10 000kw)	农村用电量（万千瓦时）Electricity Consumed in Rural Areas (10 000 kwh)	化肥施用折纯量（吨）Consumption of Chemical Fertilizers (ton)	农药使用量（吨）Consumption of Agricultural Pesticides (ton)	农用塑料薄膜使用量（吨）Consumption of Plastic Film (ton)
镇平县	Zhenping	107.29	17283.91	41963	821	935
内乡县	Neixiang	81.31	22480.91	27472	461	788
淅川县	Xichuan	51.36	24028.42	41242	634	1139
社旗县	Sheqi	93.04	7190.45	64533	1353	1276
唐河县	Tanghe	249.28	31857.87	98036	2858	1914
新野县	Xinye	178.76	22938.08	84765	2420	6726
桐柏县	Tongbai	86.94	7286.65	33818	348	676
邓州市	Dengzhou	201.43	28271.50	172081	2637	3135
商丘市	**Shangqiu**					
民权县	Minquan	95.40	17538.46	43859	1323	2398
睢县	Suixian	93.12	8236.16	53400	770	1112
宁陵县	Ningling	64.50	21665.36	43780	1113	972
柘城县	Zhecheng	85.24	26260.57	49290	620	230
虞城县	Yucheng	111.92	48609.52	157411	3161	2104
夏邑县	Xiayi	102.36	53724.88	111399	1534	2414
永城市	Yongcheng	137.13	35180.92	170865	1751	1853
信阳市	**Xinyang**					
罗山县	Luoshan	84.77	10109.00	36361	657	812
光山县	Guangshan	48.74	27618.11	38677	579	422
新县	Xinxian	28.19	6689.00	10451	332	168
商城县	Shangcheng	37.88	21597.11	18425	372	341
固始县	Gushi	137.70	38340.99	113842	3823	4534
潢川县	Huangchuan	59.43	21270.54	38448	395	1551
淮滨县	Huaibin	77.21	16356.64	49711	1289	2556
息县	Xixian	120.15	18618.70	62362	1719	1137
周口市	**Zhoukou**					
扶沟县	Fugou	106.78	19196.82	62611	1725	3542
西华县	Xihua	109.48	21525.46	116150	3520	977
商水县	Shangshui	95.23	20320.12	80882	957	2086
沈丘县	Shenqiu	83.60	30377.59	107458	2117	2334
郸城县	Dancheng	113.73	32516.86	132898	1974	1690
太康县	Taikang	171.00	19293.78	113516	2876	2934
鹿邑县	Luyi	103.36	12652.68	96926	991	679
项城市	Xiangcheng	71.98	30750.28	44522	1400	1170
驻马店市	**Zhumadian**					
西平县	Xiping	122.11	37335.50	66012	318	1223
上蔡县	Shangcai	151.98	27825.70	97040	977	998
平舆县	Pingyu	166.93	8578.83	53808	487	920
正阳县	Zhengyang	229.53	7133.13	119893	310	1051
确山县	Queshan	102.83	17167.19	66588	935	2489
泌阳县	Biyang	150.89	9871.98	62034	356	2249
汝南县	Runan	147.41	10063.21	85048	805	1200
遂平县	Suiping	110.63	8076.05	59849	500	492
新蔡县	Xincai	144.75	9729.84	79277	2421	1182

26−7 各县(市)主要农作物播种面积(2019年)

Sown Area of Major Farm Products by County and City (2019)

单位：千公顷 (1 000 hectares)

县 市	County and city	粮 食 Food	#谷物 Grain	#小麦 Wheat	#玉米 Corn	#豆类 Beans	棉 花 Cotton	油 料 Oil-bearing Crops
郑 州 市	**Zhengzhou**							
中 牟 县	Zhongmu	28.43	26.65	12.47	14.19	0.72	0.51	8.68
巩 义 市	Gongyi	43.13	41.72	22.67	18.59	0.53	0.33	2.58
荥 阳 市	Xingyang	49.89	48.76	27.11	21.58	0.30		1.98
新 密 市	Xinmi	56.19	52.65	27.59	25.06	1.78	0.04	2.99
新 郑 市	Xinzheng	47.80	46.12	24.58	21.53	0.78	0.01	5.74
登 封 市	Dengfeng	51.09	47.19	24.89	22.29	1.91	0.27	2.03
开 封 市	**Kaifeng**							
杞 县	Qixian	121.13	113.29	65.18	48.11	4.29	2.90	21.51
通 许 县	Tongxu	66.78	64.31	39.59	24.71	1.75	0.33	8.47
尉 氏 县	Weishi	108.29	102.42	65.61	36.08	3.24	1.53	27.51
兰 考 县	Lankao	100.73	96.83	59.33	37.31	1.57	1.05	16.68
洛 阳 市	**Luoyang**							
孟 津 县	Mengjin	51.46	46.69	26.57	18.04	0.72	0.31	2.15
新 安 县	Xinan	46.90	41.71	21.48	19.47	2.54	0.06	3.34
栾 川 县	Luanchuan	9.51	8.41	2.62	5.79	0.82	0.01	0.37
嵩 县	Songxian	47.49	39.35	20.11	18.98	3.46	0.31	4.55
汝 阳 县	Ruyang	43.26	37.72	19.89	17.12	1.74	0.21	4.12
宜 阳 县	Yiyang	89.05	75.29	42.97	28.12	7.73	1.17	17.45
洛 宁 县	Luoning	61.96	48.55	30.33	15.41	9.72	0.05	2.38
伊 川 县	Yichuan	78.85	69.35	38.81	23.68	2.47	0.49	3.53
偃 师 市	Yanshi	40.42	39.15	21.50	17.21	0.78	0.10	0.88
平 顶 山 市	**Pingdingshan**							
宝 丰 县	Baofeng	51.93	50.30	26.55	23.75	1.34	0.01	4.83
叶 县	Yexian	122.65	115.51	59.01	56.49	4.75	0.15	10.62
鲁 山 县	Lushan	62.61	59.81	30.79	28.46	0.79		7.76
郏 县	Jiaxian	62.69	52.13	30.85	21.27	4.81	0.19	6.36
舞 钢 市	Wugang	32.06	30.15	16.26	13.89	1.53		1.53
汝 州 市	Ruzhou	94.81	91.96	47.93	43.48	0.95	0.27	6.24
安 阳 市	**Anyang**							
安 阳 县	Anyang	63.36	62.99	31.56	31.43	0.19	0.15	0.11
汤 阴 县	Tangyin	72.95	71.55	38.05	33.39	0.78	0.14	1.81
滑 县	Huaxian	206.53	205.17	120.80	84.16	0.52	0.44	25.14
内 黄 县	Neihuang	96.34	94.93	63.07	31.84	0.25	0.09	22.09
林 州 市	Linzhou	58.16	50.24	17.56	29.25	2.30	0.55	3.48
鹤 壁 市	**Hebi**							
浚 县	Xunxian	99.99	99.63	55.42	44.13	0.13	0.10	12.83
淇 县	Qixian	41.63	41.03	20.55	20.45		0.04	0.40

26-7 续表 1 continued

单位：千公顷 (1 000 hectares)

县 市	County and city	粮 食 Food	#谷物 Grain	#小麦 Wheat	#玉米 Corn	#豆类 Beans	棉 花 Cotton	油 料 Oil-bearing Crops
新 乡 市	**Xinxiang**							
新 乡 县	Xinxiang	39.01	35.68	20.66	14.90	3.31	0.04	2.70
获 嘉 县	Huojia	55.11	49.93	26.73	18.12	5.16	0.03	0.03
原 阳 县	Yuanyang	140.53	138.37	71.14	54.32	1.33	0.25	11.18
延 津 县	Yanjin	81.42	79.58	55.37	24.20	0.16		30.75
封 丘 县	Fengqiu	113.69	110.04	65.44	44.55	1.30	0.45	14.38
长 垣 市	Changyuan	106.67	103.69	56.00	45.46	2.60	0.30	9.41
卫 辉 市	Weihui	66.17	65.79	32.71	32.91	0.17		3.02
辉 县 市	Huixian	95.20	94.09	48.65	45.13	0.26		6.47
焦 作 市	**Jiaozuo**							
修 武 县	Xiuwu	30.44	14.79	15.18	14.72	0.35	0.01	0.26
博 爱 县	Boai	27.76	13.32	13.50	13.27	0.71		0.57
武 陟 县	Wuzhi	70.51	30.62	37.88	26.47	1.45	0.03	9.38
温 县	Wenxian	39.65	17.07	21.98	17.07	0.12	0.06	3.60
沁 阳 市	Qinyang	45.58	20.95	23.06	20.92	1.21	0.00	1.27
孟 州 市	Mengzhou	36.48	13.91	22.28	13.88	0.12	0.05	9.76
濮 阳 市	**Puyang**							
清 丰 县	Qingfeng	152.23	141.94	83.53	49.03	9.61	0.01	11.13
南 乐 县	Nanle	83.46	79.92	50.97	28.95	0.55	0.01	1.69
范 县	Fanxian	67.89	65.89	36.27	29.38	0.75	0.07	1.06
台 前 县	Taiqian	62.15	55.00	29.48	11.69	6.87	0.07	0.76
濮 阳 县	Puyang	38.07	31.73	18.87	12.86	5.17	0.78	4.46
许 昌 市	**Xuchang**							
鄢 陵 县	Yanling	76.71	73.59	42.67	30.92	2.68	0.08	1.38
襄 城 县	Xiangcheng	90.33	61.78	45.09	16.29	14.11	0.25	3.87
禹 州 市	Yuzhou	97.71	87.56	47.85	39.70	2.18	0.09	5.14
长 葛 市	Changge	80.13	76.76	40.31	36.45	3.02		2.72
漯 河 市	**Luohe**							
舞 阳 县	Wuyang	80.52	72.18	42.04	30.14	7.06	0.06	9.00
临 颍 县	Linying	76.23	56.79	41.22	15.56	16.39	0.14	1.23
三 门 峡 市	**Sanmenxia**							
渑 池 县	Mianchi	42.57	32.73	21.35	10.43	7.22	0.08	6.40
卢 氏 县	Lushi	31.63	25.73	13.70	11.94	5.00		0.33
义 马 市	Yima	2.23	2.01	0.99	1.00	0.09		0.19
灵 宝 市	Lingbao	53.34	45.63	24.81	20.82	6.01	1.05	3.34
南 阳 市	**Nanyang**							
南 召 县	Nanzhao	28.55	25.67	8.36	10.08	1.54		10.83
方 城 县	Fangcheng	161.31	148.31	82.37	65.69	10.54	0.41	56.58
西 峡 县	Xixia	24.70	22.30	10.85	11.13	1.14		2.85

26-7 续表 2 continued

单位：千公顷 (1 000 hectares)

县 市 County and city	粮 食 Food	#谷物 Grain	#小麦 Wheat	#玉米 Corn	#豆类 Beans	棉 花 Cotton	油 料 Oil-bearing Crops
镇 平 县 Zhenping	98.45	95.52	52.56	42.36	1.58		22.50
内 乡 县 Neixiang	72.85	70.15	34.78	34.73	0.31	0.03	19.73
淅 川 县 Xichuan	64.12	59.22	34.57	21.10	3.02	0.39	39.83
社 旗 县 Sheqi	125.20	115.93	63.99	51.94	6.18	0.21	25.90
唐 河 县 Tanghe	231.16	216.75	142.58	68.23	7.64	0.10	54.12
新 野 县 Xinye	80.50	76.97	52.95	23.26	2.58		32.36
桐 柏 县 Tongbai	46.86	44.63	16.55	11.09	1.61		19.79
邓 州 市 Dengzhou	217.07	205.02	138.18	58.55	9.94	0.51	61.72
商 丘 市 Shangqiu							
民 权 县 Minquan	107.88	104.66	68.00	36.66	1.91	0.34	19.83
睢 县 Suixian	101.89	97.89	57.38	40.51	2.41	0.25	11.64
宁 陵 县 Ningling	76.12	72.77	48.13	24.63	1.68		22.24
柘 城 县 Zhecheng	117.13	114.79	65.99	48.81	1.61	0.41	2.07
虞 城 县 Yucheng	146.53	145.20	77.13	68.07	0.74	1.74	10.54
夏 邑 县 Xiayi	157.92	153.56	81.88	71.68	2.34	0.32	4.33
永 城 市 Yongcheng	209.20	170.67	112.00	58.33	38.87	0.12	1.88
信 阳 市 Xinyang							
罗 山 县 Luoshan	95.53	93.65	28.39	0.05	0.89	0.03	18.16
光 山 县 Guangshan	68.88	67.35	14.47		0.99	0.35	30.77
新 县 Xinxian	14.35	13.74	1.26	0.01	0.09	0.02	12.88
商 城 县 Shangcheng	41.83	40.63	8.41	0.03	0.81	0.06	10.46
固 始 县 Gushi	152.00		37.33	3.31	0.15	0.07	19.43
潢 川 县 Huangchuan	98.39	98.07	37.05	0.05	0.13		11.21
淮 滨 县 Huaibin	100.71	97.69	55.40	2.73	1.11	0.08	18.26
息 县 Xixian	162.41	159.97	92.86	12.01	1.27	0.15	15.42
周 口 市 Zhoukou							
扶 沟 县 Fugou	104.69	91.19	64.84	26.20	13.20	0.45	7.63
西 华 县 Xihua	131.65	119.18	73.73	45.45	11.35	0.26	8.45
商 水 县 Shangshui	161.21	141.01	80.05	60.88	16.96	0.37	11.43
沈 丘 县 Shenqiu	136.86	125.62	72.85	52.77	7.18	0.02	9.88
郸 城 县 Dancheng	177.37	153.69	89.06	64.63	12.28	0.21	6.76
太 康 县 Taikang	198.00	186.65	109.31	77.34	8.83	0.78	6.62
鹿 邑 县 Luyi	143.07	127.27	72.87	54.41	14.75	0.09	5.80
项 城 市 Xiangcheng	138.52	119.33	75.57	43.76	17.12	0.35	10.44
驻 马 店 市 Zhumadian							
西 平 县 Xiping	141.36	140.96	72.15	68.81	0.27		7.90
上 蔡 县 Shangcai	168.72	159.95	98.62	61.17	7.72	0.19	26.56
平 舆 县 Pingyu	132.32	124.12	80.77	43.35	6.00		25.95
正 阳 县 Zhengyang	158.41	155.14	130.32	6.65	1.60		107.45
确 山 县 Queshan	97.32	92.26	56.42	31.59	1.85		39.56
泌 阳 县 Biyang	124.93	118.93	74.89	41.40	1.17		51.27
汝 南 县 Runan	128.49	123.94	86.60	37.32	3.43		49.39
遂 平 县 Suiping	101.94	99.45	54.12	45.33	1.34	0.01	11.84
新 蔡 县 Xincai	152.27	148.75	86.80	59.46	2.29	0.24	27.36

26−8 各县(市)主要农作物产量(2019年)

Output of Major Farm Products by County and City (2019)

县 市	County and city	粮食产量 (万吨) Output of Grain (10 000tons)	#谷物 Cereal	#小麦 Wheat	#玉米 Corn	#豆类 Beans	棉花产量 (吨) Output of Cotton (ton)	油料产量 (吨) Output of Oil-bearing Crops (ton)	园林水果产量 (吨) Output of Fruits (ton)
郑州市	**Zhengzhou**								
中牟县	Zhongmu	17.61	16.55	7.75	8.80	0.19	566	42212	18331
巩义市	Gongyi	16.98	16.37	8.37	7.86	0.11	309	5422	29146
荥阳市	Xingyang	28.09	27.32	15.40	11.88	0.04		5828	67785
新密市	Xinmi	22.20	20.80	11.71	9.10	0.25	25	8393	19734
新郑市	Xinzheng	26.53	25.79	13.95	11.84	0.21	12	20117	78033
登封市	Dengfeng	20.11	17.64	8.53	9.11	0.32	303	4738	21462
开封市	**Kaifeng**								
杞县	Qixian	71.66	68.48	41.96	26.53	1.06	4072	119845	22404
通许县	Tongxu	40.78	40.12	25.77	14.35	0.20	511	39158	109731
尉氏县	Weishi	64.46	62.13	41.56	20.08	0.59	2065	129361	77053
兰考县	Lankao	57.60	55.28	35.42	19.65	0.48	2009	79274	137549
洛阳市	**Luoyang**								
孟津县	Mengjin	25.44	22.48	13.18	8.56	0.11	287	10993	69471
新安县	Xinan	21.92	19.06	9.77	9.11	0.57	196	8912	56298
栾川县	Luanchuan	4.16	3.85	1.05	2.80	0.16	8	710	6705
嵩县	Songxian	19.28	15.77	8.01	7.68	0.55	330	9730	72469
汝阳县	Ruyang	18.22	15.29	7.89	7.01	0.43	421	11604	13589
宜阳县	Yiyang	39.95	36.55	18.32	17.02	2.01	1429	73068	182058
洛宁县	Luoning	27.70	22.19	13.00	7.63	2.58	35	4349	345093
伊川县	Yichuan	40.15	34.19	18.63	12.64	0.44	527	8567	10888
偃师市	Yanshi	25.06	24.55	12.56	11.91	0.14	150	2090	70131
平顶山市	**Pingdingshan**								
宝丰县	Baofeng	28.17	27.66	15.45	12.21	0.36	21	14773	10263
叶县	Yexian	70.29	67.60	35.23	32.37	1.37	146	39723	49392
鲁山县	Lushan	23.99	22.71	12.10	10.33	0.19	1	20350	90556
郏县	Jiaxian	35.75	31.12	18.28	12.84	1.30	220	23405	12651
舞钢市	Wugang	17.66	17.01	9.44	7.57	0.45		4994	11496
汝州市	Ruzhou	46.17	44.83	24.68	20.03	0.28	295	19987	43581
安阳市	**Anyang**								
安阳县	Anyang	42.96	42.62	21.70	20.92	0.06	160	420	4078
汤阴县	Tangyin	47.38	46.68	24.55	22.09	0.25	190	7274	40718
滑县	Huaxian	161.52	160.57	93.42	67.02	0.13	563	116005	161021
内黄县	Neihuang	63.69	62.54	41.57	20.97	0.07	146	103849	253717
林州市	Linzhou	24.50	21.16	7.88	12.48	0.41	692	4799	19799
鹤壁市	**Hebi**								
浚县	Xunxian	75.98	75.76	42.08	33.66	0.04	229	42070	24222
淇县	Qixian	29.79	28.89	15.07	13.80		69	908	7665

26−8 续表 1 continued

县 市	County and city	粮食产量 (万吨) Output of Grain (10 000tons)	#谷物 Cereal	#小麦 Wheat	#玉米 Corn	#豆类 Beans	棉花产量 (吨) Output of Cotton (ton)	油料产量 (吨) Output of Oil-bearing Crops (ton)	园林水果产量 (吨) Output of Fruits (ton)
新乡市	**Xinxiang**								
新乡县	Xinxiang	27.90	26.87	15.36	11.41	1.02	36	10388	4380
获嘉县	Huojia	38.19	36.01	19.18	12.56	2.07	28	143	13011
原阳县	Yuanyang	89.58	88.26	47.10	33.54	0.42	194	46881	29283
延津县	Yanjin	53.07	51.97	38.42	13.55	0.06		148337	24660
封丘县	Fengqiu	75.20	71.71	48.11	23.57	0.34	535	65547	29632
长垣市	Changyuan	75.86	74.75	43.18	30.50	0.81	354	38025	15812
卫辉市	Weihui	42.20	41.88	22.57	19.20	0.05		11002	74318
辉县市	Huixian	61.68	61.34	32.80	28.49	0.06		19561	53411
焦作市	**Jiaozuo**								
修武县	Xiuwu	22.23	10.65	11.39	10.60	0.10	8	921	9254
博爱县	Boai	20.76	9.70	10.65	9.68	0.21		1289	15800
武陟县	Wuzhi	54.13	23.06	30.25	19.45	0.45	42	53304	33487
温县	Wenxian	31.77	13.26	18.05	13.26	0.04	58	20186	23731
沁阳市	Qinyang	34.20	15.47	17.98	15.45	0.41	14	5278	31541
孟州市	Mengzhou	27.32	10.13	17.05	10.12	0.03	124	49849	23475
濮阳市	**Puyang**								
清丰县	Qingfeng	100.88	96.68	57.48	31.16	2.81	14	43429	11992
南乐县	Nanle	60.49	57.88	38.14	19.74	0.24	8	7913	153700
范县	Fanxian	50.33	48.51	28.33	20.17	0.26	69	4688	8824
台前县	Taiqian	40.59	38.73	19.95	8.54	1.68	199	3122	8966
濮阳县	Puyang	22.68	21.05	13.02	8.03	1.29	995	18932	64089
许昌市	**Xuchang**								
鄢陵县	Yanling	56.12	54.97	33.46	21.51	1.00	75	6966	5107
襄城县	Xiangcheng	59.26	46.59	33.92	12.44	4.10	251	13325	19873
禹州市	Yuzhou	56.39	51.58	29.38	22.21	0.39	74	12978	19855
长葛市	Changge	57.68	56.37	31.44	24.93	1.05		9580	4604
漯河市	**Luohe**								
舞阳县	Wuyang	56.84	54.11	31.56	22.55	1.89	56	37627	18362
临颍县	Linying	51.67	45.02	31.60	13.42	4.56	161	4562	3754
三门峡市	**Sanmenxia**								
渑池县	Mianchi	18.11	14.81	9.15	5.34	1.35	96	17358	205665
卢氏县	Lushi	13.03	11.01	5.57	5.42	1.44		968	89251
义马市	Yima	0.98	0.89	0.43	0.45	0.02		538	835
灵宝市	Lingbao	23.18	20.77	11.27	9.50	1.40	1016	7407	1634373
南阳市	**Nanyang**								
南召县	Nanzhao	15.23	13.44	3.63	4.10	0.37		58233	13804
方城县	Fangcheng	73.01	68.92	40.39	28.46	1.21	579	292323	114393
西峡县	Xixia	10.34	9.31	3.66	5.39	0.15		8900	602681

26-8 续表 2 continued

县市	County and city	粮食产量 (万吨) Output of Grain (10 000tons)	#谷物 Cereal	#小麦 Wheat	#玉米 Corn	#豆类 Beans	棉花产量 (吨) Output of Cotton (ton)	油料产量 (吨) Output of Oil-bearing Crops (ton)	园林水果产量 (吨) Output of Fruits (ton)
镇平县	Zhenping	52.60	51.46	28.44	22.71	0.28		82658	10183
内乡县	Neixiang	39.58	37.58	19.91	17.31	0.03	38	85925	56236
淅川县	Xichuan	29.49	26.81	16.15	7.82	0.41	579	117786	70419
社旗县	Sheqi	65.57	61.49	30.98	30.51	1.03	267	136088	19292
唐河县	Tanghe	135.00	128.71	98.17	26.82	0.94	255	220110	68181
新野县	Xinye	53.33	52.00	37.16	14.60	0.55		176665	14387
桐柏县	Tongbai	24.82	24.36	7.13	4.11	0.11		71278	18465
邓州市	Dengzhou	122.48	118.41	82.85	30.62	2.66	499	288854	39182
商丘市	**Shangqiu**								
民权县	Minquan	73.33	71.70	49.07	22.63	0.50	443	100509	187108
睢县	Suixian	68.54	67.01	41.57	25.44	0.78	327	59725	32402
宁陵县	Ningling	51.87	50.67	35.02	15.65	0.51		114892	296009
柘城县	Zhecheng	80.84	79.60	49.19	30.40	0.64	531	9238	17284
虞城县	Yucheng	100.12	99.27	56.81	42.45	0.16	2254	52864	577684
夏邑县	Xiayi	107.23	105.74	60.85	44.89	0.47	421	20555	306623
永城市	Yongcheng	134.46	124.51	83.16	41.35	9.95	315	7907	272559
信阳市	**Xinyang**								
罗山县	Luoshan	70.52	69.91	11.81	0.03	0.08	31	50902	7833
光山县	Guangshan	54.25	53.86	6.00		0.09	373	77198	36829
新县	Xinxian	11.39	11.10	0.42	0.01	0.01	21	27982	3305
商城县	Shangcheng	28.96	28.68	3.33	0.02	0.07	89	32274	7708
固始县	Gushi	111.67		17.11	2.01	0.03	70	62454	14902
潢川县	Huangchuan	68.50	68.38	15.88	0.03	0.01		32968	3580
淮滨县	Huaibin	57.49	56.33	28.17	1.68	0.11	85	63533	35692
息县	Xixian	96.84	96.08	49.55	7.80	0.12	162	49722	20606
周口市	**Zhoukou**								
扶沟县	Fugou	68.89	64.94	48.78	16.02	3.76	480	40795	25456
西华县	Xihua	85.70	82.79	55.60	27.20	2.21	284	44824	177309
商水县	Shangshui	109.98	102.33	60.36	41.93	5.43	480	32017	51146
沈丘县	Shenqiu	93.93	89.26	54.79	34.48	2.28	30	42769	110629
郸城县	Dancheng	114.06	105.72	67.16	38.56	2.38	341	32402	18982
太康县	Taikang	132.12	128.22	82.41	45.81	2.52	1485	44967	42779
鹿邑县	Luyi	96.30	92.50	54.00	37.30	3.90	140	20703	12382
项城市	Xiangcheng	91.85	86.98	56.82	30.17	3.31	593	24563	47820
驻马店市	**Zhumadian**								
西平县	Xiping	97.29	97.16	54.11	43.05	0.04		37756	17810
上蔡县	Shangcai	110.83	108.41	72.54	35.79	1.78	240	95608	8969
平舆县	Pingyu	87.50	86.05	59.10	26.95	0.84		65930	5853
正阳县	Zhengyang	95.34	94.17	78.19	3.50	0.21		485379	14037
确山县	Queshan	57.15	54.47	35.56	15.84	0.29		189190	8037
泌阳县	Biyang	70.93	68.18	44.99	21.75	0.23		217499	53394
汝南县	Runan	83.70	82.28	61.44	20.82	0.65		246468	9023
遂平县	Suiping	64.56	63.57	38.80	24.77	0.25	17	47343	25639
新蔡县	Xincai	94.08	93.28	57.98	33.90	0.25	194	96972	20531

26–9 各县(市)畜牧业生产情况(2019年)

Statistics on Animal Husbandry by County and City (2019)

县 市	County and city	猪出栏头数(万头) Slaughtered Fattened Hogs (10 000 heads)	牛出栏头数(万头) Slaughtered Fattened Cattles (10 000 heads)	羊出栏只数(万只) Slaughtered Fattened Sheep and Goats (10 000 heads)	猪肉产量(万吨) Output of pork (10 000 ton)	禽蛋产量(万吨) Poultry Eggs (10 000 ton)	猪年末头数(万头) Hogs (year-end) (10 000 heads)	牛年末头数(万头) Cattles (year-end) (10 000 heads)	羊年末只数(万只) Sheep and Goats (year-end) (10 000 heads)
郑州市	**Zhengzhou**								
中牟县	Zhongmu	2.36	0.13	0.75	0.18	0.06	0.46	0.64	0.77
巩义市	Gongyi	24.84	0.30	4.65	1.86	0.77	13.35	0.52	3.68
荥阳市	Xingyang	8.07	0.92	3.42	0.65	2.29	3.58	0.99	3.25
新密市	Xinmi	12.06	0.22	3.25	0.92	2.48	10.25	0.24	5.04
新郑市	Xinzheng	17.44	0.71	3.83	1.37	2.62	3.68	0.77	2.97
登封市	Dengfeng	17.90	0.55	7.04	1.39	1.99	14.95	0.59	8.42
开封市	**Kaifeng**								
杞县	Qixian	74.14	5.58	37.38	5.53	8.50	66.23	8.14	35.76
通许县	Tongxu	54.04	0.48	24.17	3.99	2.57	33.69	2.74	24.59
尉氏县	Weishi	78.76	4.58	46.59	5.96	6.48	43.21	13.04	45.44
兰考县	Lankao	25.55	1.74	38.96	2.00	8.39	14.64	2.65	30.44
洛阳市	**Luoyang**								
孟津县	Mengjin	15.86	0.87	4.50	1.34	1.14	10.81	2.58	8.11
新安县	Xinan	13.99	0.70	9.29	1.16	1.32	11.76	1.50	8.93
栾川县	Luanchuan	3.63	0.56	2.04	0.31	0.90	4.87	0.30	1.51
嵩县	Songxian	10.98	3.32	16.84	0.93	2.08	9.57	5.64	12.47
汝阳县	Ruyang	10.93	0.84	7.07	0.82	2.05	11.19	1.01	7.88
宜阳县	Yiyang	23.59	1.39	13.46	1.83	1.30	15.26	2.27	16.11
洛宁县	Luoning	8.37	5.77	14.48	0.65	1.54	9.02	8.82	9.16
伊川县	Yichuan	21.52	2.03	5.32	1.58	1.87	21.41	4.71	8.69
偃师市	Yanshi	0.44	0.05	0.15	0.03	1.29	0.18	0.09	0.14
平顶山市	**Pingdingshan**								
宝丰县	Baofeng	28.06	0.71	7.63	2.18	0.89	22.15	1.81	7.69
叶县	Yexian	91.30	4.01	69.62	6.88	3.57	56.05	2.83	37.95
鲁山县	Lushan	18.10	1.69	17.56	1.41	2.27	12.50	2.28	14.48
郏县	Jiaxian	19.79	2.98	17.44	1.54	1.24	8.92	3.67	10.24
舞钢市	Wugang	19.53	0.32	7.52	1.52	0.97	13.90	0.59	8.91
汝州市	Ruzhou	62.60	3.70	20.67	4.72	5.31	53.01	5.77	36.01
安阳市	**Anyang**								
安阳县	Anyang	9.45	0.08	2.04	0.88	0.73	4.78	0.14	2.10
汤阴县	Tangyin	28.22	0.63	10.95	2.59	2.48	8.94	0.62	5.14
滑县	Huaxian	37.25	0.96	23.76	2.91	5.60	30.12	2.03	15.60
内黄县	Neihuang	35.27	0.68	24.97	3.29	5.12	16.22	0.95	22.36
林州市	Linzhou	45.04	0.13	5.28	3.45	1.11	30.48	0.31	5.26
鹤壁市	**Hebi**								
浚县	Xunxian	50.00	0.86	16.89	3.83	4.18	26.87	1.09	20.16
淇县	Qixian	39.80	0.12	2.13	3.17	3.37	23.31	0.66	3.66

26-9 续表 1 continued

县 市 County and city	猪出栏头数（万头）Slaughtered Fattened Hogs (10 000 heads)	牛出栏头数（万头）Slaughtered Fattened Cattles (10 000 heads)	羊出栏只数（万只）Slaughtered Fattened Sheep and Goats (10 000 heads)	猪肉产量（万吨）Output of pork (10 000 ton)	禽蛋产量（万吨）Poultry Eggs (10 000 ton)	猪年末头数（万头）Hogs (year-end) (10 000 heads)	牛年末头数（万头）Cattles (year-end) (10 000 heads)	羊年末只数（万只）Sheep and Goats (year-end) (10 000 heads)
新乡市 Xinxiang								
新乡县 Xinxiang	7.75	0.47	2.84	0.60	1.44	2.08	0.84	2.98
获嘉县 Huojia	21.48	0.17	3.07	1.60	1.97	8.05	0.39	3.20
原阳县 Yuanyang	36.13	0.97	20.74	2.74	3.76	10.41	4.60	12.82
延津县 Yanjin	20.04	0.74	8.20	1.48	1.32	11.73	1.48	3.94
封丘县 Fengqiu	59.30	2.48	20.52	4.41	4.78	32.77	3.83	12.87
长垣市 Changyuan	22.29	0.79	10.67	1.76	2.96	14.71	0.97	5.96
卫辉市 Weihui	49.92	0.70	10.96	3.73	4.20	15.07	1.55	14.08
辉县市 Huixian	74.14	1.70	8.70	5.54	7.46	29.47	3.16	6.49
焦作市 Jiaozuo								
修武县 Xiuwu	15.77	1.04	2.53	1.16	1.39	9.95	0.96	2.92
博爱县 Boai	11.51	0.51	2.38	0.88	1.14	7.29	0.92	2.62
武陟县 Wuzhi	25.41	1.98	10.57	1.97	4.05	5.27	1.34	6.76
温县 Wenxian	10.95	0.53	3.70	0.84	2.04	4.85	0.66	4.41
沁阳市 Qinyang	14.45	0.87	5.45	1.11	1.04	10.09	1.02	4.71
孟州市 Mengzhou	19.61	0.64	4.35	1.53	1.42	4.58	0.95	4.14
濮阳市 Puyang								
清丰县 Qingfeng	27.76	0.14	8.74	2.13	1.58	12.85	0.17	5.10
南乐县 Nanle	24.98	1.56	8.53	2.03	9.44	10.09	0.43	5.09
范县 Fanxian	11.17	0.70	24.30	0.87	3.48	6.84	0.96	11.34
台前县 Taiqian	4.74	0.62	4.72	0.37	1.39	5.74	0.87	4.42
濮阳县 Puyang	31.68	0.97	63.50	2.44	9.23	40.56	1.76	38.66
许昌市 Xuchang								
鄢陵县 Yanling	51.80	0.48	9.24	3.88	2.36	35.40	0.20	5.58
襄城县 Xiangcheng	39.83	3.59	19.41	2.99	3.22	26.86	5.80	16.92
禹州市 Yuzhou	51.28	1.47	31.45	3.82	0.77	41.65	1.43	21.44
长葛市 Changge	54.57	1.02	13.25	4.10	5.29	30.11	1.28	9.55
漯河市 Luohe								
舞阳县 Wuyang	54.45	0.56	13.82	4.07	2.20	38.14	0.44	9.83
临颍县 Linying	58.74	0.38	4.54	4.35	4.57	40.42	0.64	4.23
三门峡市 Sanmenxia								
渑池县 Mianchi	21.59	2.68	15.91	1.76	1.70	18.11	5.63	12.38
卢氏县 Lushi	6.37	1.19	4.31	0.52	0.53	3.52	3.83	5.02
义马市 Yima	5.90	0.03	0.82	0.48	0.05	5.54	0.04	0.61
灵宝市 Lingbao	22.87	1.76	10.30	1.86	1.22	22.05	4.88	12.91
南阳市 Nanyang								
南召县 Nanzhao	7.18	0.60	14.48	0.57	1.27	5.31	1.48	10.91
方城县 Fangcheng	60.05	3.82	26.99	4.52	2.41	43.66	4.99	29.09
西峡县 Xixia	11.18	1.41	23.85	0.88	0.86	6.34	2.46	14.02

26-9 续表 2 continued

县 市	County and city	猪出栏头数(万头) Slaughtered Fattened Hogs (10 000 heads)	牛出栏头数(万头) Slaughtered Fattened Cattles (10 000 heads)	羊出栏只数(万只) Slaughtered Fattened Sheep and Goats (10 000 heads)	猪肉产量(万吨) Output of pork (10 000 ton)	禽蛋产量(万吨) Poultry Eggs (10 000 ton)	猪年末头数(万头) Hogs (year-end) (10 000 heads)	牛年末头数(万头) Cattles (year-end) (10 000 heads)	羊年末只数(万只) Sheep and Goats (year-end) (10 000 heads)
镇平县	Zhenping	14.03	0.98	17.51	1.11	2.65	11.74	2.78	17.36
内乡县	Neixiang	91.90	4.84	62.95	6.96	2.06	68.07	7.67	41.88
淅川县	Xichuan	8.52	1.51	20.33	0.68	0.95	6.12	2.38	11.22
社旗县	Sheqi	53.24	5.27	17.49	4.02	1.81	48.43	7.54	20.91
唐河县	Tanghe	81.69	11.69	37.88	6.15	5.06	76.87	16.40	38.18
新野县	Xinye	18.24	6.66	23.36	1.46	2.65	14.98	11.56	19.84
桐柏县	Tongbai	11.59	1.72	13.14	0.92	1.26	5.79	3.28	11.24
邓州市	Dengzhou	93.99	10.38	64.24	7.07	6.28	91.92	17.17	44.05
商丘市	**Shangqiu**								
民权县	Minquan	21.39	4.63	57.39	1.74	5.28	20.05	5.72	54.65
睢县	Suixian	37.70	1.26	25.56	2.84	5.71	22.22	1.26	14.05
宁陵县	Ningling	55.26	0.96	23.23	4.17	2.69	51.78	2.00	16.01
柘城县	Zhecheng	35.26	4.05	46.12	2.67	4.76	25.55	3.81	37.59
虞城县	Yucheng	18.06	5.10	43.53	1.52	8.29	17.28	15.05	33.48
夏邑县	Xiayi	59.33	2.80	34.88	4.51	5.97	40.57	3.45	42.70
永城市	Yongcheng	41.70	2.13	76.71	3.26	12.52	36.11	2.19	48.15
信阳市	**Xinyang**								
罗山县	Luoshan	30.95	0.27	3.72	2.37	2.43	29.77	0.92	4.38
光山县	Guangshan	8.40	0.35	2.16	0.65	1.94	10.43	1.03	3.79
新县	Xinxian	2.98	0.83	2.54	0.23	0.69	3.61	1.33	4.33
商城县	Shangcheng	7.87	0.29	4.26	0.60	1.37	3.61	0.53	4.53
固始县	Gushi	69.04	1.65	38.89	5.27	12.50	42.04	1.09	31.04
潢川县	Huangchuan	52.45	0.87	5.20	3.98	8.50	23.93	1.32	3.67
淮滨县	Huaibin	9.63	1.12	13.26	0.74	4.35	11.52	1.78	9.81
息县	Xixian	22.80	1.87	7.00	1.74	2.40	27.83	3.34	7.18
周口市	**Zhoukou**								
扶沟县	Fugou	47.02	0.93	9.46	3.43	2.94	43.35	1.04	12.63
西华县	Xihua	73.06	1.13	28.91	5.53	6.34	50.35	2.70	38.59
商水县	Shangshui	55.50	1.37	43.79	4.21	5.93	54.70	2.93	26.67
沈丘县	Shenqiu	57.68	2.05	69.06	4.42	6.18	42.72	4.08	62.05
郸城县	Dancheng	48.60	2.75	37.84	3.54	7.00	46.21	5.54	43.16
太康县	Taikang	75.45	2.33	66.89	5.70	6.00	64.94	4.07	35.46
鹿邑县	Luyi	63.83	0.86	21.80	4.82	4.27	51.59	1.05	17.83
项城市	Xiangcheng	47.01	2.66	18.67	3.43	4.87	44.76	4.56	23.73
驻马店市	**Zhumadian**								
西平县	Xiping	94.47	0.94	18.68	7.20	5.43	59.15	1.28	13.65
上蔡县	Shangcai	62.23	2.34	17.66	4.67	3.11	50.24	3.06	13.84
平舆县	Pingyu	48.73	1.42	25.78	3.66	2.61	37.45	2.58	18.70
正阳县	Zhengyang	112.08	0.84	4.74	8.65	2.95	73.03	2.51	3.51
确山县	Queshan	50.08	4.88	37.27	3.78	2.51	43.16	9.77	31.38
泌阳县	Biyang	78.63	25.88	29.34	6.21	2.76	42.39	40.82	30.76
汝南县	Runan	62.59	3.28	38.01	4.71	2.94	46.75	4.25	22.45
遂平县	Suiping	69.85	1.54	12.83	5.28	4.33	47.79	1.84	9.20
新蔡县	Xincai	60.04	3.85	29.07	4.56	3.15	50.79	3.85	19.49

26−10 各县(市、区)财政、金融主要指标(2019年)

Main Indicators of Finance by County and Distict (2019)

单位：亿元 (100 million yuan)

县市区 County and District	一般公共预算收入 General Public Budget Revenue	一般公共预算支出 General Public Budget Expenditure	#教育 Education	#农林水事务 Farming Forestry Water Conservancy Operating	金融机构存款余额 Deposits of Financial Institutions	金融机构贷款余额 Loans of Financial Institutions
郑州市 Zhengzhou						
中原区 Zhongyuan	30.64	43.45	8.39	0.26		
二七区 Erqi	32.71	45.90	8.10	0.98		
管城区 Guancheng	29.57	44.45	6.84	0.47		
金水区 Jinshui	65.76	70.32	17.15	0.65		
上街区 Shangjie	14.83	23.66	2.92	0.16		
惠济区 Huiji	22.52	24.36	5.76	1.29		
中牟县 Zhongmu	57.27	101.43	16.51	9.74	621.66	463.07
巩义市 Gongyi	48.21	91.26	12.97	10.46	489.52	278.94
荥阳市 Xingyang	50.04	77.46	12.72	6.02	410.63	297.53
新密市 Xinmi	37.19	72.70	12.74	7.52	483.93	244.54
新郑市 Xinzheng	80.44	119.74	17.47	13.74	681.42	640.27
登封市 Dengfeng	29.45	58.58	11.18	8.31	350.20	203.11
开封市 Kaifeng						
龙亭区 Longting	2.17	5.66	0.75	0.25		
顺河区 Shunhe	1.63	7.08	1.21	0.34		
鼓楼区 Gulou	2.09	5.33	0.88	0.23		
禹王台区 Yuwangtai	2.11	5.32	0.84	0.27		
祥符区 Xiangfu	10.96	47.06	8.04	8.18	208.00	118.81
杞县 Qixian	16.97	61.82	11.51	6.26	240.41	117.18
通许县 Tongxu	10.54	36.68	5.48	4.41	178.36	93.45
尉氏县 Weishi	25.83	65.92	10.65	9.62	291.89	153.76
兰考县 Lankao	25.20	78.53	12.79	12.84	274.84	210.70
洛阳市 Luoyang						
老城区 Laocheng	7.48	10.90	1.28	0.10		
西工区 Xigong	18.12	20.63	2.26	0.15		
瀍河区 Chanhe	6.71	10.78	1.61	0.19		
涧西区 Jianxi	28.79	31.82	3.46	0.08		
吉利区 Jili	9.51	9.46	1.24	1.01		
洛龙区 Luolong	21.16	32.67	4.46	1.19		
孟津县 Mengjin	18.03	35.79	5.82	3.11	183.79	93.58
新安县 Xinan	26.57	39.29	7.93	4.77	239.90	150.97
栾川县 Luanchuan	22.02	31.00	6.87	5.58	193.16	106.73
嵩县 Songxian	9.22	39.78	8.25	8.47	183.66	78.02
汝阳县 Ruyang	11.78	31.12	7.18	4.77	137.00	76.71
宜阳县 Yiyang	13.87	40.01	8.89	3.56	192.46	123.67
洛宁县 Luoning	11.78	34.28	6.86	5.74	138.15	68.63
伊川县 Yichuan	24.16	49.02	11.04	5.36	415.05	673.77
偃师市 Yanshi	24.58	40.53	9.65	3.22	352.39	171.30
平顶山市 Pingdingshan						
新华区 Xinhua	6.39	13.50	2.30	0.36		
卫东区 Weidong	4.60	12.09	2.07	0.42		
石龙区 Shilong	4.40	7.74	1.04	0.58		
湛河区 Zhanhe	6.96	14.34	2.81	0.95		
宝丰县 Baofeng	14.34	37.26	5.02	4.66	206.92	164.06
叶县 Yexian	8.39	45.99	7.63	9.27	232.89	91.87
鲁山县 Lushan	8.16	47.04	9.90	9.51	268.00	86.28
郏县 Jiaxian	9.68	31.85	5.38	4.21	177.80	97.36
舞钢市 Wugang	11.65	24.01	4.29	4.37	188.53	115.30
汝州市 Ruzhou	33.20	70.05	15.25	3.16	348.12	261.84

26−10 续表 1　continued

单位：亿元　(100 million yuan)

县市区	County and District	一般公共预算收入 General Public Budget Revenue	一般公共预算支出 General Public Budget Expenditure	#教育 Education	#农林水事务 Farming Forestry Water Conservancy Operating	金融机构存款余额 Deposits of Financial Institutions	金融机构贷款余额 Loans of Financial Institutions
安　阳　市	**Anyang**						
文　峰　区	Wenfeng	7.81	11.96	2.54	0.24		
北　关　区	Beiguan	8.69	11.32	2.60	0.46		
殷　都　区	Yindu	20.51	29.12	5.43	3.23		
龙　安　区	Longan	8.02	19.67	2.96	1.63		
安　阳　县	Anyang	7.59	28.21	5.56	4.46	408.94	204.81
汤　阴　县	Tangyin	16.06	35.15	7.80	6.48	178.66	109.07
滑　　县	Huaxian	13.82	71.28	15.48	10.19	399.16	169.59
内　黄　县	Neihuang	10.25	40.91	7.58	7.51	193.15	91.16
林　州　市	Linzhou	30.26	66.60	12.83	7.71	574.82	256.62
鹤　壁　市	**Hebi**						
鹤　山　区	Heshan	3.78	8.12	1.16	0.90		
山　城　区	Shancheng	8.03	14.42	2.92	0.89		
淇　滨　区	Qibin	12.01	20.15	2.98	1.48		
浚　　县	Xunxian	8.20	36.65	5.39	5.34	187.24	131.77
淇　　县	Qixian	10.74	22.13	3.44	3.04	114.84	141.44
新　乡　市	**Xinxiang**						
红　旗　区	Hongqi	9.60	13.98	3.00	0.81		
卫　滨　区	Weibin	2.96	7.34	1.07	0.18		
凤　泉　区	Fengquan	3.83	6.37	1.19	0.51		
牧　野　区	Muye	5.70	9.60	2.02	0.30		
新　乡　县	Xinxiang	10.37	22.58	3.83	2.31	197.33	135.67
获　嘉　县	Huojia	6.50	20.99	4.65	3.28	141.02	51.50
原　阳　县	Yuanyang	11.01	40.66	6.14	9.32	185.40	132.64
延　津　县	Yanjin	5.69	27.62	5.21	4.64	135.13	51.61
封　丘　县	Fengqiu	7.01	43.79	8.20	10.18	218.50	56.13
长　垣　市	Changyuan	30.30	61.92	12.81	8.20	491.02	241.52
卫　辉　市	Weihui	11.91	35.33	6.41	4.83	179.66	93.66
辉　县　市	Huixian	23.46	45.83	9.67	6.89	370.49	199.24
焦　作　市	**Jiaozuo**						
解　放　区	Jiefang	13.63	14.09	1.87	0.92		
中　站　区	Zhongzhan	8.39	10.05	1.64	0.39		
马　村　区	Macun	6.22	7.65	1.43	0.61		
山　阳　区	Shanyang	14.72	10.66	1.70	0.27		
修　武　县	Xiuwu	15.17	22.78	3.44	2.34	115.35	85.67
博　爱　县	Boai	10.00	24.24	3.92	2.44	146.61	93.37
武　陟　县	Wuzhi	15.59	35.26	6.69	4.27	227.60	143.50
温　　县	Wenxian	9.12	22.71	3.53	2.70	161.22	87.37
沁　阳　市	Qinyang	17.84	32.31	4.60	3.17	191.19	137.13
孟　州　市	Mengzhou	15.99	27.20	3.91	3.39	155.17	102.04

26-10 续表 2 continued

单位：亿元 (100 million yuan)

县市区 County and District	一般公共预算收入 General Public Budget Revenue	一般公共预算支出 General Public Budget Expenditure	#教育 Education	#农林水事务 Farming Forestry Water Conservancy Operating	金融机构存款余额 Deposits of Financial Institutions	金融机构贷款余额 Loans of Financial Institutions
濮　阳　市 Puyang						
华　龙　区 Hualong	13.42	18.29	3.05	0.67		
清　丰　县 Qingfeng	9.40	46.36	9.46	7.88	184.40	94.41
南　乐　县 Nanle	7.38	34.05	6.62	7.05	145.50	70.97
范　　县 Fanxian	8.17	37.52	6.18	9.89	186.28	70.94
台　前　县 Taiqian	4.66	43.27	7.20	16.37	135.92	62.70
濮　阳　县 Puyang	15.01	75.94	13.57	14.09	297.06	192.96
许　昌　市 Xuchang						
魏　都　区 Weidu	12.71	19.70	3.92	0.40		
建　安　区 Jianan	23.67	51.92	9.48	6.23		
鄢　陵　县 Yanling	12.87	38.82	8.16	4.78	222.93	140.46
襄　城　县 Xiangcheng	20.54	47.47	9.36	6.32	309.98	200.61
禹　州　市 Yuzhou	23.02	65.67	12.68	6.95	421.17	255.17
长　葛　市 Changge	32.20	52.03	11.09	5.03	342.95	231.31
漯　河　市 Luohe						
源　汇　区 Yuanhui	6.86	17.30	2.26	2.01		
郾　城　区 Yancheng	6.68	23.02	4.63	2.47		
召　陵　区 Zhaoling	5.69	20.92	3.42	2.32		
舞　阳　县 Wuyang	12.56	34.73	5.65	6.59	179.88	56.34
临　颍　县 Linying	16.71	45.08	8.48	4.68	202.11	112.40
三　门　峡　市 Sanmenxia						
湖　滨　区 Hubin	10.02	13.95	3.13	0.82		
陕　州　区 Shanzhou	20.22	32.87	4.97	5.27		
渑　池　县 Mianchi	28.92	39.80	7.09	4.99	163.19	75.26
卢　氏　县 Lushi	8.13	43.10	6.01	13.98	157.24	82.79
义　马　市 Yima	16.40	20.33	3.27	0.62	123.95	76.65
灵　宝　市 Lingbao	23.91	52.40	8.13	5.62	342.62	178.35
南　阳　市 Nanyang						
宛　城　区 Wancheng	8.88	32.50	8.34	4.91		
卧　龙　区 Wolong	13.02	40.81	10.08	5.36		
南　召　县 Nanzhao	6.85	38.29	8.56	6.77	167.92	89.66
方　城　县 Fangcheng	11.07	51.13	11.95	6.77	251.53	124.57
西　峡　县 Xixia	16.51	35.48	10.06	5.12	234.69	140.36
镇　平　县 Zhenping	10.04	48.02	10.30	7.95	328.37	133.82
内　乡　县 Neixiang	11.80	40.83	9.31	7.41	270.31	159.57
淅　川　县 Xichuan	10.03	60.64	10.97	10.60	268.61	148.49
社　旗　县 Sheqi	6.61	38.53	8.65	8.03	182.18	91.60
唐　河　县 Tanghe	10.20	65.02	11.22	11.49	358.94	147.21
新　野　县 Xinye	8.34	35.55	7.09	5.94	254.00	139.11
桐　柏　县 Tongbai	10.13	33.13	7.54	7.20	164.40	65.96
邓　州　市 Dengzhou	18.02	82.20	16.37	12.71	429.97	257.32

26-10 续表 3 continued

单位：亿元 (100 million yuan)

县市区	County and District	一般公共预算收入 General Public Budget Revenue	一般公共预算支出 General Public Budget Expenditure	#教育 Education	#农林水事务 Farming Forestry Water Conservancy Operating	金融机构存款余额 Deposits of Financial Institutions	金融机构贷款余额 Loans of Financial Institutions
商丘市	**Shangqiu**						
梁园区	Liangyuan	11.13	35.64	5.59	3.51		
睢阳区	Suiyang	11.58	39.17	7.31	4.80		
民权县	Minquan	10.90	46.83	7.52	9.10	242.12	136.56
睢县	Suixian	9.04	44.17	7.66	7.87	222.20	91.12
宁陵县	Ningling	6.54	37.13	6.99	7.02	169.67	130.94
柘城县	Zhecheng	9.71	50.72	10.25	9.33	253.69	110.38
虞城县	Yucheng	10.83	55.19	9.37	8.87	308.97	126.72
夏邑县	Xiayi	10.01	56.69	9.44	10.31	329.61	108.27
永城市	Yongcheng	45.00	84.15	13.79	13.08	594.10	339.52
信阳市	**Xinyang**						
浉河区	Shihe	12.95	31.03	7.30	3.06		
平桥区	Pingqiao	11.65	36.26	10.93	6.31		
罗山县	Luoshan	7.40	42.62	7.43	8.18	274.04	83.86
光山县	Guangshan	6.42	56.74	12.84	7.47	300.82	119.43
新县	Xinxian	6.63	29.52	6.55	5.81	155.56	71.32
商城县	Shangcheng	7.18	45.58	10.61	8.56	267.00	90.06
固始县	Gushi	15.57	81.56	22.44	17.34	526.08	208.97
潢川县	Huangchuan	7.69	60.56	10.58	12.41	271.70	273.10
淮滨县	Huaibin	7.79	50.46	8.47	14.15	221.71	82.88
息县	Xixian	8.10	79.92	11.69	15.57	309.09	119.93
周口市	**Zhoukou**						
川汇区	Chuanhui	6.43	23.39	4.43	0.88		
淮阳区	Huaiyang	8.27	42.78	7.58	6.71		
扶沟县	Fugou	8.30	46.34	9.47	6.95	226.61	74.84
西华县	Xihua	8.03	60.35	11.98	10.30	254.49	91.36
商水县	Shangshui	15.42	65.88	15.21	10.26	308.68	91.43
沈丘县	Shenqiu	12.00	71.19	14.49	11.45	332.37	177.52
郸城县	Dancheng	10.01	66.77	13.87	11.67	320.20	85.20
太康县	Taikang	12.19	77.60	13.78	11.17	331.16	119.49
鹿邑县	Luyi	15.53	56.33	7.77	6.72	332.81	151.07
项城市	Xiangcheng	13.41	60.47	11.13	6.62	366.16	117.07
驻马店市	**Zhumadian**						
驿城区	Yicheng	18.40	47.81	10.66	5.23		
西平县	Xiping	12.53	49.28	8.48	7.21	286.92	133.08
上蔡县	Shangcai	10.05	71.52	15.27	14.87	385.98	125.96
平舆县	Pingyu	11.32	55.01	10.20	6.75	305.98	136.56
正阳县	Zhengyang	8.16	49.98	8.91	5.94	283.61	123.30
确山县	Queshan	12.26	35.85	8.13	8.26	131.57	37.28
泌阳县	Biyang	12.66	68.52	11.70	7.36	256.55	107.03
汝南县	Runan	9.77	50.76	9.55	8.62	260.74	101.81
遂平县	Suiping	12.31	38.24	7.65	6.12	202.24	137.45
新蔡县	Xincai	12.07	57.53	10.87	10.85	301.65	157.86

26-11 各县(市)义务教育主要指标(2019年)

Main Indicators of Compulsory Education by County and City (2019)

县市	County and City	校数（所）Nunber of Schools (unit)			在校学生数（人）Student Enrollment (person)			专任教师数（人）Full-time Teachers (person)		
		合计 Total	小学 Primary Schools	初中 Junior Secondary School	合计 Total	小学 Primary Schools	初中 Junior Secondary School	合计 Total	小学 Primary Schools	初中 Junior Secondary School
郑州市	**Zhengzhou**									
中牟县	Zhongmu	178	139	39	165251	118471	46780	8093	4845	3248
巩义市	Gongyi	98	70	28	79562	55385	24177	5813	3091	2722
荥阳市	Xingyang	79	57	22	75007	51085	23922	4842	2849	1993
新密市	Xinmi	148	114	34	101113	69329	31784	6543	3944	2599
新郑市	Xinzheng	166	128	38	167192	118493	48699	6934	3852	3082
登封市	Dengfeng	143	92	51	163891	89997	73894	8487	3174	5313
开封市	**Kaifeng**									
杞县	Qixian	194	145	49	143886	100617	43269	8814	5170	3644
通许县	Tongxu	98	70	28	83371	59086	24285	4717	2794	1923
尉氏县	Weishi	204	167	37	139377	98993	40384	6768	4007	2761
兰考县	Lankao	255	202	53	122794	87325	35469	7362	4576	2786
洛阳市	**Luoyang**									
孟津县	Mengjin	83	62	21	46835	30418	16417	3287	1636	1651
新安县	Xinan	142	117	25	58174	38258	19916	3272	1694	1578
栾川县	Luanchuan	57	40	17	44553	31023	13530	2515	1343	1172
嵩县	Songxian	126	106	20	82205	54213	27992	4112	2336	1776
汝阳县	Ruyang	83	59	24	76290	52655	23635	4103	2300	1803
宜阳县	Yiyang	98	62	36	78266	52057	26209	4986	2714	2272
洛宁县	Luoning	97	61	36	55542	36563	18979	3713	1895	1818
伊川县	Yichuan	164	118	46	125595	87882	37713	7319	4225	3094
偃师市	Yanshi	74	45	29	56186	38644	17542	4604	2352	2252
平顶山市	**Pingdingshan**									
宝丰县	Baofeng	139	118	21	84957	56391	28566	4099	2489	1610
叶县	Yexian	186	161	25	113488	79721	33767	7007	4297	2710
鲁山县	Lushan	279	236	43	156086	97245	58841	7638	4701	2937
郏县	Jiaxian	129	104	25	85737	56912	28825	5540	3251	2289
舞钢市	Wugang	56	43	13	42667	31135	11532	2224	1407	817
汝州市	Ruzhou	443	385	58	178206	125601	52605	8623	4982	3641
安阳市	**Anyang**									
安阳县	Anyang	182	157	25	68965	44871	24094	3174	1898	1276
汤阴县	Tangyin	157	132	25	78024	52425	25599	3974	2228	1746
滑县	Huaxian	343	292	51	220560	160772	59788	10292	6704	3588
内黄县	Neihuang	235	197	38	122558	82303	40255	6094	3517	2577
林州市	Linzhou	240	193	47	158573	109502	49071	7218	3789	3429
鹤壁市	**Hebi**									
浚县	Xunxian	195	171	24	92577	65355	27222	4949	3263	1686
淇县	Qixian	81	67	14	38540	27187	11353	2160	1119	1041

26-11 续表 1 continued

县市	County and City	校数(所) Number of Schools (unit) 合计 Total	小学 Primary Schools	初中 Junior Secondary School	在校学生数(人) Student Enrollment (person) 合计 Total	小学 Primary Schools	初中 Junior Secondary School	专任教师数(人) Full-time Teachers (person) 合计 Total	小学 Primary Schools	初中 Junior Secondary School
新乡市	**Xinxiang**									
新乡县	Xinxiang	95	73	22	50576	34130	16446	3135	1605	1530
获嘉县	Huojia	132	104	28	58392	39977	18415	3346	1722	1624
原阳县	Yuanyang	226	178	48	111372	76009	35363	6443	4002	2441
延津县	Yanjin	155	118	37	74643	47475	27168	4719	2272	2447
封丘县	Fengqiu	230	179	51	113242	77238	36004	7316	4126	3190
长垣市	Changyuan	264	227	37	149103	99986	49117	7526	4609	2917
卫辉市	Weihui	134	105	29	84034	54389	29645	4575	2824	1751
辉县市	Huixian	183	144	39	146637	98039	48598	5423	2477	2946
焦作市	**Jiaozuo**									
修武县	Xiuwu	70	54	16	28728	19975	8753	2303	1421	882
博爱县	Boai	67	46	21	44667	32012	12655	3006	1354	1652
武陟县	Wuzhi	164	133	31	82130	60105	22025	5375	3216	2159
温县	Wenxian	99	76	23	45063	31450	13613	2979	1830	1149
沁阳市	Qinyang	113	85	28	53249	35866	17383	3461	1960	1501
孟州市	Mengzhou	63	42	21	29854	21562	8292	2239	1211	1028
濮阳市	**Puyang**									
清丰县	Qingfeng	171	149	22	85754	62664	23090	5612	3747	1865
南乐县	Nanle	150	129	21	82694	60503	22191	5490	3620	1870
范县	Fanxian	133	113	20	72377	49852	22525	3977	2607	1370
台前县	Taiqian	105	91	14	58128	42569	15559	3458	2012	1446
濮阳县	Puyang	246	217	29	144451	110074	34377	9216	6558	2658
许昌市	**Xuchang**									
鄢陵县	Yanling	164	140	24	87579	60013	27566	5655	3673	1982
襄城县	Xiangcheng	185	160	25	112128	73348	38780	7061	4606	2455
禹州市	Yuzhou	302	227	75	158134	106878	51256	10035	4985	5050
长葛市	Changge	164	130	34	99690	67767	31923	6458	3443	3015
漯河市	**Luohe**									
舞阳县	Wuyang	157	136	21	57966	40251	17715	3537	1973	1564
临颍县	Linying	206	169	37	76752	51073	25679	5128	2361	2767
三门峡市	**Sanmenxia**									
渑池县	Mianchi	68	44	24	45858	31063	14795	3336	1604	1732
卢氏县	Lushi	60	33	27	37699	23123	14576	2668	1380	1288
义马市	Yima	16	10	6	11875	9219	2656	1171	661	510
灵宝市	Lingbao	119	92	27	74010	52577	21433	5663	3317	2346
南阳市	**Nanyang**									
南召县	Nanzhao	94	59	35	98375	68241	30134	5802	3305	2497
方城县	Fangcheng	277	234	43	179269	119125	60144	9404	5348	4056
西峡县	Xixia	116	85	31	68542	44947	23595	4409	2661	1748

26-11 续表 2 continued

县市 County and City	校数（所）Nunber of Schools (unit) 合计 Total	小学 Primary Schools	初中 Junior Secondary School	在校学生数（人）Student Enrollment (person) 合计 Total	小学 Primary Schools	初中 Junior Secondary School	专任教师数（人）Full-time Teachers (person) 合计 Total	小学 Primary Schools	初中 Junior Secondary School
镇平县 Zhenping	192	155	37	144103	101093	43010	9001	5557	3444
内乡县 Neixiang	145	121	24	105819	68407	37412	5806	3250	2556
淅川县 Xichuan	136	112	24	93936	61294	32642	6655	3505	3150
社旗县 Sheqi	126	96	30	103283	71025	32258	6229	3687	2542
唐河县 Tanghe	268	222	46	191014	136180	54834	11133	6651	4482
新野县 Xinye	121	96	25	122945	82722	40223	7025	4401	2624
桐柏县 Tongbai	72	47	25	73312	45696	27616	4913	2688	2225
邓州市 Dengzhou	363	298	65	254889	172489	82400	13781	7685	6096
商丘市 Shangqiu									
民权县 Minquan	198	146	52	114525	81602	32923	7324	3978	3346
睢县 Suixian	301	244	57	106076	73442	32634	6259	3501	2758
宁陵县 Ningling	169	139	30	84956	62421	22535	5393	3596	1797
柘城县 Zhecheng	207	145	62	114523	79514	35009	9708	6039	3669
虞城县 Yucheng	320	273	47	166860	116165	50695	10561	6350	4211
夏邑县 Xiayi	319	279	40	133418	97161	36257	9408	6224	3184
永城市 Yongcheng	367	308	59	233318	155427	77891	11113	6940	4173
信阳市 Xinyang									
罗山县 Luoshan	159	132	27	91011	58165	32846	5631	3582	2049
光山县 Guangshan	197	153	44	103049	64683	38366	7485	4151	3334
新县 Xinxian	53	31	22	40423	24924	15499	3051	1465	1586
商城县 Shangcheng	126	95	31	77485	47795	29690	5908	3569	2339
固始县 Gushi	234	179	55	188272	121422	66850	12280	7472	4808
潢川县 Huangchuan	130	100	30	91008	61490	29518	5424	3259	2165
淮滨县 Huaibin	111	84	27	92922	62196	30726	6115	3890	2225
息县 Xixian	178	140	38	130635	85943	44692	8467	5058	3409
周口市 Zhoukou									
扶沟县 Fugou	136	111	25	78657	51735	26922	5898	3264	2634
西华县 Xihua	185	153	32	95615	66249	29366	6931	4036	2895
商水县 Shangshui	250	193	57	141798	94803	46995	10013	5709	4304
沈丘县 Shenqiu	264	200	64	150487	103280	47207	11615	6895	4720
郸城县 Dancheng	396	338	58	192358	125935	66423	11886	7862	4024
太康县 Taikang	329	265	64	188635	130635	58000	11418	7159	4259
鹿邑县 Luyi	255	200	55	140860	99919	40941	10121	6038	4083
项城市 Xiangcheng	218	162	56	156998	108202	48796	10704	5849	4855
驻马店市 Zhumadian									
西平县 Xiping	220	191	29	75742	53920	21822	5749	3442	2307
上蔡县 Shangcai	439	387	52	181734	119028	62706	11351	6980	4371
平舆县 Pingyu	137	108	29	134217	96123	38094	7026	4592	2434
正阳县 Zhengyang	238	208	30	122110	85492	36618	7329	4330	2999
确山县 Queshan	153	132	21	69954	46604	23350	4861	3123	1738
泌阳县 Biyang	177	146	31	131535	89499	42036	8028	4725	3303
汝南县 Runan	188	164	24	93224	64704	28520	6287	4082	2205
遂平县 Suiping	167	148	19	70539	49816	20723	4692	2890	1802
新蔡县 Xincai	295	247	48	148025	101670	46355	8341	5395	2946

26-12 各县(市)卫生主要指标(2019年)

Main Indicators of Sanitation by County and City (2019)

县 市	County and City	卫生机构床位数(张) Number of Beds in Health Institutions (unit)	卫生技术人员(人) Medical Technical Personnel (person)	执业医师(人) Medical practitioner (person)	助理医师(人) Assistant doctor of the operation (person)	注册护士(人) Registered Nurse (person)
郑州市	**Zhengzhou**					
中牟县	Zhongmu	3519	4028	1232	413	1707
巩义市	Gongyi	3989	5402	1682	438	2336
荥阳市	Xingyang	2879	3974	1130	387	1658
新密市	Xinmi	5458	4768	1419	302	2275
新郑市	Xinzheng	6377	7006	2122	608	3022
登封市	Dengfeng	5278	4844	1508	502	2043
开封市	**Kaifeng**					
杞县	Qixian	3820	4141	1057	820	1424
通许县	Tongxu	2624	2863	738	394	1182
尉氏县	Weishi	4863	4164	1148	621	1747
兰考县	Lankao	6003	6023	1510	677	2185
洛阳市	**Luoyang**					
孟津县	Mengjin	1923	2190	656	277	771
新安县	Xinan	2512	2306	675	217	949
栾川县	Luanchuan	2120	1917	539	171	831
嵩县	Songxian	3722	2849	822	397	1145
汝阳县	Ruyang	2292	2127	585	186	878
宜阳县	Yiyang	4570	3566	835	490	1367
洛宁县	Luoning	3113	1988	538	275	786
伊川县	Yichuan	4528	4854	1266	710	2275
偃师市	Yanshi	3748	3401	1090	465	1353
平顶山市	**Pingdingshan**					
宝丰县	Baofeng	2600	2786	776	428	1009
叶县	Yexian	2997	3112	747	611	965
鲁山县	Lushan	4097	3294	832	392	1318
郏县	Jiaxian	3298	3534	953	442	1359
舞钢市	Wugang	1655	1723	528	116	732
汝州市	Ruzhou	6743	6158	1622	655	2262
安阳市	**Anyang**					
安阳县	Anyang	1103	1266	415	372	299
汤阴县	Tangyin	1720	2191	624	530	559
滑县	Huaxian	6717	6302	1673	1030	2575
内黄县	Neihuang	3698	3218	853	539	1065
林州市	Linzhou	4818	4214	1285	719	1379
鹤壁市	**Hebi**					
浚县	Xunxian	2579	1897	629	428	479
淇县	Qixian	2142	2076	582	158	931

26-12 续表 1 continued

县市 County and City	卫生机构床位数（张）Number of Beds in Health Institutions (unit)	卫生技术人员（人）Medical Technical Personnel (person)	执业医师（人）Medical practitioner (person)	助理医师（人）Assistant doctor of the operation (person)	注册护士（人）Registered Nurse (person)
新乡市 Xinxiang					
新乡县 Xinxiang	1266	1430	400	278	515
获嘉县 Huojia	2676	2095	638	191	756
原阳县 Yuanyang	3480	3669	970	544	1547
延津县 Yanjin	2721	2075	534	298	818
封丘县 Fengqiu	3912	2976	762	396	1143
长垣市 Changyuan	4419	5160	1557	745	2060
卫辉市 Weihui	4982	4827	1477	331	2293
辉县市 Huixian	3349	3320	985	512	1194
焦作市 Jiaozuo					
修武县 Xiuwu	1564	1502	469	286	495
博爱县 Boai	2388	1570	524	310	425
武陟县 Wuzhi	3497	3153	875	503	1241
温县 Wenxian	2202	2078	597	173	770
沁阳市 Qinyang	1733	2264	716	252	819
孟州市 Mengzhou	2130	2119	631	215	867
濮阳市 Puyang					
清丰县 Qingfeng	3137	2399	625	272	856
南乐县 Nanle	2652	1786	437	273	687
范县 Fanxian	1919	1901	474	204	650
台前县 Taiqian	2218	2096	482	344	901
濮阳县 Puyang	5930	4615	1230	1086	1519
许昌市 Xuchang					
鄢陵县 Yanling	3311	2916	785	447	1114
襄城县 Xiangcheng	3675	3223	799	361	1267
禹州市 Yuzhou	5235	5721	1664	689	2241
长葛市 Changge	2540	3387	958	423	1266
漯河市 Luohe					
舞阳县 Wuyang	2763	2499	653	248	981
临颍县 Linying	3200	3158	823	300	1392
三门峡市 Sanmenxia					
渑池县 Mianchi	2171	1914	513	191	727
卢氏县 Lushi	2113	1734	447	240	680
义马市 Yima	1757	1536	444	83	757
灵宝市 Lingbao	2866	3634	1206	502	1343
南阳市 Nanyang					
南召县 Nanzhao	2927	3175	687	429	1261
方城县 Fangcheng	4786	3054	781	415	1065
西峡县 Xixia	2991	2224	871	112	990

26-12 续表 2 continued

县市 County and City	卫生机构床位数（张）Number of Beds in Health Institutions (unit)	卫生技术人员（人）Medical Technical Personnel (person)	执业医师（人）Medical practitioner (person)	助理医师（人）Assistant doctor of the operation (person)	注册护士（人）Registered Nurse (person)
镇平县 Zhenping	3731	2709	632	525	810
内乡县 Neixiang	3568	2834	707	455	995
淅川县 Xichuan	2659	2723	743	249	970
社旗县 Sheqi	2560	2517	695	445	908
唐河县 Tanghe	4871	4572	1109	528	1875
新野县 Xinye	3117	2734	660	397	1025
桐柏县 Tongbai	2389	2143	463	227	798
邓州市 Dengzhou	8249	5766	1408	583	2386
商丘市 Shangqiu					
民权县 Minquan	4334	3085	788	465	1108
睢县 Suixian	4337	4580	914	434	1832
宁陵县 Ningling	2187	3468	708	504	999
柘城县 Zhecheng	5109	5064	1251	813	1987
虞城县 Yucheng	3782	4465	1044	998	1207
夏邑县 Xiayi	4303	4251	1029	558	1748
永城市 Yongcheng	7472	6840	1568	793	2535
信阳市 Xinyang					
罗山县 Luoshan	2700	2391	703	227	1021
光山县 Guangshan	3362	2739	775	313	1005
新县 Xinxian	1053	1214	315	116	449
商城县 Shangcheng	2649	2398	753	341	928
固始县 Gushi	7246	5784	1547	631	2232
潢川县 Huangchuan	2889	2360	696	560	807
淮滨县 Huaibin	2624	2272	620	321	863
息县 Xixian	3320	3167	781	371	1228
周口市 Zhoukou					
扶沟县 Fugou	3485	3324	754	481	1259
西华县 Xihua	3512	3437	766	430	1208
商水县 Shangshui	4368	4119	1109	715	1518
沈丘县 Shenqiu	4760	4443	1158	773	1352
郸城县 Dancheng	4822	5663	1312	646	2268
太康县 Taikang	7872	5470	1271	860	2144
鹿邑县 Luyi	5563	4804	1106	969	1748
项城市 Xiangcheng	3678	3157	741	372	1229
驻马店市 Zhumadian					
西平县 Xiping	3531	3377	843	453	1324
上蔡县 Shangcai	6385	4522	1195	496	1803
平舆县 Pingyu	5870	4453	1042	512	2049
正阳县 Zhengyang	3108	2730	793	343	1036
确山县 Queshan	2635	2355	531	231	1144
泌阳县 Biyang	4249	3051	792	448	1110
汝南县 Runan	2426	2812	774	359	1126
遂平县 Suiping	2967	2606	685	276	1047
新蔡县 Xincai	4081	4149	1007	673	1444

26−13 各县(市)社会保险和低保参保人数(2019年)

Number of People Participated in Basic Insurance and Lowest Cost-of-Living by County and City (2019)

单位：人 (person)

县 市	County and city	城镇职工基本养老保险参保人数 Number of Employees Participating in Basic Endowment Insurance in Urban Area	城乡居民基本养老保险参保人数 Number of Residents Participating in Basic Endowment Insurance in Urban and Rural Area	基本医疗保险参保人数 Number of People Participating in Basic Medical Insurance	城乡居民基本医疗保险参保人数 Number of Residents Participating in Basic Medical Insurance in Urban and Rural Area	城镇居民最低生活保障人数 Number of Urban Residents with Minimum Living Security	农村居民最低生活保障人数 Number of Rural Residents with Minimum Living Security
郑州市	**Zhengzhou**						
中牟县	Zhongmu	118756	266630	540319	470712	200	2605
巩义市	Gongyi	128726	408330	738198	661132	706	11199
荥阳市	Xingyang	91387	328758	628003	564886	426	6766
新密市	Xinmi	105675	421563	761039	678304	420	6286
新郑市	Xinzheng	115811	333847	643836	564511	1489	7003
登封市	Dengfeng	78969	378734	679369	605447	133	6132
开封市	**Kaifeng**						
杞县	Qixian	15580	595027	889487	858112	2017	49592
通许县	Tongxu	27807	334366	611756	587338	2717	23844
尉氏县	Weishi	89600	644060	803141	770337	1508	20182
兰考县	Lankao	82000	523561	835281	790281	2458	22518
洛阳市	**Luoyang**						
孟津县	Mengjin	19448	276644	445109	406240	1177	6477
新安县	Xinan	70471	292024	514068	467348	19030	176190
栾川县	Luanchuan	25498	207850	331865	294162	372	7174
嵩县	Songxian	38642	338639	582702	550834	1337	21037
汝阳县	Ruyang	24500	268297	481044	460383	1872	11297
宜阳县	Yiyang	48024	410000	707308	653963	2117	34316
洛宁县	Luoning	18168	257024	460187	409697	969	12777
伊川县	Yichuan	54661	445144	803380	760217	3892	31481
偃师市	Yanshi	61514	338196	585108	540446	1230	9716
平顶山市	**Pingdingshan**						
宝丰县	Baofeng	27211	308171	507024	472579	2151	11621
叶县	Yexian	62849	481000	734768	699140	3850	23106
鲁山县	Lushan	39594	502422	896115	852086	3735	21707
郏县	Jiaxian	38482	340800	584654	556874	3779	15771
舞钢市	Wugang	72778	146100	294905	264523	1010	6008
汝州市	Ruzhou	79760	645370	1026065	972424	3733	37720
安阳市	**Anyang**						
安阳县	Anyang	30074	328347	523985	497156	43	8237
汤阴县	Tangyin	40060	289360	468478	434656	1867	6294
滑县	Huaxian	99931	800751	1354551	1295973	1274	37853
内黄县	Neihuang	40215	476000	795327	765544	422	12139
林州市	Linzhou	100424	601530	1005558	946278	1270	16116
鹤壁市	**Hebi**						
浚县	Xunxian	46736	310831	646361	614854	1108	14162
淇县	Qixian	40161	108048	269082	247447	939	7414

26−13 续表1 continued

单位：人 (person)

县 市 County and city	城镇职工基本养老保险参保人数 Number of Employees Participating in Basic Endowment Insurance in Urban Area	城乡居民基本养老保险参保人数 Number of Residents Participating in Basic Endowment Insurance in Urban and Rural Area	基本医疗保险参保人数 Number of People Participating in Basic Medical Insurance	城乡居民基本医疗保险参保人数 Number of Residents Participating in Basic Medical Insurance in Urban and Rural Area	城镇居民最低生活保障人数 Number of Urban Residents with Minimum Living Security	农村居民最低生活保障人数 Number of Rural Residents with Minimum Living Security
新乡市 Xinxiang						
新乡县 Xinxiang	69970	161993	342600	300739	286	5564
获嘉县 Huojia	31817	231048	393177	362797	574	8022
原阳县 Yuanyang	29946	266487	657839	473170	1509	17854
延津县 Yanjin	43746	255448	450914	415455	697	16556
封丘县 Fengqiu	55872	489566	730803	697800	1641	25136
长垣市 Changyuan	41831	237720	473686	406153	2650	8863
卫辉市 Weihui	89165	489395	805855	753452	433	15281
辉县市 Huixian	70917	492800	867525	824190	5518	23482
焦作市 Jiaozuo						
修武县 Xiuwu	19448	124206	234608	210911	226	3566
博爱县 Boai	42124	184603	338991	335250	1436	9370
武陟县 Wuzhi	34490	355093	649797	605104	1427	14908
温县 Wenxian	32364	250387	427240	394267	1208	7781
沁阳市 Qinyang	43345	263412	466592	421000	2415	13059
孟州市 Mengzhou	36489	220220	363572	327593	1546	10250
濮阳市 Puyang						
清丰县 Qingfeng	12270	381423	686598	650877	1105	16769
南乐县 Nanle	28911	314094	533619	509442	893	10450
范县 Fanxian	25366	305098	527730	507630	1596	20075
台前县 Taiqian	12790	184880	376776	362029	336	12705
濮阳县 Puyang	46998	648009	1115774	1068754	3226	63614
许昌市 Xuchang						
鄢陵县 Yanling	9917	415510	631170	630240	6025	7655
襄城县 Xiangcheng	49935	503080	789855	753766	391	12020
禹州市 Yuzhou	92676	714190	1165747	1081996	6654	24158
长葛市 Changge	49151	414384	694899	638584	1157	8405
漯河市 Luohe						
舞阳县 Wuyang	34329	315300	528302	494095	551	9427
临颍县 Linying	12510	376608	645000	592700	617	16548
三门峡市 Sanmenxia						
渑池县 Mianchi	66070	162820	328793	274657	1251	8426
卢氏县 Lushi	33421	212313	359818	338232	859	22273
义马市 Yima	38881	28356	90825	78236	4648	
灵宝市 Lingbao	80042	430581	717170	662691	974	15563
南阳市 Nanyang						
南召县 Nanzhao	21166	324000	618345	586337	3983	36460
方城县 Fangcheng	33191	579400	1066960	1005383	3736	60814
西峡县 Xixia	77062	213631	469332	414610	943	11330

26-13 续表2 continued

单位：人 (person)

县 市 County and city	城镇职工基本养老保险参保人数 Number of Employees Participating in Basic Endowment Insurance in Urban Area	城乡居民基本养老保险参保人数 Number of Residents Participating in Basic Endowment Insurance in Urban and Rural Area	基本医疗保险参保人数 Number of People Participating in Basic Medical Insurance	城乡居民基本医疗保险参保人数 Number of Residents Participating in Basic Medical Insurance in Urban and Rural Area	城镇居民最低生活保障人数 Number of Urban Residents with Minimum Living Security	农村居民最低生活保障人数 Number of Rural Residents with Minimum Living Security
镇平县 Zhenping	48922	594873	959058	907452	3710	56878
内乡县 Neixiang	48505	362075	629100	618562	1944	19319
淅川县 Xichuan	46150	318900	647860	606000	2221	40825
社旗县 Sheqi	65489	342654	659254	617528	10295	38674
唐河县 Tanghe	91147	724252	1219814	1157841	4183	55218
新野县 Xinye	70112	427000	725215	678198	3091	19785
桐柏县 Tongbai	26099	229909	429138	395609	1696	20107
邓州市 Dengzhou	79288	931200	1564867	1564866	1840	49153
商丘市 Shangqiu						
民权县 Minquan	29287	501000	906875	869206	651	15450
睢县 Suixian	59369	472400	819927	785240	1222	22905
宁陵县 Ningling	26351	325293	628475	603468	2246	35017
柘城县 Zhecheng	57000	480000	950600	919000	10742	53965
虞城县 Yucheng	554839	438860	1070988	1068750	3958	44583
夏邑县 Xiayi	23001	736314	1140517	1100772	4134	45534
永城市 Yongcheng	63890	883000	1378030	1371175	4548	44954
信阳市 Xinyang						
罗山县 Luoshan	43695	395000	696125	663113	10524	32143
光山县 Guangshan	42176	437773	834682	796254	2060	24103
新县 Xinxian	31428	192300	343082	319007	7268	18746
商城县 Shangcheng	59652	410531	709586	677050	3930	25669
固始县 Gushi	85175	964265	1586028	1515028	17602	61825
潢川县 Huangchuan	29300	423200	850891	806230	5329	30843
淮滨县 Huaibin	36795	367652	671466	645666	5739	26899
息县 Xixian	25600	642313	1104352	948916	9658	57772
周口市 Zhoukou						
扶沟县 Fugou	53776	417106	691228	651698	6294	23430
西华县 Xihua	37949	440990	877506	836149	5542	34082
商水县 Shangshui	64250	592490	1115116	1073606	6480	48289
沈丘县 Shenqiu	59917	725154	1220789	1171789	3350	31040
郸城县 Dancheng	68740	690634	1377289	1337758	3983	48923
太康县 Taikang	78225	792207	1449054	1397521	5568	48669
鹿邑县 Luyi	85775	1116356	1123856	779636	9668	52763
项城市 Xiangcheng	99497	689567	1131836	1088797	2662	16671
驻马店市 Zhumadian						
西平县 Xiping	52104	512310	764902	723869	2919	21309
上蔡县 Shangcai	42312	774326	1199183	1156042	7111	65531
平舆县 Pingyu	28574	555782	959387	923776	13000	38266
正阳县 Zhengyang	40500	479800	734000	730000	5511	24950
确山县 Queshan	37220	292757	504694	473905	2268	14093
泌阳县 Biyang	40704	528000	763692	732733	621	27951
汝南县 Runan	57605	517000	756855	718387	2671	21446
遂平县 Suiping	14491	324000	511041	471345	1260	10605
新蔡县 Xincai	58579	567040	1117865	1083548	10721	43329

全国及各省、区、市主要统计指标

Main Indicators of the whole Nation and 31 Provinces (Municipality, Autonomous, Regions)

27-1 全国及各省区市人口、工资及投资(2019年)

Population, Wage and Investment by Province and Region (2019)

地　区	Region	常住人口 (万人) Number of the resident population (10 000 persons)	在岗职工平均工资 (元) Average Wage of Staff and Workers (yuan)	#国有经济 State-Owned Units	#城镇集体经济 Urban Collective Owned Units	固定资产投资增速 (%) Investment in Fixed Assets (%)	#房地产 Real Estate
全　　国	**National**	**140005**	**93383**	**102709**	**64499**	**5.4**	**9.9**
北　　京	Beijing	2154	173205	195783	69344	-2.4	-0.9
天　　津	Tianjin	1562	111602	144333	50286	13.9	12.5
河　　北	Hebei	7592	75775	77119	49664	6.1	-2.9
山　　西	Shanxi	3729	72207	70628	54405	9.3	20.3
内 蒙 古	Inner Mongolia	2540	83277	83988	83103	6.8	18.0
辽　　宁	Liaoning	4352	75264	74539	44007	0.5	9.0
吉　　林	Jilin	2691	76401	78033	64360	-16.3	11.9
黑 龙 江	Heilongjiang	3751	72603	68073	64527	6.3	1.4
上　　海	Shanghai	2428	151772	174728	84587	5.1	4.9
江　　苏	Jiangsu	8070	98669	137322	94575	5.1	9.4
浙　　江	Zhejiang	5850	101996	149036	67020	10.1	7.4
安　　徽	Anhui	6366	82127	103921	67704	9.2	11.7
福　　建	Fujian	3973	84374	111211	79508	5.9	14.8
江　　西	Jiangxi	4666	76131	89791	57636	9.2	3.0
山　　东	Shandong	10070	84089	101279	57402	-8.4	14.1
河　　南	**Henan**	**9640**	**68305**	**78036**	**58287**	**8.0**	**6.4**
湖　　北	Hubei	5927	81524	91665	55560	10.6	8.9
湖　　南	Hunan	6918	77563	87187	54756	10.1	12.7
广　　东	Guangdong	11521	100689	137123	62239	11.1	10.0
广　　西	Guangxi	4960	79516	85909	58120	9.5	27.0
海　　南	Hainan	945	84656	95461	58338	-9.2	-22.1
重　　庆	Chongqing	3124	89714	114570	63376	5.7	4.5
四　　川	Sichuan	8375	86855	101190	55877	8.6	15.4
贵　　州	Guizhou	3623	87970	93814	60996	1.0	27.3
云　　南	Yunnan	4858	91811	106514	79192	8.5	27.8
西　　藏	Tibet	351	123045	139406	68428	-2.1	39.9
陕　　西	Shaanxi	3876	82114	83109	61511	2.5	10.4
甘　　肃	Gansu	2647	77336	83141	52623	6.6	12.7
青　　海	Qinghai	608	93506	101025	76188	5.0	15.5
宁　　夏	Ningxia	695	88153	90536	71719	-10.3	-10.3
新　　疆	Xinjiang	2523	82052	78812	74047	2.5	3.9
河南为全国%	**Henan as % of the Country**	**6.9**	**73.1**	**76.0**	**90.4**		
河南居全国位次	**Rank of Henan in the Country**	**3**	**31**	**26**	**20**	**12**	**22**

27–2 全国及各省区市生产总值(2019年)

Gross Domestic Product by Province and Region (2019)

地区	Region	生产总值(亿元) Gross Domestic Products (100 million yuan)	第一产业 Primary Industry	第二产业 Secondary Industry	第三产业 Tertiary Industry	生产总值增速(%) Growth Rate of GDP (%)	第一产业 Primary Industry	第二产业 Secondary Industry	第三产业 Tertiary Industry
全国	**National**	**990865.10**	**70466.70**	**386165.30**	**534233.10**	**6.1**	**3.1**	**5.7**	**6.9**
北京	Beijing	35371.28	113.69	5715.06	29542.53	6.1	-2.5	4.5	6.4
天津	Tianjin	14104.28	185.23	4969.18	8949.87	4.8	0.2	3.2	5.9
河北	Hebei	35104.52	3518.44	13597.26	17988.82	6.8	1.6	4.9	9.4
山西	Shanxi	17026.68	824.72	7453.09	8748.87	6.2	2.1	5.7	7.0
内蒙古	Inner Mongolia	17212.53	1863.19	6818.88	8530.46	5.2	2.4	5.7	5.4
辽宁	Liaoning	24909.45	2177.77	9531.24	13200.44	5.5	3.5	5.7	5.6
吉林	Jilin	11726.82	1287.32	4134.82	6304.68	3.0	2.5	2.6	3.3
黑龙江	Heilongjiang	13612.68	3182.45	3615.21	6815.02	4.2	2.4	2.7	5.9
上海	Shanghai	38155.32	103.88	10299.16	27752.28	6.0	-5.0	0.5	8.2
江苏	Jiangsu	99631.52	4296.28	44270.51	51064.73	6.1	1.3	5.9	6.6
浙江	Zhejiang	62351.74	2097.38	26566.60	33687.76	6.8	2.0	5.9	7.8
安徽	Anhui	37113.98	2915.70	15337.90	18860.38	7.5	3.2	8.0	7.7
福建	Fujian	42395.00	2596.23	20581.74	19217.03	7.6	3.5	8.3	7.3
江西	Jiangxi	24757.50	2057.56	10939.83	11760.11	8.0	3.0	8.0	9.0
山东	Shandong	71067.53	5116.44	28310.92	37640.17	5.5	1.1	2.6	8.7
河南	**Henan**	**54259.20**	**4635.40**	**23605.79**	**26018.01**	**7.0**	**2.3**	**7.5**	**7.4**
湖北	Hubei	45828.31	3809.09	19098.62	22920.60	7.5	3.2	8.0	7.8
湖南	Hunan	39752.12	3646.95	14946.98	21158.19	7.6	3.2	7.8	8.1
广东	Guangdong	107671.07	4351.26	43546.43	59773.38	6.2	4.1	4.7	7.5
广西	Guangxi	21237.14	3387.74	7077.43	10771.97	6.0	5.6	5.7	6.2
海南	Hainan	5308.93	1080.36	1099.03	3129.54	5.8	2.5	4.1	7.5
重庆	Chongqing	23605.77	1551.42	9496.84	12557.51	6.3	3.6	6.4	6.4
四川	Sichuan	46615.82	4807.23	17365.33	24443.26	7.5	2.8	7.5	8.5
贵州	Guizhou	16769.34	2280.56	6058.45	8430.33	8.3	5.7	9.8	7.8
云南	Yunnan	23223.75	3037.62	7961.58	12224.55	8.1	5.5	8.6	8.3
西藏	Tibet	1697.82	138.19	635.62	924.01	8.1	4.6	7.0	9.2
陕西	Shaanxi	25793.17	1990.93	11980.75	11821.49	6.0	4.4	5.7	6.5
甘肃	Gansu	8718.30	1050.48	2862.42	4805.40	6.2	5.8	4.7	7.2
青海	Qinghai	2965.95	301.90	1159.75	1504.30	6.3	4.6	6.3	6.5
宁夏	Ningxia	3748.48	279.93	1584.72	1883.83	6.5	3.2	6.7	6.8
新疆	Xinjiang	13597.11	1781.75	4795.50	7019.86	6.2	5.3	3.7	8.1
河南为全国%	**Henan as % of the Country**	**5.5**	**6.6**	**6.1**	**4.9**				
河南居全国位次	**Rank of Henan in the Country**	**5**	**3**	**5**	**7**	**10**	**23**	**8**	**16**

注：生产总值按当年价格计算。生产总值指数按可比价格计算。
a) GDP in this table are calculated at current prices. The indices in this table are calculated at comparable prices.

27-3 全国及各省区市物价指数(2019年)
Price Indices by Province and Region (2019)

(上年=100) (Preceding Year=100)

地区	Region	居民消费价格总指数 General Consumer Price Index	固定资产投资价格指数 Price Indices of Investment In Fixed Assets	农业生产资料价格指数 General Price Index of Agricultural Means of Production	工业生产者出厂价格指数 Producer Price Indices for Industrial Products	工业生产者购进价格指数 Purchasing Price Indices for Industrial Producers
全国	**National**	**102.9**	**102.6**	**104.6**	**99.7**	**99.3**
北京	Beijing	102.3	102.1		99.6	99.6
天津	Tianjin	102.7	101.7		99.3	98.8
河北	Hebei	103.0	103.0	103.1	100.2	102.1
山西	Shanxi	102.7	104.0	104.7	99.7	101.1
内蒙古	Inner Mongolia	102.4	101.7	102.0	102.1	101.1
辽宁	Liaoning	102.4	103.1	103.6	99.5	100.8
吉林	Jilin	103.0	102.6	108.3	98.9	99.2
黑龙江	Heilongjiang	102.8	100.8	105.6	98.2	100.3
上海	Shanghai	102.5	101.4		98.8	98.7
江苏	Jiangsu	103.1	101.3	104.2	98.9	97.2
浙江	Zhejiang	102.9	102.1	102.9	98.9	97.1
安徽	Anhui	102.7	102.3	102.3	100.3	99.9
福建	Fujian	102.6	101.5	102.2	100.6	99.0
江西	Jiangxi	102.9	102.4	105.5	98.9	98.2
山东	Shandong	103.2	102.8	107.6	99.7	99.2
河南	**Henan**	**103.0**	**103.2**	**103.8**	**100.2**	**101.2**
湖北	Hubei	103.1	104.0	103.0	100.2	99.3
湖南	Hunan	102.9	101.7	102.5	99.6	100.2
广东	Guangdong	103.4	104.2	104.1	100.2	99.2
广西	Guangxi	103.7	102.4	104.6	99.3	99.5
海南	Hainan	103.4	103.3	104.3	97.4	103.1
重庆	Chongqing	102.7	103.4		99.8	100.1
四川	Sichuan	103.2	101.6	109.0	100.4	100.6
贵州	Guizhou	102.4	102.3	103.2	99.8	99.4
云南	Yunnan	102.5	102.3	103.9	100.0	99.0
西藏	Tibet	102.3		100.2	98.9	
陕西	Shaanxi	102.9	102.6	103.3	100.8	100.3
甘肃	Gansu	102.3	102.6	101.1	98.3	99.0
青海	Qinghai	102.5	102.5	103.5	98.5	98.2
宁夏	Ningxia	102.1	102.0	104.0	99.4	97.5
新疆	Xinjiang	101.9	102.8	102.6	98.5	100.0
河南居全国位次	**Rank of Henan in the Country**	**8**	**6**	**13**	**6**	**3**

27−4 全国及各省区市城乡居民收支(2019年)

Income and Expenditure of Urban and Rural Residents by Province and Region (2019)

单位：元 (yuan)

地区	Region	居民人均可支配收入 Per Capita Annual Disposable Income	城镇居民 Urban Households	农村居民 Rural Households	居民人均消费支出 Per Capita Consumption Expenditures	城镇居民 Urban Households	农村居民 Rural Households
全国	**National**	**30733**	**42359**	**16021**	**21559**	**28063**	**13328**
北京	Beijing	67756	73849	28928	43038	46358	21881
天津	Tianjin	42404	46119	24804	31854	34811	17843
河北	Hebei	25665	35738	15373	17987	23483	12372
山西	Shanxi	23828	33262	12902	15863	21159	9728
内蒙古	Inner Mongolia	30555	40782	15283	20743	25383	13816
辽宁	Liaoning	31820	39777	16108	22203	27355	12030
吉林	Jilin	24563	32299	14936	18075	23394	11457
黑龙江	Heilongjiang	24254	30945	14982	18111	22165	12495
上海	Shanghai	69442	73615	33195	45605	48272	22449
江苏	Jiangsu	41400	51056	22675	26697	31329	17716
浙江	Zhejiang	49899	60182	29876	32026	37508	21352
安徽	Anhui	26415	37540	15416	19137	23782	14546
福建	Fujian	35616	45620	19568	25314	30946	16281
江西	Jiangxi	26262	36546	15796	17650	22714	12497
山东	Shandong	31597	42329	17775	20427	26731	12309
河南	**Henan**	**23903**	**34201**	**15164**	**16332**	**21972**	**11546**
湖北	Hubei	28319	37601	16391	21567	26422	15328
湖南	Hunan	27680	39842	15395	20479	26924	13969
广东	Guangdong	39014	48118	18818	28995	34424	16949
广西	Guangxi	23328	34745	13676	16418	21591	12045
海南	Hainan	26679	36017	15113	19555	25317	12418
重庆	Chongqing	28920	37939	15133	20774	25785	13112
四川	Sichuan	24703	36154	14670	19338	25367	14056
贵州	Guizhou	20397	34404	10756	14780	21402	10222
云南	Yunnan	22082	36238	11902	15780	23455	10260
西藏	Tibet	19501	37410	12951	13029	25637	8418
陕西	Shaanxi	24666	36098	12326	17465	23514	10935
甘肃	Gansu	19139	32323	9629	15879	24454	9694
青海	Qinghai	22618	33830	11499	17545	23799	11343
宁夏	Ningxia	24412	34328	12858	18297	24161	11465
新疆	Xinjiang	23103	34664	13122	17397	25594	10318
河南为全国%	**Henan as % of the Country**	**77.8**	**80.7**	**94.7**	**75.8**	**76.9**	**90.4**
河南居全国位次	**Rank of Henan in the Country**	**23**	**26**	**16**	**26**	**28**	**21**

27−5 全国及各省区市主要农产品产量(2019年)

Output of Major Farm Products by Province and Region (2019)

单位：万吨 (10 000 tons)

地区	Region	粮食 Grain	棉花 Cotton	油料 Oilbearing Crops	水果(含果用瓜) Fruits (include fruit with melon)	肉类 Meat	奶类 Milk
全国	**National**	**66384.34**	**588.90**	**3492.98**	**27400.84**	**7758.78**	**3297.60**
北京	Beijing	28.76		0.31	59.90	5.14	26.41
天津	Tianjin	223.25	1.81	0.41	57.43	30.43	47.37
河北	Hebei	3739.24	22.74	119.54	1391.48	433.40	433.81
山西	Shanxi	1361.80	0.30	13.70	862.67	91.02	92.29
内蒙古	Inner Mongolia	3652.54	0.01	228.68	280.41	264.56	582.92
辽宁	Liaoning	2429.95		97.67	820.70	367.89	134.74
吉林	Jilin	3877.93		81.78	153.95	243.22	39.97
黑龙江	Heilongjiang	7503.01		11.54	164.96	237.10	467.02
上海	Shanghai	95.89	0.01	0.81	48.07	10.82	29.74
江苏	Jiangsu	3706.20	1.57	94.32	983.60	274.53	62.36
浙江	Zhejiang	592.15	0.81	31.93	744.11	94.27	15.52
安徽	Anhui	4054.00	5.55	161.38	706.32	402.83	33.76
福建	Fujian	493.90		22.03	727.21	255.15	14.99
江西	Jiangxi	2157.45	6.57	120.78	693.27	299.79	7.28
山东	Shandong	5357.00	19.60	288.95	2840.24	704.02	234.49
河南	**Henan**	**6695.36**	**2.71**	**645.45**	**2589.66**	**560.42**	**208.55**
湖北	Hubei	2724.98	14.36	313.95	1010.23	349.20	13.38
湖南	Hunan	2974.84	8.18	239.20	1061.99	459.42	6.30
广东	Guangdong	1240.80		110.22	1768.62	412.12	13.94
广西	Guangxi	1332.00	0.11	71.63	2472.13	380.04	8.71
海南	Hainan	144.96		8.69	456.15	67.06	0.23
重庆	Chongqing	1075.15		65.19	476.39	163.81	4.19
四川	Sichuan	3498.50	0.28	367.35	1136.70	559.53	66.77
贵州	Guizhou	1051.24	0.04	103.01	441.98	205.87	5.29
云南	Yunnan	1870.03		62.51	860.32	405.87	66.74
西藏	Tibet	103.92		5.71	2.38	28.38	48.16
陕西	Shaanxi	1231.13	0.76	60.10	2012.79	109.53	159.66
甘肃	Gansu	1162.58	3.27	63.18	710.09	101.67	44.71
青海	Qinghai	105.54		28.88	3.69	37.41	35.45
宁夏	Ningxia	373.15		7.66	258.64	33.53	183.44
新疆	Xinjiang	1527.07	500.20	66.41	1604.75	170.75	209.43
河南为全国%	**Henan as % of the Country**	**10.1**	**0.5**	**18.5**	**9.5**	**7.2**	**6.3**
河南居全国位次	**Rank of Henan in the Country**	**2**	**9**	**1**	**2**	**2**	**6**

27-6 全国及各省区市规模以上工业主要统计指标(2019年)

Main Indicators of Enterprises Above Designed Size by Province and Region (2019)

地区	Region	原油(万吨) Crude Oil (10 000 tons)	发电量(亿千瓦小时) Electricity (100 million kwh)	原煤(万吨) Coal (10 000 tons)	成品钢材(万吨) Steel (10 000 tons)	水泥(万吨) Cement (10 000 tons)	农用化肥(万吨) Chemical Fertilizers (10 000 tons)	增加值增速(%) Indices of Value-Added of Industry (%)
全国	**National**	**19101.4**	**71422.1**	**374552.5**	**120477.4**	**235012.1**	**5731.2**	**5.7**
北京	Beijing		431.2	36.1	170.7	318.8		3.1
天津	Tianjin	3111.9	713.0		5455.0	687.7	16.4	3.4
河北	Hebei	550.0	3117.7	5075.2	28409.6	10523.8	186.7	5.6
山西	Shanxi		3238.0	97109.4	5594.2	5257.5	400.6	5.3
内蒙古	Inner Mongolia	11.8	5327.3	103523.7	2563.8	3377.7	515.4	6.1
辽宁	Liaoning	1053.3	1996.0	3292.0	7254.4	4677.4	38.1	6.7
吉林	Jilin	385.7	871.8	1217.0	1544.2	1815.0	29.0	3.1
黑龙江	Heilongjiang	3110.0	1057.2	5195.0	782.0	1989.6	46.6	2.8
上海	Shanghai	39.1	792.6		1819.7	441.5	1.0	0.4
江苏	Jiangsu	151.4	5015.4	1102.7	14211.4	16072.3	200.6	6.2
浙江	Zhejiang		3351.0		3468.2	13441.0	50.4	6.6
安徽	Anhui		2769.4	10989.5	3158.4	14018.8	271.3	7.3
福建	Fujian		2406.4	831.7	3737.7	9475.0	90.3	8.8
江西	Jiangxi		1241.9	441.2	2795.7	9691.3	29.8	8.5
山东	Shandong	2237.8	5586.4	11875.6	9289.4	14643.0	425.5	1.2
河南	**Henan**	**251.1**	**2765.8**	**10873.3**	**3838.0**	**10496.6**	**416.5**	**7.8**
湖北	Hubei	53.6	2896.4	38.5	3771.6	11626.0	569.6	7.8
湖南	Hunan		1505.5	1374.7	2451.6	11251.2	59.5	8.3
广东	Guangdong	1475.1	4726.3		4510.5	16895.5	15.8	4.7
广西	Guangxi	50.3	1781.2	356.6	3346.7	12093.0	34.8	4.5
海南	Hainan	30.5	318.8			2019.0	65.6	4.2
重庆	Chongqing		761.6	1150.8	1136.4	6757.7	83.6	6.2
四川	Sichuan	8.4	3671.0	3296.4	3308.2	14184.6	451.9	8.0
贵州	Guizhou		2106.3	12969.5	707.7	11061.1	372.4	9.6
云南	Yunnan		3251.9	4779.6	2323.3	12907.4	296.9	8.1
西藏	Tibet		71.0			1080.9		3.0
陕西	Shaanxi	3543.2	2118.6	63412.4	2037.5	6642.7	127.6	5.2
甘肃	Gansu	58.1	1479.6	3663.1	936.7	4450.1	22.6	5.2
青海	Qinghai	228.0	790.5	1007.2	180.6	1348.8	560.7	7.0
宁夏	Ningxia		1697.8	7168.0	306.2	1889.7	45.4	7.6
新疆	Xinjiang	2752.1	3564.2	23773.3	1367.9	3877.1	306.5	5.0
河南为全国%	**Henan as % of the Country**	**1.3**	**3.9**	**2.9**	**3.2**	**4.5**	**7.3**	
河南居全国位次	**Rank of Henan in the Country**	**10**	**13**	**8**	**8**	**13**	**6**	**7**

27−7 全国及各省区市贸易外经和财政主要指标(2019年)

Main Indicators of Internal and Foreign Trade、Government Finance by Province and Region (2019)

地区	Region	社会消费品零售总额(亿元) Total Retail Sales of Consumer Goods (100 million yuan)	进出口贸易总额(亿元) Total Value of Import and Export Trade (100 million yuan)	#出口 Total Value of Exports	公共财政预算收入(亿元) Public Budget Revenue (100 million yuan)	公共财政预算支出(亿元) Public Budget Expenditure (100 million yuan)
全国	**National**	**411649.02**	**315504.75**	**172342.34**	**101076.82**	**203758.87**
北京	Beijing	12270.10	28669.44	5169.21	5817.10	7408.25
天津	Tianjin	5516.05	7346.33	3017.89	2410.25	3508.71
河北	Hebei	17934.19	4001.87	2370.59	3742.67	8313.71
山西	Shanxi	7909.15	1447.03	806.97	2347.56	4713.13
内蒙古	Inner Mongolia	7610.63	1095.76	376.84	2059.74	5097.89
辽宁	Liaoning	15008.59	7256.41	3130.64	2651.96	5761.44
吉林	Jilin	7777.23	1302.56	324.23	1116.86	3933.42
黑龙江	Heilongjiang	9898.42	1866.37	349.64	1262.64	5011.55
上海	Shanghai	13497.21	34053.06	13725.37	7165.10	8179.28
江苏	Jiangsu	35291.19	43383.83	27211.93	8802.36	12573.62
浙江	Zhejiang	27176.41	30838.68	23075.35	7048.00	10052.99
安徽	Anhui	13377.65	4738.47	2785.66	3182.54	7391.02
福建	Fujian	15749.69	13309.85	8280.66	3052.72	5097.25
江西	Jiangxi	8421.64	3512.64	2497.18	2486.51	6402.58
山东	Shandong	35770.58	20421.95	11131.10	6526.64	10736.82
河南	**Henan**	**23476.13**	**5713.71**	**3756.55**	**4041.89**	**10163.93**
湖北	Hubei	20224.23	3944.84	2486.02	3388.39	7967.73
湖南	Hunan	17239.54	4343.11	3076.90	3006.99	8091.76
广东	Guangdong	42664.46	71457.02	43396.28	12651.46	17314.12
广西	Guangxi	8872.98	4695.19	2597.58	1811.89	5849.02
海南	Hainan	1808.31	905.87	343.72	814.13	1859.08
重庆	Chongqing	8667.34	5793.22	3713.27	2134.88	4847.79
四川	Sichuan	20144.32	6766.53	3892.77	4070.69	10349.59
贵州	Guizhou	4174.17	453.57	327.15	1767.36	5921.40
云南	Yunnan	7539.18	2323.88	1037.27	2073.53	6770.09
西藏	Tibet	649.33	48.76	37.45	222.00	2180.88
陕西	Shanxi	9598.73	3516.04	1873.34	2287.73	5721.56
甘肃	Gansu	3692.40	379.86	131.33	850.23	3956.72
青海	Qinghai	880.75	37.25	20.21	282.14	1863.74
宁夏	Ningxia	984.49	240.62	148.92	423.55	1438.40
新疆	Xinjiang	3361.61	1641.03	1250.32	1577.60	5269.06
河南为全国%	**Henan as % of the Country**	**5.7**	**1.8**	**2.2**	**4.0**	**5.0**
河南居全国位次	**Rank of Henan in the Country**	**5**	**12**	**9**	**8**	**5**

注：1. 社会消费品零售总额来源于《中国统计提要-2020》。河南数据已根据第四次经济普查结果进行调整。
2. 财政收支为地方本级收支，数据来源于《中国统计提要-2020》。河南数据已根据河南省财政厅财政总决算进行调整。

a) The data of total retail sales of consumer goods are from China Statistical Abstract-2020. The data of Henan have been adjusted according to the results of the fourth economic census.

b) Government revenue and expenditures is corresponding level.Data are from China statistical abstract - 2020. The data of Henan have been adjusted according to the financial budget of finance department of Henan province.

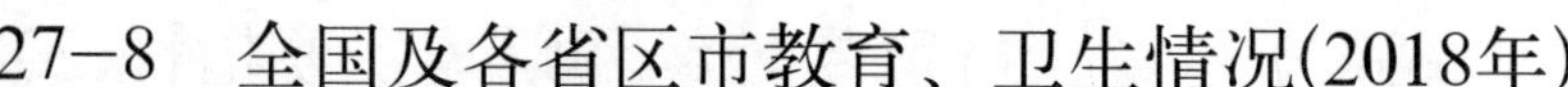

27-8 全国及各省区市教育、卫生情况(2018年)

Main Indicator on Education and Public Health by Province and Region (2018)

地区	Region	在校学生数(万人) Student Enrollment (10 000 persons) 普通高等学校 Institutions of Higher Education	普通中学 Regular Secondary Schools	小学 Primary Schools	卫生机构数(个) Health Institutions (unit)	卫生机构床位数(张) Number of Beds in Health Institutions (unit)	执业(助理)医师数(人) Licensed (Assistant) Doctors (person)
全国	**National**	**3032**	**7241**	**10561**	**1007545**	**8806956**	**3866916**
北京	Beijing	60	46	94	10336	127777	105866
天津	Tianjin	54	46	70	5962	68262	46420
河北	Hebei	147	439	679	84651	430079	228583
山西	Shanxi	80	180	229	42162	218441	105741
内蒙古	Inner Mongolia	47	107	136	24564	161083	78094
辽宁	Liaoning	104	162	195	34238	313847	123873
吉林	Jilin	70	107	119	22198	170332	79027
黑龙江	Heilongjiang	78	147	128	20375	262575	93517
上海	Shanghai	53	61	83	5597	146454	74743
江苏	Jiangsu	187	347	573	34796	516015	254659
浙江	Zhejiang	107	242	367	34119	350191	205515
安徽	Anhui	124	328	462	26435	347395	138406
福建	Fujian	86	200	334	27788	202211	99458
江西	Jiangxi	113	326	411	37029	267135	96445
山东	Shandong	218	528	739	83616	629722	315311
河南	**Henan**	**232**	**684**	**1012**	**70735**	**640008**	**251429**
湖北	Hubei	150	251	376	35515	403300	153642
湖南	Hunan	141	370	529	57230	506330	190495
广东	Guangdong	205	573	1033	53899	545196	291057
广西	Guangxi	108	330	495	33679	277357	115091
海南	Hainan	21	54	85	5411	49764	23928
重庆	Sichuan	83	173	206	21057	231806	83293
四川	Chongqing	166	414	556	83756	631763	221689
贵州	Guizhou	77	278	388	28509	264986	89798
云南	Yunnan	86	275	385	25587	311899	114031
西藏	Tibet	4	21	34	6940	17063	9317
陕西	Shaanxi	112	181	278	35404	265814	108685
甘肃	Gansu	52	141	194	26697	181172	62807
青海	Qinghai	7	35	50	6513	41443	17402
宁夏	Ningxia	14	45	58	4397	40971	20755
新疆	Xinjiang	43	151	261	18351	186426	67875
河南为全国%	**Henan as % of the Country**	**7.7**	**9.4**	**9.6**	**7.0**	**7.3**	**6.5**
河南居全国位次	**Rank of Henan in the Country**	**1**	**1**	**2**	**4**	**1**	**4**

中国统计出版社有限公司最新图书简目

（仅供参考,以实际出版为准）

统计资料

中国统计年鉴　中国统计摘要　中国第三产业统计年鉴
中国第三次全国农业普查综合资料　国际统计年鉴　金砖国家联合统计手册
中国-东盟国家统计手册　中国农村统计年鉴　中国县域统计年鉴
中国农产品价格调查年鉴　中国城市统计年鉴　中国价格统计年鉴
中国贸易外经统计年鉴　中国零售和餐饮连锁企业统计年鉴　中国商品交易市场统计年鉴
大中型批发零售和住宿餐饮企业统计年鉴　中国住户调查年鉴　中国工业统计年鉴
中国环境统计年鉴　中国能源统计年鉴　中国建筑业统计年鉴
中国房地产统计年鉴　投资领域统计年鉴　中国对外直接投资统计公报
中国人口和就业统计年鉴　中国劳动统计年鉴　中国社会统计年鉴
中国科技统计年鉴　中国高技术产业统计年鉴　全国企业创新调查年鉴
中国文化及相关产业统计年鉴　2018年时间利用调查资料　中国妇女儿童状况统计资料
中国基本单位统计年鉴　中国教育统计年鉴　中国教育经费统计年鉴
中国民族统计年鉴　中国残疾人事业统计年鉴　长江经济带发展统计年鉴

省级综合统计年鉴系列

北京 天津 河北 山西 内蒙古 辽宁 吉林 黑龙江 上海 江苏 浙江 安徽 福建 江西 山东 河南 湖北 湖南 广东 广西 海南 重庆 四川 贵州 云南 西藏 陕西 甘肃 青海 宁夏 新疆 新疆生产建设兵团

市(县)级综合统计年鉴系列

滨海新区 石家庄 唐山 邯郸 保定 沧州 邢台 廊坊 承德 衡水 秦皇岛 张家口 太原 大同 阳泉 长治 晋城 朔州 晋中 运城 忻州 临汾 吕梁 呼和浩特 鄂尔多斯 包头 沈阳 大连 长春 延吉 四平 白山 通化 哈尔滨 齐齐哈尔 黑龙江垦区 上海浦东新区 南京 无锡 徐州 常州 苏州 南通 连云港 淮安 盐城 扬州 镇江 泰州 宿迁 江阴 丹阳 海门 张家港 杭州 宁波 温州 嘉兴 湖州 绍兴 金华 衢州 舟山 台州 丽水 合肥 安庆 福州 厦门 宁德 漳州 龙岩 莆田 泉州 三明 南平 南昌 九江 上饶 新余 抚州 赣州 景德镇 济南 青岛 枣庄 潍坊 聊城 郑州 洛阳 平顶山 三门峡 南阳 商丘 信阳 济源 汝州 武汉 十堰 荆州 宜昌 荆门 咸宁 黄冈 长沙 鹰潭 广州 深圳 惠州 东莞 汕尾 湛江 肇庆 南宁 柳州 桂林 贵港 梧州 来宾 河池 防城港 海口 三亚 儋州 成都 内江 贵阳 黔南 毕节 昆明 文山 德宏 西安 延安 安康 铜川 汉中 商洛 银川 兰州 庆阳 乌鲁木齐 昌吉 阿勒泰 兵团一师、二师、三师、四师、六师、七师、八师、十师、十三师、十四师

调查年鉴系列

天津 内蒙古 上海 河南 湖北 湖南 广东 广西 重庆 四川 云南 甘肃 宁夏 南宁 贵港 昆明

统计方法应用/实用手册

Python数据分析基础（第二版）　非参数统计（第五版）　现代金融投资统计分析（第四版）
国民经济核算初级教程（第二版）　国民经济核算教程（第五版）　概率统计基础
全国统计专业技术资格考试系列考试用书：统计业务知识（第四版修订版）　统计业务知识学习指导与习题
全国统计专业技术资格考试系列考试用书：统计相关知识（第四版）　统计相关知识学习指导与习题

统计通俗读物/统计科普图书

领导干部统计知识问答　统计公文写作及会议办理实用手册　大数据在统计工作中的应用案例汇编
中国国民经济核算知识问答（修订版）　地区生产总值核算国际比较研究　新中国统计制度方法的发展与改革

重点图书

中国农业统计资料1949-2019　第四次全国经济普查地图集　中国经济普查年鉴2018
新编英汉汉英统计大词典　中国国民经济核算体系2016　国民经济行业分类注释
挑大学选专业2020—考研择校指南　挑大学选专业2020—高考志愿填报指南　中华医学统计百科全书

发行部电话：（010）63376907　63376908　63376909　同椇行书店电话：（010）68783171　68783172

地址：北京市丰台区西三环南路甲6号　邮政编码：100073　网址：http://www.zgtjcbs.com